The World as a Village

...Imagine that the Earth is a village of only 1,000 people rather than a world with 6+ billion inhabitants.

While it would not be easy to walk the Earth and get a sense of its many cultures and societies, we could walk through a village of 1,000 people and get a feeling for the diversity there.

HERE IS WHAT WE WOULD SEE:

310 people under the age of 15
70 people over the age of 65
294 living on less than $1 a day
   (average yearly income for
   villagers: $5,180)
1 physician
180 illiterate adults (out of
   a total of 690 adults)

---

147 people speaking Mandarin
62 people speaking Hindi
60 people speaking Spanish
58 people speaking English
35 people speaking Bengali
35 people speaking Arabic

---

328 Christians
196 Muslims
128 Hindus
60 Buddhists
140 followers of other faiths
123 nonreligious
25 atheists

---

144 telephones
99 different newspapers
277 televisions (53 with cable)
40 cellular telephones
9 fax machines
58 personal computers
8 Internet hosts

...And if you came back in a year there would be 1014 people in the village.

Sociology around the world

The countries that are identified on this map are cited in the book, either in the context of research studies or in relevant statistical data. Refer to the subject index for specific page references.

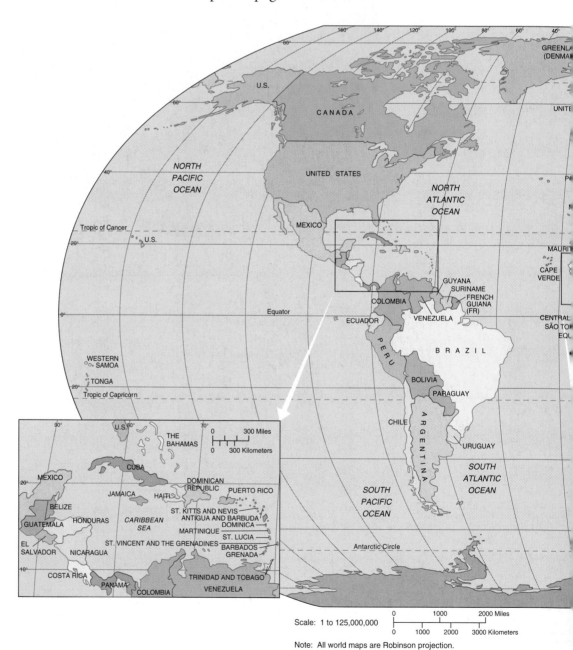

Scale: 1 to 125,000,000

Note: All world maps are Robinson projection.

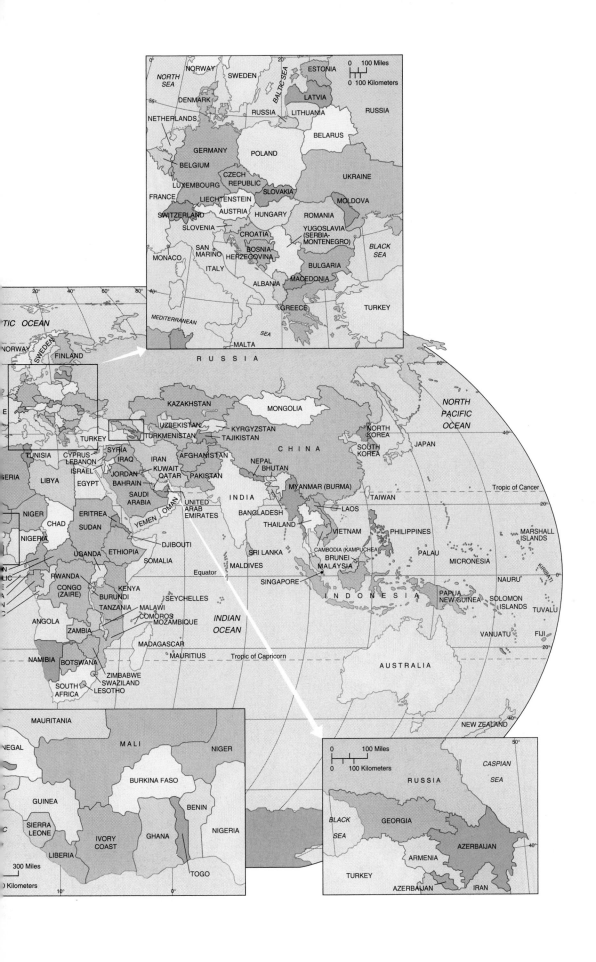

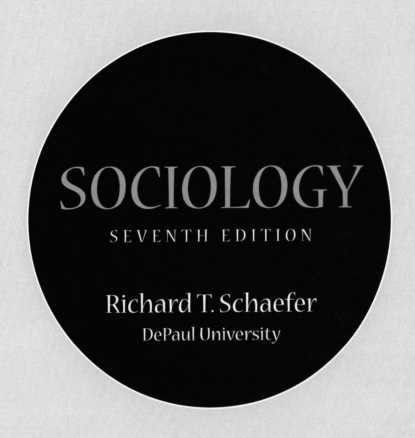

SOCIOLOGY

SEVENTH EDITION

Richard T. Schaefer
DePaul University

Boston   Burr Ridge, IL   Dubuque, IA   Madison, WI   New York   San Francisco   St. Louis
Bangkok   Bogotá   Caracas   Lisbon   London   Madrid
Mexico City   Milan   New Delhi   Seoul   Singapore   Sydney   Taipei   Toronto

McGraw-Hill Higher Education

A Division of The **McGraw-Hill** Companies

SOCIOLOGY

Published by McGraw-Hill, an imprint of The McGraw-Hill Companies, Inc., 1221 Avenue of the Americas, New York, NY 10020. Copyright © 2001, 1998, 1995, 1992, 1989, 1986, 1983, by The McGraw-Hill Companies, Inc. All rights reserved. No part of this publication may be reproduced or distributed in any form or by any means, or stored in a database or retrieval system, without the prior written consent of The McGraw-Hill Companies, Inc., including, but not limited to, in any network or other electronic storage or transmission, or broadcast for distance learning.

Some ancillaries, including electronic and print components, may not be available to customers outside the United States.

This book is printed on acid-free paper.

domestic   1 2 3 4 5 6 7 8 9 0 VNH/VNH 0 9 8 7 6 5 4 3 2 1 0
international   1 2 3 4 5 6 7 8 9 0 VNH/VNH 0 9 8 7 6 5 4 3 2 1 0

ISBN 0-07-232137-7 (student edition)
ISBN 0-07-235729-0 (annotated instructor's edition)

Editorial director: *Phillip A. Butcher*
Sponsoring editor: *Sally Constable*
Senior developmental editor: *Rhona Robbin*
Marketing manager: *Leslie Kraham*
Project manager: *Kimberly D. Hooker*
Production supervisor: *Debra B. Sylvester*
Freelance design coordinator: *Laurie J. Entringer*
Supplemental coordinator: *Jason Greve*
Media technology producer: *Kimberly Stark*
Photo research coordinator: *Sharon Miller*
Photo researchers: *Elyse Rieder and Elsa Peterson*
Cover illustrations: *Nip Rogers; José Ortega; Roxana Villa; Charlene Potts © The Stock Illustration Source, Inc.*
Compositor: *GTS Graphics, Inc.*
Typeface: *10/12 Minion*
Printer: *Von Hoffman Press, Inc.*

Library of Congress Cataloging-in-Publication Data
Schaefer, Richard T.
    Sociology / Richard T. Schaefer.—7th ed.
        p.   cm.
    Includes index
    ISBN 0-07-232137-7 (student ed. : alk. paper)—ISBN 0-07-235729-0 (annotated instructor's ed. : alk. paper)
    1. Sociology.   2. Social problems.   3. United States—Social policy.   I. Title.
HM403 .S63 2001
301—dc21   00-037213

INTERNATIONAL EDITION ISBN 0071180095

Copyright © 2001. Exclusive rights by The McGraw-Hill Companies, Inc. for manufacture and export.
This book cannot be re-exported from the country to which it is sold by McGraw-Hill.
The International Edition is not available in North America.

www.mhhe.com

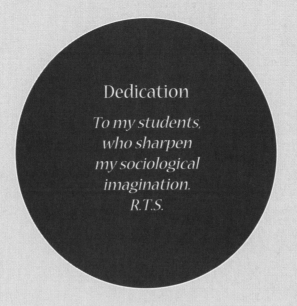

Dedication

*To my students,
who sharpen
my sociological
imagination.
R.T.S.*

About the Author

RICHARD T. SCHAEFER:
Professor, DePaul University;
B.A. Northwestern University
M.A., Ph.D. University of Chicago

Growing up in Chicago at a time when neighborhoods were going through transitions in ethnic and racial composition, Richard T. Schaefer found himself increasingly intrigued by what was happening, how people were reacting, and how these changes were affecting neighborhoods and people's jobs. His interest in social issues caused him to gravitate to sociology courses at Northwestern University, where he eventually received a B.A. in sociology.

"Originally as an undergraduate I thought I would go on to law school and become a lawyer. But after taking a few sociology courses, I found myself wanting to learn more about what sociologists studied, and fascinated by the kinds of questions they raised." This fascination led him to obtain his M.A. and Ph.D. in sociology from the University of Chicago. Dr. Schaefer's continuing interest in race relations led him to write his master's thesis on the membership of the Ku Klux Klan and his doctoral thesis on racial prejudice and race relations in Great Britain.

Dr. Schaefer went on to become a professor of sociology. He has taught introductory sociology for 30 years to students in colleges, adult education programs, nursing programs, and even a maximum-security prison. Dr. Schaefer's love of teaching is apparent in his interaction with his students. "I find myself constantly learning from the students who are in my classes and from reading what they write. Their insights into the material we read or current events that we discuss often become part of future course material and sometimes even find their way into my writing."

Dr. Schaefer is author of the third edition of *Sociology: A Brief Introduction* (McGraw-Hill, 2000). Dr. Schaefer is also the author of *Racial and Ethnic Groups,* now in its eighth edition, and *Race and Ethnicity in the United States,* second edition. His articles and book reviews have appeared in many journals, including *American Journal of Sociology; Phylon: A Review of Race and Culture; Contemporary Sociology; Sociology and Social Research; Sociological Quarterly;* and *Teaching Sociology.* He served as president of the Midwest Sociological Society in 1994–1995.

Dr. Schaefer's advice to students is to "look at the material and make connections to your own life and experiences. Sociology will make you a more attentive observer of how people in groups interact and function. It will also make you more aware of peoples' different needs and interests—and perhaps more ready to work for the common good, while still recognizing people's individuality."

Contents
in Brief

Contents

Boxes

 Sociology in the Global Community

 Research in Action

Social Policy
Sections

Preface

"What has sociology got to do with me or with my life?" Any student might well ask this question before signing up for a sociology course. Here are some things for that student to consider: Are you influenced by what you see on television? Do you use the Internet? Do you know someone with a tattoo? Did you neglect to vote in the last election? Are you familiar with binge drinking on campus? Do you use alternative medicine? These are just a few of the everyday life situations described in this book that sociology can shed light on, revealing patterns and meanings.

Sociology also looks at large social issues. It seeks to unravel the factors behind the transfer of thousands of jobs from the United States to the developing countries of the Third World. It assesses the ways in which the availability of computer technology and the Internet may increase or reduce inequality. Sociology investigates the social forces that promote prejudice, the persistence of slavery today, the issues surrounding bilingual education, the social networks established by women, the process of growing old in different cultures, and the factors that lead someone to join a social movement and work for social change. These issues, along with many others, are of great interest to me, but it is the sociological explanations for them that I find especially compelling. The introductory sociology class provides the ideal laboratory in which to confront our society and our global neighbors.

After more than 30 years of teaching sociology to students in colleges, adult education programs, nursing programs, an overseas program based in London, and even a maximum-security prison, I am firmly convinced that the discipline can play a valuable role in teaching critical thinking skills. Sociology can help students to better understand the workings of their own lives as well as of their society and other cultures. The distinctive emphasis on social policy found in this text shows students how to use the sociological imagination in examining such public policy issues as sexual harassment, the AIDS crisis, welfare reform, the death penalty, and privacy and censorship in an electronic age.

My hope is that, through their reading of this book, students will begin to think like sociologists and will be able to use sociological theories and concepts in evaluating human interactions and institutions. From the introduction of the concept of sociological imagination in Chapter 1—which draws on a study that a colleague and I conducted of the food bank system of the United States—this text stresses the distinctive way in which sociologists examine and question even the most familiar patterns of social behavior.

The first six editions of *Sociology* have been well received; it is currently used in more than 500 colleges and universities. *Sociology*, Seventh Edition, brings the research into the twenty-first century and introduces a number of features designed to appeal to today's students. One thing that remains unchanged, however, is the steady focus on three especially important points:

- **Comprehensive and balanced coverage of theoretical perspectives throughout the text.** Chapter 1 introduces, defines, and contrasts the functionalist, conflict, and interactionist perspectives. We explore their distinctive views of such topics as television (Chapter 1), social institutions (Chapter 5), deviance (Chapter 7), the family (Chapter 13), education (Chapter 15), and health and medicine (Chapter 18).
- **Strong coverage of issues pertaining to gender, age, race, ethnicity, and class in all chapters.** Examples of such coverage include social policy sections on bilingualism (Chapter 3), rethinking welfare (Chapter 8), immigration policy (Chapter 10), and sexual harassment (Chapter 6); a chapter opener on the "beauty myth" (Chapter 11); boxes on urban poverty and joblessness (Chapter 8), prejudice against Arab Americans and Muslim Americans (Chapter 10), domestic violence (Chapter 13), the role of grandparents (Chapter 13), and squatter settlements and gated communities (Chapter 19); and sections on the social construction of race (Chapter 10), the treatment of women in education (Chapter 15), and the contingency or temporary workforce (Chapter 17).
- **Use of cross-cultural material throughout the text.** Chapter 9 treats the topic of stratification from a global perspective. This chapter introduces world systems analysis, dependency theory, and modernization theory, and examines multinational corporations and the global economy. Every chapter presents global material and makes use of cross-cultural examples. Among the topics examined are:

The global "McDonaldization of society" (Chapter 3)
Neglect of children in Eastern European orphanages (Chapter 4)

Police power in Japan (Chapter 7)
The status of women around the world
(Chapter 11)
Issues of aging around the world (Chapter 12)
Transmission of cultural values (Chapter 15)
Affirmative action in South Africa (Chapter 17)
Population policy in China (Chapter 20)
Homelessness worldwide (Chapter 19)
The global disconnect in technology (Chapter 22)

I take great care to introduce the basic concepts and research methods of sociology and to reinforce this material in all chapters. The most recent data are included, making this book more current than all previous editions.

Content and Organization

Sociology is divided into 22 chapters that study human behavior from the perspective of sociologists. Part One ("The Sociological Perspective") sets the scene. The opening chapter ("Understanding Sociology") presents a brief history of the discipline and introduces the basic theories and perspectives employed in sociology. Chapter 2 ("Sociological Research") describes the major research methods.

The next five chapters (Part Two: "Organizing Social Life") focus on key sociological concepts. Chapter 3 ("Culture") illustrates how sociologists study the behavior we have learned and share. Chapter 4 ("Socialization") reveals how humans are most distinctively social animals who learn the attitudes and behavior viewed as appropriate in their particular cultures. We examine social interaction and social structure in Chapter 5 and the workings of groups and organizations in Chapter 6. Chapter 7 ("Deviance and Social Control") reviews how we conform to and deviate from established norms.

Part Three, "Social Inequality," considers the social hierarchies present in societies. Chapters 8 and 9 introduce us to the presence of social inequality in the United States (8) and worldwide (9). Chapter 10 ("Racial and Ethnic Inequality"), and Chapter 12 ("Stratification by Age") analyze specific types of inequality.

Part Four examines the major social institutions of human society. Marriage, kinship, and divorce are some of the topics examined in Chapter 13 ("The Family and Intimate Relationships"). Other social institutions that we consider are religion (Chapter 14), education (Chapter 15), government and politics (Chapter 16), the economy and work (Chapter 17), and health and medicine (Chapter 18)

The final chapters of the text, constituting Part Five ("Changing Society"), introduce major themes in our changing world. In Chapter 19 we examine the importance of communities and urbanization in our lives.

Chapter 20 deals with population and environmental issues. In Chapter 21 we look at collective behavior and social movements. Finally, Chapter 22 ("Social Change and Technology") presents a sociological analysis of the process of change, with a special focus on technology and the future.

Special Features

Poster Art

Each chapter opens with a reproduction of a poster or piece of graphic art that illustrates a key theme or concept of the chapter. Accompanying captions help readers to grasp the relevance of the artwork to the chapter.

Chapter Opener

The chapter openers convey the excitement and relevance of sociological inquiry by means of lively excerpts from writings of sociologists and others who explore sociological topics. These openers are designed to expose students to vivid writing on a broad range of topics and to stimulate their sociological imagination. For example, Chapter 3 begins with Horace Miner's classic take on Nacirema culture. Chapter 5 opens with a description of Zimbardo's mock prison study. Cornel West's musings on being a single father introduce Chapter 13. Later, in Chapter 20, Kai Erikson reflects on the value of sociology in understanding the connection between the population and the environment.

Chapter Overview

The opener is followed by a chapter overview that describes the content of the chapter in narrative form.

Key Terms

I have given careful attention to presenting understandable and accurate definitions of each key term. These terms are highlighted in bold italics when they are introduced. A list of key terms and definitions in each chapter—with page references—follows the end of the chapter. In addition, the glossary at the end of the book includes the definitions of the textbook's key terms and the page references for each term.

Research in Action

These sections, which appear in almost every chapter, present sociological findings on topics such as binge drinking, school-related violence, grandparents and divorce, and gated communities.

Sociology in the Global Community

These sections, which appear in almost every chapter, provide a global perspective on topics such as disability as a master status, slavery in the twenty-first century, police power in Japan, and population policy in China.

Eye on the Media

New to this edition, these sections illustrate how the media affect, and are affected by, social trends and events. Topics featured in these sections include the social construction of rock music as a social problem, the lack of diversity on network television, and political activism on the Internet.

Taking Sociology to Work

New to this edition, these sections profile individuals who majored in sociology and use its principles in their work. While these people work in a variety of occupations and professions, they all share a conviction that their background in sociology has been valuable in their careers.

Illustrations

The photographs, cartoons, figures, and tables are closely linked to the themes of the chapters. The maps, titled Mapping Life Nationwide and Mapping Life Worldwide, show the prevalence of social trends. A world map highlighting those countries used as examples in the text appears in the front matter to this book.

Social Policy Sections

The social policy sections that close all but one of the chapters play a critical role in helping students to think like sociologists. They apply sociological principles and theories to important social and political issues being debated by policymakers and the general public. Among the 10 sections new to this edition are bilingual education (Chapter 3), the death penalty (Chapter 7), reproductive technology (Chapter 13), school choice (Chapter 15), campaign financing (Chapter 16), and financing health care (Chapter 18). All the policy sections now present a global perspective.

Cross Reference Icons

When the text discussion refers to a concept introduced earlier in the book, an icon in the margin points the reader to the exact page.

Chapter Summaries

Each chapter includes a brief numbered summary to aid students in reviewing the important themes.

Critical Thinking Questions

After the summary, each chapter includes critical thinking questions that will help students analyze the social world in which they participate. Critical thinking is an essential element in the sociological imagination.

Additional Readings

An annotated list of books concludes each chapter; these works have been selected as additional readings because of their sociological soundness and their accessibility for introductory students. A list of sociological journals and periodicals is included as well.

Internet Connection Exercises

Two exercises in each chapter take students online to analyze social issues relevant to chapter topics. Throughout the text an icon signals where more information and/or updates are available on the book's website.

Endpapers

The front endpaper features a description of what the world would look like if it were a village of a thousand people. The back endpaper summarizes the applications used in the book to illustrate sociology's major theoretical approaches.

⬤ What's New in the Seventh Edition?

The most important changes in this edition include the following (refer as well to the chapter-by-chapter list of changes on pp. xxv–xxvii and to the *Visual Preview* on pp. xxxiii–xxxvi.):

Content

- Two additional chapters formed by splitting "Education and Religion" and "Government and the Economy" into separate chapters
- Inviting new openers drawing on the vivid writings of sociologists and others writing on sociological topics
- Focus on technology's impact throughout the book and especially in Chapter 22 ("Social Change and Technology")

- Two new box topics: "Eye on the Media" boxes that illustrate how the media affect and are affected by social events; "Taking Sociology to Work" boxes that profile people who studied sociology and use it on the job

Pedagogy

- Internet Connection exercises and Web icons (designating topics that are amplified on the book's website)
- Consistent heading structure in social policy sections (The Issue, The Setting, Sociological Insights, Policy Initiatives) to make the material more accessible to students
- Discussion questions at the end of boxes and social policy sections
- Cross reference icons
- More examples relevant to students' lives
- More cross-cultural examples, including a global focus in the social policy boxes
- More direct and engaging writing style

Map and Illustration Program

- Expanded map program: Two kinds of maps, "Mapping Life Nationwide" and "Mapping Life Worldwide," are featured throughout the text
- Map of the world at the beginning of the book shows readers the countries referenced in the text
- Use of poster art at the beginning of each chapter to illustrate key sociological concepts
- "Sticker" captions within figures draw attention to major points in the graphs
- Front endpaper featuring "The World as a Village" serves as a wonderful discussion prompt

This edition has been thoroughly updated. It includes the most recent data and research findings, many of which were published in the last three years. Recent data from the Census Bureau, Bureau of Labor Statistics, Current Population Reports, the Population Reference Bureau, the World Bank, the United Nations Development Programme, and the Centers for Disease Control have been incorporated.

A more complete, chapter-by-chapter listing of the most significant new material in this edition follows.

What's New in Each Chapter

CHAPTER 1 Understanding Sociology

- Excerpt from Katherine Irwin's article on tattooing
- Expanded discussion of conflict perspective, with more emphasis on feminist and racial views

- Discussion of how the different social sciences approach the issue of handgun control
- Section detailing how features in the book help to develop the sociological imagination

CHAPTER 2 Sociological Research

- Excerpt from *Streetwise* by Elijah Anderson
- Global box on a study of China's "sent-down" policy
- Gun control case study (with figure) to illustrate scientific method
- Section on qualitative and quantitative research and ethnography
- Field experiment study of police action in domestic assault cases
- Discussion of effects of race and gender in conducting research
- Section on how technological advances have affected sociological research

CHAPTER 3 Culture

- Excerpt from *Nacirema* by Horace Miner
- Discussion of role of technology in cultural diffusion
- Discussion of "McDonaldization of society"
- Section on nonverbal communication
- Media box on rock music as a social problem
- Illustration of pickpocket argot
- Example of culture shock on Navajo reservation
- Research box on dominant ideology of poverty in the United States
- Social policy section on bilingualism.

CHAPTER 4 Socialization

- Excerpt from *Peer Power* by Patricia A. Adler and Peter Adler
- Additional examples of twin studies
- Box on raising Amish children
- Discussion of Dionne quintuplets as example of total institutionalization
- Media box on television as a worldwide agent of socialization
- Coverage of peer harassment
- Discussion of impact of Internet and other forms of technology on socialization
- Cross-cultural examples added to social policy section on child care

CHAPTER 5 Social Interaction and Social Structure

- Excerpt from Philip Zimbardo's prison study
- Section on role strain
- Discussion of online groups and role of technology in networking
- Research box on women's social networks
- Discussion of gender/occupational role conflict
- Global aspects of AIDS crisis added to social policy section
- Discussion of how taking medication for HIV affects social interaction

CHAPTER 6 Groups and Organizations

- Excerpt from *The McDonaldization of Society* (New Century Edition) by George Ritzer
- Discussion of teenage in-group/out-group conflicts, including Columbine High School tragedy
- Expanded discussion of coalitions (including transracial community organizations and the anti-tobacco coalition)
- Research box on pizza delivery employees as a secondary group
- Global box on how formal organizations differ according to cultural setting
- Section on technology's impact on the workplace, including trend toward the virtual office

CHAPTER 7 Deviance and Social Control

- Excerpt from *The Boiler Room and Other Telephone Sales Scams* by Robert J. Stevenson
- Box on binge drinking in college
- Media box on TV crime coverage
- Section on social stigma
- Section on deviance and technology, with figure on digital piracy
- Feminist view of crime statistics
- Social policy section on the death penalty worldwide, with a global map

CHAPTER 8 Stratification and Social Mobility in the United States

- Excerpt from *No Shame in My Game* by Katherine S. Newman
- Media box on social class representation in the movie *Titanic*
- Section on Lenski's view of stratification
- Research box on William Julius Wilson's study of urban poverty

- Comparison of CEOs' salaries around the world
- Discussion of monetary value of women's unpaid labor
- Discussion of the "digital divide" among haves and have-nots
- Social policy section on welfare reform in North America and Europe

CHAPTER 9 Social Inequality Worldwide

- Excerpt from *Nike Culture* by Robert Goldman and Stephen Papson
- Discussion of student anti-sweatshop movement
- Expanded and updated account of status of women in Mexico, including charges of sexual harassment in U.S.-owned companies
- Description of Human Rights Index, with figure
- Table comparing multinational corporations revenues with entire countries' GNPs

CHAPTER 10 Racial and Ethnic Inequality

- Excerpt from article "Of Race and Risk" by Patricia J. Williams
- Media box on diversity issues in network TV
- Expanded discussion of hate groups, including Internet sites and map showing state policies
- Expanded discussion of institutional discrimination, including racial divide in computer technology and affirmative action
- Illustration of changing race and ethnicity in USA from 1500–2050
- Global map of major migration patterns in 1990s

CHAPTER 11 Stratification by Gender

- Excerpt from *The Beauty Myth* by Naomi Wolf
- Feminist perspective on gender stratification
- Expanded discussion of gender differences in meeting family obligations
- Research box on female hockey players and male nurses
- Comparison of women's labor force participation around the world
- Global box on the symbolism of the head scarf and veil in Islamic society
- Discussion of status of feminism today

CHAPTER 12 Stratification by Age

- Excerpt from "Wishing For Maybes" by Nancy Moser in *Generation to Generation*, by Sandra Martz and Shirley Coe, eds.

- Discussion of importance of networks in lives of older people
- New table summarizing theories of aging
- Research box on cumulative disadvantage theory
- Media box on televised physician-assisted suicide
- Section on "sandwich generation"

CHAPTER 13 The Family and Intimate Relationships

- Excerpt from *The War Against Parents* by Sylvia Ann Hewlett and Cornel West
- Focus on "intimate relationships" as well as "family"
- Media box on TV portrayal of family life
- Discussion of dating and love relationships on campus
- Section on interactionist view of family
- Global box on domestic violence
- Section on stepfamilies
- Expanded discussion of single-parent families, with new material on single fathers
- Research box on role of grandparents in times of divorce
- Update on cohabitation studies
- Social policy section on reproductive technology and the ethical and legal issues it raises

CHAPTER 14 Religion

- Excerpt from *For This Land* by Vine Deloria Jr.
- Separate chapter on religion
- Case studies of religious cults (the Aum in Japan and Falun Gong in China)
- Discussion of religion's role in providing social services
- Impact of the Internet on religion
- Research box on "doing religion"
- Global box on the rise of the megachurch

CHAPTER 15 Education

- Excerpt from *Savage Inequalities* by Jonathan Kozol
- Separate chapter on education
- Section on social control in schools
- Impact of taking courses on the Internet
- Global box on schooling in Vietnam
- Section on home schooling
- Section on adult education
- Social policy section on school choice

CHAPTER 16 Government

- Excerpt from *Diversity in the Power Elite* by Richard L. Zweigenhaft and G. William Domhoff
- Separate chapter on government
- Discussion of inroads of capitalism in communist countries
- Media box on political activism on the Internet
- Discussion of media differences in coverage of female vs. male political candidates
- Research box on why young people do not vote
- Discussion (illustrated by a figure) of influence of tobacco money on legislation
- Social policy section on campaign financing

CHAPTER 17 The Economy and Work

- Excerpt from *The End of Work* by Jeremy Rifkin
- Separate chapter on the economy and work
- Discussion of technology's impact in the workplace
- Media box on portrayal of the working classes
- Section on occupations and professions
- Discussion of Marx's work on alienation
- Section on the changing workforce
- Global box on the mismatch of jobs and skills worldwide
- Discussion of affirmative action in South Africa

CHAPTER 18 Health and Medicine

- Excerpt from *The Scalpel and the Silver Bear* by Dr. Lori Arviso Alvord
- Coverage of the concept of "zero health disparities"
- Global box on organ donation in Japan
- Expanded coverage of mental illness
- Discussion of the link between class and health in the workplace
- Social policy section on financing health care worldwide

CHAPTER 19 Communities and Urbanization

- Excerpt from *The Celebration Chronicles* by Andrew Ross
- Case study of technology in Blacksburg, VA
- Overview of major influences on cities in the past and predictions about future changes
- Global box on squatter settlements
- Social policy section on homelessness worldwide

CHAPTER 20 Population and the Environment

- Excerpt from *A New Species of Trouble* by Kai Erikson
- Global box on China's one-child policy
- Discussion of Iran's new family planning policies
- Discussion of sampling techniques in the 2000 census
- Section on environmental justice
- Impact of AIDS on Africa

CHAPTER 21 Collective Behavior and Social Movements

- Excerpt from *Urban Legends* by Richard Roeper
- Media box on virtual social movements on the Internet
- New section on the spillover effects of social movements
- Section on the impact of technology on collective behavior

CHAPTER 22 Social Change and Technology

- Excerpt from *The Nudist on the Late Shift* by Po Bronson
- Section on global social change today (with analysis of the Soviet collapse)
- A look at "chaos theory"
- Expanded discussion of the Internet, and utilization differences by race
- Global box on "global disconnect" in Internet technology
- World map of distribution of Internet hosts
- Discussion of opposition to genetically modified food
- Social policy section, revamped with global emphasis, on privacy and censorship in a technological age

● Support for Instructors

PRINT RESOURCES

Annotated Instructor's Edition

An annotated instructor's edition (AIE) of the text, prepared by Mark Kassop of Bergen Community College in New Jersey, offers page-by-page annotations to assist instructors in using textbook material. These include several categories: Let's Discuss (ideas for classroom discussion); Student Alerts (which anticipate common student misconceptions); Policy Pointers (which show tie-ins between important concepts and social policy applications); Theory (examples of the application of the functionalist, conflict, interactionist, and labeling perspectives); Methods (examples of the use of surveys, observation, experiments, and existing sources); Global View (examples of cross-cultural material); Race/Ethnicity (material on racial and ethnic minorities in the United States); Gender (material on women, men, and gender issues); and Contemporary Culture (examples of popular culture).

Instructor's Resource Manual

This manual, prepared by Richard T. Schaefer and Mark Kassop, provides sociology instructors with detailed key points, additional lecture ideas (among them alternative social policy issues), class discussion topics, essay questions, topics for student research (along with suggested research materials for each topic), and suggested additional readings (unlike those in the text itself, these are meant for instructors rather than students). Media materials are suggested for each chapter, including videotapes and films.

Two Test Banks

The two test banks that accompany the text were written by Mark Kassop. In addition to short-answer questions, multiple-choice questions and essay questions are included for each chapter; they will be useful in testing students on basic sociological concepts, application of theoretical perspectives, and recall of important factual information. Correct answers and page references are provided for all multiple-choice questions.

In addition to the printed format, the test banks are available on disk and on CD-ROM for computerized test construction.

Sociology Update

The newsletter *Sociology Update,* written by Richard T. Schaefer, has been a unique supplementary feature since the first edition. This newsletter is projected to come out semiannually in January and September. It is intended primarily for instructors but may be photocopied for students. *Sociology Update* will provide the most recent data, research findings, and public policy developments useful in updating text discussions. It is available both in print and on the book's web page.

Primis Customized Readers

An array of first-rate readings are available to adopters in a customized electronic database. Some are classic articles from the sociological literature; others are provocative pieces written especially for McGraw-Hill by leading sociologists.

Internet Guide

A guide to sociology surfing on the Internet assists students in using the many dimensions and services of the World Wide Web.

Dushkin/McGraw-Hill

Any of the Dushkin publications can be packaged with this text at a discount: Annual Editions, Taking Sides, Sources, Global Studies. For more information, please visit the website at **http://www.dushkin.com.**

DIGITAL RESOURCES

PageOut: The Course Website Development Center

PageOut was designed for the professor just beginning to explore web options. In less than an hour, even the novice computer user can create a course website with a template provided by McGraw-Hill (no programming knowledge required). PageOut lets you offer your students instant access to your syllabus, lecture notes, and original material. Students can even check their grades online. And, you can pull any of the McGraw-Hill content from the Schaefer website and Online Learning Center into your website. PageOut also provides a discussion board where you and your students can exchange questions and post announcements, as well as an area for students to build personal web pages.

To find out more about PageOut: The Course Website Development Center, ask your McGraw-Hill representative for details, or fill out the form at **www.mhhe.com/pageout.**

Online Learning Center Website

Instructors (and students) are invited to visit the book's Online Learning Center, the text-specific website, at **www.mhhe.com/schaefer.** Here you and your students will find an extensive variety of resources and activities, including quizzes, key terms, chapter overviews, learning objec-

tives, PowerPoint slides, and more. It's also possible to link directly to Internet sites from the Online Learning Center. And, you can use any of the material from the Online Learning Center in a course website that you create using PageOut. An icon appears in the boxes, policy sections, and Internet Connection exercises throughout the text, reminding students and instructors to visit the Online Learning Center home page for current material and activities relating to these popular sections.

PowerWeb

Offered free with the text, PowerWeb is a turnkey solution for adding the Internet to a course. PowerWeb is a password-protected website developed by Dushkin/McGraw-Hill, which offers instructors (and students):

- Course-specific materials
- Refereed course-specific web links and articles
- Student study tools—quizzing, review forms, time management tools, web research
- Interactive exercises
- Weekly updates with assessment
- Informative and timely world news
- Access to Northern Light Research Engine (received multiple Editor's Choice awards for superior capabilities from *PC Magazine*)
- Material on how to conduct web research
- Message board for instructors
- Daily news feed of topic-specific news

For further information, visit the PowerWeb website at **http://mhhe/NewMedia/dushkin/index.html#powerweb.**

PowerPoint Slides

Adopters of *Sociology* can also receive a set of 140 color PowerPoint slides, especially developed for this edition by Richard T. Schaefer. These slides include figures, tables, and maps drawn from academic and governmental sources, a few of which reproduce material from the textbook. Instructors are welcome to generate overhead transparencies from the slides if they wish to do so.

Presentation Manager

This CD-ROM includes the contents of the instructor's resource manual, test banks, PowerPoint slides, and more for instructors' convenience in customizing multimedia lectures.

SocCity

SocCity is a veritable melting pot of sociology cyber-sources, information, and Internet activities for students and instructors alike. Just click on any of the four buttons on the left side of your screen and get started (**www.mhhe.com/socscience/sociology**).

Annual Editions Online

Annual Editions Online offers online access to a wide range of current, carefully selected articles from the Dushkin/McGraw-Hill Annual Editions series. Each online article is supported with a built-in assessment in the form of online quizzes, article review forms, and well-researched Internet links of interest. An instructor's resource guide with testing suggestions for each volume is available to qualified instructors.

VIDEO RESOURCES

McGraw-Hill offers adopters a variety of videotapes that are suitable for classroom use in conjunction with the textbook.

Support for Students

Making the Grade

This CD-ROM, packaged free with the text, provides students with an excellent resource that offers enrichment, review, and self-testing. The following components are included:

- Internet primer
- Study skills primer
- Guide to electronic research
- 20 multiple-choice questions per chapter that are graded automatically
- Learning assessment
- Link to the book's website

Online Learning Center Website

Students (and instructors) are invited to visit the book's Online Learning Center, the text-specific website, at **www.mhhe.com/schaefer**. Here you will find an extensive variety of resources and activities, including quizzes, key terms, chapter overviews, learning objectives, PowerPoint slides, and more. It's also possible to link directly to Internet sites from the Online Learning Center. An icon appears in the boxes, policy sections, and Internet Connection exercises throughout the text, remind-

ing students and instructors to visit the Online Learning Center home page for current material and activities relating to these popular sections.

PowerWeb

Offered free with the text, PowerWeb is a password-protected website developed by Dushkin/McGraw-Hill, giving students:

- Web links and articles
- Study tools—quizzing, review forms, time management tools, web research
- Interactive exercises
- Weekly updates with assessment
- Informative and timely world news
- Access to Northern Light Research Engine (received multiple Editor's Choice awards for superior capabilities from *PC Magazine*)
- Material on how to conduct web research
- Daily news feed of topic-specific news

Student's Guide

The student's guide includes standard features such as detailed key points, definitions of key terms, multiple-choice questions, fill-in questions, and true–false questions. Some chapters include a "Name that sociologist" section. Perhaps the most distinctive feature is the social policy exercise, which is closely tied to the social policy section in the text. All study guide questions are keyed to specific pages in the textbook, and page references are provided for key points and definitions of key terms.

Acknowledgments

Virginia Joyner and Elizabeth Morgan collaborated with me on the seventh edition, bringing fresh insight into presenting the sociological imagination. Robert P. Lamm had been part of all the previous comprehensive editions of *Sociology*, and his contributions are still apparent.

I deeply appreciate the contributions to this book made by my editors. Rhona Robbin, a senior development editor at McGraw-Hill, has continually and successfully challenged me to make each edition better than its predecessor.

I have recieved strong support and encouragement from Phillip Butcher, editorial director; Sally Constable, sponsoring editor; and Leslie Kraham, marketing manager. Additional guidance and support were provided by Kate Purcell, editorial assistant; Amy Hill and Kimberly Hooker, project managers; Laurie Entringer, designer;

Elyse Rieder, photo editor; and Elsa Peterson and Judy Broder, permissions editors, who also assisted in obtaining the poster art. I would also like to express appreciation to Karen Nelson for assistance in preparing the reference list.

I would also like to acknowledge the contributions of the following individiduals: Mark Kassop of Bergen Community College in New Jersey for his work on the instructor's resource manual, student's guide, and test banks, as well as the annotations that appear in the annotated instructor's edition; Kenrick Thompson of Arkansas State University for preparing the test items for the *Making the Grade* CD-ROM that is packaged with each copy of the text; and John Tenuto of the College of Lake County in Illinois for developing the Internet exercises in the text and for his contributions to the annotated instructor's edition.

As is evident from these acknowledgments, the preparation of a textbook is truly a team effort. The most valuable member of this effort continues to be my wife, Sandy. She provides the support so necessary in my creative and scholarly activities.

I have had the good fortune to be able to introduce students to sociology for many years. These students have been enormously helpful in spurring on my own sociological imagination. In ways I can fully appreciate but cannot fully acknowledge, their questions in class and queries in the hallway have found their way into this textbook.

Richard T. Schaefer
schaeferrt@aol.com

As a full-service publisher of quality educational products, McGraw-Hill does much more than just sell textbooks to your students. We create and publish an extensive array of print, video, and digital supplements to support instruction on your campus. Orders of new (versus used) textbooks help us to defray the cost of developing such supplements, which is substantial. Please consult your local McGraw-Hill representative to learn about the availability of the supplements that accompany Sociology. If you are not sure who your representative is, you can find him or her by using the Rep Locator at www.mhhe.com.

Academic Reviewers

This edition continues to reflect many insightful suggestions made by reviewers of the first six hardcover editions and the three paperback brief editions. The current edition has benefited from constructive and thorough evaluations provided by sociologists from both two-year and four-year institutions.

Jan AbuShakrah
Portland Community College

Patti Adler
University of Colorado

Cynthia D. Anderson
Iowa State University

Therese Baker
California State University, San Marcos

Chet Ballard
Valdosta State University

Judith Barker
Ithaca College

John W. Bedell
California State University, Fullerton

Kathleen Bennet DeMarrais
Northern Arizona University

Mary Bernstein
Arizona State University

H. B. (Keo) Cavalcanti
University of Richmond

Larry Clarke
Shoreline Community College

Linda Cook
Houston Community College

Ione Y. DeOllos
Ball State University

Jan Fiola
Moorhead State University

Michael Goslin
Tallahassee Community College

Lillian O. Holloman
Prince George's Community College

Mark Kassop
Bergen Community College

Janet Kroon
University of South Dakota

David R. Maines
Oakland University

Rebecca Matthews
University of Iowa

Peter Meiksins
Cleveland State University

Kenneth J. Mietus
Western Illinois University

Joel I. Nelson
University of Minnesota

Timothy J. Owens
Purdue University

Pete A. Padilla
Arizona State University

Earl Piercy
Trukee Meadows Community College

Diane Pike
Augsburg College

Ferris J. Ritchey
University of Alabama, Birmingham

Nathan Rousseau
Muskingum College

Jon Schlenker
University of Maine, Augusta

Kerry Strand
Hood College

John Tenuto
College of Lake County

Jacquelyn Troup
Cerritos College

Steven Vassar
Minnesota State University

Gina Walls
Parkland Community College

Elaine Wethington
Cornell University

Eric R. Wright
Indiana University-Purdue University, Indianapolis

Stephen Zehr
University of Southern Indiana

A Visual Preview of the Seventh Edition

The seventh edition of *Sociology* continues its tradition of teaching students how to think critically about society and their own lives from a wide range of classical and contemporary sociological perspectives.

New Intriguing Chapter Openers

Chapter openers convey the excitement and relevance of sociological inquiry by means of lively excerpts from writings of sociologists and others who explore sociological topics.

Helpful Chapter Overviews

Chapter overviews provide a bridge between the chapter-opening excerpt and the content of the chapter.

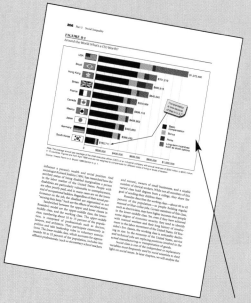

New Provocative Chapter-Opening Art

Each chapter opens with a reproduction of a poster or piece of graphic art that illustrates a key theme or concept of the chapter. Accompanying captions help readers grasp the relevance of the artwork to the chapter.

New Innovative "Sticker" Captions

Captions within figures draw attention to major points in the graphs.

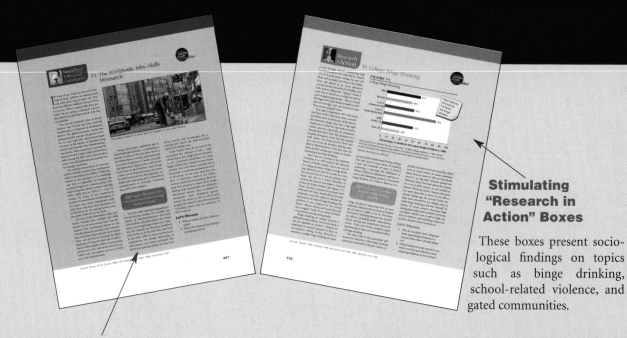

Stimulating "Research in Action" Boxes

These boxes present sociological findings on topics such as binge drinking, school-related violence, and gated communities.

Timely "Sociology in the Global Community" Boxes

These boxes provide a global perspective on topics such as disability as a master status, slavery in the twenty-first century, and police power in Japan.

New Motivational "Taking Sociology to Work" Interviews

"Taking Sociology to Work" boxes profile individuals who majored in sociology and use its principles in their work.

New Thought-Provoking Eye on the Media Boxes

These sections illustrate how the media affect—and are affected by—social trends and events. Topics featured in these boxes include constructing rock music as a social problem, the lack of diversity on network television, and political activism on the Internet.

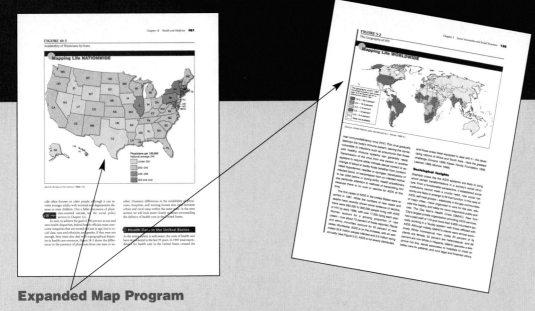

Expanded Map Program

Two kinds of maps—"Mapping Life Nationwide" and "Mapping Life Worldwide"—are featured throughout the text. A map of the world at the beginning of the book shows readers the countries referenced in the text.

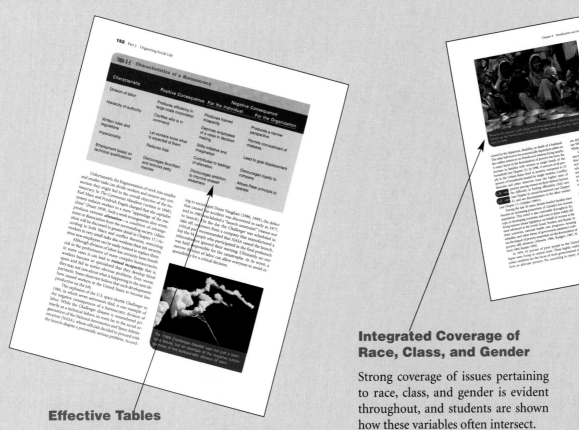

Effective Tables

Easy-to-read tables present the latest findings and summarize important concepts.

Integrated Coverage of Race, Class, and Gender

Strong coverage of issues pertaining to race, class, and gender is evident throughout, and students are shown how these variables often intersect.

Distinctive Social Policy Sections

These discussions, 10 of which are new to this edition, provide a socio-logical perspective on contemporary social issues such as welfare reform, immigration, and affirmative action. In this edition, these sections provide a global view of the issues and are organized around a consistent heading structure to make the material more accessible.

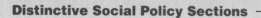

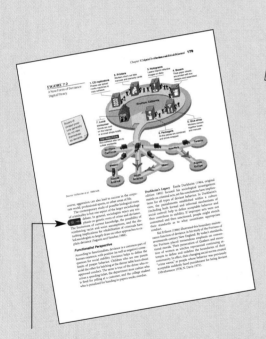

New Helpful Cross-Reference System

Key concepts that have been introduced at an earlier point in the text are highlighted with an icon that includes a page number for review purposes.

New Internet Connection Exercises

Two exercises at the end of each chapter take students online to analyze social issues relevant to chapter content. Web icons featured throughout the book signal that related information and exercises are on the book's website.

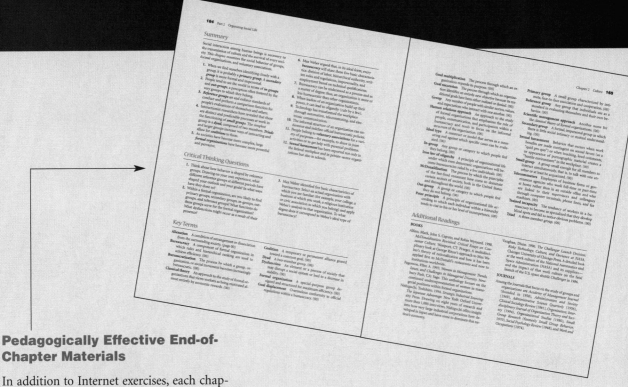

Pedagogically Effective End-of-Chapter Materials

In addition to Internet exercises, each chapter concludes with a point-by-point summary, glossary of key terms with page references, critical thinking questions, and suggested readings.

Practical Career Guide

"Careers in Sociology" appears as an appendix at the end of Chapter 1 and provides a glimpse of the opportunities available to those with degrees in sociology.

xxxvii

A Wealth of Media Resources

New SocCity Website

SocCity is a veritable melting pot of sociology cybersources, information, and Internet activities for students and instructors (**www.mhhe.com/socscience/sociology**). Just click on any of the four buttons on the left side of your screen to get started!

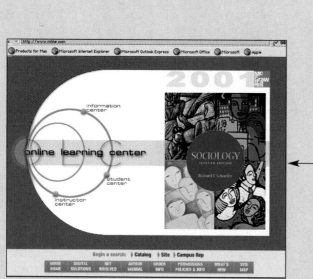

New Making the Grade

This CD-ROM, packaged free with the text, provides students with an excellent resource that offers enrichment, review, and self-testing.

New Online Learning Center

The Online Learning Center is a text-specific website (**www.mhhe.com/schaefer**) that offers students and professors a variety of resources and activities. Material from this website can be used in creating the PageOut website.

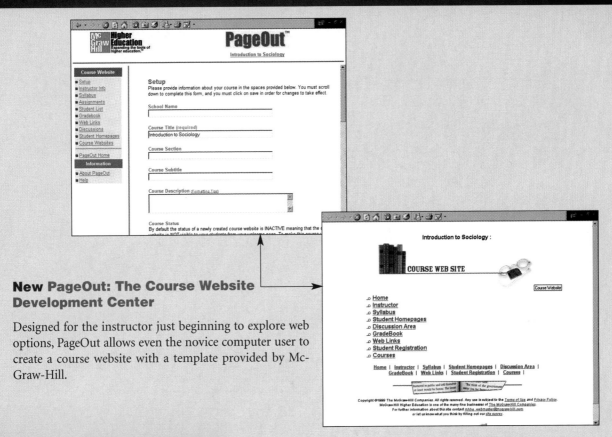

New PageOut: The Course Website Development Center

Designed for the instructor just beginning to explore web options, PageOut allows even the novice computer user to create a course website with a template provided by McGraw-Hill.

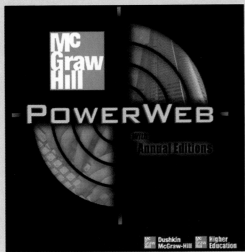

New PowerWeb

Offered free with the text, PowerWeb is a turnkey solution for adding the Internet to a course. A password-protected website developed by Dushkin/McGraw-Hill, PowerWeb offers instructors and students course-specific materials, Web links and articles, student study tools, and more.

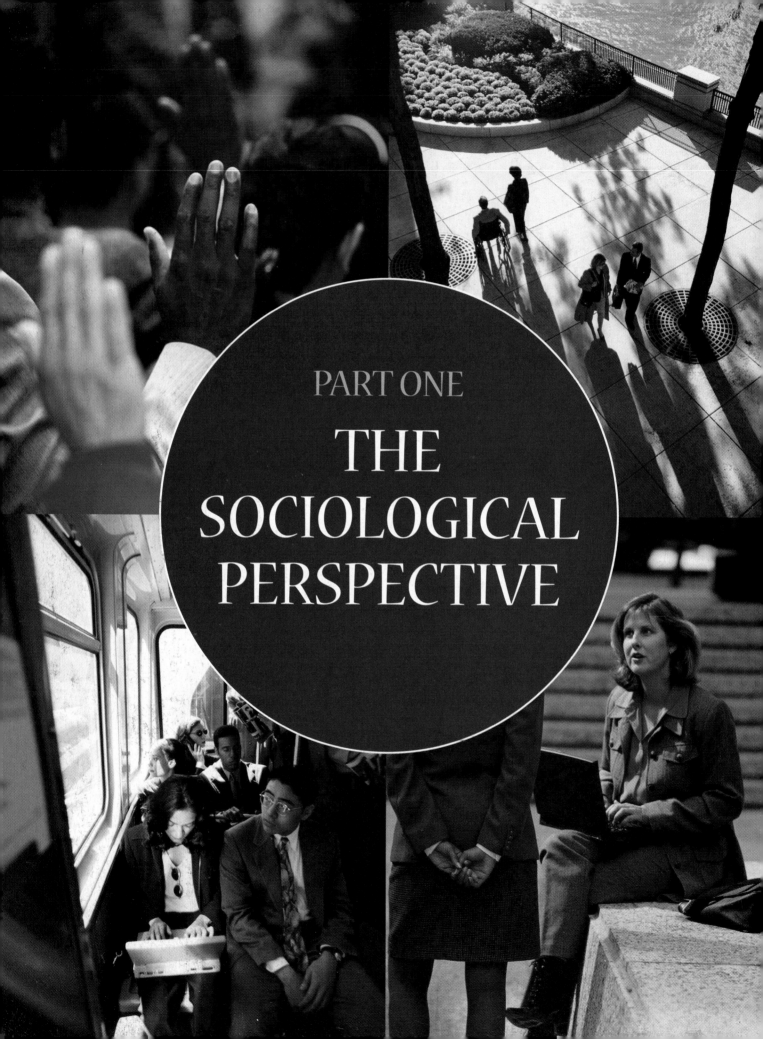

PART ONE

THE SOCIOLOGICAL PERSPECTIVE

Part One introduces the fundamental theories and research methods used by sociologists and other social scientists to understand social behavior. Chapter 1 defines the sociological imagination; compares sociology with other social sciences; discusses the origins and founders of sociology; and presents the functionalist, conflict, and interactionist approaches that will be utilized throughout the book. Chapter 2 outlines the basic principles and steps of the scientific method, examines the methods through which sociologists generate data for their research, and explores the ethical issues that sociologists face as they study human behavior. These discussions of sociological theory and research provide the foundation for our study of the organization of social life (Part Two), social inequality (Part Three), social institutions (Part Four), and social change (Part Five).

UNDERSTANDING SOCIOLOGY

UNGNDOMS-
FESTIVALEN
8–10. JULI
6–8. JULI

SEMINARHOLDERE:
KEN HENDERSON
EGIL SVARTDAHL
MIKAEL HOLTER
KARL INGE TANGEN
TOM AUNE
SANG I MØTENE;
LOVSANGSTEAM FRA
FILADELFIA SARPSBORG

BALSAM, BETANICA
TALERE: MAL FLETCHER
TOM ERLANDSEN
MØTESANG: AGAPE

FELLESDAGER
10–12. JULI
TALERE:
MAL FLETCHER
EGIL SVARTDAHL

PINSEVENNENES
SOMMERSTEVNE
13–17 JULI
TALERE:
EGIL SVARTDAHL
TOM ERLANDSEN

Sociology places us in the context of groups, cultures, and societies. We interact with others both in relatively formal environments like the workplace and in more informal settings such as the youth festival promoted in this poster from Norway.

first walked into the Blue Mosque in the spring of 1996, when I came to accompany a friend getting her first tattoo. Before entering the clean, comfortable, and friendly shop, I had never thought about getting permanent body art myself. In fact, I had specifically promised my family that I would never become tattooed. After watching my friend go through the experience, I changed my mind and began wondering what forms of body modification I could sport myself. The shop's congenial atmosphere made it easy to return several times while choosing my own piercings and eventually my own tattoo. During my visits, I formed friendships with all the artists, and started dating and eventually married the shop's owner, Lefty. Our home became a stopping ground for tattooists traveling through town and a social center for the shop. . . .

My tattoo recreational life became a research interest after Lefty and I took a vacation to California. Renting a car and roaming the California coastline, we visited a score of tattoo shops, talked about the meaning of tattoos in society, and noted the many changes taking place in the tattoo industry. At the end of one of these conversations, Lefty mentioned that someone should do a study chronicling these changes. As a graduate student in Sociology looking for a dissertation topic, I quickly stepped up to the research task and Lefty willingly assumed the responsibility of key informant. . . .

As a tattooist's wife and a shop regular, I gained a unique view of this social world. Over the two-year participant observation study, I visited the shop between one hundred to two hundred times and was present during thousands of conversations between the tattoo artists at home and at social occasions. . . .

While at home and during social functions, I focused on the social world of professional tattooists while listening to daily conversations regarding their interactions with clients, their hopes, their frustrations, and their goals. The first time tattooees at the Blue Mosque were a unique set made up equally of men and women, ranging in age (18–60) more than heavily tattooed clients of the shop, and were more likely to be middle or upper middle class. My observations reflect the largely conventional, middle class experience of getting a first tattoo *(Irwin 1999a).* ■

What makes tattooing an appropriate subject for study in sociology? Uniting all sociological studies is their focus on *patterns* of human behavior. Katherine Irwin's tattoo research, for example, tracked the dramatic change in what it meant to get a tattoo in the 1990s, as opposed to earlier periods, when tattooing was primarily associated with fringe groups like biker gangs, punk rockers, and skinheads. Tattoo clients of the 1990s, Irwin found, increasingly fit the image of avant-garde or hip individuals, seeking to make a statement about their identities but not to cut themselves off from mainstream society. By continuing to interact with that society, whether as students, or employees, or just members of conventional families, they were in fact making tattooing appear less unconventional. The tattoo has gradually become a badge of trendy social status, instead of a symbol of outcast status (Irwin 1998, 1999b).

Sociologists are not concerned with what one individual does or does not do, but with what people do as members of a group or interacting with one another, and what that means for the individuals and for society as a whole. Tattooing is, in fact, a subject that sociologists can study in any number of ways. They might examine its history (going back as far as 30,000 years) or its use in different groups and cultures. One study, for example, specifically looks at how the tattoos of prison gang members communicate their status, rank, and personal accomplishments (Mascia-Lees and Sharpe 1992; Phelan and Hunt 1998).

As a field of study, then, sociology is extremely broad in scope. You will see throughout this book the range of topics sociologists investigate—from suicide to TV viewing habits, from Amish society to global economic patterns, from peer pressure to pickpocketing techniques. Sociology looks at how others influence our behavior as well as how major social institutions like the government, religion, and the economy affect us.

This chapter will explore the nature of sociology as a field of inquiry and an exercise of the "sociological imagination." We'll look at the discipline as a science and consider its relationship to other social sciences. We will evaluate the contributions of three pioneering thinkers—Émile Durkheim, Max Weber, and Karl Marx—to the development of sociology. Next we will discuss a number of important theoretical perspectives used by sociologists, and then we'll examine practical applications of the discipline for human behavior and organizations. Finally, we will consider the ways sociology helps us to develop our sociological imagination. ■

What Is Sociology?

Sociology is the systematic study of social behavior and human groups. It focuses primarily on the influence of social relationships on people's attitudes and behavior and on how societies are established and change. This textbook deals with such varied topics as families, the workplace, street gangs, business firms, political parties, genetic engineering, schools, religions, and labor unions. It is concerned with love, poverty, conformity, discrimination, illness, technology, and community.

The Sociological Imagination

In attempting to understand social behavior, sociologists rely on an unusual type of creative thinking. C. Wright Mills (1959) described such thinking as the *sociological imagination*—an awareness of the relationship between an individual and the wider society. This awareness allows all of us (not just sociologists) to comprehend the links between our immediate, personal social settings and the remote, impersonal social world that surrounds us and helps to shape us.

A key element in the sociological imagination is the ability to view one's own society as an outsider would, rather than only from the perspective of personal experiences and cultural biases. Consider something as simple as the practice of eating while walking. In the United States we think nothing of seeing people consuming ice cream cones or sodas or candy bars as they walk along. Sociologists would see this as a pattern of acceptable behavior because others regard it as acceptable. Yet sociologists need to go beyond one culture to place the practice in perspective. This "normal" behavior is quite unacceptable elsewhere. For example, in Japan people do not eat while walking. Streetside sellers and vending machines dispense food everywhere, but the Japanese will stop to eat or drink whatever they buy before they continue on their way. In their eyes, to engage in another activity while eating shows disrespect for the food preparation, even if the food comes out of a vending machine.

The sociological imagination allows us to go beyond personal experiences and observations to understand broader public issues. Unemployment, for example, is unquestionably a personal hardship for a man or woman without a job. However, C. Wright Mills pointed out that

Do you consider talking on a cell phone while driving "normal" behavior? Some cultural practices are so new that their acceptability in a society is still being determined.

when unemployment is a social problem shared by millions of people, it is appropriate to question the way that a society is structured or organized. Similarly, Mills advocated using the sociological imagination to view divorce not simply as the personal problem of a particular man or woman, but rather as a societal problem, since it is the outcome of many marriages. And he was writing this in the 1950s, when the divorce rate was but a fraction of what it is today (I. Horowitz 1983).

Sociological imagination can bring new understanding to daily life around us. Since 1992, sociologists David Miller and Richard Schaefer (this textbook's author) have studied the food bank system of the United States, which distributes food to hungry individuals and families. On the face of it, food banks seem above reproach. After all, as Miller and Schaefer learned in their research, more than one out of four children in the United States are hungry. One-third of the nation's homeless people report eating one meal per day or less. What could be wrong with charities redistributing to pantries and shelters food that just a decade ago was destined for landfills? In 1997, for example, Second Harvest, a food distribution organization, distributed one billion pounds of food from hundreds of individual and corporate donors to more than 50,000 food pantries, soup kitchens, and social service agencies.

Many observers would uncritically applaud the distribution of tons of food to the needy. But let's look deeper. While supportive of and personally involved in such efforts, Miller and Schaefer (1993) have drawn on the sociological imagination to offer a more probing view of these activities. They note that powerful forces in our

society—such as the federal government, major food retailers, and other large corporations—have joined in charitable food distribution arrangements. Perhaps as a result, the focus of such relief programs is too restricted. The homeless are to be fed, not housed; the unemployed are to be given meals, not jobs. Relief efforts assist hungry individuals and families without challenging the existing social order (for example, by demanding a redistribution of wealth). Of course, without these limited successes in distributing food, starving people might assault patrons of restaurants, loot grocery stores, or literally die of starvation on the steps of city halls and across from the White House. Such critical thinking is typical of sociologists, as they draw on the sociological imagination to study a social issue—in this case, hunger in the United States (Second Harvest 1997; Vladimiroff 1998).

Sociology and the Social Sciences

Is sociology a science? The term *science* refers to the body of knowledge obtained by methods based upon systematic observation. Just like other scientific disciplines, sociology engages in organized, systematic study of phenomena (in this case, human behavior) in order to enhance understanding. All scientists, whether studying mushrooms or murderers, attempt to collect precise information through methods of study that are as objective as possible. They rely on careful recording of observations and accumulation of data.

Feeding the homeless seems entirely benevolent, but if we look deeper into this charitable action we might conclude that its focus is too narrow. The homeless also need shelter; the unemployed need jobs. Exercising the sociological imagination enables us to think critically as we examine social issues.

Of course, there is a great difference between sociology and physics, between psychology and astronomy. For this reason, the sciences are commonly divided into natural and social sciences. **Natural science** is the study of the physical features of nature and the ways in which they interact and change. Astronomy, biology, chemistry, geology, and physics are all natural sciences. **Social science** is the study of various aspects of human society. The social sciences include sociology, anthropology, economics, history, psychology, and political science.

These academic disciplines have a common focus on the social behavior of people, yet each has a particular orientation. Anthropologists usually study past cultures and preindustrial societies that continue today, as well as the origins of men and women; this knowledge is used to examine contemporary societies, including even industrial societies. Economists explore the ways in which people produce and exchange goods and services, along with money and other resources. Historians are concerned with the peoples and events of the past and their significance for us today. Political scientists study international relations, the workings of government, and the exercise of power and authority. Psychologists investigate personality and individual behavior. So what does sociology focus on? It emphasizes the influence that society has on people's attitudes and behavior and the ways in which people shape society. Humans are social animals; therefore, sociologists scientifically examine our social relationships with people.

Let's consider how the different social sciences might approach the hotly debated issue of handgun control.

Interest in guns passes easily from parent to child, as this photo illustrates. Sociologists are curious about such things as how people learn to use guns, what types of people use them, and how gun use in one country compares with that in another.

Table 1-1	Gun Ownership in the United States	
Sex		
Men	47%	
Women	27	
Race		
Whites	40%	
Non-Whites	19	
Age		
18–29	28%	
30–49	37	
50–64	46	
65+	36	
Region		
South	46%	
Midwest	39	
East	29	
West	33	

Note: Based on a national survey February 1999.
Source: Gallup Poll in M. Gillespie 1999.

Many people today, concerned about the misuse of firearms in the United States, are calling for restrictions on the purchase and use of handguns. Political scientists would look at the impact of political action groups, such as the National Rifle Association (NRA), on lawmakers. Historians would examine attitudes toward firearms and how guns were used over time in our country and elsewhere. Anthropologists would focus on the use of weapons in a variety of cultures as means of protection as well as symbols of power. Psychologists would look at individual cases and assess the impact handguns have on their owners as well as on individual victims of gunfire. Economists would be interested in how firearm manufacture and sales affect communities. Sociologists would gather data to inform policymakers. For example, they would examine data from different states to evaluate the effect of gun restrictions on the incidence of firearm accidents or violent crimes involving firearms. They might also look at the kind of data shown in Table 1-1, which gives an idea of who owns handguns in the United States. What explanations can be offered for the significant gender, racial, age, and geographic differences in gun ownership? How would these differences affect the formulation of social policy by city, state, and federal governments? Sociologists might also look at data that show how the United States compares to other nations in handgun ownership and use.

Sociologists put their imagination to work in a

variety of areas. Table 1-2 presents a list of the specializations within contemporary sociology. Throughout this textbook, the sociological imagination will be used to examine the United States (and other societies) from the viewpoint of respectful but questioning outsiders.

Sociology and Common Sense

Sociology focuses on the study of human behavior. Yet we all have experience with human behavior and at least some knowledge of it. All of us might well have theories about why people get tattoos, for example, or why people become homeless. Our theories and opinions typically come from "common sense"—that is, from our experiences and conversations, from what we read, from what we see on television, and so forth.

In our daily lives, we rely on common sense to get us through many unfamiliar situations. However, this commonsense knowledge, while sometimes accurate, is not always reliable, because it rests on commonly held beliefs rather than on systematic analysis of facts. It was once considered "common sense" to accept that the earth was flat—a view rightly questioned by Pythagoras and Aristotle. Incorrect commonsense notions are not just a part of the distant past; they remain with us today.

In the United States, "common sense" tells us that an "epidemic" of teen pregnancies accounts for most unwed births today, creating a drag on the welfare system. "Common sense" tells us that people panic when faced with natural disasters, such as floods and earthquakes, or even in the wake of tragedies such as the 1995 Oklahoma City bombing. However, these particular "commonsense" notions—like the notion that the earth is flat—are untrue; neither of them is supported by sociological research. The proportion of unwed mothers in their teens is declining; in fact, women who are not in their teens account for most of the unwed mothers, and they make up an estimated 93 percent of women on welfare. (Luker 1996, 1999). Disasters do not generally produce panic. In the aftermath of disasters and even explosions, greater social organization and structure emerge to deal with a community's problems. In the United States, for example, an emergency "operations group" often coordinates public services and even certain services normally performed by the private sector, such as food distribution. Decision making becomes more centralized in times of disaster.

Like other social scientists, sociologists do not accept something as a fact because "everyone knows it." Instead, each piece of information must be tested and recorded, then analyzed in relationship to other data. Sociology relies on scientific studies in order to describe and understand a social environment. At times, the findings of sociologists may seem like common sense because they deal

Table 1-2	Specializations within Sociology

Aging/Social Gerontology
Alcohol and Drugs
Applied Sociology/Evaluation Research
Biosociology
Collective Behavior/Social Movements
Community/Rural Sociology
Comparative Historical Sociology
Criminal Justice/Corrections
Criminology/Delinquency
Cultural Sociology
Demography
Development/Social Change
Deviant Behavior/Social Disorganization
Disabilities
Economy and Society
Education
Environmental Sociology
History of Sociology/Social Thought
Human Ecology
Industrial Sociology
Law and Society
Leisure/Sports/Recreation
Marriage and the Family
Mass Communication/Public Opinion
Medical Sociology
Methodology: Qualitative and Quantitative
   Approaches
Migration and Immigration
Occupations/Professions
Political Sociology
Race/Ethnic/Minority Relations
Religion
Sex and Gender
Small Groups
Social Control
Social Networks
Social Organization/Formal/Complex
Social Psychology
Socialization
Sociological Practice/Social Policy
Sociology of Art/Literature
Sociology of Knowledge/Science
Sociology of Language/Social Linguistics
Sociology of Markets
Sociology of Mental Health
Sociology of Work
Stratification/Mobility
Theory
Urban Sociology
Visual Sociology

Source: American Sociological Association 2000.

fective theory may have both explanatory and predictive power. That is, it can help us to develop a broad and integrated view of the relationships among seemingly isolated phenomena as well as to understand how one type of change in an environment leads to others.

Émile Durkheim (1951, original edition 1897) looked into suicide data in great detail and developed a highly original theory about the relationship between suicide and social factors. He was primarily concerned not with the personalities of individual suicide victims, but rather with suicide *rates* and how they varied from country to country. As a result, when he looked at the number of reported suicides in France, England, and Denmark in 1869, he also examined the populations of these nations to determine their rates of suicide. He found that whereas England had only 67 reported suicides per million inhabitants, France had 135 per million and Denmark had 277 per million. The question then became: "Why did Denmark (rather than France) have a comparatively high rate of reported suicides?"

Durkheim went much deeper into his investigation of suicide rates, and the result was his landmark work *Suicide,* published in 1897. Durkheim refused to automatically accept unproven explanations regarding suicide, including the beliefs that cosmic forces or inherited tendencies caused such deaths. Instead, he focused on such problems as the cohesiveness or lack of cohesiveness of religious and occupational groups.

Durkheim's research suggested that suicide, while a solitary act, is related to group life. Protestants had much higher suicide rates than Catholics did; the unmarried had much higher rates than married people did; soldiers were more likely to take their lives than civilians were. In addition, it appeared that there were higher rates of suicide in times of peace than in times of war and revolution, and in times of economic instability and recession rather than in times of prosperity. Durkheim concluded that the suicide rates of a society reflected the extent to which people were or were not integrated into the group life of the society.

Émile Durkheim, like many other social scientists, developed a theory to explain how individual behavior can be understood within a social context. He pointed out the influence of groups and societal forces on what had always been viewed as a highly personal act. Clearly, Durkheim offered a more *scientific* explanation for the causes of suicide than that of sunspots or inherited tendencies. His theory has predictive power, since it suggests that suicide rates will rise or fall in conjunction with certain social and economic changes.

Of course, a theory—even the best of theories—is not a final statement about human behavior. Durkheim's theory of suicide is no exception; sociologists continue to examine factors that contribute to differences in suicide

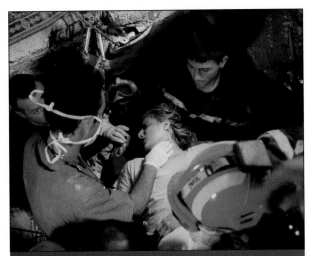

Do disasters produce panic or an organized, structured response? Common sense might tell us the former, but, in fact, disasters bring out a great deal of structure and organization to deal with their aftermath. A French rescue team is pulling this young woman from the rubble caused by a devastating earthquake in Turkey in 1999. Even Greece, Turkey's traditional "enemy," sent relief workers to aid in this disaster. The favor was returned when an earthquake struck Athens later that year.

with facets of everyday life. The difference is that such findings have been *tested* by researchers. Common sense now tells us that the earth is round. But this particular commonsense notion is based on centuries of scientific work upholding the breakthrough made by Pythagoras and Aristotle.

What Is Sociological Theory?

Why do people commit suicide? One traditional commonsense answer is that people inherit the desire to kill themselves. Another view is that sunspots drive people to take their own lives. These explanations may not seem especially convincing to contemporary researchers, but they represent beliefs widely held as recently as 1900.

Sociologists are not particularly interested in why any one individual commits suicide; they are more concerned with the social forces that systematically cause some people to take their own lives. In order to undertake this research, sociologists develop a theory that offers a general explanation of suicidal behavior.

We can think of theories as attempts to explain events, forces, materials, ideas, or behavior in a comprehensive manner. Within sociology, a **theory** is a set of statements that seeks to explain problems, actions, or behavior. An ef-

rates around the world and to a particular society's rate of suicide. For example, although the overall rate of suicide in New Zealand is only marginally higher than in the United States, the suicide rate among young people is 41 percent higher in New Zealand. Sociologists and psychiatrists from that country suggest that their remote, sparsely populated society maintains exaggerated standards of masculinity that are especially difficult for young males. Gay adolescents who fail to conform to their peers' preference for sports are particularly vulnerable to suicide (Shenon 1995b; for a critique of Durkheim's work, see Douglas 1967).

The Development of Sociology

People have always been curious about sociological matters—such as how we get along, what we do, and whom we select as our leaders. Philosophers and religious authorities of ancient and medieval societies made countless observations about human behavior. They did not test or verify these observations scientifically; nevertheless, these observations often became the foundation for moral codes. Several of the early social philosophers predicted that a systematic study of human behavior would one day emerge. Beginning in the nineteenth century, European theorists made pioneering contributions to the development of a science of human behavior.

Early Thinkers: Comte, Martineau, and Spencer

The nineteenth century was an unsettling time for intellectuals in France. The French monarchy had been deposed earlier in the revolution of 1789, and Napoleon had subsequently suffered defeat in his effort to conquer Europe. Amidst this chaos, philosophers considered how society might be improved. Auguste Comte (1798–1857), credited with being the most influential of these philosophers of the early 1800s, believed that a theoretical science of society and systematic investigation of behavior were needed to improve society. He coined the term *sociology* to apply to the science of human behavior.

Writing in the 1800s, Comte feared that the excesses of the French Revolution had permanently impaired France's stability. Yet he hoped that the study of social behavior in a systematic way would eventually lead to more rational human interactions. In Comte's hierarchy of sciences, sociology was at the top. He called it the "queen" and its practitioners "scientist-priests." This French theorist did not simply give sociology its name; he also presented a rather ambitious challenge to the fledgling discipline.

Scholars were able to learn of Comte's works largely through translations by the English sociologist Harriet

Harriet Martineau was an early pioneer of sociology who studied social behavior both in her native England and in the United States.

Martineau (1802–1876). But Martineau was a pathbreaker in her own right as a sociologist. She offered insightful observations of the customs and social practices of both her native Britain and the United States. Martineau's book *Society in America* (1962, original edition 1837) examines religion, politics, child rearing, and immigration in the young nation. Martineau gives special attention to social class distinctions and to such factors as gender and race.

Martineau's writings emphasized the impact that the economy, law, trade, and population could have on the social problems of contemporary society. She spoke out in favor of the rights of women, the emancipation of slaves, and religious tolerance. In Martineau's (1896) view, intellectuals and scholars should not simply offer observations of social conditions; they should act upon their convictions in a manner that will benefit society. In line with this view, Martineau conducted research on the nature of female employment and pointed to the need for further investigation of this important issue (Lengermann and Niebrugge-Brantley 1998).

Another important contributor to the discipline of sociology was Herbert Spencer (1820–1903). A relatively prosperous Victorian Englishman, Spencer (unlike Martineau) did not feel compelled to correct or improve society; instead, he merely hoped to understand it better. Drawing on Charles Darwin's study *On the Origin of Species,* Spencer applied the concept of evolution of the species to societies in order to explain how they change, or evolve, over time. Similarly, he adapted Darwin's evolutionary view of the "survival of the fittest" by arguing that it is "natural" that some people are rich while others are poor.

Spencer's approach to societal change was extremely popular in his own lifetime. Unlike Comte, Spencer suggested that societies are bound to change; therefore, one need not be highly critical of present social arrangements or work actively for social change. This position appealed to many influential people in England and the United States who had a vested interest in the status quo and were suspicious of social thinkers who endorsed change.

Émile Durkheim

Émile Durkheim made many pioneering contributions to sociology, including his important theoretical work on suicide. The son of a rabbi, Durkheim (1858–1917) was educated in both France and Germany. He established an impressive academic reputation and was appointed as one of the first professors of sociology in France. Above all, Durkheim will be remembered for his insistence that behavior must be understood within a larger social context, not just in individualistic terms.

As one example of this emphasis, Durkheim (1947, original edition 1912) developed a fundamental thesis to help understand all forms of society through intensive study of the Arunta, an Australian tribe. He focused on the functions that religion performed for the Arunta and underscored the role that group life plays in defining that which we consider religious. Durkheim concluded that, like other forms of group behavior, religion reinforces a group's solidarity.

Another of Durkheim's main interests was the consequences of work in modern societies. In his view, the growing division of labor found in industrial societies as workers became much more specialized in their tasks led to what he called *anomie.* **Anomie** refers to the loss of direction that a society feels when social control of individual behavior has become ineffective. The state of anomie occurs when people have lost their sense of purpose or direction, often during a time of profound social change. In a period of anomie, people are so confused and unable to cope with the new social environment that they may resort to taking their own lives.

Durkheim was concerned about the dangers that alienation, loneliness, and isolation might pose for modern industrial societies. He shared Comte's belief that sociology should provide direction for social change. As a result, he advocated the creation of new social groups— between the individual's family and the state—which

would ideally provide a sense of belonging for members of huge, impersonal societies.

Like many other sociologists, Durkheim's interests were not limited to one aspect of social behavior. Later in this book, we will consider his thinking on crime and punishment, religion, and the workplace. Few sociologists have had such a dramatic impact on so many different areas within the discipline.

Max Weber

Another important early theorist was Max Weber (pronounced "VAY-ber"). Born in Germany in 1864, Weber took his early academic training in legal and economic history, but he gradually developed an interest in sociology. Eventually, he became a professor at various German universities. Weber taught his students that they should employ **Verstehen,** the German word for "understanding" or "insight," in their intellectual work. He pointed out that we cannot analyze much of our social behavior by the kinds of objective criteria we use to measure weight or temperature. To fully comprehend behavior, we must learn the subjective meanings people attach to their actions—how they themselves view and explain their behavior.

For example, suppose that a sociologist was studying the social ranking of individuals in a fraternity. Weber would expect the researcher to employ *Verstehen* to determine the significance of the fraternity's social hierarchy for its members. The researcher might examine the effects of athleticism or grades or social skills or seniority on standing within the fraternity. He or she would seek to learn how the fraternity members relate to other members of higher or lower status. While investigating these questions, the researcher would take into account people's emotions, thoughts, beliefs, and attitudes (L. Coser 1977).

We also owe credit to Weber for a key conceptual tool: the ideal type. An **ideal type** is a construct, a made-up model that serves as a measuring rod against which actual cases can be evaluated. In his own works, Weber identified various characteristics of bureaucracy as an ideal type (discussed in detail in Chapter 5). In presenting this model of bureaucracy, Weber was not describing any particular business, nor was he using the term *ideal* in a way that suggested a positive evaluation. Instead, his purpose was to provide a useful standard for measuring how bureaucratic an actual organization is (Gerth and Mills 1958). Later in this textbook, we use the concept of ideal type to study the family, religion, authority, and economic systems and to analyze bureaucracy.

Although their professional careers coincided, Émile Durkheim and Max Weber never met and probably were unaware of each other's existence, let alone ideas. This was certainly not true of the work of Karl Marx. Durkheim's thinking about the impact of the division of labor in industrial societies was related to Marx's writings, while Weber's concern for a value-free, objective sociology was a direct response to Marx's deeply held convictions. Thus, it is not surprising that Karl Marx is viewed as a major figure in the development of sociology as well as several other social sciences (see Figure 1-1).

Karl Marx

Karl Marx (1818–1883) shared with Durkheim and Weber a dual interest in abstract philosophical issues and the concrete reality of everyday life. Unlike the others, Marx was so critical of existing institutions that a conventional academic career was impossible, and although he was born and educated in Germany, he spent most of his life in exile.

Marx's personal life was a difficult struggle. When a paper that he had written was suppressed, he fled his native land for France. In Paris, he met Friedrich Engels (1820–1895), with whom he formed a lifelong friendship. They lived at a time when European and North American economic life was increasingly being dominated by the factory rather than the farm.

In 1847, Marx and Engels attended secret meetings in London of an illegal coalition of labor unions, known as the Communist League. The following year, they prepared a platform called *The Communist Manifesto,* in which they argued that the masses of people who have no resources other than their labor (whom they referred to as the *proletariat*) should unite to fight for the overthrow of capitalist societies. In the words of Marx and Engels:

> The history of all hitherto existing society is the history of class struggles. . . . The proletarians have nothing to lose but their chains. They have a world to win. WORKING MEN OF ALL COUNTRIES UNITE! (Feuer 1959:7, 41).

After completing *The Communist Manifesto,* Marx returned to Germany, only to be expelled. He then moved to England, where he continued to write books and essays. Marx lived there in extreme poverty. He pawned most of his possessions, and several of his children died of malnutrition and disease. Marx clearly was an outsider in British society, a fact that may well have affected his view of Western cultures.

In Marx's analysis, society was fundamentally divided between classes that clash in pursuit of their own class interests. When he examined the industrial societies

FIGURE 1-1

Early Social Thinkers

	Émile Durkheim **1858–1917**	**Max Weber** **1864–1920**	**Karl Marx** **1818–1883**
Academic training	Philosophy	Law, economics, history, philosophy	Philosophy, law
Key works	1893—*The Division of Labor in Society*	1904–1905—*The Protestant Ethic and the Spirit of Capitalism*	1848—*The Communist Manifesto*
	1897—*Suicide: A Study in Sociology*	1922—*Wirtschaft und Gesellschaft*	1867—*Das Kapital*
	1912—*Elementary Forms of Religious Life*		

of his time, such as Germany, England, and the United States, he saw the factory as the center of conflict between the exploiters (the owners of the means of production) and the exploited (the workers). Marx viewed these relationships in systematic terms; that is, he believed that an entire system of economic, social, and political relationships maintained the power and dominance of the owners over the workers. Consequently, Marx and Engels argued that the working class needed to overthrow the existing class system. Marx's influence on contemporary thinking has been dramatic. Marx's writings inspired those who were later to lead communist revolutions in Russia, China, Cuba, Vietnam, and elsewhere.

Even apart from the political revolutions that his work fostered, Marx's influence on contemporary thinking has been dramatic. Marx emphasized the *group* identifications and associations that influence an individual's place in society. This area of study is the major focus of contemporary sociology. Throughout this textbook, we will consider how membership in a particular gender classification, age group, racial group, or economic class affects a person's attitudes and behavior. In an important sense, we can trace this way of understanding society back to the pioneering work of Karl Marx.

Modern Developments

Sociology today builds on the firm foundation developed by Émile Durkheim, Max Weber, and Karl Marx. However, the discipline of sociology has certainly not remained stagnant over the last century. While Europeans have continued to make contributions to the discipline, sociologists from throughout the world and especially the United States have advanced sociological theory and research. Their new insights have helped them to better understand the workings of society.

Charles Horton Cooley (1864–1929) was typical of the sociologists who came to prominence in the early 1900s. Cooley was born in Ann Arbor, Michigan, and received his graduate training in economics but later became a sociology professor at the University of Michigan. Like other early sociologists, he had become interested in this "new" discipline while pursuing a related area of study.

Cooley shared the desire of Durkheim, Weber, and Marx to learn more about society. But to do so effectively, Cooley preferred to use the sociological perspective to look first at smaller units—intimate, face-to-face groups such as families, gangs, and friendship networks. He saw these groups as the seedbeds of society in the sense that they shape people's ideals, beliefs, values, and social nature. Cooley's work increased our understanding of groups of relatively small size.

In the early 1900s, many leading sociologists in the United States saw themselves as social reformers dedicated to systematically studying and then improving a corrupt society. They were genuinely concerned about the lives of immigrants in the nation's growing cities, whether these immigrants came from Europe or from the rural American south. Early female sociologists, in particular, often took active roles in poor urban areas as leaders of community centers known as *settlement houses.* For example, Jane Addams (1860–1935), an active member of the American Sociological Society, cofounded the famous Chicago settlement, Hull House.

Addams and other pioneering female sociologists commonly combined intellectual inquiry, social service work, and political activism—all with the goal of assisting the underprivileged and creating a more egalitarian society. For example, working with the Black journalist and educator Ida B. Wells, Addams successfully prevented the implementation of a racial segregation policy in the Chicago public schools. Addams' efforts to establish a juvenile court system and a women's trade union also reflect the practical focus of her work (Addams 1910, 1930; Deegan 1991; Lengermann and Niebrugge-Brantley 1998).

By the middle of the twentieth century, however, the focus of the discipline had shifted. Sociologists for the most part restricted themselves to theorizing and gathering information; the aim of transforming society was left to social workers and others. This shift away from social reform was accompanied by a growing commitment to

A postage stamp honored social reformer Jane Addams, an early pioneer both in sociology and in the settlement house movement.

scientific methods of research and to value-free interpretation of data. Not all sociologists were happy with this emphasis. A new organization, the Society for the Study of Social Problems, was created in 1950 to deal more directly with social inequality and other social problems.

Sociologist Robert Merton (1968) made an important contribution to the discipline by successfully combining theory and research. Born in 1910 of Slavic immigrant parents in Philadelphia, Merton subsequently won a scholarship to Temple University. He continued his studies at Harvard, where he acquired his lifelong interest in sociology. Merton's teaching career has been based at Columbia University.

Merton produced a theory that is one of the most frequently cited explanations of deviant behavior. He noted different ways in which people attempt to achieve success in life. In his view, some may not share the socially agreed-upon goal of accumulating material goods or the accepted means of achieving this goal. For example, in Merton's classification scheme, "innovators" are people who accept the goal of pursuing material wealth but use illegal means to do so, including robbery, burglary, and extortion. Merton bases his explanation of crime on individual behavior—influenced by society's approved goals and means—yet it has wider applications. It helps to account for the high crime rates among the nation's poor, who may see no hope of advancing themselves through traditional roads to success. Chapter 7 discusses Merton's theory in greater detail.

Merton also emphasized that sociology should strive to bring together the "macro-level" and "micro-level" approaches to the study of society. *Macrosociology* concentrates on large-scale phenomena or entire civilizations. Thus, Émile Durkheim's cross-cultural study of suicide is an example of macro-level research. More recently, macrosociologists have examined international crime rates (see Chapter 7), the stereotype of Asian Americans as a "model minority" (see Chapter 10), and the population patterns of Islamic countries (see Chapter 20). By contrast, *microsociology* stresses study of small groups and often uses experimental study in laboratories. Sociological research on the microlevel has included studies of how divorced men and women, for example, disengage from significant social roles (see Chapter 5); of how conformity can influence the expression of prejudiced attitudes (see Chapter 7); and of how a teacher's expectations can affect a student's academic performance (see Chapter 15).

Contemporary sociology reflects the diverse contributions of earlier theorists. As sociologists approach such topics as divorce, drug addiction, and religious cults, they can draw on the theoretical insights of the discipline's pioneers. A careful reader can hear Comte, Durkheim, Weber, Marx, Cooley, Addams, and many others speaking through the pages of current research. Sociology has also broadened

beyond the intellectual confines of North America and Europe. Contributions to the discipline now come from sociologists studying and researching human behavior in other parts of the world. In describing the work of today's sociologists, it is helpful to examine a number of influential theoretical approaches (also known as *perspectives*).

Major Theoretical Perspectives

Sociologists view society in different ways. Some see the world basically as a stable and ongoing entity. They are impressed with the endurance of the family, organized religion, and other social institutions. Some sociologists see society as composed of many groups in conflict, competing for scarce resources. To other sociologists, the most fascinating aspects of the social world are the everyday, routine interactions among individuals that we sometimes take for granted. These three views, the ones most widely used by sociologists, are the functionalist, conflict, and interactionist perspectives. They will provide an introductory look at the discipline.

Functionalist Perspective

Think of society as a living organism in which each part of the organism contributes to its survival. This view is the *functionalist perspective,* which emphasizes the way that parts of a society are structured to maintain its stability.

Talcott Parsons (1902–1979), a Harvard University sociologist, was a key figure in the development of functionalist theory. Parsons had been greatly influenced by the work of Émile Durkheim, Max Weber, and other European sociologists. For over four decades, Parsons dominated sociology in the United States with his advocacy of functionalism. He saw any society as a vast network of connected parts, each of which helps to maintain the system as a whole. The functionalist approach holds that if an aspect of social life does not contribute to a society's stability or survival—if it does not serve some identifiably useful function or promote value consensus among members of a society—it will not be passed on from one generation to the next.

Let's examine prostitution as an example of the functionalist perspective. Why is it that a practice so widely condemned continues to display such persistence and vitality? Functionalists suggest that prostitution satisfies needs of patrons that may not be readily met through more socially acceptable forms such as courtship or marriage. The "buyer" receives sex without any responsibility for procreation or sentimental attachment; at the same time, the "seller" makes a living through this exchange.

Such an examination leads us to conclude that prostitution does perform certain functions that society seems to need. However, this is not to suggest that prostitution is a desirable or legitimate form of social behavior. Functionalists do not make such judgments. Rather, advocates of the functionalist perspective hope to explain how an aspect of society that is so frequently attacked can nevertheless manage to survive (K. Davis 1937).

Manifest and Latent Functions

Your college catalog typically states various functions of the institution. It may inform you, for example, that the university intends to "offer each student a broad education in classical and contemporary thought, in the humanities, in the sciences, and in the arts." However, it would be quite a surprise to find a catalog that declared, "This university was founded in 1895 to keep people between the ages of 18 and 22 out of the job market, thus reducing unemployment." No college catalog will declare that this is the purpose of the university. Yet societal institutions serve many functions, some of them quite subtle. The university, in fact, *does* delay people's entry into the job market.

Robert Merton (1968) made an important distinction between manifest and latent functions. *Manifest functions* of institutions are open, stated, conscious functions. They involve the intended, recognized consequences of an aspect of society, such as the university's

Military chaplains fill a function in society by providing inspiration and solace to those serving their country. This Navy chaplain is leading a field prayer service for the soldiers stationed in Kosovo in 1999 as part of the NATO-led peacekeeping military force.

role in certifying academic competence and excellence. By contrast, *latent functions* are unconscious or unintended functions and may reflect hidden purposes of an institution. One latent function of universities is to hold down unemployment. Another is to serve as a meeting ground for people seeking marital partners.

Dysfunctions

Functionalists acknowledge that not all parts of a society contribute to its stability all the time. A *dysfunction* refers to an element or a process of society that may actually disrupt a social system or lead to a decrease in stability.

We consider many dysfunctional behavior patterns, such as homicide, as undesirable. Yet we should not automatically interpret dysfunctions as negative. The evaluation of a dysfunction depends on one's own values or, as the saying goes, on "where you sit." For example, the official view in prisons in the United States is that inmates' gangs should be eradicated because they are dysfunctional to smooth operations. Yet some guards have actually come to view the presence of prison gangs as functional for their jobs. The danger posed by gangs creates a "threat to security," requiring increased surveillance and more overtime work for guards (Hunt et al. 1993:400).

Conflict Perspective

In contrast to functionalists' emphasis on stability and consensus, conflict sociologists see the social world in continual struggle. The *conflict perspective* assumes that social behavior is best understood in terms of conflict or tension between competing groups. Such conflict need not be violent; it can take the form of labor negotiations, party politics, competition between religious groups for members, or disputes over the federal budget.

Throughout most of the 1900s, the functionalist perspective had the upper hand in sociology in the United States. However, the conflict approach has become increasingly persuasive since the late 1960s. The widespread social unrest resulting from battles over civil rights, bitter divisions over the war in Vietnam, the rise of the feminist and gay liberation movements, the Watergate scandal, urban riots, and confrontations at abortion clinics offered support for the conflict approach—the view that our social world is characterized by continual struggle between competing groups. Currently, the discipline of sociology accepts conflict theory as one valid way to gain insight into a society.

The Marxist View

As we saw earlier, Karl Marx viewed struggle between social classes as inevitable, given the exploitation of workers under capitalism. Expanding on Marx's work,

The conflict perspective views our social world as a continual struggle between competing groups. This Native American is protesting the use of the word "Indians" by a National Football League team. By making up other team names that other groups might find offensive, he invites you to put yourself in his shoes.

sociologists and other social scientists have come to see conflict not merely as a class phenomenon but as a part of everyday life in all societies. Thus, in studying any culture, organization, or social group, sociologists want to know who benefits, who suffers, and who dominates at the expense of others. They are concerned with the conflicts between women and men, parents and children, cities and suburbs, and Whites and Blacks, to name only a few. Conflict theorists are interested in how society's institutions—including the family, government, religion, education, and the media—may help to maintain the privileges of some groups and keep others in a subservient position. Their emphasis on social change and redistribution of resources makes conflict theorists more "radical" and "activist" than functionalists (Dahrendorf 1958).

A Racial View: W. E. B. Du Bois

One important contribution of conflict theory is that it has encouraged sociologists to view society through the eyes of those segments of the population that rarely influence decision making. Early Black sociologists such as W. E. B. Du Bois (1868–1963) conducted research that they hoped would assist the struggle for a racially egalitarian society. Du Bois believed that knowledge was essential in combating prejudice and achieving tolerance and justice. Sociology, Du Bois contended, had to draw on scientific principles to study social problems such as those experienced by Blacks in the United States. In addition, Du Bois made a major contribution to sociology through his in-depth studies of urban life—both White and Black.

Du Bois had little patience for theorists such as Herbert Spencer who seemed content with the status quo. He advocated basic research on the lives of Blacks that would separate opinion from fact, and he documented their relatively low status in Philadelphia and Atlanta. Du Bois believed that the granting of full political rights to Blacks was essential to their social and economic progress in the United States. Many of his ideas challenging the status quo did not find a receptive audience within either the government or the academic world. As a result, Du Bois became increasingly involved with organizations whose members questioned the established social order, and

The ideas of W. E. B. Du Bois challenged the status quo in both academic and political circles. The first Black person to receive a doctorate from Harvard University, he later helped organize the National Association for the Advancement of Colored People (NAACP).

he helped to found the National Association for the Advancement of Colored People, better known as the NAACP (Green and Driver 1978).

The addition of diverse views within sociology in recent years has led to some helpful research, especially for African Americans. For many years, African Americans were understandably wary of participating in medical research studies, because those studies had been used for such purposes as justifying slavery or determining the impact of untreated syphilis. Now, however, African American sociologists and other social scientists are working to involve Blacks in useful ethnic medical research in such areas as diabetes and sickle cell anemia, two disorders that strike Black populations especially hard (St. John 1997).

The Feminist View

While feminist theory builds in important ways on the conflict perspective, it is also sensitive to the need for social integration advocated by functionalists. Like other conflict theorists, feminist scholars see gender differences as a reflection of the subjugation of one group (women) by another group (men). Drawing on the work of Marx and Engels, contemporary feminist theorists often view women's subordination as inherent in capitalist societies. Some radical feminist theorists, however, view the oppression of women as inevitable in *all* male-dominated societies, including those labeled as *capitalist, socialist,* and *communist* (Tuchman 1992).

As is true of the work of African American sociologists, feminist scholarship in sociology has broadened our understanding of social behavior by taking it beyond the White male point of view. For example, a family's social standing is no longer defined solely by the husband's position and income. Feminist scholars have not only challenged stereotyping of women; they have argued for a gender-balanced study of society in which women's experiences and contributions are as visible as those of men (Brewer 1989; Komarovsky 1991; P. England 1999).

The feminist perspective has given sociologists new views of familiar social behavior. For example, past research on crime rarely considered women, and when it did, the studies tended to focus on "traditional" crimes by women like shoplifting. Such a view tended to ignore the role that women play in all types of crime as well as the disproportionate role that they play as *victims* of crime. Research conducted by Meda Chesney-Lind and Noelie Rodriguez (1993) showed that nearly all women in prison had suffered physical and/or sexual abuse when they were young; half had been raped. Contributions by both feminist and minority scholars have enriched all the sociological perspectives.

Interactionist Perspective

Workers interacting on the job, encounters in public places like bus stops and parks, behavior in small groups—these are all aspects of microsociology that catch the attention of interactionists. Whereas functionalist and conflict theorists both analyze large-scale society-wide patterns of behavior, the *interactionist perspective* generalizes about everyday forms of social interaction in order to understand society as a whole. In the 1990s, for example, the workings of juries became a subject of public scrutiny. High-profile trials ended in verdicts that left some people shaking their heads. Long before jury members were being interviewed on their front lawns following trials, interactionists tried to better understand behavior in the small-group setting of a jury deliberation room, as shown in Box 1-1.

Interactionism is a sociological framework for viewing human beings as living in a world of meaningful objects. These "objects" may include material things, actions, other people, relationships, and even symbols.

While functionalist and conflict approaches were initiated in Europe, interactionism developed first in the United States. George Herbert Mead (1863–1931) is widely regarded as the founder of the interactionist perspective. Mead taught at the University of Chicago from 1893 until his death. His sociological analysis, like that of Charles Horton Cooley, often focused on human interactions within one-to-one situations and small groups. Mead was interested in observing the most minute forms of communication—smiles, frowns, nodding of one's head—and in understanding how such individual behavior was influenced by the larger context of a group or society. Despite his innovative views, Mead only occasionally wrote articles, and never a book. He was an extremely popular teacher, and most of his insights have come to us through edited volumes of lectures that his students published after his death.

The interactionist perspective is sometimes referred to as the *symbolic interactionist perspective,* because interactionists see symbols as an especially important part of human communication. Members of a society share the social meanings of symbols. In the United States, for example, a salute symbolizes respect, while a clenched fist signifies defiance. However, another culture might use different gestures to convey a feeling of respect or defiance.

Consider the different ways various societies portray suicide without the use of words. People in the United States point a finger at the head (shooting); urban Japanese bring a fist against the stomach (stabbing); and the South Fore of Papua, New Guinea, clench a hand at the throat (hanging). These types of symbolic interaction are classified as forms of **nonverbal communication,** which can include many other gestures, facial expressions, and postures.

Imagine you have been selected for a jury. How do you think you and the other jury members will arrive at a unanimous decision? How do opinions form? And how do they get changed? Your interaction with your fellow jurors is crucial in the decision-making process.

Few small groups have received as much attention in the United States in the 1990s as juries. Among the juries that have aroused great interest are the jury in the case of four Los Angeles police officers accused of beating Rodney King, the juries in the two trials of Erik and Lyle Menedez for the killings of their parents, and the jury that acquitted O. J. Simpson of double homicide charges. Well before these highly publicized trials, social scientists were studying how juries reach their decisions.

Interactionists employ four types of research: interviews with jury members who attempt to reconstruct how they reached a verdict; observation of jurors as they sit through and react to events in the courtroom; observation of actual jury deliberations (permitted by presiding judges in a few instances); and experiments that use volunteers to create mock juries. We'll consider here some findings about the influence of fellow jurors on decision making, the likelihood of finding defendants guilty, the effect that jury size has on outcomes, and recent changes in the jury experience.

In a 1957 motion picture, *Twelve Angry Men*, actor Henry Fonda played a juror who begins as the lone voice favoring acquittal of a criminal defendant, but in the end convinces the entire jury of the defendant's innocence. While the movie made for great drama, more recent research suggests that jurors generally do not change their minds after the first ballot. For example, a study of 225 cases indicated that if a majority of jurors votes to convict a defendant on the first ballot, there is only a 5 percent chance that the defendant will later be acquitted.

A jury's decision making may even occur before the first ballot. Despite judges' instructions to the contrary, many jurors form tentative verdict preferences early in a trial. Studies suggest that jurors with initial feelings of guilty or not guilty give disproportionate weight to supporting testimony that

> As with other small groups, participation in a jury can be an intense experience, especially in a long, combative criminal trial with a focus on violence and bloodshed.

reinforces their initial verdict preferences, while discounting testimony that undermines this preference.

Most research on jury decision making in criminal trials has focused on how juries decide if a defendant is guilty or not guilty. However, in a significant number of criminal cases, a defendant is tried on several counts, or there is a possibility of deciding that he or she is not guilty by reason of insanity. A number of studies have shown that jurors are more likely to convict a defendant on some charge if they are given several alternatives to an absolute verdict of not guilty.

Researchers have given special attention to comparisons of 6-person and 12-person juries. State legislatures have shown an interest in reducing jury size to save money and expedite courtroom proceedings; social scientists have explored how this might affect a jury's decision making. In one study of criminal cases, the size of a jury had no impact on the likelihood of conviction when the defendant appeared not to be guilty. However, when the defendant's guilt seemed more obvious, 12-person juries were more reluctant to convict than 6-person juries.

Research on jury members needs to deal with changes in the experience of being a juror. For example, the rise in violent crime in the United States and improved methods of documenting the crime scene now mean that jurors are more likely to be exposed to images and descriptions of graphic violence and gore. Mental health professionals and social scientists have documented the trauma jurors sometimes suffer that can trigger classic symptoms of stress, such as depression, anxiety, weight loss, sleep loss, and disruptions in close social relationships. As with other small groups, participation in a jury can be an intense experience, especially in a long, combative criminal trial with a focus on violence and bloodshed.

Let's Discuss

1. Does it appear that jurors enter the deliberations with totally open minds? Why or why not?
2. What effect does smaller jury size have on decision making? What might be the reason for this?

Sources: Abramson 1994; Hare 1992; MacCoun 1989; Roan 1995; Sabini 1992.

Since Mead's teachings have become well known, sociologists have expressed greater interest in the interactionist perspective. Many have moved away from what may have been an excessive preoccupation with the large-scale (macro) level of social behavior and have redirected their attention toward behavior that occurs in small groups (micro-level). Erving Goffman (1922–1982) popularized a particular type of interactionist method known as the ***dramaturgical approach.*** The dramaturgist compares everyday life to the setting of the theater and stage. Just as actors project certain images, all of us seek to present particular features of our personalities while we hide other qualities. Thus, in a class, we may feel the need to project a serious image; at a party, we want to look relaxed and friendly.

The Sociological Approach

Which perspective should a sociologist use in studying human behavior? Functionalist? Conflict? Interactionist?

Sociology makes use of all three perspectives (see Table 1-3), since each offers unique insights into the same issue. Think about how Katherine Irwin went about studying the tattoo culture in the United States today (described in the chapter opening). She focused on the tattoo's use as a symbol of hip social status (functionalist perspective), and she examined the tensions between a parent and a child who decides to get tattooed, and the disapproval an employer might show toward a tattooed employee (conflict perspective). Research into the actual process of getting tattooed, including the negotiations between the tattoo artist and the tattooee, made use of the interactionist perspective. As another example, Box 1-2 shows how television might look from the functionalist, conflict, and interactionist points of view.

No one approach to a particular issue is "correct." This textbook assumes that we can gain the broadest understanding of our society by drawing on all three perspectives in the study of human behavior and institutions. These perspectives overlap as their interests coincide but can diverge according to the dictates of each approach and of the issue being studied. A sociologist's theoretical orientation influences his or her approach to a research problem in important ways.

Table 1-3 Comparing Major Theoretical Perspectives

	Functionalist	Conflict	Interactionist
View of society	Stable, well integrated	Characterized by tension and struggle between groups	Active in influencing and affecting everyday social interaction
Level of analysis emphasized	Macro	Macro	Micro analysis as a way of understanding the larger macro phenomena
Key concepts	Manifest functions Latent functions Dysfunction	Inequality Capitalism Stratification	Symbols Nonverbal communication Face-to-face
View of the individual	People are socialized to perform societal functions	People are shaped by power, coercion, and authority	People manipulate symbols and create their social worlds through interaction
View of the social order	Maintained through cooperation and consensus	Maintained through force and coercion	Maintained by shared understanding of everyday behavior
View of social change	Predictable, reinforcing	Change takes place all the time and may have positive consequences	Reflected in people's social positions and their communications with others
Example	Public punishments reinforce the social order	Laws reinforce the positions of those in power	People respect laws or disobey them based on their own past experience
Proponents	Émile Durkheim Talcott Parsons Robert Merton	Karl Marx W. E. B. Du Bois C. Wright Mills	George Herbert Mead Charles Horton Cooley Erving Goffman

1-2 Functionalist, Conflict, and Interactionist Views of Television

Television to most of us is that box sitting on the shelf or table that diverts us, occasionally entertains us, and sometimes puts us to sleep. But sociologists would look much deeper at the medium. Here is what they would find using the three sociological perspectives.

FUNCTIONALIST VIEW

In examining any aspect of society, including television, functionalists emphasize the contribution it makes to overall social stability. Functionalists regard television as a powerful force in communicating the common values of our society and in promoting an overall feeling of unity and social solidarity:

- Television vividly presents important national and international news. On a local level, television communicates vital information on everything from storm warnings and school closings to locations of emergency shelters.
- Television programs transmit valuable learning skills (*Sesame Street*) and factual information (the National Geographic series on PBS).
- Television "brings together" members of a community or even a nation by showing important events and ceremonies (inaugurations, press conferences, parades, and state funerals) and

through coverage of disasters such as the 1986 *Challenger* explosion and the 1995 bombing in Oklahoma City.
- Television contributes to economic stability and prosperity by promoting and advertising services and (through shopping channels) as a direct marketplace for products.

> On a local level, television communicates vital information on everything from storm warnings and school closings to locations of emergency shelters.

CONFLICT VIEW

Conflict theorists argue that the social order is based on coercion and exploitation. They emphasize that television reflects and even exacerbates many of the divisions of our society and world, including those based on gender, race, ethnicity, and social class:

- Television is a form of big business in which profits are more important than the quality of the product (programming).
- Television's decision makers are overwhelmingly White, male, and

prosperous; by contrast, television programs tend to ignore the lives and ambitions of subordinate groups, among them working-class people, African Americans, Hispanics, gays and lesbians, people with disabilities, and older people.
- Television distorts the political process, as candidates with the most money (often backed by powerful lobbying groups) buy exposure to voters and saturate the air with attack commercials.
- By exporting *Beverly Hills 90210*, *Baywatch*, and other programs around the world, U.S. television undermines the distinctive traditions and art forms of other societies and encourages their cultural and economic dependence on the United States.

INTERACTIONIST VIEW

In studying the social order, interactionists are especially interested in shared understandings of everyday behavior. Consequently, interactionists examine television on the microlevel by focusing on how day-to-day social behavior is shaped by television:

- Television literally serves as a baby-sitter or a "playmate" for many

Applied and Clinical Sociology

Many early sociologists—notably, Jane Addams and George Herbert Mead—were quite concerned with social reform. They wanted their theories and findings to be relevant to policymakers and to people's lives in general. For instance, Mead was the treasurer of Hull House for many years, where he applied his theory to improving the lives of those who were powerless (especially immigrants). He also served on committees dealing with Chicago's labor problems and public education (D. Miller 1973). Today, *applied sociology* is the use of the discipline of sociology with the specific intent of yielding practical applications for human behavior and organizations.

Often, the goal of such work is to assist in resolving a social problem. For example, in the last 30 years, seven presidents of the United States have established commissions to delve into major societal concerns facing our nation. Sociologists have been called upon to apply their expertise to studying such issues as violence, pornography, crime, immigration, and population. In Europe, both academic and governmental research departments are offering increasing financial support for applied studies.

A vivid example of applied sociology is the growing local community research movement. One pioneering institution in this effort is the Center for the Study of Local Issues, a research unit of Anne Arundel Community College, located in Arnold, Maryland. The center encour-

children and even infants for long periods of their lives.

- Friendship networks can emerge from shared viewing habits or from recollections of a cherished series from the past, while family members and friends often gather for parties centered on the broadcasting of popular events such as the Super Bowl or the Academy Awards.

- The frequent appearance of violence in news and entertainment programming creates feelings of fear and may actually contribute to manifestations of aggression in interpersonal relations.

- The power of television encourages political leaders and even entertainment figures to carefully manipulate symbols (through public appearances) and attempt to convey self-serving definitions of social reality.

Despite their differences, functionalists, conflict theorists, and interactionists would agree that there is much more to television than simply "entertainment." They would also agree that television and other popular forms of culture are worthy subjects for serious study by sociologists.

Go Packers! The Glory Years Sports Bar & Grill in Green Bay, Wisconsin, is a place where loyal fans gather to watch televised Green Bay Packer football games. This is one way television can promote interaction among people.

Let's Discuss

1. What functions does television serve? What might be some "dysfunctions"?

2. From the conflict perspective, what effect does the export of U.S. television programs have on other parts of the world?

ages both students and faculty to apply social scientific research methods in studying community issues such as employment opportunities for people with disabilities.

In another example of local community research, sociologists at DePaul University in Chicago and their students are examining the impact of the opening of a Motorola cellular phone plant with 3,000 employees in the small town of Harvard, Illinois. This rural, agriculture-based community has only 6,500 residents and is 80 miles from Chicago (well outside the suburban fringe). Some residents of Harvard view the arrival of Motorola as a great boost to the local economy, but others are fearful of the power of a Fortune 500 company with $33 billion in assets. In studying the social and economic impact of Mo-

torola on Harvard, the DePaul researchers are interested not only in the influence a huge corporation can have on a town but in whether the lifestyle of a rural Illinois community can influence the corporate boardroom (Koval et al. 1996; see also Pestello et al. 1996).

Growing interest in applied sociology has led to such specializations as medical sociology and environmental sociology. The former includes research on how health care professionals and patients deal with disease. As one example, medical sociologists have studied the social impact of the AIDS crisis on families, friends, and communities (see Chapter 5). Environmental sociologists examine the relationship between human societies and the physical environment. One focus of their work is the issue of "environmental justice"

23

(see Chapter 20), which has been raised because researchers and community activists have found that hazardous waste dumps are especially likely to be found in poor and minority neighborhoods (M. Martin 1996).

The growing popularity of applied sociology has led to the rise of the specialty of clinical sociology. Louis Wirth (1931) wrote about clinical sociology more than 60 years ago, but the term itself has become popular only in recent years. While applied sociology may simply be evaluative, *clinical sociology* is dedicated to altering social relationships (as in family therapy) or to restructuring social institutions (as in the reorganization of a medical center).

The Sociological Practice Association was founded in 1978 to promote the application of sociological knowledge to intervention for individual and social change. This professional group has developed a procedure for certifying clinical sociologists—much as physical therapists or psychologists are certified. In 1989 the American Sociological Association began publishing a new journal of clinical sociology, *Sociological Practice Review.*

Applied sociologists generally leave it to others to act on their evaluations. By contrast, clinical sociologists take direct responsibility for implementation and view those with whom they work as their clients. This specialty has become increasingly attractive to sociology graduate students because it offers an opportunity to apply intellectual learning in a practical way. Up to now, a shrinking job market in the academic world has made such alternative career routes appealing.

Applied and clinical sociology can be contrasted with *basic* (or *pure*) *sociology,* which seeks a more profound knowledge of the fundamental aspects of social phenomena. This type of research does not necessarily hope to generate specific applications, although such ideas may result once findings are analyzed. When Durkheim studied suicide rates, he was not primarily interested in discovering a way to eliminate suicide. In this sense, his research was an example of basic rather than applied sociology.

Developing the Sociological Imagination

In this book, we will be illustrating the sociological imagination in several different ways—by showing theory in practice and research in action; by speaking across race, gender, class, and national boundaries; and by highlighting social policy throughout the world.

Theory in Practice

We will illustrate how the three sociological perspectives—functionalist, conflict, and interactionist—are helpful in understanding today's issues, whether it be cap-

ital punishment or financing health care. Sociologists do not necessarily declare "here I am using functionalism," but their research and approaches do tend to draw on one or more theoretical frameworks, as will become clear in the pages to follow.

Research in Action

Sociologists actively investigate a variety of issues and social behavior. We have already seen that such research might involve the meaning of tattoos and decision making in the jury box. Often the research has direct applications to improving people's lives, as in the case of increasing the participation of African Americans in diabetes testing. Throughout the rest of the book, the research performed by sociologists and other social scientists will shed light on group behavior of all types.

Speaking across Race, Gender, Class, and National Boundaries

Sociologists include both men and women, people from a variety of socioeconomic backgrounds (some privileged and many not), and individuals from a wealth of ethnic, national, and religious origins. In their work, sociologists seek to draw conclusions that speak to all people—not just the affluent or powerful. This is not always easy. Insights into how a corporation can increase its profits tend to attract more attention and financial support than do, say, the merits of a needle exchange program for low-income, inner-city residents. Yet sociology today, more than ever, seeks to better understand the experiences of *all* people. In Box 1-3, we take a look at how a woman's role in public places is defined differently from that of a man in different parts of the world.

Social Policy throughout the World

One important way we can use the sociological imagination is to enhance our understanding of current social issues throughout the world. Beginning with Chapter 2, which focuses on research, each chapter will conclude with a discussion of a contemporary social policy issue. In some cases, we will examine a specific issue facing national governments. For example, government funding of child care centers will be discussed in Chapter 4, Socialization; sexual harassment in Chapter 6, Groups and Organizations; and the search for shelters in Chapter 19, Communities and Urbanization. These social policy sections will demonstrate how fundamental sociological concepts can enhance our critical thinking skills and help us to better understand current public policy debates taking place around the world.

1-3 Women in Public Places Worldwide

By definition, a public place, such as a sidewalk or a park, is open to all persons. Even some private establishments, such as restaurants, are intended to belong to people as a whole. Yet sociologists and other social scientists have found that societies define access to these places differently for women and men.

In many Middle Eastern societies, women are prohibited from public places and are restricted to certain places in the house. In such societies, the coffeehouse and the market are considered male domains. Some other societies, such as Malagasy, strictly limit the presence of women in "public places" yet allow women to conduct the haggling that is a part of shopping in open-air markets. In some West African societies, women actually control the marketplace. In various eastern European countries and Turkey, women appear to be free to move about in public places, but the coffeehouse remains the exclusive preserve of males. Similarly in Taiwan today, wine houses are the exclusive domains of businessmen; even female managers are unwelcome. Contrast this with coffeehouses and taverns in North America, where women and men mingle freely and even engage each other in conversation as total strangers.

While casual observers may view both private and public space in the United States as gender-neutral, private all-male clubs do persist, and even in public spaces women experience some inequality. Erving Goffman, an interactionist, conducted classic studies of public spaces, which he found to be innocuous settings for routine interactions, such as "helping" encounters when a person is lost and asks for directions. But sociologist Carol Brooks Gardner has offered a

> Women are well aware that a casual helping encounter with a man in a public place can too easily lead to undesired sexual queries or advances.

feminist critique of Goffman's work: "Rarely does Goffman emphasize the habitual disproportionate fear that women can come to feel in public toward men, much less the routine trepidation that ethnic and racial minorities and the disabled can experience" (1989:45). Women are well aware that a casual helping encounter with a man in a public place can too easily lead to undesired sexual queries or advances.

Whereas Goffman suggests that street re-

marks about women occur rarely—and that they generally hold no unpleasant or threatening implications—Gardner (1989:49) counters that "for young women especially, . . . appearing in public places carries with it the constant possibility of evaluation, compliments that are not really so complimentary after all, and harsh or vulgar insults if the woman is found wanting." She adds that these remarks are sometimes accompanied by tweaks, pinches, or even blows, unmasking the latent hostility of many male-to-female street remarks.

According to Gardner, many women have a well-founded fear of the sexual harassment, assault, and rape that can occur in public places. She concludes that "public places are arenas for the enactment of inequality in everyday life for women and for many others" (1989:56).

Let's Discuss

1. How would a coffeehouse in Turkey differ from one in Seattle, Washington? What might account for these differences?
2. How does Carol Gardner's view of women in public places differ from that of Erving Goffman?

Sources: Cheng and Liao 1994; Gardner 1989, 1990, 1995; Goffman 1963b, 1971; Rosman and Rubel 1994; D. Spain 1992.

In addition, sociology has been used to evaluate the success of programs or the impact of changes brought about by policymakers and political activists. Chapter 8, Stratification and Social Mobility in the United States, includes a discussion of research on the effectiveness of welfare reform experiments. Chapter 18, Health and Medicine, considers the issue of financing health care in the United States and other nations, partly by drawing on studies showing that some people may be vulnerable to a lower quality of medical care than others. These discussions will underscore the many practical applications of sociological theory and research.

Sociologists expect the next quarter of a century to be perhaps the most exciting and critical period in the history of the discipline. This is because of a growing recognition—both in the United States and around the world—that current social problems *must* be addressed before their magnitude overwhelms human societies. We can expect sociologists to play an increasing role in the government sector by researching and developing public policy alternatives. It seems only natural for this textbook to focus on the connection between the work of sociologists and the difficult questions confronting the policymakers and people of the United States.

Summary

Sociology is the systematic study of social behavior and human groups. In this chapter, we examine the nature of sociological theory, the founders of the discipline, theoretical perspectives of contemporary sociology, and applications of sociology and consider ways to exercise the "sociological imagination."

1. An important element in the *sociological imagination*—which is an awareness of the relationship between an individual and the wider society—is the ability to view our own society as an outsider might, rather than from the perspective of our limited experiences and cultural biases.

2. Knowledge that relies on "common sense" is not always reliable. Sociologists must test and analyze each piece of information that they use.

3. In contrast to other *social sciences,* sociology emphasizes the influence that groups can have on people's behavior and attitudes and the ways in which people shape society.

4. Sociologists employ *theories* to examine the relationships between observations or data that may seem completely unrelated.

5. Nineteenth-century thinkers who contributed sociological insights included Auguste Comte, a French philosopher; Harriet Martineau, an English sociologist; and Herbert Spencer, an English scholar.

6. Other important figures in the development of sociology were Émile Durkheim, who pioneered work on suicide; Max Weber, who taught the need for "insight" in intellectual work; and Karl Marx, who emphasized the importance of the economy and of conflict in society.

7. In the twentieth century, the discipline of sociology is indebted to the U.S. sociologists Charles Horton Cooley and Robert Merton.

8. *Macrosociology* concentrates on large-scale phenomena or entire civilizations, whereas *microsociology* stresses study of small groups.

9. The *functionalist perspective* of sociology emphasizes the way that parts of a society are structured to maintain its stability. Social change should be slow and evolutionary.

10. The *conflict perspective* assumes that social behavior is best understood in terms of conflict or tension between competing groups. Social change, spurred by conflict and competition, should be swift and revolutionary.

11. The *interactionist perspective* is primarily concerned with fundamental or everyday forms of interaction, including symbols and other types of nonverbal communication. Social change is ongoing, as individuals get shaped by society and in turn shape it.

12. Sociologists make use of all three perspectives, since each offers unique insights into the same issue.

13. *Applied sociology*—the use of the discipline with the specific intent of yielding practical applications for human behavior and organizations—can be contrasted with *basic sociology,* which seeks to gain a more profound knowledge of the fundamental aspects of social phenomena.

14. This textbook makes use of the sociological imagination by showing theory in practice and research in action; by speaking across race, gender, class, and national boundaries; and by highlighting social policy around the world.

Critical Thinking Questions

1. What aspects of the social and work environment in a fast-food restaurant would be of particular interest to a sociologist because of his or her "sociological imagination"?

2. What are the manifest and latent functions of a health club?

3. How might the interactionist perspective be applied to a place where you have been employed or to an organization you joined?

Key Terms

Anomie   The loss of direction felt in a society when social control of individual behavior has become ineffective. (page 13)

Applied sociology   The use of the discipline of sociology with the specific intent of yielding practical applications for human behavior and organizations. (22)

Basic sociology   Sociological inquiry conducted with the objective of gaining a more profound knowledge of the fundamental aspects of social phenomena. Also known as *pure sociology*. (24)

Clinical sociology   The use of the discipline of sociology with the specific intent of altering social relationships and facilitating change. (24)

Conflict perspective   A sociological approach that assumes that social behavior is best understood in terms of conflict or tension between competing groups. (17)

Dramaturgical approach   A view of social interaction that examines people as if they were theatrical performers. (20)

Dysfunction   An element or a process of society that may disrupt a social system or lead to a decrease in stability. (17)

Functionalist perspective   A sociological approach that emphasizes the way that parts of a society are structured to maintain its stability. (16)

Ideal type   A construct or model that serves as a measuring rod against which actual cases can be evaluated. (13)

Interactionist perspective   A sociological approach that generalizes about fundamental or everyday forms of social interaction. (19)

Latent functions   Unconscious or unintended functions; hidden purposes. (17)

Macrosociology   Sociological investigation that concentrates on large-scale phenomena or entire civilizations. (16)

Manifest functions   Open, stated, and conscious functions. (17)

Microsociology   Sociological investigation that stresses study of small groups and often uses laboratory experimental studies. (16)

Natural science   The study of the physical features of nature and the ways in which they interact and change. (9)

Nonverbal communication   The sending of messages through the use of posture, facial expressions, and gestures. (19)

Science   The body of knowledge obtained by methods based upon systematic observation. (8)

Social science   The study of various aspects of human society. (9)

Sociological imagination   An awareness of the relationship between an individual and the wider society. (7)

Sociology   The systematic study of social behavior and human groups. (7)

Theory   In sociology, a set of statements that seeks to explain problems, actions, or behavior. (11)

Verstehen   The German word for "understanding" or "insight"; used to stress the need for sociologists to take into account people's emotions, thoughts, beliefs, and attitudes. (13)

Additional Readings

Borgatta, Edgar F., and Marie L. Borgatta, eds. 1992. *Encyclopedia of Sociology*. New York: Macmillan. A four-volume work that includes more than 350 signed essays on subjects ranging from "adulthood" to "work orientation." This encyclopedia is a good place to begin further reading or research.

Du Bois, W. E. B. 1996. *The Philadelphia Negro: A Social Study*. With a new introduction by Elijah Anderson. Philadelphia: Temple University Press. The reissuing of this classic work, which first appeared in 1899, documents the timelessness of Du Bois' observations a century ago.

Glassner, Barry. 1999. *The Culture of Fear*. New York: Basic Books. Glassner looks at how people's fears of crime, drug use, and other social problems are growing, even though the social reality often does not match the public perceptions.

Levin, Jack. 1999. *Sociological Snapshots 3: Seeing Social Structure and Change in Everyday Life*. Thousand Oaks, CA: Pine Forge Press. The sociological imagination is employed to look at everything from elevator culture and television soap operas to religious cults and the death penalty.

McDonald, Lynn. 1994. *Women Founders of the Social Sciences*. Ottawa, Can.: Carlton University Press. The author examines the important but often overlooked contributions of such pioneers as Mary Wollstonecraft, Harriet Martineau, Beatrice Webb, Jane Addams, and many more.

Internet Connection

Note: While all the URLs listed were current as of the printing of this book, these sites often change. Please check our website (http://www.mhhe.com/schaefer) for updates.

1. Sociology is a unique and exciting discipline due, in part, to its multiple areas of specialization (see Table 1-1 in the chapter). To learn more, visit the American Sociological Association's "Sections" webpage (**http://www.asanet.org/Sections/general.htm**) and A Sociological Tour Through Cyberspace (**http://www.trinity.edu/~mkearl/**). On both sites, you will discover further information about sociologists and the wide variety of topics they study. At the latter site, explore three different areas of study from "Excercising the Sociological Imagination."

    (a) Which social issues, institutions, and experiences do the areas of study focus upon?

    (b) What new historical facts, sociological terms, and statistical information did you learn?

    (c) What kind of research projects and possibilities do each of these areas of study offer? Why are these areas of study important?

    (d) How do the three areas you chose compare to one another? Do they complement one another in any way?

    (e) Consider the list from Table 1-1 and the two websites above. Which area of specialization are you most interested in? Why?

2. The chapter illuminates the differences among the conflict, functionalist, and interactionist perspectives by demonstrating how each views the role of television in our society. It is now your turn to apply these sociological perspectives. The Transparency homepage (**http://www.transparencynow. com**) offers commentary on the nightly news, the sociological dimensions of situation comedies, and the themes of science fiction. Log on to the site and select two of the articles listed. Read, reflect on, and summarize the findings or opinions expressed in both works.

    (a) What is the main point of each of the articles?

    (b) From which of the three sociological perspectives is each piece written? Be sure to offer specific support for your contentions.

    (c) Do you agree or disagree with each analysis? Why?

    (d) How do the ideas and conclusions of the two articles compare?

    (e) Did reading these works offer you a new insight into a favorite television show or movie?

    (f) Did reading these works offer a new insight into the sociological perspectives?

Appendix | CAREERS IN SOCIOLOGY

An undergraduate degree in sociology doesn't just serve as excellent preparation for future graduate work in sociology. It also provides a strong liberal arts background for entry-level positions in business, social services, foundations, community organizations, not-for-profit groups, law enforcement, and other types of governmental jobs. Many fields—among them marketing, public relations, and broadcasting—now require investigative skills and an understanding of diverse groups found in today's multiethnic and multinational environment. Moreover, a sociology degree requires accomplishment in oral and written communication, interpersonal skills, problem solving, and critical thinking—all job-related skills that may give sociology graduates an advantage over those who pursue more technical degrees (Benner and Hitchcock 1986; Billson and Huber 1993). Consequently, while few occupations specifically require an undergraduate degree in sociology, such academic training can be an important asset in entering a wide range of occupations (American Sociological Association, 1993, 1995a). Just to bring this home, a number of chapters highlight a real-life professional who describes how the study of sociology has helped in his or her career. Look for the "Taking Sociology to Work" boxes.

The accompanying figure summarizes sources of employment for those with BA or BS degrees in sociology. It shows that the areas of human services, the not-for-profit sector, business, and government offer major career opportunities for sociology graduates. Undergraduates who know where their career interests lie are well advised to enroll in sociology courses and specialties best suited for those interests. For example, students hoping to become health planners would take a class in medical sociology; students seeking employment as social science research assistants would focus on courses in statistics and methods. Internships, such as placements at city planning agencies and survey research organizations, afford another way for sociology students to prepare for careers. Studies show that students who choose an internship placement have less trouble finding jobs, obtain better jobs, and enjoy greater job satisfaction than students without internship placements (Salem and Grabarek 1986).

Many college students view social work as the field

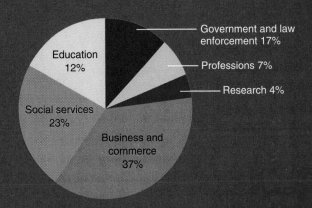

Source: Schaefer 1998b.

most closely associated with sociology. Traditionally, social workers received their undergraduate training in sociology and allied fields such as psychology and counseling. After some practical experience, social workers would generally seek a master's degree in social work (MSW) to be considered for supervisory or administrative positions. Today, however, some students choose (where it is available) to pursue an undergraduate degree in social work (BSW). This degree prepares graduates for direct service positions such as caseworker or group worker.

Many students continue their sociological training beyond the bachelor's degree. More than 250 universities in the United States have graduate programs in sociology that offer PhD and/or master's degrees. These programs differ greatly in their areas of specialization, course requirements, costs, and research and teaching opportunities available to graduate students (American Sociological Association 1997a).

Higher education is an important source of employment for sociologists with graduate degrees. About 75 percent of recent PhD recipients in sociology sought employment in colleges and universities. These sociologists teach not only majors committed to the discipline but also students hoping to become doctors, nurses, lawyers, police officers, and so forth.

For sociology graduates interested in academic careers, the road to a PhD degree (or doctorate) can be long and difficult. This degree symbolizes competence in original research; each candidate must prepare a book-length study known as a *dissertation*. Typically, a doctoral student

Sociology students put in many years and a great deal of work on the way to a PhD. Fortunately, the job market for instructors is looking much better than in years past as the size of the college student population steadily grows.

in sociology will engage in four to seven years of intensive work, including the time required to complete the dissertation. Yet even this effort is no guarantee of a job as a sociology professor.

The good news is that over the next 10 years, the demand for instructors is expected to increase because of high rates of retirement among faculty from the baby-boom generation, as well as the anticipated slow but steady growth in the college student population in the United States. Nonetheless, anyone who launches an academic career must be prepared for considerable uncertainty and competition in the college job market (American Sociological Association 1995a; B. Huber 1985).

Of course, not all people working as sociologists teach or hold doctoral degrees. Take government, for example. The Census Bureau relies on people with sociological training to interpret data for other government agencies and the general public. Virtually every agency depends on survey research—a field in which sociology students can specialize—in order to assess everything from community needs to the morale of the agency's own workers. In addition, people with sociological training can put their academic knowledge to effective use in probation and parole, health sciences, community development, and recreational services. Some people working in government or private industry have a master's degree (MA or MS) in sociology; others have a bachelor's degree (a BA or BS).

Currently, about 22 percent of the members of the American Sociological Association use their sociological skills outside the academic world, whether in social service agencies or in marketing positions for business firms. A renewed interest in applied sociology has led to the hiring of an increasing number of sociologists with graduate degrees by businesses, industry, hospitals, and nonprofit organizations. Indeed, studies show that many sociology graduates are making career changes from social service areas to business and commerce. As an undergraduate major, sociology is excellent preparation for employment in many parts of the business world (Billson 1994).

Whether you take a few courses in sociology or actually complete a degree, you will benefit from the critical thinking skills developed in this discipline. Sociologists emphasize the value of being able to analyze, interpret, and function within a variety of working situations; this is an asset in virtually any career. Moreover, given the rapid technological change evident in the 1990s and the expanding global economy, all of us will need to adapt to substantial social change, even in our own careers. Sociology provides a rich conceptual framework that can serve as a foundation for flexible career development and can assist us in taking advantage of new employment opportunities (American Sociological Association 1995a, 1995b).

CHAPTER

2

SOCIOLOGICAL RESEARCH

How America Knows What America Needs

This Is Your Future. Don't Leave It Blank.

U.S. Department of Commerce
Economics and Statistics Administration
U.S. CENSUS BUREAU

USCENSUSBUREAU

United Sta
Census
2000

Good social research collects data using the established scientific method. This poster encourages all people to respond to census takers from the federal government for the Census 2000.

Many blacks perceive whites as tense or hostile to them in public. They pay attention to the amount of eye contact given. In general, black males get far less time in this regard than do white males. Whites tend not to "hold" the eyes of a black person. It is more common for black and white strangers to meet each other's eyes for only a few seconds, and then to avert their gaze abruptly. Such behavior seems to say, "I am aware of your presence," and no more. Women especially feel that eye contact invites unwanted advances, but some white men feel the same and want to be clear about what they intend. This eye work is a way to maintain distance, mainly for safety and social purposes. Consistent with this, some blacks are very surprised to find a white person who holds their eyes longer than is normal according to the rules of the public sphere. As one middle-aged white female resident commented:

Just this morning, I saw a [black] guy when I went over to Mr. Chow's to get some milk at 7:15. You always greet people you see at 7:15, and I looked at him and smiled. And he said "Hello" or "Good morning" or something. I smiled again. It was clear that he saw this as surprising.

Many people, particularly those who see themselves as more economically privileged than others in the community, are careful not to let their eyes stray, in order to avoid an uncomfortable situation. As they walk down the street they pretend not to see other pedestrians, or they look right at them without speaking, a behavior many blacks find offensive.

Moreover, whites of the Village often scowl to keep young blacks at a social and physical distance. As they venture out on the streets of the Village and, to a lesser extent, of Northton, they may plant this look on their faces to ward off others who might mean them harm. Scowling by whites may be compared to gritting [looking "tough"] by blacks as a coping strategy. At times members of either group make such faces with little regard for circumstances, as if they were dressing for inclement weather. But on the Village streets it does not always storm, and such overcoats repel the sunshine as well as the rain, frustrating many attempts at spontaneous human communication. *(Anderson 1990: 208, 220–221)* ■

his study of "eye work" was part of extensive research into life on the street that sociologist Elijah Anderson conducted in two adjacent neighborhoods of Philadelphia—"the Village," a racially mixed area with mixed incomes, and "Northton," mostly Black and low-income. Anderson became intrigued with the nature of social interaction between strangers on the street shortly after moving into the Village community in 1975. Over the next 14 years he undertook a formal study. He focused on how such a diverse group of people related to one another in everyday life. In particular, he was interested in their "public behavior," including the way they used eye contact in their daily encounters.

Like any good scientist, Anderson was thorough in his research. He interviewed residents, videotaped street scenes, took extensive notes, photographed settings, and hung out for hours at a time in the local bars, laundromats, and corner stores in the course of his observations. As a Black man, he was also able to draw on his own experiences with the Whites in his neighborhood. Anderson systematically traced how social changes—including gentrification of previously low-income areas, increasing drug use and crime, and declining city services—affected social relations and the ways people negotiated public spaces. Three of his books, *A Place on the Corner* (1978), *Streetwise* (1990), and *Code of the Streets* (1999), came out of this research, and he hopes other researchers will make use of his database for their own studies.

Effective sociological research can be quite thought-provoking. It may suggest many new questions about social interactions that require further study, such as why we make assumptions about people's intentions based merely on their gender or age or race. In some cases, rather than raising additional questions, a study will simply confirm previous beliefs and findings.

This chapter will examine the research process used in conducting sociological studies. We will first look at the steps that make up the scientific method in doing research. Then we will take a look at various techniques commonly used in sociological research, such as experiments, observations, and surveys. We will pay particular attention to the ethical challenges sociologists face in studying human behavior and to the debate raised by Max Weber's call for "value neutrality" in social science research. We will also examine the role that technology plays in research today. The social policy section considers the difficulties in researching human sexuality. Finally, the chapter appendixes provide guidelines for understanding tables and graphs and writing up research.

Whatever the area of sociological inquiry and whatever the perspective of the sociologist—whether functionalist, conflict, interactionist, or any other—there is one crucial requirement: imaginative, responsible research that meets the highest scientific and ethical standards. ■

What Is the Scientific Method?

Like all of us, sociologists are interested in the central questions of our time. Is the family falling apart? Why is there so much crime in the United States? Are we lagging behind in our ability to feed the world population? Such issues concern most people, whether or not they have academic training. However, unlike the typical citizen, the sociologist has a commitment to the use of the scientific method in studying society. The *scientific method* is a systematic, organized series of steps that ensures maximum objectivity and consistency in researching a problem.

Many of us will never actually conduct scientific research. Why, then, is it important that we understand the scientific method? Because it plays a major role in the workings of our society. Residents of the United States are constantly being bombarded with "facts" or "data." A television news report informs us that "one in every two marriages in this country now ends in divorce," yet Chapter 13 will show that this assertion is based on misleading statistics. Almost daily, advertisers cite supposedly scientific studies to prove that their products are superior. Such claims may be accurate or exaggerated. We can make better evaluations of such information—and will not be fooled so easily—if we are familiar with the standards of scientific research. These standards are quite stringent and demand as strict adherence as possible.

The scientific method requires precise preparation in developing useful research. Otherwise, the research data collected may not prove useful. There are five basic steps in the scientific method that sociologists and other researchers follow: (1) defining the problem, (2) reviewing the literature, (3) formulating the hypothesis, (4) selecting the research design and then collecting and analyzing data, and (5) developing the conclusion (see Figure 2-1). We'll use an actual example to illustrate the workings of the scientific method.

FIGURE 2-1

The Scientific Method

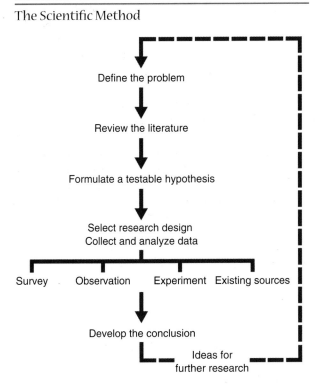

The scientific method allows sociologists to objectively and logically evaluate the facts collected. This can lead to further ideas for sociological research.

Defining the Problem

The picture of assault weapons aimed at children has become all too familiar a sight in schoolrooms across the nation in recent years. Schoolyard shootings, accidents involving guns, drive-by shootings, and terrorist violence have all precipitated concern about the misuse of weapons and sparked a debate about how much to curtail firearms. Opinions vary widely. Those who own and safely use firearms don't want their privileges taken away. In some parts of the nation, gun manufacture is a major industry and source of employment. And for every story of improper use of guns there are accounts of citizens who use them responsibly for recreation or to protect themselves and their property. In the midst of all these opinions there is a need to know "the facts." That is where social scientists have a role to play. In this case study we'll take a look at the research undertaken to assess the effect of the ban on assault weapons passed by Congress in 1994 (Roth and Koper 1999a, 1999b).

The first step in any research project is to state as clearly as possible what you hope to investigate—that is, *define the problem*. In this instance, researchers Jeffrey Roth and Christopher Koper were interested in knowing if the ban worked. Did it result in a decrease in gun at-

tacks? Early on, any social science researcher must develop an operational definition of each concept being studied. An *operational definition* is an explanation of an abstract concept that is specific enough to allow a researcher to measure the concept. For example, a sociologist interested in status might use membership in exclusive social clubs as an operational definition of status. Someone studying prejudice might consider a person's unwillingness to hire or work with members of minority groups as an operational definition of prejudice. Jeffrey Roth and Christopher Koper had to develop two operational definitions: they had to (1) define what weapons were or were not covered by the ban and (2) determine what constituted "success" for the legislation.

Their research is a clear example of applied sociology seeking to evaluate the effectiveness of public policies, but they also drew upon theoretical perspectives. Firearms, whatever one's opinion, serve a variety of functions, and not all of them are criminal. One estimate suggests that 40 percent of all gun owners use them for recreational purposes, 20 percent in the line of work, and 40 percent for self-protection (J. Wright 1995). Roth and Koper, in effect, had to sort out the different functions of firearms and specifically measure the impact of one piece of legislation on the dysfunctional use of assault weapons. Other researchers might define the issue of gun control from a different perspective. For example, one might use the conflict approach to see how powerful interests work to prevent changes in gun licensing procedures. Interactionists might look at behavior patterns in gun clubs or interaction among gun enthusiasts.

Reviewing the Literature

By conducting a *review of the literature*—the relevant scholarly studies and information—researchers refine the problem under study, clarify possible techniques to be used in collecting data, and eliminate or reduce avoidable mistakes. Government control of firearms is relatively recent, but there is no lack of relevant research. For example, the researchers found material in the respected *Journal of the American Medical Association* that considered the impact of an earlier ban on the import of several models of assault rifles. That study found that while sales surged and prices increased prior to imposition of the ban, criminal use declined, suggesting that high prices and hoarding made the guns less accessible to criminal users. Other research material concluded that certain types of crime such as burglary in the home or small business may be reduced if law-abiding citizens are armed. Roth and Koper were interested in seeing which findings would be replicated (American Medical Association Council on Scientific Affairs 1992; Cook and Leitzel 1996; J. Lott 1998).

Functionalists would point out that not all firearms are used for criminal purposes. In fact, it is estimated that 40 percent of all gun owners use them for recreation.

Formulating the Hypothesis

After reviewing earlier research and drawing on the contributions of sociological theorists, the researchers then *formulate the hypothesis*. A **hypothesis** is a speculative statement about the relationship between two or more factors known as *variables*. Income, religion, occupation, and gender can all serve as variables in a study. We can define a **variable** as a measurable trait or characteristic that is subject to change under different conditions.

Researchers who formulate a hypothesis generally must suggest how one aspect of human behavior influences or affects another. The variable hypothesized to cause or influence another is called the **independent variable.** The second variable is termed the **dependent variable** because its action "depends" on the influence of the independent variable.

Roth and Koper hypothesized that banning certain assault weapons would make them less available and thus would reduce the number of crimes involving such weapons. The independent variable is the enactment of

the federal legislation. The researchers would look closely at any data prior to and following the legislation. The dependent variables influenced by the independent variable are the availability of weapons and incidence of crime. These variables proved to be complicated because the researchers had to differentiate between weapons covered by the ban and similar weapons not affected by the ban. Furthermore, measuring crime is limited to *reported* crime; the researchers acknowledged they could not measure incidents that were unreported to law enforcement agencies. Roth and Koper recognized that the announcement of an impending ban on assault weapons would increase demand for them and drive up the price. Therefore, they hypothesized that speculators, rather than potential criminals, would be most likely to buy the weapons prior to the ban.

Identifying independent and dependent variables—in this case, passing a law and measuring the outcome—is a critical step in clarifying cause-and-effect relationships in society. As shown in Figure 2-2, *causal logic* involves the relationship between a condition or variable and a particular consequence, with one event leading to the other. Under causal logic, the degree of integration into society may be

FIGURE 2-2

Causal Logic

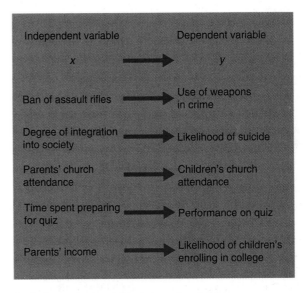

An independent variable is hypothesized to cause or influence another variable (a dependent variable). In *causal logic* an independent variable (often designated by the symbol x) influences a dependent variable (generally designated as y); thus, x leads to y. For example, parents who attend church regularly (x) are more likely to have children who are churchgoers (y). Notice that the first two pairs of variables are taken from studies already described in this textbook.

Whether it is the census or any other type of research, sampling methods have a direct impact on the accuracy of the results.

directly related to or produce a greater likelihood of suicide (refer back to Durkheim's study of suicide in Chapter 1). Similarly, the time students spend reviewing material for a quiz may be directly related to or produce a greater likelihood of getting a high score on the quiz.

p. 9

A *correlation* exists when a change in one variable coincides with a change in the other. Correlations are an indication that causality *may* be present; they do not necessarily indicate causation. For example, data indicate that working mothers are more likely to have delinquent children than are mothers who do not work outside the home. This correlation is actually caused by a third variable: family income. Lower-class households are more likely to have a full-time working mother; at the same time, reported rates of delinquency are higher in this class than in other economic levels. Consequently, while having a mother who works outside the home is correlated with delinquency, it does not *cause* delinquency. Sociologists seek to identify the *causal* link between variables; this causal link is generally advanced by researchers in their hypotheses.

Collecting and Analyzing Data

How do you test a hypothesis to determine if it is supported or refuted? You need to collect information, using one of the research designs described later in the chapter. The research design guides the researcher in collecting and analyzing data.

Selecting the Sample

In most studies, social scientists must carefully select what is known as a *sample*. A *representative sample* is a selection from a larger population that is statistically typical of that population. There are many kinds of samples, but the one social scientists most frequently use is the random sample. In a *random sample,* every member of an entire population being studied has the same chance of being selected. Thus, if researchers want to examine the opinions of people listed in a city directory (a book that, unlike the telephone directory, lists all households), they might call every 10th or 50th or 100th name listed. This would constitute a random sample. The advantage of using specialized sampling techniques is that sociologists do not need to question everyone in a population.

It is all too easy to confuse the careful scientific techniques used in representative sampling with the many *nonscientific* polls that receive much more media attention. For example, television viewers and radio listeners are encouraged to place "800" and "900" calls or use e-mail to give their views on today's headlines or on political contests. Obviously the results of such polls reflect nothing more than the views of those who happened to see the television program (or hear the radio broadcast) and took the time, perhaps at some cost, to register their opinions. These data do not necessarily reflect (and indeed may distort) the views of the broader population. Not everyone has access to a television or radio or has the time to watch or listen to a program or has the means and/or inclination to make a toll call or to send e-mail. Similar problems are raised by "mail-back" questionnaires found in many magazines and by "mall intercepts" where shoppers are asked about some issue. Even when these techniques include answers from tens of thousands of people, their accuracy will be far less than that of a carefully selected representative sample of 1,500 respondents (S. Roberts 1994b).

Sociology in the Global Community

2-1 "Sent-down" in China

Imagine arriving at school and learning that the entire college was being closed and that, in fact, the government was closing all universities. Furthermore, since there was no school for you to attend, you were now being taken to the countryside to work on farms so the country could increase agricultural production. This is basically what happened to students in China from 1967 to 1978 during a period historians refer to as the Cultural Revolution, when China was trying to rid itself of outside influences. During this time, 17 million young urban people—about a third of the youth entering the labor force—were the victims of the government's "send-down" policy. They were forced to live and work in rural areas rather than attend school or work at government jobs they may have held.

Sociologists Xueguang Zhou and Liren Hou of Duke University were interested in what impact these state policies had on the people's lives. To learn more, the researchers decided to interview those who were "sent-down" as well as comparable people who were not sent to rural areas. They did their representative sampling in several stages: first selecting cities from different geographical areas, then systematically selecting blocks

> 17 million young urban people were the victims of the government's "send-down" policy.

within those cities, and finally randomly selecting and interviewing adults within the blocks. The accumulated a sample of 2,793 people, of whom 855 had been sent-down.

Zhou and Hou found that those who stayed in rural areas more than six years were likely to marry later, have fewer children, and hold poorer jobs than those who spent less time or those who stayed in urban areas.

While these differences may be expected, some findings were surprising. For example, those who were sent-down for only a few years were more likely to graduate from college than those young people who were never sent-down. The researchers argue that many of the youths who left "early" from rural areas were well-connected politically and therefore probably came from more prosperous backgrounds. Also, these young people may have resolved to quickly overcome the adverse effects of the state policy.

Let's Discuss

1. How did the researchers make sure their sample was representative? Do you think selecting names from a phone book would produce the same results?
2. Describe the independent and dependent variables in this study. (Refer back to page 37 if you need to.)

Source: Zhou and Hou 1999.

Sampling has become a hot issue in census taking. Every 10 years the U.S. government seeks to count every resident; the results determine everything from political representation to allocation of at least $180 billion in federal aid to the states. The effort to count every household has always been difficult and inevitably results in some inaccuracies. For example, the number of households "missed" in the 1990 census amounted to some 4 to 5 million people. As federal dollars grow in importance, the "undercount," as it is called, has taken on greater significance. That is why the Bureau of the Census proposed using sampling in the 2000 census as a means to estimate data for those households that fail to respond to initial efforts to collect data. But sampling has political consequences. The undercounted people most likely to be added to the population count by the use of "sampling" are minorities and poor people, who traditionally support Democrats. In 1999 the Supreme Court ruled that sampling may not be used to determine congressional apportionment, but is acceptable in other census surveys used to determine allocations for government programs (J. Greenburg 1999).

Sampling is a complex aspect of research design. In Box 2-1, we consider the approach some researchers took when trying to create an appropriate sample of people in the world's most populous nation—China. We'll also see how they made use of data from the sample.

Ensuring Validity and Reliability

The scientific method requires that research results be both valid and reliable. *Validity* refers to the degree to which a measure or scale truly reflects the phenomenon under study. A valid measure of the ban on assault rifles depended on gathering accurate data. Firearms vary in numerous specific ways. Fortunately for the researchers the legislation clarified in exacting detail just what the ban covered. But this meant Roth and Koper had to become knowledgeable about such matters as where the ammunition magazine was placed, whether the barrel was threaded, and the weight of firearms loaded as opposed to unloaded. All these factors and more determined whether the data collected were relevant to their study or not.

Reliability refers to the extent to which a measure provides consistent results. Reliability was less of a concern with Roth and Koper since the process for reporting gun sales, clearance checks for permits, and reporting of crime incidents were already well-established prior to the beginning of their social research. However, they looked closely at data collection from different states to see if they could detect any potential reliability problems.

Developing the Conclusion

Scientific studies, including those conducted by sociologists, do not aim to answer all the questions that can be raised about a particular subject. Therefore, the conclusion of a research study represents both an end and a beginning. It terminates a specific phase of the investigation, but it should also generate ideas for future study. Both Roth and Koper see a need to continue the research to gauge the lasting impact of the assault rifle ban.

Supporting Hypotheses

Sociological studies do not always generate data that support the original hypothesis. In many instances, a hypothesis is refuted, and researchers must reformulate their conclusions. Unexpected results may also lead sociologists to reexamine their methodology and make changes in the research design.

Roth and Koper's research applied an understanding of social behavior to the impact of social policies. In the short term it appears that fewer of the banned weapons were used in crimes (see Figure 2-3). When the ban went into effect the number of assault weapon traces placed by law enforcement agencies decreased dramatically. This seems to confirm the findings of the earlier research published in the *Journal of the American Medical Association.* Following the ban there did not appear to be a reduction in multiple-gunshot victims, so characteristic of rapid-fire assault rifles. However, other evidence suggests that the 1994 ban may have contributed to a reduction in

FIGURE 2-3

Impact of Assault Rifle Ban

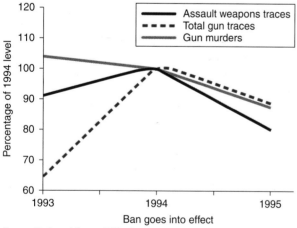

Source: Roth and Koper 1999a:6.

the *overall* gun murder rate of about 11 percent and to fewer murders of police officers by criminals armed with assault weapons.

Controlling for Other Factors

A **control variable** is a factor held constant to test the relative impact of the independent variable. For example, if researchers wanted to know how adults in the United States feel about restrictions on smoking in public places, they would probably attempt to use a respondent's smoking behavior as a control variable. That is, how do smokers versus nonsmokers feel about smoking in public places? Consequently, the researchers would compile separate statistics on how smokers and nonsmokers feel about antismoking regulations.

In Summary: The Scientific Method

Let us briefly summarize the process of the scientific method through a review of the example. Roth and Koper *defined a problem* (the question of what effect the assault weapon ban had on crime). They *reviewed the literature* (other studies of firearms control) and *formulated a hypothesis* (the ban of certain assault weapons would make them less available and thus would reduce crimes involving such weapons). They *collected and analyzed the data,* making sure the data were valid and reliable. Finally, they *developed the conclusion:* in the short term, at least, it appears that fewer banned weapons were used in crime than before the ban went into effect.

Major Research Designs

An important aspect of sociological research is deciding how data should be collected. A **research design** is a detailed plan or method for obtaining data scientifically. Selection of a research design is a critical step for sociologists and requires creativity and ingenuity. This choice will directly influence both the cost of the project and the amount of time needed to collect the results of the research. Sociologists regularly use surveys, observation, experiments, and existing sources to generate data for their research.

Surveys

Almost all of us have responded to surveys of one kind or another. We may have been asked what kind of detergent we use, which presidential candidate we intend to vote for, or what our favorite television program is. A **survey** is a study, generally in the form of an interview or questionnaire, that provides sociologists with information concerning how people think and act. Among the United

Research in Action

2-2 Framing Survey Questions about the Holocaust

In 1992, Jewish Americans and others were shocked when a survey reported that one out of five people in the United States doubted that the Holocaust had occurred. The survey, commissioned by the American Jewish Committee, was conducted by the respected research firm of Roper Starch Worldwide. The question read,

> As you know, the term *Holocaust* usually refers to the killing of millions of Jews in Nazi death camps during World War II. Does it seem possible or does it seem impossible to you that the Nazi extermination of the Jews never happened?

Confused by the wording of this question? That is not surprising, for imbedded in it is a difficult double negative ("*impossible . . . never*"). Some 22 percent of the respondents thought it possible that the Nazi extermination of Jews never happened, while another 22 percent did not know if it was possible or impossible (Morin 1994:37).

A storm of controversy followed the release of these distressing data. Many researchers argued that the confusing question may have caused some people to give answers entirely the opposite of what they had intended. Eventually, in 1994, pollster Burns W. Roper publicly apologized at a conference of professional poll takers. Roper admitted that the question about the Holocaust was so poorly worded that it tainted any results. "We should never have approved that question, and we certainly

> Many researchers argued that the confusing question may have caused some people to give answers entirely the opposite of what they had intended.

never should have written it," admitted Roper (Kifner 1994a:A20).

In his remarks before the American Association for Public Opinion Research, Roper concluded that the faulty wording of a single question "served to misinform the public, to scare the Jewish community needlessly, and to give aid and comfort to the neo-Nazis who have a commitment to Holocaust denial." In a subsequent survey conducted in March 1994, Roper researchers asked 991 adults in the United States,

> Does it seem possible to you that the Nazi extermination of the Jews never happened, or do you feel certain that it happened?

In this survey, 91 percent of respondents said they were certain that the Holocaust had happened, while 8 percent were not sure and only 1 percent said it never happened. Through use of a less confusing question, the Roper organization documented the fact that only a tiny minority of people in the United States deny that the Nazi extermination of the Jews took place.

Let's Discuss

1. What made the original wording of the Holocaust question so confusing? If you had been asked the question in that form, how do you think you would have responded?
2. What were some of the unintended consequences of the faulty wording?

Sources: Kagay 1994; Kifner 1994a; P. Novick 1999.

States' best-known surveys of opinion are the Gallup poll and the Harris poll. As anyone who watches the news during presidential campaigns knows, these polls have become a staple of political life.

When you think of surveys, you may recall seeing many "person on the street" interviews on local television news shows. While such interviews can be highly entertaining, they are not necessarily an accurate indication of public opinion. First, they reflect the opinions of only those people who happen to be at a certain location. Such a sample can be biased in favor of commuters, middle-class shoppers, or factory workers, depending on which street or area the newspeople select. Second, television interviews tend to attract outgoing people who are willing to appear on the air, while they frighten away others who may feel intimidated by a camera. As we've seen, a survey must be based on precise, representative

sampling if it is to genuinely reflect a broad range of the population.

In preparing to conduct a survey, sociologists must not only develop representative samples; they must exercise great care in the wording of questions. An effective survey question must be simple and clear enough for people to understand it. It must also be specific enough so that there are no problems in interpreting the results. Even questions that are less structured ("What do you think of programming on educational television?") must be carefully phrased to solicit the type of information desired. Surveys can be indispensable sources of information, but only if the sampling is done properly and the questions are worded accurately. Box 2-2 illustrates the controversy that can develop when a survey on a sensitive subject contains poorly worded questions.

There are two main forms of surveys: the **interview** and the **questionnaire**. Each of these has its own advantages. An interviewer can obtain a high response rate because people find it more difficult to turn down a personal request for an interview than to throw away a written questionnaire. In addition, a skillful interviewer can go beyond written questions and "probe" for a subject's underlying feelings and reasons. On the other hand, questionnaires have the advantage of being cheaper, especially when large samples are used.

Studies have shown that characteristics of the interviewer have an impact on survey data. For example, women interviewers tend to receive more feminist responses from female subjects than do male researchers, and African American interviewers tend to receive more detailed responses about race-related issues from Black subjects than do White interviewers. The possible impact of gender and race only indicates again how much care social research requires (D. Davis 1997; L. Huddy et al. 1997).

Observation

Investigators who collect information through direct participation and/or observation of a group, tribe, or community under study are engaged in **observation.** This method allows sociologists to examine certain behaviors and communities that could not be investigated through other research techniques.

Observation research is the most common form of **qualitative research,** which relies on what is seen in field or naturalistic settings more than on statistical data. Generally, such studies focus on small groups or communities

rather than large groups or whole nations. An increasingly popular form of qualitative research in sociology today is ethnography. **Ethnography** refers to efforts to describe an entire social setting through extended, systematic observation. Elijah Anderson's study, described at the beginning of this chapter, involved not just understanding behavior of pedestrians but also understanding all facets of life in two urban neighborhoods. Anthropologists rely heavily on ethnography. Much as an anthropologist seeks to understand the people of some Polynesian island, the sociologist as an ethnographer seeks to understand and present to us an entire way of life in some setting.

Quantitative research collects and reports data primarily in numerical form. Most of the survey research discussed so far in this book has been this type of research. While quantitative research can make use of larger samples than qualitative research, it can't look at a topic in as great depth. Neither type of research is necessarily better; indeed usually we are best informed when we rely on studies using a variety of research designs that look at both qualitative and quantitative aspects of the same subject.

In some cases, the sociologist actually "joins" a group for a period of time to get an accurate sense of how it operates. This is called *participant observation.* In the tattoo study described in Chapter 1 as well as in p. 6 Anderson's study of "eye work," the researcher was a participant observer.

During the late 1930s, in a classic example of participant-observation research, William F. Whyte moved into a low-income Italian neighborhood in Boston. For nearly four years, he was a member of the social circle of "corner boys" that he describes in *Street Corner Society.* Whyte revealed his identity to these men and joined in their conversations, bowling, and other leisure-time activities. His goal was to gain greater insight into the community that these men had established. As Whyte (1981:303) listened to Doc, the leader of the group, he "learned the answers to questions I would not even have had the sense to ask if I had been getting my information solely on an interviewing basis." Whyte's work was especially valuable, since, at the time, the academic world had little direct knowledge of the poor and tended to rely for information on the records of social service agencies, hospitals, and courts (Adler et al. 1992).

The initial challenge that Whyte faced—and that every participant

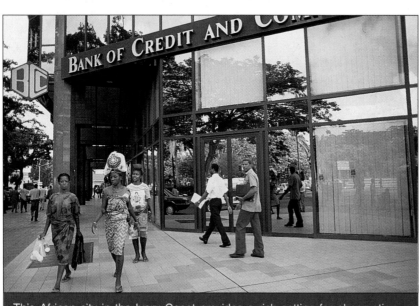
This African city in the Ivory Coast provides a rich setting for observation research. An ethnographer would take note of the interaction of Western and African cultures in the everyday street life.

observer encounters—was to gain acceptance into an unfamiliar group. It is no simple matter for a college-trained sociologist to win the trust of a religious cult, a youth gang, a poor Appalachian community, or a circle of skid row residents. It requires a great deal of patience and an accepting, nonthreatening type of person.

Observation research poses other complex challenges for the investigator. Sociologists must be able to fully understand what they are observing. In a sense, then, researchers such as William F. Whyte or Elijah Anderson must learn to see the world as the group sees it in order to fully comprehend the events taking place around them.

This raises a delicate issue. If the research is to be successful, the observer cannot allow the close associations or even friendships that in-

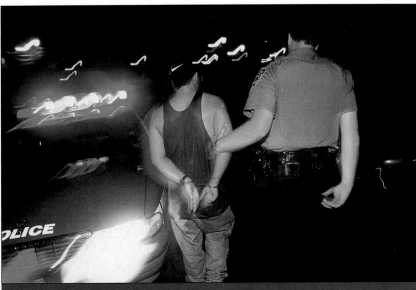

Does arresting someone for domestic assault deter future incidents of violence? An experiment in Miami, Florida, studied this question by making use of control and experimental groups.

evitably develop to influence the subjects' behavior or the conclusions of the study. Anson Shupe and David Bromley (1980), two sociologists who have used participant observation, have likened this challenge to that of "walking a tightrope." Even while working hard to gain acceptance from the group being studied, the participant observer *must* maintain some degree of detachment.

Managers may rely on observation research to improve working conditions or productivity. For example, when Norway's shipping industry was faced with severe cutbacks, a team of researchers worked aboard a merchant ship as part of an effort to improve the social organization and efficiency of Norway's fleet. Similarly, when faced with growing competition in the photocopying industry, Xerox Corporation employed a research team to propose cost-cutting measures to managers and union leaders. In each case, the methodology of participant observation proved useful in solving practical problems (W. Whyte 1989).

Experiments

When sociologists want to study a possible cause-and-effect relationship, they may conduct experiments. An *experiment* is an artificially created situation that allows the researcher to manipulate variables.

In the classic method of conducting an experiment, two groups of people are selected and matched for similar characteristics such as age or education. The researchers then assign the subjects to one of two groups—the experimental or the control group. The *experimental group* is exposed to an independent variable; the *control group* is not. Thus, if scientists were testing a new type of antibiotic drug, they would administer that drug to an experimental group but not to a control group.

Sociologists don't often rely on this classic form of experiment because it generally involves manipulating human behavior in an inappropriate manner. However, sociologists do conduct a variation of laboratory-type experiments by trying to recreate experimental conditions in the field. For example, they may compare children's performance in two schools that use different curricula. Another area of investigation that has led to several experimental studies in the field is an examination of police action in domestic assault cases. Emergency calls to a household where domestic violence is occurring account for a significant part of a police officer's work. Sociologists Anthony Pate and Edwin Hamilton (1992) studied cases in Dade County (Miami) Florida in which officers did or did not arrest the violent suspect and then looked at the effect of the arrest or nonarrest on future incidents of assault in the household. In other words, they compared cases where no arrest was made (the control group) with incidents where the suspect was arrested (experimental group). They found that an arrest did have a deterrent effect if the suspect was employed. Pate and Hamilton concluded that while an arrest may be a sobering experience for any individual, the impact of being taken to a police station is greater if a person is employed and is forced to explain what is happening in his or her personal life to a boss.

In some experiments, as in observation research, the presence of a social scientist or other observer may affect the behavior of people being studied. The recognition of this phenomenon grew out of an experiment conducted during the 1920s and 1930s at the Hawthorne plant of the Western Electric Company. A group of researchers set out to determine how to improve the productivity of workers at the plant. The investigators manipulated such variables as the lighting and working hours to see what impact changes in them had on productivity. To their surprise, they found that *every* step they took seemed to increase productivity. Even measures that seemed likely to have the opposite effect, such as reducing the amount of lighting in the plant, led to higher productivity.

Why did the plant's employees work harder even under less favorable conditions? Their behavior apparently was influenced by the greater attention being paid to them in the course of the research and by the novelty of being subjects in an experiment. Since that time, sociologists have used the term **Hawthorne effect** to refer to subjects of research who deviate from their typical behavior because they realize that they are under observation (S. Jones 1992; Lang 1992; Pelton 1994).

How do people respond to being observed? Evidently these employees at the Hawthorne plant enjoyed the attention paid them when researchers observed them at work. No matter what variables were changed, the workers increased their productivity every time, including when the level of lighting was *reduced.*

Use of Existing Sources

Sociologists do not necessarily have to collect new data in order to conduct research and test hypotheses. The term **secondary analysis** refers to a variety of research techniques that make use of publicly accessible information and data. In the case study of the effect of the ban on certain assault rifles, the researchers made use of existing data. Generally, in conducting secondary analysis, researchers utilize data in ways unintended by the initial collectors of information. For example, census data are compiled for specific uses by the federal government but are valuable for marketing specialists in locating everything from bicycle stores to nursing homes.

Sociologists consider secondary analysis to be *nonreactive,* since it does not influence people's behavior. As an example, Émile Durkheim's statistical analysis of suicide neither increased nor decreased human self-destruction. Subjects of an experiment or observation research are of-

ten aware that they are being watched—an awareness that can influence their behavior—but this is not the case with secondary analysis. Researchers, then, can avoid the Hawthorne effect by using secondary analysis.

There is one inherent problem, however: the researcher who relies on data collected by someone else may not find exactly what is needed. Social scientists studying family violence can use statistics from police and social service agencies on *reported* cases of spouse abuse and child abuse. Yet such government bodies have no precise data on *all* cases of abuse.

Many social scientists find it useful to study cultural, economic, and political documents, including newspapers, periodicals, radio and television tapes, the Internet, scripts, diaries, songs, folklore, and legal papers, to name some examples (see Table 2-1). In examining these sources, researchers employ a technique known as **content analysis,** which is the systematic coding and objective recording of data, guided by some rationale.

Using content analysis, Erving Goffman conducted a pioneering exploration of how advertisements in 1979 portrayed women as inferior to men. Women typically were shown being subordinate to or dependent on others or being instructed by men. They used caressing and touching gestures more than men. Even when presented in leadership-type roles, women were likely to be shown in seductive poses or gazing out into space. Similarly, researchers today are analyzing films to look at the increase

Table 2-1	Existing Sources Used in Sociological Research

Most Frequently Used Sources

Census data

Crime statistics

Birth, death, marriage, and divorce statistics

Other Sources

Newspapers and periodicals

Personal journals, diaries, e-mail, and letters

Records and archival material of religious organizations, corporations, and other organizations

Transcripts of radio programs

Videotapes of motion pictures and television programs

Webpages

Song lyrics

Scientific records (such as patent applications)

Speeches of public figures (such as politicians)

Votes cast in elections or by elected officials on specific legislative proposals

Attendance records for public events

Videotapes of social protests and other public events

Literature, including folklore

in smoking in motion pictures, despite increased public health concerns. This type of content analysis can have clear social policy implications if it draws the attention of the motion picture industry to the message it may be delivering (especially to young people) that smoking is acceptable, even desirable. For example, a 1999 content analysis found that tobacco use appeared in 89 percent of the 200 most popular movie rentals (Goffman 1979; Kang 1997; and Roberts et al. 1999).

These examples underscore the value of using existing sources in studying contemporary material. Researchers have learned, in addition, that such analysis can be essential in helping us to understand social behavior

from the distant past. For example, sociologist Karen Barkey (1991) examined village court records from the seventeenth-century Ottoman Empire (centered in modern-day Turkey) to assess the extent of peasant rebellions against the empire and, more specifically, its tax policies. Barkey could hardly have relied on surveys, observations, or experiments to study the Ottoman Empire; like other scholars studying earlier civilizations, she turned to secondary analysis.

Ethics of Research

A biochemist cannot inject a serum into a human being unless the serum has been thoroughly tested. To do otherwise would be both unethical and illegal. Sociologists must also abide by certain specific standards in conducting research—a **code of ethics.** The professional society of the discipline, the American Sociological Association (ASA), first published the *Code of Ethics* in 1971 (most recently revised in 1997), which put forth the following basic principles:

1. Maintain objectivity and integrity in research.
2. Respect the subject's right to privacy and dignity.
3. Protect subjects from personal harm.
4. Preserve confidentiality.
5. Seek informed consent when data are collected from research participants or when behavior occurs in a private context.
6. Acknowledge research collaboration and assistance.
7. Disclose all sources of financial support (American Sociological Association 1997a).

Content analysis of recent films finds this unstated message: smoking is cool. In this still from *Fight Club*, Brad Pitt is shown enjoying his cigarette. If the movie industry is made aware of the extent of smoking in films and the message that sends to young viewers, perhaps it will try to alter the message.

On the surface, the basic principles of the ASA's *Code of Ethics* probably seem clear-cut. How could they lead to any disagreement or controversy? However, many delicate ethical questions cannot be resolved simply by reading the seven points above. For example, should a sociologist engaged in participant-observation research *always* protect the confidentiality of subjects? What if the subjects are members of a religious cult allegedly engaged in unethical and possibly illegal activities? What if the sociologist is interviewing political activists and is questioned by a grand jury about his or her research?

Most sociological research uses *people* as sources of information—as respondents to survey questions, subjects of observation, or participants in experiments. In all cases, sociologists need to be certain that they are not invading the privacy of their subjects. Generally, this is handled by assuring those involved of anonymity and by guaranteeing that personal information disclosed will remain confidential. However, a study by William Zellner raised important questions about the extent to which sociologists can threaten people's right to privacy.

Accident or Suicide?

An ethical issue—with the right to know posed against the right to privacy—became apparent in research on automobile accidents in which fatalities occur. Sociologist William Zellner (1978) wanted to learn if fatal car crashes are sometimes suicides that have been disguised as accidents in order to protect family and friends (and perhaps to collect otherwise unredeemable insurance benefits). These acts of "autocide" are by nature covert.

In his efforts to assess the frequency of such suicides, Zellner sought to interview the friends, coworkers, and family members of the deceased. He hoped to obtain information that would allow him to ascertain whether the deaths were accidental or purposeful. Zellner told the people approached for interviews that his goal was to contribute to a reduction of future accidents by learning about the emotional characteristics of accident victims. He made no mention of his suspicions of autocide, out of fear that potential respondents would refuse to meet with him.

Zellner eventually concluded that at least 12 percent of all fatal single-occupant crashes are suicides. This information could be valuable for society, particularly since some of the probable suicides actually killed or critically injured innocent bystanders in the process of taking their own lives. Yet the ethical questions still must be faced. Was Zellner's research unethical because he misrepresented the motives of his study and failed to obtain his subjects' informed consent? Or was his deception justified by the social value of his findings?

The answers to these questions are not immediately apparent. Zellner appeared to have admirable motives and took great care in protecting confidentiality. He did not reveal names of suspected suicides to insurance companies, though Zellner did recommend that the insurance industry drop double indemnity (payment of twice the person's life insurance benefits in the event of accidental death) in the future.

Zellner's study raised an additional ethical issue: the possibility of harm to those who were interviewed. Subjects were asked if the deceased had "talked about suicide" and if they had spoken of how "bad or useless" they were. Could these questions have led people to guess the true intentions of the researcher? Perhaps, but according to Zellner, none of the informants voiced such suspicions. More seriously, might the study have caused the bereaved to *suspect* suicide—when before the survey they had accepted the deaths as accidental? Again, there is no evidence to suggest this, but we cannot be sure.

Given our uncertainty about this last question, was the research justified? Was Zellner taking too big a risk in asking the friends and families of the deceased victims if they had spoken of suicide before their death? Does the right to know outweigh the right to privacy in this type of

Are some people who die in single-occupant car crashes actually suicides? One sociological study of possible "autocides" concluded that at least 12 percent of such accident victims have in fact committed suicide. But the study also raised some ethical questions concerning the right to know and the right to privacy.

situation? And who has the right to make such a judgment? In practice, as in Zellner's study, it is the *researcher*, not the subjects of inquiry, who makes the critical ethical decisions. Therefore, sociologists and other investigators bear the responsibility for establishing clear and sensitive boundaries for ethical scientific investigation.

Preserving Confidentiality

Like journalists, sociologists occasionally find themselves subject to questions from law enforcement authorities because of knowledge they have gained in conducting research. This uncomfortable situation raises profound ethical questions.

In May 1993, Rik Scarce, a doctoral candidate in sociology at Washington State University, was jailed for contempt of court. Scarce had declined to tell a federal grand jury what he knew—or even whether he knew anything—about a 1991 raid on a university research laboratory by animal rights activists. At the time, Scarce was conducting research for a book about environmental protestors and knew at least one suspect in the break-in. Curiously, although chastised by a federal judge, Scarce won respect from fellow prison inmates who regarded him as a man who "wouldn't snitch" (Monaghan 1993:A8).

The American Sociological Association supported Scarce's position when he appealed his sentence. Ultimately, Scarce maintained his silence, the judge ruled that nothing would be gained by further incarceration, and Scarce was released after serving 159 days in jail. In January 1994, the U.S. Supreme Court announced without comment that it had declined to hear Scarce's case on appeal. The Court's failure to consider his case led Scarce (1994, 1995) to argue that federal legislation is needed to clarify the rights of scholars and members of the press to preserve the confidentiality of research subjects.

Neutrality and Politics in Research

The ethical considerations of sociologists lie not only in the methods they use but also in the way they interpret results. Max Weber (1949, original edition 1904) recognized that personal values would influence the questions that sociologists select for research. In his view, that was perfectly acceptable, but under no conditions could a researcher allow his or her personal feelings to influence the *interpretation* of data. In Weber's phrase, sociologists must practice **value neutrality** in their research.

As part of this neutrality, investigators have an ethical obligation to accept research findings even when the data run counter to their own personal views, to theoretically based explanations, or to widely accepted beliefs. For example, Émile Durkheim challenged popular conceptions when he reported that social (rather than supernatural) forces were an important factor in suicide.

Some sociologists believe that it is impossible for scholars to prevent their personal values from influencing their work. If that is true, then Weber's insistence on value-free sociology may lead the public to accept sociological conclusions without exploring the biases of the researchers. Furthermore, drawing on the conflict perspective, Alvin Gouldner (1970), among others, has suggested that sociologists may use objectivity as a sacred justification for remaining uncritical of existing institutions and centers of power. These arguments are attacks not so much on Weber himself as on how his goals have been incorrectly interpreted. As we have seen, Weber was quite clear that sociologists may bring values to their subject matter. In his view, however, they must not confuse their own values with the social reality under study (Bendix 1968).

Let's consider what might happen when researchers bring their own biases to the investigation. A man investigating the impact of intercollegiate sports, for example, may focus only on the highly visible revenue-generating sports of football and basketball and neglect the so-called "minor sports" such as tennis or soccer that are more likely to involve women athletes. Despite the early work of W.E.B. Du Bois and Jane Addams, sociologists still need to be reminded that the discipline often fails to adequately consider *all* people's social behavior. In her book *The Death of White Sociology* (1973) Joyce Ladner called attention to the tendency of mainstream sociology to treat the lives of African Americans as a social problem. More recently, feminist sociologist Shulamit Reinharz (1992) has argued that sociological research should not only be inclusive but also be open to bringing about social change and drawing on relevant research by nonsociologists. Both Reinharz and Ladner maintain that research should always analyze whether women's unequal social status has affected the study in any way. For example, one might broaden the study of firearms control to consider how the implications of gun control differ for women than for men. Do women need concealed handguns for safety, or are they more likely to be victimized by criminals wielding these weapons? The issue of value neutrality does not mean you can't have opinions, but it does mean you must work to overcome any biases, however unintentional, that you may bring to the research.

Peter Rossi (1987:73) admits that "in my professional work as a sociologist, my liberal inclinations have led me to undertake applied social research in the hope that . . . my research might contribute to the general liberal aim of social reform. . . ." Yet, in line with Weber's view of value neutrality, Rossi's commitment to rigorous research methods and objective interpretation of data has sometimes led him to controversial findings not necessarily

A homeless woman living in Chicago. Sociologist Peter Rossi came under attack by the Chicago Coalition for the Homeless for finding in a carefully researched study that the city's homeless population was far below the Coalition's estimate. The Coalition accused Rossi of hampering their efforts at social reform.

supportive of his own liberal values. For example, when Rossi and a team of researchers carefully attempted to measure the extent of homelessness in Chicago in the mid-1980s, they arrived at estimates of the city's homeless population far below those offered (with little firm documentation) by the Chicago Coalition for the Homeless. Coalition members bitterly attacked Rossi for hampering social reform efforts by minimizing the extent of homelessness. Having been involved in similar controversies before, Rossi (1987:79) concludes that "in the short term, good social research will often be greeted as a betrayal of one or another side to a particular controversy." But he insists that such applied research is exciting to do and can make important long-term contributions to our understanding of social problems.

Technology and Sociological Research

Advances in technology have affected all aspects of life, and sociological research is no exception. The increased speed and capacity of computers have enabled sociologists to handle much larger sets of data. In the recent past, only people with large grants or major institutional support could easily work with census data. Now anyone with a desktop computer and modem can access information to learn more about social behavior. Moreover, data from foreign countries concerning crime statistics and health

care are just as available as information from our own country.

The Internet affords an excellent opportunity to communicate with fellow researchers as well as to locate useful information on social issues posted on websites. There has been an astounding growth in sociological publications to the point where in 1997 there were 30,153 sociology books and articles published. As difficult as it was to determine this number, it would be impossible to calculate all the sociological postings on Internet mailing lists or World Wide Web sites. Of course, you need to apply the same critical scrutiny to Internet material that you would use on any printed resource (Sociological Abstracts 1998).

Researchers usually rely on computers to deal with quantitative data—that is, numerical measures—but electronic technology is also assisting us with qualitative data, such as information obtained in observation research. Numerous software programs such as *Ethnograph* and *Nud*ist* allow the researcher not only to record his or her observations, like a word processing program, but also to identify common behavioral patterns or similar concerns expressed in interviews. For example, after observing students in a college cafeteria and recording your observations over several weeks, you could then group all your observations related to certain variables, such as "sorority" or "study group" (Dohan and Sanchez-Jankowski 1998).

How useful is the Internet for conducting survey research? That's unclear as yet. It is relatively easy to send out or post on an electronic bulletin board a questionnaire and solicit responses. It is an inexpensive way to reach large numbers of potential respondents and get a quick return of responses. However, there are some obvious dilemmas. How do you protect a respondent's anonymity? Second, how do you define the potential audience? Even if you know to whom you sent the questionnaire, the respondents may forward it on to others.

In 1999 Harris Interactive, a major polling company, inaugurated Harris Poll Online to conduct public opinion polling and marketing research. As a trial, they conducted a 1998 election survey using Internet responses and were able to get accurate results by controlling for characteristics (gender, age, income, race, region of country, and so forth) of the respondents. Now they have a database of 5.2 million

Taking Sociology to Work

KILJOONG KIM:
Associate Statistician, Nielsen Media Research

www.mhhe.com/schaefer

Much of what we see on television is influenced by what Nielsen Media Research learns about our viewing habits. Kiljoong Kim uses his statistical skills to help select the samples and to analyze the data that come from the monitoring devices placed on the TVs of the sample population. The media networks use this information to decide what programming appeals to what kinds of audiences.

Kim says that one of the things he examines in television ratings is how they differ across racial groups. As he notes, "the top 25 shows for Whites are drastically different from the top 25 shows for African Americans." But Kim is intrigued by how results of the 2000 census may change things, since people who used to inaccurately classify themselves as Black or White are now given options to designate themselves as biracial or multiracial for the first time in history. "That's one of the reasons sociology is getting more interesting. Things are constantly changing, including the composition of this society by race. It certainly has an impact on my professional career."

Kim's undergraduate training at the University of Wisconsin was in quantitative analysis. "I had to learn about computers and demography (like census data). Being a sociology major was very helpful for what I do now." After a year of doing educational research Kim realized that a lot of people in the same field had advanced degrees. He went on to get his master's degree in sociology at DePaul University, where he is currently teaching classes in statistics and quantitative research in sociology.

Kim's advice for students: Broaden your horizons. Don't feel pressured to declare a major right away, but try out different courses and see what you like. That's how he discovered sociology. Kim sees the value of studying math along with sociology, which is not surprising, given the type of work that he does.

respondents, of whom 600,000 live in other countries. The ability to deliver and receive 50,000 five-minute surveys per hour results in a dramatic savings in cost. The only problem is that half of all households in the United States are not connected to the Internet. That means certain segments of the population, generally the poor and less educated, are unavailable as potential respondents. Figure 2-4 looks at some of the concerns and possible solutions presented by Internet polling. Social scientists are closely monitoring this new technology to see how it might revolutionize one type of research design (J. Simons 1999; H. Taylor and G. Terhanian 1999a; Terhanian 2000).

Computers have tremendously extended the range and capability of sociological research, from allowing large amounts of data to be stored and analyzed to facilitating communication with other researchers via websites, newsgroups, and e-mail.

49

FIGURE 2-4

A Dialogue: Will Using the Internet to Sample Public Attitudes Work?

☞ There is no comprehensive list of e-mail addresses.

☞ True, so we would build a list asking people to apply.

☞ But half the households don't have access to the Internet.

☞ The proportion is growing rapidly, and we can compensate by oversampling.

☞ People who agree to receive questionnaires may not be representative of the general public.

☞ Yes, but by asking people for their characteristics (age, race, gender, and so forth), we can weight their responses accordingly. And just think about it: after the initial computer expenses, this system is fast and inexpensive.

☞ Yes, but can we say the results are reliable?

☞ We don't know much now, so we do need to run some parallel telephone surveys to test the reliability of these initial Internet-based surveys.

SOCIAL POLICY AND SOCIOLOGICAL RESEARCH

Studying Human Sexuality

www.mhhe.com/schaefer

The Issue

Here's a scene from *Veronica's Closet,* the NBC sitcom:

Veronica and her ex-husband, Bryce, share joint custody of their dog, Buddy. Veronica knocks on the door of Bryce's apartment to exchange the dog, and is surprised when a young woman named Pepper answers. Pepper tells Veronica that Bryce has just recently hired her. Veronica asks sarcastically, "By the hour or for the whole night?" Pepper ignores the slur and responds energetically that she is Bryce's new assistant. Veronica then relents, "When I first saw you, I just thought—she's sleeping with my ex-husband." Pepper, in a young, bubbly voice, replies excitedly "Oh, I am!" (Kunkel et al. 1999:21)

You can find similar scenes from dozens of TV shows today. Human sexuality is a topic of drama and comedy as well as life. Certainly, it is an important aspect of human behavior. As we will see, however, it is a difficult topic to research because of all the preconceptions, myths, and beliefs we bring to the topic of sexuality. Yet, in this age of devastating sexually transmitted diseases, there is no time more important to increase our scientific understanding of human sexuality.

The Setting

We have few reliable national data on patterns of sexual behavior in the United States. Until recently, the only comprehensive study of sexual behavior was the famous two-volume Kinsey Report prepared in the 1940s

Research into sexual behavior in the United States is complicated by the sensitivity of the subject and the reluctance of government agencies to provide funding. Sociologists had to raise private funds to finance the National Health and Social Life Survey (NHSLS), a nationwide study of the sexual practices of adults.

FIGURE 2-5

Views on Sex before Marriage

Proportion agreeing that it is not wrong at all if a man and a woman have sexual relations before marriage.

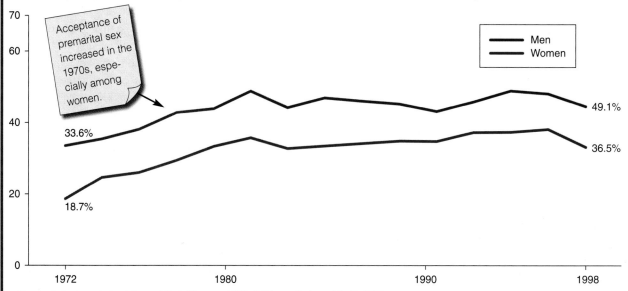

Source: Author's analysis of General Social Surveys, 1972–1998; see Davis and Smith 1999.

(Kinsey et al. 1948, 1953). While the Kinsey Report is still widely quoted, the volunteers interviewed for the report were not representative of the nation's adult population. Since then, social scientific studies of sexual behavior have typically been rather limited in scope but still useful. For example, every two years the general public is interviewed as a part of the federally funded General Social Survey. In Figure 2-5, we see how attitudes about premarital sexual behavior have changed since the early 1970s.

In part, we have few reliable data on patterns of sexual behavior because it is difficult for researchers to obtain accurate information about this sensitive subject. Moreover, until AIDS emerged in the 1980s, there was little scientific demand for data on sexual behavior, except for specific areas such as contraception. Finally, even though the AIDS crisis has reached dramatic proportions (as will be discussed in the social policy section of Chapter 5), government funding for studies of sexual behavior is controversial. Because the General Social Survey described above concerns *attitudes* rather than *behavior* of human sexuality, its funding has not been in jeopardy.

Sociological Insights

The controversy surrounding research on human sexual behavior raises the issue of value neutrality. And

this becomes especially delicate when one considers the relationship of sociology to the government. The federal government has become the major source of funding for sociological research. Yet Max Weber urged that sociology remain an autonomous discipline and not become unduly influenced by any one segment of society. According to his ideal of value neutrality, sociologists must remain free to reveal information that is embarrassing to government or, for that matter, is supportive of government institutions. Thus, researchers investigating a prison riot must be ready to examine objectively not only the behavior of inmates but also the conduct of prison officials before and during the outbreak. Conflict theorists and feminists, among others, are critical of some research that claims to be objective. In turn, their research is occasionally criticized for not sufficiently addressing Weber's concern for value neutrality. In any case, maintaining objectivity may be difficult if sociologists fear that findings critical of government institutions will jeopardize their chances of obtaining federal support for new research projects.

Although the American Sociological Association's *Code of Ethics* expects sociologists to disclose all funding sources, the code does not address the issue of whether sociologists who accept funding from a particular agency may also accept their perspective on what needs to be studied. Lewis Coser (1956:27) has argued that as sociologists in the United States have increasingly turned from basic sociological research to applied research for government agencies and the private sector, "they have relinquished to a large extent the freedom to choose their own problems, substituting the problems of their clients for those which might have interested them on purely theoretical grounds." Viewed in this light, the importance of government funding for sociological studies raises troubling questions for those who cherish Weber's ideal of value neutrality in research. As we'll see in the next section, applied sociological research on human sexuality has run into barriers constructed by government funding agencies.

Policy Initiatives

In 1987 the federal National Institute of Child Health and Human Development sought proposals for a national survey of sexual behavior. Sociologists responded with various proposals that a review panel of scientists approved for funding. However, in 1991, led by Senator Jesse Helms and other conservatives, the U.S. Senate voted 66–34 to forbid funding any survey on adult sexual practices. Helms appealed to popular fears by arguing that such surveys of sexual behavior were intended to "legitimize homosexual lifestyles" and to support "sexual decadence." Two years earlier, a similar debate in Great Britain had led to the denial of government funding for a national sex survey (A. Johnson et al. 1994; Laumann et al. 1994a:36).

Despite the vote by the U.S. Senate, sociologists Edward Laumann, John Gagnon, Stuart Michaels, and Robert Michael developed the National Health and Social Life Survey (NHSLS) to better understand the sexual practices of adults in the United States. The researchers raised $1.6 million of *private* funding to make their study possible.

The researchers made great efforts to ensure privacy during the NHSLS interviews, as well as confidentiality of responses and security in maintaining data files. Perhaps because of this careful effort, the interviewers did not typically experience problems even though they were asking people about their sexual behavior. All interviews were conducted in person, although there was also a confidential form that included questions about such sensitive subjects as family income and masturbation. The researchers used several techniques to test the accuracy of subjects' responses, such as asking

redundant questions at different times in different ways during the 90-minute interview. These careful procedures helped establish the validity of the NHSLS findings (see Table 2-2).

Today, research on human sexuality is not the only target of policymakers. Congress began in 1995 considering passage of the Family Privacy Protection Act, which would force all federally funded researchers to obtain written consent from parents before surveying young people on such issues as drug use, antisocial behavior, and emotional difficulties, as well as sexual behavior. Researchers around the country suggest that this legal requirement will make it impossible to survey representative samples of young people. They note that when parents are asked to return consent forms, only about half do so, even though no more than 1 to 2 percent actually object to the survey. Moreover, the additional effort required to

Table 2-2 Selected Findings from the National Health and Social Life Survey (NHSLS)

- Women are more likely to have their first experience of sexual intercourse because of "affection for partner" (48 percent), while men do so because of "curiosity/readiness for sex" (51 percent).
- The most likely place to meet a spouse is at school (23 percent); the most likely place to meet a cohabitant is at a private party, social club, or gym (19 percent).
- Adults in the United States have sex, on average, about once a week. However, about one-third of adults have sex only a few times a year or not at all.
- While 22 percent of women reported that they had been coerced into a sexual encounter at some time, only 3 percent of men admitted that they had ever coerced a woman into a sexual encounter.
- Some 2.8 percent of men and 1.5 percent of women stated that they were homosexual or bisexual. In the nation's 12 largest cities, more than 9 percent of men identified themselves as gay, compared to 3 to 4 percent in the suburbs of those cities and only 1 percent in rural areas.

Sources: Laumann et al. 1994a, 1994b.

get all the forms returned raises research costs by 25-fold (Elias 1996).

Despite the difficulties of fighting such political battles, the authors of the NHSLS believe that their research was important. These researchers argue that using data from their survey allows us to more easily address such public policy issues as AIDS, sexual harassment, rape, welfare reform, sex discrimination, abortion, teenage pregnancy, and family planning.

Let's Discuss

1. Why is human sexuality a difficult subject to research?
2. How does value neutrality become an important issue in research sponsored by the government?
3. Describe the efforts that the NHSLS researchers made to ensure that their study was confidential and the results were reliable and valid. If you were to conduct a survey in your community of people who engage in premarital sex, how would you set it up?

Appendix I

UNDERSTANDING TABLES AND GRAPHS

Tables allow social scientists to summarize data and make it easier for them to develop conclusions. A ***cross-tabulation*** is a type of table that illustrates the relationship between two or more characteristics.

During 1999, the Gallup organization polled 1,018 people in the United States, ages 18 and over. Each respondent was interviewed and asked: "Are you for or against the legalization of marijuana?" There is no way that, without some type of summary, analysts in the Gallup organization could examine hundreds of individual responses and reach firm conclusions. However, through use of the cross-tabulation presented in the accompanying table, we can quickly see that older people are less likely to favor legalization of marijuana than are younger people.

Graphs, like tables, can be quite useful for sociologists. Illustration A (on page 54) shows a type of pictorial graph that often appears in newspapers and magazines. It documents that in 1996 the United States had more than 12 times the number of personal computers per 1,000 people than did Mexico and nearly twice as many as Canada. However, this graph relies on a visual misrepresentation. Through use of two dimensions—length and width—the graph inflates the presence of personal computers in the United States. Although the U.S. "computer" should appear 12 times as large as the Mexican computer, it actually appears much larger. Thus, Illustration A misleads readers about the comparison among the three nations. Illustration B, a bar graph, makes a more accurate comparison.

Attitudes on Legalization of Marijuana			
Age of Respondent	For	Against	No Opinion
18–29 years	44%	54%	2%
30–49 years	30	68	2
50–64 years	21	78	1
65 years and older	11	85	4

Source: D. Moore 1999 for Gallup Poll.

PERSONAL COMPUTERS IN CANADA, MEXICO, AND THE UNITED STATES

Illustration A (*misleading*)

Computers per 1,000 persons: Canada   Mexico   United States
                                     271   37   406

Illustration B (*more representative*)

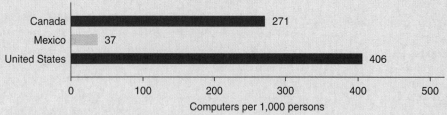

Source: For data, World Bank 2000:226–227.

Appendix II

WRITING A LIBRARY RESEARCH REPORT

Let's say that you have decided to write a report on cohabitation (unmarried couples living together). How do you go about doing the necessary library research? Students must follow procedures similar to those used by sociologists in conducting original research. First, you must define the problem that you wish to study—perhaps in this case, how much cohabitation occurs and what its impact is on marital happiness later. The next step is to review the literature, which generally requires library research.

The following steps will be helpful in finding information:

1. Check this textbook and other textbooks that you own. Don't forget to begin with the materials closest at hand. At the end of each chapter of this textbook is a listing of books, journals, and electronic sources of information (including CD-ROMs and sites on the Internet and Web).

2. Use the library catalog. Most academic libraries now use computerized systems that access not only the college library's collection but also books and magazines from other libraries available through interlibrary loans. These systems allow you to search for books by author or title. You can use title searches to locate books by subject as well. For example, if you search the title base for the keyword "cohabitation," you will learn where books with that word somewhere in the title are located in the library's book stacks. Near these books will be other works on cohabitation that may not happen to have that word in the title. You may also want to search other related key words, such as "unmarried couples."

3. Investigate using computerized periodical indexes if available in your library. *Sociological Abstracts* online covers most sociological writing since 1974. A recent search found more than 420 articles having to do with cohabitation. Some dealt with laws about cohabitation while others focused on trends in other countries. Expanded Academic Index covers general-interest periodicals (*Time, Ms., National Review, Atlantic Monthly,* and so forth) for the most recent four years; it also indexes the *New York Times* for the last six months. These electronic systems may be connected to a printer, allowing you to produce your own printout complete with bibliographic information and sometimes even abstracts of articles.

4. Consult the *Encyclopedia of the Social Sciences,* which concentrates on material of interest to social scientists. Each article includes references for further information.

5. Examine government documents. The United States government, states and cities, and the United Nations publish information on virtually every subject of interest to social science researchers. Publications of the Census Bureau, for example, include tables showing the number of unmarried couples living together and some social characteristics of these households. Many university libraries have access to a wide range of government reports. Consult the librarian for assistance in locating such materials.

6. Use newspapers. Major newspapers publish indexes annually or even weekly that are useful in locating information about specific events or issues. Newspaper Abstracts Ondisc is a computerized index to eight major newspapers in the United States, with coverage beginning in 1985.

7. Ask people, organizations, and agencies concerned with the topic for information and assistance. Be as specific as possible in making requests. You might receive very different information on the issue of cohabitation from talking with marriage counselors and with clergy from different religions.

8. If you run into difficulties, consult the instructor, teaching assistant, or librarian.

Once you have completed all research, the task of writing the report can begin. Here are a few tips:

- Be sure the topic you have chosen is not too broad. You must be able to cover it adequately in a reasonable amount of time and a reasonable number of pages.
- Develop an outline for your report. You should have an introduction and a conclusion that relate to each other—and the discussion should proceed logically throughout the paper. Use headings within the paper if they will improve clarity and organization.
- Do not leave all the writing until the last minute. It is best to write a rough draft, let it sit for a few days, and then take a fresh look before beginning revisions.
- If possible, read your paper *aloud.* Doing so may be helpful in locating sections or phrases that don't make sense.

Remember that you *must* cite all information you have obtained from other sources. If you use an author's exact words, it is essential that they be placed in quotation marks. Even if you reworked someone else's ideas, you must indicate the source of these ideas.

Some professors may require that students use footnotes in research reports. Others will allow students to employ the form of referencing used in this textbook, which follows the format of the American Sociological Association. If you see "(Merton 1968:27)" listed after a statement or paragraph, it means that the material has been adapted from page 27 of a work published by Merton in 1968 and listed in the reference section at the back of this textbook.

Summary

Sociologists are committed to the use of the scientific method in their research efforts. In this chapter, we examine the basic principles of the scientific method and study various techniques used by sociologists in conducting research.

1. There are five basic steps in the *scientific method:* defining the problem, reviewing the literature, formulating the hypothesis, selecting the research design and then collecting and analyzing data, and developing the conclusion.

2. Whenever researchers wish to study abstract concepts, such as intelligence or prejudice, they must develop workable *operational definitions.*

3. A *hypothesis* usually states a possible relationship between two or more variables.

4. By using sampling techniques, sociologists avoid having to test everyone in a population.

5. According to the scientific method, research results must possess both *validity* and *reliability.*

6. The two principal forms of *survey* research are the *interview* and the *questionnaire.*

7. *Observation* allows sociologists to study certain behaviors and communities that cannot be investigated through other research methods.

8. When sociologists wish to study a cause-and-effect relationship, they may conduct an **experiment.**

9. Sociologists also make use of existing sources as in *secondary analysis* and *content analysis.*

10. The *Code of Ethics* of the American Sociological Association calls for objectivity and integrity in research, respect for the subject's privacy, and confidentiality.

11. Max Weber urged sociologists to practice *value neutrality* in their research by ensuring that their personal feelings do not influence the interpretation of data.

12. Technology today plays an important role in sociological research, whether it be a computer database or information from the Internet.

13. Despite failure to obtain government funding, researchers developed the National Health and Social Life Survey (NHSLS) to better understand the sexual practices of adults in the United States.

Critical Thinking Questions

1. Suppose that your sociology instructor has asked you to do a study of homelessness. Which research technique (survey, observation, experiment, existing sources) would you find most useful? How would you use that technique to complete your assignment?

2. How can a sociologist genuinely maintain value neutrality while studying a group that he or she finds repugnant (for example, a White supremacist organization, a satanic cult, or a group of prison inmates convicted of rape)?

3. Why is it important for sociologists to have a code of ethics?

Key Terms

Causal logic   The relationship between a condition or variable and a particular consequence, with one event leading to the other. (page 37)

Code of ethics   The standards of acceptable behavior developed by and for members of a profession. (45)

Content analysis   The systematic coding and objective recording of data, guided by some rationale. (44)

Control group   Subjects in an experiment who are not introduced to the independent variable by the researcher. (43)

Control variable   A factor held constant to test the relative impact of an independent variable. (40)

Correlation   A relationship between two variables whereby a change in one coincides with a change in the other. (38)

Cross-tabulation   A table that shows the relationship between two or more variables. (53)

Dependent variable   The variable in a causal relationship that is subject to the influence of another variable. (37)

Ethnography   The study of an entire social setting through extended systematic observation. (42)

Experiment   An artificially created situation that allows the researcher to manipulate variables and introduce control variables. (43)

Experimental group   Subjects in an experiment who are exposed to an independent variable introduced by a researcher. (43)

Hawthorne effect   The unintended influence that observers or experiments can have on their subjects. (44)

Hypothesis   A speculative statement about the relationship between two or more variables. (37)

Independent variable   The variable in a causal relationship that, when altered, causes or influences a change in a second variable. (37)

Interview   A face-to-face or telephone questioning of a respondent to obtain desired information. (41)

Observation   A research technique in which an investigator collects information through direct involvement with and observation of a group, tribe, or community. (42)

Operational definition   An explanation of an abstract concept that is specific enough to allow a researcher to measure the concept. (36)

Qualitative research   Research that relies on what is seen in field or naturalistic settings more than on statistical data. (42)

Quantitative research   Research that collects and reports data primarily in numerical form. (42)

Questionnaire   A research instrument employed to obtain desired information from a respondent. (41)

Random sample   A sample for which every member of the entire population has the same chance of being selected. (38)

Reliability   The extent to which a measure provides consistent results. (39)

Representative sample   A selection from a larger population that is statistically typical of that population. (38)

Research design   A detailed plan or method for obtaining data scientifically. (40)

Scientific method   A systematic, organized series of steps that ensures maximum objectivity and consistency in researching a problem. (35)

Secondary analysis   A variety of research techniques that make use of publicly accessible information and data. (44)

Survey   A study, generally in the form of interviews or questionnaires, that provides sociologists and other researchers with information concerning how people think and act. (40)

Validity   The degree to which a scale or measure truly reflects the phenomenon under study. (39)

Value neutrality   Objectivity of sociologists in the interpretation of data. (47)

Variable   A measurable trait or characteristic that is subject to change under different conditions. (37)

Additional Readings

BOOKS

American Sociological Association. 1997. *Style Guide,* 2d ed. Washington, DC: ASA. This concise handbook (39 pages) provides guidance in writing clearly as well as citation format, including referencing electronic sources such as the Internet.

Denzin, Norman K., and Yvonna S. Lincoln (eds.). 1994. *Handbook of Qualitative Research.* Thousand Oaks, CA: Sage. The 36 articles in this anthology cover newer techniques used in conducting observation and biographical research, as well as ethical issues facing researchers.

Ericksen, Julia A. 1999. *Kiss and Tell: Surveying Sex in the Twentieth Century.* Cambridge, MA: Harvard University Press. Evaluates the methodology of the hundreds of surveys of human sexuality conducted by sociologists and other social scientists.

JOURNALS

Among the journals that focus on methods of sociological and other social scientific research are the following: *Irb: A Review of Human Subjects Research* (founded in 1979), *Journal of Contemporary Ethnography* (1971), *Qualitative Sociology* (1977), *Social Science Research* (1972), and *Sociological Methods and Research* (1972).

Many sociological journals are now available on the Internet, but one specific journal on research is available only online. You can locate *Sociological Research Online* at **http://www.socresonline.org.uk/socresonline/.**

Internet Connection

Note: While all the URLs listed were current as of the printing of this book, these sites often change. Please check our website (http://www.mhhe.com/schaefer) for updates.

1. Ever since the pioneering work of thinkers such as Émile Durkheim, the collection and analysis of statistical data have been core to sociological research. Engage in secondary analysis of your own community's census data (**http://factfinder. census.gov/**). Link to "Community Profiles" and follow these directions: First, browse the "Select Geography" section and find the area of your hometown. Second, go to the "Select Profile" option, and choose "Social Characteristics." Finally, view the profile.

   (a) What is the total population for your community?

   (b) How many persons are enrolled in elementary school, high school, and college? How many persons from your hometown or city have a bachelor's degree? How many have a graduate or professional degree?

   (c) How many persons age 16 to 64 have a disability?

   (d) What is the ancestry and language spoken at home for those living around you?

   (e) Considering all this information, how would you describe your community?

   (f) Which of the statistics surprised you the most? Why?

   (g) What new information did you learn about your community? Did this exercise in secondary analysis change the way you see your environment?

2. The Gallup Poll (**http://www.gallup.com/poll/ soc_issues.asp** and **http://www.gallup.com/poll/ lifestyle.asp**) offers an examination of lifestyles and opinions in the United States. Direct your webbrowser to these two sites.

   (a) How are people spending their leisure time?

   (b) What are their religious experiences, practices, and beliefs today?

   (c) How much do they exercise?

   (d) How do people feel about current politicians and future candidates?

   (e) What is their opinion of school violence, race relations, and drugs?

   (f) What are their attitudes toward abortion?

   (g) How confident are citizens in their social institutions?

   (h) What do these results reflect about life in the United States today? Were you surprised by any of the findings?

   (i) How do you stand on these issues in comparison with those polled?

   Next, click on the "FAQ" button to learn about the scientific research methods employed by The Gallup Organization.

   (j) How important is the sample size? How are questions constructed? How is the sample of respondents selected?

   (k) Considering what you learned in the chapter, how would you evaluate and rate the methods used by The Gallup Organization?

PART TWO

ORGANIZING
SOCIAL LIFE

MADD

Sociologist Peter Berger (1963:18–

19) once observed that the "sociologist is a person intensively, endlessly,

shamelessly interested" in the doings of people. In Part Two, we begin our

study of the organization of social life within human communities and

societies.

Chapter 3 examines the basic element of any society: its culture. It con-

siders the development of culture, cultural universals, and variations among

cultures. Chapter 4 presents the lifelong socialization process through which

we acquire culture and are introduced to social structure. Chapter 5 exam-

ines social interaction and the major aspects of social structure: statuses,

roles, groups, and institutions. Chapter 6 focuses on the impact of groups and

organizations on social behavior. Chapter 7 examines attempts to enforce

acceptance of social norms, as well as behavior that violates norms.

CULTURE

One of many stalls selling comic books that line the streets near a railroad station in Bombay, India. At first glance, the comic books may look different from those in the United States, but closer inspection reveals some common themes—adventure, romance, beauty, and crime.

Nacirema culture is characterized by a highly developed market economy which has evolved in a rich natural habitat. While much of the people's time is devoted to economic pursuits, a large part of the fruits of these labors and a considerable portion of the day are spent in ritual activity. The focus of this activity is the human body, the appearance and health of which loom as a dominant concern in the ethos of the people. While such concern is certainly not unusual, its ceremonial aspects and associated philosophy are unique.

The fundamental belief underlying the whole system appears to be that the human body is ugly and that its natural tendency is to debility and disease. Incarcerated in such a body, man's only hope is to avert these characteristics through the use of the powerful influences of ritual and ceremony. Every household has one or more shrines devoted to this purpose. The more powerful individuals in this society have several shrines in their houses, and, in fact, the opulence of a house is often referred to in terms of the number of such ritual centers it possesses. . . .

While each family has at least one such shrine, the rituals associated with it are not family ceremonies but are private and secret. The rites are normally only discussed with children, and then only during the period when they are being initiated into these mysteries. I was able, however, to establish sufficient rapport with the natives to examine these shrines and to have the rituals described to me.

The focal point of the shrine is a box or chest which is built into the wall. In this chest are kept the many charms and magical potions without which no native believes he could live. These preparations are secured from a variety of specialized practitioners. The most powerful of these are the medicine men, whose assistance must be rewarded with substantial gifts. However, the medicine men do not provide the curative potions for their clients, but decide what the ingredients should be and then write them down in an ancient and secret language. This writing is understood only by the medicine men and by the herbalists who, for another gift, provide the required charm *(Miner 1956)*. ■

nthropologist Horace Miner cast his observant eyes on the intriguing behavior of the Nacirema. If we look a bit closer, however, some aspects of this culture may seem familiar, for what Miner is describing is actually the culture of the United States ("Nacirema" is "American" spelled backward). The "shrine" is the bathroom, and we are correctly informed that in this culture a measure of wealth is often how many bathrooms are in one's house. The bathroom rituals make use of charms and magical potions (beauty products and prescription drugs) obtained from specialized practitioners (such as hair stylists), herbalists (pharmacists), and medicine men (physicians). Using our sociological imagination we could update the Nacirema "shrine" to 2001 by describing blow-dryers, braided dental floss, Water Piks, and hair gel.

We begin to appreciate how to understand behavior when we step back and examine it thoughtfully, objectively—whether it is our own "Nacirema" culture or another one. Take the case of Fiji, an island in the Pacific. A recent study showed that for the first time eating disorders were showing up among the young people there. This was a society where, traditionally, "you've gained weight" was a compliment and "your legs are skinny" was a major insult. Having a robust, nicely rounded body was the expectation for both men and women. What happened to change this cultural ideal? With the introduction of cable television in 1995, many Fiji islanders, especially girls, have come to want to look like not their mothers and aunts but the thin-waisted stars of *Melrose Place* and *Beverly Hills 90210*. By understanding life in Fiji, we can also come to understand our own society much better (Becker 1995; Becker and Burwell 1999).

The study of culture is basic to sociology. In this chapter we will examine the meaning of culture and society as well as the development of culture from its roots in the prehistoric human experience to the technological advances of today. The major aspects of culture—including language, norms, sanctions, and values—will be defined and explored. We will see how cultures develop a dominant ideology, and how functionalist and conflict theorists view culture. The discussion will focus both on general cultural practices found in all societies and on the wide variations that can distinguish one society from another. The social policy section will look at the conflicts in cultural values that underlie current debates over bilingualism. ■

The children in this Indonesian village are drawn to the house with the television. What effect do you think watching *Friends* would have on them? Using our sociological imagination to look at the influence of television on other cultures can help us to understand TV's impact on our own culture.

Culture and Society

Culture is the totality of learned, socially transmitted customs, knowledge, material objects, and behavior. It includes the ideas, values, customs, and artifacts (for example, CDs, comic books, and birth control devices) of groups of people. Therefore, patriotic attachment to the flag of the United States is an aspect of culture, as is national addiction to the tango in Argentina.

Sometimes people refer to a particular person as "very cultured" or to a city as having "lots of culture." That use of the term *culture* is different from our use in this textbook.

In sociological terms, *culture* does not refer solely to the fine arts and refined intellectual taste. It consists of all objects and ideas within a society, including ice cream cones, rock music, and slang words. Sociologists consider both a portrait by Rembrandt and a portrait by a billboard painter to be aspects of a culture. A tribe that cultivates soil by hand has just as much of a culture as a people that relies on computer-operated machinery. Each people has a distinctive culture with its own characteristic ways of gathering and preparing food, constructing homes, structuring the family, and promoting standards of right and wrong.

Sharing a similar culture helps to define the group or society to which we belong. A fairly large number of people are said to constitute a *society* when they live in the same territory, are relatively independent of people outside their area, and participate in a common culture. The city of Los Angeles is more populous than many nations of the world, yet sociologists do not consider it a society in its own right. Rather, it is seen as part of—and dependent on—the larger society of the United States.

A society is the largest form of human group. It consists of people who share a common heritage and culture. Members of the society learn this culture and transmit it from one generation to the next. They even preserve their distinctive culture through literature, art, video recordings, and other means of expression. If it were not for the social transmission of culture, each generation would have to reinvent television, not to mention the wheel.

Having a common culture also simplifies many day-to-day interactions. For example, when you buy an airline ticket, you know you don't have to bring along hundreds of dollars in cash. You can pay with a credit card. When you are part of a society, there are many small (as well as more important) cultural patterns that you take for granted. You assume that theaters will provide seats for the audience, that physicians will not disclose confidential information, and that parents will be careful when crossing the street with young children. All these assumptions reflect the basic values, beliefs, and customs of the culture of the United States.

Language is a critical element of culture that sets humans apart from other species. Members of a society generally share a common language, which facilitates day-to-day exchanges with others. When you ask a hardware store clerk for a flashlight, you don't need to draw a picture of the instrument. You share the same cultural term for a small, battery-operated, portable light. However, if you were in England and needed this item, you would have to ask for an "electric torch." Of course, even within the same society, a term can have a number of different meanings. In the United States, *grass* signifies both a plant eaten by grazing animals and an intoxicating drug.

Development of Culture around the World

We've come a long way from our prehistoric heritage. As we begin a new millennium, we can transmit an entire book around the world via the Internet, clone cells, and prolong lives through organ transplants. The human species has produced such achievements as the ragtime compositions of Scott Joplin, the poetry of Emily Dickinson, the paintings of Vincent Van Gogh, the novels of Jane Austen, and the films of Akira Kurosawa. We can peer into the outermost reaches of the universe, and we can analyze our innermost feelings. In all these ways, we are remarkably different from other species of the animal kingdom.

The process of expanding culture has been under way for thousands of years. The first archeological evidence of humanlike primates places our ancestors back many millions of years. About 700,000 years ago, people built hearths to harness fire. Archeologists have uncovered tools that date back about 100,000 years. From 35,000 years ago we have evidence of paintings, jewelry, and statues. By that time, marriages, births, and deaths had already developed elaborate ceremonies (Haviland 1999; Harris 1997).

Tracing the development of culture is not easy. Archeologists cannot "dig up" weddings, laws, or government, but they are able to locate items that point to the emergence of cultural traditions. Our early ancestors were primates that had characteristics of human beings. These curious and communicative creatures made important advances in the use of tools. Recent studies of chimpanzees in the wild have revealed that they frequently use sticks and other natural objects in ways learned from other members of the group. However, unlike chimpanzees, our ancestors gradually made tools from increasingly durable materials. As a result, the items could be reused and refined into more effective implements.

Cultural Universals

Despite their differences, all societies have developed certain common practices and beliefs, known as *cultural universals.* Many cultural universals are, in fact, adaptations to meet essential human needs, such as people's need for food, shelter, and clothing. Anthropologist George Murdock (1945:124) compiled a list of cultural universals. Some of these include athletic sports, cooking, funeral ceremonies, medicine, and sexual restrictions.

The cultural practices listed by Murdock may be universal, but the manner in which they are expressed varies from culture to culture. For example, one society may let its members choose their own marriage partners. Another may encourage marriages arranged by the parents.

Sports are a cultural universal, but the variety of expression is endless. Shown here: traditional Japanese archery and camel racing in Saudi Arabia.

Not only does the expression of cultural universals vary from one society to another, it also may change dramatically over time within a society. Thus, the most popular styles of dancing in the United States today are sure to be different from the styles dominant in the 1950s or the 1970s. Each generation, and each year for that matter, most human cultures change and expand through the processes of innovation and diffusion.

Innovation

The process of introducing an idea or object that is new to culture is known as *innovation.* Innovation interests sociologists because of the social consequences that introducing something new can have in any society. There are two forms of innovation: discovery and invention. A *discovery* involves making known or sharing the existence of an aspect of reality. The finding of the DNA molecule and the identification of a new moon of Saturn are

both acts of discovery. A significant factor in the process of discovery is the sharing of newfound knowledge with others. By contrast, an *invention* results when existing cultural items are combined into a form that did not exist before. The bow and arrow, the automobile, and the television are all examples of inventions, as are Protestantism and democracy.

Diffusion and Technology

You don't have to sample gourmet food to eat "foreign" foods. Breakfast cereal comes originally from Germany, candy from the Netherlands, chewing gum from Mexico, and the potato chip from the America of the Indians. The United States has also "exported" foods to other lands. Residents of many nations enjoy pizza, which was popularized in the United States. However, in Japan they add squid, in Australia it is eaten with pineapple, and in England people like kernels of corn with the cheese.

Just as a culture does not always discover or invent its foods, it may also adopt ideas, technology, and customs from other cultures. Sociologists use the term *diffusion* to refer to the process by which a cultural item is spread from group to group or society to society. Diffusion can occur through a variety of means, among them exploration, military conquest, missionary work, the influence of the mass media, tourism, and the Internet.

Early in human history, culture changed rather slowly through discovery. Then, as the number of discoveries in a culture increased, inventions became possible. The more inventions there were, the more rapidly additional inventions could be created. In addition, as diverse cultures came into contact with one another, they could each take advantage of the other's innovations. Thus, when people in the United States read a newspaper, we look at characters invented by the ancient Semites, printed by a process invented in Germany, on a material invented in China (Linton 1936).

Nations tend to feel a loss of identity when they accept culture from outside. Many societies try to defend against what they regard as an invasion of too much culture from foreign countries, especially the economically dominant United States. Countries throughout the world decry U.S. exports, from films to language to Bart Simpson. Movies produced in the United States account for 65 percent of the global box office. Magazines as diverse as *Cosmopolitan* and *Reader's Digest* sell two issues abroad for every one they sell in the United States. *The X-Files* airs in 60 countries. These examples of canned culture all facilitate the diffusion of cultural practices. As Figure 3-1 shows, countries like Canada have made attempts to monitor and regulate diffusion (Farhi and Rosenfeld 1998).

FIGURE 3-1

What Is Canadian?

Canadians try to ward against U.S. influence by controlling what is played on the radio. The government requires that 35 percent of a station's programming in the daytime be Canadian. But what is Canadian? A complicated set of rules gives points based on whether the artist, the composer, the lyricist, or the production is Canadian. A song that earns two points meets the government requirements. Canadian Celine Dion singing "My Heart Will Go On" would not be classified as Canadian.

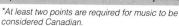

Celine Dion		Lenny Kravitz
Canadian	**Nationality**	Not Canadian
"My Heart Will Go On"	**Song**	"American Woman"
Not Canadian	**Lyricist**	Canadian
Not Canadian	**Composer**	Canadian
1 point*		2 points*

*At least two points are required for music to be considered Canadian.

Source: DePalma 1999.

Technology in its many forms has now increased the speed by which aspects of culture are shared and has broadened the distribution of cultural elements. Sociologist Gerhard Lenski has defined **technology** as "information about how to use the material resources of the environment to satisfy human needs and desires" (Nolan and Lenski 1999:41). Today's technological developments no longer have to await publication in journals with limited circulation. Press conferences, often simultaneously carried on the Internet, now trumpet new developments.

Technology not only accelerates the diffusion of scientific innovations but also transmits culture. Later in Chapter 22, we will discuss the concern in many parts of the world that the English language and North American culture dominate the Internet and World Wide Web. Control, or at least dominance, of technology influences the direction of diffusion of culture. Websites abound with the most superficial aspects of U.S. culture but little information about the pressing issues faced by citizens of other nations. People all over the world find it easier to visit electronic chat rooms about daytime television soaps like *All My Children* than to learn about their own government's policies on day care or infant nutrition programs.

Sociologist William F. Ogburn (1922) made a useful distinction between the elements of material and nonmaterial culture. **Material culture** refers to the physical or technological aspects of our daily lives, including food items, houses, factories, and raw materials. **Nonmaterial culture** refers to ways of using material objects and to cus-

toms, beliefs, philosophies, governments, and patterns of communication. Generally, the nonmaterial culture is more resistant to change than the material culture. Consequently, Ogburn introduced the term **culture lag** to refer to the period of maladjustment when the nonmaterial culture is still adapting to new material conditions. For example, the ethics of using the Internet, particularly privacy and censorship issues, have not yet caught up with the explosion in Internet use and technology (see the social policy section in Chapter 22).

Diffusion can involve a single word like "cyber" or an entirely new orientation toward living, which may be transmitted through advances in electronic communication. Sociologist George Ritzer (1995b) coined the term "McDonaldization of society" to describe how the principles of fast-food restaurants developed in the United States have come to dominate more and more sectors of societies throughout the world. For example, hair salons and medical clinics now take walk-in appointments. In Hong Kong, sex selection clinics offer a menu of items—from fertility enhancement to methods of increasing the likelihood of producing a child of the desired sex. Religious groups from evangelical preachers on local stations or websites to priests at the Vatican Television Center use marketing techniques similar to those that sell "happy meals."

McDonaldization is associated with the bringing together of cultures, so that we see more and more similarities in cultural expression. In Japan, for example, African

entrepreneurs have found a thriving market for hip-hop fashions popularized by teens in the United States. In Austria, the McDonald's organization itself has drawn on the Austrians' love of coffee, cake, and conversation to create the McCafe as part of its fast-food chain. Many observers believe that McDonaldization and the use of technology to spread elements of culture through diffusion both serve to reduce regional and national distinctiveness in all aspects of a society's culture (Alfino et al. 1998; T. Clark 1994; Ritzer 1995b; Rocks 1999). (Cultural diffusion via the media is discussed in more detail in Chapter 4.)

Elements of Culture

Each culture considers its own distinctive ways of handling basic societal tasks as "natural." But, in fact, methods of education, marital ceremonies, religious doctrines, and other aspects of culture are learned and transmitted through human interactions within specific societies. Parents in India are accustomed to arranging marriages for their children, whereas parents in the United States leave marital decisions up to their offspring. Lifelong residents of Naples consider it natural to speak Italian, whereas lifelong residents of Buenos Aires feel the same way about Spanish. We'll now take a look at the major aspects of culture that shape the way the members of a society live—language, norms, sanctions, and values.

Language

The English language makes extensive use of words dealing with war. We speak of "conquering" space, "fighting" the "battle" of the budget, "waging a war" on drugs, making a "killing" on the stock market, and "bombing" an examination; something monumental or great is "the bomb." An observer from an entirely different and warless culture could gauge the importance that war and the military have had on our lives simply by recognizing the prominence that militaristic terms have in our language (Haviland 1999). In the old West, words such as *gelding, stallion, mare, piebald,* and *sorrel* were all used to describe one animal—the horse. Even if we knew little of this period of history, we could conclude from the list of terms that horses were quite important in this culture. The Slave Indi-

ans of northern Canada, who live in a rather frigid climate, have 14 terms to describe ice, including 8 for different kinds of "solid ice" and others for "seamed ice," "cracked ice," and "floating ice." Clearly, language reflects the priorities of a culture (Basso 1972).

Language is, in fact, the foundation of every culture. *Language* is an abstract system of word meanings and symbols for all aspects of culture. It includes speech, written characters, numerals, symbols, and gestures and expressions of nonverbal communication. Figure 3-2 shows where the major languages of the world are spoken.

Language, of course, is not an exclusively human attribute. Although they are incapable of human speech, primates such as chimpanzees have been able to use symbols to communicate. However, even at their most advanced level, animals operate with essentially a fixed set of signs with fixed meanings. By contrast, humans can manipulate symbols in order to express abstract concepts and rules and to expand human cultures.

Unlike some other elements of culture, language permeates all parts of society. Certain cultural skills, such as cooking or carpentry, can be learned without the use of language through the process of imitation. However, is it possible to transmit complex legal and religious systems to the next generation by observing how they are performed? You could bang a gavel as a judge does, but you would never be able to understand legal reasoning without language. Therefore, people invariably depend on language for the use and transmission of the rest of a culture.

It's back to the classroom for these business executives. Conducting business overseas in today's global economy requires language skills.

FIGURE 3-2

Languages of the World

Mapping Life WORLDWIDE

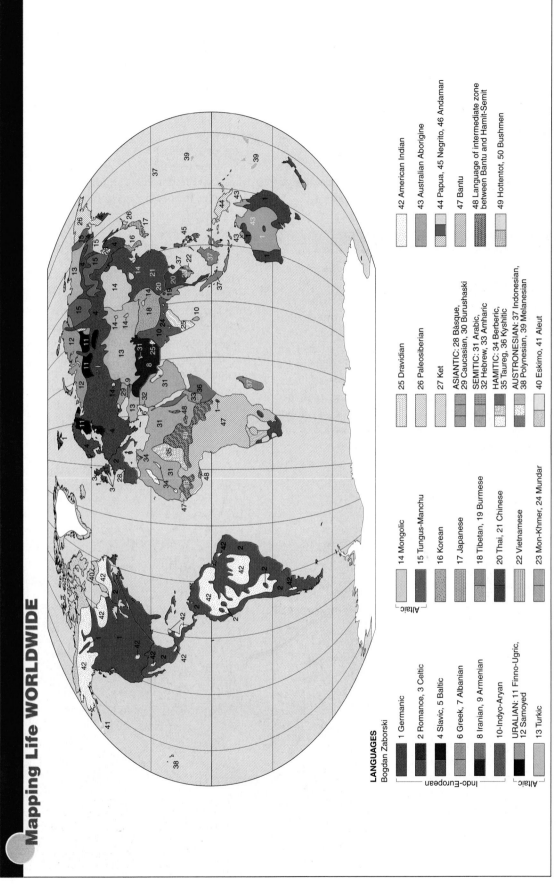

LANGUAGES
Bogdan Zaborski

Indo-European
1 Germanic
2 Romance, 3 Celtic
4 Slavic, 5 Baltic
6 Greek, 7 Albanian
8 Iranian, 9 Armenian
10 Indyo-Aryan

URALIAN: 11 Finno-Ugric, 12 Samoyed

Altaic
13 Turkic

Altaic
14 Mongolic
15 Tungus-Manchu
16 Korean
17 Japanese
18 Tibetan, 19 Burmese
20 Thai, 21 Chinese
22 Vietnamese
23 Mon-Khmer, 24 Mundar

25 Dravidian
26 Paleosiberian
27 Ket
ASIANTIC: 28 Basque, 29 Caucasian, 30 Burushaski
SEMITIC: 31 Arabic, 32 Hebrew, 33 Amharic
HAMITIC: 34 Berberic, 35 Taureg, 36 Kyshitic
AUSTRONESIAN: 37 Indonesian, 38 Polynesian, 39 Melanesian
40 Eskimo, 41 Aleut

42 American Indian
43 Australian Aborigine
44 Papua, 45 Negrito, 46 Andaman
47 Bantu
48 Language of intermediate zone between Bantu and Hamit-Semit
49 Hottentot, 50 Bushmen

Source: Espenshade 1990:25.

While language is a cultural universal, striking differences in the use of language are evident around the world. This is the case even when two countries use the same spoken language. For example, an English-speaking person from the United States who is visiting London may be puzzled the first time an English friend says "I'll ring you up." The friend means "I'll call you on the telephone." Similarly, the meanings of nonverbal gestures vary from one culture to another. Whereas residents of the United States attach positive meanings to the commonly used "thumbs up" gesture, this gesture has only vulgar connotations in Greece (Ekman et al. 1984).

Sapir-Whorf Hypothesis

Language does more than simply describe reality; it also serves to *shape* the reality of a culture. For example, most people in the United States cannot easily make the verbal distinctions about ice that are possible in the Slave Indian culture. As a result, they are less likely to notice such differences.

The **Sapir-Whorf hypothesis,** named for two linguists, describes the role of language in interpreting our world. According to Sapir and Whorf, since people can conceptualize the world only through language, language *precedes* thought. Thus, the word symbols and grammar of a language organize the world for us. The Sapir-Whorf hypothesis also holds that language is not a "given." Rather, it is culturally determined and leads to different interpretations of reality by focusing our attention on certain phenomena.

In a literal sense, language may color how we see the world. Berlin and Kay (1991) have noted that humans possess the physical ability to make millions of color distinctions, yet languages differ in the number of colors that are recognized. The English language distinguishes between yellow and orange, but some other languages do not. In the Dugum Dani language of New Guinea's West Highlands, there are only two basic color terms—*modla* for "white" and *mili* for "black." By contrast, there are 11 basic terms in English. Russian and Hungarian, though, have 12 color terms. Russians have terms for light blue and dark blue, while Hungarians have terms for two different shades of red.

Gender-related language can reflect—although in itself it will not determine—the traditional acceptance of men and women in certain occupations. Each time we use a term such as *mailman, policeman,* or *fireman,* we are implying (especially to young children) that these occupations can be filled only by males. Yet many women work as *letter carriers, police officers,* and *firefighters*—a fact that is being increasingly recognized and legitimized through the use of such nonsexist language (Henley et al. 1985; Martyna 1983).

Language can also transmit stereotypes related to race. Look up the meanings of the adjective *black* in dic-

tionaries published in the United States. You will find *dismal, gloomy* or *forbidding, destitute of moral light or goodness, atrocious, evil, threatening, clouded with anger.* By contrast, dictionaries list *pure* and *innocent* among the meanings of the adjective *white.* Through such patterns of language, our culture reinforces positive associations with the term (and skin color) *white* and a negative association with *black.* Is it surprising, then, that a list preventing people from working in a profession is called a *blacklist,* while a lie that we think of as somewhat acceptable is called a *white lie?*

Language can shape how we see, taste, smell, feel, and hear. It also influences the way we think about the people, ideas, and objects around us. A culture's most important norms, values, and sanctions are communicated to people through language. That's why the introduction of a new language into a society is such a sensitive issue in many parts of the world (see the social policy section of this chapter).

Nonverbal Communication

You know the appropriate distance to stand from someone when you talk informally. You know the circumstances under which it is appropriate to touch others, with a pat on the back or by taking someone's hand. If you are in the midst of a friendly meeting and one member suddenly sits back, folds his arms, and turns down the corners of his mouth, you know at once that trouble has arrived. These are all examples of *nonverbal communication,* the use of gestures and facial expressions to communicate.

We are not born with these gestures and expressions.

Nonverbal communication can take many forms. A particularly striking example arose out of the horrors of slavery in the United States. People sympathetic to the plight of escaping slaves would hang quilts with patterns similar to this one to indicate a "safe house" or to "point" in the right direction. In this example, the pattern emphasizes the triangles in the upper left corner, pointing in a westerly direction.

BURT CONSTABLE:
Newspaper Columnist and Reporter

As a columnist at Chicago's *Daily Herald,* Burt Constable does light-hearted takes on things for the most part, but he also tackles serious issues that require weeks of research. So within one week he may write about a local helicopter crash, Christmas card options, and the tobacco industry. "The stories that stick out most in my mind are the stories dealing with people. . . . These stories are more rewarding than the big events of the day."

Constable majored in journalism at Northwestern with a minor in sociology and graduated in 1980. He freely acknowledges that he "entered college with a black and white background; sociology provided all the grays for me." He grew up in a rural, all-White, Protestant community. The sociology classes he took were eye-opening, especially an upper-class course called "Sex" (which he says he took "for all the wrong reasons"). That class explored gender differences, abortion issues, gay issues, sexual harassment, gender perception, and so on. "Many of my ideas as a columnist come back from that class." Another important class was "Problems with Contemporary Cities," which looked at such issues as housing, crime, and government funding.

Constable credits sociology with helping him to write, deal with other human beings, and understand office politics. "It's also taught me to go into interviews with an open mind, to probe, to keep digging for the causes behind a problem." Sociology gave him the confidence to ask more questions and never be satisfied that the story is done.

Constable's advice to sociology students is to learn from one another, especially in the small groups with teaching assistants. "Some of that has stuck with me much longer than the textual stuff."

We learn them, just as we learn other forms of language, from people who share our same culture. This is as true for the basic expressions of smiling, laughter, and crying as it is for more complex emotions such as shame or distress (Fridlund et al. 1987).

Like other forms of language, nonverbal communication is not the same in all cultures. For example, sociological research at the microlevel documents that people from various cultures differ in the degree to which they touch others during the course of normal social interaction.

Norms

"Wash your hands before dinner." "Thou shalt not kill." "Respect your elders." All societies have ways of encouraging and enforcing what they view as appropriate behavior while discouraging and punishing what they consider to be improper behavior. *Norms* are established standards of behavior maintained by a society.

In order for a norm to become significant, it must be widely shared and understood. For example, in movie theaters in the United States, we typically expect that people will be quiet while the film is shown. Because of this norm, an usher can tell a member of the audience to stop talking so loudly. Of course, the application of this norm can vary, depending on the particular film and type of audience. People attending a serious artistic film will be more likely to insist on the norm of silence than those attending a slapstick comedy or horror movie.

Types of Norms

Sociologists distinguish between norms in two ways. First, norms are classified as either formal or informal. *Formal norms* generally have been written down and specify strict rules for punishment of violators. In the United States, we often formalize norms into laws, which must be very precise in defining proper and improper behavior. Sociologist Donald Black (1995) has termed *law* to be "governmental social control," establishing laws as formal norms enforced by the state. Laws are just one example of formal norms. The requirements for a college major and the rules of a card game are also considered formal norms.

By contrast, *informal norms* are generally understood but are not precisely recorded. Standards of proper dress are a common example of informal norms. Our society has no specific punishment or sanction for a person who comes to school, say, wearing a monkey suit. Making fun of the nonconforming student is the most likely response.

Norms are also classified by their relative importance to society. When classified in this way, they are known as *mores* and *folkways.*

Mores (pronounced "MOR-ays") are norms deemed highly necessary to the welfare of a society, often because they embody the most cherished principles of a people. Each society demands obedience to its mores; violation can lead to severe penalties. Thus, the United States has strong mores against murder, treason, and child abuse that have been institutionalized into formal norms.

Not so long ago someone who wore jeans to work in a law firm would have caused quite a stir. Today, however, "casual Fridays" have become an informal norm in the workplace.

Folkways are norms governing everyday behavior. Folkways play an important role in shaping the daily behavior of members of a culture. Consider, for example, something as simple as footwear. In Japan it is a folkway for youngsters to wear flip-flop sandals while learning to walk. A study of Japanese adults has found that, even barefoot, they walk as if wearing flip-flops—braking their thigh muscles and leaning forward as they step. This folkway may even explain why Japan produces so few competitive runners (Stedman 1998).

Society is less likely to formalize folkways than mores, and their violation raises comparatively little concern. For example, walking up a "down" escalator in a department store challenges our standards of appropriate behavior, but it will not result in a fine or a jail sentence.

In many societies around the world, folkways exist to reinforce patterns of male dominance. Various folkways reveal men's hierarchical position above women within the traditional Buddhist areas of southeast Asia. In the sleeping cars of trains, women do not sleep in upper berths above men. Hospitals that house men on the first floor do not place women patients on the second floor. Even on clotheslines, folkways dictate male dominance: women's attire is hung lower than that of men (Bulle 1987).

Acceptance of Norms

People do not follow norms, whether mores or folkways, in all situations. In some cases, they can evade a norm because they know it is weakly enforced. It is illegal for U.S. teenagers to drink alcoholic beverages, yet drinking by minors is common throughout the nation. (In fact, teenage alcoholism is one of our country's most serious social problems.)

In some instances, behavior that appears to violate society's norms may actually represent adherence to the norms of a particular group. Teenage drinkers conform to the standards of a peer group. Conformity to group norms also governed the behavior of the members of a religious cult associated with the Branch Davidians. In 1993, after a deadly gun battle with federal officials, nearly 100 members of the cult defied government orders to abandon their compound near Waco, Texas. After a 51-day standoff, the Department of Justice ordered an assault on the compound and 86 cult members died.

Norms are violated in some instances because one norm conflicts with another. For example, suppose that you live in an apartment building and one night hear the screams of the woman next door, who is being beaten by her husband. If you decide to intervene by ringing their doorbell or calling the police, you are violating the norm of "minding your own business" while, at the same time, following the norm of assisting a victim of violence.

Even when norms do not conflict, there are always exceptions to any norm. The same action, under different circumstances, can cause one to be viewed either as a hero or as a villain. Secretly taping telephone conversations is normally considered illegal and abhorrent. However, it can be done with a court order to obtain valid evidence for a criminal trial. We would heap praise on a government agent who uses such methods to convict an organized crime baron. In our culture, we tolerate killing another human being if it is in self-defense, and we actually reward killing in warfare.

Acceptance of norms is subject to change as the political, economic, and social conditions of a culture are transformed. For example, under traditional norms in the United States, a woman was expected to marry, rear children, and remain at home if her husband could support the family without her assistance. However, these norms have been changing in recent decades, in part as a result of the contemporary feminist movement (see Chapter 11). As support for traditional norms weakens, people feel free to violate them more frequently and openly and are less likely to be punished for doing so.

Sanctions

Suppose that a football coach sends a 12th player onto the field. Or imagine a college graduate showing up in shorts for a job interview at a large bank. Or consider a driver who neglects to put any money into a parking meter. These people have violated widely shared and understood norms. So what happens? In each of these situations, the person will receive sanctions if his or her behavior is detected.

Sanctions are penalties and rewards for conduct concerning a social norm. Note that the concept of *reward* is included in this definition. Conformity to a norm can lead to positive sanctions such as a pay raise, a medal, a word of gratitude, or a pat on the back. Negative sanctions include fines, threats, imprisonment, and stares of contempt.

Table 3-1 summarizes the relationship between norms and sanctions. As you can see, the sanctions that are associated with formal norms (those written down and codified) tend to be formalized as well. If a coach sends too many players onto the field, the team will be penalized 15 yards. The driver who fails to put money in the parking meter will be given a ticket and expected to pay a fine. But sanctions for violations of informal norms can vary. The college graduate who comes to the bank interview in shorts will probably lose any chance of getting the job; on the other hand, he or she might be so brilliant the bank officials will overlook the unconventional attire.

Table 3-1	Norms and Sanctions	
Norms	**Sanctions**	
	Positive	**Negative**
Formal	Salary bonus	Demotion
	Testimonial dinner	Firing from a job
	Medal	Jail sentence
	Diploma	Expulsion
Informal	Smile	Frown
	Compliment	Humiliation
	Cheers	Belittling

Applying sanctions entails first *detecting* violations of norms or obedience to norms. A person cannot be penalized or rewarded unless someone with the power to provide sanctions is aware of the person's actions. Therefore, if none of the officials in the football game realizes that there is an extra player on the field, there will be no penalty. If the police do not check the parking meter, there will be no fine or ticket. Furthermore, there can be *improper* application of sanctions in certain situations. The referee may make an error in counting the number of football players and levy an undeserved penalty on one team for "too many players on the field."

The entire fabric of norms and sanctions in a culture reflects that culture's values and priorities. The most cherished values will be most heavily sanctioned; matters regarded as less critical, on the other hand, will carry light and informal sanctions.

Values

We each have our own personal set of standards—which may include such things as caring or fitness or success in business—but we also share a general set of objectives as members of a society. Cultural *values* are these collective conceptions of what is considered good, desirable, and proper—or bad, undesirable, and improper—in a culture. They indicate what people in a given culture prefer as well as what they find important and morally right (or wrong). Values may be specific, such as honoring one's parents and owning a home, or they may be more general, such as health, love, and democracy. Of course, the members of a society do not uniformly share its values. Angry political debates and billboards promoting conflicting causes tell us that much. In Box 3-1 we explore how rock music has divided opinions, to the extent that some people regard the music as a social problem.

Values influence people's behavior and serve as criteria for evaluating the actions of others. There is often a direct relationship among the values, norms, and sanctions of a culture. For example, if a culture highly values the institution of marriage, it may have norms (and strict sanctions) that prohibit the act of adultery. If a culture views private property as a basic value, it will probably have stiff laws against theft and vandalism.

The values of a culture may change, but most remain relatively stable during any one person's lifetime. Socially shared, intensely felt values are a fundamental part of our lives in the United States. Sociologist Robin Williams (1970) has attempted to offer a list of basic values. His list includes achievement, efficiency, material comfort, nationalism, equality, and the supremacy of science and reason over faith. Obviously, not all 273 million people in this

3-1 Knockin' Rock—Making Music a Social Problem

In 1990 rock artist Judas Priest was sued by the parents of two boys who carried out a suicide pact. The parents claimed that the lyrics of Priest's song "Beyond the Realms of Death" encouraged the boys to opt out of life. That case was dismissed, but it symbolizes the antagonism that rock music has aroused in society, creating a cultural divide between generations.

In fact, rock music has come under attack for decades as the source of all sorts of evils—sexual promiscuity, teen pregnancy, drug use, satanism, suicide, abuse of women, and communism, to name just a few. Critics, who generally come from the religious and political right, point to the obscene lyrics of heavy metal, the anger of rap songs, the decadent lifestyles of rock artists, and the explicit movements and gestures of the performers as causes of deviant behavior in the youth generation.

The criticisms have had an impact. The U.S. Senate held hearings about obscene music, and record companies instigated voluntary labeling, to alert buyers to explicit lyrics. Cities and towns have canceled public performances of controversial rock musicians (Marilyn Manson was even paid $40,000 *not* to play in South Carolina). In the 1950s Ed Sullivan instructed his TV camera crew to show Elvis Presley only from the waist up while he was performing. Anxious parents today attempt to monitor the music their kids buy and the music videos they watch. In a word, rock music has been made into a social problem.

But is rock truly a social problem in that it causes undesirable behavior? Sociologist Deena Weinstein thinks not. In her research she found "no sociologically credible evidence that rock caused sexual promiscuity,

rape, drug abuse, satanism, and suicide. Indeed, there is clear evidence that it is not the cause of such behaviors" (1999). That is not to say that rock music has no part to play in these problems. According to Weinstein, rock music functions as a symbolic rebellion. It reflects the values of those who cherish the music, and these may be values that other groups in society want to inhibit. Rock music legitimizes the "disapproved" behaviors by giving them a symbolic form and making them public. Weinstein acknowledges, however, that symbols can have "complex and varied relations to behavior."

> Rock music has come under attack for decades as the source of all sorts of evils—sexual promiscuity, teen pregnancy, drug use, satanism, suicide, abuse of women, and communism, to name just a few.

Weinstein shows how the symbolic function of rock has changed over succeeding generations, matching the concerns and values of each youth generation. In the 1950s early "rock'n'roll" expressed the rebellion of teenagers against a society conforming to respectable middle-class codes. In the 1960s rock provided an outlet for feelings of political rebellion and a desire for consciousness expansion. The 1970s and 1980s gave rise to a number of distinct styles catering to special audiences. For example, the defiant rap music and the satanic appeals of heavy metal symbolized the alienation of marginalized youth.

In every decade, rock's detractors have tended to be the older generation—generally

The satanic lyrics of the rock vocalist Marilyn Manson give symbolic expression to the alienation felt by young people pushed to the margins of society.

white, middle class, politically conservative, and religious. They are intent on preserving the cultural values they hold dear and passing these on intact and unchanged to the generations to follow. Bewildered by rapid social changes and a youth culture resisting adult authority, the older generation makes rock into a convenient scapegoat for all their own fears and failures. The result is that they are more concerned with "killing the messenger" than paying attention to the message embedded in rock's symbolic rebellion. But, as Weinstein (1999) points out, "what could be more gratifying for a young symbolic rebel than to be thought of by the adult world as really important, as really dangerous?"

Let's Discuss

1. Describe how rock music today reflects the values of the youth generation.
2. How would a conflict theorist and a functionalist look at the interplay of rock music and its supporters and detractors?

Sources: Weinstein 1999, 2000.

country agree on one set of goals, and we should not look on such a list as anything more than a starting point in defining the national character. Nevertheless, a review of 27 different attempts to describe the "American value system," including the works of anthropologist Margaret Mead and

sociologist Talcott Parsons, revealed an overall similarity to the values identified by Williams (Devine 1972).

Cultures that seem similar may actually have quite different values. Take the issue of gays in the military. In 1993, President Bill Clinton's plan to lift the ban on lesbians and gay men in the U.S. armed forces aroused strong opposition both inside and outside the military. Yet, only a year earlier, Canada had ended a similar ban. Of 17 major allies of the United States, only three (Great Britain, Greece, and Portugal) explicitly ban gays from their military forces. A Danish air force general was puzzled over the controversy in the United States, noting, "I don't understand why you have a debate on it. . . . Nobody cares about it" (Lancaster 1992:14).

Each year more than 350,000 entering college students at 700 two-year and four-year colleges fill out a questionnaire surveying their attitudes. Because this survey focuses on an array of issues, beliefs, and life goals, it is commonly cited as a barometer of the values of the United States. The respondents are asked what various values are personally important to them. Over the last 33 years, the value of "being very well-off financially" has shown the strongest gain in popularity; the proportion of first-year college students who endorse this value as "essential" or "very important" rose from 44 percent in 1967 to 73 percent in 1999 (see Figure 3-3). By contrast, the value that has shown the most striking decline in endorsement by students is "developing a meaningful philosophy of life." While this value was the most popular in the 1967 survey, endorsed by more than 80 percent of the respondents, it had fallen to sixth place on the list by 1999 and was endorsed by only 40 percent of students entering college.

During the 1980s and 1990s, there was growing support for values having to do with money, power, and status. At the same time, there was a decline in support for

certain values having to do with social awareness and altruism, such as "helping others." According to the 1997 nationwide survey, only 38 percent of first-year college students stated that "influencing social values" was an "essential" or a "very important" goal. The proportion of students for whom "helping to promote racial understanding" was an essential or very important goal reached a record high of 42 percent in 1992 but fell to 28 percent in 1999. Clearly, like other aspects of culture, such as language and norms, a nation's values are not necessarily fixed.

Culture and the Dominant Ideology

Both functionalist and conflict theorists agree that culture and society are in harmony with each other, but for different reasons. Functionalists maintain that stability requires a consensus and the support of society's members; consequently, there are strong central values and common norms. This view of culture became popular in sociology beginning in the 1950s. It was borrowed from British anthropologists who saw cultural traits as all working toward stabilizing a culture. From a functionalist perspective, a cultural trait or practice will persist if it performs functions that society seems to need or contributes to overall social stability and consensus. We saw in Chapter 1 that this view helps explain why p. 14 widely condemned social practices such as prostitution continue to survive.

Conflict theorists agree that a common culture may exist, but they argue that it serves to maintain the privileges of certain groups. Moreover, while protecting their own self-interests, powerful groups may keep others in a subservient position. The term ***dominant ideology*** describes the set of cultural beliefs and practices that help to maintain powerful social, economic, and political interests. This concept was first used by Hungarian Marxist Georg Lukacs (1923) and Italian Marxist Antonio Gramsci (1929), but it did not gain an audience in the United States until the early 1970s. In Karl Marx's view, a capitalist society has a dominant ideology that serves the interests of the ruling class.

From a conflict perspective, the dominant ideology has major social significance. Not only do a society's most powerful groups and institutions control wealth and property; even more important, they control the means of producing beliefs about reality through religion, education, and the media. For example, if all of a society's most important institutions tell women that they should be subservient to men, this dominant ideol-

FIGURE 3-3

Life Goals of First-year College Students in the United States, 1966–1999

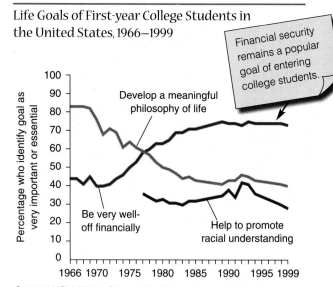

Sources: UCLA Higher Research Institute, as reported in Astin et al. 1994; Sax et al. 1999.

Research in Action

3-2 Dominant Ideology and Poverty

Why do we think people are poor? *Individualistic* explanations emphasize personal responsibility: Poor people lack the proper work ethic, lack ability, or are unsuited to the workplace because of problems like drinking or drug abuse. *Structural* explanations, on the other hand, lay the blame for poverty on such external factors as inferior educational opportunities, prejudice, and low wages in some industries. Past research documents that people in the United States generally go along with the individualistic explanation. In short, the dominant ideology holds that people are poor largely because of their own shortcomings.

How pervasive is this view, however? Do the poor and rich alike subscribe to it? In seeking answers, sociologists have conducted studies of how various groups of people view poverty. The research has shown that people with lower incomes are more likely than the wealthy to see the larger socioeconomic system as the cause of poverty. In part this structural view, focusing on the larger job market, relieves them of some personal responsibility for their plight, but it also reflects the social reality

that they are close to. On the other hand, the wealthy tend to embrace the dominant individualistic view because continuation of the socioeconomic status quo is in their best interests. They also prefer to regard their own success as the result of their own accomplishments, with little or no help from external factors.

> ...the dominant ideology holds that people are poor largely because of their own shortcomings.

Sociologist John Morland (1996) surveyed 2,628 people in metropolitan Los Angeles representing a mix of Whites, African Americans, and Latinos. As expected, he found that members of racial and ethnic minorities are more likely to support structural explanations of poverty than are Whites. He found this is true even among those Blacks and Latinos who are better off economically. Apparently, they are familiar with the historical reality of race-based dis-

crimination, and they can identify with the struggles of fellow group members.

Interestingly, while racial and ethnic minorities tend to support structural explanations more than Whites, they do not reject the individualistic view. This "dual consciousness" among minorities suggests that structural and individualistic explanations need not be considered mutually exclusive.

Is the dominant ideology on poverty widespread? Yes, but it appears that the individualist ideology is dominant in U.S. society not because of a lack of alternatives, but because those who see things differently lack the political influence and status needed to get the ear of the mainstream culture.

Let's Discuss

1. Distinguish between individualistic and structural explanations of poverty in the United States. Which is the dominant ideology?
2. Does support for the dominant ideology about poverty divide along income lines among racial and ethnic minorities? Why or why not?

Sources: Bobo 1991; Morland 1996.

ogy will help to control women and keep them in a subordinate position (Abercrombie et al. 1980, 1990; R. Robertson 1988).

A growing number of social scientists believe it is not easy to identify a "core culture" in the United States. For support, they point to the lack of consensus on national values, the diffusion of cultural traits, the diversity within our culture, and the changing views of young people (refer back to Figure 3-3). Yet there is no way of denying that certain expressions of values have greater influence than others, even in so complex a society as the United States (Abercrombie et al. 1980, 1990; Archer 1988; Wuthnow and Witten 1988). Box 3-2 illustrates that there is a dominant ideology about poverty that derives its strength from the more powerful segments of society.

Neither the functionalist nor the conflict perspective can alone explain all aspects of a culture. For example, we can trace the custom of tossing rice at a bride and groom back to the wish to have children and to the view of rice as

a symbol of fertility, rather than to the powerlessness of the proletariat. Nevertheless, certain cultural practices in our society and others clearly benefit some to the detriment of many. These practices may indeed promote social stability and consensus—but at whose expense?

Cultural Variation

Each culture has a unique character. Inuit tribes in northern Canada—wrapped in furs and dieting on whale blubber—have little in common with farmers in Southeast Asia, who dress for the heat and subsist mainly on the rice they grow in their paddies. Cultures adapt to meet specific sets of circumstances, such as climate, level of technology, population, and geography. This adaptation to different conditions shows up in differences in all elements of culture, including norms, sanctions, values, and language. Thus, despite the presence of cultural universals such as courtship and religion, there is still great diversity among the world's many cultures. Moreover, even within a single nation, certain segments of the populace develop cultural patterns that differ from the patterns of the dominant society.

Aspects of Cultural Variation

Subcultures

Residents of a retirement community, workers on an offshore oil rig, rodeo cowboys, street gangs, goth music fans—all are examples of what sociologists refer to as *subcultures*. A **subculture** is a segment of society that shares a distinctive pattern of mores, folkways, and values that differs from the pattern of the larger society. In a sense, a subculture can be thought of as a culture existing within a larger, dominant culture. The existence of many subcultures is characteristic of complex societies such as the United States.

You can get an idea of the impact of subcultures within the United States by considering the variety of seasonal traditions in December. The religious and commercial celebration of the Christmas holiday is an event well-entrenched in the dominant culture of our society. However, the Jewish subculture observes Hanukkah, African Americans have begun to observe the relatively new holiday of Kwanzaa, and some people join in rituals celebrating the winter solstice.

Members of a subculture participate in the dominant culture, while at the same time engaging in unique and distinctive forms of behavior. Frequently, a subculture will develop an **argot,** or specialized language, that distinguishes it from the wider society. For example, if you were to join a band of pickpockets you would need to learn what the dip, dish, and tailpipe are expected to do (see Figure 3-4).

Argot allows "insiders," the members of the subculture, to understand words with special meanings. It also establishes patterns of communication that "outsiders" can't understand. Sociologists associated with the interac-

Cultures vary because they need to adapt to the special conditions of their environment. Peruvians who live in the high Andes near the equator must adapt to a climate that can range from hot to cold within a single day. These women in Cuzco wear layers of clothing and cover their heads both for warmth and for protection from the high-altitude sun.

Retirement communities represent a fast-growing subculture in the United States today.

tionist perspective emphasize that language and symbols offer a powerful way for a subculture to feel cohesive and maintain its identity.

Subcultures develop in a number of ways. Often a subculture emerges because a segment of society faces

FIGURE 3-4

The Argot of Pickpockets

Source: Gearty 1996.

problems or even privileges unique to its position. Sub-cultures may be based on common age (teenagers or old people), region (Appalachians), ethnic heritage (Cuban Americans), occupation (firefighters), or beliefs (deaf activists working to preserve deaf culture). Certain subcultures, such as computer "hackers," develop because of a shared interest or hobby. In still other subcultures, such as that of prison inmates, members have been excluded from conventional society and are forced to develop alternative ways of living.

Functionalist and conflict theorists agree that variation exists within a culture. Functionalists view subcultures as variations of particular social environments and as evidence that differences can exist within a common culture. However, conflict theorists suggest that variation often reflects the inequality of social arrangements within a society. A conflict perspective would view the challenge to dominant social norms by African American activists, the feminist movement, and the disability rights movement as a reflection of inequity based on race, gender, and disability status. Conflict theorists also argue that subcultures sometimes emerge when the dominant society unsuccessfully tries to suppress a practice, such as the use of illegal drugs.

Countercultures

By the end of the 1960s, an extensive subculture had emerged in the United States composed of young people turned off by a society they believed was too materialistic

and technological. This group primarily included political radicals and "hippies" who had "dropped out" of mainstream social institutions. These young men and women rejected the pressure to accumulate more and more cars, larger and larger homes, and an endless array of material goods. Instead, they expressed a desire to live in a culture based on more humanistic values, such as sharing, love, and coexistence with the environment. As a political force, this subculture opposed the United States' involvement in the war in Vietnam and encouraged draft resistance (Flacks 1971; Roszak 1969).

When a subculture conspicuously and deliberately *opposes* certain aspects of the larger culture, it is known as a **counterculture** (Zellner 1995). Countercultures typically thrive among the young, who have the least investment in the existing culture. In most cases, a 20-year-old can adjust to new cultural standards more easily than someone who has spent 60 years following the patterns of the dominant culture.

In the wake of the Oklahoma City bombing in 1995,

"IT'S ENDLESS. WE JOIN A COUNTER-CULTURE; IT BECOMES THE CULTURE. WE JOIN ANOTHER COUNTER-CULTURE; IT BECOMES THE CULTURE..."

Cultures change. Aspects we once regarded as unacceptable—such as men wearing earrings and people wearing jeans in the workplace—and associated with fringe groups are now widely accepted.

people around the United States learned of a right-wing counterculture: armed militias. These militias, established in some 40 states, together have anywhere from 10,000 to 40,000 members. Militia leaders claim that their paramilitary training and arms caches are essential measures of self-defense against what they see as an oppressive federal government that is violating the rights of U.S. citizens. Nevertheless, many militias have ties to right-wing, White supremacist groups that often espouse anti-Semitic conspiracy theories (R. Serrano 1996).

Culture Shock

In the Navajo town of Window Rock, Arizona, a zoo with 78 animals has sparked an unusual controversy. Traditionalists among the reservation's 175,000 inhabitants maintain that the zoo violates Navajo culture, which holds animals in great respect and by custom does not enclose any animals. These Navajo are offended by the sight of zoo animals in cages. On the other side of the controversy are less traditional reservation inhabitants and the zoo's curator and veterinarian, who are both White. They are worried that many of the animals would not survive if they were released. This controversy illustrates culture

shock between two cultures within the same society; each one is encountering unfamiliar aspects of a different culture (Robbins 1999).

Anyone who feels disoriented, uncertain, out of place, even fearful, when immersed in an unfamiliar culture may be experiencing **culture shock.** For example, a resident of the United States who visits certain areas in China and wants local meat for dinner may be stunned to learn that the specialty is dog meat. Similarly, someone from a strict Islamic culture may be shocked upon first seeing the comparatively provocative dress styles and open displays of affection that are common in the United States and various European cultures.

All of us, to some extent, take for granted the cultural practices of our society. As a result, it can be surprising and even disturbing to realize that other cultures do not follow our "way of life." The fact is that customs that seem strange to us are considered normal and proper in other cultures, which may see *our* mores and folkways as odd.

Culture shock over conflicting value systems is not limited to contacts between traditional and modern societies. We can experience culture shock at home. A conservative, churchgoing older person, for example, might feel bewildered or horrified at a goth concert.

Women in certain areas of Thailand traditionally elongated their necks by wearing layers of coils. The custom began dying out until the Thai people discovered that tourists would pay money to be "shocked" by the practice. These girls are members of the "Long Neck" tribe.

Attitudes toward Cultural Variation

Ethnocentrism

Many everyday statements reflect our attitude that our culture is best. We use terms such as *underdeveloped, backward,* and *primitive* to refer to other societies. What "we" believe is a religion; what "they" believe is superstition and mythology (Spradley and McCurdy 1980).

It is tempting to evaluate the practices of other cultures on the basis of our own perspectives. Sociologist William Graham Sumner (1906) coined the term **ethnocentrism** to refer to the tendency to assume that one's culture and way of life constitute the norm or are superior to all others. The ethnocentric person sees his or her own group as the center or defining point of culture and views all other cultures as deviations from what is "normal."

Those westerners who are contemptuous of India's Hindu religion and culture because of its view of cattle as sacred are engaged in ethnocentrism. As another manifestation of ethnocentrism, people in one culture may dismiss as unthinkable the mate selection or child-rearing practices of another culture. We might, in fact, be tempted to view the Nacirema culture from an ethnocentric point of view—until we learn it is our own culture that Miner describes (see the chapter opening).

Conflict theorists point out that ethnocentric value judgments serve to devalue groups and to deny equal opportunities. Psychologist Walter Stephan notes a typical example of ethnocentrism in New Mexico's schools. Both Hispanic and Native American cultures teach children to look down when they are being criticized by adults, yet many "Anglo" (non-Hispanic White) teachers believe that you should look someone in the eye when you are being criticized. "Anglo teachers can feel that these students are being disrespectful," notes Stephan. "That's the kind of misunderstanding that can evolve into stereotype and prejudice" (Goleman 1991:C8).

Functionalists note that ethnocentrism serves to maintain a sense of solidarity by promoting group pride. Denigrating other nations and cultures can enhance our own patriotic feelings and belief that our way of life is superior. Yet this type of social stability is established at the expense of other peoples. Of course, ethnocentrism is hardly limited to citizens of the United States. Visitors from many African cultures are surprised at the disrespect that children in the United States show their parents. People from India may be repelled by our practice of living in the same household with dogs and cats. Many Islamic fundamentalists in the Arab world and Asia view the United States as corrupt, decadent, and doomed to destruction. All these people may feel comforted by membership in cultures that, in their view, are superior to ours.

Cultural Relativism

While ethnocentrism evaluates foreign cultures using the familiar culture of the observer as a standard of correct behavior, **cultural relativism** views people's behavior from the perspective of their own culture. It places a priority on understanding other cultures, rather than dismissing them as "strange" or "exotic." Unlike ethnocentrism, cultural relativism employs the kind of value neutrality in scientific study that Max Weber saw as so important (see Chapter 2).

p. 47

Cultural relativism stresses that different social contexts give rise to different norms and values. Thus, we must examine practices such as polygamy, bullfighting, and monarchy within the particular contexts of the cultures in which they are found. While cultural relativism does not suggest that we must unquestionably *accept* every cultural variation, it does require a serious and unbiased effort to evaluate norms, values, and customs in light of their distinctive culture.

Applying cultural relativism can raise delicate questions. In 1989, a Chinese immigrant was convicted in a New York court of bludgeoning his wife to death with a hammer. However, the judge acquitted the man of the most serious charges against him and sentenced him to only five years' probation, on the basis that cultural considerations warranted leniency. The wife had confessed to having had an extramarital affair; in such situations, as an expert on Chinese culture testified at the trial, husbands in China often exact severe punishment on their wives. In posttrial hearings, the judge declared that the defendant "took all his Chinese culture with him to the United States" and therefore was not fully responsible for his violent conduct. In response to this ruling, Brooklyn district attorney Elizabeth Holtzman angrily insisted, "There should be one standard of justice, not one that depends on the cultural background of the defendant. . . . Anyone who comes to this country must be prepared to live by and obey the laws of this country" (Rosario and Marcano 1989:2).

There is an interesting extension of cultural relativism, referred to as *xenocentrism*. **Xenocentrism** is the belief that the products, styles, or ideas of one's society are *inferior* to those that originate elsewhere (W. Wilson et al. 1976). In a sense, it is a reverse ethnocentrism. For example, people in the United States often assume that French fashions or Japanese electronic devices are superior to our own. Are they? Or are people unduly charmed by the lure of goods from exotic places? Such fascination with overseas products can be damaging to competitors in the United States. Some companies have responded by creating products that *sound* European like Häagen-Dazs ice cream (made in Teaneck, New Jersey). Conflict theorists are most likely to consider the economic impact of xenocentrism in the developing world. Consumers in developing nations frequently turn their backs on locally produced goods and instead purchase items imported from Europe or North America.

How one views one's culture—whether from an ethnocentric point of view or through the lens of cultural relativism—has important consequences in the area of social policy. A hot issue today is the extent to which a nation should accommodate nonnative language speakers by sponsoring bilingual programs. We'll take a close look at this issue in the next section.

The Issue

In Sri Lanka, English-speaking Tamils seek to break away from the Sinhalese-speaking majority. Romanian radio announces that in areas where 20 percent of the people speak Hungarian, bilingual road and government signs will be used. In schools from Miami to Boston to Chicago, school administrators strive to deliver education to their Creole-speaking Haitian students. All over the world, nations are having to face the problem of how to deal with residential minorities who speak a language different from that of the mainstream culture.

Bilingualism refers to the use of two or more languages in a particular setting, such as the workplace or educational facilities, treating each language as equally legitimate. Thus, a program of bilingual education may instruct children in their native language while gradually introducing them to the language of the host society. If the curriculum is also bicultural, it will teach children about the mores and folkways of both the dominant culture and the subculture. To what degree should schools in the United States present the curriculum in a language other than English? This issue has prompted a great deal of debate among educators and policymakers.

The Setting

Languages know no political boundaries. Despite the portrayal of dominant languages in Figure 3-1 (page

70), minority languages are common in many nations. For example, while Hindi is the most widely spoken language in India and English is widely used for official purposes, there are still 18 other languages officially recognized in this nation of about one billion people. According to a report released by the Bureau of the Census, almost 32 million residents of the United States—that's about one out of every seven people—speak a language other than English as their primary language. Indeed, 50 different languages are each spoken by at least 30,000 residents of this country (Instituto del Tercer Mundo 1997).

Schools throughout the world must deal with incoming students speaking many languages. Do bilingual programs in the United States help these children to learn English? It is difficult to reach firm conclusions because bilingual programs in general vary so widely in their approach. They differ in the length of the transition to English and how long they allow students to remain in bilingual classrooms. However, according to a major overview of 11 different studies on bilingual education, children with limited English proficiency who are taught using at least some of their native language perform significantly better on standardized tests than similar children who are taught only in English. Yet bilingual programs are an expense that many communities and states are unwilling to pay and are quick to cut back (J. Greene 1998; see also A. Pyle 1998).

Support for bilingualism or bilingual education does not mean that parents are unwilling for their children to become fluent in the dominant language. A survey in Los Angeles found that 83 percent of Latino parents in suburban Los Angeles favor English instruction for their children as soon as possible. This desire is certainly understandable from an economic perspective. Research shows that earnings of immigrants with English language skills, as opposed to those without these skills, are 8.3 percent higher in Australia, 12.2 percent higher in Canada, and 16.9 percent higher in the United States (R. Porter 1997).

Sociological Insights

For a long time, people in the United States demanded conformity to a single language. In a sense, this demand coincides with the functionalist view that language serves to unify members of a society. Immigrant children from Europe and Asia—including young Italians, Jews, Poles, Chinese, and Japanese—were expected to learn English once they entered school. In some cases, immigrant children were actually forbidden to speak their native languages on school grounds. There was little respect granted to immigrants' cultural traditions; a young person would often be teased about his or her "funny" name, accent, or style of dress.

Recent decades have seen challenges to this pattern of forced obedience to our dominant ideology. Beginning in the 1960s, active movements for Black pride and ethnic pride insisted that people regard the traditions of *all* racial and ethnic subcultures as legitimate and important. Conflict theorists explain this development as a case of subordinated language minorities seeking opportunities of self-expression. Partly as a result of these challenges, society began to view bilingualism as an asset. It seemed to provide one way of assisting millions of non–English-speaking people in the United States to *learn* English in order to function more effectively within the society.

The perspective of conflict theory also helps us understand some of the attacks on bilingual programs. Many of them stem from an ethnocentric point of view, which holds that any deviation from the majority is bad. This attitude tends to be expressed by those who wish to stamp out foreign influence wherever it occurs, especially in our schools. This view does not take into account that success in bilingual education may actually have beneficial results, such as decreasing the number of high school dropouts and increasing the number of Hispanics in colleges and universities.

Policy Initiatives

Bilingualism has policy implications largely in two areas—efforts to maintain language purity and programs to enhance bilingual education. Nations vary dramatically in their tolerance for a variety of languages. China continues to tighten its cultural control over Tibet by extending instruction of Mandarin, a Chinese dialect, from high school into the elementary schools, which will now be bilingual along with Tibetan. Even more forceful is Indonesia, which has a large Chinese-speaking minority;

public display of Chinese-language signs or books is totally banned. By contrast, nearby Singapore establishes English as the medium of instruction but allows students to take their mother tongue as a second language, be it Chinese, Malay, or Tamil (M. Farley 1998).

In many nations, language dominance is a regional issue—for example, in Miami or along the border of Texas, where Spanish speaking is prevalent. A particularly virulent bilingual hot spot is Quebec—the French-speaking province of Canada. The Québécois, as they are known, represent 80 percent of the province's population, but only 25 percent of Canada's total population. A law implemented in 1978 mandated education in French for all Quebec's children except those whose parents or siblings had learned English elsewhere in Canada. While special laws like this one have advanced French in the province, dissatisfied Québécois have moved for secession to form their own separate country. In 1995, the people of Quebec voted to remain united with Canada by only the narrowest of margins (50.5 percent). Language and related cultural areas both unify and divide this nation of 30 million people (Schaefer 2000).

Policymakers in the United States have been somewhat ambivalent in dealing with the issue of bilingualism. In 1965, the Elementary and Secondary Education Act (ESEA) provided for bilingual, bicultural education. Then, in the 1970s, the federal government took an active role in establishing the proper form for bilingual programs. However, more recently, federal policy has been less supportive of bilingualism. Local school districts have been forced to provide an increased share of funding for their bilingual programs. In 1998 voters in California approved a proposition that would in effect dismantle bilingual education: it requires instruction in English for 1.4 million children who are not fluent in the language.

In the United States, there have been repeated efforts (most recently in 1997) to introduce a constitutional amendment to make English the official language of the nation. A major force behind the proposed amendment and other efforts to restrict bilingualism is U.S. English, a nationwide organization founded in 1983 that now claims to have one million members. Its adherents say they feel like strangers in their own neighborhoods, aliens in their own country. By contrast, Hispanic leaders see the U.S. English campaign as a veiled expression of racism.

Despite such challenges, U.S. English seems to be making headway in its efforts to oppose bilingualism. By 1999, 25 states had officially declared English to be their official language (see Figure 3-5). The actual impact of these measures, beyond their symbolism, is unclear. A 1988 Arizona constitutional amendment, for example, has been subject to several rulings and has yet to be implemented.

Let's Discuss

1. How might someone with an ethnocentric point of view look at bilingualism?

2. Describe how conflict theorists would explain recent developments in bilingual programs in the United States.
3. Why is the province of Quebec in Canada considered a "bilingual hot spot"?

FIGURE 3-5

States with Official English Laws

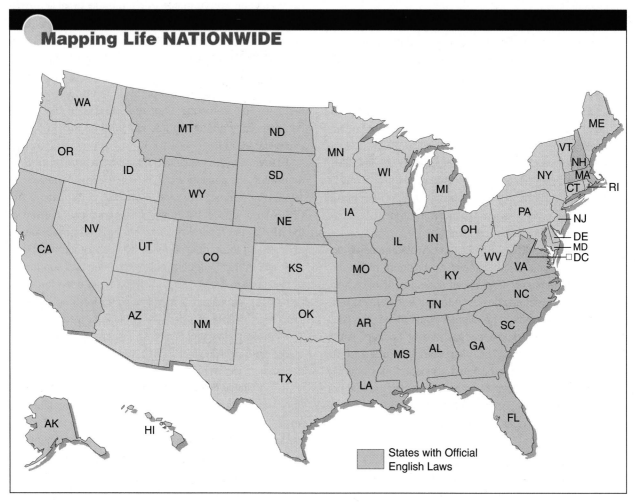

Source: U.S. English 1999.

Summary

Culture is the totality of learned, socially transmitted customs, knowledge, material objects, and behavior. This chapter examines the basic elements that make up a culture, social practices common to all cultures, and variations that distinguish one culture from another.

1. Sharing a similar culture helps to define the group or society to which we belong.
2. Anthropologist George Murdock has compiled a list of *cultural universals,* general practices found in every culture, including courtship, family, games, language, medicine, religion, and sexual restrictions.
3. Human culture is constantly expanding through *innovation,* including both *discovery* and *invention.*
4. *Diffusion*—the spread of cultural items from one place to another—also changes cultures. But societies resist ideas that seem too foreign as well as those that are perceived as threatening to their own values and beliefs.
5. *Language,* an important element of culture, includes speech, written characters, numerals, symbols, and gestures and other forms of nonverbal communication. Language both describes culture and shapes it for us.
6. Sociologists distinguish between *norms* in two ways. They are classified as either *formal* or *informal* norms and as *mores* or *folkways.*

7. The more cherished *values* of a culture will receive the heaviest sanctions; matters that are regarded as less critical, on the other hand, will carry light and informal sanctions.
8. The *dominant ideology* of a culture describes the set of cultural beliefs and practices that help to maintain powerful social, economic, and political interests.
9. In a sense, a *subculture* can be thought of as a culture existing within a larger, dominant culture. *Countercultures* are subcultures that deliberately oppose aspects of the larger culture.
10. People who measure other cultures by the standard of their own engage in *ethnocentrism.* Using *cultural relativism* allows us to view people from the perspective of their own culture.
11. The social policy of *bilingualism* calls for programs that use two or more languages, treating each as equally legitimate. It is supported by those who want to ease the transition of nonnative language speakers into a host society; it is opposed by those who adhere to a single cultural tradition in language.

Critical Thinking Questions

1. Select three cultural universals from George Murdock's list (see p. 66) and analyze them from a functionalist perspective. Why are these practices found in every culture? What functions do they serve?
2. Drawing on the theories and concepts presented in the chapter, apply sociological analysis to one subculture with which you are familiar. Describe the norms, values, argot, and sanctions evident in that subculture.
3. In what ways is the dominant ideology of the United States evident in the nation's literature, music, movies, theater, television programs, and sporting events?

Key Terms

Argot Specialized language used by members of a group or subculture. (page 78)

Bilingualism The use of two or more languages in particular settings, such as workplaces or educational facilities, treating each language as equally legitimate. (82)

Counterculture A subculture that deliberately opposes certain aspects of the larger culture. (79)

Cultural relativism The viewing of people's behavior from the perspective of their own culture. (81)

Cultural universals General practices found in every culture. (66)

Culture The totality of learned, socially transmitted customs, knowledge, material objects, and behavior. (65)

Culture lag Ogburn's term for a period of maladjustment during which the nonmaterial culture is still adapting to new material conditions. (68)

Culture shock The feeling of surprise and disorientation that is experienced when people witness cultural practices different from their own. (80)

Diffusion The process by which a cultural item is spread from group to group or society to society. (67)

Discovery The process of making known or sharing the existence of an aspect of reality. (67)

Dominant ideology A set of cultural beliefs and practices that helps to maintain powerful social, economic, and political interests. (76)

Ethnocentrism The tendency to assume that one's own culture and way of life represent the norm or are superior to all others. (80)

Folkways Norms governing everyday social behavior whose violation raises comparatively little concern. (73)

Formal norms Norms that generally have been written down and that specify strict rules for punishment of violators. (72)

Informal norms Norms that generally are understood but are not precisely recorded. (72)

Innovation The process of introducing new elements into a culture through either discovery or invention. (67)

Invention The combination of existing cultural items into a form that did not previously exist. (67)

Language An abstract system of word meanings and symbols for all aspects of culture. It also includes gestures and other nonverbal communication. (69)

Law Governmental social control. (72)

Material culture The physical or technological aspects of our daily lives. (68)

Mores Norms deemed highly necessary to the welfare of a society. (72)

Nonmaterial culture Cultural adjustments to material conditions, such as customs, beliefs, patterns of communication, and ways of using material objects. (68)

Norms Established standards of behavior maintained by a society. (72)

Sanctions Penalties and rewards for conduct concerning a social norm. (74)

Sapir-Whorf hypothesis A hypothesis concerning the role of language in shaping cultures. It holds that language is culturally determined and serves to influence our mode of thought. (69)

Society A fairly large number of people who live in the same territory, are relatively independent of people outside it, and participate in a common culture. (66)

Subculture A segment of society that shares a distinctive pattern of mores, folkways, and values that differs from the pattern of the larger society. (78)

Technology Information about how to use the material resources of the environment to satisfy human needs and desires. (68)

Values Collective conceptions of what is considered good, desirable, and proper—or bad, undesirable, and improper—in a culture. (74)

Xenocentrism The belief that the products, styles, or ideas of one's society are inferior to those that originate elsewhere. (81)

Additional Readings

BOOKS

DeVita, Philip B., and James D. Armstrong, eds. 1998. *Distant Mirrors: America as a Foreign Culture.* 2d ed. Belmont, CA: West/Wadsworth. Nineteen essays by scholars from Europe, Africa, Asia, and Latin America who conduct observation research about U.S. society and culture from the outsider's perspective.

Kraybill, Donald B., and Steven M. Nott. 1995. *Amish Enterprises: From Plows to Profits.* Baltimore: Johns Hopkins University Press. An examination of how the Amish have adapted to capitalism in the United States while maintaining their distinctive values and subculture.

Weinstein, Deena. 2000. *The Music and Its Culture.* Cambridge, MA: Da Capo. A sociologist examines the subculture associated with "heavy metal" music and efforts to curtail this subculture.

Zellner, William M. 1995. *Countercultures: A Sociological Analysis.* New York: St. Martin's. An overview of six countercultures found in the United States: the Unification Church, the Church of Scientology, satanists, skinheads, survivalists, and the Ku Klux Klan.

JOURNALS

Among the journals that focus on issues of culture and language are *Academic Questions* (the journal of the National Association of Scholars, founded in 1988), *American Anthropologist* (1988), *Cross-Cultural Research* (1994), *Cultural Survival Quarterly* (1977), *Ethnology* (1962), *International Journal of the Sociology of Language* (1974), *MultiCultural Social Change* (1979), and *Theory, Culture, and Society* (1982).

Internet Connection

Note: While all the URLs listed were current as of the printing of this book, these sites often change. Please check our website (http://www.mhhe.com/schaefer) for updates.

1. This chapter discusses how language, in general, serves as the foundation for culture. One type of language is the nonverbal sign language used to communicate to the deaf. To learn more about American Sign Language, visit Sign Language Dictionary Online (**http://dww.deafworldweb.org/asl).** Use the series of letters/words in the left-hand corner to see moving picture demonstrations of signing. Try signing your own name.
   (a) What is "Gestuno"? Why was it created?
   (b) How do "foreign" sign languages differ from ASL?
   (c) What role do facial gestures play in sign language, according to the "Introductions" section of the site?
   (d) What is a "Sign Area" and where is it generally located, according to the "Culture and Language" section?
   (e) Click on the "ASL Stories" link and read/watch the story of "The Lamp." What is the moral of the story? Was watching a story in sign language different from hearing an oral version? Why or why not?

   (f) Some people question the legitimacy of signing as a valid language. What is your perspective?

2. We all belong to subcultures, segments of society that share a distinctive pattern of mores, folkways, and values differing from the pattern of the larger society. One example of subcultures is online gaming groups. Log on to the Rebel Squadron homepage (**http://www.rebelsquadrons.org/),** a site for international Star Wars fans who come together via the computer and play simulation games.
   (a) What is the age range for all members of this subculture group?
   (b) Which countries do members come from?
   (c) Do the members have an argot? If so, what are some of their specialized terms and words?
   (d) Examine the club "Bylaws." What are the mission statement and shared goals of the gamers? What norms are members expected to observe? What possible sanctions can be levied against deviants?
   (e) How does one join the group? What are the requirements for becoming an insider?
   (f) In what ways are "online" subcultures different from traditional ones? In what ways are they the same?

Schools can sometimes be stressful arenas of socialization. This poster informs schoolchildren in Japan that they can call a hotline and receive advice concerning stress, bullying by classmates, and corporal punishment from their teachers.

In sixth grade, the popular girls' clique split into two subgroups, whose leaders were Tiffany and Emily. The girls from the two groups liked each other, but the leaders did not. Tiffany was jealous of the attention Emily got from her followers and from the popular boys, wanting center stage all to herself. Emily resented Tiffany's intrusions and manipulations. They polarized their groups against each other.

By spring, Tiffany could no longer control her hatred. She persuaded one of the less popular boys to steal Emily's backpack, empty it, and take it into the rest room and smear it with excrement. Emily discovered her backpack missing, searched for it, and alerted her teacher. The backpack was finally found in the boys' rest room (where it could not be traced back to Tiffany), clogging up a toilet, soaking in urine and feces. Although the school administrators interviewed numerous people to try to uncover the truth, they were never able to solve the crime.

Tiffany used Emily's anguish to ridicule her, portray her as weak, and turn the bulk of the popular people (boys and girls) against her. The following year Emily's parents sent her to boarding school.

*   *   *

One day Larry, Brad, and Trevor were at Rick's house. Larry had just turned twelve and had a lot of birthday money in his wallet. Brad noticed Larry's wallet lying on Rick's bed and climbed on top of it. He motioned Trevor to join him. From his perch, Brad asked Larry where his wallet was, and when Larry could not find it, Brad accused Rick of stealing it. Despite Rick's fervent denials, Brad eventually convinced Larry of Rick's guilt, whipping him into a frenzy of anger and outrage. Larry tore Rick's room apart looking for his wallet. Brad slyly showed Trevor the wallet he was sitting on, inviting him to join him in conspiratorial silence.

Brad's accusations, Larry's fear for his money and anger at Rick, and Rick's pathetic denials escalated to the point where Larry began threatening to break Rick's things if he did not turn over the wallet. Helplessly, Rick professed innocence and ignorance. Larry broke Rick's lamp. Then he smashed the telephone in Rick's room (a birthday gift) to the floor, shattering it. He stomped on video games. Rick wailed and cried. Larry ran out of the room, moving to the kitchen to find more things to destroy, his anger out of control. Rick followed him, screaming, terrified. As Larry was about to throw down a blender, Rick's mother came home and stopped him. Assessing the situation, she sent the three boys home. Searching the house, she found the wallet on the bed and called Larry's mother.

The next day in school, Brad and Trevor bragged exultantly to everybody about their caper. Rick was out of the group. *(Adler and Adler 1998:2–3)* ■

Patricia and Peter Adler's intensive research into preadolescent culture began with their own children, when they were five and nine. As participant observers, the parents jumped into the lives of their children, their children's friends, and children of their own friends as well as other children in their community over a period of eight years. They uncovered a dynamic peer culture—one in which the preadolescents' interactions help determine such things as status, popularity, friendships, and activities. In their book *Peer Power*, the Adlers show that children are active agents in creating their social world and getting socialized into it; they are not just the passive objects of socialization by parents, teachers, and other authority figures in their lives. These researchers found that while each child has his or her own special issues and experiences, the influence of the peer culture forms lifelong patterns.

Sociologists, in general, are interested in the patterns of behavior and attitudes that emerge *throughout* the life course, from infancy to old age. These patterns are part of the process of ***socialization,*** whereby people learn the attitudes, values, and behaviors appropriate for members of a particular culture. Socialization occurs through human interactions. We learn a great deal from those people most important in our lives—immediate family members, best friends, and teachers. But we also learn from people we see on the street, on television, and in films and magazines. From a microsociological perspective, socialization helps us to discover how to behave "properly" and what to expect from others if we follow (or challenge) society's norms and values. From a macrosociological perspective, socialization provides for the transmission of a culture from one generation to the next and thereby for the long-term continuance of a society.

Socialization affects the overall cultural practices of a society, and it also shapes our self-images. For example, in the United States, a person who is viewed as "too heavy" or "too short" does not conform to the ideal cultural standard of physical attractiveness. An unfavorable evaluation of someone's appearance by others can significantly influence the person's self-esteem. In this sense, socialization experiences can help shape our personalities. In everyday speech, the term ***personality*** is used to refer to a person's typical patterns of attitudes, needs, characteristics, and behavior.

This chapter will examine the role of socialization in human development. It begins by analyzing the debate concerning the interaction of heredity and environmental factors. We pay particular attention to how people develop perceptions, feelings, and beliefs about themselves. The chapter will also explore the lifelong nature of the socialization process, as well as important agents of socialization, among them the family, schools, and the media. Finally, the social policy section will focus on the socialization experience of group child care for young children. ■

The Role of Socialization

What makes us who we are? Is it the genes we are born with? Or the environment in which we grow up? Researchers have traditionally clashed over the relative importance of biological inheritance and environmental factors in human development—a conflict called the *nature versus nurture* (or *heredity versus environment*) debate. Today, most social scientists have moved beyond this debate, acknowledging instead the *interaction* of these variables in shaping human development. However, we can better appreciate how heredity and environmental factors interact and influence the socialization process if we first examine situations in which one factor operates almost entirely without the other (Homans 1979).

Environment: The Impact of Isolation

In the 1994 Hollywood film *Nell*, Jodie Foster played a young woman hidden from birth by her mother in a backwoods cabin. Raised without normal human contact, Nell crouches like an animal, screams wildly, and speaks or sings in a language all her own. This movie was drawn from the actual account of an emaciated 16-year-old boy who mysteriously appeared in 1828 in the town square of Nuremberg, Germany (Lipson 1994).

The Case of Isabelle

Some viewers may have found the story of Nell difficult to believe, but the painful childhood of Isabelle was all too real. For the first six years of her life, Isabelle lived in almost total seclusion in a darkened room. She had little contact with other people, with the exception of her mother, who could neither speak nor hear. Isabelle's mother's parents had been so deeply ashamed of Isabelle's illegitimate birth that they kept her hidden away from the world. Ohio authorities finally discovered the child in 1938, when Isabelle's mother escaped from her parents' home, taking her daughter with her.

When she was discovered at age six, Isabelle could not speak. She could merely make various croaking sounds. Her only communications with her mother were simple gestures. Isabelle had been largely deprived of the typical interactions and socialization experiences of childhood. Since she had actually seen few people, she initially showed a strong fear of strangers and reacted almost like a wild animal when confronted with an unfamiliar person.

These children in a Romanian orphanage enjoy little adult contact and spend much of their time confined to cribs. This neglect can result in adjustment problems later in life.

As she became accustomed to seeing certain individuals, her reaction changed to one of extreme apathy. At first, it was believed that Isabelle was deaf, but she soon began to react to nearby sounds. On tests of maturity, she scored at the level of an infant rather than a six-year-old.

Specialists developed a systematic training program to help Isabelle adapt to human relationships and socialization. After a few days of training, she made her first attempt to verbalize. Although she started slowly, Isabelle quickly passed through six years of development. In a little over two months, she was speaking in complete sentences. Nine months later, she could identify both words and sentences. Before Isabelle reached the age of nine, she was ready to attend school with other children. By her 14th year, she was in sixth grade, doing well in school, and emotionally well-adjusted.

Yet, without an opportunity to experience socialization in her first six years, Isabelle had been hardly human in the social sense when she was first discovered. Her inability to communicate at the time of her discovery—despite her physical and cognitive potential to learn—and her remarkable progress over the next few years underscore the impact of socialization on human development (K. Davis 1940, 1947).

Isabelle's experience is important for researchers because it is one of few cases of children reared in total isolation. Unfortunately, however, there are many cases of children raised in extremely neglectful social circumstances. Recently, attention has focused on infants and

young children in orphanages in the formerly communist countries of Eastern Europe. For example, in Romanian orphanages, babies lie in their cribs for 18 or 20 hours a day, curled against their feeding bottles and receiving little adult care. Such minimal attention continues for the first five years of their lives. Many of them are fearful of human contact and prone to unpredictable antisocial behavior. This situation came to light as families in North America and Europe began adopting 18,000 of these children. The adjustment problems for about 20 percent of them were often so dramatic that the adopting families suffered guilty fears of being ill-fit adoptive parents. Many of them have asked for assistance in dealing with the children. Slowly, efforts are being made to introduce the deprived youngsters to feelings of attachment that they never had experienced before (V. Groza et al. 1999; M. Talbot 1998).

Increasingly, researchers are emphasizing the importance of early socialization experiences for humans who grow up in more normal environments. We now know that it is not enough to care for an infant's physical needs; parents must also concern themselves with children's social development. If, for example, children are discouraged from having friends, they will miss out on social interactions with peers that are critical for emotional growth.

Primate Studies

Studies of animals raised in isolation also support the importance of socialization in development. Harry Harlow (1971), a researcher at the primate laboratory of the University of Wisconsin, conducted tests with rhesus monkeys that had been raised away from their mothers and away from contact with other monkeys. As was the case with Isabelle, the rhesus monkeys raised in isolation were found to be fearful and easily frightened. They did not mate, and the females who were artificially inseminated became abusive mothers. Apparently, isolation had had a damaging effect on the monkeys.

A creative aspect of Harlow's experimentation was his use of "artificial mothers." In one such experiment, Harlow presented monkeys raised in isolation with two substitute mothers—one cloth-covered replica and one covered with wire that had the ability to offer milk. Monkey after monkey went to the wire mother for the life-giving milk, yet spent much more time clinging to the more motherlike cloth model. In this study, the monkeys valued the artificial mothers that provided a comforting physical sensation (conveyed by the terry cloth) more highly than those that provided food. It appears that the infant monkeys developed greater social attachments from their need for warmth, comfort, and intimacy than from their need for milk.

While the isolation studies discussed above may seem to suggest that inheritance can be dismissed as a factor in the social development of humans and animals, studies of twins provide insight into a fascinating interplay between hereditary and environmental factors.

The Influence of Heredity

Oskar Stohr and Jack Yufe are identical twins who were separated soon after their birth and raised on different continents in very different cultural settings. Oskar was reared as a strict Catholic by his maternal grandmother in the Sudetenland of Czechoslovakia. As a member of the Hitler Youth movement in Nazi Germany, he learned to hate Jews. By contrast, his brother Jack was reared in Trinidad by the twins' Jewish father. Jack joined an Israeli kibbutz (a collective settlement) at age 17 and later served in the Israeli army. But when they were reunited in middle age, some startling similarities emerged:

Both were wearing wire-rimmed glasses and mustaches, both sported two pocket shirts with epaulets. They share idiosyncrasies galore: they like spicy foods and sweet liqueurs, are absent-minded, have a habit of falling asleep in front of the television, think it's funny to sneeze in a crowd of strangers, flush the toilet before using it, store rubber bands on their wrists, read magazines from back to front, dip buttered toast in their coffee (Holden 1980).

The twins also were found to differ in many important respects: Jack is a workaholic; Oskar enjoys leisure-time activities. Whereas Oskar is a traditionalist who is domineering toward women, Jack is a political liberal who is much more accepting of feminism. Finally, Jack is extremely proud of being Jewish, while Oskar never mentions his Jewish heritage (Holden 1987).

Oskar and Jack are prime examples of the interplay of heredity and environment. For a number of years, researchers at the Minnesota Center for Twin and Adoption Research have been studying pairs of identical twins reared apart to determine what similarities, if any, they show in personality traits, behavior, and intelligence. Thus far, the preliminary results from the available twin studies indicate that both genetic factors and socialization experiences are influential in human development. Certain characteristics, such as twins' temperaments, voice patterns, and nervous habits, appear to be strikingly similar even in twins reared apart, suggesting that these qualities may be linked to hereditary causes. However, identical twins reared apart differ far more in their attitudes, values, types of mates chosen, and even drinking habits; these qualities, it would seem, are influenced by environmental patterns. In examining clusters of personality traits among such twins, the Minnesota studies have found marked similarities in their tendency toward leadership or dominance, but significant differences in their need for intimacy, comfort, and assistance.

Researchers have also been impressed with the similar scores on intelligence tests of twins reared apart in *roughly similar* social settings. Most of the identical twins register scores even closer than those that would be expected if the same person took a test twice. At the same time, however, identical twins brought up in *dramatically different* social environments score quite differently on intelligence tests—a finding that supports the impact of socialization on human development (McGue and Bouchard 1998).

We need to be cautious when reviewing the studies of twin pairs and other relevant research. Widely broadcast findings have often been based on extremely small samples and preliminary analysis. For example, one study (not involving twin pairs) was frequently cited as confirming genetic links with behavior. Yet the researchers had to retract their conclusions after they increased the sample from 81 to 91 cases and reclassified two of the original 81 cases. After these change, the initial findings were no longer valid. Critics add that the studies on twin pairs have not provided satisfactory information concerning the extent to which these separated identical twins may have had contact with each other, even though they were "raised apart." Such interactions—especially if they were extensive—could call into question the validity of the twin studies (Kelsoe et al. 1989).

Psychologist Leon Kamin fears that overgeneralizing from the Minnesota twin results—and granting too much importance to the impact of heredity—may lead to blaming the poor and downtrodden for their unfortunate condition. As the debate over nature versus nurture continues, we can certainly anticipate numerous efforts to replicate the research and clarify the interplay between hereditary and environmental factors in human development (Horgan 1993; Leo 1987; Plomin 1989; Wallis 1987:67).

Sociobiology

Do the *social* traits that human groups display have biological origins? As part of the continuing debate on the relative influences of heredity and the environment, there has been renewed interest in sociobiology in recent years. **Sociobiology** is the systematic study of the biological bases of social behavior. Sociobiologists basically apply naturalist Charles Darwin's principles of natural selection to the study of social behavior. They assume that particular forms of behavior become genetically linked to a species if they contribute to its fitness to survive (van den Berghe 1978). In its extreme form, sociobiology suggests that *all* behavior is the result of genetic or biological factors and that social interactions play no role in shaping people's conduct.

Sociobiology does not seek to describe individual behavior on the level of "Why is Fred more aggressive than Jim?" Rather, sociobiologists focus on how human nature is affected by the genetic composition of a group of people who share certain characteristics (such as men or women, or members of isolated tribal bands). In general, sociobiologists have stressed the basic genetic heritage that *all* humans share and have shown little interest in speculating about alleged differences between racial groups or nationalities (Wilson 1975, 1978).

Some researchers insist that intellectual interest in sociobiology will only deflect serious study of the more significant factor influencing human behavior—socialization. Yet Lois Wladis Hoffman (1985), in her presidential address to the Society for the Psychological Study of Social Issues, argued that sociobiology poses a valuable challenge to social scientists to better document their own research. Interactionists, for example, could show how social behavior is not programmed by human biology but instead adjusts continually to the attitudes and responses of others.

Conflict theorists (like functionalists and interactionists) believe that people's behavior rather than their genetic structure defines social reality. Conflict theorists fear that the sociobiological approach could be used as an argument against efforts to assist disadvantaged people, such as schoolchildren who are not competing successfully (M. Harris 1997).

Edward O. Wilson, a zoologist at Harvard University,

has argued that there should be parallel studies of human behavior with a focus on both genetic and social causes. Certainly most social scientists would agree that there is a biological basis for social behavior. But there is less support for the most extreme positions taken by certain advocates of sociobiology (S. Begley 1998; Gove 1987; Wilson 1975, 1978; see also Lopreato 1992; Nielsen 1994; R. Wright 1995).

The Self and Socialization

We all have various perceptions, feelings, and beliefs about who we are and what we are like. How do we come to develop these? Do they change as we age?

We were not born with these understandings. Building on the work of George Herbert Mead (1964b), sociologists recognize that we create our own designation: the self. The **self** is a distinct identity that sets us apart from others. It is not a static phenomenon but continues to develop and change throughout our lives.

Sociologists and psychologists alike have expressed interest in how the individual develops and modifies the sense of self as a result of social interaction. The work of sociologists Charles Horton Cooley and George Herbert Mead, pioneers of the interactionist approach, has been especially useful in furthering our understanding of these important issues (Gecas 1982).

p. 17

Sociological Approaches to the Self

Cooley: Looking-Glass Self

In the early 1900s, Charles Horton Cooley advanced the belief that we learn who we are by interacting with others. Our view of ourselves, then, comes not only from direct contemplation of our personal qualities but also from our impressions of how others perceive us. Cooley used the phrase **looking-glass self** to emphasize that the self is the product of our social interactions with other people.

The process of developing a self-identity or self-concept has three phases. First, we imagine how we present ourselves to others—to relatives, friends, even strangers on the street. Then we imagine how others evaluate us (attractive, intelligent, shy, or strange). Finally, we develop some sort of feeling about ourselves, such as respect or shame, as a result of these impressions (Cooley 1902:152; Howard 1989:249).

A subtle but critical aspect of Cooley's looking-glass self is that the self results from an individual's "imagination" of how others view him or her. As a result, we can develop self-identities based on *incorrect* perceptions of how others see us. A student may react strongly to a teacher's criticism and decide (wrongly) that the instructor views the student as stupid. This misperception can easily be converted into a negative self-identity through the following process: (1) the teacher criticized me, (2) the teacher must think that I'm stupid, (3) I *am* stupid. Yet self-identities are also subject to change. If the student receives an "A" at the end of the course, he or she will probably no longer feel stupid.

Mead: Stages of the Self

George Herbert Mead continued Cooley's exploration of interactionist theory. Mead (1934, 1964a) developed a useful model of the process by which the self emerges, defined by three distinct stages: the preparatory stage, the play stage, and the game stage.

During the *preparatory stage,* children merely imitate the people around them, especially family members with whom they continually interact. Thus, a small child will bang on a piece of wood while a parent is engaged in carpentry work or will try to throw a ball if an older sibling is doing so nearby.

As they grow older, children become more adept at using symbols to communicate with others. **Symbols** are the gestures, objects, and language that form the basis of human communication. By interacting with relatives and friends, as well as by watching cartoons on television and looking at picture books, children in the preparatory stage begin to understand the use of symbols. Like spoken languages, symbols vary from culture to culture and even between subcultures. Raising one's eyebrows may mean astonishment in North America, but in Peru it means "money" or "pay me," while in the Pacific island nation of Tonga it means "yes" or "I agree" (R. Axtell 1990).

Mead was among the first to analyze the relationship of symbols to socialization. As children develop skill in communicating through symbols, they gradually become more aware of social relationships. As a result, during the *play stage,* the child becomes able to pretend to be other people. Just as an actor "becomes" a character, a child becomes a doctor, parent, superhero, or ship captain.

Mead, in fact, noted that an important aspect of the play stage is role playing. **Role taking** is the process of mentally assuming the perspective of another, thereby enabling one to respond from that imagined viewpoint. For example, through this process, a young child will gradually learn when it is best to ask a parent for favors. If the parent usually comes home from work in a bad mood, the child will wait until after dinner when the parent is more relaxed and approachable.

In Mead's third stage, the *game stage,* the child of about eight or nine years old no longer just plays roles but begins to consider several actual tasks and relationships simultaneously. At this point in development, children grasp not only their own social positions, but also those of

"Say cheese!" Children imitate the people around them, especially family members they continually interact with, during the *preparatory stage* described by George Herbert Mead.

others around them—just as in a football game the players must understand their own and everyone else's positions. Consider a girl or boy who is part of a scout troop out on a weekend hike in the mountains. The child must understand what he or she is expected to do, but also must recognize the responsibilities of other scouts as well as the leaders. This is the final stage of development under Mead's model; the child can now respond to numerous members of the social environment.

Mead uses the term **generalized others** to refer to the attitudes, viewpoints, and expectations of society as a whole that a child takes into account. Simply put, this concept suggests that when an individual acts, he or she takes into account an entire group of people. For example, a child will not act courteously merely to please a particular parent. Rather, the child comes to understand that courtesy is a widespread social value endorsed by parents, teachers, and religious leaders.

At the game stage, children can take a more sophisticated view of people and the social environment. They now understand what specific occupations and social positions are and no longer equate Mr. Williams only with the role of "librarian" or Ms. Franks only with "principal." It has become clear to the child that Mr. Williams can be a librarian, a parent, and a marathon runner at the same time and that Ms. Franks is one of many principals in our society. Thus, the child has reached a new level of sophistication in his or her observations of individuals and institutions.

Mead: Theory of the Self

Mead is best known for his theory of the self. According to Mead (1964b), the self begins as a privileged, central position in a person's world. Young children picture themselves

Double Dutch jump roping contests require contestants to carry out several tasks at once and to understand the roles of others—characteristics of the *game stage* outlined by George Herbert Mead.

as the focus of everything around them and find it difficult to consider the perspectives of others. For example, when shown a mountain scene and asked to describe what an observer on the opposite side of the mountain sees (such as a lake or hikers), young children describe only objects visible from their own vantage point. This childhood tendency to place ourselves at the center of events never entirely disappears. Many people with a fear of flying automatically assume that if any plane goes down, it will be the one they are on. And who reads the horoscope section in the paper without looking at their own horoscope first? And why else do we buy lottery tickets if we do not imagine ourselves winning?

As people mature, the self changes and begins to reflect greater concern about the reactions of others. Parents, friends, co-workers, coaches, and teachers are often among those who play a major role in shaping a person's self. Mead used the term ***significant others*** to refer to those individuals who are most important in the development of the self (Schlenker 1985). Many young people, for example, find themselves drawn to the same kind of work their parents engage in.

In some instances, studies concerning significant others have generated controversy among researchers. For example, it has often been argued that African American adolescents are more "peer-oriented" than their White counterparts because of presumed weaknesses in Black families. However, investigations indicate that these hasty conclusions were based on limited studies focusing on less affluent Blacks. In fact, there appears to be little difference in who African Americans and Whites from similar economic backgrounds regard as their significant others (Giordano et al. 1993; Juhasz 1989).

Goffman: Presentation of the Self

How do we manage our "self"? How do we display to others who we are? Erving Goffman, a sociologist associated with the interactionist perspective, suggested that many of our daily activities involve attempts to convey impressions of who we are.

Early in life, the individual learns to slant his or her presentation of the self in order to create distinctive appearances and satisfy particular audiences. Goffman (1959) refers to this altering of the presentation of the self as ***impression management.*** Box 4-1 provides an everyday example of this concept by describing how students engage in impression management after getting their examination grades.

In examining such everyday social interactions, Goffman makes so many explicit parallels to the theater that his view has been termed the ***dramaturgical approach.*** According to this perspective, people resemble performers in action. For example, a clerk may try to appear busier than he or she actually is if a supervisor happens to be watching. A customer in a singles' bar may try to look as if he or she is waiting for a particular person to arrive.

Goffman (1959) has also drawn attention to another aspect of the self—***face-work.*** How often do you initiate some kind of face-saving behavior when you feel embarrassed or rejected? In response to a rejection at the singles'

4-1 Impression Management by Students after Exams

When you get an exam back, you probably react differently with fellow classmates, depending on the grades that you and they earned. This is all part of impression management, as sociologists Daniel Albas and Cheryl Albas (1988) demonstrated. They explored the strategies that college students use to create desired appearances after receiving their grades on exams. Albas and Albas divide these encounters into three categories: those between students who have all received high grades (Ace–Ace encounters), those between students who have received high grades and those who have received low or even failing grades (Ace–Bomber encounters), and those between students who have all received low grades (Bomber–Bomber encounters).

Ace–Ace encounters occur in a rather open atmosphere because there is comfort in sharing a high mark with another high achiever. It is even acceptable to violate the norm of modesty and brag when among other Aces since, as one student admitted, "It's much easier to admit a high mark to someone who has done better than you, or at least as well."

Ace–Bomber encounters are often sensitive. Bombers generally attempt to avoid such exchanges because "you . . . emerge looking like the dumb one" or "feel like you are lazy or unreliable." When forced into interactions with Aces, Bombers work to appear gracious and congratulatory. For their part, Aces offer sympathy and support for the dissatisfied Bombers and even rationalize their own "lucky" high scores. To help

> When forced into interactions with Aces, Bombers work to appear gracious and congratulatory.

Bombers save face, Aces may emphasize the difficulty and unfairness of the examination.

Bomber–Bomber encounters tend to be closed, reflecting the group effort to wall off the feared disdain of others. Yet, within the safety of these encounters, Bombers openly share their disappointment and engage in expressions of mutual self-pity that they themselves call "pity parties." They devise

face-saving excuses for their poor performances, such as "I wasn't feeling well all week" or "I had four exams and two papers due that week." If the grade distribution in a class included particularly low scores, Bombers may blame the professor, who will be attacked as a sadist, a slave driver, or simply an incompetent.

As is evident from these descriptions, students' impression management strategies conform to society's informal norms regarding modesty and consideration for less successful peers. In classroom settings, as in the workplace and in other types of human interactions, efforts at impression management are most intense when status differentials are more pronounced as in encounters between the high-scoring Aces and the low-scoring Bombers.

Let's Discuss

1. How does an Ace present the self in encounters with other Aces? How does this presentation differ from an encounter with a Bomber?
2. What social norms govern the students' impression management strategies?

Sources: Albas and Albas 1988; Bobo 1991; Feagin 1975; Morland 1996.

---

bar, a person may engage in face-work by saying, "There really isn't an interesting person in this entire crowd." We feel the need to maintain a proper image of the self if we are to continue social interaction.

Goffman's approach is generally regarded as an insightful perspective on everyday life, but it is not without its critics. Writing from a conflict perspective, sociologist Alvin Gouldner (1970) sees Goffman's work as implicitly reaffirming the status quo, including social class inequalities. Using Gouldner's critique, one might ask if women and minorities are expected to deceive both themselves and others while paying homage to those in power. In considering impression management and other concepts developed by Goffman, sociologists must remember that by describing social reality, one is not necessarily endorsing its harsh impact on many individuals and groups (S. Williams 1986).

Goffman's work represents a logical progression of the sociological efforts begun by Cooley and Mead on how personality is acquired through socialization and how we manage the presentation of our self to others. Cooley stressed the process by which we come to create a self; Mead focused on how the self develops as we learn to interact with others; Goffman emphasized the ways in which we consciously create images of ourselves for others.

Psychological Approaches to the Self

Psychologists have shared the interest of Cooley, Mead, and other sociologists in the development of the self. Early work in psychology, such as that of Sigmund Freud (1856–1939), stressed the role of inborn drives—among them the drive for sexual gratification—in channeling human behavior. More recently, psychologists such as

Jean Piaget and Lawrence Kohlberg have emphasized the stages through which human beings progress as the self develops.

Like Charles Horton Cooley and George Herbert Mead, Freud believed that the self is a social product and that aspects of one's personality are influenced by others (especially one's parents). However, unlike Cooley and Mead, he suggested that the self has components that are always fighting with each other. According to Freud, our natural impulsive instincts are in constant conflict with societal constraints. Part of us seeks limitless pleasure, while another part seeks out rational behavior. By interacting with others, we learn the expectations of society and then select behavior most appropriate to our own culture. (Of course, as Freud was well aware, we sometimes distort reality and behave irrationally.)

Research on newborn babies by the Swiss child psychologist Jean Piaget (1896–1980) has underscored the importance of social interactions in developing a sense of self. Piaget found that newborns have no self in the sense of a looking-glass image. Ironically, though, they are quite self-centered; they demand that all attention be directed toward them. Newborns have not yet separated themselves from the universe of which they are a part. For these babies, the phrase "you and me" has no meaning; they understand only "me." However, as they mature, children are gradually socialized into social relationships even within their rather self-centered world.

In his well-known *cognitive theory of development,* Piaget (1954) identifies four stages in the development of children's thought processes. In the first, or *sensorimotor,* stage, young children use their senses to make discoveries. For example, through touching they discover that their hands are actually a part of themselves. During the second, or *preoperational,* stage, children begin to use words and symbols to distinguish objects and ideas. The milestone in the third, or *concrete operational,* stage is that children engage in more logical thinking. They learn that even when a formless lump of clay is shaped into a snake, it is still the same clay. Finally, in the fourth, or *formal operational,* stage, adolescents are capable of sophisticated abstract thought and can deal with ideas and values in a logical manner.

Piaget has suggested that moral development becomes an important part of socialization as children develop the ability to think more abstractly. When children learn the rules of a game such as checkers or jacks, they are learning to obey societal norms. Those under eight years old display a rather basic level of morality: rules are rules, and there is no concept of "extenuating circumstances." However, as they mature, children become capable of greater autonomy and begin to experience moral dilemmas as to what constitutes proper behavior.

According to Jean Piaget, social interaction is the key to development. As they grow older, children give increasing attention to how other people think and why they act in particular ways. In order to develop a distinct personality, each of us needs opportunities to interact with others. As we saw earlier, Isabelle was deprived of the chance for normal social interactions, and the consequences were severe (Kitchener 1991).

Socialization and the Life Course

The Life Course

Adolescents among the Kota people of the Congo in Africa paint themselves blue, Mexican American girls go on a daylong religious retreat before dancing the night away, Egyptian mothers step over their newborn infants seven times, students at the Naval Academy throw hats in

Body painting is a ritual marking the passage to puberty among young people in Liberia in northern Africa.

the air. These are all ways of celebrating ***rites of passage,*** a means of dramatizing and validating changes in a person's status. The Kota rite marks the passage to adulthood. The color blue, viewed as the color of death, symbolizes the death of childhood. Hispanic girls celebrate reaching womanhood with a *quinceañera* ceremony at age 15. In the Cuban American community of Miami, the popularity of the *quinceañera* supports a network of party planners, caterers, dress designers, and the Miss Quinceañera Latina pageant. For thousands of years, Egyptian mothers have welcomed their newborns to the world in the Soboa ceremony by stepping over the seven-day-old infant seven times. The Naval Academy seniors celebrate their graduation from college by hurling their hats skyward (D. Cohen 1991; Garza 1993; McLane 1995; Quadagno 1999).

These specific ceremonies mark stages of development in the life course. They indicate that the socialization process continues throughout all stages of the human life cycle. Sociologists and other social scientists use the life-course approach in recognition that biological changes mold but do not dictate human behavior from birth until death.

In the culture of the United States, each individual has a "personal biography" that is influenced by events both in the family and in the larger society. While the completion of religious confirmations, school graduations, marriage, and parenthood can all be regarded as rites of passage in our society, people do not necessarily experience them at the same time. The timing of these events depends on such factors as one's gender, economic background, where one lives (central city, suburb, or rural area), and even when one was born.

Sociologists and other social scientists have moved away from identifying specific life stages that we are all expected to pass through at some point. Indeed, people are much less likely to follow an "orderly" progression of life events (leaving school, then obtaining their first job, then getting married) than they were in the past. For example, in 1997, 25 percent of students attending four-year colleges in the United States were 25 years or older. Some of these students undoubtedly started college *after* beginning a first job and *after* marrying. With such changes in mind, researchers are increasingly reluctant to offer sweeping generalizations about stages in the life course (Bureau of the Census 1999a:202).

We encounter some of the most difficult socialization challenges (and rites of passage) in the later years of life. Assessing one's accomplishments, coping with declining physical abilities, experiencing retirement, and facing the inevitability of death may lead to painful adjustments. Old age is further complicated by the negative way that many societies, including the United States, view and treat the elderly. The common stereotypes of the elderly as helpless and dependent may well weaken an older person's self-image. However, as we will explore more fully in Chapter 12, many older people continue to lead active, productive, fulfilled lives—whether within the paid labor force or as retirees.

Anticipatory Socialization and Resocialization

The development of a social self is literally a lifelong transformation that begins in the crib and continues as one prepares for death. Two types of socialization occur at many points throughout the life course: anticipatory socialization and resocialization.

Anticipatory socialization refers to the processes of socialization in which a person "rehearses" for future positions, occupations, and social relationships. A culture can function more efficiently and smoothly if members become acquainted with the norms, values, and behavior associated with a social position before actually assuming that status. Preparation for many aspects of adult life begins with anticipatory socialization during childhood and adolescence and continues throughout our lives as we prepare for new responsibilities.

You can see the process of anticipatory socialization in the families of snakers (a term they prefer to *snake charmers*) in India. At the age of five or six, the son of a snaker begins to touch the snakes he has observed all his life. The boy will soon learn how to catch snakes and will become familiar with the habits of each species. In snaker families, it is a matter of intense pride when a boy follows in the footsteps of his father, his grandfather, and earlier male ancestors (Skafte 1979).

Anticipatory socialization also takes place as high school students start to consider what colleges they may attend. Traditionally, this meant looking at publications received in the mail or making campus visits. However, with new technology, more and more students are using the Web to begin their college experience. Colleges are investing more time and money in developing attractive websites. Before long, students will be able to take "virtual" campus walks and hear audio clips of everything from the alma mater to a sample zoology lecture.

Occasionally, assuming new social and occupational positions requires us to *unlearn* a previous orientation. ***Resocialization*** refers to the process of discarding former behavior patterns and accepting new ones as part of a transition in one's life. Often resocialization occurs when there is an explicit effort to transform an individual, as happens in reform schools, therapy groups, prisons, religious conversion settings, and political indoctrination camps. The process of resocialization typically involves considerable

stress for the individual, much more so than socialization in general or even anticipatory socialization (Gecas 1992).

Resocialization is particularly effective when it occurs within a total institution. Erving Goffman (1961) coined the term **total institutions** to refer to institutions, such as prisons, the military, mental hospitals, and convents, that regulate all aspects of a person's life under a single authority. Because the total institution is generally cut off from the rest of society, it provides for all the needs of its members. Quite literally, the crew of a merchant vessel at sea becomes part of a total institution. So elaborate are its requirements, and so all-encompassing are its activities, a total institution often represents a miniature society.

Goffman (1961) has identified four common traits of total institutions:

- All aspects of life are conducted in the same place and are under the control of a single authority.
- Any activities within the institution are conducted in the company of others in the same circumstances—for example, novices in a convent or army recruits.
- The authorities devise rules and schedule activities without consulting the participants.
- All aspects of life within a total institution are designed to fulfill the purpose of the organization. Thus, all activities in a monastery are centered on prayer and communion with God (Davies 1989; P. Rose et al. 1979).

People often lose their individuality within total institutions. For example, a person entering prison may experience the humiliation of a **degradation ceremony** as he or she is stripped of clothing, jewelry, and other personal possessions (Garfinkel 1956). Even the person's self is taken away to some extent; the prison inmate loses a name and becomes known to authorities as a number. From this point on, scheduled daily routines allow for little or no personal initiative. The individual becomes secondary and rather invisible in the overbearing social environment.

Back in 1934, the world was gripped by the birth of quintuplets to Olivia and Elzire Dionne in Canada. In the midst of the Depression, people wanted to hear and see all they could about these five girls, born generations before fertility drugs made multiple births more common. What seemed like a heartwarming story turned out to be a tragic case of Goffman's total institutionalization. The government of Ontario soon took the quintuplets from their home and set them up in a facility complete with an observation gallery overlooking their playground. Each month, 10,000 tourists paid an entry fee to view the five little "Cinderellas." When the girls left the nine-room compound, it was always to raise money for some worthwhile cause or to merchandise some product. Within their compound, even their parents and their older sib-

How would you like to be "on view" for thousands of tourists? That was the fate of the Dionne quintuplets during the 1930s in Canada. The five little girls were removed from their parents and kept under sharp watch in a nine-room compound called "Quintland"—a form of a *total institution*.

lings had to make appointments to see them. A child psychiatrist responsible for their child rearing ordered they never be spanked—or hugged (to prevent the chance of infection).

After nine years, the quintuplets were reunited with their family. But the legacy of total institutionalization persisted. Sharp divisions and jealousies had developed between the five girls and other siblings. The parents were caught up in charges of doing too much or too little for all their children. In 1997 the three surviving quintuplets made public a poignant letter to the parents of recently born septuplets in Iowa:

We three would like you to know we feel a natural affinity and tenderness for your children. We hope your children receive more respect than we did. Their fate should be no different from that of other children. Multiple births

should not be confused with entertainment, nor should they be an opportunity to sell products. . . .

Our lives have been ruined by the exploitation we suffered at the hands of the government of Ontario, our place of birth. We were displayed as a curiosity three times a day for millions of tourists. . . .

We sincerely hope a lesson will be learned from examining how our lives were forever altered by our childhood experiences. If this letter changes the course of events for these newborns, then perhaps our lives will have served a higher purpose (Dionne et al. 1997:39).

It is to be hoped that the Iowa septuplets won't find themselves in the position of the Dionne women in 1998, waging a lawsuit against the government for the way they were raised in an institutional environment.

Agents of Socialization

As we have seen, the culture of the United States is defined by rather gradual movements from one stage of socialization to the next. The continuing and lifelong socialization process involves many different social forces that influence our lives and alter our self-images.

The family is the most important agent of socialization in the United States, especially for children. We'll also give particular attention in this chapter to five other agents of socialization: the school, the peer group, the mass media, the workplace, and the state. The role of religion in socializing young people into society's norms and values will be explored in Chapter 14.

Family

Children in Amish communities are raised in a highly structured and disciplined manner. But they are not immune to the temptations posed by their peers in the non-Amish world—"rebellious" acts such as dancing, drinking, and riding in cars. Still, Amish families don't get too concerned; they know the strong influence they ultimately exert over their offspring (see Box 4-2). The same is true for the family in general. It is tempting to say that the "peer group" or even the "media" really raise kids these days, especially when the spotlight falls on young people involved in shooting sprees and hate crimes. Almost all available research, however, shows that the role of the family in socializing a child cannot be underestimated (W. Williams 1998; for a different view see J. Harris 1998).

The lifelong process of learning begins shortly after birth. Since newborns can hear, see, smell, taste, and feel heat, cold, and pain, they are constantly orienting themselves to the surrounding world. Human beings, especially family members, constitute an important part of their so-

cial environment. People minister to the baby's needs by feeding, cleansing, carrying, and comforting the baby.

The caretakers of a newborn are not concerned with teaching social skills per se. Nevertheless, babies are hardly asocial. An infant enters an organized society, becomes part of a generation, and typically joins a family. Depending on how they are treated, infants can develop strong social attachments and dependency on others.

Most infants go through a relatively formal period of socialization generally called *habit training*. Caregivers impose schedules for eating and sleeping, for terminating breast or bottle feeding, and for introducing new foods. In these and other ways, infants can be viewed as objects of socialization. Yet they also function as socializers. Even as the behavior of a baby is being modified by interactions with people and the environment, the baby is causing others to change their behavior patterns. He or she converts adults into mothers and fathers, who, in turn, assist the baby in progressing into childhood (Rheingold 1969).

As both Charles Horton Cooley and George Herbert Mead noted, the development of the self is a critical aspect of the early years of one's life. In the United States, such social development includes exposure to cultural assumptions regarding gender and race. African American parents, for example, have learned that children as young as two years old can absorb negative messages about Blacks in children's books, toys, and television shows—all of which are designed primarily for White consumers (Linn and Poussaint 1999).

The term **gender roles** refers to expectations regarding the proper behavior, attitudes, and activities of males and females. For example, we traditionally think of "toughness" as masculine—and desirable only in men—while we view "tenderness" as feminine. As we will see in Chapter 11, other cultures do not necessarily assign these qualities to each gender in the way that our culture does.

As the primary agents of childhood socialization, parents play a critical role in guiding children into those gender roles deemed appropriate in a society. Other adults, older siblings, the mass media, and religious and educational institutions also have noticeable impact on a child's socialization into feminine and masculine norms. A culture or subculture may require that one sex or the other take primary responsibility for socialization of children, economic support of the family, or religious or intellectual leadership.

The differential gender roles absorbed in early childhood often help define a child's popularity later on. In the extract that opened this chapter, the Adlers give a picture of the dynamics of "in" and "out" groups among both girls and boys. Patricia Adler has found that boys typically achieve high status on the basis of their athletic ability, "coolness," toughness, social skills, and success in relationships with girls. By contrast, girls owe their

Jacob is a typical teenager in his Amish community in Lancaster County, Pennsylvania. At 14 he is in his final year of schooling. Over the next few years he will become a full-time worker on the family farm, taking breaks only for three-hour religious services each morning. When he is a bit older, Jacob may bring a date in his family's horse-drawn buggy to a community "singing." But he will be forbidden to date outside his own community and can marry only with the deacon's consent. Jacob is well aware of the rather different way of life of the "English" (the Amish term for non-Amish people). One summer he and his friends hitchhiked late at night to a nearby town to see a movie, breaking several Amish taboos. His parents learned of his adventure, but like most Amish they are confident that their son will choose the Amish way of life. What is this way of life and how can the parents be so sure of its appeal?

Jacob and his family live in a manner very similar to their ancestors, members of the conservative Mennonite church who migrated to North America from Europe in the eighteenth and nineteenth centuries. Schisms in the church after 1850 led to a division between those who wanted to preserve the "old order" and those who favored a "new order" with more progressive methods and organization. Today the old order Amish live in about 50 communities in the United States and Canada. Estimates put their number at about 80,000 with approximately 75 percent living in three states—Ohio, Pennsylvania, and Indiana.

The old order Amish live a "simple" life and reject most aspects of modernization and contemporary technology. That's why they spurn such conveniences as electricity, automobiles, radio, and television. The Amish maintain their own schools and traditions, and they do not want their children socialized into many norms and values of the dominant culture of the United States. Those who stray too far from Amish mores may be excommunicated and shunned by all other members of the community—a practice of social control called Meiding. Sociologists

> The old order Amish live a "simple" life and reject most aspects of modernization and contemporary technology.

sometimes use the term "secessionist minorities" to refer to groups like the Amish who reject assimilation and coexist with the rest of society primarily on their own terms.

Life for Amish youth attracts particular attention since their socialization pushes them to forgo movies, radio, television, cosmetics, jewelry, musical instruments of any kind, and motorized vehicles. Yet, like Jacob did, Amish youth often test their subculture's boundaries during a period of discovery called *rumspringe*, a term that literally means "running around." Amish young people attend barn dances where taboos like drinking, smoking, and driving cars are commonly broken. Parents often react by looking the other way, sometimes literally. For example, when they

hear radio sounds from a barn or a motorcycle entering the property in the middle of the night, they don't immediately investigate and punish their offspring. Instead, they will pretend not to notice, secure in the comfort that their children almost always return to the traditions of the Amish lifestyle. Occasionally, young people go too far. For example, in 1997 a motorcycle gang of 10 Amish youth were caught selling drugs, including cocaine, in suburban Philadelphia. But cases like this are so rare that they make headlines when they happen. Research shows that only about 20 percent of Amish youth leave the fold, generally to join a more liberal Mennonite group, and rarely does a baptized adult ever leave. The socialization of Amish youth moves them gently but firmly into becoming Amish adults.

Let's Discuss

1. What makes Amish parents so sure that their children will choose to remain in the Amish community?
2. How would a functionalist and a conflict theorist look at Amish traditions?

Sources: Kephart and Zellner 1998; Meyers 1992; Remnick 1998.

popularity to their parents' status and their own physical appearance, social skills, and academic success (Adler and Adler 1998; P. Adler et al. 1992).

Like other elements of culture, socialization patterns are not fixed. The last 30 years, for example, have witnessed a sustained challenge to traditional gender-role socialization in the United States, due in good part to the efforts of the feminist movement (see Chapter 11). Nevertheless, despite such changes, children growing up today are hardly free of traditional gender roles.

Parents do not work in isolation of other agents of socialization. As we'll see later, the media play a critical role, one that parents feel increasing pressure to monitor. One result of parental concern is the television rating system, which many find too bewildering to be useful (see Figure 4-1). Besides these ratings, parents can refer to the long-established motion picture rating systems (P, PG, PG-17, R, etc.) as well as ratings for video games ranging from "C" for early childhood to "A" for adults only.

Interactionists remind us that socialization concern-

FIGURE 4-1

Rating TV Shows

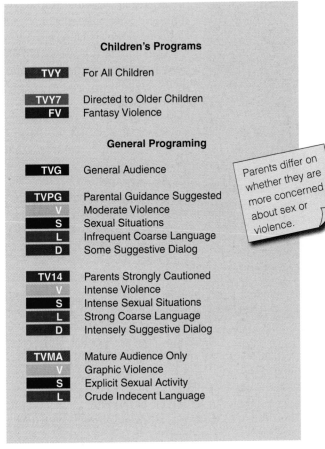

Children's Programs

TVY	For All Children
TVY7	Directed to Older Children
FV	Fantasy Violence

General Programing

TVG	General Audience
TVPG	Parental Guidance Suggested
V	Moderate Violence
S	Sexual Situations
L	Infrequent Coarse Language
D	Some Suggestive Dialog
TV14	Parents Strongly Cautioned
V	Intense Violence
S	Intense Sexual Situations
L	Strong Coarse Language
D	Intensely Suggestive Dialog
TVMA	Mature Audience Only
V	Graphic Violence
S	Explicit Sexual Activity
L	Crude Indecent Language

Parents differ on whether they are more concerned about sex or violence.

Source: Federal Communications Commission 1998.

ing not only masculinity and femininity, but also marriage and parenthood, begins in childhood as a part of family life. Children observe their parents as they express affection, deal with finances, quarrel, complain about in-laws, and so forth. This represents an informal process of anticipatory socialization. The child develops a tentative model of what being married and being a parent are like. We will explore socialization for marriage and parenthood more fully in Chapter 13.

School

Where did you learn the national anthem? Who taught you about the heroes of the American Revolution? Where were you first tested on your knowledge of your culture? Like the family, schools have an explicit mandate to socialize people in the United States—and especially children—into the norms and values of our culture.

As conflict theorists Samuel Bowles and Herbert Gintis (1976) have observed, schools in this country fos-

ter competition through built-in systems of reward and punishment, such as grades and evaluations by teachers. Consequently, a child who is working intently to learn a new skill can sometimes come to feel stupid and unsuccessful. However, as the self matures, children become capable of increasingly realistic assessments of their intellectual, physical, and social abilities.

Functionalists point out that, as agents of socialization, schools fulfil the function of teaching children the values and customs of the larger society. Conflict theorists agree but add that schools can reinforce the divisive aspects of society, especially those of social class. For example, higher education in the United States is quite costly despite the existence of financial aid programs. Students from affluent backgrounds have an advantage in gaining access to universities and professional training. At the same time, less affluent young people may never receive the preparation that would qualify them for the best-paying and most prestigious jobs. The contrast between the functionalist and conflict views of education will be discussed in more detail in Chapter 15.

In teaching students the values and customs of the larger society, schools in the United States have traditionally socialized children into conventional gender roles. Professors of education Myra Sadker and David Sadker (1985:54; 1995) note that "although many believe that classroom sexism disappeared in the early '70s, it hasn't." A report released in 1992 by the American Association of University Women—which summarized 1,331 studies of girls in school—concludes that schools in the United States favor boys over girls.

According to this report, girls show a disturbing pattern of *downward* intellectual mobility compared with boys, because they are treated differently. Teachers praise boys more than girls and offer boys more academic assistance. Boys receive praise for the intellectual content of their work, whereas girls are more likely to be praised for being neat. Teachers reward boys for assertiveness (for example, calling out answers without raising their hands) while reprimanding girls for similar behavior. Finally, girls often are not expected or encouraged to pursue high-level mathematics or science courses. The report concludes that girls are less likely than boys to reach their academic potential and insists that "the system must change" (American Association of University Women 1992:84; Bailey and Campbell 2000).

In other cultures as well, schools serve socialization functions. During the 1980s, for example, Japanese parents and educators were distressed to realize that children were gradually losing the knack of eating with chopsticks. This became a national issue in 1997 when school lunch programs introduced plastic sporks (combined fork and spoon, used frequently in the United States). National

This Japanese school maintains the Japanese cultural practice of eating with chopsticks. When school lunch programs introduced the "spork" (combined plastic spoon and fork) in the late 1990s, Japanese parents raised a fuss and forced a return to the traditional chopsticks.

leaders, responding to the public outcry, banished sporks in favor of *hashi* (chopsticks). On a more serious note, Japanese schools have come under increasing pressure in recent years as working parents have abdicated more and more responsibility to educational institutions. To rectify the imbalance, the Japanese government in 1998 promoted a guide to better parenting, calling on parents to read more with their children, allow for more playtime, limit TV watching, and plan family activities, among other things (Gauette 1998).

Peer Group

Ask 13-year-olds who matters most in their lives and they are likely to answer "friends." As a child grows older, the family becomes somewhat less important in social development. Instead, peer groups increasingly assume the role of Mead's significant others. Within the peer group, young people associate with others who are approximately their own age and who often enjoy a similar social status.

Peer groups can ease the transition to adult responsibilities. At home, parents tend to dominate; at school, the teenager must contend with teachers and administrators. But within the peer group, each member can assert himself or herself in a way that may not be possible elsewhere. Nevertheless, almost all adolescents in our culture remain economically dependent on their parents, and most are emotionally dependent as well.

Teenagers imitate their friends in part because the peer group maintains a meaningful system of rewards and punishments. The group may encourage a young person to follow pursuits that society considers admirable, as in a school club engaged in volunteer work in hospitals and nursing homes. On the other hand, the group may encourage someone to violate the culture's norms and values by driving recklessly, shoplifting, engaging in acts of vandalism, and the like.

Peers can be the source of harassment as well as support, as the chapter opening extract showed. This problem has received considerable attention in Japan, where bullying in school is a constant fact of life. Groups of students act together to humiliate, disgrace, or torment a specific student, a practice known in Japan as *ijime*. Most students go along with the bullying out of fear that they might be the target some time. In some cases the *ijime* has led to a child's suicide. In 1998 the situation became so desperate that a volunteer association set up a 24-hour telephone hotline in Tokyo just for children (see the chapter opening poster). The success of this effort convinced the government to sponsor a nationwide hotline system (Sugimoto 1997; Matsushita 1999).

Gender differences are noteworthy in the social world of adolescents. Males are more likely to spend time in *groups* of males, while females are more likely to interact with a *single* other female. This pattern reflects differences in levels of emotional intimacy; teenage males are less likely to develop strong emotional ties than are females. Instead, males are more inclined to share in group activities. These patterns are evident among adolescents in many societies besides the United States (Dornbusch 1989:248).

Mass Media and Technology

In the last 75 years, media innovations—radio, motion pictures, recorded music, television, and the Internet—have become important agents of socialization. Television, in particular, is a critical force in the socialization of children in the United States. Remarkably, 32 percent of children in the United States under the age of 7 have their own television, and 53 percent of all children ages 12 to 18 have their own sets. Little wonder that the American Academy of Pediatrics has urged parents to not allow children under 2 years old to watch television. Parents should

incidents on television are initiated by "good" characters, who are likely to be perceived as positive role models (J. Federman 1998; L. Mifflin 1999).

Television, however, is not always a negative socializing influence. Even critics of the medium concede this. Creative programming such as *Sesame Street* can assist children in developing basic skills essential for schooling. Plus, many shows manage to get out positive messages. Safe sex got a plug on *Party of Five*, and an episode of *Felicity* presented an accurate portrayal of date rape and its aftermath. Over four years in the late 1980s and early 1990s, the story lines of 160 prime-time shows got across a message about using designated drivers in drinking situations. Partly as a result, surveys showed that 67 percent of Americans were aware of the concept of the designated driver; moreover, nationwide drunk

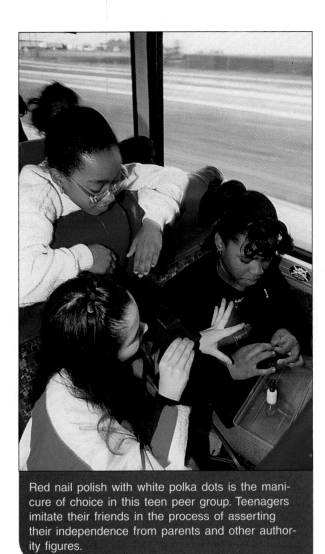

Red nail polish with white polka dots is the manicure of choice in this teen peer group. Teenagers imitate their friends in the process of asserting their independence from parents and other authority figures.

also avoid using any kind of media as an electronic babysitter and should try to create an "electronic media–free" environment in their children's rooms. Unfortunately, at whatever age we view television, it seriously misrepresents the realities of day-to-day life, as Table 4-1 shows (Rideout et al. 1999).

Television has certain characteristics that distinguish it from other agents of socialization. It permits imitation and role playing but does not encourage more complex forms of learning. Watching television is, above all, a passive experience; one sits back and waits to be entertained. Critics of television are further alarmed by the programming that children view as they sit for hours in front of a television set. It is generally agreed that children (as well as adults) are exposed to a great deal of violence on television. Despite recent attention to the issue, a 1998 study showed that the situation had not changed over the last two years. Of particular concern is that 40 percent of violent

Table 4-1 Distorted Viewing: Television Characters versus Reality

	Proportion of All Prime-Time Television Characters	Proportion of U.S. Population
Male	63%	49%
Female	37	51
Children, ages 0–12	4	19
Older people, ages 60 and over	8	17
White	84	76
Hispanic	2	9
Wear glasses	14	38
Are overweight	10	68
Drink alcoholic beverages	7	61
Smoke cigarettes	2	26
Have been crime victims	18	5

Note: Data adapted from *USA Today* study of television, Bureau of the Census, NIDA Household Survey, National Association to Advance Fat Acceptance, and Roper Survey.

Sources: Adapted from Gable 1993a, 1993b.

4-3 From *Ulitsa Sezam* to *The X-Files*

Television is a powerful agent of socialization in almost every society today. The question is, What message is being delivered, especially to children? Many people are concerned that the message has a distinctly Western flavor, especially of U.S. culture. They have good reason to worry—as of 1993, the United States controlled 75 percent of the world's television programming. *Baywatch* reaches viewers in some 140 countries. It's not surprising that U.S. values, U.S. ways of doing things, even "American English" (as opposed to "British English") are spreading rapidly and threatening to erode local national cultures. The situation leads critics to complain, "The global culture emanates primarily from one source, a global village called Los Angeles" (quoted in Son 1996). At the same time that we are the biggest exporter of TV programming, we are the smallest importer—foreign programs use up less than 2 percent of TV airtime in the United States. As a result, other nations learn a lot about us, but we know little about them.

Some countries are making an attempt to broadcast their own culture as a way to socialize children into *their* society. The Children's Television Network, based in the United States, has coproduced local versions of *Sesame Street* in 18 nations. The one in Russia—called *Ulitsa Sezam*—places its characters, including a Big Bird–like Zeliboba and Bert and Ernie types known as Vlas and Yenik, in a courtyard looked over by a kindly caretaker, Aunt Dasha. She spins Russian folktales and hands out homespun wisdom that draws on the culture of prerevolutionary Russia. Russian parents welcome *Ulitsa Sezam* into their homes, especially since 20 percent of all day care centers have closed in the recent turbulent economic times. In April 1998 an Israeli/Palestinian coproduction of *Sesame Street* debuted in Israel, aimed at encouraging mutual respect among Jewish and Arab children.

In some developing countries, locally produced soap operas have attempted to convey specific social messages. For example,

"Can you show me how to get to Sesame Street?" Palestinian and Israeli Muppets interact in a jointly produced *Sesame Street* that debuted in Israel in 1998. The program aims to encourage mutual respect among Jewish and Arab children.

Nigeria's *Cock Crow at Dawn* encourages villages to adopt modern agricultural practices, while India's *Hum Log (O We People)* has promoted family planning and higher status for women. One survey revealed that three-fourths of Indian viewers approved of the messages being dramatized in *Hum Log*.

> *Baywatch* reaches viewers in some 140 countries.

But these accomplishments in local programming are rare. A number of European countries have tried, largely without success, to impose quotas on U.S. programs. Canada actually mandates the amount of national programming that media outlets must provide. The Canadian government also gives tax breaks to national production companies, and the Canada Television and Cable Production Fund distributes $150 million to underwrite production costs. Still, viewers favor the U.S. shows—*The X-Files*, *E.R.*, *Friends*, and so on·

Developing countries are particularly vulnerable to the avalanche of foreign programming because many of them have no home-based television production industry. They are at the mercy of the broadcast whims of large satellite cable networks (such as CNN). As a result, the United Nations' 1996 Human Development Report warns that market forces are having a more dramatic effect on cultures today than government repression. Programs broadcast on the world's more than 1.2 billion sets can be seen as "a new form of cultural domination through the incentives and values they inculcate" in a socialization process (quoted in Son 1996). Things won't change soon. It is estimated that it will be 5 to 10 years before networks in Asia, for example, begin to tailor products for local markets.

Let's Discuss

1. How do U.S. television programs affect socialization in other parts of the world?
2. Why is it important for countries to have their own local programming?

Sources: W. Brown and Cody 1991; Hockstader 1996; MacLeod 1996; H. Schneider 1997; Selig 1998; Son 1996.

driving fatalities dropped by 32 percent between 1988 and 1997 (Cox 1999).

Another benefit is that television programs and even commercials can expose young people to unfamiliar lifestyles and cultures. Not only do children in the United States learn about life in "faraway lands," but also inner-city children learn about the lives of farm children and vice versa. The same goes for children living in other countries. Unfortunately, the dominance of the United States in the television industry has some global consequences, as we see in Box 4-3.

While we have focused on television as an agent of socialization, it is important to note that similar issues have been raised regarding the content of popular music

p. 75

(especially rock music and "rap"), music videos, motion pictures, and Internet websites. These forms of entertainment, like television, serve as powerful agents of socialization for many young people in the United States and elsewhere. Continuing controversy about the content of music, music videos, and films has sometimes led to celebrated court battles, as certain parents' organizations and religious groups challenge the intrusion of these media into the lives of children and adolescents. In recent years, people have expressed concern about the type of material that children can access on the Internet, especially pornography.

Finally, sociologists and other social scientists have begun to consider the impact of technology on socialization, especially as it applies to family life. The Silicon Valley Cultures Project studied families in California's Silicon Valley (a technological corridor) for 10 years beginning in 1991. While these families may not be typical, they probably represent a lifestyle that more and more households will approximate. This study has found that technology in the form of e-mail, webpages, cellular phones, voice mail, digital organizers, and pagers is allowing householders to let outsiders do everything from grocery shopping to soccer pools. The researchers are also finding that families are socialized into multitasking (doing more than one task at a time) as the social norm; devoting one's full attention to one task—even eating or driving—is less and less common on a typical day (Silicon Valley Cultures Project 1999).

Workplace

Learning to behave appropriately within an occupation is a fundamental aspect of human socialization. In the United States, working full-time confirms adult status; it is an indication to all that one has passed out of adolescence. In a sense, socialization into an occupation can represent both a harsh reality ("I have to work in order to buy food and pay the rent") and the realization of an ambition ("I've always wanted to be an airline pilot") (W. Moore 1968:862).

It used to be that "going to work" began with the end of our formal schooling, but that is no longer the case, at least not in the United States. More and more young people work today, and not just for a parent or relative. Adolescents generally seek jobs in order to make spending money; 80 percent of high school seniors said little or none of what they earn goes to family expenses. And these teens rarely look on their employment as a means of exploring vocational interests or getting on-the-job training.

Some observers feel that the increasing number of teenagers who are working earlier in life and for longer hours are now finding the workplace almost as important an agent of socialization as school. In fact, a number of educators complain that student time at work is adversely affecting schoolwork. Figure 4-2 shows data from two international studies. The level of teenage employment in the United States, the highest among industrial countries, may provide one explanation for why U.S. high school students lag behind other countries in international achievement tests (R. Cooper 1998).

This boy's day doesn't end when school lets out. So many teenagers now work after school, the workplace has become another important agent of socialization for that age group.

FIGURE 4-2

Teenagers on the Job and in School—International Comparisons

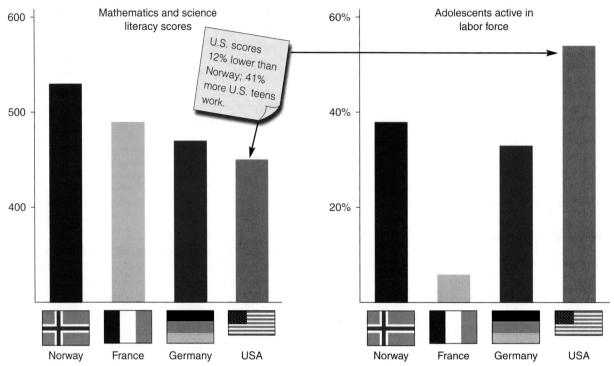

Sources: Commission on Behavioral and Social Sciences and Education 1998; Third International Mathematics and Science Study 1998.

Socialization in the workplace becomes different when it involves a more permanent shift from an afterschool job to full-time employment. Wilbert Moore (1968:871–80) has divided occupational socialization into four phases. The first phase is *career choice,* which involves selection of academic or vocational training appropriate for the desired job. The second phase, *anticipatory socialization,* may last only a few months or extend for a period of years. In a sense, young people experience anticipatory socialization throughout childhood and adolescence as they observe their parents at work.

The third phase of occupational socialization—*conditioning and commitment*—occurs in the work-related role. *Conditioning* consists of reluctantly adjusting to the more unpleasant aspects of one's job. Most people find that the novelty of a new daily schedule quickly wears off and then realize that parts of the work experience are rather tedious. *Commitment* refers to the enthusiastic acceptance of pleasurable duties that comes with recognition of the positive tasks of an occupation.

In Moore's view, if a job proves to be satisfactory, the person will enter a fourth stage of socialization, which he calls *continuous commitment.* At this point, the job becomes an indistinguishable part of the person's self-identity. Violation of proper conduct becomes unthinkable. A person may choose to join professional associations, unions, or other groups that represent his or her occupation in the larger society.

Occupational socialization can be most intense during the transition from school to job, but it continues through one's work history. Technological advances may alter the requirements of the position and necessitate some degree of resocialization. Many men and women today change occupations, employers, or places of work many times during their adult years. Therefore, occupational socialization continues throughout a person's years in the labor market.

The State

Social scientists have increasingly recognized the importance of the state as an agent of socialization because of its growing impact on the life course. Traditionally, family members have served as the primary caregivers in our culture, but in the twentieth century, the family's protective function has steadily been transferred to outside agencies such as hospitals, mental health clinics, and insurance companies (Ogburn and Tibbits 1934). The state runs many of these agencies or licenses and regulates them.

In the past, heads of households and local groups such as religious organizations influenced the life course most significantly. However, in the 1990s, national interests are increasingly influencing the individual as a citizen and an economic actor. For example, labor unions and political parties serve as intermediaries between the individual and the state.

The state has had a noteworthy impact on the life course by reinstituting the rites of passage that had disappeared in agricultural societies and in periods of early in-

dustrialization. For example, government regulations stipulate the ages at which a person may drive a car, drink alcohol, vote in elections, marry without parental permission, work overtime, and retire. These regulations do not constitute strict rites of passage: most 18-year-olds choose not to vote, and most people choose their age of retirement without reference to government dictates. Still, the state shapes the socialization process by regulating the life course to some degree and by influencing our views of appropriate behavior at particular ages (Mayer and Schoepflin 1989).

In the social policy section that follows, we will see that the state is under pressure to become a provider of child care, which would give it a new and direct role in the socialization of infants and young children.

SOCIAL POLICY AND SOCIALIZATION

Day Care around the World

www.mhhe.com/schaefer

The Issue

The rise in single-parent families, increased job opportunities for women, and the need for additional family income have all propelled an increasing number of mothers of young children into the paid labor force of the United States. In 1996, 63 percent of all mothers with children under the age of six were part of the labor force. Who, then, takes care of the children of these women during work hours?

For 30 percent of all preschoolers with employed mothers, the solution has become group child care programs. Day care centers have become the functional equivalent of the nuclear family, performing some of the nurturing and socialization functions previously handled only by family members (Abelson 1997). But how does group day care compare to care in the home? And what is the state's responsibility to assure quality care?

The Setting

In 1997, the United States was transfixed by the murder trial in Massachusetts of British au pair Louise Woodward for the death of an eight-month-old boy in her care. Eventually convicted but given a suspended sentence, Woodward brought attention to the complex problem of child care. Many were critical of the behavior of the 19-year-old au pair; others questioned the mother's (but rarely the father's) desire to work outside the home. Yet few people in the United States, Great Britain, or elsewhere can afford the luxury of having a parent stay at

home or paying for high-quality live-in child care. For millions of mothers and fathers, finding the right kind of child care is a challenge to parenting and to the pocketbook.

Researchers have found that high-quality child care centers do not adversely affect the socialization of children; in fact, good day care benefits children. The value of preschool programs was documented in a series of studies conducted by the National Institute of Child Health and Human Development in the United States and the University of North London in England. They found no significant differences in infants who had received extensive nonmaternal care as compared with those who had been cared for solely by their mothers. The researchers also reported that more infants in the United States are being placed in child care outside the home and that, overall, the quality of these arrangements is better than had been found in previous studies. It is difficult, however, to generalize about child care since there is so much variability among day care providers and even among policies from one state to another; see Figure 4-3 (NICHD 1999a, 1999b; North Carolina Abecedarian Project 2000).

Sociological Insights

Studies assessing the quality of child care outside of the home reflect the microlevel of analysis and the interest that interactionists have in the impact of face-to-face interaction. They also explore macro-level implications for the functioning of social institutions like the family. But some of the issues surrounding day care have also been of interest from the conflict perspective.

FIGURE 4-3

Quality of State Child Care Policies

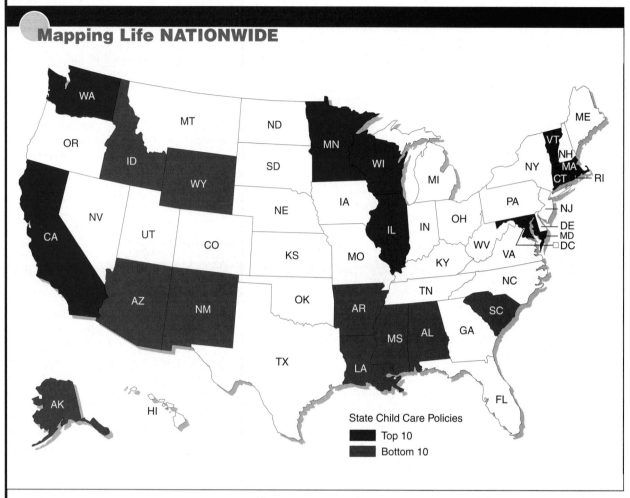

Mapping Life NATIONWIDE

State Child Care Policies

- Top 10
- Bottom 10

Note: Judgments based on child-to-adult ratios, number of accredited centers, safety requirements, tax breaks, and perceived commitment by governor. Panel selected top 10; author, using the same database, selected the bottom 10.

Source: Holcomb, Dreisbach, and Willer 1999.

Quality day care in the United States is not equally available to all families. Parents in wealthy neighborhoods have an easier time finding day care than those in poor or working-class communities. And their chances of finding quality care are much better as well. In a study covering 36 states, Harvard researchers Bruce Fuller and Xiaoyan Liang (1993) found wide disparities in the availability of child care. In the richest communities, there is one preschool teacher for every 45 children ages three to five; in the poorest communities, there is one teacher for every 77 children. *Affordable* child care is also a problem. Viewed from a conflict perspective, child care costs are an especially serious burden for lower-class families. Indeed, the poorest

families spend 25 percent of their income for preschool child care, while families who are *not* poor pay only 6 percent or less of their income for day care.

Feminists echo the concern of conflict theorists that high-quality child care receives little governmental support because it is regarded as "merely a way to let women work." Nearly all child care workers (95 percent) are women; many find themselves in low-status, minimum-wage jobs. The average salary of a child care worker in the United States in 1998 was only $10,710—less than counter workers typically make at many McDonald's—and there are few fringe benefits. Although parents may complain of child care costs, the staff, in effect, subsidizes children's care by working for low wages. Not surprisingly,

People in Sweden pay higher taxes than do United States citizens, but they have access to excellent preschool day care at little or no cost.

and free after-school care is widely available. By contrast, in the United States, the total cost of child care typically falls on the individual family and can run more than $5,000 per year for a three- to four-year-old in urban areas and up to $7,800 in downtown sections (Daycare Action Council 2000; *New York Times* 1993a; Topolnicki 1993).

There is a long way to go in making quality child care more affordable and more accessible, not just in the United States, but throughout the world. Government day care facilities in Mexico have lengthy waiting lists. In an attempt to reduce government spending, France is considering cutting back the budgets of subsidized nurseries, even though waiting lists already exist and the French public heartily disapproves of any cutbacks (L. King 1998; Simons 1997; Women's International Network 1995).

Experts in child development view such reports as a vivid reminder of the need for greater governmental and private-sector support for child care. Edward Zigler, director of the Bush Center on Child Development at Yale University, concludes, "It's not just that we're not doing anything. It's that we're perfectly satisfied in this country to every day put children in settings that compromise their growth and development. It's a tragedy, and the cost to this country is going to be immense" (Baker 1994:26).

there is high turnover among child care workers (Bureau of the Census 1998c:419; Schmitt 1998).

Policy Initiatives

Policies regarding child care outside the home vary throughout the world. Most developing nations do not have the economic base to provide subsidized child care. Working mothers largely rely on relatives or take their children to work. Even those industrial countries with elaborate programs of subsidized child care occasionally fall short of the needs for quality supervised child care.

When policymakers decide that publicly funded child care is desirable, they must determine the degree to which taxpayers should subsidize it. A number of European nations, including the Netherlands and Sweden, impose higher taxes than the United States while providing excellent preschool care at little or no cost. In 1991, about half of all Danish children ages three to six attended public child care programs. Parents pay a maximum of 30 percent of the costs. In France, where child care providers enjoy status and good wages, virtually all children ages three to five attend free schooling,

Let's Discuss

1. Is it desirable to expose young children to the socializing influence of day care?
2. In the view of conflict theorists, why does child care receive little government support?
3. Should the costs of day care programs be paid by government, by the private sector, or entirely by parents?

Summary

Socialization is the process whereby people learn the attitudes, values, and actions appropriate for members of a particular culture. This chapter examines the role of socialization in human development; the way in which people develop perceptions, feelings, and beliefs about themselves; the lifelong nature of the socialization process; and the important agents of socialization.

1. Socialization affects the overall cultural practices of a society, and it also shapes the images that we hold of ourselves.

2. Heredity and environmental factors interact in influencing the socialization process. *Sociobiology* is the systematic study of the biological bases of social behavior.

3. In the early 1900s, Charles Horton Cooley advanced the belief that we learn who we are by interacting with others, a phenomenon he calls the *looking-glass self.*

4. George Herbert Mead, best known for his theory of the *self,* proposed that as people mature, their selves begin to reflect their concern about reactions from others—both *generalized others* and *significant others.*

5. Erving Goffman has shown that many of our daily activities involve attempts to convey distinct impressions of who we are, a process called *impression management.*

6. Socialization proceeds throughout the life course. Some societies mark stages of development with formal *rites of passage.* In the culture of the United States, significant events such as marriage and parenthood serve to change a person's status.

7. As the primary agents of socialization, parents play a critical role in guiding children into those *gender roles* deemed appropriate in a society.

8. Like the family, schools in the United States have an explicit mandate to socialize people—and especially children—into the norms and values of our culture.

9. Peer groups and the mass media, especially television, are important agents of socialization for adolescents.

10. We are most fully exposed to occupational roles through observing the work of our parents, of people whom we meet while they are performing their duties, and of people portrayed in the media.

11. The state shapes the socialization process by regulating the life course and by influencing our views of appropriate behavior at particular ages.

12. As more and more mothers of young children have entered the labor market of the United States, the demand for child care has increased dramatically and poses policy questions for nations around the world.

Critical Thinking Questions

1. Should social research in areas such as sociobiology be conducted even though many investigators believe that this analysis is potentially detrimental to large numbers of people?
2. Drawing on Erving Goffman's dramaturgical approach, discuss how the following groups engage in impression management: athletes, college instructors, parents, physicians, politicians.
3. How would functionalists and conflict theorists differ in their analyses of socialization by the mass media?

Key Terms

Anticipatory socialization   Processes of socialization in which a person "rehearses" for future positions, occupations, and social relationships. (page 99)

Cognitive theory of development   Jean Piaget's theory explaining how children's thought progresses through four stages. (98)

Degradation ceremony   An aspect of the socialization process within total institutions, in which people are subjected to humiliating rituals. (100)

Dramaturgical approach   A view of social interaction that examines people as if they were theatrical performers. (96)

Face-work   The efforts of people to maintain the proper image and avoid embarrassment in public. (96)

Gender roles   Expectations regarding the proper behavior, attitudes, and activities of males and females. (101)

Generalized others   The attitudes, viewpoints, and expectations of society as a whole that a child takes into account in his or her behavior. (95)

Impression management   The altering of the presentation of the self in order to create distinctive appearances and satisfy particular audiences. (96)

Looking-glass self   A concept that emphasizes the self as the product of our social interactions with others. (94)

Personality   In everyday speech, a person's typical patterns of attitudes, needs, characteristics, and behavior. (91)

Resocialization The process of discarding former behavior patterns and accepting new ones as part of a transition in one's life. (99)

Rites of passage Rituals marking the symbolic transition from one social position to another. (99)

Role taking The process of mentally assuming the perspective of another, thereby enabling one to respond from that imagined viewpoint. (95)

Self A distinct identity that sets us apart from others. (94)

Significant others Those individuals who are most important in the development of the self, such as parents, friends, and teachers. (96)

Socialization The process whereby people learn the attitudes, values, and behaviors appropriate for members of a particular culture. (91)

Sociobiology The systematic study of biological bases of social behavior. (94)

Symbols The gestures, objects, and language that form the basis of human communication. (95)

Total institutions Institutions that regulate all aspects of a person's life under a single authority, such as prisons, the military, mental hospitals, and convents. (100)

Additional Readings

BOOKS

Adler, Patricia A. and Peter Adler. 1998. *Peer Power: Preadolescent Culture and Identity.* New Brunswick, NJ: Rutgers University Press. Based on eight years of observation research, sociologists discuss the role of peer groups and family as they relate to popularity, social isolation, bullying, and boy–girl relationships.

Dennis, Everette E., ed. 1996. *Children and the Media.* Rutgers, NJ: Transaction. The contributors to this anthology examine such subjects as educational programming, the treatment of children as news subjects, and the handling of issues affecting children in the mass media.

Goffman, Erving. 1959. *The Presentation of Self in Everyday Life.* New York: Doubleday. Goffman demonstrates his interactionist theory that the self is managed in everyday situations in much the same way that a theatrical performer carries out a stage role.

Pollack, William. 1998. *Real Boys: Rescuing Our Sons from the Myths of Boyhood.* New York: Henry Holt. A clinical psychologist looks at the disenchantment experienced by so many boys because their true emotions are kept hidden.

Tobien, Josph J., David Y. H. Wu, and Dana H. Davidson. 1989. *Preschool in Three Cultures: Japan, China, and the United States.* New Haven, CT: Yale University Press. A comparative look at formal early childhood education in three nations, drawing upon the views of parents, teachers, and administrators.

JOURNALS

Among the journals that deal with socialization issues are *Adolescence* (founded in 1966), *Ethology and Sociobiology* (1979), *Journal of Personality and Social Psychology* (1965), and *Young Children* (1945).

Internet Connection

Note: While all the URLs listed were current as of the printing of this book, these sites often change. Please check our website (www.mhhe.com/schaefer) for updates.

1. The mass media play an active role in socialization, with popular children's programs being one way that young people learn the attitudes, values, and actions appropriate to their society. Visit the Teletubbies homepage (**http://www.bbc.co.uk/education/teletubbies/tubbies.html**).

   (a) What is "waving bye-bye" and what does it encourage in children?

   (b) Choose three of the activities for parents and children provided in the "Come and See" section and complete them. What lessons and values do the three activities aim to teach children? Why would it be important for children to learn such lessons?

   (c) In the "Tubby Grown-Ups" link, read the FAQ (frequently asked questions). How did the creators of the Teletubbies come up with the idea? Why are some segments of the show repeated in each episode, according to the creators and producers?

   (d) Thinking back on your own childhood, were there any television programs like this that helped socialize you? In what ways?

   (e) There is a great deal of debate about violence in the media and its impact on children. What is your opinion? What evidence can you give to support your view?

   (f) In what ways can socialization through the media be positive? In what ways can it be negative?

2. Erving Goffman researched the total institution, providing examples such as prisons, concentration camps, and military boot camps. Alcatraz Island, located in San Francisco Bay, was one of the most famous prisons in the United States. Log on to the virtual museum dedicated to Alcatraz (**http://www.nps.gov/alcatraz**). Take an online tour of the island and read about its history.

   (a) When was Alcatraz a federal prison?

   (b) Who were some of the famous criminals sentenced to its shores? Who was the "Birdman of Alcatraz"?

   (c) Did anyone ever escape from the prison-island?

   (d) In what ways was Alcatraz different from other prisons in terms of socialization, rules, living arrangements, and activities?

   (e) In what ways did Alcatraz exemplify Goffman's four traits of total institutions?

   (f) What are some reasons Alcatraz ultimately closed?

   (g) Why was the island occupied by Native Americans for nearly two years?

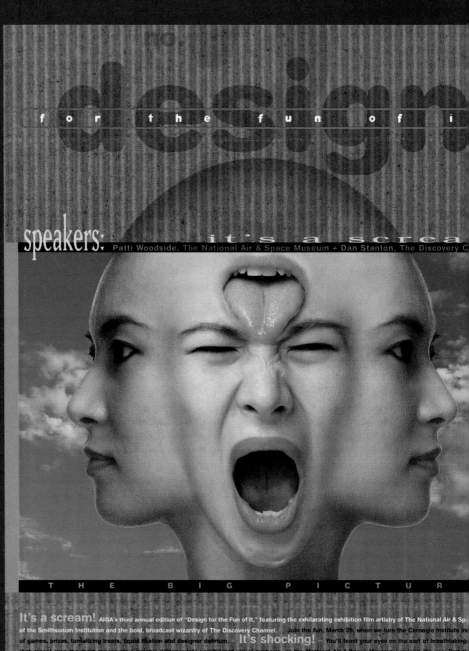

Social interaction is shaped by social structure. The same person might express herself very differently in different social settings, as suggested by this poster for a professional meeting.

The quiet of a summer Sunday morning in Palo Alto, California was shattered by a screeching squad car siren as police swept through the city picking up college students in a surprise mass arrest. Each suspect was charged with a felony, warned of his constitutional rights, spread-eagled against the car, searched, handcuffed and carted off in the back seat of the squad car to the police station for booking.

After being fingerprinted and having identification forms prepared for his "jacket" (central information file), each prisoner was left isolated in a detention cell to wonder what he had done to get himself into this mess. After a while, he was blindfolded and transported to the "Stanford County Prison." Here he began the induction process of becoming a prisoner—stripped naked, skin searched, deloused, and issued a uniform, bedding, soap and towel. By late afternoon when nine such arrests had been completed, these youthful "first offenders" sat in dazed silence on the cots in their barren cells.

These men were part of a very unusual kind of prison, an experimental or mock prison, created by social psychologists for the purpose of intensively studying the effects of imprisonment upon volunteer research subjects. . . .

At the end of only six days we had to close down our mock prison because what we saw was frightening. It was no longer apparent to most of the subjects (or to us) where reality ended and their roles began. The majority had indeed become prisoners or guards, no longer able to clearly differentiate between role playing and self. There were dramatic changes in virtually every aspect of their behavior, thinking and feeling. In less than a week the experience of imprisonment undid (temporarily) a lifetime of learning; human values were suspended, self-concepts were challenged and the ugliest, most base, pathological side of human nature surfaced. We were horrified because we saw some boys (guards) treat others as if they were despicable animals, taking pleasure in cruelty, while other boys (prisoners) became servile, dehumanized robots who thought only of escape, of their own individual survival and of their mounting hatred for the guards. *(Zimbardo 1974:61, 62; 1972:4)* ■

n this description of a study directed by the social psychologist Philip Zimbardo, college students adopted predictable patterns of social interaction (those expected of guards and prisoners) when they were placed in a mock prison. Sociologists use the term *social interaction* to refer to the ways in which people respond to one another, whether face to face or over the telephone or computer. In the mock prison, social interactions between guards and prisoners were highly impersonal. The guards addressed the prisoners by number rather than name, and wore reflector sunglasses that made eye contact with them impossible.

As in many real-life prisons, the simulated prison at Stanford University had a social structure in which guards held virtually total control over prisoners. The term *social structure* refers to the way in which a society is organized into predictable relationships. The social structure of Zimbardo's mock prison influenced the interactions between the guards and prisoners. Zimbardo (1992:576) notes that it was a real prison "in the minds of the jailers and their captives." His simulated prison experiment, first conducted more than 25 years ago, has subsequently been repeated (with similar findings) both in the United States and in other countries.

The concepts of social interaction and social structure, which are closely linked to each other, are central to sociological study. Sociologists observe patterns of behavior closely to understand and accurately describe the social interactions of a community or society and the social structure in which they take place.

This chapter begins by considering how social interaction shapes the way we view the world around us. The chapter will focus on the four basic elements of social structure: statuses, social roles, groups, and institutions. Groups are important because much of our social interaction occurs in them. Social institutions such as the family, religion, and government are a fundamental aspect of social structure. We will contrast the functionalist, conflict, and interactionist approaches to the study of social institutions. We will also examine the typologies developed by Ferdinand Tönnies and Gerhard Lenski for comparing modern societies with simpler forms of social structure. The social policy section will consider the AIDS crisis and its implications for social institutions throughout the world. ∎

Social Interaction and Reality

According to sociologist Herbert Blumer (1969:79), the distinctive characteristic of social interaction among people is that "human beings interpret or 'define' each other's actions instead of merely reacting to each other's actions." In other words, our response to someone's behavior is based on the *meaning* we attach to his or her actions. Reality is shaped by our perceptions, evaluations, and definitions.

These meanings typically reflect the norms and values of the dominant culture and our socialization experiences within that culture. As interactionists emphasize, the meanings that we attach to people's behavior are shaped by our interactions with them and with the larger society. Consequently, social reality is literally constructed from our social interactions (Berger and Luckmann 1966).

Defining and Reconstructing Reality

How do we define our social reality? As an example, let us consider something as simple as how we regard tattoos (refer back to Chapter 1). Even as recently as a few years ago, most of us in the United States considered tattoos as something "weird" or "kooky." We associated them with fringe countercultural groups, such as punk rockers, bike gangs, and skinheads. A tattoo elicited an automatic negative response among many people. Now, however, so many people, including society's trendsetters, are tattooed and the ritual of getting a tattoo has become so legitimized, the mainstream culture regards tattoos differently. At this point, as a result of increased social interactions with those people, tattoos look perfectly at home to us in a number of settings.

The ability to define social reality reflects a group's power within a society. Indeed, one of the most crucial aspects of the relationship between dominant and subordinate groups is the ability of the dominant or majority group to define a society's values. Sociologist William I. Thomas (1923), an early critic of theories of racial and gender differences, saw that the "definition of the situation" could mold the thinking and personality of the individual. Writing from an interactionist perspective, Thomas observed that people respond not only to the objective features of a person or situation but also to the meaning that the person or situation has for them. For example, in Philip Zimbardo's mock prison experiment, student "guards" and "prisoners" accepted the definition of the situation (including the traditional roles and behavior associated with being a guard or prisoner) and acted accordingly.

As we have seen throughout the last 40 years—first in the civil rights movement of the 1960s and since then among such groups as women, the elderly, gays and lesbians, and people with disabilities—an important aspect of the process of social change involves *re*defining or *re*constructing social reality. Members of subordinate groups begin to challenge traditional definitions and instead perceive and experience reality in a new way. For example, the world champion boxer Muhammad Ali began his career as the creation of a White male syndicate, which sponsored his early matches when he was known as Cassius Clay. Soon, however, the young boxer rebelled against those who would keep him or his race down. He broke the old stereotypes of self-effacing Black athletes. He insisted on his own political views (including refusing to serve in the Vietnam War), his own religion (Black Muslim), and his own name (Muhammad Ali). Not only did Ali change the world of sports, he also had a hand in altering the world of race relations (Remnick 1998).

In challenging racist stereotypes of African Americans, boxing champion Muhammad Ali helped to redefine their social reality. Today, courageous in the face of degenerative disease, he is reconstructing the social reality of disabled Americans. Ali was honored at the opening of the summer Olympic games in Atlanta, where he lit the ceremonial torch.

Viewed from a sociological perspective, Ali was redefining social reality by looking much more critically at the racist thinking and terminology that restricted him and other African Americans.

Negotiated Order

As we have seen, people can reconstruct social reality through a process of internal change as they take a different view of everyday behavior. Yet people also reshape reality by negotiating changes in patterns of social interaction. The term *negotiation* refers to the attempt to reach agreement with others concerning some objective. Negotiation does not involve coercion; it goes by many names, including *bargaining, compromising, trading off, mediating, exchanging, "wheeling and dealing,"* and *collusion.* It is through negotiation as a form of social interaction that society creates its social structure (Strauss 1977; see also G. Fine 1984).

Negotiation occurs in many ways. As interactionists point out, some social situations, such as buying groceries, involve no mediation, while other situations require significant amounts of negotiation. For example, we may negotiate with others regarding time ("When should we arrive?"), space ("Can we have a meeting at your house?"), or even assignment of places while waiting for concert tickets. In traditional societies, impending marriage often leads to negotiations between the families of the husband and wife. For example, anthropologist Ray Abrahams (1968) has described how the Labwor people of Africa arrange for an amount of property to go from the groom's to the bride's family at the time of marriage. In the view of the Labwor, such bargaining over an exchange of cows and sheep culminates not only in a marriage but, more important, in the linking of two clans or families.

While such family-to-family bargaining is common in traditional cultures, negotiation can take much more elaborate forms in modern industrial societies. Consider the tax laws of the United States. From a sociological perspective, such laws are formal norms (reflected in federal and state codes). The entire tax code undergoes revision through negotiated outcomes involving many competing interests, including big business, foreign nations, and political action committees (see Chapter 16). On an individual level, taxpayers, if audited, will mediate with agents of the

JANE LEVINE: AIM Advertising

As part of a small four-person ad agency in New York City, Jane Levine has no title, but takes on whatever needs to be done—whether it be customer service, handling accounts, production, creative work, or proofreading. "There is no typical work week," she says. "My job is task-oriented, from pitching new business to buying media."

Jane has found that her sociology background helps her out every day, especially in regard to what she learned about groups. "Being able to look at a group or a situation and understand it makes me a better communicator," a crucial quality in sales. "I deal with important people in business, and I'm able to understand where they're coming from—ultimately, it's a sale." She also credits the study of sociology with allowing her to have a much more open mind. "I'm much more accepting and inquisitive about other people and cultures. It has opened my mind, from food to music to people to architecture."

Jane received her degree in sociology from Salisbury State in 1986. The instructor of her introductory course also wrote the textbook she used. "I thought that was the coolest thing ever. I really studied and got into it." She appreciated the "different slant" that sociology offered. Today Jane claims that "sociology has had a major, positive effect on my life." Her advice to students: "If you're interested, you should definitely pursue other classes in sociology."

Internal Revenue Service. Changes in the taxpayers' individual situations will occur through such negotiations. The tax structure of the United States can hardly be viewed as fixed; rather, it reflects the sum of negotiations for change at any time (Maines 1977, 1982; J. Thomas 1984).

Negotiations underlie much of our social behavior. Most elements of social structure are not static and are therefore subject to change through bargaining and exchanging. For this reason, sociologists use the term *negotiated order* to underscore the fact that the social order is continually being constructed and altered through negotiation. *Negotiated order* refers to a social structure that derives its existence from the social interactions through which people define and redefine its character.

We can add negotiation to our list of cultural universals

pp. 66–67

because all societies provide guidelines or norms in which negotiations take place. The recurring role of negotiation in social interaction and social structure will be apparent as we examine statuses, social roles, groups, networks, and institutions (Strauss 1977).

Elements of Social Structure

We can examine predictable social relationships in terms of five elements: statuses, social roles, groups, social networks, and social institutions. These elements make up social structure just as a foundation, walls, and ceilings make up a building's structure. The elements of social structure are developed through the lifelong process of socialization, described in Chapter 4.

Statuses

We normally think of a person's "status" as having to do with influence, wealth, and fame. However, sociologists use *status* to refer to any of the full range of socially defined positions within a large group or society—from the lowest to the highest position. Within our society, a person can occupy the status of president of the United States, fruit picker, son or daughter, violinist, teenager, resident of Minneapolis, dental technician, or neighbor. Clearly, a person holds more than one status simultaneously.

Ascribed and Achieved Status

Sociologists view some statuses as *ascribed*, while they categorize others as *achieved* (see Figure 5-1). An *ascribed status* is "assigned" to a person by society without regard for the person's unique talents or characteristics. Generally, this assignment takes place at birth; thus, a person's racial background, gender, and age are all considered ascribed statuses. These characteristics are biological in origin but are significant mainly because of the social meanings they have in our culture. Conflict theorists are especially interested in ascribed statuses, since these statuses often confer privileges or reflect a person's membership in a subordinate group. The social meanings of race and ethnicity, gender, and age will be analyzed more fully in Chapters 10–12.

In most cases, there is little that people can do to change an ascribed status. But we can attempt to change the traditional constraints associated with such statuses. As an example, the Gray Panthers—an activist political group founded in 1971 to work for the rights of older

FIGURE 5-1

Social Statuses

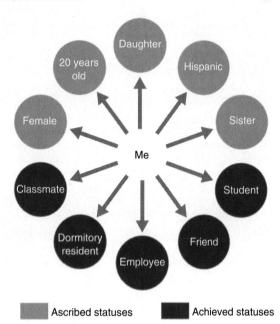

■ Ascribed statuses ■ Achieved statuses

The person in this figure—"me"—occupies many positions in society, each of which involves distinct statuses. How would you define your statuses?

people—have tried to modify society's negative and confining stereotypes of the elderly (see Chapter 12). As a result of their work and that of other groups supporting older citizens, the ascribed status of "senior citizen" is no longer as difficult for millions of older people.

An ascribed status does not necessarily have the same social meaning in every society. In a cross-cultural study, sociologist Gary Huang (1988) confirmed the long-held view that respect for the elderly is an important cultural norm in China. In many cases, the prefix "old" is used respectfully: calling someone "old teacher" or "old person" is like calling a judge in the United States "your honor." Huang points out that positive age-seniority distinctions in language are absent in the United States; consequently, we view the term *old man* as more of an insult than a celebration of seniority and wisdom.

Unlike ascribed statuses, an **achieved status** comes to us largely through our own efforts. Both "bank president" and "prison guard" are achieved statuses, as are "lawyer," "pianist," "advertising executive," and "social worker." You must do something to acquire an achieved status—go to school, learn a skill, establish a friendship, or invent a new product. As we see in the next section, our achieved status is heavily influenced by our ascribed status. Being male, for example, will decrease the likelihood that a person would consider being a child care worker.

Master Status

Each person holds many different statuses; some may connote higher social positions, and some, lower positions. How is one's overall social position viewed by others in light of these conflicting statuses? According to sociologist Everett Hughes (1945), societies deal with such inconsistencies by agreeing that certain statuses are more important than others. A **master status** is a status that dominates others and thereby determines a person's general position within society. For example, Arthur Ashe, who died of AIDS in 1993, had a remarkable career as a tennis star; but at the end of his life, his status as a well-known personality with AIDS may have outweighed his statuses as a retired athlete, an author, and a political activist. As we will see in Box 5-1, throughout the world many people with disabilities find that their status as "disabled" is given undue weight and overshadows their actual ability to perform successfully in meaningful employment.

Our society gives such importance to race and gender that they often dominate our lives. Indeed, such ascribed statuses often influence achieved status. The African American activist Malcolm X (1925–1965), an eloquent and controversial advocate of Black power and Black pride in the early 1960s, recalled that his feelings and perspectives changed dramatically while in eighth grade. His English teacher, a White man, advised him that his goal of becoming a lawyer was "no realistic goal for a nigger" and encouraged him instead to become a carpenter. Malcolm X (1964:37) found that his position as a Black man (ascribed status) was an obstacle to his dream of becoming a lawyer (achieved status). In the United States, ascribed statuses of race and gender can function as master statuses that have an important impact on one's potential to achieve a desired professional and social status.

Social Roles

What Are Social Roles?

Throughout our lives, we are acquiring what sociologists call *social roles*. A **social role** is a set of expectations for people who occupy a given social position or status. Thus, in the United States, we expect that cab drivers will know how to get around a city, that secretaries will be reliable in handling phone messages, and that police officers will take action if they see a citizen being threatened. With each distinctive social status—whether ascribed or achieved—come particular role expectations. However, actual performance varies from individual to individual. One secretary may assume extensive administrative responsibilities, while another may focus on clerical duties. Similarly, in Philip Zimbardo's mock prison experiment, some students were brutal and sadistic as guards, but others were not.

5-1 Disability as a Master Status

Throughout history and around the world, people with disabilities have often been subjected to cruel and inhuman treatment. For example, in the early twentieth century, the disabled were frequently viewed as subhuman creatures who were a menace to society. As one result, many state legislatures in this country passed compulsory sterilization laws aimed at "handicapped people." In Japan more than 16,000 women with disabilities were involuntarily sterilized with government approval from 1945 to 1995. Sweden recently apologized for the same action taken against 62,000 of its citizens in the 1970s.

Today, such blatantly hostile treatment of people with disabilities has generally given way to a *medical model,* which views the disabled as chronic patients. Increasingly, however, people concerned with the rights of the disabled have criticized this model as well. In their view, it is the unnecessary and discriminatory barriers present in the environment—both physical and attitudinal—that stand in the way of people with disabilities more than any biological limitations do. Applying a *civil rights model,* activists emphasize that those with disabilities face widespread prejudice, discrimination, and segregation. For example, most voting places are inaccessible to wheelchair users and fail to provide ballots that can be used by those unable to read print.

Drawing on the earlier work of Erving Goffman, contemporary sociologists have suggested that society has attached a stigma to many forms of disability and that this stigma leads to prejudicial treatment. Indeed, people with disabilities frequently observe that the nondisabled see them only as blind, wheelchair users, and so forth, rather than as complex human beings with individual strengths and weaknesses, whose blindness or use of a wheelchair is merely one aspect of their lives. A review of studies of people with disabilities disclosed that

> In Japan more than 16,000 women with disabilities were involuntarily sterilized with government approval from 1945 to 1995.

most academic research on the subject does not differentiate gender—thereby perpetuating the view that a disability overrides other personal characteristics. Consequently, disability serves as a master status.

Without question, people with disabilities occupy a subordinate position in the United States. By 1970, a strong political movement for disability rights had emerged across the United States. Women and men involved in this movement are working to challenge negative views of disabled people

and to modify the social structure by reshaping laws, institutions, and environments so that people with disabilities can be fully integrated into mainstream society.

The effort to overcome the master status is global in nature. The African nation of Botswana has plans to assist its disabled, most of whom live in rural areas and are in need of special services relating to mobility and economic development. Kenya, however, fails to outlaw discrimination against people with disabilities, even though its constitution outlaws discrimination on the basis of other characteristics, including sex, tribe, race, place of origin, creed, or religion. In many countries, disability rights activists are targeting issues essential to overcoming master status and to being a full citizen, such as employment, housing, and access to public buildings.

Let's Discuss

1. Does your campus present barriers to disabled students? If so, what kind of barriers—physical, attitudinal, or both? Describe some of them.
2. Why do you think nondisabled people see disability as the most important characteristic of a disabled person? What can be done to help people see beyond the wheelchair and the seeing-eye dog?

Sources: M. Fine and Asch 1988; Goffman 1963a; Gove 1980; H. Hahn 1993; D. Murphy 1997; *Newsday* 1997; Ponczek 1998; Shapiro 1993.

Roles are a significant component of social structure. Viewed from a functionalist perspective, roles contribute to a society's stability by enabling members to anticipate the behavior of others and to pattern their own actions accordingly. Yet social roles can also be dysfunctional by restricting people's interactions and relationships. If we view a person *only* as a "police officer" or a "supervisor," it will be difficult to relate to this person as a friend or neighbor.

Role Conflict

Imagine the delicate situation of a woman who has worked for a decade on an assembly line in an electrical

plant and has recently been named supervisor of the unit she worked in. How is this woman expected to relate to her longtime friends and co-workers? Should she still go out to lunch with them, as she has done almost daily for years? Is it her responsibility to recommend the firing of an old friend who cannot keep up with the demands of the assembly line?

Role conflict occurs when incompatible expectations arise from two or more social positions held by the same person. Fulfillment of the roles associated with one status may directly violate the roles linked to a second status. In the example above, the newly promoted supervisor will

Imagine you are a journalist walking down this street as you witness the mugging going on here. What do you do? Try to stop the crime? Or take a picture for your magazine? This was the role conflict that Sarah Leen, a professional photographer, experienced when she stopped to change a lens and take a picture of this scene. At the same time, Leen felt fear for her own safety. People in certain professions—among them, journalism—commonly experience role conflict during disasters, crimes, and other distressing situations.

Role Strain

Role conflict describes the situation of a person dealing with the challenge of occupying two social positions simultaneously. However, even a single position can cause problems. Sociologists use the term **role strain** to describe difficulties that result from the differing demands and expectations associated with the same social position.

In the opening example, social psychologist Philip Zimbardo unexpectedly experienced role strain. He initially saw himself merely as a college professor directing an imaginative experiment in which students played the roles of either guard or inmate. However, he soon found that as a professor, he is also expected to look after the welfare of the students or at least not to endanger them. Eventually he resolved the role strain by making the difficult decision to terminate the experiment. Twenty-five years later, in a television interview, he was still reflecting on the challenge of this role strain (CBS News 1998).

experience a serious conflict between certain social and occupational roles.

Role conflicts call for important ethical choices. In the example just given, the new supervisor has to make a difficult decision about how much allegiance she owes her friend whose work is unsatisfactory. Our culture tells us that success is more important than friendship. If friends are holding us back, we should leave them and pursue our ambitions. Yet, at the same time, we are told that abandoning our friends is contemptible. The supervisor must decide whether she will risk her promotion out of concern for her friend.

One common type of role conflict occurs when individuals move into occupations that are not common among people with their ascribed status. Male preschool teachers and female police officers experience this type of role conflict. In the latter case, female officers must strive to reconcile their workplace role in law enforcement with the societal view of women, which does not embrace many skills needed in police work. And while female police officers encounter sexual harassment, as women do throughout the labor force, they must also deal with the "code of silence," an informal norm that precludes their implicating fellow officers in wrongdoing (S. Martin 1994; C. Fletcher 1995).

National Park Service employees also experience role strain. For generations their primary role was to assist visitors to enjoy the beauty that the park system offers. However, increasingly, the social problems of the larger society, ranging from traffic jams to crime, have intruded, as more and more people seek to "escape" the routine workday world. Employees now find themselves torn between encouraging tourists to explore activities and curtailing activities that might interfere with the enjoyment of others, or even worse, actually harm the park. Park employees in parts of Africa face similar role strain. Photo safaris generate huge revenues for countries such as Kenya, but national wildlife refuges also are a target for people who traffic in illegal animal skins or ivory. Park employees have to carry out two very different demands at the same time—to be welcoming ambassador to visitors and a government enforcer of poaching laws.

Role Exit

Often, when we think of assuming a social role, we focus on the preparation and anticipatory socialization that a person undergoes for that role. This is true if a person is about to become an attorney, a chef, a spouse, or a par-

National Park rangers, hired to assist tourists and protect the pristine environment they patrol, experience role strain when big-city traffic, crime, and recreational pursuits spill across park boundaries. In 1999 rangers at Yosemite National Park arrested a parachutist who jumped from El Capitan in a well-publicized protest against park regulations forbidding such stunts.

their role exit as a gradual, evolutionary process that had no single turning point. The last stage of role exit involves the *creation of a new identity.*

Many of you participated in a role exit when you made the transition from high school to college. You left behind the role of offspring living at home and took on the role of a somewhat independent college student living with peers in a dorm. Sociologist Ira Silver (1996) has made a study of the central role that material objects play in this transition. The objects that students choose to leave home (like stuffed animals and dolls) are associated with their prior identities. They may remain deeply attached to these objects but do not want them to be seen as part of their new identities at college. The objects they bring with them symbolize how they now see themselves and how they wish to be perceived. CDs, tapes, and wall posters, for example, all are calculated to say, "This is me."

ent. Yet, until recently, social scientists have given less attention to the adjustments involved in *leaving* social roles.

Sociologist Helen Rose Fuchs Ebaugh (1988) developed the term ***role exit*** to describe the process of disengagement from a role that is central to one's self-identity and reestablishment of an identity in a new role. Drawing on interviews with 185 people—among them ex-convicts, divorced men and women, recovering alcoholics, ex-nuns, former doctors, retirees, and transsexuals—Ebaugh (herself a former nun) studied the process of voluntarily exiting from significant social roles.

Ebaugh has offered a four-stage model of role exit. The first stage begins with *doubt*—as the person experiences frustration, burnout, or simply unhappiness with an accustomed status and the roles associated with this social position. The second stage involves a *search for alternatives.* A person unhappy with his or her career may take a leave of absence; an unhappily married couple may begin what they see as a temporary separation.

The third stage of role exit is the *action stage* or *departure.* Ebaugh found that the vast majority of her respondents could identify a clear turning point that made them feel it was essential to take final action and leave their job, end their marriage, or engage in another type of role exit. However, 20 percent of respondents saw

Groups

In sociological terms, a ***group*** is any number of people with similar norms, values, and expectations who interact with one another. The members of a women's college basketball team, of a hospital's business office, or of a symphony orchestra constitute a group. However, the entire staff of a large hospital would not be considered a group, since the staff members rarely interact with one another at one time. Perhaps the only point at which they all come together is an annual party.

Every society is composed of many groups in which daily social interaction takes place. We seek out groups to establish friendships, to accomplish certain goals, and to fulfill social roles that we have acquired. We'll explore the various types of groups in which people interact in detail in Chapter 6, where sociological investigations of group behavior will also be examined.

Groups play a vital part in a society's social structure. Much of our social interaction takes place within groups and is influenced by their norms and sanctions. Being a teenager or a retired person takes on special meanings when you interact within groups designed for people with that particular status. The expectations associated with

The pictures in this student's room in India may signify his attempt to create a new identity, the final stage in role exit.

many social roles, including those accompanying the statuses of brother, sister, and student, become more clearly defined in the context of a group.

New technology has broadened the definition of groups to include those who interact electronically—a significant number of Americans. About half of all U.S. teenagers now go online; 83 percent of them exchange e-mail, and 42 percent visit chat rooms. Not all the people they and their parents converse with are real. At some websites, *chatterbots*—fictitious correspondents created by artificial intelligence programs—respond to questions as if a human were replying. While answering product or service-related questions, the chatterbot may begin "chatting" with an online consumer about family or the weather. Ultimately, such conversations may develop into a group that includes other online correspondents, both real and artificial. New groups organized around old interests, such as antique collection or bowling, have already arisen from this type of virtual reality (Kantrowitz and Wingert 1999; D. Pescovitz 1999; Van Slambrouck 1999).

For the human participant, such online exchanges offer a new opportunity to alter one's image—what Goffman (1959) refers to as impression management. How might you present yourself to an online discussion group?

Social Networks and Technology

Groups do not merely serve to define other elements of the social structure, such as roles and statuses; they also are an intermediate link between the individual and the larger society. We are all members of a number of different groups and through our acquaintances make connections with people in different social circles. This connection is known as a ***social network***—that is, a series of social relationships that links a person directly to others and therefore indirectly to still more people. Social networks may constrain people by limiting the range of their interactions, yet these networks may also empower people by making available vast resources (Marsden 1992).

Involvement in social networks—commonly known as *networking*—is especially valuable in finding employment. For example, while looking for a job one year after finishing school, Albert Einstein was successful only when a classmate's father put him in touch with his future employer. These kinds of contacts, even if they are weak and distant, can be crucial in establishing social networks and facilitating transmission of information.

With advances in technology, we can now maintain social networks electronically. We don't need face-to-face contacts for knowledge sharing anymore. It is not uncommon for those looking for employment or for a means of identifying someone with common interests to first turn to the Internet. Sociologist Manuel Castells (1996, 1997, 1998) views the emerging electronic social networks as fundamental to new organizations and the growth of existing businesses and associations.

A study released in 2000 documented a rise in the amount of time people are spending online in their homes. The increase suggests that face-to-face interactions may well be declining, since there are only so many hours in anyone's day. Indeed, a third of the respondents said they spent more than five hours a week online while at home. Of those heavy users, 8 percent reported attending fewer social events as a result of their surfing, and 13 percent said they were spending less time with family and friends. However, the Internet can also promote social contacts, especially among those who have few opportunities, such as the disabled and the geographically isolated. Significantly, the number of retired people who frequent chatrooms created for older users has increased sharply. Participants at websites such as ThirdAge report that they have formed new online friendships to replace old ones formed at the workplace (Galant 2000; Nie and Erbring 2000). In Chapter 22, we will examine further the ways in which computer technology has assisted the formation of larger and even international social networks.

In the workplace, networking pays off more for men than for women because of the traditional presence of

Research in Action

5-2 Women's Social Networks

While sociologists have rightly given a good deal of attention to "old boy networks," there has been growing interest in the social networks created by women.

Sociologist Pierette Hondagneu-Sotelo conducted observation research and interviews among Hispanic women (primarily Mexican immigrants) who live in San Francisco and are employed as domestic workers in middle- and upper-class homes. These women engage in what sociologist Mary Romero has called "job work." This term refers to work performed when a domestic worker maintains several employers and cleans each home on a weekly or biweekly basis for a flat rate of pay for the work completed (in Spanish, *por el trabajo*) as opposed to being paid an hourly rate for the job (*por la hora*). Job work typically brings low pay, there is no reimbursement for transportation costs, and there are no health care benefits.

At first glance, we might expect that women engaged in such job work would be isolated from each other since they work alone. However, Hondagneu-Sotelo found that these Hispanic women have created strong social networks. Through interactions in various social settings—such as picnics, baby showers, church events, and informal gatherings at women's homes—

they share such valuable information as cleaning tips, remedies for work-related physical ailments, tactics for negotiating better pay and gratuities, and advice on how to leave undesirable jobs.

Networking has also been useful for members of the A Team, a social network of 12 to 14 women who are senior health care professionals in the Boston area. The A Team began in 1977 through a series of ca-

> The A Team began in 1977 through a series of casual lunches attended by young women who were beginning careers in a health care field dominated by middle-aged men.

sual lunches attended by young women who were beginning careers in a health care field dominated by middle-aged men.

By 1984, many members of the A Team had advanced to middle-management or more senior positions in local hospitals or state government. But the group realized that women still did not hold any chief executive officer (CEO) positions in hospitals in

the Boston area. Because members felt that their qualifications matched those of the men being named as CEOs, they joined forces in an all-out effort to help each other gain the contacts they believed would lead to top posts. The A Team networked with headhunters, hospital trustees, women executives in other industries, and local politicians; held seminars to educate members on such topics as how to analyze financial statements; and continued informal networking efforts (including phoning friends and former associates to recommend colleagues).

The results of this networking were impressive. As of 1995, many women from the A Team hold top executive posts in hospitals and other health care institutions in the Boston area.

Let's Discuss

1. Have you ever participated in a job- or school-related network? If so, did you benefit from the opportunities it offered? In what way?

2. Suppose you want to land a professional job in the field of your choice. What people or organizations might help you to reach your goal? How would you get started?

Sources: Gabor 1995: Hondagneu-Sotelo 1994; Reskin and Padavic 1994; Romero 1998.

men in leadership positions. A 1997 survey of executives found that 63 percent of men use networking to find new jobs compared to 41 percent of women. Thirty-one percent of the women use classified advertisements to find jobs, compared to only 13 percent of the men (Carey and McLean 1997). Still, as we see in Box 5-2, women at all levels of the paid labor force are beginning to make effective use of social networks. A study of women who were leaving the welfare rolls to enter the paid workforce found that networking was an effective tool in their search for employment. Informal networking also helped them to locate child care and better housing—both of which are key to successful employment (Henly 1999).

In a recent study of informal networks among middle-aged managers at four Fortune 500 firms, Herminia Ibarra (1995) of the Harvard Business School noted the impact of

race on networking. Whereas White managers often participate in all-White social networks, African American managers are more likely to be part of racially integrated networks—in part because there are comparatively fewer Blacks with whom to network. With this reality in mind, African Americans have established a diverse array of national organizations to assist their networking efforts. Among these are the National Black MBA Association, the National Association of Black Women Entrepreneurs, the Black Filmmaker Foundation, Rocks (which is dedicated to mentoring junior Black officers within the U.S. Army), and the Black Girls Coalition (which brings together African American fashion models). Race and gender clearly play a role in face-to-face networking, but electronic networking allows one to assume different or, at least, ambiguous social identities (Moskos 1991; S. Turkle 1995; L. Williams 1994).

Social Institutions

The mass media, the government, the economy, the family, and the health care system are all examples of social institutions found in our society. *Social institutions* are organized patterns of beliefs and behavior centered on basic social needs, such as replacing personnel (the family) and preserving order (the government).

By studying social institutions, sociologists gain insight into the structure of a society. For example, the institution of religion adapts to the segment of society that it serves. Church work has a very different meaning for ministers who serve a skid row area, a naval base, and a suburban middle-class community. Religious leaders assigned to a skid row mission will focus on tending to the ill and providing food and shelter. By contrast, clergy in affluent suburbs will be occupied with counseling those considering marriage and divorce, arranging youth activities, and overseeing cultural events.

Functionalist View

One way to understand social institutions is to see how they fulfill essential functions. Anthropologist David F. Aberle and his colleagues (1950) and sociologists Raymond Mack and Calvin Bradford (1979) have identified five major tasks, or functional prerequisites, that a society or relatively permanent group must accomplish if it is to survive (see Table 5-1):

1. *Replacing personnel.* Any group or society must replace personnel when they die, leave, or become incapacitated. This is accomplished through such means as immigration, annexation of neighboring groups of people, acquisition of slaves, or normal sexual reproduction of members. The Shakers, a religious sect that came to the United States in 1774, are a conspicuous example of a group that has *failed* to replace personnel. Their religious beliefs commit the Shakers to celibacy; to survive, the group must recruit new members. At first, the Shakers proved quite successful in attracting members and reached a peak of about 6,000 members in the United States during the 1840s. However, as of 1999, the only Shaker community left in this country was a farm in Maine with seven members (Swanson 1999).

2. *Teaching new recruits.* No group can survive if many of its members reject the established behavior and responsibilities of the group. Thus, finding or producing new members is not sufficient. The group must encourage recruits to learn and accept its values and customs. This learning can take place formally within schools (where learning is a manifest function) or informally through interaction

and negotiation in peer groups (where instruction is a latent function).

3. *Producing and distributing goods and services.* Any relatively permanent group or society must provide and distribute desired goods and services for its members. Each society establishes a set of rules for the allocation of financial and other resources. The group must satisfy the needs of most members at least to some extent, or it will risk the possibility of discontent and, ultimately, disorder.

4. *Preserving order.* The native people of Tasmania, a large island just south of Australia, are now extinct. During the 1800s, they were destroyed by the hunting parties of European conquerors, who looked upon the Tasmanians as half-human. This annihilation underscores a critical function of every group or society—preserving order and protecting itself from attack. The Tasmanians were unable to defend them-

Table 5-1 Functions and Institutions

Functional Prerequisite	Social Institutions
Replacing personnel	Family Government (immigration)
Teaching new recruits	Family (basic skills) Economy (occupations) Education (schools) Religion (sacred teachings)
Producing and distributing goods and services	Family (food preparation) Economy Government (regulations regarding commerce) Health care system
Preserving order	Family (child rearing, regulation of sexuality) Government Religion (morals)
Providing and maintaining a sense of purpose	Government (patriotism) Religion

Sister Marie, who belongs to the last surviving Shaker community in the United States, checks the supplies in a refrigerator at the group's home in Maine. The Shakers have found no effective way to replace their personnel—an essential task if a group is to become a permanent part of society.

tect itself from external attack by amassing a frightening arsenal of weaponry, while another may make determined efforts to remain neutral in world politics and to promote cooperative relationships with its neighbors. No matter what its particular strategy, any society or relatively permanent group must attempt to satisfy all these functional prerequisites for survival. If it fails on even one condition, as the Tasmanians did, the society runs the risk of extinction.

Conflict View

Conflict theorists do not concur with the functionalist approach to social institutions. While both perspectives agree that institutions are organized to meet basic social needs, conflict theorists object to the implication that the outcome is necessarily efficient and desirable.

selves against the more developed European technology of warfare, and an entire people was wiped out.

5. *Providing and maintaining a sense of purpose.* People must feel motivated to continue as members of a society in order to fulfill the previous four requirements. The behavior of U.S. prisoners of war (POWs) while in confinement during the war in Vietnam is a testament to the importance of maintaining a sense of purpose. While in prison camps, some of these men mentally made elaborate plans for marriage, family, children, reunions, and new careers. A few even built houses in their minds—right down to the last doorknob or water faucet. By holding on to a sense of purpose—their intense desire to return to their homeland and live normal lives—the POWs refused to allow the agony of confinement to destroy their mental health.

Many aspects of a society can assist people in developing and maintaining a sense of purpose. For some people, religious values or personal moral codes are most crucial; for others, national or tribal identities are especially meaningful. Whatever these differences, in any society there remains one common and critical reality. If an individual does not have a sense of purpose, he or she has little reason to contribute to a society's survival.

This list of functional prerequisites does not specify how a society and its corresponding social institutions will perform each task. For example, one society may pro-

From a conflict perspective, the present organization of social institutions is no accident. Major institutions, such as education, help to maintain the privileges of the most powerful individuals and groups within a society, while contributing to the powerlessness of others. As one example, public schools in the United States are financed largely through property taxes. This allows more affluent areas to provide their children with better-equipped schools and better-paid teachers than low-income areas can afford. As a result, children from prosperous communities are better prepared to compete academically than children from impoverished communities. The structure of the nation's educational system permits and even promotes such unequal treatment of school children.

Conflict theorists argue that social institutions such as education have an inherently conservative nature. Without question, it has been difficult to implement educational reforms that promote equal opportunity—whether in the area of bilingual education, school desegregation, or mainstreaming of students with disabilities. From a functionalist perspective, social change can be dysfunctional, since it often leads to instability. However, from a conflict view, why should we preserve the existing social structure if it is unfair and discriminatory?

Social institutions also operate in gendered and racist environments, as conflict theorists, as well as feminists and interactionists, have pointed out. In schools, offices,

Donated computers are an attempt to redress the inherent inequality between rich and poor school systems in the United States. Philadelphia School Superintendent David Mornbeck, left, and IBM Chairman and CEO Louis Gerstner, Jr., watch as elementary school students try one of the computers IBM donated to Philadelphia schools.

and governmental institutions, assumptions are made about what people can do that reflect the sexism and racism of the larger society. For instance, many people assume that women cannot make tough decisions—even those in the top echelons of corporate management. (This process of stigmatization is discussed more fully in the policy section of Chapter 17.) Others assume that all Black students at elite colleges represent affirmative action admissions. Inequality based on gender, economic status, race, and ethnicity thrives in such an environment—to which we might add discrimination based on age, physical disability, and sexual orientation. The truth of this assertion can be seen in routine decisions to advertise jobs and provide or withhold fringe benefits like child care and parental leave.

To describe the interlocking models of oppression that are built into most institutions, feminist sociologist Patricia Hill Collins (1971) coined the phrase *matrix of domination*. Unless activists and policymakers intervene to restructure decision making in these institutions, those in less advantaged groups will remain at the bottom.

Interactionist View

Social institutions affect our everyday behavior, whether we are driving down the street or waiting in a long shopping line. Sociologist Mitchell Duneier (1994a, 1994b)

studied the social behavior of the word processors, all women, who work in the service center of a large Chicago law firm. Duneier was interested in the informal social norms that emerge in this work environment and the rich social network that these female employees had created.

The Network Center, as it is called, is merely a single, windowless room in a large office building where the firm occupies seven floors. This center is staffed by two shifts of word processors, who work either from 4:00 P.M. to midnight or midnight to 8:00 A.M. Each word processor works in a cubicle with just enough room for her keyboard, terminal, printer, and telephone. Work assignments for the word processors are placed in a central basket and then completed according to precise procedures.

At first glance, we might think that these women labor with little social contact, apart from limited work breaks and occasional conversations with their supervisor. However, drawing on the interactionist perspective, Duneier learned that despite working in a large office, these women find private moments to talk (often in the halls or outside the washroom) and share a critical view of the law firm's attorneys and day-shift secretaries. Indeed, the word processors routinely suggest that their assignments represent work that the "lazy" secretaries should have completed during the normal workday. Duneier (1994b) tells of one word processor who resented the lawyers' superior attitude and pointedly refused to recognize or speak with any attorney who would not address her by name.

Interactionist theorists emphasize that our social behavior is conditioned by the roles and statuses that we accept, the groups to which we belong, and the institutions within which we function. For example, the social roles associated with being a judge occur within the larger context of the criminal justice system. The status of "judge" stands in relation to other statuses, such as attorney, plaintiff, defendant, and witness, as well as to the social institution of government. While the symbolic aspects of courts and jails are awesome, the judicial system derives its continued significance from the roles people carry out in social interactions (Berger and Luckmann 1966).

Social Structure in Global Perspective

Modern societies are complex, especially when compared with earlier social arrangements. Sociologists Ferdinand Tönnies and Gerhard Lenski have offered important typologies for contrasting modern societies with simpler forms of social structure.

Tönnies's *Gemeinschaft* and *Gesellschaft*

Ferdinand Tönnies (1855–1936) was appalled by the rise of an industrial city in his native Germany during the late 1800s. In his view, this city marked a dramatic change from the ideal type of a close-knit community, which Tönnies (1988, original edition 1887) termed *Gemeinschaft*, to that of a impersonal mass society known as *Gesellschaft*.

The **Gemeinschaft** (pronounced guh-MINE-shoft) community is typical of rural life. It is a small community in which people have similar backgrounds and life experiences. Virtually everyone knows one another, and social interactions are intimate and familiar, almost as one might find among kinfolk. There is a commitment to the larger social group and a sense of togetherness among community members. People relate to others in a personal way, not just as "clerk" or "manager." With this more personal interaction comes less privacy: we know more about everyone.

Do you think many visitors to this museum know each other? Strangers who congregate together can be part of a *Gesellschaft*.

"I'd like to think of you as a person, David, but it's my job to think of you as personnel."

In a *Gesellschaft*, people are likely to relate to one another in terms of their roles rather than their individual backgrounds.

Social control in the *Gemeinschaft* community is maintained through informal means such as moral persuasion, gossip, and even gestures. These techniques work effectively because people are genuinely concerned about how others feel toward them. Social change is relatively limited in the *Gemeinschaft*; the lives of members of one generation may be quite similar to those of their grandparents.

By contrast, the **Gesellschaft** (pronounced guh-ZELL-shoft) is an ideal type characteristic of modern urban life. Most people are strangers and feel little in common with other community residents. Relationships are governed by social roles that grow out of immediate tasks, such as purchasing a product or arranging a business meeting. Self-interests dominate, and there is generally little consensus concerning values or commitment to the group. As a result, social control must rely on more formal techniques, such as laws and legally defined punishments. Social change is an important aspect of life in the *Gesellschaft*; it can be strikingly evident even within a single generation.

Table 5-2 summarizes the differences between the *Gemeinschaft* and the *Gesellschaft* as described by Tönnies. Sociologists have used these terms to compare social structures stressing close relationships with those that emphasize less personal ties. It is easy to view *Gemeinschaft* with nostalgia as a far better way of life than the "rat race" of contemporary existence. However, the more intimate relationships of the *Gemeinschaft* come with a price. The prejudice and discrimination found within

Table 5-2 **Comparison of *Gemeinschaft* and *Gesellschaft***

Gemeinschaft	*Gesellschaft*
Rural life typifies this form.	Urban life typifies this form.
People share a feeling of community that results from their similar backgrounds and life experiences.	People perceive little sense of commonality. Their differences in background appear more striking than their similarities.
Social interactions, including negotiations, are intimate and familiar.	Social interactions, including negotiations, are more likely to be task-specific.
There is a spirit of cooperation and unity of will.	Self-interests dominate.
Tasks and personal relationships cannot be separated.	The task being performed is paramount; relationships are subordinate.
There is little emphasis on individual privacy.	Privacy is valued.
Informal social control predominates.	Formal social control is evident.
There is less tolerance of deviance.	There is greater tolerance of deviance.
Emphasis is on ascribed statuses.	There is more emphasis on achieved statuses.
Social change is relatively limited.	Social change is very evident—even within a generation.

Gemeinschaft can be quite confining; more emphasis is placed on such ascribed statuses as family background than on people's unique talents and achievements. In addition, *Gemeinschaft* tends to be distrustful of the individual who seeks to be creative or just to be different.

Lenski's Sociocultural Evolution Approach

Sociologist Gerhard Lenski takes a very different view of society and social structure. Rather than distinguishing between two opposite types of societies, as Tönnies had, Lenski sees human societies as undergoing change according to a dominant pattern, known as ***sociocultural evolution.*** This term refers to the "process of change and development in human societies that results from cumulative growth in their stores of cultural information" (Lenski et al. 1995:75). In the sections that follow, we will examine the consequences of sociocultural evolution for the social structure of a society.

In Lenski's view, a society's level of technology is critical to the way it is organized. He defines ***technology*** as "information about the ways in which the material resources of the environment may be used to satisfy human needs and desires" (Nolan and Lenski 1999:414). The available technology does not completely define the form that a particular society and its social structure take. Nevertheless, a

low level of technology may limit the degree to which it can depend on such things as irrigation or complex machinery.

Preindustrial Societies

We can categorize preindustrial societies according to the way in which the social institution of the economy is organized. The first type of preindustrial society to emerge in human history was the ***hunting-and-gathering society,*** in which people simply rely on whatever foods and fibers are readily available. Technology in such societies is minimal. People are organized in groups and are constantly on the move in search of food. There is little division of labor into specialized tasks.

Hunting-and-gathering societies are composed of small, widely dispersed groups. Each group consists almost entirely of people related to one another. As a result, kinship ties are the source of authority and influence, and the social institution of the family takes on a particularly important role. Tönnies would certainly view such societies as examples of *Gemeinschaft.* Since resources are scarce, there is relatively little inequality in terms of material goods. Social differentiation within the hunting-and-gathering society is based on such ascribed statuses as gender, age, and family background. The last hunting-and-gathering societies were located in the southern tip of South America and in the Kalahari Desert of southwest

Africa; they had virtually disappeared by the close of the twentieth century (Nolan and Lenski 1999).

Horticultural societies, in which people plant seeds and crops rather than subsist merely on available foods, emerged about 10,00 to 12,000 years ago. Members of horticultural societies are much less nomadic than hunters and gatherers. They place greater emphasis on the production of tools and household objects. Yet technology within horticultural societies remains rather limited. They cultivate crops with the aid of digging sticks or hoes (J. Wilford 1997).

The last stage of preindustrial development is the *agrarian society,* which emerged about 5,000 years ago. As in horticultural societies, members of agrarian societies are primarily engaged in the production of food. However, the introduction of new technological innovations such as the plow allows farmers to dramatically increase their crop yield. They can cultivate the same fields over generations, thereby allowing the emergence of still larger settlements.

The social structure of the agrarian society continues to rely on the physical power of humans and animals (as opposed to mechanical power). Nevertheless, the social structure has more carefully defined roles than in horticultural societies. Individuals focus on specialized tasks, such as repair of fishing nets or work as a blacksmith. As human settlements become more established and stable, social institutions become more elaborate and property rights take on greater importance. The comparative permanence and greater surpluses of agrarian society make it more feasible to create artifacts such as statues, public monuments, and art objects and to pass them on from one generation to the next.

Industrial Societies

Although the industrial revolution did not topple monarchs, it produced changes every bit as significant as those resulting from political revolutions. The industrial revolution, which took place largely in England during the period 1760 to 1830, was a scientific revolution focused on the application of nonanimal (mechanical) sources of power to labor tasks. It involved changes in the social organization of the workplace, as people left the homestead and began working in central locations such as factories.

As the industrial revolution proceeded, a new form of social structure emerged. An *industrial society* is a society that depends on mechanization to produce its goods and services. Industrial societies relied on new inventions that facilitated agricultural and industrial production and on new sources of energy such as steam. Many societies underwent an irrevocable shift from an agrarian-oriented economy to an industrial base. No longer did an individual or a family typically make an entire product. Instead, specialization of tasks and manufacturing of goods be-

came increasingly common. Workers, generally men but also women and even children, left the home to labor in central factories.

The process of industrialization had distinctive social consequences. Families and communities could not continue to function as self-sufficient units. Individuals, villages, and regions began to exchange goods and services and become interdependent. As people came to rely on the labor of members of other communities, the family lost its unique position as the source of power and authority. The need for specialized knowledge led to more formalized education, and education emerged as a social institution distinct from the family.

Postindustrial and Postmodern Societies

When the sociocultural evolutionary approach first appeared in the 1960s, it paid relatively little attention to how maturing industrialized societies may change with the emergence of even more advanced forms of technology. More recently, in evaluating the increasingly rapid pace of technological and social change, Gerhard Lenski and his collaborators have observed,

The only things that might conceivably slow the rate of technological innovation in the next several decades are nuclear war, collapse of the world economy, or an environmental catastrophe. Fortunately, none of these appears likely in that time frame. (Lenski et al. 1995:441)

Lenski and other sociologists have studied the significant changes in the occupational structure of industrial societies as they shift from manufacturing to service economies. Social scientists call these technologically advanced nations *postindustrial societies.* Sociologist Daniel Bell (1999) defines *postindustrial society* as a society whose economic system is engaged primarily in the processing and control of information. The main output of a postindustrial society is services rather than manufactured goods. Large numbers of people become involved in occupations devoted to the teaching, generation, or dissemination of ideas.

Taking a functionalist perspective, Bell views this transition from industrial to postindustrial society as a positive development. He sees a general decline in organized working-class groups and a rise in interest groups concerned with such national issues as health, education, and the environment. Bell's outlook is functionalist because he portrays postindustrial society as basically consensual. Organizations and interest groups will engage in an open and competitive process of decision making. The level of conflict between diverse groups will diminish, and there will be much greater social stability.

Conflict theorists take issue with Bell's analysis of postindustrial society. For example, Michael Harrington

(1980), who alerted the nation to the problems of the poor in his book *The Other America*, was critical of the significance that Bell attached to the growing class of white-collar workers. Harrington conceded that scientists, engineers, and economists are involved in important political and economic decisions, but he disagreed with Bell's claim that they have a free hand in decision making, independent of the interests of the rich. Harrington followed in the tradition of Marx by arguing that conflict between social classes will continue in postindustrial society.

More recently, sociologists have gone beyond discussion of postindustrial societies to the ideal type of postmodern society. A *postmodern society* is a technologically sophisticated society that is preoccupied with consumer goods and media images (Brannigan 1992). Such societies consume goods and information on a mass scale. Postmodern theorists take a global perspective and note the ways that aspects of culture cross national boundaries. For example, residents of the United States may listen to reggae music from Jamaica, eat sushi and other types of Japanese food, and wear clogs from Sweden (Lyotard 1993).

The emphasis of postmodern theorists is on observing and describing newly emerging cultural forms and patterns of social interaction. Within sociology, the postmodern view offers support for integrating the insights of various theoretical perspectives—functionalism, conflict theory, interactionism, and labeling theory—while also incorporating feminist theories and other contemporary approaches. Indeed, feminist sociologists argue optimistically that, with its indifference to hierarchies and distinctions, postmodernism will discard traditional values of male dominance in favor of gender equality. Yet others contend that despite new technology, postindustrial and postmodern societies can be expected to experience the

problems of inequality that plague industrial societies (Ritzer 1995a; Sale 1996; Smart 1990; B. Turner 1990; van Vucht Tijssen 1990).

Ferdinand Tönnies and Gerhard Lenski present two visions of society's social structure. While different, both approaches are useful, and this textbook will draw on both. The sociocultural evolutionary approach emphasizes a historical perspective. It does not picture different types of social structures coexisting within the same society. Consequently, according to this approach, one would not expect a single society to include hunters and gatherers along with a postmodern culture. By contrast, sociologists frequently observe that a *Gemeinschaft* and a *Gesellschaft* can be found in the same society. For example, a rural New Hampshire community less than 100 miles from Boston is linked to the metropolitan area by the technology of the modern information age.

The work of Tönnies and Lenski reminds us that a major focus of sociology has been to identify changes in social structure and the consequences for human behavior. At the macrolevel, we see society shifting to more advanced forms of technology. The social structure becomes increasingly complex, and new social institutions emerge to assume some functions previously performed by the family. On the microlevel, these changes affect the nature of social interactions between people. Each individual takes on multiple social roles, and people come to rely more on social networks rather than solely on kinship ties. As the social structure becomes more complex, people's relationships tend to become more impersonal, transient, and fragmented. In the social policy section that follows, we will examine the impact of the AIDS crisis on the social structure and social interaction in the United States and other nations.

SOCIAL POLICY AND SOCIAL STRUCTURE

The AIDS Crisis

www.mhhe.com/schaefer

The Issue

In his novel *The Plague*, Albert Camus (1948:34) wrote, "There have been as many plagues as wars in history, yet always plagues and wars take people equally by surprise." Regarded by many as the distinctive plague of the modern era, AIDS certainly caught major social institutions—particularly the government, the health care system, and the economy—by surprise when it initially became noticed by medical practitioners in the 1970s. It has since spread around the world. While there are en-

couraging new therapies to treat people, there is currently no way to eradicate AIDS by medical means. Therefore, it is essential to protect people by reducing the transmission of the fatal virus. But how is this to be done? And whose responsibility is it? What role do social institutions have?

The Setting

AIDS is the acronym for *acquired immune deficiency syndrome*. Rather than being a distinct disease, AIDS is actually a predisposition to disease caused by a virus, the hu-

FIGURE 5-2

The Geography of HIV

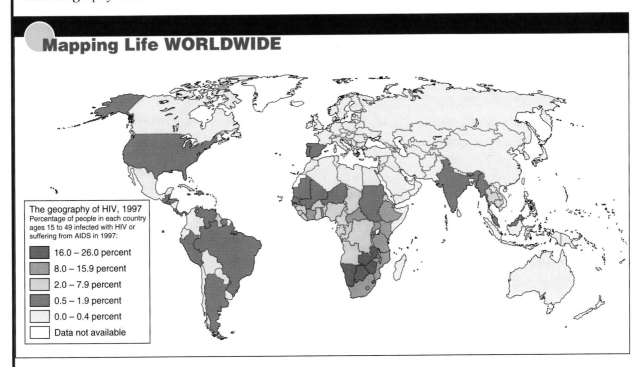

Source: United Nations data reproduced by L. Altman 1998:A1.

man immunodeficiency virus (HIV). This virus gradually destroys the body's immune system, leaving the carrier vulnerable to infections such as pneumonia that those with healthy immune systems can generally resist. Transmission of the virus from one person to another appears to require either intimate sexual contact or exchange of blood or bodily fluids (whether from contaminated hypodermic needles or syringes, transfusions of infected blood, or transmission from an infected mother to her child before or during birth). Health practitioners pay particular attention to methods of transmitting HIV because there is no cure or vaccine for AIDS at this time.

The first cases of AIDS in the United States were reported in 1981. While the numbers of new cases and deaths have recently shown some evidence of decline, there were 650,000 to 900,000 people living with AIDS or HIV by early 1999, with over 17,000 dying each year. Women account for a growing proportion of new cases—now about 70 percent of those reported. Racial and ethnic minorities account for 50 percent of new cases. Worldwide, AIDS is on the increase, with an estimated 33.6 million people infected and 2.6 million dying annually (see Figure 5-2). AIDS is not evenly distributed,

and those areas least equipped to deal with it—the developing nations of Africa and South Asia—face the greatest challenge (Cimons 1999; Kaiser Family Foundation 1999; Leeman 1999; Morrow 1999).

Sociological Insights

Dramatic crises like the AIDS epidemic are likely to bring about certain transformations in a society's social structure. From a functionalist perspective, if established social institutions cannot meet a crucial need, new social networks are likely to emerge to fill that function. In the case of AIDS, self-help groups—especially in the gay communities of major cities—have organized to care for the sick, educate the healthy, and lobby for more responsive public policies. The Gay Men's Health Crisis (GMHC), New York City's largest private organization providing AIDS services, has a paid staff of 179 and more than 6,600 volunteers typically working in a "buddy system" with those afflicted with AIDS. Although initially GMHC's clients were almost exclusively White homosexual men, today 20 percent of its clients are female, 32 percent are heterosexual, and 66 percent are non-White or Hispanic. GMHC operates a telephone hot line, sends advocates to hospitals to insist on better care for patients, and runs legal and financial clinics as well as therapy and support groups for people with AIDS and their loved ones (Gay Men's Health Crisis 2000).

In the 1990s, the label of "person with AIDS" or "HIV-positive" often functioned as a master status. Indeed, people with AIDS or infected with the virus face a powerful dual stigma. Not only are they associated with a lethal and contagious disease, but they have a disease that disproportionately afflicts already stigmatized groups, such as gay males and intravenous drug users. This linkage with stigmatized groups delayed recognition of the severity of the AIDS epidemic; the media took little interest in the disease until it seemed to be spreading beyond the gay community. Viewed from a conflict perspective, policymakers were slow to respond to the AIDS crisis because those in high-risk groups—gay men and IV drug users—were comparatively powerless. However, studies in the United States show that people with the virus and with AIDS who receive appropriate medical treatment are living longer than before. This may put additional pressure on policymakers to address the issues raised by the spread of AIDS (Epstein 1997; Shilts 1987).

On the microlevel of social interaction, observers widely forecast that AIDS would lead to a more conservative sexual climate—among both homosexuals and heterosexuals—in which people would be much more cautious about involvement with new partners. Yet it appears that many sexually active people in the United States have not heeded precautions about "safe sex." According to the 1993 nationwide Youth Risk Behavior Survey, only 59 percent of males and 46 percent of females reported that they or their partner used a condom during their last experience of sexual intercourse. Data from studies conducted in the early 1990s indicated that only women and African Americans had significantly increased their use of condoms (Centers for Disease Control and Prevention 1995).

Another interactionist concern is the tremendous impact on one's daily routine of taking the appropriate medication. As Figure 5-3 shows, tens of thousands of AIDS patients are having to reorder their lives around their medical regimens. Even patients without the symptoms of HIV find the concentrated effort that is needed to fight the disease—taking 95 doses of 16 different medications every 24 hours—extremely taxing. Think for a moment about the effect such a regimen would have on your own life, from eating and sleeping to work, study, child care, and recreation.

Policy Initiatives

Given the absence of a medical cure or vaccine, policy initiatives emphasize the need for more information about how AIDS is contracted and spread. In an address before the American Sociological Association, Canadian sociologist Barry Adam (1992) argued that sociologists can make an important contribution to AIDS-related research. He outlined four directions for such sociological research:

- How is information about AIDS produced and distributed? Is the distribution of information about how to have "safer sex" being limited or even censored?
- How does an AIDS "folklore"—false information about remedies and cures—emerge and become integrated into a community? Why do certain communities and individuals resist or ignore scientific information about the dangers of AIDS?
- How are medical and social services made available to people with AIDS? Why are these services often denied to the poorest patients?
- How is *homophobia* (fear of and prejudice against homosexuality) related to fears concerning AIDS? In what ways does homophobia correlate with other forms of bias?

Adam's questions underscore the impact of the AIDS crisis on social interaction and social structure. Addressing these questions will allow policymakers to better assess such initiatives as sex education programs in schools, needle exchange programs, and policies regarding AIDS testing.

AIDS has struck all societies, but not all nations can respond in the same manner. In some nations, cultural practices may prevent people from considering the AIDS epidemic realistically. They are less likely to take the necessary preventive measures, including more open discussion of sexuality, homosexuality, and drug use. Prevention has shown signs of working among target groups, such as drug users, pregnant women, and gay men and lesbians, but these initiatives are few and far between in developing nations. The prescribed treatment for a pregnant woman to reduce mother-to-baby transmission of AIDS costs about $1,000—many times the average annual income in much of the world where risk of AIDS is greatest. Africa, for example, accounts for 90 percent of the world's AIDS deaths. Even more costly is the medication for adult patients with HIV, which costs $71,000 a year (Pear 1997; Sawyer 2000; Specter 1998; Sternberg 1999).

The issues that divide rich and poor nations also manifest themselves within industrial nations. Despite efforts to expand medical coverage, the U.S. federal

FIGURE 5-3

Daily Dosing for AIDS

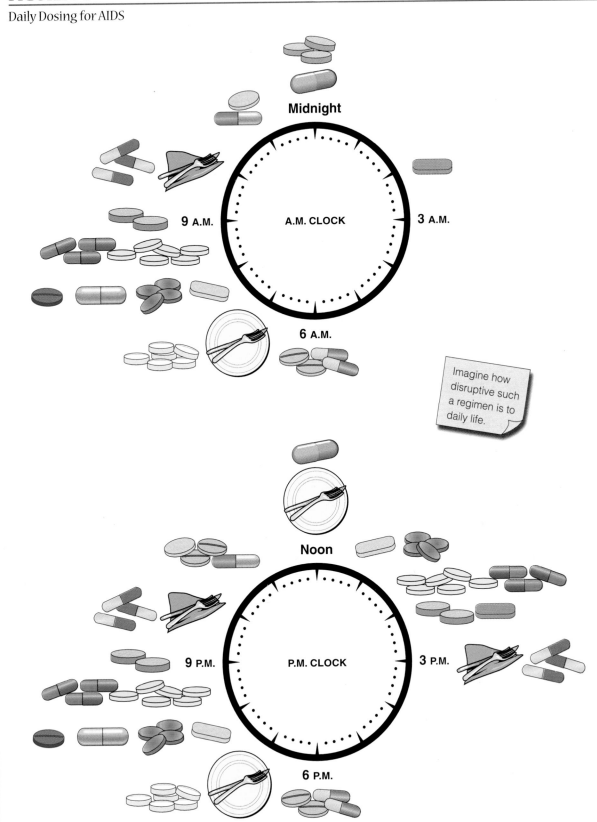

Note: Regimen may vary due to individual reactions to medications taken together. Shapes and colors of the 16 different prescriptive drugs are symbolic rather than realistic.

Source: Schaefer in consultation with Roxane Laboratories 2000.

government announced in 1997 that it could not expand Medicaid to cover low-income people who are infected with the HIV virus but do not have full-blown AIDS. Drug treatment for HIV now costs about $10,000 a year per person; adding other medical costs (excluding home care) brings yearly expenses to $20,000. Critics contend that to have a policy that covers people only when they are completely disabled by AIDS is counterproductive to keeping people in the labor force. However, in much of the developing world, policymakers are facing even graver questions as increased proportions of the workforce and the next generation are affected with AIDS (Gay Men's Health Crisis 2000; Sternberg 1999).

Let's Discuss

1. Has information on how to avoid getting AIDS been made available to you? Do you personally know of a case in which such information was withheld from someone or censored? If so, why and by whom?
2. Have you come across AIDS "folklore" (misinformation) on your campus or in your neighborhood? If so, how widespread do you think it is?
3. If you were a sociologist who wanted to understand why some people knowingly ignore the dangers of AIDS, how would you go about studying the problem?

Summary

Social interaction refers to the ways in which people respond to one another. *Social structure* refers to the way in which a society is organized into predictable relationships. This chapter examines the basic elements of social structure—statuses, social roles, groups, and institutions.

1. We shape our social reality based on what we learn through our social interactions. Social change comes from redefining or reconstructing social reality. Sometimes change is *negotiated.*
2. An *ascribed status* is generally assigned to a person at birth, whereas an *achieved status* is attained largely through one's own effort.
3. In the United States, ascribed statuses, such as race and gender, can function as *master statuses* that have an important impact on one's potential to achieve a desired professional and social status.
4. With each distinctive status—whether ascribed or achieved—come particular *social roles,* the set of expectations for people who occupy that status.
5. Much of our patterned behavior takes place within *groups* and is influenced by the norms and sanctions established by groups. Groups serve as links to *social networks* and their vast resources.

6. The mass media, the government, the economy, the family, and the health care system are all examples of *social institutions* found in the United States.
7. One way to understand social institutions is to see how they fulfill essential functions, such as replacing personnel, training new recruits, and preserving order.
8. The conflict perspective argues that social institutions help to maintain the privileges of the powerful while contributing to the powerlessness of others.
9. Interactionist theorists emphasize that our social behavior is conditioned by the roles and statuses that we accept, the groups to which we belong, and the institutions within which we function.
10. Ferdinand Tönnies distinguished the close-knit community of *Gemeinschaft* from the impersonal mass society know as *Gesellschaft.*
11. Gerhard Lenski views human societies as changing historically along one dominant pattern, which he calls *sociocultural evolution.*
12. The AIDS crisis affects every social institution, including the family, the schools, the health care system, the economy, and the government.

Critical Thinking Questions

1. People in certain professions seem particularly susceptible to role conflict. For example, journalists commonly experience role conflict during disasters, crimes, and other distressing situations. Should they offer assistance to the needy or cover breaking news as reporters? Select two other professions and discuss the types of role conflict they might experience.

2. The functionalist, conflict, and interactionist perspectives can all be used in analyzing social institutions. What are the strengths or weaknesses in each perspective's analysis of social institutions?

3. In what ways does HIV serve to underscore issues of race, class, and gender in the United States today?

Key Terms

Achieved status   A social position attained by a person largely through his or her own efforts. (page 122)

Agrarian society   The most technologically advanced form of preindustrial society. Members are primarily engaged in the production of food but increase their crop yield through such innovations as the plow. (133)

Ascribed status   A social position "assigned" to a person by society without regard for the person's unique talents or characteristics. (121)

Gemeinschaft   Close-knit communities, often found in rural areas, in which strong personal bonds unite members. (131)

Gesellschaft   Communities, often urban, that are large and impersonal, with little commitment to the group or consensus on values. (131)

Group   Any number of people with similar norms, values, and expectations who interact with one another. (125)

Homophobia   Fear of and prejudice against homosexuality. (136)

Horticultural societies   Preindustrial societies in which people plant seeds and crops rather than subsist merely on available foods. (133)

Hunting-and-gathering society   A preindustrial society in which people rely on whatever foods and fibers are readily available in order to live. (132)

Industrial society   A society that depends on mechanization to produce its goods and services. (133)

Master status   A status that dominates others and thereby determines a person's general position within society. (122)

Negotiated order   A social structure that derives its existence from the social interactions through which people define and redefine its character. (121)

Negotiation   The attempt to reach agreement with others concerning some objective. (120)

Postindustrial society   A society whose economic system is primarily engaged in the processing and control of information. (133)

Postmodern society   A technologically sophisticated society that is preoccupied with consumer goods and media images. (134)

Role conflict   Difficulties that occur when incompatible expectations arise from two or more social positions held by the same person. (123)

Role exit   The process of disengagement from a role that is central to one's self-identity and reestablishment of an identity in a new role. (125)

Role strain   Difficulties that result from the differing demands and expectations associated with the same social position. (124)

Social institutions   Organized patterns of beliefs and behavior centered on basic social needs. (128)

Social interaction   The ways in which people respond to one another. (119)

Social network   A series of social relationships that links a person directly to others and therefore indirectly to still more people. (126)

Social role   A set of expectations for people who occupy a given social position or status. (122)

Social structure   The way in which a society is organized into predictable relationships. (119)

Sociocultural evolution   The process of change and development in human societies that results from cumulative growth in their stores of cultural information. (132)

Status   A term used by sociologists to refer to any of the full range of socially defined positions within a large group or society. (121)

Technology   Information about the ways in which the material resources of the environment may be used to satisfy human needs and desire. (132)

Additional Readings

Bell, Daniel. 1999. *The Coming of Post-Industrial Society: A Venture in Social Forecasting.* New York: Basic Books. Updated with a new foreword, this book describes the current economic trend away from growing food or making products for a living and toward the provision of services and information as a livelihood.

Conrad, Phillip Kottak. 1999. *Assault on Paradise: Social Change in a Brazilian Village.* 3d ed. New York: McGraw-Hill. An anthropologist describes how a traditional fishing village is transformed into a tourist-oriented economy networked tightly to the outside world.

Epstein, Steven. 1996. *Impure Science: AIDS, Activism, and the Politics of Knowledge.* Berkeley, CA: University of California Press. A sociologist examines AIDS research from the perspective of how it has been influenced by social and political forces.

Kephart, William M., and William M. Zellner. 1998. *Extraordinary Groups: An Examination of Unconventional Life-Styles.* 6th ed. New York: St. Martin's. Among the groups described in this very readable book are the Amish, the Oneida community, the Mormons, Hasidic Jews, Jehovah's Witnesses, and the Romani (commonly known as Gypsies).

Internet Connection

NOTE: While all the URLs listed were current as of the printing of this book, these sites often change. Please check our website (http://www.mhhe.com/schaefer) for updates.

1. Disability is a master status that supersedes race, religion, and gender. Visit the ALS Survival Guide (**http://www.lougehrigsdisease.net/index.html**) to learn about the social, psychological, medical, and emotional aspects of Lou Gehrig's disease (amyotrophic lateral sclerosis). Pay special attention to the Guest Speaker articles and the Vital Statistics sections.

   (a) What are the symptoms and causes of ALS? What is the life expectancy of someone with ALS?

   (b) Who was Lou Gehrig, and why is he associated with ALS? Was ALS Gehrig's master status?

   (c) In terms of age, race, and gender, who is at most risk of developing ALS?

   (d) What are some of the social and physical challenges confronting those with ALS? What are some of the challenges facing their families?

   (e) How are ALS patients treated by other people? Can you see similarities to the way those with AIDS are treated? Can ALS be considered a master status?

   (f) What new research is being conducted on ALS? Do you believe that enough attention and resources are being focused on the disease? Why or why not?

   (g) Have the media had an impact on the way you view people with disabilities? How so?

2. The Amish are a living example of a traditional, intimate *Gemeinschaft* community. Visit the online photo gallery at (**http://www.hp.com/abouthp/features/amish/gallery**), then read the answers to frequently asked questions about the Amish at (**http://www.800padutch.com/atafaq.html**).

   (a) What is the history of the Amish? Why did they leave Europe? In which regions of the United States do the Amish live today?

   (b) How do the Amish view modern technologies, such as cars and electricity? What kind of work do they do? How do they receive medical care?

   (c) How and why do Amish schools differ from most American schools? What is dating like for Amish teens? Is it similar to your own dating experience?

   (d) What is shunning, and how do the Amish use it to control deviance?

   (e) Apply the typology in Table 5-2 (page 130) to the Amish. Which features of a *Gemeinschaft* society do the Amish exhibit?

   (f) Would you like to live as the Amish do? Which aspects of their lifestyle appeal to you? Which do not?

   (g) Did your visit to these two websites dispel any misconceptions about the Amish that you might have acquired from television or the movies?

A poster advertises the London Fire Brigade's parachute team, a group of fire fighters trained to skydive in unison at special events. Formed in 1987, the all-volunteer group is dedicated to the promotion of fire safety.

The McDonaldization of Society

New Century Edition

GEORGE RITZER

ay Kroc, the genius behind the franchising of McDonald's restaurants, was a man with big ideas and grand ambitions. But even Kroc could not have anticipated the astounding impact of his creation. McDonald's is the basis of one of the most influential developments in contemporary society. Its reverberations extend far beyond its point of origin in the United States and in the fast-food business. It has influenced a wide range of undertakings, indeed the way of life, of a significant portion of the world. And that impact is likely to expand at an accelerating rate.

However, this is not a book about McDonald's, or even about the fast-food business. . . . Rather, McDonald's serves here as the major example, the paradigm, of a wide-ranging process I call *McDonaldization*. . . . As you will see, McDonaldization affects not only the restaurant business but also education, work, health care, travel, leisure, dieting, politics, the family, and virtually every other aspect of society. McDonaldization has shown every sign of being an inexorable process, sweeping through seemingly impervious institutions and regions of the world.

The success of McDonald's itself is apparent: In 1998, its total sales reached $36 billion, with operating income of $3.1 billion. The average U.S. outlet has sales of approximately $1.6 million in a year. McDonald's, which first began franchising in 1955, had 24,800 restaurants throughout the world by the end of 1998. Martin Plimmer, a British commentator, archly notes: "There are McDonald's everywhere. There's one near you, and there's one being built right now even nearer to you. Soon, if McDonald's goes on expanding at its present rate, there might even be one in your house. You could find Ronald McDonald's boots under your bed. And maybe his red wig, too."

McDonald's is such a powerful model that many businesses have acquired nicknames beginning with Mc. Examples include "McDentists" and "McDoctors," meaning drive-in clinics designed to deal quickly and efficiently with minor dental and medical problems; "McChild" care centers, meaning child care centers such as Kinder-Care; "McStables," designating the nationwide race horse-training operation of Wayne Lucas; and "McPaper," designating the newspaper *USA TODAY*. (Ritzer 2000:1–2, 10) ∎

I
n this excerpt from *The McDonaldization of Society,* sociologist George Ritzer contemplates the enormous influence of a well-known fast-food restaurant on modern-day culture and social life. Ritzer defines **McDonaldization** as "the process by which the principles of the fast-food restaurant are coming to dominate more and more sectors of American society as well as the rest of the world" (Ritzer 2000:1). In his book, he shows how the business principles on which the fast-food industry is founded—efficiency, calculability, predictability, and control—have changed not only the way Americans do business, but the way they live their lives.

Despite the runaway success of McDonald's and its imitators, and the advantages these enterprises bring to millions of people around the world, Ritzer is critical of their effect on society. The waste and environmental degradation created by billions of disposable containers and the dehumanized work routines of fast-food crews are two of the disadvantages he cites in his critique. Would the modern world be a better one, Ritzer asks, if it were less McDonaldized?

This chapter considers the impact of groups and organizations on social interaction. It will begin by noting the distinctions between various types of groups, with particular attention given to the dynamics of small groups. We will examine how and why formal organizations came into existence and describe Max Weber's model of the modern bureaucracy. We'll also look at technology's impact on the organization of the workplace. The social policy section will focus on the issue of sexual harassment, which has become a major concern of both governmental and private-sector organizations. ■

Understanding Groups

In everyday speech, people use the term *group* to describe any collection of individuals, whether three strangers sharing an elevator or hundreds attending a rock concert. However, in sociological terms a **group** is any number of people with similar norms, values, and expectations who interact with one another. College sororities and fraternities, dance companies, tenants' associations, and chess clubs are all considered examples of groups. The important point is that members of a group share some sense of belonging. This characteristic distinguishes groups from mere *aggregates* of people, such as passengers who happen to be together on an airplane flight, or from *categories* who share a common feature (such as being retired) but otherwise do not act together.

Consider the case of a college *a cappella* singing group. It has agreed-upon values and social norms. All members want to improve their singing skills and schedule lots of performances. In addition, like many groups, the singing ensemble has both a formal and an informal structure. The members meet regularly to rehearse; they choose leaders to run the rehearsals and manage their affairs. At the same time, some group members may take on unofficial leadership roles by coaching new members in singing techniques and performing skills.

The study of groups has become an important part of sociological investigation because they play such a key role in the transmission of culture. As we interact with others, we pass on our ways of thinking and acting—from language and values to ways of dressing and leisure activities.

Types of Groups

Sociologists have made a number of useful distinctions between types of groups—primary and secondary groups, in-groups and out-groups, and reference groups.

Primary and Secondary Groups

Charles Horton Cooley (1902:2357) coined the term **primary group** to refer to a small group characterized by intimate, face-to-face association and cooperation. The members of a street gang constitute a primary group; so do members of a family living in the same household, as well as "sisters" in a college sorority.

Primary groups play a pivotal role both in the socialization process (see Chapter 4) and in the development of roles and statuses (see Chapter 5). Indeed, primary groups can be instrumental in a person's day-to-day existence.

When we find ourselves identifying closely with a group, it is probably a primary group. However, people in the United States participate in many groups that are not characterized by close bonds of friendship, such as large college classes and business associations. The term **secondary group** refers to a formal, impersonal group in which there is little social intimacy or mutual understanding (see Table 6-1). The distinction between primary and secondary groups is not always clear-cut. Some social clubs may become so large and impersonal that they no longer function as primary groups.

pp. 125–126

Table 6-1	Comparison of Primary and Secondary Groups	
Primary Group	**Secondary Group**
Generally small	Usually large
Relatively long period of interaction	Short duration, temporary
Intimate, face-to-face association	Little social intimacy or mutual understanding
Some emotional depth in relationships	Relationships generally superficial
Cooperative, friendly	More formal and impersonal

Secondary groups often emerge in the workplace among those who share special understandings about their occupation. Almost all of us have come in contact with people who deliver food, but, using observation research, two sociologists have given us new understanding of the secondary group ties that emerge in this occupation (see Box 6-1).

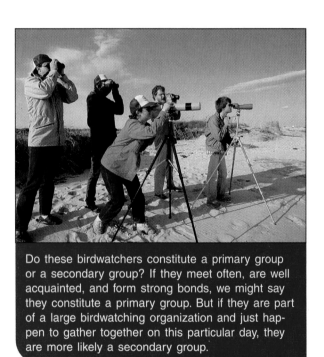

Do these birdwatchers constitute a primary group or a secondary group? If they meet often, are well acquainted, and form strong bonds, we might say they constitute a primary group. But if they are part of a large birdwatching organization and just happen to gather together on this particular day, they are more likely a secondary group.

In-Groups and Out-Groups

A group can hold special meaning for members because of its relationship to other groups. People in one group sometimes feel antagonistic to or threatened by another group, especially if the group is perceived as being different culturally or racially. Sociologists identify these "we" and "they" feelings by using two terms first employed by William Graham Sumner (1906:1213): *in-group* and *out-group*.

An **in-group** can be defined as any group or category to which people feel they belong. Simply put, it comprises everyone who is regarded as "we" or "us." The in-group may be as narrow as one's family or as broad as an entire society. The very existence of an in-group implies that there is an out-group viewed as "they" or "them." More formally, an **out-group** is a group or category to which people feel they do not belong.

One typical consequence of in-group membership is a feeling of distinctiveness and superiority among members, who see themselves as better than people in the out-group. A double standard held by members of the in-group can enhance this sense of superiority. Proper behavior for the in-group is simultaneously viewed as unacceptable behavior for the out-group. Sociologist Robert Merton (1968:480–88) describes this process as the conversion of "in-group virtues" into "out-group vices." This

"So long, Bill. This is my club. You can't come in."

An exclusive social club is an in-group whose members consider themselves superior to others.

Research in Action

6-1 Pizza Delivery Employees as a Secondary Group

We all tend to take pizza delivery for granted. We may not even take note of the person who brings the pizza to our door. But sociologists Patrick Kinkade and Michael Katovich did. Using an interactionist perspective they explored the social relationships that developed among urban pizza delivery drivers as they socialized during work while waiting for orders and after work in bars. In fact, one of the researchers spent 18 months as a pizza delivery person at three locales in Ft. Worth, Texas. What they found was that pizza deliverers form a tight network based on the ordinary transactions and the occasional dangerous interactions of their profession.

Within their culture, the pizza delivery drivers take risks and receive minimal rewards. While attacks on them are usually publicized, they are not documented statistically. But the drivers themselves are well aware of the possible dangers and talk to one another a great deal about them. During the observation period, two drivers were robbed and eight others were "tailed," resulting in four automobile accidents.

The researchers found that the world of this secondary group is "hypermasculine," with racist and sexist overtones. The drivers uniformly characterized the dangers to their safety as coming from members of racial and ethnic communities, even when there was no evidence of this. The drivers also regularly boasted of their sexual prowess and told and retold accounts of sexual favors they received from customers.

Among the 106 drivers studied by the researchers, five types emerged:

- *The comedian.* This individual uses humor to neutralize or trivialize the anxiety felt over runs into neighborhoods perceived as high-risk.

> Within their culture, the pizza delivery drivers take risks and receive minimal rewards.

- *The adventurer.* The adventurer claims to invite problems and actually looks forward to testing himself in dangerous situations.
- *The denier.* This individual attempts to neutralize anxiety by suggesting a problem does not exist or is exaggerated.
- *The fatalist.* This person recognizes and admits the risk of danger but simply accepts it without making any effort to neutralize it.

- *The pro.* The pro generally has had a long history in the delivery business, having worked for several pizza services and, commonly, having been an assistant manager, if not a manager, at one of the other stores.

In general, the researchers found through observation and interview that urban pizza deliverers derive more satisfaction from their secondary group membership than from monetary rewards. Group membership and identity, therefore, are very important. The study shows how people, especially in urban environments, make use of secondary groups to "carve out a niche" in the larger social world. They accept their identity as a delivery person and assume a particular type that they feel comfortable with.

Let's Discuss

1. Have you ever belonged to a work-related secondary group? If so, was your membership in the group a rewarding experience?
2. Think about a secondary group to which you belong. Can you identify any common role types? If so, describe them.

Source: Kinkade and Katovich 1997.

---

differential standard is apparent in worldwide discussions of terrorism. When a group or a nation takes aggressive actions, it usually justifies them as necessary, even if civilians are hurt and killed. Opponents are quick to label such actions with the emotion-laden term of "terrorist" and seek condemnation from the world community. Yet these same people may themselves retaliate with actions that hurt civilians, which the first group will then condemn.

Conflict between in-groups and out-groups can turn violent on a personal as well as a political level. In 1999 two disaffected students at Columbine High School in Littleton, Colorado, launched an attack on the school that left 15 students and teachers dead, including themselves. The gunmen, members of an out-group that other students referred to as the Trenchcoat Mafia, apparently resented the taunting of an in-group referred to as the Jocks. Similar episodes have occurred in schools across the nation, where rejected adolescents, overwhelmed by personal and family problems, peer group pressure, academic responsibilities, or media images of violence, have struck out against more popular classmates. In-group members who actively provoke out-group members may have their own problems, including limited time and attention from working parents. Sociologists David Stevenson and Barbara Schneider (1999), who studied 7,000 teenagers, found that despite many opportunities for group membership, young people

In William Golding's novel *Lord of the Flies*, a group of boys from an English prep school is marooned on a tropical island after their plane crashes, killing all the adults on board. Written as a fable about human nature, the novel describes the breakdown of social order among the boys, who divide into in- and out-groups and begin warring on one another. This frame from Peter Brook's film version dramatizes one of their savage confrontations.

In many cases, people model their behavior after groups to which they do not belong. For example, a college student majoring in finance may read *The Wall Street Journal*, study the annual reports of corporations, and listen to midday stock market news on the radio. **p. 99** The student is engaging in the process of anticipatory socialization by using financial experts as a reference group to which he or she aspires.

Often, two or more reference groups influence us at the same time. Our family members, neighbors, and coworkers all shape different aspects of our self-evaluation. In addition, certain reference group attachments change during the life cycle. A corporate executive who quits the rat race at age 45 to become a social worker will find new reference groups to use as standards for evaluation. We shift reference groups as we take on different statuses during our lives.

spend an average of three-and-a-half hours alone every day. While youths may claim they want privacy, they also crave attention, and striking out at members of an in-group or out-group, be they the wrong gender, race, or friendship group, seems to be one way to get it.

Reference Groups

Both in-groups and primary groups can dramatically influence the way an individual thinks and behaves. Sociologists use the term *reference group* when speaking of any group that individuals use as a standard for evaluating themselves and their own behavior. For example, a high school student who aspires to join a social circle of hip-hop music devotees will pattern his or her behavior after that of the group. The student will begin dressing like these peers, listening to the same tapes and CDs, and hanging out at the same stores and clubs.

Reference groups have two basic purposes. They serve a normative function by setting and enforcing standards of conduct and belief. Thus, the high school student who wants the approval of the hip-hop crowd will have to follow the group's dictates to at least some extent. Reference groups also perform a comparison function by serving as a standard against which people can measure themselves and others. An actor will evaluate himself or herself against a reference group composed of others in the acting profession (Merton and Kitt 1950).

Studying Small Groups

Studying small groups is an important aspect of sociological research. The term *small group* is used to refer to a group small enough for all members to interact simultaneously, that is, to talk with one another or at least be acquainted. Certain primary groups, such as families, may also be classified as small groups. However, many small groups differ from primary groups in that they do not necessarily offer the intimate personal relationships characteristic of primary groups. For example, a manufacturer may bring together its seven-member regional sales staff twice a year for an intensive sales conference. The salespeople, who live in different cities and rarely see one another, constitute a small secondary group, not a primary group.

We may think of small groups as being informal and unpatterned; yet, interactionist researchers have revealed that there are distinct and predictable processes at work in the functioning of small groups. A long-term ethnographic study of street gangs in Chicago revealed an elaborate structure resembling that of a family business. A street gang is composed of several geographically based units called *sets*, each of which possesses a leader, lower-ranking officers, and a rank-and-file membership. Besides staffing the economic network of the drug trade, gang members develop relationships with tenant leaders in public housing projects and participate in non-delinquent social activities important to the maintenance of their authority in the neighborhood (Venkatesh 1997).

Size of a Group

At what point does a collection of people become too large to be called a small group? That is not clear. If there are more than 20 members, it is difficult for individuals to interact regularly in a direct and intimate manner. But even within a range of 2 to 20 people, group size can substantially alter the quality of social relationships. For example, as the number of group participants increases, the most active communicators become even more active relative to others. Therefore, a person who dominates a group of 3 or 4 members will be relatively more dominant in a 15-person group.

Group size also has noticeable social implications for members who do not assume leadership roles. In a larger group, each member has less time to speak, more points of view to absorb, and a more elaborate structure within which to function. At the same time, an individual has greater freedom to ignore certain members or viewpoints than he or she would in a smaller group. Clearly, it is harder to disregard someone in a 4-person workforce than in an office with 30 employees or a college band with 50 members.

German sociologist Georg Simmel (1858–1918) is credited as the first sociologist to emphasize the importance of interaction processes within groups. Reflecting on group size, Simmel (1950, original edition 1917) suggested that smaller groups have distinctive qualities and patterns of interaction that inevitably disappear as they expand in size. Larger groups, in Simmel's view, develop particular forms of interaction that are unnecessary in small groups.

The simplest of all social groups or relationships is the **dyad,** or two-member group. A wife and a husband constitute a dyad, as does a business partnership or a singing duo. In a dyad, one is able to achieve a special level of intimacy that cannot be duplicated in larger groups. However, as Simmel (1950) noted, a dyad, unlike any other group, can be destroyed by the loss of a single member. Therefore, the threat of termination hangs over a dyadic relationship perhaps more than over any other type.

Obviously, the introduction of one additional person

Groups come in all sizes. This group of puppeteers, a secondary group, has 120 members.

to a dyad dramatically transforms the character of the small group. The dyad now becomes a three-member group, or **triad.** The new member has at least three basic ways of interacting with and influencing the dynamics of the group. The new person may play a *unifying* role within a triad. When a married couple has its first child, the baby may serve to bind the group closer together. A newcomer may also play a *mediating* role within a three-person group. If two roommates in an apartment are perpetually sniping at each other, the third roommate may attempt to remain on good terms with each and arrange compromise solutions to problems. Finally, a member of a triad can choose to employ a *divide-and-rule* strategy. This is the case, for example, with a coach who hopes to gain greater control over two assistants by making them rivals (Nixon 1979).

Coalitions

As groups grow to the size of triads or larger, we can expect coalitions to develop. A **coalition** is a temporary or permanent alliance geared toward a common goal. Coalitions can be broad-based or narrow, and can take on many different objectives. Sociologist William Julius Wilson (1999) has described community-based organizations in Texas that include Whites and Latinos, working class and affluent, who have banded together to work for improved sidewalks, better drainage systems, and comprehensive street paving. Out of this type of coalition building, Wilson hopes, will emerge better interracial understanding.

Some coalitions are intentionally short lived. In 1997,

Some members of the Congressional Black Caucus take to the microphones to make their point. The Caucus is an example of a coalition, an alliance geared toward a common goal. It was formed in 1970 by the Black members of the House of Representatives.

Congress deadlocked over a proposed settlement between the major tobacco companies and 40 state governments, which would have reimbursed states for the medical costs created by long-term tobacco use. The prospect of continued delays, no settlement, or even further lawsuits against cigarette manufacturers prompted the formation of an unusual coalition. For a brief time the major tobacco companies joined the Campaign for Tobacco-Free Kids, the American Cancer Society, and the Association of Trial Lawyers of America to reach a settlement in excess of $360 billion. Shortly after the settlement was announced, coalition members returned to their decades-long fight against each other (R. Pear 1997).

The effects of group size and coalition on group dynamics are but two of the many aspects of the small group that sociologists have studied. Another area, conformity and deviance, is examined in Chapter 7. While it is clear that small-group encounters have a considerable influence on our lives, we are also deeply affected by much larger groupings of people, as we'll see in the next section.

Understanding Organizations

Formal Organizations and Bureaucracies

As contemporary societies have shifted to more advanced forms of technology and their social structures have be-

come more complex, our lives have become increasingly dominated by large secondary groups referred to as *formal organizations* and designed for a specific purpose. A *formal organization* is a special-purpose group designed and structured for maximum efficiency. The United States Postal Service, the Boston Pops orchestra, and the college you attend are all examples of formal organizations. Organizations vary in their size, specificity of goals, and degree of efficiency, but they all are structured in such a way as to facilitate the management of large-scale operations. They also have a bureaucratic form of organization (described in the next section of the chapter).

In our society, formal organizations fulfill an enormous variety of personal and societal needs and shape the lives of every one of us. In fact, formal organizations have become such a dominant force that we must create organizations to supervise other organizations, such as the Securities and Exchange Commission (SEC) to regulate the brokerage companies. It sounds much more exciting to say that we live in the "computer age" than in the "age of formal organization"; however, the latter is probably a more accurate description of our times (Azumi and Hage 1972; Etzioni 1964).

Ascribed statuses such as gender, race, and ethnicity influence how we see ourselves within formal organizations. For example, a study of women lawyers in the nation's largest law firms found significant differences in these women's self-images. In firms in which fewer than 15 percent of partners were women, the female lawyers were likely to believe that "feminine" traits were strongly devalued and that masculinity was equated with success. As one female attorney put it, "Let's face it: this is a man's environment, and it's sort of Jock City, especially at my firm." Women in firms where female lawyers were well represented in positions of power (where more than 15 percent of partners were women) had a stronger desire for and higher expectations of promotion (Ely 1995:619). (The impact of race, ethnicity, and gender on people's experiences and career prospects will be examined more fully in Chapters 9 and 10.)

Characteristics of a Bureaucracy

A *bureaucracy* is a component of formal organization in which rules and hierarchical ranking are used to achieve

Taking Sociology to Work

JAMES P. SCHADT:
Former Chief Executive Officer of *Reader's Digest*

www.
mhhe
.com
/schaefer

"What do large groups of people want? If you can provide what they want, you should produce it, and they will buy it. This is the basic job of a consumer products company." This is how Jim Schadt describes the most important part of his job as CEO of *Reader's Digest* and, before that, Cadbury Beverages (Schweppes, Dr. Pepper, 7-Up, Canada Dry, and so on). Jim got his BA in sociology in 1960 from Northwestern University, where he concentrated in the study of human groups and statistics.

He acknowledges that "this has helped me to understand behavior patterns, especially consumers' and market research." For instance, at one point *Reader's Digest* conducted a big study of the media habits of 4,000 people in five countries. What he discovered was that the consumers' media interests did not follow demographic patterns (age, gender, and class groups, for example) but fell into behavioral groups of similar lifestyles and values—such as busy single parents looking for ways to sim-

plify their lives, or people who were seeking spiritual support and guidance, or homemakers of all economic groups interested in cooking and gardening.

As the leader of his company, Jim found it was important to be sensitive to how different groups can be from one another, whether they are employees or customers. "While the consumers' interest and your product are very similar across national and cultural lines, you will need to alter your message for different groups in order to reach your customers." *Reader's Digest* does 65 to 70 percent of its business abroad.

Jim feels strongly that studying human behavior in college makes it easier to be an effective leader of large organizations or communities, and is more important for leadership than if you study physical sciences or chemical engineering, for example. His advice to sociology students: "Keep asking questions about the connection of sociology to real life."

efficiency. Rows of desks staffed by seemingly faceless people, endless lines and forms, impossibly complex language, and frustrating encounters with red tape—all these unpleasant images have combined to make *bureaucracy* a dirty word and an easy target in political campaigns. As a result, few people want to identify their occupation as "bureaucrat" despite the fact that all of us perform various bureaucratic tasks. Elements of bureaucracy enter into almost every occupation in an industrial society such as the United States.

Complaints about bureaucracy are not limited to the United States. In 1993, the bureaucratic nature of the United Nations' humanitarian efforts in Somalia came under attack. The five international agencies designated to run relief efforts in Somalia had more than 12,000 employees, of whom only 116 were serving in the impoverished, war-torn African nation. Moreover, like many bureaucracies, the relief apparatus was slow in dealing with a drastic problem. In the words of a former United Nations worker in Somalia, "The average U.N. person takes 15 days to reply to a fax. . . . 3,000 people can die in 15 days" (Longworth 1993:9).

In order to develop a more useful and objective definition of bureaucracy, let us consider the writings of Max Weber (1947, original edition 1922). This pioneer of sociology, who was introduced in Chapter 1, first directed researchers to the significance of bureaucratic structure. In an important sociological advance, Weber emphasized

the basic similarity of structure and process found in the otherwise dissimilar enterprises of religion, government, education, and business.

Weber saw bureaucracy as a form of organization quite different from the family-run business. For analytical purposes, he developed an ***ideal type*** of bureaucracy that would reflect the most characteristic aspects of all human organizations. By *ideal type* Weber meant a construct or model that could serve as a measuring rod against which specific cases could be evaluated. In actuality, perfect bureaucracies do not exist; no real-world organization corresponds exactly to Weber's ideal type.

p. 11

Weber proposed that whether the purpose is to run a church, a corporation, or an army, the ideal bureaucracy can be seen as having five basic characteristics. A discussion of those characteristics, as well as the ***dysfunctions*** (or potential negative consequences) of a bureaucracy, follows. (Table 6-2 summarizes the discussion.)

1. Division of Labor Specialized experts are employed in each position to perform specific tasks. In your college bureaucracy, the admissions officer does not do the job of registrar; the guidance counselor doesn't see to the maintenance of buildings. By working at a specific task, people are more likely to become highly skilled and carry out a job with maximum efficiency. This emphasis on specialization is so basic a part of our lives that we may not realize that it is a fairly recent development in Western culture.

Table 6-2 Characteristics of a Bureaucracy

Characteristic	Positive Consequence	Negative Consequence For the Individual	For the Organization
Division of labor	Produces efficiency in large-scale corporation	Produces trained incapacity	Produces a narrow perspective
Hierarchy of authority	Clarifies who is in command	Deprives employees of a voice in decision making	Permits concealment of mistakes
Written rules and regulations	Let workers know what is expected of them	Stifle initiative and imagination	Lead to goal displacement
Impersonality	Reduces bias	Contributes to feelings of alienation	Discourages loyalty to company
Employment based on technical qualifications	Discourages favoritism and reduces petty rivalries	Discourages ambition to improve oneself elsewhere	Allows Peter principle to operate

Unfortunately, the fragmentation of work into smaller and smaller tasks can divide workers and remove any connection they might feel to the overall objective of the bureaucracy. In *The Communist Manifesto* (written in 1848), Karl Marx and Friedrich Engels charged that the capitalist system reduces workers to a mere "appendage of the machine" (Feuer 1959). Such a work arrangement, they wrote, produces extreme *alienation*—a condition of estrangement or dissociation from the surrounding society. (Alienation will be discussed in greater detail in Chapter 17.) According to both Marx and conflict theorists, restricting workers to very small tasks also weakens their job security, since new employees can be easily trained to replace them.

Although division of labor has certainly been beneficial in the performance of many complex bureaucracies, in some cases it can lead to *trained incapacity;* that is, workers become so specialized that they develop blind spots and fail to notice obvious problems. Even worse, they may not care about what is happening in the next department. Some observers believe that such developments have caused workers in the United States to become less productive on the job.

The explosion of the U.S. space shuttle *Challenger* in 1986, in which seven astronauts died, is one example of the negative consequences of a bureaucratic division of labor. While the *Challenger* disaster is remembered primarily as a technical failure, its roots lay in the social organization of the National Aeronautics and Space Administration (NASA), whose officials decided to proceed with the launch despite a potentially serious problem. Accord-

ing to sociologist Diane Vaughan (1996, 1999), the defect that caused the accident was discovered as early as 1977, and in 1985 was labeled a "launch constraint" (reason not to launch). On the day the *Challenger* was scheduled to take off, engineers from a company that manufactured a critical part recommended that NASA cancel the launch, but the 34 people who participated in the final prelaunch teleconference ignored their warning. Ultimately, no one was held responsible for the catastrophe. At its worst, a narrow division of labor can allow everyone to avoid responsibility for a critical decision.

The 1986 *Challenger* disaster was not just a technical failure, but an example of the negative consequences of the bureaucratic division of labor.

2. Hierarchy of Authority Bureaucracies follow the principle of hierarchy; that is, each position is under the supervision of a higher authority. A president heads a college bureaucracy; he or she selects members of the administration, who in turn hire their own staff. In the Roman Catholic church, the pope is the supreme authority; under him are cardinals, bishops, and so forth.

3. Written Rules and Regulations What if your sociology professor gave you an A for having such a friendly smile? It would certainly be a pleasant surprise, but it would also be "against the rules."

Rules and regulations, as we all know, are an important characteristic of bureaucracies. Ideally, through such procedures, a bureaucracy ensures uniform performance of every task. This prohibits you from receiving an A for a nice smile, but it also guarantees you that you will receive essentially the same treatment as other students.

Through written rules and regulations, bureaucracies generally offer employees clear standards as to what is considered an adequate (or exceptional) performance. In addition, procedures provide a valuable sense of continuity in a bureaucracy. Individual workers will come and go, but the structure and past records give the organization a life of its own that outlives the services of any one bureaucrat.

Of course, rules and regulations can overshadow the larger goals of an organization and become dysfunctional. If blindly applied, they will no longer serve as a means to achieving an objective but instead will become important (and perhaps too important) in their own right. This would certainly be the case if a hospital emergency room physician failed to treat a seriously injured person because he or she had no valid proof of U.S. citizenship. Robert Merton (1968) has used the term ***goal displacement*** to refer to overzealous conformity to official regulations.

4. Impersonality Max Weber wrote that in a bureaucracy, work is carried out *sine ira et studio,* "without hatred or passion." Bureaucratic norms dictate that officials perform their duties without the personal consideration of people as individuals. This is intended to guarantee equal treatment for each person; however, it also contributes to the often cold and uncaring feeling associated with modern organizations.

We typically think of big government and big business when we think of impersonal bureaucracies. But today even small firms have telephone systems greeting callers with an electronic menu. E-mail addresses are sought under the guise of efficiency, but they also make it less likely that a response will be direct and personal.

5. Employment Based on Technical Qualifications Within a bureaucracy, hiring is based on technical qualifi-

cations rather than on favoritism, and performance is measured against specific standards. Written personnel policies dictate who gets promoted, and people often have a right to appeal if they believe that particular rules have been violated. Such procedures protect bureaucrats against arbitrary dismissal, provide a measure of security, and encourage loyalty to the organization.

In this sense, the "impersonal" bureaucracy can be an improvement over nonbureaucratic organizations. College faculty members, for example, are ideally hired and promoted according to their professional qualifications, including degrees earned and research published, and not because of favors they do the college president. Once they are granted tenure, their jobs are protected against the whims of a president or dean.

Although any bureaucracy ideally will value technical and professional competence, personnel decisions do not always follow this ideal pattern. Dysfunctions within bureaucracy have become well publicized, particularly because of the work of Laurence J. Peter. According to the ***Peter principle,*** every employee within a hierarchy tends

These members of the Puerto Rico Symphony Orchestra must be technically proficient and professionally trained, or they will never make beautiful music together. Technical qualification is one of the characteristics of a well-structured bureaucracy.

to rise to his or her level of incompetence (Peter and Hull 1969). This hypothesis, which has not been directly or systematically tested, reflects a possible dysfunctional outcome of structuring advancement on the basis of merit. Talented people receive promotion after promotion until, sadly, they finally achieve positions that they cannot handle with their usual competence (Blau and Meyer 1987).

Bureaucratization as a Process

The five characteristics of bureaucracy, developed by Max Weber more than 75 years ago, describe an ideal type rather than offer a precise definition of an actual bureaucracy. Not every formal organization will possess all of Weber's characteristics. In fact, there can be wide variation among actual bureaucratic organizations. In Box 6-2, we consider how some bureaucracies actually function in different cultural settings, including Weber's native country of Germany.

Sociologists have used the term **bureaucratization** to refer to the process by which a group, organization, or social movement becomes increasingly bureaucratic. Normally, we think of bureaucratization in terms of large organizations. In a typical citizen's nightmare, one may have to speak to 10 or 12 individuals in a corporation or government agency to find out which official has jurisdiction over a particular problem. Callers can get transferred from one department to another until they finally hang up in disgust. Bureaucratization also takes place within small-group settings.

The sociologist Jennifer Bickman Mendez (1998) studied domestic houseworkers employed in central California by a nationwide franchise. She found that housekeeping tasks were minutely defined, to the point that employees had to follow 22 written steps for cleaning a bathroom. Complaints and special requests went not to the workers, but to an office-based manager. The impersonality and efficiency of this bureaucratic system is yet another example of the McDonaldization of the workplace.

Oligarchy: Rule by a Few

Conflict theorists have examined the bureaucratizing influence on social movements. German sociologist Robert Michels (1915) studied socialist parties and labor unions in Europe before World War I, and found that such organizations were becoming increasingly bureaucratic. The emerging leaders of these organizations—even some of the most radical—had a vested interest in clinging to power. If they lost their leadership posts, they would have to return to full-time work as manual laborers.

Through his research, Michels originated the idea of the **iron law of oligarchy**, which describes how even a democratic organization will develop into a bureaucracy ruled by a few (the oligarchy). Why do oligarchies emerge? People who achieve leadership roles usually have the skills, knowledge, or charismatic appeal (as Weber noted) to direct, if not control, others. Michels argues that the rank and file of a movement or organization look to leaders for direction and thereby reinforce the process of rule by a few. In addition, members of an oligarchy are strongly motivated to maintain their leadership roles, privileges, and power.

Michels's insights continue to be relevant today. Contemporary labor unions in the United States and Western Europe bear little resemblance to those organized after spontaneous activity by exploited workers. Conflict theorists have pointed to the longevity of union leaders, who are not always responsive to the needs and demands of membership and seem more concerned with maintaining their own positions and power.

At least one study, however, raises questions about Michels's views. Based on her research on "pro-choice" organizations, which endorse the right to legal abortions, sociologist Suzanne Staggenborg (1988) disputes the

Sociology in the Global Community

6-2 The Varying Cultures of Formal Organizations

The U.S. negotiator in a business deal with a German company is running late for an appointment in Berlin. He barges into his German counterpart's office, leans across the desk, extends a hand, booms out "Good to see you, Franz!" and proceeds to regale Franz with an amusing story about his taxi ride to the office. Unwittingly, he has violated four rules of polite behavior in German organizations: punctuality, personal space, privacy, and proper greetings. In German formal organizations, meetings take place on time, business is not mixed with pleasure or joking, greetings are formal, and the casual use of first names is frowned on.

Now picture a formal business meeting that takes place in a corporation in France. A Japanese negotiating team enters the conference room, but is dismayed to find a round table. The Japanese do not use round tables in business settings. They prefer to sit facing the opposite side and have a prescribed seating order, with the power position in the middle, flanked by interpreters, key advisers, note takers, and finally the most junior personnel at the ends. The French negotiators get down to business and make direct offers, for which they expect quick answers from the Japanese team. But the protocol in Japanese organizations is to nurture business relationships first and conduct indirect negotiations until the real decision making can take place later in private.

What these examples show is that formal organizations are influenced by national cultures. They reflect the ways we all have been socialized. Geert Hofstede, an international management scholar based in the Netherlands, calls these ingrained patterns of thinking, feeling, and acting *mental programs* (or "software of the mind"). If business is to be successful, the participants have to have some understanding of the customs, values, and procedures of other cultures. In the examples above, this holds true equally for the Germans *and* the U.S. citizens, for the French *and* the Japanese.

Hofstede explored some of the cross-cultural differences in formal organizations by means of a study of IBM employees in 50 different countries. Since the respondents to his survey were matched in almost every respect *except for nationality*, he felt the national differences in their answers would show up clearly. He found four dimensions in which the countries differed:

1. *Power distance.* This refers to the degree to which a culture thinks it is appropriate to distribute power unequally and to accept the decisions of power holders. At one extreme on this dimension are the Arab countries, Guatemala, Malaysia, and the Philippines, each of which tolerates hierarchy and inequality and believes the actions of authorities should not be challenged. At the opposite end of this

> The Japanese do not use round tables in business settings.

scale are Austria, Denmark, Israel, and New Zealand.
2. *Uncertainty avoidance.* Cultures differ in how much they can tolerate uncertainty and adapt to change. Those that feel threatened by uncertainty will establish more structure; examples include Greece, Portugal, and Uruguay. At the other extreme are countries that minimize rules and rituals, accept dissent, and take risks in trying new things: Denmark, Ireland, Jamaica, and Singapore can be found among these nations.
3. *Individualism/collectivism.* This dimension refers to how cultures vary in encouraging people to be unique and independent versus conforming and interdependent. In other words, what is the balance between allegiance to the self or to the group? Guatemala, Indonesia, Pakistan, and West Africa all take a collectivist orientation:

absolute loyalty to the group and an emphasis on belonging. On the other hand, Australia, Belgium, the Netherlands, and the United States are highly individualistic societies, valuing the autonomy of the individual.
4. *Masculinity/femininity.* To what extent do cultures prefer achievement, assertiveness, and acquisition of wealth (masculinity) to nurturance, social support, and quality of life (femininity)? Countries high in the masculinity index include Austria, Italy, Japan, and Mexico. High-scoring feminine cultures include Chile, Portugal, Sweden, and Thailand.

Hofstede's data come with some baggage attached. His respondents were for the most part males working in one large multinational corporation. Their point of view may be unique to their gender and level of education. Moreover, he collected his data in 1974; since then economic and political changes are sure to have affected cultural patterns. Still, his work is valuable for showing the cultural differences within the range of his respondents and for alerting all of us, and especially those in the business community, of the need to understand the cultural settings of formal organizations.

Let's Discuss

1. Which of the four business negotiating styles (American, German, Japanese, French) would you feel most comfortable with in a business setting? Do your classmates' answers differ based on their nationality or cultural background?
2. Analyze your campus culture. How much power distance is there between students, professors, and administrators? How much individualism is tolerated on your campus? How much pressure is there to conform?

Sources: Frazee 1997; Hofstede 1997; Lustig and Koester 1999.

assertion that formal organizations with professional leaders inevitably become conservative and oligarchical. Indeed, she notes that many formal organizations in the pro-choice movement appear to be more democratic than informal groups; the routinized procedures that they follow make it more difficult for leaders to grab excessive power (see also E. Scott 1993).

While the "iron law" may sometimes help us to understand the concentration of formal authority within organizations, sociologists recognize that there are a number of checks on leadership. Groups often compete for power within a formal organization. For example, in an automotive corporation, divisions manufacturing heavy machinery and passenger cars compete against each other for limited research and development funds. Moreover, informal channels of communication and control can undercut the power of top officials of an organization.

Bureaucracy and Organizational Culture

How does bureaucratization affect the average individual who works in an organization? The early theorists of formal organizations tended to neglect this question. Max Weber, for example, focused on management personnel within bureaucracies, but he had little to say about workers in industry or clerks in government agencies.

According to the *classical theory* of formal organizations, also known as the *scientific management approach,* workers are motivated almost entirely by economic rewards. This theory stresses that productivity is limited only by the physical constraints of workers. Therefore, workers are treated as a resource, much like the machines that began to replace them in the twentieth century. Management attempts to achieve maximum work efficiency through scientific planning, established performance standards, and careful supervision of workers and production. Planning under the scientific management approach involves efficiency studies but not studies of workers' attitudes or feelings of job satisfaction.

It was not until workers organized unions—and forced management to recognize that they were not objects—that theorists of formal organizations began to revise the classical approach. Along with management and administrators, social scientists became aware that informal groups of workers have an important impact on organizations (Perrow 1986). An alternative way of considering bureaucratic dynamics, the *human relations approach,* emphasizes the role of people, communication, and participation within a bureaucracy. This type of analysis reflects the interest of interactionist theorists in small-group behavior. Unlike planning under the scientific management approach, planning based on the human relations perspective focuses on workers' feelings, frustrations, and emotional need for job satisfaction. In Box 6-2 on page 155, we saw how understanding human relations in the corporate structure can enhance doing business abroad.

The gradual move away from a sole focus on physical aspects of getting the job done—and toward the concerns and needs of workers—led advocates of the human relations approach to stress the less formal aspects of bureaucratic structure. Informal structures and social networks within organizations develop partly as a result of people's ability to create more direct forms of communication than under the formal structure. Charles Page (1946) has used the term *bureaucracy's other face* to refer to the unofficial activities and interactions that are such a basic part of daily organizational life.

A series of classic studies illustrates the value of the human relations approach. The p. 44 Hawthorne studies alerted sociologists to the fact that research subjects may alter their behavior to match the experimenter's expectations. The major focus of the Hawthorne studies, however, was the role of social factors in workers' productivity. One aspect of the research investigated the switchboard-bank wiring room, where 14 men were making parts of switches for telephone equipment. The researchers discovered that these men were producing far below their physical capabilities. This was especially surprising because they would earn more money if they produced more parts.

Why was there such an unexpected restriction of output? The men feared that if they produced switch parts at a faster rate, their pay rate might be reduced or some might lose their jobs. As a result, this group of workers established their own (unofficial) norm for a proper day's work. They created informal rules and sanctions to enforce it. Yet management was unaware of such practices and actually believed that the men were working as hard as they could (Roethlisberger and Dickson 1939; for a different perspective, see S. Vallas 1999).

Recent research has underscored the impact of informal structures within organizations. Sociologist James Tucker (1993) studied everyday forms of resistance by temporary employees working in short-term positions. Tucker points out that informal social networks can offer advice to a temporary employee on how to pursue a grievance. For example, a female receptionist working for an automobile dealer was being sexually harassed both physically and verbally by a male supervisor. Other female employees, who were aware of the supervisor's behavior, suggested that she complain to the manager of the dealership. Although the manager said there was little that he could do, he apparently spoke with the supervisor and the harassment stopped. We will examine sexual harassment within organizations in the social policy section.

Technology's Impact on the Workplace

In 1968, Stanley Kubrick's motion picture *2001: A Space Odyssey* dazzled audiences with its futuristic depiction of travel to Jupiter. As we approach 2001, it is clear that we have not lived up to this target of outer space exploration. However, what about the portrayal of computers? In *2001* a mellow-voiced computer named HAL is very efficient and helpful to the crew, only to try to take over the entire operation and destroy the crew in the process. While computers may now successfully compete against chess champions, they are as far short of achieving the artificial intelligence of HAL as earthlings are of accomplishing manned travel to Jupiter.

Still, the computer today is a commanding presence in our lives, and in the workplace in particular. It is not just that the computer makes tedious, routine tasks easier, so that with little effort secretaries can electronically correct the spelling of their documents. It has affected the workplace in far more dramatic ways.

Automation

Jeremy Rifkin (1996)—the president of the Foundation on Economic Trends—notes that computer-generated automation has completely transformed the nature of manufacturing. By the year 2005, less than 12 percent of the paid labor force of the United States will be on the factory floor; by 2020, less than 2 percent of the global workforce will be performing factory work. Moreover, automation is reshaping the service sector of the economy in a similar way, leading to substantial reductions in employees ("downsizing") and the increasing use of temporary or contingent workers (see Chapter 17).

Telecommuting

Increasingly, the workforce is turning into *telecommuters* in many industrial countries. *Telecommuters* are employees of business firms or government agencies who work full-time or part-time at home rather than in an outside office and who are linked to their supervisors and colleagues through computer terminals, phone lines, and fax machines (see Chapter 17). Two 1999 studies confirmed the importance of this trend. One national survey showed that next to on-site day care, most office workers want virtual offices that allow them to work off-site. Another study estimated that by 2005, at least 25 percent of the U.S. workforce will be telecommuters or home office workers (Carey and Jerding 1999; Nie 1999).

What are the social implications of this shift toward the virtual office? From an interactionist perspective, the workplace is a major source of friendships; restricting face-to-face social opportunities could destroy the trust that is created by face-to-face "handshake agreements." Thus, telecommuting may move society further along the continuum from *Gemeinschaft* to *Gesellschaft*. On a more positive note, telecommuting may be the first social change that pulls fathers and mothers back into the home rather than pushing them out. The trend, if it continues, should also increase autonomy and job satisfaction for many employees (Nie 1999).

Electronic Communication

Electronic communication in the workplace has generated some heat lately. On the one hand, e-mailing is a highly convenient way to push messages around, especially with the CC (carbon copy) button. It's democratic too—lower-status employees are more likely to participate in e-mail discussion than in face-to-face communications, which gives organizations the benefit of the experiences and views of more of their workforce. But e-mailing is almost too easy to use. It is estimated that more than 6.6 trillion e-mail messages a year now move through U.S. computers. At Computer Associates, a software company, managers were receiving 300 e-mails a day each and people were e-mailing colleagues in the next cubicle. To deal with the electronic chaos, the company's CEO took the unusual step of banning all e-mails from 9:30 to 12 and 1:30 to 4. Other companies have limited the number of CCs that can

Telecommuters are linked to their supervisors and colleagues through computer terminals, phone lines, and fax machines.

be sent and banned systemwide messages (Gwynne and Dickerson 1997; Sproull and Kiesler 1991).

There are other problems with e-mail. It doesn't convey body language, which in face-to-face communication can soften insensitive phrasing and make unpleasant messages (such as a reprimand) easier to take. It also leaves a permanent record, and that can be a problem if messages are written thoughtlessly. In an antitrust case that the federal government brought against Microsoft in 1998, the prosecutors used as evidence e-mail sent to and from Microsoft's CEO Bill Gates. Finally, as will be discussed in detail in Chapter 22, companies can monitor e-mail as a means of "watching" their employees. Dartmouth professor Paul Argenti advises those who use e-mail, "Think before you write. The most important thing to know is what not to write" (Gwynne and Dickerson 1997:90).

Voluntary Associations

By 1995, there were more than 22,000 voluntary associations in the United States. *Voluntary associations* are organizations established on the basis of common interest, whose members volunteer or even pay to participate. The Girl Scouts of America, the American Jewish Congress, the Kiwanis Club, and the League of Women Voters are all considered voluntary associations; so, too, are the American Association of Aardvark Aficionados, the Cats on Stamps Study Group, the Mikes of America, the New York Corset Club, and the William Shatner Fellowship. The nation's largest voluntary association, the American Automobile Association, has 32 million members; the smallest, the School Bus Manufacturers Institute, has only 5 (Burek 1992; Fisher and Schwartz 1995).

The variety of voluntary associations in the United States was evident in 1988 on the campus of Gallaudet University in Washington, D.C., when students and alumni shut down the school and eventually forced the board of trustees to appoint the university's first deaf president. Among the voluntary associations that supported the naming of a deaf president were the National Association of the Deaf, DeafPride, the Alexander Graham Bell Association for the Deaf, the National Black Deaf Advocates, the American Society for Deaf Children, and the Convention

of American Instructors for the Deaf (Christiansen and Barnartt 1995:148).

The categories of "formal organization" and "voluntary association" are not mutually exclusive. Large voluntary associations such as the Lions Club and the Masons have structures similar to those of profit-making corporations. At the same time, certain formal organizations, such as the Young Men's Christian Association (YMCA) and the Peace Corps, have philanthropic and educational goals usually found in voluntary associations. Interestingly, the Democratic Party and the United Farm Workers union are considered examples of voluntary associations. While membership in a political party or union can be a condition of employment and therefore not genuinely voluntary, political parties and labor unions are usually included in discussions of voluntary associations.

Participation in voluntary associations is not unique to the United States. This textbook's author attended a carnival in London featuring bungee-jumping, at which participants were expected to jump from a height of 180 feet. Skeptics were given assurances of the attraction's safety by being told that the proprietor belonged to a voluntary association: the British Elastic Rope Sports Association. In a cross-cultural study, three Canadian sociologists examined membership in voluntary associations in 15 countries. Religious memberships were found to be prominent in the United States, Canada, the Netherlands, Ireland, and Northern Ireland. By contrast, union partici-

The AARP is a voluntary association of people aged 50 and older, both retired and working, that advocates for the needs of older Americans. A huge organization, it has been instrumental in maintaining Social Security benefits to retirees. Here AARP volunteers staff a phone bank in an effort to get out the vote in Des Moines, Iowa.

pation was highest in Great Britain, Norway, and Sweden. While people's country of residence may influence the types of voluntary associations they join, membership in such organizations is clearly a common social pattern (Curtis et al. 1992).

Voluntary associations can provide support to people in preindustrial societies. During the post–World War II period, migration from rural areas of Africa to the cities was accompanied by a growth in voluntary associations, including trade unions, occupational societies, and mutual aid organizations developed along old tribal ties. As pp. 131–132 people moved from the *Gemeinschaft* of the countryside to the *Gesellschaft* of the city, these voluntary associations provided immigrants with substitutes for the extended groups of kinfolk that they had had in their villages (Little 1988).

A common voluntary association in nonindustrial societies is the military association, which may be compared to our own American Legion or Veterans of Foreign Wars posts. These associations unite members through their experiences in the military, glorify the activities of war, and perform certain services for the community. Membership in such associations is usually voluntary and based on the achieved criterion of participation in a war. Among the North American Plains Indians, such military societies were common. The Cheyenne Indians, for example, originally had five military associations: the Fox, the Dog, the Shield, the Elk, and the Bowstring. Although these associations featured distinctive costumes, songs, and dances, they were alike in their internal organization. Each was headed by four leaders, who were among the Cheyenne's most important war chiefs (Ember and Ember 1993:359–360).

Membership in voluntary associations is not random. The most consistent predictor of participation is socioeconomic status—that is, a person's income, education, and occupation. People of higher socioeconomic status are more likely to belong to and participate actively in such organizations. Partly, this reflects the cost of group memberships, which may exclude people with limited income from joining (Sills 1968:365–366; J. Williams et al. 1973).

Reflecting the occupational patterns of the larger society, voluntary associations in the United States are largely segregated by gender. Half of them are exclusively female, and one-fifth are all-male. The exclusively male associations tend to be larger and more heterogeneous in terms of background of members. As noted in Chapter 5, membership in all-male associations holds more promise for making desirable business contacts than membership in all-female groups (McPherson and Smith-Lovin 1986). Although participation varies across the population of the United States, most people belong to at least one voluntary association (see Figure 6-1), while more than one-fourth maintain three or more memberships.

Sociologists have applied functionalist analysis to the study of voluntary associations. David Sills (1968:373–376) has identified several key functions that these groups serve within our society. First, they mediate between individuals and government. Professional associations such as the American Medical Association mediate between their members and government in such matters as licensing and legislation. Second, voluntary associations give people training in organizational skills that is invaluable for future officeholders—and for better performance within most jobs. Third, organizations such as the National Association for the Advancement of Colored People (NAACP), the National Women's Political Caucus, and the American Association of Retired Persons (AARP) help to bring traditionally disadvantaged and underrepresented groups into the political mainstream. In 1993, the National Association of Twentysomethings was established to provide its members (ages 18 through 29) with employment information and counseling, financial planning, and health insurance. Finally, voluntary associations assist in governing. During the influx of South Asian and Cuban refugees in the late 1970s and early 1980s, religious and charitable groups became deeply involved in helping the federal government resettle refugees.

FIGURE 6-1

Membership in Voluntary Associations

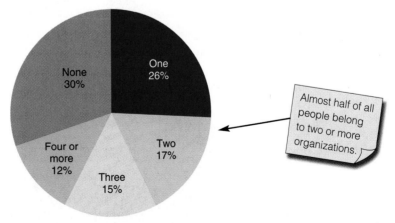

Source: J. Davis and Smith 1999:336.

The importance of voluntary associations—and especially of their unpaid workers (or volunteers)—is increasingly being recognized. Traditionally, unpaid work has been devalued in the United States, even though the skill levels, experience, and training demands are often comparable with those of wage labor. Viewed from a conflict perspective, the critical difference has been that a substantial amount of volunteer work is performed by women. Feminists and conflict theorists agree that, like the unpaid child care and household labor of homemakers, the effort of volunteers has been too often ignored by scholars—and awarded too little respect by the larger society—because it is viewed as "women's work." Failure to recognize women's volunteerism thereby obscures a critical contribution women make to a society's social structure (Daniels 1987, 1988).

Curiously, although membership in voluntary associations in the United States is high, people tend to add and drop affiliations rather quickly. This reflects the fact that a decision to enter a voluntary association typically involves only limited personal objectives (Babchuk and Booth 1969). As de Tocqueville wrote, people in the United States are "forever forming associations."

Organizational Change

Just as individuals and relationships change, so too do organizations, both formal and voluntary. The most obvious changes often involve personnel: a new president of the United States is elected, an executive is fired, a star athlete retires. However, sociologists are most interested in how the organization itself changes.

These changes often relate to other social institutions, particularly the government. Its regulatory statutes, licensing procedures, tax laws, and contracting for goods and services directly influence the structure of formal organizations. Government policies relating to affirmative action (see Chapter 17) or disability rights (see Chapter 5) influence the internal decisions of organizations and may even require the hiring of new personnel.

In addition, an organization's goals may change over time along with its leaders and structure. A church starts a basketball league; an oil company purchases a movie studio; a chewing tobacco firm begins to manufacture ballpoint pens. Such actions take place when an organization decides that its traditional goals are no longer adequate. It must then modify its previous objectives or cease to exist.

Goal Multiplication

If an organization concludes that its goals must change, it will typically establish additional goals or expand upon its traditional objectives. For example, in the 1970s many colleges began continuing education programs to meet the needs of potential students holding full-time jobs and wishing to take classes at night. In the 1980s, the Elderhostel movement opened college campuses in the United States to older people who could live and learn along with much younger college students.

Goal multiplication takes place when an organization expands its purposes. Generally, this is the result of changing social or economic conditions that threaten the organization's survival. The YMCA has practiced such goal multiplication. Reflecting its name, the Young Men's Christian Association had a strong evangelistic focus during its beginnings in the United States in the 1850s. Bible study and tent revival meetings were provided by the early YMCAs. However, in the early 1900s, the YMCA began to diversify its appeal. It attempted to interest members by offering gymnasium facilities and residence quarters. Gradually, women, Lutherans, Roman Catholics, Jews, and the "unchurched" were accepted and even recruited as members.

The Young Men's Christian Association (YMCA) has experienced goal multiplication in recent decades. Its range of activities currently includes social service programs for people with disabilities, day care centers, fitness classes for office workers, residence dormitories for college students and single adults, and senior citizens' facilities.

The most recent phase of goal multiplication at the YMCA began in the 1960s. In larger urban areas, the organization became involved in providing employment training and juvenile delinquency programs. As a result, the YMCA received substantial funding from the federal government. This was a dramatic change for an organization whose income had previously come solely from membership fees and charitable contributions.

In the 1980s, the YMCA continued to serve the poor, as evidenced by the building of a new facility in 1984 in the Watts section of Los Angeles—the first major private construction in the area since the riots of 1965. Yet the organization also maintains a lucrative branch in Beverly Hills and has expanded rapidly to serve middle-class residents of cities and suburbs. The YMCA's impressive range of activities currently includes social service programs for the disabled, day care centers, fitness classes for office workers, residence dormitories for college students and single adults, "learning for living" classes for adults, and senior citizens' facilities (Schmidt 1990).

These transitions in the YMCA were not always smooth. At times, major contributors and board members withdrew support because of opposition to organizational changes; they preferred the YMCA to remain as it had been. However, the YMCA has survived and grown by expanding its goals from evangelism to general community service (Etzioni 1964:13; Zald 1970).

Goal Succession

Unlike goal multiplication, *goal succession* occurs when a group or organization has either realized or been denied its goal. It must then identify an entirely new objective that can justify its existence. Cases of goal succession are rare because most organizations never fully achieve their goals. If they do, as in the case of a committee supporting a victorious candidate for public office, they usually dissolve.

Sociologist Peter Blau (1964:241–246), who coined the term *succession of goals,* noted that organizations do not necessarily behave in a rigid manner when their goals are achieved or become irrelevant. Rather, they may shift toward new objectives. A case in point is the Foundation for Infantile Paralysis, popularly known for its annual March of Dimes campaign. For some time, the foundation's major goals were to support medical research on polio and to provide assistance for victims of the disease. However, in 1955 the Salk vaccine was found to be an effective protection against paralytic polio. This left the foundation, so to speak, "unemployed." A vast network of committed staff members and volunteers was suddenly left without a clear rationale for existence. The group might have disbanded at this point, but instead it selected a new goal—combating arthritis and birth defects—and took on a new name (Etzioni 1964; Sills 1957).

Goal succession can also occur when programs seem to succeed through failure. For example, government agencies that are responsible for enforcing drug laws continue to exist because they fail to put drug pushers out of business. Likewise, prisons fail to rehabilitate inmates, thereby guaranteeing the steady return of many clients.

SOCIAL POLICY AND ORGANIZATIONS

Sexual Harassment

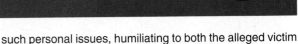

The Issue

In 1991, Clarence Thomas, awaiting confirmation to the Supreme Court, was accused of repeatedly harassing a former aide, law professor Anita Hill. In 1994, 29 women filed a federal lawsuit against a Mitsubishi automobile plant, accusing the company of fostering a climate of sexual harassment. Three years later, the company settled the lawsuit with 27 of the women for $9.5 million, and then for another $34 million with 350 other women. In 1998, Kathleen Willey said President Bill Clinton sexually groped her in the Oval Office, at a time when she was a White House volunteer and seeking a paid position there. Rarely have news reporters had to deal with such personal issues, humiliating to both the alleged victim and the offender alike.

The courts recognize two kinds of sexual harassment. *Sexual harassment* occurs (1) when work benefits are made contingent on sexual favors (as a "quid pro quo") or (2) when touching, lewd comments, or appearance of pornographic material creates a "hostile environment" in the workplace, making it unpleasant for reasonable people to do their work. In 1998 the Supreme Court ruled that harassment also applied to people of the same sex in the workplace. The "quid pro quo" type of harassment is fairly easy to identify in a court of law. But the issue of hostile environment has become the subject of considerable debate in courts and in the general public (L. Greenhouse 1998a; T. Lewin 1998b).

The Setting

Sexual harassment is not new, but it has received increased attention in many parts of the world as growing numbers of women enter the paid labor force and growing numbers of people in positions of influence pay attention to victims' stories. In a recent 10-year period, the proportion of women participating in the labor force has grown by at least 12 percent in Ireland, the Netherlands, South Korea, and the United States. In 1998, 15 million more U.S. women worked than in 1980, making them close to half the labor force (Bureau of the Census 1998c:409; Cloud 1998).

Women of all ages and racial and ethnic groups—and men as well—have been the victims of sexual harassment. Such harassment may occur as a single encounter or as a repeated pattern of behavior. In a national survey in the United States conducted in December 1992, 32 percent of women indicated that they had been sexually harassed in their work outside

Sexual harassment can be as subtle as an unwanted hand on the shoulder. Repeated actions of this kind can lead to a "hostile environment."

the home, compared with 23 percent in a similar survey in October 1991. These numbers may at first suggest that there has been a dramatic increase in sexual harassment, but in fact they may simply represent a shift in attitudes concerning such abuses. Martha Burt, director of social services research at the Urban Institute, observes, "People now are more willing to label these behaviors as being sexual harassment, people are more willing to talk about it, and people are more [angry] about it" (R. Morin 1993:37).

Sociological Insights

In the United States, sexual harassment must be understood in the context of continuing prejudice and discrimination against women (see Chapter 10). Whether it occurs in the federal bureaucracy, in the corporate world, or in universities, sexual harassment generally takes place in organizations in which the hierarchy of authority finds White males at the top and women's work is valued less than men's. One survey in the private sector found that African American women were three times more likely than White women to experience sexual harassment. From a conflict perspective, it is not surprising that women—and especially women of color—are most likely to become victims of sexual harassment. These groups are typically an organization's most vulnerable employees in terms of job security (J. Jones 1988).

Many bureaucracies have traditionally given little attention to the pervasive sexual harassment in their midst; the emotional costs of this discrimination suffered by (largely female) employees have not been a major concern. However, more regulations prohibiting sexual harassment have been issued as managers and executives confront the costs of sexual harassment *for the organization*. Given Mitsubishi's experience (noted at the beginning of the section), many formal organizations are developing zero tolerance for sexual harassment. Nine out of 10 companies now have rules and regulations dealing with the issue. However, many of these are weak and constitute only a single paragraph in the company handbook (Cloud 1998).

Policy Initiatives

Sexual harassment is still not defined by federal law. Its legal standing developed as an offshoot of Title VII of the Civil Rights Act of 1964, which prohibits employment discrimination based on sex. It was not until 1976 that a court accepted cases of sexual harassment, even of the "quid pro quo" variety, as being relevant to the Civil Rights Act.

In the 1986 case of *Meritor Savings Bank v. Vinson,* the Supreme Court unanimously held that sexual harassment by a supervisor violates federal law against sex discrimination in the workplace, as outlined in the 1964 Civil Rights Act. If sufficiently severe, sexual harassment constitutes a violation of the law even if the unwelcome sexual demands are not linked to concrete employment benefits such as a raise or a promotion. The justices ruled that the existence of a hostile or abusive work environment—in which a woman feels degraded as the result of unwelcome flirtation or obscene joking—may in itself constitute illegal sex discrimination. A federal judge subsequently ruled that the public display of photographs of nude and partly nude women at a workplace constitutes sexual harassment (Domino 1995).

In 1992, the Supreme Court extended the scope of sexual harassment from the workplace to school settings. While some regarded this broadening of the law as the end of spontaneous and warm feelings between the sexes, others countered that informal rules of power allowed supervisors to harass subordinates, including students. Women are the main targets of such incidents, most of which are not even reported to administrators. Even the hallways of high schools are dangerous territory for female students. According to a 1999 national survey, 83 percent of female students and 60 percent of males in grades 8 through 11 reported being sexually harassed. Because of these experiences and other forms of sexual harassment, 33 percent of the female students stated that they wanted to avoid going to school, and were less inclined to speak in class (Mauro 1999).

Over 15,800 sexual harassment claims are filed annually with the Equal Employment Opportunity Commission. But there is confusion about where to draw the lines. By 1998, 26 percent of women surveyed felt that sexual harassment was a "big problem," but 52 percent also felt that "we have gone too far in making common interactions between employees into cases of sexual harassment" (Cloud 1998:49).

The policy for dealing with sexual harassment in the United States is still evolving as courts at all levels hear cases and reach conclusions that are not necessarily consistent. The confusion will continue, but the old patriarchal system in which male bosses behaved as they pleased with female subordinates is ending. Organizations are developing their own formal regulations in anticipation of the problems they may face, in an effort to create a climate that is nonhostile for all workers. And most large formal organizations have initiated sensitivity and diversity training, to facilitate employees' awareness of situations that might lead to complaints of harassment or intolerance. To be effective, such training must be ongoing and an integral part of an organization's behavioral norms. Occasional antibigotry lectures and one-shot sessions on the theme of "Let's avoid harassment" are unlikely to accomplish the desired results (Fernandez 1999).

The battle against sexual harassment is being fought not only in the United States but around the world. In 1991, the European Economic Community established a code of conduct that holds employers ultimately responsible for combating such behavior. In 1992, France joined many European countries in banning sexual harassment. That same year, in an important victory for Japan's feminist movement, a district court ruled that a small publishing company and one of its male employees had violated the rights of a female employee because of crude remarks that led her to quit her job. The complainant had charged that her male supervisor had spread rumors about her, telling others that she was promiscuous. When she attempted to get him to stop making such comments, she was advised to quit her job. In the view of the complainant's lawyer, "Sexual harassment is a big problem in Japan, and we hope this will send a signal to men that they have to be more careful" (Kanagae 1993; Perlez 1996; Pollack 1996; Weisman 1992:A3).

Let's Discuss

1. Have you ever been sexually harassed, either at work or at school? If so, did you complain about it? What was the outcome?
2. In the instances of sexual harassment you are personally familiar with, was there a difference in power between the victim and the person being harassed? If so, was the difference in power based on gender, age, status, or race?
3. Have you ever received training in avoiding sexual harassment at school or in the workplace? Do you think this type of training is effective in preventing the problem?

Summary

Social interaction among human beings is necessary to the transmission of culture and the survival of every society. This chapter examines the social behavior of groups, formal organizations, and voluntary associations.

1. When we find ourselves identifying closely with a group, it is probably a *primary group.* A *secondary group* is more formal and impersonal.

2. People tend to see the world in terms of *in-groups* and *out-groups*, a perception often fostered by the very groups to which they belong.

3. *Reference groups* set and enforce standards of conduct and perform a comparison function for people's evaluations of themselves and others.

4. Interactionist researchers have revealed that there are distinct and predictable processes at work in the functioning of *small groups.* The simplest group is a *dyad,* composed of two members. *Triads* and larger groups increase ways of interacting and allow for *coalitions* to form.

5. As societies have become more complex, large *formal organizations* have become more powerful and pervasive.

6. Max Weber argued that, in its ideal form, every *bureaucracy* will share these five basic characteristics: division of labor, hierarchical authority, written rules and regulations, impersonality, and employment based on technical qualifications.

7. Bureaucracy can be understood as a process and as a matter of degree; thus, an organization is more or less bureaucratic than other organizations.

8. When leaders of an organization build up their power, it can lead to oligarchy (rule by a few).

9. The informal structure of an organization can undermine and redefine official bureaucratic policies.

10. Technology has transformed the workplace through automation, telecommuting, and electronic communication.

11. People belong to *voluntary associations* for a variety of purposes—for example, to share in joint activities or to get help with personal problems.

12. *Sexual harassment* has been reported not only in the federal workplace and in private-sector organizations but also in schools.

Critical Thinking Questions

1. Think about how behavior is shaped by reference groups. Drawing on your own experience, what different reference groups at different periods have shaped your outlook and your goals? In what ways have they done so?

2. Within a formal organization, are you likely to find primary groups, secondary groups, in-groups, out-groups, and reference groups? What functions do these groups serve for the formal organization? What dysfunctions might occur as a result of their presence?

3. Max Weber identified five basic characteristics of bureaucracy. Select an actual organization with which you are familiar (for example, your college, a business at which you work, a religious institution or civic association to which you belong) and apply Weber's analysis to that organization. To what degree does it correspond to Weber's ideal type of bureaucracy?

Key Terms

Alienation   A condition of estrangement or dissociation from the surrounding society. (page 152)

Bureaucracy   A component of formal organization in which rules and hierarchical ranking are used to achieve efficiency. (150)

Bureaucratization   The process by which a group, organization, or social movement becomes increasingly bureaucratic. (154)

Classical theory   An approach to the study of formal organizations that views workers as being motivated almost entirely by economic rewards. (156)

Coalition   A temporary or permanent alliance geared toward a common goal. (149)

Dyad   A two-member group. (149)

Dysfunction   An element or a process of society that may disrupt a social system or lead to a decrease in stability. (151)

Formal organization   A special-purpose group designed and structured for maximum efficiency. (150)

Goal displacement   Overzealous conformity to official regulations within a bureaucracy. (153)

Goal multiplication   The process through which an organization expands its purpose. (160)

Goal succession   The process through which an organization identifies an entirely new objective because its traditional goals have been either realized or denied. (161)

Group   Any number of people with similar norms, values, and expectations who interact with one another. (145)

Human relations approach   An approach to the study of formal organizations that emphasizes the role of people, communication, and participation within a bureaucracy and tends to focus on the informal structure of the organization. (156)

Ideal type   A construct or model that serves as a measuring rod against which specific cases can be evaluated. (151)

In-group   Any group or category to which people feel they belong. (146)

Iron law of oligarchy   A principle of organizational life under which even democratic organizations will become bureaucracies ruled by a few individuals. (154)

McDonaldization   The process by which the principles of the fast-food restaurant have come to dominate certain sectors of society, both in the United States and throughout the world. (145)

Out-group   A group or category to which people feel they do not belong. (146)

Peter principle   A principle of organizational life according to which each individual within a hierarchy tends to rise to his or her level of incompetence. (153)

Primary group   A small group characterized by intimate, face-to-face association and cooperation. (145)

Reference group   Any group that individuals use as a standard in evaluating themselves and their own behavior. (148)

Scientific management approach   Another name for the *classical theory* of formal organizations. (156)

Secondary group   A formal, impersonal group in which there is little social intimacy or mutual understanding. (145)

Sexual harassment   Behavior that occurs when work benefits are made contingent on sexual favors (as a "quid pro quo") or when touching, lewd comments, or appearance of pornographic material creates a "hostile environment" in the workplace. (161)

Small group   A group small enough for all members to interact simultaneously, that is, to talk with one another or at least be acquainted. (148)

Telecommuters   Employees of business firms or government agencies who work full-time or part-time at home rather than in an outside office and who are linked to their supervisors and colleagues through computer terminals, phone lines, and fax machines. (157)

Trained incapacity   The tendency of workers in a bureaucracy to become so specialized that they develop blind spots and fail to notice obvious problems. (152)

Triad   A three-member group. (149)

Voluntary associations   Organizations established on the basis of common interest, whose members volunteer or even pay to participate. (158)

Additional Readings

BOOKS

Alfino, Mark, John S. Caputo, and Robin Wynyard. 1998. *McDonaldization Revisited: Critical Essays on Consumer Culture.* Westport, CT: Praeger. A multidisciplinary look at George Ritzer's approach to Max Weber's theory of rationalization and how it has been applied first to McDonald's restaurants and now to institutions worldwide.

Fagenson, Ellen A. 1993. *Women in Management: Trends, Issues, and Challenges in Managerial Diversity.* Newbury Park, CA: Sage. This anthology focuses on the continued underrepresentation of women in managerial positions within formal organizations.

Nishiguchi, Toshihiro. 1994. *Strategic Industrial Sourcing: The Japanese Advantage.* New York: Oxford University Press. Drawing on eight years of research and more than 1,000 interviews, Nishiguchi offers insight into how very large industrial corporations have developed in Japan and have come to dominate that nation's economy.

Vaughan, Diane. 1996. *The Challenger Launch Decision: Risky Technology, Culture, and Deviance at NASA.* Chicago: University of Chicago Press. A detailed look at the work culture of the National Aeronautics and Space Administration (NASA) and its suppliers—and the impact of that work culture on the fatal launch of the U.S. space shuttle *Challenger* in 1986.

JOURNALS

Among the journals that focus on the study of groups and organizations are *Academy of Management Journal* (founded in 1958), *Administration and Society* (1969), *Administrative Science Quarterly* (1956), *Clinical Sociology Review* (1981), *Organization: Interdisciplinary Journal of Organization Theory and Society* (1994), *Organizational Studies* (1980), *Small Group Research* (formerly *Small Group Behavior*, 1970), *Social Psychology Review* (1948), and *Work and Occupations* (1974).

Internet Connection

Note: While all the URLs listed were current as of the printing of this book, these sites often change. Please check our website (http://www.mhhe.com/schaefer) for updates.

1. Max Weber outlined the characteristics of bureaucracies: division of labor, hierarchy of authority, written rules and communications, impersonality, and employment based on technical qualifications. A modern twist on Weber's thinking can be found in the work of George Ritzer. To learn more about Ritzer's ideas regarding the McDonaldization of society, log onto Lycos (**http://www.lycos.com**) and enter the name George Ritzer in the search engine. Visit the sites that deal with McDonaldization and answer the following questions.

    (a) What does Ritzer mean by McDonaldization? How are fast-food techniques relevant to the wider culture?

    (b) Define the terms *efficiency, calculability, predictability,* and *control.* What examples of each concept does the site offer? Can you think of other examples?

    (c) Where else do you see "McDonaldization" in our society?

    (d) What does the "irrationality of rationality" mean?

    (e) In what ways does Ritzer's work parallel Weber's?

    (f) What arguments could be made by those who might disagree with Weber and Ritzer? Is there anything good or beneficial about living in a rationalized society?

2. Imagine you are a news reporter. Your assignment is to write a retrospective on the space shuttle *Challenger,* which exploded in 1986. As part of your research, link to NASA information on the *Challenger* at (**http://www.hq.nasa.gov/office/pao/History/sts51l.html**). There you will find transcripts from the mission's voice recorder, crew biographies, a space shuttle reference manual, and copies of the Report of the Presidential Commission on the Space Shuttle Challenger Accident.

    (a) Who were the *Challenger*'s crew members? What were their backgrounds and accomplishments? Why was this mission special in terms of the composition of its crew?

    (b) What would have been the goals of the *Challenger* mission had disaster not struck?

    (c) According to the Rogers Report, what was the direct cause of the accident? What were the contributing causes?

    (d) Why does the report call the shuttle disaster "an accident rooted in history"? Do you believe the explosion should be called an accident, considering the contributing causes?

    (e) Relate the causes of the accident to this chapter's discussion of bureaucracies and their dysfunctions.

    (f) What recommendations did the Presidential Commission make to reduce the chances of another disaster? What is your opinion of those recommendations?

    (g) Have Americans again become too complacent about the dangers of space travel?

Cigarette smoking has become stigmatized in the United States. These two billboards remind smokers that their habit is socially isolating (top) and life-threatening (bottom).

When asked, jokingly, "What are you doing on the telephone?" one salesman retorted, "Boiling." Another chimed in, "We're boiling away." The term *boiler room,* however, is only recognized by experienced telephone salesmen. Like other members of deviant groups whose style of deviance is attributed by outsiders but rarely self-acknowledged (hippies, pool sharks, and white-collar criminals), boilers are not, except in jest, referred to as such but rather in terms borrowed from the conventional sales world: telephone sales agents, telemarketing reps, brokers, or inside salesmen.

When the term is occasionally used in sales talks given by management, a form of deviance disavowal is practiced. The working definition of a boiler room becomes all the negative characteristics of the industry mapped onto the competition. There are many negative characteristics. These are the result of the difficulties involved in negotiating sales over the telephone. Boiler rooms offer a range of disreputabilities, any of which clearly establishes telephone salesmen as members of a deviant occupation, each of which may be more or less dominant in a particular setting, and few of which are experienced in pure form. The disreputabilities are:

1. Some rooms engage in outright fraud (the scams), thus breaking numerous local, state, and federal ordinances.

2. No boiler room delivers all of what is promised to customers. Although this is sometimes a matter of degree (i.e., product claims exceeding capabilities), it is often a difference in kind—a nondelivery or nonusable, sometimes dangerous, product or fictitious services.

Because all boiler rooms are organized as businesses, most of the routine behavior therein is no different from that in other kinds of sales or administrative work. In performing their jobs, telephone salesmen learn a great deal about the formal and imagined attributes of the products they sell, but they rarely have a chance to see what is vended or shipped. Such matters are categorically defined as "not their concern," and information control networks are extremely active *(Stevenson 1998:76, 77).* ∎

I n this excerpt from his book *The Boiler Room and Other Telephone Sales Scams*, sociologist Robert J. Stevenson describes how swindlers whose sole aim is to fleece unsuspecting customers and employees masquerade as reputable telemarketers. In writing his book, Stevenson drew upon participant observation research he did over a nine-year period. During that time he observed a variety of scams, from the sale of purported rare coins to a bogus travel agency and a phony training institute. While on the job, he picked up the argot used by "hot" (successful) pitchmakers (see Chapter 4) and observed how new hires were socialized into their deviant roles through pressure from managers and competition with others. Many, he found, were otherwise respectable workers who had lost their jobs and were struggling to maintain their incomes. Few suspected what they were getting into when they agreed to take the job.

Conformity to the boss's wishes and deviance from accepted business practices are both responses to pressure from others, either real or imagined. In the United States, people are socialized to have mixed feelings about both conforming and nonconforming behavior. The term *conformity* can conjure up images of mindless imitation of one's peer group—whether a circle of teenagers wearing "phat pants" or a group of businesspeople dressed in similar gray suits. Yet the same term can also suggest that an individual is cooperative or a "team player." What about those who do not conform? They may be respected as individualists, leaders, or creative thinkers who break new ground. Or they may be labeled as "troublemakers" and "weirdos" (Aronson 1999).

This chapter examines the relationship between conformity, deviance, and social control. It begins by distinguishing between conformity and obedience and then looks at two experiments regarding conforming behavior and obedience to authority. The informal and formal mechanisms used by societies to encourage conformity and discourage deviance are analyzed. We give particular attention to the legal order and how it reflects underlying social values.

The second part of the chapter focuses on theoretical explanations for deviance, including the functionalist approach employed by Émile Durkheim and Robert Merton; the interactionist-based theories; labeling theory, which draws upon both the interactionist and the conflict perspectives; and conflict theory.

The third part of the chapter focuses on crime, a specific type of deviant behavior. As a form of deviance subject to official, written norms, crime has been a special concern of policymakers and the public in general. We will take a look at various types of crime found in the United States, the ways crime is measured, and international crime rates. Finally, the social policy section considers the use of the death penalty in the United States and in the rest of the world. ■

Social Control

As we saw in Chapter 3, each culture, subculture, and group has distinctive norms governing what it deems appropriate behavior. Laws, dress codes, bylaws of organizations, course requirements, and rules of sports and games all express social norms.

How does a society bring about acceptance of basic norms? The term **social control** refers to the techniques and strategies for preventing deviant human behavior in any society. Social control occurs on all levels of society. In the family, we are socialized to obey our parents simply because they are our parents. Peer groups introduce us to informal norms, such as dress codes, that govern the behavior of members. Colleges establish standards they expect of their students. In bureaucratic organizations, workers encounter a formal system of rules and regulations. Finally, the government of every society legislates

and enforces social norms—including norms regarding "proper" and "improper" expressions of sexual intimacy.

Most of us respect and accept basic social norms and assume that others will do the same. Even without thinking, we obey the instructions of police officers, follow the day-to-day rules at our jobs, and move to the rear of elevators when people enter. Such behavior reflects an effective process of socialization to the dominant standards of a culture. At the same time, we are well aware that individuals, groups, and institutions *expect* us to act "properly." If we fail to do so, we may face punishment through informal **sanctions** such as fear and ridicule, or formal sanctions such as jail sentences or fines. p. 74 ◄
The challenge to effective social control is that people often receive competing messages about how to behave. While the state or government may clearly define acceptable behavior, friends or fellow employees may encourage quite different behavior patterns. Box 7-1 presents the

Research in Action

7-1 College Binge Drinking

www.mhhe.com/schaefer

Scott Krueger was an outstanding high school student. Not only did he compile a 97.6 grade-point average; he was well liked, well rounded, and close to his family. Scott was placed in so many advanced courses, friends at his school in Buffalo, New York, took to calling him "Skippy." When it came time to decide on a college, he had his pick of engineering schools—Penn, Cornell, Michigan, MIT. Scott finally decided on MIT after an overnight visit convinced him that "they weren't all geeks" there.

One night in September 1997, after Scott had been at MIT little more than a month, he told his sister he had to get off the phone. His fraternity pledge class had a big night ahead, one in which the class had to drink a certain amount collectively, he explained. Several hours later Scott lay comatose in a hospital emergency room, his hair matted with vomit. His blood-alcohol level was 4.1—five times the drunken driving standard in Massachusetts. A few days later he died, another college-age victim of alcohol poisoning from binge drinking.

Scott was not unusual in his behavior. According to a 1999 study by the Harvard School of Public Health, about two out of five college students indulge in binge drinking (defined as at least five drinks in a row for men and four in a row for women). For those who live in a Greek fraternity or sorority, the rates are even higher—four out of five are binge drinkers (see Figure 7-1). These numbers represent an increase from 1993 and 1997 data, despite efforts on many campuses across the nation to educate students about the risks of binge drinking. The problem is not confined to the United States—Britain, Russia, and South Africa all report regular "drink 'til you drop" alcoholic consumption among young people.

Binge drinking on campus presents a difficult social problem. On the one hand, it can be regarded as *deviant*, violating the standards of conduct expected of those in an academic setting. In fact, Harvard researchers consider binge drinking the most

FIGURE 7-1

College Binge Drinking

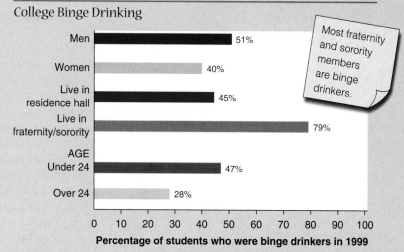

Percentage of students who were binge drinkers in 1999

Note: Based on a national survey of more than 14,000 college students in 1999. Binge drinking is defined as one drinking session of at least five drinks for men or four drinks for women during the two weeks prior to the self-administered questionnaire.

Source: Wechsler et al. 2000:23.

serious public health hazard facing colleges. Not only does it cause about 50 fatalities a year and hundreds of cases of alcohol poisoning; it increases the likelihood of falling behind in schoolwork, getting injured, and damaging property. Occasional binge drinkers are 5 times as likely as non-

> About two out of five college students indulge in binge drinking.

binge drinkers to experience five or more alchohol-related problems; frequent bingers are 22 times as likely to do so. Moreover, this kind of drinking behavior has secondary effects, including public disturbances, drunk driving, and unwelcome sexual advances. Three out of four students report experiencing at least one secondhand effect of binge drinking.

The other side of this potentially self-destructive behavior is that binge drinking represents *conformity* to the peer culture, es-

pecially in fraternities and sororities, which serve as social centers on many campuses. Most students seem to take an "everybody does it—no big deal" attitude toward the behavior. Many find that taking five drinks in a row is fairly typical. As one student at Boston University noted, "Anyone that goes to a party does that or worse. If you talk to anyone college age, it's normal." Some colleges and universities are taking steps to make binge drinking a bit less "normal" by means of *social control*—banning kegs, closing fraternities and sororities, encouraging liquor retailers not to sell in high volume to students, and expelling students after three alcohol-related infractions.

Let's Discuss

1. Why do you think most college students regard binge drinking as a normal rather than a deviant behavior?

2. Which method of social control do you think would be most effective in stopping binge drinking on your campus?

Sources: Glauber 1998; Goldberg 1998; McCormick and Kalb 1998; Wechsler et al. 2000.

172

latest research on a behavior that is officially frowned upon, but nevertheless engaged in by many college students: binge drinking.

Functionalists contend that people must respect social norms if any group or society is to survive. In their view, societies literally could not function if massive numbers of people defied standards of appropriate conduct. By contrast, conflict theorists maintain that "successful functioning" of a society will consistently benefit the powerful and work to the disadvantage of other groups. They point out, for example, that widespread resistance to social norms was necessary to overturn the institution of slavery in the United States.

Conformity and Obedience

Techniques for social control operate on both the group level and the societal level. People whom we regard as our peers or as our equals influence us to act in particular ways; the same is true of people who hold authority over us or occupy awe-inspiring positions. Stanley Milgram (1975) made a useful distinction between these two important levels of social control.

Milgram defined **conformity** as going along with peers—individuals of our own status, who have no special right to direct our behavior. By contrast, **obedience** is defined as compliance with higher authorities in a hierarchical structure. Thus, a recruit entering military service will typically *conform* to the habits and language of other recruits and will *obey* the orders of superior officers. Students will *conform* to the drinking behavior of their peers and will *obey* the requests of campus security officers.

Conformity to Prejudice

We often think of conformity in terms of rather harmless situations, such as members of an expensive health club who all work out in elaborate and costly sportswear. But researchers have found that people may conform to the attitudes and behavior of their peers even when such conformity means expressing intolerance toward others. Fletcher Blanchard, Teri Lilly, and Leigh Ann Vaughn (1991) conducted an experiment at Smith College and found that statements people overhear others make influence their own expressions of opinion on the issue of racism.

A student confederate of the researchers approached 72 White students as each was walking across the campus to get responses for an opinion poll she said she was conducting for a class. At the same time, a second White student—actually another confederate working with the researchers—was stopped and asked to participate in the survey. Both students were then asked how Smith College should respond to anonymous racist notes actually sent

to four African American students in 1989. The confederate always answered first. In some cases, she condemned the notes; in others, she justified them.

Blanchard and his colleagues (1991:102–103) conclude that "hearing at least one other person express strongly antiracist opinions produced dramatically more strongly antiracist public reactions to racism than hearing others express equivocal opinions or opinions more accepting of racism." A second experiment demonstrated that when the confederate expressed sentiments justifying racism, subjects were much *less* likely to express antiracist opinions than were those who heard no one else offer opinions. In these experiments, social control (through the process of conformity) influenced people's attitudes, or at least the expression of those attitudes. In the next section, we will see that social control (through the process of obedience) can alter people's behavior.

Obedience to Authority

If ordered to do so, would you comply with an experimenter's instruction to give people increasingly painful electric shocks? Most people would say no; yet, the research of social psychologist Stanley Milgram (1963, 1975) suggests that most of us *will* obey such orders. In Milgram's words (1975:xi), "Behavior that is unthinkable in an individual . . . acting on his own may be executed without hesitation when carried out under orders."

Milgram placed advertisements in New Haven, Connecticut, newspapers to recruit subjects for what was announced as a learning experiment at Yale University. Participants included postal clerks, engineers, high school teachers, and laborers. They were told that the purpose of the research was to investigate the effects of punishment on learning. The experimenter, dressed in a gray technician's coat, explained that in each testing, one subject would be randomly selected as the "learner" while another would function as the "teacher." However, this lottery was rigged so that the "real" subject would always be the teacher while an associate of Milgram's served as the learner.

At this point, the learner's hand was strapped to an electric apparatus. The teacher was taken to an electronic "shock generator" with 30 lever switches. Each switch was labeled with graduated voltage designations from 15 to 450 volts. Before beginning the experiment, subjects were given sample shocks of 45 volts to convince them of the authenticity of the experiment.

The experimenter instructed the teacher to apply shocks of increasing voltage each time the learner gave an incorrect answer on a memory test. Teachers were told that "although the shocks can be extremely painful, they cause no permanent tissue damage." In reality, the learner did not receive any shocks.

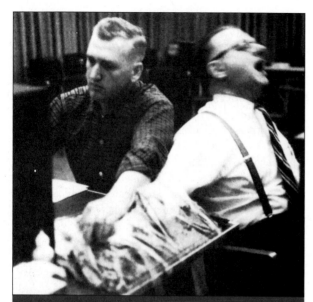

In one of Stanley Milgram's experiments, a supposed "victim" received an electric shock when his hand rested on a shock plate. At the 150-volt level, the "victim" would demand to be released, and would refuse to place his hand on the shock plate. The experimenter would then order the actual subject to force the "victim's" hand onto the plate, as shown in the photo. Though 40 percent of the true subjects stopped complying with Milgram at this point, 30 percent did force the "victim's" hand onto the shock plate, despite his pretended agony.

The learner deliberately gave incorrect answers and acted out a prearranged script. For example, at 150 volts, the learner would cry out, "Experimenter, get me out of here! I won't be in the experiment any more!" At 270 volts, the learner would scream in agony. When the shock reached 350 volts, the learner would fall silent. If the teacher wanted to stop the experiment, the experimenter would insist that the teacher continue, using such statements as "The experiment requires that you continue" and "You have no other choice; you *must* go on" (Milgram 1975:19–23).

The results of this unusual experiment stunned and dismayed Milgram and other social scientists. A sample of psychiatrists had predicted that virtually all subjects would refuse to shock innocent victims. In their view, only a "pathological fringe" of less than 2 percent would continue administering shocks up to the maximum level. Yet almost *two-thirds* of participants fell into the category of "obedient subjects."

Why did these subjects obey? Why were they willing to inflict seemingly painful shocks on innocent victims who had never done them any harm? There is no evidence that these subjects were unusually sadistic; few seemed to enjoy administering the shocks. Instead, in Milgram's

view, the key to obedience was the experimenter's social role as a "scientist" and "seeker of knowledge."

Milgram pointed out that in the modern industrial world, we are accustomed to submitting to impersonal authority figures whose status is indicated by a title (professor, lieutenant, doctor) or by a uniform (the technician's coat). The authority is viewed as larger and more important than the individual; consequently, the obedient individual shifts responsibility for his or her behavior to the authority figure. Milgram's subjects frequently stated, "If it were up to me, I would not have administered shocks." They saw themselves as merely doing their duty (Milgram 1975).

From an interactionist perspective, one important aspect of Milgram's findings is the fact that subjects in follow-up studies were less likely to inflict the supposed shocks as they were moved physically closer to their victims. Moreover, interactionists emphasize the effect of *incrementally* administering additional dosages of 15 volts. In effect, the experimenter negotiated with the teacher and convinced the teacher to continue inflicting higher levels of punishment. It is doubtful that anywhere near the two-thirds rate of obedience would have been reached had the experimenter told the teachers to administer 450 volts immediately to the learners (B. Allen 1978; Katovich 1987).

Milgram launched his experimental study of obedience to better understand the involvement of Germans in the annihilation of six million Jews and millions of other people during World War II. In an interview conducted long after the publication of his study, he suggested that "if a system of death camps were set up in the United States of the sort we had seen in Nazi Germany, one would be able to find sufficient personnel for those camps in any medium-sized American town" (CBS News 1979:7–8).

Informal and Formal Social Control

The sanctions used to encourage conformity and obedience—and to discourage violation of social norms—are carried out through informal and formal social control. As the term implies, people use *informal social control* casually to enforce norms. Examples of informal social control include smiles, laughter, raising an eyebrow, and ridicule (see Chapter 3).

In the United States and many other cultures, one common and yet controversial example of informal social control is parental use of corporal punishment. Adults often view spanking, slapping, or kicking children as a proper and necessary means of maintaining authority. Child development specialists counter that corporal punishment is inappropriate because it teaches children to solve problems through violence; they warn that slapping and spanking can escalate into more serious forms of abuse. Yet, despite a 1998 policy statement by the American Academy of Pediatrics that corporal punishment is not effective and can indeed be harmful, 59 percent of pediatricians support the use of corporal punishment, at least in certain situations. Our culture widely accepts this form of informal social control (Wolraich et al. 1998).

Sometimes informal methods of social control are not adequate to enforce conforming or obedient behavior. In those cases, **formal social control** is carried out by authorized agents, such as police officers, physicians, school administrators, employers, military officers, and managers of movie theaters. It can serve as a last resort when socialization and informal sanctions do not bring about desired behavior. An increasingly significant means of formal social control in the United States is to jail people. During the course of a year, 5.5 million adults undergo some form of correctional supervision—jail, prison, probation, or parole. Put another way, almost one out of every 30 adult Americans is subject to this very formal type of social control every year (Department of Justice 1999b).

Societies vary in deciding which behaviors will be subjected to formal social control and how severe the sanctions will be. In the nation of Singapore, chewing of gum is prohibited, feeding birds can lead to fines of up to $640, and there is even a $95 fine for failing to flush the toilet. Singapore deals with serious crimes especially severely. The death penalty is mandatory for murder, drug trafficking, and crimes committed with firearms. Japan has created a special prison for reckless drivers. While some are imprisoned for vehicular homicide, others serve prison time for drunken driving and fleeing the scene of an accident (S. Efron 1998; Elliott 1994).

Another controversial example of formal social control is the use of surveillance techniques. In 1992, police in Great Britain began to install closed-circuit television systems on "high streets" (the primary shopping and business areas of local communities) in an effort to reduce street crime. Within two years, 300 British towns had installed or made plans to install such surveillance cameras, and the use of public surveillance had spread to the United States. Supporters of surveillance believe that it will make the public feel more secure. Moreover, it can be cheaper to install and maintain cameras than to put more police officers on street patrol. For critics, however, the use of surveillance cameras brings to mind the grim, futuristic world presented by Britain's own George Orwell (1949) in his famous novel *1984*. In the world of *1984*, an all-seeing "Big Brother" represented an authoritarian government that watched people's every move and took immediate action against anyone who questioned the oppressive regime (Halbfinger 1998; Uttley 1993).

"Big Brother" is watching you! In an attempt to reduce street crime, the city of Baltimore installed a video surveillance camera in its business district. Some residents are comforted by the camera's presence, but critics charge that it is inappropriate to a free society.

Law and Society

Some norms are so important to a society they are formalized into laws controlling people's behavior. *Law* may be defined as governmental social control (Black 1995). Some laws, such as the prohibition against murder, are directed at all members of society. Others, such as fishing and hunting regulations, primarily affect particular categories of people. Still others govern the behavior of social institutions (corporate law and laws regarding the taxing of nonprofit enterprises).

Sociologists have become increasingly interested in the creation of laws as a social process. Laws are created in response to perceived needs for formal social control. Sociologists have sought to explain how and why such perceptions arise. In their view, law is not merely a static body of rules handed down from generation to generation.

Rather, it reflects continually changing standards of what is right and wrong, of how violations are to be determined, and of what sanctions are to be applied (Schur 1968).

Sociologists representing varying theoretical perspectives agree that the legal order reflects underlying social values. Therefore, the creation of criminal law can be a most controversial matter. Should it be against the law to employ illegal immigrants in a factory (see Chapter 10), to have an abortion (see Chapter 11), or to smoke on an airplane? Such issues have been bitterly debated because they require a choice among competing values. Not surprisingly, laws that are unpopular—such as the prohibition of alcohol under the Eighteenth Amendment in 1919 and the widespread establishment of a 55-mile-per-hour speed limit on highways—become difficult to enforce owing to lack of consensus supporting the norms.

Socialization is actually the primary source of conforming and obedient behavior, including obedience to law. Generally, it is not external pressure from a peer group or authority figure that makes us go along with social norms. Rather, we have internalized such norms as valid and desirable and are committed to observing them. In a profound sense, we want to see ourselves (and to be seen) as loyal, cooperative, responsible, and respectful of others. In the United States and other societies around the world, people are socialized both to want to belong and to fear being viewed as different or deviant.

Control theory suggests that our connection to members of society leads us to systematically conform to society's norms. According to sociologist Travis Hirschi and other control theorists, we are bonded to our family members, friends, and peers in a way that leads us to follow the mores and folkways of our society, while giving little conscious thought to whether we will be sanctioned if we fail to conform. Through socialization, we develop sufficient self-control that further pressure to obey social norms is unnecessary. While control theory does not effectively explain the rationale for every conforming act, it nevertheless reminds us that while the media may focus on crime and disorder, most members of most societies conform to and obey basic norms (Gottfredson and Hirschi 1990; Hirschi 1969).

Deviance

What Is Deviance?

For sociologists, the term *deviance* does not mean perversion or depravity. ***Deviance*** is behavior that violates the standards of conduct or expectations of a group or society (Wickman 1991:85). In the United States, alcoholics, compulsive gamblers, and the mentally ill would all be classified as deviants. Being late for class is categorized as a deviant act; the same is true of dressing too casually for a formal wedding. On the basis of the sociological definition, we are all deviant from time to time. Each of us violates common social norms in certain situations.

Is being overweight an example of deviance? In the United States and many other cultures, unrealistic standards of appearance and body image place a huge strain on people—especially on adult women and girls—based on how they look. Journalist Naomi Wolf (1992) has used the term *the beauty myth* to refer to an exaggerated ideal of beauty, beyond the reach of all but a few females, which has unfortunate consequences. In order to shed their "deviant" image and conform to (unrealistic) societal norms, many women and girls become consumed with adjusting their appearances. For example, in a *People* magazine "health" feature, a young actress stated that she knows it is

The current ideal of feminine beauty in the United States is the wafer-thin physique of a fashion model, epitomized by actress Calista Flockhart. In an effort to live up to the ideal, many young girls develop eating disorders.

Sanctions   Penalties and rewards for conduct concerning a social norm. (171)

Social constructionist perspective   An approach to deviance that emphasizes the role of culture in the creation of the deviant identity. (184)

Social control   The techniques and strategies for preventing deviant human behavior in any society. (171)

Societal-reaction approach   Another name for *labeling theory.* (184)

Stigma   A label used to devalue members of deviant social groups. (177)

Victimization surveys   Questionnaires or interviews used to determine whether people have been victims of crime. (190)

Victimless crimes   A term used by sociologists to describe the willing exchange among adults of widely desired, but illegal, goods and services. (187)

White-collar crimes   Crimes committed by affluent individuals or corporations in the course of their daily business activities. (186)

Additional Readings

BOOKS

Cole, David. 1999. *No Equal Justice: Race and Class in the American Criminal Justice System.* New York: The New Press. A readable account of the role of race and social class in the arrest and conviction of criminal suspects in the United States. Written from the point of view of a law professor.

Currie, Elliott. 1998. *Crime and Punishment in America.* New York: Henry Holt and Co. Sociologist Elliott Currie analyzes the increase in the prison population in light of changes in laws and sentencing procedures. He also considers some policy alternatives to the existing ways of handling criminal violence.

Finkenauer, James O., and Patricia W. Gavin. 1999. *Scared Straight: The Panacea Phenomenon Revisited.* Prospect Heights, IL: Waveland Press. A critical look at programs in which prisoners speak to juveniles in an effort to scare them away from crime. Drawing on data from both the United States and Norway, the authors find such programs have had little success, but remain immensely popular with the general public.

Gamson, Joshua. 1998. *Freaks Talk Back: Tabloid Talk Shows and Sexual Nonconformity.* Chicago: University of Chicago Press. A sociologist looks at the presentation of socially dysfunctional or stigmatized behaviors on television talk shows.

Kleinknecht, William. 1996. *The New Ethnic Mobs: The Changing Face of Organized Crime in America.* New York: Free Press. A journalist considers how organized crime in the United States has incorporated members of various racial and ethnic groups in leadership positions and has spread its illegal activities around the world.

JOURNALS

Among the journals that focus on issues of social control, deviance, and crime are *Crime and Delinquency* (founded in 1955), *Criminology* (1961), *Deviant Behavior* (1979), and *Law and Society Review* (1966).

Internet Connection

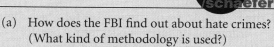

Note: While all the URLs listed were current as of the printing of this book, these sites often change. Please check our website (http://www.mhhe.com/schaefer) for updates.

1. Crime statistics are of vital importance to sociologists. Learn more about hate crimes and the way statistics on them are collected by visiting the FBI's website (**http://www.fbi.gov/**). Click on "Uniform Crime Reports" and then "Hate Crime Statistics: 1998."

   (a) How does the FBI find out about hate crimes? (What kind of methodology is used?)

   (b) How many bias-motivated criminal incidents were reported in the last year? How many of those crimes were motivated by race? By religion? By sexual orientation? By disability?

   (c) Looking at Table 1: Single Bias Incidents, which racial group had the most victims and which the least? Which religion had the most victims and which the least?

7-3 Police Power in Japan

It is midnight in Tokyo. Downtown streets are filled with pedestrians, strollers abound in the park, bicycles sit unchained on the street, many front doors are unlocked, and children under eight years of age are even seen riding alone on the subway. As much of a culture shock as this may be to a visitor from the United States, an additional surprise comes the next morning when virtually no crimes are reported. Tokyo has the lowest rates of murder, rape, robbery, and theft of any major city in the world. A comparison of crime rates in the United States and Japan per 100,000 inhabitants shows that the United States has about six times as many serious crimes. Yet Japan has fewer police officers per capita: 1 for every 557 residents, compared with 1 for every 357 residents in the United States.

Why is there so little crime in Japan? The country's low rate of unemployment and comparatively egalitarian distribution of wealth contribute to social cohesiveness and harmony. Moreover, the cultural values of the Japanese help to promote law-abiding behavior and cooperation with police officers. As part of their early socialization, children are encouraged to respect authority figures and place great value on self-discipline. Throughout Japan, there is persistent community disapproval of wrongdoing, and socially deviant behavior is not excused. Indeed, Japanese culture ostracizes offenders and demands that they confess and show remorse.

Still another factor contributing to low crime rates is the absolute trust that the Japanese have in the police. Once or twice a year, the police knock on every door in Japan to speak with residents or business owners about conditions in the building and neighborhood. Japanese people do not regard this as harassment, but rather as an example of the police taking a personal interest in their welfare.

Small police boxes, known as *kobans,* are located in all urban neighborhoods and are staffed by two officers at all times. The *koban* officials are the first line of police response to a crime or crisis, yet they more of-

> Tokyo has the lowest rates of murder, rape, robbery, and theft of any major city in the world.

ten function as sources of information about locations and addresses in Tokyo's confusing maze of streets. Consequently, the Japanese tend to look favorably on the *koban* system, rather than fearing its social control functions.

In recent years, the power of Japan's police has come under fire. International human rights groups criticize the police for such practices as conducting investigations without allowing suspects access to a lawyer and jailing suspects for up to 23 days without filing criminal charges. Yet there are no broad public demands for curtailing the power of the police.

In Japan, every urban neighborhood has a *koban,* or miniature police station. Officers who are stationed there can respond quickly to crimes, crises, and requests for directions from pedestrians.

Let's Discuss

1. Do you trust the police in your community as much as the Japanese do their police? Why or why not?
2. Would you like to live in a country like Japan, with its low crime rate, high degree of social cohesiveness, and respect for authority?

Sources: Kerbo and McKinstry 1998; Kristof 1995, 1996; Kyodo News International 1998b; Shelley 1992; Struck 2000.

forms of violence. When coupled with sharp disparities between poor and affluent citizens, significant unemployment, and substantial alcohol and drug abuse, all these factors combine to produce a climate conducive to crime.

There are, however, disturbing increases in violent crime evident in other Western societies. For example, crime in Russia has skyrocketed since the overthrow of Communist party rule (with its strict controls on guns and criminals) in 1991. Whereas there were fewer than 260 homicides in Moscow in 1978 and again in 1988, there are now more than 1,000 homicides per year. Organized crime has filled a power vacuum in Moscow since the end of communism; one result is that gangland shootouts and premeditated "contract hits" have become more common. Some prominent reformist politicians have been targeted as well. Russia is the only nation in the world that incarcerates a higher proportion of its citizens than the United States. Russia imprisons 580 per 100,000 of its adults on a typical day compared to 550 in the United States, fewer than 100 in Mexico or Britain, and only 16 in Greece (Currie 1998; Shinkai and Zvekic 1999).

Television shows that feature scenes like this arrest in Kansas City, shown on *Cops,* have become staples of prime-time television. The constant barrage of crime-related programming has distorted viewers' perceptions of the crime rate.

cross-national comparisons. Nevertheless, with some care, we can offer preliminary conclusions about how crime rates differ around the world.

During the 1980s and 1990s, violent crimes were much more common in the United States than in western Europe. Murders, rapes, and robberies were reported to the police at much higher rates in the United States. Yet the incidence of certain other types of crime appears to be higher elsewhere. For example, England, Italy, Australia, and New Zealand all have higher rates of car theft than in the United States, while the Czech Republic has a higher burglary rate. Brazil has a homicide rate twice that of the United States. In Box 7-3, we examine the reasons for Japan's overall low crime rate (Rotella 1999; Russell 1995).

Why are rates of violent crime so much higher in the United States? While there is no simple answer to this question, sociologist Elliot Currie (1985, 1998) has suggested that our society places greater emphasis on individual economic achievement than do other societies. At the same time, many observers have noted that the culture of the United States has long tolerated, if not condoned, many

groups have not always trusted law enforcement agencies, they have often refrained from contacting the police. Feminist sociologists and others have noted that many women do not report rape or spousal abuse out of fear that officials will regard the crime as their fault. Partly because of the deficiencies of official statistics, the National Crime Survey was initiated in 1972. The Bureau of Justice Statistics, in compiling this report, seeks information from law enforcement agencies but also interviews members of 45,400 households annually and asks if they have been victims of a specific set of crimes during the preceding year. In general, *victimization surveys* question ordinary people, not police officers, to learn how much crime occurs. As shown in Figure 7-3, data from these surveys reveal a fluctuating crime rate with significant declines in both the 1980s and 1990s.

Unfortunately, like other crime data, victimization surveys have particular limitations. They require first that victims understand what has happened to them and also that victims disclose such information to interviewers. Fraud, income tax evasion, and blackmail are examples of crimes that are unlikely to be reported in victimization studies. Nevertheless, 93 percent of all households have been willing to cooperate with investigators for the National Crime Survey (C. Ringel 1997).

International Crime Rates

It if is difficult to develop reliable crime data in the United States, it is even more difficult to make useful

FIGURE 7-3

Victimization Rates, 1973–1998

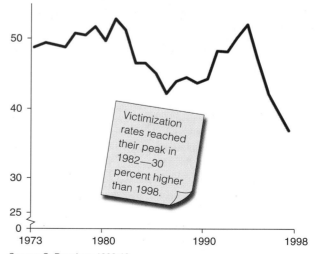

Source: C. Rennison 1999:10.

 **Eye on the Media** 7-2 Crime Wave on the Airways

 www.mhhe.com/schaefer

"A local man kills his wife and children, then shoots himself. . . . The latest on this gruesome crime tonight, on the ten o'clock news."

"Police drag a local pond in search of a missing schoolteacher. Who is the suspect they have taken into custody? Find out tonight on the late-night news."

"An elderly man bludgeoned to death on an early morning walk. D. A. Robert McNamara calls it a 'senseless crime.' Neighbors react, next on the evening news."

Night after night, the first story reported on the TV news is a violent crime. Was it always this way? Not according to the Center for Media and Public Affairs, which estimates that from 1992 to 1996, network coverage of murders alone rose more than sevenfold. While in 1992 the three major networks paid little attention to crime, over the next four years the topic became their number one concern. *Washington Post* columnist Howard Kurtz has dubbed the trend toward increased crime coverage "an unprecedented electronic crime wave."

Not only are TV news shows devoting more airtime to violent crimes; they tend to stress the sensational aspects of these events. Camera crews focus on the crime scene—police barricades, flashing lights, and bodies being removed to the dismay of stunned onlookers. Reporters dutifully interview the neighbors, who confide that they are concerned about their families' safety, and have become more careful about locking their doors at night. Less footage is devoted to the outcome of criminal investigations—the apprehension of suspects and the trial, conviction, and sentencing of those found guilty.

Other types of television coverage reinforce the grisly impressions created by the evening news. Crime shows like *Cops* and *America's Most Wanted* are among the most popular on TV, staples of prime-time Saturday night. Viewers seem to have an insatiable appetite for these shows, which feature file footage from dashboard-mounted video cameras in police cruisers, dramatizations of actual crimes, and appeals for information on the whereabouts of suspects. Televised trials, most notably that of O. J. Simpson, have held viewers spellbound for months at a time. And TV dramas like *NYPD Blue* feature violent crimes in almost every episode. Little wonder that makers of

> From 1992 to 1996, network coverage of murders alone rose more than sevenfold.

home security devices find television a good medium in which to advertise their wares.

This constant barrage of crime-related programming seems to have had an effect on public perceptions of crime. In a 1981 survey, 44 percent of Americans interviewed said they felt "very safe" when walking alone at night in their neighborhoods. But by 1996, only 29 percent of those surveyed responded the same way to that question. In fact, over half the respondents to another survey said they were afraid to walk alone at night in certain places close to home. The fear of being victimized is most likely related to TV viewing. According to researchers at Texas A&M University and Sam Houston State University, two-thirds of Americans

they questioned said they got most of their information on crime from TV.

The public's heightened fear of crime runs counter to actual crime statistics, which show that crime has been decreasing over the last decade. Between 1993 and 1996, for instance, the murder rate declined 20 percent. Analysts at the Center for Media and Public Affairs blame the TV networks for the disparity between reality and public perceptions. "Journalists decided crime was news—and they made it a public concern and a political concern," explains Bob Lichter. TV executives deny they have made a conscious decision to play up crime. "Are we going out there trying to fill the newscast with crime stories? That's not true," protests Bill Wheatley of NBC News. "We do not sit around and say, 'Hey, maybe we'll get a bigger audience if we show them more crime,' " says Jeff Fager of *CBS Evening News*. But Paul Friedman of *World News Tonight* is more frank. "You worry when the other guy increased his audience because he paid more attention to the Simpson case than you did, so the next time a big sensational murder comes along, you second-guess yourself about how much you should be covering it."

Let's Discuss

1. Do TV stations in your area concentrate on violent crime in their news reports? In what ways?
2. How safe do you feel in your own home and neighborhood? Do you know anyone who has been the victim of a violent crime?

Sources: S. Allan 1999; Fishman and Cavender 1998; P. Johnson 1997; R. Morin 1997; Schiraldi 1999.

committing crimes outside the prison population. It remains to be seen whether this pattern will continue, but even with current declines, reported crimes remain well above those of other nations and exceed the reported rates in the United States of just 20 years earlier.

While the crime rates have declined, the people's fear of crime seems to have increased. A 1999 survey showed that only 2 percent of adult Americans believe that violent

crime rates are decreasing significantly (R. Morin 1999). Box 7-2 discusses the mass media's portrayal of crime and its relationship to the public perception that crime is a pressing national problem.

Sociologists have several ways of measuring crime. Historically, they have relied on official statistics, but underreporting has always been a problem with such measures. Because members of racial and ethnic minority

(d) In what kinds of places do hate crimes occur? What are Group I cities and Group A offenses? Were any hate crimes reported in the state, city, or town where you live?

(e) Did any of these statistics surprise you? Why or why not?

(f) What are some of the limitations of using government-collected data such as the Uniform Crime Reports?

2. Breaking news about the application of the death penalty, as well as the debate surrounding it, can be found by logging on to **http://headlines.yahoo.com/ Full_Coverage/US/Death_Penalty.**

(a) Has the death penalty been used within the last month, or will it be used within the next month? If so, what were the circumstances under which the penalty was imposed?

(b) Why has the state of Texas been accelerating its use of the death penalty in recent years?

(c) Who is Mumia Abu-Jamal?

(d) Using the links provided at this website, learn about the history of the death penalty. Which Supreme Court case suspended the use of the death penalty in the 1970s? What were some of the reasons for the Court's decision?

(e) What are some of the arguments made on both sides of the death penalty debate? What evidence is cited to support each side?

(f) What is your own stance regarding the death penalty? What facts can you cite to support your position?

PART THREE

SOCIAL INEQUALITY

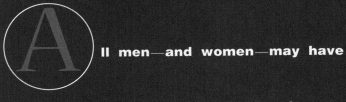**ll men—and women—may have**

been created equal but they don't live in perfect equality. Part Three focuses

on the structure and processes of social inequality. Chapter 8 examines the

important sociological concepts of stratification and social mobility, as well

as inequality based on social class, with special emphasis on the United

States. In Chapter 9, we consider stratification and social mobility abroad and

give particular attention to the unequal relationship between the world's

industrialized and developing nations. Chapter 10 deals with issues of preju-

dice and discrimination against racial and ethnic groups. Chapter 11 dis-

cusses inequality based on gender and the position of women as an oppressed

majority. Chapter 12 analyzes the aging process from a sociological perspec-

tive and examines inequality based on age.

CHAPTER 8

STRATIFICATION AND SOCIAL MOBILITY IN THE UNITED STATES

presents **WorkWorld**™

Internet & High-Tech Career Expo

Real Jobs.   **Real Companies.**   **Real Easy.**

Before entering:

1

Select Location

2 Choose:
 Exhibitor
● Opportunity Seeker

► **ENTER**

As the twenty-first century begins, high-tech jobs symbolize unlimited opportunity. But these opportunities do not exist for millions of less skilled people. Even the ability to do job searches online, as reflected in this website for Hotjobs.com, is very limited for these people.

I n the early 1990s, the McDonald's Corporation launched a television ad campaign featuring a young black man named Calvin, who was portrayed sitting atop a Brooklyn stoop in his Golden Arches uniform while his friends down the sidewalk passed by, giving him a hard time about holding down a "McJob." After brushing off their teasing with good humor, Calvin is approached furtively by one young black man who asks, *sotto voce,* whether Calvin might help him get a job too. He allows that he could use some earnings and that despite the ragging he has just given Calvin, he thinks the uniform is really pretty cool—or at least that having a job is pretty cool. . . .

Americans have always been committed to the moral maxim that work defines the person. We carry around in our heads a rough tally that tells us what kinds of jobs are worthy of respect and what kinds are to be disdained, a pyramid organized by the income a job carries, the sort of credentials it takes to secure a particular position, the qualities of an occupation's incumbents—and we use this system of stratification (ruthlessly at times) to boost the status of some and humiliate others. . . .

Kimberly, a 20-year-old African American woman, began working at Burger Barn when she was 16 and discovered firsthand how her "friends" would turn on her for taking a low-wage job. Fortunately, she found a good friend at work who steadied her with a piece of advice:

Say it's a job. You are making money. Right? Don't care what nobody say. You know? If they don't like it, too bad. They sitting on the corner doing what they are doing. You got to work making money. You know? Don't bother with what anybody has to say about it.

Kim's friend and adviser, a Burger Barn veteran who had long since come to terms with the insults of his peers, called upon a general status hierarchy that places the working above the nonworking as a bulwark against the slights. The advice Kim gleaned from her friend and her manager made a big difference in helping her to see that she deserves her dignity.

Kids come in here . . . they don't have enough money. I'll be like, "You don't have enough money; you can't get [the food you ordered]." One night this little boy came in here and cursed me out. He [said], "That's why you are working at [Burger Barn]. You can't get a better job. . . ." I was upset and everything. I started crying. [My manager] was like, "Kim, don't bother with him. I'm saying, *you got a job.* You know. It is a *job.*" (Newman 1999:86, 102). ■

Contrary to popular belief, the majority of poor people in the United States do work. They just don't earn enough to lift themselves out of poverty. And they are very often overlooked by social scientists and policymakers, who tend to focus on the jobless poor in addressing issues of poverty. Katherine Newman, an anthropologist and professor of urban studies at Harvard University, aimed to counteract this neglect and misapprehension with her poignant look at the everyday life of the working poor, *No Shame in My Game.* The working poor—Black, White, Latino—are, in fact, a significant segment of the labor force.

Newman and her researchers followed the lives of 200 workers in large fast-food restaurants in New York City's Harlem over the course of a year and a half. They also tracked what happened to 100 unsuccessful job-seekers in the community. Their research techniques included interviews, visits to homes and schools, observation through on-site work at the restaurants, and personal diaries kept by the subjects of the study. The study threw light on the plight of the working poor—the struggle to get a job and to keep it, the stigma of taking low-level jobs, the long hours for low pay, the conflicting demands of family and school—and put a human face on this largely "invisible" population. In the course of doing so, Newman revealed layers of hierarchy even within the lower social class.

Ever since people first began to speculate about the nature of human society, their attention has been drawn to the differences between individuals and groups within any society. The term *social inequality* describes a condition in which members of a society have different amounts of wealth, prestige, or power. Some degree of social inequality characterizes every society.

When a system of social inequality is based on a hierarchy of groups, sociologists refer to it as *stratification:* a structured ranking of entire groups of people that perpetuates unequal economic rewards and power in a society. These unequal rewards are evident not only in the distribution of wealth and income, but even in the distressing mortality rates of impoverished communities. Stratification involves the ways in which one generation passes on social inequalities to the next, thereby producing groups of people arranged in rank order from low to high.

Stratification is a crucial subject of sociological investigation because of its pervasive influence on human interactions and institutions. It inevitably results in social inequality because certain groups of people stand higher in social rankings, control scarce resources, wield power, and receive special treatment. As we will see in this chapter, the consequences of stratification are evident in the unequal distribution of wealth and income within industrial societies. The term *income* refers to salaries and wages. By contrast, *wealth* is an inclusive term encompassing all of a person's material assets, including land, stocks, and other types of property.

This chapter focuses on the unequal distribution of socially valued rewards within human societies. First, we will examine three general systems of stratification. We will pay particular attention to Karl Marx's theories of class and to Max Weber's analysis of the components of stratification. In addition, we will consider and compare functionalist and conflict theorists' explanations for the existence of stratification.

The second part of the chapter will explain how sociologists measure social class. We will examine the consequences of stratification in terms of wealth and income, health, educational opportunities, and other aspects of life. In the third part of the chapter, the movement of individuals up and down the social hierarchies of the United States will be examined. Finally, in the social policy section, we will address the issue of welfare reform in North America and Europe. ■

Understanding Stratification

Systems of Stratification

Look at the three general systems of stratification examined here—slavery, castes, and social classes—as ideal types useful for purposes of analysis. Any stratification system may include elements of more than one type. For example, prior to the Civil War, you could find in the southern states of the United States social classes dividing Whites as well as the institutionalized enslavement of Blacks.

To understand these systems better, it may be helpful to review the distinction between *achieved status* and *ascribed status,* described in Chapter 5. **Ascribed status** is a social position "assigned" to a person without regard for that person's pp. 121–122 unique characteristics or talents. By contrast, **achieved status** is a social position attained by a person largely through his or her own effort. The two are closely linked. The nation's most affluent families generally inherit wealth and status, while many members of racial and ethnic minorities inherit disadvantaged status. Age and gender, as well, are ascribed statuses that influence a person's wealth and social position.

Slavery

The most extreme form of legalized social inequality for individuals or groups is *slavery*. What distinguishes this oppressive system of stratification is that enslaved individuals are *owned* by other people. They treat these human beings as property, just as if they were household pets or appliances.

Slavery, an ascribed status, has varied in the way it has been practiced. In ancient Greece, the main source of slaves consisted of captives of war and piracy. Although succeeding generations could inherit slave status, it was not necessarily permanent. A person's status might change depending on which city-state happened to triumph in a military conflict. In effect, all citizens had the potential of becoming slaves or of being granted freedom, depending on the circumstances of history. By contrast, in the United States and Latin America, racial and legal barriers were established to prevent the freeing of slaves. As Box 8-1 shows, millions of people around the world continue to live as slaves.

Castes

Castes are hereditary systems of rank, usually religiously dictated, that tend to be fixed and immobile. The caste system is generally associated with Hinduism in India and other countries. In India there are four major castes, called *varnas*. A fifth category of outcastes, referred to as *untouchables,* is considered to be so lowly and unclean as to have no place within this system of stratification. There are also many minor castes. Caste membership is an ascribed status (at birth, children automatically assume the same position as their parents). Each caste is quite sharply defined, and members are expected to marry within that caste.

Caste membership generally determines one's occupation or role as a religious functionary. An example of a lower caste in India is the *Dons,* whose main work is the undesirable job of cremating bodies. The caste system promotes a remarkable degree of differentiation. Thus, the single caste of chauffeurs has been split into two separate subcastes: drivers of luxury cars have a higher status than drivers of economy cars.

In recent decades, industrialization and urbanization have taken their toll on India's rigid caste system. Many villagers have moved to urban areas where their low-caste status is unknown. Schools, hospitals, factories, and pub-

Jacob Lawrence's painting, *Harriet Tubman* Series No. 9, graphically illustrates the torment of slavery as once practiced in the United States. Slavery is the most extreme form of legalized social inequality.

lic transportation facilitate contacts between different castes that were previously avoided at all costs. In addition, the government has tried to reform the caste system. India's constitution, adopted in 1950, includes a provision abolishing discrimination against untouchables, who had traditionally been excluded from temples, schools, and most forms of employment. Yet the caste system prevails, and its impact is now evident in electoral politics, as various political parties compete for the support of frustrated untouchable voters who constitute one-third of India's electorate. For the first time India has someone from an untouchable background serving in the symbolic but high-status position of president. Meanwhile, however, dozens of low-caste people continue to be killed for overstepping their lowly status in life (C. Dugger 1999; U. Schmetzer 1999).

Social Classes

A *class system* is a social ranking based primarily on economic position in which achieved characteristics can influence social mobility. In contrast to slavery and caste systems, the boundaries between classes are imprecisely defined, and one can move from one stratum, or level, of society to another. Yet class systems maintain stable stratification hierarchies and patterns of class divisions, and they too are marked by unequal distribution of wealth and power.

Income inequality is a basic characteristic of a class system. In 1998, the median household income in the United States was $38,885. In other words, half of all households had higher incomes in that year and half had lower incomes. Yet this fact may not fully convey the in-

Sociology in the Global Community

www.mhhe.com/schaefer

8-1 Slavery in the Twenty-first Century

More than 100 million people around the world were still enslaved at the end of the twentieth century, according to estimates by Britain's Anti-Slavery International, the world's oldest human rights organization. And yet the 1948 Universal Declaration of Human Rights, which is supposedly binding on all members of the United Nations, holds that "No one shall be held in slavery or servitude; slavery and the slave trade shall be prohibited in all their forms" (Masland 1992:30, 32).

The United States considers any person a slave who is unable to withdraw his or her labor voluntarily from an employer. In many parts of the world, however, bonded laborers are imprisoned in virtual lifetime employment as they struggle to repay small debts. Indeed, the Bonded Labor Liberation Front has found workers paying off debts that are eight *centuries* old.

The Swiss-based human rights group Christian Solidarity International has focused worldwide attention on the plight of slaves in the West African nation of Sudan. The organization solicits funds and uses them to buy slaves their freedom—at about $50 a slave. Several thousand members of the Dinka tribe have now regained their freedom that way. Some people believe that this program only encourages the Sudanese to enter the slave trade in order to receive payments, but the entire situation dramatically shows that slavery in the world did not end in the 1800s.

While contemporary slavery may be most obvious in Third World countries, it also afflicts the industrialized nations of the West. Throughout Europe, guest workers and maids are employed by masters who hold

> More than 100 million people around the world were still enslaved at the end of the century.

their passports, subject them to degrading working conditions, and threaten them with deportation if they protest. Similar tactics are used to essentially imprison young women from Eastern Europe who have been brought (through deceptive promises) to work in the sex industries of Belgium, France, Germany, Greece, the Netherlands, and Switzerland.

Within the United States, illegal immigrants are forced to labor for years under terrible conditions to pay off debts or out of fear of being turned over to immigration authorities. In New York City, dozens of deaf Mexican immigrants were forced to peddle trinkets in the subways and streets. In Florida and South Carolina, young women were lured from overseas with offers of landscaping jobs only to find themselves prostitutes in agricultural migrant camps. In Los Angeles, Thai immigrants were forced to work in a sweatshop an average of 84 hours a week at the meager wage of $1.60 per hour, supposedly to pay off debts as high as $30,000 to the smugglers who brought them into California. This series of events finally led in 1998 to the creation of a federal task force to investigate and prosecute modern-day slavery in the United States.

Let's Discuss

1. Why are many bonded laborers around the world in the position of slaves?
2. If you were in the position of an illegal immigrant working for what amounts to slave labor, what would you do? Should those who seek the help of the authorities be deported?

Sources: Bales 1999; I. Fisher 1999; McDonnell and Becker 1996; Navarro 1998; *New York Times* 1997; Scheer 1998; C. Tyler 1991.

---

come disparities in our society. In 1994, about 70,000 tax returns reported incomes in excess of $1 million. At the same time, about 15 million households reported incomes under $5,000. The people with the highest incomes, generally those heading private companies, earn well above even affluent wage earners. In Figure 8-1, we see how much better heads of U.S. corporations are reimbursed than CEOs (chief executive officers) in other industrial countries (Bureau of the Census 1997a:344; 1999 inc:v).

Sociologist Daniel Rossides (1997) has conceptualized the class system of the United States using a five-class model: the upper class, the upper-middle class, the lower-middle class, the working class, and the lower class. While the lines separating social classes in his model are not so sharp as the divisions between castes, he shows that mem-

bers of the five classes differ significantly in ways other than income level.

Rossides categorized about 1 to 2 percent of the people of the United States as *upper-class,* a group limited to the very wealthy. These people associate in exclusive clubs and social circles. By contrast, the *lower class,* consisting of approximately 20 to 25 percent of the population, disproportionately consists of Blacks, Hispanics, single mothers with dependent children, and people who cannot find regular work or must make do with low-paying work. This class lacks both wealth and income and is too weak politically to exercise significant power.

Both of these classes, at opposite ends of the nation's social hierarchy, reflect the importance of ascribed status and achieved status. Ascribed statuses such as race clearly

FIGURE 8-1

Around the World: What's a CEO Worth?

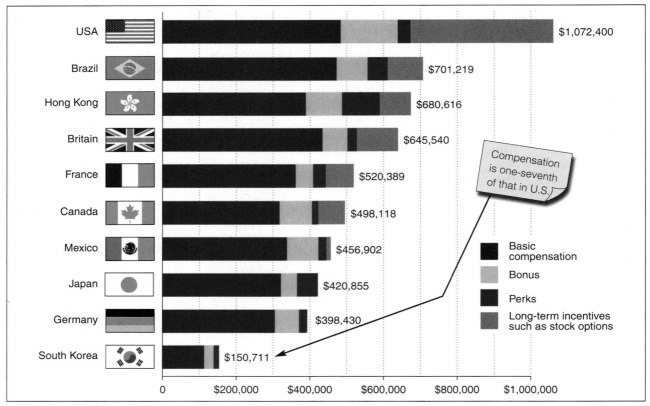

Note: The average annual pay package of the chief executive officer (CEO) of an industrial company with annual revenues of $250 million to $500 million in 10 countries. Figures are from April 1998 and are not weighted to compensate for different costs of living or levels of taxation.

Source: Towers Perrin in A. Bryant 1999:Section 4, p. 1.

influence a person's wealth and social position. And sociologist Richard Jenkins (1991) has researched how the ascribed status of being disabled marginalizes a person in the labor market of the United States. People with disabilities are particularly vulnerable to unemployment, are often poorly paid, and in many cases are on the lower end of occupational ladders. Regardless of their actual performance on the job, the disabled are stigmatized as not "earning their keep." Such are the effects of ascribed status.

Sandwiched between the upper and lower classes in Rossides's model are the upper-middle class, the lower-middle class, and the working class. The *upper-middle class,* numbering about 10 to 15 percent of the population, is composed of professionals such as doctors, lawyers, and architects. They participate extensively in politics and take leadership roles in voluntary associations. The *lower-middle class,* which accounts for approximately 30 to 35 percent of the population, includes less affluent professionals (such as elementary school teachers

and nurses), owners of small businesses, and a sizable number of clerical workers. While not all members of this varied class hold degrees from a college, they share the goal of sending their children there.

Rossides describes the *working class*—about 40 to 45 percent of the population—as people holding regular manual or blue-collar jobs. Certain members of this class, such as electricians, may have higher incomes than people in the lower-middle class. Yet, even if they have achieved some degree of economic security, they tend to identify with manual workers and their long history of involvement in the labor movement of the United States. Of Rossides's five classes, the working class is noticeably declining in size. In the economy of the United States, service and technical jobs are replacing positions involved in the actual manufacturing or transportation of goods.

Social class is one of the independent or explanatory variables most frequently used by social scientists to shed light on social issues. In later chapters, we will analyze the relationships between social class and divorce patterns (Chapter 13), religious behavior (Chapter 14), and formal schooling (Chapter 15), as well as other relationships in which social class is a variable.

Perspectives on Stratification

Sociologists have engaged in heated debates and reached varying conclusions about stratification and social inequality. No theorist stressed the significance of class for society—and for social change—more strongly than Karl Marx. Marx viewed class differentiation as the crucial determinant of social, economic, and political inequality. By contrast, Max Weber questioned Marx's emphasis on the overriding importance of the economic sector and argued that stratification should be viewed as having many dimensions.

Karl Marx's View of Class Differentiation

Sociologist Leonard Beeghley (1978:1) aptly noted that "Karl Marx was both a revolutionary and a social scientist." Marx was concerned with stratification in all types of human societies, beginning with primitive agricultural tribes and continuing into feudalism. But his main focus was on the effects of economic inequality on all aspects of nineteenth-century Europe. The plight of the working class made him feel that it was imperative to strive for changes in the class structure of society.

In Marx's view, social relations during any period of history depend on who controls the primary mode of economic production, such as land or factories. Differential access to scarce resources shapes the relationship between groups. Thus, under the feudal estate system, most production was agricultural, and the land was owned by the nobility. Peasants had little choice but to work according to terms dictated by those who owned the land.

Using this type of analysis, Marx examined social relations within *capitalism*—an economic system in which the means of production are largely in private hands and the main incentive for economic activity is the accumulation of profits (Rosenberg 1991). Marx focused on the two classes that began to emerge as the estate system declined—the bourgeoisie and the proletariat. The *bourgeoisie,* or capitalist class, owns the means of production, such as factories and machinery, while the *proletariat* is the working class. In capitalist societies, the members of the bourgeoisie maximize profit in competition with other firms. In the process, they exploit workers, who must exchange their labor for subsistence wages. In Marx's view, members of each class share a distinctive culture. He was most interested in the culture of the proletariat, but he also examined the ideology of the bourgeoisie, through which it justifies its dominance over workers.

According to Marx, exploitation of the proletariat will inevitably lead to the destruction of the capitalist system because the workers will revolt. But, first, the working class must develop *class consciousness*—a subjective awareness of common vested interests and the need for collective political action to bring about social change. Workers must often overcome what Marx termed *false consciousness,* or an attitude held by members of a class that does not accurately reflect its objective position. A worker with false consciousness may adopt an individualistic viewpoint toward capitalist exploitation ("*I* am being exploited by *my* boss"). By contrast, the class-conscious worker realizes that *all* workers are being exploited by the bourgeoisie and have a common stake in revolution (Vanneman and Cannon 1987).

For Karl Marx, class consciousness is part of a collective process whereby the proletariat comes to identify the bourgeoisie as the source of its oppression. Revolutionary leaders will guide the working class in its class struggle. Ultimately, the proletariat will overthrow the rule of the bourgeoisie and the government (which Marx saw as representing the interests of capitalists) and will eliminate private ownership of the means of production. In his rather utopian view, classes and oppression will cease to exist in the postrevolutionary workers' state.

How accurate were Marx's predictions? He failed to anticipate the emergence of labor unions, whose power in collective bargaining weakens the stranglehold that capitalists maintain over workers. Moreover, as contemporary conflict theorists note, he did not foresee the extent to which political liberties and relative prosperity could contribute to "false consciousness." Many people have come to view themselves as individuals striving for improvement within "free" societies with substantial mobility—rather than as downtrodden members of social classes facing a collective fate. Finally, Marx did not predict that Communist party rule would be established and later overthrown in the former Soviet Union and throughout Eastern Europe. Still, the Marxist approach to the study of class is useful in stressing the importance of stratification as a determinant of social behavior and the fundamental separation in many societies between two distinct groups, the rich and the poor.

Max Weber's View of Stratification

Unlike Karl Marx, Max Weber insisted that no single characteristic (such as class) totally defines a person's position within the stratification system. Instead, writing in 1916, he identified three analytically distinct components of stratification: class, status, and power (Gerth and Mills 1958).

Weber used the term *class* to refer to people who have a similar level of wealth and income. For example, certain workers in the United States try to support their families through jobs that pay the federal minimum wage (such as the working poor described in the chapter opener). According to Weber's definition, these wage earners constitute a class because they have the same economic position and fate. While Weber agreed with Marx on the importance of the economic dimension of stratification, he argued that the actions of individuals and groups could not be understood *solely* in economic terms.

Weber used the term ***status group*** to refer to people who rank the same in prestige or lifestyle. An individual gains status through membership in a desirable group, such as the medical profession. But status is not the same as economic class standing. In our culture, a successful pickpocket may be in the same income class as a college professor. Yet the thief is widely regarded as a member of a low-status group, while the professor holds high status.

For Weber, the third major component of stratification reflects a political dimension. ***Power*** is the ability to exercise one's will over others. In the United States, power stems from membership in particularly influential groups, such as corporate boards of directors, government bodies, and interest groups. Conflict theorists generally agree that two major sources of power—big business and government—are closely interrelated (see Chapters 16 and 17).

In Weber's view, then, each of us has not one rank in society but three. Our position in a stratification system reflects some combination of class, status, and power. Each factor influences the other two, and in fact the rankings on these three dimensions often tend to coincide. John F. Kennedy came from an extremely wealthy family, attended exclusive preparatory schools, graduated from Harvard University, and went on to become president of the United States. Like Kennedy, many people from affluent backgrounds achieve impressive status and power.

At the same time, these dimensions of stratification may operate somewhat independently in determining a person's position. Harry S Truman was a hat maker in his native town of Independence, Missouri, but he used a political power base to work his way up to the presidency of the United States. A widely published poet may achieve high status while earning a relatively modest income. Successful professional athletes have little power but enjoy a relatively high position in terms of class and status. To understand the workings of a culture more fully, sociologists must carefully evaluate the ways in which it distributes its most valued rewards, including wealth and income, status, and power (Duberman 1976; Gerth and Mills 1958).

Is Stratification Universal?

Must some members of society receive greater rewards than others? Do people need to feel socially and economically superior to others? Can social life be organized

How does it feel sitting in the chairperson's seat? In the United States a great deal of power resides with corporate boards of directors.

without structured inequality? These questions have been debated for centuries, especially among political activists. Utopian socialists, religious minorities, and members of recent countercultures have all attempted to establish communities that, to some extent or other, would abolish inequality in social relationships.

Social science research has found that inequality exists in all societies—even the simplest. For example, when anthropologist Gunnar Landtman (1968, original edition 1938) studied the Kiwai Papuans of New Guinea, he initially noticed little differentiation among them. Every man in the village did the same work and lived in similar housing. However, on closer inspection, Landtman observed that certain Papuans—the men who were warriors, harpooners, and sorcerers—were described as "a little more high" than others. By contrast, villagers who were female, unemployed, or unmarried were considered "down a little bit" and were barred from owning land.

Stratification is universal in that all societies maintain some form of differentiation among members. Depending on its values, a society may assign people to distinctive ranks based on their religious knowledge, skill in hunting, beauty, trading expertise, or ability to provide health care. But why has such inequality developed in human societies? And how much differentiation among people, if any, is actually essential?

Functionalist and conflict sociologists offer contrasting explanations for the existence and necessity of social stratification. Functionalists maintain that a differential system of rewards and punishments is necessary for the efficient operation of society. Conflict theorists argue that competition for scarce resources results in significant political, economic, and social inequality.

Functionalist View

Would people go to school for many years to become physicians if they could make as much money and gain as much respect working as street cleaners? Functionalists say no, which is partly why they believe that a stratified society is universal.

In the view of Kingsley Davis and Wilbert Moore (1945), society must distribute its members among a variety of social positions. It must not only make sure that these positions are filled but also see that they are staffed by people with the appropriate talents and abilities. Rewards, including money and prestige, are based on the importance of a position and the relative scarcity of qualified personnel. Yet this assessment often devalues work performed by certain segments of society, such as women's work as homemakers or occupations traditionally filled by women or low-status work in fast-food outlets.

Davis and Moore argue that stratification is universal and that social inequality is necessary so that people will be motivated to fill functionally important positions. But, critics say, unequal rewards are not the only means of encouraging people to fill critical positions and occupations. Personal pleasure, intrinsic satisfaction, and value orientations also motivate people to enter particular careers. Functionalists agree but note that society must use some type of reward to motivate people to enter unpleasant or dangerous jobs, as well as jobs that require a long training period. This response does not justify stratification systems in which status is largely inherited, such as slave or caste societies. Similarly, it is difficult to explain the high salaries our society offers to professional athletes or entertainers on the basis of how critical these jobs are to the survival of society (R. Collins 1975; Kerbo 1996; Tumin 1953, 1985).

Even if stratification is inevitable, the functionalist explanation for differential rewards does not explain the wide disparity between the rich and the poor. Critics of the functionalist approach point out that the richest 10 percent of households account for 20 percent of the nation's income in Sweden, 25 percent in France, and 30 percent in the United States. In their view, the level of income inequality found in contemporary industrial societies cannot be defended—even though these societies have a legitimate need to fill certain key occupations (World Bank 2000:238–239).

Conflict View

The writings of Karl Marx are at the heart of conflict theory, as we saw in Chapter 1. Marx p. 12 viewed history as a continuous struggle between the oppressors and the oppressed that would ultimately culminate in an egalitarian, classless society. In terms of stratification, he argued that the dominant class under capitalism—the bourgeoisie—manipulated the economic and political systems in order to maintain control over the exploited proletariat. Marx did not believe that stratification was inevitable, but he did see inequality and oppression as inherent in capitalism (E. Wright et al. 1982).

Like Marx, contemporary conflict theorists believe that human beings are prone to conflict over such scarce resources as wealth, status, and power. However, where Marx focused primarily on class conflict, more recent theorists have extended this analysis to include conflicts based on gender, race, age, and other dimensions. British sociologist Ralf Dahrendorf is one of the most influential contributors to the conflict approach.

Dahrendorf (1959) modified Marx's analysis of capitalist society to apply to *modern* capitalist societies. For Dahrendorf, social classes are groups of people who share common interests resulting from their authority relationships. In identifying the most powerful groups in society, he includes not only the bourgeoisie—the owners of the means of production—but also the managers of industry, legislators, the judiciary, heads of the government bureaucracy, and others. In that respect, Dahrendorf has merged Marx's emphasis on class conflict with Weber's recognition that power is an important element of stratification (Cuff et al. 1990).

Conflict theorists, including Dahrendorf, contend that the powerful of today, like the bourgeoisie of Marx's time, want society to run smoothly so that they can enjoy their privileged positions. Because the status quo suits those with wealth, status, and power, they have a clear interest in preventing, minimizing, or controlling societal conflict.

One way for the powerful to maintain the status quo is to define and disseminate the society's dominant ideology. In Chapter 3, we noted that the term p. 76 **dominant ideology** describes a set of cultural beliefs and practices that helps to maintain powerful social, economic, and political interests. For Karl Marx, the dominant ideology in a capitalist society serves the interests of the ruling class. From a conflict perspective, the social significance of the dominant ideology is that a society's most powerful groups and institutions not only control wealth and property, but, even more important, they control the means of producing beliefs about reality through religion, education, and the media (Abercrombie et al. 1980, 1990; Robertson 1988).

The powerful, such as leaders of government, also use limited social reforms to buy off the oppressed and reduce the danger of challenges to their dominance. For example, minimum wage laws and unemployment compensation unquestionably give some valuable assistance to needy men and women. Yet these reforms also serve to pacify those who might otherwise rebel. Of course, in the view of conflict theorists, such maneuvers can never entirely eliminate conflict, since workers will continue to demand equality, and the powerful will not give up their control of society.

Conflict theorists see stratification as a major source of societal tension and conflict. They do not agree with Davis and Moore that stratification is functional for a society or that it serves as a source of stability. Rather, conflict sociologists argue that stratification will inevitably lead to instability and to social change (R. Collins 1975; L. Coser 1977).

Lenski's Viewpoint

Let's return to the question posed earlier—"Is stratification universal?"—and consider the sociological response. Some form of differentiation is found in every culture, from the most primitive to the most advanced industrial societies of our time. Sociologist Gerhard Lenski, in his

p. 132 ← sociocultural evolution approach (refer back to Chapter 5), described how economic systems change as their level of technology becomes more complex, beginning with hunting and gathering and culminating eventually with industrial society. In subsistence-based, hunting-and-gathering societies, people focus on survival. While inequality and differentiation are evident, a stratification system based on social class does not emerge because there is no real wealth to be claimed.

As a society advances in technology, it becomes capable of producing a considerable surplus of goods. The emergence of surplus resources greatly expands the possibilities for inequality in status, influence, and power and allows a well-defined rigid social class system to develop. In order to minimize strikes, slowdowns, and industrial sabotage, the elites may share a portion of the economic surplus with the lower classes, but not enough to reduce their power and privilege.

As Lenski argued, the allocation of surplus goods and services controlled by those with wealth, status, and power reinforces the social inequality that accompanies stratification systems. While this reward system may once have served the overall purposes of society, as functionalists con-

tend, the same cannot be said for the large disparities separating the haves from the have-nots in current societies. In contemporary industrial society, the degree of social and economic inequality far exceeds the need to provide for goods and services (Lenski 1966; Nolan and Lenski 1999).

Stratification by Social Class

Measuring Social Class

We're continually assessing how wealthy people are by looking at the cars they drive, the houses they live in, the clothes they wear, and so on. Yet it is not so easy to locate an individual within our social hierarchies as it would be in slavery or caste systems of stratification. To determine someone's class position, sociologists generally rely on the objective method.

The *objective method* of measuring social class views class largely as a statistical category. Researchers assign individuals to social classes on the basis of criteria such as occupation, education, income, and residence. The key to the objective method is that the *researcher,* rather than the person being classified, identifies an individual's class position.

The first step in using this method is to decide what indicators or causal factors will be measured objectively, whether wealth, income, education, or occupation. The prestige ranking of occupations has proved to be a useful indicator of a person's class position. For one thing, it is much easier to determine accurately than income or wealth. The term *prestige* refers to the respect and admiration that an occupation holds in a society. "My daughter, the physicist" connotes something very different from "my daughter, the waitress." Prestige is independent of the particular individual who occupies a job, a characteristic that distinguishes it from esteem. *Esteem* refers to the reputation that a specific person has earned within an occupation. Therefore, one can say that the position of president of the United States has high prestige, even though it has been occupied by people with varying degrees of esteem. A hairdresser may have the esteem of his clients, but he lacks the prestige of a corporation president.

Table 8-1 ranks the prestige of a number of well-known occupations. In a series of national surveys, sociologists assigned prestige rankings to about 500 occupations, ranging from physician to newspaper vendor. The highest possible prestige score was 100, and the lowest was 0. Physician, lawyer, dentist, and college professor were the most highly regarded occupations. Sociologists have used such data to assign prestige rankings to virtually all jobs and have found a stability in rankings from 1925 to 1991. Similar studies in other countries have also devel-

Table 8-1   Prestige Rankings of Occupations

Occupation	Score	Occupation	Score
Physician	86	Secretary	46
Lawyer	75	Insurance agent	45
Dentist	74	Bank teller	43
College professor	74	Nurse's aide	42
Architect	73	Farmer	40
Clergy	69	Correctional officer	40
Pharmacist	68	Receptionist	39
Registered nurse	66	Barber	36
High school teacher	66	Child care worker	35
Accountant	65	Hotel clerk	32
Airline pilot	60	Bus driver	32
Police officer and detective	60	Truck driver	30
Prekindergarten teacher	55	Salesworker (shoes)	28
Librarian	54	Garbage collector	28
Firefighter	53	Waiter and waitress	28
Social worker	52	Bartender	25
Electrician	51	Farm worker	23
Funeral director	49	Janitor	22
Mail carrier	47	Newspaper vendor	19

Sources: J. Davis and Smith 1998:1,242–1,246; Nakao and Treas 1990, 1994; NORC 1994.

oped useful prestige rankings of occupations (Hodge and Rossi 1964; Lin and Xie 1988; Treiman 1977).

Studies of social class tend to neglect the occupations and incomes of *women* as determinants of social rank. In an exhaustive study of 589 occupations, sociologists Mary Powers and Joan Holmberg (1978) examined the impact of women's participation in the paid labor force on occupational status. Since women tend to dominate the relatively low-paying occupations, such as bookkeepers and secretaries, their participation in the workforce leads to a general upgrading of the status of most male-dominated occupations. More recent research conducted in both the United States and Europe has assessed the occupations of husbands *and* wives in determining the class positions of families. (Sørensen 1994). With more than half of all married women now working outside the home (see Chapter 11), this approach seems long overdue, but it also raises some questions. For example, how is class or status to be judged in dual-career families—by the occupation regarded as having greater prestige, the average, or some other combination of the two occupations?

Sociologists—and, in particular, feminist sociologists in Great Britain—are drawing on new approaches in assessing women's social class standing. One approach is to focus on the individual (rather than the family or household) as the basis of categorizing a woman's class position. Thus, a woman would be classified based on her own occupational status rather than that of her spouse (O'Donnell 1992).

Another feminist effort to measure the contribution of women to the economy reflects a more clearly political agenda. International Women Count Network, a global grassroots feminist organization, has sought to give a monetary value to women's unpaid work. Besides providing symbolic recognition of women's role in labor, this value would also be used to calculate pension programs and benefits that are based on wages received. In 1995 the United Nations placed an $11 trillion price tag on unpaid labor by women, largely in child care, housework, and agriculture. Whatever the figure today, the continued undercounting of many workers' contribution to a family and to an entire economy makes virtually all measures of stratification in need of reform (United Nations Development Programme 1995; Wages for Housework Campaign 1999).

Another complication in measuring social class is that advances in statistical methods and computer technology have multiplied the factors used to define class under the objective method. No longer are sociologists limited to annual income and education in evaluating a person's class position. Today, studies are published that use as criteria the value of homes, sources of income, assets, years in present occupations, neighborhoods, and considerations regarding dual careers. Adding these variables will not necessarily paint a different picture of class differentiation in the United States, but it does allow sociologists to measure class in a more complex and multidimensional way.

Whatever the technique used to measure class, the sociologist is interested in real and often dramatic differences in power, privilege, and opportunity in a society. The study of stratification is a study of inequality. Nowhere is this more evident than in the distribution of wealth and income.

Consequences of Social Class

Wealth and Income

By all measures, income in the United States is distributed unevenly. Nobel prizewinning economist Paul Samuelson has described the situation in the following words: "If we made an income pyramid out of a child's blocks, with each layer portraying $500 of income, the peak would be far higher than Mount Everest, but most people would be within a few feet of the ground" (Samuelson and Nordhaus 1998:344).

Recent data support Samuelson's analogy. As Figure 8-2 shows, in 1999 the top fifth (or 20 percent of the nation)—earning $102,300 or more—accounted for 50 percent of total after-tax income. By contrast, the bottom fifth—earning $8,800 or less—accounted for only 4 percent of after-tax income.

There has been modest redistribution of income in the United States over the past 70 years. From 1929 through 1970, the government's economic and tax policies

FIGURE 8-2

Comparison of Distribution of Income and Wealth in the United States

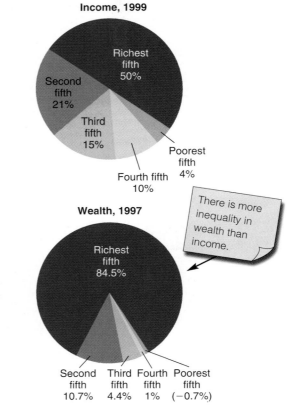

Income, 1999

Wealth, 1997

There is more inequality in wealth than income.

Note: Data on wealth do not add to 100 percent due to rounding.

Sources: Income data (after-tax family income) are from the Congressional Budget Office cited in Shapiro and Greenstein 1999. Data on wealth are from Wolff 1999.

shifted income somewhat to the poor. However, in the last three decades—and especially during the 1980s—federal budgetary policies favored the affluent. Moreover, while the salaries of highly skilled workers and professionals have continued to rise, the wages of less skilled workers have *decreased* when controlled for inflation. As a result, the income gap between the richest and poorest groups in the United States is widening. (Bernstein et al. 2000; Kennickell et al. 2000; Plotnick et al. 1998).

Survey data show that only 38 percent of people in the United States believe that government should take steps to reduce the income disparity between the rich and the poor. By contrast, 80 percent of people in Italy, 66 percent in Germany, and 65 percent in Great Britain support governmental efforts to reduce income inequality. It is not surprising, then, that many European countries provide more extensive "safety nets" to assist and protect the disadvantaged. By

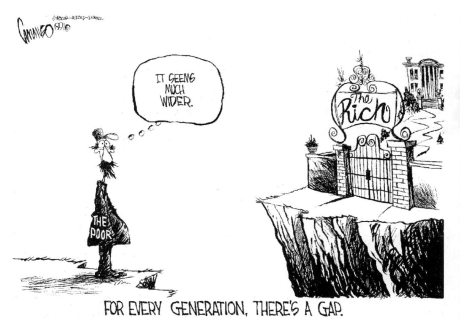

FOR EVERY GENERATION, THERE'S A GAP.

contrast, the strong cultural value placed on individualism in the United States leads to greater possibilities for both economic success and failure (Lipset 1996).

Wealth in the United States is much more unevenly distributed than income. As Figure 8-2 shows, in 1997 the richest fifth of the population held 85 percent of the nation's wealth. Government data indicate that more than one out of every 100 households had assets over $2.4 million, while one-fifth of all households were in debt and therefore had a negative net worth. Researchers have also found a dramatic disparity in wealth between African Americans and Whites. This disparity is evident even when educational backgrounds are held constant: the households of college-educated Whites have about three times as much wealth as the households of college-educated Blacks (Hurst et al. 1996; Kennickell et al. 2000; Oliver and Shapiro 1995).

Poverty

Approximately one out of every nine people in this country lives below the poverty line established by the federal government. Indeed, in 1997, 36 million people were living in poverty. The economic boom of the 1990s passed these people by. A 1999 Bureau of the Census report showed that one in five households had trouble meeting basic needs—everything from paying the utility bills to buying dinner. In this section, we'll consider just how we define "poverty" and who is included in that category (K. Bauman 1999; Dalaker and Naifeh 1998).

Studying Poverty   The efforts of sociologists and other social scientists to better understand poverty are complicated

by the difficulty of defining it. This problem is evident even in government programs that conceive of poverty in either absolute or relative terms. *Absolute poverty* refers to a minimum level of subsistence; no family should be expected to live below it. This standard theoretically remains unchanged from year to year. Policies concerning minimum wages, housing standards, or school lunch programs for the poor imply a need to bring citizens up to some predetermined level of existence. For example, in 1997 the federal minimum wage rate was raised to $5.15 an hour. Even so, when one takes inflation into account, this standard was actually lower than what workers were guaranteed at any time from 1956 through 1982 (Bureau of the Census 1999a:497).

By contrast, *relative poverty* is a floating standard of deprivation by which people at the bottom of a society, whatever their lifestyles, are judged to be disadvantaged *in comparison with the nation as a whole.* Most of our country's current social programs view poverty in relative terms. Therefore, even if the poor of the 1990s are better off in absolute terms than the poor of the 1930s or 1960s, they are still seen as deserving special assistance from government.

One commonly used measure of relative poverty is the federal government's *poverty line,* a money income figure adjusted annually to reflect the consumption requirements of families based on their size and composition. The poverty line serves as an official definition of which people are poor. In 1998, for example, any family of four with a combined income of $16,660 or less fell below the poverty line. This definition determines which individuals and families will be eligible for certain government benefits (Dalaker 1999:1).

In the 1990s, there was growing debate over the validity of the poverty line as a measure of poverty and a standard for allocating government benefits. Some critics charge that the poverty line is too low; they note that the federal government continues to use 20-year-old nutritional standards in assessing people's level of poverty. If the poverty line is too low, then government data will underestimate the extent of poverty in the United States, and many deserving poor citizens will fail to receive benefits.

Other observers dispute this view. They argue that the poverty line may actually overestimate the number of low-income people because it fails to consider noncash benefits (such as Medicare, Medicaid, food stamps, public housing, and health care and other fringe benefits provided by some

Table 8-2 Who Are the Poor in the United States?

Group	Percentage of the Population of the United States	Percentage of the Poor of the United States
Under 18 years old	26	39
18 to 65 years old	61	51
Over 65 years old	13	10
Whites (non-Hispanic)	83	46
Blacks	12	26
Hispanics	11	24
Asians and Pacific Islanders	4	4
Married couples and families with male householders	82	43
Families with female householders	18	57

Notes: Data are for 1998, as reported by the Bureau of the Census in 1999.

Sources: Bureau of the Census 1997a:17–19, 58; Dalaker 1999:vii.

employers). In response, the Bureau of the Census has considered several different definitions of poverty; they showed at most a 1.4 percent lower rate. That is, if the official poverty threshold places 13 percent of the population in the category of the poor, the poverty estimate including *all* these noncash benefits would account for about 11.6 percent of the population (K. Short et al. 1999; Uchitelle 1999).

Who Are the Poor? Not only does the category of the poor defy any simple definition, it counters common stereotypes about "poor people." For example, many people in the United States believe that the vast majority of the poor are able to work but will not. Yet many poor adults *do* work outside the home, although only a portion (13 percent of all low-income adults) work full-time throughout the year. About 58 percent of poor adults do not work, primarily because they are ill or disabled, are maintaining a home, or are retired (Dalaker 1999:17).

A sizable number of the poor live in urban slums, but a majority live outside these poverty areas. Poverty is no stranger in rural areas, ranging from Appalachia to hard-hit farming regions to Native American reservations. Included among the poor of the United States are elderly people, children living in single-parent families with their mothers, and over 10,000 men in military service who cannot adequately support their large families. Table 8-2 provides additional statistical information regarding these low-income people in the United States. (The situation of the most destitute poor in the United States and worldwide, the homeless, will be examined in the social policy section of Chapter 18.)

Since World War II, an increasing proportion of the poor people of the United States have been women—many of whom are divorced or never-married mothers. Currently, almost two out of every three adults classified as poor by the federal government are women. In 1959, female householders accounted for 26 percent of the nation's poor; by 1998, that figure had risen to 57 percent (see Table 8-2). This alarming trend, known as the *feminization of poverty,* is evident not just in the United States but around the world.

About half of all women in the United States living in poverty are "in transition," coping with an economic crisis

Poverty hits women particularly hard throughout the world, a situation known as the "feminization of poverty." Shown here are women and children in India.

caused by the departure, disability, or death of a husband. The other half tend to be economically dependent either on the welfare system or on friends and relatives living nearby. A major factor in the feminization of poverty has been the increase in families with women as single heads of the household (see Chapter 13). In 1998, 13 percent of all people in the United States lived in poverty, compared to 33 percent of households headed by single mothers. Conflict theorists and other observers trace the higher rates of poverty among women to three distinct factors: the difficulty in finding affordable child care (see Chapter 4), sexual harassment (see Chapter 6), and sex discrimination in the labor market (see Chapter 11) (Dalaker 1999:2).

p. 109
p. 161

During the last 20 years, female-headed families have become an increasing proportion of Canada's low-income population. This trend is also noticeable throughout Europe, in developing countries, and even in three widely differing nations whose legislation on behalf of women is the most advanced in the world: Israel, Sweden, and Russia. In these countries, national health care programs, housing subsidies, and other forms of government assistance cushion the impact of poverty somewhat, yet the feminization of poverty still advances (Abowitz 1986; Rodgers 1987; H. Scott 1985; Stanley 1995).

In 1995, 45 percent of poor people in the United States were living in central cities. These highly visible urban residents are the focus of most governmental efforts to alleviate poverty. Yet, according to many ob-

servers, the plight of the urban poor is growing worse, owing to the devastating interplay of inadequate education and limited employment prospects. Traditional employment opportunities in the industrial sector are largely closed to the unskilled poor. Past and present discrimination heightens these problems for low-income urban residents who are Black and Hispanic (Baugher and Lamison-White 1996:vii).

Sociologist William Julius Wilson (1980, 1987, 1989, 1996) and other social scientists have used the term ***underclass*** to describe the long-term poor who lack training and skills. While estimates vary depending on the definition, in 1990 the underclass comprised more than 3 million adults in the United States, not including the elderly. In central cities, about 49 percent of the underclass are African American, 29 percent are Hispanic, 17 percent are White, and 5 percent are "other" (O'Hare and Curry-White 1992).

Conflict theorists, among others, have expressed alarm at the portion of the nation's population living on this lower rung of the stratification hierarchy and at society's reluctance to address the lack of economic opportunities for these people. Often, portraits of the underclass seem to "blame the victims" for their own plight while ignoring other factors that push people into poverty. In Box 8-2 we consider Wilson's latest research into the persistence of urban poverty.

Poverty, of course, is not a new phenomenon. Yet the concept of the underclass describes a chilling development: individuals and families, whether employed or unemployed, who are beyond the reach of any safety net provided by existing social programs. Moreover, membership in the underclass is not an intermittent condition but a long-term attribute. The underclass is understandably alienated from the larger society and engages sporadically in illegal behavior. These illegal acts do little to encourage society to address the long-term problems of the underclass.

Analyses of the poor reveal that they are not a static social class. The overall composition of the poor changes continually, with some individuals and families moving above the poverty level after a year or two while others slip below it. Still, there are hundreds of thousands of people who remain in poverty for many years at a time. African Americans are more likely than Whites to be "persistently

8-2 When Work Disappears

Woodlawn, an urban neighborhood on Chicago's South Side, used to boast more than 800 commercial and industrial establishments. Today, some 50 years later, there are about 100 left, mostly barber shops, thrift stores, and small catering businesses. One Woodlawn resident described the changes on returning after an absence of many years: "I was just really appalled. . . . those resources are just gone, completely. . . . And . . . housing, everybody has moved, there are vacant lots everywhere" (Wilson 1996:5). Another South Side resident noted, "Jobs were plentiful in the past. You could walk out of the house and get a job. . . . Now, you can't find anything. . . . The majority they want to work but they can't find work" (p. 36). When opportunities cease to exist, discouragement sets in. An unmarried welfare mother of three put it this way: "Sometimes you can try and then you say 'I'm tired of trying' " (p. 77).

It has been more than 30 years since President Lyndon Johnson launched a series of federal programs known as the "war on poverty." Yet poverty is still with us as we move past the year 2000, and efforts continue to identify its causes and solutions. Sociologist and past president of the American Sociology Association William Julius Wilson has undertaken a major study of poverty using surveys, interviews, and existing census data from 1987 to the present. His Urban Poverty and Family Life Study (UPFLS) has investigated Chicago neighborhoods with poverty rates of at least 20 percent.

Wilson and his colleagues have noted that the jobless increasingly dominate low-income neighborhoods. As time passes, there are fewer and fewer middle-class households. The absence of full-time workers is especially noticeable in African American poor neighborhoods. As a local community becomes more jobless, it is less able to support neighborhood services such as a pharmacy or hardware store or even a movie theater. As a result, these poverty

neighborhoods become increasingly marginal to the economic, social, and cultural life of the city. Wilson sees this as a movement away from what the historian Albert Spear (1967) termed an *institutional ghetto* (where viable social institutions did exist) to the *jobless ghetto* of today.

What drives the persistence of poverty in urban areas? According to Wilson, it is primarily the exodus of decent-paying jobs, especially in the manufacturing sector. In the last several decades, almost all improvements in productivity have been associated with improved technology and skilled workers. Manufacturers no longer rely so much on assembly-line workers, who often enjoyed not only employment but also labor union fringe benefits and some protec-

> When opportunities cease to exist, discouragement sets in.

tion from layoffs. A generation ago, the typical ghetto resident might have worked as a machine operator or assembler, but today's resident, if even successful in finding wage labor, is working as a waiter or janitor (see the chapter opening). Not only have good-paying jobs disappeared from the urban center, but the new jobs that are available tend to be professional, managerial, and technical positions requiring years of post-secondary education.

For women, especially Black women, the situation is even worse. Wilson found that African American women were significantly isolated from people who were working, had some college education, or were married. This makes it even more difficult for people to move beyond the poverty areas into the larger economy and the better employment opportunities found there. Thus, in Wilson's view, it is the economy and the social structure that supports it, not the poor, that need reforming.

William Julius Wilson, a sociologist at Harvard University, specializes in the study of urban poverty.

Reflecting on inner-city joblessness, Wilson proposes some initiatives, such as national performance standards in education in order to upgrade the minimum level of schooling that the youth in poverty areas receive. His research also shows the clear need for expansion of child care and other family support mechanisms. In addition, he calls for developing metropolitan solutions to bridge the central cities and suburbs. Wilson admits that these approaches are not likely to meet with political acceptance or be easily adopted, but they do underscore the idea that there is no simple solution to reducing poverty in urban areas if viable employment opportunities disappear.

Let's Discuss

1. Has a community you lived in or near seen jobs disappear? What changes took place in a neighborhood as a result?
2. What causes joblessness in urban areas? What can be done to counter it?

Source: Wilson 1996, 1999.

poor." Over a 20-year period, 12 percent of Whites lived below the poverty line for 5 or more consecutive years, and 5 percent of Whites lived below the poverty line for 7 or more consecutive years. In this same 20-year period, African Americans were twice as likely as Whites to experience long poverty spells. Two studies in 1998 documented that Hispanics are also displaying chronic or long-term periods of poverty. Both Hispanics and Blacks are less likely than Whites to leave the welfare rolls as a result of welfare reform discussed in the policy section of this chapter (J. DeParle 1998; Gottschalk et al. 1994; M. Naifeh 1998).

Explaining Poverty   Why is it that pervasive poverty continues within a nation of such vast wealth? Sociologist Herbert Gans (1995) has applied functionalist analysis to the existence of poverty and argues that various segments of society actually *benefit* from the existence of the poor. Gans has identified a number of social, economic, and political functions that the poor perform for society, among them the following:

- The presence of poor people means that society's dirty work—physically dirty or dangerous, dead-end and underpaid, undignified and menial jobs—will be performed at low cost.
- Poverty creates jobs for occupations and professions that "service" the poor. It creates both legal employment (public health experts, welfare caseworkers) and illegal jobs (drug dealers, numbers "runners").

- The identification and punishment of the poor as deviants uphold the legitimacy of conventional social norms and "mainstream values" regarding hard work, thrift, and honesty (see Chapter 7). p. 178
- Within a relatively hierarchical society, the existence of poor people guarantees the higher status of the more affluent. As psychologist William Ryan (1976) has noted, affluent people may justify inequality (and gain a measure of satisfaction) by "blaming the victims" of poverty for their disadvantaged condition.
- Because of the lack of political power, the poor often absorb the costs of social change. Under the policy of deinstitutionalization, mental patients released from long-term hospitals have been "dumped" primarily into low-income communities and neighborhoods. Similarly, halfway houses for rehabilitated drug abusers are often rejected by more affluent communities and end up in poorer neighborhoods.

In Gans's view, then, poverty and the poor actually satisfy positive functions for many nonpoor groups in the United States.

Stratification and Life Chances

Max Weber saw class as closely related to people's *life chances*—that is, their opportunities to provide themselves with material goods, positive living conditions, and favorable life experiences (Gerth and Mills 1958). Life chances are reflected in such measures as housing, education, and health. Occupying a higher position in a society improves your life chances and brings greater access to social rewards. By contrast, people in the lower social classes are forced to devote a larger proportion of their limited resources to the necessities of life.

The affluent and powerful not only have more material possessions than others; they also benefit in many nonmaterial ways. This fact was brought home to us by the hit motion picture *Titanic*, which showed that one's "life" chances had literal consequences in determining who would survive the ship's sinking in 1912 (see Box 8-3). We can also see the effects of life chances in education. Children from high-income families with low high school achievement in the

Functionalists point out that some people, such as these New York City social workers (standing), actually *benefit* from the existence of poverty. Many occupations and professions "service" the poor.

8-3 Social Class in the Movie *Titanic* and on the *SS Titanic*

The movie *Titanic* has been phenomenally successful. Millions of people in the United States, Japan, Germany, China, and elsewhere in the world have paid to see the film. By 2000, box office sales had surpassed 1.8 billion dollars internationally, making it the most successful motion picture ever. While the special effects depicting the ship's breakup on an iceberg were spectacular, film audiences were mainly drawn to the story of how aristocratic 17-year-old Rose, facing a loveless marriage to a society figure, became attracted to working-class Jack.

They were not traveling together on that ill-fated maiden voyage of the *Titanic*. Rose was ensconced in first-class luxury while

Jack was traveling in third-class, or steerage, thanks to a ticket he won in a poker game. Still, for purposes of the plot, they managed to meet on board. Jack had to borrow a suit and act "properly" in order to pass the class line and gain entrance to the stuffy first-class dining room. But Rose had no trouble leaving her rich friends for a bawdy evening among those in the lower decks.

The story of Rose and Jack was attractive because it was so romantic. After all, it typified a social class fantasy of the rich and poor falling in love and then struggling to

> The first attempt to alert steerage passengers to the need to head to the boat deck came at least 45 minutes after the other passengers were alerted.

survive. The theme of love between social class misfits is not new to motion pictures—consider Eliza Doolittle and Professor Henry Higgins in *My Fair Lady* and Vivian Ward and Edward Lewis in *Pretty Woman*. However, the fictional tale of Rose and Jack is particularly ironic because it uses as a backdrop a real tragedy that reinforces the fact that social inequality outweighs any iceberg.

When the *Titanic* sank in 1912, 1,502 passengers and crew members perished and only 705 survived. The luxury liner was sup-

posed to be "unsinkable," but there were still contingency plans for leading passengers to lifeboats in case of emergency. There was one glitch: These procedures were established only for first- and second-class passengers. Approximately 62 percent of the first-class passengers came away alive; even one-third of the first-class male passengers survived, despite a rule of "women and children first." In third class, only 25 percent of the passengers survived. Did the crew and the White Star Line purposely make the 381 steerage passengers expendable? There is no reason to think that, but, like all poorer people on land, they were given less thought and sometimes no thought at all. The first attempt to alert steerage passengers to the need to head to the boat deck came at least 45 minutes after the other passengers were alerted. Clogged passageways made it difficult for steerage passengers to find the lifeboats without being carefully guided. The real-life counterparts of Jack had little chance to survive the calamity. Stratification does make a difference for a person's life chances.

Let's Discuss

1. If you were a passenger on the *Titanic*, how would you be able to distinguish the upper and lower classes? What features on board kept the classes separate?
2. Why did so many more first-class passengers survive the ship's sinking than did lower-class passengers?

Sources: Butler 1998; Riding 1998; K. Crouse 1999.

United States are more likely to attend college than are children from less affluent families with the highest levels of achievement. This gap in educational opportunities has remained significant since 1972 (National Center for Education Statistics 1997).

In the United States, there are clear financial consequences associated with having (or not having) a college degree. For example, according to a 1999 study by the Bureau of the Census, a male with a college degree typically earned $55,057 annually while a male high

school graduate earned only $28,742 a year (Bureau of the Census 1999:36).

Class position also affects health in important ways. In fact, class is increasingly being viewed as an important predictor of health, as the affluent avail themselves of improved health services while such advances bypass poor people. The chances of a child's dying during the first year of life are much higher in poor families than among the middle class. This higher infant mortality rate results in part from the inadequate nutrition received by low-income expectant mothers. Even when they survive infancy, the poor are more likely than the affluent to suffer from serious, chronic illnesses such as arthritis, bronchitis, diabetes, and heart disease. In addition, the poor are less likely to be protected from the high costs of illness by private health insurance. They may have jobs without health insurance; may work part-time and not be eligible for employee health benefits; or may simply be unable to afford the premiums (E. Goode 1999; D. Williams and Collins 1995).

All these factors contribute to differences in the death rates of the poor and the affluent. Studies published in the 1990s, drawing on health data in the United States from 1986 through 1993, document the impact of class (as well as gender and race) on mortality. Among people whose family incomes were less than $9,000, the death rates per 1,000 people 25 to 64 years old were as follows: Black men, 19.5; White men, 16.0; Black women, 7.6; White women, 6.5. By contrast, among people whose family incomes were $25,000 or more, the comparable death rates were Black men, 3.6; White men, 2.4; Black women, 2.3; White women, 1.6. The researchers add that the gap in the death rate between Blacks and Whites is widening. Ill health among the poor only serves to increase the likelihood that the poor will remain impoverished (Federman et al. 1996; Pappas et al. 1993; see also Guralnik et al. 1993).

Like disease, crime can be particularly devastating when it attacks the poor. According to the 1994 National Crime Victimization Survey, people in low-income families were more likely to be assaulted, raped, or robbed than were the most affluent people. Furthermore, if accused of a crime, a person with low income and status is likely to be represented by an overworked public defender. Whether innocent or guilty, such a person may sit in jail for months, unable to raise bail (Perkins and Klaus 1996).

Even the administration of state lotteries underscores differences in life chances. A lottery participant is six times more likely to be struck by lightning than to win the jackpot, yet states target low-income residents in their lottery promotions. Lottery terminals are more heavily concentrated in poor neighborhoods than in wealthy communities. Lottery advertisements are most frequent at the beginning of each month, when Social Security and public assistance checks arrive. Based on studies of lottery purchases, state lottery executives view the poor as more likely than the affluent to spend a high portion of their earnings for the very unlikely chance of becoming an instant millionaire (Novak and Schmid 1999).

Some people have hoped that the Internet revolution would help level the playing field by making information and markets uniformly available. Unfortunately, however, not everyone is able to get onto the "infohighway," and so yet another aspect of social inequality has emerged—the *digital divide*. The poor, minorities, and those who live in rural communities and inner cities are not getting connected at home or at work. A recent government study found that despite falling computer prices, the Internet gap between the haves and have-nots has not narrowed. For example, while 42 percent of all households have a computer, these computers are in about 80 percent of households with family incomes over $75,000 and in fewer than 16 percent in which families make less than $20,000. As wealthier people start to buy high-speed Internet connections, they will be able to take advantage of even more sophisticated interactive services and the digital divide will grow even larger (National Telecommunications Information Administration 1999).

Wealth, status, and power may not ensure happiness, but they certainly provide additional ways of coping with one's problems and disappointments. For this reason, the opportunity for advancement is of special significance to those who are on the bottom of society looking up. These people want the rewards and privileges that are granted to high-ranking members of a culture.

Social Mobility

Ronald Reagan's father was a barber, and Jimmy Carter began as a peanut farmer, yet each man eventually achieved the most powerful and prestigious position in our country. The rise of a child from a poor background to the presidency—or to some other position of great prestige, power, or financial reward—is an example of social mobility. The term *social mobility* refers to movement of individuals or groups from one position of a society's stratification system to another. But how significant—how frequent, how dramatic—is mobility in a class society such as the United States?

Open versus Closed Class Systems

Sociologists use the terms *open class system* and *closed class system* to indicate the amount of social mobility in a society. An *open system* implies that the position of each individual is influenced by the person's *achieved* status. An open class system encourages competition among members of society. The United States is moving toward this ideal type as it attempts to reduce barriers faced by women, racial and ethnic minorities, and people born in lower social classes.

At the other extreme of social mobility is the *closed system,* which allows little or no possibility of moving up. The slavery and caste systems of stratification are examples of closed systems. In such societies, social placement is based on *ascribed* statuses, such as race or family background, which cannot be changed.

Types of Social Mobility

An airline pilot who becomes a police officer moves from one social position to another of the same rank. Each occupation has the same prestige ranking: 60 on a scale ranging from a low of 0 to a high of 100 (see Table 8-1 on page 211). Sociologists call this kind of movement **horizontal mobility.** However, if the pilot were to become a lawyer (prestige ranking of 75), he or she would experience **vertical mobility,** the movement from one social position to another of a different rank. Vertical mobility can also involve moving *downward* in a society's stratification system, as would be the case if the airline pilot becomes a bank teller (ranking of 43). Pitirim Sorokin (1959, original edition 1927) was the first sociologist to distinguish between horizontal and vertical mobility. Most sociological analysis, however, focuses on vertical rather than horizontal mobility.

One way of examining vertical social mobility is to contrast intergenerational and intragenerational mobility. **Intergenerational mobility** involves changes in the social position of children relative to their parents. Thus, a plumber whose father was a physician provides an example of downward intergenerational mobility. A film star whose parents were both factory workers illustrates upward intergenerational mobility.

Intragenerational mobility involves changes in social position within a person's adult life. A woman who enters the paid labor force as a teacher's aide and eventually becomes superintendent of the school district experiences upward intragenerational mobility. A man who becomes a taxicab driver after his accounting firm goes bankrupt undergoes downward intragenerational mobility.

Social Mobility in the United States

The belief in upward mobility is an important aspect of our society. Does this mean that the United States is indeed the land of opportunity? Not unless such ascriptive characteristics as race, gender, and family background have ceased to be significant in determining one's future prospects.

The Impact of Occupational Structure

Two sociological studies conducted a decade apart offer insight into the degree of mobility in the nation's occupational structure (Blau and Duncan 1967; Featherman and Hauser 1978). Taken together, these investigations lead to several noteworthy conclusions. First, occupational mobility (both intergenerational and intragenerational) has been common among males. Approximately 60 to 70 percent of sons are employed in higher-ranked occupations than their fathers.

Second, although there is a great deal of mobility in the United States, much of it covers a very "short distance." That is, people who reach an occupational level different from that of their parents usually advance or fall back only one or two out of a possible eight occupational levels. Thus, the child of a laborer may become an artisan or a technician, but he or she is less likely to become a manager or professional. The odds against reaching the top are extremely high unless one begins from a relatively privileged position.

Third, as the later study by Featherman and Hauser (1978) documents, occupational mobility among African Americans remains sharply limited by racial discrimination (see Chapter 10). Even when the researchers compared Black and White males who had similar levels of schooling, parental background, and early career experience, the achievement levels of Blacks were less than those of Whites. The researchers have also noted that Blacks are more likely than Whites to be downwardly mobile and less likely to be upwardly mobile. Featherman and Hauser offer evidence of a modest decline in the significance of race; yet, we must regard their conclusions with some caution, since they did not consider households with no adult male present or individuals who were not counted in the labor force.

The Impact of Education

Another conclusion of both studies is that education plays a critical role in social mobility. The impact of formal schooling on adult status is even greater than that of family background (although, as we saw in our discussion of stratification and life chances, family background influences the likelihood that one will receive higher education). Furthermore, education represents an important means of intergenerational mobility. Three-fourths of college-educated men achieved some upward mobility, compared with only 12 percent of those who received no schooling (see also J. Davis 1982).

Education's impact on mobility has diminished somewhat in the last decade, however. An undergraduate degree—a B.A. or a B.S.—serves less as a guarantee of upward mobility than it did in the past simply because more and more entrants into the job market now hold such a degree. Moreover, intergenerational mobility is declining, since there is no longer such a stark difference between generations. In earlier decades many high school–educated parents successfully sent their children to college, but today's college students are increasingly likely to have college-educated parents (Hout 1988).

Research suggests that for the poor, social mobility is becoming more and more difficult to achieve. In addition to Wilson's work on the underclass described in Box 8-2, studies by sociologist Greg Duncan (1994; Duncan and Yeung 1995) and by economist Ann Huff Stevens (1994) report that in the late 1980s, the opportunity to advance out of poverty narrowed significantly for poor people in general and especially for young women and African American children.

The Impact of Gender

Studies of mobility, even more than those of class, have traditionally ignored the significance of gender, but some research findings are now available that explore the relationship between gender and mobility.

Women's employment opportunities are much more limited than men's (as Chapter 11 will show). Moreover, according to recent research, women whose skills far exceed the jobs offered them are more likely than men to withdraw entirely from the paid labor force. This withdrawal violates an assumption common to traditional mobility studies: that most people will aspire to upward mobility and seek to make the most of their opportunities.

Ernestina Galindo has broken the mold—she runs her own tortilla factory in Austin, Texas. While entrepreneurship may still be easier for men, women often try it because they encounter resistance to advancement in larger corporations.

In contrast to men, women have a rather large range of clerical occupations open to them. But the modest salary ranges and limited prospects for advancement in many of these positions mean there is not much possibility of upward mobility. Moreover, self-employment as shopkeepers, entrepreneurs, independent professionals, and the like—an important road to upward mobility for men—is difficult for women, who find it hard to secure the necessary financing. Although sons commonly follow in the footsteps of their fathers, women are unlikely to move into their fathers' positions. Consequently, gender remains an important factor in shaping social mobility within the United States. Women in the United States (and in other parts of the world) are especially likely to be trapped in poverty and unable to rise out of their low-income status (P. Smith 1994).

In recent decades, many male workers in the United States have experienced downward mobility, including unemployment. (As we will see in Chapter 17, this has resulted in part from corporate "downsizing" and "restructuring" as well as plant closings.) For the first time since World War II, college-educated men in their late 40s and 50s—who may have assumed they were in their prime earning years—are experiencing a significant decline in wages. Some have lost high-level jobs at major corporations and have shifted (after periods of unemployment) to lower-paying positions at small companies or to self-employment.

The social policy section that follows takes into consideration the very limited prospects of mobility experienced by those on welfare. Can they find jobs that allow them to leave the welfare system, or are they doomed to remain trapped in poverty year after year? We'll see how governments at home and abroad have dealt with this difficult issue.

Rethinking Welfare in North America and Europe

The Issue

- After five years on public assistance, Claudia Melgosa of Glendale, California, is a welfare success story. The 28-year-old mother of two has landed a job at a storage company and moved up to a $9-an-hour customer service position. However, Carlos Sabala of nearby Santa Monica works in a hotel for $7.18 and worries about being edged back into unemployment by the stiff competition for low-wage jobs (Ellis and Ellingwood 1998).
- Helene Desegrais, a single mother in Paris, France, waited for four months to obtain a place in government-subsidized day care for her daughter. Now she can seek a full-time job, but she is concerned about government threats to curtail such services to keep taxes down (Simons 1997).
- Marcia Missouri of Worcester, Massachusetts, tacks up a handwritten advertisement in the public housing project in which she lives to say that she is available to clean yards and braid hair for a few extra dollars. The sign lists a friend's phone number; she doesn't have a phone of her own (Vobejda and Havenmann 1997).

These are the faces of people living on the edge—often women with children seeking to make a go of it amidst changing social policies. Governments in all parts of the world are searching for the right solution to welfare: How much subsidy should they provide? How much responsibility should fall on the shoulders of the poor?

The Setting

By the 1990s, there was intense debate in the United States over the issue of welfare. Welfare programs were costly, and there was widespread concern (however unfounded) that welfare payments discouraged recipients from seeking jobs. Both Democrats and Republicans vowed to "end welfare as we know it" (Pear 1996:20).

In late 1996, in a historic shift in federal policy, the Personal Responsibility and Work Opportunity Reconciliation Act was passed, ending the long-standing federal guarantee of assistance to every poor family that meets eligibility requirements. It set a lifetime limit of five years of welfare benefits for recipients and required that all able-bodied adults work after two years of benefits (although hardship exceptions are allowed). The federal government would give block grants to the states to use as they wish in assisting poor and needy residents, and it would permit states to experiment with ways to move people off welfare (R. Wolf 1996). In 1997, the Clinton administration created the "Welfare to Work Partnership," a nonprofit group intended to encourage businesses to hire welfare recipients.

Other countries vary widely in their commitment to social service programs. But most industrialized nations devote higher proportions of their expenditures to housing, social security, welfare, and unemployment compensation than the United States does. In Switzerland in 1997, 71 percent of central-government spending went to these social service areas; in Ireland, 60 percent; while in the United States the figure stood at 54 percent. In good part, this is because the United States has such a comparatively high level of military spending. A study by sociologist Greg Duncan (1994) of welfare programs in the United States and seven European nations found that a higher proportion of the poor escape poverty in Europe than in the United States. Apparently, the greater benefits facilitate upward mobility (World Bank 2000:256–257).

Sociological Insights

Many sociologists tend to view the debate over welfare throughout industrialized nations from a conflict perspective: the "haves" in positions of policymaking listen to the interests of other "haves," while the cries of the "have-nots" are drowned out. Critics of so-called welfare reform believe that the nation's economic problems are unfairly being blamed on welfare spending and the poor. From a conflict perspective, this backlash against welfare recipients reflects deep fears and hostility toward the nation's urban and predominantly African American and Hispanic underclass.

Those critical of the backlash note that "welfare scapegoating" conveniently ignores the lucrative federal handouts that go to *affluent* individuals and families. For example, while federal housing aid to the poor was being cut drastically in the 1980s, the amount of tax deductions for mortgage interest and property taxes more than doubled. The National Association of Home Builders, an ardent defender of the mortgage-interest deduction, estimates that it costs the federal government $60 billion a year in lost taxes. This deduction generally benefits affluent taxpayers who own their own homes. According to one study, more than 44 percent of the benefits from this tax break go to the 5 percent of taxpayers with the highest incomes, who together save themselves $22 billion annually (Goodgame 1993; Johnston 1996).

Those who take a conflict perspective also urge policy-makers and the general public to look closely at *corporate welfare,* the tax breaks, direct payments, and grants that the government makes to corporations, rather than focus on the comparatively small allowances be-

Moving off welfare often requires job training. The "workfare" program illustrated here is preparing workers for construction jobs.

ing given to welfare mothers and their children. According to a 1998 estimate by the public-interest group Essential Information, these breaks to corporations cost U.S. taxpayers more than $125 billion, while programs to assist the poor cost $75 billion. But any suggestion to curtail such "corporate welfare" brings a strong response from special-interest groups much more powerful than any coalition on behalf of the poor (Lilliston 1994; Bartlett and Steele 1998).

Policy Initiatives

As of mid-1999, almost three years after the law changed the welfare system, 6.8 million people had left welfare, reducing the welfare rolls to 7.3 million. The Welfare to Work Partnership had found some 410,000 jobs in 10,000 companies that joined the partnership through 1999. Remarkably, the former welfare recipients in these businesses were *less* likely to leave their jobs than were other employees. The low turnover helps offset the costs of training (Department of Health and Human Services 1999; Welfare to Work Partnership 1999).

The government likes to highlight success stories such as that of Claudia Melgosa (described at the beginning of this section). It is true that people who previously depended on tax dollars are now working and paying taxes themselves. But skeptics say that it is much too soon to see if "workfare" will be successful.

They point to the new jobs being generated during a booming economy as an unrealistic test of the system. Furthermore, the hard-core jobless, those people harder to train or people encumbered by drug or alcohol abuse, physical disabilities, or child care needs, are not going to subsist easily even in a successful economy. A 1999 survey showed that the biggest needs of welfare-to-work employees were child care and transportation—services rarely provided by employers. At the same time that suggestions mount to provide such services for former welfare recipients, the working poor, like Carlos Sabala above, complain that "we get nothing" (Fuller and Kagan 2000; Welfare to Work Partnership 1999).

European countries have witnessed many of the same citizen demands as found in North America: Keep our taxes low, even if it means reducing services to the poor. However, nations in eastern and central Europe have faced a special challenge since the end of communism. The governments in those nations had traditionally provided an impressive array of social services, but they differed from capitalist systems in several important respects. First, the communist system was premised on full employment, so there was no need to provide unemployment insurance; social services focused on the old and the disabled. Second, subsidies, such as for housing and even utilities, played an important role. With new competition from the West and tight budgets, some of these countries (as well as Sweden, despite its long history of social welfare programs) are beginning to realize that a system of universal coverage is no longer affordable and must be replaced by more targeted programs. Some of these countries' residents have sought refuge in western Europe, putting new demands on social service systems there just as people are calling for a moratorium on higher taxes (World Bank 1997:55–57; Kuptsch and Mazie 1999).

Both in North American and Europe, people are beginning to turn to private means to support themselves. For instance, they are investing money for their later years rather than depending on government social security programs. But that solution only works if you have a job and can save money. Increasing proportions of people are seeing the gap between themselves and the affluent growing with fewer government programs aimed to assist them. Solutions are frequently left to the private sector, while government policy initiatives at the national level all but disappear.

Let's Discuss

1. How does the level of spending for social services in the United States compare with that of European countries? What accounts for the differences?
2. Do you think welfare recipients should be required to work? What kind of support should they be given?
3. Has the welfare system that went into law in the United States in 1996 been successful? Why or why not?

Summary

Stratification is the structured ranking of entire groups of people that perpetuates unequal economic rewards and power in a society. In this chapter, we examine three general systems of stratification, the explanations offered by functionalist and conflict theorists for the existence of social inequality, the relationship between stratification and social mobility, and stratification within the world system.

1. Some degree of ***social inequality*** characterizes all cultures.
2. Systems of ***stratification*** include ***slavery, castes,*** and social ***class.***
3. Karl Marx saw that differences in access to the means of production created social, economic, and political inequality and distinct classes of owners and laborers.
4. Max Weber identified three analytically distinct components of stratification: ***class, status,*** and ***power.***
5. Functionalists argue that stratification is necessary so that people will be motivated to fill society's important positions; conflict theorists see stratification as a major source of societal tension and conflict.
6. One consequence of social class in the United States is that both ***wealth*** and ***income*** are distributed unevenly.
7. The category of the "poor" defies any simple definition and counters common stereotypes about "poor people." The long-term poor who lack training and skills form an ***underclass.***
8. Functionalists find that the poor satisfy positive functions for many of the nonpoor in the United States.
9. One's ***life chances***—opportunities for obtaining material goods, positive living conditions, and favorable life experiences—are related to one's social class. Occupying a higher social position improves a person's life chances.
10. ***Social mobility*** is more likely to be found in an ***open system*** that emphasizes achieved status than in a ***closed system*** that focuses on ascribed characteristics. Race, gender, and family background are important factors in mobility.
11. Many governments are struggling with how much of their tax dollars to spend on welfare programs. The trend in the United States is to put welfare recipients to work.

Critical Thinking Questions

1. Sociologist Daniel Rossides has conceptualized the class system of the United States using a five-class model. According to Rossides, the upper-middle class and the lower-middle class together account for about 40 percent of the nation's population. Yet studies suggest that a higher proportion of respondents identify themselves as "middle class." Drawing on the model presented by Rossides, suggest why members of both the upper class and the working class might prefer to identify themselves as "middle class."

2. Sociological study of stratification generally is conducted at the macrolevel and draws most heavily on the functionalist and conflict perspectives. How might sociologists use the *interactionist* perspective to examine social class inequalities within a college community?

3. Imagine that you have opportunity to spend a year in a developing country studying inequality in that nation. How would you draw on the research designs of sociology (surveys, observation, experiments, existing sources) to better understand and document stratification in this developing country?

Key Terms

Absolute poverty   A standard of poverty based on a minimum level of subsistence below which families should not be expected to live. (page 213)

Achieved status   A social position attained by a person largely through his or her own efforts. (203)

Ascribed status   A social position "assigned" to a person by society without regard for the person's unique talents or characteristics. (203)

Bourgeoisie   Karl Marx's term for the capitalist class, comprising the owners of the means of production. (207)

Capitalism   An economic system in which the means of production are largely in private hands and the main incentive for economic activity is the accumulation of profits. (207)

Castes   Hereditary systems of rank, usually religiously dictated, that tend to be fixed and immobile. (204)

Class   A group of people who have a similar level of wealth and income. (207)

Class consciousness   In Karl Marx's view, a subjective awareness held by members of a class regarding their common vested interests and need for collective political action to bring about social change. (207)

Class system   A social ranking based primarily on economic position in which achieved characteristics can influence social mobility. (204)

Closed system   A social system in which there is little or no possibility of individual mobility. (219)

Dominant ideology   A set of cultural beliefs and practices that helps to maintain powerful social, economic, and political interests. (209)

Esteem   The reputation that a particular individual has earned within an occupation. (210)

False consciousness   A term used by Karl Marx to describe an attitude held by members of a class that does not accurately reflect their objective position. (207)

Horizontal mobility   The movement of an individual from one social position to another of the same rank. (220)

Income   Salaries and wages. (203)

Intergenerational mobility   Changes in the social position of children relative to their parents. (220)

Intragenerational mobility   Changes in a person's social position within his or her adult life. (220)

Life chances   People's opportunities to provide themselves with material goods, positive living conditions, and favorable life experiences. (217)

Objective method   A technique for measuring social class that assigns individuals to classes on the basis of criteria such as occupation, education, income, and place of residence. (210)

Open system   A social system in which the position of each individual is influenced by his or her achieved status. (219)

Power   The ability to exercise one's will over others. (208)

Prestige   The respect and admiration that an occupation holds in a society. (210)

Proletariat   Karl Marx's term for the working class in a capitalist society. (207)

Relative poverty   A floating standard of deprivation by which people at the bottom of a society, whatever their lifestyles, are judged to be disadvantaged in comparison with the nation as a whole. (213)

Slavery   A system of enforced servitude in which people are legally owned by others and in which enslaved status is transferred from parents to children. (204)

Social inequality   A condition in which members of a society have different amounts of wealth, prestige, or power. (203)

Social mobility   Movement of individuals or groups from one position of a society's stratification system to another. (219)

Status group   People who have the same prestige or lifestyle, independent of their class positions. (208)

Stratification   A structured ranking of entire groups of people that perpetuates unequal economic rewards and power in a society. (203)

Underclass   Long-term poor people who lack training and skills. (215)

Vertical mobility   The movement of a person from one social position to another of a different rank. (220)

Wealth   An inclusive term encompassing all of a person's material assets, including land and other types of property. (203)

Additional Readings

BOOKS

Bales, Kevin. 1999. *Disposable People: New Slavery in the Global Economy.* Berkeley: University of California Press. Considers the more than 27 million people around the world who are victims of coerced labor. Offers case studies of Brazil, India, Mauritania, Thailand, the United States, and parts of Europe.

Blank, Rebecca M. 1997. *It Takes a Nation: A New Agenda for Fighting Poverty.* Princeton, NJ: Princeton University Press. An economist confronts some of the common myths about welfare, critically evaluates proposals that were part of the welfare reform program of 1996, and closes with her own suggestions for addressing poverty in the United States.

Braun, Denny. 1997. *The Rich Get Richer.* 2d ed. Chicago: Nelson-Hall. A sociologist looks at growing inequality within the United States, as well as throughout the world, with a special focus on the rise of multinational corporations.

Herman, Andrew. 1999. *The "Better Angels" of Capitalism: Rhetoric, Narrative, and Moral Identity among Men of the American Upper Class.* Boulder, CO: Westview Press. An ethnographic study of wealthy men in the United States, which notes how they are able to persuade themselves and others of the legitimacy of their power and privilege.

Oliver, Melvin L. and Thomas M. Shapiro. 1995. *Black Wealth/White Wealth: New Perspectives on Racial Inequality.* New York: Rutledge. A detailed examination of the massive differences in wealth between African Americans and Whites, regardless of education and occupation.

JOURNALS

Among the journals that focus on issues of stratification, social class, and social mobility are *American Journal of Economics and Sociology* (founded in 1941), *Humanity and Society* (1977), *Journal of Poverty* (1997), and *Review of Black Political Economy* (1970). See also the *Current Population Reports* series published by the Bureau of the Census (available at www.census.gov).

Internet Connection

Note: While all the URLs listed were current as of the printing of this book, these sites often change. Please check our website (http://www.mhhe.com/schaefer) for updates.

1. This chapter highlights the different social experiences of the rich and the poor. Visit the Internet site Forbes: The World's Richest People **(http://www.forbes.com/tool/toolbox/billnew/)** for a virtual trip to the top of the social class system.

   (a)   Who is the richest person in the world according to the site?

   (b)   How did he/she become a billionaire?

   (c)   What is this person's educational level?

   (d)   How many women are on the "World's Richest" list?

   (e)   How did the people on the list become billionaires?

   (f)   What kinds of activities do they pursue for leisure?

   (g)   What facts did you learn about their daily work and home lives?

   (h)   Click on a region of the world map to see which countries have billionaires. Which country has the most billionaires? Which has the fewest? Why is this so?

(i) Next, visit the Internet site Inside Out (**http://www.c3.hu/collection/homeless/**). Homeless persons on the streets of Budapest were asked by researchers to photograph and comment on their daily lives and environments. This website is the result. Choose two of the persons, view their pictures, and read their experiences. How is life different for those at the bottom of the social class system in comparison to those at the top?

(j) What challenges do they face each day?

(k) What are some of their values and norms? What is important to them?

(l) What goals do they have for the future?

(m) How do they have fun?

(n) What worries do homeless persons have that you do not have?

2. The chapter details the welfare reform that has occurred over the last few years in the United States. Log on to the Welfare Reform State Links page (**http://www.acf.dhhs.gov/news/welfare/ stlinks.htm**) and choose "Illinois" from the list of states offered.

(a) What is TANF? What did it replace?

(b) What are the goals of the Illinois reformed welfare system?

(c) What are the responsibilities of those on welfare?

(d) Can you think of additional goals and responsibilities not mentioned?

(e) After reflecting on the statistics offered, does it appear that the new welfare system is working? Why or why not?

(f) Make a list of three strong points and three weaknesses of the Illinois system, and choose another state that interests you (perhaps your home state). How does this second state compare to Illinois in terms of program policies, goals, and success?

(g) Which state do you think has the better system?

(h) If the president appointed you to improve the U.S. welfare system, what changes would you make? Why?

CHAPTER

9

SOCIAL INEQUALITY WORLDWIDE

The digital revolution has come to Jodhpur, India, despite the fact that the per capita gross national product is only $370 (compared to $20,870 in Great Britain, India's former colonizer).

nstantly recognized throughout the world, the *Nike swoosh* sometimes seems to be everywhere—on shirts and caps and pants. The icon is no longer confined to shoes as sponsorship deals have plastered the *swoosh* across jerseys and sporting arenas of all manner, from basketball to football to volleyball to track to soccer to tennis to hockey. *Nike*'s growth strategy is based on penetrating new markets in apparel while making acquisitions in sporting goods. The value of the *swoosh* now runs so deep that visitors to remote, rural, and impoverished regions of the Third World report finding peasants sewing crude *swoosh* imitations on to shirts and caps, not for the world market but for local consumption. . . . As the *Nike* symbol has grown ascendant in the marketplace of images, *Nike* has become the sign some people love to love and the sign others love to hate. . . .

Nike is a transnational corporation that links national economies into a complex web of global production arrangement. . . . Almost all production of shoes, apparel and accessories is outsourced to contract suppliers in developing nations while the home office in Beaverton, Oregon designs, develops, and markets the branded goods. . . .

It is very difficult to compete in today's athletic footwear industry without engaging in the outsourcing of labor to relatively unskilled laborers in impoverished nations. Companies in the athletic footwear industry depend on the existence of poor Asian nations where there is a ready surplus of labor force in need of work and wages, even if those wages are below the poverty line. . . .

Nike speaks the language of universal rights, concern for children, transcendence over the categories of age, race, gender, disability or any social stereotype. As moral philosophy, its images speak out against racism, sexism, and ageism. *Nike*'s imagery celebrates sport, athletic activity, and play as universally rewarding categories. Playing makes for healthier, more productive citizens, and better self-actualized human beings. However, no matter what its imagery suggests, *Nike*, like any other capitalist firm, must operate within the relationships and constraints of competitive capitalist marketplaces. No matter how many P.L.A.Y. commercials *Nike* runs on TV, there will still be haunting images of production practices in Pakistan, Indonesia, and Vietnam. As the world grows more unified, it becomes increasingly difficult to suppress entirely those gaps between image and practice, between humanism and capitalism, between moral philosophy and the bottom line of corporate profit growth. *(Goldman and Papson 1998:2, 6–8, 184)* ■

s sociologists Robert Goldman and Stephen Papson note in their book *Nike Culture,* the Nike symbol (the swoosh) and philosophy ("Just do it") have swept the world. People in all parts of the globe pay up to hundreds of dollars for a pair of Air Jordan shoes, and teams in all kinds of sporting arenas wear the Nike logo. Unfortunately, there is another side to Nike's global dominance. Its products are made in harsh sweatshop conditions for very little compensation, mostly in the developing nations. One group critical of Nike's practices claimed in 1996 that the 45 Indonesian workers who participated in making a $70 pair of Air Pegasus shoes shared a total of $1.60. Other stories of Vietnamese and Chinese women who are subject to health and safety hazards, pitifully underpaid, and physically harassed by shop floor managers have also helped to fuel concern about human rights violations.

Students protesting sweatshop labor in developing countries mock Nike with its own slogan: "Just do it."

This concern has recently given rise to a nationwide coalition called United Students Against Sweatshops, based on college campuses across the country. Because this is an issue that combines women's rights, immigrant rights, environmental concerns, and human rights, it has linked disparate groups on campus. Nike is not their only target. Many apparel manufacturers contract out their production to take advantage of cheap labor and overhead costs. The student movement—ranging from sit-ins and "knit-ins" to demonstrations and building occupation—has been aimed at ridding campus stores of all products made in sweatshops, both at home and abroad. Pressed by their students, many colleges and universities have agreed to adopt anti-sweatshop codes governing the products they make and stock on campus. And Nike and Reebok, partly in response to student protests,

have raised the wages of some 100,000 workers in their Indonesian factories (to about 20 cents an hour—still far below what is needed to raise a family) (Appelbaum and Dreier 1999).

The global corporate culture of the apparel industry focuses our attention on worldwide stratification, as seen in the enormous gap between those enjoying wealth and those destitute from poverty.

This chapter will focus on stratification around the world, beginning with an examination of who controls the world marketplace. The impact of colonialism and neocolonialism on social inequality will be studied, as will world systems analysis, the immense power of multinational corporations, and the consequences of modernization. After this macro-level examination of the disparity between rich and poor countries, we will focus on stratification *within* the nations of the world through discussions of the distribution of wealth and income, comparative perspectives on prestige, and comparative social mobility. To better understand inequality in another country, we will present a case study of stratification in Mexico. Finally, in the social policy section, we will address the issue of international human rights and the violations of human rights evident around the world. ∎

Stratification in the World System

Kwabena Afari is a pineapple exporter in Ghana. But for years his customers had to show a great deal of ingenuity to get in touch with him. First a call had to be placed to Accra, the capital city. Someone there would call the post office in Afari's hometown. Then the post office would send a messenger to his home. Afari has recently solved his problem by getting a cellular phone, but his longtime dilemma symbolizes the problems of the roughly 600 million people who live in sub-Saharan Africa and are being left behind by the trade and foreign investment transforming the global economy. One African entrepreneur notes, "It's not that we have been left behind. It's that we haven't even started" (Buckley 1997:8).

It is true that technology, the information highway, and innovations in telecommunications have all made the world a smaller and more unified place. Yet while the world marketplace is gradually shrinking in space and tastes, the profits of business are not being equally shared. There remains a substantial disparity between the world's "have" and "have-not" nations. For example, in 1995, the average value of goods and services produced per citizen (per capita gross national product) in the United States, Japan, Switzerland, and Norway was more than $25,000. By contrast, the figure was under $200 in six poorer countries. The 140 developing nations accounted for 78 percent of the world's population but possessed only about 16 percent of all wealth (Haub and Cornelius 1999). These contrasts are illustrated in Figure 9-1. Three forces discussed below are particularly responsible for the domination of the world marketplace by a few nations: the legacy of colonialism, the advent of multinational corporations, and modernization.

Colonialism, Neocolonialism, and World Systems Analysis

Colonialism is the maintenance of political, social, economic, and cultural domination over a people by a foreign power for an extended period of time (W. Bell 1981b). In simple terms, it is rule by outsiders. The long reign of the British Empire over much of North America, parts of Africa, and India is an example of colonial domination. The same can be said of French rule over Algeria, Tunisia, and other parts of North Africa. Relations between the colonial nation and colonized people are similar to those between the dominant capitalist class and the proletariat as described by Karl Marx.

By the 1980s, colonialism had largely disappeared. Most of the world's nations that were colonies before World War I had achieved political independence and established their own governments. However, for many of these countries, the transition to genuine self-rule was not yet complete. Colonial domination had established patterns of economic exploitation that continued even after nationhood was achieved—in part because former colonies were unable to develop their own industry and technology. Their dependence on more industrialized nations, including their former colonial masters, for managerial and technical expertise, investment capital, and manufactured goods kept former colonies in a subservient position. Such continuing dependence and foreign domination constitute *neocolonialism.*

The economic and political consequences of colonialism and neocolonialism are readily apparent. Drawing on the conflict perspective, sociologist Immanuel Wallerstein (1974, 1979, 1999) views the global economic system as divided between nations that control wealth and those from which resources are taken. Neocolonialism allows industrialized societies to accumulate even more capital.

Wallerstein has advanced a *world systems analysis* to describe the unequal economic and political relationships in which certain industrialized nations (among them the United States, Japan, and Germany) and their global corporations dominate the *core* of the system. At the *semiperiphery* of the system are countries with marginal economic status, such as Israel, Ireland, and South Korea. Wallerstein suggests that the poor developing countries of Asia, Africa, and Latin America are on the *periphery* of the world economic system. Core nations and their corporations control and exploit the developing nations' economies, much as the old colonial empires ruled their colonies (Chase-Dunn and Grimes 1995).

Wallerstein's world systems analysis is the most widely used version of *dependency theory.* According to this theory, even as developing countries make economic advances, they remain weak and subservient to core nations and corporations within an increasingly intertwined global economy. This allows industrialized nations to continue to exploit developing countries for their own gain. In a sense, dependency theory applies the conflict perspective on a global scale.

In the view of world systems analysis and dependency theory, a growing share of the human and natural resources of developing countries is being redistributed to the core industrialized nations. In part, this is because developing countries owe huge sums of money to industrialized nations as a result of foreign aid, loans, and trade deficits. This global debt crisis has intensified the Third World dependency begun under colonialism, neocolonialism, and multinational investment. International financial institutions are pressuring indebted countries to adopt austerity measures so they can meet their interest payments. The result is that developing nations may be forced to devalue their currencies, freeze workers' wages, increase privatization of industry, and reduce government services and employment.

FIGURE 9-1

Gross National Product per Capita, 1999

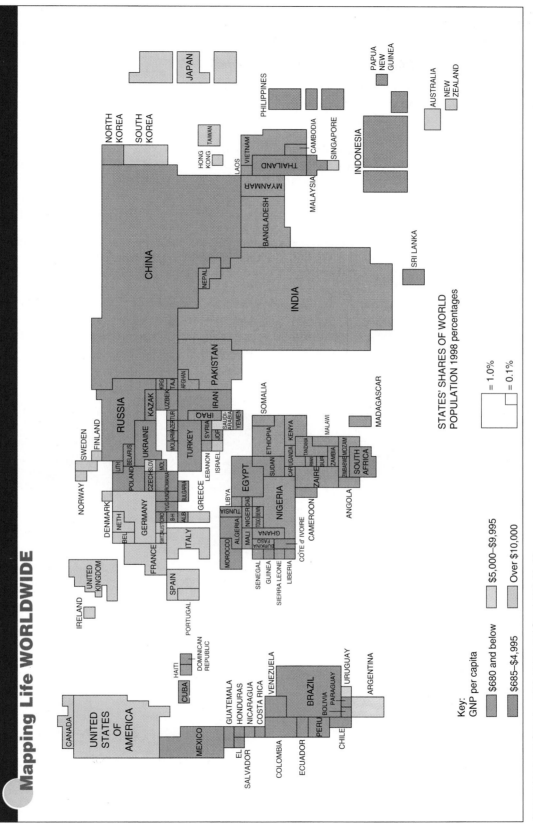

Mapping **Life WORLDWIDE**

STATES' SHARES OF WORLD
POPULATION 1998 percentages

☐ = 1.0%
☐ = 0.1%

Key:
GNP per capita

$680 and below
$685–$4,995
$5,000–$9,995
Over $10,000

Sources: Haub and Cornelius 1999; Kidron and Segal 1995:28–29.

This stylized map reflects the different sizes in population of the world's nations. The color for each country shows the 1998 estimated *gross national product* (the total value of goods and services produced by the nation in a given year) per capita. As the map shows, some of the world's most populous countries—such as India, Indonesia, Bangladesh, and Pakistan—are among the nations with the lowest standard of living as measured by per capita gross national product.

In addition to their political and economic impact, colonialism and neocolonialism have an important cultural component. The colonized people lose their native values and begin to identify with the culture of the colonial power. People may discard or neglect their native language as they attempt to emulate their colonizers. Those opposed to contemporary neocolonialism see every consumer product, book, film, or television program designed by a colonial nation as an attack on the traditions and cultural autonomy of the dependent people. Even the popularity of *Titanic* or *The X-Files* may be viewed as a threat to native cultures when such programs dominate their media at the expense of local art forms. Sembene Ousmane, one of Africa's most prominent writers and filmmakers, noted, "[Today] we are more familiar with European fairy tales than with our own traditional stories" (World Development Forum 1990:4).

p. 67

Multinational Corporations

A key role in neocolonialism today is played by worldwide corporate giants. The term **multinational corporations** refers to commercial organizations that are headquartered in one country but do business throughout the world. Such private trade and lending relationships are not new; merchants have conducted business abroad for hundreds of years, trading gems, spices, garments, and other goods. However, today's multinational giants are not merely buying and selling overseas; they are also *producing* goods all over the world, as we saw in the case of Nike (Wallerstein 1974).

Moreover, today's "global factory" (the factories throughout the developing world run by multinational corporations) now has the "global office" alongside it. Multinationals based in core countries are beginning to establish reservations services, centers to process insurance claims, and data processing centers in the periphery nations. As service industries become a more important part of the international marketplace, many companies have concluded that the low costs of overseas operations more than offset the expense of transmitting information around the world.

Do not underestimate the size of these global corporations. Table 9-1 shows that the total revenues of multinational businesses are on a par with the total value of goods and services exchanged in *entire nations*. Foreign sales represent an important source of profit for multinational corporations, a fact that encourages them to expand into other

Table 9-1   Comparing Multinational Corporations and Nations

Corporation	Revenues ($ millions)	Comparable Nation (or City)	Gross National Product ($ millions)
1. General Motors (USA)	$161,315	Hong Kong	$158,300
2. Daimler Chrysler (Germany)	154,615	Norway	152,100
3. Ford Motor (USA)	144,416	Indonesia	138,500
4. Wal-Mart (USA)	139,208		
5. Mitsui (Japan)	109,372	Portugal	106,400
8. Exxon (USA)	100,697	Israel	95,200
11. Royal Dutch/Shell (Brit./Neth.)	93,692	Singapore	95,100
14. IBM (USA)	81,667	Philippines	78,900
29. Philip Morris (USA)	57,813	New Zealand	55,800
31. Sony (Japan)	53,157	Czech Republic	51,800
36. Nestlé (Switzerland)	49,504	Algeria	46,500

Notes: Revenues are generally for 1996, except some corporate fiscal years that end March 30, 1997. GNP data are for either 1995 or 1996 and are based on local currencies converted to prevailing U.S. dollar equivalencies.

Sources: For corporate data: J. Kahn 1999. For GNP data: World Bank 2000:230–231.

countries (in many cases, the developing nations). The economy of the United States is heavily dependent on foreign commerce, much of which is conducted by multinationals. Almost one out of five manufacturing jobs in the United States has to do with the export of goods to foreign countries (Bureau of the Census 1997a:751).

Multinational corporations can actually help the developing nations of the world. They bring jobs and industry to areas where subsistence agriculture previously served as the only means of survival. Multinationals promote rapid development through diffusion of inventions and innovations from industrial nations. Viewed from a functionalist perspective, the combination of skilled technology and management provided by multinationals and the relatively cheap labor available in developing nations is ideal for a global enterprise. Multinationals can take maximum advantage of technology while reducing costs and boosting profits.

The international ties of multinational corporations also facilitate the exchange of ideas and technology around the world. They make the nations of the world more interdependent. And these ties may prevent certain disputes from reaching the point of serious conflict. A country cannot afford to sever diplomatic relations, or engage in warfare, with a nation that is the headquarters for its main business suppliers or is a key outlet for exports.

Conflict theorists challenge this favorable evaluation of the impact of multinational corporations. They emphasize that multinationals exploit local workers to maximize profits. Starbucks—the international coffee retailer based in Seattle—gets some of its coffee from farms in

Guatemala. But to earn enough money to buy a pound of Starbucks' coffee, a Guatemalan farmworker would have to pick 500 pounds of beans, representing five days of work (Entine and Nichols 1996).

The pool of cheap labor in the developing world prompts multinationals to move factories out of core countries. An added bonus for the multinationals is that the developing world discourages strong trade unions. Organized labor in industrialized countries insists on decent wages and humane working conditions, but governments seeking to attract or keep multinationals may develop a "climate for investment" that includes repressive antilabor laws restricting union activity and collective bargaining. If labor's demands in factories run by multinational corporations become threatening, the firm will simply move its plant elsewhere, leaving a trail of unemployment behind. Nike, for example, moved its factories from the United States to Korea to Indonesia to Vietnam, seeking the lowest labor costs. Conflict theorists conclude that, on the whole, multinational corporations have a negative social impact on workers in both industrialized and developing nations.

Workers in the United States and other core countries are beginning to recognize that their own interests are served by helping to organize workers in developing nations. As long as multinationals can exploit cheap labor abroad, they will be in a strong position to reduce wages and benefits in industrialized countries. With this in mind, in the 1990s, labor unions, religious organizations, campus groups, and other activists mounted public campaigns to pressure companies such as Nike, Starbucks, Reebok, the Gap, and Wal-Mart to improve the wages and working conditions in their overseas operations (Cavanagh and Broad 1996).

Several sociologists who have surveyed the effects of foreign investment conclude that, although it may initially contribute to a host nation's wealth, it eventually increases economic inequality within developing nations. This is true in both income and ownership of land. The upper and middle classes benefit most from economic expansion, while the lower classes are less likely to benefit. Multinationals invest in limited areas of an economy and in restricted regions of a nation. Although certain sectors of the host nation's economy expand, such as hotels and expensive restaurants, this very expansion appears to retard growth in agriculture and other economic sectors. Moreover,

As these billboards show, multinational corporations have arrived in Vietnam. Multinationals take advantage of cheap labor in developing countries but they also help diffuse technology to those nations.

The Laboring American Dream

There is similar criticism of *modernization theory,* a functionalist approach that proposes that modernization and development will gradually improve the lives of people in developing nations. According to this theory, while countries develop at uneven rates, development in peripheral countries will be assisted by the innovations transferred from the industrialized world. Critics of modernization theory, including dependency theorists, counter that any such technology transfer only increases the dominance of core nations over developing countries and facilitates further exploitation.

Contemporary sociologists emphasize that both industrialized and developing countries are "modern." Current researchers are increasingly viewing modernization as movement along a series of social indicators—among them degree of urbanization, energy use, literacy, political democracy, and use of birth control. Clearly, these are often

multinational corporations often buy out or force out local entrepreneurs and companies, thereby increasing economic and cultural dependence (Bornschier et al. 1978; Chase-Dunn and Grimes 1995; P. Evans 1979; Wallerstein 1979).

Modernization

Millions of people around the world are witnessing a revolutionary transformation of their day-to-day life. Contemporary social scientists use the term *modernization* to describe the far-reaching process by which peripheral nations move from traditional or less developed institutions to those characteristic of more developed societies.

Wendell Bell (1981a), whose definition of modernization we are using, notes that modern societies tend to be urban, literate, and industrial. They have sophisticated transportation and media systems. Families tend to be organized within the nuclear family unit rather than the extended-family model (see Chapter 13). Members of societies that have undergone modernization shift allegiance from such traditional sources of authority as parents and priests to newer authorities such as government officials.

Many sociologists are quick to note that terms such as *modernization* and even *development* contain an ethnocentric bias. The unstated assumptions behind these terms are that "they" (people living in developing countries) are struggling to become more like "us" (in the core industrialized nations). Viewed from a conflict perspective, such use of these terms perpetuates the dominant ideology of capitalist societies.

subjective indicators; even in industrialized nations, not all observers would agree that wider use of birth control represents an example of "progress" (Armer and Katsillis 1992; Hedley 1992).

Current modernization studies generally take a convergence perspective. Using the indicators noted above, researchers focus on how societies are moving closer together despite traditional differences. Initially, such modernization studies emphasized the convergence between the United States and the (former) Soviet Union or between capitalist North America and the socialist democracies of western Europe. Now, however, this convergence perspective increasingly includes the developing countries of the Third World. Researchers recognize the interdependence of core industrialized nations and the developing world—as well as the continuing exploitation of the latter countries by the former. From a conflict perspective, modernization in developing countries often perpetuates their dependence on and continued exploitation by more industrialized nations. Conflict theorists view such a continuing dependence on foreign powers as an example of contemporary neocolonialism (Adelman 1993; C. Kerr 1960; O'Donnell 1992).

Stratification within Nations: A Comparative Perspective

At the same time that the gap between rich and poor nations is widening, so too is the gap between rich and poor citizens within nations. As discussed earlier, stratification in developing nations is closely related to their relatively weak and dependent position in the global economy. Local elites work hand in hand with multinational corporations and prosper from such alliances. At the same time, the economic system with its prevailing developmental values creates and perpetuates the exploitation of industrial and agricultural workers. That's why foreign investment in developing countries tends to increase economic inequality (Bornschier et al. 1978; Kerbo 1996). As Box 9-1 makes clear, inequality within a society is also evident in industrialized nations such as Japan.

Distribution of Wealth and Income

In at least 15 nations around the world, the most affluent 10 percent of the population receives at least 40 percent of all income: Brazil (the leader at 48 percent), Chile, Colombia, Guatemala, Honduras, Lesotho, Mali, Mexico, Panama, Papua New Guinea, Portugal, Senegal, Sierra Leone, South Africa, and Zimbabwe (World Bank 2000:238–239). Figure 9-2 compares the distribution of income in selected industrialized and developing nations.

The decade of the 1980s was particularly cruel for many developing countries. Some nations—including Zambia, Bolivia, and Nigeria—saw per capita income plummet as dramatically as it did in the United States during the Great Depression of the 1930s. With these trends in mind, researcher Alan Durning (1990:26) observed that the term "developing nation" has become a cruel misnomer: Many of the world's less affluent nations are disintegrating rather than developing.

Women in developing countries find life especially difficult. Karuna Chanana Ahmed, an anthropologist from India who has studied women in developing nations, calls women the most exploited among oppressed people. Women face sex discrimination beginning at birth. They are commonly fed less than male children, are denied educational opportunities, and are often hospitalized only when critically ill. Whether inside or outside the home, women's work is devalued. When economies fail, as they did in Asian countries in the late 1990s, women are the first to be laid off from work (J. Anderson and Moore 1993; Kristof 1998).

Surveys show a significant degree of *female infanticide* (the killing of baby girls) in China and rural areas of India. Only one-third of Pakistan's sexually segregated schools are for women, and one-third of these schools have no buildings. In Kenya and Tanzania, it is illegal for a woman to own a house. In Saudi Arabia, women are prohibited from driving, walking alone in public, and socializing with men outside their families (C. Murphy 1993). We will explore women's second-class status throughout the world more fully in Chapter 11.

What factors have contributed to the recent difficulties of developing nations? Certainly runaway population growth has hurt the standard of living of many Third World peoples. So, too, has the accelerating environmental decline evident in the quality of air, water, and other natural resources. (We will examine population growth and environmental decline in more detail in Chapter 20.) Still another factor has been the developing nations' collective debt of $1.3 trillion. If we add to a nation's debt repayment the estimates of money being invested elsewhere by wealthy citizens, the annual outflow of funds may reach $100 billion (Durning 1990; Kerbo 1996).

Unfortunately, the massive exodus of money from poorer regions of the world only intensifies their destruction of natural resources. From a conflict view, less affluent nations are being forced to exploit their mineral deposits, forests, and fisheries to meet their debt obligations while offering subsistence labor to local workers. The poor turn to the only means of survival available to them: marginal lands. They plow mountain slopes, burn plots in tropical forests, and overgraze grasslands—often knowing that their actions are destructive to the environment. But they see no alternative in their agonizing fight for simple survival (Durning 1990; Waring 1988).

Prestige

Sociologists have recognized that comparative research is essential in determining whether observed patterns of stratification are unique to a single nation, are restricted to a particular type of society (such as industrial or developing nations), or are applicable to a wide range of societies (Kalleberg 1988). We have seen that societies as different as Brazil, Mexico, the United States, and Japan all share a marked inequality in the distribution of income (refer to Figure 9-2). But a person's class position, defined largely in economic terms and reflecting p. 210 his or her level of wealth and income, is but one component of stratification.

By ranking the prestige of various occupations, sociologists can gain a deeper understanding of another aspect of inequality. But are perceptions in the United States regarding the prestige of occupations comparable to those held in other societies? In an effort to study stratification from a cross-cultural perspective, sociologist Donald Treiman (1977) examined the reputation that certain jobs had in 53 different nations. People were asked to rate occupations and the results were tabulated along a scale ranging from 0 to 100, with higher scores being more prestigious. Treiman found a high degree of correlation or similarity in all contemporary societies, including both industrialized and nonindustrialized nations.

Research in Action

9-1 Inequality in Japan

A tourist visiting Japan may at first experience a bit of culture shock after noticing the degree to which everything in Japanese life is ranked: corporations, universities, even educational programs. These rankings are widely reported and accepted. Moreover, the ratings shape day-to-day social interactions: Japanese find it difficult to sit, talk, or eat together unless the relative rankings of those present have been established, often through the practice of *meishi* (the exchange of business cards).

The apparent preoccupation with ranking and formality suggests an exceptional degree of stratification. Yet researchers have determined that Japan's level of income inequality is among the *lowest* of major industrial societies (see Figure 9-2 on page 239). Whereas the pay gap between Japan's top corporate executives and the nation's lowest-paid workers is about 8 to 1, the comparable figure for the United States would be 37 to 1. In addition, Japanese law prohibits the lucrative stock options received by top U.S. executives.

> Even in developing countries, women are twice as likely to be managers as in Japan.

This relative level of income equality in Japanese society is rather recent; it dates back to post-World War II economic changes, including extensive land reform and the breakup of powerful holding companies. Among the factors that initially contributed to a lower level of inequality in Japan had been an expanding economy combined with a labor shortage. However, during the 1990s the gap between rich and poor began to grow as a result of a severe economic recession and tax laws that let the rich hold on to more of their money.

One factor that still works against inequality is that Japan is rather homogeneous—certainly when compared with the United States—in terms of race, ethnicity, nationality, and language. Japan's population is 98 percent Japanese. But there is discrimination against the nation's Chinese

While women constitute more than 40 percent of Japan's work force, they are generally restricted to subordinate positions.

and Korean minorities, and the *Burakumin* constitute a low-status subculture who encounter extensive prejudice. We will discuss these groups in the next chapter (Box 10-1).

Perhaps the most pervasive form of inequality in Japan is gender discrimination. Japanese girls do not receive the same encouragement to achieve in education that boys do. It should be no surprise, then, that Japanese women occupy a subordinate position in higher education. Whereas 80 percent of the nation's male college students are in four-year universities, two-thirds of female students are in women's junior colleges that promote traditional domestic roles for women. Even when Japanese women enter four-year universities, they often major in home economics, nutrition, or literature.

Overall, women earn only about 64 percent of men's wages. Fewer than 10 percent of Japanese managers are female—a ratio that is one of the lowest in the world. Even in developing countries, women are twice as likely to be managers as in Japan.

In 1985, Japan's parliament—at the time, 97 percent male—passed an Equal Employment bill that encourages employers to end

sex discrimination in hiring, assignment, and promotion policies. However, feminist organizations were dissatisfied because the law lacked strong sanctions. In a landmark ruling issued in late 1996, a Japanese court for the first time held an employer liable for denying promotions due to sex discrimination. The court ordered a Japanese bank to pay 12 female employees a total of almost $1 million and added that 11 of the women must immediately be promoted to management posts.

On the political front, Japanese women have made progress but remain underrepresented. In a study of women in government around the world, the Inter-Parliamentary Union found that, as of 1999, Japan ranked near the bottom of the countries studied, with less than 5 percent of its national legislators female.

Let's Discuss

1. What factors contribute to the relatively low level of income inequality in Japan?
2. Describe the types of gender discrimination found in Japan. Why do you think Japanese women occupy such a subordinate social position?

Sources: Abegglen and Stalk 1985; French 2000; Inter-Parliamentary Union 1999; Jordan 1996b; Kerbo 1996; Kristof 1995c; Magnier 1999; Nakane 1970; Sterngold 1992; Strom 2000.

FIGURE 9-2

Distribution of Income in Nine Nations

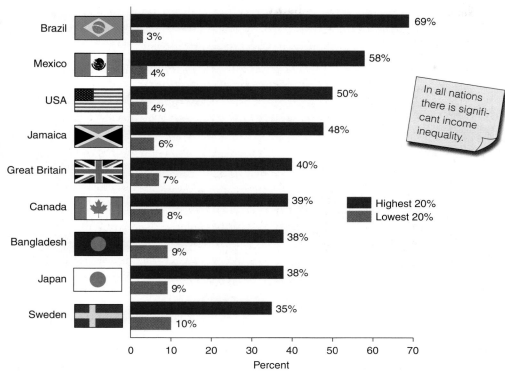

Note: Data are considered comparable although based on statistics covering 1986 to 1999.

Sources: World Bank 1997:54–56; 2000:238–239. U.S. data from the Congressional Budget Office cited in Shapiro and Greenstein 1999.

Treiman's pioneering research inspired subsequent efforts to gather and compare data from many societies using the objective method of measuring stratification differences. In one important study, sociologists Nan Lin and Wen Xie (1988) interviewed a random sample of residents of Beijing, the capital of the People's Republic of China, to study occupational prestige. The researchers recognized the potential bias of sampling those who live in one of China's most cosmopolitan cities. Forty-seven percent of the 1,774 respondents questioned were professionals, managers, or administrators—whereas this was true of only 23 percent of residents of other urban areas. Still, given the constraints on acquiring social scientific data in China, this study offers unique insights regarding stratification in the world's most populous nation.

Lin and Xie found that physicians ranked near the top of the occupational hierarchy, while police officers were near the middle, and garbage collectors were close to the bottom—a finding similar to the results of surveys in the United States. Teachers and professors, however, received much lower prestige ratings in

p. 211

China, reflecting the low wages they receive relative to other occupations. The Chinese respondents gave a much higher prestige rating to textile workers than did respondents in the United States. Textile workers in China evidently fare much better relative to other workers than they do in the United States or Europe.

As one part of their analysis, the researchers compared the prestige rankings of male and female respondents. Although China has officially maintained a national policy of gender equality since 1949, it has not been able to eliminate occupational segregation by gender. Partly as a result, the prestige rankings of Chinese men and women seemed to reflect the structure of occupational opportunity. Males, for example, gave higher ratings than females to such occupations as natural scientist, athlete, driver, and mechanic—all of which are more likely to be held by males. Each gender showed a tendency to rate more highly those occupations most open to it.

Treiman's cross-cultural research reminds us that prestige distinctions are universal; the study of China by Lin and Xie underscores this finding. Even a society that

Internet start-up companies are now enjoying the prestige that blue chip corporations like General Motors used to command. These two casually dressed young men are the founders of Excite, the company that developed a popular Internet search engine.

has experienced revolutionary movements and decades of Communist party rule still stratifies itself in its ranking of prestigious occupations.

Social Mobility

Mobility in Industrial Nations

Studies of intergenerational mobility in industrialized nations have found the following patterns:

1. There are substantial similarities in the ways that parents' positions in stratification systems are transmitted to their children.
2. As in the United States, mobility opportunities in other nations have been influenced by structural factors, such as labor market changes that lead to the rise or decline of an occupational group within the social hierarchy.
3. Immigration continues to be a significant factor shaping a society's level of intergenerational mobility (Ganzeboom et al. 1991; Haller et al. 1990; Hauser and Grusky 1988).

Cross-cultural studies suggest that intergenerational mobility has been increasing in recent decades, at least among men. Dutch sociologists Harry Ganzeboom and Ruud Luijkx joined by sociologist Donald Treiman of the United States (1989) examined surveys of mobility in 35 industrial and developing nations. They found that almost

all the countries studied had witnessed increased intergenerational mobility between the 1950s and 1980s. In particular, they noted a common pattern of movement away from agriculture-based occupations.

Mobility in Developing Nations

Mobility patterns in industrialized countries are usually associated with intergenerational and intragenerational mobility. However, within developing nations, macro-level social and economic changes often overshadow micro-level movement from one occupation to another. For example, there is typically a substantial wage differential between rural and urban areas, which leads to high levels of migration to the cities. Yet the urban industrial sectors of developing countries generally cannot provide sufficient employment for all those seeking work. When migrants find that they are unable to move upward within the conventional economy, the informal or underground economies described in Box 9-2 become more attractive as a source of employment and financial rewards (Thirlwall 1989:103).

The amount of social movement in a society—both upward and downward—is rather limited in societies characterized by slavery and caste systems of stratification. For example, a study of agricul- p. 204 tural households in central India between 1975 and 1983 found that, on average, 84 percent of those who were poor in any year had been poor in the previous year. Over the nine-year period of study, 44 percent of households had been poor for six or more years, and 19 percent were poor in all nine years (World Bank 1990:135).

Recent research on social mobility has persuasively pursued a conflict view: Cross-national differences in mobility are influenced by the differing relations of countries to the world economy. Drawing on Wallerstein's world systems analysis, researchers argue that there is likely to be greater inequality and less mobility in the developing countries than in the core industrialized nations (Ries 1992:187).

Gender Differences and Mobility

Only recently have researchers begun to investigate the impact of gender on the mobility patterns of developing nations. Many aspects of the development process—especially modernization in rural areas and the rural-to-

Sociology in the Global Community

9-2 The Informal Economy

Do you know someone who takes in tips and doesn't report the income? Have you traded services with someone—say, a haircut for help with a computer problem? These are aspects of an **informal economy,** the transfer of money, goods, or services that are not reported to the government. Participants in this type of economy avoid taxes, regulations, and minimum wage provisions, as well as expenses incurred for bookkeeping and financial reporting. Anthropologists studying developing nations and preindustrial societies have long acknowledged the existence of informal social networks that make, sell, and trade goods and services. Only recently have these networks been identified as common to all societies.

In industrial societies, the informal economy embraces transactions that are individually quite small but that can be quite significant when taken together. One major segment of this economy involves illegal transactions—such as prostitution, sale of illegal drugs, gambling, and bribery—leading some observers to describe it as an "underground economy." Yet the informal economy also includes unregulated child care services and the unreported income of craftspeople, street vendors, and employees who receive substantial tips. According to estimates, the informal economy may account for as much as 10 to 20 percent of all economic activity in the United States.

Although these informal economic trans-actions take place in virtually all societies—both capitalist and socialist—the pattern in developing countries differs somewhat from the informal economy of industrialized nations. In the developing world, governments often set up burdensome business regulations that an overworked bureaucracy must administer. When requests for licenses and permits pile up, holding up business projects, legitimate entrepreneurs find they need to "go

> When requests for licenses and permits pile up, holding up business projects, legitimate entrepreneurs find they need to "go underground" in order to get anything done.

underground" in order to get anything done. In Latin America, for example, the underground economy is estimated to account for about one-third of the gross domestic product of the area. Informal industrial enterprises, such as textile factories and repair shops, tend to be labor-intensive. Underground entrepreneurs cannot rely on advanced machinery, since a firm's assets can be confiscated for failure to operate within the open economy.

Viewed from a functionalist perspective, the bureaucratic regulations have contributed to the rise of an efficient informal economy in certain countries. Nevertheless, these regulatory systems are dysfunctional for overall political and economic well-being. Since informal firms typically operate in remote locations to avoid detection, they cannot easily expand even when they become profitable. Given the limited protection for their property and contractual rights, participants in the informal economy are less likely to save and invest their income.

Informal economies have been criticized for promoting highly unfair and dangerous working conditions. A study of the underground economy of Spain found that workers' incomes were low, there was little job security, and safety and health standards were rarely enforced. Both the Spanish government and the nation's trade unions seemed to ignore the exploitation of participants in the informal economy. Still, especially in the developing world, the existence of a substantial underground economy simply reflects the absence of an economic system that is accessible to all residents.

Let's Discuss

1. What conditions contribute to the creation of an informal economy?
2. Describe an informal economy that you have observed or been a part of. Which perspective—functionalist, conflict, or interactionist—do you think best fits the notion of informal economy.

Sources: Ferman et al. 1987; Hershey 1988; Lemkow 1987; Weigard 1992.

urban migration described above—may result in the modification or abandonment of traditional cultural practices and even marital systems. The effects on women's social standing and mobility are not necessarily positive. As a country develops and modernizes, women's vital role in food production deteriorates, jeopardizing both their autonomy and their material well-being. The movement of families to the cities weakens women's ties to relatives who can provide food, financial assistance, and social support (Alam 1985; Boserup 1977; Tiano 1987).

One recent effort to investigate gender and mobility took place in Sri Lanka in Southeast Asia. Researchers ex-amined the impact of foreign aid—in the form of plans to improve agricultural production, irrigation, and rural electrification—on the local population. Virtually all the foreign aid programs were more successful in increasing the incomes of men than of women. Where women's incomes did rise, it was usually in such occupations as rubber and tea cultivation, in which women earn almost 40 percent less than their male counterparts. Overall, foreign aid in Sri Lanka had the unintended consequence of increasing income inequality between male and female workers; similar conclusions were reached in studies conducted in India and Malaysia (Stoeckel and Sirisena 1988).

Chinese immigrants at work in a restaurant in Georgia. Immigrants to industrialized nations may enjoy higher wages but often must accept more menial forms of employment than they had in their native land.

Studies of the distribution of wealth and income within various countries, comparative studies of prestige, and cross-cultural research on mobility consistently reveal that stratification based on class, gender, and other factors shows up within a wide range of societies. Clearly, a worldwide view of stratification must include not only the sharp contrast between wealthy and impoverished nations but also the layers of hierarchies *within* industrialized societies and developing countries.

Stratification in Mexico: A Case Study

Colonialism, neocolonialism, and the domination and exploitation of a peripheral developing country by a core industrialized nation can be clearly seen in the history of Mexico. In this section we will look in some detail at the dynamics of stratification in this country.

In the 1520s, the Aztec Indian tribe that ruled Mexico was overthrown by Spain, and Mexico remained a Spanish colony until the 1820s. In 1836, Texas declared its independence from Mexico, and by 1846, Mexico was at war with the United States. As a result of its defeat, Mexico was forced to surrender over half its territory, including the area of today's California, New Mexico, and northern Arizona. In the 1860s, France sought to turn Mexico into a colony under the Austrian prince Maximilian, but ultimately withdrew after bitter resistance led by a Mexican

Indian who served as the nation's president, Benito Juárez.

Finally, in the twentieth century, as we will explore more fully in this case study, there has been a close cultural, economic, and political relationship between Mexico and the United States, but it has clearly been a relationship in which the United States is the dominant party. According to Wallerstein's analysis, the United States is at the core while neighboring Mexico is still on the periphery of the world economic system.

As of 1999, Mexico had 100 million residents, making it the eleventh most populous nation in the world. The population is concentrated in the nation's three largest cities: Mexico City (the fifth-largest city in the world), Guadalajara, and Monterrey. Indeed, one of every four Mexicans lives in these urban areas. Population growth is a critical issue in Mexico; by the year 2025, the population is expected to expand to about 125 million. Such rapid growth will inevitably intensify Mexico's already serious economic and environmental problems (Haub and Cornelius 1999; Holt 1999; World Resources Institute et al. 1996).

If we compare Mexico to the United States, the overall differences in the standard of living and in life chances are quite dramatic. The *gross domestic product*—the value of all final goods and services produced within a country—is a commonly used measure of an average resident's economic well-being. In 1996, the gross domestic product per person in the United States came to $27,821; in Mexico, it was a mere $7,776. About 90 percent of U.S. youths who are of high-school age are in school compared to 51 percent in Mexico. At birth, people in the United States can expect to live an average of 76 years, while life expectancy in Mexico is 72 years (Bureau of the Census 1999c:836; World Bank 2000:241).

Although Mexico is unquestionably a poor country, the gap between its richest and poorest citizens is one of the widest in the world (refer back to Figure 9-2). In 2000, judged by the standards of the United Nations, 40 percent of the population survived on $2 per day. At the same time, the wealthiest 10 percent of Mexico's people account for 43 percent of the entire nation's income. According to a *Forbes* magazine portrait of the world's wealthiest individuals, Mexico had the fourth-largest number of people on the list—behind only the United

States, Germany, and Japan (Castañeda 1995; World Bank 2000:237, 239).

Political scientist Jorge Castañeda (1995:71) calls Mexico a "polarized society with enormous gaps between rich and poor, town and country, north and south, white and brown (or *criollos* and *mestizos*)." He adds that the country is also divided along lines of class, race, religion, gender, and age. We will examine stratification within Mexico by focusing on race relations and the plight of Mexican Indians, the status of Mexican women, Mexico's economy and environment, and emigration to the United States and its impact on the U.S.–Mexican "borderlands."

Race Relations in Mexico: The Color Hierarchy

On January 1, 1994, rebels from an armed insurgent group called the Zapatista National Liberation Army seized four towns in the state of Chiapas in southern Mexico. The rebels—who named their organization after Emiliano Zapata, a farmer and leader of the 1910 revolution against a corrupt dictatorship—were backed by 2,000 lightly armed Mayan Indians and peasants. Zapatista leaders declared that they had turned to armed insurrection to protest economic injustices and discrimination against the region's Indian population. The Mexican government mobilized the army to crush the revolt, but was forced to retreat as news organizations broadcast pictures of the confrontation around the world. A cease-fire was declared after only 12 days of fighting, but 196 people had already died. Negotiations between the Mexican government and the Zapatista National Liberation Army collapsed in 1996, with sporadic violence ever since (J. Preston 1998).

While many factors contributed to the Zapatista revolt, the subordinate status of Mexico's Indian population throughout the country was surely important. As of early 1996, while accounting for an estimated 15 percent of Mexico's population, Mexican Indians held no important offices in the central government and only a few of the more than 600 seats in the national assembly. Fully 60 percent of Mexican Indians over the age of 12 were unemployed; most of those who did hold jobs earned less than the minimum wage of about $2.50 *per day*. Only 12 percent of Indians complete even a sixth-grade education (DePalma 1995a, 1996; McMahon 1995). The plight of Mexico's Indians is explored further in Figure 9-3.

The subordinate status of Mexico's Indians is but one reflection of the nation's color hierarchy, which links social class to the appearance of racial purity. At the top of this hierarchy are the *criollos*, the 10 percent of the population who are typically White, well-educated members of the business and intellectual elites with familial roots in Spain. In the middle is the large, impoverished *mestizo* majority, most of whom have brown skin and a mixed racial lineage as a result of intermarriage. At the bottom of the color hierarchy are the destitute, full-blooded Mexican Indian minority and a small number of Blacks, some descended from 200,000 African slaves brought to Mexico. This color hierarchy is an important part of day-to-day life—enough so that some Mexicans in the cities use hair dyes, skin lighteners, and blue or green contact lenses to appear more White and European. Ironically, however, nearly all Mexicans are considered part Indian because of centuries of intermarriage (Castañeda 1995; DePalma 1995a).

Many observers take note of widespread denial of prejudice and discrimination against people of color in Mexico. Schoolchildren are taught that the election of Benito Juárez, a Zapotec Indian, as president of Mexico in the nineteenth century proves that all Mexicans are equal. In addition, Mexico's National Commission of Human Rights has *never* received a complaint alleging racial discrimination and has no process for handling such a complaint. With such denial

Mexican women mourn the 1994 death of a member of the Zapatista National Liberation Army, an insurgent group protesting economic injustices and discrimination against the Indian population in the state of Chiapas.

FIGURE 9-3

Relative Position of Indians in Mexico, 1990

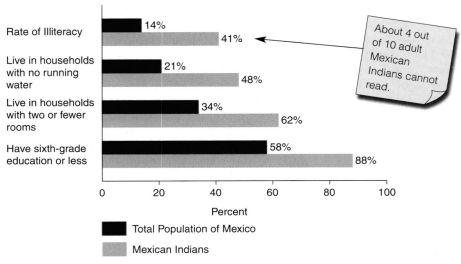

Rate of Illiteracy — 14% / 41%

About 4 out of 10 adult Mexican Indians cannot read.

Live in households with no running water — 21% / 48%

Live in households with two or fewer rooms — 34% / 62%

Have sixth-grade education or less — 58% / 88%

Percent

■ Total Population of Mexico

■ Mexican Indians

Source: Data from 1990 Mexican census as reported in McMahon 1995; and World Bank 1995.

in mind, there has been a marked growth in the last decade of formal organizations and voluntary associations representing indigenous Indians. The Zapatista revolt in Chiapas was an even more dramatic indication that those at the bottom of Mexico's color hierarchy are weary of inequality and injustice (DePalma 1995a, 1996; Stavenhagen 1994).

The Status of Women in Mexico

In 1975, Mexico City hosted the first international conference on the status of women convened by the United Nations. Much of the focus was on the situation of women in developing countries; in that regard, the situation is mixed. Women now constitute 33 percent of the labor force, an increase in the past 20 years but still behind industrial countries. Unfortunately, Mexican women are even more mired in the lowest-paying jobs than their counterparts in industrial nations. In the political arena, women are rarely seen in top decision-making positions, but they have increased their representation in the national legislature to 18 percent, ranking Mexico at 25th among 179 nations worldwide (Inter-Parliamentary Union 1999; World Bank 2000).

Feminist sociologists emphasize that even when they work outside the home, Mexican women often don't get recognized as active and productive household members, while men are typically viewed as the heads of households. As one consequence, women find it difficult to obtain credit and technical assistance in many parts of the country and to

Women account for just a small proportion of elected officials and cabinet ministers in Mexico.

inherit land in rural areas. Within manufacturing and service industries, women generally receive little training and tend to work in the least-automated and least-skilled jobs—in good part because there is little expectation that women will pursue career advancement, organize for better working conditions, or become active in labor unions (Kopinak 1995; Martelo 1996; see also G. Young 1993).

As is true in many developing countries, women in Mexico are more vulnerable than men to contracting the HIV virus and developing AIDS. Their subordinate social and economic position makes it difficult for them to assess their risk of infection from male sexual partners and, even more important, to negotiate taking precautions. Interestingly, abortion is widely available in Mexico. Despite laws prohibiting abortion except in cases of rape or when necessary to save the woman's life, there are an estimated 400,000 abortions each year. Some women obtain abortions from practitioners of folk medicine, but many attempt to self-abort and then seek medical attention to prevent serious injury (Delriozolezzi 1995; Honey 1994).

In recent decades, Mexican women have begun to organize to address an array of economic, political, and health issues. Since women continue to serve as the household managers for their families, even when they work outside the home, they are well aware of the consequences of the inadequate public services in their lower-income urban neighborhoods. As far back as 1973, women in Monterrey—the nation's third-largest city—began protesting the continuing disruptions of the city's water supply. After individual complaints to city officials and the water authority proved fruitless, social networks of female activists began to emerge. These activists sent delegations to confront politicians, organized protest rallies, and blocked traffic as a means of getting media attention. Their efforts brought improvement in Monterrey's water service, but the issue of reliable and safe water remains a concern in Mexico and many developing countries (V. Bennett 1995).

Mexico's Economy and Environment

Mexico strongly lobbied for acceptance of the North American Free Trade Agreement (NAFTA), ultimately signed in 1993, which provided for the dismantling of almost all trade barriers among the United States, Canada, and Mexico. Mexico hoped its struggling economy would receive a major boost from such a favorable linkage to the world's largest consumer market, the United States. Indeed, in 1995 Mexico recorded its first trade surplus with the United States since 1990. Still, any benefit from NAFTA was dramatically undercut in 1994 by the collapse of the *peso,* Mexico's unit of currency. This collapse reflected a widespread loss of confidence as a result of internal political unrest (the Zapatista revolt, discussed earlier) and the assassination of a leading political figure who had spearheaded economic reform. Although U.S. investment in Mexico has increased since the signing of NAFTA, the implementation of the agreement has meant little in the day-to-day economic struggles of the average Mexican (DePalma 1995b; Robberson 1995). We will examine the impact of NAFTA more fully in Chapter 17.

Adding to the pressures on low-income Mexicans, the nation's Social Security system is in a state of crisis and could soon go bankrupt. During the last 50 years, this system has evolved into a "cradle-to-grave" security blanket covering hospital births, child care, lifetime medical care, retirement pensions, and funeral costs for 37 million Mexicans. However, the recent economic crisis has intensified the financial pressures on the system. It is difficult in any case to support a population with more older people

Vigorous government efforts to control pollution in Mexico City have had some success, but conditions for pollution remain ideal in this large city located in a mountain valley some 7,300 feet above sea level.

than ever before—some of whom need long-term and expensive hospitalization because of heart disease and cancer (DePalma 1995c).

Mexico's recession has also hampered efforts to address the nation's serious environmental problems. Not only was the government reluctant to introduce new measures, but citizens could not afford new cars equipped to improve air quality. At the beginning of the 1990s, air pollutants hit emergency levels in Mexico City half the year. Despite opposition from oil companies, the government gradually introduced stronger controls. For example, the "Today You Can't Drive" program took 20 percent of all vehicles without catalytic converters off the road each weekday.

By 2000 there was reason to be optimistic. Mexico City was experiencing five emergency pollution days per year compared to 177 in 1992. This is a dramatic turnaround, especially since the capital's location in a high mountain valley provides ideal conditions for the persistence of pollution. Another encouraging development is that the United States and Mexico signed comprehensive agreements to work together to curb air and water pollution across their common border, which includes massive industrial development on the Mexican side (Saldaña 1999; Smith 2000).

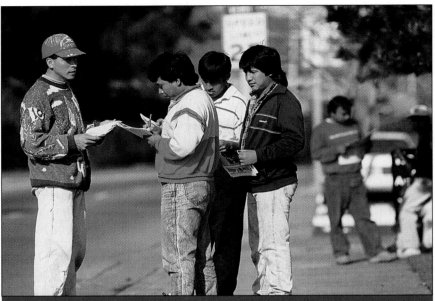

Illegal immigrants from Mexico on a California street, looking for work. The borderlands along the boundary between the United States and Mexico mix the cultures of the two countries.

The Borderlands

Air and water pollution are but two of the many ways in which the problems of Mexico and the United States intertwine. Growing recognition of the borderlands reflects the increasingly close and complex relationship between these two countries. The term *borderlands* refers to the area of a common culture along the border between Mexico and the United States. Legal and illegal emigration from Mexico to the United States, day laborers crossing the border regularly to go to jobs in the United States, the implementation of the North American Free Trade Agreement, and the exchange of media across the border all make the notion of separate Mexican and U.S. cultures obsolete in the borderlands (Heyck 1994).

The economic position of the borderlands is rather complicated, as we can see in the emergence of the *maquiladoras* on the Mexican side. These are foreign companies that establish operations in Mexico yet are ex-

empt from Mexican taxes and are not required to provide insurance or benefits for their workers. The *maquiladoras* have sucked manufacturing jobs from other parts of North America to Mexico. As of late 1999, one million new jobs had been created in the *maquiladoras*, with daily wages of $5 to $15 a day. Moreover, since many of these firms come from the United States and sell their products to Mexico's vast domestic market, their operations deepen the impact of U.S. consumer culture on Mexico's urban and rural areas (*Migration News* 1999c; Wood 1999).

The *maquiladoras* have contributed to Mexico's economic development, but not without some cost. Conflict theorists note that unregulated growth allows the owners to exploit the workers with jobs that lack security, possibilities for advancement, and decent wages. Moreover, many of the U.S.-owned companies require female job applicants to take a urine test to screen out those who are pregnant, a violation of Mexican law as well as the NAFTA agreement and the source of numerous cases of sex discrimination. Social activists also complain that tens of thousands of Mexicans work on *maquiladora* assembly lines for much lower wages, such as $1 an hour, raising again the issue of sweatshop labor noted earlier in the chapter (S. Dillon 1998; Dougherty and Holthouse 1999).

When people in the United States think about the borderlands, they generally think about immigration. As we'll see in the social policy section of Chapter 10, immigration is a controversial political issue in the United States—especially immigration across the Mexican border. For its part, Mexico is concerned about the priorities and policies of its powerful northern neighbor. From Mexico's point of view, the United States too often regards Mexico simply as a reserve pool of easily available cheap labor. The United States encourages Mexicans to cross the border when workers are needed but discourages and "cracks down" on immigrants when they are not. Some people, then, see immigration more as a labor market issue than a law enforcement issue. Viewed from the perspective of Immanuel Wallerstein's world systems analysis and dependency theory, this is yet another example of a core industrialized nation exploiting a peripheral developing country.

The social impact of emigration to the United States is felt throughout Mexico. According to sociological research, the earliest emigrants were typically married men of working age who came from the middle of the stratification system. They had enough financial resources to afford the costs and risks of emigration, yet experienced enough financial strain that entering the United States remained attractive. Over time, kinship ties to migrants multiplied and emigration became less class-selective, with entire families making the trek to the United States. More recently, the occupational backgrounds of Mexican

emigrants have widened further, reflection not only changes in U.S. immigration policy but also the continuing crisis in the Mexican economy (Massey 1998).

Many Mexicans who have come to the United States send some part of their earnings back across the border to family members still in Mexico. This substantial flow of money, sometimes referred to as "remittances" or "migradollars," is estimated by the International Monetary Fund at a minimum of $6 billion annually and accounts for 3 percent of Mexico's gross domestic product. Sociologist Douglas Massey points out that if these funds went solely into the purchase of consumer goods, this would underscore the view of dependency theory that Mexico's economy is little more than an extension of the economy of the United States. In fact, however, some of these "migradollars" are used by Mexicans to establish and maintain small business enterprises, such as handicraft workshops and farms. Consequently, the transfer of "migradollars" does stimulate the local and national economies of Mexico (Durand et al. 1996; *Migration News* 1999b).

We now turn to an examination of how social inequality takes on an especially ugly face in the form of human rights abuse.

SOCIAL POLICY AND SOCIAL INEQUALITY WORLDWIDE

Universal Human Rights

The Issue

One October evening in 1999 three men broke into the house of Digna Ochoa y Placido, a human rights lawyer in Mexico. The men tied her up, interrogated her about the members of political and environmental organizations she represented, and threatened her life. When she managed to free herself she found her phone line cut, her gas line open, and her office ransacked. Ochoa had already been abducted several months earlier and received several death threats for her environmental work on behalf of farmer ecologists who opposed logging interests (*Amnesty Now* 2000).

Poised on the third millennium, the world seemed capable of many mighty feats—ranging from explorations of distant solar systems to refinement of tiny genes within human cells. Yet at the same time came constant reminders of how quickly people and their fundamental human rights can be trampled. The end of Soviet dominance of eastern Europe set off bitter and sometimes violent clashes among racial, ethnic, and religious groups

in Bosnia, Kosovo, Serbia, and former republics of the Soviet Union itself. Fundamentalists in Afghanistan have imposed their strict laws on much of their population. Hutus and Tutsis massacred one another in a virulent civil war in central Africa. Iraq's mistreated Kurdish minority continued to fight for its rights, as did the Mexican peasants of Indian heritage. A peace agreement between Israel and the Palestinians did not end hostilities or killings in that troubled area.

Human rights refers to universal moral rights belonging to all people because they are human. The most important elaboration of human rights appears in the Universal Declaration of Human Rights, adopted by the United Nations in 1948. This declaration prohibits slavery, torture, and degrading punishment; grants everyone the right to a nationality and its culture; affirms freedom of religion and the right to vote; proclaims the right to seek asylum in other countries to escape persecution; and prohibits arbitrary interference with one's privacy and arbitrary taking of a person's property. It also emphasizes that mothers and children are entitled to special care and assistance.

What steps, if any, can the world community take to ensure the protection of these rights? And is it even possible to agree on what those rights are?

The Setting

The 1990s tragically brought the term *ethnic cleansing* into the world's vocabulary. Within the former Yugoslavia, Serbs initiated a policy intended to "cleanse" Muslims from parts of Bosnia-Herzegovina and ethnic Albanians from the province of Kosovo. Hundreds of thousands of people have been killed in the fighting in this area, while many others have been uprooted from their homes. Moreover, there have been reports of substantial numbers of rapes of Muslim, Croatian, and Kosovar women by Serbian soldiers. In 1996 a United Nations tribunal indicted eight Bosnian Serb military and police officers for rape, marking the first time that sexual assault was treated as a war crime under international law (Simons 1996c; see also Fein 1995).

Drawing on the principles of the Universal Declaration of Human Rights, in 1995 the United Nations Human Rights Commission condemned Iraq, Iran, and the Sudan for serious human rights violation, including summary executions, cases of torture, and discrimination against women. The commission adopted resolutions expressing concern over human rights abuses in Haiti, Zaire, and Myanmar and only narrowly rejected a resolution to investigate the state of human rights in China (*New York Times* 1995a).

At first, the United States opposed a binding obligation to the Universal Declaration of Human Rights. The government feared that the declaration would cause international scrutiny of the nation's own domestic civil rights controversies (at a time when racial segregation by law was still common). By the early 1960s, however, the United States began to use the declaration to promote democracy abroad (Forsythe 1990).

Sociological Insights

By its very title, the Universal Declaration of Human Rights emphasizes that such rights should be *universal*. But cultural relativism encourages understanding and respecting the distinctive norms, values, and customs of each culture. In some situations, conflicts arise between human rights standards and local social practices that rest on alternative views of human dignity. For example, is India's caste system an inherent violation of human rights? What about the many cultures of the world that view the subordinate status of women as an essential element in their traditions? Should human rights be interpreted differently in different parts of the world?

In 1993 the United States rejected such a view. In a speech at the World Conference on Human Rights, Secretary of State Warren Christopher insisted that the Universal Declaration of Human Rights set a single standard for acceptable behavior around the world. However, in the late 1990s certain Asian and African nations were reviving arguments about cultural relativism in an attempt to block sanctions by the United Nations Human Rights Commission (Crossette 1996b; Donnelly 1989; Sciolino 1993).

It is not often that a nation makes the bold statement that Christopher did. Policymakers, including those in the United States, more frequently look at human rights issues from an economic perspective. Functionalists would point out how much more quickly we become embroiled in "human rights" concerns when oil is at stake, as in the Middle East, or military alliances come into play, as in Europe. The United States is less likely to want to interfere in an area where its economic concerns are modest (as in Africa) or where it is seeking to advance an economic agenda (as in China).

This intersection of economics and human rights issues has led to the creation of a Human Rights Index, using a database that weighs measures of human rights violations in a country against its level of economic development. Human rights abuses include such indicators as the denial of minority and women's rights, the presence of political prisoners, and the use of torture. Because poverty and a position at the periphery of the world economic system make equality difficult to achieve, the index is adjusted to reflect the level of a nation's development. Figure 9-4 highlights the best nations and the worst offenders in this index of 194 nations. In this list, Mexico ranks 20, Russia 32, and the United States 92—almost in the middle.

The feminist perspective has been particularly useful in unraveling human rights issues. Women's groups emerged as a strong and effective lobby at the World Conference on Human Rights held in Vienna in 1993. The next year the U.S. State Department focused for the first time on worldwide treatment of women in its annual human rights report, painting a grim picture of discrimination and abuse. In a major speech at the 1995 World Conference on Women in Beijing, China, Hillary Rodham Clinton stated that women's rights can no longer be discussed separately from human rights. She cited the killing of female babies, the selling of women and girls into slavery and prostitution, and wartime rape as abuses that must be addressed (S. Greenhouse 1994; Riding 1993; P. Tyler 1995a, 1995b).

p. 81

FIGURE 9-4

Human Rights Index

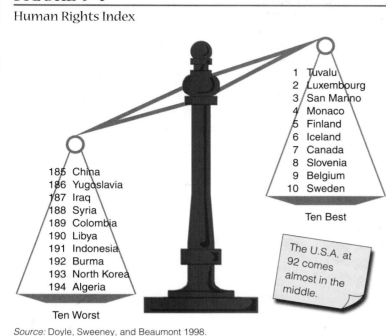

1 Tuvalu
2 Luxembourg
3 San Marino
4 Monaco
5 Finland
6 Iceland
7 Canada
8 Slovenia
9 Belgium
10 Sweden

Ten Best

185 China
186 Yugoslavia
187 Iraq
188 Syria
189 Colombia
190 Libya
191 Indonesia
192 Burma
193 North Korea
194 Algeria

Ten Worst

The U.S.A. at 92 comes almost in the middle.

Source: Doyle, Sweeney, and Beaumont 1998.

Policy Initiatives

Human rights come wrapped up in international diplomacy. For that reason, many national policymakers hesitate to interfere in human rights issues, especially if they conflict with what are regarded as more pressing national concerns. Stepping up to fill the gap are international organizations such as the United Nations and nongovernmental organizations (NGOs) like Médecins sans Frontières and Amnesty International. Most initiatives come from these international bodies.

Médecins sans Frontières (Doctors Without Borders), the world's largest independent emergency medical aid organization, won the 1999 Nobel Peace Prize for its work in countries worldwide. Founded in 1971 and based in Paris, the organization has 5,000 doctors and nurses working in 80 countries. "Our intention is to highlight current upheavals, to bear witness to foreign tragedies and reflect on the principles of humanitarian aid," explains Dr. Rony Brauman, the organization's president (Spielmann 1992:12; also see Daley 1999).

Among the endangered peoples of the world are many indigenous (native or tribal) peoples whose settlement preceded immigration from other countries and colonialism. They include nomadic Bedouins of the Arabic peninsula, the Inuit (Eskimo) of North America, the Sami (or Lapp) of northern Scandinavia, the Ainu of Japan, the Aborigines of Australia, and Brazil's Yanomani Indians. Indigenous peoples are organizing to defend their way of life, assisted by voluntary associations in the core industrialized nations. As one result of this activism, the United Nations has established a working group to draft a Universal Declaration of the Right of Indigenous Peoples (Durning 1993).

Amnesty International monitors human rights violations around the world. Founded in 1966, the organization has chapters in many countries and 400,000 members in the United States alone. It works

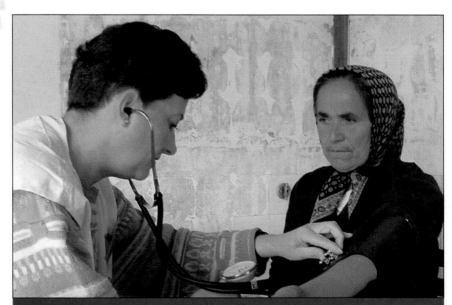

International nongovernmental organizations sometimes step in when governmental and diplomatic initiatives fail to address human rights abuses. This Albanian doctor treating a Serb woman in Kosovo is a member of Médecins sans Frontières, an independent emergency medical aid organization.

for the release of men and women detained for their conscientiously held beliefs, their color, ethnic origin, sex, religion, or language—provided they have neither used nor advocated violence. The winner of the 1977 Nobel Prize for Peace, Amnesty International opposes all forms of torture and capital punishment and advocates prompt trials of all political prisoners.

Women's rights got a boost from the World Conference on Women. In 1995 the conference delegates agreed on a "platform of action" calling on governments around the world to improve the status of girls, better the economic situation of women, and protect women from increasing levels of violence.

In recent years, there has been growing awareness of lesbian and gay rights as an aspect of universal human rights In 1994, Amnesty International USA (1994:2) published a pioneering report in which it acknowledged that "homosexuals in many parts of the world live in constant fear of government persecution." The report examined abuses in Brazil, Greece, Mexico, Iran, the United States, and other countries, including cases of torture, imprisonment, and extrajudicial execution. Later in 1994

the United States issued an order that would allow lesbians and gay men to seek political asylum in the United States if they can prove they have suffered government persecution in their home countries solely because of their sexual orientation (Johnston 1994). We'll look at lesbian and gay rights in more detail in Chapter 21.

Ethnic cleansing in the former Yugoslavia; human rights violations in Iraq, Iran, and the Sudan; persecution of the Aborigines of Australia and other indigenous peoples; violence against women inside and outside the family; governmental torture of lesbians and gay men—all these are vivid reminders that social inequality today can have life-and-death consequences. Universal human rights remain an ideal and not a reality.

Let's Discuss

1. Why are there varying definitions of human rights?
2. Does it surprise you that the U.S. does not rank very high in human rights (Figure 9-4)? Why do you think this is the case?
3. How have feminist groups broadened the debate over universal human rights?

Summary

We can easily see worldwide stratification both in the gap between rich and poor nations and in the inequality *within* countries around the world. This chapter examines stratification within the world economic system, the impact of multinational corporations on developing countries, modernization, and the distribution of wealth and income in various nations.

1. As of 1995, the 140 developing nations accounted for 78 percent of the world's population but only 16 percent of all wealth.
2. Former colonized nations are kept in a subservient position, subject to foreign domination, through the process of **neocolonialism.**
3. Drawing on the conflict perspective, the world systems analysis of sociologist Immanuel Wallerstein views the global economic system as divided between nations that control wealth (*core nations*) and those from which capital is taken (*periphery nations*).
4. According to **dependency theory,** even as developing countries make economic advances, they remain weak and subservient to core nations and corporations within an increasingly intertwined global economy.
5. **Multinational corporations** bring jobs and industry to developing nations, but they also tend to exploit the workers there in order to maximize profits.
6. Many sociologists are quick to note that terms such as **modernization** and even *development* contain an ethnocentric bias.
7. According to **modernization theory,** development in peripheral countries will be assisted by the innovations transferred from the industrialized world.
8. Social mobility is more limited in developing nations than in the core nations.
9. While Mexico is unquestionably a poor country, the gap between its richest and poorest citizens is one of the widest in the world.
10. The subordinate status of Mexico's Indians is but one reflection of the nation's color hierarchy, which links social class to the appearance of racial purity.
11. Growing recognition of the **borderlands** reflects the increasingly close and complex relationship between Mexico and the United States.
12. **Human rights** need to be identified and abuses of these rights need to be corrected in countries throughout the world.

Critical Thinking Questions

1. In what ways is the informal economy evident in your college community and in the city or town where you grew up? Drawing on the functionalist, conflict, and interactionist perspectives, analyze the informal economy as you have seen it in these communities.
2. Imagine that you had the opportunity to spend a year in Mexico studying inequality in that nation. How would you draw on the research designs of sociology (surveys, observation, experiments, existing sources) to better understand and document stratification in Mexico?
3. How active should the U.S. government be in addressing violations of human rights in other countries? At what point, if any, does concern for human rights turn into ethnocentrism by failing to respect the distinctive norms, values, and customs of another culture?

Key Terms

Borderlands The area of a common culture along the border between Mexico and the United States. (246)

Colonialism The maintenance of political, social, economic, and cultural dominance over a people by a foreign power for an extended period of time. (232)

Dependency theory An approach that contends that industrialized nations continue to exploit developing countries for their own gain. (232)

Human rights Universal moral rights belonging to all people because they are human. (247)

Informal economy Transfers of money, goods, or services that are not reported to the government. (241)

Modernization The far-reaching process by which peripheral nations move from traditional or less developed institutions to those characteristic of more developed societies. (236)

Modernization theory A functionalist approach that proposes that modernization and development will gradually improve the lives of people in peripheral nations. (236)

Multinational corporations Commercial organizations that, while headquartered in one country, own or control other corporations and subsidiaries throughout the world. (234)

Neocolonialism Continuing dependence of former colonies on foreign countries. (232)

World systems analysis A view of the global economic system as divided between certain industrialized nations that control wealth and developing countries that are controlled and exploited. (232)

Additional Readings

BOOKS

Gereffi, Gary, and Miquel Korenziewicz, eds. 1994. *Commodity Chains and Global Capitalism.* New York: Praeger. The contributors to this volume look at the relationship among a variety of global economy networks that are overtaking the nation-state.

LaFeber, Walter. 1999. *Michael Jordan and the New Global Capitalism.* New York: W. W. Norton. Considers the growing intersection of culture and capital on an international scale.

Waring, Marilyn. 1988. *If Women Counted: A New Feminist Economics.* San Francisco: Harper and Row. Waring, a social scientist from New Zealand, considers how women's labor is overlooked in the global economy.

Weigard, Bruce. 1992. *Off the Books: A Theory and Critique of the Underground Economy.* Dix Hills, N.Y.: General-Hall. An examination of the social consequence of people's participation in activities outside the mainstream economy.

The World Bank. *World Development Report.* New York: Oxford University Press. Published annually by the International Bank for Reconstruction and Development (the United Nations agency more commonly referred to as the World Bank), this volume provides a vast array of social and economic indicators regarding world development.

JOURNALS

Among the journals that consider issues of worldwide stratification, uneven development, and universal human rights are *Holocaust and Genocide Studies* (founded in 1987), *Human Rights Quarterly* (1978), *International Journal of Urban and Regional Research* (1976), *International Labor Review* (1921), *Journal of Developing Areas* (1965), *Latin American Research Review* (1956), *Review of Income and Wealth* (1954), and *World Development* (1973).

Internet Connection

Note: While all the URLs listed were current as of the printing of this book, these sites often change. Please check our website (http://www.mhhe.com/schaefer) for updates.

1. Universal human rights have become a major concern for politicians, sociologists, and activist groups. Direct your web browser to (**http://headlines.yahoo.com/Full_Coverage/World/Human_Rights/**) and learn about recent events in the area of human rights.
   (a) What news stories dominate the headlines?
   (b) Does it appear that human rights are more or less being respected according to these headlines? What examples can you give to support your answer?
   (c) According to the Universal Declaration of Human Rights, what rights should all persons enjoy? Can you think of any to add to this list?
   (d) Which rights do you feel are the most important? Why?
   (e) What examples from your text or from current events show violation of any of these specific human rights?
   (f) According to the Human Rights Watch World Report 2000, how well does the United States do in respecting universal human rights? What might improve matters in the United States?
   (g) What is Amnesty International? When and why was it founded? What are its goals and mission statements? What are its current campaigns?
   (h) What role might television and the Internet play in improving the observance of human rights?

2. Mali is one of the poorest countries in the world (see Figure 9-1). Take an online field trip to Mali courtesy of Oxfam (**http://www.oxfamamerica.org/global/mali/index.htm**).
   (a) Where is Mali?
   (b) What is "mankala"?
   (c) What purpose does the tea ceremony serve in Mali culture?
   (d) Why is dancing important?
   (e) What are the birth rate, population growth rate, death rate, and life expectancy ages for men and women? How does Mali compare to the United States in terms of these numbers?
   (f) What kinds of work are most people in the Mali labor force engaged in?
   (g) What surprised you most about your "field trip" to Mali?
   (h) Imagine that you were selected to improve conditions in Mali. Which problems would receive priority attention, and why? What realistic solutions would you offer to alleviate the poverty and hunger in Mali?
   (i) Do you think the United States does enough to assist countries like Mali? Why or why not?

CHAPTER 10

RACIAL AND ETHNIC INEQUALITY

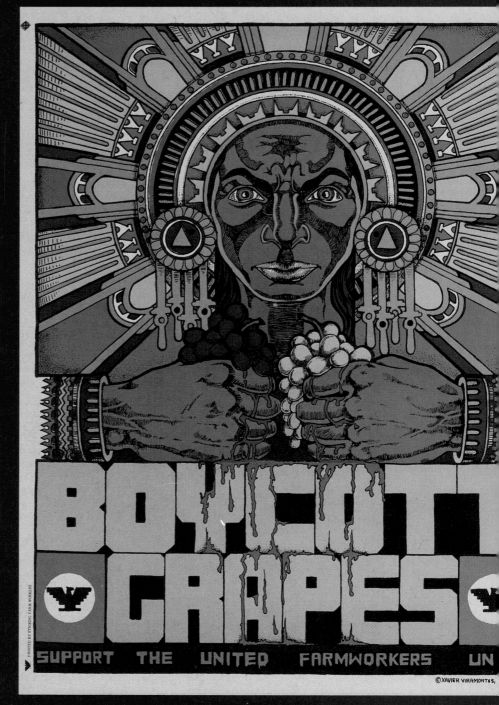

BOYCOTT GRAPES

SUPPORT THE UNITED FARMWORKERS UN

©XAVIER VIRAMONTES,

PRINTED BY STERLING FARM WORKERS

This 1973 poster encouraged consumers to boycott grapes in support of the predominantly Mexican United Farm Workers Union, on strike to protest treatment of migrant farm workers in California. The godlike Aztec figure, shown with the "blood" of grapes dripping through his fingers, suggests the anger striking fieldworkers must have felt over their low pay and substandard living conditions.

Several years ago, at a moment when I was particularly tired of the unstable lifestyle that academic careers sometimes require, I surprised myself and bought a real house. Because the house was in a state other than the one where I was living at the time, I obtained my mortgage by telephone. I am a prudent little squirrel when it comes to things financial, always tucking away stores of nuts for the winter, and so I meet the criteria of a quite good credit risk. My loan was approved almost immediately. . . .

I should also note that I speak a Received Standard English, regionally marked as Northeastern perhaps, but not easily identifiable as black. With my credit history, my job as a law professor and, no doubt, with my accent, I am not only middle class but apparently match the cultural stereotype of a good white person. It is thus, perhaps, that the loan officer of the bank, whom I had never met, had checked off the box on the fair housing form indicating that I was white.

Race shouldn't matter, I suppose, but it seemed to in this case, so I took a deep breath, crossed out "white" and sent the contract back. That will teach them to presume too much, I thought. A done deal, I assumed. But suddenly the transaction came to a screeching halt. The bank wanted more money, more points, a higher rate of interest. Suddenly I found myself facing great resistance and much more debt. To make a long story short, I threatened to sue under the act in question [the Fair Housing Act], the bank quickly backed down and I procured the loan on the original terms.

What was interesting about all this was that the reason the bank gave for its new-found recalcitrance was not race, heaven forbid. . . . The reason they gave was that property values in that neighborhood were suddenly falling. They wanted more money to buffer themselves against the snappy winds of projected misfortune.

Initially, I was surprised, confused. The house was in a neighborhood that was extremely stable. I am an extremely careful shopper; I had uncovered absolutely nothing to indicate that prices were falling. It took my realtor to make me see the light. "Don't you get it," he sighed. "This is what always happens." . . .

"I'll bet you'll keep your mouth shut the next time they plug you into the computer as white," laughed a friend when he heard my story. *(Williams 1997)* ∎

S ome people believe that racial discrimination is a thing of the past in the United States—that it ended decades ago with the passage of civil rights legislation. But the experience of Patricia J. Williams, a professor of law at Columbia University, is a vivid reminder that race continues to shape the lives of even professional African Americans. Indeed, millions of African Americans, Asian Americans, Hispanic Americans, and many other racial and ethnic minorities have experienced the often bitter contrast between the "American dream" and the grim realities of poverty, prejudice, and discrimination. According to a recent national study, discrimination in mortgage lending actually *increased* between 1995 and 1999 (Turner and Skidmore 1999). Like class, the social definitions of race and ethnicity still affect people's place and status in a stratification system, not only in this country but throughout the world. High incomes and hard-earned professional credentials do not always override racial and ethnic stereotypes or protect those who fit them from the sting of racism.

This chapter focuses primarily on the meaning of race and ethnicity. We begin by identifying the basic characteristics of a minority group and distinguishing between racial and ethnic groups. The next section of the chapter will examine the dynamics of prejudice and discrimination. After considering the functionalist, conflict, and interactionist perspectives on race and ethnicity, we'll take a look at patterns of intergroup relations, particularly in the United States. Finally, the social policy section will explore issues related to immigration worldwide. ■

Minority, Racial, and Ethnic Groups

Sociologists frequently distinguish between racial and ethnic groups. The term *racial group* is used to describe a group that is set apart from others because of obvious physical differences. Whites, African Americans, and Asian Americans are all considered racial groups in the United States. While race does turn on physical differences, it is the culture of a particular society that constructs and attaches social significance to these differences, as we will see later. Unlike racial groups, an *ethnic group* is set apart from others primarily because of its national origin or distinctive cultural patterns. In the United States, Puerto Ricans, Jews, and Polish Americans are all categorized as ethnic groups.

Minority Groups

A numerical minority is any group that makes up less than half of some larger population. The population of the United States includes thousands of numerical minorities, including television actors, green-eyed people, tax lawyers, and descendants of the Pilgrims who arrived on the *Mayflower.* However, these numerical minorities are not considered to be minorities in the sociological sense; in fact, the number of people in a group does not necessarily determine its status as a social minority (or dominant group). When sociologists define a minority group, they are primarily concerned with the economic and political power, or powerlessness, of that group. A *minority group* is a subordinate group whose members have significantly less control or power over their own lives than the members of a dominant or majority group have over theirs.

Sociologists have identified five basic properties of a minority group—unequal treatment, physical or cultural traits, ascribed status, solidarity, and in-group marriage (Wagley and Harris 1958):

1. Members of a minority group experience unequal treatment as compared to members of a dominant group. For example, the management of an apartment complex may refuse to rent to African Americans, Hispanics, or Jews. Social inequality may be created or maintained by prejudice, discrimination, segregation, or even extermination.

2. Members of a minority group share physical or cultural characteristics that distinguish them from the dominant group. Each society arbitrarily decides which characteristics are most important in defining the groups.

3. Membership in a minority (or dominant) group is not voluntary; people are born into the group. Thus, race and ethnicity are considered *ascribed* statuses. pp. 121–22

4. Minority group members have a strong sense of group solidarity. William Graham Sumner, writing in 1906, noted that people make distinctions between members of their own group (the *in-group*) and everyone else (the *out-group*). In-groups and out-groups were discussed in Chapter 6. When a group is the object of long-term prejudice and discrimination, the feeling of "us versus them" can and often does become extremely intense.

5. Members of a minority generally marry others from the same group. A member of a dominant group is often unwilling to marry into a supposedly inferior minority. In addition, the minority group's sense of solidarity encourages marriages within the group and discourages marriages to outsiders.

Race

The term *racial group* refers to those minorities (and the corresponding dominant groups) set apart from others by obvious physical differences. But what is an "obvious" physical difference? Each society determines which differences are important while ignoring other characteristics that could serve as a basis for social differentiation. In the United States, we see differences in both skin color and hair color. Yet people learn informally that differences in skin color have a dramatic social and political meaning, while differences in hair color do not.

When observing skin color, people in the United States tend to lump others rather casually into such categories as "Black," "White," and "Asian." More subtle differences in skin color often go unnoticed. However, this is not the case in other societies. Many nations of Central America and South America have color gradients distinguishing people on a continuum from light to dark skin color. Brazil has approximately 40 color groupings, while in other countries people may be described as "Mestizo Hondurans," "Mulatto Colombians," or "African Panamanians." What we see as "obvious" differences, then, are subject to each society's social definitions.

The largest racial minorities in the United States are African Americans (or Blacks), Native Americans (or American Indians), and Asian Americans (Japanese Americans, Chinese Americans, and other Asian peoples). Figure 10-1 provides information about the population and distribution of racial and ethnic groups in the United States over the past five centuries.

Biological Significance of Race

Viewed from a biological perspective, the term *race* would refer to a genetically isolated group with distinctive gene frequencies. But it is impossible to scientifically define or identify such a group. Consequently, contrary to popular belief, there are no "pure races." Nor are there physical traits—whether skin color or baldness—that can be used to describe one group to the exclusion of all others. If scientists examine a smear of human blood under a microscope, they cannot tell whether it came from a Chinese or

FIGURE 10-1

Racial and Ethnic Groups in the United States, 1500–2050 (Projected)

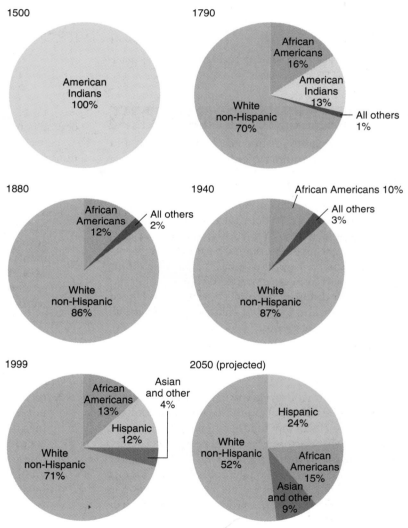

Sources: Author's estimate; Bureau of the Census 1975, 2000a; Thornton 1987.

The racial and ethnic composition of what is today the United States has been undergoing change not just for the last 50 years, but for the last 500. Five centuries ago the land was populated only by indigenous Native Americans.

a Navajo, a Hawaiian or an African American. There is, in fact, more genetic variation *within* races than across them.

Migration, exploration, and invasion have led to intermingling of races. Scientific investigations indicate that the percentage of North American Blacks with White ancestry ranges from 20 percent to as much as 75 percent. Recent DNA findings suggest that some Blacks today can even claim Thomas Jefferson as their ancestor. Such statistics undermine a fundamental assumption of life in the United States: that we can accurately categorize individuals as "Black" or "White" (Herskovits 1930; D. Roberts 1975).

Some people would like to find biological explanations to help social scientists understand why certain peoples of the world have come to dominate others (refer back to the discussion of sociobiology in Chapter 4). Given the absence of pure racial groups, there can be no satisfactory biological answers for such social and political questions.

Social Construction of Race

In the southern part of the United States, it was known as the "one-drop rule." If a person had even a single drop of "Black blood," that person was defined and viewed as Black, even if he or she *appeared* to be White. Clearly, race had social significance in the South, enough so that White legislators established official standards about who was "Black" and "White."

The one-drop rule was a vivid example of the *social construction of race*—the process by which people come to define a group as a race based in part on physical characteristics, but also on historical, cultural, and economic factors. It is an ongoing process subject to some debate, especially in a diverse society like the United States, where each year increasing numbers of children are born to parents of different racial backgrounds. Census Bureau estimates indicate that about 7 percent of the U.S. population could claim multiple racial ancestry in 1999; by the year 2030 the percentage of the population is expected to climb to 21 percent. Among Asian Americans the percentage of people claiming mixed ancestry is expected to reach 36 percent; among Native Americans, 89 percent; among Whites, 21 percent; among Blacks, 14 percent; and among Hispanics, 45 percent (Edmonson and Passel 1999).

Still, mixed racial ancestry is an identity that is not clearly defined in a society that literally thinks in "black" and "white" terms. Facing this social reality, the U.S. Census Bureau considered adding a "biracial" category to Census 2000. But trial studies showed that people were confused by this "new" term, and relatively few chose it. As a compromise, the Census 2000 for the first time allowed people to check off as many racial categories as they wish, so that one could, for example, check off "White," "American Indian," *and* "African American." Sociologists and others are eagerly awaiting the results of this opportunity for people to individually express their blended racial identity.

A dominant or majority group has the power not only to define itself legally but to define a society's values. Sociologist William I. Thomas (1923), an early critic of theories of racial and gender differences, saw that the "definition of the situation" could mold the personality of the individual. To put it another way, Thomas, writing from the interactionist perspective, observed that people respond not only to the objective features of a situation or person but also to the *meaning* that situation or person has for them. Thus, we can create false images or stereotypes that become real in their consequences. *Stereotypes* are unreliable generalizations about all members of a group that do not recognize individual differences within the group.

In the last 30 years, critics have pointed out the power of the mass media to perpetuate false racial and ethnic stereotypes. Television is a prime example: Almost all the leading dramatic roles are cast as Whites, even in urban-based programs like *Friends*. Blacks tend to be featured mainly in crime-based dramas. (See Box 10-3 on p. 272–273 for further discussion of the distorted picture of American society presented on prime-time television programs.)

Self-Fulfilling Prophecy

In certain situations, we may respond to stereotypes in such a way that false definitions end up being accurate. In this phenomenon, called the *self-fulfilling prophecy,* a person or group that is described as having particular characteristics begins to display those very traits. When teachers and counselors tell a bright child from a working-class family that he would make a good carpenter or mechanic, for instance, they may discourage him from thinking of college or a profession. Seeing himself through their eyes as a tradesperson, he may well grow up to become a blue-collar worker. In assessing the impact of self-fulfilling prophecies, we can refer back to labeling theory, which emphasizes `pp. 183–84` how a person comes to be labeled as deviant and even to accept a self-image of deviance.

Self-fulfilling prophecies can be especially devastating for minority groups (see Figure 10-2 on next page). The dominant group in a society believes that subordinate group members lack the ability to perform in important and lucrative positions. So it denies them the training needed to become scientists, executives, or physicians, effectively locking the subordinate group into society's inferior jobs. The false definition has become real: in terms of employment, the minority has become inferior because it was originally defined as inferior and was prevented from achieving equality.

Because of this vicious circle, talented people from minority groups may come to see the worlds of entertainment and professional sports as their only hope for

FIGURE 10-2

The Self-fulfilling Prophecy

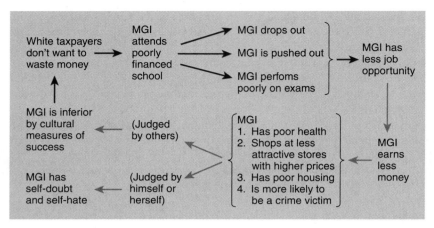

The self-validating effects of definitions made by the dominant group are shown in this figure. A minority group individual attends a poorly financed school and is left unequipped to perform jobs that offer high status and high pay. He or she then gets a low-paying job and must settle for a lifestyle far short of society's standards. Since the person shares these standards, he or she may begin to feel self-doubt and self-hatred. This last phase of the cycle has been called into question in recent research.

Note: MGI stands for "minority group individual." Arrows represent direction of negative cumulative effect.

Source: Schaefer 2000:21.

The popular Puerto Rican recording star Ricky Martin performs his hit song "Livin' la Vida Loca" on the *Today* show in Rockefeller Center. Entertainment, as opposed to corporate or government leadership, is a field in which Latinos have enjoyed some success.

achieving wealth and fame. It is no accident that successive waves of Irish, Jewish, Italian, Black, and Hispanic performers and athletes have made their mark on our society. Unfortunately, these very successes may convince the dominant group that its original stereotypes are valid—that these are the *only* areas of society in which minorities can excel. Furthermore, athletics and the arts are well-known in our society as highly competitive arenas. For every Gloria Estefan, Sammy Sosa, or Oprah Winfrey who "makes it," many, many more will end up disappointed (Allport 1979; Merton 1968).

Sociologist Harry Edwards (1984:9–13) agrees that the self-fulfilling prophecy of "innate Black athletic superiority" can have damaging consequences. Edwards points out that although this perception of athletic prowess may channel many African Americans into sports, only about 2,500 of them, at best, currently make a living in professional sports. In his view, Blacks should no longer put football playbooks ahead of textbooks, and the Black community should abandon its "blind belief in sport as an extraordinary route to social and economic salvation" (see also Gates 1991).

African Americans and other minorities do not always passively accept harmful stereotypes and self-fulfilling prophecies. In the 1960s and 1970s, many subordinate minorities in the United States rejected traditional definitions and replaced them with feelings of pride, power, and strength. "Black is beautiful" and "Red power" movements among Blacks and Native Americans were efforts to take control of their own lives and self-images. However, although a minority can make a determined effort to redefine a situation and resist stereotypes, the definition that remains most important is the one used by a society's

10-1 Social Construction of Race and Ethnicity in Japan

To those who watched the 1998 Winter Olympics in Nagano, those who tour Japan, and those who do business there from abroad, Japan seems very homogeneous, with outward civility to all races or nationalities.

This picture of tolerance, however, disguises significant inequality along racial and ethnic lines in Japan. These distinctions may be difficult to discern because, after all, 96 percent of the population is Japanese, but for the racial and ethnic minorities, the historical and contemporary discrimination is very real. The largest minority is the Burakumins, followed by resident Koreans. The two million Burakumins represent an interesting case because physically they are indistinguishable from the Japanese. Their ancestors were part of the lowest group in a quasi-caste system originating four centuries ago, and they have lived in segregated communities ever since. Identified by their station in life and viewed as a distinct socially constructed race, the Burakumins continue to face discrimination in marriage, employment, and education, as well as other areas. One study showed that one-third declared their rights were being violated in such areas as work, school, or choosing a marriage partner. It is not unusual for employers or families to hire private detectives if they suspect a prospective employee or in-law is a Burakumin. In 1969,

the Japanese government passed legislation to counter discrimination and provided special incentives to increase the numbers of Burakumins continuing their schooling. Despite these efforts, a variety of groups today find it necessary to work on behalf of the Burakumins. Some use established policymaking channels, while others take much more militant positions.

There has also been growing controversy concerning Japan's treatment of its Korean minority—a more visible subordinate group

> It is not unusual for employers or families to hire private detectives if they suspect a prospective employee or in-law is a Burakumin.

to outsiders. About 700,000 Koreans live in Japan, of whom more than 85 percent were born there. It is not easy for Koreans to obtain Japanese citizenship; without citizenship, they cannot vote, cannot work as teachers or government officials, and must carry alien registration cards at all times. Only about half of the Korean males finish high school, compared to 97 percent of the general population.

Koreans in Japan disproportionately work for low wages, without safety standards, and without any real hope of advance-

ment. Moreover, because discrimination is so common, fewer than 5 percent of Koreans use their own names in business circles. Similarly, many young Koreans use Japanese aliases to conceal their heritage in schools.

Over time, the government of Japan has taken a more conciliatory attitude toward resident Koreans. In 1993, after years of bitter debate, Japan's parliament agreed to end the mandatory fingerprinting of most Koreans and other foreign residents required under the nation's Alien Registration Law. Nevertheless, Korean residents—many of whose families have lived in Japan for generations—still have no right to work in government jobs or to learn about their heritage in public schools. The nation's Supreme Court did rule in 1995 that local governments could permit resident Koreans to vote. Though this step was hailed as a major victory, there is little movement to make it a national policy.

Let's Discuss

1. Has anyone in your family ever been denied a job or an education because of his or her race or ethnicity? If so, explain the circumstances.
2. Did one of your ancestors ever change the family surname to escape discrimination based on ethnicity? If so, when and under what circumstances? Did the change make a difference in your family's social standing?

Sources: Kerbo and McKinstry 1998; T. Neary 1997; Sugimoto 1997.

powerful groups. In this sense, the historic White, Anglo-Saxon, Protestant norms of the United States still shape the definitions and stereotypes of racial and ethnic minorities. The power of race to be a defining characteristic even shows up in societies that seem outwardly homogeneous, as Box 10-1 shows.

Ethnicity

An ethnic group, unlike a racial group, is set apart from others because of its national origin or distinctive cultural patterns. Among the ethnic groups in the United States

are peoples with a Spanish-speaking background, referred to collectively as *Hispanics* or *Latinos,* such as Puerto Ricans, Mexican Americans, Cuban Americans, and other Latin Americans. Other ethnic groups in this country include Jewish, Irish, Italian, and Norwegian Americans. While these groupings are convenient, they serve to obscure differences within these ethnic categories (as in the case of Hispanics) as well as to overlook the mixed ancestry of so many ethnic people in the United States.

The distinction between racial and ethnic minorities is not always clear-cut. Some members of racial minorities, such as Asian Americans, may have significant

261

West Indians show pride in their heritage at the annual West Indian Day parade in New York City. Many racial and ethnic minorities hold parades and celebrations to preserve and display their unique culture.

In recent years, college campuses across the United States have been the scene of bias-related incidents. Student-run newspapers and radio stations have ridiculed racial and ethnic minorities; threatening literature has been stuffed under the doors of minority students; graffiti endorsing the views of White supremacist organizations such as the Ku Klux Klan have been scrawled on university walls. In some cases, there have even been violent clashes between groups of White and Black students (Bunzel 1992; Schaefer 2000).

Prejudice can result from **ethnocentrism**—the tendency to assume that one's culture and way of life represent the norm or are superior to all others. Ethnocentric people judge other cultures by the standards of their own group, which leads quite easily to prejudice against cultures viewed as inferior.

pp. 80–81

cultural differences from other groups. At the same time, certain ethnic minorities, such as Hispanics, may have obvious physical differences that set them apart from other residents of the United States.

Despite categorization problems, sociologists continue to feel that the distinction between racial groups and ethnic groups is socially significant. That is because in most societies, including the United States, physical differences tend to be more visible than ethnic differences. Partly as a result of this fact, stratification along racial lines is more resistant to change than stratification along ethnic lines. Members of an ethnic minority sometimes can become, over time, indistinguishable from the majority—although this process may take generations and may never include all members of the group. By contrast, members of a racial minority find it much more difficult to blend in with the larger society and to gain acceptance from the majority.

Prejudice and Discrimination

False definitions of individuals and groups are perpetuated by prejudice. **Prejudice** is a negative attitude toward an entire category of people, often an ethnic or racial minority. If you resent your roommate because he or she is sloppy, you are not necessarily guilty of prejudice. However, if you immediately stereotype your roommate on the basis of such characteristics as race, ethnicity, or religion, that is a form of prejudice.

One important and widespread form of prejudice is **racism,** the belief that one race is supreme and all others are innately inferior. When racism prevails in a society, members of subordinate groups generally experience prejudice, discrimination, and exploitation. In 1990, as concern mounted about racist attacks in the United States, Congress passed the Hate Crimes Statistics Act. This law directs the Department of Justice to gather data on crimes motivated by the victim's race, religion, ethnicity, or sexual orientation.

In 1998 a total of 9,235 hate crimes were reported to authorities. Some 58 percent of these crimes against persons involved racial bias, while 16 percent reflected bias based on sexual orientation; 16 percent, religious bias; and 10 percent, ethnic bias. As Figure 10-3 shows, laws against such crimes vary from state to state (Department of Justice 1999a:58–59).

A particularly horrifying hate crime made the front pages in 1998: In Jasper, Texas, three White men with possible ties to race-hate groups tied up a Black man, beat him with chains, and then dragged him behind their truck until his body was dismembered. Numerous groups in the United States have been victims of hate crimes as well as generalized prejudice. In Box 10-2 on p. 264, we examine prejudice against Arab Americans and Muslims living in the United States.

The activity of organized hate groups appears to be increasing, both in reality and in virtual reality. While

FIGURE 10-3

Hate Crime Laws in the United States

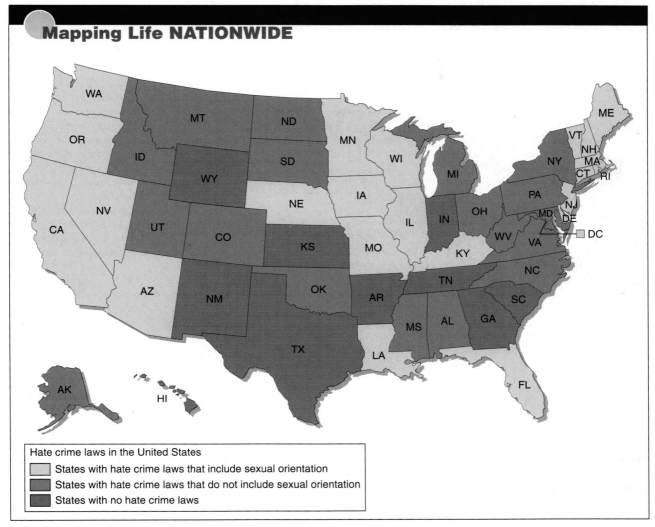

Source: National Gay and Lesbian Task Force 1999.

only a few hundred such groups may exist, there were at least 2,000 websites advocating racial hatred on the Internet in 1999. Particularly troubling were sites disguised as video games for young people, or as "educational sites" about crusaders against prejudice, like Martin Luther King, Jr. The technology of the Internet has allowed race-hate groups to expand far beyond their traditional southern base to reach millions (J. Sandberg 1999).

Discriminatory Behavior

John and Glenn are alike in almost every way—about the same age, they are both Big Ten college graduates with good jobs. But they find they have different experiences in

everyday routines, such as walking into a store. John gets instant attention from the same sales staff that ignores Glenn, even though he has been waiting five minutes. When Glenn is locked out of his car, passersby ignore him, while John receives many offers of help. At an employment agency, Glenn is lectured on laziness and told he will be monitored "real close"; John is encouraged.

What accounts for these differences in the everyday life experiences of two men? Very simply, John is White and Glenn is Black. The two were part of an experiment, conducted by the television newsmagazine *Primetime Live*, to assess the impact of race on the day-to-day lives of residents in a typical U.S. city. Over a three-week period reporters closely monitored the two men, who had been trained to

Research in Action

10-2 Prejudice against Arab Americans and Muslim Americans

As marginal groups with little political power, Arab Americans and Muslim Americans are vulnerable to prejudice and discrimination. The 1995 bombing of a federal office building in Oklahoma City was at first mistakenly attributed to Middle East terrorism. Many Arabic and Islamic schoolchildren in the United States were targeted and blamed for the attack. One fifth-grade boy was told, "Go back where you came from!" His mother, an attorney and a second-generation Syrian American, asked where her children were supposed to go. One was born in Texas, the other in Oklahoma.

Sociologists have observed two trends in the United States over the last 20 years. First, the numbers of people in the United States who are Arab or who practice the Muslim faith have increased dramatically. Second, the open expression of hostility toward Arab and Muslim people has also increased. Obviously, the coinciding of these two trends has made life unpleasant for many of these people.

For nearly 30 years news events have fueled anti-Arab and anti-Muslim feelings within the United States and contributed to stereotyping: the 1972 terrorist killings of Israeli athletes at the Olympic Games in

> One fifth-grade boy was told, 'Go back where you came from!'

Germany, the 1979 seizure of U.S. hostages by Iran, the 1990 invasion of Kuwait by Iraq, the 1993 bombing of the World Trade Center in New York City, and fears of Y2K terrorism in 1999. Media coverage of such issues has provided little insight into Arab cultures and Islamic religious practices.

Instead, as content analysis of the media has documented, Arabs and Muslims are repeatedly presented as almost cartoonlike figures, whether camel drivers, outrageously wealthy sheiks, or deranged terrorists. Even Disney's 1993 animated film *Aladdin* referred to Arabs as "barbaric." The movie depicted an Arabic guard threatening to cut off a young girl's hand for stealing food but did not point out that such punishment would violate Islamic law.

"Profiling" at airports has put some citizens under special surveillance. Fearing terrorists, a number of airlines use appearance and ethnic-sounding names to identify and take aside Arab Americans (or those who match the "profile") and search their belongings. Muslim women who choose to don head scarves or *hijbab* in keeping with their tradition to dress modestly encounter harassment from strangers in the street. Many employers insist that the women shed

Sources: El-Badry 1994; Henneberger 1995; Lindner 1998; Power 1998; Shaheen 1999.

Muslim men stop to pray in the midst of a Muslim Day parade in Manhattan, New York. The Muslim population in the United States has increased dramatically over the past two decades, but is often misunderstood and stereotyped by the media.

present themselves in an identical manner. Not once or twice, but "every single day," said program host Diane Sawyer, John and Glenn were treated differently (ABC News 1992).

Prejudice often leads to **discrimination,** the denial of opportunities and equal rights to individuals and groups based on some type of arbitrary bias. Say that a White corporate president with a prejudice against Asian Americans has to fill an executive position. The most qualified candidate for the job is a Vietnamese American. If the president refuses to hire this candidate and instead selects an inferior White candidate, he or she is engaging in an act of racial discrimination.

Prejudiced *attitudes* should not be equated with discriminatory *behavior*. Although the two are generally related, they are not identical,

the covering if they wish to get a job or expect to be promoted. These citizens find it difficult to understand such attitudes in a nation founded on religious freedom.

In the United States, many people inaccurately lump together Arab Americans and Muslims. While these groups overlap, many Arab Americans are Christians (as is true of many Arabs living in the Middle East) and many Muslims (such as African Americans, Iranians, and Pakistanis) are non-Arabs. Currently, there are an estimated 870,000 Arab Americans, and their numbers are rising. Many cling to the culture of their nation of origin, which can vary considerably. For example, Arabs constitute an ethnic group in 22 nations of North Africa and the Middle East, including Morocco, Syria, Iraq, Saudi Arabia, and Somalia.

At present, about 6 million Muslims live in the United States, of whom about 42 per-

cent are African American, 24 percent are South Asian, 12 percent are Arab, and 22 percent are "other." Muslims are followers of Islam, the world's largest faith after Christianity. Islam is based on the teachings found in the Koran (or Al-Qur'an) of the seventh-century prophet Mohammed. Islamic believers are divided into a variety of faiths and sects, such as Sunnis and Shiites, which are sometimes antagonistic toward one another (just as there are religious rivalries among Christians and among Jews).

The first known mosque in the United States was founded in 1929. Today, there are more than 1,100 mosques in this country, of which 80 percent have been established in the last 25 years. The largest group of Muslims in the United States, African Americans, is divided between those who follow mainstream Islamic doctrine and those who follow the teachings of the controversial Na-

tion of Islam (headed by Minister Louis Farrakhan). The Muslim population of the United States is growing significantly, owing to high birthrates, substantial immigration of Muslims, and conversion of non-Muslims. By the year 2000, according to estimates by sociologists and others, Muslims in this country will outnumber Presbyterians, Methodists, Lutherans, and Jews.

Let's Discuss

1. Recall the last time you saw a Muslim or Arab character portrayed on television or in the movies. Describe the character. Did the role fit the typical stereotype of Muslims and Arabs?
2. What can be done to promote better understanding of Arab and Muslim Americans and counter prejudice and discrimination against them?

and either condition can be present without the other. A prejudiced person does not always act on his or her biases. The White president, for example, might choose—despite his or her stereotypes—to hire the Vietnamese American. This would be prejudice without discrimination. On the other hand, a White corporate president with a completely respectful view of Vietnamese Americans might refuse to hire them for executive posts out of fear that biased clients would take their business elsewhere. In this case, the president's action would constitute discrimination without prejudice.

Discrimination persists even for the most educated and qualified minority group members from the best family backgrounds. Despite their talents and experiences, they sometimes encounter attitudinal or organizational bias that prevents them from reaching their full potential. The term *glass ceiling* refers to an invisible barrier that blocks the promotion of a qualified individual in a work environment because of the individual's gender, race, or ethnicity (Schaefer 2000; H. Yamagata et al. 1997).

In early 1995, the federal Glass Ceiling Commission issued the first comprehensive study of barriers to promotion in the United States. The commission found that

glass ceilings continue to block women and minority group men from top management positions in the nation's industries. While White men constitute about 43 percent of the paid labor force, they hold about 95 of every 100 senior management posts. According to the report, the existence of this glass ceiling results principally from the fears and prejudices of many middle- and upper-level White male managers, who believe that the inclusion of women and minority group men in management circles will threaten their own prospects for advancement (Department of Labor 1995a, 1995b).

Institutional Discrimination

Discrimination is practiced not only by individuals in one-to-one encounters but also by institutions in their daily operations. Social scientists are particularly concerned with the ways in which structural factors such as employment, housing, health care, and government operations maintain the social significance of race and ethnicity. *Institutional discrimination* refers to the denial of opportunities and equal rights to individuals and groups that results from the normal operations of a society. This

In November 1999, *Lethal Weapon* star Danny Glover charged the city of New York with discrimination after several municipally licensed cabs passed him by. A former cabdriver himself, Glover declared that the Big Apple's cabbies needed diversity training.

kind of discrimination consistently affects certain racial and ethnic groups more than others.

The U.S. Commission on Civil Rights (1981:9–10) has identified various forms of institutional discrimination, including:

- Rules requiring that only English be spoken at a place of work, even when it is not a business necessity to restrict the use of other languages.
- Preferences shown by law and medical schools in the admission of children of wealthy and influential alumni, nearly all of whom are White.
- Restrictive employment-leave policies, coupled with prohibitions on part-time work, that make it difficult for the heads of single-parent families (most of whom are women) to obtain and keep jobs.

Computer technology represents another area of institutional discrimination. As technology increases globally, access to this technology will be crucial in determining who moves ahead and who stays behind. It is apparent in the United States that a racial divide does indeed exist in this area. African Americans are much less likely to have a computer in their home than are Whites. The difference has consequences in schooling. While three-quarters of Whites in college and high school have access to a home computer, fewer than one-third of Blacks do. Similarly, while 43 percent of all households in the United States have a home computer, only 30 percent of Hispanic households do. These fundamental differences in access will only increase in significance as better-paying jobs and even information itself become tied more and more to computer technology (Hoffman and Novak 1998; Wilhelm 1998).

In some cases, even ostensibly neutral institutional standards can turn out to have discriminatory effects. African American students at a midwestern state university protested a policy under which fraternities and sororities that wished to use campus facilities for a dance were required to post $150 security deposits to cover possible damages. The Black students complained that this policy had a discriminatory impact on minority student organizations. Campus police countered that the university's policy applied to all student groups interested in using these facilities. However, since overwhelmingly White fraternities and sororities at the school had their own houses that they used for dances, the policy indeed affected only African American and other minority organizations.

There have been attempts to eradicate or compensate for discrimination in the United States. The 1960s saw the passage of many pioneering civil rights laws, including the landmark 1964 Civil Rights Act (which prohibits discrimination in public accommodations and publicly owned facilities on the basis of race, color, creed, national origin, and gender). In two important rulings in 1987, the Supreme Court held that federal prohibitions against racial discrimination protect members of all ethnic minorities—including Hispanics, Jews, and Arab Americans—even though they may be considered White.

For more than 20 years, affirmative action programs have been instituted to overcome past discrimination. ***Affirmative action*** refers to positive efforts to recruit minority members or women for jobs, promotions, and educational opportunities. However, many people have resented these programs, arguing that advancing one group's cause merely shifts the discrimination to another group. Thus, by giving priority to African Americans in school admissions, for example, more qualified White

DELORES CLEARY:
Assistant Professor,
Central Washington University

Delores Cleary, a Native American woman, left her reservation for Seattle at age 25 with her husband and two children. Shortly after her move, she started taking classes at the local community college. Her first class happened to be an introduction to sociology course. "I just loved sociology and kept taking classes." Her enthusiasm eventually led to a B.A. from Central Washington University in 1989 and a master's and Ph.D. from Washington State in 1994.

She currently teaches three classes a week; conducts research on Native American issues having to do with identity, gambling, and poverty; and is actively involved in community service. Recently she won a large grant to develop an interdisciplinary year-long course on racism. Everything she learned in her academic career applies to what she does now. In the classroom, she emphasizes "the intersection of race, gender, and sexual orientation that impacts people's place in the social structure," to which she brings her own experience. As chair of an Indian parent committee, she finds that her sociology background helps her to negotiate conflict and plan and organize social change.

Cleary claims that the study of sociology "has empowered me to really take control of my life and make change and become a contributing member of society, to benefit humanity." She advises today's students that reading the text and taking the class will help to make changes in their lives, "to understand their place in the world and in American society."

---

candidates may be overlooked. In many parts of the country and many sectors of the economy, affirmative action is being rolled back, even though it was never fully implemented. Affirmative action is discussed in the policy section of Chapter 17.

Discriminatory practices continue to pervade nearly all areas of life in the United States today. In part, this is because various individuals and groups actually *benefit* from racial and ethnic discrimination in terms of money, status, and influence. Discrimination permits members of the majority to enhance their wealth, power, and prestige at the expense of others. Less qualified people are hired and promoted simply because they are members of the dominant group. Such individuals and groups will not surrender these advantages easily. We'll turn now to a closer look at this functionalist analysis, as well as the conflict and interactionist perspectives.

Studying Race and Ethnicity

Relations among racial and ethnic groups lend themselves to analysis from the three major perspectives of sociology. Viewing race from the macrolevel, functionalists observe that racial prejudice and discrimination serve positive functions for dominant groups, whereas conflict theorists see the economic structure as a central factor in the exploitation of minorities. The micro-level analysis of interactionist researchers stresses the manner in which everyday contact between people from different racial and ethnic backgrounds contributes to tolerance or leads to hostility.

Functionalist Perspective

What possible use could racial bigotry have for society? Functionalist theorists, while agreeing that racial hostility is hardly to be admired, point out that it indeed serves positive functions for those practicing discrimination.

Anthropologist Manning Nash (1962) has identified three functions that racially prejudiced beliefs have for the dominant group:

1. Such views provide a moral justification for maintaining an unequal society that routinely deprives a minority of its rights and privileges. Southern Whites justified slavery by believing that Africans were physically and spiritually subhuman and devoid of souls (Hoebel 1949).

2. Racist beliefs discourage the subordinate minority from attempting to question its lowly status, which would be to question the very foundations of society.

3. Racial myths encourage support for the existing order by introducing the argument that any major societal change (such as an end to discrimination) would only bring greater poverty to the minority and lower the majority's standard of living. As a result, Nash suggests, racial prejudice grows when a society's value system (for example, one underlying a colonial empire or a regime perpetuating slavery) is being threatened.

Although racial prejudice and discrimination may serve the interests of the powerful, such unequal treatment can also be dysfunctional to a society and even to its dominant group. Sociologist Arnold Rose (1951) outlines four dysfunctions associated with racism:

1. A society that practices discrimination fails to use the resources of all individuals. Discrimination limits the search for talent and leadership to the dominant group.
2. Discrimination aggravates social problems such as poverty, delinquency, and crime and places the financial burden to alleviate these problems on the dominant group.
3. Society must invest a good deal of time and money to defend its barriers to full participation of all members.
4. Racial prejudice and discrimination often undercut goodwill and friendly diplomatic relations between nations.

Conflict Perspective

Conflict theorists would certainly agree with Arnold Rose that racial prejudice and discrimination have many harmful consequences for society. Sociologists such as Oliver Cox (1948), Robert Blauner (1972), and Herbert M. Hunter (2000) have used the *exploitation theory* (or *Marxist class theory*) to explain the basis of racial subordination in the United States. As we saw in Chapter 8, Karl Marx viewed the exploitation of the lower class as a basic part of the capitalist economic system. From a Marxist point of view, racism keeps minorities in low-paying jobs, thereby supplying the capitalist ruling class with a pool of cheap labor. Moreover, by forcing racial minorities to accept low wages, capitalists can restrict the wages of *all* members of the proletariat. Workers from the dominant group who demand higher wages can always be replaced by minorities who have no choice but to accept low-paying jobs.

The conflict view of race relations seems persuasive in a number of instances. Japanese Americans were the object of little prejudice until they began to enter jobs that brought them into competition with Whites. The movement to keep Chinese immigrants out of the United States became most fervent during the latter half of the nineteenth century, when Chinese and Whites fought over dwindling work opportunities. Both the enslavement of Blacks and the extermination and removal westward of Native Americans were, to a significant extent, economically motivated.

A sign in a shop window in Los Angeles advertises the proprietor's prejudice against immigrants. According to the functionalist perspective, open displays of racial and ethnic bigotry are an attempt to maintain the power of the dominant group in society.

However, the exploitation theory is too limited to explain prejudice in its many forms. Not all minority groups have been economically exploited to the same extent. In addition, many groups (such as the Quakers and the Mormons) have been victimized by prejudice for other than economic reasons. Still, as Gordon Allport (1979:210) concludes, the exploitation theory correctly "points a sure finger at one of the factors involved in prejudice, . . . rationalized self-interest of the upper classes."

Interactionist Perspective

A Latina is transferred from a job on an assembly line to a similar position working next to a White man. At first, the White man is patronizing, assuming that she must be incompetent. She is cold and resentful; even when she needs assistance, she refuses to admit it. After a week, the growing tension between the two leads to a bitter quarrel. Yet, over time, each slowly comes to appreciate the other's strengths and talents. A year after they begin working together, these two workers become respectful friends. This is an example of what interactionists call the *contact hypothesis* in action.

The **contact hypothesis** states that interracial contact between people of equal status in cooperative circumstances will cause them to become less prejudiced and to abandon previous stereotypes. People begin to see one another as individuals and discard the broad generalizations characteristic of stereotyping. Note the factors of *equal status* and *cooperative circumstances*. In the example above, if the two workers had been competing for one vacancy as a supervisor, the racial hostility between them might have worsened (Allport 1979; Schaefer 2000; Sigelman et al. 1996).

As Latinos and other minorities slowly gain access to better-paying and more responsible jobs in the United States, the contact hypothesis may take on even greater significance. The trend in our society is toward increasing contact between individuals from dominant and subordinate groups. This may be one hope of eliminating—or at least reducing—racial and ethnic stereotyping and prejudice. Another may be the establishment of interracial coalitions, an idea suggested by sociologist William Julius Wilson (1999). To work, such coalitions would obviously need to be built on an equal role for all members.

Contact between individuals occurs on the microlevel. We turn now to a consideration of intergroup relations on a macrolevel.

Patterns of Intergroup Relations

Racial and ethnic groups can relate to one another in a wide variety of ways, ranging from friendships and intermarriages to genocide, from behaviors that require mutual approval to behaviors imposed by the dominant group.

One devastating pattern of intergroup relations is **genocide**—the deliberate, systematic killing of an entire people or nation. This term is used to refer to the killing of 1 million Armenians by Turkey beginning in 1915 (Melson 1986). It is most commonly applied to Nazi Germany's extermination of 6 million European Jews, as well as gays, lesbians, and the Romani people ("Gypsies"), during World War II. The term *genocide* is also appropriate in describing the United States' policies toward Native Americans in the nineteenth century. In 1800, the Native American (or American Indian) population of the United States was about 600,000; by 1850, it had been reduced to 250,000 through warfare with the cavalry, disease, and forced relocation to inhospitable environments.

The *expulsion* of a people is another extreme means of acting out racial or ethnic prejudice. In 1979, Vietnam expelled nearly one million ethnic Chinese, partly as a result of centuries of hostility between Vietnam and

Ethnic Albanian women mourn the death of a man killed by Serbs in the province of Kosovo. Such "ethnic cleansings" have met with worldwide condemnation.

neighboring China. In a more recent example of expulsion (which had aspects of genocide), Serbian forces began a program of "ethnic cleansing" in 1991 in the newly independent states of Bosnia and Herzegovina. Throughout the former nation of Yugoslavia, the Serbs drove more than 1 million Croats and Muslims from their homes. Some were tortured and killed, others abused and terrorized, in an attempt to "purify" the land for the remaining ethnic Serbs. In 1999, Serbs were again the focus of worldwide condemnation as they sought to "cleanse" the province of Kosovo of ethnic Albanians.

Genocide and expulsion are extreme behaviors. More typical intergroup relations as they occur in North America and throughout the world follow four identifiable patterns: (1) amalgamation, (2) assimilation, (3) segregation, and (4) pluralism. Each pattern defines the dominant group's actions and the minority group's responses. Intergroup relations are rarely restricted to only one of the four patterns, although invariably one does tend to dominate. Therefore, think of these patterns primarily as ideal types.

Amalgamation

Amalgamation describes the end result when a majority group and a minority group combine to form a new group. Through intermarriage over several generations, various groups in the society combine to form a new group. This can be expressed as A + B + C → D, where A, B, and C represent different groups present in a society, and D signifies the end result, a unique cultural-racial group unlike any of the initial groups (Newman 1973).

The belief in the United States as a "melting pot" became very compelling in the first part of the twentieth century, particularly since that image suggested that the nation had an almost divine mission to amalgamate various groups into one people. However, in actuality many residents were not willing to have Native Americans, Jews, African Americans, Asian Americans, and Irish Roman Catholics as a part of the melting pot. Therefore, this pattern does not adequately describe dominant–subordinate relations existing in the United States.

Assimilation

Many Hindus in India complain about Indian citizens who copy the traditions and customs of the British. In Australia, Aborigines who have become part of the dominant society refuse to acknowledge their darker-skinned grandparents on the street. In the United States, some Italian Americans, Polish Americans, Hispanics, and Jews have changed their ethnic-sounding family names to names typically found among White, Protestant families.

Assimilation is the process by which a person forsakes his or her own cultural tradition to become part of a different culture. Generally, it is practiced by a minority group member who wants to conform to the standards of the dominant group. Assimilation can be described as an ideology in which A + B + C → A. The majority A dominates in such a way that members of minorities B and C imitate A and attempt to become indistinguishable from the dominant group (Newman 1973).

Assimilation can strike at the very roots of a person's identity as he or she seeks to blend in with the dominant group. Alphonso D'Abuzzo, for example, changed his name to Alan Alda. This process is not unique to the United States: Joyce Frankenberg of Great Britain changed her name to Jane Seymour. Name changes, switches in religious affiliation, and dropping of native languages can obscure one's roots and heritage. Moreover, assimilation does not necessarily bring acceptance for the minority group individual. A Chinese American may speak flawless English, attend a Protestant church faithfully, and know the names of all members of the Baseball Hall of Fame. Yet he or she is still *seen* as different and may therefore be rejected as a business associate, a neighbor, or a marriage partner.

Segregation

Separate schools, separate seating sections on buses and in restaurants, separate washrooms, even separate drinking fountains—these were all part of the lives of African Americans in the South when segregation ruled earlier in the twentieth century. *Segregation* refers to the physical separation of two groups of people in terms of residence, workplace, and social events. Generally, a dominant group imposes it on a minority group. Segregation is rarely complete, however. Intergroup contact inevitably occurs even in the most segregated societies. Elijah Anderson's (1990, 1999) participant observation research pp. 34–35 reflects the social tensions that arise from such strained circumstances.

From 1948 (when it received its independence) to 1990, the Republic of South Africa severely restricted the movement of Blacks and other non-Whites by means of a wide-ranging system of segregation known as *apartheid.* Apartheid even included the creation of homelands where Blacks were expected to live. However, decades of local resistance to apartheid, combined with international pressure, led to marked political changes in the 1990s. In 1994, a prominent Black activist, Nelson Mandela, was elected as South Africa's president, the first election in which Blacks (the majority of the nation's population) were allowed to vote. Mandela had spent almost 28 years in South African prisons for his anti-apartheid activities. His election as South Africa's president was widely viewed as the final blow to the oppressive policy of apartheid.

"Ho, ho, ho" apparently works in any language. As Japanese Americans assimilated the norms and values of mainstream U.S. culture, they created their own "Shogun Santa." This one can be found in the Little Tokyo neighborhood of Los Angeles.

South Africa is far from being the only country in which segregation has been common. Until civil rights laws came into play in the latter half of this century, segregation was the rule in many parts of the United States. Housing practices still often force subordinate racial and ethnic groups into certain neighborhoods, usually undesirable ones. While members of a minority group may voluntarily seek to separate themselves from the dominant majority, this is not the primary factor contributing to segregation. The central causes of residential segregation in the United States appear to be the prejudices of Whites and the resulting discriminatory practices in the housing and lending markets. Data consistently show that Blacks, Hispanics, and (to a somewhat lesser extent) Asians face segregation in the nation's metropolitan areas. Such housing segregation is evident around the world: Studies in Sweden, for example, document that

migrants from Chile, Greece, and Turkey are confined to segregated areas of Swedish cities (Andersson-Brolin 1988; Doig et al. 1993).

Pluralism

In a pluralistic society, a subordinate group does not have to forsake its lifestyle and traditions. *Pluralism* is based on mutual respect among various groups in a society for one another's cultures. It allows a minority group to express its own culture and still to participate without prejudice in the larger society. Earlier, we described amalgamation as A + B + C → D, and assimilation as A + B + C → A. Using this same approach, we can conceive of pluralism as A + B + C → A + B + C. All the groups are able to coexist in the same society (Newman 1973).

In the United States, pluralism is more of an ideal than a reality. There are distinct instances of pluralism: the ethnic neighborhoods in major cities, such as Koreatown, Little Tokyo, Andersonville (Swedish Americans), and Spanish Harlem. Yet there are also limits to such cultural freedom. In order to survive, a society must promote a certain consensus among its members regarding basic ideals, values, and beliefs. Thus, if a Rumanian migrating to the United States wants to move up the occupational ladder, he or she cannot avoid learning the English language.

Switzerland exemplifies a modern pluralistic state. The absence both of a national language and of a dominant religious faith leads to a tolerance for cultural diversity. In addition, various political devices safeguard the interests of ethnic groups in a way that has no parallel in the United States. By contrast, Great Britain has found it difficult to achieve cultural pluralism in a multiracial society. East Indians, Pakistanis, and Blacks from the Caribbean and Africa are experiencing prejudice and discrimination within the dominant White British society. There is pressure to cut off all Asian and Black immigration and to expel, even by a few, those non-Whites currently living in Britain (see the social policy section in this chapter).

Race and Ethnicity in the United States

Few societies have a more diverse population than the United States; the nation is truly a multiracial, multiethnic society. Of course, this has not always been the case. The population of what is now the United States has changed dramatically since the arrival of European settlers in the 1600s, as Figure 10-1 showed. Immigration, colonialism, and in the case of Blacks, slavery

10-3 The Color of Network TV

In late spring 1999, as the television networks prepared their schedules for the 1999–2000 season, an article in the *Los Angeles Times* hit the broadcasting industry like a bombshell. In every new prime-time series—26 of them—set to debut in the coming season, the *Times* reported, all the leading characters, as well as the vast majority of the supporting casts, would be White. The public response was immediate. The NAACP, alarmed by the "virtual whitewash in programming," threatened a lawsuit, and a national coalition of Latino groups urged viewers to boycott network TV (Braxton 1999:F10).

Incredibly, network executives seemed surprised by the news of the all-White season. It wasn't deliberate, explained director–actor Edward James Olmos; network executives simply weren't aware of the problem. In the aftermath of the article's publication, producers, writers, executives, and advertisers blamed each other for the oversight. Television programming was dictated by advertisers, a former executive claimed; if advertisers said they wanted blatantly biased programming, the networks would provide it. Jery Isenberg, chairman of the Caucus for Producers, Writers & Directors, blamed the networks, saying that writers

would produce a series about three-headed Martians if the networks told them to.

Beyond these lame excuses, real reasons can be found for the departure from the diversity of past shows and seasons. In recent years the rise of both cable TV and the Internet has fragmented the broadcast entertainment market, siphoning viewers away from the general-audience sitcoms and dramas of the past. With the proliferation of cable channels such as Black Entertainment Television

> The NAACP, alarmed by the "virtual whitewash in programming," threatened a lawsuit.

(BET) and the Spanish-language Univision, and websites that cater to every imaginable taste, there no longer seems a need for broadly popular series such as *The Cosby Show*, whose tone and content appealed to Whites as well as Blacks in a way the newer series do not. The result of these sweeping technological changes has been a sharp divergence in viewer preferences. In current lists of the top 10 network shows among Blacks, Whites, and Latinos, the only show that appeals to all three groups is *Monday Night Football*.

While BET and Univision were grabbing minority audiences and offering new outlets for minority talent, network executives and writers remained overwhelmingly White. Not surprisingly, these mainstream writers and producers, most of whom live far from ethnically and racially diverse inner-city neighborhoods, tend to write and prefer stories about people like themselves. Marc Hirschfeld, an NBC executive, claims some White producers have told him they don't know how to write for Black characters. Steven Bochco, producer of *NYPD Blue*, is a rare exception. Bochco's upcoming series, *City of Angels*, has a cast that is mostly non-White, like the people Bochco grew up with in an inner-city neighborhood.

The networks' first response to the bad press was to move some token Black or ethnic characters into the casts of the all-White series set for the fall season. By January 2000, 13 percent of prime-time characters were African American and another 3 percent were from other minority groups. But in the minds of many industry professionals, that measure fell short of the mark. Jesse L. Martin, an African American actor featured on *Ally McBeal*, told a reporter that in his opinion, adding a few Black faces to an all-White cast would not be enough.

Sources: Braxton 1999; Hoffman 1997; Lowry et al. 1999; Wood 2000.

determined the racial and ethnic makeup of our present-day society.

The diversity of the United States is evident in statistics on the general population, especially in the urban centers. But one would not necessarily know that Americans are a diverse people from watching television. In 1977 the U.S. Civil Rights Commission reported that minorities were underrepresented on TV, and tended to be cast in crime-based series set in urban areas. Remarkably, a generation later the situation has not changed much. A token African American doctor or ethnic family may appear in the afternoon soap operas, but nighttime TV programs are overwhelmingly White (see Box 10–3, Eye on the Media). In the following sections we will attempt to paint a truer picture of American society than the one seen on television.

Racial Groups

The largest racial minorities in the United States include African Americans, Native Americans, and Asian Americans.

African Americans

"I am an invisible man," wrote Black author Ralph Ellison in his novel *Invisible Man* (1952:3). "I am a man of substance, of flesh and bone, fiber and liquids—and I might even be said to possess a mind. I am invisible, understand, simply because people refuse to see me."

Over four decades later, many African Americans still feel invisible. Despite their large numbers, they have long been treated as second-class citizens. Currently, by the

Sharon D. Johnson of the Writers Guild of America agreed. She doubted the networks would take the more meaningful step of hiring Black writers, though, because writers simply aren't as visible to the public as actors.

In the long run, industry observers believe, the networks will need to integrate their ranks before they achieve true diversity in programming. Adonis Hoffman, director of the Corporate Policy Institute, has urged network executives to throw open their studios and boardrooms to minorities. Hoffman thinks such a move would empower Black writers and producers to present a true-to-life portrait of African Americans. There are some signs of agreement from the networks. According to Doug Herzog, president of Fox Entertainment, incorporating diversity into network programming requires a well-conceived long-term strategy. Real progress, he says, means incorporating diversity from within.

Why should it matter that minority groups aren't visible on network television, if they are well represented on BET and Univision? The answer is that if they are not, Whites as well as minorities will see a distorted picture of their society every time they turn on network TV. In Hoffman's

words, "African Americans, Latinos and Asians, while portrayed as such, are not merely walk-ons in our society—they are woven into the fabric of what has made this country great." (Hoffman 1997:M6)

Let's Discuss

1. Do you watch network TV? If so, how well do you think it reflects the diversity of American society?

2. Have you seen a movie or TV show recently that portrayed members of a minority group in a sensitive and realistic way—as real people rather than stereotypes or token walk-ons? If so, describe the show.

standards of the federal government, more than 1 out of every 4 Blacks—as opposed to 1 out of every 11 Whites—is poor.

Contemporary institutional discrimination and individual prejudice against African Americans are rooted in the history of slavery in the United States. While many other subordinate groups have had little wealth and income, as sociologist W. E. B. Du Bois (1909) and others have noted, enslaved Blacks were in an even more oppressive situation because, by law, they could not own property and could not pass on the benefits of their labor to their children. In bondage, the Africans were forced to assimilate and were stripped of much of their African tribal heritage. Yet the destruction of African cultures was not complete; some aspects survived in oral literature, reli-

gious customs, and music. Black resistance to slavery included many slave revolts, such as those led by Denmark Vesey in South Carolina in 1822 and Nat Turner in Virginia in 1831. Still, most Blacks remained subject to the arbitrary and often cruel actions of their White owners (Herskovits 1941, 1943).

The end of the Civil War did not bring genuine freedom and equality for Blacks. The Southern states passed "Jim Crow" laws to enforce official segregation, and they were upheld as constitutional by the Supreme Court in 1896. In addition, Blacks faced the danger of lynching campaigns, often led by the Ku Klux Klan, during the late nineteenth and early twentieth centuries. From a conflict perspective, Whites maintained their dominance formally through legalized segregation and informally by

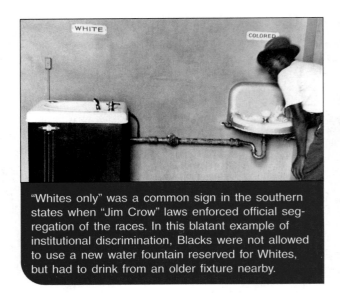

"Whites only" was a common sign in the southern states when "Jim Crow" laws enforced official segregation of the races. In this blatant example of institutional discrimination, Blacks were not allowed to use a new water fountain reserved for Whites, but had to drink from an older fixture nearby.

Table 10-1	Relative Economic Positions of African Americans and Whites, 1998–1999	
Characteristic	**African Americans**	**Whites**
Four-year college education, people 25 and over	14.7%	25.0%
Median family income	$28,602	$46,754
Unemployment rate	8.1%	3.5%
People below the poverty line	26.5%	11.0%

Note: Data, where available, are for White non-Hispanics.
Sources: Bureau of the Census 1999a:51; Bureau of Labor Statistics 2000.

means of vigilante terror and violence (Franklin and Moss 1994).

A turning point in the struggle for Black equality came in the unanimous Supreme Court decision in the 1954 case of *Brown v. Board of Education of Topeka, Kansas.* The Court outlawed segregation of public school students, ruling that "separate educational facilities are inherently unequal." In the wake of the *Brown* decision, there was a surge of activism on behalf of Black civil rights, including boycotts of segregated bus companies and sit-ins at restaurants and lunch counters that refused to serve Blacks.

During the decade of the 1960s, a vast civil rights movement emerged, with many competing factions and strategies for change. The Southern Christian Leadership Conference (SCLC), founded by Dr. Martin Luther King, Jr., used nonviolent civil disobedience to oppose segregation. The National Association for the Advancement of Colored People (NAACP) favored use of the courts to press for equality for African Americans. But many younger Black leaders, most notably Malcolm X, turned toward an ideology of Black power. Proponents of **Black power** rejected the goal of assimilation into White, middle-class society. They defended the beauty and dignity of Black and African cultures and supported the creation of Black-controlled political and economic institutions (Ture and Hamilton 1992).

Despite numerous courageous actions to achieve Black civil rights, Black and White America are still separate, still unequal. From birth to death, Blacks suffer in terms of their life chances. Life remains

pp. 217–19

difficult for millions of poor Blacks, who must attempt to survive in ghetto areas shattered by high unemployment and abandoned housing. The economic position of Blacks is shown in Table 10-1. As the table il-

lustrates, the median household income of Blacks is only 61 percent that of Whites, and the unemployment rate among Blacks is more than twice that of Whites.

There have been economic gains for *some* African Americans—especially middle-class men and women—over the last 35 years. For example, data compiled by the Department of Labor show that the number of African Americans in management areas of the labor market increased nationally from 2.4 percent of the total in 1958 to 7.2 percent in 1998. Yet Blacks still represent only 5 percent or less of all physicians, engineers, scientists, lawyers, judges, and marketing managers. In another area important for developing role models, African Americans and Hispanics together account for only 12 percent of all editors and reporters in the United States (Bureau of the Census 1999a:424).

In many respects, the civil rights movement of the 1960s left institutionalized discrimination against African Americans untouched. Consequently, in the 1970s and 1980s, Black leaders worked to mobilize African American political power as a force for social change. Between 1970 and 1997, the number of African American elected officials increased by almost sixfold. Even so, Blacks remain significantly *underrepresented.* This underrepresentation is especially distressing in view of the fact that sociologist W. E. B. Du Bois observed over 90 years ago that Blacks could not expect to achieve equal social and economic opportunities without first gaining political rights (Bureau of the Census 1999a:298; Green and Driver 1978).

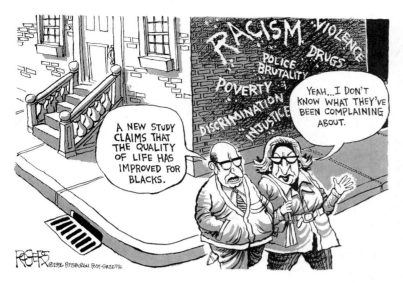

Native Americans

There are approximately 2 million Native Americans. They represent a diverse array of cultures, distinguishable by language, family organization, religion, and livelihood. The outsiders who came to the United States—European settlers and their descendants—came to know the native people as "American Indians." By the time the Bureau of Indian Affairs (BIA) was organized as part of the *War* Department in 1824, Indian–White relations had already included three centuries of mutual misunderstanding. Many bloody wars during the nineteenth century wiped out a significant part of the nation's Indian population. By the end of the nineteenth century, schools for Indians operated by the BIA or church missions prohibited the practice of Native American cultures. Yet, at the same time, such schools did little to make the children effective competitors in White society.

Today, life remains difficult for members of the 554 tribal groups in the United States, whether they live in cities or on reservations. For example, one Native American teenager in six has attempted suicide—a rate four times higher than the rate for other teenagers. Traditionally, some Native Americans chose to assimilate and abandon all vestiges of their tribal cultures to escape certain forms of prejudice. However, by the

1990s, an increasing number of people in the United States were openly claiming an identity as Native American. Since 1960, the federal government's count of Native Americans has tripled, to an estimated 2.4 million. According to the 1990 census, there has been a 16 percent increase in Native Americans during the 1990s. Demographers believe that more and more Native Americans who previously concealed their identity are no longer pretending to be White (Bureau of the Census 1999a).

The introduction of gambling on Indian reservations threatens to become still another battleground between Native Americans and the dominant White society. By 1998, one-third of all tribes were operating off-track betting, casino tables for such games as blackjack and roulette, slot machines, high-stakes bingo, sports betting, and video games of chance. The gamblers—who are overwhelmingly *not* Native Americans—typically travel long distances to wager money at the new casinos. While gambling on reservations generates $6 billion annually, the profits are not evenly spread among tribes. Much of Native America is untouched by casino windfalls. According to 1998 estimates, the overall unemployment rate on reservations is over 30 percent, compared to 4 percent for the general population (Egan 1998; Harrah's Entertainment 1996; Schaefer 2000). Some Native Americans oppose gambling on moral grounds and

A Native American dealer works a blackjack table in a casino in Pueblo San Felipe, New Mexico. Casinos are one of the few sources of employment and income on many Native American reservations.

Like many racial and ethnic minority groups in the United States, Native Americans keep certain aspects of their traditional culture (such as the cradle board) while adopting some customs and practices from the dominant culture (such as the stroller).

feel that it is being marketed in a manner incompatible with Native American culture. Yet, some reservations have managed profits from gambling well and have invested them in projects for the betterment of the entire reservation. At the same time, established White gambling interests, particularly in Nevada and New Jersey, have begun efforts to pressure Congress to restrict Native American casinos—even though these casinos generate only 5 percent of the nation's overall gambling revenues.

Asian Americans

Asian Americans are a diverse group, one of the fastest-growing segments of the population of the United States. Among the many groups of Americans of Asian descent are Chinese Americans, Japanese Americans, and Korean Americans.

Asian Americans are held up as a model or ideal minority group, supposedly because, despite past suffering from prejudice and discrimination, they have succeeded economically, socially, and educationally without resorting to confrontations with Whites. The existence of a model minority seems to reaffirm the notion that anyone can get ahead in the United States with talent and hard work and implies that those minorities that don't succeed are somehow responsible for their failures. Viewed from a conflict perspective, this becomes yet another instance of "blaming the victims" (Hurh and Kim 1989).

This concept of a model minority ignores the diversity among Asian Americans: There are rich and poor

Japanese Americans, rich and poor Filipino Americans, and so forth. In fact, Southeast Asians living in the United States have the highest rate of welfare dependency of any racial or ethnic group. For every Asian American family with an annual income of $75,000 or more, there is another earning less than $35,000 a year. Moreover, even when Asian Americans are clustered at the higher-paying end of the stratification system, the glass ceiling may limit how far up they can go (Bureau of the Census 1999b).

Chinese Americans   Unlike African slaves and Native Americans, the Chinese were initially encouraged to immigrate to the United States. From 1850 to 1880, more than 200,000 Chinese immigrated to this country, lured by job opportunities created by the discovery of gold. However, as employment possibilities decreased and competition for mining grew, the Chinese became the target of a bitter campaign to limit their numbers and restrict their rights. Chinese laborers were exploited, then discarded.

In 1882, Congress enacted the Chinese Exclusion Act, which prevented Chinese immigration and even forbade Chinese in the United States to send for their families. As a result, the Chinese population steadily declined until after World War II. More recently, the descendants of the nineteenth-century immigrants have been joined by a new influx from Hong Kong and Taiwan. The groups of immigrants sometimes form sharp contrasts in their degree of assimilation, desire to live in Chinatowns, and feelings about this country's relations with the People's Republic of China (Kwong and Lum 1988).

Currently, about 1.65 million Chinese Americans live in the United States. Some Chinese Americans have entered lucrative occupations. In 1996, the state of Washington elected Gary Locke, a Chinese American, as the first Asian American governor of a state on the mainland United States. Such accomplishments have led to the popular concept that the strides made by Chinese Americans (and other Asian Americans) constitute a success story.

Yet many Chinese immigrants struggle to survive under living and working conditions that belie the "model minority" stereotype. New York City's Chinatown district is filled with illegal sweatshops in which recent immigrants—many of them Chinese women—work for minimal wages. Even in "legal" factories in the garment industry, hours are long and rewards are limited. A seamstress typically works 11 hours per day, 6 days a week, and earns about $10,000 a year. Other workers, such as hemmers and cutters, earn only $5,000 per year (Finder 1995; Lum and Kwong 1989).

Japanese Americans   There are approximately 800,000 Japanese Americans in the United States. As a people, they are relatively recent arrivals to this nation. In 1880 there were only 148 Japanese in the United States, but by 1920 there were more than 110,000. The early Japanese immigrants—who are called the *Issei*—were usually males seeking employment opportunities. Many Whites saw them (along with Chinese immigrants) as a "yellow peril" and subjected them to widespread prejudice and discrimination.

In 1941, the attack on Pearl Harbor by Japan—by then allied with Hitler's Germany—had severe repercussions for Japanese Americans. The federal government decreed that all Japanese Americans on the West Coast must leave their homes and report to "evacuation camps." They became, in effect, scapegoats for the anger that other people in the United States felt concerning Japan's role in World War II. By August 1943, in an unprecedented application of guilt by virtue of ancestry, 113,000 Japanese Americans were forced to live in hastily built camps. In striking contrast, only a few German Americans and Italian Americans were sent to evacuation camps (Hosokawa 1969).

This mass detention was costly for the interned Japanese Americans. The Federal Reserve Board estimates losses of nearly half a billion dollars, or more than $4,500 per person(about $27,000 per person in today's terms). Moreover, the psychological effect on these citizens—including the humiliation of being labeled as "disloyal"—was immeasurable. Eventually, the Japanese born in the United States, the *Nisei,* were allowed to enlist in the Army and serve in a segregated combat unit in Europe. Others resettled in the East and Midwest to work in factories.

In 1983, a federal commission recommended government payments to all surviving Japanese Americans who were held in detention camps. The commission reported that the detention was motivated by "race prejudice, war hysteria, and a failure of political leadership." It added that "no documented acts of espionage, sabotage, or fifth-column activity were shown to have been committed" by Japanese Americans (Pear 1983). In 1988, President Ronald Reagan signed the Civil Liberties Act, which required the federal government to issue individual apologies for all violations of Japanese Americans' constitutional rights and established a $1.25 billion trust fund to pay reparations to the approximately 77,500 surviving Japanese Americans who had been interned (Takezawa 1995).

Korean Americans   The population of Korean Americans is now nearly as large as that of Japanese Americans. Yet Korean Americans are often overshadowed by the larger groups from Asia.

Today's Korean American community is the result of three waves of immigration. The initial wave, of a little more than 7,000 immigrants, arrived between 1903 and 1910, when laborers migrated to Hawaii. The second wave followed the end of the Korean War, accounting for about 14,000 immigrants from 1951 through 1964. Most of these immigrants were wives of U.S. servicemen and war orphans. The third wave, continuing to the present, has reflected the admissions priorities set up in the 1965 Immigration Act. These well-educated immigrants arrive in the United States with professional skills. However, because of language difficulties and discrimination, many must settle at least initially for positions of lower responsibility than those they held in Korea and must suffer through a period of disenchantment. Stress, loneliness, and family strife may accompany the pain of adjustment (Hurh and Kim 1994).

Korean American women commonly participate in the paid labor force, as do many Asian American women. About 60 percent of Korean American women born in the United States and half of those born abroad work in the labor force. These figures may not seem striking compared with data for White women, but the cultural differences make the figures more significant. In Korea, the woman is expected to serve as mother and homemaker only. Although these roles carry over to the United States, women are pressed to support their families while their husbands struggle to establish themselves financially. Many Korean American men begin small service and retail businesses and gradually involve their wives in the business. The situation is made more difficult by the hostility that Korean American–run businesses often encounter from their prospective customers (Hurh 1998; Kim 1999).

In the early 1990s, the apparent friction between Korean Americans and another subordinate racial group, African Americans, attracted nationwide attention. In New York City, Los Angeles, and Chicago, the scene was replayed in which a Korean American merchant confronted a Black person allegedly threatening or robbing a store. The Black neighborhood responded with hostility to what they perceived as the disrespect and arrogance of the Korean American entrepreneur. In South Central Los Angeles, the only shops in which to buy groceries, liquor, or gasoline are owned by Korean immigrants, who have largely replaced the White businesspeople. African Americans were well aware of the dominant role that Korean Americans play in their local retail market. During the 1992 riots in South Central, small businesses owned by Koreans were a particular target. More than 1,800 Korean businesses were looted or burned during the riots; Korean establishments suffered $347 million in property damage (Kim 1999).

Such friction is not new; earlier generations of Jewish, Italian, and Arab merchants encountered similar hostility from what to outsiders seems an unlikely source—another oppressed minority. The contemporary conflict was dramatized in Spike Lee's 1989 movie *Do the Right Thing,* in which African Americans and Korean Americans clashed. The situation stems from Korean Americans' being the latest immigrant group to cater to the needs of inner-city populations abandoned by those who moved up the economic ladder.

Ethnic Groups

Unlike racial minorities, members of subordinate ethnic groups are generally not hindered by physical differences from assimilating into the dominant culture of the United States. However, members of ethnic minority groups still face many forms of prejudice and discrimination. Take the cases of the country's largest ethnic groups—Hispanics, Jews, and White ethnics.

Hispanics

The various groups included under the general terms *Hispanics* and *Latinos* together represent the largest ethnic minority in the United States. It was estimated in 2000 that there were more than 30 million Hispanics in this country, including 19 million Mexican Americans, over 3 million Puerto Ricans, and smaller numbers of Cuban Americans and people of Central or South American origin. This latter group represents the fastest-growing and most diverse segment of the Hispanic community (Bureau of the Census 1999a).

According to Census Bureau data, the Hispanic population now outnumbers the African American population in 4 of the 10 largest cities of the United States: Los Angeles, Houston, Phoenix, and San Antonio. Hispanics are now the majority of residents in such cities as Miami, Florida; El Paso, Texas; and Santa Ana, California. The rise in the Hispanic population of the United States—fueled by Hispanics' comparatively high birthrates and level of immigration—could intensify debates over such controversial public policy issues as bilingualism and immigration (S. Roberts 1994).

The various Hispanic groups share a heritage of Spanish language and culture, which can cause serious problems for assimilation in the United States. An intelligent student whose first language is Spanish may be presumed slow or even unruly by English-speaking schoolchildren, and frequently by English-speaking teachers as well. The labeling of Hispanic children as being underachievers, as having learning disabilities, or as suffering from emotional

problems can act as a self-fulfilling prophecy for some of the children. Bilingual education has been introduced in many school districts as a means of easing the educational difficulties experienced by Hispanic children and others whose first language is not English.

The educational difficulties of Hispanic students certainly contribute to the generally low economic status of Hispanics. By 1998, only 11 percent of Hispanic adults had completed college, compared with 25 percent of Whites. The median household income of Hispanics was 64 percent that of Whites. In that same year, 8.3 million Hispanics (or 26 percent of all Hispanics in the United States) lived below the poverty line (Bureau of the Census 1999a:51, 54).

Mexican Americans The largest Hispanic population comprises Mexican Americans, who can be further subdivided into those descended from the residents of the territories annexed after the Mexican-American War of 1848 and those who have immigrated from Mexico to the United States. The opportunity for a Mexican to earn in one hour what it would take an entire day to earn in Mexico has pushed millions of legal and illegal immigrants north.

Aside from the family, the most important social organization in the Mexican American (or Chicano) community is the church, specifically the Roman Catholic church. The strong identification with the Catholic faith has reinforced the already formidable barriers between Mexican Americans and their predominantly White and Protestant neighbors of the Southwest. At the same time, the Catholic church helps many immigrants develop a sense of identity and assists their assimilation into the norms and values of the dominant culture of the United States. The complexity of the Mexican American community is underscored by the fact that Protestant churches—especially those that endorse expressive, open worship—have gained increasing support among Mexican Americans (Herrmann 1994; Kanellos 1994).

Puerto Ricans The second-largest segment of Hispanics in the United States is composed of Puerto Ricans. Since 1917, residents of Puerto Rico have held the status of American citizens. Many have migrated to New York and other eastern cities. Unfortunately, Puerto Ricans experience serious poverty both in the United States and on the island. Those living in the continental United States have barely half the family income of Whites. As a result, a reverse migration began in the 1970s; more Puerto Ricans were leaving for the island than were coming to the mainland (Lemann 1991).

Politically, Puerto Ricans in the United States have not been as successful as Mexican Americans in organizing for their rights. For many mainland Puerto Ricans—as for many residents of the island—the paramount po-

Members of the Hispanic sorority Sigma Lambda Gamma smile for the camera at Eastern Michigan University. In the United States, about 11 percent of Hispanic adults are college graduates.

litical issue is the destiny of Puerto Rico itself. Should it continue in its present commonwealth status, petition for admission to the United States as the 51st state, or attempt to become an independent nation? This question has divided Puerto Rico for decades and remains a central issue in Puerto Rican elections. In a 1998 referendum, voters supported a "none of the above" option, effectively favoring continuing the commonwealth status over statehood, with little support for independence.

Cuban Americans Cuban immigration into the United States dates back as far as 1831, but it began in earnest following Fidel Castro's assumption of power after the 1959 Cuban revolution. The first wave of 200,000 Cubans included many professionals with relatively high levels of schooling; these men and women were largely welcomed as refugees from communist tyranny. However, more recent waves of immigrants have aroused growing concern, partly because they are less likely to be skilled professionals.

Throughout the various waves of immigration from

Cuba since the revolution, Cuban Americans have been encouraged to locate across the United States. Nevertheless, many continue to settle in (or return to) metropolitan Miami, Florida, with its warm climate and proximity to Cuba. As of 1990, 53 percent of all Cuban Americans lived in Miami, 15 percent lived in New York City, and 5 percent lived in Los Angeles. While Hispanics comprised only 4 percent of Miami's population in 1950, today they constitute a majority of residents, and most of this Hispanic population is Cuban American (Winsberg 1994).

The Cuban experience in the United States has been mixed. Some detractors worry about the vehement anticommunism of Cuban Americans and about the apparent growth of a Cuban organized crime syndicate that engages in the drug trade and ganglike violence. Recently, Cuban Americans in Miami have expressed concern over what they view as the indifference of the city's Roman Catholic hierarchy. Like other Hispanics, Cuban Americans are underrepresented in leadership positions within the church. Finally—despite many individual success stories—as a group, Cuban Americans in Miami remain behind "Anglos" (Whites) in their income, rate of employment, and proportion of professionals (Firmat 1994; Llanes 1982).

Jewish Americans

Jews constitute almost 3 percent of the population of the United States. They play a prominent role in the worldwide Jewish community because the United States has the world's largest concentration of Jews. Like the Japanese, many Jewish immigrants came to this country and became white-collar professionals in spite of prejudice and discrimination.

Anti-Semitism—that is, anti-Jewish prejudice—in the United States has often been vicious, although rarely so widespread and never so formalized as in Europe. In many cases, Jews have been used as scapegoats for other people's failures. This was clearly indicated in a study of World War II veterans (Bettelheim and Janowitz 1964). The researchers found that men who had experienced downward mobility (for example, job failure) were more likely to blame their setbacks on Jewish Americans than on their own shortcomings.

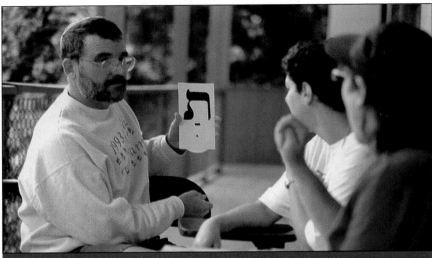

For practicing Jews, the Hebrew language is an important part of religious instruction. This teacher is showing flashcards of Hebrew alphabetic characters to deaf students.

As is true for other minorities discussed in this chapter, Jewish Americans face the choice of maintaining ties to their long religious and cultural heritage or becoming as indistinguishable as possible from gentiles. Many Jews have tended to assimilate, as is evident from the rise in marriages between Jews and Christians. A study conducted for the Council of Jewish Federations reported that since 1985, slightly more than half of Jews who married chose to marry a non-Jew. Moreover, of those children of intermarriages who receive religious instruction, 72 percent are reared in faiths other than Judaism. These trends worry Jewish leaders, some of whom fear for the long-term future of the Jewish people (*Religion Watch* 1991).

Jews have not achieved equality in the United States. Despite high levels of education and professional training, they are still conspicuously absent from the top management of large corporations (except for the few firms founded by Jews). Until the late 1960s, many prestigious universities maintained restrictive quotas that limited Jewish enrollment. Private social clubs and fraternal groups frequently limit membership to gentiles (non-Jews), a practice upheld by the Supreme Court in the 1964 case of *Bell v. Maryland.*

The Anti-Defamation League (ADL) of B'nai B'rith, founded in 1913, makes an annual survey of reported anti-Semitic incidents. Although the number has fluctuated, the 1994 tabulation reached the highest level in the 17 years during which the ADL has been recording such incidents. It dropped slightly the next three years, but still the total of harassment, threats, episodes of vandalism, and assaults came to 1,571 incidents reported in 1997. Some incidents were inspired and carried out by neo-Nazi skinheads—groups of young people who champion racist and anti-Semitic ideologies. Particularly disturbing has been the number of reported anti-Semitic incidents on college campuses. In 1997, 104 incidents were reported on 80 campuses. Anti-Jewish graffiti, anti-Semitic speakers, and swastikas affixed to predominantly Jewish fraternities were among the documented incidents (Anti-Defamation League of B'nai B'rith 1998). Such threatening behavior only intensifies the fears of many Jewish Americans, who find it difficult to forget the Holocaust—the extermination of 6 million Jews by the Nazi Third Reich during the late 1930s and 1940s.

White Ethnics

A significant segment of the population of the United States is made up of White ethnics whose ancestors have come from Europe within the last 100 years. The nation's White ethnic population includes about 58 million people who claim at least partial German ancestry, 39 million Irish Americans, 15 million Italian Americans, and 9 million Polish Americans, as well as immigrants from other European nations. Some of these people continue to live in close-knit ethnic neighborhoods, while others have largely assimilated and left the "old ways" behind (Bureau of the Census 1999a:56).

To what extent are White ethnics found among the nation's elite? Sociologists Richard Alba and Gwen Moore (1982) conducted interviews with 545 people who held important positions in powerful social, economic, and political institutions. They found that White Anglo-Saxon Protestants were overrepresented among the nation's elite, while White ethnics were underrepresented (although not so dramatically as were African Americans, Hispanics, Asian Americans, and Native Americans). Some ethnic minorities appeared to have risen to key positions in particular areas of the elite structure. For example, Irish Catholics were well represented among labor leaders.

White ethnics and racial minorities have often been antagonistic to one another because of economic competition—an interpretation in line with the conflict approach to sociology. As Blacks, Hispanics, and Native Americans emerge from the lower class, they will initially be competing with working-class Whites for jobs, housing, and educational opportunities. In times of high unemployment or inflation, any such competition can easily generate intense intergroup conflict.

In many respects, the plight of White ethnics raises the same basic issues as that of other subordinate people in the United States. How ethnic can people be—how much can they deviate from an essentially White, Anglo-Saxon, Protestant norm—before society punishes them

for a willingness to be different? Our society does seem to reward people for assimilating. Yet, as we have seen, assimilation is no guarantee of equality or freedom from discrimination. In the social policy section that follows, we will focus on immigrants, people who inevitably face the question of whether to strive for assimilation.

SOCIAL POLICY AND RACE AND ETHNICITY

Global Immigration

The Issue

Worldwide immigration is at an all-time high. Each year, two to four million people move from one country to another. As of the mid-1990s, immigrants totaled about 125 million, representing 2 percent of the global population (Martin and Widgren 1996). Their constantly increasing numbers and the pressure they put on job opportunities and welfare capabilities in the countries they enter raise troubling questions for many of the world's economic powers. Who should be allowed in? At what point should immigration be curtailed?

The Setting

The migration of people is not uniform across time or space. At certain times, wars or famines may precipitate large movements of people either temporarily or permanently. Temporary dislocations occur when people wait until it is safe to return to their home areas. However, more and more migrants who cannot make adequate livings in their home nations are making permanent moves to developed nations. Figure 10-4 shows the destinations of the major migration streams: into North America, the oil-rich areas of the Middle East, and the industrial economies of

FIGURE 10-4

Major Migration Patterns of the 1990s

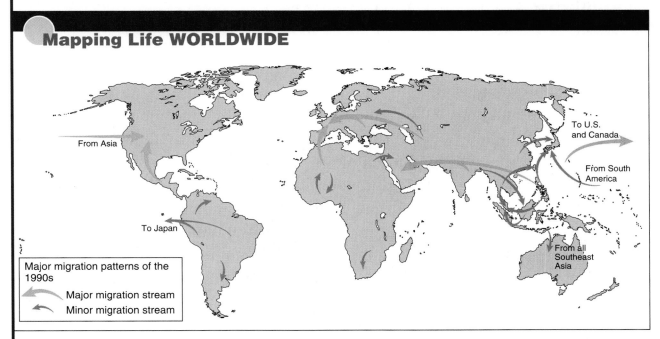

Source: Martin and Widgren 1996:21.

western Europe and Asia. Currently, seven of the world's wealthiest nations (including Germany, France, the United Kingdom, and the United States) shelter about one-third of the world's migrant population, but less than one-fifth of the total world population. As long as there are disparities in job opportunities among countries, there is little reason to expect this international migration trend to end.

Countries like the United States that have long been a destination for immigrants have a history of policies to determine who has preference to enter. Often, clear racial and ethnic biases are built into these policies. In the 1920s, U.S. policy gave preference to people from western Europe, while making it difficult for residents of southern and eastern Europe, Asia, and Africa to enter the country. During the late 1930s and early 1940s, the federal government refused to lift or loosen restrictive immigration quotas in order to allow Jewish refugees to escape the terror of the Nazi regime. In line with this policy, the *S.S. St. Louis,* with more than 900 Jewish refugees on board, was denied permission to land in the United States in 1939. This ship was forced to sail back to Europe, where it is estimated that at least a few hundred of its passengers later died at the hands of the Nazis (Morse 1967; G. Thomas and Witts 1974).

Since the 1960s, policies in the United States have encouraged immigration of people with relatives here as well as of people who have needed skills. This change has significantly altered the pattern of sending nations. Previously, Europeans dominated, but for the last 40 years, immigrants have come primarily from Latin America and Asia (see Figure 10-5). This means that an ever-growing proportion of the United States will be Asian or Hispanic. To a large degree, fear and resentment of this growing racial and ethnic diversity is a key factor in opposition to immigration. In many nations, people are very concerned that the new arrivals do not reflect the cultural and racial heritage of the nation.

Sociological Insights

Despite people's fears about it, immigration provides many valuable functions. For the receiving society, it alleviates labor shortages, such as in the areas of health care and technology in the United States. In 1998, Congress debated not whether individuals with technological skills should be allowed into the country, but just how much to increase the annual number. For the sending nation, migration can relieve economies unable to support large numbers of people. Often overlooked is the large amount of money that immigrants send *back* to their home nations. For example, worldwide immigrants from Portugal alone

FIGURE 10-5

Immigration in the United States, 1820s–1990s

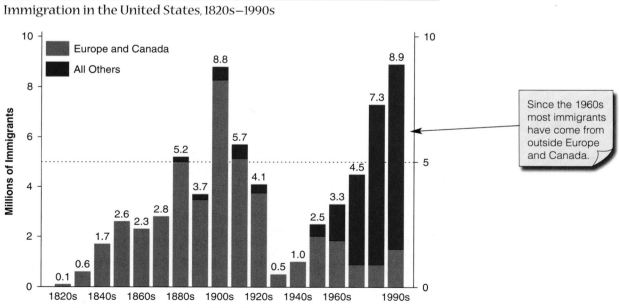

Source: Immigration and Naturalization Service 1999a, 1999b. Projection for the 1990s by the author based on Immigration and Naturalization data.

send more than $4 billion annually back to their home country (World Bank 1995).

There has been considerable research, particularly in the United States, on the impact of immigration on a nation's economy. Studies generally show that it has a positive impact on the economy, although areas experiencing high concentrations of immigrants may find it difficult to meet short-term social service needs. When migrants with skills or educational potential leave developing countries, it can be dysfunctional for those nations. No amount of payments back home can make up for the loss of valuable human resources from poor nations (Martin and Midgley 1999).

Conflict theorists note how much of the debate over immigration is phrased in economic terms. But this debate is intensified when the arrivals are of different racial and ethnic background from the host population. For example, Europeans often refer to "foreigners," but the term does not necessarily mean one of foreign birth. In Germany, "foreigners" refers to people of non-German ancestry, even if they were born in Germany; it does not refer to people of German ancestry born in another country who may choose to come to their "mother country." Fear and dislike of "new" ethnic groups divide countries throughout the world. In 1998, the One Nation Party of Australia sought office on a platform of removing all illegal immigrants and seizing their property to cover deportation costs (Martin and Widgren 1996; *Migration News* 1998b).

Policy Initiatives

The long border with Mexico provides ample opportunity for illegal immigration into the United States. Throughout the 1980s, there was a growing perception that the United States had lost control of its borders. Feeling public pressure for immigration control, Congress ended a decade of debate by approving the Immigration Reform and Control Act of 1986. The act marked a historic change in immigration policy. For the first time, hiring of illegal aliens was outlawed, and employers caught violating the law became subject to fines and even prison sentences. Just as significant a change was the extension of amnesty and legal status to many illegal immigrants already living in the United States. More than a decade later, however, the 1986 immigration law appears to have had mixed results. Substantial numbers of illegal immigrants con-

tinue to enter the country each year, with an estimated 5 million present at any given time (Martin and Midgley 1999).

In part because the 1986 immigration law failed to end illegal immigration, there has been increasing pressure in several states for further governmental action. Most dramatically, in November 1994, California's voters overwhelmingly approved Proposition 187, a controversial initiative that (among other provisions) calls for withholding social services and schooling opportunities from illegal immigrants. Constitutional challenges to the law resulted in blocking of all the measure's provisions.

Indeed, the entire world feels the overwhelming impact of economic globalization on immigration patterns. Europe is also wrestling with policy initiatives. The European Union agreement of 1997 gives the governing commission authority to propose Europewide legislation on immigration beginning in 2002. However, the policies must be accepted unanimously, which seems unlikely. An EU policy that would allow immigrants to live and work in one EU country would allow them to work anywhere. The immigration issue is expected to complicate efforts by the sending nations (such as Turkey) to become members of the EU (Light 1999; Sassen 1999).

The intense debate over immigration reflects deep value conflicts in the culture of many nations. One strand of our culture, for example, has traditionally emphasized egalitarian principles and a desire to help people in their time of need. At the same time, however, hostility to potential immigrants and refugees—whether Chinese in the 1880s, European Jews in the 1930s and 1940s, or Mexicans, Haitians, and Arabs today—reflects not only racial, ethnic, and religious prejudice, but also a desire to maintain the dominant culture of the in-group by keeping out those viewed as outsiders.

Let's Discuss

1. Did you or your ancestors immigrate to the United States from another nation? If so, when and where did your family come from, and why? Did they face discrimination?

2. Do you live, work, or study with recent immigrants to the United States? If so, are they well accepted in your community, or do they face prejudice and discrimination?

3. What is your opinion of the recent backlash against illegal immigrants in California?

Summary

The social dimensions of race and ethnicity are important factors in shaping people's lives in the United States and other countries. In this chapter, we examine the meaning of race and ethnicity and study the major racial and ethnic minorities of the United States.

1. A *racial group* is set apart from others by obvious physical differences, whereas an *ethnic group* is set apart primarily because of national origin or distinctive cultural patterns.
2. When sociologists define a *minority group,* they are primarily concerned with the economic and political power, or powerlessness, of the group.
3. In a biological sense, there are no "pure races" and no physical traits that can be used to describe one group to the exclusion of all others.
4. The meaning that people give to the physical differences between races gives social significance to race, leading to *stereotypes* and *self-fulfilling prophecy.*
5. *Prejudice* often leads to *discrimination,* but the two are not identical, and each can be present without the other.
6. *Institutional discrimination* results from the normal operations of a society.

7. Functionalists point out that discrimination is both functional and dysfunctional in society. Conflict theorists explain racial subordination by *exploitation theory.* Interactionists focus on the microlevel of race relations, posing *contact hypothesis* as a means of reducing prejudice and discrimination.
8. Four patterns describe typical intergroup relations in North America and elsewhere: *amalgamation, assimilation, segregation,* and *pluralism.*
9. In the United States, the most highly rewarded pattern of intergroup relations is assimilation. Pluralism remains more of an ideal than a reality.
10. Contemporary prejudice and discrimination against African Americans are rooted in the history of slavery in the United States.
11. Asian Americans are commonly viewed as a "model minority," a stereotype not necessarily beneficial to members of this group.
12. The various groups included under the general term *Hispanics* represent the largest ethnic minority in the United States.
13. The increase of immigration worldwide has raised questions in individual nations about how to control the process.

Critical Thinking Questions

1. Which sociological perspective would be most helpful in discussing the riots in Los Angeles in 1992? Apply this perspective in exploring the causes of the rioting and the implications of these events for racial and ethnic relations in the United States.
2. The text states that "in the United States, pluralism is more of an ideal than a reality." Can the community in which you grew up and the college you attend be viewed as genuine examples of pluralism?

Examine the relations between dominant and subordinate racial and ethnic groups in your hometown and your college.
3. What are some of the similarities and differences in the position of African Americans and Hispanics as minorities in the United States? What are some of the similarities and differences in the position of Asian Americans and Jewish Americans?

Key Terms

Affirmative action   Positive efforts to recruit minority group members or women for jobs, promotions, and educational opportunities (266)

Amalgamation   The process by which a majority group and a minority group combine through intermarriage to form a new group. (270)

Anti-Semitism   Anti-Jewish prejudice. (279)

Apartheid   The policy of the South African government designed to maintain the separation of Blacks and other non-Whites from the dominant Whites. (270)

Assimilation   The process by which a person forsakes his or her own cultural tradition to become part of a different culture. (270)

Black power   A political philosophy promoted by many younger Blacks in the 1960s that supported the creation of Black-controlled political and economic institutions. (274)

Contact hypothesis   An interactionist perspective which states that interracial contact between people of equal status in cooperative circumstances will reduce prejudice. (269)

Discrimination   The process of denying opportunities and equal rights to individuals and groups because of prejudice or other arbitrary reasons. (264)

Ethnic group   A group that is set apart from others because of its national origin or distinctive cultural patterns. (257)

Ethnocentrism   The tendency to assume that one's own culture and way of life represent the norm or are superior to all others. (262)

Exploitation theory   A Marxist theory that views racial subordination in the United States as a manifestation of the class system inherent in capitalism. (268)

Genocide   The deliberate, systematic killing of an entire people or nation. (269)

Glass ceiling   An invisible barrier that blocks the promotion of a qualified individual in a work environment because of the individual's gender, race, or ethnicity. (265)

Institutional discrimination   The denial of opportunities and equal rights to individuals and groups that results from the normal operations of a society. (265)

Issei   The early Japanese immigrants to the United States. (277)

Minority group   A subordinate group whose members have significantly less control or power over their own lives than the members of a dominant or majority group have over theirs. (257)

Nisei   Japanese born in the United States who were descendants of the Issei. (277)

Pluralism   Mutual respect between the various groups in a society for one another's cultures, which allows minorities to express their own cultures without experiencing prejudice. (271)

Prejudice   A negative attitude toward an entire category of people, such as a racial or ethnic minority. (262)

Racial group   A group that is set apart from others because of obvious physical differences. (257)

Racism   The belief that one race is supreme and all others are innately inferior. (262)

Segregation   The act of physically separating two groups; often imposed on a minority group by a dominant group. (270)

Self-fulfilling prophecy   The tendency of people to respond to and act on the basis of stereotypes, leading to validation of false definitions. (259)

Stereotypes   Unreliable generalizations about all members of a group that do not recognize individual differences within the group. (259)

Additional Readings

BOOKS

O'Hearn, Claudine Chiawei, ed. 1998. *Half and Half: Writers on Growing Up Biracial and Bicultural.* New York: Parthenon Books. Eighteen essayists address the difficulties of fitting into, and the benefits of being part of, two worlds.

Pollard, Kevin M., and William P. O'Hare. 1999. *America's Racial and Ethnic Minorities. Population Bulletin* 54. This brief publication (48 pages) provides an overview of contemporary racial and ethnic groups, as well as a discussion of changing definitions of race.

Schaefer, Richard T. 2000. *Racial and Ethnic Groups.* 8th ed. New York: Prentice Hall. Comprehensive in its coverage of race and ethnicity, this text also discusses women as a subordinate minority and examines dominant–subordinate relations in Canada, Northern Ireland, Israel and the Palestinian territory, Mexico, and South Africa.

Sniderman, Paul S., and Edward G. Carmines. 1997. *Reaching Beyond Race.* Cambridge, MA: Harvard University Press. Using surveys, two political scientists intensively examine White attitudes on race and measure opposition to affirmative action and other policies.

JOURNALS

Among the journals that focus on issues of race and ethnicity are *Amerasian Journal* (founded in 1971), *The Black Scholar* (1969), *Contemporary Jewry* (1978), *Ethnic and Racial Studies* (1978), *Hispanic Journal of Behavioral Studies* (1979), *Journal of Refugee Studies* (1988), and *Race and Society* (1997). Local publications produced by racial and ethnic communities are also useful.

Internet Connection

Note: While all the URLs listed were current as of the printing of this book, these sites often change. Please check our website (http://www.mhhe.com/schaefer) for updates.

1. Unfortunately, prejudice sometimes leads to the tragedy of genocide. Visit the PBS website, The Triumph of Evil: How the West Ignored Warnings of the 1994 Rwanda Genocide and Turned Its Back on the Victims (**http://www.pbs.org/wgbh/ pages/frontline/shows/evil/**). Use your sociological imagination to reflect on the timeline and the photographs, interviews, and articles presented there.

   (a) According to Alain Destaxhe, how is *genocide* defined? How can it be compared to other social crimes?

   (b) According to Destaxhe's description, which three world historical events would qualify as instances of genocide?

   (c) In what ways do the photographs and descriptions of events in Rwanda parallel other cases of genocide in the twentieth century? In what ways are they unique?

   (d) What historical and social forces led up to the genocide in Rwanda? Who were some of the major figures involved?

   (e) How would a conflict theorist view the bloodshed in Rwanda?

   (f) How many days did the killings in Rwanda go on? What was the response of the United States and the United Nations? Should the United States have done more to stop the killings in Rwanda?

   (g) How did events in Somalia impact these official reactions to events in Rwanda?

   (h) Why do you think the United States and the United Nations took a more active role in opposing "ethnic cleansing" in the former nation of Yugoslavia in 1999, but not in Rwanda in 1994?

   (i) In your opinion, did the U.S. media give the Rwandan genocide enough attention? Why or why not?

2. Hate Watch (**http://hatewatch.org**) is one of many online sites dedicated to raising awareness of hate crimes and hate groups. Spend some time exploring both its Activist Center and its list of hate groups. Warning: Occasionally, linking with these websites may generate return e-mail from the organizations represented on the sites.

   (a) Which groups are most likely to become the victims of hate crimes? Give some examples of hate crimes that have been reported recently in the news. Are intergroup relations improving, or are they getting worse?

   (b) Choose one of the activist groups listed in the Activist Center. What is the group's name? Its mission or goal?

   (c) What specific measures does the group advocate to eradicate or prevent hate crimes? Do you think the group's efforts will be helpful? Why or why not?

   (d) Choose one of the hate groups listed under Online Bigotry: Hate by Category. What is the group's name, and what symbols does it use to represent itself? From an interactionist approach, what does each symbol's shape, form, and color say about the group?

   (e) What is the group's mission or goal? Through what means does the group seek to reach its goals?

   (f) When did the group come into existence? Who are its members and leaders?

   (g) Do you think Hate Watch is justified in labeling this group as racist or bigoted? Why or why not?

   (h) In what ways has the Internet become a tool for both activist and racist groups?

   (i) What specific steps should society take to deal with the social problem of hate crimes? What specific steps can *you* take?

STRATIFICATION
BY GENDER

In 1989 a militant group called the Guerrilla Girls called attention to sexism in the art world with this poster, which protests the underrepresentation of female artists at the world-famous Metropolitan Museum of Art in New York City. This poster and others dealing with sexism in the arts can be viewed at www.guerrillagirls.com.

A t last, after a long silence, women took to the streets. In the two decades of radical action that followed the rebirth of feminism in the early 1970s, Western women gained legal and reproductive rights, pursued higher education, entered the trades and the professions, and overturned ancient and revered beliefs about their social role. A generation on, do women feel free?

The affluent, educated, liberated women of the First World, who can enjoy freedoms unavailable to any women ever before, do not feel as free as they want to. And they can no longer restrict to the subconscious their sense that this lack of freedom has something to do with—with apparently frivolous issues, things that really should not matter. Many are ashamed to admit that such trivial concerns—to do with physical appearance, bodies, faces, hair, clothes—matter so much. But in spite of shame, guilt, and denial, more and more women are wondering if . . . something important is indeed at stake that has to do with the relationship between female liberation and female beauty.

The more legal and material hindrances women have broken through, the more strictly and heavily and cruelly images of female beauty have come to weigh upon us. . . .

During the past decade, women breached the power structure; meanwhile, eating disorders rose exponentially and cosmetic surgery became the fastest-growing medical specialty. During the past five years, consumer spending doubled, pornography became the main media category, ahead of legitimate films and records combined, and thirty-three thousand American women told researchers that they would rather lose ten to fifteen pounds than achieve any other goal. More women have more money and power and scope and legal recognition than we have ever had before; but in terms of how we feel about ourselves *physically,* we may actually be worse off than our unliberated grandmothers. Recent research consistently shows that inside the majority of the West's controlled, attractive, successful working women, there is a secret "underlife" poisoning our freedom; infused with notions of beauty, it is a dark vein of self-hatred, physical obsessions, terror of aging, and dread of lost control. *(Wolf 1992:9–10)* ■

I n this excerpt from Naomi Wolf's book *The Beauty Myth,* a feminist confronts the power of a false ideal of womanhood. Though in recent decades, American women have broken legal and institutional barriers that once limited their educational opportunities and career advancement, Wolf writes, psychologically they are still enslaved by unrealistic standards of appearance. The more freedom women have gained, in fact, the more obsessed they seem to have become with the ideal of the emaciated supermodel—an ideal that few women can ever hope to attain without jeopardizing their health or resorting to expensive cosmetic surgery.

Wolf implies that the Beauty Myth is a societal control mechanism that is meant to keep women in their place—as subordinates to men at home and on the job. Indeed, the term *trophy wife* reduces the conventionally beautiful woman to the role of status symbol of a successful man. But men too are captive to unrealistic expectations regarding their physical appearance. In hopes of attaining the brawny, muscular physique characteristic of body builders and profes-

sional wrestlers, more and more men are now taking steroids or electing to undergo cosmetic surgery.

The Beauty Myth is but one example of how cultural norms may lead to differentiation based on gender. Such differentiation is evident in virtually every human society about which we have information. We saw in Chapters 8, 9, and 10 that most societies establish hierarchies based on social class, race, and ethnicity. This chapter will examine the ways in which societies stratify their members on the basis of gender. It will begin by looking at how various cultures, including our own, assign women and men to particular social roles. Then it will consider sociological explanations for gender stratification.

Next, the chapter will focus on the unique situation of women as an oppressed majority. It will analyze the social, economic, and political aspects of women's subordinate position and consider the consequences of gender stratification for men and minority women. The chapter will also examine the emergence of the contemporary feminist movement. Finally, the social policy section will analyze the intense and continuing controversy over abortion. ■

Social Construction of Gender

Gender is such a routine part of our everyday activities that we typically take it for granted and only take notice when someone deviates from conventional behavior and expectations. How many air passengers do you think feel a start when the captain's voice from the cockpit belongs to a female? Or consider another example: A father announces that he will be late for work because his son has a routine medical checkup. We are likely to wonder how he found himself in this situation. Is he a single father struggling to bring up his son by himself? Could his wife have such pressing business that she cannot adjust her schedule to perform the appropriate parental duties? Consciously or unconsciously, we are likely to assume that these parental duties are, in fact, *maternal* duties.

Although a few people begin life with an unclear sexual identity, the overwhelming majority begin with a definite sex and quickly receive societal messages about how to behave. Many societies have established social distinctions between females and males that do not inevitably result from biological differences between the sexes (such as women's reproductive capabilities).

In studying gender, sociologists are interested in the gender-role socialization that leads females and males to

behave differently. In Chapter 5, *gender roles* were defined as expectations regarding the proper behavior, attitudes, and activities of males and females. The application of traditional gender roles leads to many forms of differentiation between women and men. Both sexes are physically capable of learning to cook and sew, yet most Western societies determine that these tasks should be performed by women. Both men and women are capable of learning to weld and fly airplanes, but these functions are generally assigned to men.

Gender roles are evident not only in our work and behavior but in how we react to others. We are constantly "doing gender" without realizing it. If the father discussed above sits in the doctor's office with his son in the middle of a workday, he will receive approving glances from the receptionist and from other patients. "Isn't he a wonderful father?" runs through their minds. But if the boy's mother leaves *her* job and sits with the son in the doctor's office, she will not receive such silent applause.

We socially construct our behavior so that male–female differences are either created or exaggerated. For example, men and women come in a variety of heights, sizes, and ages. Yet traditional norms regarding marriage and even casual dating tell us that in heterosexual couples, the man should be older, taller, and wiser than the woman. As we will

When Fannie Barnes first took the controls of a San Francisco cable car, she probably raised a few eyebrows. No female before had ever been a "gripman" in the cable car system.

pected to play with trucks, blocks, and toy soldiers; girls are given dolls and kitchen goods. Boys must be masculine—active, aggressive, tough, daring, and dominant—whereas girls must be feminine—soft, emotional, sweet, and submissive. These are all traditional gender-role patterns that have been influential in the socialization of children in the United States.

An important element in traditional views of proper "masculine" and "feminine" behavior is fear of homosexuality. In Chapter 5, we defined *homophobia* as fear of and prejudice against homosexuality. Homophobia contributes significantly to rigid gender-role socialization, since many people stereotypically associate male homosexuality with femininity and lesbianism with masculinity. Consequently, men and women who deviate from traditional expectations about gender roles are often presumed to be gay. Despite the advances made by the gay liberation movement (which will be explored in Chapter 21), the continuing stigma attached to homosexuality in our culture places pressure on all males (whether gay or not) to exhibit only narrow "masculine" behavior and on all females (whether lesbian or not) to exhibit only narrow "feminine" behavior (Seidman 1994; see also Lehne 1995).

It is *adults,* of course, who play a critical role in guiding children into those gender roles deemed appropriate in a society. Parents are normally the first and most crucial agents of socialization. But other adults, older siblings, the

see throughout this chapter, such social norms help to reinforce and legitimize patterns of male dominance.

In recent decades, women have increasingly entered occupations and professions previously dominated by men. Yet our society still focuses on "masculine" and "feminine" qualities as if men and women must be evaluated in these terms. Clearly, we continue to "do gender," and this social construction of gender continues to define significantly different expectations for females and males in the United States (Lorber 1994; L. Rosenbaum 1996; C. West and Zimmerman 1987).

Gender Roles in the United States

Gender-Role Socialization

Male babies get blue blankets, while females get pink ones. Boys are ex-

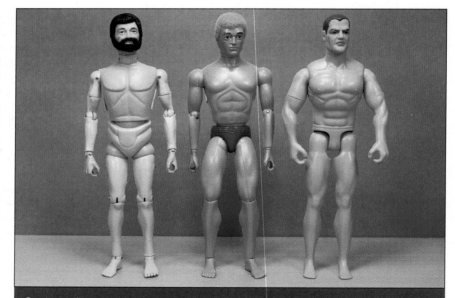

Society often exaggerates male–female differences in appearance and behavior. In 1964, the G.I. Joe doll (left) had a realistic appearance, but by 1992 (middle) it had begun to acquire the exaggerated muscularity characteristic of professional wrestlers (right). The change intensified the contrast with ultra-thin female figures, like the Barbie doll (Angier 1998).

pp. 101–02 ◀ mass media, and religious and educational institutions also exert an important influence on gender-role socialization in the United States and elsewhere. Researchers Sandnabba and Ahlberg (1999) found that in Finland, parents' responses to children's cross-gender behavior varied with the child's gender. Girls who engaged in "boyish" behavior were more accepted than boys whose behavior was seen as "girlish."

Women's Gender Roles

How does a girl come to develop a feminine self-image whereas a boy develops one that is masculine? In part, they do so by identifying with females and males in their families and neighborhoods and in the media. If a young girl regularly sees female characters on television working as defense attorneys and judges, she may believe that she herself can become a lawyer. And it will not hurt if women that she knows—her mother, sister, parents' friends, or neighbors—are lawyers. By contrast, if this young girl sees women portrayed in the media only as models, nurses, and secretaries, her identification and self-image will be quite different. Even if she does become a professional, she may secretly regret falling short of the media stereotype—a shapely, sexy young woman in a bathing suit (Wolf 1992).

Television is far from being alone in stereotyping women. Studies of children's books published in the United States in the 1940s, 1950s, and 1960s found that females were significantly underrepresented in central roles and illustrations. Virtually all female characters were portrayed as helpless, passive, incompetent, and in need of a strong male caretaker. By the 1980s, there was somewhat less stereotyping in children's books, with some female characters shown to be active. Nevertheless, boys were still shown engaged in active play three times as often as girls (Kortenhaus and Demarest 1993).

Social research on gender roles reveals some persistent differences between men and women in North America and Europe. Women experience a mandate to both marry and be a mother. Often, marriage is viewed as the true entry into adulthood. And women are expected not only to become mothers but to *want* to be mothers. Obviously, men play a role in these events, but they do not appear to be as critical in identifying the life course for a man. Society defines men's roles by economic success. While women may achieve recognition in the labor force, it is not as important to their identity as it is for men (Doyle and Paludi 1998; Russo 1976).

Traditional gender roles have most severely restricted females. Throughout this chapter, we will see how women have been confined to subordinate roles within the political and economic institutions of the United States. Yet it is also true that gender roles have restricted males.

Media stereotypes can influence the way girls and boys see themselves and their future roles in society. Today, stories featuring strong women like Xena, the Warrior Princess, are extremely popular among young girls, reflecting the influence of the women's movement on gender roles.

Men's Gender Roles

During the game I always played the outfield. Right field. Far right field. And there I would stand in the hot sun wishing I was anyplace else in the world (Fager et al. 1971).

This is the childhood recollection of a man who, as a boy, disliked sports, dreaded gym classes, and had particular problems with baseball. Obviously, he did not conform to the socially constructed male gender role and no doubt paid the price for it.

Men's roles are socially constructed in much the same way as women's roles are. Family, peers, and the media all influence how a boy or a man comes to view his appropriate role in society. Robert Brannon (1976) and James Doyle (1995) have identified five aspects of the male gender role:

- Antifeminine element—show no "sissy stuff," including any expression of openness or vulnerability.

- Success element—prove one's masculinity at work and sports.
- Aggressive element—use force in dealing with others.
- Sexual element—initiate and control all sexual relations.
- Self-reliant element—keep cool and unflappable.

No systematic research has established all these elements as a common aspect among boys and men, but specific studies have confirmed individual elements.

Being antifeminine is basic to men's gender roles. Males who do not conform to the socially constructed gender role face constant criticism and even humiliation both from children when they are boys and from adults as men. It can be agonizing to be treated as a "chicken" or a "sissy"—particularly if such remarks come from one's father or brothers. At the same time, boys who successfully adapt to cultural standards of masculinity may grow up to be inexpressive men who cannot share their feelings with others. They remain forceful and tough—but as a result they are also closed and isolated (Faludi 1999; McCreary 1994; G. Sheehy 1999).

In the last 35 years, inspired in good part by the contemporary feminist movement (examined later in the chapter), increasing numbers of men in the United States have criticized the restrictive aspects of the traditional male gender role. Some men have taken strong public positions in support of women's struggle for full equality and have even organized voluntary associations such as the National Organization of Men Against Sexism (NOMAS), founded in 1975 to support positive changes for men. Nevertheless, the traditional male gender role remains well entrenched as an influential element of our culture (Messner 1997; NOMAS 1999).

One recent reflection of the persistence of traditional gender roles has been the rise of the Promise Keepers, an evangelical Christian men's ministry that in the mid-1990s drew more than 700,000 men to stadiums across North America to hear inspirational messages. At Promise Keeper events, men "promise" to return to the home and assume their "rightful" place as head of the household. The Promise Keepers have been criticized for their reassertion of male dominance and their exclusion of women and gay men.

Many of the same criticisms have been directed against the October 1995 Million Man March on Washington, D.C., organized by controversial minister Louis Farrakhan of the Nation of Islam. The march encouraged African American men to accept responsibility for their families and communities; it received strong support in Black communities around the United States. For some, the Promise Keepers and the Million Man March represent welcome efforts to reassess the traditional male role; for others, they represent an unwelcome return to conventional norms of male dominance (Miller and Schaefer 1998).

Cross-Cultural Perspective

To what extent do actual biological differences between the sexes contribute to the cultural differences associated with gender? This question brings us back to the debate over "nature versus nurture." In assessing the alleged and real differences between men and women, it is useful to examine cross-cultural data. pp. 91–94

The research of anthropologist Margaret Mead points to the importance of cultural conditioning—as opposed to biology—in defining the social roles of males and females. In *Sex and Temperament,* Mead (1963, original edition 1935; 1973) describes typical behaviors of each sex in three different cultures in New Guinea:

In one [the Arapesh], both men and women act as we expect women to act—in a mild parental responsive way; in the second [the Mundugumor], both act as we expect men to act—in a fierce initiating fashion; and in the third [the Tchambuli], the men act according to our stereotypes for women—are catty, wear curls, and go shopping—while the women are energetic, managerial, unadorned partners (Mead 1963: preface to 1950 ed.).

If biology determined all differences between the sexes, then cross-cultural differences, such as those described by Mead, would not exist. Her findings confirm the influential role of culture and socialization in gender-role differentiation. There appears to be no innate or biological reason to designate completely different gender roles for men and women.

In any society, gender stratification requires not only individual socialization into traditional gender roles within the family, but also the promotion and support of these traditional roles by other social institutions such as religion and education. Moreover, even with all major institutions socializing the young into conventional gender roles, every society has women and men who resist and successfully oppose these stereotypes: strong women who become leaders or professionals, gentle men who care for children, and so forth. It seems clear that differences between the sexes are not dictated by biology. Indeed, the maintenance of traditional gender roles requires constant social controls—and these controls are not always effective.

Cultural conditioning is important in the development of gender role differences. This sister and brother from Sudest Island in Papua New Guinea expect women to be the honorary heads of the family.

arrangement of gender roles as arising out of this need to establish a division of labor between marital partners.

Parsons and Bales contended that women take the expressive, emotionally supportive role and men the instrumental, practical role, with the two complementing each other. *Instrumentality* refers to emphasis on tasks, focus on more distant goals, and a concern for the external relationship between one's family and other social institutions. *Expressiveness* denotes concern for maintenance of harmony and the internal emotional affairs of the family. According to this theory, women's interest in expressive goals frees men for instrumental tasks, and vice versa. Women become "anchored" in the family as wives, mothers, and household managers; men are anchored in the occupational world outside the home. Of course, Parsons and Bales offered this framework in the 1950s, when many more women were full-time homemakers than is true today. These theorists did not explicitly endorse traditional gender roles, but they implied that dividing tasks between spouses was functional for the family unit.

Given the typical socialization of women and men in the United States, the functionalist view is initially persuasive. However, it would lead us to expect girls and women with no interest in children to become baby-sitters and mothers. Similarly, males who love spending time with children might be "programmed" into careers in the business world. Such differentiation might harm the individual who does not fit into prescribed roles, while also depriving society of the contributions of many talented people who are confined by gender stereotyping. Moreover, the functionalist approach does not convincingly explain why men should be categorically assigned to the instrumental role and women to the expressive role.

Explaining Stratification by Gender

Cross-cultural studies indicate that societies dominated by men are much more common than those in which women play the decisive role. Sociologists have turned to all the major theoretical perspectives to understand how and why these social distinctions are established. Each approach focuses on culture, rather than biology, as the primary determinant of gender differences. Yet, in other respects, there are wide disagreements between advocates of these sociological perspectives.

The Functionalist View

Functionalists maintain that gender differentiation has contributed to overall social stability. Sociologists Talcott Parsons and Robert Bales (1955) argued that to function most effectively, the family requires adults who will specialize in particular roles. They viewed the traditional

The Conflict Response

Viewed from a conflict perspective, this functionalist approach masks underlying power relations between men and women. Parsons and Bales never explicitly presented the expressive and instrumental tasks as unequally valued by society, yet this inequality is quite evident. Although social institutions may pay lip service to women's expressive skills, it is men's instrumental skills that are most highly rewarded—whether in terms of money or prestige. Consequently, according to feminists and conflict theorists, any division of labor by gender into instrumental and expressive tasks is far from neutral in its impact on women.

Conflict theorists contend that the relationship between females and males has traditionally been one of unequal power, with men in a dominant position over women. Men may originally have become powerful in preindustrial times because their size, physical strength, and freedom from childbearing duties allowed them to

Conflict theorists emphasize that men's work is uniformly valued, while women's work (whether unpaid labor in the home or wage labor) is devalued. These women are making tents in a factory in Binghamton, New York.

dominate women physically. In contemporary societies, such considerations are not so important, yet cultural beliefs about the sexes are long established, as anthropologist Margaret Mead and feminist sociologist Helen Mayer Hacker (1951, 1974) both stressed. Such beliefs support a social structure that places males in controlling positions.

In this sense, traditional gender roles do not simply assign various qualities and behaviors to females and males. They also send messages about these roles. Feminist author Letty Cottin Pogrebin (1981:40) suggests that the two crucial messages of gender-role stereotypes are that "boys are better" and "girls are meant to be mothers." In order for a system of male dominance to maintain itself, she argues, children must be socialized to accept traditional gender-role divisions as natural and just. Sociologist Barbara Bovee Polk (1974:418), in describing the "conflicting cultures approach" to gender differences, observes that "masculine values have higher status and constitute the dominant and visible culture of the society. They . . . provide the standard for adulthood and normality." According to this view, women are oppressed because they constitute an alternative subculture that deviates from the prevailing masculine value system.

Thus, conflict theorists see gender differences as a reflection of the subjugation of one group (women) by another group (men). If we use an analogy to Marx's analysis of class conflict, we can say that males are like the bourgeois, or capitalists; they control most of the society's wealth, prestige, and power.

pp. 15–16, 207

Females are like the proletarians, or workers; they can acquire valuable resources only by following the dictates of their "bosses." Men's work is uniformly valued, while women's work (whether unpaid labor in the home or wage labor) is devalued.

The Feminist Perspective

A significant component of the conflict approach to gender stratification draws on feminist theory. While use of that term is comparatively recent, the critique of women's position in society and culture goes back to some of the earliest works that have influenced sociology. Among the most important are Mary Wollstonecraft's *A Vindication of the Rights of Women* (originally published in 1792), John Stuart Mill's *The Subjection of Women* (originally published in 1869), and Friedrich Engels's *The Origin of Private Property, the Family, and the State* (originally published in 1884).

Engels, a close associate of Karl Marx, argued that women's subjugation coincided with the rise of private property during industrialization. Only when people moved beyond an agrarian economy could males "enjoy" the luxury of leisure and withhold rewards and privileges from women. Drawing on the work of Marx and Engels, contemporary feminist theorists often view women's subordination as part of the overall exploitation and injustice that they see as inherent in capitalist societies. Some radical feminist theorists, however, view the oppression of women as inevitable in *all* male-dominated societies, whether they be labeled "capitalist," "socialist," or "communist" (Feuer 1959; Tuchman 1992).

Feminist sociologists would find little to disagree with in the conflict theorists' perspective. But the feminist perspective would argue that the very discussion of women and society, however well meaning, has been distorted by the exclusion of women from academic thought, including sociology. In Chapter 1 we noted the many accomplishments of Jane Addams, but she generally worked outside the discipline. Her work focused on what we would now call applied sociology and social work. At the time, her efforts, while valued as humanitarian, were seen as unrelated to the research and conclusions being reached in academic circles, which, of course, were male academic circles (M. Andersen 1997).

For most of the history of sociology, studies were

conducted on male subjects or about male-led groups and organizations, and the findings were generalized to all people. For example, for many decades studies of urban life focused on street corners, neighborhood taverns, and bowling alleys—places where men typically congregated. While the insights were valuable, they did not give a true impression of city life because they overlooked the areas where women were likely to gather, such as at playgrounds with their children or at grocery stores (L. Lofland 1975).

Since men and women have had different life experiences, the issues they approach are different, and even when they choose similar concerns, they approach them from different perspectives. For example, women who enter politics today typically do so for different reasons from men. Men often embark on a political career to make business contacts or build on them, a natural extension of their livelihood; women generally become involved because they want to help. This difference is relevant to the likelihood of their future success. The areas in which women achieve political recognition revolve around such social issues as day care, the environment, education, and child protection—areas that do not attract a lot of big donors. Men focus on tax policies, business regulation, and trade agreements—issues that do excite big donors. Sometimes women do become concerned with these issues, such as former Representative Pat Schroeder of Colorado, who became an acknowledged authority on military spending. But then they must constantly reassure voters they still are concerned about "family issues." Male politicians who occasionally focus on the "bread and butter" issues, however, are seen as enlightened and ready to govern (G. Collins 1998).

Feminist theorists (including conflict theorists) emphasize that male dominance in the United States goes far beyond the economic sphere. Throughout this textbook, we examine disturbing aspects of men's behavior toward women. The ugly realities of rape, wife battering (see Chapter 13), sexual harassment (Chapter 6), and street harassment all illustrate and intensify women's subordinate position. Even if women reach economic parity with men, even if women win equal representation in government, genuine equality between the sexes cannot be achieved if these attacks remain as common as they are today.

Both functionalist and conflict theorists acknowledge that it is not possible to change gender roles drastically without dramatic revisions in a culture's social structure. Functionalists perceive potential for social disorder, or at least unknown social consequences, if all aspects of traditional gender stratification are disturbed. Yet, for conflict theorists, no social structure is ultimately desirable if it is

maintained by oppressing a majority of its citizens. These theorists argue that gender stratification may be functional for men—who hold power and privilege—but it is hardly in the interests of women (R. Collins 1975; Schmid 1980).

The Interactionist Approach

While functionalists and conflict theorists studying gender stratification typically focus on macrolevel social forces and institutions, interactionist researchers often examine gender stratification on the microlevel of everyday behavior. As an example, studies show that men initiate up to 96 percent of all interruptions in cross-sex (male–female) conversations. Men are more likely than women to change topics of conversation, to ignore topics chosen by members of the opposite sex, to minimize the contributions and ideas of members of the opposite sex, and to validate their own contributions. These patterns reflect the conversational (and, in a sense, political) dominance of males. Moreover, even when women occupy a prestigious position, such as that of physician, they are more likely to be interrupted than their male counterparts are (A. Kohn 1988; Tannen 1990; C. West and Zimmerman 1983).

In certain studies, all participants are advised in advance of the overall finding that males are more likely than females to interrupt during a cross-sex conversation. After learning this information, men reduce the

Studies show that as many as 96 percent of all interruptions in cross-sex (male–female) conversations are initiated by men.

frequency of their interruptions, yet they continue to verbally dominate conversations with women. At the same time, women reduce their already low frequency of interruption and other conversationally dominant behaviors.

These findings regarding cross-sex conversations have been frequently replicated. They have striking implications when one considers the power dynamics underlying likely cross-sex interactions—employer and job seeker, college professor and student, husband and wife, to name only a few. From an interactionist perspective, these simple, day-to-day exchanges are one more battleground in the struggle for sexual equality—as women try to "get a word in edgewise" in the midst of men's interruptions and verbal dominance (Tannen 1994a, 1994b).

Nordic countries have the highest proportion of female political representatives in the world. In March 1996 Swedish Prime Minister Goran Persson posed with members of his new government, half of whom were women.

Women: The Oppressed Majority

Many people—both male and female—find it difficult to conceive of women as a subordinate and oppressed group. Yet take a look at the political structure of the United States: Women remain noticeably underrepresented. For example, in mid-2000, only 3 of the nation's 50 states had a female governor (Arizona, New Hampshire, New Jersey). Women have made slow but steady progress in certain political arenas. In 1981, out of 535 members of Congress, there were only 21 women—19 in the House of Representatives and 2 in the Senate. By contrast, the Congress that took office in January 1999 had 67 women: 58 in the House and 9 in the Senate. Yet the leadership of Congress still remains overwhelmingly male (Center for the American Woman and Politics 1999).

In October 1981, Sandra Day O'Connor was sworn in as the nation's first female Supreme Court justice. In 1993, women achieved two significant breakthroughs: Janet Reno became the nation's first female attorney general and Ruth Bader Ginsburg joined Justice O'Connor on the Supreme Court. Still, no woman has ever served as president of the United States, vice president, speaker of the House of Representatives, or chief justice of the Supreme Court. (We will examine women's involvement in politics and government in more detail in Chapter 16.)

This lack of women in decision-making positions is evidence of women's powerlessness in the United States.

In Chapter 10, we identified five basic properties that define a minority or subordinate group. If we apply this model to the situation of women in this country, we find that a numerical majority group fits our definitions of a subordinate minority (Dworkin 1982; Hochschild 1973).

1. Women experience unequal treatment. In 1997, the median income for year-round, male workers was $43,709; for comparable female workers, it was only $29,261 (Bureau of the Census 1999a:482). Though they are not segregated from men, women are the victims of prejudice and discrimination in the paid labor force, in the legal system, and in other areas of society. Moreover, women are increasingly dominating the ranks of the impoverished, leading to what has been called the *feminization of poverty*. pp. 214–15

2. Women obviously share physical and cultural characteristics that distinguish them from the dominant group (men).

3. Membership in this subordinate group is involuntary.

4. Through the rise of contemporary feminism, women are developing a greater sense of group solidarity, as we will see later in the chapter.

5. Women are not forced to marry within the group, yet many women feel that their subordinate status is most irrevocably defined within the institution of marriage.

Sexism and Sex Discrimination

Just as African Americans are victimized by racism, women suffer from the sexism of our society. ***Sexism*** is the ideology that one sex is superior to the other. The term is generally used to refer to male prejudice and discrimination against women. In Chapter 10, we noted that Blacks can suffer from both individual acts of racism and institutional discrimination. ***Institutional discrimination*** was defined as the denial of opportunities and equal rights to individuals or groups that results from the normal operations of a society. In the same sense, women suffer both from individual acts of sexism (such as sexist remarks and acts of violence) and from institutional sexism.

It is not simply that particular men in the United States are biased in their treatment of women. All the major institutions of our society—including the government, armed forces, large corporations, the media, the universities, and the medical establishment—are controlled by men. These institutions, in their "normal," day-to-day operations, often discriminate against women and perpetuate sexism. For example, if the central office of a nationwide bank sets a policy that single women are a bad risk for loans—regardless of their incomes and investments—the institution will discriminate against women in state after state. It will do so even at bank branches in which loan officers hold no personal biases concerning women, but are merely "following orders." We will examine institutional discrimination against women within the educational system in Chapter 15.

Our society is run by male-dominated institutions, yet with the power that flows to men come responsibility and stress. Men have higher reported rates of certain types of mental illness than women do and greater likelihood of death due to heart attack or strokes (see Chapter 18). The pressure on men to succeed—and then to remain on top in a competitive world of work—can be especially intense. This is not to suggest that gender stratification is as damaging to men as it is to women. But it is clear that the power and privilege men enjoy are no guarantee of well-being.

The Status of Women Worldwide

The Hindu society of India makes life especially harsh for widows. When Hindu women marry, they join their husband's family. If the husband dies, the widow is the "property" of that family. In many cases, she ends up working as an unpaid servant; in others she is simply abandoned and left penniless. Ancient Hindu scriptures portray widows as "inauspicious" and advise that "a wise man should avoid her blessings like the poison of a snake" (J. Burns 1998:10). Such attitudes die slowly in the villages, where most Indians live.

Though Westerners tend to view Muslim societies as being similarly harsh toward women, that perception is actually an overgeneralization. Muslim countries are exceedingly varied and complex, and do not often fit the stereotypes created by the Western media. For a detailed discussion of the status of Muslim women today, see Box 11-1.

These are but a few reflections of women's second-class status throughout the world. It is estimated that women grow half the world's food, but they rarely own land. They constitute one-third of the world's paid labor force but are generally found in the lowest-paying jobs. Single-parent households headed by women—which appear to be on the increase in many nations—are typically found in the poorest sections of the population. Indeed, the feminization of poverty has become a global phenomenon. As in the United States, women worldwide are underrepresented politically.

A detailed overview of the status of the world's women, issued by the United Nations in 1995, noted that "too often, women and men live in different worlds—worlds that differ in access to education and

Women have second-class status around the world. These women are processing raw silk by hand in India.

11-1 The Head Scarf and the Veil: Complex Symbols

"My mother wears a *djellabah* [a robelike outergarment] and a veil. I have never worn them. But so what? I still cannot get divorced as easily as a man, and I am still a member of my family group and responsible to them for everything that I do. What is the veil? A piece of cloth" (Fernea and Fernea 1979:77).

The Moroccan woman who made this comment to a Western scholar several decades ago worked as a linguist and bought her clothes in Paris. She was saying, in essence, that despite a dramatic change in the clothing many Moroccan women wore, their roles and their status in the family had not changed. She was right about the strong cultural continuity in Moroccan society; for her and for millions of other Muslim women, traditions were much the same then as they had been for centuries. But as interactionists would point out, the veil is much more than a piece of cloth. Like a flag, it represents values that are sacred to Islamic society.

The wearing of a veil or head scarf, which is common to many but not all Middle Eastern societies, is based on a verse from the Koran: "Prophet, enjoin your wives, your daughters and the wives of true believers to draw their veils close round them . . . so that they may be recognized and not molested." The injunction to cover one's body in the presence of men to whom one is not closely related is based on a view of women as bearers of the family's honor. To protect their chastity from men's predatory sexual advances, women must keep themselves out of harm's way. Wearing a veil in public is intended to do just that, to signal others that they are not to touch the wearer. A man who ignores that signal does so at his

peril, for his action shames not just the woman, but her whole family.

The veil is also a way of maintaining a family's social status. Unlike rich families, poor families depend on their wives' and daughters' presence in the fields and markets, where a veil and robe can hamper a woman's ability to work. Thus in some regions of North Africa, Muslim women have never worn the veil. Nor do women veil themselves in small communities, where everyone knows everyone else. Only in the city is a woman required to wear a veil.

In effect, the veil represents a rejection of the Beauty Myth, which is so prevalent in Western societies. While a Muslim woman's

> In effect, the veil represents a rejection of the Beauty Myth, which is so prevalent in Western societies.

beauty is valued, it is not to be seen or exploited by the whole world. By covering themselves almost completely, Muslim women assure themselves and their families that their physical persons will not play a role in their contacts outside the family. Rather, these women will be known only for their faith, their intellect, and their personalities.

In the twentieth century, the veil was politicized by modernization movements that pitted Western cultural values against traditional Islamic values. In Turkey, for instance, the rise to power of Mustafa Attaturk in 1923 sparked a process of sweeping social change, in which government officials attempted to subordinate traditional ethnic and religious influences to their nationalis-

tic goals. They substituted Latin for Arabic in written documents, and purged the spoken language of Persian and Arabic words. Though women weren't forbidden to wear the veil, they were not allowed to veil themselves in public places like schools. Not surprisingly, many Muslims resented these forced social changes. In recent decades, revolutionary movements in countries like Iran and Afghanistan have reinstituted the veil and other Islamic traditions.

In Turkey, however, a modified version of the veil has recently become the symbol of militant feminists. Among educated young women who study at the universities, the new veil signifies an intention to transcend the traditional roles of wife and mother. Women who are professionals, writers, intellectuals, and activists wear it as a public statement of their aspirations.

Westerners may think the Turkish feminists' adoption of the veil is strange. Together with some Muslim feminists, people from the West tend to see the veil as a symbol of women's second-class status. But to many Muslim women it makes sense. The veil allows young women to leave their homes in the countryside and mix with strange men in the great universities of the city, without violating Islamic custom. To many Muslim women, the veil is no less than a means of liberation.

Let's Discuss

1. Consider life in a society in which women wear veils. Can you see any advantages, from the woman's point of view? From the man's?
2. Do you find the Western emphasis on physical beauty oppressive? If so, in what ways?

Sources: C. Cancel 1997; Fernea 1998; Fernea and Fernea 1977, 1979; N. Gole 1997; Read and Bartkowski 1999.

work opportunities, and in health, personal security, and leisure time." While acknowledging that much has been done in the last 20 years to sharpen people's awareness of gender inequities, the report identified a number of areas of continuing concern:

• Despite advances in higher education for women, women still face major barriers when they attempt to use their educational achievements to advance in the workplace. For example, women rarely hold more than 1 to 2 percent of top executive positions.

FIGURE 11-1

Women's Participation in the Paid Labor Force by Country, 1960s–1990s

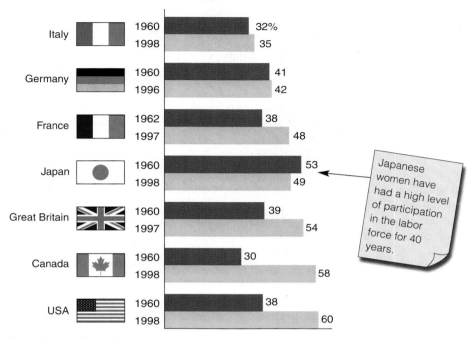

Source: Bureau of Labor Statistics 1999a.

- Women almost always work in occupations with lower status and pay than men. In both developing and developed countries, many women work as unpaid family laborers. (Figure 11-1 shows the labor force participation of women in seven industrialized countries.)
- Despite social norms regarding support and protection, many widows around the world find that they have little concrete support from extended family networks.
- In many African and a few Asian nations, traditions mandate the cutting of female genitals, typically by practitioners who fail to use sterilized instruments. This can lead either to immediate and serious complications from infection or to long-term health problems.
- While males outnumber females as refugees, refugee women have unique needs, such as protection against physical and sexual abuse (United Nations 1995:xvi, xvii, xxii, 11, 46, 70).

Moreover, according to a *Human Development Report* issued by the United Nations in 1995, there are twice as many illiterate women in developing countries as illiterate men. As noted above, some societies do not allow women to attend school. Of 1.3 billion people living in poverty around the world, 70 percent are female (Horne 1995).

What conclusions can we make about women's equality worldwide? First, as anthropologist Laura Nader (1986:383) has observed, even in the relatively more egalitarian nations of the West, women's subordination is "institutionally structured and culturally rationalized, exposing them to conditions of deference, dependency, powerlessness, and poverty." While the situation of women in Sweden and the United States is significantly better than in Saudi Arabia and Bangladesh, women nevertheless remain in a second-class position in the world's most affluent and developed countries.

Second, there is a link between the wealth of industrialized nations and the poverty of the developing countries. Viewed from a pp. 231–36 conflict perspective, the economies of developing nations are controlled and exploited by industrialized countries and multinational corporations based in those countries. Much of the exploited labor in developing nations, especially in the nonindustrial sector, is performed by women. Women workers typically toil long hours for low pay, but contribute significantly to their fami-lies' incomes. Consequently, the affluence of Western industrialized nations has come, in part, at the expense of women in Third World countries (Jacobson 1993).

Women in the Workforce of the United States

"Does your mother work?" "No, she's just a housewife." This familiar exchange reminds us of women's traditional role in the United States, and it reminds us that women's work has generally been viewed as unimportant. The U.S. Commission on Civil Rights (1976:1) concluded that the passage in the Declaration of Independence proclaiming that "all men are created equal" has been taken too literally for too long. This is especially true with respect to opportunities for employment.

A Statistical Overview

Women's participation in the paid labor force of the United States in-

To escape gender bias, more and more women are opening their own businesses. Women own about a third of all businesses in the United States—about 8 million in all.

creased steadily throughout the twentieth century (see Figure 11-2). No longer is the adult woman associated solely with the role of homemaker. Instead, millions of women—married and single, with and without children—are working outside the home. In 1998, more than 60 percent of adult women in the United States held jobs outside the home, as compared with 38 percent in 1960. A majority of women are now members of the paid labor force, not full-time homemakers. Indeed, 55 percent of new mothers return to the labor force within a year of giving birth. As recently as 1971, only 31 percent went back to work (Bureau of Labor Statistics 1999a; Fiore 1997).

Yet women entering the job market find their options restricted in important ways. Particularly damaging is occupational segregation, or confinement to sex-typed "women's jobs." For example, in 1997, women accounted for 99 percent of all secretaries, 97 percent of all dental assistants, and 81 percent of all librarians. Entering such sex-typed occupations places women in "service" roles that parallel the traditional gender-role standard under

FIGURE 11-2

Trends in U.S. Women's Participation in the Paid Labor Force, 1890–1998

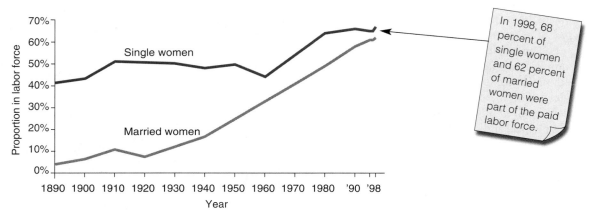

In 1998, 68 percent of single women and 62 percent of married women were part of the paid labor force.

Sources: Bureau of the Census 1975; 1999a:417.

which housewives "serve" their husbands. Women are *underrepresented* in occupations historically defined as "men's jobs," which often carry much greater financial rewards and prestige than women's jobs. For example, in 1997, women accounted for approximately 46 percent of the paid labor force of the United States. Yet they constituted only 10 percent of all engineers, 17 percent of all dentists, 26 percent of all physicians, and 29 percent of all computer systems analysts (see Table 11-1). In Box 11-2, we consider unique situations that run *against* sex-typing: male nurses and female hockey players.

In the last 35 years, however, there has been a dramatic shift in the proportion of women entering many professions traditionally dominated by men. Over the period 1960 to 1996, the proportion of people earning degrees who were female rose from 1 percent to 39 percent in dentistry, from 3 percent to 43 percent in law, and from 6 percent to 38 percent in medicine (Bureau of the Census 1999a:206). Certainly these changes reflect the impact of the women's liberation movement (discussed later in the chapter).

Women from all groups and men from minority groups sometimes encounter attitudinal or organizational bias that prevents them from reaching their full potential. As we saw in Chapter 10, the term **glass ceiling** refers to an invisible barrier that blocks the promotion of a qualified individual in a work environment because of the individual's gender, race, or ethnicity. A recent study of the *Fortune* 1,000 largest corporations in the United States showed that only 9 percent of the seats on their boards of directors were held by women. Indeed, 16 percent of these corporations still did not have even one woman on the board (Catalyst 1999).

One response to the "glass ceiling" and other gender bias in the workplace is to start your own business and work for yourself. This route to success, traditionally taken by men from immigrant and racial minority groups, has become more common among women as they have increasingly sought paid employment outside the home. According to data released in 1998, women own an impressive 8 million businesses in the United States. Yet, according to an earlier study, while women own about one-third of all business firms, they account for only 11 percent of all business revenues. In good part, this is because they typically form small businesses. In fact, 81 percent of all businesses owned by women have no employees (Bureau of the Census 1996a; Dickerson 1998).

The workplace patterns described here have one crucial result: Women earn much less money than men in the paid labor force of the United States. In 1998, the median weekly earnings of full-time female workers were about 76 percent of those for full-time male workers. Given these data, it is hardly surprising to learn that many women are living in poverty, particularly when they must function as heads of households. In the discussion of poverty in Chapter 8, we noted that female heads of households and their children accounted for most of the nation's poor people living in families. Yet not all women are in equal danger of experiencing poverty. As will be discussed more fully later in the chapter, women who are members of racial and ethnic minorities suffer from "double jeopardy": stratification by race and ethnicity as well as by gender (Bureau of Labor Statistics 1999b).

Social Consequences of Women's Employment

"What a circus we women perform every day of our lives. It puts a trapeze artist to shame." These words by the writer Anne Morrow Lindbergh attest to the lives of women today who try to juggle their work and family lives. This situation has many social consequences. For one thing, it

Table 11-1 U.S. Women in Selected Occupations, 1998
Women as Percentage of All Workers in the Occupation

Underrepresented		Overrepresented	
Airline pilots	3	High school teachers	57
Firefighters	3	Social workers	68
Engineers	11	Cashiers	78
Clergy	12	File clerks	80
Police	16	Librarians	83
Dentists	19	Elementary teachers	84
Physicians	27	Registered nurses	93
Computer systems analysts	27	Receptionists	96
Mail carriers	30	Child care workers	97
College teachers	42	Secretaries	98
Pharmacists	44	Dental hygienists	99

Source: Bureau of the Census 1999a:424–426.

11-2 Female Ice Hockey Players and Male Nurses

When you sit down to watch ice hockey, you expect to watch men playing. When you are being assisted by a nurse, you expect it to be a woman. And, indeed, in almost every case you would be correct, but not always.

Nationwide, about 7.5 percent of all nurses are male. Sociologist E. Joel Heikes (1991) wondered what characteristics male nurses exhibit when entering a traditionally female occupation; consequently, he conducted in-depth interviews with male registered nurses employed in hospital settings in Austin, Texas. Heikes reports that male nurses in Austin felt more visible than female nurses and typically responded by overachieving. Although they did not feel polarized from the female nurses, they did feel socially isolated as "tokens" in the workplace. Typically, they were excluded from traditionally female gatherings, such as female nurses' baby and bridal showers. Such social isolation did not reduce the male nurses' skills training, but it excluded them from informal

interactions in which they could have "networked" with female nurses and learned more about the day-to-day workings of the hospital.

Stereotyping was also evident in Austin: Male nurses were commonly mistaken for physicians. Even though being mistaken for someone of higher status may appear to be

> Like male nurses, female hockey players are rare specimens, although they have actually been around almost as long as male players.

advantageous, it can often have negative connotations for the male nurse. It is a constant reminder of his deviant position in a traditionally female occupation. The implicit message is that men should be doctors rather than nurses. Indeed, when correctly

identified as nurses, men face a much more serious form of stereotyping. Because of the persistence of traditional gender roles, it is assumed that all male nurses must be gay. Many male nurses told Heikes that they felt a need to deny this stigmatized identity.

More recently, sociologist Christine Williams (1992, 1995) examined the under-representation of men in four predominantly female professions: nursing, elementary school teaching, librarianship, and social work. Drawing on in-depth interviews with 99 men and women in these professions in four cities in the United States, Williams found that the experience of tokenism is very different for women and men. While men in these traditionally female professions commonly experience negative stereotyping, they nevertheless benefit from hidden *advantages* stemming from their status as men, such as receiving early and disproportionate encouragement to become administrators. By contrast,

Sources: Bureau of the Census 1999a; DeSimone 2000; Elliot 1997; Heikes 1991; Lillard 1998; Theberge 1997; Zimmer 1988.

puts pressure on child care facilities and on public financing of day care and even on the fast food industry, which provides many of the meals women used to prepare during the day. For another, it raises questions about what responsibility male wage earners have in the household.

Who does do the housework when women become productive wage earners? Studies indicate that there continues to be a clear gender gap in the performance of housework, although the differences are narrowing. Still, as shown in Figure 11-3 (p. 306), the most recent study finds women doing more housework and spending more time on child care than men, whether it be on a workday or when off work. Taken together, then, a woman's workday on and off the job is much longer than a man's. A recent development over the last 20 years is women's involvement in elder care. According to a Department of Labor (1998) study, 72 percent of caregivers are women, typically spending around 18 hours per week caring for a parent.

Sociologist Arlie Hochschild (1989, 1990) has used

the phrase "second shift" to describe the double burden—work outside the home followed by child care and housework—that many women face and few men share equitably. On the basis of interviews with and observations of 52 couples over an eight-year period, Hochschild reports

women in traditionally male professions often find that their advancement is limited and their token status is hardly an asset.

Like male nurses, female hockey players are rare specimens, although they have actually been around almost as long as male players. A photograph of the daughter of Lord Stanley, founder of the coveted Stanley Cup given to the champions in professional hockey, shows her playing the sport in 1890. A rivalry between U.S. and Canadian women's teams goes back to 1916. But women were never taken very seriously as hockey players—until quite recently. Since 1990, the number of female hockey players registered on U.S. hockey teams has increased eightfold. By the end of the decade the number of women's teams had risen from 149 in 1990 to 1,268. And in 1998, women made their first appearance on the rink in the Olympics, where the U.S. team took a gold medal.

While increasing numbers of women have come into their own in ice hockey, they still are put down for not being as "tough and strong" as male hockey players. Hockey rules do not allow women to body check, which calls for shoving an opponent hard into the boards on the side of the rink. Their game relies more on finesse than strength. Using both observation and interviews, sociologist Nancy Theberge (1997) studied a female Canadian league. She found that while the players generally acknowledge that the game is more skill-oriented without body checking, they favor including body checking in women's hockey to make the sport more professional. They reason that if they can make a living at the sport, then they should accept the risk of injury that comes with "hard checks." Ironically, their willingness to accept a more intense level of the game comes at a time when many people feel that men's professional hockey has become too physical and too violent; hard body checking leads to the fights that accompany many games.

Theberge found that even without body checking, injury and pain were routine features of the lives of female hockey players. She notes, "For these athletes, overcoming injury and pain is a measure of both ability and commitment." Some observers, however, find it troubling that as women's involvement in ice hockey grows, the pressure increases to develop a system that normalizes injury and pain in the sport.

Let's Discuss

1. Have you ever played a sport or worked in a job that was stereotyped as being more appropriate for the opposite sex? If so, how comfortable were you with your role?
2. Do you think women's hockey rules should be amended to allow body checking? Why or why not? Should men's hockey rules be amended to discourage checking?

that the wives (and not their husbands) drive home from the office while planning domestic schedules and play dates for children—and then begin their second shift. Drawing on national studies, she concludes that women spend 15 fewer hours in leisure activities each week than their husbands do. In a year, these women work an extra month of 24-hour days because of the "second shift"; over a dozen years, they work an extra year of 24-hour days. Hochschild found that the married couples she studied were fraying at the edges, and so were their careers and their marriages. Juggling so many roles means that more things can go wrong for women, which contributes to stress. A study by a Harvard sociologist found that married women are 50 percent more likely than married men to complain of being in a bad mood (Kessler 1998).

With such reports in mind, many feminists have advocated greater governmental and corporate support for pp. 109–11 child care, more flexible family leave policies, and other reforms designed to ease the burden on the nation's families.

Even professional women, with all the advantages of advanced degrees, still encounter significant problems in combining careers and family life. A survey of 902 female graduates of Harvard University's business, law, and medical schools asked if they felt they have been successful in combining career and family. Eighty-five percent of respondents answered affirmatively. Yet 53 percent of the women questioned said that they had *changed* their jobs or specialties as a result of family obligations, while 25 percent of those with M.B.A. degrees had left the paid labor force completely (Swiss and Walker 1993).

Most studies of gender, child care, and housework focus on the time actually spent by women and men performing these duties. However, sociologist Susan Walzer (1996) was interested in whether there are gender differences in the amount of time that parents spend *thinking* about the care of their children. Drawing on interviews with 25 couples, Walzer found that mothers are much more involved than fathers in the invisible, mental labor associated with taking care of a baby. For example, while

Sociologist Arlie Hochschild has used the phrase "second shift" to describe the double burden—work outside the home followed by child care and housework—that many women face and few men share equitably.

involved in work outside the home, mothers are more likely to think about their babies and to feel guilty if they become so consumed with the demands of their jobs that they *fail* to think about their babies.

A study of Canadian married couples by sociologist Susan Shaw (1988) offers insight into the rather different ways in which men and women view housework. Specifically, men are more likely than women to view these activities as "leisure"—and are less likely to see them as "work." Because they think of these tasks basically as women's work, men perceive themselves as having more freedom of choice in engaging in housework and child care. Choosing to do a task makes it seem more like play than work.

Given the stresses of performing most of the housework, why do married women accept this arrangement? Psychologist Mary Clare Lennon and sociologist Sarah Rosenfield (1994) studied this issue by using as secondary data interviews of adults from 13,017 households in a national sample. In that survey, almost 61 percent of women and more than 67 percent of men suggested that this uneven distribution of housework is fair to both spouses. According to the researchers, those married women with the fewest alternatives and financial prospects outside of marriage are most likely to accept unequal household arrangements as fair. Apparently, the more dependent a particular wife is, the more she will do to preserve (and justify) the marital relationship. In a striking finding, Lennon and Rosenfield report that those women who *do* view unequal housework as unjust experience more symptoms of depression. All in all, the continuing disparity in household labor has a rather significant meaning in terms of power relationships within the family (a subject examined more fully in Chapter 13).

Women: Emergence of a Collective Consciousness

The feminist movement of the United States was born in upstate New York, in a town called Seneca Falls, in the summer of 1848. On July 19, the first women's rights convention began, attended by Elizabeth Cady Stanton, Lu-

FIGURE 11-3

Gender Differences in Child Care and Housework, 1997

Hours in Child Care

Workdays	MEN	WOMEN
1977	1.8	3.3
1997	2.3	3.0

Non-Workdays	MEN	WOMEN
1977	5.2	7.3
1997	6.4	8.3

Hours in Housework

Workdays	MEN	WOMEN
1977	1.2	3.7
1997	2.2	3.1

Non-Workdays	MEN	WOMEN
1977	4.2	7.2
1997	5.1	6.1

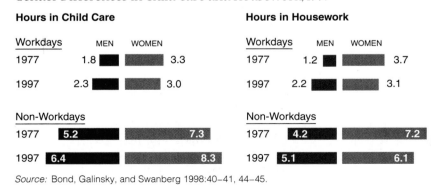

Women still spend more time on child care and housework than their male counterparts.

Source: Bond, Galinsky, and Swanberg 1998:40–41, 44–45.

cretia Mott, and other pioneers in the struggle for women's rights. This first wave of *feminists,* as they are currently known, battled ridicule and scorn as they fought for legal and political equality for women. They were not afraid to risk controversy on behalf of their cause; in 1872, Susan B. Anthony was arrested for attempting to vote in that year's presidential election.

Ultimately, the early feminists won many victories, among them the passage and ratification of the Nineteenth Amendment to the Constitution, which granted women the right to vote in national elections beginning in 1920. But suffrage did not lead to other reforms in women's social and economic position, and the women's movement became a much less powerful force for social change in the early and middle twentieth century.

The second wave of feminism in the United States emerged in the 1960s and came into full force in the 1970s. In part, the movement was inspired by three pioneering books arguing for women's rights: Simone de Beauvoir's *The Second Sex,* Betty Friedan's *The Feminine Mystique,* and Kate Millett's *Sexual Politics.* In addition, the general political activism of the 1960s led women—

Minority women face not only gender bias but racial-ethnic bias in the workplace. Faye Wattleton, former president of Planned Parenthood, broke through both barriers.

many of whom were working for Black civil rights or against the war in Vietnam—to reexamine their own powerlessness as women. The sexism often found within allegedly progressive and radical political circles made many women decide that they needed to establish their own movement for "women's liberation" (Evans 1980; Firestone 1970; J. Freeman 1973, 1975).

More and more women became aware of sexist attitudes and practices—including attitudes they themselves had accepted through socialization into traditional gender roles—and began to challenge male dominance. A sense of "sisterhood," much like the class consciousness that Marx hoped would emerge in the proletariat, became evident. Individual women identified their interests with those of the collectivity *women.* No longer were they "happy" in submissive, subordinate roles ("false consciousness" in Marxist terms).

National surveys today, however, show that while women generally endorse feminist positions, they do not necessarily accept the label of "feminist." Close to 40 percent of women considered themselves feminists in 1989; the proportion dropped to about 20 percent in 1998. Feminism as a unified political cause, requiring one to accept a similar stance on everything from abortion to sexual harassment to pornography to welfare, has fallen out of favor. Both women and men prefer to express their views on these complex issues individually rather than under a convenient umbrella like "feminism." Still, feminism is very much alive in the growing acceptance of women in nontraditional roles and even the basic acknowledgment that a married mother not only can be working outside the home but also perhaps belongs in the labor force. A majority of women say that given the choice, they would prefer to work outside the home rather than stay home and take care of a house and family, and about one-quarter of women prefer Ms. to Miss or Mrs. (Bellafante 1998; P. Geyh 1998).

The women's movement has undertaken public protests on a wide range of issues. Feminists have endorsed passage of the equal rights amendment, government subsidies for child care (see Chapter 4), affirmative action for women and minorities (see Chapter 16), federal legislation outlawing sex discrimination in education (see Chapter 15), greater representation of women in government (see Chapter 16), and the right to legal abortions (discussed in the social policy section of this chapter). Feminists have condemned violence against women in the family (see Chapter 13), sexual harassment in organizations (see Chapter 6), the retreat from affirmative action (see Chapter 17), forced sterilization of poor and minority women, sexist advertising and pornography, and discrimination against lesbians and gay men (see Chapter 13). The Taking Sociology to Work box on page 308 describes the efforts of one member of the women's

Taking Sociology to Work

STACEY KARP:
President of San Francisco Chapter of NOW (National Organization for Women)

Stacey Karp got involved with NOW when she took a semester off from the University of Wisconsin to work with the San Francisco chapter. After graduating in 1996, she moved to the Bay Area and continued to volunteer for NOW—and soon found herself in the president's position. The work is unpaid for the most part, but Karp feels the experience she is gaining is invaluable.

"My job is to oversee the entire chapter, with its 1,200 members; to set policies; and to be the spokesperson for those policies." In the course of a day, Karp will typically write press releases, attend government hearings, lobby elected officials, talk to constituents, and, if necessary, organize a protest of some sort. One protest Karp participated in was directed against the Promise Keepers, an organization dedicated to having men take responsibility for their families. According to Karp, "in reality the PK is about having men be in *control* of their families—having men make all the decisions and having women be submissive."

Karp chose sociology as her major because she's always been interested in people. "It was a great way to be able to study people, to understand what statistics mean, and to learn how to take action to involve people." A sociology of gender course got Karp interested in women's issues, which then led her to minor in women's studies.

Karp's advice to students: If you are interested in sociology, don't be concerned about what kind of career your degree will lead to. "Pretty much *everything* has to do with sociology. It's all about the study of people and how our society works."

movement, Stacey Karp, president of the San Francisco chapter of NOW.

Minority Women: Double Jeopardy

Many women experience differential treatment not only because of gender but because of race and ethnicity as well. These citizens face a "double jeopardy"—that of subordinate status twice defined. A disproportionate share of this low-status group are also impoverished, so that the double jeopardy effectively becomes a triple jeopardy. The litany of social ills continues for many if we consider old age, ill health, disabilities, and the like.

Feminists have addressed themselves to the particular needs of minority women. The question for African American women, Latinas, Asian American women, and others appears to be whether they should unify with their "brothers" against racism or challenge them for their sexism. One answer is that, in a truly just society, both sexism and racism must be eradicated.

The discussion of gender roles among African Americans has always provoked controversy. Advocates of Black nationalism contend that feminism only distracts women from full participation in the Black struggle. The existence of feminist groups among Blacks, in their view, simply divides the Black community and thereby serves the dominant White society. By contrast, Black feminists such as Florynce Kennedy argue, in turn, that little is to be gained by adopting or maintaining the gender-role divisions of the dominant society. African American journalist Patricia Raybon (1989) has noted that the media commonly portray Black women in a negative light: as illiterate, as welfare mothers, as prostitutes, and so forth. Black feminists emphasize that it is not solely Whites and White-dominated media that focus on these negative images; Black men (most recently, Black male rap artists) have also been criticized for the way they portray African American women.

The plight of Latinas is usually considered part of either the Latino or the feminist movement, ignoring the distinctive experience of Mexican American, Cuban, Puerto Rican, and Central and South American women. In the past, these women have been excluded from decision making in the two institutions that most directly affect their daily lives: the family and the church. The Hispanic family, especially in the lower class, feels the pervasive tradition of male domination. The Roman Catholic church relegates women to supportive roles while reserving the leadership positions for men (De Andra 1996).

We can see that activists among minority women do not agree on whether priority should be granted to fighting for sexual equality or to eliminating inequality among racial and ethnic groups. Neither component of inequality can be ignored. Helen Mayer Hacker (1973:11), who pioneered research on both Blacks and women, stated before the American Sociological Association, "As a partisan observer, it is my fervent hope that in fighting the twin battles of sexism and racism, Black women and Black men will [create] the outlines of the good society for all Americans" (see also Zia 1993).

SOCIAL POLICY AND GENDER STRATIFICATION

The Battle over Abortion from a Global Perspective

The Issue

Few issues seem to stir as much intense conflict as abortion. A critical victory in the struggle for legalized abortion in the United States came in 1973 when the Supreme Court granted women the right to terminate pregnancies. This ruling, known as *Roe v. Wade,* was based on a woman's right to privacy. The Court's decision was generally applauded by pro-choice groups, which believe women have the right to make their own decisions about their bodies and should have access to safe and legal abortion. It was bitterly condemned by those opposed to abortion. For these pro-life groups, abortion is a moral and often a religious issue. In their view, human life actually begins at the moment of conception rather than at the moment of a baby's delivery. On the basis of this judgment, the fetus is a human life, not a potential person. Termination of this life is viewed as essentially an act of murder.

The Setting

Until about 25 years ago, it was very difficult for a woman to terminate a pregnancy legally in the United States and most other industrialized nations. Beginning in the

Advocates on both sides see abortion as a life-and-death issue. Pro-life advocates regard the fetus as a life, while pro-choice supporters express outrage at violent attacks on abortion clinics and abortion providers.

late 1960s, a few state governments reformed statutes and made it easier for a woman to obtain legal abortions. However, with abortion permissible in only a small minority of states, and only under certain conditions, a large number of women continued to have illegal abortions, with 10,000 dying annually in botched procedures. That was the impetus for establishing abortion as legal and bringing the issue to the Supreme Court. Today in the United States, about 3 in every 10 pregnancies ends in an abortion (Centers for Disease Control 2000; Lewin 1997; Miller 1998).

The debate that has followed *Roe v. Wade* revolves around prohibiting abortion altogether or, at the very least, putting limits on it. In 1979, for example, Missouri required parental consent for minors wishing to obtain an abortion, and the Supreme Court upheld this law. Parental notification and parental consent have become especially sensitive issues in the debate over abortion. The respected Alan Guttmacher Institute estimates that over 1 million teenagers in the United States become pregnant each year and that 42 percent of them decide to have abortions. Pro-life activists argue that the parents of these teenagers should have the right to be notified about—and to permit or prohibit—these abortions. In their view, parental authority deserves full support at a time when the traditional nuclear family is embattled. However, pro-choice activists counter that many pregnant teenagers come from troubled families where they have been abused. These young women may have good reason to avoid discussing such explosive issues with their parents (Salholz 1990).

Changing technology has had its impact. "Day-after" pills are available in some nations; these pills can abort the fertilized egg the day after conception. In the United States, doctors, guided by ultrasound, can now end a pregnancy as early as eight days after conception. Pro-life activists are concerned that use of this ultrasound technology will allow people to terminate pregnancies of unwanted females in nations where a premium is placed on male offspring.

As of 1998, the people of the United States appeared to support their right to legal abortion, but with reservations. According to a national survey, 58 percent of respondents stated that abortion is "sometimes the best course in a bad situation." At the same time, 50 percent regard abortion as "the same thing as murdering a child," while 38 percent think that "the fetus is not really a child" (Goldberg and Elder 1998).

By the 1990s, abortion had also become a controversial issue in western Europe. As in the United States, many European nations bowed to public opinion and liberalized abortion laws in the 1970s, although Ireland, Belgium, and Malta continue to prohibit abortion. Austria, Denmark, Greece, the Netherlands, Norway, and Sweden have laws that allow a woman to have an abortion on request. Other countries have much more restrictive legislation, especially concerning abortions in the later stages of pregnancy. Inspired by their counterparts in the United States, antiabortion activists have become more outspoken in Great Britain, France, Spain, Italy, and Germany. In a victory for antiabortion forces, Germany's highest court ruled in 1993 that a liberal abortion law passed in 1992 was unconstitutional because the state was required to protect human life (Kinzer 1993; M. Simons 1989; Warner 1996).

Sociological Insights

Sociologists see gender and social class as largely defining the issues surrounding abortion. The intense conflict over abortion reflects broader differences over women's position in society. Sociologist Kristin Luker (1984) has offered a detailed study of activists in the pro-choice and pro-life movements. Luker interviewed 212 activists in California, overwhelmingly women, who spent at least five hours a week working for one of these movements. According to Luker, each group has a consistent, coherent view of the world. Feminists involved in defending abortion rights typically believe that men and women are essentially similar; they support women's full participation in work outside the home and oppose all forms of sex discrimination. By contrast, most antiabortion activists believe that men and women are fundamentally different. In their view, men are best suited for the public world of work, whereas women are best suited for the demanding and crucial task of rearing children. These activists are troubled by women's growing participation in work outside the home, which they view as destructive to the family and ultimately to society as a whole.

In terms of social class, the first major restriction on the legal right to terminate a pregnancy affected poor people. In 1976, Congress passed the Hyde Amendment, which banned the use of Medicaid and other federal funds for abortions. The Supreme Court upheld this legislation in 1980. State laws also restrict the use of public funds for abortions (see Figure 11-4). Another obstacle facing the poor is access to abortion providers: In the face of vocal pro-life public sentiment, fewer and fewer hospitals throughout the world are even allowing their physicians to perform abortions except in extreme cases. In the United States, there were 3,000 hospitals permitting abortion in 1982 compared to fewer than 2,300 in 1998. Moreover, abortion providers in clinics are intimidated by death threats and actual murders. For many of the poor in rural areas, this reduction in service makes it more costly to locate and travel to a facility that will accommodate their wishes. Viewed from a conflict perspective, this is one more financial burden that falls especially heavily on low-income women (Bush 1993; Lewin 1992; Rubin 1998).

Policy Initiatives

The Supreme Court currently supports the general right to terminate a pregnancy by a narrow 5–4 majority. While pro-life activists continue to hope for an overruling of *Roe v. Wade,* they have focused in the interim on weakening the decision through such issues as limiting the use of fetal tissue in medical experiments and prohibiting late-term abortions, termed "partial-birth" abortions by pro-life supporters. The Supreme Court continues to hear cases involving such restrictions. In 1998 the Court gave the states the authority (22 have done so) to prohibit abortions at the point where the fetus is viable outside the mother's womb—a definition that continues to be redefined by developments in medical technology (L. Greenhouse 1998b).

Increasingly, pro-choice advocates are turning to the state courts for favorable decisions on the right to an abortion. Some state constitutions actually provide stronger privacy rights than does the U.S. Constitution. Taking advantage of these provisions, activists have won several pro-choice victories. While pro-life forces continue to lobby at state levels, their most visible success has come at the national level. In 1999, the U.S. House of Representatives passed the Unborn Victims of Violence Act, which would elevate all stages of prenatal development—even an embryo—to the legal standing of a person. A presidential veto and Supreme Court rejection of this legislation are both likely, but such actions show that both pro- and anti-choice legal efforts are far from over in the United States (National Abortion and Reproductive Rights Action League Foundation 1999b).

What is the policy in other countries? In some countries the practice varies from the law. For example, in many areas of Australia, laws permit the procedure only to save the life of the mother, yet 50 percent of all pregnancies in that nation are terminated by abortion. In 1998, an officer arrested two doctors for violating the law. Observers say he was unfamiliar with the widespread tolerance of abortion,

FIGURE 11-4

Restrictions on Public Funding for Abortion

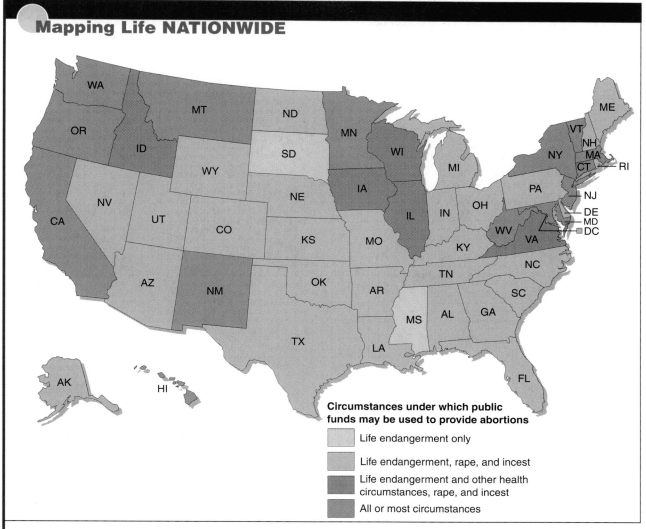

Mapping Life NATIONWIDE

Circumstances under which public funds may be used to provide abortions

- Life endangerment only
- Life endangerment, rape, and incest
- Life endangerment and other health circumstances, rape, and incest
- All or most circumstances

Note: Data as of December 15, 1998.

Source: National Abortion and Reproductive Rights Action League Foundation 1999b.

but senior officials and the courts are now having to deal with the case. Pro-choice Australians are seeking to reform laws to conform to the practice, but pro-life people are using the unusual situation to argue for enforcement of existing laws (Coatney 1998).

The policies of the United States and developing nations are intertwined. Throughout the 1980s and 1990s, antiabortion members of Congress have often successfully blocked foreign aid to countries that might use the funds to encourage abortion. And yet these developing nations generally have the most restrictive abortion laws. As shown in Figure 11-5, it is primarily in Africa, Latin America, and parts of Asia that women are not able to terminate a pregnancy upon request. As might be expected, illegal abortions are most common in these nations. In general, the more restrictive a nation's legislation on abortion, the higher its rate of unsafe abortions, for pregnancies may typically be terminated by unskilled health providers or by the pregnant women themselves. According to the World Health Organization (1998), of the 80,000 women's deaths globally that result from abortions, 95 percent are in poor nations, where they occur in defiance of the law.

FIGURE 11-5

The Global Divide on Abortion

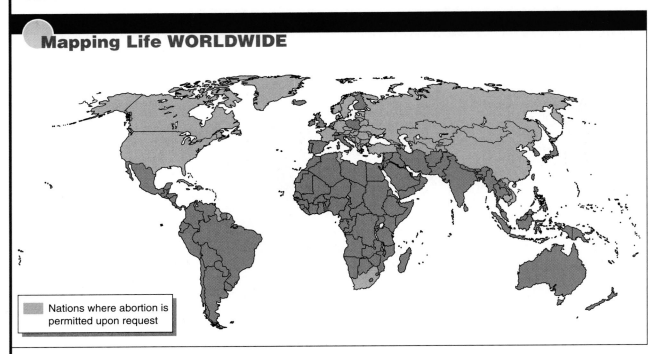

Mapping Life WORLDWIDE

Nations where abortion is permitted upon request

Note: Data current as of May 1998.

Source: United Nations Population Division, Department of Economy and Social Affairs 1998b.

Let's Discuss

1. Do you know anyone who has undergone an illegal abortion? If so, what were the circumstances? Was the woman's health endangered by the procedure?

2. Do you think teenage girls should have to get their parents' consent before having an abortion? Why?

3. Under what circumstances should abortions be allowed? Explain your reasoning.

Summary

Gender is an ascribed status that provides a basis for social differentiation. This chapter examines the social construction of gender, theories of stratification by gender, women as an oppressed majority group, and the double jeopardy of minority women.

1. The social construction of gender continues to define significantly different expectations for females and males in the United States.

2. *Gender roles* show up in our work and behavior and in how we react to others.

3. Females have been more severely restricted by traditional gender roles, but these roles have also restricted males.

4. The research of anthropologist Margaret Mead points to the importance of cultural conditioning in defining the social roles of males and females.

5. Functionalists maintain that sex differentiation contributes to overall social stability, whereas conflict theorists contend that the relationship between females and males has been one of unequal power, with men in a dominant position over women. This dominance also shows up in everyday interactions.

6. As one example of their micro-level approach to the study of gender stratification, interactionists have analyzed men's verbal dominance over women through conversational interruptions.

7. Although numerically a majority, in many respects women fit the definition of a subordinate minority group within the United States.
8. Women around the world experience ***sexism*** and ***institutional discrimination.***
9. As women have taken on more and more hours of paid employment outside the home, they have been only partially successful in getting their husbands to take a greater role in homemaking duties, including child care.
10. Many women agree with the positions of the feminist movement but reject the label of "feminist."
11. Minority women experience double jeopardy through differential treatment based on both gender and race and ethnicity.
12. The issue of abortion has bitterly divided the United States (as well as other nations) and pitted pro-choice activists against pro-life activists.

Critical Thinking Questions

1. Sociologist Barbara Bovee Polk suggests that women are oppressed because they constitute an alternative subculture that deviates from the prevailing masculine value system. Does it seem valid to view women as an "alternative subculture"? In what ways do women support and deviate from the prevailing masculine value system evident in the United States?
2. In what ways is the social position of White women in the United States similar to that of African American women, Hispanic women, and Asian American women? In what ways is a woman's social position markedly different, given her racial and ethnic status?
3. Imagine that you were asked to study political activism among women. How might you employ surveys, observations, experiments, and existing sources to better understand such activism?

Key Terms

Expressiveness   A term used to refer to concern for maintenance of harmony and the internal emotional affairs of the family. (295)

Gender roles   Expectations regarding the proper behavior, attitudes, and activities of males and females. (291)

Glass ceiling   An invisible barrier that blocks the promotion of a qualified individual in a work environment because of the individual's gender, race, or ethnicity. (303)

Homophobia   Fear of and prejudice against homosexuality. (292)

Institutional discrimination   The denial of opportunities and equal rights to individuals and groups that results from the normal operations of a society. (299)

Instrumentality   A term used to refer to emphasis on tasks, focus on more distant goals, and a concern for the external relationship between one's family and other social institutions. (295)

Sexism   The ideology that one sex is superior to the other. (299)

Additional Readings

BOOKS

Epstein, Cynthia Fuchs, Carroll Seron, Bonnie Oglensky, and Robert Saute. 1999. *The Part-Time Paradox: Time Norms, Professional Life, Family and Gender.* New York: Routledge. The authors explore the conflict and tension between the time demands of career and family life; they also examine the choice of part-time work as a solution.

Faludi, Susan. 1999. *Stiffed: The Betrayal of the American Man.* New York: William Morrow. A journalist finds that American men, though still the dominant sex, feel misunderstood and underappreciated.

Nelson, Mariah Burton. 1994. *The Stronger Women Get, the More Men Love Football: Sexism and the American Culture of Sports.* New York: Avon Books. A columnist and former professional basketball player considers the social consequences of male domination of sports.

Pipher, Mary. 1994. *Reviving Ophelia: Saving the Selves of Adolescent Girls.* New York: Ballantine. A clinical psychologist asks why adolescent girls stifle their inner selves, despite feminist advances.

Pollock, William. 1998. *Real Boys: Rescuing Our Sons from the Myths of Boyhood.* New York: Henry Holt. A researcher at Harvard Medical School explores why boys are confused by conventional expectations of masculinity.

Richardson, Laurel, Verta Taylor, and Nancy Whittier, eds. 1997. *Feminist Frontiers IV.* New York: McGraw-Hill. This book's 53 selections cover a broad range of concerns, including inequality, family life, domestic violence, and national and international politics.

JOURNALS

Among the journals that focus on issues of gender stratification are *Gender and Society* (founded in 1987), *Journal of African American Men* (1995), *Journal of Men's Studies* (1992), *Journeymen* (1991), *Sex Roles* (1975), *Signs: Journal of Women in Culture and Society* (1975), *Women: A Cultural Review* (1990), *Women's Review of Books* (1983), *Women's Studies* (1972), and *Women's Studies International Forum* (1978).

Internet Connection

Note: While all the URLs listed were current as of the printing of this book, these sites often change. Please check our website (http://www.mhhe.com/schaefer) for updates.

1. Gender and sex issues find expression in the debate over reproductive rights. This chapter provides multiple perspectives on the complex issue of abortion. Learn more about both pro-life and pro-choice groups and their perspectives by logging onto (**http://dir.yahoo.com/Health/Reproductive_ Health/Abortion/Organizations/**).

   (a) Choose one pro-choice and one pro-life organization from the lists provided on the website. Compare and contrast the two groups. What is the goal or mission of each organization? When and why did it form? What kinds of support and services does it offer?

   (b) What is each organization's position on abortion, and why? What actions, laws, and social policies does each support? Do you think the group's objectives are reasonable and realistic? Why or why not?

   (c) If the organizations offer statistics, examine them. How do the statistics offered by one organization compare to the statistics offered by the other?

   (d) Using an interactionist approach, examine the symbols and language each organization uses. How is abortion referred to? What images of abortion are used, and why?

   (e) Which of the two organizations you selected does a better job of presenting its position? In what way?

   (f) What is your own position on reproductive rights? Why?

2. Gender inequality is rooted in social institutions, a fact that is evident in the way women are presented on television, in the movies, and in advertisements. Visit the website About-Face: Gallery of Offenders (**http://www.about-face.org/gallery/index.html**). Choose "The Light" link, and then "New Top Ten Offenders," "Facts," and "Making Progress Gallery of Winners." Study each of the pictures from the ads, and read the accompanying opinions and critiques.

   (a) Which of the statistics and facts given on this site surprised you the most? Why?

   (b) Which of the 10 offender advertisements do you think is the most offensive? Why? What aspect of the ad specifically demonstrates gender inequality or sexism?

   (c) Do you think any of the advertisements in the Offenders section do not belong there? If so, explain why.

   (d) Compare the ads in the Making Progress section to the ads in the New Top Ten Offenders section. How do the words, images, and symbols in the two groups of ads differ?

   (e) Can you think of examples of advertisements that have sexualized men? Describe them.

   (f) What arguments could advertisers make in defense of their creations?

   (g) What are some of the social consequences of sexism in advertisements?

   (h) What suggestions does the website make for ending the sexualization of women in the media? Can you think of other methods?

STRATIFICATION BY AGE

Society typically expects older people to slow down and "take it easy." This ad for McDonalds in Germany turns that notion on its head. The poster reads: "With the flavor of freedom and adventure."

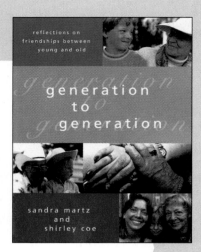

On bad days, I wish I'd never answered the phone that Tuesday night.

It was a fluke we were home in the first place. Manny was in the car, within seconds of tooting the horn at me, while I rummaged through my desk looking for the tickets to the travelogue we were late for. *If only I hadn't forgotten the tickets; if only I'd cleaned my desk the week before; if only . . .*

It solved nothing to think of the *if onlys.* I was in the house, the phone rang, I answered it. And our lives were changed. . . .

"Mom, Jake's left! He's gone. Sarah's crying, Jon threw up, and the soup boiled over. I can't deal with it, Mom. Can I bring the kids over? Please?"

I stopped looking for the tickets. I heard Manny toot the horn. We wouldn't be late for the travelogue. We weren't going.

"Bring them over," I said.

That was nine months ago.

To be perfectly honest—a trait that is more and more dear to me—if we had missed that particular phone call, there would've been another. Life-changing phone calls are persistent and inevitable.

On good days I look at our grandchildren, Sarah and Jonathan, and smile at the fine job they're doing coloring their pictures or setting the table. And when they climb into my lap at night and nuzzle their downy cheeks against mine, I praise God for the love He brought into our lives.

This dizzying combination of regret and gratitude is natural now. The tranquility of our retirement years has been replaced by the chaos and tedium of raising two small children. Loud voices. Rigid schedules.

It's harder on Manny. Even though I'd long ago left behind thoughts of homework and skinned knees, I was infinitely more prepared to take on the responsibility of our grandchildren than he was. He'd never witnessed the day-to-day dealings of broken shoelaces and sack lunches with our own daughter. He'd been at work. But work was over for him. He paid his dues, and his lofty dreams of retirement—our lofty dreams—were cut short as we backtracked twenty years to the sights and sounds of parenthood. . . .

The children are no longer visitors. Their Barbie dolls and race cars are at home on the shelves in the family room, right next to my needlepoint and Manny's fishing magazines. There is an odd comfort in the sounds of their footfalls. Their laughter weaves its way through the rungs of the chairs and echoes in the cookie jar. They belong here. They are ours. *(N. Moser 1998:158, 159, 160)* ■

As this excerpt suggests, the distinctions between generations are getting more and more blurred. We are not automatically "old" when we turn 60, or when we become grandparents as Nancy Moser discovered. She and her husband Manny saw the years fall away when they reassumed the responsibilities of parenthood in raising their grandchildren. At the same time they had to put their retirement dreams on hold. Her essay, which appears in the anthology *Generation to Generation,* is aptly titled "Wishing for Maybes." While the Mosers' situation is not typical of people their age, it is certainly not unusual. More than 3 million children under age 18 in the United States are living in a home maintained by their grandparents (Bryson and Casper 1999).

People are becoming increasingly aware that age—like race or gender—is socially constructed. We tend to view age as an ascribed status, and this view dominates our perceptions of others. Rather than simply suggesting that a particular driver is not compe- tent, someone may say, "Those old codgers shouldn't be on the road." In such instances, elderly people are categorized by age in a way that obscures individual differences. Many social observers today feel that stereotypical attitudes toward age and aging won't change until we look at the life course as a continuum, rather than a series of finite stages with predictable consequences.

This chapter looks at the process of aging in terms of the life course. It examines aging around the world but focuses primarily on the position of older people within the age stratification system of the United States. After exploring various theories to explain the impact of aging on the individual and society, we will take a look at role transitions throughout the life course, including the role of the "sandwich generation," which finds itself caring for both children and parents. We will pay particular attention to the effects of prejudice and discrimination on older people and the rise of a political consciousness among the elderly. Finally, the social policy section examines the controversy surrounding the issue of "the right to die." ■

Aging and Society

The Sherpas—a Tibetan-speaking, Buddhist people in Nepal—live in a culture that idealizes old age. Almost all elderly members of the Sherpa culture own their homes, and most are in relatively good physical condition. Typically, older Sherpas value their independence and prefer not to live with their children. Among the Fulani of Africa, however, older men and women move to the edge of the family homestead. Since this is where people are buried, the elderly sleep over their own graves, for they are already viewed as socially dead. Like gender stratification, age stratification varies from culture to culture. One society may treat older people with great reverence, while another sees them as unproductive and "difficult" (M. C. Goldstein and Beall 1981; Stenning 1958; Tonkinson 1978).

It is understandable that all societies have some system of age stratification and associate certain social roles with distinct periods in one's life (see Box 12-1). Some of this age differentiation seems inevitable; it would make little sense to send young children off to war or to expect most older citizens to handle physically demanding tasks such as loading goods at shipyards. However, as is the case with stratification by gender, age stratification in the United States goes far beyond the physical constraints of human beings at different ages.

This elderly Sherpa living in Nepal is honored among his people for his age. Not all old people are so lucky—in many cultures being old is considered next to dead.

Sociology in the Global Community

12-1 Aging Worldwide: Issues and Consequences

www.mhhe.com/schaefer

An electric water kettle is wired so that people in another location can determine if it has been used in the previous 24 hours. This may seem a zany bit of modern technology, but it symbolizes a change taking place around the globe—the growing needs of an aging population. Welfare Network Ikebukuro Honcho has installed these wired hot pots in Japan so that volunteers can monitor if the elderly have used the devices to prepare their morning tea. An unused pot initiates contacts to see if the older person needs help. This technological monitoring system is an indication of the tremendous growth of Japan's elderly population and, of particular social significance, the increasing numbers who live *alone*.

Around the world, there are more than 419 million people aged 65 or over; they represent about 7 percent of the world's population. In an important sense, the aging of the world's population represents a major success story that has unfolded during the later stages of the twentieth century. Through the efforts of both national governments and international agencies, many societies have drastically reduced the incidence of diseases and their rates of death. Consequently, these nations—especially the

industrialized countries of Europe and North America—have increasingly higher proportions of older members.

The overall population of Europe is older than that of any other continent. As the proportion of older people in Europe continues to rise, many governments that have long prided themselves on their social welfare programs are examining ways to shift a larger share of the costs of caring for the elderly to the private sector and chari-

> An unused pot initiates contacts to see if the older person needs help.

ties. Germany and France have instituted or are weighing plans to raise the age at which retirees will qualify for pensions.

In most developing countries, people over 60 are likely to be in poorer health than their counterparts in industrialized nations. Yet few of these nations are in a position to offer extensive financial support to the elderly. Ironically, modernization in the developing world, while bringing with it many social and economic advances, has undercut the traditionally high status of the elderly. In

many cultures, the earning power of younger adults now exceeds that of older family members.

In 1996, the United Nations cosponsored an international conference that examined social and economic policies dealing with the "Oldest Old"—those people age 80 and over. This rapidly increasing group deserves special attention. First, the oldest old in both industrialized and developing countries will probably have to depend for their security on a declining proportion of the population that is of working age. Second, in their search for support systems from either family or government, the oldest old may be forced to migrate, which will affect the immigration policies of many nations. Finally, the needs of the oldest old may intensify the pressures on their children (older workers) to postpone retirement for 5 or 10 additional years.

Let's Discuss

1. For an older person, how might life in Pakistan differ from life in France?
2. Do you know an aged person who lives alone? What arrangements have been made (or should be made) for care in case of emergency?

Sources: Crossette 1996; Hani 1998; Haub and Cornelius 1999; Longworth 1996; M. Specter 1998; Strom 2000a.

"Being old" is a master status that commonly overshadows all others in the United States. The insights of labeling theory help us analyze the consequences of aging. Once people are labeled "old," this designation has a major impact on how others perceive them and even on how they view themselves. Negative stereotypes of the elderly contribute to their position as a minority group subject to discrimination, as we'll see later in the chapter.

p. 183

The model of five basic properties of a minority or subordinate group (introduced in Chapter 10) can be applied to older people in the United States to clarify their subordinate status:

p. 257

1. The elderly experience unequal treatment in employment and may face prejudice and discrimination.

2. The elderly share physical characteristics that distinguish them from younger people. In addition, their cultural preferences and leisure-time activities often differ from those of the rest of society.

3. Membership in this disadvantaged group is involuntary.

4. Older people have a strong sense of group solidarity, as is reflected in the growth of senior citizens' centers, retirement communities, and advocacy organizations.

5. Older people generally are married to others of comparable age.

There is one crucial difference between older people and other subordinate groups, such as racial and ethnic minorities or women: *All* of us who live long enough will eventually assume the ascribed status of being an older person (M. Barron 1953; J. Levin and Levin 1980; Wagley and Harris 1958).

Explaining the Aging Process

Aging is one important aspect of socialization—the life-long process through which an individual learns the cultural norms and values of a particular society. There are no clear-cut definitions for different periods of the aging cycle in the United States. Thus, while *old age* has typically been regarded as beginning at 65, which corresponds to the retirement age for many workers, not everyone in the United States accepts this definition. With life expectancy being extended, writers are beginning to refer to people in their 60s as the "young old" to distinguish them from those in their 80s and beyond (the "old old").

The particular problems of the elderly have become the focus for a specialized area of research and inquiry known as gerontology. *Gerontology* is the scientific study of the sociological and psychological aspects of aging and the problems of the aged. It originally developed in the 1930s, as an increasing number of social scientists became aware of the plight of the elderly.

Gerontologists rely heavily on sociological principles and theories to explain the impact of aging on the individual and society. They also draw upon the disciplines of psychology, anthropology, physical education, counseling, and medicine in their study of the aging process. Two influential views of aging—disengagement theory and activity theory—can be best understood in terms of the sociological perspectives of functionalism and interactionism, respectively. The conflict perspective also contributes to our sociological understanding of aging.

Functionalist Approach: Disengagement Theory

Elaine Cumming and William Henry (1961) introduced an explanation of the impact of aging during one's life course known as *disengagement theory.* This theory, based on a study of elderly people in good health and relatively comfortable economic circumstances, contends that society and the aging individual mutually sever many of their relationships. In keeping with the functionalist perspective, disengagement theory emphasizes that passing social roles on from one generation to another ensures social stability.

According to this theory, the approach of death forces people to drop most of their social roles—including those of worker, volunteer, spouse, hobby enthusiast, and even reader. Younger members of society then take on

these functions. The aging person, it is held, withdraws into an increasing state of inactivity while preparing for death. At the same time, society withdraws from the elderly by segregating them residentially (retirement homes and communities), educationally (programs designed solely for senior citizens), and recreationally (senior citizens' social centers). Implicit in disengagement theory is the view that society should *help* older people to withdraw from their accustomed social roles.

Since it was first outlined more than three decades ago, disengagement theory has generated considerable controversy. Some gerontologists have objected to the implication that older people want to be ignored and "put away"—and even more to the idea that they should be encouraged to withdraw from meaningful social roles. Critics of disengagement theory insist that society *forces* the elderly into an involuntary and painful withdrawal from the paid labor force and from meaningful social relationships. Rather than voluntarily seeking to disengage, older employees find themselves pushed out of their jobs—in many instances, even before they are entitled to maximum retirement benefits (Boaz 1987).

Although functionalist in its approach, disengagement theory ignores the fact that postretirement employment has been *increasing* in recent decades. In the United States, fewer than half of all employees actually retire from their career jobs. Instead, most move into a "bridge job"—employment that bridges the period between the end of a person's career and his or her retirement. Unfortunately, the elderly can easily be victimized in such "bridge jobs." Psychologist Kathleen Christensen (1990), warning of "bridges over troubled water," emphasizes that older employees do not want to end their working days as minimum-wage jobholders engaged in activities unrelated to their career jobs (Doeringer 1990; Hayward et al. 1987).

Interactionist Approach: Activity Theory

Ask Ruth Vitow if she would like to trade in her New York City custom lampshade business for a condo in Florida, and you will get a quick response: "Deadly! I'd hate it." Vitow is in her nineties and vows to give up her business "when it gives me up." James Russell Wiggins has been working at a weekly newspaper in Maine since 1922. At age 95 he is now the editor. Vitow and Wiggins are among the 3.7 percent of people age 90 or above still in the nation's workforce (Mehren 1999:A21).

How important is staying actively involved for older people, whether at a job or in other pursuits? A tragic disaster in Chicago in 1995 showed that it can be a matter of life and death. An intense heat wave lasting more than a week—with a heat index exceeding 115 degrees on two consecutive days—resulted in 733 heat-related deaths.

A. DAVID ROBERTS:
Social Worker

D ave Roberts admits to being a "people person," a trait that sociology courses fostered by showing how "everybody has differences; there are little bits of different cultures in all of us." He also had the benefit of "a lot of great teachers" at Florida State University, including Dr. Jill Quadagno in an "Aging" course. It was this class that sparked his interest in aging issues, which led to a certificate in gerontology in addition to a sociology degree in 1998. He realized that there was a good job market in working with the aging baby boom generation.

Volunteer work with the Meals on Wheels program steered him toward working with the elderly. Today Roberts is a social worker in a nursing home, where he is responsible for patients' care plans. In the course of this work, he meets regularly with patients, family members, and medical residents.

Roberts finds that the concept of teamwork he learned in group projects in college has helped him in this job. Also, the projects he had to do in school taught him to work on a schedule. Perhaps most importantly, sociology has helped him "to grow as a person to explore different angles, different theories. . . . I'm a better person."

His advice for sociology students: "Just give it a chance; they throw everything into an intro course. Don't get overwhelmed; take it as it comes."

About three-fourths of the deceased were 65 and older. Subsequent analysis showed that older people who lived alone had the highest risk of dying, suggesting that support networks for the elderly literally help save lives. Older Hispanics and Asian Americans had lower death rates from the heat wave than did other racial and ethnic groups. Their stronger social networks probably resulted in more regular contact with family members and friends during this critical time (Schaefer 1998a).

Often seen as an opposing approach to disengagement theory, *activity theory* argues that the elderly person who remains active and socially involved will be best-adjusted. Proponents of this perspective acknowledge that a 70-year-old person may not have the ability or desire to perform various social roles that he or she had at age 40. Yet they contend that old people have essentially the same need for social interaction as any other group.

The improved health of older people—sometimes overlooked by social scientists—has strengthened the arguments of activity theorists. Illness and chronic disease are no longer quite the scourge of the elderly that they once were. The recent emphasis on fitness, the availability of better medical care, greater control of infectious diseases, and the reduction of fatal strokes and heart attacks have combined to mitigate the traumas of growing old. Accumulating medical research also points to the importance of remaining socially involved. Among those who decline in their mental capacities later in life, deterioration is most rapid in old people who withdraw from social relationships and activities (Liao et al. 2000; National Institute on Aging 1999b).

The Days Inn motel chain hires many retirees to work full- or part-time as reservationists. *Activity theory* argues that the elderly person who remains active will be best-adjusted.

Admittedly, many activities open to the elderly involve unpaid labor, for which younger adults may receive salaries. Such unpaid workers include hospital volunteers (versus aides and orderlies), drivers for charities such as the Red Cross (versus chauffeurs), tutors (as opposed to teachers), and craftspeople for charity bazaars (as opposed to carpenters and dressmakers). However, some companies have recently initiated programs to hire retirees for full-time or part-time work. For example, about 130 of the 600 reservationists at the Days Inn motel chain are over 60 years of age.

Disengagement theory suggests that older people find satisfaction in withdrawal from society. Functionally speaking, they conveniently recede into the background and allow the next generation to take over. Proponents of activity theory view such withdrawal as harmful for both the elderly and society and focus on the potential contributions of older people to the maintenance of society. In their opinion, aging citizens will feel satisfied only when they can be useful and productive in society's terms—primarily by working for wages (Civic Ventures 1999; Dowd 1980; Quadagno 1999).

The Conflict Approach

Conflict theorists have criticized both disengagement theory and activity theory for failing to consider the impact of social structure on patterns of aging. Neither approach, they say, attempts to question why social interaction "must" change or decrease in old age. In addition, these perspectives, in contrast to the conflict perspective, often ignore the impact of social class on the lives of the elderly.

The privileged position of the upper class generally leads to better health and vigor and to less likelihood of dependency in old age. Affluence cannot forestall aging indefinitely, but it can soften the economic hardships faced in later years. By contrast, working-class jobs often carry greater hazards to health and a greater risk of disability; aging will be particularly difficult for those who suffer job-related injuries or illnesses. Working-class people also depend more heavily on Social Security benefits and private pension programs. During inflationary times, their relatively fixed incomes from these sources barely keep pace with escalating costs of food, housing, utilities, and other necessities (Atchley 1985).

Conflict theorists have noted that the transition from

Table 12-1 Theories of Aging

Sociological Perspective	View of Aging	Social Roles	Portrayal of Elderly
Functionalist	Disengagement	Reduced	Socially isolated
Interactionist	Activity	Changed	Involved in new networks
Conflict	Competition	Relatively unchanged	Victimized, organized to confront victimization

agricultural economies to industrialization and capitalism has not always been beneficial for the elderly. As a society's production methods change, the traditionally valued role of older people within the economy tends to erode. Their wisdom is no longer relevant. Although pension plans, retirement packages, and insurance benefits may be developed to assist older people, those whose wealth allows them access to investment funds can generate the greatest income for their later years.

According to the conflict approach, the treatment of older people in the United States reflects the many divisions in our society. The low status of older people is seen in prejudice and discrimination against them, age segregation, and unfair job practices—none of which are directly addressed by either disengagement or activity theory.

The three perspectives considered here take different views of the elderly. Functionalists portray them as socially isolated with reduced social roles; interactionists see older people as involved in new networks of people in a change of social roles; conflict theorists regard older people as victimized by social structure, with their social roles relatively unchanged but devalued. Table 12-1 summarizes these perspectives.

Role Transitions throughout the Life Course

As we have seen in Chapter 4 and throughout this textbook, socialization is a lifelong process. p. 91 We simply do not experience things the same way at different points in the life course. For example, one study found that even falling in love differs depending on where we are in the life course. Young unmarried adults tend to treat love as a noncommittal game or else as an obsession characterized by possessiveness and dependency. People over the age of 50 are much more likely to see love as involving commitment, and they tend to take a practical approach to finding a partner who meets a set of rational criteria. The life course, then, affects the manner in which we relate to one another (Montgomery and Sorell 1997).

How we move through the life course varies dramatically, depending on the individual. Some people, for instance, start their own households in their early 20s, while others are well into their 30s before beginning a permanent relationship with someone else. Still, it is possible to identify a series of developmental periods, with critical transitions between the various stages, as shown in the model devised by psychologist Daniel Levinson (Figure 12-1). In the following sections, we will focus on major transitions associated with the later stages of the life course: the sandwich generation, retirement, and death and dying.

The Sandwich Generation

The first transitional period identified by Levinson begins at about age 17 and extends to age 22. It marks the time at which an individual gradually enters the adult world, perhaps by moving out of the parental home, beginning a career, or entering a marriage. The second transitional period, the midlife transition, typically begins at about age 40. Men and women often experience a stressful period of self-evaluation, commonly known as the *midlife crisis,* in which they realize that they have not achieved basic goals and ambitions and have little time left to do so. Thus, Levinson (1978, 1996) found that most adults surveyed experienced tumultuous midlife conflicts within the self and with the external world.

Not all the challenges at this time of life come from career or one's partner. During the late 1990s growing attention focused on the *sandwich generation*—adults who simultaneously try to meet the competing needs of their parents and of their own children. Caregiving goes in two directions: (1) to children who even as young adults may still require significant direction and (2) to aging parents whose health and economic problems may demand intervention by their adult children. According to a national survey in 1997, almost one-fourth of all households in the United States are providing informal, unpaid care for an older friend or relative. The average caregiver spends 18 hours a week in this assistance. Understandably, this constitutes a significant amount of time for the 40 percent of the caregivers who still have children under 18 (J. Chatzky 1999; National Alliance for Caregiving 1997; Velkoff and Lawson 1998).

The last major transition identified by Levinson occurs after age 60, and this is a time when dramatic changes take place in people's everyday lives, as we will now see.

FIGURE 12-1

Developmental and Transitional Periods in Adulthood

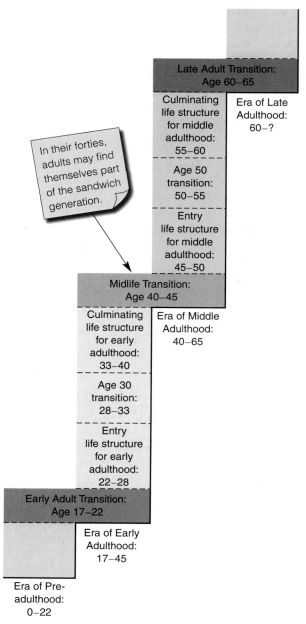

Source: D. Levinson 1996:18.

Adjusting to Retirement

Retirement is a rite of passage that marks a critical transition from one phase of a person's life to another. Typically, there are symbolic events associated with this rite of passage, such as retirement gifts, a retirement party, and special moments on the "last day on the job." The prere-

Three generations in this family celebrate their March birthdays together. While we all move through the life course in individual ways, it is possible to identify certain developmental periods with critical transitions between the stages.

tirement period itself can be emotionally charged, especially if the retiree is expected to train his or her successor (Atchley 1976).

For both men and women in the United States, the average age of retirement has declined since 1950, while at the same time longevity has increased. The quality of health has also improved. According to a study released in 2000, in any given year after age 65, the elderly are now less likely to have a hospital stay or need nursing services than they were in 1993 (Liao et al. 2000).

Gerontologist Robert Atchley (1976) has identified several phases of the retirement experience:

- *Preretirement,* a period of anticipatory socialization as the person prepares for retirement
- *The near phase,* when the person establishes a specific departure date from his or her job
- *The honeymoon phase,* an often-euphoric period in which the person pursues activities that he or she never had time for before

- *The disenchantment phase,* in which retirees feel a sense of letdown or even depression as they cope with their new lives, which may include illness or poverty
- *The reorientation phase,* which involves the development of a more realistic view of retirement alternatives
- *The stability phase,* a period in which the person has learned to deal with life after retirement in a reasonable and comfortable fashion
- *The termination phase,* which begins when the person can no longer engage in basic, day-to-day activities such as self-care and housework

As this analysis demonstrates, retirement is not a single transition but rather a series of adjustments that vary from one person to another. The length and timing of each phase will vary for each individual, depending on such factors as his or her financial and health status. In fact, a person will not necessarily go through all the phases identified by Atchley. For example, people who were forced to retire or who face financial difficulties may never experience a "honeymoon phase." A significant number of retirees continue to be part of the paid labor force of the United States, often taking part-time jobs to supplement their pension income. This is certainly the expectation of baby boomers, as Figure 12-2 shows.

FIGURE 12-2

Retirement Expectations

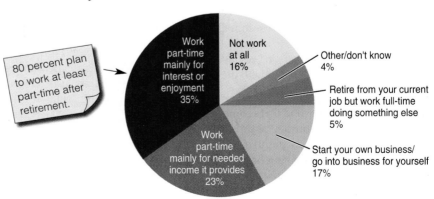

Note: Survey of the baby boom generation (people born from 1946 to 1964) conducted in 1998.
Source: AARP 1998.

Like other aspects of life in the United States, the experience of retirement varies according to gender, race, and ethnicity. White males are most likely to benefit from a structure of retirement wages as well as to have participated in a formal retirement preparation program. As a result, anticipatory socialization for retirement is most systematic for White men. By contrast, members of racial and ethnic minority groups—especially African Americans—are more likely to exit the paid labor force through disability than through retirement. Because of their comparatively lower incomes and smaller savings, men and women from racial and ethnic minority groups work intermittently after retirement more often than do older Whites (National Institute on Aging 1999a; Quadagno 1999).

Death and Dying

Among the role transitions that typically (but not always) come later in life is death. Until recently, death was viewed as a taboo topic in the United States. However, psychologist Elisabeth Kübler-Ross (1969) through her pioneering book *On Death and Dying* has greatly encouraged open discussion of the process of dying.

Drawing on her work with 200 cancer patients, Kübler-Ross identified five stages of the experience of dying that a person may undergo:

1. When people finally realize that they are dying, they first *deny* the truth to themselves, their families, and their friends.
2. When denial can no longer be maintained, it is followed by a period of *anger,* which can be directed at almost anyone or anything.
3. In the stage of *bargaining*—often relatively brief— people talk about the unfulfilled goals they will pursue if they somehow recover. In effect, they are hoping to bargain with God for additional time.
4. When people realize that these deals are not realistic, they enter a stage of *depression* and experience a pervasive sense of loss.
5. The final stage, *acceptance,* is not always reached by the dying patient. Those who accept death are not happy about the prospect, but have come to terms with their fate and are ready to die in peace.

As Kübler-Ross (1969:113) notes: "It is as if the pain had gone, the struggle is over, and there comes a time for 'the final rest before the long journey' as one patient phrased it."

Despite its continued popular appeal, the Kübler-Ross five-stage theory of dying has been challenged. Researchers often can't substantiate these stages. Moreover, this model relies on an assumption that the dying person clearly recognizes that death is nearing. Yet more than 20 percent of people in the United States age 65 and over die

in nursing homes; for them and many others, an array of chronic, debilitative, degenerative diseases can mask death. Finally, critics of Kübler-Ross emphasize that even if this five-stage model is accurate for the United States, it does not apply to other cultures that deal with death quite differently (Marshall and Levy 1990; Retsinas 1988).

Functionalists would see those who are dying as fulfilling distinct social functions. Gerontologist Richard Kalish (1985) lists among the tasks of the dying: completing unfinished business, such as settling insurance and legacy matters; restoring harmony to social relationships and saying farewell to friends and family; dealing with medical care needs; and making funeral plans and other arrangements for survivors after death occurs. In accomplishing these tasks, the dying person actively contributes to meeting society's needs for smooth intergenerational transitions, role continuity, compliance with medical procedures, and minimal disruption of the social system despite loss of one of its members.

This functionalist analysis brings to mind the cherished yet controversial concept of a "good death." One researcher described a "good death" among the Kaliai, a people of the South Pacific, in which the dying person "called all his kinsmen to gather around him, disposed of his possessions after repaying the obligations owed by him and forgiving any obligations of others to him, and then informed those gathered that it was time for him to die" (Counts 1977:370).

The "good death" among the Kaliai has its parallel in Western societies, where we may refer to a "natural death," an "appropriate death," or a "death with dignity." In the Western ideal of a "good death," friends and family surround the dying person, there is minimal technological interference with the natural dying process, the dying person's pain and discomfort are controlled, and there is an orderly and meaningful closure for the dying person and his or her loved ones. While this Western ideal makes the experience of dying as positive as possible, some critics fear that acceptance of the "good death" concept may direct individual efforts and social resources away from attempts to extend life. Some people do argue that fatally ill older people should not only passively accept death but should forgo further treatment in order to reduce health care expenditures. As we will see in the social policy section, such issues are at the heart of current debates over the "right to die" and physician-assisted suicide (Kearl 1989; Marshall and Levy 1990).

Recent studies in the United States suggest that, in many varied ways, people have broken through the historic taboos about death and are attempting to arrange certain aspects of the idealized "good death." For example, bereavement practices—once highly socially structured— are becoming increasingly varied and therapeutic. More and more people are actively addressing the inevitability

Coffins in Ghana sometimes reflect the way the dead lived their lives. This Methodist burial service is for a woman who died at age 85, leaving behind 11 children, 82 grandchildren, and 60 great-grandchildren. Her coffin, designed as a mother hen, features 11 chicks nestling between the wings (Secretan 1995).

of death by making wills, leaving "living wills" (health care proxies that explain their feelings about the use of life-support equipment), donating organs, and providing instructions for family members about funerals, cremations, and burials. Given medical and technological advances and a breakthrough in open discussion and negotiation regarding death and dying, it is more possible than ever that "good deaths" can become a social norm in the United States (M. LaGanga 1999; J. Riley 1992).

Age Stratification in the United States

The "Graying of America"

When Lenore Schaefer, a ballroom dancer, tried to get on the *Tonight Show,* she was told she was "too young": she was in her early 90s. When she turned 101, she made it. But even at that age, Lenore is no longer unusual in our society. Today, people over 100 constitute, proportionately, the country's fastest-growing age group. They are part of the increasing proportion of the population of the United States composed of older people (Krach and Velkoff 1998; Rimer 1998).

As Figure 12-3 shows, men and women aged 65 and over constituted only 4 percent of the nation's population in the year 1900, but by 2001 this figure had reached 14 per-

cent. It is currently projected to level off by the year 2050. However, the "old old" segment of the population (that is, people 85 years old and over) is growing at an ever-faster rate.

In 1990, 14 percent of Whites were over the age of 65, compared with 8 percent of African Americans, 6 percent of Asian Americans, and 5 percent of Hispanics. These differences reflect the shorter life spans of these latter groups, as well as immigration patterns among Asians and Hispanics. Yet people of color are increasing their presence among the elderly population of the United States. In 1995, 15 percent of all people 65 years and older were people of color; by the year 2050, this figure is projected to rise to 34 percent (Treas 1995).

The "graying of America" is not a uniform trend. The highest proportion of older people are found in Florida, Pennsylvania, Rhode Island, Iowa, West Virginia, and Arkansas. However, many more states are undergoing an aging trend. In 1996, Florida was the state most populated by the elderly, with 18.5 percent of the population over the age of 65. Yet, as Figure 12-4 shows, in about 25 years, more than half of the states will have a greater proportion of elderly than Florida does now.

While the United States is noticeably graying, the nation's older citizens are in a sense getting younger, owing to

FIGURE 12-3

Actual and Projected Growth of the Elderly Population of the United States

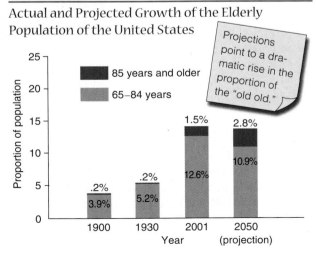

Projections point to a dramatic rise in the proportion of the "old old."

Sources: Bureau of the Census 1975; Bureau of the Census data in Yax 1999.

FIGURE 12-4

26 Floridas by 2025

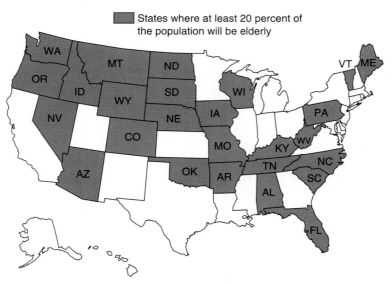

States where at least 20 percent of the population will be elderly

Source: Bureau of the Census in Yax 1999.

improved health and nutrition. Researchers at the National Institute on Aging (1999b) have found a decrease in chronic disability in every age category. From the perspective of activity theory, this is obviously a welcome change that should be encouraged (Horn and Meer 1987).

Clearly, the graying of the United States is a phenomenon that can no longer be ignored—either by social scientists or by government policymakers. Advocacy groups on behalf of the elderly have emerged and spoken out on a wide range of issues (as we will see later in the chapter). Politicians court the votes of older people, since they are the age group most likely to register and most likely to vote. In fact, they are the only age group that has actually increased their turnout rate over the last 25 years (L. Feldman 1999; LaGanga 2000).

Wealth and Income

There is significant variation in wealth and poverty among the nation's older people. Some individuals and couples find themselves poor in part because of fixed pensions and skyrocketing health care costs (see Chapter 18). Nevertheless, as a group, older people in the United States are

neither homogeneous nor poor. The typical elderly person enjoys a standard of living that is much higher than at any point in the nation's past. Class differences among the elderly remain evident but tend to narrow somewhat: Those older people who enjoyed middle-class incomes while younger tend to remain better off after retirement than those who previously had lower incomes, but the financial gap lessens a bit (Arber and Ginn 1991; Duncan and Smith 1989).

To some extent, older people owe their overall improved standard of living to a greater accumulation of wealth—in the form of home ownership, private pensions, and other financial assets. But much of the improvement is due to more generous Social Security benefits. While modest when compared with other countries' pension programs, Social Security nevertheless provides 38 percent of all income received by older people in the United States. Currently, about one-eighth of the nation's elderly population lives below the poverty line; without Social Security, that figure would rise to half. At the extreme end of poverty are those groups who were more likely to be poor at earlier points in the life cycle: female-headed households and racial and ethnic minorities (Duncan and Smith 1989; Hess 1990).

Women account for 59 percent of people in the United States 65 years old and over and 72 percent of those 85 and over. Older women experience a double burden: They are female in a society that favors males, and

Life begins at 65 for these retirees in Georgetown, Texas, checking out a model of Sun City, a retirement community with full services.

This Native American woman carries a *triple* burden: she is female in a society that favors male, elderly in a society that values youth, and a minority member in a society that favors Whites.

they are elderly in a society that values youth. The social inequities that women experience throughout their lifetimes, as noted earlier in the chapter, only intensify as they age. As a result, in 1990 about half of older women living alone received some form of public assistance—whether Medicaid, food stamps, or subsidized or public housing.

Viewed from a conflict perspective, it is not surprising that older women experience a double burden; the same is true of elderly members of racial and ethnic minorities. For example, in 1997 the proportion of older Hispanics with incomes below the poverty line (23.8 percent) was more than twice as large as the proportion of older Whites (9.0 percent). Moreover, 26 percent of older African Americans were below the federal government's poverty line (Dalaker and Naifeh 1998:3–5).

Economic inequality is not a static condition, for people move in and out of poverty. Race and ethnicity, however, are ascribed characteristics. And while people may move up and down the social ladder, those who *begin* life with greater resources have more opportunities to acquire additional resources. Women and minorities, and especially minority women, are less likely to accumulate savings or even have adequate pension plans for their older years. (See Box 12-2.)

Ageism

It "knows no one century, nor culture, and is not likely to go away any time soon." This is how physician Robert Butler (1990:178) described prejudice and discrimination against the elderly, which he called **ageism**. Ageism reflects a deep uneasiness among young and middle-aged people about growing old. For many, old age symbolizes disease, disability, and death; seeing the elderly serves as a reminder that *they* may someday become old and infirm. Ageism was popularized by Maggie Kuhn, a senior citizen who took up the cause of elderly rights after she was forced to retire from her position at the United Presbyterian Church. Kuhn formed the Gray Panthers in 1971, a national organization dedicated to the fight against age discrimination. Later in this chapter, we'll look at other successful efforts of the elderly to organize (R. Thomas 1995).

With ageism all too common in the United States, it is hardly surprising that older people are barely visible on television. A content analysis of 1,446 fictional television characters revealed that only 2 percent were age 65 and over—even though this age group accounts for about 13 percent of the nation's population. A second study found older women particularly underrepresented on television (Robinson and Skill 1993; Vernon et al. 1990).

Competition in the Labor Force

In the United States in the year 1900, fully two-thirds of men aged 65 and over were found in the paid labor force, working either full-time or part-time. As recently as 1950, 46 percent of older men were in the labor force, but by 1990 this figure had dropped to 16 percent. Even among the "young old" (those 65 to 69 years of age), labor force participation has declined from 60 percent in 1950 to less than 30 percent in 1990 (Taeuber 1992). Despite these falling percentages, younger adults continue to view older workers as "job stealers," a biased judgment similar to that directed against illegal immigrants. This mistaken belief not only intensifies age conflict but leads to age discrimination. p. 283

While firing people simply because they are old violates federal laws, courts have upheld the right to lay off older workers for economic reasons. Critics contend that later the same firms hire young, cheaper workers to replace the experienced, older workers. Norman Matloff (1998), a computer science professor at the University of California, finds rampant age discrimination in the computer software industry, supposedly an understaffed field. Employers shunt aside mid-career programmers because they

12-2 Theory of Cumulative Disadvantage

Steve, a White male, grew up in a middle-class family in Pittsburgh. His parents, while not well off, were able to send him through college. Steve worked nights to pay his way through graduate school and obtained a masters in business. He joined a brokerage business and worked his way up the corporate ladder. By the time he retired at 65 as a vice president of the company, Steve had accumulated a nest egg of savings through stock and bond purchases, owned a house in an affluent suburb of Philadelphia, and could look forward to substantial monthly pension payments as well as Social Security.

Contrast Steve's life course with that of James, a Black male from Chicago's South Side. James was raised by a single mother, who generally depended on welfare payments to put food on the table. James actually liked the structure of school but felt pressure to contribute income to the family, so he dropped out of high school to work as an inventory clerk in a warehouse, for little more than minimum wage. When the warehouse closed he bounced around from job to job, with long periods of unemployment.

Health problems also sidelined him. James was never able to save money or to buy a home or an apartment; he felt lucky just to make the rent each month. He never worked anyplace long enough to earn a pension. In his old age James must make do with whatever Social Security income he is entitled to.

James's story illustrates the increasing inequality faced by aging racial and ethnic

> While senior citizens as a group have made economic strides, members of racial minorities have not kept pace.

group members as a result of diminished life chances. While senior citizens as a group have made economic strides, members of racial minorities have not kept pace. Sociologist Angela O'Rand has advanced the notion of *cumulative disadvantage* over the life course to explain what is happening. Two biases work against minority group members: First, they are less likely than Whites to have steady work histories, which would al-

low them to accumulate wealth (such as a home) that can serve as a valuable nest egg in later years. For example, about 42 percent of African Americans own a home compared to 64 percent of Whites. The second bias is related to the first. Members of racial minorities are less likely than Whites to be served by pension programs that provide steady income during retirement.

In short, those who are advantaged early in life have more opportunity to receive formal schooling, to obtain a job that leads to advancement up the ladder, to save for retirement, and to have access to dependable retirement savings programs. Their *advantages* accumulate over the life course, while the *disadvantages* suffered by racial and ethnic groups accumulate.

Let's Discuss

1. How did your grandparents' life chances affect the quality of life in their later years?
2. Would a conflict theorist agree with the notion of cumulative disadvantage? Why or why not?

Sources: Oliver and Shapiro 1995; A. O'Rand 1996.

command higher salaries than recent college graduates. Companies defend their actions on the grounds that the older workers lack skills in the latest software programs.

A controlled experiment conducted in 1993 by the American Association of Retired Persons confirmed that older people often face discrimination when applying for jobs. Comparable résumés for two applicants—one 57 years old and the other 32 years old—were sent to 775 large firms and employment agencies around the United States. In situations for which positions were actually available, the younger applicant received a favorable response 43 percent of the time. By contrast, the older applicant received favorable responses less than half as often (only 17 percent of the time). One *Fortune* 500 corporation asked the younger applicant for more information, while it informed the older applicant that no appropriate positions were open (Bendick et al. 1993).

In contrast to the negative stereotypes, researchers have found that older workers can be an *asset* for

employers. According to a study issued in 1991, older workers can be retrained in new technologies, have lower rates of absenteeism than younger employees, and are often more effective salespeople. The study focused on two corporations based in the United States (the hotel chain Days Inns of America and the holding company Travelers Corporation of Hartford) and a British retail chain—all of which have long-term experience in hiring workers age 50 and over. An official of the private fund that commissioned the study concluded, "We have here the first systematic hard-nosed economic analysis showing older workers are good investments" (Telsch 1991:A16).

The Elderly: Emergence of a Collective Consciousness

During the 1960s, students at colleges and universities across the country, advocating "student power," collectively demanded a role in the governance of educational

States (behind only the Roman Catholic church and the American Automobile Association) and represents one out of every four registered voters in the United States. The AARP has endorsed voter registration campaigns, nursing home reforms, and pension reforms. As an acknowledgment of its difficulties in recruiting members of racial and ethnic minority groups, AARP began a Minority Affairs Initiative. The spokeswoman of this initiative, Margaret Dixon, became AARP's first African American president in 1996 (Fountain 1996; Mehren and Rosenblatt 1995; see also C. Morris 1996).

People grow old in many different ways. Not all the elderly face the same challenges or enjoy the same resources. While the AARP lobbies to protect the elderly in general, other groups work in more specific ways. For example, the National Committee to Preserve Social Security and Medicare, founded in 1982, successfully lobbied Congress to keep Medicare benefits for the ailing poor elderly. Other large special interest groups represent retired federal employees, retired teachers, and retired union workers (Quadagno 1999).

Still another manifestation of the new awareness of older people is the formation of organizations for elderly homosexuals. One such group, Senior Action in a Gay Environment (SAGE), was established in New York City in 1978 and now oversees a nationwide network of local community groups. Like more traditional senior citizens' groups, SAGE sponsors workshops, classes, dances, and food deliveries to the homebound. At the same time, SAGE must deal with special concerns. Many gay couples find that nursing homes won't allow them to share a room. In addition, nearly 90 percent of gay seniors today

Older job applicants must deal with negative stereotypes, despite the fact that older workers are often found to be a good investment for a company: they can learn new technologies, are absent less often than younger employees, and have proved to be effective in sales.

institutions. In the following decade, the 1970s, many older people became aware that *they* were being treated as second-class citizens and also turned to collective action.

The largest organization representing the nation's elderly is the American Association of Retired Persons (AARP), founded in 1958 by a retired school principal who was having difficulty getting insurance because of age prejudice. Many of AARP's services involve discounts and insurance for its 31.5 million members, but the organization also functions as a powerful lobbying group.

The potential power of AARP is enormous; it is the third-largest voluntary association in the United

Members of SAGE, Senior Action in a Gay Environment, take part in a gay pride demonstration in New York City. This nationwide organization focuses on the speical needs of gay seniors.

have no children, and more than two-thirds live alone—twice the percentage of heterosexual seniors. It's not surprising that SAGE has surfaced to deal with these large-scale special needs (R. Bragg 1999; SAGE 1999).

The elderly in the United States are better off today financially and physically than ever before. Many of them have strong financial assets and medical care packages that will take care of most any health need. But, as we have seen, a significant segment is impoverished, faced with the prospect of declining health and mounting medical bills. And some older people may now have to add being aged to a lifetime of discrimination. As in all other stages of the life course, the aged constitute a diverse group in the United States and around the world.

We will now turn to a topic that many older persons find of intense interest—the right to die. But as we will see, this issue is highly controversial.

SOCIAL POLICY AND AGE STRATIFICATION

The Right to Die Worldwide

The Issue

On August 4, 1993, Dr. Jack Kevorkian, a retired pathologist, helped a 30-year-old Michigan man with Lou Gehrig's disease commit suicide in a van. Thomas Hyde, Jr. died after inhaling carbon monoxide through a mask designed by Dr. Kevorkian; in doing so, he became the 17th person to commit suicide with Kevorkian's assistance. They physician was openly challenging a Michigan law (aimed at him) that makes it a felony crime—punishable by up to four years in jail—to assist in a suicide. Since then Kevorkian has assisted in numerous other suicides, but it was not until he did it on television in 1998 that charges brought against him resulted in a guilty verdict (see Box 12-3).

The issue of physician-assisted suicide is but one aspect of the larger debate in the United States and other countries over the ethics of suicide and euthanasia. The term **euthanasia** has been defined as the "act of bringing about the death of a hopelessly ill and suffering person in a relatively quick and painless way for reasons of mercy" (Council on Ethical and Judicial Affairs, American Medical Association 1992:2, 229). This type of mercy killing reminds us of the ideal of "good death" discussed earlier in the chapter. The debate over euthanasia and assisted suicide often focuses on cases involving older people, though it can involve younger adults with terminal and degenerative diseases (as in the case of Thomas Youk and Thomas Hyde, Jr.) or even children.

The Setting

Many societies are known to have practiced **senilicide**—"killing of the old"—because of extreme difficulties in providing basic necessities such as food and shelter. In a study of the treatment of the elderly in 41 nonindustrialized societies, Anthony Glascock (1990) found that some form of "death-hastening" behavior was present in 21 of them. Killing of the elderly was evident in 14 of these societies, while abandoning of older people was evident in 8 societies. Typically, such death hastening occurs when older people become decrepit and are viewed as "already dead." Death hastening in these nonindustrialized cultures is open and socially approved. Family members generally make decisions, often after open consultation with those about to die.

Currently, public policy in the United States does not permit *active euthanasia* (such as a deliberate injection of lethal drugs to a terminally ill patient) or physician-assisted suicide. Although suicide itself is no longer a crime, assisting suicide is illegal in at least 29 states. There is greater legal tolerance today for *passive euthanasia* (such as disconnecting life-support equipment from a comatose patient).

Sociological Insights

While formal norms concerning euthanasia may be in flux, informal norms seem to permit mercy killings. According to an estimate by the American Hospital Association, as many as 70 percent of all deaths in the United States are quietly negotiated, with patients, family members, and physicians agreeing not to use life-support technology. In an informal poll of internists, one in five reported that he or she had assisted or helped cause the death of a patient. In a period in which AIDS-related deaths are common, an AIDS underground is known to share p. 134 information and assistance regarding suicide (Gibbs 1993; Martinez 1993).

Conflict theorists ask questions about the values raised by such decisions. By endorsing physician-assisted suicide, are we devaluing the disabled through an acceptance

Eye on the Media

www.mhhe.com/schaefer

12-3 Death by Doctor on Television

In 1998, the television newsprogram *60 Minutes*, known for its pathbreaking visual stories, created a stir when it aired a videotape made by Dr. Jack Kevorkian that shows him assisting the suicide of Thomas Youk. Youk, 52 years old, was suffering from incurable Lou Gehrig's disease and was terrified of choking to death in the course of his illness. The tape shows the doctor administering a lethal injection of potassium chloride, which Kevorkian calls his "medicide." It produces death by stopping the heart.

> The tape shows the doctor administering a lethal injection of potassium chloride, which Kevorkian calls his "medicide."

The CBS show, which drew huge ratings, brought the issue of physician-assisted "mercy killing" right into people's homes. Some media observers questioned the wisdom of showing the tape provided by Kevorkian. The "in-your-face" publicity tactic led to a successful prosecution of Kevorkian by the state of Michigan, after four earlier attempts to find him guilty failed. Kevorkian's medical license was re-

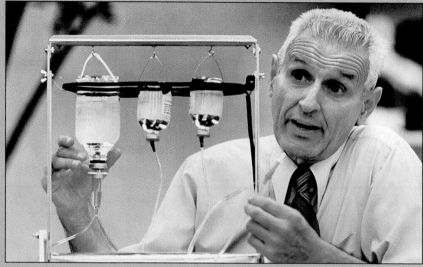

Dr. Jack Kevorkian with the apparatus that administers a lethal injection to those who want assistance in suicide.

voked by the state in June 1998, and he is now awaiting the outcome of his appeal.

Let's Discuss

1. If you were the producer of *60 Minutes*, would you air Dr. Kevorkian's videotape? Why or why not?

2. Thomas Youk signed a consent form for the doctor to carry out the lethal injection. Should that be enough to shield Kevorkian from prosecution by the state?

Source: P. Belluck 1999.

---

of their premature death? Critics note that we all are only temporarily able-bodied; disease or a speeding automobile can place any one of us among the disabled. By establishing a precedent for ending the lives of selected disabled people, we may unwittingly contribute to negative social views and labeling of all disabled people. Further reflecting the conflict perspective, gerontologist Elizabeth Markson (1992:6) argues that the "powerless, poor or undesirable are at special risk of being 'encouraged' to choose assisted death."

Critics of euthanasia charge that many of its supporters are guilty of ageism and other forms of bias. In a society that commonly discriminates against the elderly and people with disabilities, medical authorities and even family members may decide too quickly that such people

should die "for their own good" or (in a view somewhat reminiscent of disengagement theory) "for the good of society." It is also feared that society may use euthanasia to reduce health care costs—rather than striving to make life better for those near the end. Older people may even feel compelled to (prematurely) end their lives to ease the emotional and financial burdens on family members and friends (Glascock 1990:45; *New York Times* 1993b; Richman 1992).

Policy Initiatives

In the industrialized world, euthanasia is widely accepted only in the Netherlands. Dutch law provides for euthanasia only after approval of a three-member commission consisting of a doctor, lawyer, and an ethicist, but the majority of physician-assisted suicides in the Netherlands don't follow these procedures. A national survey in 1999 showed that 92 percent of that nation's people accept euthanasia and physician-assisted suicide (R. Moseley 1999).

In the United States, the only state to pass a law permitting assisted suicide is Oregon, with its Death with Dignity Act in 1997. Similar measures have failed to win support in at least 20 other states. While only 15 terminally ill people have ended their lives with lethal medication under Oregon's law, the legislation—the only such law in the world—has encountered sharp opposition throughout the country. In 1999, the U.S. Congress passed a measure that effectively overrules Oregon's law by preventing federally controlled drugs from being used to end a life. The law does allow for use of drugs to control pain, which could hasten death. The whole complex issue of assisted suicide—backed by the American Medical Association but opposed by other medical groups—is headed for appeals (R. Pear 1999; S. Verhovek 1999).

Advances in technology allow us to prolong life in ways that were unimaginable decades ago. But should people be forced or expected to prolong lives that are unbearably painful or that are, in effect, "lifeless"? Unfortunately, medical and technological advances cannot provide answers to complex ethical, legal, and political questions.

Let's Discuss

1. Why do you think "death-hastening" behavior is common in nonindustrialized countries?
2. In what ways are conflict theory and disengagement theory relevant in the debate over the "right to die"?
3. Do you think someone should be allowed to choose to die? Why or why not?

Summary

Age, like gender and race, is an ascribed status that forms the basis for social differentiation. This chapter examines theories regarding the aging process, role transitions in the life course, age stratification in the United States, the growing political activism of the nation's elderly population, and controversy surrounding the right to die.

1. Like other forms of stratification, age stratification varies from culture to culture.
2. "Being old" is a master status that seems to overshadow all others in the United States.
3. The particular problems of the aged have become the focus for a specialized area of research and inquiry known as *gerontology.*
4. *Disengagement theory* implicitly suggests that society should help older people withdraw from their accustomed social roles, whereas *activity theory* argues that the elderly person who remains active and socially involved will be best-adjusted.
5. From a conflict perspective, the low status of older people is reflected in prejudice and discrimination against them and unfair job practices.
6. As we age, we go through role transitions, including the role of the sandwich generation, adjustment to retirement, and preparation for death.
7. An increasing proportion of the population of the United States is composed of older people.
8. *Ageism* reflects a deep uneasiness on the part of younger people about growing old.
9. The American Association of Retired Persons (AARP) works as a powerful lobbying group backing legislation that will benefit senior citizens.
10. The "right to die" often entails physician-assisted suicide, a very controversial issue worldwide.

Critical Thinking Questions

1. Are there elderly students at your college or university? How are they treated by younger students and by faculty members? Is there a subculture of older students? How do younger students view faculty members in their fifties and sixties?
2. Is age segregation functional or dysfunctional for older people in the United States? Is it functional or dysfunctional for society as a whole? What are the manifest functions, the latent functions, and the dysfunctions of age segregation?
3. Imagine that you were asked to study political activism among older people. How might you employ surveys, observations, experiments, and existing sources to better understand such activism?

Key Terms

Activity theory   An interactionist theory of aging that argues that elderly people who remain active and socially involved will be best-adjusted (322)

Ageism   Prejudice and discrimination against the elderly. (329)

Disengagement theory   A functionalist theory of aging that contends that society and the aging individual mutually sever many of their relationships. (321)

Euthanasia   The act of bringing about the death of a hopelessly ill and suffering person in a relatively quick and painless way for reasons of mercy. (332)

Gerontology   The scientific study of the sociological and psychological aspects of aging and the problems of the aged. (321)

Midlife crisis   A stressful period of self-evaluation that begins about age 40. (324)

Sandwich generation   The generation of adults who simultaneously try to meet the competing needs of their parents and their own children. (324)

Senilicide   The killing of the aged. (332)

Additional Readings

BOOKS

Dychtwald, Ken. 1999. *Age Power: How the 21st Century Will Be Ruled by the New Old.* New York: Putnam. A gerontologist projects social patterns and aging into the future.

Howe, Neil, and Bill Strauss. 1993. *13th Gen: Abort, Retry, Ignore, Fail?* New York: Vintage. A heavily illustrated view of the lifestyles and beliefs of the thirteenth generation in the United States (people born between 1961 and 1981).

Posner, Richard. 1995. *Aging and Old Age.* Chicago: University of Chicago Press. A former law professor and the chief judge of a federal appeals court, Posner analyzes old age in the U.S., the voting patterns of the elderly, ageism, physician-assisted suicide, and social service programs intended to assist older people.

Quadagno, Jill. 1999. *Aging and the Life Course: An Introduction to Social Gerontology.* New York: McGraw-Hill. A sociological overview not only of the elderly but of the entire process of aging.

JOURNALS

Among the journals that focus on issues of aging and age stratification are *Ageing and Society* (founded in 1981), *Ageing International (1994), Contemporary Gerontology* (1994), *Death Studies* (1976), *Generations* (1976), *The Gerontologist* (1961), *Journal of Aging and Ethnicity* (1996), *Journal of Applied Gerontology* (1982), *Journal of Cross-Cultural Gerontology* (1986), *Journal of Gerontology* (1946), *Research on Aging* (1979), and *Youth and Society* (1968).

Internet Connection

Note: While all the URLs listed were current as of the printing of this book, these sites often change. Please check our website (http://www.mhhe.com/schaefer) for updates.

1. The policy in the United States toward medical care for the elderly has undergone revisions and challenges in recent years. Examine these two sites to add to your knowledge of the issue: the official U.S. government site for Medicare information (**http://www.medicare.gov**) and the *Washington Post*'s Medicare Prognosis (**http://www.washingtonpost.com/wp-srv/politics/special/medicare/medicare.htm**).
    (a) Who is eligible for Medicare under the current system?
    (b) How is Medicare funded?
    (c) How much is spent each year through Medicare?
    (d) What social problems does Medicare aim to alleviate?
    (e) What is the difference between Medicare and Medicaid?
    (f) How does Medicare Part A compare to Medicare Part B?
    (g) What kinds of medical and health needs are covered by Medicare? What kinds are not?
    (h) What is MediGap?
    (i) How will changes in the population, "the graying of America," and increased life expectancy rates affect Medicare?
    (j) On the *Washington Post* site, be sure to participate in "Poll Taker" and compare your opinion on which political party can best protect the Medicare system with that of other Americans.
    (k) Based on all you learned from the book and websites, what do you think the future of Medicare in the United States will be? Why?

2. Debate rages in the United States regarding euthanasia and physician-assisted suicide. Religious Tolerance.org offers multiple perspectives and statistics on the issue (**http://www.religioustolerance.org/euthanas.htm**).
    (a) What does the term "euthanasia" mean? Where did it originate?
    (b) What is the difference between passive euthanasia, active euthanasia, physician-assisted suicide, and involuntary euthanasia according to the site?
    (c) How do various religious organizations view the issue?
    (d) What are some of the arguments offered by those on differing sides of this issue?
    (e) What is the "Death with Dignity Law" in the state of Oregon? What is its current status? Under what circumstances and conditions can a person seek to end his or her life?
    (f) According to the study by the Center for Disease Control and Prevention, headed by Dr. Arthur Chin, what have been the results in Oregon? What were the demographics of those who exercised their right to die?
    (g) According to the polls, what attitudes do Americans hold toward euthanasia and physician-assisted suicide?
    (h) What is your opinion of the issue in general and the Oregon law in particular? Why do you hold that opinion?
    (i) Use your sociological imagination and discuss/compare how a functionalist and a conflict theorist would view such a law.
    (j) What is the legal standing of euthanasia in Australia, Colombia, Canada, the Netherlands, and Japan?

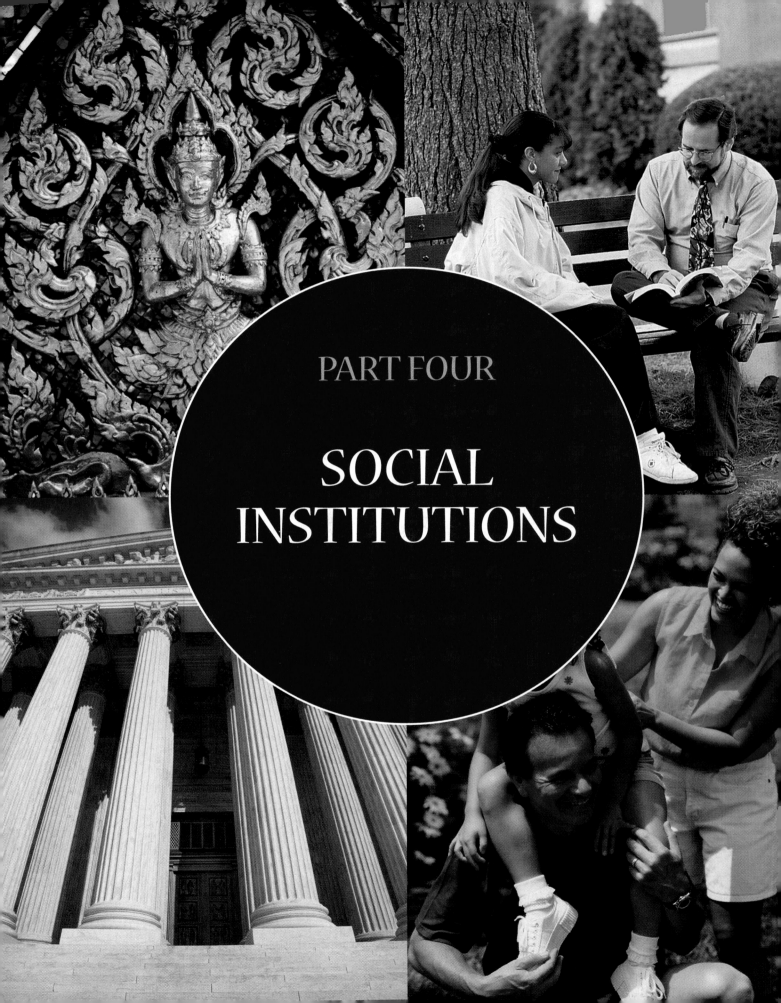

PART FOUR

SOCIAL INSTITUTIONS

Part Four considers sociological analysis of major social institutions, including the family, religion, education, government, the economy, and the health care system. As noted earlier in the text, *social institutions* are organized patterns of beliefs and behavior centered on basic social needs.

Chapter 13 focuses on the functions of the family and intimate relationships and their importance as cultural universals. Chapter 14 discusses the dimensions, functions, and organization of religion, and Chapter 15 considers the functions of education, schools as social organizations, and recent trends in education. Chapter 16 looks at government and politics, with particular emphasis on types of governments. Chapter 17 examines economic systems, aspects of work, and the changing economy. Chapter 18 analyzes sociological perspectives on health and illness, the health care system, and mental illness.

CHAPTER

13

THE FAMILY AND INTIMATE RELATIONSHIPS

New technology has sparked a demand for testing services to determine who is and who is not the father of a child. When billboards advertising these services appeared in the United States in 1997, some people found them amusing while others perceived them as further evidence of the problems confronting the family.

From the time of the breakdown of my marriage to Cliff's mother in 1979 to my marriage to Elleni in 1990, I was forced to deal with a difficult but nonetheless standard set of problems. My ex-wife was awarded custody of two-year-old Cliff and then decided to move to Atlanta. I had no recourse, legal or otherwise. And yet in my struggle to build a close relationship with my son, I now had to cope with an almost impossible set of barriers. Hundreds of miles separated me from Cliff, and I had limited visitation rights—a few specified weekends during the year plus three months in the summer. Besides which, what would I do with my son during our precious time together? My bachelor homes did not provide a supportive context for a four-year-old or a nine-year-old—there were no kids on the block, no basketball hoop in the back yard. But I wrestled with these problems and over time developed a strategy that worked, albeit imperfectly.

I hit upon this great solution for the summers. I would take Cliff back to Sacramento, back to the loving, child-centered home that had been so good to me and my siblings a generation ago. It required a lot of stretching and bending of the rules, but I organized life so that I really could take two and a half months out of the year. It meant postponing book deadlines and taming an almost impossible travel schedule, but it was well worth it. Those summers in Sacramento stand out like jewels in my memory. My parents' home turned out to be a profoundly healing place in which Cliff and I could reach out to one another. It provided the deeply needed (and yet so hard to contrive) rhythms and routines of normal family life. Three meals a day; regular bedtimes; clean clothes; a bevy of cousins—Kahnie, Phillip and Phyllis, Cornel and Erika—just around the corner, on tap for casual play; bicycles and baseball gear in the garage all ready to be put to use whenever a grownup was available. And hovering in the backgrounds, loving, eagle-eyed grandparents. . . . The evening meal was particularly important, as all three generations gathered for a cookout in the backyard. Conversation and laughter flowed, advice was sought and help was freely offered, jokes and stories were traded, and the children, spellbound, hung on the edges, absorbing the spirit and the meaning of family life.

The rest of the year was a struggle. I maintained regular telephone contact with Cliff, calling him several times a week just to hear his voice and shoot the breeze. But in the rushed, tantalizing visits around Thanksgiving, Christmas, and Easter, it was always hard not to lapse into the role of being a "good-time dad," showering gifts on him in an attempt to make up for real time or a deeper agenda. *(Hewlett and West 1998: 21–22)* ■

In this excerpt from *The War Against Parents* philosophy scholar Cornel West underscores how deeply family life has been altered by divorce, one of many social factors that have gradually but inevitably turned the traditional nuclear family on its head. The family of today is not what it was a century ago or even a generation ago. New roles, new gender distinctions, new child-rearing patterns have all combined to create new forms of family life. Today, for example, we are seeing more and more women take the breadwinner's role, whether married or as a single parent. Blended families—the result of divorces and remarriages—are almost the norm. And many people are seeking intimate relationships outside marriage, whether it be in gay partnerships or in cohabiting arrangements.

This chapter addresses family and intimate relationships in the United States as well as in other parts of the world. As we will see, family patterns differ from one culture to another and even within the same culture. A *family* can be defined as a set of people related by blood, marriage (or some other agreed-upon relationship), or adoption who share the primary responsibility for reproduction and caring for members of society.

In this chapter, we will see that the family is universal—found in every culture—however varied in its organization. We will look at the family and intimate relationships from the functionalist, conflict, and interactionist points of view and at the variations in marital patterns and family life, including different family forms of child rearing. We'll pay particular attention to the increasing number of people in dual-income or single-parent families. We will examine divorce in the United States and consider such diverse lifestyles as cohabitation, remaining single, lesbian and gay relationships, and marriage without children. The social policy section will look at controversial issues surrounding the use of reproductive technology. ■

Global View of the Family

Among Tibetans, a woman may be simultaneously married to more than one man, usually brothers. This system allows sons to share the limited amount of good land. A Hopi woman may divorce her husband by placing her belongings outside the door. A Trobriand Island couple signals marriage by sitting in public on a porch eating yams provided by the bride's mother. She continues to provide cooked yams for a year while the groom's family offers in exchange such valuables as stone axes and clay pots (W. Haviland 1999).

As these examples illustrate, there are many variations in "the family" from culture to culture. Yet the family as a social institution is present in all cultures. Moreover, certain general principles concerning its composition, kinship patterns, and authority patterns are universal.

Composition: What Is the Family?

If we were to take our information on what a family is from what we see on television, we might come up with some very strange scenarios (see Box 13-1). The media don't always help us get a realistic view of the family. Moreover, many people still think of the family in very narrow terms—as a married couple and their unmarried children living together, like the family in the old *Cosby Show* or *Family Ties* or *Growing Pains*. However, this is but one type of family, what sociologists refer to as a ***nuclear family.*** The

In wedding ceremonies in Sumatra, Indonesia, the bride's headdress indicates her village and her social status—the more elaborate the headdress, the higher her status. After she is married, the bride and her husband live with her maternal family, and all property passes from mother to daughter.

Eye
on the Media   13-1 The Family in TV Land

www.
mhhe
.com
/schaefer

Put an alien creature from outer space in front of a television, and it would have no idea of what family life is like in the United States. It would conclude that most adults are men, most adults are not married, almost no one is over age 50, very few adults have children, most mothers don't work for pay, and child care is simply not an issue. When parents are depicted, they are either not around for the most part or they are clueless. The baby boomers in *Everybody Loves Raymond* treat their parents like meddling invaders, which is also how the teenage generation treats their boomer parents in *Dawson's Creek*. Even the cartoon show *Rugrats*, aimed at young children, portrays talking babies as making their way in the world on their own.

The fact is that *Friends, Third Rock from the Sun, Frasier, Sports Night, Ally McBeal,* and similar programs present fantasy lives that most households find fascinating, but not exactly true to their lives. Eight out of 10 adults in the United States think that almost no TV family is like their own; nearly half find no TV family like theirs.

These conclusions come out of a content analysis of prime-time TV programming conducted by Katharine Heintz-Knowles, a communications professor at the University of Washington and the mother of three children, who knows first-hand what a work–family conflict looks like. She has had to deal with finding sitters on short notice, taking children to work with her when a sitter was unavailable, and missing meetings to tend to a sick child. In fact, she acknowledges that her "life today is one big work–family conflict" (Gardner 1998:13). But when she watched television, she didn't see much of her life reflected on the screen.

Her study, called "Balancing Acts:

Television Reality versus Social Reality

	Adult TV Characters	U.S. Adult Population
Women	38%	51%
Over age 50	14%	38%
Parents of minor children	15%	32%

Work/Family Issues on Prime-Time TV," carried out content analysis of 150 episodes of 92 different programs on commercial networks over a two-week period. She found that of the 820 TV characters studied, only 38 percent were women, only 15 percent could be identified as parents of minor children, and only 14 percent were over age 50 (see the table for how these percentages compare to the adult U.S. population). Only

> Eight out of 10 adults in the United States think that almost no TV family is like their own.

3 percent of the TV characters faced recognizable conflicts between work and family, and no TV family made use of a child care center. Commenting on this study, TV personality Rosie O'Donnell (1998) noted, "Television may bring the realities of violence and natural disaster into our lives, but it rarely captures the reality of work and family life. . . . And heaven forbid a person over the age of 30 and bigger than a size four ever showed up on Melrose Place."

Because television is the major storyteller in our lives today, its programs can shape our attitudes and beliefs. Unfortunately, television gives a distorted view of family life in the United States, not only to our hypothetical alien, but also to viewers at home and in other societies on planet Earth. If very few shows depict real-life challenges in family life and possible solutions, then viewers may well go away thinking their own problems are unique and insoluble. By confronting these issues, television could call attention to what needs to be changed—both on an individual level and on a societal level—and offer hope for solutions. It appears, however, that most TV programmers offer up a fantasy world in order to satisfy people who seek entertainment and escape from their everyday lives.

Let's Discuss

1. How well does television portray the social reality of your family life?
2. Take the role of a television producer. What kind of show would you create to reflect family life today?

Sources: Blanco 1998; National Partnership for Women and Families 1998; O'Donnell 1998.

term nuclear family is well chosen, since this type of family serves as the nucleus, or core, upon which larger family groups are built. Most people in the United States see the nuclear family as the preferred family arrangement. Yet, as Figure 13-1 shows, by 1997 only about a third of the nation's family households fit this model.

The proportion of households in the United States composed of married couples with children at home has decreased steadily over the last 30 years, and this trend is expected to continue. At the same time, there have been increases in the number of single-parent households (see Figure 13-1). Similar trends are evident in other industri-

FIGURE 13-1

Types of Family Households in the United States, 1980, 1997, and 2010

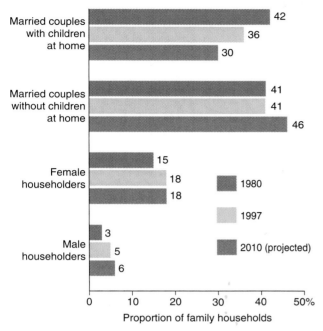

Note: "Children" refers to children under 18. Not included are unrelated people living together with no children present. Because of rounding numbers may not total 100 percent.

Source: Bureau of the Census 1998c:61, 62.

alized nations, including Canada, Great Britain, and Japan (see Figure 13-2).

A family in which relatives—such as grandparents, aunts, or uncles—live in the same home as parents and their children is known as an ***extended family.*** While not common, such living arrangements do exist in the United States. The structure of the extended family offers certain advantages over that of the nuclear family. Crises such as death, divorce, and illness put less strain on family members, since there are more people who can provide assistance and emotional support. In addition, the extended family constitutes a larger economic unit than the nuclear family. If the family is engaged in a common enterprise—a farm or a small business—the additional family members may represent the difference between prosperity and failure.

In considering these differing family types, we have limited ourselves to the form of marriage that is characteristic of the United States—monogamy. The term ***monogamy*** describes a form of marriage in which one woman and one man are married only to each other. Some observers, noting the high rate of divorce in the

United States, have suggested that "serial monogamy" is a more accurate description of the form that monogamy takes in the United States. Under ***serial monogamy,*** a person may have several spouses in his or her life but only one spouse at a time.

Some cultures allow an individual to have several husbands or wives simultaneously. This form of marriage is known as ***polygamy.*** In fact, most societies throughout the world, past and present, have preferred polygamy to monogamy. Anthropologist George Murdock (1949, 1957) sampled 565 societies and found that more than 80 percent had some type of polygamy as their preferred form. While polygamy steadily declined through most of the twentieth century, in at least five countries in Africa 20 percent of men are still in polygamous marriages (Population Reference Bureau 1996).

There are two basic types of polygamy. According to Murdock, the most common—endorsed by the majority of cultures he sampled—was ***polygyny.*** Polygyny refers to the marriage of a man to more than one woman at the same time. The various wives are often sisters, who are expected to hold similar values and have already had experience sharing a household. In polygynous societies, relatively few men actually have multiple spouses. Most individuals live in typical monogamous families; having multiple wives is viewed as a mark of status.

The other principal variation of polygamy is ***polyandry,*** under which some women have more than one husband at the same time. As we saw earlier, this is the case in the culture of the Todas of southern India. Polyandry, however, tends to be exceedingly rare in the world today. It has been accepted by some extremely poor societies that practice female infanticide (the killing of baby girls) and thus have a relatively small number of women. Like many other societies, polyandrous cultures devalue the social worth of women.

In 1999 controversy over polygamy erupted in Russia. The president of the Russian republic of Ingushetia signed a decree legalizing polygyny for the mostly Islamic population. It allows men whose wives didn't produce sons or were childless to take on additional wives. The president pointed out that each additional marriage must be approved by all spouses and the wives' relatives, and that the system is advantageous for women who might not otherwise find a husband. But women in other parts of Russia were deeply offended by the decree. One female democratic activist claimed it "plays into the hands of those who have always considered Russia to be a barbaric country" (R. Paddock 1999:A28). Another problem is that polygyny is incompatible with the Russian Constitution, which prohibits the practice but provides for no penalty.

FIGURE 13-2

The Nuclear Family in Industrialized Nations, 1960 and 1990

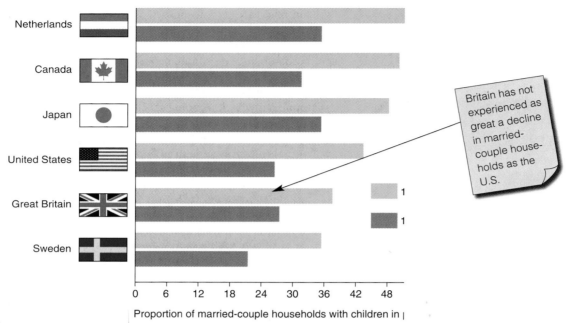

Proportion of married-couple households with children in |

Source: Bureau of Labor Statistics data in Sorrentino 1990 and author's estimate.

Kinship Patterns: To Whom Are We Related?

Many of us can trace our roots by looking at a family tree or listening to elderly family members tell us about their lives—and about the lives of ancestors who died long before we were even born. Yet a person's lineage is more than simply a personal history; it also reflects societal patterns that govern descent. In every culture, children encounter relatives to whom they are expected to show an emotional attachment. The state of being related to others is called **kinship.** Kinship is culturally learned and is not totally determined by biological or marital ties. For example, adoption creates a kinship tie that is legally acknowledged and socially accepted.

The family and the kin group are not necessarily the same. While the family is a household unit, kin do not always live together or function as a collective body on a daily basis. Kin groups include aunts, uncles, cousins, in-laws, and so forth. In a society such as the United States, the kinship group may come together only rarely, as for a wedding or funeral. However, kinship ties frequently create obligations and responsibilities. We may feel compelled to assist our kin and feel free to call upon relatives for many types of aid, including loans and baby-sitting.

How are kinship groups identified? The principle of descent assigns people to kinship groups according to their relationship to an individual's mother or father. There are three primary ways of determining descent. The United States follows the system of **bilateral descent,** which means that both sides of a person's family are regarded as equally important. For example no higher value is given to the brothers of one's father as opposed to the brothers of one's mother.

Most societies—according to Murdock, 64 percent—give preference to one side of the family or the other in tracing descent. **Patrilineal** (from Latin pater, "father") **descent** indicates that only the father's relatives are important in terms of property, inheritance, and emotional ties. Conversely, in societies that favor **matrilineal** (from Latin mater, "mother") **descent,** only the mother's relatives are significant.

New forms of reproductive technology (discussed in the policy section) will force a new way of looking at kinship. Today a combination of biological and social processes can "create" a family member, requiring that more distinctions be made about who is related to whom (C. Cussins 1998).

Authority Patterns: Who Rules?

Imagine that you have recently married and must begin to make decisions about the future of your new family. You and your spouse face many questions. Where will you live? How will you furnish your home? Who will do the cooking, the shopping, the cleaning? Whose friends will be invited to dinner? Each time a decision must be made, an issue is raised: Who has the power to make the decision? In simple terms, who rules the family? The conflict perspective examines these questions in the context of traditional gender stratification, under which men have held a dominant position over women.

p. 295

Societies vary in the way that power within the family is distributed. If a society expects males to dominate in all family decision making, it is termed a **patriarchy**. Frequently, in patriarchal societies, such as Iran, the eldest male wields the greatest power, although wives are expected to be treated with respect and kindness. A woman's status in Iran is typically defined by her relationship to a male relative, usually as a wife or daughter. In many patriarchal societies women find it more difficult to obtain a divorce than a man does (G. Farr 1999). By contrast, in a **matriarchy**, women have greater authority than men. Matriarchies, which are very uncommon, emerged among Native American tribal societies and in nations in which men were absent for long periods of time for warfare or food gathering.

A third type of authority pattern, the **egalitarian family**, is one in which spouses are regarded as equals. This does not mean, however, that each decision is shared in such families. Wives may hold authority in some spheres, husbands in others. Many sociologists believe the egalitarian family has begun to replace the patriarchal family as the social norm in the United States.

Studying the Family

Do we really need the family? A century ago, Friedrich Engels (1884), a colleague of Karl Marx, described the family as the ultimate source of social inequality because of its role in the transfer of power, property, and privilege. More recently, conflict theorists have argued that the family contributes to societal injustice, denies opportunities to women that are extended to men, and limits freedom in sexual expression and selection of a mate. By contrast, the functionalist perspective focuses on the ways in which the family gratifies the needs of its members and contributes to the stability of society. The interactionist view considers more intimate, face-to-face relationships.

Functionalist View

There are six paramount functions performed by the family, first outlined more than 60 years ago by sociologist William F. Ogburn (Ogburn and Tibbits 1934):

1. **Reproduction.** For a society to maintain itself, it must replace dying members. In this sense, the family contributes to human survival through its function of reproduction.
2. **Protection.** Unlike the young of other animal species, human infants need constant care and economic security. The extremely long period of dependency for children places special demands on older family members. In all cultures, it is the family that assumes ultimate responsibility for the protection and upbringing of children.

Smile—it's family reunion time! The state of being related to others is called kinship. Kin groups include aunts, uncles, cousins, and so forth, as shown in this family from Slovakia.

3. **Socialization.** Parents and other kin monitor a child's behavior and transmit the norms, values, and language of a culture to the child (see Chapters 3 and 4).

p. 101 ◀

4. **Regulation of sexual behavior.** Sexual norms are subject to change over time (for instance, changes in customs for dating) and across cultures (Islamic Saudi Arabia compared with more permissive Denmark). However, whatever the time period or cultural values in a society, standards of sexual behavior are most clearly defined within the family circle. The structure of society influences these standards. In male-dominated societies, for example, formal and informal norms generally permit men to express and enjoy their sexual desires more freely than women may.

5. **Affection and companionship.** Ideally, the family provides members with warm and intimate relationships and helps them feel satisfied and secure. Of course, a family member may find such rewards outside the family—from peers, in school, at work—and may perceive the home as an unpleasant place. Nevertheless, unlike other institutions, the family is obligated to serve the emotional needs of its members. We expect our relatives to understand us, to care for us, and to be there for us when we need them.

6. **Providing of social status.** We inherit a social position because of the "family background" and reputation of our parents and siblings. The family unit presents the newborn child with an ascribed status of race and ethnicity that helps to determine his or her place within a society's stratification system. Moreover, family resources affect children's ability to pursue certain opportunities such as higher education and specialized lessons.

The family has traditionally fulfilled a number of other functions, such as providing religious training, education, and recreational outlets. Ogburn argued that other social institutions have gradually assumed many of these functions. Although the family once played a major role in religious life—with the reading of the Bible and the singing of hymns commonly taking place at home—this function has largely shifted to churches, synagogues, and other religious organizations. Similarly, education once took place at the family fireside; now it is the responsibility of professionals working in schools and colleges. Even the family's traditional recreational function has been transferred to outside groups such as Little Leagues, athletic clubs, and Internet chat rooms.

Conflict View

Conflict theorists view the family not as a contributor to social stability, but as a reflection of the inequality in wealth and power found within the larger society. Feminist theorists and conflict theorists note that the family has traditionally legitimized and perpetuated male dominance. Throughout most of human history—and in a very wide range of societies—husbands have exercised overwhelming power and authority within the family. Indeed, not until the "first wave" of contemporary feminism in the United States in the mid-1800s was there a substantial challenge to the historic status of wives and children as the legal property of husbands.

p. 17 ◀

While the egalitarian family has become a more common pattern in the United States in recent decades—owing in good part to the activism of feminists beginning in the late 1960s and early 1970s—male dominance within the family has hardly disappeared. Sociologists have found that women are significantly more likely to leave their jobs when their husbands find better employment opportunities than men

We inherit our social status from our family. It is not hard to guess that this young man has a big step up the social and economic ladder compared with a child from a disadvantaged family.

Sociology in the Global Community

13-2 Domestic Violence

www.mhhe.com/schaefer

"It's the same every Saturday night. The husband comes home drunk and beats her." This is how Tania Kucherenko describes her downstairs neighbors in Moscow after turning a deaf ear to the screams of terror and the sounds of furniture being overthrown and glass breaking. "There's nothing we can do. It's best not to interfere." Contempt for women runs deep in Russia, where women who dare to leave their husbands risk losing their legal status, a place to live, and the right to work (Bennett 1997:A1).

Wife battering, child abuse, abuse of the elderly, and other forms of domestic violence are an ugly reality of family life across the world. In Japan, Tanzania, and Chile, more than half the women report physical abuse by a partner. While estimates are difficult to find on a topic so hidden from public view, an estimate in 2000 concluded that around the world one-third of all women have been beaten, or coerced into sex, or otherwise physically abused in their lifetime.

Drawing on studies conducted throughout the world, we can make the following generalizations:

- Women are most at risk of violence from the men they know.
- Violence against women is evident in all socioeconomic groups.
- Family violence is at least as dangerous as assaults committed by strangers.
- Though women sometimes exhibit violent behavior toward men, most acts of violence that cause injury are perpetrated by men against women.
- Violence within intimate relationships tends to escalate over time.

This billboard in Poland reads, "Because he had to let off steam." It is a reminder to Poles that domestic violence is a serious problem in their country, affecting both wives and children.

- Emotional and psychological abuse can be at least as debilitating as physical abuse.
- Use of alcohol exacerbates family violence but does not cause it.

Using the conflict and feminist models, researchers have found that in relationships where the inequality is greater between men and women, the likelihood of assault on

> The situation of battered women is so intolerable that it has been compared to that of prison inmates.

wives increases dramatically. This suggests that much of the violence between intimates, even when sexual in nature, is about power rather than sex.

The situation of battered women is so intolerable that it has been compared to that of prison inmates. Criminologist Noga Avni (1991) interviewed battered women at a shelter in Israel and found that their day-to-day lives with their husbands or lovers shared many elements of life in an oppres-

sive total institution, as described by Erving Goffman (1961). Physical barriers are imposed on these women; by threatening further violence, men are able to restrict women to their homes, damaging both their self-esteem and their ability to cope with repeated abuse. Moreover, as in a total institution, battered women are cut off **p. 100** ← from external sources of physical and emotional assistance and moral support. In Avni's view, society could more effectively aid victims of domestic violence if it better understood the essential imprisonment of these women. Women in these situations have few economic alternatives, and they fear that their children may also be victimized if they don't submit to the abuse.

The family can be a dangerous place not only for women but also for children and the elderly. In 1996, public agencies received more than three million reports of child abuse and/or neglect. That means reports were filed on about 1 out of every 25 children. Another national study found that approximately 450,000 elderly persons, or 1 in every 90, were abused or neglected in that same year.

Let's Discuss

1. How does the degree of equality in a relationship correlate to the likelihood of domestic violence? How might conflict theorists explain this?
2. Do you know of a family that experienced domestic violence? Did the victim(s) seek outside help, and was that help effective?

Sources: American Bar Association 1999; American Humane Association 1999; Gelles and Cornell 1990; Heise et al. 1999; National Center on Elder Abuse 1998; Straus 1994.

are when their wives receive desirable job offers (Bielby and Bielby 1992). And unfortunately, many husbands reinforce their power and control over wives and children through acts of domestic violence. (Box 13-2 considers cross-cultural findings about violence within the home.)

Conflict theorists also view the family as an economic

349

unit that contributes to societal injustice. The family is the basis for transferring power, property, and privilege from one generation to the next. The United States is widely viewed as a "land of opportunity," yet social mobility is restricted in important ways. Children "inherit" the privileged or less-than-privileged social and economic status of their parents (and, in some cases, of earlier generations as well). As conflict theorists point out, the social class of their parents significantly influences children's socialization experiences and the protection they receive. This means that the socioeconomic status of a child's family will have a marked influence on his or her nutrition, health care, housing, educational opportunities, and, in many respects, life chances as an adult. For that reason, conflict theorists argue that the family helps to maintain inequality.

p. 220

Interactionist View

Interactionists focus on the microlevel of family and other intimate relationships. They are interested in how individuals interact with one another, whether they are cohabiting partners or long-time married couples. For example, a study of both Black and White two-parent households found that when fathers are more involved with their children (such as reading, helping with homework, restricting television viewing) children have fewer behavior problems, get along better with others, and are more responsible (Mosley and Thompson 1995).

Another interactionist study might examine the role of the stepparent. The increased number of single parents who remarry has sparked an interest in those who are helping to raise other people's children. While no young girl or boy may dream about one day becoming a stepmom or stepdad, this is hardly an unusual occurrence today. Studies have found that stepmothers are more likely to accept the blame for bad relations with their stepchildren, whereas stepfathers are less likely to accept responsibility. Interactionists theorize that stepfathers (like most fathers) may simply be unaccustomed to interaction directly with children when the mother isn't there (Bray and Kelly 1999; Furstenberg and Cherlin 1991).

Marriage and Family

Currently, close to 90 percent of all men and women in the United States marry at least once during their lifetimes. Historically, the most consistent aspect of family life in this country has been the high rate of marriage. In fact, despite the high rate of divorce, there are indications of a miniboom in marriages in the United States of late, fueled by a strong economy and a return to traditional values (Parker 1998).

When fathers interact regularly with their children, it's a win/win situation. The fathers get close to their offspring, and studies show that the children end up with fewer behavior problems.

In this part of the chapter, we will examine various aspects of love, marriage, and parenthood in the United States and contrast them with cross-cultural examples. We're used to thinking of romance and mate selection as strictly a matter of individual preference. Yet, sociological analysis tells us that social institutions and distinctive cultural norms and values also play an important role.

Courtship and Mate Selection

"My rugby mates would roll over in their graves," says Tom Buckley of his online courtship and subsequent marriage to Terri Muir. But Tom and Terri are hardly alone these days in turning to the Internet for matchmaking services. By the end of 1999 more than 2,500 websites were helping people find mates. You could choose from oneandonly.com or 2ofakind.com or cupidnet.com, among others. One service alone claims 2 million subscribers. Tom and Terri carried on their romance via

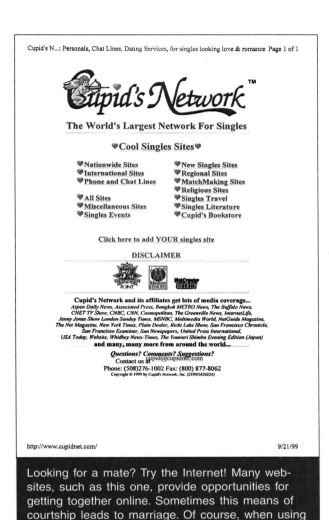

Looking for a mate? Try the Internet! Many websites, such as this one, provide opportunities for getting together online. Sometimes this means of courtship leads to marriage. Of course, when using the Internet to meet people it is always wise to proceed cautiously.

e-mail for a year before they met. According to Tom, "E-mail made it easier to communicate because neither one of us was the type to walk up to someone in the gym or a bar and say, 'You're the fuel to my fire' " (B. Morris 1999:D1).

Internet romance is only the latest courtship practice. In the central Asian nation of Uzbekistan and other traditional cultures that favor arranged marriages, courtship is defined largely through the interaction of two sets of parents. They arrange spouses for their children. Typically, a young Uzbekistani woman will be socialized to eagerly anticipate her marriage to a man whom she has met only once, when he is presented to her family at the time of the final inspection of her dowry. In the United States, by contrast, courtship is conducted primarily by individuals who may have a romantic interest in each other. In our culture, courtship often requires these individuals to rely heavily on intricate games, gestures, and signals. Despite such differences, courtship—whether in the United States, Uzbekistan, or elsewhere—is influenced by the norms and values of the larger society (C. J. Williams 1995).

Take our choice of a mate. Why are we drawn to a particular person in the first place? To what extent are these judgments shaped by the society around us?

Aspects of Mate Selection

Many societies have explicit or unstated rules that define potential mates as acceptable or unacceptable. These norms can be distinguished in terms of endogamy and exogamy. **Endogamy** (from the Greek *endon*, "within") specifies the groups within which a spouse must be found and prohibits marriage with others. For example, in the United States, many people are expected to marry within their own racial, ethnic, or religious group and are strongly discouraged or even prohibited from marrying outside the group. Endogamy is intended to reinforce the cohesiveness of the group by suggesting to the young that they should marry someone "of our own kind."

By contrast, **exogamy** (from the Greek *exo*, "outside") requires mate selection outside certain groups, usually one's own family or certain kinfolk. The **incest taboo**, a social norm common to virtually all societies, prohibits sexual relationships between certain culturally specified relatives. For people in the United States, this taboo means that we must marry outside the nuclear family. We cannot marry our siblings, and in most states we cannot marry our first cousins.

Endogamous restrictions may be seen as preferences for one group over another. In the United States, such preferences are most obvious in racial barriers. Until the 1960s, some states outlawed interracial marriages. This practice was challenged by Richard Loving (a White man) and Mildred Jeter Loving (a part-Black, part–Native American woman), who married in 1958. Eventually, in 1967, the Supreme Court ruled that it was unconstitutional to prohibit marriage solely on the basis of race. The decision struck down statutes in Virginia and 16 other states.

The number of marriages between African Americans and Whites in the United States has increased by more than six times in recent decades, jumping from 51,000 in 1960 to 330,000 in 1998. Moreover, 25 percent of married Asian American women and 12 percent of married Asian American men are married to a person who is not of Asian descent. Marriage across ethnic lines is even greater among Hispanics; 28 percent of all married Hispanics have a non-Hispanic spouse. While all these examples of exogamy are impressive, endogamy is still the social norm in the United States (Bureau of the Census 1998a, 1999a:58).

Survey data show that some Whites still oppose interracial marriages. According to the 1998 General Social Survey, 13 percent of Whites favor a law against racial intermarriage. By contrast, only 4 percent of Blacks felt the same way (Davis and Smith 1999).

Interracial unions force a society to reconsider its definitions of race and ethnicity. In Chapter 10, p. 259 we noted that race is socially constructed in the United States and around the world. As increasing proportions of children in this country come from biracial or multiracial backgrounds, traditional definitions of race and ethnicity will no longer be as relevant. As we saw in Chapter 10, the sensitive issue of racial labels became a legislative concern in the mid-1990s, when the Bureau of the Census considered how to ask people about their racial backgrounds in the 2000 census. Several voluntary associations representing mixed-race children requested that the census offer a new category of "multiracial" or "biracial" so that they would no longer be forced to define themselves as solely "White," "Black," "Asian," or "American Indian." In the end it was decided to let people check off several categories they felt applied to them but not to provide the "multiracial" or "biracial" classification (R. Schaefer 2000).

The Love Relationship

Whatever else "love" is, most people would agree it is complicated. Listen to what a Yale University junior has to say on the subject:

Love isn't in the air these days, at least not in New Haven . . . my peers and I find ourselves in a new world of romance, and we're feeling a little out of our league. We are children of the Age of Divorce, born into the AIDS crisis, reared on Madonna, *Friends,* and *Beverly Hills 90210.* No wonder we're confused. We know we want this thing called love. More than previous generations, though, we're unsure of what love is and how to get it—and we're not so sure that finding it will be worth the trouble (Rodberg 1999:1–2).

Another student claims that "love, like everything else, must be pondered, and we have too many other things to ponder—no matter how much we profess to want love" (quoted in Rodberg 1999:4).

For a variety of reasons, hinted at in these quotations, this generation of college students seems more likely to "hook up" or cruise in large packs than engage in the romantic dating relationships of their parents and grandparents. Still, at some point in their adult lives the great majority of today's students will meet someone they "love" and enter into a long-term relationship that focuses on creating a family.

In the United States, love is important in the courtship process. Living in their own home makes the affectional bond between husband and wife especially important. The couple is expected to develop its own emotional ties, free of the demands of other household members for affection. Sociologist William Goode (1959) observed that spouses in a nuclear family have to rely heavily on each other for the companionship and support that might be provided by other relatives in an extended-family situation.

Parents in the United States tend to value love highly as a rationale for marriage, and they encourage their children to develop intimate relationships based on love and affection. In addition, songs, films, books, magazines, television shows, and even cartoons and comic books reinforce the theme of love. At the same time, our society expects parents and peers to help a person confine his or her search for a mate to "socially acceptable" members of the opposite sex.

Traditional gender-role socialization has made it easier for women to express love and other feelings of social intimacy than it is for men. The qualities identified with intimacy—emotional warmth, expressiveness, vulnera-

Interracial unions, which are becoming increasingly common and accepted, are blurring definitions of race. Would the children of this interracial couple be considered Black or White?

bility, and sensitivity—are associated with the female but not the male gender role. Studies show that men are more likely than women to base their perceptions of love and intimacy on sex, on providing practical help, and on simply being in the presence of a loved one (Cancian 1986; L. Thompson and Walker 1989).

Most people in the United States may take the importance of falling in love for granted, but love-and-marriage is by no means a cultural universal. In fact, in many cultures (both today and in the past) love and marriage are unconnected and are sometimes at odds with one another. For example, feelings of love are not a prerequisite for marriage among the Yaruros of inland Venezuela or in other cultures where there is little freedom for mate selection. The Yaruro male of marriageable age doesn't engage in the kind of dating behavior so typical of young people in the United States. Rather, he knows that, under the traditions of his culture, he must marry one of his mother's brothers' daughters or one of his father's sisters' daughters. The young man's choice is further limited because one of his uncles selects the eligible cousin that he must marry (Freeman 1958; Lindholm 1999).

Many of the world's cultures give priority in mate selection to factors other than romantic feelings. In societies with *arranged marriages,* often engineered by parents or religious authorities, economic considerations play a significant role. The newly married couple is expected to develop a feeling of love *after* the legal union is formalized, if at all.

Even within the United States, some subcultures carry on the arranged marriage practices of their native cultures. Young people among the Sikhs and Hindus who have immigrated from India and among Islamic Muslims and Hasidic Jews allow their parents or designated matchmakers to find spouses within their ethnic community. As one young Sikh declared, "I will definitely marry who my parents wish. They know me better than I know myself" (Segall 1998:48). Young people who have emigrated without their families often turn to the Internet to find partners who share their background and goals. Matrimonial ads for the Indian community run on such websites as SuitableMatch.com and INDOLINK.com. Speaking of arranged marriages, one Hasidic Jewish woman noted that "the system isn't perfect, and it doesn't work for everyone, but this is the system we know and trust, the way we couple, and the way we learn to love. So it works for most of us" (p. 53).

Variations in Family Life and Intimate Relationships

Within the United States, social class, race, and ethnicity create variations in family life. Understanding these variations will give us a more sophisticated understanding of contemporary family styles in our country.

Social Class Differences

Various studies have documented the differences in family organization among social classes in the United States. The upper class emphasis lineage and maintenance of family position. If you are in the upper class, you are not simply a member of a nuclear family but rather a member of a larger family tradition (think of "the Rockefellers" or "the Kennedys"). As a result, upper-class families are quite concerned about what they see as "proper training" for children.

Lower-class families do not often have the luxury of worrying about the "family name"; they must first struggle to pay their bills and survive the crises often associated with life in poverty. Such families are more likely to have only one parent in the home, creating special challenges in child care and financial needs. Children in lower-class families typically assume adult responsibilities—including marriage and parenthood—at an earlier age than children of affluent homes. In part, this is because they may lack the money needed to remain in school.

Social class differences in family life are less striking than they once were. In the past, family specialists agreed that there were pronounced contrasts in child-rearing practices. Lower-class families were found to be more authoritarian in rearing children and more inclined to use physical punishment. Middle-class families were more permissive and more restrained in punishing their children. However, these differences may have narrowed as more and more families from all social classes have turned to the same books, magazines, and even television talk shows for advice on rearing children (M. Kohn 1970; Luster et al. 1989).

Among the poor, women often play a significant role in the economic support of the family. Men may earn low wages, may be unemployed, or may be entirely absent from the family. In 1997, 31.6 percent of all families headed by women with no husband present were below the government poverty line. This compared with only 5.2 percent for married couples (Dalaker and Naifeh 1998:vii).

Many racial and ethnic groups appear to have distinctive family characteristics. However, racial and class factors are often closely related. In examining family life among racial and ethnic minorities, keep in mind that certain patterns may result from class as well as cultural factors.

Racial and Ethnic Differences

The subordinate status of racial and ethnic minorities in the United States profoundly affects their family life. For example, the lower incomes of African Americans, Native Americans (or American Indians), most Hispanic groups, and selected Asian American groups take a toll on creating and maintaining successful marital unions. The economic restructuring of the last 50 years described by sociologist William Julius Wilson (1996) and others has especially affected people living in inner cities and p. 216 ◄

desolate rural areas such as reservations. Further, the immigration policy of the United States has complicated the successful relocation of intact families from Asia and Latin America (Doob 1999).

Political leaders and the media have tended not only to emphasize the problems of minority families but to "blame the victims," thereby ignoring the impact of generations of prejudice and discrimination. For example, in the aftermath of the 1992 race riots in Los Angeles, instead of focusing on structural sources of unrest such as the declining employment opportunities in central-city neighborhoods, the lack of available health care, and the rise of organized gang activity, Vice President Dan Quayle pointed to the breakdown of family values, especially among African Americans (as evidenced by the absence of adult males in many Black families). He criticized the media for presenting a positive portrayal of a television character (Murphy Brown) who chose to have a child while remaining unmarried. Quayle's message was clear: The cause of the riots was within Los Angeles, and its Black and Hispanic residents were at fault (R. Schaefer 2000).

The African American family suffers from many negative and inaccurate stereotypes. It is true that a significantly higher proportion of Black than White families have no husband present in the home (see Figure 13-3). Yet Black single mothers are often part of stable, functioning kin networks, despite the pressures of sexism and racism. Members of these networks—predominantly female kin such as mothers, grandmothers, and aunts—ease financial strains by sharing goods and services. In addition to these strong kinship bonds, Black family life has emphasized deep religious commitment and high aspirations for achievement. The strengths of the Black family were evident during slavery, when Blacks demonstrated a remarkable ability to maintain family ties despite the fact that they enjoyed no legal protections and, in fact, were often forced to separate (Morehouse Research Institute and Institute for American Values 1999).

Sociologists have also taken note of differences in family patterns among other racial and ethnic groups. For example, Mexican American men have been described as exhibiting a sense of virility, of personal worth, and of pride in their maleness that is called **machismo.** Mexican Americans are also described as being more familistic than many other subcultures. **Familism** refers to pride in the extended family, expressed through the maintenance of close ties and strong obligations to kinfolk outside the immediate family. However, these family patterns are changing in response to changes in the social class standing, educational achievements, and occupations held by Mexican Americans. As Mexican Americans and other groups assimilate into the dominant culture of the United

FIGURE 13-3

One-Parent Families among Whites, African Americans, Hispanics, and Asians or Pacific Islanders in the United States

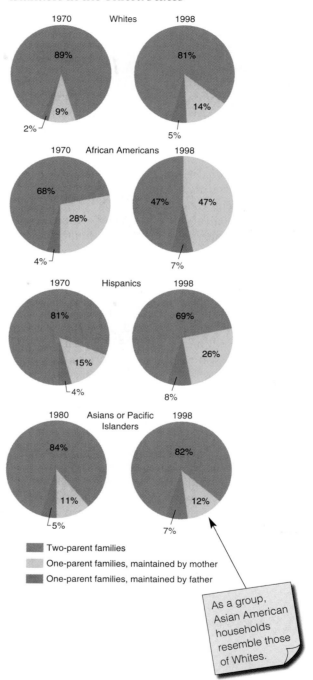

Two-parent families
One-parent families, maintained by mother
One-parent families, maintained by father

As a group, Asian American households resemble those of Whites.

Note: "Children" refers to children under 18. Not included are unrelated people living together with no children present. Early data for Asian Americans are for 1980. Because of rounding numbers may not total 100 percent.

Source: Bureau of the Census 1994:63; 1999a:63.

Korean family ties often provide a huge economic boost. Not only do family members work together in family businesses such as the husband and wife pictured here; they also contribute financial resources through a rotating credit association known as a kye.

States, their family lives take on some of the positive and negative aspects associated with White households (Becerra 1999; Vega 1995).

Distinctive family patterns are also evident among the more than two million Greek Americans—especially those who have migrated to the United States in recent years. Generally, Greek families have left agricultural areas in their homelands to settle in urban centers where there is already a Greek American community. This community typically centers on a Greek Orthodox church that helps to maintain the traditional old world culture. Gender roles are sharply defined within a patriarchal and close-knit community. Even as adolescents, young Greek Americans are closely watched by parents, who play an active role in mate selection. However, as assimilation proceeds among second- or third-generation Greek Americans, these distinctive family dynamics begin to fade (G. Kourvetaris 1999; Pula 1995).

Within a racial or ethnic minority, family ties can serve as an economic boost. For example, Korean immigrants to the United States generally begin small service or retail businesses involving all adult family members. To obtain the funds needed to begin a business, they often pool their resources through a kye (pronounced KAY)—an association (not limited to kinfolk) that grants money to members on a rotating basis so they can gain access to even more additional capital. The kye

allows Korean Americans to start small businesses long before other minorities in similar economic circumstances. Such rotating credit associations are not unique to Korean Americans; other Asian Americans as well as West Indians living in the United States also have used them (H. Lee 1999).

Child-Rearing Patterns in Family Life

The Nayars of southern India acknowledge the biological role of fathers, but the mother's eldest brother is responsible for her children (Gough 1974). By contrast, uncles play only a peripheral role in child care in the United States. Caring for children is a universal function of the family, yet the ways in which different societies assign this function to family members can vary significantly. Even within the United States, child-rearing patterns are varied. We'll take a look here at parenthood and grandparenthood, adoption, dual-income families, single-parent families, and stepfamilies. (See Figure 13-4 for an idea of how children in the United States are distributed by type of family.)

FIGURE 13-4

Living Arrangements of Children in the United States by Type of Family, 1998

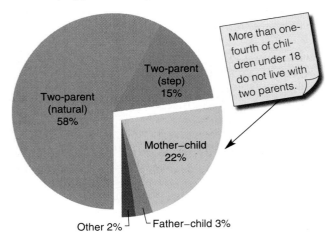

More than one-fourth of children under 18 do not live with two parents.

Two-parent (natural) 58%

Two-parent (step) 15%

Mother–child 22%

Other 2%

Father–child 3%

Source: Bureau of the Census 1998d.

Parenthood and Grandparenthood

The socialization of children is essential to the maintenance of any culture. Consequently, parenthood is one of the most important (and most p. 101 demanding) social roles in the United States. Sociologist Alice Rossi (1968, 1984) has identified four factors that complicate the transition to parenthood and the role of socialization. First, there is little anticipatory socialization for the social role of caregiver. The normal school curriculum gives scant attention to the subjects most relevant to successful family life—such as child care and home maintenance. Second, only limited learning occurs during the period of pregnancy itself. Third, the transition to parenthood is quite abrupt. Unlike adolescence, it is not prolonged; unlike socialization for work, you cannot gradually take on the duties of caregiving. Finally, in Rossi's view, our society lacks clear and helpful guidelines for successful parenthood. There is little consensus on how parents can produce happy and well-adjusted offspring—or even on what it means to be "well-adjusted." For these reasons, socialization for parenthood involves difficult challenges for most men and women in the United States.

One recent development in family life in the United States has been the extension of parenthood, as adult children continue to (or return to) live at home. In 1995, more than half of all children ages 18 to 24 and one out of eight of those ages 25 to 34 lived with their parents. Some of these adult children are still pursuing an education, but in many instances, financial difficulties are at the heart of these living arrangements. While rents and real estate prices skyrocketed in the 1990s, salaries for younger workers did not keep pace, and many found themselves unable to afford their own homes. Moreover, with many marriages now ending in divorce—most commonly in the first seven years of marriage—divorced sons and daughters are returning to live with their parents, sometimes with their own children (Bureau of the Census 1997a:58).

Is this living arrangement a positive development for family members? Social scientists have just begun to examine this phenomenon, sometimes called the "boomerang generation" or the "full-nest syndrome" in the popular press. One survey in Virginia seemed to show

Even though parenthood is a crucial social role, society generally provides few clear guidelines for successful parenting. Shown here are some successes: a mother from the United States with her children and a family boating on a river in India.

that neither the parents nor their adult children were happy about continuing to live together. The children often felt resentful and isolated, but the parents also suffered: Learning to live without children in the home is an essential stage of adult life and may even be a significant turning point for a marriage (Berkeley Wellness Letter 1990; Mogelonsky 1996).

As life expectancy increases in the United States, more and more parents are becoming grandparents and even great-grandparents. After interviewing many grandparents, sociologists Andrew Cherlin and Frank Furstenberg Jr. (1992) identified three principal styles of grandparenting:

1. More than half (55 percent) of grandparents surveyed functioned as "specialists in recreational care-giving." They enriched their grandchildren's lives through recreational outings and other special activities.
2. More than one-fourth (29 percent) carried on a "ritualistic" (primarily symbolic) relationship with their grandchildren. In some instances, this was because the grandparents lived far away from their grandchildren and could see them only occasionally.
3. About one-sixth (16 percent) of grandparents surveyed were actively involved in everyday routine care of their grandchildren and exercised substantial authority over them.

Later in this chapter, we will look further at the increasing number of households where children are raised by a grandparent.

Adoption

In a legal sense, **adoption** is a "process that allows for the transfer of the legal rights, responsibilities, and privileges of parenthood" to a new legal parent or parents (E. Cole 1985:638). In many cases, these rights are transferred from a biological parent or parents (often called birth parents) to an adoptive parent or parents.

Viewed from a functionalist perspective, government has a strong interest in encouraging adoption. Policymakers, in fact, have both a humanitarian and a financial stake in the process. In theory, adoption offers a stable family environment for children who otherwise might not receive satisfactory care. Moreover, government data show that unwed mothers who keep their babies tend to be of lower socioeconomic status and often require public assistance to support their children. Government can lower its social welfare expenses if children are transferred to economically self-sufficient families. From a conflict perspective, however, such financial considerations raise the ugly specter of adoption's serving as a means whereby af-

fluent (often infertile) couples "buy" the children of the poor (C. Bachrach 1986).

The largest single category of adoption in the United States is adoption by relatives. In most cases, a stepparent adopts the children of a spouse. There are two legal methods of adopting an unrelated person: adoptions arranged by licensed agencies and private agreements sanctioned by the courts (M. Groves 1999).

In some cases the adopters are not married. An important court decision in 1995 in New York held that a couple does not have to be married to adopt a child. Under this ruling, unmarried heterosexual couples, lesbian couples, and gay male couples can all legally adopt children in New York. Writing for the majority, Chief Justice Judith Kaye argued that by expanding the boundaries of who can be legally recognized as parents, the state may be able to assist more children in securing "the best possible home." With this ruling, New York became the third state (after Vermont and Massachusetts) to recognize the right of unmarried couples to adopt children (Dao 1995).

Dual-Income Families

The idea of a family consisting of a wage-earning husband and a wife who stays at home has largely given way to the *dual-income household*. Among married people between the ages of 25 and 34, 96 percent of the men and 72 percent of the women are in the labor force. Why has there been such a rise in the number of dual-income couples? A major factor is economic need. In 1997, the median income for households with both partners employed was 80 percent more than in households in which only one person was working outside the home ($54,192, compared with $29,780). Of course, not all of a family's second wage is genuine additional income because of such work-related costs as child care. Other factors contributing to the rise of the dual-income model include the nation's declining birthrate (see Chapter 18), the increase in the proportion of women with a college education, the shift in the economy of the United States from manufacturing to service industries, and the impact of the feminist movement in changing women's consciousness (Bureau of the Census 1998e:5; 1999a:416).

Dual-income families raise issues about quality of life—marital relationships, child care, and standard of living. Television programming hasn't aided the process. As we saw in Box 13-1, real-life work–family conflicts are rarely portrayed. Sociologist Arlie Hochschild (1989, 1990) has used the phrase "second shift" to describe the double burden—work outside the home followed by child care and housework—that many women carry and few men share equitably. More recently, Hochschild has referred to the failure of corporate and p. 304

Dad takes breakfast duty while Mom rushes off to work in this "dual-income" family. An increasing proportion of couples in the United States reject the traditional nuclear family model of husband as breadwinner and wife as homemaker.

public policies to ease the work–family dilemma as the "stalled revolution." As noted in the social policy section of Chapter 4, there is still not enough quality day care available.

p. 111

Single-Parent Families

In the United States of the late nineteenth century, immigration and urbanization made it increasingly difficult to maintain *Gemeinschaft* communities where everyone knew one another and shared responsibility for unwed mothers and their children. In 1883, the Florence Crittenton Houses were founded in New York City—and subsequently established around the nation—as refuges for prostitutes (then stigmatized as "fallen women"). Within a few years, the Crittenton homes began accepting unwed mothers as residents. By the early 1900s, sociologist W. E. B. Du Bois (1911) had noted that the institutionalization of unwed mothers was occurring in segregated facilities. At the time that he was writing, there were seven homes of various types nationwide for unwed Black mothers as well as one Crittenton home reserved for that purpose.

In recent decades, the stigma attached to "unwed mothers" and other single parents has significantly diminished. *Single-parent families,* in which there is only one parent present to care for the children, can hardly be viewed as a rarity in the United States. In 1998, a single parent headed about 19 percent of White families with children under 18, 31 percent of Hispanic families with children, and 54 percent of African American families with children (Bureau of the Census 1999a:62).

The lives of single parents and their children are not inevitably more difficult than life in a traditional nuclear family. It is as inaccurate to assume that a single-parent family is necessarily "deprived" as it is to assume that a two-parent family is always secure and happy. Nevertheless, life in a single-parent family can be extremely stressful, in both economic and emotional terms.

A family headed by a single mother faces especially difficult problems when the mother is a teenager. Even though teenage pregnancy rates declined during the 1990s, teenagers in the United States still become pregnant, give birth, and have abortions at much higher rates than adolescents in almost any other industrialized nation. Many adults with traditional attitudes toward sexuality and family life have suspected that the availability of birth control and sex education in the United States and other developed countries leads to increases in pregnancy among teenagers. However, researchers point out that the lowest rates of pregnancy among teenagers are found in countries with liberal attitudes toward sex, easily accessible birth control services for young people, and comprehensive sex education programs (Bruce et al. 1995; Bureau of the Census 1998c; F. Furstenberg et al. 1999; Ventura et al. 1999).

Why do teenagers in the United States get pregnant so often? Drawing on two decades of social science research, sociologist Kristin Luker (1996:11) observes:

The short answer to why teenagers get pregnant and especially to why they continue those pregnancies is that a fairly substantial number of them just don't believe what adults tell them, be it about sex, contraception, marriage, or babies. They don't believe in adult conventional wisdom.

Why might low-income teenage women wish to have children and face the obvious financial difficulties of motherhood? Viewed from an interactionist perspective, these women tend to have low self-esteem and limited options; a child may provide a sense of motivation and purpose for a teenager whose economic worth in our society is limited at best. Given the barriers that many young women face

Taking Sociology to Work

BARBARA CORRY::
Founder of Peace Offerings

www.mhhe.com/schaefer

Barbara Corry's own exposure to domestic violence when she was a child led her to found Peace Offerings, a California-based organization that Barbara describes as "dedicated to ending domestic violence through education." She deals with recovery issues for all members of the family—the women, the batterers, and the children living in the home. The pamphlets that she writes are used by shelters, social service agencies, and churches throughout the country. In order to launch Peace Offerings, Corry had to stretch herself in entrepreneurial ways, learning how to fundraise, set up a website, and recruit and train volunteers.

Corry's minor in sociology as an undergraduate student at DePaul University gave her an overview of the field. It helped her refine where her interests lay. "I chose to do a master's program in sociology that was applied work, not just ivory tower theorizing. The program addressed social problems from the perspective of finding solutions." She studied domestic violence through various courses in criminology, social problems, deviance, and gender.

Sociology gives her an understanding of the social problems within a society, a community, a family. "Sociologists are able to see between the cracks. They are able to understand why some families don't work as they should." For example, some children who grow up in violent homes go on to batter later in life because they have learned inequality and violence as a way to interact in a family. "My coursework also taught me what was going on in my own life," she says.

Her advice for sociology students: "Be creative with your job options. Take a topic that you are interested in and be entrepreneurial. You can develop a good expertise with marketable skills that are sociologically grounded."

---

because of their gender, race, ethnicity, and class, many teenagers may believe that they have little to lose and much to gain by having a child.

According to a widely held stereotype, "unwed mothers" and "babies having babies" in the United States are predominantly African American. However, this view is not entirely accurate. While African Americans account for a disproportionate share of births to unmarried women and to teenagers, the majority of all babies born to unmarried teenage mothers are born to White adolescents. Moreover, since 1990, birthrates among Black teenagers have declined more than any other group (Ventura et al. 1998a).

While 76 percent of single parents in the United States are mothers, the number of households headed by single fathers has more than quadrupled over the period 1980 to 1998. The stereotypes of single fathers are that they raise only boys or older children. In fact, about 44 percent of children living in such households are girls; almost one-third of single fathers care for preschoolers. Whereas single mothers often develop social networks, single fathers are typically more isolated. In addition, they must deal with schools and social service agencies more accustomed to women as custodial parents (Bureau of the Census 1999a:62; D. Johnson 1993).

What about single fathers who do not head the household? This is typically an understudied group for sociological purposes, but a study of low-income unmarried fathers in Philadelphia came up with some unexpected findings. When asked what their lives would be like without having children, they responded that they would be dead or in jail. This was true even of those fathers who had very little to do with their children. Apparently, the mere fact of fathering children prompts men to get jobs, stay in the community, and stay healthy. Many of these men were upset that they have to hand over money without having a say in how it is spent or in some cases even having legal access to their offspring (P. Cohen 1998).

Stepfamilies

Approximately one-third of all people in the United States will marry, divorce, and then remarry. The rising rates of divorce and remarriage have led to a noticeable increase in stepfamily relationships. In 1980, 9 percent of all family households with children present included a stepparent; by 1990, that figure had almost tripled to 24 percent (Bureau of the Census 1995a:64; Cherlin and Furstenberg 1994).

Stepfamilies are an exceedingly complex form of family organization. Here is how one 13-year-old boy described his family.

Tim and Janet are my stepbrother and sister. Josh is my stepdad. Carin and Don are my real parents, who are divorced. And Don married Anna and together they had Ethan and Ellen, my half-sister and brother. And Carin married Josh and had little Alice, my half-sister (Bernstein 1988).

Most households in the United States do not consist of two parents living with their unmarried children.

The exact nature of these blended families has social significance for adults and children alike. Certainly resocialization is required when an adult becomes a stepparent or a child becomes a stepchild and stepsibling. Moreover, an important distinction must be made between first-time stepfamilies and households where there have been repeated divorces, breakups, or changes in custodial arrangements.

In evaluating the rise of stepfamilies, some observers have assumed that children would benefit from remarriage because they would be gaining a second custodial parent and potentially would enjoy greater economic security. However, after reviewing many studies on stepfamilies, sociologist Andrew Cherlin (1999:421) concluded that "the well-being of children in stepfamily households is no better, on average, than the well-being of children in divorced, single-parent households." Stepparents can play valuable and unique roles in their stepchildren's lives, but their involvement does not guarantee an improvement.

● Divorce

"Do you promise to love, honor, and cherish . . . until death do you part?" Every year, people of all social classes and racial and ethnic groups make this legally binding agreement. Yet an increasing number of these promises shatter in divorce. While rates may vary among states, divorce is a nationwide phenomenon, as Figure 13-5 shows.

Statistical Trends in Divorce

Just how common is divorce? Surprisingly, this is not a simple question; divorce statistics are difficult to interpret.

The media frequently report that one out of every two marriages ends in divorce. But this figure is misleading, since many marriages last for decades. It is based on a comparison of all divorces that occur in a single year (regardless of when the couples were married) against the number of new marriages in the same year. As the second column of Table 13-1 indicates, there were about 51 divorces in the United States in 1999 for every 100 new marriages. But that could, in fact, represent 51 divorces for every 3,000 marriages in the decades leading up to 1999.

We get a more accurate perspective on divorce if we examine the number of divorces per married women ages 14 to 44 (see the third column in Table 13-1). Using these statistics, we can see that the number of divorces per 1,000 married women in this age group has almost doubled over the past 39 years. Nevertheless, about half of every 10 marriages remain intact; about two-thirds of divorced women and three-fourths of divorced men eventually remarry. Women are less likely to remarry because many retain custody of children after a divorce, which complicates establishing a new adult relationship (Bianchi and Spain 1996).

Some people regard the nation's high rate of remarriage as an endorsement of the institution of marriage, but it does lead to the new challenges of a remarriage kin network composed of current and prior marital relationships. This network can be particularly complex if children are involved or if an ex-spouse remarries.

The current high divorce rate of the United States is not the result of a sudden explosion; rather, signs of such a tendency showed up early in the nation's history. Residents

Table 13-1	Divorce Rates in the United States	
Year	Divorces per 100 Marriages Performed	Divorces per 1,000 Married Women 14 to 44 Years Old
1920	13.4	10.0
1930	17.0	10.0
1940	16.9	14.0
1950	23.1	17.0
1960	25.8	16.0
1970	32.8	26.0
1980	49.7	40.0
1999	50.6	30.3

Sources: Bureau of the Census 1997a:56; National Center for Health Statistics 1974, 1990, 2000; and author's estimates.

FIGURE 13-5

Divorce

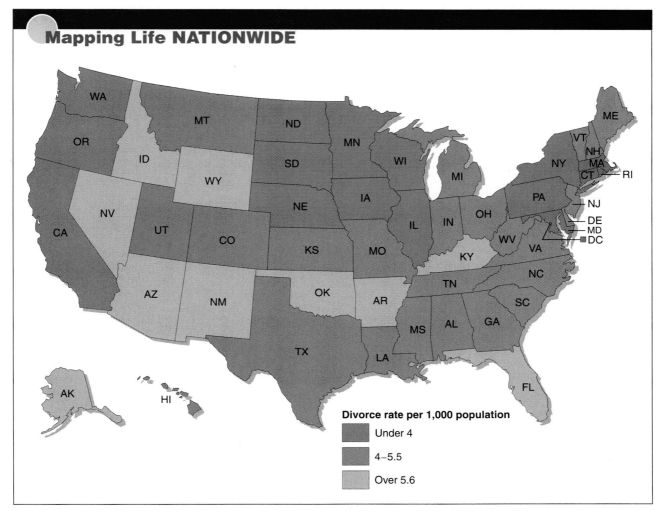

Mapping Life NATIONWIDE

Divorce rate per 1,000 population

■ Under 4

■ 4–5.5

□ Over 5.6

Variation among states results from a number of factors, including grounds for divorce, ease in getting married, and age distribution of the population.

of colonial America could receive divorces more easily than their counterparts anywhere in the Western world. The divorce rate in the United States remained fairly stable between 1920 and 1965, almost tripled between 1965 and 1975, and has remained steady ever since. How does the rate compare with those of other nations? The divorce rate of the United States actually declined by 13 percent over the period 1980 to 1995, compared with increases of 10 percent in Canada, 27 percent in Sweden, and 150 percent in the Netherlands. Even so, the current divorce rates of these three nations are barely half as high as the rate of the United States (Bureau of the Census 1998c:832).

Factors Associated with Divorce

Perhaps the most important factor in the increase in divorce throughout the twentieth century has been the greater social *acceptance* of divorce. It's no longer considered necessary to endure an unhappy marriage. Most importantly, various religious denominations have relaxed negative attitudes toward divorce, and most religious leaders no longer treat it as a sin. The growing acceptance of divorce is a worldwide phenomenon. In 1998, a few months after a highly publicized divorce by pop superstar Seiko Matsuda, the prime minister of Japan released a

When a couple with children gets divorced, an important legal decision must be made as to legal custody. Who has the right to make important decisions about the children and to have legal responsibility for them? While joint custody between the mother and father is growing in popularity, the social reality is that most children remain in the care of their mother most of the time. About one-quarter of divorced fathers see their children weekly, but an almost equal proportion have not seen their children in over a year.

Add to this picture, sporadic contact with grandparents. If many parents rarely see their children following divorce, what is the likelihood that grandparents can maintain the type of contact they would like? While data on this subject are not complete, it seems that kinship ties become even more fragile beyond the immediate family following a breakup. Indeed, if children are young at the time of divorce and remarriage soon occurs, the new stepgrandparents often come to view the children as their own grandchildren. Obviously, this creates tension and jealousy on the part of the natural grandparents, who now view the family scene from a distance.

Yet sometimes they are successful in maintaining stronger ties than even their own adult son or daughter has with their children. There is a growing trend in the United States for families *maintained* by grandparents. By 1998, 5.6 percent of all children lived in households maintained by a grandparent. In 37 percent of these over 4 million households, grandparents raised the children without either parent present. It is the parent-absent households that have been experiencing the greatest increase.

What do we know about the over 1 million families solely maintained by grand-

> There is a growing trend in the United States for families maintained by grandparents.

parents? They face many of the challenges of parent–child households. In the majority of cases, a grandparent is working and has to juggle work and home responsibilities. But in some ways the challenges are even greater than in parent–child families. These grandparents had been through child rearing at a much younger age and presumably were not anticipating doing it again. Since they are past their prime earning years, their households tend to be poorer, to receive more public assistance, and to have less health insurance than comparable families with children. They tend to raise older children—at least six years of age.

This growing phenomenon of grandparent-maintained families raises some important issues. First, sociologists need to assess quality-of-life issues and the parenting skills of grandparents unexpectedly parenting again. In the meantime, grandparents and their grandchildren would benefit greatly from the extension of policies and programs intended to help traditional parent–child families in times of need. The welfare policies that require recipients to get jobs have spawned employer-based or subsidized child care and family-friendly policies. These now need to be extended to grandparents who care for their grandchildren. Unfortunately, most agencies are currently ill-equipped to deal with the grandparent-maintained household.

Let's Discuss

1. Why is the number of grandparent-maintained households increasing?
2. How do grandparent-maintained households differ from parent-maintained households? In what ways are they similar?

Sources: Cherlin and Furstenberg 1992; Coontz 1997; Hall and Jerding 1999.

---

survey showing that 54 percent of those polled supported uncontested divorce, compared to 20 percent in 1979 (Kyodo News International 1998a).

A few other factors deserve mention:

- Many states have adopted more liberal divorce laws in the last two decades. No-fault divorce laws, allowing a couple to end their marriage without fault on either side (such as specifying adultery), accounted for an initial surge in the divorce rate after they were introduced in the 1970s, although they appear to have had little effect beyond that.
- Divorce has become a more practical option in newly formed families, since they now tend to have fewer children than in the past.

- A general increase in family incomes, coupled with the availability of free legal aid for some poor people, has meant that more couples can afford costly divorce proceedings.
- As society provides greater opportunities for women, more and more wives are becoming less dependent on their husbands—both economically and emotionally. They may then feel more able to leave if the marriage seems hopeless.

Impact of Divorce on Children

Divorce is traumatic for all involved, as Cornel West made clear in the excerpt that opened this chapter. But it has special meaning for the more than 1 million children whose parents divorce each year. Of course, for some of these children, divorce signals the welcome end to being witness to a very dysfunctional relationship. A national sample conducted by sociologists Paul Amato and Alan Booth (1997) found that in about a third of divorces, the children benefit from parental separation because it lessens their exposure to conflict. But in about 70 percent of all divorces, they found that the parents engaged in a low level of conflict; in these cases, the realities of divorce appear to be harder for the children to bear than living with the marital unhappiness. Other researchers, using differing definitions of conflict, have found greater unhappiness for children living in homes with marital differences. Still, it would be simplistic to assume that children are automatically better off following the breakup of their parents' marriage. Clearly, the interests of the parents do not necessarily serve children well.

Divorce can obviously be a painful experience for both female and male children, but we should avoid labeling young people as "children of divorce" as if this *parental* experience is the singular event defining the life of a girl or boy. Large-scale studies in the United States and Great Britain have shown that some of the alleged negative effects of divorce actually resulted from conditions (such as poverty) that existed *before* the parental separation. Moreover, if divorce does not lower children's access to resources and does not increase stress, its impact on children may be neutral or even positive. Divorce does not ruin the life of every child it touches, though its effect on a child is not always benign (Cherlin 1999). Divorces involving children also have an impact on family members beyond the nuclear family. In Box 13-3, we consider recent research on the role of grandparents in divorce.

In recent years, concern about the high rate of divorce in the United States and its impact on children has led policymakers to reconsider existing divorce laws. Louisiana's "covenant marriages" have received considerable publicity. Beginning in 1997, couples in that state have had the option of entering a legal union that requires premarital counseling and sets strict limits on divorce; for example, a marriage can dissolve only after a two-year separation or after documented adultery or abuse. It is very early to assess the impact of this system on marital longevity. Seventeen states have considered a similar arrangement, but only Arizona has adopted even a modified form of the procedure. Yet even if few states take up Louisiana's initiative, the nation appears willing to enter into a discussion of what educational and parenting programs can reduce marital breakup (Nock et al. 1999).

Diverse Lifestyles

Marriage is no longer the presumed route from adolescence to adulthood. In fact, it has lost much of its social significance as a rite of passage. The nation's marriage rate has dipped by 43 percent since 1960 because people are postponing marriage until later in life and more couples, including same-sex couples, are deciding to form partnerships without marriage (Popenoe and Whitehead 1999).

Cohabitation

Saint Paul once wrote, "It is better to marry than to burn." However, as journalist Tom Ferrell (1979) has suggested, more people than ever "prefer combustible to connubial bliss." One of the most dramatic trends of recent years has been the tremendous increase in male–female couples who choose to live together without marrying, thereby engaging in what is commonly called *cohabitation.*

The number of such households in the United States rose sixfold in the 1960s and increased another 48 percent just between 1990 and 1998. According to a 1999 Census Bureau report, at any given time, about 1 out of 10 opposite-sex couples are unmarried. Half of all people between the ages of 25 and 40 have cohabited. If current trends continue, that will soon be true of half of all people in the United States between the ages of 25 and 50 (Bureau of the Census 1999a:60; Clark and Fields 1999).

We can also find increases in cohabitation in Canada, France, Sweden, Denmark, and Australia. Data released in Great Britain indicate that more than 12 percent of people ages 18 to 24 are cohabiting. One report notes that in Sweden it is almost universal for couples to live together before marriage. Demographers in Denmark call the practice of

This young couple in England are cohabiting, an increasingly popular alternative to marriage in many countries today.

living together *marriage without papers.* In Australia, these couples are known as *de factos* (Blanc 1984; Levinson 1984; O'Donnell 1992; Thomson and Colella 1992).

Some countries have governmental policies that do not encourage marriage. For example, Sweden offers no married-couple allowance for tax purposes, no tax deduction for raising children, and no way for couples to jointly file their income taxes. Not surprisingly, many Swedish couples choose to cohabit rather than to marry. About half of the babies in Sweden are born to unmarried mothers—although there are proportionately many fewer unmarried *teenage* mothers in Sweden than in the United States (*Economist* 1995).

People commonly associate cohabitation only with college campuses or sexual experimentation. But according to a study in Los Angeles, working couples are almost twice as likely to cohabit as college students are. And census data show that in 1997, 36 percent of unmarried couples had one or more children present in the household. These cohabitants are more like spouses than dating partners. Moreover, in contrast to the common perception that people who cohabit have never been married, researchers report that about half of all people involved in cohabitation in the United States have been previously married. Cohabitation serves as a temporary or permanent alternative to matrimony for many men and women who have experienced their own divorces or the inability of their parents to remain married (Popenoe and Whitehead 1999).

Recent research has documented significant increases in cohabitation among older people in the United States. For example, census data indicate that in 1980, there were 340,000 opposite-sex couples who were unmarried, living together, and over the age of 45. By 1998, there were 985,000 such couples—nearly three times as many. Older couples may choose cohabitation rather than marriage for many reasons: because of religious differences, to preserve the full Social Security benefits they receive as single people, out of fear of commitment, to avoid upsetting children from previous marriages, because one partner or both are not legally divorced, or because one or both have lived through a spouse's illness and death and do not want to experience that again. But some older couples simply see no need for marriage and report being happy living together as they are (Bureau of the Census 1999a:60).

Remaining Single

Looking at TV programs today, as Box 13-1 pointed out, you would be justified in thinking most households are composed of singles. While this is not the case, it is true that more and more people in the United States are *postponing* entry into first marriages. In 1998, 70 percent of all women 20 to 24 years of age had never married, com-

pared with only 36 percent in 1970. As of 1998, one out of every four households in the United States (accounting for over 26 million people) was a single-member household. Even so, fewer than 5 percent of women and men in the United States are likely to remain single throughout their lives (Bureau of the Census 1999a:60).

The trend toward maintaining a single lifestyle for a longer period of time is related to the growing economic independence of young people. This is especially significant for women. In 1890, women accounted for only one-sixth of the paid labor force; they are now more than two-thirds of it. Freed from financial needs, women don't necessarily have to marry to enjoy a satisfying life. p. 302 ◄

There are many reasons why a person may choose not to marry. (Just ask *Ally McBeal*'s Renee, Fish, Elaine, Cage, and, of course, Ally.) Singleness is an attractive option for those who do not want to limit their sexual intimacy to one lifetime partner. Also, some men and women do not want to become highly dependent on any one person—and do not want anyone depending heavily on them. In a society that values individuality and self-fulfillment, the single lifestyle can offer certain freedoms that married couples may not enjoy.

Remaining single represents a clear departure from societal expectations; indeed, it has been likened to "being single on Noah's Ark." A single adult must confront the inaccurate view that he or she is always lonely, is a workaholic, is immature, and is automatically affluent. These stereotypes help support the traditional assumption in the United States and most other societies that to be truly happy and fulfilled, a person must get married and raise a family. To help counter these societal expectations, singles have formed numerous support groups, such as Alternative to Marriage Project (www.unmarried.org).

Lesbian and Gay Relationships

We were both raised in middle-class families, where the expectation was we would go to college, we would become educated, we'd get a nice white-collar job, we'd move up and own a nice house in the suburbs. And that's exactly what we've done (*New York Times* 1998:B2).

Sound like an average family? The only break with traditional expectations in this case is that the "we" described here is a gay couple.

The lifestyles of lesbians and gay men vary greatly. Some live in long-term, monogamous relationships. Some couples live with children from former heterosexual marriages or adopted children. Some live alone, others with roommates. Others remain married and do not publicly acknowledge their homosexuality. Researchers for the Na-

Lesbian and gay couples are pushing for domestic partnership legislation, which would allow them the traditional partnership benefits enjoyed by married couples.

tional Health and Social Life Survey—who interviewed more than 3,400 adults in the United States in 1992—found that 2.8 percent of the men and 1.4 percent of the women reported some level of homosexual or bisexual identity (Laumann et al. 1994b:293).

Census data collected in 1998 in preparation for Census 2000 indicated that about 2 percent of all households consisted of same-gender couples. In half of these households, the census respondents chose to classify themselves as "married," despite state laws that preclude legal same-sex marriage. This means that out of more than 2 billion same-sex households, a million couples view themselves as married, not merely living together (Clark and Fields 1999; Fields and Clark 1999).

The contemporary lesbian and gay rights movement has given an increasing number of lesbians and gay men the support to proclaim their sexual and affectional orientation. Gay activists were distressed in 1986 when a divided Supreme Court ruled, by a 5–4 vote, that the Constitution does not protect homosexual relations between consenting

adults, even within the privacy of their own homes. Nevertheless, as of 2000, 10 states, the District of Columbia, and more than 165 cities and counties in the United States had adopted civil rights laws protecting lesbians and gay men against discrimination in such areas as employment, housing, and public accommodations (ACLU 2000).

Gay activist organizations emphasize that despite the passage of laws protecting the civil rights of lesbians and gay men, lesbian couples and gay male couples are prohibited from marrying—and therefore from gaining traditional partnership benefits—in all 50 states of the United States. With such inequities in mind, 18 municipalities have passed legislation allowing for registration of domestic partnerships and 49 cities provide employee benefits that extend to domestic partnerships. Under such policies, a ***domestic partnership*** may be defined as two unrelated adults who reside together, agree to be jointly responsible for their dependents, basic living expenses, and other common necessities, and share a mutually caring relationship. Domestic partnership benefits can apply to such areas as inheritance, parenting, pensions, taxation, housing, immigration, workplace fringe benefits, and health care. While the most passionate support for domestic partnership legislation has come from lesbian and gay male activists, the majority of those eligible for such benefits would be cohabiting heterosexual couples (ACLU 1999).

Domestic partnership legislation, however, faces strong opposition from conservative religious and political groups. In the view of opponents, support for domestic partnership undermines the historic societal preference for the nuclear family. Advocates of domestic partnership counter that such relationships fulfill the same functions for the individuals involved and for society as the traditional family and should enjoy the same legal protections and benefits. The gay couple quoted at the beginning of this section consider themselves a family unit, just like the nuclear family that lives down the street in their West Hartford, Connecticut, suburb. They cannot understand why they have been denied a family membership at their municipal swimming pool and why they have to pay more than a married couple (*New York Times* 1998).

According to a 1998 General Social Survey, 58 percent of respondents believe that homosexuality between two adults is always wrong while fully 28 percent feel it is not wrong. Sharp divisions in public opinion persist (Davis and Smith 1999).

Marriage without Children

There has been a modest increase in childlessness in the United States. According to data from the census, about 19 percent of women in 1998 will complete their childbearing years without having borne any children, compared to 10 percent in 1980. As many as 20 percent of women in their 30s expect to remain childless (Bachu 1999).

Childlessness within marriage has generally been viewed as a problem that can be solved through such means as adoption and artificial insemination. Some couples, however, choose not to have children and regard themselves as child-free, not childless. They do not believe that having children automatically follows from marriage, nor do they feel that reproduction is the duty of all married couples.

Economic considerations have contributed to this shift in attitudes; having children has become quite expensive. According to a government estimate in 1998, the average middle-class family will spend $148,450 to feed, clothe, and shelter a child from birth to age 17. If the child attends college, that amount could double, depending on the college chosen. Aware of the financial pressures, some couples are having fewer children than they otherwise might, and others are weighing the advantages of a child-free marriage (Bureau of the Census 1999a:470).

As more couples are childless, they are beginning to question current practices in the workplace. While applauding employers' efforts to provide child care and flexible work schedules, some couples p. 109 nevertheless express concern about tolerance of employees who leave early to take children to doctors, ballgames, or after-school classes. In a 1994 survey of 14,000 workers, 20 percent said that "they were made to work longer hours, tackle more difficult assignments, or in other ways cover for parents they worked with" (L. Williams 1994:11). As more dual-career couples enter the paid labor force and struggle to balance career and familial responsibilities, there may be increasing conflicts with employees who have no children.

Meanwhile, many childless couples who desperately want children are willing to try any means necessary to get pregnant. The social policy section that follows explores the controversy surrounding recent advances in reproductive technology.

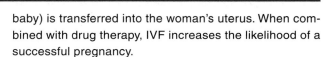

SOCIAL POLICY AND THE FAMILY

Reproductive Technology

The Issue

The 1997 feature film *Gattaca* told the story of a future United States in which genetic engineering enhanced people's genes. Those who were not "enhanced" in the womb—principally those whose parents could not afford the treatments—suffer discrimination and social hurdles throughout their lives. To borrow a line from the movie, "Your genes are your résumé."

Far-fetched? Perhaps, but today we are witnessing common aspects of reproductive technology that were regarded as so much science fiction just a generation ago. "Test tube" babies, frozen embryos, surrogate mothers, sperm and egg donation, and cloning of human cells are raising questions about the ethics of creating and shaping human life. To what extent should social policy encourage or discourage innovative reproductive technology?

The Setting

In an effort to overcome infertility, many couples turn to a recent reproductive advance known as in vitro fertilization (IVF). In this technique, an egg and a sperm are combined in a laboratory dish. If the egg is fertilized, the resulting embryo (the so-called test tube

baby) is transferred into the woman's uterus. When combined with drug therapy, IVF increases the likelihood of a successful pregnancy.

The procedure also makes *multiple* births more likely. Between 1980 and 1997, the rate of triplets or larger multiples of babies born to the same mother at the same time has increased more than 400 percent. Obviously, this results in substantially larger medical and child care expenses for the parents and presents unique and difficult parenting challenges (Martin and Park 1999).

While using technology to enhance the ability to reproduce is a recent phenomenon, the first successful artificial insemination actually took place in 1884 in Philadelphia. However, the ability to preserve sperm, beginning in the 1970s, made the process much simpler, since it eliminated the inconvenience of matching ovulation cycles with sperm donations (Rifkin 1998).

Sociological Insights

Replacing personnel is a functional prerequisite p. 128 that the family as a social institution performs. Obviously, advances in reproductive technology allow childless couples to fulfill their personal, and societal, goals. The new technology also allows opportunities not previously considered. A small but growing number of same-sex couples are using donated sperm or eggs to have genetically related children and fulfill their desire to have children and a family (Bruni 1998).

Sometimes it is difficult to define relationships. For example, in 1995, one California couple, John and Luanne Buzzanca, hired a married woman to carry a child to term for them—a child conceived of the sperm and egg of anonymous, unrelated donors. One month before birth, John filed for divorce and claimed he had no parental responsibilities, including child support. Eventually the court ruled that the girl baby had no legal parents; she is temporarily living with Luanne, who may seek to adopt the baby. While this is an unusual case, it suggests the type of functional confusion that can arise in trying to establish kinship ties (Weiss 1998).

In the future depicted in *Gattaca,* the poor were at a disadvantage in being able to genetically control their lives. The conflict perspective would note that in the world today, the technologies available are often accessible only to the most affluent. Just as techniques were being perfected, insurance companies announced they were terminating coverage of advanced fertility treatments, such as in vitro fertilization, beginning in 1998. For the many infertile couples who do not even investigate advanced procedures, cost is a major factor, according to a survey conducted by the Centers for Disease Control and Prevention. In vitro fertilization can cost about $10,000 for each procedure, and there is no guarantee that the procedure will succeed (E. Stephen 1999).

Conflict theorists further note the irony that while lower-class women have broad access to contraceptive coverage, they have limited access to infertility treatments. Sociologists Leslie King and Madonna Harrington Meyer (1997) conclude that class differences in access to reproductive services lead to a dualistic fertility policy in the United States, one that encourages births among the more affluent and discourages births among the poor, particularly those on Medicaid.

Today it is possible to know the sex of the unborn. Coupled with the ability to legally abort a fetus, this knowledge allows parents to reduce the likelihood of having a baby of an "unwanted sex." This practice has been common in countries with a patriarchal tradition, such as India. Now, however, it is even becoming possible to *preselect* the sex of a baby. Beginning in 1998, for the cost of about $2,500, couples could purchase

the expertise that would sort the sperm that is more likely to produce a baby of a desired sex. Feminist theorists are watching these developments closely. They are concerned that in societies where men enjoy a higher status, this technology will be used to effectively reduce the presence of women. Initial indications in the United States suggest that couples using this procedure are just as likely to try to engineer a girl as a boy, but this development needs to be monitored in the twenty-first century (L. Belkin 1999).

Interactionists observe that the quest for information and social support connected with reproductive technology has created new social networks. Like other special-interest groups, couples with infertility problems band together to

The possibility of cloning humans in the future, eerily foreshadowed in Andy Warhol's *The Twenty Marilyns,* poses major ethical dilemmas.

share information, offer support to one another, and demand better treatment. They develop social networks—sometimes through voluntary associations or Internet support groups—where they share information about new medical techniques, insurance plans, and the merits of particular physicians and hospitals. One Internet self-help group, Mothers of Supertwins, offers supportive services for mothers but also lobbies for improved counseling at infertility clinics to better prepare couples for the demands of many babies at one time (MOST 1999).

Policy Initiatives

In Japan, some infertile couples have caused a controversy by using eggs or sperm donated by siblings for in vitro fertilization. This violates an ethical (though not legal) ban on "extramarital fertilization," the use of genetic material from anyone other than a spouse for conception. While opinion is divided on this issue, most Japanese agree that there should be government guidelines on reproductive technology. Many nations, including England and Australia, bar payments to egg donors, resulting in very few donors in these countries. Even more countries limit how many times a man can donate sperm. Because the United States has no such restrictions, infertile foreigners who can afford the costs view this country as a land of opportunity (Efron 1998; Kolata 1998).

The legal and ethical issues connected with reproductive technology are immense. Many people feel we should be preparing for the possibility of a human clone. At this time, however, industrial societies are hard-pressed to deal with present advances in reproductive technology, much less future ones. Already, reputable hospitals are mixing donated sperm and eggs to create embryos that are frozen for future use. This raises the possibility of genetic screening as couples choose what they regard as the most "desirable" embryo—a "designer baby" in effect. Couples can select (some would say adopt) a frozen embryo that matches their requests in terms of race, sex, height, body type, eye color, intelligence, ethnic and religious background, and even national origin (S. Begley 1998; Rifkin 1998).

Let's Discuss

1. What are some of the innovations in reproductive technology in recent years? What ethical and legal issues do they raise?
2. Do you think the ability to preselect the sex of a baby will result in an imbalance between the sexes? Why or why not?
3. If you were writing legislation to regulate reproductive technology, what guidelines (if any) would you include?

Summary

The *family,* in its many varying forms, is present in all human cultures. This chapter examines the state of marriage, the family, and other intimate relationships in the United States and considers alternatives to the traditional nuclear family.

1. There are many variations in the family from culture to culture and even within the same culture.
2. The structure of the *extended family* can offer certain advantages over that of the *nuclear family.*
3. We determine kinship by descent from both parents (*bilateral descent*), from the father (*patrilineal*), or from the mother (*matrilineal*).
4. Sociologists do not agree on whether the *egalitarian family* has replaced the *patriarchal family* as the social norm in the United States.
5. Sociologists have identified six basic functions of the family: reproduction, protection, socialization, regulation of sexual behavior, companionship, and the providing of social status.
6. Conflict theorists argue that the family contributes to societal injustice and denies opportunities to women that are extended to men.
7. Interactionists focus on the microlevel—on how individuals interact in the family and other intimate relationships.
8. Mates are selected in a variety of ways. Some marriages are arranged. Some people are able to choose their mates. Some societies require choosing a mate within a certain group (*endogamy*) or outside certain groups (*exogamy*).
9. In the United States, there is considerable variation in family life associated with social class, race, and ethnic differences.
10. Currently, the majority of all married couples in the United States have two partners active in the paid labor force.

11. Among the factors that contribute to the rising divorce rate in the United States are the greater social acceptance of divorce and the liberalization of divorce laws in many states.

12. More and more people are living together without marrying, thereby engaging in what is called *cohabitation.* People are also staying single longer in general or deciding not to have children within marriage.

13. While many municipalities in the United States have passed *domestic partnership* legislation, such proposals continue to face strong opposition from conservative religious and political groups.

14. Reproductive technology has advanced to such an extent that ethical questions have arisen about the creation and shaping of human life.

Critical Thinking Questions

1. During recent political campaigns, there has been extensive discussion of "family values." What does this term mean to you? Why is it used by candidates in an election year? Are there ways in which government should act to strengthen family life in the United States? Should government act to promote the nuclear family model? Or should it give equal support to all types of families, including single-parent households and families headed by gay and lesbian parents?

2. In an increasing proportion of couples in the United States, both partners work outside the home. What are the advantages and disadvantages of the dual-income model for women, for men, for children, and for the society as a whole?

3. Given the high rate of divorce in the United States, is it more appropriate to view divorce as dysfunctional or as a normal part of our marriage system? What are the implications of viewing divorce as normal rather than as dysfunctional?

Key Terms

Adoption   In a legal sense, a process that allows for the transfer of the legal rights, responsibilities, and privileges of parenthood to a new legal parent or parents. (357)

Bilateral descent   A kinship system in which both sides of a person's family are regarded as equally important. (346)

Cohabitation   The practice of living together as a male–female couple without marrying. (363)

Domestic partnership   Two unrelated adults who have chosen to share one another's lives in a relationship of mutual caring, who reside together, and who agree to be jointly responsible for their dependents, basic living expenses, and other common necessities. (365)

Egalitarian family   An authority pattern in which the adult members of the family are regarded as equals. (347)

Endogamy   The restriction of mate selection to people within the same group. (351)

Exogamy   The requirement that people select mates outside certain groups. (351)

Extended family   A family in which relatives—such as grandparents, aunts, or uncles—live in the same home as parents and their children. (345)

Familism   Pride in the extended family, expressed through the maintenance of close ties and strong obligations to kinfolk. (354)

Family   A set of people related by blood, marriage (or some other agreed-upon relationship), or adoption who share the responsibility for reproducing and caring for members of society. (343)

Incest taboo   The prohibition of sexual relationships between certain culturally specified relatives. (351)

Kinship   The state of being related to others. (346)

Machismo   A sense of virility, personal worth, and pride in one's maleness. (354)

Matriarchy   A society in which women dominate in family decision making. (347)

Matrilineal descent   A kinship system that favors the relatives of the mother. (346)

Monogamy   A form of marriage in which one woman and one man are married only to each other. (345)

Nuclear family   A married couple and their unmarried children living together. (343)

Patriarchy   A society in which men dominate family decision making. (347)

Patrilineal descent   A kinship system that favors the relatives of the father. (346)

Polyandry   A form of polygamy in which some women have more than one husband at the same time. (345)

Polygamy   A form of marriage in which an individual can have several husbands or wives simultaneously. (345)

Polygyny   A form of polygamy in which a husband can have several wives at the same time. (345)

Serial monogamy   A form of marriage in which a person can have several spouses in his or her lifetime but only one spouse at a time. (345)

Single-parent families   Families in which there is only one parent present to care for children. (358)

Social institutions   Organized patterns of beliefs and behavior centered on basic social needs. (339)

Additional Readings

BOOKS

Coontz, Stephanie. 1997. *The Way We Really Are: Coming to Terms with America's Changing Families.* New York: Basic Books. A family historian considers how much and how little family organization has changed in the United States.

Hochschild, Arlie Russell. 1997. *Time Bind: When Work Becomes Home and Home Becomes Work.* New York: Metropolitan Books, Henry Holt. The author of *The Second Shift* describes the crunch that is taking place in time commitments to work and home and the social consequences it can have on both.

Luker, Kristin. 1996. *Dubious Conceptions: The Politics of Teenage Pregnancy.* Cambridge, MA: Harvard University Press. A sociologist analyzes attitudes toward unwed mothers in the United States, including the current "demonization" of these young women.

Mindel, Charles H., Robert W. Habenstein, and Roosevelt Wright, Jr., eds. 1999. *Ethnic Families in America: Patterns and Variations.* 4th ed. Upper Saddle River, NJ: Prentice Hall. This collection of 19 essays covers family as a social institution in a variety of ethnic contexts, including Cuban American, Asian Indian, Native American, and the Amish.

Salinger, Adrienne. 1999. *Living Solo.* Kansas City, MO: Andrews McMeel Publishing. A photojournalist examines the lives of single people, investigating their inner lives, dwelling places, and somewhat eccentric indulgences.

Zimbrana, Ruth E., ed. 1995. *Understanding Latino Families: Scholarship, Policy, and Practice.* Thousand Oaks, CA: Sage. An anthology with 10 specially written chapters focusing on family life among Latinos.

JOURNALS

Among the journals focusing on the family are *Family Planning Perspectives* (founded in 1969), *Family Relations* (1951), *International Family Planning Perspectives* (1975), *Journal of Comparative Family Studies* (1970), *Journal of Family Issues* (1980), *Journal of Family Violence* (1986), and *Journal of Marriage and the Family* (1938).

Internet Connection

Note: While all the URLs listed were current as of the printing of this book, these sites often change. Please check our website (http://www.mhhe.com/schaefer) for updates.

1. The Organization of Parents Through Surrogacy (OPTS), Inc., offers an online site at **http://www.opts.com/.**
   (a) What are the mission and perspective of OPTS?
   (b) Click on the "Legislative Alert" section to read about new laws affecting surrogacy. What is OPTS's stance on these laws?
   (c) What are the laws in your own state regarding this issue?
   (d) Do you support the goals of existing laws and the proposed laws? Why or why not?
   (e) What was the "Buzzanca Custody Case" (see "In the Spotlight" section)? Do you agree with the outcome?
   (f) Read the material in the "Viewpoints" and article sections. What are some of the social, political, moral, and legal issues faced by those considering surrogacy? What do you think about these issues?
   (g) How does surrogacy compare to other reproductive technologies?
   (h) What are the pros and cons of surrogacy?

2. The Stepfamily Network at **http://www.stepfamily. net/index.htm** aims to educate members of stepfamilies and professionals. Click on "Feature Article" and "Your Questions" to read current and past offerings.
   (a) What are some of the unique challenges faced by stepfamilies regarding such issues as discipline and vacation time?
   (b) How do stepparents deal with holidays such as Mother's and Father's Day?
   (c) If you come from a blended family, do you recognize some of the issues presented on this Internet site? If you do not come from a blended family, how does your home life compare? Are some of the challenges and issues applicable to all families?
   (d) Visit the "Kids' Korner Art Gallery" and explore the drawings of stepchildren. What themes are found in the art?
   (e) What emotions are the children trying to express through their work?
   (f) How do these drawings relate to this book's discussion of children of divorce and the rise of stepfamilies?

In this billboard distributed by Volkswagen of France, the figure of Jesus at the Last Supper says to his apostles, "Rejoice, my friends, for a new Golf is born." While an image of Jesus is sacred for Christians, it is used here in a secular manner—to advertise cars.

G rowing up in a small mixed-blood community of seven hundred on the eastern edge of the Pine Ridge Reservation in South Dakota, I uncritically accepted the idea that the old Dakota religion and Christianity were both "true" and in some mysterious way compatible with each other. There were, to be sure, Christian fundamentalists with their intolerance and the old traditional Indians who kept their practices hidden, but the vast majority of the people in the vicinity more or less assumed that a satisfactory blend had been achieved that guaranteed our happiness.

Although my father was an Episcopal priest with a large number of chapels in a loosely organized Episcopal missionary district known (to Episcopalians) as "Corn Creek," he was far from an orthodox follower of the white man's religion. I always had the feeling that within the large context of "religion," which in a border town meant the Christian milieu, there was a special area in his spiritual life in which the old Dakota beliefs and practices reigned supreme. He knew thirty-three songs; some of them social, some ancient, and several spiritual songs used in a variety of ceremonial contexts. Driving to his chapels to hold Christian services he would open the window of the car and beat the side of the door with his hand for the drum beat and sing song after song. . . .

When I went to college I was exposed to a much larger canvas of human experience upon which various societies had left their religious mark. My first reaction was the belief that most of the religious traditions were simply wrong, that a few of them had come close to describing religious reality, but that it would take some intensive study to determine which religious traditions would best assist human beings in succeeding in the world. It was my good fortune to have as a religion and philosophy professor a Christian mystic who was trying to prove the deepest mysteries of the faith. He also had some intense personal problems which emerged again and again in his beliefs, indicating to me that religion and the specific individual path of life were always intertwined.

Over several years and many profound conversations he was able to demonstrate to me that each religious tradition had developed a unique way to confront some problems and that they had something in common if only the search for truth and the elimination of many false paths. But his solution, after many years, became untenable for me. I saw instead religion simply as a means of organizing a society, articulating some reasonably apparent emotional truths, but ultimately becoming a staid part of social establishments that primarily sought to control human behavior and not fulfill human individual potential. It seemed as if those religions that placed strong emphasis on certain concepts failed precisely in the areas in which they claimed expertise. Thus religions of "love" could point to few examples of their efficacy; religions of "salvation" actually saved very few. The more I learned about world religions, the more respect I had for the old Dakota ways. *(Deloria 1999:273– 75)* ■

In this excerpt from *For This Land,* Vine Deloria—a Standing Rock Sioux—reveals his deep personal ties to the religion of his ancestors, undiluted by the overlays of missionary Christian theology. Even though his father is an Episcopal priest, Deloria is keenly aware of how tribal beliefs intrude and color his father's religious sensibility. He is also aware of the fact that Native American rites and customs have been appropriated by a generation of non-Indians seeking a kind of New Age "magic." For Deloria, Indian spiritual beliefs are an integral part of the Native American culture and help to define that culture. Mixing those beliefs with the beliefs of other religions or systems of thought threatens to undermine the strength of the culture.

Religion plays a major role in people's lives, and religious practices of some sort are evident in every society. That makes religion a *cultural universal,* along with other general practices found in every culture such as dancing, food preparation, the family, and personal names. p. 66 At present, an estimated 4 billion people belong to the world's many religious faiths (see Figure 14-1).

When religion's influence on other social institutions in a society diminishes, the process of *secularization* is said to be underway. During this process, religion will survive in the private sphere of individual and family life (as in the case of many Native American families); it may even thrive on a personal level. But, at the same time, other social institutions—such as the economy, politics, and education—maintain their own sets of norms independent of religious guidance (Stark and Iannaccone 1992).

This chapter focuses on religion as it has emerged in modern industrial societies. It begins with a brief overview of the approaches that Émile Durkheim first introduced and those that later sociologists have used in studying religion. We will explore religion's role in societal integration, social support, social change, and social control. We'll examine three important dimensions of religious behavior—belief, ritual, and experience—as well as the basic forms of religious organization. We will pay particular attention to the emergence of new religious movements. Finally, the social policy section will examine the controversy over religion in public schools. ■

Durkheim and the Sociological Approach to Religion

If a group believes that it is being directed by a "vision from God," sociologists will not attempt to prove or disprove this revelation. Instead, they will assess the effects of the religious experience on the group. What sociologists are interested in is the social impact of religion on individuals and institutions (M. McGuire 1981:12).

Émile Durkheim was perhaps the first sociologist to recognize the critical importance of religion in human societies. He saw its appeal for the individual, but—more important—he stressed the *social* impact of religion. In Durkheim's view, religion is a collective act and includes many forms of behavior in which people interact with others. p. 9 As in his work on suicide, Durkheim was not so interested in the personalities of religious believers as he was in understanding religious behavior within a social context.

Durkheim defined *religion* as a "unified system of beliefs and practices relative to sacred things." In his view, religion involves a set of beliefs and practices that are uniquely the property of religion—as opposed to other social institutions and ways of thinking. Durkheim (1947, original edition 1912) argued that religious faiths distinguish between certain events that transcend the ordinary and the everyday world. He referred to these realms as the *sacred* and the *profane.*

The *sacred* encompasses elements beyond everyday life that inspire awe, respect, and even fear. People become a part of the sacred realm only by completing some ritual, such as prayer or sacrifice. Believers have faith in the sacred; this faith allows them to accept what they cannot understand. By contrast, the *profane* includes the ordinary and commonplace. It can get confusing, however, because the same object can be either sacred or profane depending on how it is viewed. A normal dining room table is profane, but it becomes sacred to Christians if it bears the elements of a communion. For Confucians and Taoists, incense sticks are not mere decorative items; they are highly valued offerings to the gods in religious ceremonies marking new and full moons.

Following the direction established by Durkheim almost a century ago, contemporary sociologists view religions in two different ways. They study the norms and values of religious faiths through examination of their substantive religious beliefs. For example, it is possible to compare the degree to which Christian faiths literally interpret the Bible, or Muslim groups follow the Qur'an (or

FIGURE 14-1

Religions

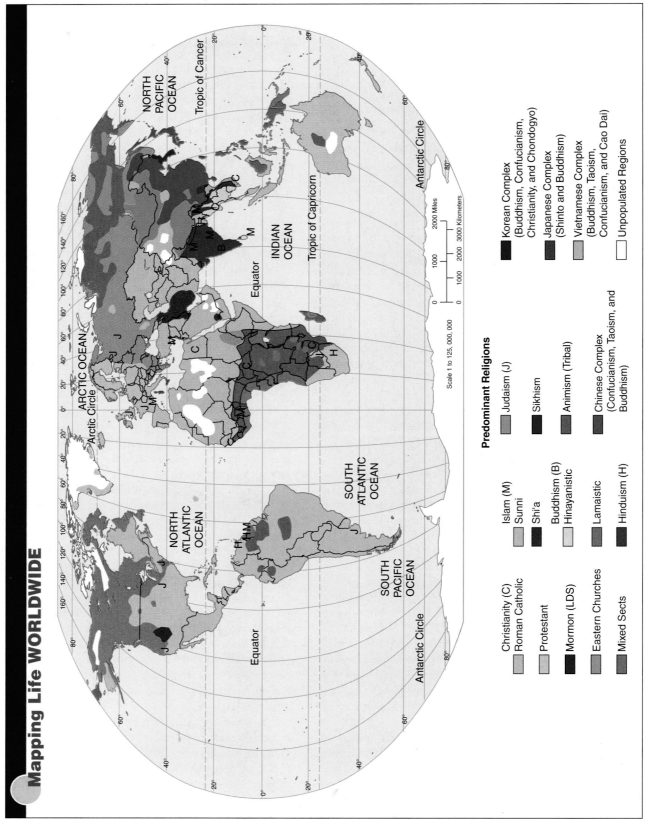

Mapping Life WORLDWIDE

Predominant Religions

Christianity (C)	Judaism (J)
Roman Catholic	Islam (M)
Protestant	Sunni
Mormon (LDS)	Shi'a
	Sikhism
Eastern Churches	Buddhism (B)
Mixed Sects	Hinayanistic
	Animism (Tribal)
	Lamaistic
	Hinduism (H)
	Chinese Complex (Confucianism, Taoism, and Buddhism)

Korean Complex (Buddhism, Confucianism, Christianity, and Chondogyo)

Japanese Complex (Shinto and Buddhism)

Vietnamese Complex (Buddhism, Taoism, Confucianism, and Cao Dai)

Unpopulated Regions

Scale 1 to 125, 000, 000

Source: Allen 1996:12–13.

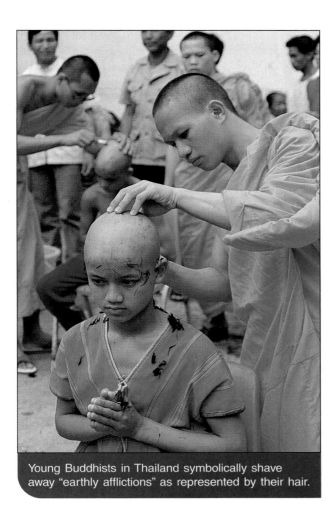

Young Buddhists in Thailand symbolically shave away "earthly afflictions" as represented by their hair.

Koran), the sacred book of Islam. At the same time, sociologists examine religions in terms of the social functions they fulfill, such as providing social support or reinforcing the social norms. By exploring both the beliefs and the functions of religion, we can better understand its impact on the individual, on groups, and on society as a whole.

The Role of Religion

Since religion is a cultural universal, it is not surprising that it plays a basic role in human societies. In sociological terms, these include both manifest and latent functions. Among its *manifest* (open and stated) functions, religion defines the spiritual world and gives meaning to the divine. Religion provides an explanation for events that seem difficult to understand, such as our relationship to what lies beyond the grave.

The *latent* functions of religion are unintended, covert, or hidden. Even though the manifest function of

p. 15

church services is to offer a forum for religious worship, they might at the same time fulfill a latent function as a meeting ground for unmarried members.

Functionalists and conflict theorists both evaluate religion's impact as a social institution on human societies. We'll consider a functionalist view of religion's role in integrating society, in social support, and in promoting social change, and then look at religion as a means of social control from the conflict perspective. Note that, for the most part, religion's impact is best understood from a macro-level viewpoint, oriented toward the larger society. The social support function is an exception: it is best viewed on the microlevel, directed toward the individual.

The Integrative Function of Religion

Émile Durkheim viewed religion as an integrative power in human society—a perspective reflected in functionalist thought today. Durkheim sought to answer a perplexing question: "How can human societies be held together when they are generally composed of individuals and social groups with diverse interests and aspirations?" In his view, religious bonds often transcend these personal and divisive forces. Durkheim acknowledged that religion is not the only integrative force—nationalism or patriotism may serve the same end.

How does religion provide this "societal glue"? Religion, whether it be Buddhism, Islam, Christianity, or Judaism, offers people meaning and purpose for their lives. It gives them certain ultimate values and ends to hold in common. Although subjective and not always fully accepted, these values and ends help a society to function as an integrated social system. For example, funerals, weddings, bar and bat mitzvahs, and confirmations serve to integrate people into larger communities by providing shared beliefs and values about the ultimate questions of life.

The integrative power of religion can be seen in the role that churches, synagogues, and mosques have traditionally played and continue to play for immigrant groups in the United States. For example, Roman Catholic immigrants may settle near a parish church that offers services in their native language, such as Polish or Spanish. Similarly, Korean immigrants may join a Presbyterian church with many Korean American members and with religious practices like those of churches in Korea. Like other religious organizations, these Roman Catholic and Presbyterian churches help to integrate immigrants into their new homeland.

Yet another example of the integrative impact of religion is provided by the Universal Fellowship of Metropolitan Community Churches. It was established in the United States in 1968 to offer a welcoming place of worship for lesbians and gay men. This spiritual community

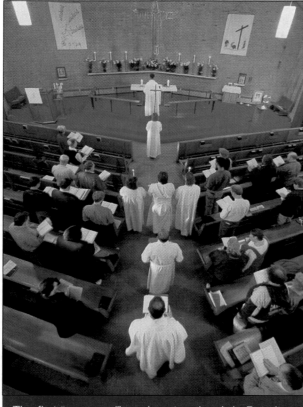

The first "gay-proud" service at a church in Detroit, Michigan, in 1996. This ecumenical Christian ministry is intended to provide a spiritual home for the gay community and to educate the straight community about homosexuals.

conflict in the former Yugoslavia. Serbia, Macedonia, and Montenegro are dominated by the Orthodox Church, and Croatia and Slovenia by the Catholic church; the embattled republic of Bosnia-Herzegovina has a 40 percent Islamic plurality. In many of these areas, the dominant political party is tied into the most influential church. p. 247

Religious conflict (though on a less violent level) has been increasingly evident in the United States as well. Sociologist James Davison Hunter (1991) has referred to the "cultural war" taking place in the United States. Christian fundamentalists, conservative Catholics, and Orthodox Jews have joined forces in many communities in a battle against their liberal counterparts for control of the secular culture. The battlefield is an array of familiar social issues, among them multiculturalism, child care (Chapter 4), abortion (Chapter 11), home schooling (Chapter 15), gay rights, and government funding for the arts. p. 109/309

Religion and Social Support

Most of us find it difficult to accept the stressful events of life—death of a loved one, serious injury, bankruptcy, divorce, and so forth. This is especially true when something "senseless" happens. How can family and friends come to terms with the death of a talented college student, not even 20 years old, from a terminal disease?

Through its emphasis on the divine and the supernatural, religion allows us to "do something" about the calamities we face. In some faiths, adherents can offer sacrifices or pray to a deity in the belief that such acts will change their earthly condition. At a more basic level, religion encourages us to view our personal misfortunes as relatively unimportant in the broader perspective of human history—or even as part of an undisclosed divine purpose. Friends and relatives of the deceased college student may see this death as being "God's will" and as having some ultimate benefit that we cannot understand. This perspective may be much more comforting than the terrifying feeling that any of us can die senselessly at any moment—and that there is no divine "answer" as to why one person lives a long and full life, while another dies tragically at a relatively early age.

Faith-based community organizations have taken on more and more responsibilities in the area of social assistance. In fact, as part of an effort to cut back on government-funded welfare programs, government leaders have advocated shifting the social "safety net" to private organizations in general and to churches and religious charities in particular. Sociologist William Julius Wilson (1999) has singled out faith-based organizations in 40 communities from California to Massachusetts as models of social re-

is especially important today, given the many organized religions openly hostile to homosexuality. Currently, the Metropolitan Community Church has 42,000 members in its local churches in 15 countries. As part of its effort to support lesbian and gay rights, the Metropolitan Community Church performs same-sex marriages, which it calls "holy union ceremonies" (L. Stammer 1999).

In some instances, religious loyalties are *dysfunctional;* they contribute to tension and even conflict between groups or nations. During the Second World War, the German Nazis attempted to exterminate the Jewish people; approximately 6 million European Jews were killed. In modern times, nations such as Lebanon (Muslims versus Christians), Israel (Jews versus Muslims as well as Orthodox versus secular Jews), Northern Ireland (Roman Catholics versus Protestants), and India (Hindus versus Muslims and, more recently, Sikhs) have been torn by clashes that are in large part based on religion.

In the 1990s, religious tensions contributed to bloody

form. These organizations identify experienced leaders and assemble them into nonsectarian coalitions devoted to community development (K. Starr 1999).

Religion and Social Change

The Weberian Thesis

Max Weber (1958a, original edition 1904) carefully examined the connection between religious allegiance and capitalist development. His findings appeared in his pioneering work *The Protestant Ethic and the Spirit of Capitalism,* first published in 1904.

Weber noted that in European nations with both Protestant and Catholic citizens, an overwhelming number of business leaders, owners of capital, and skilled workers were Protestant. In his view, this was no mere coincidence. Weber pointed out that the followers of John Calvin (1509–1564), a leader of the Protestant Reformation, emphasized a disciplined work ethic, this-worldly concerns, and a rational orientation to life that have become known as the ***Protestant ethic.*** One by-product of the Protestant ethic was a drive to accumulate savings that could be used for future investment. This "spirit of capitalism," to use Weber's phrase, contrasted with the moderate work hours, leisurely work habits, and lack of ambition that he saw as typical of the times (Winter 1977; Yinger 1974).

Few books on the sociology of religion have aroused as much commentary and criticism as *The Protestant Ethic and the Spirit of Capitalism.* It has been hailed as one of the most important theoretical works in the field and as an excellent example of macro-level analysis. Like Durkheim, Weber demonstrated that religion is not solely a matter of intimate personal beliefs. He stressed that the collective nature of religion has social consequences for society as a whole.

Weber provides a convincing description of the origins of European capitalism. But this economic system has subsequently been adopted by non-Calvinists in many parts of the world. Contemporary studies in the United States show little or no difference in achievement orientation between Roman Catholics and Protestants. Apparently, the "spirit of capitalism" has become a gener-

Did somebody say McDonald's? Probably not among the Orthodox Jews in Israel. They object to the fact that the establishment is open on Friday night and Saturday (the Jewish Sabbath). Secular Jews living in Jerusalem, on the other hand, have no objections. This is but a small skirmish amid intense conflicts between Orthodox and secular Jews in Israel today.

alized cultural trait rather than a specific religious tenet (Greeley 1989).

Conflict theorists caution that Weber's theory—even if it is accepted—should not be regarded as an analysis of mature capitalism as reflected in the rise of multinational corporations that cross national p. 234 boundaries. The primary disagreement between Max Weber and Karl Marx concerned not the origins of capitalism but its future. Unlike Marx, Weber believed that capitalism could endure indefinitely as an economic system. He added, however, that the decline of religion as an overriding force in society opened the way for workers to express their discontent more vocally (R. Collins 1980).

Liberation Theology

Sometimes the clergy can be found in the forefront of activism. Many religious activists, especially in the Roman Catholic church in Latin America, support ***liberation theology***—the use of a church in a political effort to eliminate poverty, discrimination, and other forms of injustice evident in a secular society. Advocates of this religious movement sometimes sympathize with Marxism. Many believe that radical change, rather than economic development in itself, is the only acceptable solution to the desperation of the masses in impoverished developing countries. Activists associated with liberation theology believe that organized religion has a moral responsibility to take a strong public stand against the oppression of the poor, racial and ethnic minorities, and women (C. Smith 1991).

The term *liberation theology* dates back to the 1973 publication of the English translation of *A Theology of Liberation*. This book was written by a Peruvian priest, Gustavo Gutierrez (1990), who lived in a slum area of Lima during the early 1960s. After years of exposure to the vast poverty around him, Gutierrez concluded that "in order to serve the poor, one had to move into political action" (R. M. Brown 1980:23).

Politically committed Latin American theologians came under the influence of social scientists who viewed the domination of capitalism and multinational corporations as central to the hemisphere's problems. One result was a new approach to theology that rejected the models developed in Europe and the United States and instead built on the cultural and religious traditions of Latin America.

While many worshippers support liberation theology, religious leaders in the Roman Catholic church are not happy with the radical movement. The official position of Pope John Paul II and others in the church hierarchy is that clergy should adhere to traditional pastoral duties and keep a distance from radical politics. The Pope specifically came out against church activists in his 1999 visit to Mexico City (S. Pagani 1999).

Liberation theology may possibly be dysfunctional, however. Some Roman Catholics have come to believe that by focusing on opposing political and governmental injustice, the clergy are no longer addressing their personal and spiritual needs. Partly as a result of such disenchantment, some Catholics in Latin America are converting to mainstream Protestant faiths or to Mormonism.

Religion and Social Control: A Conflict View

Liberation theology is a relatively recent phenomenon and marks a break with the traditional role of churches. It was this role that Karl Marx opposed. In his view, religion *impeded* social change by encouraging oppressed people to focus on other-worldly concerns rather than on their immediate poverty or exploitation. Marx described religion as an "opiate" particularly harmful to oppressed peoples. He felt that religion often drugged the masses into submission by offering a consolation for their harsh lives on earth: the hope of salvation in an ideal afterlife. For example, during the period of slavery in the United States, White masters forbade Blacks to practice native African religions, while encouraging

them to adopt the Christian religion. Christianity taught the slaves that obedience would lead to salvation and eternal happiness in the hereafter. Viewed from a conflict perspective, Christianity may have pacified certain slaves and blunted the rage that often fuels rebellion (M. McGuire 1992; Yinger 1970).

Marx acknowledged that religion plays an important role in propping up the existing social structure. The values of religion, as already noted, reinforce other social institutions and the social order as a whole. From Marx's perspective, however, religion's promotion of stability within society only helps to perpetuate patterns of social inequality. In a society with several religious faiths, the dominant religion will represent the ruling economic and political class. Marx was concerned that religion would reinforce social control within an oppressive society. He argued that religion's focus on heavenly concerns diverted attention from earthly problems and from needless suffering created by unequal distribution of valued resources (Harap 1982).

According to Marx, religion reinforces the interests of those in power. For example, India's traditional caste system defined the social structure of that society, at least among the Hindu majority. The caste system was almost certainly the creation of the priesthood, but it also served the interests of India's political rulers by granting a certain religious legitimacy to social inequality. Contemporary Christianity, like the Hindu faith, reinforces traditional patterns of behavior that call for the subordination of the powerless.

p. 204

The role of women in the church is another example of uneven distribution of power. Assumptions about gender roles leave women in a subservient position both within Christian churches and at home. In fact, women find it as difficult to achieve leadership positions in many churches as they do in large corporations. In 1997, 86 percent of all clergy in the United States were male. Female clergy are more likely to serve in subsidiary pastoral roles and to wait longer for desirable assignments. While women play a significant role as volunteers in community churches, men continue to make the major theological and financial judgments for nationwide church organizations. Like Marx, conflict theorists argue that to whatever extent religion actually does influence social behavior, it reinforces existing patterns of dominance and inequality (Bureau of the Census 1998c:417; J. Dart 1997).

From a Marxist perspective, religion functions as an "agent of de-politicization" (J. Wilson 1973). In simpler terms, religion keeps people from seeing their lives and societal conditions in political terms—for example, by obscuring the overriding significance of conflicting economic interests. Marxists suggest that by inducing a "false

When Raedora Steward-Dodd found out that the American Baptist Church ordains women, she decided to exchange her Texas police officer badge for the robes of a Baptist minister. Female clergy don't often have an easy time, however. They are more likely to serve in subsidiary pastoral roles and to wait longer for desirable assignments than male clergy.

p. 207 consciousness" among the disadvantaged, religion lessens the possibility of collective political action that can end capitalist oppression and transform society.

Religious Behavior

All religions have certain elements in common, yet these elements are expressed in the distinctive manner of each faith. The patterns of religious behavior, like other patterns of social behavior, are of great interest to sociologists, since they underscore the relationship between religion and society.

Religious beliefs, religious rituals, and religious experience all help to define what is sacred and to differentiate the sacred from the profane. Let us now examine these three dimensions of religious behavior.

Belief

Some people believe in life after death, in supreme beings with unlimited powers, or in supernatural forces. *Religious beliefs* are statements to which members of a particular religion adhere. These views can vary dramatically from religion to religion.

The Adam and Eve account of creation found in Genesis, the first book of the Old Testament, is an example of a religious belief. Many people in the United States strongly adhere to this biblical explanation of creation and even insist that it be taught in public schools. These people, known as *creationists,* are worried by the secularization of society and oppose teaching that directly or indirectly questions biblical scripture.

Ritual

Religious rituals are practices required or expected of members of a faith. Rituals usually honor the divine power (or powers) worshipped by believers; they also remind adherents of their religious duties and responsibilities. Rituals and beliefs can be interdependent; rituals generally involve the affirmation of beliefs, as in a public or private statement confessing a sin (Roberts 1995). Like any social institution, religion develops distinctive normative patterns to structure people's behavior. Moreover, there are sanctions attached to religious rituals, whether rewards (pins for excellence at church schools) or penalties (expulsion from a religious institution for violation of norms).

In the United States, rituals may be very simple, such as saying grace at a meal or observing a moment of silence to commemorate someone's death. Yet certain rituals, such as the process of canonizing a saint, are quite elaborate. Most religious rituals in our culture focus on services conducted at houses of worship. Thus, attendance at a service, silent and spoken reading of prayers, and singing of spiritual hymns and chants are common forms of ritual behavior that generally take place in group settings. From an interactionist perspective, these rituals serve as important face-to-face encounters in which people reinforce their religious beliefs and their commitment to their faith. One way to think of religious rituals is as how people "do religion" together, as Box 14-1 describes.

For Muslims, a very important ritual is the *hajj,* a pilgrimage to the Grand Mosque in Mecca, Saudi Arabia. Every Muslim who is physically and financially able is expected to make this trip at least once. Each year 2 million pilgrims go to Mecca during the one-week period indicated by the Islamic lunar calendar. Muslims from all over the

Candidates for the priesthood prostrate themselves prior to ordination in Notre Dame Cathedral in Paris. Prostration signifies the initiate has separated himself from his old life and humbled himself sufficiently to accept a higher authority. Such examples of "doing religion" help people solidify their faith in face-to-face encounters.

rather slight, such as the feeling of exaltation a person receives from hearing a choir sing Handel's "Hallelujah Chorus." But many religious experiences are more profound, such as a Muslim's experience on a *hajj*. In his autobiography, the late African American activist Malcolm X (1964:338) wrote of his *hajj* and how deeply moved he was by the way that Muslims in Mecca came together across lines of race and color. For Malcolm X, the color blindness of the Muslim world "proved to me the power of the One God."

Still another profound religious experience is being "born again"—that is, at a turning point in one's life making a personal commitment to Jesus. According to a 1997 national survey, more than 44 percent of people in the United States claimed that they had a born-again Christian experience at some time in their lives—a figure that translates into nearly 80 million adults. An earlier survey found that Baptists (61 percent) were the most likely to report such experiences; by contrast, only 18 percent of

world make the *hajj,* including those in the United States, where many tours are arranged to facilitate this ritual.

Some rituals induce an almost trancelike state. The Plains Indians eat or drink peyote, a cactus containing the powerful hallucinogenic drug mescaline. Similarly, the ancient Greek followers of the god Pan chewed intoxicating leaves of ivy in order to become more ecstatic during their celebrations. Of course, artificial stimulants are not necessary to achieve a religious "high." Devout believers, such as those who practice the pentecostal Christian ritual of "speaking in tongues," can reach a state of ecstasy simply through spiritual passion.

Experience

In sociological study of religion, the term *religious experience* refers to the feeling or perception of being in direct contact with the ultimate reality, such as a divine being, or of being overcome with religious emotion. A religious experience may be

The representation of religion can take many forms. This motorcycle club organizes itself as a strong Christian group, even though its attire and lifestyle may be objectionable to many Christians.

Research in Action

14-1 Doing Religion

More than 100 people in a Black congregation are packed into the living room of an old house. Led by the pastor's wife and four dancing women, the worshippers are singing, dancing, waving their arms. The church is rocking, and the pace doesn't stop for three hours. Across town a White congregation is singing the same hymns, but no one is dancing. The mood is mellow and the drummer looks almost embarrassed to be there. Sharon Bjorkman uncovered these contrasting styles in the course of fieldwork researching forms of worship in churches in the Chicago area. This observation research was part of a nationwide study conducted by the Hartford Institute for Religion Research.

Bjorkman was interested in going beyond the doctrinal background of a particular church and observing the physical actions of the people attending services and those conducting them. As Durkheim noted, defining what is sacred in a religion is a collective act. Using the interactionist perspective, Bjorkman took notes on what happened at services, who participated, and what or who motivated them to do so.

The first thing that she discovered was the disadvantage of being an outsider. For example, not "knowing the ropes," she was unprepared for the strenuous physical activity in the Black church. In the churches she visited she didn't know whether to carry a Bible or what version to use. As Bjorkman notes, you need to be socialized to know what is expected of you in a church service. Depending on the socialization church

> The church is rocking, and the pace doesn't stop for three hours.

members receive, usually through example and reprimand, they will be active or passive, loud or quiet, meditative or demonstrative.

The church leader plays a key role in shaping the congregation's actions. Leaders decide the format of services, including what songs are sung, what instruments are used, and how much to involve the worshippers. In services that call for testimonies from the congregation, the leader would actively solicit certain members and badger

them if need be. The same tactic applied to "altar calls" where congregants would come forward to confess sins or seek blessings.

As important as church leaders are, they would have little influence if the individual members chose not to cooperate. Worship styles, then, are jointly developed by leaders and members. Generally, Bjorkman found, leaders would take small incremental steps to "train" their members to accept a particular style of service.

This study illustrates the crucial part that human relations play within formal organizations. Religious rituals are not just dry formal procedures dictated by a rote program of service. They evolve out of the active participation of leaders and members "doing religion" together.

Let's Discuss

1. What accounts for differing forms of church rituals, even within the same denomination?
2. Do you attend a church regularly? What style of worship does the church leader set? How does that affect your feelings about your religion?

Sources: Bjorkman 1999; Ammerman et al. 1998.

Catholics and 11 percent of Episcopalians stated that they had been born again. The collective nature of religion, as emphasized by Durkheim, is evident in these statistics. The beliefs and rituals of a particular faith can create an atmosphere either friendly or hostile to this type of religious experience. Thus, a Baptist would be encouraged to come forward and share such experiences with others, whereas an Episcopalian who claimed to have been born again would receive much less support (Princeton Religious Research Center 1998).

Religious Organization

The collective nature of religion has led to many forms of religious association. In modern societies, religion has become increasingly formalized. Specific structures such as churches and synagogues are constructed for religious worship; individuals are trained for occupational roles within various fields. These developments make it possible to distinguish clearly between the sacred and secular parts of one's life—a distinction that could not be made in earlier societies in which religion was largely a family activity carried out in the home.

Sociologists find it useful to distinguish between four basic forms of organization: the ecclesia, the denomination, the sect, and the new religious movement or cult. We can see differences among these types of organizations in such factors as size, power, degree of commitment expected from members, and historical ties to other faiths.

Ecclesiae

An *ecclesia* (plural, *ecclesiae*) is a religious organization that claims to include most or all of the members of a society and is recognized as the national or official reli-

 **Sociology in the Global Community**

 www.mhhe.com/schaefer

14-2 The Emergence of the Megachurch

The Yoido Full Gospel Church in Seoul, South Korea, has six daily services in a facility with 13,000 seats. Unable to serve all of its 700,000 members, the church reaches 30,000 other worshipers via closed-circuit television, and 50,000 tune in from 20 satellite congregations across the metropolitan area. Worshippers listen to the sermons of Pastor David Cho and join in with 11 choirs, accompanied by a pipe organ or a 24-piece orchestra.

Not as large but still impressive is the Harvest Christian Fellowship in Riverside, California, which attracts up to 20,000 churchgoers. Clear glass and modern music have replaced stained glass windows and hymns. While Christian, the sermons are just as likely to make references to Elvis and Oprah as to Jacob and Abraham.

The 6,000-seat temple of the Protestant Works and Mission Church near Abidjan, Ivory Coast, is as impressive as any modern structure in Africa. The mix of Baptist and Jehovah's Witness teachings has found a reception among locals in a largely Muslim nation.

These are just three examples of the growing emergence worldwide of megachurches, large worship centers only loosely affiliated, if at all, with existing denominations. Within the United States alone, the number of megachurches with 2,000 people attending each week has grown from 10 in 1970 to over 500 in 1999.

Megachurches that begin with denominational ties frequently break them when they become financially self-sufficient. They often break away not so much on the basis of doctrinal issues as from a desire to be viewed as unique and to be free of church hierarchy.

Sociologists have observed the significant impact on religious organizations of these megachurches, whose growth is sometimes defined by the size of the parking lot. Their size often provokes hostility from more traditional churches that fear being overwhelmed or, in some cases, from the preexisting dominant faith (such as Buddhism in South Korea and Islam in the Ivory Coast). Some people view the megachurch as the latest intrusion of European/North American culture into the local landscape, especially in Latin America and Africa.

Megachurches appeal particularly to younger people, who seem prepared to

> The sermons are just as likely to make references to Elvis and Oprah as to Jacob and Abraham.

shop around for religious faith just as they would a college or automobile. The very size of the megachurch facility may attract someone used to working in large bureaucracies or dealing with huge supermarkets or large medical clinics or shopping malls. People comfortable in these settings may find the anonymity of a huge religious place of worship preferable to the intimacy of a small church with 50 to 100 members genuinely interested in getting to know them as individuals.

In addition, these megachurches in North America and developing nations often attract the growing number of self-identified born-again or charismatic Christians who do not feel welcome in more traditional faiths. Their size allows these megachurches to offer programs that cater to specific needs, such as singles or people with chronic health issues. Perhaps most importantly, the megachurch is willing to use the latest marketing tools, multimedia presentations, and motivational techniques to reach out to those who feel disenchanted with traditional denominations.

Let's Discuss

1. What impact are the megachurches having on other religious organizations?
2. Do you prefer small congregations to megachurches? Why or why not?

A megachurch in Houston, Texas.

Sources: Carey and Mosemak 1999; M. Luo 1999; Maxwell 1992; Ostling 1993; Schaller 1990.

It is difficult to distinguish sects from cults. A ***new religious movement (NRM)*** or ***cult*** is a generally small, secretive religious group that represents either a new religion or a major innovation of an existing faith. NRMs are similar to sects in that they tend to be small and are often viewed as less respectable than more established faiths.

However, unlike sects, NRMs normally do not result from schisms or breaks with established ecclesiae or denominations. Some cults, such as those focused on UFO sightings, may be totally unrelated to the existing faiths in a culture. Even when a cult does accept certain fundamental tenets of a dominant faith—such as belief in Jesus as divine or Muhammad as a messenger of God—it will offer new revelations or new insights to justify its claim to be a more advanced religion (Stark and Bainbridge 1979, 1985).

Like sects, NRMs may undergo transformation over time into other types of religious organizations. An example is the Christian Science church, which began as a new religious movement under the leadership of Mary Baker Eddy. Today, this church exhibits the characteristics of a denomination. NRMs tend to be in the early stages of what may develop into a denomination, or they may just as easily fade away through loss of members or weak leadership (Richardson and van Driel 1997).

Case Studies on Cults: Aum Supreme Truth and Falun Gong

Cults have a long history and are global in scope. Two cults in Asia are currently attracting worldwide attention—the Aum in Japan and the Falun Gong in China.

Few people, even in Japan, had heard of the Aum Supreme Truth (or *Shinrikyo*) before March 1995. That was when Aum supporters released deadly nerve gas in the Tokyo subway system, killing 12 and injuring more than 5,000 people. Aum's charismatic leader, Shoko Asahara, studied Buddhism and Hinduism in the Himalayas before founding his own religion in Japan in 1987, combining Buddhist elements with Christianity. He promises his followers that they will develop supernatural powers, but they must submit to arbitrary and strict rules of behavior described as being part of an ancient tradition.

The Aum cult manifests a siege mentality: It is convinced that outside groups are intent on destroying the organization. Asahara called on his followers to join in a final world revolution against Japan's enemies. To prepare for this Armageddon, the group built chemical factories and stockpiled various lethal chemicals, including the sarin gas used in the Tokyo subway. The Aum group has been accused as well of other gas attacks and assorted murders. Many Aum followers have been convicted, while Asahara is still on trial for being the mastermind of the doomsday cult's crimes.

Membership in the cult has fallen off from a peak of 10,000 to about 2,100 today, and the cult has had to declare bankruptcy. In September 1999 the cult announced that it was suspending external activities, and in December a spokesman for the cult apologized, for the first time, for its attacks. Meanwhile, the Japanese government passed legislation late in 1999 that will enable it to conduct surveillance of groups whose members attempted or carried out indiscriminate murders in the past 10 years—in effect, specifically targeting the Aum cult (Gaouette 1999; Takahara 1999; *New York Times* 1999b).

While Japan has been dealing with its cult problem, China has been encountering its own version—although on the face of it, one that is far more innocent. To the casual observer, the followers of Falun Gong (literally, "the Law of the Wheel Breathing Exercise") simply perform slow-motion exercises to music from a tape recorder. But the Falun Gong (pronounced *fah-luhn gung*) is essentially a religious movement that borrows heavily from Buddhist and Taoist philosophies and styles itself as a school of

Practitioners of Falun Gong combine meditation with marital arts exercises, borrowing from Buddhist and Taoist philosophies. Falun Gong's phenomenal growth in China has raised alarms among the Communist leadership, who want no competition for the control of the masses.

qigong (pronounced *chee-gong*), a traditional Chinese practice that uses meditation and martial arts exercises to channel unseen forces and improve health. Founded in 1992 by Li Hongzhi, its adherents—primarily middle-aged women, retirees, and students—number in the tens of millions today.

The group's rapid growth and strong appeal have worried the Communist Chinese leadership. The Communist party mistrusts any group whose value system it cannot control. In addition, since Marxism is basically the state "religion," the Chinese authorities might be seeing Falun Gong as a form of liberation theology, meant to rouse the masses. These fears seemed confirmed when 10,000 members of Falun Gong suddenly materialized in Beijing in April of 1999 to demand official recognition from the government. Several months later the government banned the group, put its exiled leader on the most wanted list, and began arresting, detaining, or dispersing thousands of people caught practicing Falun Gong. Apparently, all traces of the organized movement are to be stamped out (Platt 1999; Eckholm 1999; McCarthy 1999).

Comparing Forms of Religious Organization

How can we determine whether a particular religious group falls into the sociological category of ecclesia, denomination, sect, or NRM? As we have seen, these types of religious organizations have somewhat different relationships to society. Ecclesiae are recognized as national churches; denominations, although not officially approved by the state, are generally widely respected. By contrast, sects as well as NRMs are much more likely to be at odds with the larger culture.

Still, ecclesiae, denominations, and sects are best viewed as ideal types along a continuum rather than as mutually exclusive categories. Table 14-1 summarizes some of the primary characteristics of these ideal types. Since the United States has no ecclesiae, sociologists studying this country's religions have naturally focused on the denomination and the sect. These religious forms have been pictured on either end of a continuum, with denominations accommodating to the secular world and sects making a protest against established religions.

Table 14-1 Characteristics of Ecclesiae, Denominations, Sects, and New Religious Movements

Characteristic	Ecclesia	Denomination	Sect	New Religious Movement (or Cult)
Size	Very large	Large	Small	Small
Wealth	Extensive	Extensive	Limited	Variable
Religious Services	Formal, little participation	Formal, little participation	Informal, emotional	Variable
Doctrines	Specific, but interpretation may be tolerated	Specific, but interpretation may be tolerated	Specific, purity of doctrine emphasized	Innovative, pathbreaking
Clergy	Well-trained, full-time	Well-trained, full-time	Trained to some degree	Unspecialized
Membership	By virtue of being a member of society	By acceptance of doctrine	By acceptance of doctrine	By an emotional commitment
Relationship to the State	Recognized, closely aligned	Tolerated	Not encouraged	Ignored or challenged

Source: Adapted from G. Vernon 1962; see also Chalfant et al. 1994.

NRMs have also been included in Table 14-1 but are outside the continuum because they generally define themselves as a new view of life rather than in terms of existing religious faiths (Chalfant et al. 1994).

Advances in electronic communications have led to still another form of religious organization: the electronic church. Facilitated by cable television and satellite transmissions, *televangelists* (as they are called) direct their messages to more people—especially in the United States—than are served by all but the largest denominations. While some televangelists are affiliated with religious denominations, most give viewers the impression that they are disassociated from established faiths.

At the close of the 1990s, the electronic church had taken on yet another dimension—the Internet. One research group estimated that in 1999, 25 million people used the Internet for religious purposes. That is equivalent to the number of adherents of the denomination of the Southern Baptist Convention. One estimate projects that by 2010, 10 to 20 percent of the U.S. population may be relying primarily or exclusively on the Internet for religious input (Barna Research Group 1998).

Much of the spiritual content on the Internet is tied to organized denominations. People use cyberspace to learn more about their faith or even just the activities of their own place of worship. But, as more and more people are discovering, the "church" we locate on the World Wide Web exists only in *virtual* reality. For some purposes, virtual religious experience simply will not do. For example, a minyan, a set quorum for Jewish prayers, requires 10 Jews gathered in one space; cyberspace doesn't

By Kevin Rechin, USA TODAY

count at this point. While Muslims can view the Kabbah, or the Holy Shrine, in Mecca on the Net, they cannot fulfill their religious obligations except by actual pilgrimage there. The Internet, then, isn't suitable for some forms of religious and spiritual expression, but it certainly has added a new dimension to religious behavior (G. Zelizer 1999).

SOCIAL POLICY AND RELIGION

Religion in the Schools

The Issue

Should public schools be allowed to sponsor organized prayers in the classroom? How about reading Bible verses? Or just a collective moment of silence? Can public school athletes offer up a group prayer in a team huddle? Should students be able to initiate voluntary prayers at school events? Should a school be allowed to post the Ten Commandments in a hallway? Each of these situations has been an object of great dissension among those

who see a role for prayer in the schools and those who want to maintain a strict separation of church and state.

Another area of controversy centers on the teaching of theories about the origin of humans and of the universe. Mainstream scientific thinking theorizes that humans evolved over billions of years from one-celled organisms, and that the universe came into being 15 billion years ago as a result of a "big bang." But these theories are challenged by people who hold to the biblical account of the creation of

How, when, and where should prayer be allowed in public schools? These students in Annandale, Virginia, celebrate National Day of Prayer *outside* their high school.

New York schools was "wholly inconsistent" with the First Amendment's prohibition against government establishment of religion. In finding that such organized school prayer violated the Constitution—even when no student was required to participate—the Court argued, in effect, that promoting religious observance was not a legitimate function of government or education. Subsequent Court decisions allow *voluntary* school prayer by students, but forbid school officials to *sponsor* any prayer or religious observance at school events. Despite these rulings, many public schools still regularly lead their students in prayer recitations or Bible reading (Firestone 1999).

The controversy over whether the biblical account of creation should be presented in school curricula recalls the famous "monkey trial" of 1925. In this trial, high school biology teacher John T. Scopes was convicted of violating a Tennessee law making it a crime to teach the scientific theory of evolution in public schools. Creationists today have gone beyond espousing fundamentalist religious doctrine; they attempt to reinforce their position regarding the origins of humanity and the universe with quasi-scientific data.

In 1987 the Supreme Court ruled that states could not compel the teaching of creationism in public schools if the primary purpose was to promote a religious viewpoint. For a while, this ruling gave priority to the theory of evolution in most public school districts, but creationists, especially in the South and Midwest, have been persistently chipping away at the dominance of evolutionary theory in the classroom. Many school districts now require that teachers entertain alternative theories to evolution and to the creation of the universe, and some discount evolution altogether.

humans and the universe some 10,000 years ago—a viewpoint known as ***creationism.*** Creationists want their theory taught in the schools as the only one or, at the very least, as an alternative to the theory of evolution.

Who has the right to decide these issues? And what is the "right" decision? Religion in the schools constitutes one of the thorniest issues in U.S. public policy today.

The Setting

Both of the issues just described go to the heart of the First Amendment's provisions on religious freedom. On the one hand, the government is required to protect the right to practice one's religion but, on the other hand, it cannot take any measures that would seem to "establish" one religion over another (the church/state separation). The controversy over prayer in public schools actually began in the 1830s when masses of Italian and Irish Catholic immigrants objected to compulsory reading of the Protestant King James Bible and the recitation of Protestant prayers in their children's schools. Religious diversity in the United States in the twentieth century added the objections of Jewish, Buddhist, Hindu, Muslim, and atheist parents to Christian practices in public schools.

In the key case of *Engle* v. *Vitale,* the Supreme Court ruled in 1962 that the use of nondenominational prayer in

Sociological Insights

Supporters of school prayer and of creationism feel that strict Court rulings force too great a separation between what Émile Durkheim called the *sacred* and the *profane.* They insist that use of nondenominational prayer can in no way lead to the establishment of an ecclesia in the United States. Moreover, they believe that school prayer—and the teaching of creationism—can provide the spiritual guidance and socialization that many children today do not receive from parents or regular church attendance. Many communities also believe that schools should transmit the dominant culture of the United States by encouraging prayer (Coeyman 1999).

According to a 1998 General Social Survey, 55 percent of adults in the United States disapprove of a Supreme Court ruling against the required reading of the Lord's Prayer or Bible verses in public schools. A national survey in 1999 showed that 68 percent of the public favors teaching creationism along with evolution in public schools, and 40 percent favors teaching *only* creationism.

No other Western society has such a large body of opinion supporting views that depart so much from contemporary scientific understanding. Perhaps this is a reflection of a deep-rooted and enduring strain of religious fundamentalism in the United States, and the fact that religious belief in general is stronger in the United States than in other Western societies (Davis and Smith 1999; G. Johnson 1999; Lewis 1999).

Opponents of school prayer and creationism argue that a religious majority in a community might impose religious viewpoints specific to its faith, at the expense of religious minorities. Viewed from a conflict perspective, organized school prayer could reinforce the religious beliefs, rituals, and interests of the powerful; violate the rights of the powerless; increase religious dissension; and threaten the cultural and religious pluralism of the United States. These critics question whether school prayer can remain truly voluntary. Drawing on the interactionist perspective and small-group research, they suggest that children will face enormous social pressure to conform to the beliefs and practices of a religious majority.

Policy Initiatives

School education is fundamentally a local issue, so most initiatives and lobbying have taken place at the local or state level. Many religious fundamentalists have been successful in pushing their agenda by getting their own candidates elected to state and local school boards. In 1999 the Kansas Board of Education caused a stir when it voted to delete from the state's science curriculum virtually any mention of evolution and to remove from standardized tests questions having to do with the theory of evolution or the "big bang" theory of the creation of the universe. While individual teachers still have leeway to teach mainstream scientific thinking, their students will not be tested on it.

That same year, however, New Mexico's Board of Education voted overwhelmingly to limit the statewide science curriculum to the teaching of evolution. It was the first state in recent years to take a firm stand against the teaching of creationism. Other states have made other changes: Alabama and Nebraska now allow for discussion of theories that challenge evolution, and Kentucky has replaced the word "evolution" with "change over time." The strategy in some states is to ensure that if evolution is taught, it is presented only as an unproved theory (Belluck 1999; Janofsky 1999).

In 1993 Alabama passed a law explicitly permitting student-led voluntary prayer in the public school. Challenges of that law have passed through the court system ever since. In 1999 a federal appellate court ruled that students could engage in personal, voluntary prayer in the schools, including prayer over the public address system and at graduation ceremonies, as long as school officials do not take a direct role (Firestone 1999).

On the federal level, most lobbying has sought to bring religion into the public schools through passage of a Constitutional amendment. According to a Gallup poll conducted in 1996, 48 percent of those who identify themselves with the religious or Christian right want an amendment to declare "that the United States is a Christian nation." Periodically, conservatives in Congress have tried to pass an amendment that would allow for organized school prayer. In 1998 the House narrowly rejected the Religious Freedom Amendment, which would permit prayer and religious gatherings to occur on school property and be led by school officials (ACLU 1999b; T. Smith 1996).

The activism of religious fundamentalists in the nation's public school system raises a more general question: Whose ideas and values deserve a hearing in classrooms? Critics see this campaign as one step toward sectarian religious control of public education.

They worry that, at some point in the future, teachers may not be able to use books, or make statements, that conflict with fundamentalist interpretations of the Bible. For advocates of a liberal education who are deeply committed to intellectual (and religious) diversity, this is a genuinely frightening prospect.

Let's Discuss

1. Was there any organized prayer in the school you attended? Do you think promoting religious observance is a legitimate function of the social institution of education?
2. How might a conflict theorist view the issue of organized school prayer?
3. In what ways have Christian fundamentalists and their allies attempted to reshape public education in the United States?

Summary

Religion is a cultural universal, found throughout the world, although in varied forms. This chapter examines the dimensions and functions of religion and types of religious organizations.

1. Émile Durkheim stressed the social impact of religion and attempted to understand individual religious behavior within the context of the larger society.
2. Religion serves the functions of integrating people in a diverse society and providing social support in time of need.
3. Max Weber saw a connection between religious allegiance and capitalistic behavior through a religious orientation known as the *Protestant ethic.*
4. *Liberation theology* uses the church in a political effort to alleviate poverty and social injustice.
5. From a Marxist point of view, religion serves to reinforce the social control of those in power. It lessens the possibility of collective political action that can end capitalist oppression and transform society.
6. Religious behavior is expressed through *beliefs, rituals,* and *religious experience.*
7. Sociologists have identified four basic types of religious organization: the *ecclesia,* the *denomination,* the *sect,* and the *new religious movement (NRM)* or *cult.* Advances in communication have led to a new type of church organization—the electronic church.
8. How much religion—if any—should be permitted in the schools is a matter of intense debate in U.S. society today.

Critical Thinking Questions

1. From a conflict point of view, explain how religion could be used to bring about social change.
2. What role do new religious movements (or cults) play in the organization of religion? Why are they so often controversial?
3. How might the electronic church—on broadcast media and the Internet—change the face of religion in the future?

Key Terms

Creationism   A literal interpretation of the Bible regarding the creation of humanity and the universe used to argue that evolution should not be presented as established scientific fact. (390)

Cultural universals   General practices found in every culture. (375)

Denomination   A large, organized religion not officially linked with the state or government. (384)

Ecclesia   A religious organization that claims to include most or all of the members of a society and is recognized as the national or official religion. (383)

Established sect   A religious group that is the outgrowth of a sect, yet remains isolated from society. (384)

Liberation theology   Use of a church, primarily Roman Catholicism, in a political effort to eliminate poverty, discrimination, and other forms of injustice evident in a secular society. (379)

Megachurches   Large worship centers affiliated only loosely, if at all, with existing denominations. (384)

New religious movement (NRM) or cult   A generally small, secretive religious group that represents either a new religion or a major innovation of an existing faith. (387)

Profane   The ordinary and commonplace elements of life, as distinguished from the sacred. (375)

Protestant ethic   Max Weber's term for the disciplined work ethic, this-worldly concerns, and rational orientation to life emphasized by John Calvin and his followers. (379)

Religion   A unified system of beliefs and practices relative to sacred things. (375)

Religious beliefs   Statements to which members of a particular religion adhere. (381)

Religious experience   The feeling or perception of being in direct contact with the ultimate reality, such as a divine being, or of being overcome with religious emotion. (382)

Religious rituals   Practices required or expected of members of a faith. (381)

Sacred   Elements beyond everyday life that inspire awe, respect, and even fear. (375)

Sect   A relatively small religious group that has broken away from some other religious organization to renew what it views as the original vision of the faith. (384)

Secularization   The process through which religion's influence on other social institutions diminishes. (375)

Additional Readings

BOOKS

King, Ursula, ed. 1995. *Religion and Gender.* Oxford, Eng.: Blackwell. A professor of religious studies offers a collection of articles on women's portrayal of and participation in religion, drawing on contributions from feminists, anthropologists, and others.

Lee, Martha F. 1996. *The Nation of Islam: An American Millenarium Movement.* Syracuse, NY: Syracuse University Press. A political scientist examines the origins of the organized religion commonly known as the "Black Muslims" and changes in this faith over the last half-century.

Stark, Rodney, and William Sims Bainbridge. 1996. *Religion, Deviance, and Social Control.* New York: Routledge. An examination of religion as a source of social control and religion's impact on deviance, beginning with Durkheim's work on suicide and continuing with such contemporary issues as drugs, alcohol, cults, and mental illness.

Zellner, William W., and Marc Petrowky, eds. 1999. *Sects, Cults, and Spiritual Communities: A Sociological Analysis.* Westport, CT: Praeger. A collection of essays profiling religious groups outside the mainstream of American spiritual organizations. Included are treatments of the Jesus People, Santería, and Scientology.

JOURNALS

The sociological study of religion is reflected in the *Journal for the Scientific Study of Religion* (founded in 1961), *Religion Watch* (monthly newsletter, 1986), *Review of Religious Research* (1958), *Social Compass* (1954), and *Sociological Analysis* (1940).

Internet Connection

Note: While all the URLs listed were current as of the printing of this book, these sites often change. Please check our website (http://www.mhhe.com/schaefer) for updates.

1. The organization of religious behavior includes such examples as ecclesiae, denominations, sects, and cults. One of the most notorious religious organizations was The People's Temple, led by Jim Jones and based in Jones-town, Guyana. On November 18, 1978, one of the worst mass suicides in history occurred when approximately 900 members of Jones's group drank poisoned punch. Pictures, source material, time lines, and articles regarding this tragedy are available at the two following web addresses: The *San Francisco Examiner*'s "Days of Darkness" (**http://www.examiner.com/jonestown/**) and CNN's "Jonestown Massacre +20: Questions Linger" (**http://www.cnn.com/US/9811/18/ jonestown.anniv.01/**). Visit both of these sites and use your sociological research skills to piece together information.

   (a) Who was Jim Jones?
   (b) What were some of the beliefs and practices of The People's Temple?
   (c) What was Jonestown like according to those who lived there?
   (d) How did the U.S. government and outsiders view Jonestown?
   (e) Would sociologists classify The People's Temple as a sect or a cult or something else entirely? Why?
   (f) What questions still remain about what really happened over 20 years ago?
   (g) What similarities exist between the Jonestown Massacre and the more recent Heaven's Gate suicide?

   (h) What are the challenges faced by sociologists who wish to draw distinctions between sects, cults, ecclesiae, and denominations? How can we tell these organizations apart?

2. Sociologists who utilize the interactionist perspective focus on the meaning of symbols. Religious holiday celebrations are an obvious source of symbolism. The following website affords the opportunity to learn more about religious holidays and observances: (**http://dir.yahoo.com/Society_and_ Culture/Religion_and_Spirituality/Holidays_ and_Observances/**). Visit this site and choose a religious group and holiday/observance you are unfamiliar with in the list. Now, activate your sociological imagination.

   (a) What is the name of the holiday? Which religious group is it associated with?
   (b) During what time of the year does the event occur? Is the timing of the event important?
   (c) How many days does it last?
   (d) What is the purpose of the celebration or observation?
   (e) What are its origins?
   (f) Has the holiday changed over time?
   (g) What are the various roles played by members during ceremonies or rituals?
   (h) What specific symbols and items are used by participants? What do those symbols/items represent?
   (i) Does the holiday reflect important beliefs and values of the religion? How so?
   (j) Does the holiday you just examined have any features in common with holidays or celebrations practiced by other religious groups you are familiar with?

CHAPTER

15

EDUCATION

Once this man dreamed of going to college.
Today he finally made it.

THE COLLEGE FUND/UNCF.
A mind is a terrible thing to waste.

Sociological Perspectives on Education

Functionalist View

Conflict View

Interactionist View

Schools as Formal Organizations

Bureaucratization of Schools

Teachers: Employees and Instructors

The Student Subculture

Adult Education

Home Schooling

Social Policy and Education: School Choice Programs

The Issue

The Setting

Sociological Insights

Policy Initiatives

Boxes

SOCIOLOGY IN THE GLOBAL COMMUNITY: Schooling in Vietnam

RESEARCH IN ACTION: Violence in the Schools

TAKING SOCIOLOGY TO WORK: Alison Streit, Administrator, Girl Scouts of America

For decades the United Negro College Fund has been reminding Americans that a mind is a terrible thing to waste. Yet millions of African Americans still receive an inferior education in dilapidated, poorly staffed inner-city schools. This poster celebrates the achievement of those who have overcome institutional barriers to a college education.

In order to find Public School 261 in District 10, a visitor is told to look for a mortician's office. The funeral home, which faces Jerome Avenue in the North Bronx, is easy to identify by its green awning. The school is next door, in a former roller-skating rink. No sign identifies the building as a school. A metal awning frame without an awning supports a flagpole, but there is no flag. . . .

Textbooks are scarce and children have to share their social studies books. The principal says there is one full-time pupil counselor and another who is here two days a week: a ratio of 930 children to one counselor. The carpets are patched and sometimes taped together to conceal an open space. "I could use some new rugs," she observes. . . .

The library is a tiny, windowless and claustrophobic room. I count approximately 700 books. Seeing no reference books, I ask a teacher if encyclopedias and other reference books are kept in classrooms.

"We don't have encyclopedias in classrooms," she replies. "That is for the suburbs."

The school, I am told, has 26 computers for its 1,300 children. There is one small gym and children get one period, and sometimes two, each week. Recess, however, is not possible because there is no playground. . . .

On the top floor of the school, a sixth grade of 30 children shares a room with 29 bilingual second graders. Because of the high class size there is an assistant with each teacher. This means that 59 children and four grown-ups—63 in all—must share a room that, in a suburban school, would hold no more than 20 children and one teacher. There are, at least, some outside windows in this room—it is the only room with windows in the school—and the room has a high ceiling. It is a relief to see some daylight. . . .

As I leave the school, a sixth grade teacher stops to talk. . . . I ask her, "Do the children, ever comment on the building?"

"They don't say," she answers, "but they know."

I ask her if they see it as a racial message.

"All these children see TV," she says. "They know what suburban schools are like. Then they look around them at their school. This was a roller-rink, you know. . . . They don't comment on it but you see it in their eyes. They understand" *(Kozol 1991:85, 86, 87, 88).* ■

In the prosperous 1980s Jonathan Kozol, the author of this passage from *Savage Inequalities,* toured public schools throughout the United States. He found that while students in affluent suburban towns were attending spacious, modern schools, children in the inner city were crowded into antiquated, decrepit buildings. An educator, Kozol challenged his readers to confront the social implications of this stark contrast in educational resources.

Education, like the family and religion, is a ***cultural universal.*** As such it is an important aspect of socialization—the lifelong process of learning the attitudes, values, and behavior considered appropriate to members of a particular culture. As we saw in Chapter 4, socialization can occur in the classroom or at home, through interactions with parents, teachers, friends, and even strangers. Exposure to books, films, television, and other forms of communication also promotes socialization. When learning is explicit and formalized—when some people consciously teach, while others adopt the role of learner—the process of socialization is called ***education.*** But students learn far more about their society at school than what is included in the curriculum.

This chapter focuses in particular on the formal systems of education that characterize modern industrial societies. We will begin with a discussion of three theoretical perspectives on education: functionalist, conflict, and interactionist. As we will see, education can both perpetuate the status quo and foster social change. An examination of schools as formal organizations—as bureaucracies and subcultures of teachers and students—follows. Two types of education that are becoming more common in the United States today, adult education and home schooling, merit special mention. The chapter closes with a social policy discussion of controversial school choice programs. ■

Sociological Perspectives on Education

Education is now a major industry in the United States. In the last few decades, an increasing proportion of people have obtained high school diplomas, college degrees, and advanced professional degrees. For example, the proportion of people 25 years of age or over with a high school diploma increased from 41 percent in 1960 to more than 83 percent in 1998. Those with a college degree rose from 8 percent in 1960 to about 24 percent in 1998 (see Figure 15-1 for international comparisons). According to projections, in 2003 some 69 million people will be enrolled in some level of education—about 27 percent of the nation's population (Bureau of the Census 1999a:163, 169).

Education has become a vast and complex social institution throughout the world. It prepares citizens for the various roles demanded by other social institutions, such as the family, government, and the economy. The functionalist, conflict, and interactionist perspectives offer distinctive ways of examining education as a social institution.

Functionalist View

Like other social institutions, education has both manifest (open, stated) and latent (hidden) functions. The most basic *manifest* function of education is the transmission of knowledge. Schools teach students how to read, speak foreign languages, and repair automobiles. Education has another important manifest function: bestowing status. Because many believe this function is performed inequitably, it will be considered later, in the section on the conflict view of education.

In addition to these manifest functions, schools perform a number of *latent* functions: transmitting culture, promoting social and political integration, maintaining social control, and serving as agents of change.

Transmitting Culture

As a social institution, education performs a rather conservative function—transmitting the dominant culture. Schooling exposes each generation of young people to the existing beliefs, norms, and values of their culture. In our society, we learn respect for social control and reverence for established institutions, such as religion, the family, and the presidency. Of course, this is true in many other cultures as well. While schoolchildren in the United States are hearing about the accomplishments of George Washington and Abraham Lincoln, British children are hearing about the distinctive contributions of Queen Elizabeth I and Winston Churchill.

In Great Britain, the transmission of the dominant culture in schools goes far beyond learning about monarchs and prime ministers. In 1996, the government's chief curriculum adviser—noting the need to fill a void left by the diminishing authority of the Church of England—proposed that British schools socialize students into a set of core values. These include honesty, respect for others, politeness, a sense of fair play,

FIGURE 15-1

Percentage of Adults 25 to 64 Who Have Completed Higher Education, 1996

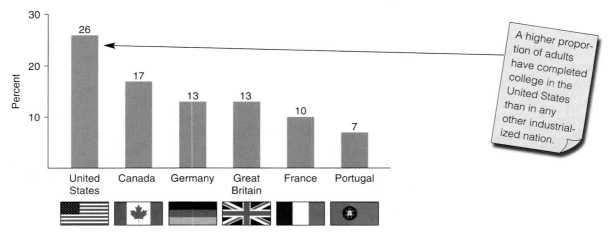

A higher proportion of adults have completed college in the United States than in any other industrialized nation.

Source: Bureau of the Census 1999a:840.

forgiveness, punctuality, nonviolent behavior, patience, faithfulness, and self-discipline (Charter and Sherman 1996).

Sometimes nations need to reassess their ways of transmitting culture. When an economic crisis hit Asian countries in 1997 and 1998, many Asian students who had been studying abroad could no longer afford to do so. South Korea, for example, had sent 42,000 college students to the United States alone in 1998. Now it had to figure out how to accommodate thousands more students pursuing higher education at home. South Koreans also began to question the content of the curriculum. Their schools traditionally teach Confucian values with a focus on rote memorization. This leads to an emphasis on accumulating facts as opposed to using reasoning. Entrance to college turns on a highly competitive exam that tests knowledge of facts. Once in college, a student has virtually no opportunity to change his or her program, and the classes continue to rely on memorization. The combination of an economic crisis and growing complaints about the educational process has caused government officials to reevaluate the educational structure. Moreover, growth in juvenile crime, although low by our standards, has led the government to introduce a new civic education program emphasizing honesty and discipline (Institute of International Education 1999; Woodard 1998).

On the college level in the United States, there has been growing controversy over the general education or basic curriculum requirements. Critics charge that standard academic curricula have failed to represent the important contributions of women and people of color to

history, literature, and other fields of study. The underlying questions raised by this debate, still to be resolved, are: Which ideas and values are essential for instruction? Which culture should be transmitted by the schools and colleges of the United States?

Promoting Social and Political Integration

Yale University requires its freshmen and sophomores to live together on campus in order to foster a sense of community among diverse groups. Many other universities have the same requirement. Education serves the latent function of promoting social and political integration by transforming a population composed of diverse racial, ethnic, and religious groups into a society whose members share—to some extent—a common identity (Touraine 1974). U.S. schools have historically played an important role in socializing the children of immigrants into the norms, values, and beliefs of the dominant culture. From a functionalist perspective, the common identity and social integration fostered by education contribute to societal stability and consensus.

In the past, the integrative function of education was most obvious through its emphasis on promoting a common language. Immigrant children were expected to learn English. In some instances, they were even forbidden to speak their native languages on school grounds. More recently, bilingualism has been defended both for its educational value and as a means of encouraging cultural diversity. However, critics argue that bilingualism undermines the social and political integration that education has traditionally promoted (see Chapter 3).

ALISON STREIT:
Administrator, Girl Scouts of America

"Everything I do has to do with a sociology class of one kind or another," says Alison Streit. She runs two programs for the Girl Scout Council based in Boston and recruits and trains volunteers to work with girls. The programs are designed to address racial, cultural, and gender issues in the lives of the Scouts, most of whom come from lower-income families.

Alison chose to major in sociology at Wesleyan University because it seemed to be "the discipline that looked most comprehensively at the world and tried to understand it and change it . . . to me it's really a worldview." She got her feminist awareness at Wesleyan, earning her BA in sociology in 1990, and expanded that awareness in graduate school at the University of California, Santa Barbara, where she got her MA in sociology in 1994. The classes about gender and race were "so fundamental to how I think about myself." Her social movements class educated her for life. "Sociology explained so much to me."

Sociology comes into play in very specific ways in Alison's job. She is much more aware of cultural differences. "I can't just talk about 'girls'; there are many different types of girls." She cites an example: during one group session, the girls were listening to music. The White girls wanted to listen to music from *Titanic;* one Black girl rolled her eyes and said, "Only White girls listen to *Titanic.*" Study of issues of diversity and inequality has prepared her for work with a lot of different communities and her own research on the girls.

Alison feels that sociology has informed her life, from the most personal aspects to the most abstract. Her advice to students is to "make the connections between sociology and the rest of your courses and every moment of your life. Sociology is relevant. Take any chapter of your textbook and ask yourself how it's relevant to your life."

This bilingual adult education class in Long Beach, California, is helping to integrate immigrant mothers and their children into mainstream society. While they are learning English, students also absorb the norms, values, and beliefs of the dominant culture.

Maintaining Social Control

In performing the manifest function of transmitting knowledge, schools go far beyond teaching such skills as reading, writing, and mathematics. Like other social institutions, such as the family and religion, education prepares young people to lead productive and orderly lives as adults by introducing them to the norms, values, and sanctions of the larger society.

Through the exercise of social control, schools teach students various skills and values essential to their future positions within the labor force. They learn punctuality, discipline, scheduling, and responsible work habits, as well as how to negotiate their way through the complexities of a bureaucratic organization. As a social institution, education reflects the interests of the family and in turn prepares young people for their participation in yet another social institution—the economy. Students are being trained for what is ahead, whether it be the assembly line or a physician's office. In effect, then, schools serve as a transitional agent of social control—between parents and employers in the life cycle of most individuals (Bowles and Gintis 1976; M. Cole 1988).

Schools direct and even restrict students' aspirations in a manner that reflects societal values and prejudices. School administrators may allocate funds for athletic programs while giving much less support to music, art, and dance. Teachers and guidance counselors may encourage male students to pursue careers in the sciences but steer equally talented female students into careers as early childhood teachers. Such socialization into traditional

pp. 103–4 ◀ gender roles can be viewed as a form of social control.

Serving as an Agent of Change

So far, we have focused on conservative functions of education—on its role in transmitting the existing culture, promoting social and political integration, and maintaining social control. Yet education can also stimulate or bring about desired social change. Sex education classes were introduced in public schools in response to the soaring pregnancy rate among teenagers. Affirmative action in admissions—giving priority to females or minorities—has been endorsed as a means of countering racial and sexual discrimination (see Chapter 10). Project Head Start—an early childhood program serving more than 790,000 children annually—has sought to compensate for the disadvantages in school readiness experienced by children from low-income families (Bureau of the Census 1999a:402).

Education also promotes social change by serving as a meeting ground where distinctive beliefs and traditions can be shared. In 1998, there were 481,000 foreign students in the United States, of whom 72 percent were from developing nations. Cross-cultural exchanges between these visitors and citizens of the United States ultimately broaden the perspective of both the hosts and their guests. The same is certainly true when students from the United States attend schools in Europe, Latin America, Africa, or the Far East (Bureau of the Census 1999a:194).

Numerous sociological studies have revealed that increased years of formal schooling are associated with openness to new ideas and more liberal social and political viewpoints. Sociologist Robin Williams points out that better-educated people tend to have greater access to factual information, more diverse opinions, and the ability to make subtle distinctions in analysis. Formal education stresses both the importance of qualifying statements (in place of broad generalizations) and the need at least to question (rather than simply accept) established truths and practices. As we saw in Chapter 2, the scientific method relies on *testing* hypotheses and reflects the questioning spirit that characterizes modern education (R. Williams et al. 1964).

Conflict View

Sociologist Christopher Hurn (1985) has compared the functionalist and conflict views of schooling. According to Hurn, the functionalist perspective portrays contemporary education as basically benign. For example, it argues that schools rationally sort and select students for future high-status positions, thereby meeting society's need for talented and expert personnel. By contrast, the conflict perspective views education as an instrument of elite domination. Schools convince subordinate groups of their inferiority, reinforce existing social class inequality, and discourage alternative and more democratic visions of society.

Criticizing the functionalist view, conflict theorists argue that the educational system socializes students into values dictated by the

In response to a rising pregnancy rate among adolescent girls, many schools have begun to offer sex education courses that promote abstinence. When schools attempt to remedy negative social trends, they are serving as an agent of social change.

powerful, that schools stifle individualism and creativity in the name of maintaining order, and that the level of change promoted by education is relatively insignificant. From a conflict perspective, the inhibiting effects of education are particularly apparent in the "hidden curriculum," creation of standards for entry into occupations, the differential way in which status is bestowed, and the treatment of women in education.

The Hidden Curriculum

Schools are highly bureaucratic organizations (as we will see later). Many teachers rely on the rules and regulations of schools to maintain order. Unfortunately, the need for control and discipline can take precedence over the learning process. Teachers may focus on obedience to the rules as an end in itself. If this occurs, students and teachers

In Tokyo's public schools, students learn adult responsibilities early on. In this classroom, classmates take turns serving the lunch.

alike become victims of what Philip Jackson (1968) has called the *hidden curriculum* (see also P. Freire 1970).

The term **hidden curriculum** refers to standards of behavior that are deemed proper by society and are taught subtly in schools. According to this curriculum, children must not speak until the teacher calls on them and must regulate their activities according to the clock or bells. In addition, they are expected to concentrate on their own work rather than assist other students who learn more slowly. A hidden curriculum is evident in schools around the world. For example, Japanese schools offer guidance sessions during lunch that seek to improve the classroom experience but also to develop healthy living skills. In effect, these sessions instill values and encourage behavior useful for the Japanese business world, such as self-discipline and openness to group problem solving and decision making (Okano and Tsuchiya 1999).

In a classroom overly focused on obedience, value is placed on pleasing the teacher and remaining quiet—rather than on creative thought and academic learning (Leacock 1969). Habitual obedience to authority may result in the type of distressing behavior documented by Stanley Milgram in his classic obedience studies (see Chapter 7).

Credentialism

Fifty years ago, a high school diploma was a minimum requirement for entry into the paid labor force of the United States; today, a college diploma is virtually the bare

minimum. This change reflects the process of **credentialism**—a term used to describe the increase in the lowest level of education needed to enter a field.

In recent decades, the number of occupations viewed as professions has risen. Credentialism is one symptom of this trend. Employers and occupational associations typically contend that such changes are a logical response to the increasing complexity of many jobs. However, in many cases, employers raise degree requirements for a position simply because all applicants have achieved the existing minimum credential (R. Collins 1979; Dore 1976; Hurn 1985).

Conflict theorists observe that credentialism may reinforce social inequality. Applicants from poor and minority backgrounds are especially likely to suffer from the escalation of qualifications, since they lack the financial resources needed to obtain degree after degree. In addition, upgrading credentials serves the self-interest of the two groups most responsible for this trend. Educational institutions profit from prolonging the investment of time and money that people make by staying in school. Moreover, as Hurn (1985) has suggested, current jobholders have a stake in raising occupational requirements. Credentialism can increase the status of an occupation and is crucial to demands for higher pay. Max Weber anticipated such possibilities as far back as 1916, concluding that the "universal clamor for the creation of educational certificates in all fields makes for the formation of a privileged stratum in businesses and in offices" (Gerth and Mills 1958:240–41).

Bestowal of Status

Both functionalist and conflict theorists agree that education performs the important function of bestowing status. As noted earlier, an increasing proportion of people in the United States are obtaining high school diplomas, college degrees, and advanced professional degrees. From a functionalist perspective, this widening bestowal of status is p. 209 beneficial not only to particular recipients but to society as a whole. In the view of Kingsley Davis and Wilbert Moore (1945) society must distribute its members among a variety of social positions. Education can contribute to this process by sorting people into appropriate levels and courses of study that will prepare them for appropriate positions within the labor force.

Conflict sociologists are far more critical of the *differential* way education bestows status. They stress that schools sort pupils according to social class background. Although the educational system helps certain poor children to move into middle-class professional positions, it denies most disadvantaged children the same educational opportunities afforded children of the affluent. In this way, schools tend to preserve social class inequalities in each new generation (Giroux 1988; Labaree 1986; Mingle 1987).

Money contributes to this disparity. For the most part, local property taxes finance public schools in the United States. Since the total value of property tends to be lower in areas with many low-income families, these school districts generally have less money available for education. For instance, in affluent Beverly Hills High

School, students who qualify have a choice of 14 advanced placement courses that carry extra weight in college admissions. But in poor neighborhoods nearby, Black and Latino students have a choice of only three such courses (Coeyman 1999; Sappenfield 1999).

Studies conducted since 1987 suggest that the funding inequities between richer and poorer districts have actually widened in recent years. Educational expenses have increased across the nation, but less affluent districts have been unable to keep pace. In recent years, there have been a growing number of legal challenges to the district-by-district school financing inequities within various states (Glaub 1990).

Even a single school can reinforce class differences by putting students in tracks. The term **tracking** refers to the practice of placing students in specific curriculum groups on the basis of test scores and other criteria. Tracking begins very early in the classroom, often in reading groups during first grade. These tracks can reinforce the disadvantages that children from less affluent families may face if they haven't been exposed to reading materials and computers and other forms of educational stimulation in their homes during early childhood years. It is estimated that about 60 percent of elementary schools in the United States and about 80 percent of secondary schools retain some form of tracking (Strum 1993).

A national study released in 1992 found that ability grouping worsens the academic prospects of lower-achieving students while it fails to improve the prospects of higher-achieving students. Moreover, tracking appears to lessen the likelihood that students will learn about and interact with others from different racial backgrounds, since ability grouping often contributes to segregation within schools (Oakes 1985).

Tracking and differential access to higher education are evident in many nations around the world. Japan's educational system mandates equality in school funding and insists that all schools use the same textbooks. Nevertheless, it is only the more affluent Japanese families who can afford to send their children to *juku,* or cram schools. These afternoon schools prepare high school students for examinations that determine admission into prestigious colleges (Efron 1997).

According to a study of teachers' attitudes toward students in the "outback" in rural Australia—an area

Private schools like Phillips Andover Academy in Massachusetts bestow a special status on their students, most of whom come from affluent White families. Conflict theorists charge that the U.S. educational system tends to reinforce social class inequalities.

Studies conducted since 1987 suggest that the funding inequities between richer and poorer school districts have actually widened in recent years.

where sheep vastly outnumber people—students are being prepared to stay in the "bush." Indeed, only a small minority seek out electives geared toward preparation for college. However, beginning in the 1980s, parents questioned this agriculture-oriented curriculum in view of rural Australia's declining employment base (M. Henry 1989).

Conflict theorists hold that the educational inequalities resulting from funding disparities and tracking are designed to meet the needs of modern capitalist societies. Samuel Bowles and Herbert Gintis (1976) argue that capitalism requires a skilled, disciplined labor force and that the educational system of the United States is structured with this objective in mind. Citing numerous studies, they offer support for what they call the ***correspondence principle.***

According to this approach, schools with students from different social classes promote the values expected of individuals in each class and perpetuate social class divisions from one generation to the next. Thus, working-class children, assumed to be destined for subordinate positions, are more likely to be placed in high school vocational and general tracks, which emphasize close supervision and compliance with authority. By contrast, young people from more affluent families are largely directed to college preparatory tracks, which stress leadership and decision-making skills—corresponding to their likely futures. While the correspondence principle continues to be persuasive, researchers have noted that the impact of race and gender on students' educational experiences may even overshadow that of class (M. Cole 1988).

Treatment of Women in Education

The educational system of the United States, like many other social institutions, has long been characterized by discriminatory treatment of women. In 1833, Oberlin College became the first institution of higher learning to admit

female students—some 200 years after the first men's college was established. But Oberlin believed that women should aspire to become wives and mothers, not lawyers and intellectuals. In addition to attending classes, female students washed men's clothing, cared for their rooms, and served them at meals. In the 1840s, Lucy Stone, then an Oberlin undergraduate and later one of the nation's most outspoken feminist leaders, refused to write a commencement address because it would have been read to the audience by a male student (Fletcher 1943; Flexner 1972).

In the twentieth century, sexism in education shows up in many ways—in textbooks with negative stereotypes of women, counselors' pressure on female students to prepare for "women's work," and unequal funding for women's and men's athletic programs. But perhaps nowhere has educational discrimination been more evident than in the employment of teachers. The positions of university professor and college administrator, which hold relatively high status in the United States, generally are filled by men. Public school teachers, who earn much lower salaries, are largely female.

Women have made great strides in one area: the proportion of women continuing their schooling. As was detailed in Chapter 11, women's access to graduate education and to medical, dental, and law schools has increased dramatically in the last few decades. Pressure from the feminist movement played a major role in opening the doors of these institutions.

In cultures where traditional gender roles remain as social norms, women's education suffers appreciably. For example, in rural China, a school with several hundred students often has only a handful of girls. Although the central government is attempting to address such inequality, the typical five- or six-year-old girl in Chinese villages is engaged in farmwork rather than schoolwork. In 1995, China's State Education Commission estimated that the nation had nearly 10 million school dropouts, most of them girls (P. Tyler 1995).

The same gender disparities can be seen in many other countries. Worldwide, illiteracy is generally below 30 percent of the adult population, except in Africa, the Middle East, and South Asia (see Figure 15-2). Yet women account for 70 percent or more of illiterate adults not only in China but in Jordan, Syria, Russia, and South Korea (D. Smith 1999; P. Tyler 1995).

Interactionist View

In George Bernard Shaw's play *Pygmalion,* later adapted into the hit Broadway musical *My Fair Lady,* flower girl Eliza Doolittle is transformed into a "lady" by Professor Henry Higgins. He changes her manner of speech and teaches her the etiquette of "high society." When she is

Although the Chinese government is attempting to address educational inequalities, girls continue to receive less education than boys—especially in rural areas.

introduced into society as an aristocrat, she is readily accepted. People treat her as a "lady" and she responds as one.

The labeling approach pp. 183—84, 259—61 and the concept of the self-fulfilling prophecy suggest that if we treat people in particular ways, they may fulfill our expectations. Children labeled as "troublemakers" come to view themselves as delinquents. A dominant group's stereotyping of racial minorities may limit their opportunities to break away from expected roles.

Can this labeling process operate in the classroom? Because of their focus on micro-level classroom dynamics, interactionist researchers have been particularly interested in this question. Howard Becker (1952)

FIGURE 15-2

Illiteracy Rates by Country and Gender, 1995

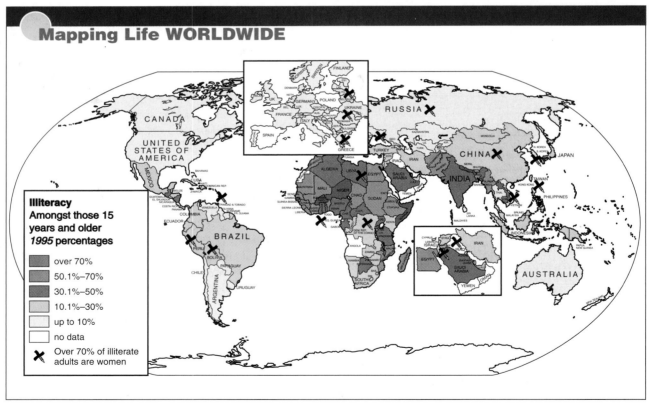

Source: UNESCO data reproduced in D. Smith 1999:70–71.

studied public schools in low-income and more affluent areas of Chicago. He noticed that administrators expected less of students from poor neighborhoods, and he wondered if teachers were accepting this view. Subsequently, in *Pygmalion in the Classroom,* psychologist Robert Rosenthal and school principal Lenore Jacobson (1968) documented what they referred to as a ***teacher-expectancy effect***—the impact that a teacher's expectations about a student's performance may have on the student's actual achievements. This appears to be especially true in lower grades (through grade three) (Brint 1998).

Between 1965 and 1966, children in a San Francisco elementary school were administered a verbal and reasoning pretest. Rosenthal and Jacobson then *randomly* selected 20 percent of the sample and designated them as "spurters"—children of whom teachers could expect superior performance. On a later verbal and reasoning test, the spurters were found to score significantly higher than before. Moreover, teachers evaluated them as more interesting, more curious, and better-adjusted than their classmates. These results were striking. Apparently, teachers' perceptions that these students were exceptional led to noticeable improvements in performance.

Studies in the United States have revealed that teachers wait longer for an answer from a student believed to be a high achiever and are more likely to give such children a second chance. In one experiment, teachers' expectations were even shown to have an impact on students' athletic achievements. Teachers obtained better athletic performance—as measured in the number of sit-ups or push-ups performed—from those students of whom they *expected* higher numbers (R. Rosenthal and Babad 1985).

The teacher-expectancy effect has been confirmed in a rather surprising setting: a training base for the Israeli army. Instructors for a combat command course were purposely given incorrect information about the "command potential" of 105 men about four days before the trainees arrived. Once the course began, the trainees who had been labeled "high in potential" did indeed learn more than others. These trainees also looked on the combat command course more favorably than the other recruits did (Eden and Shani 1982).

Despite these findings, some researchers continue to question the accuracy of this self-fulfilling prophecy because of the difficulties in defining and measuring teacher expectancy. Further studies are needed to clarify the relationship between teacher expectations and actual student performance. Nevertheless, interactionists emphasize that ability alone may not be so completely predictive of academic success as one might think (Brint 1998).

Schools as Formal Organizations

Nineteenth-century educators would be amazed at the scale of schools in the United States as we head into the twenty-first century. For example, California's public school system, the largest in the nation, currently enrolls as many children as there were in the entire country's secondary schools in 1950 (Bureau of the Census 1975:368; 1999a:179).

In many respects, today's schools, when viewed as an example of a formal organization, are similar to factories, hospitals, and business firms. Like these organizations, schools do not operate autonomously; they are influenced by the market of potential students. This is especially true of private schools, but could have broader impact if acceptance of voucher plans and other types of school choice programs increases (see the social policy section at the end of this chapter). The parallels between schools and other types of formal organizations will become more apparent as we examine the bureaucratic nature of schools, teaching as an occupational role, and the student subculture (Dougherty and Hammack 1992).

Bureaucratization of Schools

It is simply not possible for a single teacher to transmit culture and skills to children of varying ages who will enter many diverse occupations. The growing number of students being served by individual schools and school systems as well as the greater degree of specialization required within a technologically complex society have combined to bureaucratize schools.

Max Weber noted five basic characteristics of bureaucracy, all of which are evident in the vast majority of schools, whether at the elementary, secondary, or even college level. **pp. 151–53**

1. **Division of labor.** Specialized experts teach particular age levels of students and specific subjects. Public elementary and secondary schools now employ instructors whose sole responsibility is to work with children with learning disabilities or physical impairments. In a college sociology department, one professor may specialize in sociology of religion, another in marriage and the family, and a third in industrial sociology.
2. **Hierarchy of authority.** Each employee of a school system is responsible to a higher authority. Teachers must report to principals and assistant principals and may also be supervised by department heads. Principals are answerable to a superintendent of schools, and the superintendent is hired and fired by a board of education. Even the students are

hierarchically organized by grade and within clubs and organizations.

3. **Written rules and regulations.** Teachers and administrators must conform to numerous rules and regulations in the performance of their duties. This bureaucratic trait can become dysfunctional; the time invested in completing required forms could instead be spent in preparing lessons or conferring with students.

4. **Impersonality.** As was noted in Chapter 6, the university has been portrayed as a giant, faceless bureaucracy that cares little for the uniqueness of the individual. As class sizes have swelled at schools and universities, it has become more difficult for teachers to give personal attention to each student. In fact, bureaucratic norms may actually encourage teachers to treat all students in the same way despite the fact that students have distinctive personalities and learning needs.

5. **Employment based on technical qualifications.** At least in theory, the hiring of teachers and college professors is based on professional competence and expertise. Promotions are normally dictated by written personnel policies; people who excel may be granted lifelong job security through tenure. Teachers have achieved these protections partly because of the bargaining power of unions (Borman and Spring 1984; W. Tyler 1985).

Functionalists take a generally positive view of the bureaucratization of education. Teachers can master the skills needed to work with a specialized clientele, since they no longer are expected to cover a broad range of instruction. The chain of command within schools is clear; students are presumably treated in an unbiased fashion because of uniformly applied rules. Finally, security of position protects teachers from unjustified dismissal. In general, then, functionalists observe that bureaucratization of education increases the likelihood that students, teachers, and administrators will be dealt with fairly—that is, on the basis of rational and equitable criteria.

By contrast, conflict theorists argue that the trend toward more centralized education has harmful consequences for disadvantaged people. The standardization of educational curricula, including textbooks, will generally reflect the values, interests, and lifestyles of the most powerful groups in our society and may ignore those of racial and ethnic minorities. In addition, the disadvantaged, more so than the affluent, will find it difficult to sort through complex educational bureaucracies and to organize effective lobbying groups. Therefore, in the view of conflict theorists, low-income and minority parents will

have even less influence over citywide and statewide educational administrators than they have over local school officials (Bowles and Gintis 1976; Katz 1971). The experiences of parents in many developing countries seem to support this view of centralized education; see Box 15-1.

In the United States, a significant countertrend to the bureaucratization of schools is the availability of education over the Internet. Increasingly, colleges and universities are reaching out via the Web, offering entire courses and even majors to students in the comfort of their homes. Online curricula provide flexibility for working students and others who may have difficulty attending conventional classes because of distance or disability. Research on this type of learning is just beginning, so the question of whether teacher–student contact can thrive online remains to be settled. Computer-mediated instruction may also have an impact on instructors' status as employees, which we will discuss next, as well as on alternative forms of education like adult education and home schooling.

A college professor takes time to confer with a student. In large classes, it is difficult for instructors to give personal attention to individual students.

Sociology in the Global Community

15-1 Schooling in Vietnam

For many people in the United States, Vietnam is still a painful memory, a distant place devastated by civil war and a long and destructive bombing campaign. Yet this country, unified following the withdrawal of U.S. troops in the 1970s, is now a peaceful and independent nation determined to rebuild its society. Like neighboring countries, Vietnam is struggling to provide its citizens basic services, including formal education. The government of Vietnam spends less than 3 percent of the gross national product on education—about half the proportion spent by industrial countries like the United States and Great Britain. Less than half of all high-school-age children in Vietnam attend school (compared to over 95 percent in the United States), and girls make up only a quarter of high school enrollments there (compared to half in the United States).

Despite these differences, Vietnamese parents' concerns are similar to those of North American parents. According to the World Bank, surveys of Vietnamese households show that parents of school-age children are significantly less satisfied with the quality of the education their children are receiving than are school administrators and local government officials. Parents, ana-

lysts suspect, may be more concerned with the outcome of their children's schooling than are school administrators, who may focus more on the quality of the services they deliver. Similar differences of opinion regarding the quality of education can be heard at school board meetings in communities across the United States.

> Less than half of all high-school-age children in Vietnam attend school (compared to over 95 percent in the United States), and girls make up only a quarter of high school enrollments there.

In Vietnam as in the United States, school administration tends to be centralized. In such systems, parents are often frustrated in their efforts to influence educators and hold them accountable for their children's learning. Under extreme conditions, students may learn very little of the prescribed curriculum. For example, in Ghana and Kenya, testing showed that a significant percentage of grade school pupils could

score little better than if they had guessed on measures of their learning. Together with parental disenchantment, such results have prompted a search for alternatives to centralized educational systems.

One response has been a move toward community-managed schools. In Nicaragua, school reform has given parents, teachers, and principals greater power over decisions regarding the staffing and educational methods used in local schools. While the results have been mixed, in general student achievement has improved. In El Salvador, a similar program has brought noticeable improvements in the quality of schooling. Parental monitoring of community-managed schools, for example, has halved the rate of teacher absenteeism there.

Let's Discuss

1. Has the quality of the public schools in your community become a subject of debate? If so, what are parents complaining about at school board meetings and other public forums?
2. Do parents in your community have any control over the kind of education their children receive? If so, how do they exercise that control?

Source: J. Knowles et al. 1998; World Bank 1999a, 1999b.

Teachers: Employees and Instructors

Whether they serve as instructors of preschoolers or graduate students, teachers are employees of formal organizations with bureaucratic structures. There is an inherent conflict in serving as a professional within a bureaucracy. The organization follows the principles of hierarchy and expects adherence to its rules; professionalism demands the individual responsibility of the practitioner. This conflict is very real for teachers, who experience all the positive and negative consequences of working in bureaucracies (refer back to Table 6-2 on page 152).

A teacher undergoes many perplexing stresses every day. While teachers' academic assignments have become more specialized, the demands on their time remain diverse and contradictory. There are conflicts inherent in serving as an instructor, a disciplinarian, and an employee

of a school district at the same time. For college professors, different types of role strain arise. While formally employed as teachers, they are expected to work on committees and are encouraged to conduct scholarly research. In many colleges and universities, security of position (tenure) is based primarily on the publication of original scholarship. As a result, instructors must fulfill goals that compete for time.

College professors rarely have to take on the role of disciplinarian, but this task has become a major focus of schoolteachers' work in the United States. Order is needed to establish an environment in which students can actually learn. Many observers sense that the nation's schools have been the scene of increasingly violent misbehavior in recent years, although these concerns may be overblown (see Box 15-2).

ittleton, Colorado; Jonesboro, Arkansas; West Paducah, Kentucky; Pearl, Mississippi; Edinboro, Pennsylvania; Springfield, Oregon—these are now more than just the names of small and medium-size cities. They resonate with the sound of gunshots, of kids killing kids on school grounds. As a result, people no longer perceive schools as safe havens. But how accurate is that impression?

Studies of school violence put the recent spate of school killings in perspective:

- A child has only a one in a million chance of being killed at school.
- The number of people shot and killed in school in the 1997–1998 school year was 40 (including adults), about average over the last six years.
- According to the Center for Disease Control, 99 percent of violent deaths of school-aged children in 1992–1994 occurred *outside* school grounds.
- Fewer students are now being found with guns in school.

- Data from the National School Safety Center at Pepperdine University suggest there has been a 27 percent decline in school-associated violent deaths from 1992 through the 1997–1998 school year.
- Twenty-three times more children are killed in gun *accidents* than in school killings.

> A child has only a one in a million chance of being killed at school.

Schools, then, are safer than neighborhoods, but people still are unnerved by the perception of an alarming rise in schoolyard violence that has been generated by heavy media coverage of the recent incidents. Some conflict theorists object to the huge outcry about recent violence in schools. After all, they note, violence in and around inner-city schools has a long history. It

seems that only when middle-class White children are the victims does school violence become a plank on the national policy agenda. When violence hits the middle class, the problem is viewed not as an extension of delinquency, but as a structural issue in need of legislative remedies, such as gun control. Meanwhile, feminists observe that virtually all the offenders are male and, in some instances, such as in the case of Jonesboro, the victims are disproportionately female. The precipitating factor for violence is often a broken-off dating relationship—yet another example of violence of men against women (or, in this case, boys against girls).

Increasingly, efforts to prevent school violence are focusing on the ways in which the socialization of young people in the United States contributes to violence. For example, the *Journal of the American Medical Association* published a study of Second Step, a violence prevention curriculum for elementary school students that teaches social skills re-

Source: Bowles 1999; Department of Education 1999; Donohue, Schiraldi, and Ziedenberg 1998; D. Grossman et al. 1997; National Center for Education Statistics 1998; S. Schaefer 1996.

Given these difficulties, does teaching remain an attractive profession in the United States? In 1999, 7 percent of first-year college students indicated that they were interested in becoming elementary school teachers and 4 percent, high school teachers. While these figures reflect a modest upturn in the appeal of teaching in recent years, they are dramatically lower than the 13 percent of first-year male students and 38 percent of first-year female students who had such occupational aspirations in 1968 (Astin et al. 1994; Sax et al. 1999).

Undoubtedly, economic considerations enter into students' feelings about the attractiveness of teaching. In 1998, the average salary for all public elementary and secondary school teachers in the United States was $39,400. This salary places teachers somewhere near the average of all wage earners in the nation. (In private industry, workers with professional responsibilities and educational qualifications comparable with teachers earn salaries ranging from $38,000 to $90,000.) By contrast, university students in Japan line up for coveted teaching jobs. By law, Japanese teachers are paid 10 per-

cent more than employees in the top-level civil service job, which places them among the top 10 percent of wage earners in the country (Bureau of the Census 1999a:179; Richburg 1985).

The status of any job reflects several factors, including the level of education required, financial compensation, and the respect given the occupation within society. The teaching profession (see Table 8-1, page 211) is feeling pressure in all three of these areas. First, the amount of formal schooling required for teaching remains high, but the public has begun to call for new competency examinations for teachers. Second, the statistics cited above demonstrate that teachers' salaries are significantly lower than those of many professionals and skilled workers. Finally, as we have seen, the overall prestige of the teaching profession has declined in the last decade. Many teachers have become disappointed and frustrated and have left the educational world for other careers in other professions. Many are simply "burned out" by the severe demands, limited rewards, and general sense of alienation that they experience on the job.

lated to anger management, impulse control, and empathy. The study evaluated the impact of the program on urban and suburban elementary school students and found that it appeared to lead to a moderate decrease in physically aggressive behavior and an increase in neutral and prosocial behavior in school. However, one can never undertake such efforts early enough. The "peaceful play" program in Illinois shows *preschoolers* how to resolve their disputes in a nonviolent fashion. Other approaches to preventing violence include stiffer regulations of gun sales and gun ownership, longer school days, and afterschool programs (to keep young people occupied during unsupervised hours).

Some people believe that a key ingredient to prevention of violence, in or out of school, is greater parental supervision and responsibility for their children. In her book *A Tribe Apart,* Patricia Hersch (1998) documents the lives of eight teens growing up in a Virginia suburb over a three-year period. Her conclusion: Children need meaningful adult relationships in their lives. Secretary of Education Richard Riley cites studies showing that youths who feel connected to their parents and schools are less likely to engage in high-risk behavior (Chaddock 1998:B7).

Let's Discuss

1. Has a shooting or other violent episode ever occurred at your school? If so, how did students react? Do you feel safer at school than at home, as experts say you are?

2. What steps have administrators at your school taken to prevent violence? Have they been effective, or should other steps be taken?

The Student Subculture

An important latent function of education relates directly to student life: Schools provide for students' social and recreational needs. Education helps toddlers and young children develop interpersonal skills that are essential during adolescence and adulthood. During high school and college years, students may meet future husbands and wives and may establish lifelong friendships.

When people observe high schools, community colleges, or universities from the outside, students appear to constitute a cohesive, uniform group. However, the student subculture is actually much more complex and diverse. High school cliques and social groups may crop up based on race, social class, physical attractiveness, placement in courses, athletic ability, and leadership roles in the school and community. In his classic community study of "Elmtown," August Hollingshead (1975) found some 259 distinct cliques in a single high school. These cliques, whose average size was five, were centered on the school itself, on recreational activities, and on religious and community groups.

We can find a similar diversity at the college level. Burton Clark and Martin Trow (1966) and, more recently, Helen Lefkowitz Horowitz (1987) have identified distinctive subcultures among college students. Here are four ideal types of subcultures that come out of their analyses:

1. The *collegiate* subculture focuses on having fun and socializing. These students define what constitutes a "reasonable" amount of academic work (and what amount of work is "excessive" and leads to being labeled as a "grind"). Members of the collegiate subculture have little commitment to academic pursuits.

2. By contrast, the *academic* subculture identifies with the intellectual concerns of the faculty and values knowledge for its own sake.

3. The *vocational* subculture is primarily interested in career prospects and views college as a means of obtaining degrees that are essential for advancement.

4. Finally, the *nonconformist* subculture is hostile to the college environment and seeks out ideas that may or may not relate to studies. It may find outlets through campus publications or issue-oriented groups.

411

Today the student subculture of many schools in the United States includes young people with disabilities. Federal legislation that took effect in 1980 promotes *mainstreaming*, maximum integration of disabled children with nondisabled children.

students must function academically and socially within universities where there are few Black faculty members or Black administrators, where harassment of Blacks by campus police is common, and where the curricula place little emphasis on Black contributions. Indeed, Feagin (1989:11) suggests that "for minority students life at a predominantly White college or university means long-term encounters with *pervasive whiteness*." In Feagin's view, African American students at such institutions experience blatant and subtle racial discrimination, which has a cumulative impact that can seriously damage the students' confidence (see also Feagin et al. 1996).

Sometimes schools can seem overwhelmingly bureaucratic, with the effect of stifling rather than nourishing intellectual curiosity in students. This concern has led many parents and policymakers to push for school choice programs—allowing parents to choose the school that suits their children's needs and forcing schools to compete for their "customers." We'll take a look at this issue in the social policy section at the end of the chapter.

Adult Education

Picture a "college student." Most likely, you will imagine someone under 25 years of age. This reflects the belief that education is something experienced and completed during the first two or three decades of life and rarely supplemented after that. However, many colleges and universities

Each college student is eventually exposed to these competing subcultures and must determine which (if any) seems most in line with his or her feelings and interests.

The typology used by these researchers reminds us that school is a complex social organization—almost like a community with different neighborhoods. Of course, these four subcultures are not the only ones evident on college campuses in the United States. For example, one might find subcultures of Vietnam veterans or former full-time homemakers at community colleges and four-year commuter institutions.

Sociologist Joe Feagin has studied a distinctive collegiate subculture: Black students at predominantly White universities. These

Students in a Los Angeles high school engage in role play designed to expose stereotypes and increase social tolerance. The student subculture at many big-city schools is highly diverse, and tension between different groups can surface in negative ways.

have witnessed a dramatic increase in the number of older students pursuing two-year, four-year, and graduate degrees. These older students are more likely to be female—and are more likely to be Black or Hispanic—than is the typical 19- or 20-year-old college student. Viewed from a conflict perspective, it is not surprising that women and minorities are overrepresented among older students; members of these groups are the most likely to miss out on higher education the first time around (F. Best and Eberhard 1990).

In 1970, only one-quarter of all students taking credit courses in colleges in the United States were 25 years old or older. However, by the

FIGURE 15-3

Age Distribution of College Students in the United States, 1970–2008

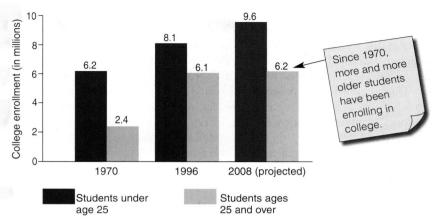

Since 1970, more and more older students have been enrolling in college.

Students under age 25
Students ages 25 and over

Source: National Center for Educational Statistics 1999: Table 174.

Many adults return to school in later life to obtain further education, advance their careers, or change their line of work. These adults are studying microbiology.

mid-1990s, this figure had risen to more than 40 percent (see Figure 15-3). Obviously, sociological models of the collegiate subculture will have to be revised significantly in light of such changes. Moreover, as the age of the "typical" college student increases, there will be a growing need for on-campus child care. This pp. 109–11 is especially true in community colleges, where the median age of students is already 31.

It should be noted that the nation's colleges *need* older students. Given the expected decrease in population in the age group 18 to 24 years old over the period 2010 through 2050, institutions of higher learning will have to find new consumers for their services in order to survive financially. This need has led colleges across the United States to develop adult education programs. Currently, about half of all adults take part in some type of adult education (Bureau of the Census 1999a:17).

One aspect of the adult education boom involves the rapidly changing nature of the business world in an age of technological innovation. Business firms have come to accept the view of education as lifelong and may encourage (or require) employees to learn job-related skills. Thus, secretaries are sent to special schools to be trained to use the latest computer software. Realtors attend classes to learn about alternative forms of financing for home buyers. In occupation after occupation, longtime workers and professionals are going back to school to adapt to the new demands of their jobs.

Not all adult education is at the college level. Each year thousands of young adults drop out of high school, sometimes because of family obligations and sometimes out of a desire to enter the workforce or the informal economy. Later these adults may recognize the desirability of a high school diploma and decide to pursue a GED (General Educational Development) diploma, which usually involves taking preparatory classes followed by a series of exams. In recent years the proportion of students who take this alternative route to finishing high school has grown steadily. During the 1990s, the percentage of high school degrees awarded to students aged 18 to 24 years who attended GED programs increased from less than 5 percent to over 10 percent. Thus far, researchers have found conflicting evidence on the effect of a GED versus a traditional degree on employment status and earnings; additional research needs to be done on this topic (Population Reference Bureau 2000).

Home Schooling

When most people think of school, they think of bricks and mortar and the teachers, administrators, and other employees who staff school buildings. But for an increasing number of students in the United States, home is the classroom and the teacher is a parent. The Department of Education estimates that nationwide, more than a million students are now being educated at home. That is about 2 percent of the K–12 school population.

In the past, families that taught their children at home lived in isolated environments or held strict religious views at odds with the secular environment of public schools. But today, home schooling is attracting a broader range of families not necessarily tied to organized

religion. Poor academic quality, peer pressure, and school violence are motivating many parents to teach their children at home. Indeed, recent publicity on school shooting sprees seems to have accelerated the move toward home schooling (*Education Week* 1999; Schnaiberg 1999b).

While supporters of home schooling feel children can do just as well or better in home schools as in public schools, critics counter that because home-schooled children are isolated from the larger community, they lose an important chance to improve their socialization skills. But proponents of home schooling claim their children benefit from contact with others besides their own age group. They also see home schools as a good alternative for children who suffer from attention deficit disorder (ADD) and learning disorders (LDs). Such children often do better in smaller classes, which present fewer distractions to disturb their concentration (National Homeschool Association 1999).

Given the lack of regulation of home schools, quality control is an issue. While home schooling is legal in all 50 states, only 34 states regulate home schools; 29 monitor students' progress through tests or evaluations. Despite the lack of uniform standards, a national study funded by the Home School Legal Defense Association reports that home-schooled students score higher than others on standardized tests, in every subject and every grade. Almost 25 percent of the students who participated in the study were working above grade level for their age. Home schooling works, particularly for those who have made a commitment to it (*Education Week* 1999; Schnaiberg 1999a).

Who are the people who are running home schools? In general, they tend to have higher-than-average incomes and educational levels. Most are two-parent families, and their children watch less television than average—both factors that are likely to support superior educational performance. The same students, with the same types of family and the same support from their parents, would probably do just as well in the public schools. As research has repeatedly shown, small classes are better than big classes, and strong parental and community involvement is key (Schnaiberg 1999a).

Home schooling, then, gives those parents who are willing to make the effort an alternative to traditional education. So do voucher programs and school choice, the subjects of the next section.

At a home school in Brunswick, Maine, a mother educates her three children. An estimated 3,500 families home-schooled their children in Maine in 1998.

School Choice Programs

The Issue

Imagine a school where every child in kindergarten reads, where third graders read *The Iliad,* where children beg to do second drafts of their writing, where classes are small, and where teachers are chosen by the school, not assigned to it. This was the vision dangled before inner-city parents in Jersey City, New Jersey, one evening in 1998 by a private company that runs publicly financed charter schools. The company representatives were making their somewhat exaggerated pitch to draw students away from the standard public schools to a new charter school. That night, hundreds of parents signed their children up, even though the school didn't have a location yet and was run

Charter schools in New Jersey, like this one in Newark, have become so popular that some of them must use a lottery to select students. While parents are happy with the educational results of these schools, critics are concerned that the most motivated students are being lured away from the regular public schools.

by a company with a track record of just two schools, each open for only one year. "The parents were willing to take the plunge, because while they didn't know fully what they were getting into, they knew they weren't pleased with what their children had" (Winerip 1998:44).

This is the world of the school choice movement, which is increasingly pitting parents against public school proponents. How far should school choice go? For example, should public funds be used to send children to private and parochial schools? Should charter schools be allowed to skim the best students off the public schools? What role should the government play in promoting school choice and in improving public education in general?

The Setting

The term *school choice programs* refers to various types of educational experiments under which parents can choose where to send their children. In the 1970s, school choice took the form of *magnet schools,* usually centralized public schools that offered special enrichment pro-

grams to entice children from their local schools. At first, they were part of an attempt to improve racial balance in the schools, but soon they became known primarily as laboratories for experiments in education. Another form of school choice is the use of *school vouchers.* They provide for the transfer of public funds to the public or private school of the parents' choice. Since the funds follow the child, it was hoped that voucher plans would stimulate the local schools to perform better in order to keep their students. The most recent school choice development has been the *charter school movement.* This nationwide effort allows parents and private educators (or anyone who has an idea for a school) to create and control a school that is chartered by the state and funded by public money. Staff hiring and curriculum decisions are in the planners' hands, although the schools are often subject to certain state rules and regulations as well.

Proponents of school choice often rely on the work of economists for support (Tucker 1993). The use of school vouchers, for example, was first advanced by economist Milton Friedman in his book *Capitalism and Freedom* (1962). The idea is to set up a sort of free-market system of education: Parents shop for the school they want, which receives that child's portion of the school budget ($7,000 in New Jersey, for example). The schools that are most popular thrive, and those that are not picked must improve to compete or else close their doors (Tashman 1992).

Support for school choice comes from a diverse sampling of the "consumers of education": liberals who oppose compulsory school assignments for their children and seek more freedom of choice, nonpolitical parents disillusioned by schools that have become too impersonal and bureaucratized, and Christian fundamentalists who view religious education as a means of combating growing secularization. A national survey done in 1999 showed that overall, about half the population of the United States favored school vouchers; among parents of children attending public schools, the idea was even more popular. In contrast, about half the population thought home schooling was "a bad thing for the nation" (Kirp 1994; Rose and Gallup 1999).

Sociological Insights

Many criticisms have been aimed at school choice programs. The analogy to business competition within a free-market economy seems deceptive to some observers. They argue that while a successful business such as Coca-Cola can expand into new markets across the United States and the world, an elementary school has a limited potential for expanding its customer base. Rather than expanding, an outstanding school will become ever more selective as parents compete to enroll their children. Most charter schools in New Jersey are so oversubscribed they use a lottery to select their students. There is concern, too, about the state of public schools whose most motivated students are skimmed off by school choice programs. They are often left with disproportionately high numbers of poorly motivated students and students with severe learning difficulties.

Critics of choice programs are also troubled by the divisive religious issue underlying the voucher policy. About two-thirds of private school students in the United States attend institutions with religious affiliations; among parents who send their children to private schools, as many as 95 percent identify religion as the number-one criterion in choosing a school. For opponents of vouchers and tuition tax credits, any government aid to parochial education—whether direct (payments to the schools) or indirect (tuition grants to students or tax credits)—violates the nation's historic separation of church and state. Moreover, drawing on the functionalist perspective, critics of school choice point out that education in the United States has traditionally promoted social and political integration. Such integration is undermined when students attend private and parochial schools and do not interact with peers across class, racial, ethnic, and religious lines (Bracey 1993; Lines 1985; V. Martinez et al. 1994).

Viewed from a conflict perspective, the social class and religious implications of school choice programs are a matter of concern—especially when such programs provide financial support for families to send children to private and parochial schools. Studies of existing choice programs suggest that the more affluent households and those with highly educated parents are especially likely to take advantage of these experiments. In part, this is because vouchers and tax credits may not cover the full cost of private school and therefore may not be useful for less affluent families. Despite these concerns and opposition by many Black civil rights groups, public opinion surveys show more support among African American than White parents for school vouchers. Black parents tend to see a voucher program, however flawed, as a welcome alternative to the public schools, in which many of them have little faith (S. Holmes 1999).

Research has just begun on the impact of school choice programs, since they are relatively new. Harvard's Program on Education Policy and Governance Center undertook the first independent evaluation of Cleveland's groundbreaking school voucher program. The study found that the program was popular with parents surveyed and that it raised the scores of students tested at the end of the first year. These results are particularly promising since the program is directed at low-income families, who receive vouchers covering up to 90 percent of private or parochial school tuition. The same researchers discovered that students who participate in Milwaukee's school choice program improve their test scores and perform better than those who don't participate in the program. A similar study of New York City's school voucher system in 1998 also found that low-income pupils using vouchers had slightly better standardized test scores than low-income students not in the program. Up to now, not much information has been available on how well charter schools are doing. But that is about to change. Massachusetts, for example, now requires charters to develop an "accountability contract" with the state involving annual site visits and evidence of academic success (Chaddock 1999; Greene et al. 1997a, 1997b; Holloway 1998; Peterson et al. 1998).

Policy Initiatives

As interest in school voucher programs grows, the controversy that surrounds them grows as well. In 1999 legal challenges were mounted against the voucher program in Cleveland, a statewide voucher program in Florida, and a proposed plan to award vouchers to private schools in Wisconsin, including those affiliated with religious groups. Plaintiffs charged that these programs violated the tradition of separation of church and state. As we saw in the last chapter, the meaning of that fundamental concept is being redefined, and the case of vouchers is no exception. Ultimately, a Supreme Court decision will be necessary to resolve the issue (Janofsky 2000).

pp. 389–92 ◀

So far, school choice policy decisions have been made only at the local and state levels. As of the year 2000, only five public voucher programs were operating in the United States—in Milwaukee, Cleveland, and the states of Florida, Minnesota, and Arizona. Each program served only a small percentage of children. Some 25 state legislatures were thinking of using public money to pay for private and parochial school tuition, however. On the federal level, a bill calling for federal subsidy of tuition vouchers for low-income families failed to pass the House of Representatives in 1997 (Janofsky 2000; Joint Center for Political and Economic Studies 1997b).

Interest in school choice is not unique to the United States. In Great Britain, New Zealand, and Sweden, policymakers have given parents a measure of freedom in selecting their children's schools, and government financing of schools is based on enrollment figures. In Australia, Denmark, and the Netherlands, there has been increasing governmental financial support for private schools (*The Economist* 1994).

Let's Discuss

1. Would you send your child to a private or charter school if the government offered you a tuition voucher? Why or why not?
2. What do you think of the idea that public schools should be able to compete with private schools? What difficulties might they face that private schools do not?
3. Which is more important, maintaining the separation of church and state or fostering educational choice by allowing students to attend religious schools at public expense? Justify your position.

Summary

Education is a cultural universal, found throughout the world, although in varied forms. This chapter examines sociological views of education and analyzes schools as an example of formal organizations.

1. Transmission of knowledge and bestowal of status are manifest functions of education. Among its latent functions are transmitting culture, promoting social and political integration, maintaining social control, and serving as an agent of social change.

2. In the view of conflict theorists, education serves as an instrument of elite domination by creating standards for entry into occupations, bestowing status unequally, and subordinating the role of women in education.

3. Teacher expectations about a student's performance can sometimes have an impact on the student's actual achievements.

4. Today, most schools in the United States are organized in a bureaucratic fashion. Weber's five basic characteristics of bureaucracy are all evident in schools.

5. Since 1970, the proportion of older adults enrolled in U.S. colleges and universities has been rising steadily, in part because of sweeping changes in business, industry, and technology. For many Americans, education has become a lifelong pursuit.

6. Home schooling has become a viable alternative to traditional public and private schools. An estimated million or more American children are now educated at home.

7. School choice and tuition voucher programs are having a direct effect on public education, forcing some schools to compete or go out of business.

Critical Thinking Questions

1. What are the functions and dysfunctions of tracking in schools? Viewed from an interactionist perspective, how would tracking of high school students influence the interactions between students and teachers? In what ways might tracking have positive and negative impacts on the self-concepts of various students?

2. Are the student subcultures identified in the text evident on your campus? What other student subcultures are present? Which subcultures have the highest (and the lowest) social status? How might functionalists, conflict theorists, and interactionists view the existence of student subcultures on a college campus?

Key Terms

Correspondence principle   The tendency of schools to promote the values expected of individuals in each social class and to prepare students for the types of jobs typically held by members of their class. (405)

Credentialism   An increase in the lowest level of education required to enter a field. (403)

Cultural universals   General practices found in every culture. (399)

Education   A formal process of learning in which some people consciously teach while others adopt the social role of learner. (399)

Hidden curriculum   Standards of behavior that are deemed proper by society and are taught subtly in schools. (403)

Teacher-expectancy effect   The impact that a teacher's expectations about a student's performance may have on the student's actual achievements. (407)

Tracking   The practice of placing students in specific curriculum groups on the basis of test scores and other criteria. (404)

Additional Readings

BOOKS

Entwistle, Doris R., Karl L. Alexander, and Linda Steffel Olson. 1997. *Children, Schools and Inequality.* Boulder, CO: Westview Press. An overview of a number of issues confronting the schools including poverty, placement tests, Head Start, tracking, and social inequality.

Feagin, Joe R., Harnán Vera, and Nikitah Imani. 1996. *The Agony of Education: Black Students at White Colleges and Universities.* New York: Routledge. An examination of the challenges faced by African Americans at predominantly White colleges.

Lemann, Nicholas. 1999. *The Big Test: The Secret History of the American Meritocracy.* New York: Farrar, Straus & Giroux. A look at the historical development of the Educational Testing Service and its role in promoting the use of standardized testing in the college admissions process.

Sadker, Myra, and David Sadker. 1995. *Failing at Fairness: How America's Schools Cheat Girls.* New York: Touchstone. The authors present a history of women's education in the United States and then critically examine the contemporary treatment of females from elementary school through graduate school.

JOURNALS

The sociology of education is reflected in *Educational Record* (founded in 1920), *Education and Urban Society* (1968), *Education Week* (1981), the *Harvard Educational Review* (1974), *Journal of Contemporary Education* (1984), *Journal of Educational Finance* (1975), *Phi Delta Kappan* (1915), and *Sociology of Education* (1927).

Internet Connection

Note: While all the URLs listed were current as of the printing of this book, these sites often change. Please check our website (http://www.mhhe.com/schaefer) for updates.

1. The American Association of University Women maintains a webpage dedicated to issues of gender inequality in education. Log onto (**http://www.aauw.org/**). While visiting this site, reflect on your own experience as a student and answer the following questions:
   - (a) What is the American Association of University Women (AAUW)? What are the organization's goals?
   - (b) What historical events helped to shape the AAUW, and what contributions has it made to society?
   - (c) Click on "Issues" and examine the Fact Sheets/Position Papers section, especially the Education reports. What is Title IX of the Education Amendments of 1972? What is the current status of women's athletics in education according to the AAUW, and what statistics support these findings? In which areas have schools made the most progress toward gender equality, and which the least? What myths still exist regarding the current status of gender equality in academics?

   - (d) What is the AAUW's position on issues such as single-sex education and school vouchers? What is your own opinion on these issues?
   - (e) What more can be done to improve gender equity in the classroom and on campus?

2. School choice and tuition vouchers are increasingly popular alternatives to the traditional educational system, but will they make a difference? Learn more about these plans by logging onto (**http://fullcoverage.yahoo.com/Full_Coverage/ US/School_Choice_and_Tuition_Vouchers/**).
   - (a) Which states currently offer tuition vouchers? Have these programs been successful? Why or why not?
   - (b) What educational problems do school choice and tuition voucher plans aim to alleviate?
   - (c) What are some of the economic, social, and political challenges in starting and maintaining school choice programs?
   - (d) Visit some of the "pro" and "con" organizations listed at the bottom of the website. What are the main reasons for opposing school choice? For advocating it? What research or evidence supports each side?
   - (e) Which side of the debate do you agree with, and why?

GOVERNMENT

Voter turnout in the United States is low compared to other Western democracies. A clothing store offered this public service advertisement to encourage citizens to vote.

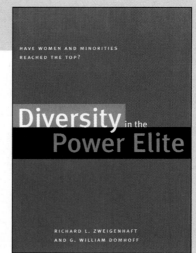

The power elite and Congress are more diverse than they were before the social movements that emerged in the 1960s brought pressure to bear on corporations, politicians, and government. Although the power elite is still composed primarily of Christian white men, there are now Jews, women, blacks, Latinos, and Asian Americans on the boards of the country's largest corporations; presidential cabinets are far more diverse than was the case forty years ago; and the highest ranks of the military are no longer filled solely by white men. In the case of elected officials in Congress, the trend toward diversity is even greater for women and all of the minority groups that we have studied. At the same time, we have shown that the assimilation of the different groups has been uneven. . . .

Ultimately we suggest that the increase in diversity at the top contains several ironies, the most important of which is related to what is perhaps the major unresolved tension in American life, between liberal individualism and the class structure. The diversification of the power elite has been celebrated, but this celebration ignores the continuing importance of the class structure. The movements that led to diversity in the power elite have succeeded to some extent, especially for women and minorities from privileged social backgrounds, but there has been no effect on the way the power elite functions or on the class structure itself. . . .

We therefore have to conclude on the basis of our findings that the diversification of the power elite did not generate any changes in an underlying class system. . . . The values of liberal individualism embedded in the Declaration of Independence, the Bill of Rights, and the civic culture were renewed by vigorous and courageous activists, but despite their efforts the class structure remains a major obstacle to individual fulfillment for the overwhelming majority of Americans. This fact is more than an irony. It is a dilemma. It combines with the dilemma of race to create a nation that celebrates equal opportunity but is, in reality, a bastion of class privilege and conservatism. *(Zweigenhaft and Domhoff 1998:176–77, 194)* ■

Half a century ago C. Wright Mills (1959), the originator of the phrase *the sociological imagination,* studied the political process in the United States and articulated the concept of the power elite. In doing so, Mills stimulated a discussion about how society's most important decisions are made. Mills made a point of stating that the power elite was composed of men. That was no accident; at the time Mills wrote, no women made life-and-death decisions on society's behalf.

Four decades after Mills opened discussion of the subject, psychologist Richard L. Zweigenhaft and sociologist G. William Domhoff returned to the question of who rules America. As the opening excerpt from their book *Diversity in the Power Elite* (1998) shows, they found only modest changes in the nation's power structure. Today, a few privileged women occupy positions in the power elite, but the majority of the nation's decision makers are still men, and virtually all of them are White.

The power elite operates within the framework of the existing political system, be it local, state, national, or international. By **political system,** sociologists mean the social institution that is founded on a recognized set of procedures for implementing and achieving society's goals, such as the allocation of valued resources. Like religion and the family, the political system is a cultural universal: It is found in every society. In the United States, the political system holds the ultimate responsibility for addressing the social policy issues examined in this textbook: child care, the AIDS crisis, sexual harassment, welfare reform, and so forth.

This chapter will present a sociological analysis of the impact of government on people's lives. We will begin with a macro-level analysis of the sources of power in a political system, and the three major types of authority. We will see how politics works in the United States, with particular attention to political socialization, citizens' participation in politics, the changing role of women in politics, and the influence of interest groups on political decision making. We'll also look at two models of power in the United States: the elite and the pluralist models. Finally, the social policy section will explore the controversy over campaign financing, an issue that vividly illustrates the close relationship between government and the moneyed interest groups that seek to influence the political process. ■

Politics and Government

An economic system does not exist in a vacuum. Someone or some group makes important decisions about how to use resources and how to allocate goods, whether it be a tribal chief or a parliament or a dictator. A cultural universal common to all economic systems, then, is the exercise of power and authority. The struggle for power and authority inevitably involves **politics,** which political scientist Harold Lasswell (1936) tersely defined as "who gets what, when, and how." In their study of politics and government, sociologists are concerned with social interactions among individuals and groups and their impact on the larger political and economic order.

Power

p. 208

Power is at the heart of a political system. According to Max Weber, **power** is the ability to exercise one's will over others. To put it another way, whoever can control the behavior of others is exercising power. Power relations can involve large organizations, small groups, or even people in an intimate association.

There are three basic sources of power within any political system—force, influence, and authority. *Force* is the actual or threatened use of coercion to impose one's will on others. When leaders imprison or even execute political dissidents, they are applying force; so, too, are terrorists when they seize or bomb an embassy or assassinate a political leader (see Box 16-1 on p. 425). *Influence,* on the other hand, refers to the exercise of power through a process of persuasion. A citizen may change his or her position regarding a Supreme Court nominee because of a newspaper editorial, the expert testimony of a law school dean before the Senate Judiciary Committee, or a stirring speech at a rally by a political activist. In each case, sociologists would view such efforts to persuade people as examples of influence. Now let's take a look at the third source of power, *authority.*

Types of Authority

The term *authority* refers to power that has been institutionalized and is recognized by the people over whom it is exercised. Sociologists commonly use the term in connection with those who hold legitimate power through elected or publicly acknowledged positions. A person's

JEANNE KOHL-WELLES:
Washington State Senator

During the socially turbulent 1960s, Jeanne Kohl-Welles was teaching at an inner-city school in Los Angeles. Her experiences there inspired in her a desire to work for social change. Kohl-Welles enrolled in graduate school, immersed herself in sociology courses, and eventually earned a PhD in sociology from UCLA.

Later, while teaching at the University of Washington, Kohl-Welles became involved in local politics. "It was something I always thought I would want to do, to play a more direct role in effecting social change and public policy," she explains. Today, as a Washington State senator, she does just that. "In 1994 I introduced legislation that required schools to establish policies on sexual harassment. Being a sociologist I recognized the need for involvement of different groups. It was very difficult to get that bill through, but we did it."

Kohl-Welles is now working on a new law that will allow women on welfare to satisfy their work requirements by going to college. Her ability to analyze social research on such issues helps her to formulate good public policy. In fact, she sees the influence of sociology in everything she does: "the way I look at things, the different programs I deal with, what legislation I work on, how I speak before different groups. Being a sociologist gives me a perspective on social groups in society, socialization, social inequities, how to remove barriers."

Her advice to students: "Be open and explore opportunities." Kohl-Welles feels that being able to use research findings and apply sociological theory to real-life situations is valuable in almost any occupation, but particularly in public policy. In her opinion, a student with both a sociology degree and an interest in government would add a great deal to any legislative staff. "What public policy makers deal with *are* social issues," she says emphatically.

---

authority is limited by the constraints of a particular social position. Thus, a referee has the authority to decide whether a penalty should be called during a football game but has no authority over the price of tickets to the game.

Max Weber (1947, original edition 1913) developed a classification system regarding authority that has become one of the most useful and frequently cited contributions of early sociology. He identified three ideal types of authority: traditional, legal-rational, and charismatic. Weber did not insist that only one type applies to a given society or organization. All can be present, but their relative importance will vary. Sociologists have found Weber's typology valuable in understanding different manifestations of legitimate power within a society.

Traditional Authority

Until the middle of this century, Japan was ruled by a revered emperor, whose power was absolute and passed down from generation to generation. In a political system based on *traditional authority,* legitimate power is conferred by custom and accepted practice. A king or queen is accepted as ruler of a nation simply by virtue of inheriting

King Bhumibol Adulyadej of Thailand reviews the Royal Honor Guard during a ceremony honoring his birthday. In a political system based on traditional authority, power is conferred according to accepted custom—in this case, on the basis of royal birth.

The horrifying bombing of a U.S. government building in Oklahoma City in April 1995 killed 168 people, but the damage went far beyond the number of deaths and injuries. This incident touched the "heartland" of the United States in a profound way; no longer could people believe that such incidents occur only in New York or Paris, Belfast or Beirut, Johannesburg or Jerusalem. Indeed, in a Gallup survey conducted in 1995 after the Oklahoma City bombing, 86 percent of respondents felt it likely that bombings or similar acts of violence would occur elsewhere in the United States in the near future.

Terrorism is the use or threat of violence against random or symbolic targets in pursuit of political aims. While terrorism often is related to international political controversies, there is purely domestic terrorism as well. For example, Chapter 11 mentioned murder and threats against physicians and other personnel of women's health clinics that offer abortions. From 1982 through early 1997, 183 abortion clinics in the United States were bombed or burned.

An essential aspect of contemporary terrorism involves use of the media. Terrorists may wish to keep secret their individual identities, but they want their political messages and goals to receive as much publicity as possible. Drawing upon Erving Goffman's dramaturgical approach, sociologist Alfred McClung Lee has likened terrorism to the theater, where certain scenes are played out

in a predictable fashion. Whether through calls to the media, anonymous manifestos, or other means, terrorists typically admit responsibility for and defend their violent acts.

For terrorists, the end justifies the means. The status quo is viewed as oppressive; desperate measures are believed essential to end the suffering of the deprived. Convinced that working through the formal political process will not effect desired political change, terrorists insist that illegal actions—often directed against innocent people—are needed. In a sense, terrorists hope to intimidate society and thereby bring about a new political order.

> From 1982 through early 1997, 183 abortion clinics in the United States were bombed or burned.

Some political commentators have argued that terrorism defies definition because one person's "terrorist" is another person's "freedom fighter." In this view, we carry our biases into our evaluation of terrorist incidents and criticize only those perpetrated by groups who do not share our political goals. Sociologists reject this critique, countering that even in warfare there are accepted rules outlawing the use of certain tactics. For example, civilian noncombatants are supposedly immune from deliberate attack and are not to be taken prisoner. If we are to set objective standards regarding

terrorism, then we should condemn *any and all people* who are guilty of certain actions, no matter how understandable or even admirable some of their goals may be.

The bombing in Oklahoma City was the work of people affiliated with militia groups hostile to the federal government. Without question, the bombing brought unprecedented governmental and media attention to a paramilitary right-wing counterculture of "weekend warriors" (refer back to Chapter 3). The members of this counterculture—overwhelmingly White, male, and Christian—are enraged by many aspects of U.S. national policy (including gun control) and, in some instances, adhere to paranoid and anti-Semitic conspiracy theories. In his 1994 book *Warrior Dreams: Paramilitary Culture in Post-Vietnam America*, sociologist James William Gibson tied the emergence of this counterculture to the U.S. military defeat in the war in Vietnam. A year before the Oklahoma City bombing, Gibson warned that the paramilitary counterculture posed a "great danger" to the United States.

Let's Discuss

1. Have you ever lived in a place where the threat of terrorism was a part of daily life, or known someone who did? What was it like?
2. Can any goal, no matter how noble, justify terrorist activity?

Sources: Gibson 1994; Herman and O'Sullivan 1990; K. Johnson and Sharn 1997; Lee 1983; R. Miller 1988; D. Moore 1995b; Paul 1987; K. Stern 1996.

the crown; a tribal chief rules because that is the accepted practice. The ruler may be loved or hated, competent or destructive; in terms of legitimacy, that does not matter. For the traditional leader, authority rests in custom, not in personal characteristics, technical competence, or even written law. People accept this authority because "this is how things have always been done." Traditional authority is absolute when the ruler has the ability to determine laws and policies.

Legal-Rational Authority

The U.S. Constitution gives Congress and our president the authority to make and enforce laws and policies. Power made legitimate by law is known as *legal-rational authority.* Leaders derive their legal-rational authority from the written rules and regulations of political systems, such as a constitution. Generally, in societies based on legal-rational authority, leaders are thought to have specific areas of competence and authority, but are not

425

thought to be endowed with divine inspiration, as in certain societies with traditional forms of authority.

Charismatic Authority

Joan of Arc was a simple peasant girl in medieval France, yet she was able to rally the French people and lead them in major battles against English invaders. How was this possible? As Weber observed, power can be legitimized by the charisma of an individual. The term *charismatic authority* refers to power made legitimate by a leader's exceptional personal or emotional appeal to his or her followers. Charisma lets a person lead or inspire without relying on set rules or traditions. In fact, charismatic authority is derived more from the beliefs of followers than from the actual qualities of leaders. So long as people *perceive* a leader as having qualities setting him or her apart from ordinary citizens, that leader's authority will remain secure and often unquestioned.

Unlike traditional rulers, charismatic leaders often become well known by breaking with established institutions and advocating dramatic changes in the social structure and the economic system. Their strong hold over their followers makes it easier to build protest movements that challenge the dominant norms and values of a society. Thus, charismatic leaders such as Jesus, Joan of Arc, Mahatma Gandhi, Malcolm X, and Martin Luther King all used their power to press for changes in accepted social behavior. But so did Adolf Hitler, whose charismatic appeal turned people toward violent and destructive ends in Nazi Germany.

Observing from an interactionist perspective, sociologist Carl Couch (1996) points out that the growth of the electronic media has facilitated the development of charismatic authority. During the 1930s and 1940s, the heads of state of the United States, Great Britain, and Germany all used radio to issue direct appeals to citizens. In recent decades, television has allowed leaders to "visit" people's homes and communicate with them. Time and again, Saddam Hussein has rallied the Iraqi people through shrewd use of television appearances. In both Taiwan and South Korea in 1996, troubled political leaders facing reelection campaigns spoke frequently to national audiences and exaggerated military threats from neighboring China and North Korea, respectively.

As was noted earlier, Weber used traditional, legal-rational, and charismatic authority as ideal types. In reality, particular leaders and political systems combine elements of two or more of these forms. Presidents Franklin D. Roosevelt, John F. Kennedy, and Ronald Reagan wielded power largely through the legal-rational basis of their authority. At the same time, they were unusually charismatic leaders who commanded the personal loyalty of large numbers of citizens.

Political Behavior in the United States

Citizens of the United States take for granted many aspects of their political system. They are accustomed to living in a nation with a Bill of Rights, two major political parties, voting by secret ballot, an elected president, state and local governments distinct from the national government, and so forth. Yet, of course, each society has its own ways of governing itself and making decisions. Just as U.S. residents expect Democratic and Republican candidates to compete for public offices, residents of the People's Republic of China and Cuba are accustomed to one-party rule by the Communist party. In this section, we will examine a number of important aspects of political behavior within the United States.

Political Socialization

Do your political views coincide with those of your parents? Did you vote in the last election? Did you register to vote, or do you plan to do so? The process by which you acquire political attitudes and develop patterns of political behavior is known as *political socialization.* This involves not only learning the prevailing beliefs of a society but also coming to accept the political system, whatever its limitations and problems.

Chapter 6 identified five functional prerequisites that a society must fulfill to survive. One of these was the need to teach recruits to accept the values and customs of the group. In a political sense, this function is crucial; each succeeding generation must be encouraged to accept a society's basic political values and its particular methods of decision making. The principal institutions of political socialization are those that also socialize us to other cultural norms: the family, schools, and the media.

Many observers see the family as playing a particularly significant role in the process. Parents pass on their political attitudes and evaluations to their sons and daughters through discussions at the dinner table and also through the example of their political involvement or apathy. Early socialization does not always determine a person's political orientation; there are changes over time and between generations. Yet research on political socialization continues to show that parents' views have an important impact on their children's outlook (M. Jennings and Niemi 1981).

Schools provide young people with information and analysis of the political world. Unlike the family and peer groups, schools are easily susceptible to centralized and uniform control. That is why totalitarian societies commonly use educational institutions to indoctrinate the students in certain political beliefs. Even in democracies, where local

and Richard Nixon in the 1960 presidential race, television has given increasing exposure to political candidates. Electronic "town meetings" and televised debates are standard fare in political campaigns today. Many speeches given by our nation's leaders are designed not for immediate listeners but for the larger television audience.

Political socialization can take different forms in different types of societies. Using observation research, sociologist Benigno Aguirre (1984) concluded that the Cuban government encouraged certain types of crowd behavior to reinforce its legitimacy. The Committees for the Defense of the Revolution—which functioned much as the Communist party did when it ruled the Soviet Union—mobilized Cubans for parades, celebrations, protests, and testimonials on behalf of deceased revolutionary leaders. Through these mobilizations, Cuba's rulers hoped to convey the political message that Fidel Castro's communist government had and deserved widespread popular support.

Participation and Apathy

In theory, a representative democracy will function most effectively and fairly if an informed and active electorate communicates its views to government leaders. Unfortunately, this is hardly the case in the United States. Virtually all citizens are familiar with the basics of the political process, and most tend to identify to some extent with a political party (see Table 16-1), but only a small minority

Children in the United States are socialized to view representative democracy as the best form of government. One part of this process is encouraging schoolchildren to vote in mock elections.

schools are not under the pervasive control of the national government, political education will generally reflect the norms and values of the prevailing political order.

In the view of conflict theorists, students in the United States learn much more than factual information about their political and economic way of life. They are socialized to view capitalism and representative democracy as the "normal" and most desirable ways of organizing a nation, a form of dominant ideology.

pp. 76–77 At the same time, schools often present competing values and forms of government in a negative fashion or simply ignore them. From a conflict perspective, this type of political education serves the interests of the powerful and ignores the significance of the social divisions found within the United States.

Like the family and schools, the mass media can have obvious effects on people's thinking and political behavior. Beginning with the debates between John Kennedy

Table 16-1   Political Party Preferences in the United States

Party Identification	Percentage of Population
Strong Democrat	13
Not very strong Democrat	22
Independent, close to Democrat	13
Independent	17
Independent, close to Republican	9
Not very strong Republican	18
Strong Republican	9

Note: Data are for 1998. Numbers do not add to 100 percent due to rounding.
Source: J. Davis and Smith 1998:83.

(often members of the higher social classes) actually participate in political organizations on a local or national level. Studies reveal that only 8 percent of the people in the United States belong to a political club or organization. Not more than one in five has *ever* contacted an official of national, state, or local government about a political issue or problem (Orum 1989).

The failure of most citizens to become involved in political parties diminishes the democratic process. Within the political system of the United States, the political party serves as an intermediary between people and government. Through competition in regularly scheduled elections, the two major parties provide for challenges to public policies and for an orderly transfer of power. An individual dissatisfied with the state of the nation or a local community can become involved in the political party process in many ways, such as by joining a political club supporting candidates for public office or working to change the party's position on controversial issues. If, however, people do not take an interest in the decisions of major political parties, public officials in a "representative" democracy will be chosen from two unrepresentative lists of candidates.

In the 1980s, it became clear that many people in the United States were beginning to be turned off by political parties, politicians, and big government. The most dramatic indication of this growing alienation comes from voting statistics. Voters of all ages and races appear to be less enthusiastic than ever about elections, even presidential contests. For example, almost 80 percent of eligible voters in the United States went to the polls in the presidential election of 1896. Yet by the 1996 election, turnout had fallen to less than 49 percent of all eligible voters.

While a few nations still command high voter turnout, it is increasingly common to hear national leaders of other countries complain of voter apathy. Japan typically enjoyed 70 percent turnout in its Upper House elections in the 1950s through mid-1980s, but by 1998 turnout was closer to 58 percent. In the 1998 British general elections, there was only a 34 percent turnout in London and 28 percent in the rest of England (A. King 1998; Masaki 1998).

Political participation makes government accountable to the voters. If participation declines, government can operate with less of a sense of accountability to society. This issue is most serious for the least powerful individuals and groups within the United States. Voter turnout has been particularly low among members of racial and ethnic minorities. According to a 1996 postelection survey, only 50.6 percent of *registered* Black voters and 26.7 percent of *registered* Hispanics reported that they had actually voted (see Table 16-2). Moreover, the poor—whose focus understandably is on survival—are traditionally underrepresented among voters as well. The low turnout found among these groups is explained, at least in part, by their common feeling of powerlessness. Yet these low voting statistics encourage political power brokers to continue to ignore the interests of the less affluent and the nation's minorities. The segment of the voting population that has shown the *most* voter apathy—the young—is highlighted in Box 16-2.

Women in Politics

In 1999, the top five statewide elected positions in Arizona were all held by women—governor, attorney general, state treasurer, secretary of state, and superintendent of

Table 16-2   Surveys of Voter Participation in the Presidential Elections of 1972 and 1996

Group	1972 (Nixon–McGovern)		1996 (Clinton–Dole–Perot)	
	Percent Registered	Percent Who Voted	Percent Registered	Percent Who Voted
Total U.S. Population	72.3	63.0	65.9	54.2
Whites	73.4	64.5	67.7	56.0
Blacks	65.5	52.1	63.5	50.6
Hispanics	44.4	37.5	35.7	26.7

Source: Casper and Bass 1998.

education. Newspapers nationwide featured this land-mark event. Of course, it was newsworthy because typically these positions are all held by men, in state after state, year after year.

Women continue to be dramatically underrepresented in the halls of government. In 1999, there were only 67 women in Congress. They accounted for 58 of the 435 members of the House of Representatives and 9 of the 100 members of the Senate. Only two states other than Arizona had female governors—New Hampshire and New Jersey (Center for the American Woman and Politics 1999).

p. 299 Sexism has been the most serious barrier to women interested in holding office. Women were not even allowed to vote in national elections until 1920, and subsequent female candidates have had to overcome the prejudices of both men and women regarding women's fitness for leadership. Not until 1955 did a majority of people state that they would vote for a qualified woman for president. Moreover, women often encounter prejudice, discrimination, and abuse after they are elected. Despite these problems, more women are being elected to political office, and more of them are identifying themselves as feminists.

But while women politicians may be enjoying more electoral success now than in the past, there is evidence that the media cover them differently from men. A content analysis of newspaper coverage of recent gubernatorial races showed that reporters wrote more often about a female candidate's personal life, appearance, or personality than a male candidate's, and less often about her political positions and voting record. Furthermore, when political issues were raised in newspaper articles, reporters were more likely to illustrate them with statements made by male candidates than by female candidates (J. Devitt 1999).

Figure 16-1 (page 432) shows the representation of women in national legislatures throughout the world. While the proportion of women has increased in the United States and many other nations, women still do not account for half the members of the national legislature in any country. Sweden ranks the highest, with 43 percent. Overall, the United States in 2000 ranked 40th among 116 nations in the proportion of women serving as national legislators (Inter-Parliamentary Union 2000).

A new dimension of women and politics emerged beginning in the 1980s. Surveys detected a growing "gender gap" in the political preferences and activities of males and females. Women were more likely to register as Democrats than as Republicans and were also more critical of the policies of the Reagan and Bush administrations. According to political analysts, the Democratic party's support for the right to choose a legal abortion,

Members of the United States' first all-female state administration pose for a historic photograph. From left, Attorney General Janet Napolitano, Superintendent of Public Instruction Lisa Graham Keegan, Treasurer Carol Springer, Governor Jane Hull, and Secretary of State Betsey Bayless, all of Arizona.

for family and medical leave legislation, and for governmental action to require insurers to cover a minimum two-day hospital stay for new mothers has attracted women voters. As one analyst put it, "Women have traditionally felt more vulnerable, and the safety net—whether it's for older women, women in poverty, or single heads of households—has been a more immediate experience in their lives. Traditionally, the Democratic party has been associated with that safety net" (Marks 1998:3).

A gender gap was still evident in the 1998 election. Data from exit polls revealed that Democrats received 51 percent of women's votes, compared with 45 percent of men's votes. While that is only a 6 percent gap, many elections are settled by such a margin, so turnout of female voters is a key to Democratic victories. When women did not turn out in the 1994 congressional elections, solid support from White male voters was an important factor in Republican success (R. Benedetto 1998; Berke 1994; Purnick 1996).

Research in Action

16-2 Why Don't Young People Vote?

In 1971, there was great optimism. All through the 1960s, young people in the United States had actively participated in a range of political issues—from pushing civil rights to protesting the Vietnam War. They were especially disturbed by the fact that young men who were barred from voting were yet being drafted to serve in the military and dying for their country. In response to these concerns, the 26th Amendment to the Constitution was ratified in 1971, lowering the voting age from 21 to 18 in federal, state, and local elections.

Now, almost 30 years later, we can consider the available research and see what happened. Frankly, what is remarkable is what did *not* happen. First, young voters (those between 18 and 21) have not united in any particular political sentiment. We can see in how the young vote the same divisions of race, ethnicity, and gender that are apparent among older age groups.

Second, while the momentum for lowering the voting age came from college campuses, the majority of young voters are not students at all. Many are already part of the workforce and either live with their parents or have established their own households.

Third, and particularly troubling, is their low voter turnout. In the 1996 presidential election, only 46 percent of the voting age population ages 18–20 was even registered.

Among these young people, only 31 percent bothered to show up at the polls. This is an even lower turnout than among non–high school graduates or the unemployed.

What is behind this voter apathy among the young? The popular explanation is that people, especially young people, are alienated from the political system, turned off by the shallowness and negativity of candidates and campaigns. True, studies document that young voters are susceptible to cyni-

> While the momentum for lowering the voting age came from college campuses, the majority of young voters are not students at all.

cism and distrust, but these are not necessarily associated with voter apathy. Numerous studies show the relationship between how people perceive the candidates and issues and their likelihood of voting is a very complex one. Communication scholars Erica Weintraub Austin and Bruce Pinkleton completed a survey of less experienced eligible voters and found that those who believe that they can see through the "lies" told by politicians via the media are *more* apt to

think their participation can make a difference. In any event, young people do vote as they age. Any disaffection with the voting booth is certainly not permanent.

Other explanations for the lower turnout among the young seem more plausible. First, the United States is virtually alone in requiring citizens to, in effect, vote twice. They must first *register* to vote, often at a time when issues are not on the front burner and candidates haven't even declared. Then they must vote on election day. Young people, who tend to be mobile and to lead hectic lives, find it difficult to track voting requirements (which vary by state) and be present where they are legally eligible to vote. Time constraints are the single biggest reason that voters gave for not voting in the 1996 election. In 1995, the motor-voter law went into effect, allowing people to register when they applied for or renewed driver's licenses, but this attempt to simplify the registration process has done little to change voting apathy. A year later, only 66 percent of the voting age population reported they were registered, the lowest rate for a presidential election since 1968.

Second, while citizens in the United States generally tend to be more active than their counterparts in other countries in politics on the community level, young people often feel unmoved by such local issues as public school

Sources: Austin and Pinkleton 1995; Bureau of the Census 1998f; Casper and Bass 1998; Clymer 2000; Cook 1991; Landers 1988; Leon 1996; Shogan 1998.

Interest Groups

Common needs or common frustrations may lead people to band together in social movements to have an effect in the political arena. Examples include the civil rights movement of the 1960s and the anti–nuclear power movement of the 1980s (Sherman and Kolker 1987). We will consider social movements in more detail in Chapter 21. People can also influence the political process through membership in interest groups (some of which, in fact, may be part of larger social movements).

An **interest group** is a voluntary association of citizens who attempt to influence public policy. The National Organization for Women (NOW) is considered an inter-

est group; so, too, are the Juvenile Diabetes Foundation and the National Rifle Association (NRA). Such groups are a vital part of the political process of the United States. Many interest groups (often known as *lobbies*) are national in scope and address a wide array of social, economic, and political issues.

One way in which interest groups influence the political process is through their political action committees. A **political action committee** (or **PAC**) is a political committee established by an interest group—say, a national bank, corporation, trade association, or cooperative or membership association—to solicit contributions for candidates or political parties.

430

financing and land use. Sometimes issues such as landlord policies or student–police relations surface in college towns, mobilizing the youth vote, but this activism often declines as the issue fades from view.

Third, the entry of young people into the electorate during the 1970s came at a time when the traditional, well-organized two-party system that actively sought out new voters, whatever age, suffered a decline. No longer are potential new voters greeted by political party faithful all too ready to guide a recruit through the voting process.

These studies do not point to easy solutions for reversing the three-decade pattern of low turnout among the newest voters. Facilitating the registration and voting process, identifying local issues of interest, grass-roots campaigning, and more careful evaluation of media campaigning may all help. We also need to continue to research potential reasons why more than 7 million people between the ages of 18 and 21 fail to even register to vote and why another million who take that step fail to vote.

"Rock the Vote" was the theme of this celebrity get-out-the-vote rally during the 1996 presidential election campaign. But neither William Baldwin (at the microphone) nor the other celebrities were very successful. Of registered voters ages 18–20, only 31 percent bothered to show up at the polls.

Let's Discuss

1. How often do you vote? If you do not vote, what accounts for your apathy? Are you too busy to register? Are community issues uninteresting to you?

2. Do you think voter apathy is a serious social problem? What might be done to increase voter participation in your age group and community?

Political action committees distribute substantial funds to candidates for public office. The potential power of PACs emerged in an analysis by this textbook's author of the position taken by U.S. senators in a crucial pair of votes in 1998. The Senate defeated a measure that would have increased the tax on a pack of cigarettes and approved a settlement with tobacco companies requiring them to pay for increased medical costs caused by the public's use of tobacco products. All tobacco companies strongly opposed both measures. As you can see in Figure 16-2, senators receiving more campaign contributions from tobacco interest PACs were much more likely to vote against these bills. In that same session of Congress, the

Senate showed little interest in reforming campaign finance, although the House did pass a measure that would curb some of the excesses.

Models of Power Structure In the United States

Who really holds power in the United States? Do "we the people" genuinely run the country through elected representatives? Or is it true that, behind the scenes, a small elite controls both the government and the economic system? It is difficult to determine the location of power in a

FIGURE 16-1

Women in National Legislatures

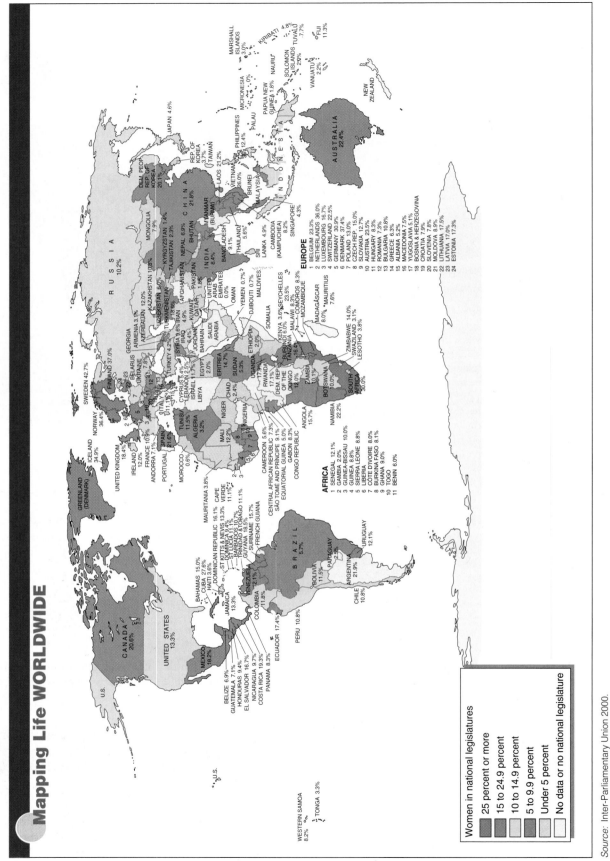

Mapping Life WORLDWIDE

Source: Inter-Parliamentary Union 2000.

Each color on the map indicates a certain percentage of women in the national legislatures, as designated by the key.

FIGURE 16-2

Tobacco Vote and Campaign Contributions

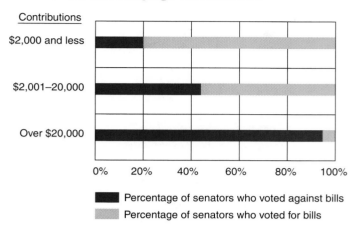

Contributions

- $2,000 and less
- $2,001–20,000
- Over $20,000

0% 20% 40% 60% 80% 100%

■ Percentage of senators who voted against bills
▨ Percentage of senators who voted for bills

The greater the campaign contribution from tobacco interest groups, the more likely senators were to vote against the legislation that tobacco interests opposed.

Source: Author's analysis of data from the Center for Responsible Politics, Federal Election Commission, and *USA Today* as cited in *USA Today* 1998, p. 16A.

society as complex as the United States. In exploring this critical question, social scientists have developed two basic views of our nation's power structure: the power elite and the pluralist models.

Power Elite Models

Karl Marx essentially believed that nineteenth-century representative democracy was a sham. He argued that industrial societies were dominated by relatively small numbers of people who owned factories and controlled natural resources. In Marx's view, government officials and military leaders were essentially servants of this capitalist class and followed their wishes. Therefore, any key decisions made by politicians inevitably reflected the interests of the dominant bourgeoisie. Like others who hold an *elite model* of power relations, Marx believed that society is ruled by a small group of individuals who share a common set of political and economic interests.

Mills's Model

Sociologist C. Wright Mills took this model a step further in his pioneering work *The Power Elite* (1956), referred to at the beginning of this

chapter. Mills described a small ruling elite of military, industrial, and governmental leaders who controlled the fate of the United States. Power rested in the hands of a few, both inside and outside government—the *power elite.*

A pyramid illustrates the power structure of the United States in Mills's model (see Figure 16-3a). At the

In December 1999, the world's largest company was created when the merger of two major oil companies, Exxon and Mobil, was approved. Some observers would call this event an example of the power elite flexing their muscles.

FIGURE 16-3

Power Elite Models

THE POWER ELITE

Corporate rich

Executive branch

Military leaders

Interest group leaders

Legislators

Local opinion leaders

Unorganized, exploited masses

Social Upper Class

THE POWER ELITE

Corporate Community

Policy-Formation Organizations

a. C. Wright Mills's model, 1956

b. William Domhoff's model, 1998

Source: Domhoff 1998, p. 3.

top are the corporate rich, leaders of the executive branch of government, and heads of the military (whom Mills called the "warlords"). Directly below are local opinion leaders, members of the legislative branch of government, and leaders of special-interest groups. Mills contended that such individuals and groups would basically follow the wishes of the dominant power elite. At the bottom of the pyramid are the unorganized, exploited masses.

This power elite model is, in many respects, similar to the work of Karl Marx. The most striking difference is that Mills felt that the economically powerful coordinate their maneuvers with the military and political establishments to serve their common interests. Yet, reminiscent of Marx, Mills argued that the corporate rich were perhaps the most powerful element of the power elite (first among "equals"). And, of course, there is a further dramatic parallel between the work of these conflict theorists. The powerless masses at the bottom of Mills's power elite model certainly bring to mind Marx's portrait of the oppressed workers of the world, who have "nothing to lose but their chains."

A fundamental element in Mills's thesis is that the power elite not only includes relatively few members but also operates as a self-conscious, cohesive unit. Although not necessarily diabolical or ruthless, the elite comprises similar types of people who regularly interact with one another and have essentially the same political and economic interests. Mills's power elite is not a conspiracy but

rather a community of interest and sentiment among a small number of influential people (A. Hacker 1964).

Admittedly, Mills failed to clarify when the elite opposes protests and when it tolerates them; he also failed to provide detailed case studies that would substantiate the interrelationship between members of the power elite. Nevertheless, his challenging theories forced scholars to look more critically at the democratic political system of the United States.

Domhoff's Model

More recently, sociologist G. William Domhoff (1998) has agreed with Mills that a powerful elite runs the United States. Significantly, he finds that it is still largely White, male, and upper class, as we saw in the chapter opening excerpt from his book with Richard L. Zweigenhaft (1998). But Domhoff stresses the role played both by elites of the corporate community and by the leaders of policy-formation organizations such as chambers of commerce and labor unions. Many of the people in both groups are also members of the social upper class.

While these groups overlap, as Figure 16-3b shows, they do not necessarily agree on specific policies. Domhoff notes that in the electoral arena two different coalitions have exercised influence. A *corporate-conservative coalition* has played a large role in both political parties and has generated support for particular candidates through direct-mail appeals. But there is also a *liberal-labor coalition* based in unions, local environmental organizations, a segment of the minority group community, liberal churches, and the university and arts communities (Zweigenhaft and Domhoff 1998).

Sociologists have come to accept the notion that a limited number of people exercise a vast amount of power. While the elite groups can be identified, their composition changes over time, as does the influence of particular groups. In the 1950s during the military build-up in the Cold War between Communist countries and Western democracies, the military was appropriately included in Mills's model as a major player. Fifty years later, the military is no longer so influential, but interest groups play a bigger role, as reflected in Domhoff's model.

Pluralist Model

Several social scientists insist that power in the United States is more widely shared than the elite models indicate. In their view, a pluralist model more accurately describes the nation's political system. According to the ***pluralist model,*** many conflicting groups within the community have access to government, so that no single group is dominant.

The pluralist model suggests that a variety of groups play a significant role in decision making. Typically, pluralists make use of intensive case studies or community studies based on observation research. One of the most famous—an investigation of decision making in New Haven, Connecticut—was reported by Robert Dahl in his book *Who Governs?* (1961). Dahl found that while the number of people involved in any important decision was rather small, community power was nonetheless diffuse. Few political actors exercised decision-making power on all issues. One individual or group might be influential in a battle over urban renewal but at the same time have little impact over educational policy. Several other studies of local politics, in such communities as Chicago and Oberlin, Ohio, further document that monolithic power structures do not operate on the level of local government.

The pluralist model, however, has not escaped serious questioning. Domhoff (1978, 1998) reexamined Dahl's study of decision making in New Haven and argued that Dahl and other pluralists had failed to trace how local elites prominent in decision making were part of a larger national ruling class. In addition, studies of community power, such as Dahl's work in New Haven, can examine decision making only on issues that become part of the political agenda. This focus fails to address the possible power of elites to keep certain matters that threaten their dominance entirely *out* of the realm of government debate.

Dianne Pinderhughes (1987) has criticized the plu-

ralist model for failing to account for the exclusion of African Americans from the political process. Drawing on her studies of Chicago politics, Pinderhughes points out that the residential and occupational segregation of Blacks and their long political disenfranchisement violated the logic of pluralism—which would hold that such a substantial minority should always have been influential in community decision making. This critique applies to many cities across the United States where other racial and ethnic minorities, among them Asian Americans, Puerto Ricans, and Mexican Americans, are relatively powerless (J. Watts 1990).

Historically, pluralists have stressed ways in which large numbers of people could participate in or influence governmental decision making. As Box 16-3 suggests, new communications technologies like the Internet are increasing the opportunity to be heard, not just in countries like the United States but in developing countries the world over. One common point of the elite and pluralist

As part of their political socialization, children may be taken to political demonstrations and rallies like this protest against the tobacco industry.

 **Eye on the Media**

16-3 Political Activism on the Internet

Pam Fielding, a lobbyist whose firm is based on the Internet, knows firsthand the power of the sprawling electronic network. While representing the National Education Association, she spearheaded an online drive to preserve the special discount schools receive from Internet service providers. When Fielding's firm urged concerned Net surfers to contact Congress about the issue, more than 20,000 e-mail messages poured in to Congress and the Federal Communications Commission. Every one of them was a personal message from a parent, a businessperson, a teacher or school administrator. "I was convinced at that moment that the Internet was the future of democracy," Fielding says (Engardio 1999:148).

Not just in the United States, but in far-flung places like China, Mexico, Indonesia, Kosovo, and Malaysia, citizens are making themselves heard through cyberactivism—the use of the Internet for political purposes. In China, 10,000 members of the fast-growing Falun Gong religious sect (see Chapter 14) surprised government officials with a mass rally organized on the web. (A similar incident took place in the United States in 1999, when thousands of protesters converged on a meeting of the World Trade Organization in Seattle—11 months after the start of an e-mail campaign.) In Kosovo, the staff of *Koha Ditore,* a dissident newspaper, took to the web after Serbian soldiers closed their office. And in Mexico, the revolutionary *Zapatista* movement (see Chapter 9) gained support from an online campaign for self-rule in the state of Chiapas.

As these incidents illustrate, organizers find the web especially useful in circumventing the restrictive controls of authoritarian regimes. Websites can be established outside a country's borders, beyond the control of government officials yet still accessible to the country's citizens. What is more, government officials who would like to clamp down on such activities are constrained by their desire to reap the commercial benefits of the web. For example, Chi-

nese officials have decided to advance information technology despite the challenges it poses, according to Elizabeth Economy of the Council on Foreign Relations. The technology is simply too important to China's economic modernization for the government to suppress it. From a conflict theory perspective, then, the Internet seems to have the potential to level the playing field for opposition groups—or at least to minimize the ruling party's clout.

Also growing in importance are borderless organizations that unite people of like mind from around the world. These are very tightly knit communities, notes Professor Juan Enriquez of Harvard University. Labor groups and environmental organizations like Greenpeace have become particularly adept at using e-mail to mobilize activists

> Not just in the United States, but in far-flung places like China, Mexico, Indonesia, Kosovo, and Malaysia, citizens are making themselves heard through cyberactivism.

quickly, wherever they are needed. The result: a completely new kind of power structure, compared to the more familiar face-to-face approach of Washington lobbyists. "The new people with power are those with credibility and an e-mail list," says political consultant Jennifer Laszlo. "You have no idea who they are, where they are, what color they are" (Engardio 1999:145).

The Internet serves grass-roots organizers at the local level, too. In California, proponents of local control of schools established a website dubbed www.localchoice2000.com. Their purpose was not just to publicize an upcoming ballot initiative, but to involve citizens—several million of them—in drafting the document. The group also sought permission to gather the signatures they needed to put the initiative on the ballot electronically,

using special PIN numbers. Supporters of these pluralist techniques argued that electronic petitions would save time and money, broaden citizen participation in government, and improve the wording of ballot initiatives.

Even conventional politicians are learning to use the web. Candidates in the year 2000 U.S. presidential elections used their websites to raise money, sign up campaign workers, and spread news among their supporters. Governor George W. Bush published a list of his campaign donors online; Senator John McCain exposed pork-barrel spending by Congress. Vice President Al Gore used his website to conduct electronic town halls, in which he answered voters' questions online. These efforts, which amounted to what the interactionist Erving Goffman called impression management (see pages 96–97), were well received. While phone calls and expensive television ads typically command a voter's attention for less than a minute, researchers found that hits on campaign websites lasted an average of eight minutes each. Acknowledging the growing importance of the Net in presidential politics, political strategist Rick Segal commented on the old adage that a presidential candidate needs a good message, a good ground game, and a good air game on TV. Now, he said, a candidate needs a good online game, too.

Let's Discuss

1. Have you ever used the Internet for political purposes—to learn about a candidate's positions or join a grass-roots political campaign, for instance? Compare the experience to more traditional organizing activities, such as phone calls, poster making, and street demonstrations. What are the advantages and disadvantages of the Internet, from your point of view?
2. Are you familiar with some of the websites of dissident political organizations abroad? Describe what you have learned from them.

Sources: Crossette 1999; Engardio 1999; Goffman 1959; Kelley 1999; Mac Farquhar 1999; Miller 1999; Van Slambrouck 1998.

436

perspectives stands out, however: Power in the political system of the United States is unequally distributed. All citizens may be equal in theory, yet those high in the na-tion's power structure are "more equal." New communications technology may or may not change that distribution of power.

SOCIAL POLICY AND THE GOVERNMENT

Campaign Financing

The Issue

November 23, 1999

Question: How do you reconcile your position on campaign finance reform with all their money you are spending on television advertisements?

Hillary Rodham Clinton: "I believe we ought to have you know, more public financing of campaigns. We don't have it yet, does that mean I shouldn't raise money?"

(Washington Transcript Service 1999:17).

In her bid for election to the U.S. Senate, Hillary Rodham Clinton was not the first politician to criticize campaign financing methods while at the same time raising millions of dollars to pay her expenses. Over the last few decades, many seasoned representatives have left office bemoaning the amount of time they had to spend raising money. Nor, as we shall see, are attempts to regulate campaign financing new.

The Setting

Regulation of campaign contributions has a long history, beginning with efforts to bar the requirement that government employees contribute to their bosses' campaign funds. More recently, the focus on both the state and national levels has been on remedying the shortcomings of the Federal Campaign Act of 1974, passed in the wake of the Watergate scandal. In that infamous fiasco, campaign contributions actually financed a break-in at the Democratic National Committee offices, and the obstruction of the ensuing criminal investigation. The Campaign Act of 1974 placed restrictions on so-called *hard money,* or donations made to specific candidates for national office. Hard money is now limited to $10,000 per organization or $2,000 per individual donor per election cycle (the primary and election being separate cycles). These limits were intended to keep national candidates or elected officials from being "bought" by the wealthy or by powerful special interest groups.

But soon after passage of the act, contributors and potential recipients—that is, politicians—found loopholes in the new law. First, the 1974 legislation did not limit *soft money*—donations to the major political parties, leadership committees, and political action committees by corporations and special interest groups. Donors quickly realized that by contributing to a party or other organization rather than an individual, they could circumvent the limits on the amount of their donations. Not only are there no limits on soft money; there are few if any requirements to report the source and amount of such funds.

Second, contributors discovered they could still spend freely on *independent expenditures,* or purchases made on behalf of a political position rather than an individual candidate. This *issue advocacy money,* as it is also called, quickly became an underhanded way of supporting a particular candidate while escaping contribution limits. To support a pro-environment or "green" candidate, for example, donors would purchase television ads expressing concern about the environment and pollution.

Ironically, the huge increase in issue advocacy money that followed passage of the 1974 act *encouraged* candidates to accumulate huge amounts of soft money, for fear they might at some point be challenged on a well-funded issue. And donors, concerned that candidates might switch their positions on an issue because the "other side" was better funded, felt even more obligated to contribute. According to 1999 data from the Federal Election Commission, the total amount of money spent by all federal candidates increased from $173 million per year immediately after passage of the Federal Election Campaign Act to over $1.03 billion in 1996. Initial reports on the 2000 presidential election show that large donations accounted for the vast majority of campaign contributions (Public Interest Research Groups 1999; see also Glasser and Eilperin 1999; Mauro and Drinkard 1999).

Sociological Insights

Functionalists would say that political contributions keep the public involved in the democratic process and connected to the candidates. Issue advocacy money also

Summary

1. Every society must have a *political system* in order to have recognized procedures for the allocation of valued resources.
2. There are three basic sources of *power* within any political system: *force, influence,* and *authority.*
3. Max Weber identified three ideal types of authority: *traditional, legal-rational,* and *charismatic.*
4. The principal institutions of *political socialization* in the United States are the family, schools, and the media.
5. Political participation makes government accountable to its citizens, but there is a great deal of apathy in both the United States and other countries.
6. Women are still underrepresented in office but are becoming more successful at winning elections to public office.
7. Sometimes people band together in *interest groups* to influence public policy.
8. Advocates of the *elite model* of the power structure of the United States see the nation as being ruled by a small group of individuals who share common political and economic interests (a *power elite*), whereas advocates of a *pluralist model* believe that power is more widely shared among conflicting groups.
9. Despite legislative efforts to reform campaign financing methods, wealthy donors and special interest groups wield enormous power in U.S. government through their contributions to candidates, political parties, and issue advocacy.

Critical Thinking Questions

1. In many places in the world, the United States is considered a model political system. Drawing on material presented in earlier chapters of this textbook, discuss the values and beliefs on which this political system is founded. Have those values and beliefs changed over time? Has the system itself changed?
2. Who really holds power in the college or university you attend? Describe the distribution of power at your school, drawing on the elite and pluralist models where they are relevant.
3. Imagine that you have joined your state representative's legislative staff as a summer intern. She has assigned you to a committee that is working on solutions to the problem of school violence, particularly recent school shootings. How could you use what you have learned about sociology to conceptualize the problem? What type of research would you suggest the committee undertake? What legislative solutions might you recommend?

Key Terms

Authority Power that has been institutionalized and is recognized by the people over whom it is exercised. (423)

Charismatic authority Power made legitimate by a leader's exceptional personal or emotional appeal to his or her followers. (426)

Elite model A view of society as ruled by a small group of individuals who share a common set of political and economic interests. (433)

Force The actual or threatened use of coercion to impose one's will on others. (423)

Influence The exercise of power through a process of persuasion. (423)

Interest group A voluntary association of citizens who attempt to influence public policy. (430)

Legal-rational authority Power made legitimate by law. (425)

Pluralist model A view of society in which many competing groups within the community have access to government so that no single group is dominant. (435)

Political action committee (PAC) A political committee established by an interest group—say, a national bank, corporation, trade association, or cooperative or membership association—to solicit contributions for candidates or political parties. (430)

Political socialization The process by which individuals acquire political attitudes and develop patterns of political behavior. (426)

Political system   The social institution that relies on a recognized set of procedures for implementing and achieving the goals of a group. (423)

Politics   In Harold D. Lasswell's words, "who gets what, when, and how." (423)

Power   The ability to exercise one's will over others. (423)

Power elite   A small group of military, industrial, and government leaders who control the fate of the United States. (433)

Traditional authority   Legitimate power conferred by custom and accepted practice. (424)

Additional Readings

BOOKS

Enloe, Cynthia. 1990. *Bananas, Beaches, and Bases: Making Feminist Sense of International Politics.* Berkeley: University of California Press. Enloe studied the lives of women on military bases and of diplomatic wives as part of her examination of the male-dominated agenda of international politics.

Kurtz, Lester R., ed. 1999. *Encyclopedia of Violence, Peace and Conflict.* San Diego, CA: Academic Press. This three-volume set includes interdisciplinary articles on topics like conflict theory, colonialism, mass media, indigenous peoples, and military culture.

Zweigenhaft, Richard L., and G. William Domhoff. 1998. *Diversity in the Power Elite.* New Haven: Yale University Press. A psychologist and a sociologist team up to consider why, although women and minorities have made inroads, the overwhelming majority of the elite of the nation continues to be White and male.

JOURNALS

Among the journals that focus on issues of government are the *American Political Science Review* (founded in 1906), *Congressional Digest* (1921), *Congressional Quarterly Weekly Report* (1943), *Insurgent Sociologist* (1969), *Social Policy* (1970), and *Terrorism* (1988).

Internet Connection

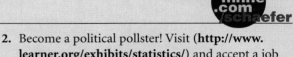

Note: While all the URLs listed were current as of the printing of this book, these sites often change. Please check our website (http://www.mhhe.com/schaefer) for updates.

1. Political Action Committees (PACs) collect and distribute funds to candidates sympathetic to special interest groups. A list of PACs can be found at the web address (**http://dir.yahoo.com/ Government/U_S__Government/Politics/ Interest_Groups/Political_Action_Committees__ PACs_/**). Choose two of the PACs named there and log onto their websites. Answer questions (a) to (c) for each PAC:
   (a) What is the PAC's name? When and why was it organized? By whom?
   (b) What causes, issues, or groups does the PAC represent? What social or political changes is it working toward?
   (c) Which political party or ideology, if any, does the PAC seem closest to? What strategies does it employ to advance its goals?
   (d) Are the two PACs you examined similar? In what ways?
   (e) What do you think conflict theorists would say about the role of interest groups in political decision making?

2. Become a political pollster! Visit (**http://www. learner.org/exhibits/statistics/**) and accept a job with the campaign of fictional mayoral candidate Stephanie Higgins.
   (a) Read "Statistics-Polls: What do the numbers tell us?" What is meant by the term *random sample*? How is a random sample selected?
   (b) Create your own sample by clicking on "Sampling the Electorate."
   (c) Learn about margin of error by reading the $+/-5\%$ section. What does the term *margin of error* mean? What other kinds of error should pollsters be mindful of? Can polling results be trusted, given the possibility for these kinds of errors?
   (d) Why are polls and statistics important in politics? In daily life?
   (e) Who won the fictional election? Has your experience with the Higgins campaign changed your view of political polls? Why or why not?

This Canadian poster from 1991 calls for blocking the lowering of trade barriers with the United States. The fear was that Canadians would lose jobs (symbolized by the empty factory in the background). The controversy over trade barriers continues today worldwide, reflecting the concern that national economies are giving way to a single global economy.

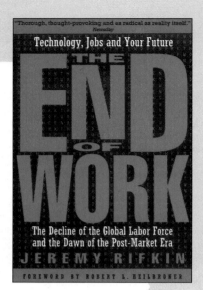

Percy Barnevik is the chief executive officer of Asea Brown Boveri, a 29-billion-dollar-a-year Swiss-Swedish builder of electric generators and transportation systems, and one of the largest engineering firms in the world. Like other global companies, ABB has recently re-engineered its operations, cutting nearly 50,000 workers from the payroll, while increasing turnover 60 percent in the same time period. Barnevik asks, "Where will all these [unemployed] people go?" He predicts that the proportion of Europe's labor force employed in manufacturing and business services will decline from 35 percent today to 25 percent in ten years from now, with a further decline to 15 percent twenty years down the road. Barnevik is deeply pessimistic about Europe's future: "If anybody tells me, wait two or three years and there will be a hell of a demand for labor, I say, tell me where? What jobs? In what cities? Which companies? When I add it all together, I find a clear risk that the 10% unemployed or underemployed today could easily become 20 to 25%." . . .

For some, particularly the scientists, engineers, and employers, a world without work will signal the beginning of a new era in history in which human beings are liberated, at long last, from a life of back-breaking toil and mindless repetitive tasks. For others, the workerless society conjures up the notion of a grim future of mass unemployment and global destitution, punctuated by increasing social unrest and upheaval. On one point virtually all of the contending parties agree. We are, indeed, entering into a new period in history—one in which machines increasingly replace human beings in the process of making and moving goods and providing services. . . .

Most workers feel completely unprepared to cope with the enormity of the transition taking place. The rash of current technological breakthroughs and economic restructuring initiatives seem to have descended on us with little warning. Suddenly, all over the world, men and women are asking if there is a role for them in the new future unfolding across the global economy. Workers with years of education, skills, and experience face the very real prospect of being made redundant by the new forces of automation and information. What just a few short years ago was a rather esoteric debate among intellectuals and a small number of social writers around the role of technology in society is now the topic of heated conversation among millions of working people. They wonder if they will be the next to be replaced by the new thinking machines. . . .

The new high-technology revolution could mean fewer hours of work and greater benefits for millions. For the first time in modern history, large numbers of human beings could be liberated from long hours of labor in the formal marketplace, to be free to pursue leisure-time activities. The same technological forces could, however, as easily lead to growing unemployment and a global depression. *(Rifkin 1995a:11–13)* ■

n his book *The End of Work,* social activist Jeremy Rifkin takes a look at what the economic world will look like after automation and high technology make human labor more and more obsolete. Economic forces have a huge impact on our lives—from something as basic as whether we can put food on the table to more soul-searching concerns such as "How can I be productive?" Rifkin's view is that we must be prepared to deal with the inevitable dysfunctions and dislocations that accompany a major transformation of the global economic system.

The term *economic system* refers to the social institution through which goods and services are produced, distributed, and consumed. As with social institutions such as the family, religion, and government, the economic system shapes other aspects of the social order and is, in turn, influenced by them. Throughout this textbook, you have been reminded of the economy's impact on social behavior—for example, individual and group behavior in factories and offices. You have studied the work of Karl Marx and Friedrich Engels, who emphasized that the economic system of a society can promote social inequality. And you learned that foreign investment in developing countries can intensify inequality among residents.

This chapter will present a sociological analysis of the impact of the economy on people's lives. We begin with macro-level analysis of capitalism and socialism as ideal types of economic systems. Next we examine aspects of work, including types of jobs, alienation in the workplace, and worker satisfaction. Then we take a look at the changing nature of the U.S. economy and the global economy as we enter the twenty-first century. Finally, the social policy section explores the controversy over affirmative action, an issue that focuses on unequal opportunities. ■

Economic Systems

The sociocultural evolution approach developed by Gerhard Lenski categorizes preindustrial societies according to the way in which the economy is organized. The principal types of preindustrial societies, as you recall, are hunting-and-gathering societies, horticultural societies, and agrarian societies.

As noted in Chapter 5, the *industrial revolution*—which took place largely in England during the period 1760 to 1830—brought about changes in the social organization of the workplace. People left their homesteads and began working in central locations such as factories. As the industrial revolution proceeded, a new form of social structure emerged: the *industrial society,* a society that depends on mechanization to produce its goods and services.

Two basic types of economic systems distinguish contemporary industrial societies: capitalism and socialism. As described in the following sections, capitalism and socialism serve as ideal types of economic systems. No nation precisely fits either model. Instead, the economy of each individual state represents a mixture of capitalism and socialism, although one type or the other is generally useful in describing a society's economic structure. China's economy, for example, is primarily socialistic, while the U.S. economy is much more capitalistic.

Capitalism

In preindustrial societies, land functioned as the source of virtually all wealth. The industrial revolution changed all that. It required that certain individuals and institutions be willing to take substantial risks in order to finance new inventions, machinery, and business enterprises. Eventually, bankers, industrialists, and other holders of large sums of money replaced landowners as the most powerful economic force. These people invested their funds in the hope of realizing even greater profits and thereby became owners of property and business firms.

The transition to private ownership of business was accompanied by the emergence of the capitalist economic system. *Capitalism* is an economic system in which the means of production are largely in private hands and the main incentive for economic activity is the accumulation of profits. In practice, capitalist systems vary in the degree to which the government regulates private ownership and economic activity (Rosenberg 1991).

Immediately following the industrial revolution, the prevailing form of capitalism was what is termed *laissez-faire* ("let them do"). Under the principle of laissez-faire, as expounded and endorsed by British economist Adam Smith (1723–1790), people could compete freely with minimal government intervention in the economy. Business retained the right to regulate itself and essentially operated without fear of government regulation (Smelser 1963).

Two centuries later, capitalism has taken on a somewhat different form. Private ownership and maximization of profits still remain the most significant characteristics of capitalist economic systems. However, in contrast to the era of laissez-faire, capitalism today features extensive government regulation of economic relations. Without restrictions, business firms can mislead consumers, endanger the safety of their workers, and even defraud the companies' investors—all in the pursuit of greater profits. That is why the government of a capitalist nation often monitors prices, sets safety standards for industries, protects the rights of consumers, and regulates collective bargaining between labor unions and management. Yet, under capitalism as an ideal type, government rarely takes over ownership of an entire industry.

Contemporary capitalism also differs from laissez-faire in another important respect: It tolerates monopolistic practices. A *monopoly* exists when a single business firm controls the market. Domination of an industry allows the firm to effectively control a commodity by dictating pricing, standards of quality, and availability. Buyers have little choice but to yield to the firm's decisions; there is no other place to purchase the product or service. Monopolistic practices violate the ideal of free competition cherished by Adam Smith and other supporters of laissez-faire capitalism.

Some capitalistic nations, such as the United States, outlaw monopolies through antitrust legislation. Such laws prevent any business from taking over so much of the competition in an industry that it gains control of the market. The U.S. federal government allows monopolies to exist only in certain exceptional cases, such as the utility and transportation industries. Even then, regulatory agencies scrutinize these officially approved monopolies and protect the public. The protracted legal battle against Microsoft points to the uneasy relationship between government and private monopolies in capitalistic countries.

Conflict theorists point out that while *pure* monopolies are not a basic element of the economy of the United States, competition is much more restricted than one might expect in what is called a *free enterprise system*. In numerous industries, a few companies largely dominate the field and keep new enterprises from entering the marketplace.

Socialism

 Socialist theory was refined in the writings of Karl Marx and Friedrich Engels. These European radicals were disturbed by the exploitation of the working class as it emerged during the industrial revolution. In their view, capitalism forced large numbers of people to exchange their labor for low wages. The owners of an industry profit from the labor of their workers, primarily because they pay workers less than the value of the goods produced.

As an ideal type, a socialist economic system attempts to eliminate such economic exploitation. Under *socialism,* the means of production and distribution in a society are collectively rather than privately owned. The basic objective of the economic system is to meet people's needs rather than to maximize profits. Socialists reject the laissez-faire philosophy that free competition benefits the general public. Instead, they believe that the central government, acting as the representative of the people, should make basic economic decisions. Therefore, government ownership of all major industries—including steel production, automobile manufacturing, and agriculture—is a major feature of socialism as an ideal type.

In practice, socialist economic systems vary in the extent to which they tolerate private ownership. For example, in Great Britain, a nation with certain aspects of both a socialist and a capitalist economy, passenger airline service is concentrated in the government-owned corporation British Airways. Yet private airline companies are allowed to compete with it.

Socialist societies differ from capitalist nations in their commitment to social service programs. For example, the U. S. government provides health care and health insurance for the elderly and poor through the Medicare and Medicaid programs. By contrast, socialist countries typically offer government-financed medical care for *all* citizens. In theory, the wealth of the people as a collectivity is used to provide health care, housing, education, and other key services for each individual and family.

Marx believed that each socialist state would eventually "wither away" and evolve into a communist society. As an ideal type, *communism* refers to an economic system under which all property is communally owned and no social distinctions are made on the basis of people's ability to produce. In recent decades, the Soviet Union, the People's Republic of China, Vietnam, Cuba, and nations in Eastern Europe were popularly thought of as examples of communist economic systems. However, this represents an incorrect usage of a term with sensitive political connotations. All nations known as communist in the twentieth century have actually fallen far short of the ideal type.

By the early 1990s, Communist parties were no longer ruling the nations of Eastern Europe. The first major challenge to Communist rule came in 1980 when Poland's Solidarity movement—led by Lech Walesa and backed by many workers—questioned the injustices of that society. While martial law initially forced Solidarity underground, it eventually negotiated the end of Communist party rule in 1989. Over the next two years, dominant Communist parties were overthrown after popular uprisings in the Soviet Union and throughout Eastern Europe. The former Soviet Union, Czechoslovakia, and Yugoslavia were subdivided to accommodate the ethnic, linguistic, and religious differences within these areas. As of 1998, China, Cuba, and Vietnam remained socialist societies ruled by Communist parties. However, even in these countries capitalism was making inroads. For example, by 1995, 60 percent of Vietnam's economic output and 25 percent of China's came from the private sector (Steinfeld 1999; World Bank 1996:15).

Cuba, in particular, is adjusting to a dual economy. While the Communist government leader Fidel Castro remains firmly committed to Marxism, the centrally controlled economy has been in ruins following the end of Soviet aid and the continued trade embargo by the United States. Reluctantly, Castro has allowed small-scale family-managed businesses, such as restaurants and craft shops, to operate and accept dollars rather than the heavily de-

Soon after the U.S. government lifted its trade embargo against Vietnam in 1994, Coca-Cola and Pepsi rushed in to corner the market. Coca-Cola made its "biggest" statement on the steps of the Opera House in Hanoi.

valued Cuban peso. This leads to an ironic situation in which government-employed teachers and doctors earn less than the small business operators, taxi drivers, and hotel workers who have access to foreign currency. This situation underscores how difficult it is to understand any nation's economy without considering its position in the global economy (J. McKinley 1999).

To assess capitalism's impact on China, consider the case of Deng Zhifang, the youngest son of the late Deng Xiaoping (who ruled China from 1978 until 1997). Deng Zhifang, an engineer trained in the United States, worked in the 1980s for a state-owned company in China. At that time, he rode a bicycle to work each day and answered his own telephone. However, now he is a property owner and international businessman worth tens of millions of dollars (Kristof 1997).

As we have seen, capitalism and socialism serve as ideal types of economic systems. In reality, the economy of each industrial society—including the United States, Great Britain, and Japan—includes certain elements of both capitalism and socialism. Whatever the differences, whether they more closely fit the ideal type of capitalism or socialism, all industrial societies rely chiefly on mechanization in the production of goods and services.

Aspects of Work

As indicated in the chapter opening, the workplace has undergone tremendous changes in the last few decades, primarily because of automation and the applications of high technology. These changes have affected the types of occupations and professions that people enter today and how satisfied they are with their jobs, as we'll now see.

Occupations and Professions

Whatever we call it—*job, work, occupation, gig, stint, position, duty,* or *vocation*—it is what we do for pay. Our paid labor relates to our social behavior in a number of ways. Preparation for work is a critical aspect of the socialization process. In addition, our work in- p. 107 fluences our social identities or what Charles Horton Cooley termed the *looking-glass self.* A person who asks, "What do you do?" expects you to indicate your occupation. We tend to define ourselves by our work. Of course, work has more than a symbolic significance. Our occupations also determine in large part our positions in the stratification system.

In the United States and other contemporary societies, the majority of the paid labor force is involved in providing services, such as health care, education, selling of goods, banking, and government. Along with the shift

Taking Sociology to Work

BINTI HARVEY:
CBS Online Reporter

Binti Harvey writes for the Online Business News Service, a financial news network that is accessed by the web. She covers technology stocks in the two columns she writes daily. In the course of her work, she often talks with the chief financial officers of multinational technology firms.

Harvey finds that her sociology degree, earned at UCLA in 1996, has been of tremendous value in her job. The first aspect is in "writing, writing, writing! Sociology gave me a really strong grasp of the fundamentals of writing. It has helped me with deadlines and to put together a comprehensive yet concise story quickly." Sociology has also helped her to take a broader look at issues and make connections. Finally, and perhaps most importantly, it has played a big role in helping her to understand others. "I'm in a lot of situations with business people who aren't comfortable with a young Black female. My sociological background has helped me understand where they're coming from, their perspective. It has helped me to help them to see me as a reporter." In Harvey's view, sociology allows people who would normally not have power to empower themselves.

Her advice to sociology students is to learn the terms but put more emphasis on learning the concepts and how to apply them to everyday life. "It's one of the few subjects that you'll encounter in college that you can apply to your daily life."

toward service industries, there has been a rise in the number of occupations viewed as professions. In popular usage, the term *professional* is frequently used to convey a positive evaluation of work ("She's a real professional") or to denote full-time paid performance in a vocation (as in "professional golfer").

Sociologists use the term **profession** to describe an occupation requiring extensive knowledge that is governed by a code of ethics. Professionals tend to have a great degree of autonomy. They are not responsible to a supervisor for every action, nor do they have to respond to the whims of a customer. In general, professionals are their own authority in determining what is best for their clients. Table 17-1 summarizes some of the characteristics used by sociologists to distinguish professions from other occupations.

It is widely agreed that medicine and law are professions, whereas driving a taxi is an occupation. But how do you categorize funeral director, firefighter, and pharmacist? In these cases it's not clear where "occupation" ends and "profession" begins. To some extent, as occupations have become more skill-based and professions tied more and more to large bureaucracies (such as doctors in an HMO), the two ideal types have converged. Moreover, a growing number of occupational groups have claimed and even demanded professional status—often in an attempt to gain greater prestige and financial rewards. In certain instances, existing professions may object to the efforts of a related vocation to achieve designation as a profession. They may fear a loss in business or clientele or a downgrade in the status of their profession as still more occupations are included. The hostility of the medical profession toward midwifery is an example of such a conflict between an established profession and an occupation that has aspired to professional status. In general, workers in nonprofessional occupations are granted low esteem, which shows up in the way these workers are portrayed in the media, or, more accurately, in the way they do not get portrayed at all (see Box 17-1).

What happens to the professional who is used to autonomy when he or she works in a large formal organization with a bureaucratic structure? There is an inherent conflict in serving as a professional p. 151 within a bureaucracy, such as being a scientist in a corporation. The formal organization, as described by Max Weber, follows the principle of hierarchy and expects loyalty and obedience. Yet professionalism demands the individual responsibility of the practitioner. Bureaucracy fosters impersonality, yet professions emphasize close relations with one's professional colleagues. Most professionals in this situation have to accept a trade-off: While they resent limitations on their freedom and initiative, they appreciate the security that the organization provides (Leicht and Fennell 1997; Hodson and Sullivan 1995; Pavalko 1972, 1988).

Work and Alienation: Marx's View

"A moron could learn this job, it's so easy," says one Burger King worker in George Ritzer's study of the fast-food industry (1996:130). Doing repetitive tasks that take minimal skills can be demoralizing and lead to a sense of alienation and isolation in the workplace. Jeremy Rifkin, as we saw in the chapter opening, took this concern a step

448

Table 17-1   Occupations and Professions Compared

Characteristic	Occupation	Profession
Systematic body of theory or abstract knowledge	No	Yes
Training	Relatively short; usually informal	Extensive and formalized
Degree of specialization	Little	Extensive
Autonomy	Little	Extensive
Self-regulatory associations	No	Yes
Relationship to public	"Customer is always right"	Client is viewed as somewhat subordinate
Formal certification	Not necessarily	Yes
Sense of community with similar jobholders	Low	High
Code of ethics	Informal	Highly developed; usually formalized

Sources: Author based on Greenwood 1957; Leicht and Fennell 1997; Pavalko 1972, 1988.

further: As work becomes more and more automated, human skills become obsolete and workers lose their jobs altogether or are forced into the low-skills service jobs (Rifkin 1996).

All the pioneers of sociological thought were concerned about the negative impact on workers as a result of the changes in the workplace brought about by the industrial revolution. Émile Durkheim (1933, original version 1893) argued that as labor becomes more and more differentiated, individuals experience *anomie,* or loss of direction. Workers can't feel the same fulfillment from performing one specialized task in a factory as they did when they were totally responsible for creating a product. It is clear that the impersonality of bureaucratic organizations can result in a cold and uncaring workplace. But the most penetrating analysis of the dehumanizing aspects of industrialization was offered by Karl Marx.

Marx believed that as the process of industrialization advanced within capitalist societies, workers were robbed of any meaningful relationship with their work. In today's terms, consider the telemarketer making a "cold call" to sell someone a credit card. Does that person feel a part of the financial institution? For Marx, the emphasis on specialization of tasks contributed to a growing sense of alienation among industrial workers. The term ***alienation*** refers to the situation of being estranged or disassociated from the surrounding society. But it wasn't just the monotonous repetition of the same tasks that concerned Marx. In his

view, an even deeper cause of alienation is the *powerlessness* of workers in a capitalist economic system. Workers have no control over their occupational tasks, the products of their labor, or the distribution of profits. Moreover, they are constantly producing property that is owned by others (the members of the capitalist class) (Erikson 1986).

The solution to the problem of workers' alienation, according to Marx, is to give workers greater control over the workplace and the products of their labor. He didn't focus on limited reforms of factory life; rather he envisioned a revolutionary overthrow of capitalist oppression. After a transition to collective ownership of the means of production (socialism) the ideal of communism would be achieved eventually. Yet the trend in capitalist societies has been toward concentration of ownership by giant corporations. Currently about 48 percent of the paid U.S. labor force is employed in business firms with more than 500 workers. Through mergers and acquisitions, such corporations become even larger, and individual workers find themselves the employees of firms with overwhelming size and power (Bureau of the Census 1999a:557).

When Karl Marx wrote about work and alienation in 1844, the physical conditions of labor were much harsher than they are today. Yet his writings inspired research into alienated labor that persists today, even as workers enjoy safer and more comfortable surroundings. The growth of the size of businesses, the emergence of huge franchise chains, and the dominance of multinational corporations

17-1 Missing Workers

Tune in your local news and you are more likely to get advice on where to find good eyeglasses than how to solve problems in the workplace. Worker issues fare no better on the national evening news programs, as a 1999 study indicates. Content analysis showed that only 2 percent of total airtime treats issues of interest to workers, including child care, the minimum wage, and workplace safety and health. For example, all three major networks together spent only 13 minutes on job safety and health even

> Tune in your local news and you are more likely to get advice on where to find good eyeglasses than how to solve problems in the workplace.

though 16 workers die each day from work-related injuries.

The media image does not improve when we turn to TV series. Over a 15-year period only 11 percent of prime-time network family series depicted heads of households as working-class characters. Those characters who are working class are likely to be shown as "immature" or "irresponsible," even if lovable, as, for example, Homer on "The Simpsons."

Why is it that the media don't tell us much about workers' issues? For one thing, the news media are owned by big corporations whose

Homer Simpson is one of the few working-class characters featured on prime-time television programs.

high-level decision makers may not favor worker-friendly presentations. Second, advertisers want a "positive environment" for their ads, meaning that media images should not clash with corporate agendas. A third factor is the background of editors, writers, producers, and others who put on the news and create TV series. Many of them live like corporate elite and have little contact with the working class, much less exposure to their problems. Finally, working-class organizations, includ-

ing even the labor unions, do not have the clout to compete with the corporate elite to get their "image" across.

Let's Discuss

1. Why are worker issues underrepresented in the media?
2. If you were to create a TV series devoted to working-class issues, what would it look like? Describe some characters and plot lines.

Sources: Fairness and Accuracy in Reporting 1990; M. Witt 1999; OSHA 1999.

have only increased the isolation of laborers (Hodson and Sullivan 1995).

Already by the 1980s the term *burnout* was increasingly being used to describe the stress experienced by a wide range of workers, including professionals, self-employed persons, and even unpaid volunteers. Marx had focused on alienation among the proletarians, whom he viewed as powerless to effect change within capitalist institutions. However, the broader concept of work-related anxiety now covers alienation even among more affluent workers who have a greater degree of control over their working conditions. From a conflict perspective, we have

masked the fact that alienation falls most heavily on the lower and working classes by making it appear endemic from the boardroom to the shop floor.

Worker Satisfaction

Most studies of alienation have focused on how structural changes in the economy serve to increase or decrease worker satisfaction. In general, people with greater responsibility for a finished product (such as white-collar professionals and managers) experience more satisfaction than those with little responsibility.

Stocking shelves may help pay the bills but is unlikely to provide high job satisfaction, especially in a large supermarket where workers have less responsibility and more anonymity.

For both women and men working in blue-collar jobs, the repetitive nature of work can be particularly unsatisfying. The automobile assembly line is commonly cited as an extreme example of monotonous work. Studs Terkel (1974:159), in his book *Working,* gives a first-person account of a spot welder's labor:

I stand in one spot, about two- or three-feet area, all night. The only time a person stops is when the line stops. We do about thirty-two jobs per car, per unit, forty-eight units per hour, eight hours a day. Thirty-two times forty-eight times eight. Figure it out, that's how many times I push that button.

Robert Blauner's (1964) classic research study revealed that printers—who often work in small shops and supervise apprentices—were more satisfied with their work than laborers on automobile assembly lines who performed repetitive tasks.

Factors in Job Satisfaction

A number of general factors can reduce the level of dissatisfaction of contemporary industrial workers. Higher wages give workers a sense of accomplishment apart from the task before them. A shortened official workweek is supposed to increase the amount of time people can devote to recreation and leisure, thereby reducing some of the discontent stemming from the workplace. However, it seems that shortened workweeks are still accompanied by a measure of worker discontent. Paid absentee hours rose throughout the 1990s, and the reasons given for the absences indicate low satisfaction. In 1995, 45 percent of absent workers cited personal illness as the reason, but by 1998, only 22 percent gave that reason. Sixteen percent cited stress and another 16 percent indicated a sense of entitlement (B. Stone 1999).

Numerous studies have shown that positive relationships with coworkers can make a boring job tolerable or even enjoyable. In his often cited "banana time" study, sociologist Donald Roy (1959) examined worker satisfaction by means of a two-month participant observation within a small group of factory machine operators. Drawing on the interactionist perspective, Roy carefully recorded the social interactions among members of his work group, including many structured "times" and "themes" designed to break up long days of simple, repetitive work. For example, the workers divided their food breaks into coffee time, peach time, banana time, fish time, Coke time, and lunch time—each of which occurred daily and involved distinctive responsibilities, jokes, and insults. Roy (1959:166) concludes that his observations "seem to support the generally accepted notion that one key source of job satisfaction lies in the informal interaction shared by members of a work group." The patterned conversation and horseplay of these workers reduced the monotony of their workdays.

Sociologist George Ritzer (1977) has suggested that the relatively positive impression many workers present is misleading. In his view, manual workers are so deeply alienated that they come to expect little from their jobs. Their satisfaction comes from nonwork tasks, and any job-related gratification results from receiving wages. Ritzer's interpretation explains why manual workers—although they say they are satisfied with their occupations—would not choose the same line of work if they could begin their lives over.

Job Satisfaction in Japan

One of the major economic developments of the 1980s was the emergence of Japan as an industrial giant. In earlier decades, many people attributed Japan's economic accomplishments to low wages combined with production of inexpensive goods. However, Japanese salaries in the

1980s were comparable to those of other industrial nations. A more likely explanation of Japan's remarkable success at that time focused instead on the unusual pride that Japanese workers felt in their products. In Japanese plants and factories, workers are expected to assume the role of quality-control inspector. Although actually involved in specialized tasks of production, employees can still identify with the finished product.

For a long time, the collectivist orientation of Japanese culture heavily influenced its capitalist economic system. An individual was perceived as an extension of his or her family, business, or community and as bound together with others in a common purpose. In contrast to U.S. firms, most Japanese companies maintained an ideal of "lifetime employment" for some of their employees. They made substantial investments in training of workers and so were reluctant to lay off employees during a business slump. The employer–employee relationship was paramount. Companies even operated reception halls, gymnasiums and swimming pools, mortgage-lending institutions, and cultural programs for the benefit of their workers.

By the close of the 1990s this situation had changed. A severe economic recession hit Japan, resulting in record unemployment. While still low compared to European countries, it meant that almost twice as many people were looking for jobs as there were job openings. Companies facing the impact of a lingering recession as well as increased competition from abroad for products set aside the notion of lifetime employment. Interactionists observed that Japanese men—accustomed to job security—were so embarrassed over losing a job that they would keep it a secret from their families for days if not weeks. Men in their 50s were now looking for work along with recent college graduates. As a result of this restructuring, the bonds that linked worker and employer are currently weakening. The feelings of worker isolation that Marx and Ritzer wrote about in Europe and North America are becoming increasingly evident in Japan (Barr 1999; Kerbo and McKinstry 1998; Strom 1999).

The Changing Economy

As advocates of the power elite model point out, the trend in capitalist societies has been toward concentration of ownership by giant corporations, especially multinational ones. For example, there were p. 234 3,882 mergers in 1998 alone, involving $1.4 trillion in business (Bureau of the Census 1999a:563).

The nature of the U.S. economy is changing in important ways, in part because the nation's economy is increasingly intertwined with and dependent upon the global economy. In 1998, foreign companies acquired 483 U.S. firms valued together at $232 billion (Bureau of the Census 1999a:563). In the following sections, we will examine developments in the global economy that have interested sociologists: the changing face of the workforce, deindustrialization, the emergence of e-commerce, and the rise of a contingency (or temporary) workforce. As these trends show, any change in the economy inevitably has social and political implications and soon becomes a concern of policymakers.

The Face of the Workforce

The workforce in the United States is constantly changing. During World War II, when men were mobilized to fight abroad, women entered the workforce in large numbers. And with the rise of the civil rights move-

When job layoffs hit Japan in the 1990s, it caused a stir because the Japanese were accustomed to the idea of lifetime employment with one firm. In this demonstration at Nissan headquarters in Tokyo in 1999, labor activists are protesting auto plant shutdowns and a 14 percent cut in the workforce. The banners on the bus read: "How can you call the mass dismissal of workers Renaissance? Stop the closure of five plants in the Nissan-Renault's large-sized restructuring."

Amazon.com's huge distribution center in Seattle, Washington. E-commerce is undercutting traditional retail shops, with inventory and shipping warehouses taking their place.

have witnessed what has been called the "temping of America."

Unemployed workers and entrants to the paid labor force accept positions as temporary or part-time workers. Some do so for flexibility and control over their work time, but others accept these jobs because they are the only ones available. Young people are especially likely to fill temporary positions. Employers find it attractive and functional to shift toward a contingency workforce because it allows them to respond more quickly to workforce demands—as well as to hire employees without having to offer the fringe benefits that full-time employees enjoy. All around the United States, large firms have come to rely on part-time or temporary workers, most of whom work part-time involuntarily. Many of these workers feel the effects of deindustrialization and shifts in the global economy. They lost their full-time jobs when companies moved operations to developing nations (Cooper 1994; Francis 1999).

It is difficult to estimate the size of the contingency workforce of the United States. Heidi Hartmann of the Institute for Women's Policy Research notes that there is no agreement among social scientists as to how to define a "contingent worker" or how many there are. According to

storeowners. Even established companies like Nike, Timex, Levi's, and Mattel are establishing their own online "stores," bypassing the retail outlets that they have courted for years to directly reach customers with their merchandise. Megamalls once replaced personal ties to stores for many shoppers; the growth of e-commerce with its "cybermalls" is just the latest change in the economy.

Some observers note that e-commerce offers more opportunities to consumers in rural areas and to those with disabilities. To its critics, however, e-commerce signals more social isolation, more alienation, and greater disconnect for the poor and disadvantaged who are not a part of the new information technology (Drucker 1999; Hansell 1999; Stoughton and Walker 1999).

The Contingency Workforce

In the past, the term "temp" typically conjured up images of a replacement receptionist or a worker covering for someone on vacation. However, in association with the deindustrialization and downsizing described above, a "contingency workforce," in which workers are hired only for as long as they are needed, has emerged in the United States, and we

one estimate, however, contingent workers constitute about one-fourth of the nation's paid labor force. In 1998, for example, about 28 percent of Microsoft's workforce was temporary. This included a large number of long-term temporaries (those who work more than one year), who have come to refer to their awkward status as "permatemps." In a 1995 survey of executives of large corporations, two-thirds indicated that they expect to use more temporary help. In many companies, management is increasingly assigning major tasks to outside firms and temporary workers through a process known as "outsourcing" (Greenhouse 1998; J. Larson 1996).

During the 1970s and 1980s, temporary workers typically held low-skill positions at fast-food restaurants, telemarketing firms, and other service industries. Today, the contingent workforce is evident at virtually *all* skill levels and in *all* industries. Clerical "temps" handle word processing and filing duties, managers are hired on a short-term basis to reorganize departments, freelance writers prepare speeches for corporate executives, and blue-collar workers are employed for a few months when a factory receives an unusually high number of orders. A significant minority of temporary employees are contract workers who are being "rented" for specific periods of time by the companies that previously downsized them—and are now working at lower salary levels without benefits or job security (Kirk 1995; Uchitelle 1996).

In some cases, employees have benefited from the rise of a contingency workforce. For example, a number of dual-career couples who share child care find it desirable to hold part-time jobs at different times of day or on different days of the week. For most workers, however, the disadvantages of temporary or part-time employment outweigh the benefits. Temporary and part-time employees generally receive lower wages and salaries than permanent, full-time workers. Contingent workers do not participate in on-the-job training programs and do not receive support for completing college or graduate school. They typically receive few (if any) fringe benefits, such as paid vacations, sick-day pay, health and life insurance, or pension benefits. Because they do not fit the traditional definition of an "employee," they are not well protected under federal labor laws. As a result, they are even more vulnerable than other workers to discrimination based on gender, race, or ethnicity—and can more easily be pressured into accepting hazardous working conditions (Cooper 1994).

Workers in the United States generally blame forces outside their control—indeed, outside the nation—for the problems they experience as a result of deindustrialization and the rise of a contingency workforce. The relocation of factories to other countries has unquestionably contributed to job loss in the United States. But as we saw in the chapter opening extract, there are growing indications that automation is substantially reducing the need for human labor in both manufacturing and service industries. By the year 2020, it is projected that less than 2 percent of the entire global labor force will be engaged in factory work (Rifkin 1996). In Chapter 22, we will look at the role of technology in promoting social and economic change.

In the struggles of part-time workers and the unemployed to make ends meet, we find government and the economy intertwined, as the government steps in with assistance, whether it be unemployment compensation, government-funded child care, or welfare. In the social policy section that follows, we examine affirmative action, a controversial issue that provides another example of the link between government and the economy.

An accountant studies a ledger in an office. Increasing numbers of educated, white-collar professionals (such as accountants) have joined low-level "temp" workers in the contingency workforce.

SOCIAL POLICY AND THE ECONOMY

Affirmative Action

The Issue

Jessie Sherrod began picking cotton in the fields of Mississippi when she was eight years old, earning $1.67 each time she worked a 12-hour day. Today, at 45, she is a Harvard-educated pediatrician who specializes in infectious diseases. But the road from the cotton fields to the medical profession was hardly an easy one. "You can't make up for 400 years of slavery and mistreatment and unequal opportunity in 20 years," she says angrily. "We had to ride the school bus for five miles . . . and pass by a white school to get to our black elementary school. Our books were used books. Our instructors were not as good. We didn't have the proper equipment. How do you make up for that?" (Stolberg 1995:A14). Some people think it should be done through affirmative action programs.

The term *affirmative action* first appeared in an executive order issued by President John F. Kennedy in 1961. That order called for contractors to "take affirmative action to ensure that applicants are employed, and that employees are treated during employment, without regard to their race, creed, color, or national origin." In 1967, the order was amended by President Lyndon Johnson to also prohibit discrimination on the basis of sex, but affirmative action remained a vague concept. Currently, **affirmative action** refers to positive efforts to recruit minority group members or women for jobs, promotions, and educational opportunities. But many people feel that affirmative action programs constitute reverse discrimination against qualified Whites and males. Does government have a responsibility to make up for past discrimination? If so, how far should it take it?

The Setting

A variety of court decisions and executive branch statements have outlawed certain forms of job discrimination based on race, sex, or both, including (1) word-of-mouth recruitment among all-White or all-male workforces, (2) recruitment exclusively in schools or colleges that are limited to one sex or are predominantly White, (3) discrimination against married women or forced retirement of pregnant women, (4) advertising in male and female "help wanted" columns when gender is not a legitimate occupational qualification, and (5) job qualifications and tests that are not substantially related to the job. Also, the lack of minority (African American, Asian, American Indian, or Hispanic) or female employees may in itself represent evidence of unlawful exclusion (Commission on Civil Rights 1981).

In the late 1970s, a number of bitterly debated cases on affirmative action reached the Supreme Court. In 1978, in the *Bakke* case, by a narrow 5–4 vote, the Supreme Court ordered the medical school of the University of California at Davis to admit Allen Bakke, a White engineer who originally had been denied admission. The justices ruled that the school had violated Bakke's constitutional rights by establishing a fixed quota system for minority students. The Court added, however, that it was constitutional for universities to adopt flexible admissions programs that use race as one factor in decision making.

Sociological Insights

Sociologists—and especially conflict theorists—view affirmative action as a legislative attempt to reduce inequality embedded in the social structure by increasing opportunities of groups such as women and African Americans that have been deprived in the past. The gap in earning power between White males and other groups (see Figure 17-2) is one indication of the inequality that needs to be addressed.

Even if they acknowledge the disparity in earnings between White males and others, many people in the United States doubt that everything done in the name of affirmative action is desirable. By 1996, a national survey suggested that the nation was fairly evenly split on this controversial issue. Forty-five percent of respondents agreed that most governmental affirmative action programs should be continued, while 43 percent contended that such programs should be abolished (Bennet 1996).

Much less documented than economic inequality are the social consequences of affirmative action policies on everyday life. Interactionists focus on situations in which some women and minorities in underrepresented professions and schools are often mistakenly viewed as products of affirmative action. Fellow students and workers may stereotype them as less qualified and see them as beneficiaries of preference over more qualified White males. Obviously, this is not necessarily the case, but such labeling may well affect social relationships. Sociologist Orlando

FIGURE 17-2

Median Income by Race, Ethnicity, and Gender, 1998

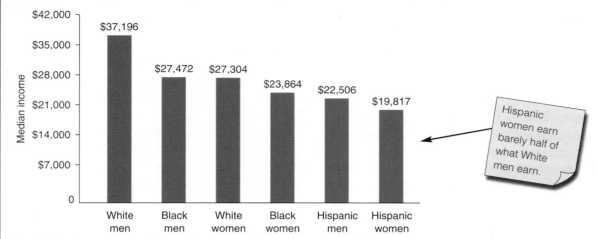

Hispanic women earn barely half of what White men earn.

Note: Median income includes all financial sources and is limited to year-round, full-time workers over 15 years of age.

Source: Bureau of the Census 1999inc:32–33.

Patterson (1998) has noted that workplace isolation experienced by minority workers inhibits their advancement up the corporate ladder; yet if efforts to increase their representation are scaled back, these problems in advancement will persist.

Has affirmative action actually helped to alleviate employment inequality on the basis of race and gender? Sociologists In Soo Son, Suzanne Model, and Gene Fisher (1989) studied income data and occupational mobility among Black male and White male workers in the period 1974 to 1981 to examine possible class polarization among Blacks. The researchers found that while Black college graduates made substantial gains as a result of affirmative action, less advantaged Blacks apparently did not benefit from it. The researchers (1989:325) conclude that the "racial parity achieved by young college-educated blacks in the 1970s will be maintained only if the government's commitment to affirmative action does not slacken."

Policy Initiatives

By the early 1990s, affirmative action had emerged as an increasingly important issue in state and national political campaigns. Generally, discussion focused on the use of quotas (or the "Q word," as it came to be known) in hiring practices. Supporters of affirmative action argue that hiring goals (or targets) establish floors for mi-

nority inclusion but do not exclude truly qualified candidates from any group. Opponents insist that these "targets" are, in fact, quotas that lead to reverse discrimination. However, affirmative action has caused very few claims of reverse discrimination by White people. Fewer than 100 of the more than 3,000 discrimination opinions in federal courts from 1990 to 1994 even raised the issue of reverse discrimination, and reverse discrimination was actually established in only six cases (*New York Times* 1995).

In the 1996 elections, California's voters approved by a 54 to 46 percent margin the California Civil Rights Initiative, also known as Proposition 209. This measure amends the state constitution to *prohibit* any program that gives preference to women and minorities in college admissions, hiring, promotion, or government contracts. In other words, it aims to abolish affirmative action programs. In 1997, the Supreme Court turned down a request to put an immediate halt to the initiative. This ruling suggests the Court is unlikely to overturn the measure. The approval of Proposition 209 by California voters has encouraged opponents of affirmative action across the nation. In early 1997, the American Civil Rights Institute was established to aggressively lobby for federal and state legislation that will abolish all preferential treatment based on race and sex in employment, government contracts, and admissions. In 1998, voters in Washington State passed an anti-affirmative action measure known as Initiative 200, and other states were considering similar measures (Wickham 1998).

There is evidence that the move against affirmative action may not be as dramatic as originally thought, however. Even when pressed to roll back preference programs, governments, including that in California, are looking for ways to increase opportunity in employment (Morello 1997). Much attention has been focused on the impact that reducing racial preference programs will have in highly competitive law and medical schools. The initial evidence is that Proposition 209 has caused a significant decline in minorities at elite institutions, particularly at UCLA and University of California at Berkeley, but most institutions are experiencing a similar decline. These changes came just as a study in the prestigious *Journal of the American Medical Association* suggests that giving preference to ethnicity dramatically increases the diversity of the student population without diluting the quality of the graduates (Davidson and Lewis 1997).

The United States is not alone in its effort to compensate for generations of inequality between racial groups. After dismantling the system of apartheid that favored Whites economically and socially, the Republic of South Africa is now trying to level the playing field. Inequality is stark: 88 percent of the nation's population is non-White, yet this group accounts for only 4 percent of the managerial ranks. The South African government has chosen the term "affirmative action" for its policy to encourage the hiring of Blacks in management positions where none existed before. Because the gaps are much greater than in the United States, there has been a virtual hiring frenzy in the limited pool of black South African managers and professionals. The subject of affirmative action in this nation almost always splits along racial lines: Blacks are infuriated that there is so much injustice to make up for, while Whites are reluctant to embrace the program meant to redress inequality. The specifics may be different from the United States, but the concerns and impatience seen in South Africa are familiar (Daley 1997).

Let's Discuss

1. Would a conflict theorist support the policy of affirmative action? Why or why not?
2. Do you think claims of reverse discrimination have any validity? What should be done about them?
3. If you were to draft legislation either supporting or abolishing affirmative action, what provisions would it include?

The First National Bank in South Africa has made an effort to hire Blacks for management positions. South Africa has used affirmative action to help close a gap in which 88 percent of the population is non-White but only 4 percent of this group fills the managerial ranks.

Summary

The *economic system* of a society has an important influence on social behavior and on other social institutions.

1. As the industrial revolution proceeded, a new form of social structure emerged: the *industrial society.*
2. Economic systems of *capitalism* vary in the degree to which the government regulates private ownership and economic activity, but all emphasize the profit motive.
3. The basic objective of a *socialist* economic system is to eliminate economic exploitation and meet people's needs.
4. Marx believed that *communism* would naturally evolve out of the socialism stage.
5. In most societies today the trend is toward an increase in jobs providing services and a rise in the number of occupations that aspire to be a *profession.*
6. Industrial jobs can lead to a sense of *alienation* in the workplace. Karl Marx expected that powerless workers would eventually overthrow the capitalist system.
7. The nature of the U.S. economy is changing. Sociologists are interested in the changing face of the workforce, the effects of *deindustrialization,* increased use of a contingency workforce, and the emergence of e-commerce.
8. Despite numerous recent *affirmative action* programs, White males continue to hold the overwhelming majority of prestigious and high-paying jobs in the United States.

Critical Thinking Questions

1. The United States has long been put forward as the model of a capitalist society. Drawing on material in earlier chapters of the textbook, discuss the values and beliefs that have led people in the United States to cherish a laissez-faire, capitalist economy. To what degree have these values and beliefs changed during the twentieth century? What aspects of socialism are now evident in the nation's economy? Have there been basic changes in our values and beliefs to support certain principles traditionally associated with socialist societies?

2. Describe some of the service workers in the college or university that you attend. Are there any issues that point toward alienation in the workplace? Does your school make much use of a contingent workforce, especially among students?

3. Imagine that you have been assigned to study possible changes in the economy of the nearest city. How could you use surveys, observation research, experiments, and existing sources to complete this task?

Key Terms

Affirmative action   Positive efforts to recruit minority group members or women for jobs, promotions, and educational opportunities. (page 459)

Alienation   The situation of being estranged or disassociated from the surrounding society. (449)

Capitalism   An economic system in which the means of production are largely in private hands, and the main incentive for economic activity is the accumulation of profits. (445)

Communism   As an ideal type, an economic system under which all property is communally owned and no social distinctions are made on the basis of people's ability to produce. (446)

Deindustrialization   The systematic, widespread withdrawal of investment in basic aspects of productivity such as factories and plants. (454)

Downsizing   Reductions taken in a company's workforce as part of deindustrialization. (455)

E-commerce   Numerous ways that people with access to the Internet can do business from their computer. (455)

Economic system   The social institution through which goods and services are produced, distributed, and consumed. (445)

Industrial society   A society that depends on mechanization to produce its goods and services. (445)

Laissez-faire   A form of capitalism under which people compete freely, with minimal government intervention in the economy. (445)

Monopoly   Control of a market by a single business firm. (446)

Profession   An occupation requiring extensive knowledge that is governed by a code of ethics. (448)

Socialism   An economic system under which the means of production and distribution are collectively owned. (446)

Trade unions   Organizations that seek to improve the material status of their members, all of whom perform a similar job or work for a common employer. (455)

Additional Readings

BOOKS

Bowen, William G., and Derek Bok. 1998. *The Shape of the River: Long-Term Consequences of Considering Race in College and University Admissions.* Princeton, NJ: Princeton University Press. A detailed statistical analysis of affirmative action leads Bowen and Bok, former presidents of Princeton and Harvard, to conclude that not only do minority students admitted to college under affirmative action policies gain from their experiences, but so do the colleges and the larger society.

Fernandez, John P. 1998. *Race, Gender and Rhetoric.* New York: McGraw-Hill. A scholar of management theory looks at the changes taking place in organizations as they become more diverse and more representative of women in decision-making positions.

Gleick, James. 1999. *Faster: The Acceleration of Just About Everything.* New York: Pantheon Books. A journalistic look at the ever-increasing pace of life in the workplace and throughout the lives of people in industrial nations.

Moore, Thomas S. 1996. *The Disposable Work Force: Worker Displacement and Employment Instability in America.* New York: Aldine de Gruyter. Drawing on a case study of a plant closing in Wisconsin, Moore examines the displacement of workers in the United States.

JOURNALS

Among the journals focusing on the economy are *Industrial and Labor Relations Review* (founded in 1947), *Insurgent Sociologist* (1969), and *Work and Occupations* (1974).

Internet Connection

Note: While all the URLs listed were current as of the printing of this book, these sites often change. Please check our website (http://www.mhhe.com/schaefer) for updates.

1. The chapter discusses the socioeconomic trend of corporate downsizing. Check the latest information regarding layoffs and downsizing at (**http://fullcoverage.yahoo.com/Full_Coverage/Business/Downsizing_and_Layoffs/**). Choose one of the corporations that recently cut jobs on a large scale.
   (a) How many jobs were lost?
   (b) Will the company help the ex-employees find new jobs?
   (c) If there was a union involved, what efforts were made to preserve jobs? Why wasn't the union effective in stopping the downsizing?
   (d) Did technology play a role in the decision to cut jobs?
   (e) How did the corporation justify the downsizing? Do you think these justifications are reasonable? Why or why not?
   (f) What alternatives besides downsizing would you propose to the corporation?
   (g) How would a functionalist view this example of downsizing as compared to a conflict theorist?
   (h) Does it appear that downsizing is slowing or increasing in the United States?
   (i) How confident do you feel about the availability and stability of jobs after your graduation from school? Has your confidence level had any impact on your choice of major or field of study?

2. The History Place™: Child Labor in America 1908–1912 (**http://www.historyplace.com/unitedstates/childlabor/index.html**) offers a virtual look at the photographs of Lewis W. Hine. Hine used his camera as a tool to document social issues and injustices such as child labor. Visit the page, examine the photos, and read the text accompanying the pictures.
   (a) How old are the children in Hine's photos?
   (b) What variety of work did these children perform?
   (c) Why did children work during this era in such occupations?
   (d) What were the challenges and dangers in their jobs?
   (e) What kinds of emotions do you see on the faces of the children?
   (f) What kinds of clothes did they wear?
   (g) Are there gender differences in terms of who did what job?
   (h) What do you imagine the daily lives of these children were like?
   (i) What feelings do you have while looking at these pictures?
   (j) Ask a grandparent or older relative if he or she worked as a child, or if his or her parents worked under such conditions. How do their experiences compare with those of the children in the photo essay? How did your own childhood compare?
   (k) Are there still countries today with child labor?
   (l) What surprised you most about the photographs and text on this website? Why?

HEALTH AND MEDICINE

WELCOME TO AMERICA

the only industrialized country besides South Africa without national healthca

This billboard protests the lack of a national health care program in the United States. The reference to South Africa was especially pointed when the poster first appeared in 1989, because of the racist apartheid regime that held sway there.

THE SCALPEL
AND THE
SILVER BEAR

The First Navajo
Woman Surgeon
Combines
Western Medicine
and
Traditional Healing

LORI ARVISO ALVORD, M.D.
AND
ELIZABETH COHEN VAN PELT

knew that Navajo people mistrusted Western medicine, and that Navajo customs and beliefs, even Navajo ways of interacting with others, often stood in direct opposition to the way I was trained at Stanford to deliver medical care. I wanted to make a difference in the lives of my people, not only by providing surgery to heal them but also by making it easier for them to understand, relate to, and accept Western medicine. By speaking some Navajo with them, by showing respect for their ways, and by being one of them, I could help them. I watched my patients. I listened to them. Slowly I began to develop better ways to heal them, ways that respected their culture and beliefs. I desired to incorporate these traditional beliefs and customs into my practice. . . .

Navajo patients simply didn't respond well to the brusque and distanced style of Western doctors. To them it is not acceptable to walk into a room, quickly open someone's shirt and listen to their heart with a stethoscope, or stick something in their mouth or ear. Nor is it acceptable to ask probing and personal questions. As I adapted my practice to my culture, my patients relaxed in situations that could otherwise have been highly stressful to them. As they became more comfortable and at ease, something even more remarkable—astonishing, even—happened. When patients were trusting and accepting before surgery, their operations seemed to be more successful. If they were anxious, distrustful, and did not understand, or had resisted treatment, they seemed to have more operative or postoperative complications. Could this be happening? The more I watched, the more I saw it was indeed true. Incorporating Navajo philosophies of balance and symmetry, respect and connectedness into my practice, benefited my patients and allowed everything in my two worlds to make sense.

Navajos believe in *hózhǫ or hózhǫ́ni*—"Walking in Beauty"—a worldview in which everything in life is connected and influences everything else. A stone thrown into a pond can influence the life of a deer in the forest, a human voice and a spoken word can influence events around the world, and all things possess spirit and power. So Navajos make every effort to live in harmony and balance with everyone and everything else. Their belief system sees sickness as a result of things falling out of balance, of losing one's way on the path of beauty. In this belief system, religion and medicine are one and the same. *(Alvord and Van Pelt 1999:13–14)* ■

n this excerpt from *The Scalpel and the Silver Bear,* Dr. Lori Arviso Alvord, the first Navajo woman to become a surgeon, describes her effort to bridge the cultural gap between Western medicine and traditional Native American healing. Dropping the impersonal clinical manner she had learned in medical school, Alvord reached out to her Navajo patients, acknowledging their faith in holistic healing practices. Her account communicates the wonder she felt as she watched their health improve. By walking in beauty, Dr. Alvord had become a healer as well as a surgeon.

Alvord's account illustrates the powerful effect of culture on both health and medicine. Culture affects the way people interact with doctors and healers, the way they relate to their families when they are sick, and even the way they think about health. In this chapter, we will consider first the relationship between culture and health. Then we will present a sociological overview of health, illness, health care, and medicine as a social institution.

We will begin by examining how functionalists, conflict theorists, interactionists, and labeling theorists look at health-related issues. Then we will study the distribution of diseases in a society by gender, social class, race and ethnicity, and age. We'll also look at the evolution of the health care system of the United States. Sociologists are interested in the roles that people play within the health care system and the organizations that deal with issues of health and sickness. Therefore, we will analyze the interactions among doctors, nurses, and patients; the role of government in providing health services to the needy; and alternatives to traditional health care. The chapter continues with an examination of mental illness in which we contrast the medical and labeling approaches to mental disorders. Finally, the social policy section will explore the issue of how to finance health care worldwide. ■

Culture and Health

In the 1970s, medical writer Lynn Payer (1988:21–22) began nine years of research for a book on the ways in which culture contributed to differences in medical care in the United States, England, France, and what was then West Germany. While her original interest in the subject was primarily journalistic, soon the matter became highly personal: A routine gynecological checkup in France revealed a grapefruit-sized fibroid tumor in her uterus. Payer had a surgical procedure known as a myomectomy to remove it, but after she moved back to the United States there was a recurrence of the fibroids, which gave her an opportunity to compare medical care in the United States and France.

Payer's French surgeon had never mentioned hysterectomy as an option, presumably because it would end her ability to have children. The surgeon had insisted that she *must* have a myomectomy. By contrast, her physicians in the United States pressured her to have a hysterectomy and claimed that a second myomectomy would be impossible. In Payer's view, the differing medical recommendations in the United States and France were influenced less by the actual facts of her condition than by the comparatively higher value placed on having children in French culture.

Payer's experience illustrates that even in industrialized nations, medical care is culturally defined. In Japan, for instance, organ transplants are rare due to cultural inhibitions against the harvesting of organs from brain-dead donors (see Box 18-1). Furthermore, researchers have shown that diseases themselves are rooted in the shared meanings of particular cultures. The term *culture-bound syndrome* refers to a disease or illness that cannot be understood apart from its specific social context (Cassidy 1982:326).

In the United States, a culture-bound syndrome known as anorexia nervosa has received increasing attention over the last 25 years. First described in England in the 1860s, this condition is characterized by an intense fear of becoming obese and a distorted image of one's body. Those suffering from anorexia nervosa (primarily young women in their teenage years or twenties) drastically reduce their body weight through self-induced semistarvation and self-induced vomiting. Anorexia nervosa is best understood in the context of Western culture, which typically views the slim, youthful body as healthy and beautiful, whereas the fat person is viewed as ugly and lacking in self-discipline (Chernin 1981; R. Hahn 1985; Prince 1985; Swartz 1985).

Other societies have their own culture-bound syndromes. For example, dyschromic spirochetosis—a disease characterized by spots of various colors on the skin—is so common in a particular South American Indian tribe that people who do not have it are regarded as abnormal. Indeed, the few single men who do not suffer from this disease are excluded from many of the tribe's social activities because they are viewed as "strange." In a 1982 study conducted in Nigeria, at least half of all students questioned reported suffering from "brain fog,"

18-1 Organ Donation in Japan

By late 1998 15-year-old Takashi Naka-zawa had been waiting a year for a life-saving lung transplant from the Japan Organ Transplant Network. Though millions of organ donor cards had been printed and distributed to Japanese citizens, not one patient on any of the organ transplant lists had received a transplant, and seven people had died waiting. Still, Nakazawa, who had just undergone emergency surgery in Los Angeles, had decided against seeking a transplant in the United States. "I am gambling that it'll be easier to receive a transplant in this country soon," he told a reporter (Negushi 1998:10).

Organ transplants are a controversial issue in Japan, where until 1997 the transfer of organs from brain-dead patients was prevented by the legal definition of death, which did not equate the end of human life with the end of brain function. Because heart, kidney, and pancreas transplants must be taken from brain-dead donors while the heart is still beating, the law virtually forbade them. And since 1968, when Dr. Juro Wada, a pioneer of transplant surgery in Japan, performed a heart transplant on a patient who later died, the government has vigorously pursued those who dared defy the law. Criminal investigations of the doctors involved were so chilling, for the next 30 years transplants were virtually unknown in Japan. Of the 33 Japanese who received heart transplants between 1984 and 1997, all underwent the operation in the United States or Europe.

But in 1997, publicity about the plight of thousands of terminally ill Japanese moved the legislature to reconsider the question of transplants. The new Organ Transplant Law provides that brain death may be determined to be the end of human life on a case-by-case basis, with the agreement of two or more doctors. It also defines the conditions under which organs may be transplanted, requiring a signed donor card and the approval of immediate family. Brain death must be diagnosed at one of only 343 au-thorized medical institutions, and both organ donors and recipients must be of a specified age. But to date, these safeguards have functioned more to restrict access to transplants than to encourage them. Superstition and distrust of Japanese doctors, who do not routinely obtain patients' informed consent, have also contributed to the shortage of organs. "The situation is very disappointing when we think of how many hopes the law raised, only to shatter them," admits Yoshio Aranami (Negushi 1998:10), who directs an organization of transplant recipients.

In February 1999 the first legal transplants from a brain-dead donor were finally performed. Japanese doctors successfully transplanted the heart, liver, kidneys, and corneas of the donor to recipients selected

> Though millions of organ donor cards had been printed and distributed to Japanese citizens, not one patient on any of the organ transplant lists had received a transplant, and seven people had died waiting.

by the Japan Organ Transplant Network. Later that year they transplanted the heart and kidneys of another donor to waiting patients. "I am thankful the second transplants have been realized relatively quickly," commented the surgeon who performed the heart transplant, Dr. Soichiro Kitamura (Kyodo News 1999:4). Officials of the transplant network noted that the waiting time for a heart transplant had dropped from 16 months for the first recipient to 29 days for the second—a hopeful sign for those on the waiting lists.

Still, the number of Japanese on the waiting lists far exceeds the number of donated organs available for transplant. In the face of the continuing shortage of organs, Japanese doctors and scientists are developing other means of saving lives. In October 1998 doctors at Okayama University Hospital performed the first lung transplant from living donors to be done in Japan. To save a terminally ill young woman, they removed part of her mother's lung and part of her sister's, and transplanted both to her body. Japanese scientists have also begun to search for radically different solutions to the organ shortage. Some are working on developing a permanent artificial heart; others are experimenting with culturing organs from live cells. But these alternatives to conventional transplants are years, many of them decades, away from becoming a reality.

The acute shortage of organ transplants in Japan is just one example of how culture influences health care. Despite the desperate need of many Japanese patients, only about 50 percent of the Japanese people approve of transplants. Hirofumi Kiuchi, an advocate of the procedure, admits that his own mother is opposed to it: "Even though a transplant saved my life, she's uncomfortable with the idea of removing organs from someone whose heart is still beating," he explains (Kunii 1997:20). This type of cultural inhibition can be seen all over the world, from the most to the least traditional societies. In the United States, where organ transplants are well accepted, cultural resistance has slowed public acceptance of traditional Asian remedies, such as herbs and acupuncture. Health, illness, medicine, and the body are all socially constructed concepts.

Let's Discuss

1. How do you feel about organ donation? Would you allow a relative's organs to be donated in the event of his or her death? Have you signed a donor card so your own organs can be donated??

2. Is there any other medical procedure, such as acupuncture, that you are uncomfortable with? If so, do you think your cultural background explains your reluctance to accept the procedure?

Sources: Associated Press 1998; Japan Times Staff 1998; Kunii 1997; Kyodo News 1999; Negushi 1998.

A young woman checks her weight on the bathroom scale. In the United States, an intense fear of becoming obese causes some young women to develop a culture-bound syndrome known as *anorexia nervosa*.

with symptoms including burning or crawling sensations. In 1993, hundreds of girls in Egypt broke out in sobs and complained of unpleasant smells and nausea. Many of them fainted and dozens of schools subsequently closed. Although investigators could not find any clinical reasons for this outbreak, similar incidents had occurred in Europe but are unknown in North America (Hedges 1993; Prince 1985; Zola 1983:39).

Culture can also influence the relative incidence of a disease or disorder. In *The Scalpel and the Silver Bear,* Dr. Lori Arviso Alvord writes of the depression and alcoholism that attended life on the reservation. These diseases, she says, are born out of "historical grief": "Navajo children are told of the capture and murder of their forefathers and mothers, and then they too must share in the legacy. . . ." Not just for the Navajo, Alvord writes, but for Black Americans as well, the weight of centuries of suffering, injustice, and loss too often manifests itself in despair and addiction (Alvord and Van Pelt 1999:12). Indeed, the rate of alcoholism mortality among Native Americans

served by the Indian Health Service is five times that of the general population of the United States (Utter 1993:190).

Sociological Perspectives on Health and Illness

From a sociological point of view, social factors contribute to the evaluation of a person as "healthy" or "sick." How, then, can we define health? We can imagine a continuum with health on one end and death on the other. In the preamble to its 1946 constitution, the World Health Organization defined **health** as a "state of complete physical, mental, and social well-being, and not merely the absence of disease and infirmity" (Leavell and Clark 1965:14). With this definition in mind, the "healthy" end of our continuum represents an ideal rather than a precise condition. Along the continuum, people define themselves as "healthy" or "sick" on the basis of criteria established by each individual, relatives, friends, coworkers, and medical practitioners. Because health is relative, we can view it in a social context and consider how it varies in different situations or cultures (Twaddle 1974; Wolinsky 1980).

Why is it that you may consider yourself sick or well when others do not agree? Who controls definitions of health and illness in our society, and for what ends? What are the consequences of viewing yourself (or being viewed) as ill or disabled? Drawing on four sociological perspectives—functionalism, conflict theory, interactionism, and labeling theory—we can gain greater insight into the social context shaping definitions of health and treatment of illness.

Functionalist Approach

Illness entails at least a temporary disruption in a person's social interactions both at work and at home. Consequently, from a functionalist perspective, "being sick" must be controlled so that not too many people are released from their societal responsibilities at any one time. Functionalists contend that an overly broad definition of illness would disrupt the workings of a society.

"Sickness" requires that one take on a social role, even if temporarily. The **sick role** refers to societal expectations about the attitudes and behavior of a person viewed as being ill. Sociologist Talcott Parsons (1951, 1972, 1975), well known for his contributions to functionalist theory (see Chapter 1), has outlined the behavior required of people considered "sick." They are exempted from their normal, day-to-day responsibilities and generally are not blamed

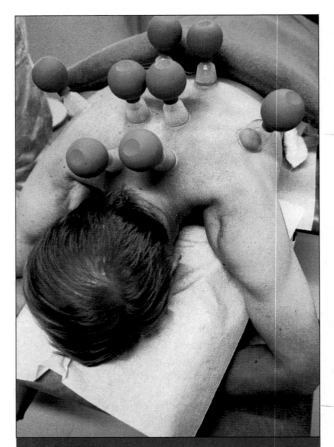

Health care takes many forms around the world. Cupping—a traditional practice used in ancient China, India, Egypt, and Greece—survives in modern Finland (left). Physiotherapists there use suction cups to draw out blood in order to lower patients' blood pressure, improve their circulation, and relieve muscular pain. In the western Pacific (right), the Malaitan people of Laulasi Island, one of the Solomon Islands, believe that a leaf called *raralu* has medicinal properties that reduce swelling. This boy has squeezed a *raralu* leaf to release its juices and used it to bandage his broken finger.

for their condition. Yet they are obligated to try to get well, and this may include seeking competent professional care. Attempting to get well is particularly important in the world's developing countries. In modern automated industrial societies, we can absorb a greater degree of illness or disability, but in horticultural or agrarian societies, the availability of workers is a much more critical concern (Conrad 1997).

According to Parsons's theory, physicians function as "gatekeepers" for the sick role, either verifying a patient's condition as "illness" or designating the patient as "recovered." The ill person becomes dependent on the doctor because the latter can control valued rewards (not only treatment of illness but also excused absences from work and school). Parsons suggests that the doctor–patient relationship is somewhat like that between parent and child. Like a parent, the physician helps the patient to return to society as a full and functioning adult (Segall 1976).

There have been a number of criticisms of the concept of the sick role. First, patients' judgments regarding their own state of health may be related to their gender, age, social class, and ethnic group. Second, the sick role may be more applicable to people experiencing short-term illnesses than those with recurring, long-term illnesses. Finally, even simple factors, such as whether a person is employed or not, seem to affect willingness to assume the sick role—as does the impact of socialization into a particular occupation or activity. For example, beginning in childhood, athletes learn to define certain ailments as "sports injuries" and therefore do not regard themselves as "sick" (Curry 1993).

Nonetheless, sociologists continue to rely on Parsons's model for functionalist analysis of the relationship between illness and societal expectations for the sick.

Conflict Approach

Functionalists seek to explain how health care systems meet the needs of society as well as those of individual patients and medical practitioners, but conflict theorists take issue with this view. They express concern that the profession of medicine has assumed a preeminence that extends well beyond whether to excuse a student from school or an employee from work. Sociologist Eliot Freidson (1970:5) has likened the position of medicine today to that of state religions yesterday—it has an officially approved monopoly of the right to define health and illness and to treat illness. Conflict theorists use the term *medicalization of society* to refer to the growing role of medicine as a major institution of social control (Conrad and Schneider 1992; McKinlay and McKinlay 1977; Zola 1972, 1983).

Social control involves techniques and strategies for regulating behavior in order to enforce the distinctive norms and values of a culture. Typically,

`pp. 171–76` ◀

we think of informal social control as occurring within families and peer groups, whereas formal social control is carried out by authorized agents such as police officers, judges, school administrators, and employers. However, viewed from a conflict perspective, medicine is not simply a "healing profession"; it is a regulating mechanism as well.

How does it manifest its social control? First, medicine has greatly expanded its domain of expertise in recent decades. Society tolerates such expansion of the boundaries of medicine because we hope that these experts can bring new "miracle cures" to complex human problems as they have to the control of certain infectious diseases. Consequently, as the medicalization of society has proceeded in the twentieth century, physicians have become much more involved in examining a wide range of issues, among them sexuality (including homosexuality), old age, anxiety, obesity, child development, alcoholism, and drug addiction. The social significance of medicalization is that once a problem is viewed using a *medical model*—once medical experts become influential in proposing and assessing relevant public policies—it becomes more difficult for "common people" to join the discussion and exert influence on decision making. It also becomes more difficult to view these issues as being shaped by social, cultural, or psychological factors, rather than simply by physical or medical factors (R. Caplan 1989; Conrad and Schneider 1992; Starr 1982).

Second, medicine serves as an agent of social control by retaining absolute jurisdiction over many health care procedures. It has even attempted to guard its jurisdiction by placing health care professionals such as chiropractors and nurse-midwives outside the realm of acceptable medicine. Despite the fact that midwives first brought professionalism to child delivery, they have been portrayed as having invaded the "legitimate" field of obstetrics. Nurse-midwives have sought licensing as a way to achieve professional respectability, but physicians continue to exert power to ensure that midwifery remains a subordinate occupation (M. Radosh 1984; P. Radosh 1986; Zia 1990; Zola 1972).

The medicalization of society is but one concern of conflict theorists as they assess the workings of health care institutions. As we have seen throughout this textbook, when analyzing any issue, conflict theorists seek to determine who benefits, who suffers, and who dominates at the expense of others. Viewed from a conflict perspective, there are glaring inequities in health care delivery within the United States. For example, poor and rural areas tend to be underserved because medical services concentrate where people are numerous and/or wealthy.

Similarly, from a global perspective, there are obvious inequities in health care delivery. Today, the United States has about 25 physicians per 1,000 people, while African nations have fewer than 1 per 1,000. This situation is only worsened by the "brain drain"—the immigration to the United States and other industrialized nations of skilled workers, professionals, and technicians who are desperately needed by their home countries. As part of this brain drain, physicians and other health care professionals have come to the United States from developing countries such as India, Pakistan, and various African states. Conflict theorists view such emigration out of the Third World as yet another way in which the world's core industrialized nations enhance their quality of life at the expense of developing countries (World Bank 1999b:90–91).

In another example of global inequities in health care, multinational corporations based in industrialized countries have reaped significant profits by "dumping" unapproved drugs on unsuspecting Third World consumers. In some cases, fraudulent capsules and tablets are manufactured and marketed as established products in developing countries. These "medications" contain useless ingredients or perhaps one-tenth of the needed dosage of a genuine medication. Even when the drugs dumped on developing countries are legitimate, the information available to physicians and patients is less likely to include warnings of health hazards and more likely to include undocumented testimonials than in industrialized nations (Silverman et al. 1992).

A midwife hands a newborn baby to its mother. Despite the fact that midwives first brought professionalism to child delivery, physicians insist on treating midwifery as a subordinate occupation.

Conflict theorists emphasize that inequities in health care resources have clear life-and-death consequences. For example, in 1999, the infant mortality rate in western Sierra Leone ranged as high as 150 infant deaths per 1,000 live births. By contrast, Japan's infant mortality rate was only 3.7 deaths per 1,000 live births and Iceland's was only 2.6. From a conflict perspective, the dramatic differences in infant mortality rates around the world (see Figure 18-1) reflect, at least in part, unequal distribution of health care resources based on the wealth or poverty of various communities and nations.

In 1998, the United States had a rate of 7 infant deaths per 1,000 live births (although it is estimated that the rate in some poor, inner-city neighborhoods in this country exceeds 30 deaths per 1,000 live births). Yet, despite the wealth of the United States, at least 22 nations have lower infant mortality rates, among them Canada, Great Britain, and Japan. Conflict theorists point out that, unlike the United States, these countries offer some form of government-supported health care for all citizens, which typically leads to greater availability and greater use of prenatal care than is the case in this country. (We will examine government's role in health care in greater detail in the social policy section of this chapter.)

Interactionist Approach

In examining health, illness, and medicine as a social institution, interactionists generally focus on micro-level study of the roles played by health care professionals and patients. They emphasize that the patient should not always be viewed as passive, but instead as an actor who often shows a powerful intent to see the physician (Alonzo 1989; Zola 1983).

Sometimes patients play an active role in health care by *failing* to follow a physician's advice. For example, some patients stop taking medications long before they should, some take an incorrect dosage on purpose, and others never even fill their prescriptions. Such noncompliance results in

FIGURE 18-1

Infant Mortality Rates, 1999

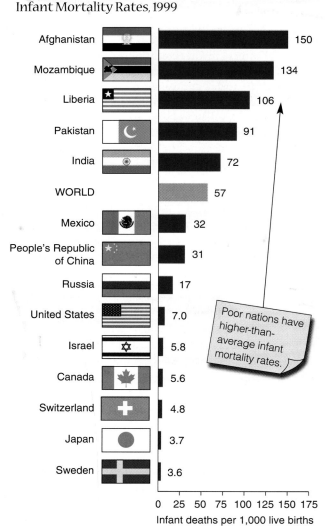

Country	Infant deaths per 1,000 live births
Afghanistan	150
Mozambique	134
Liberia	106
Pakistan	91
India	72
WORLD	57
Mexico	32
People's Republic of China	31
Russia	17
United States	7.0
Israel	5.8
Canada	5.6
Switzerland	4.8
Japan	3.7
Sweden	3.6

Poor nations have higher-than-average infant mortality rates.

Infant deaths per 1,000 live births

Source: Haub and Cornelius 1999.

Research in Action

18-2 How Race and Ethnicity Affect Views of Patient Autonomy

Should patients be told the seriousness of their illness? Should they be included in the decisions about what medical care they receive? In the last 25 years, the principle of patient autonomy has become a fundamental ideal of medical care in the United States. According to this principle, "people have the right to make informed decisions about their medical care; consequently, they need the truth about their diagnosis, their prognosis, and the risks and benefits of possible treatments." While the ideal of patient autonomy has won wide acceptance from physicians, policymakers, and the general public, some critics argue that the current focus on patient autonomy reflects an ethnocentric cultural bias by ignoring other values, such as family integrity and physician responsibility.

The question of how race and ethnicity influence attitudes toward patient autonomy was studied by a team of researchers, including an internal medicine specialist and ethicist, anthropologists, translators, a statistician, and a law professor. The researchers administered questionnaires to 800 people age 65 or over in 31 senior citizen centers in Los Angeles County. An equal number came from European American, African American, Korean American, and Mexican American backgrounds.

The major finding of the study was that there are marked differences by race and ethnicity in attitudes toward patient autonomy. While 88 percent of African Americans and 87 percent of European Americans believe that a patient should be informed of a diagnosis of cancer, the same is true of only

65 percent of Mexican Americans and 47 percent of Korean Americans. Moreover, 69 percent of European Americans and 63 percent of African Americans believe that a patient should be informed of a terminal prognosis, as compared with 48 percent of Mexican Americans and 35 percent of Korean Americans.

One reason why Korean Americans are especially opposed to hearing a terminal prognosis is their belief in the unity of mind and body. Anthropologist Kyeyoung Park, a consultant on the study, noted that that kind of truth-telling is like a death sentence

> Navajos believe that physicians and other healers should never offer a terminal diagnosis or use any negative language that could trouble or hurt a patient.

to traditional Koreans because of their view that the body will react to ominous news received by the mind. As a result, many Korean Americans believe that doctors should always be optimistic and positive in their communications with patients.

Similarly, a separate study of residents of a Navajo Indian reservation in Arizona revealed that Navajo culture places a high value on thinking and speaking in a positive way. For Navajos, language can shape reality. Consequently, Navajos believe that physicians and other healers should never

offer a terminal diagnosis or use any negative language that could trouble or hurt a patient. One highly regarded medicine man noted that the mention of death to a patient "is sharper than any needle" (Carrese and Rhodes 1995:828).

In the Los Angeles study, Korean Americans and Mexican Americans were especially likely to believe that the family (and not the patient) should be told of a terminal diagnosis and should make any decisions about the use of life-supporting technology. In the view of Dr. Leslie Blackhall, the director of the study, physicians trained in the United States "may have lost sight of the fact that, for many cultures, the family unit is more important than the individual in decision-making." With such racial and ethnic differences in mind, the authors of the study conclude that physicians should ask patients if they wish to be informed about their illness and involved in decisions about their care—or if they prefer that family members be given such information and responsibility (Blackhall et al. 1995:825).

Let's Discuss

1. How has terminal illness been handled in your family? Have relatives who were dying been told the truth about their condition, or has it been withheld from them? Do you think your family's cultural background influenced the decision?
2. Which is more important, the patient's right to know or the patient's faith in the chance of recovery?

Sources: Blackhall et al. 1995; Carrese and Rhodes 1995; Monmaney 1995.

part from the prevalence of self-medication in our society; many people are accustomed to self-diagnosis and self-treatment. On the other hand, patients' active involvement in their health care can sometimes have very *positive* consequences. Some patients read books about preventive health care techniques, attempt to maintain healthful and nutritious diets, carefully monitor any side effects of medication, and adjust dosage based on such perceived side effects.

The interactionist perspective has been especially helpful in unraveling cultural differences that affect health care in a multicultural society such as that of the United States (see Box 18-2). For example, when Community Action for Women's Health began surveying Native Americans in Los Angeles in 1994 concerning their health care needs, the researchers found that the respondents regarded the surveys as too intrusive and offered little cooperation. Subsequently, questions were asked orally and answers were written on forms with the image of a traditional medicine wheel printed on them. The researchers then received much greater cooperation, presumably because the respondents felt that the medical team shared their cultural beliefs (*Los Angeles Times* 1995).

Labeling Approach

Labeling theory helps us to understand why certain people are *viewed* as deviants, "bad kids," or criminals whereas others whose behavior is similar are not. Labeling theorists also suggest that the designation "healthy" or "ill" generally involves social definition by others. Just as police officers, judges, and other regulators of social control have the power to define certain people as criminals, health care professionals (especially physicians) have the power to define certain people as "sick." Moreover, like labels that suggest nonconformity or criminality, labels associated with illness commonly reshape how others treat us and how we see ourselves. Our society attaches serious consequences to labels that suggest less-than-perfect physical or mental health (Becker 1963; C. Clark 1983; H. Schwartz 1987).

pp. 183–84

An example from history illustrates perhaps the ultimate extreme in labeling social behavior as a sickness. As enslavement of Africans in the United States came under increasing attack in the nineteenth century, medical authorities provided new rationalizations for this oppressive practice. Noted physicians published articles stating that the skin color of Africans deviated from "healthy" white skin coloring because Africans suffered from congenital leprosy. Moreover, the continuing efforts of enslaved Africans to escape from their White masters were classified as an example of the "disease" of drapetomania (or "crazy runaways"). The prestigious *New Orleans Medical and Surgical Journal* suggested that the remedy for this "disease" was to treat slaves kindly as one might treat children. Apparently, these medical authorities would not entertain the view that it was quite healthy and sane to flee slavery or join in a slave revolt (Szasz 1971).

By the late 1980s, the power of a label—"person with AIDS"—had become quite evident. As we saw in our discussion of the late Arthur Ashe (see page 122), this label often functions as a master status that overshadows all other aspects of a person's life. Once someone is told that he or she has tested positive for HIV, the virus associated with AIDS, that person is forced to confront immediate and difficult questions: Should I tell my family members, my sexual partner(s), my friends, my coworkers, my employer? How will these people respond? As discussed in the social policy section of Chapter 5, people's intense fear of this disease has led to prejudice and discrimination—even social ostracism—against those who have (or are suspected of having) AIDS. Consequently, a person who has AIDS must deal with not only the serious medical consequences of the disease, but also the distressing social consequences associated with the label.

According to labeling theorists, a variety of life experiences can come to be viewed as illnesses or not. Recently, premenstrual syndrome, posttraumatic disorders, and hyperactivity have been "labeled" medically recognized disorders. Disagreements continue in the medical community over whether chronic fatigue syndrome constitutes a medical illness. Following the 1991 Gulf War against Iraq, more than 21,000 U.S. soldiers and other personnel reported a variety of symptoms ranging from fatigue and rashes to respiratory disorders. These symptoms have come to be called the Gulf War Syndrome (or Illness), although the government has yet to officially rec-

In 1994, former Olympic diving champion Greg Louganis revealed that he had AIDS. The label "person with AIDS" often functions as a master status, overshadowing all other aspects of a person's life.

ognize a clear link between the combat situation and subsequent symptoms.

Probably the most noteworthy recent medical example of labeling is the case of homosexuality. For years, psychiatrists classified being gay or lesbian as a mental disorder subject to treatment, not as a lifestyle. This official sanction by the psychiatry profession became an early target of the growing gay and lesbian rights movement in the United States. In 1974, members of the American Psychiatric Association voted to drop homosexuality from the standard manual on mental disorders (Adam 1995; Charmaz and Paterniti 1999; Monteiro 1998).

An Overview

As you know by now, the four sociological approaches described above should not be regarded as mutually exclusive. In the study of health-related issues, they share certain common themes. First, any person's health or illness is more than an organic condition, since it is subject to the interpretation of others. Owing to the impact of culture, family and friends, and the medical profession, health and illness are not purely biological occurrences but are sociological occurrences as well. Second, since members of a society (especially industrial societies) share the same health delivery system, health is a group and societal concern. Although health may be defined as the complete well-being of an individual, it is also the result of his or her social environment. As we shall see in the next section, such factors as a person's social class, race and ethnicity, gender, and age can influence the likelihood of contracting a particular disease (Cockerham 1998).

These U.S. Marines wore gas masks while in combat situations in the Gulf War in 1991. Many soldiers who were not protected complained later of a number of symptoms, ranging from fatigue to rashes to respiratory disorders. These symptoms came to be labeled the Gulf War Syndrome.

Social Epidemiology and Health

Social epidemiology is the study of the distribution of disease, impairment, and general health status across a population. In its earliest period, epidemiology concentrated on the scientific study of epidemics, focusing on how they started and spread. Contemporary social epidemiology is much broader in scope, concerned not only with epidemics but also with nonepidemic diseases, injuries, drug addiction and alcoholism, suicide, and mental illness. Epi-demiology draws on the work of a wide variety of scientists and researchers, among them physicians, sociologists, public health officials, biologists, veterinarians, demographers, anthropologists, psychologists, and meteorologists.

Researchers in social epidemiology commonly use two concepts: incidence and prevalence. *Incidence* refers to the number of *new* cases of a specific disorder occurring within a given population during a stated period of time, usually a year. For example, the incidence of AIDS in the United States in 1997 was 58,492 cases. By contrast, *prevalence* refers to the total number of cases of a specific disorder that exist at a given time. The prevalence of AIDS in the United States in January 2000 was about 270,000 cases (Centers for Disease Control and Prevention 2000).

When incidence figures are presented as rates, or as the number of reports per 100,000 people, they are called *morbidity rates.* (The term *mortality rate,* you will recall, refers to the incidence of *death* in a given population.) Sociologists find morbidity rates useful because they reveal that a specific disease occurs more frequently among one segment of a population than another. As we shall see, social class, race, ethnicity, gender, and age can all affect a population's morbidity rates. In 1999 the U.S. Department of Health and Human Services, recognizing the inequality inherent in U.S. morbidity and mortality rates, launched the Campaign for 100% Access and Zero Health Disparities, an ambitious undertaking (Bureau of Primary Health Care 1999).

Social Class

Social class is clearly associated with differences in morbidity and mortality rates. Studies in the United States and other countries have consistently shown that people in the lower classes have higher rates of mortality and disability (see Figure 18-2). A study published in 1998 documents the impact of class on mortality. The authors concluded that Americans whose family incomes were less than $10,000 could expect to die seven years sooner than those with incomes of at least $25,000 (Pamuk et al. 1998:5).

Numerous studies document the impact of social class on health. An examination of data from 11 countries in North America and Europe found strong associations between household income and health, and between household income and life expectancy, when comparing families of similar size. Moreover, drawing on secondary analysis of U.S. census data, researchers from the Harvard School of Public Health found that higher overall mortality rates—as well as higher incidence of infant mortality and deaths from coronary heart disease, cancer, and homicide—were associated with lower incomes. In the parts of the United States where income inequality was most pronounced, the gaps between the health of rich and poor people were the greatest (Atkinson and Micklewright 1992; Kennedy et al. 1996).

Why is class linked to health? Crowded living conditions, substandard housing, poor diet, and stress all contribute to the ill health of many low-income people in the United States. In certain instances, poor education may lead to a lack of awareness of measures necessary to maintain good health. Yet financial strains are certainly a major factor in the health problems of less affluent people in the United States. Given the high costs of quality medical care—which we will explore more fully later in the chapter—the poor have significantly less access to health care resources.

Another factor in the link between class and health is evident at the workplace: The occupations of people in the working and lower classes of the United States tend to be more dangerous than those of more affluent citizens. Miners, for example, must face the possibility of injury or death due to explosions and cave-ins; they are also likely to develop respiratory diseases such as black lung. Workers in textile mills may contract a variety of illnesses caused by exposure to toxic substances, including one disease commonly known as *brown lung disease* (R. Hall 1982). In recent years, the nation has learned of the perils of asbestos poisoning, a particular worry for construction workers.

In the view of Karl Marx and contemporary conflict theorists, capitalist societies such as the United States care more about maximizing profits than they do about the health and safety of industrial workers. As a result, government agencies do not take forceful action to regulate conditions in the workplace, and workers suffer many preventable, job-related injuries and illnesses.

Research shows that the lower classes are more vulnerable to environmental pollution than the affluent; this is the case not only where the lower classes work but also where they live. Undergraduates at Occidental College confirmed this pattern in 1995 in a study of Los Angeles County. Drawing on secondary data (including high-tech mapping techniques and census data), the student researchers found that the poor, African Americans, Hispanics, Asian Americans, and Native Americans were especially likely to be living near the county's 82 potential environmental hazards (Moffatt 1995).

Race and Ethnicity

Health profiles of many racial and ethnic minorities reflect the social inequality evident in the United States. The poor economic and environmental conditions of groups such as African Americans, Hispanics, and Native Americans are manifested in high morbidity and mortality rates for these groups. So dramatic are these differences that the federal government in 1998 launched an initiative to end long-standing racial and ethnic health disparities by the year 2010. It is true that some afflictions, such as sickle-cell anemia among Blacks, have a clear genetic basis. But in most instances, environmental factors contribute to the differential rates of disease and death.

Compared to Whites, African American men are twice as likely to suffer from heart disease. Black men younger than 65 are twice as likely to be stricken by

FIGURE 18-2

Days of Disability by Family Income

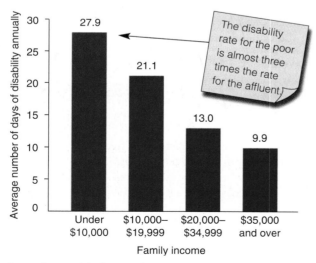

Source: Bureau of the Census 1999a:145.

prostate cancer. The stomach cancer rate for Hispanics is two to three times higher, and they suffer from diabetes at a rate twice the national average. Native Americans suffer from diabetes at a rate almost three times the national average. Chinese Americans are more than four times as likely to get liver cancer; and Hepatitis B is much more common among Asian Americans than among the rest of the population. According to the government, these disparities seem to stem from the fact that minorities are less likely to get regular medical checkups, be immunized, or get routinely tested for cancer.

In many respects, the mortality rates for African Americans are distressing. Compared with Whites, Blacks have higher death rates from diseases of the heart, pneumonia, diabetes, and cancer. The death rate from strokes is twice as high among African Americans. Such epidemiological findings reflect in part the fact that a higher proportion of Blacks are found among the nation's lower classes. According to the National Center for Health Statistics (1998), Whites can expect to live 76.8 years. By contrast, life expectancy for Blacks is 70.2 years.

As noted earlier, infant mortality is regarded as a primary indicator of health care, but there is a significant gap in the United States between the infant mortality rates of African Americans and Whites. Generally, the rate of infant deaths is more than twice as high among Blacks; indeed, African Americans account for 15 percent of all live births in the nation but 30 percent of infant deaths. Hispanics and Native Americans have infant mortality rates lower than African Americans but higher than Whites (National Center for Health Statistics 1997b, 1999; see also Morehouse Medical Treatment Effectiveness Center 1999).

Health care also reflects social and ethnic differences. According to a recent study, African Americans (and, to a lesser extent, Hispanics and Asian Americans) are less likely to receive expensive heart procedures than White patients. The study was based on examination of hospital discharge records of 131,000 patients who had sought care for chest pains or heart disease between 1986 and 1988. Some of the reasons cited for the differential treatment of patients included the severity of illness, income, age, and the hospital where patients were treated. African Americans, Hispanics, and Asian Americans are more likely than Whites to be treated at smaller community hospitals that rarely or never perform cardiac procedures. Dr. David Carlisle, lead researcher in the study, noted, "Ethnic differences do exist [in the quality of health care received] and they probably are more serious than we thought" (Carlisle et al. 1995; Shuit 1995).

Drawing on the conflict perspective, sociologist Howard Waitzkin (1986) suggests that racial tensions contribute to the medical problems of Blacks. In his view, the stress resulting from racial prejudice and discrimina-

tion helps to explain the higher rates of hypertension found among African Americans (and Hispanics) compared with Whites. Hypertension is twice as common in Blacks as in Whites; it is believed to be a critical factor in Blacks' high mortality rates from heart disease, kidney disease, and stroke (Morehouse Medical Treatment Effectiveness Center 1999).

Gender

A large body of research indicates that, in comparison with men, women experience a higher prevalence of many illnesses, though they tend to live longer. There are variations—for example, men are more likely to have parasitic diseases whereas women are more likely to become diabetic—but, as a group, women appear to be in poorer health than men. The apparent inconsistency between the ill health of women and their greater longevity deserves an explanation, and researchers have advanced a theory. Women's lower rate of cigarette smoking (reducing their risk of heart disease, lung cancer, and emphysema), lower consumption of alcohol (reducing the risk of auto accidents and cirrhosis of the liver), and lower rates of employment in dangerous occupations explain about one-third of their greater longevity than men—

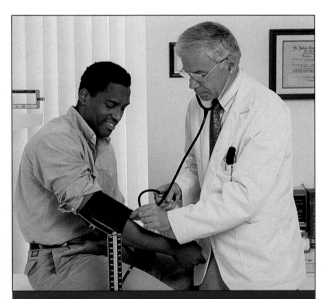

African American men are twice as likely as Whites to suffer from heart disease, yet are less likely than others to have regular checkups. Minority group members are not always comfortable going to physicians, who are more likely than not to be White males. Moreover, many of them lack health insurance, and cannot afford to pay cash for health care.

despite women's otherwise poorer health record. Moreover, some clinical studies suggest that the genuine differences in morbidity between women and men may be less pronounced than the data show. Researchers argue that women are much more likely than men to seek treatment, to be diagnosed as having diseases, and thus to have their illnesses reflected in data examined by epidemiologists.

From a conflict perspective, women have been particularly vulnerable to the medicalization of society, with everything from birth to beauty treated in an increasingly medical context. Such medicalization may contribute to women's higher morbidity rates as compared with those of men. Ironically, while women have been especially affected by medicalization, medical researchers have often excluded women from clinical studies. Female physicians and researchers charge that sexism is at the heart of such research practices and insist that there is a desperate need for studies with female subjects. With such issues in mind, in 1992 the National Institutes of Health (NIH) established an Office of Research on Women. Its task is to ensure that adequate numbers of women serve both as researchers and as participants in taxpayer-supported studies (Bates 1999; McDonald 1999).

Age

Health is the overriding concern of the elderly. Most older people in the United States report having at least one chronic illness, but only some of these conditions are potentially life threatening or require medical care. At the same time, health problems can affect the quality of life of older people in important ways. Almost half of older people in the United States are troubled by arthritis, and many have visual or hearing impairments that can interfere with the performance of everyday tasks.

Older people are also especially vulnerable to certain types of mental health problems. Alzheimer's disease, the leading cause of dementia in the United States, afflicts an estimated 4 million older people. While some individuals with Alzheimer's exhibit only mild symptoms, the risk of severe problems resulting from this disease rises substantially with age. Only 10 percent of people age 65 or over have symptoms of Alzheimer's, but that figure rises to 48 percent of people age 85 and over (Alzheimer's Association 1999).

Not surprisingly, older people in the United States use health services more often than younger people. In 1997, younger people age 15 to 24 visited physicians an average of less than two times a year, compared to more than six annual visits for those 75 and over. Similar discrepancies are evident in rates of hospitalization. Twenty-three percent of people hospitalized in the United States were age 75 and over, while people age 15 to 24 accounted for only 9 percent of those hospitalized. Beyond issues of differential health care, it is obvious that the disproportionate use of the health care system in the United States by older people is a critical factor in all discussions about the cost of health care and possible reforms of the health care system (Bureau of the Census 1999a:134, 138).

While improving health care may be a central issue for the elderly, public attention has focused on the appropriateness of physician-assisted suicide. This issue—first brought to national attention by Dr. Jack Kevorkian during a 1989 television appearance on the *Donahue* show—is but one aspect of the larger debate in the United States and other countries over the ethics of suicide and euthanasia. The term ***euthanasia*** has been defined as the "act of bringing about the death of a hopelessly ill and suffering person in a relatively quick and painless way for reasons of mercy" (Council on Ethical and Judicial Affairs, American Medical Association 1992:2,229). The debate over euthanasia and assisted sui-

As people age and become more susceptible to chronic diseases, some of them lose the ability to care for themselves. This Alzheimer's patient is being fed by his spouse.

FIGURE 18-3

Availability of Physicians by State

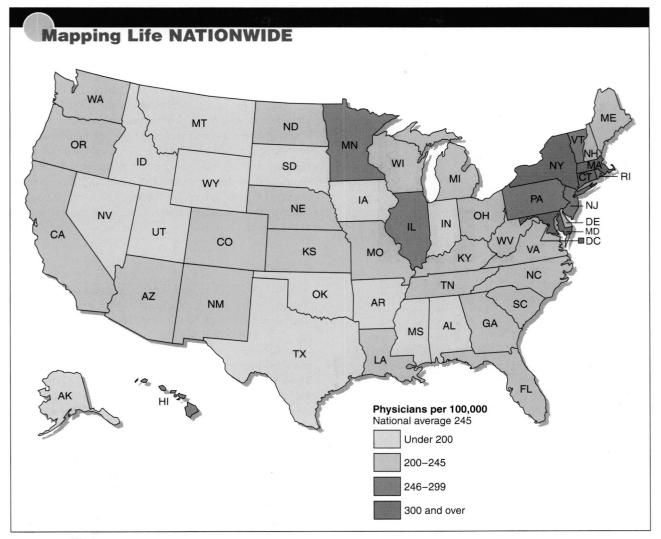

Mapping Life NATIONWIDE

Physicians per 100,000
National average 245

- Under 200
- 200–245
- 246–299
- 300 and over

Source: Bureau of the Census 1999a:133.

cide often focuses on older people, although it can involve younger adults with terminal and degenerative diseases or even children. (For a fuller discussion of physician-assisted suicide, refer to the social policy section in Chapter 12.)

In sum, to achieve the goal of 100 percent access and zero health disparities, federal health officials must overcome inequities that are rooted not just in age, but in social class, race and ethnicity, and gender. If that were not enough, they must also deal with a geographical disparity in health care resources. Figure 18-3 shows the differences in the presence of physicians from one state to an-

other. Dramatic differences in the availability of physicians, hospitals, and nursing homes also exist between urban and rural areas within the same state. In the next section we will look more closely at issues surrounding the delivery of health care in the United States.

Health Care in the United States

As the entire nation is well aware, the costs of health care have skyrocketed in the last 35 years. In 1997 total expenditures for health care in the United States crossed the

FIGURE 18-4

Total Health Care Expenditures in the United States, 1970–2008 (projected)

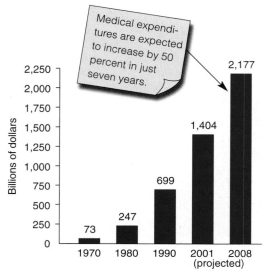

Medical expenditures are expected to increase by 50 percent in just seven years.

Source: Health Care Financing Administration 1999.

trillion-dollar threshold—more than four times the 1980 figure (see Figure 18-4). The amount we now spend on health care equals that spent on education, defense, prisons, farm subsidies, food stamps, and foreign aid combined. By the year 2008, total expenditures for health care in the United States are expected to exceed $2.1 trillion.

The rising costs of medical care are especially burdensome in the event of catastrophic illnesses or confinement in a nursing home. Bills of tens of thousands of dollars are not unusual in the treatment of cancer, Alzheimer's dis-

ease, and other chronic illnesses requiring custodial care. As of 2000, drugs used in the United States to combat the HIV virus associated with AIDS could easily cost about $65,000 per patient per year. Health costs in the United States have escalated in part because of increasing use of expensive technology. For example, the CAT scanner, a direct descendant of the X-ray machine, uses a computer to integrate pictures shot from various angles into a single, multidimensional image of a skull (Sawyer 2000).

Clearly the health care system of the United States has moved far beyond the days when general practitioners living in a neighborhood or community typically made house calls and charged modest fees for their services. How did health care become big business involving nationwide hospital chains and marketing campaigns? How have these changes reshaped typical interactions between doctors, nurses, and patients? We will address these questions in the next section of the chapter.

A Historical View

Today, state licensing and medical degrees confer an authority on medical professionals, which is maintained from one generation to the next. However, health care in the United States has not always followed this model. The "popular health movement" of the 1830s and 1840s emphasized preventive care and what is termed "self-help." There was strong criticism of "doctoring" as a paid occupation. New medical philosophies or sects established their own medical schools and challenged the authority and methods of more traditional doctors. By the 1840s, most states had repealed medical licensing laws. However, through the leadership of the American Medical Association (AMA), founded in 1848, "regular" doctors attacked lay practitioners, sectarian doctors, and female physicians in general. (For a different view, see Navarro 1984).

The emergence of massive, organized philanthropy in the early twentieth century had a critical impact in reshaping and centralizing medicine. Beginning in 1903, extensive foundation support was allocated to create a respectable medical profession. A researcher employed by the Carnegie Corporation was sent to tour the nation to determine which medical schools should receive funding. Numerous medical schools that he found unworthy of financial aid were forced to close. Among them were six of the nation's eight Black medical schools and most of the alternative schools that had been open to female students. In state after state, tough licensing laws restricted medical practice to traditional doctors from approved institutions. As one result, babies could no longer be delivered by midwives in most states; the practice of obstetrics was restricted to physicians (Ehrenreich and English 1973).

Once authority was institutionalized through standardized programs of education and licensing, it was conferred upon all who successfully completed these programs. The authority of the physician no longer depended on lay attitudes or the person occupying the sick role; it was increasingly built into the structure of the medical profession and the health care system. As the institutionalization of health care proceeded, the medical profession gained control over both the market for its services and the various organizational hierarchies that govern medical practice, financing, and policymaking. By the 1920s, physicians controlled hospital technology, the division of labor of health personnel, and, indirectly, other professional practices such as nursing and pharmacy (R. Coser 1984).

Physicians, Nurses, and Patients

The preeminence of physicians within the health care system of the United States has traditionally given them a position of dominance in their dealings with both patients and nurses. The functionalist and interactionist perspectives combine to offer a framework for understanding the professional socialization of physicians as it relates to patient care. Functionalists suggest that established physicians and medical school professors serve as mentors or role models who transmit knowledge, skills, and values to the passive learner—the medical student. Interactionists emphasize that students are molded by the medical school environment as they interact with their classmates. Both approaches argue that the typical training of physicians in the United States leads to rather dehumanizing physician–patient encounters. As Dr. Lori Arviso Alvord writes in *The Scalpel and the Silver Bear,* "I had been trained by a group of physicians who placed much more emphasis on their technical abilities and clinical skills than on their abilities to be caring and sensitive" (Alvord and Van Pelt 1999:13). Despite many efforts to formally introduce a humanistic dimension of patient care into the medical school curriculum, patient overload and cost-containment efforts of hospitals tend to undercut positive relations. Moreover, widespread publicity about malpractice suits and high medical costs has further strained the physician–patient relationship (Becker et al. 1961; Merton et al. 1957; Mizrahi 1986).

Interactionists have closely examined how compliance and negotiation occur between physician and patient. They concur with Talcott Parsons's view that the relationship is generally asymmetrical, with doctors holding a position of dominance and control of rewards. Just as physicians have maintained dominance in their interactions with patients, doctors have similarly controlled interactions with nurses. Despite their training and professional status, nurses commonly take orders from physicians. Traditionally, the relationship between doctors and nurses has paralleled the male dominance of the United States: Most physicians have been male, whereas virtually all nurses have been female (refer back to Box 11–2 on page 304, which focuses on male nurses within a traditionally female profession).

Like other women in subordinate roles, nurses have been expected to perform their duties without challenging the authority of men. Psychiatrist Leonard Stein (1967) refers to this process as the *doctor–nurse game.* According to the rules of this "game," the nurse must never disagree openly with the physician. When she has recommendations concerning a patient's care, she must communicate them indirectly in a deferential tone. For example, if asked by a hospital's medical resident, "What sleeping medication has been helpful to Mrs. Brown in the past?" (an indirect request for a recommendation), the nurse will respond with a disguised recommendation statement, such as "Pentobarbital mg 100 was quite effective night before last." Her careful response allows the physician to authoritatively restate the same prescription as if it were *his* idea.

Like nurses, female physicians have traditionally found themselves in a subordinate position because of gender. According to 1995 data, while 39 percent of all medical students in the United States were female, 79 percent of all medical school faculty members were male. Moreover, as of 1994, there were only four female deans of medical schools. However, a study published in 1996 reported that when differences of medical specialty, number of hours worked, and practice setting were taken into account, female and male doctors were earning almost the same amount of money. Male physicians continue to earn more than their female colleagues, in good part because female physicians are more often found in lower-paying specialties such as general practice and pediatrics (L. Baker 1995; Barzansky et al. 1995).

A recent study of male and female medical residents suggests that the increasing number of women physicians may alter the traditional doctor–patient relationship. Male residents were found to be more focused on the intellectual challenges of medicine and the prestige associated with certain medical specialties. By contrast, female residents were more likely to express a commitment to caring for patients and devoting time to them. In terms of the functionalist analysis of gender stratification offered by sociologists Talcott Parsons and Robert Bales, male residents took the *instrumental,* achievement-oriented role, while female residents took the *expressive,* interpersonal-oriented role. As women continue to enter and move higher in the hierarchies of the medical profession, there will surely be sociological studies to see if these apparent gender differences persist (Geckler 1995).

p. 295

Patients have traditionally relied on medical personnel to inform them of health care issues, but increasingly they are now turning to the media for health care information. Recognizing this change, pharmaceutical firms are advertising their prescription drugs directly to potential customers through television and magazine advertisements. The Internet is also a growing source for patient information.

Medical professionals are understandably suspicious of these new sources of information. The American Academy of Pediatrics published a study in 1998 that investigated websites with information on treating childhood diarrhea. They found that only 20 percent of the sources of information conformed to current recommended medical practices. The study noted that even if the source of information was a major medical center, it did not improve the likelihood of compliance. The Academy concluded, reflecting its professional stake in the issue, that patients need to be "warned" not to use Internet medical information. However, there is little doubt that web research is transforming an increasing proportion of patient–physician encounters, as patients arrive for their doctor's appointments armed with the latest printout from the Internet (Kolata 2000; McClung et al. 1998).

The Role of Government

The first significant involvement of the federal government in the field of health care came with the 1946 Hill-Burton Act, which provided subsidies for building and improving hospitals, especially in rural areas. An even more important change came with the enactment of two wide-ranging government assistance programs: Medicare, which is essentially a compulsory health insurance plan for the elderly; and Medicaid, which is a noncontributory federal and state insurance plan for the poor. These programs greatly expanded federal involvement in health care financing for needy men, women, and children. In addition, over 1,000 government-subsidized community health centers are located in low-income, medically underserved communities (Blendon 1986).

Given rates of illness and disability among elderly people, Medicare has had a particularly noteworthy impact on the health care system of the United States. Initially, Medicare simply reimbursed health care providers such as physicians and hospitals for the costs of their services. However, as the overall costs of Medicare increased dramatically, the federal government introduced a price-control system in 1983. All illnesses were classified into 468 diagnostic-related groups (DRGs); a reimbursement rate was set for each condition and remained fixed regardless of the individual needs of any patient. In effect, the federal government told hospitals and doctors that it would no longer

be concerned with their costs in treating Medicare patients; it would reimburse them only to a designated level.

The DRG system of reimbursement has contributed to the controversial practice of "dumping," under which patients whose treatment may be unprofitable are transferred by private hospitals to public facilities. Many private hospitals in the United States have begun to conduct "wallet biopsies" to investigate the financial status of potential patients; those judged as undesirable are then refused admission or are dumped. A federal law passed in 1987 made it illegal for any hospital receiving Medicare funds to dump patients, but the practice continues. Since dumping was outlawed, fewer than 9 percent of the known violators have actually been penalized (Feinglass 1987; Sherrill 1995:67).

Alternatives to Traditional Health Care

In traditional forms of health care, people rely on physicians and hospitals for treatment of illness. Yet at least one out of every three adults in the United States attempts to maintain

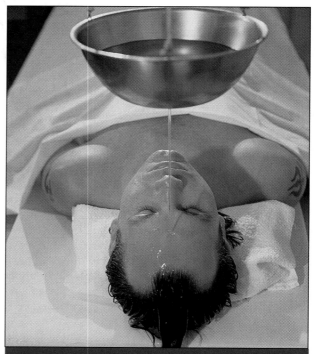

Oil dripping, an ancient Indian practice, is used in holistic medicine, an approach to health care that emphasizes treatment of the whole person—physical, mental, emotional, and spiritual. A 20-minute drip of warm, herb-infused oil is often prescribed for those who suffer from insomnia, hypertension, and digestive problems.

good health or respond to illness through use of alternative health care techniques. For example, in recent decades there has been growing interest in *holistic* (this term is also spelled *wholistic*) medical principles first developed in China. **Holistic medicine** refers to therapies in which the health care practitioner considers the person's physical, mental, emotional, and spiritual characteristics. The individual is regarded as a totality, rather than as a collection of interrelated organ systems. Treatment methodologies include massage, chiropractic medicine, acupuncture (which involves the insertion of fine needles into surface points), respiratory exercises, and the use of herbs as remedies. Nutrition, exercise, and visualization may also be used to treat ailments generally treated through medication or hospitalization (Sharma and Bodeker 1998).

The Navajo concept of *hózhǫ́* (Walking in Beauty) is another example of a holistic approach to health (see the chapter introduction, page 468). Practitioners of holistic medicine do not necessarily function totally outside the traditional health care system. Some, like Dr. Lori Arviso Alvord, have medical degrees and rely on X-rays and EKG machines for diagnostic assistance. Other holistic clinics, often referred to as *wellness clinics,* reject the use of medical technology. The recent resurgence of holistic medicine comes amidst a widespread recognition of the value of nutrition and the dangers of overreliance on prescription drugs (especially those used to reduce stress, such as Valium).

The medical establishment—professional organizations, research hospitals, and medical schools—has generally served as a stern protector of traditionally accepted health care techniques. However, a major breakthrough occurred in 1992 when the federal government's National Institutes of Health—the nation's major funding source for biomedical research—opened an Office of Alternative Medicine, empowered to accept grant requests. Potential areas of study include herbal medicine, mind–body control techniques, and the use of electromagnetism to heal bones. A national study published in *The Journal of the American Medical Association* indicates that 46 percent of the general public uses alternative medicine. Most of it is not covered by insurance. Indeed, out-of-pocket expenses for alternative medicine match all out-of-pocket expenses for traditional physician services (Eisenberg et al. 1998; Stolberg 2000).

While many observers applaud the use of alternative medical procedures, conflict theorists note the difference between those who can afford to use alternatives *in addition to* conventional medicine and those who have no choice. For example, Cubans have recently begun to rely more on traditional cures, such as sitting on cobalt blocks to ease circulatory problems, in response to a shortage of government resources. Likewise, in low-income neighborhoods in the United States, people rely on alternative care techniques out of necessity, not choice (Kovaleski 1999).

In some cases, movements for political change have generated health care alternatives. For example, as part of the larger feminist movement beginning in the 1960s, women became more vocal in their dissatisfaction with the traditional health care system. Marked by the appearance of the book *Our Bodies, Ourselves* (Boston Women's Health Book Collective 1969, 1992), the contemporary women's health movement emerged out of the realization that women are by far the most frequent users of health services for themselves, their children, and other dependent family members. Activists agree that women should assume more responsibility for decisions concerning their health. The movement therefore has taken many forms, including organizations working for changes in the health care system, women's clinics, and "self-help" groups.

Although the women's health movement supports greater access to health care for all people in the United States, it focuses on specific women's health issues such as menstruation, childbirth, abortion rights (see Chapter 11), and menopause. Women's health groups have expressed concern about the hazards of oral contraceptives and the intrauterine device (IUD)—hazards that they feel have been concealed by drug companies and the medical establishment. Activists generally favor a greater voice for women in maternity care, the establishment of midwifery centers, and full representation of female consumers on health policymaking boards. The women's health movement has demanded increased entry of women into medical school and hospital administrative positions. Some activists have gone so far as to endorse the exclusion of male medical students from obstetrics and gynecological specialties. Clearly, feminists are resisting the social-control aspects of the male-dominated medical hierarchy (Legato 1998; Sherwin 1992; M. Zimmerman 1987; Zola 1983).

The goals of the women's health movement are ambitious, but the health care system has proved to be fairly resistant to change. Conflict theorists point out that physicians, medical schools, hospitals, and drug companies all have a vested interest in keeping women in a rather dependent and uninformed position as health care consumers. Despite an increase in female doctors, women remain underrepresented in key positions in the health care system of the United States (R. Sidel and Sidel 1984).

Mental Illness in the United States

Terms such as *mental illness* and *insanity* evoke dramatic and often inaccurate images of emotional problems. The media routinely emphasize the most violent behavior of those with disturbances, but mental health and mental

Taking Sociology to Work

ERIKA MILES:
Director, Health Programs, CVS.com

"Health care has always fascinated me, and I was lucky enough to discover medical sociology," says Erika Miles. Right after graduating from Colgate University in 1992, Erika worked three years for the Robert Wood Johnson Foundation as a quantitative research assistant, doing studies on physician behavior and underserved populations. Just as Miles was starting graduate school, she discovered the Internet and was hooked. She dropped her graduate studies, taught herself web design, and started doing Internet marketing for various pharmaceutical companies. At CVS.com, an online pharmacy in Seattle, she develops corporate strategies for working with pharmaceutical companies, health care providers, and other Internet companies.

Developing websites in health care has a lot to do with sociology, according to Miles. "Much of the work is really thinking about how people work, act, and react to their surroundings, their families, and their work environments—and how all that relates to their health." She also does "a ton of qualitative and quantitative research," and credits her undergraduate sociology courses with helping her with that aspect of her work.

Erika basically just fell into being a sociology major after starting out with a 200-level course on peace and social change movements, which she loved. "Sociology just made sense, which is more than I can say for a lot of other classes I took." Miles believes that a sociology degree has great potential because it can apply to many different fields. "It is a degree that really helps you learn how to think about the people around you."

Miles's advice to students is to take research classes and write a thesis, whether they are required to or not. "That is really where you get to apply what you've learned."

---

illness can more appropriately be viewed as a continuum of behavior that we ourselves move along. Using a less sensational definition, a person can be considered to have a mental disorder "if he or she is so disturbed that coping with routine, everyday life is difficult or impossible" (J. Coleman and Cressey 1980:315). The term *mental illness* should be reserved for a disorder of the brain that disrupts a person's thinking, feeling, and ability to interact with others (National Alliance for the Mentally Ill 2000).

How prevalent is mental illness? The World Bank finds that in industrial economies, mental disorders account for 4 of the 10 leading causes of disability. In the United States, the Surgeon General estimates that every year, one out of every five Americans suffers from some form of mental illness. The most common disorders include depression, anxiety disorders, and obsessive-compulsive disorders (National Institute of Mental Health 1999).

People in the United States have traditionally maintained a negative and suspicious view of those with mental disorders. Holding the status of "mental patient" or even "former mental patient" can have unfortunate and undeserved consequences. For example, during the 1972 election campaign, it was learned that the Democratic vice presidential nominee, Senator Thomas Eagleton of Missouri, had once received treatment for depression. Public reaction was so strong that presidential nominee George McGovern was forced to drop Eagleton from the Democratic ticket.

Politics is not the only arena where people viewed as mentally ill experience second-class treatment. Voting rights are denied in some instances, acceptance for jury duty is problematic, and past emotional problems are an issue in divorce and custody cases. Moreover, content analysis of network television programs shows mentally ill characters uniformly portrayed in a demeaning and derogatory fashion; many are labeled as "criminally insane," "wackos," or "psychos." From an interactionist perspective, a key social institution is shaping social behavior by manipulating symbols and thereby intensifying people's fears about the mentally ill (Burton 1990; DeFleur and Dennis 1981; Link 1987).

Theoretical Models of Mental Disorders

In studying mental illness, we can draw on both a medical model and a more sociological approach derived from labeling theory. Each model offers distinctive assumptions regarding treatment of people with mental disorders.

According to the *medical model*, mental illness is rooted in biological causes that can be treated through medical intervention. Problems in brain structure or in the biochemical balance in the brain, sometimes due to injury and sometimes to genetic inheritance, are thought to be at the bottom of these disorders. The Surgeon General of the United States (1999), Dr. David Satcher, has released an exhaustive report on mental health in which he declares that the accumulated weight of scientific evidence leaves no doubt about the physical origins of mental illness.

That is not to say that social factors do not contribute

to mental illness. Just as culture affects the incidence and prevalence of illness in general, its treatment, and the expression of certain culture-bound syndromes, so too it can affect mental illness. In fact, the very definition of mental illness differs from one culture to the next. In mainstream American culture, for instance, hallucinations are considered to be highly abnormal. But in many traditional cultures, they are seen as evidence of divine favor, and confer a special status on those who experience them. As we have noted throughout this textbook, a given behavior may be viewed as normal in one society, disapproved of but tolerated in a second, and labeled as "sick" and heavily sanctioned in a third.

Social setting can have a profound effect on the expression and severity of mental illness, as well as on the prognosis for recovery. Of two patients who suffer from the same disorder, one may make an excellent recovery with the help of a supportive family, while another who comes from a troubled family may suffer repeated relapses. In some cases, the social setting may be so stressful that it provokes mental illness. People who have been exposed to the horrors of war, for example, often suffer from terrifying flashbacks to violent scenes they have witnessed.

In contrast to the medical model, labeling theory suggests that mental illness is not really an "illness," since the individual's problems arise from living in society and not from physical maladies. For example, the Surgeon General's report (1999:5) notes that "bereavement symptoms" of less than two months' duration do not qualify as a mental disorder, but beyond that they may be redefined. Sociologists would see this approach to bereavement as labeling by those with the power to affix labels rather than as an acknowledgment of a biological condition.

Psychiatrist Thomas Szasz (1974), in his book *The Myth of Mental Illness,* which first appeared in 1961, advanced the view that numerous personality disorders are not "diseases," but simply patterns of conduct labeled as disorders by significant others. The response to Szasz's challenging thesis was sharp: the commissioner of the New York State Department of Hygiene demanded his dismissal from his university position because Szasz did not "believe" in mental illness. But many sociologists embraced his model as a logical extension of examining individual behavior in a social context.

War can be hazardous to your mental health. Many people who once lived in war zones, like these Rwandans fleeing the horrors of genocide, later suffer from symptoms of severe mental trauma, including depression, nightmares, and flashbacks to violent events.

Although labeling will not typically "make sane people insane," it undoubtedly causes mentally ill patients to feel that they are devalued by the larger society. And the more they believe they are being negatively labeled, the more difficult they will find it to interact with others. Some mentally ill people may keep their problems and treatment a secret and may withdraw from social contacts. Such coping strategies to deal with labeling can lead to negative consequences in terms of employment, social support networks, and self-esteem (Cockerham 1998; for a different view, see Gove 1980; Link et al. 1989).

The medical model is persuasive because it pinpoints causes of mental illness and treatment for disorders. Yet proponents of the labeling perspective maintain that mental illness is a distinctively social process, whatever other processes are involved. From a sociological perspective, the ideal approach to mental illness integrates the insights of labeling theory with those of the medical approach (Scheff 1999).

Patterns of Care

For most of human history, those suffering from mental disorders were deemed the responsibility of their families. Yet mental illness has been a matter of governmental concern much longer than physical illness has. This is because severe emotional disorders threaten stable social relationships and entail prolonged incapacitation.

As early as the 1600s, European cities began to confine the insane in public facilities along with the poor and criminals. This development brought resistance from prisoners, who were indignant at being forced to live with "lunatics." The isolation of the mentally ill from others in the same facility and from the larger society made physicians the central and ultimate authority for their welfare.

In the United States, the period of the 1840s and 1850s was the "age of the asylum." Before 1810, only a few states had institutions for the mentally ill, but by 1860, 28 of the nation's 33 states had such public facilities. The asylum was put forward as a humanitarian and even utopian institution that would rehabilitate the suffering and serve as a model facility for the rest of society. Its social structure emphasized discipline, neatness, fixed schedules, and work assignments for patients. Existing relationships were deemphasized; families were discouraged from visiting with patients because they would disrupt hospital routines (Perrucci 1974; Rothman 1971).

At a community mental health center, outpatients create a newsletter for their day program. In the 1980s, community-based mental health care replaced hospitalization as the typical form of treatment for people with serious mental illnesses.

The residential mental hospital is an example of a total institution in which people are removed from the larger society for an appreciable period of time. p. 100 Drawing on the work of Erving Goffman, Harold Garfinkel (1956) revealed that people in total institutions undergo "degradation ceremonies" that strip them of their identities, destroy personal dignity, and often lead to confusion and distress. From a functionalist perspective, the crowding and depersonalization inherent in mental hospitals are dysfunctional to the resolution of emotional problems.

A major policy development in caring for those with mental disorders came with the passage of the 1963 Community Mental Health Centers Act. The CMHC program, as it is known, was significant in increasing federal government involvement in the treatment of the mentally ill. It also marked acceptance of the view that community-based mental health centers (which treat clients on an outpatient basis, thereby allowing them to continue working and living at home) provide more effective treatment than the institutionalized programs of state and county mental hospitals.

The expansion of the federally funded CMHC program decreased inpatient care. Consequently, by the 1980s, community-based mental health care had replaced hospitalization as the typical form of treatment. The deinstitutionalization of the mentally ill reached dramatic proportions across the United States. Whereas state mental hospitals had held almost 560,000 long-term patients in 1955, by 1994 they held fewer than 70,000 patients. Deinstitutionalization was often defended as a social reform that would effectively reintegrate the mentally ill into the outside world. However, the authentic humanitarian concern behind deinstitutionalization proved to be convenient for politicians whose goal was simply cost cutting (Bureau of the Census 1999a:144; Grob 1995).

Ironically, in a marked shift from public policy over the last three decades, several states have recently made it easier to involuntarily commit mental patients to hospitals. These changes have come in part because community groups and individual residents have voiced increasing fear and anger about the growing number of mentally ill homeless people living in their midst (and often on the streets). All too often, the severely mentally ill end up in jail or prison after committing crimes that lead to their prosecution. Indeed, family members of mentally ill men and women complain that they cannot get adequate treatment for their loved ones until they have committed violent acts. Nevertheless, civil liberties advocates and voluntary associations consisting of mentally ill people worry about the risks of denying people their constitutional rights, and cite horror stories about the abuses people experience during institutionalization (Marquis and Morain 1999; Shogren 1994).

SOCIAL POLICY AND HEALTH

Financing Health Care Worldwide

The Issue

Cindy Martin died in 1990 at age 26, after four months of surgery and intensive care at Presbyterian Hospital in Pittsburgh. In the aftermath of her death, her husband's insurance company received a bill for $1.25 million. While accountants attempted to untangle the costs of seven surgical procedures performed on Cindy Martin—including heart, liver, and kidney transplants—this case underscored troubling issues regarding the high cost of health care. Who should pay for the expensive medical procedures of the 1990s? What role, if any, should government play in providing medical care and health insurance for its citizens (Freudenheim 1990)?

In many developing nations of the world, health care issues center on very basic needs of primary care. The goals established at the UN's World Health Assembly in 1981 were modest by North American standards: safe water in the home or within 15 minutes' walking distance; immunization against major infectious diseases; availability of essential drugs within an hour's walk or travel; and the presence of trained personnel for pregnancy and childbirth. While significant progress has been made in some areas, many developing countries have seen little improvement; in some places, health care has deteriorated (World Bank 1997). The focus of this social policy section, however, is on those industrialized (or developed) nations where the availability of health care is really not an issue. The question is more one of accessibility and affordability. What steps are being taken to make the available services reachable?

The Setting

The United States is now the only Western industrial democracy that does not treat health care as a basic right. According to the Bureau of the Census, in 1999 some 44 million people in the United States had no health insurance the entire year. The uninsured typically include self-employed people with limited incomes, illegal immigrants, and single and divorced mothers who are the sole providers for their families. African Americans and Hispanics are less likely than Whites to carry private health insurance. Although people with lower incomes are least likely to be covered, substantial numbers of households at all income levels go without coverage for some or most of any given year (Campbell 1999).

National health insurance is a general term for legislative proposals that focus on ways to provide the entire population with health care services. First discussed by government officials in the United States in the 1930s, it has come to mean many different things, ranging from narrow health insurance coverage with minimal federal subsidies to broad coverage with large-scale federal funding.

Opponents of national health insurance insist that it would be extremely costly and would lead to significant tax increases. Defenders counter, however, that other countries have maintained broad governmental health coverage for decades:

- Great Britain's National Health Service is almost totally tax-supported, and health care services are free to all citizens.
- Under Sweden's national health system, medical care is delivered primarily by publicly funded hospitals and clinics, while a national health insurance system sets fees for health care services and reimburses providers of health care.

THE SOUND OF DISASTER

- Although Canadians rely on private physicians and hospitals for day-to-day treatment, health care is guaranteed as a right for all citizens. Income taxes finance public medical insurance, medical fees are set by the government, and private health insurance is prohibited.

Ironically, while these countries offer extensive health coverage for all citizens, the United States has higher health care costs than any other nation: an average annual cost of $3,701 per person, compared with $1,665 in Canada and only $1,246 in Great Britain (Bureau of the Census 1997a:835; Lassey et al. 1997). As Figure 18-5 shows, most industrial nations finance a substantially larger share of health care costs through public expenditures than does the United States.

Sociological Insights

As conflict theorists suggest, the health care system, like other social institutions, resists basic change. In general, those who receive substantial wealth and power through the workings of an existing institution will have a strong incentive to keep things as they are. In this case, private insurance companies are benefiting finan-

cially from the current system and have a clear interest in opposing certain forms of national health insurance. In addition, the American Medical Association (AMA), one of Washington's most powerful lobbying groups, has been successfully fighting national health insurance since the 1930s. Overall, there are more than 200 political action committees (PACs) that represent the medical, pharmaceutical, and insurance industries. These PACs contribute millions of dollars each year to members of Congress and use their influence to block any legislation that would threaten their interests (Dolbeare 1982; Kemper and Novak 1991).

Policy Initiatives

Early in the 1990s, the U.S. Congress dismissed the idea of any sort of national health insurance. While virtually everyone agreed that the existing fee-for-service system was too costly, a major move to centralize financing, and hence control, of health care was deemed unacceptable. Yet, even without legislative reform, major changes have been occurring in the United States.

As of 1997, managed care plans (as opposed to traditional health insurance) enrolled 85 percent of all workers, up from 52 percent just since 1993 (Findlay 1998). These managed care plans limit one's choice of physicians

FIGURE 18-5

Government Expenditure for Health Care

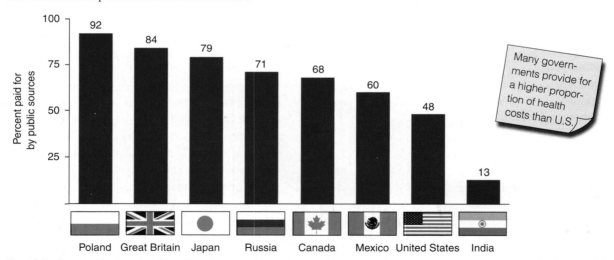

Note: Author's calculation based on World Bank data for years 1990–1995 as percent of GDP health expenditure paid by all public sources versus private sources.
Source: World Bank 1999b:90–91.

The proportion of health care paid directly by the government, as opposed to patients themselves or their employers through insurance, varies widely among nations. In many countries, a much higher proportion is paid by the government than in either Canada or the United States.

and treatment but cover most medical costs. ***Health maintenance organizations (HMOs),*** which provide comprehensive medical services for a preestablished fee, are playing a prominent role in managed care. The number of people in the United States enrolled in HMOs has risen from 6 million in 1980 to 164 million in 1997 (American Association of Health Plans 1998a; Eckholm 1994; Kelly and Levy 1995).

The health system is unquestionably undergoing "corporatization," as for-profit health care companies (often linking insurers, hospitals, and groups of physicians) are achieving increasing dominance. Conflict theorists have long argued that an underlying and disturbing aspect of capitalism in the United States is that illness may be exploited for profit. Critics of the corporatization of health care worry that the growing pressures on physicians and other health care providers to make cost-effective decisions may lead to inadequate and even life-threatening patient care (Sherrill 1995).

There are growing concerns about the quality of care people receive through managed care plans such as HMOs, especially the elderly and minorities, who are less likely to be able to afford private insurance plans. According to a national survey, people in managed care feel they spend less time with physicians, find it more difficult to see specialists, and generally sense that the overall quality of health care has deteriorated (Appleby 1999).

The U.S. health delivery system has undergone change, but for the most part independent of government intervention. What has happened in other industrial countries that have traditionally relied on a more publicly financed and centrally controlled health care system? Uniformly, these nations are increasingly concerned with cost control and efforts to improve the efficiency and effectiveness of health services. Aging populations and technological breakthroughs have provided new opportunities for health care delivery, but have also entailed new costs. National health insurance programs have tended to increase the share of patient costs and to reduce the range of procedures covered. These steps have also been accompanied by reduced reimbursement of professionals and hospitals.

Another pattern in industrial countries, although less universal, is greater attention to unequal health care delivery. Addressing this problem, however, often creates difficulties. Great Britain, for example, in attempting to meet the needs of previously underserved rural areas, has closed facilities in London and other metropolitan areas and tried to reassign medical staff to rural

The great majority of Americans who have medical insurance now belong to managed care plans. Many have questioned the quality of managed care, complaining that they see the doctor less often under such plans than in the past.

areas. Another trend actually runs counter to the other two trends: acknowledgment of patients' rights to have a greater voice in the type of care they receive and who administers it (Mechanic and Rochefort 1996).

Medical services have always been distributed according to the ability to pay for services and the availability of facilities and personnel. As governments throughout the world take greater responsibility for health care and as care becomes increasingly expensive, governments can be expected to give more and more attention to controlling expenditures. While the U.S. federal government has not been as heavily involved as other nations, the introduction of payment according to DRGs and the institution of managed care plans have introduced a degree of control previously unknown in the United States (Mechanic and Rochefort 1996).

Let's Discuss

1. Are you and your family covered by a health insurance plan? If not, why aren't you covered? Has anyone in your family ever required a medical procedure he or she couldn't pay for?

2. Have you ever belonged to a health maintenance organization? If so, how satisfied were you with the care you received? Were you ever denied a specific treatment because it was too costly?

3. Should health care be a basic right of all Americans?

Summary

The meanings of **health,** sickness, and disease are shaped by social definitions of behavior. This chapter considers the relationship between culture and health, several sociological perspectives on health and illness, the distribution of diseases in a society, the evolution of the U.S. health care system, and the sociological dimension of mental health and mental illness. It closes with a discussion of how health care is financed worldwide.

1. The effect of culture on health can be seen in the existence of **culture-bound syndromes,** as well as in cultural differences in medical care and the **incidence** and **prevalence** of certain diseases.

2. According to Talcott Parsons's functionalist perspective, physicians function as "gatekeepers" for the **sick role,** either verifying a person's condition as "ill" or designating the person as "recovered."

3. Conflict theorists use the term *medicalization of society* to refer to medicine's growing role as a major institution of social control.

4. Labeling theorists suggest that the designation of a person as "healthy" or "ill" generally involves social definition by others. These definitions affect how others see us and how we view ourselves.

5. Contemporary **social epidemiology** is concerned not only with epidemics but also with nonepidemic diseases, injuries, drug addition and alcoholism, suicide, and mental illness.

6. Studies have consistently shown that people in the lower classes have higher rates of mortality and disability.

7. Racial and ethnic minorities have higher rates of morbidity and mortality than do Whites. Women tend to be in poorer health than men but live longer. Older people are especially vulnerable to mental health problems, like Alzheimer's disease.

8. The preeminent role of physicians within the health care system of the United States has given them a position of dominance in their dealings with nurses and patients.

9. Many people seek alternative health care techniques, such as **holistic medicine** and self-help groups.

10. Mental disorders may be viewed from two different perspectives, the medical model and the sociological model, which is based on labeling theory. In the United States, society has traditionally taken a negative, suspicious attitude toward people with mental disorders.

11. In the developed world, an aging population and technological breakthroughs have made health care both more extensive and more costly. At the same time, developing nations struggle to provide primary care for a burgeoning population. Throughout the world, an important issue is who is to pay for this care.

Critical Thinking Questions

1. Sociologist Talcott Parsons has argued that the doctor–patient relationship is somewhat like that between parent and child. Does this view seem accurate? Should the doctor–patient relationship become more egalitarian? How might functionalist and conflict theorists differ in their views of the power of physicians within the health care system of the United States?

2. Relate what you have learned about the medical and sociological models of mental illness to the process of classifying a person as mentally ill. How would the process differ under the two models? Draw on Erving Goffman's concept of stigmatization (see Chapter 5).

3. Relate what you have learned about social epidemiology to the question of universal health care coverage. If the United States were to adopt a system of universal coverage, what might be the effect on the incidence and prevalence of disease among Americans of all classes, races and ethnicities, genders, and ages? What might be the ultimate effect of such changes on health care costs?

Key Terms

Culture-bound syndrome   A disease or illness that cannot be understood apart from its specific social context. (469)

Euthanasia   The act of bringing about the death of a hopelessly ill and suffering person in a relatively quick and painless way for reasons of mercy. (480)

Health   As defined by the World Health Organization, a state of complete physical, mental, and social well-being, and not merely the absence of disease and infirmity. (471)

Health maintenance organization (HMO)   An organization that provides comprehensive medical services for a preestablished fee. (490)

Holistic medicine   A means of health maintenance using therapies in which the health care practitioner considers the person's physical, mental, emotional, and spiritual characteristics. (485)

Incidence   The number of new cases of a specific disorder occurring within a given population during a stated period of time. (477)

Mental illness   A disorder of the brain that disrupts a person's thinking, feeling, and ability to interact with others. (486)

Morbidity rates   The incidence of diseases in a given population. (477)

Mortality rate   The incidence of death in a given population. (477)

Prevalence   The total number of cases of a specific disorder that exist at a given time. (477)

Sick role   Societal expectations about the attitudes and behavior of a person viewed as being ill. (471)

Social epidemiology   The study of the distribution of disease, impairment, and general health status across a population. (477)

Additional Readings

BOOKS

Bosk, Charles L. 1992. *All God's Mistakes: Genetic Counseling in a Pediatric Hospital.* Chicago: University of Chicago Press. Drawing on observation research, Bosk provides an inside look at how a genetic counseling team interacts with parents and with one another.

Cockerham, William C. 1999. *Health and Social Change in Russia and Eastern Europe.* New York: Routledge. An examination of the sociological causes of the decline in life expectancy—unusual in an industrialized society—that began in the 1960s in the countries of the former Soviet Union.

Guillemin, Jeanne. 1999. *Anthrax: The Investigation of a Deadly Outbreak.* Berkeley: University of California Press. A sociologist describes her social-epidemiological investigation into the mystery-shrouded outbreak of anthrax in the Soviet Union in 1979.

Lassey, Marie L., William R. Lassey, and Martin J. Jinks. 1997. *Health Care Systems around the World: Charac-teristics, Issues, Reforms.* Upper Saddle River, NJ: Prentice Hall. A comparative look at health care delivery in 13 countries, including Canada, China, Japan, Mexico, Russia, and Sweden.

Leavitt, Judith Walzer. 1996. *Typhoid Mary: Captive in the Public's Health.* Boston: Beacon. A professor of the history of medicine and women's studies examines how scientists discovered that a healthy body could carry typhoid, using a notorious case study from the early 1900s.

JOURNALS

Among the journals dealing with issues of health, illness, and health care are *Health: An Interdisciplinary Journal for the Social Study of Health, Illness, and Medicine* (founded in 1997), *Journal of Gender, Culture, and Health* (1996), *Journal of Health and Social Behavior* (1965), *Millbank Memorial Quarterly* (1923), and *Social Science and Medicine* (1967).

Internet Connection

Note: While all the URLs listed were current as of the printing of this book, these sites often change. Please check our website (http://www.mhhe.com/schaefer) for updates.

1. The CDC (Centers for Disease Control and Prevention) and the NCHS (National Center for Health Statistics) offer a link to FASTATS A to Z (**http://www.cdc.gov/nchs/fastats/fastats.htm**), a comprehensive online database of health statistics. From the extensive menu, select and review the statistics for topics you are interested in, but be sure to include the following: AIDS/HIV, Alcohol Use, Deaths/Mortality, Health Insurance Coverage, Immunization, Men's Health, and Women's Health. (Unless otherwise noted, all statistics given are for the United States.)

   (a) For the year listed, how many deaths were there in the United States from AIDS/HIV? How many new cases were reported?

(b)   How many alcohol-induced deaths were there in the United States in 1997? How many deaths from liver disease? During a one-month period in 1996, what percentage of persons age 12 years and older consumed alcohol?

(c)   Overall, how many deaths were there in the United States in 1997? What was the death rate in the United States in that year? Name the 10 leading causes of death in the United States, in order of importance.

(d)   How many Americans under age 65 have no health insurance coverage? How many Americans belong to HMOs?

(e)   What percentage of Americans is vaccinated against diphtheria, polio, and measles?

(f)   What is the leading cause of death for American men? For American women? For both men and women between the ages of 25 and 44? Name the most common chronic and acute medical conditions in the United States.

(g)   Which of the statistics you read at this site surprised you the most? Why?

2. The policy section of this chapter enumerates the challenges in financing health care worldwide. In the United States, a public debate regarding the pros and cons of health maintenance organizations (HMOs) has received much attention from policy-makers and the press. Link to and examine the following websites: Yahoo's Full Coverage (**http://fullcoverage.yahoo.com/Full_Coverage/ US/Health_Care_Debate**) and CNN's The HMO Debate (**http://www.cnn.com/HEALTH/specials/ HMOs/**).

(a)   What are the benefits of belonging to an HMO? The limitations and costs? What are the main issues in the public debate over HMOs?

(b)   What legislation is currently being considered, or has just been passed, regarding HMOs? Does it favor health insurance providers, patients and consumers, both, or neither?

(c)   Define the terms *authorization, capitation, gatekeeping,* and *preexisting condition.* How does an HMO differ from a PPO and a POS (point of service) plan?

(d)   Read some of the postings made by visitors to the website. What kinds of experiences do they describe? Do you agree or disagree with the opinions expressed in the postings? Explain.

(e)   Take the online poll offered at the CNN site. How do your opinions compare to those of others who have taken the poll?

(f)   Considering all you have learned from both your textbook and these websites, would you rather have an HMO, a PPO, or a POS health insurance plan? Explain your answer.

PART FIVE

CHANGING SOCIETY

Throughout this textbook, we have been reminded that sociologists are vitally concerned with changes in cultures, social institutions, and social behavior. Part Five will focus more directly on change as a characteristic aspect of human societies.

Chapter 19 describes changes in human communities, with particular emphasis on urbanization and metropolitan growth. This chapter also examines the diversity of suburban and rural communities. Chapter 20 considers changing patterns of population growth and their social consequences in the United States and throughout the world. The chapter also focuses on the environmental issues that confront our planet as we move through the twenty-first century. Chapter 21 offers sociological analysis of collective behavior and social movements. In Chapter 22, we examine sociological views of social change, with special emphasis on technological changes and the ways in which they are reshaping our future.

COMMUNITIES AND URBANIZATION

The homeless are among the socially overlooked poor in urban centers around the world. In 1990, an artists' collective collaborated with activists in Chicago to create personalized billboards covered with the signatures of homeless people who lived nearby. The poignant message of the signs acknowledged the homeless as individuals, raising their profile in the community.

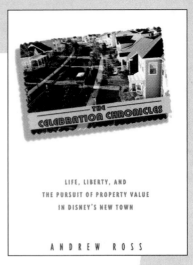

THE
CELEBRATION CHRONICLES

LIFE, LIBERTY, AND
THE PURSUIT OF PROPERTY VALUE
IN DISNEY'S NEW TOWN

ANDREW ROSS

O f all the amenities Celebration would offer—summarized in the five cornerstones of Place, Health, Education, Community, and Technology—the promise of a "sense of community" is the least easy to plan, guarantee, or put a price on. Hiring professionals to deliver the promise and ensure its upkeep is the natural offshoot of a corporate society where layers of experts are added yearly to monitor and manage activities that people used to do for themselves. The corporate concept of a community manager would have been as bizarre as a bug-eyed Martian to the idealized small towns of yore, whose close-knit civic virtue and neighborliness Celebration was designed to restore. Nowadays, there are managers for everything, even things that are supposed to have been lost, like our fabled sense of community.

"Community" is one of the most emotionally ubiquitous and versatile touchstones of American life. As a result, it is one of the more overused words in our daily lexicon, relentlessly mined for all sorts of social, religious, and commercial purposes, and in most instances no more meaningful than a sugary advertising cliché. . . .

In the last twenty years, "community" has become a competitive feature in the consumer housing industry, where developers bundle it into the package of amenities on offer. Customers can buy into a "strong" community where others appear to be weak or disorganized or in decline. Community then acquires value as a therapeutic asset that can be purchased by those who, among all the groups in society, probably have least need for its restorative virtues. Celebration's planners set out to raise the bar in the industry by offering a deluxe, next-generation version of the all-inclusive community package, far beyond the "enclaving" model that promised a safe retreat from the hustle and bustle of the city, and the "lifestyle" model that threw in golf and other sports. Celebration's packaging was expected to set the new standard for community-in-depth models of marketing. The demand for such a place rests on the perception that community is everywhere else an endangered species, especially in the nowhere of suburbia. Move to a real town, goes the pitch, and you'll see the difference it makes in your social life. *(Ross 1999:218–220)* ■

In this excerpt from *The Celebration Chronicles,* Andrew Ross, a professor of American Studies, debunks the promise of prepackaged community used to market the Disney-planned town called Celebration. A brand-new place, built from the ground up in a cypress swamp in Florida, Celebration is designed to resemble an old-fashioned home town, from its Victorian-style houses with their front porches clustered close to the street to its quaint-looking shops in the downtown business district. Families nostalgic for the small-town life their grandparents once knew have flocked to the place, some of them moving hundreds of miles or leaving good jobs and thriving businesses behind. But community is an elusive concept, an intangible that cannot necessarily be manufactured overnight. Ross reports that the teenagers who live in Celebration have taken to miming Disney's robotic theme-park characters in front of visitors who come to admire the town (Grief 2000).

This chapter explores the important role that communities of all sorts, from planned towns like Celebration to suburbs and big-city neighborhoods, play in people's lives. Communities give people the feeling that they are a part of something larger than themselves—or sometimes, as in the case of Celebration's teens, the feeling that they are just going through the motions. In sociological terms, a ***community*** may be formally defined as a spatial or political unit of social organization that gives people a sense of belonging. That sense of belonging can be based either on shared residence in a particular city or neighborhood or on a common identity, like that of gays and lesbians (Dotson 1991; see also Hillery 1955).

Anthropologist George Murdock (1949) has observed that there are only two truly universal units of human social organization: the family and the community. This chapter explores the importance of communities from a sociological perspective. We will begin with the successive development of early communities, preindustrial cities, and industrial and postindustrial cities. We will examine the dramatic urbanization evident around the world in the twentieth century, and contrast two different views of urban growth. Then we'll look at the three types of communities found in the United States—central cities, suburbs, and rural areas. Later in the chapter, we will consider a new type of community brought about by technological change: the online community. Finally, in the social policy section, we will analyze the distressing phenomenon of homelessness in the United States and elsewhere. ■

In the Disney-planned town of Celebration, Florida, homes are clustered close together, inviting neighbors to socialize over the traditional white picket fences.

How Did Communities Originate?

Early Communities

For most of human history, people used very basic tools and knowledge to survive. They satisfied their need for an adequate food supply through hunting, foraging for fruits or vegetables, fishing, and herding. In comparison with later industrial societies, early civilizations were much more dependent on the physical environment and much less able to alter that environment to their advantage. The emergence of horticultural societies, in which people actually cultivated food rather than merely gathering fruits and

p. 133

vegetables, led to many dramatic changes in human social organization.

Significantly, it was no longer necessary to move from place to place in search of food. Because people had to remain in specific locations to cultivate crops, more stable and enduring communities began to develop. Ultimately, as agricultural techniques became more and more sophisticated, a cooperative division of labor involving both family members and others developed. It gradually became possible for people to produce more food than they actually needed for themselves. They could give food, perhaps as part of an exchange, to others who might be involved in nonagricultural labor. This transition from subsistence to surplus represented a critical step in the emergence of cities.

Eventually, people produced enough goods to cover both their own needs and those of people not engaged in agricultural tasks. Initially, the surplus was limited to agricultural products, but it gradually evolved to include all types of goods and services. Residents of a city came to rely on community members who provided craft products and means of transportation, gathered information, and so forth (Lenski et al. 1995).

With these social changes came an even more elaborate division of labor, as well as a greater opportunity for differential rewards and privileges. So long as everyone was engaged in the same tasks, stratification was limited to such factors as gender, age, and perhaps the ability to perform the task (a skillful hunter could win unusual respect from the community). However, the surplus allowed for expansion of goods and services, leading to greater differentiation, a hierarchy of occupations, and social inequality. Therefore, surplus was a precondition not only for the establishment of cities but also for the division of members of a community into social classes (see Chapter 8). The ability to produce goods for other communities marked a fundamental shift in human social organization.

Preindustrial Cities

It is estimated that, beginning about 10,000 B.C., permanent settlements free from dependence on crop cultivation emerged. Yet, by today's standards of population, these early communities would barely qualify as cities. The *preindustrial city,* as it is termed, generally had only a few thousand people living within its borders and was characterized by a relatively closed class system and limited mobility. Status in these early cities was usually based on ascribed characteristics such as family background, and education was limited to members of the elite. All the residents relied on perhaps 100,000 farmers and their own part-time farming to provide them with the needed

This painting shows twelfth-century traders in a port city on the Mediterranean Sea. Such early settlements represented one type of preindustrial city.

agricultural surplus. The Mesopotamian city of Ur had a population of about 10,000 and was limited to roughly 220 acres of land, including the canals, the temple, and the harbor.

Why were these early cities so small and relatively few in number? A number of key factors restricted urbanization:

Reliance on animal power (both humans and beasts of burden) as a source of energy for economic production. This limited the ability of humans to make use of and alter the physical environment.

Modest levels of surplus produced by the agricultural sector. Between 50 and 90 farmers may have been required to support one city resident (Davis 1995, originally published in 1949).

Problems in transportation and storage of food and other goods. Even an excellent crop could easily be lost as a result of such difficulties.

Hardships of migration to the city. For many peasants, migration was both physically and economically impossible. A few weeks of travel was out of the question without more sophisticated techniques of food storage.

Dangers of city life. Concentrating a society's population in a small area left it open to attack from outsiders, as well as more susceptible to extreme damages from plagues and fires.

Gideon Sjoberg (1960) examined the available information on early urban settlements of medieval Europe, India, and China. He identified three preconditions of city life: advanced technology in both agricultural and nonagricultural areas, a favorable physical environment, and a well-developed social organization.

For Sjoberg, the criteria for defining a "favorable" physical environment are variable. Proximity to coal and iron helps only if a society knows how to use these natural resources. Similarly, proximity to a river is particularly beneficial only if a culture has the means to transport water efficiently to the fields for irrigation and to the cities for consumption.

A sophisticated social organization is also an essential precondition for urban existence. Specialized social roles bring people together in new ways through the exchange of goods and services. A well-developed social organization ensures that these relationships are clearly defined and generally acceptable to all parties. Admittedly, Sjoberg's view of city life is an ideal type, since inequality did not vanish with the emergence of urban communities.

Industrial and Postindustrial Cities

Imagine how life could change by harnessing the energy of air, water, and other natural resources to power society's tasks. Advances in agricultural technology led to dramatic changes in community life, but so did the process of in-

p. 133 ◄ dustrialization. The *industrial revolution*, which began in the middle of the eighteenth century, focused on the application of nonanimal sources of power to labor tasks. Industrialization had a wide range of effects on people's lifestyles as well as on the structure of communities. Emerging urban settlements became centers not only of industry but also of banking, finance, and industrial management.

The factory system that developed during the industrial revolution led to a much more refined division of labor than was evident in early preindustrial cities. The many new occupations that were created produced a complex set of relationships among workers. Thus, the *industrial city* was not merely more populous than its preindustrial predecessors; it was also based on very different principles of social organization. Sjoberg outlined the contrasts between preindustrial and industrial cities, as summarized in Table 19-1.

In comparison with preindustrial cities, industrial cities have a more open class system and more mobility. After initiatives in industrial cities by women's rights groups, labor unions, and other political activists, formal education gradually became available to many children from poor and working-class families. While ascribed characteristics such as gender, race, and ethnicity remained important, a talented or skilled individual had a greater opportunity to better his or her social position. In these and other respects, the industrial city is genuinely a "different world" from the preindustrial urban community.

In the latter part of the twentieth century, a new type of urban community emerged. The **postindustrial city** is a city in which global finance and the electronic flow of information dominate the economy. Production is decentralized and often takes place outside of urban centers, but control is centralized in multinational corporations whose influence transcends urban and even national boundaries. Social change is a constant feature of the postindustrial city. Economic and spatial restructuring seems to occur each decade if not more frequently. In the postindustrial world, cities are forced into increasing competition for economic opportunities, which deepens the plight of the urban poor (E. Phillips 1996; D. Smith and Timberlake 1993).

Sociologist Louis Wirth (1928, 1938) argued that a relatively large and permanent settlement leads to distinctive patterns of behavior, which he called **urbanism.** He identified three critical factors contributing to urbanism: the size of the population, population density, and the heterogeneity (variety) of the population. A frequent result of urbanism, according to Wirth, is that we become insensitive to events around us and restrict our attention to primary groups to which we are emotionally attached. Today, people living in postindustrial cities are developing new types of attachments through the use of electronic communication: see the case study of the Blacksburg Electronic Village, pages 517–19.

Urbanization

The 1990 census was the first to demonstrate that more than half the population of the United States lives in urban areas of 1 million or more residents. In only three states (Mississippi, Vermont, and West Virginia) do more than half the residents live in rural areas. Clearly, urbanization has become a central aspect of life in the United States (Bureau of the Census 1991c).

Urbanization shows up throughout the world. In 1920, only 14 percent of the world's people lived in urban areas, but by 1990 that proportion had risen to 43 percent, and by the year 2025 it is expected to be as high as 61 percent (World Resources Institute et al. 1996). Historian Kenneth Jackson (1996:E15) notes,

Table 19-1   **Comparing Types of Cities**

Preindustrial Cities (through 18th century)	Industrial Cities (18th through mid-20th century)	Postindustrial Cities (beginning late 20th century)
Closed class system—pervasive influence of social class at birth	Open class system—mobility based on achieved characteristics	Wealth based on ability to obtain and use information
Economic realm controlled by guilds and a few families	Relatively open competition	Corporate power dominates
Beginnings of division of labor in creation of goods	Elaborate specialization in manufacturing of goods	Sense of place fades, transitional networks emerge
Pervasive influence of religion on social norms	Influence of religion limited to certain areas as society becomes more secularized	Religion becomes more fragmented; greater openness to new religious faiths
Little standardization of prices, weights, and measures	Standardization enforced by custom and law	Conflicting views of prevailing standards
Population largely illiterate, communication by word of mouth	Emergence of communication through posters, bulletins, and newspapers	Emergence of extended electronic networks
Schools limited to elites and designed to perpetuate their privileged status	Formal schooling open to the masses and viewed as a means of advancing the social order	Professional, scientific, and technical personnel are increasingly important

Sources: Based on Sjoberg 1960:323–328; E. Phillips 1996:132–135.

At the turn of the century, only 14 percent of us called a city home and just 11 places on the planet had a million inhabitants. Now there are 400 cities with populations of at least one million and 20 megacities of more than 10 million.

During the nineteenth and early twentieth centuries, rapid urbanization occurred primarily in European and North American cities; however, since World War II, there has been an urban "explosion" in the world's developing countries (see Figure 19-1). Such rapid growth is evident in the rising number of "squatter settlements," areas occupied by the very poor on the fringe of cities, described in Box 19-1.

Some metropolitan areas have spread so far that they have connected with other urban centers. Such a densely populated area, containing two or more cities and their suburbs, has become known as a *megalopolis.* An example is the 500-mile corridor stretching from Boston south to Washington, D.C., and including New York City, Philadelphia, and Baltimore, which accounts for one-sixth of the total population of the United States. Even

FIGURE 19-1

Urbanization around the World, 1998

Mapping Life WORLDWIDE

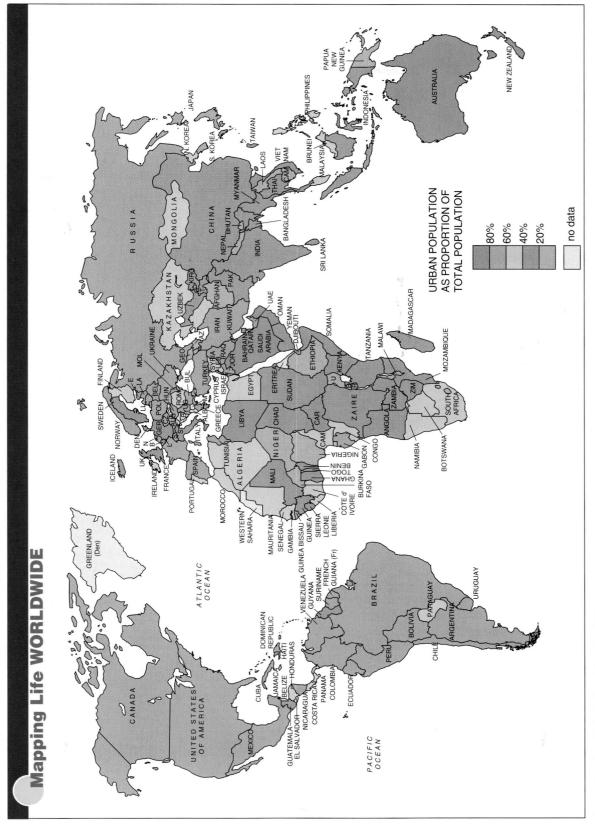

URBAN POPULATION
AS PROPORTION OF
TOTAL POPULATION

80%
60%
40%
20%

no data

Source: Based on data in Haub and Cornelius 1999.

19-1 Squatter Settlements

Bariadas, favelas, bustees, kampungs, and bidonvilles: The terms vary depending on the nation and language, but the meaning is the same—"squatter settlements." In *squatter settlements,* areas occupied by the very poor on the fringe of cities, housing is constructed by the settlers themselves from discarded material, including crates from loading docks and loose lumber from building projects. While the term "squatter settlement" has wide use, many observers prefer to use a less pejorative term, such as "autonomous settlements."

This type of settlement is very typical of cities in the world's developing nations. In such countries, new housing has not kept pace with the combined urban population growth resulting from births and migration from rural areas. In addition, squatter settlements are swelled by city dwellers forced out of housing by astronomical jumps in rent. By definition, squatters living on vacant land are trespassers and can be legally evicted. However, given the large number of poor people who live in such settlements (by UN estimates, 40 or 50 percent of inhabitants of cities in many developing nations), governments generally look the other way.

Obviously squatters live in substandard housing, yet this is only one of the many problems they face. Residents do not receive most public services, since their presence cannot be legally recognized. Police and fire protection, paved streets, and sanitary sewers are virtually nonexistent. In some countries, squatters may have trouble voting or enrolling their children in public schools.

Despite such conditions, squatter settlements are not always as bleak as they may appear from the outside. Rather than disorganized collections of people, you can often find a well-developed social organization. A thriving "informal economy" typically de-

> Squatter settlements are not always as bleak as they may appear from the outside.

velops: residents establish small, home-based businesses such as grocery stores, jewelry shops, and the like. Rarely, however, can any but the most ambitious entrepreneurs climb out of poverty through success in this underground economy.

Local churches, men's clubs, and women's clubs are often established in specific neighborhoods within the settlements. In addition, certain areas may form governing councils or membership associations. These governing bodies may face the usual problems of municipal governments, including charges of corruption and factional splits. Yet, in many cases, they seem to serve their constituents effectively. In Peru, squatters hold annual elections, whereas the rest of the nation has not held local elections for more than 70 years.

Squatter settlements remind us that respected theoretical models of social science in the United States may not directly apply to other cultures. The various ecological models of urban growth, for example, would not explain metropolitan expansion that locates the poorest people on the urban fringes. Furthermore, solutions that are logical for a highly industrialized nation may not be relevant in the developing nations. Planners in developing nations, rather than focusing on large-scale solutions to urban problems, must think in terms of basic amenities, such as providing water taps or electrical power lines to the ever-expanding squatter settlements.

Let's Discuss

1. Do you know of any "squatters" in your own community? If so, describe them and the place where they live.
2. Given the number of homeless people in the United States, why aren't there more squatters?

Sources: Castells 1983; Patton 1988; Yap 1998.

when it is divided into autonomous political jurisdictions, the megalopolis can be viewed as a single economic entity. The megalopolis is also evident in Great Britain, Germany, Italy, Egypt, India, Japan, and China.

Functionalist View: Urban Ecology

Human ecology is concerned with the interrelationships between people and their spatial setting and physical environment. Human ecologists have long been interested in how the physical environment shapes people's lives (for example, rivers can serve as a barrier to residential expansion) and also how people influence the surrounding environment (air conditioning has accelerated growth of major metropolitan areas in the Southwest). *Urban ecol-*

ogy focuses on such relationships as they emerge in urban areas. Although the urban ecological approach examines social change in cities, it is nevertheless functionalist in its orientation because it emphasizes that different elements in urban areas contribute to stability.

Early urban ecologists such as Robert Park (1916, 1936) and Ernest Burgess (1925) concentrated on city life but drew on the approaches used by ecologists in studying plant and animal communities. With few exceptions, urban ecologists trace their work back to the *concentric-zone theory* devised in the 1920s by Burgess (see Figure 19-2). Using the city of Chicago as an example, Burgess proposed a theory for describing land use in industrial cities. At the center, or nucleus, of such a city is the central business district. Large department stores, hotels, theaters, and financial institutions occupy this highly valued land. Surrounding this urban center are succeeding zones that contain other types of land use and that illustrate the growth of the urban area over time.

Note that the creation of zones is a *social* process, not the result of nature alone. Families and business firms compete for the most valuable land; those possessing the most wealth and power are generally the winners. The concentric-zone theory proposed by Burgess also represented a dynamic model of urban growth. As urban growth proceeded, each zone would move even farther from the central business district.

Because of its functionalist orientation and its emphasis on stability, the concentric-zone theory tended to understate or ignore certain tensions apparent in metropolitan areas. For example, the growing use by the affluent of land in a city's peripheral areas was uncritically approved, while the arrival of African Americans in White neighborhoods in the 1930s was described by some sociologists in terms such as "invasion" and "succession." Moreover, the urban ecological perspective gave little thought to gender inequities, such as the establishment of men's softball and golf leagues in city parks without any programs for women's sports. Consequently, the urban ecological approach has been criticized for its failure to address issues of gender, race, and class.

By the middle of the twentieth century, urban populations had spilled beyond the traditional city limits. No longer could urban ecologists focus exclusively on *growth* in the central city, for large numbers of urban residents were abandoning the cities to live in suburban areas. As a response to the emergence of more than one focal point in some metropolitan areas, C. D. Harris and Edward Ullman (1945) presented the **multiple-nuclei theory** (see Figure 19-2). In their view, all urban growth does not radiate outward from a central business district. Instead, a metropolitan area may have many centers of development, each of which reflects a particular urban need or activity. Thus, a city may have a financial district, a manufacturing zone, a waterfront area, an entertainment center, and so forth. Certain types of business firms and certain types of housing will naturally cluster around each distinctive nucleus (Schwab 1993).

The rise of suburban shopping malls is a vivid example of the phenomenon of multiple nuclei within metropolitan areas. Initially, all major retailing in cities was located in the central business district. Each residential neighborhood had its own grocers, bakers, and butchers, but people traveled to the center of the city to make major purchases at department stores. However, as major metropolitan areas expanded and the suburbs became more populous, an increasing number of people began to shop nearer their homes. Today, the suburban mall is a significant retailing and social center for communities across the United States.

In a refinement of multiple-nuclei theory, contemporary urban ecologists have begun to study what journalist Joel Garreau (1991) has called "edge cities." These communities, which have grown up on the outskirts of major metropolitan areas, are economic and social centers with identities of their own. By any standard of measurement—height of buildings, amount of office space, presence of medical facilities, presence of leisure-time facilities, or, of course, population—edge cities qualify as independent cities rather than large suburbs.

We can see the blurring of edge cities and suburbs with central cities in the case of Schaumburg, Illinois.

FIGURE 19-2

Comparison of Ecological Theories of Urban Growth

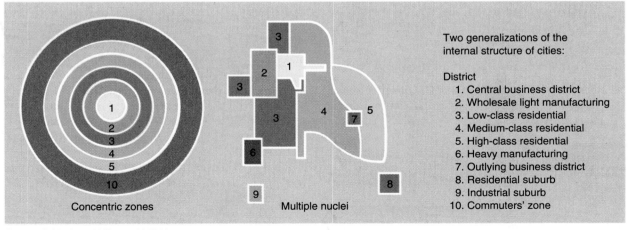

Two generalizations of the internal structure of cities:

District
1. Central business district
2. Wholesale light manufacturing
3. Low-class residential
4. Medium-class residential
5. High-class residential
6. Heavy manufacturing
7. Outlying business district
8. Residential suburb
9. Industrial suburb
10. Commuters' zone

Concentric zones   Multiple nuclei

Source: C. Harris and Ullmann 1945:13.

Though the African country of Kenya is mostly rural, Nairobi, a city with almost a million residents, is a modern urban area with international business connections. According to world systems analysis, the cities of developing nations exist on the periphery of the global economy, controlled and exploited by the more powerful industrialized nations.

Established as a German immigrant community in the 1840s, Schaumburg became a commuter suburb of Chicago after World War II. However, the opening of a major shopping mall in 1971, coupled with the arrival of corporations such as Motorola relocating from the central city, placed Schaumburg firmly on the map. Its population jumped from 18,730 in 1970 to about 74,000 in 1996. Despite a surge in population and job opportunities over this period, Schaumburg continued to resemble many rapidly expanding edge cities in that it had no traditional Main Street or central business district. To remedy this, Schaumburg began construction in 1996 of a town square called Olde Schaumburg, complete with shops, restaurants, a library, ponds, parks, and a waterfall (Pasternak 1998).

Conflict View: New Urban Sociology

While acknowledging the descriptive value of urban ecological models, contemporary sociologists point out that metropolitan growth is not governed by waterways and rail lines, as a purely ecological interpretation might suggest. From a conflict perspective, communities are human creations that reflect people's needs, choices, and decisions—but some people have more influence over these decisions than others. Drawing on conflict theory, an approach that has come to be called the *new urban sociology* considers the interplay of local, national, and worldwide forces and

their effect on local space, with special emphasis on the impact of global economic activity (Gottdiener and Hutchison 2000).

New urban sociologists note that ecological approaches typically have avoided examining the social forces, largely economic in nature, that have guided urban growth. For example, central business districts may be upgraded or abandoned, depending on whether urban policymakers grant substantial tax exemptions to developers. The suburban boom in the post–World War II era was fueled by federal housing policies that channeled investment capital into the construction of single-family homes rather than to affordable rental housing in the cities. Similarly, while some observers suggest that the growth of sun-belt cities is due to a "good business climate," new urban sociologists counter that this term is actually a euphemism for hefty state and local government subsidies and antilabor policies (Gottdiener and Feagin 1988; M. Smith 1988).

The new urban sociology draws generally on the conflict perspective and more specifically on sociologist Immanuel Wallerstein's *world systems analysis.* Wallerstein argues that certain industrialized nations (among them, the United States, Japan, and Germany) p. 232 hold a dominant position at the *core* of the global economic system. At the same time, the poor developing countries of Asia, Africa, and Latin America are on the *periphery* of the global economy, where they are controlled and exploited by core industrialized nations. Through use of world systems analysis, new urban sociologists consider urbanization from a global perspective. They view cities not as independent and autonomous entities but rather as the outcome of decision-making processes directed or influenced by a society's dominant classes and by core industrialized nations. New urban sociologists note that the rapidly growing cities of the world's developing countries have been shaped by the historical impact of colonialism followed by a global economy controlled by core nations and multinational corporations (Gottdiener and Feagin 1988; D. Smith 1995).

The urban ecologists of the 1920s and 1930s were not ignorant of the role that the larger economy played in urbanization, but their theories emphasized the impact of local rather than national or global forces. By contrast, through a broad, global emphasis on social inequality and

Residential neighborhoods in Las Vegas sprawl across the desert to the foothills. Like other urban areas in the United States, this sunbelt city has mushroomed in size through the construction of mostly single-family suburban homes.

struct and support such housing. But affluent people *are* interested in growth and *can* somehow find capital to build new shopping centers, office towers, and ballparks.

Why, then, can't they provide the capital for affordable housing, ask new urban sociologists? Part of the answer is that developers, bankers, and other powerful real estate interests view housing in quite a different manner from tenants and most homeowners. For a tenant, an apartment is shelter, housing, a home. But for developers and investors—many of them large (and sometimes multinational) corporations—an apartment is simply a housing investment. These financiers and owners are primarily concerned with maximizing profit, not with solving social problems (Feagin 1983; Gottdiener and Hutchison 2000).

As we have seen throughout this textbook—in studying such varied issues as deviance, race and ethnicity, and aging—no single theoretical approach necessarily offers sociologists the only valuable perspective. As is shown in Table 19-2, urban ecology and new urban sociology offer significantly different ways of viewing urbanization that enrich our understanding of this complex phenomenon.

conflict, new urban sociologists are interested in such topics as the existence of an underclass (refer back to Chapter 8), the power of multinational corporations (refer back to Chapter 9), and deindustrialization (refer back to Chapter 17), as well as issues to be examined later in this chapter, such as urban fiscal crises, residential segregation, and homelessness.

In an illustration of the new urban sociology, Joe Feagin has likened urban development to a game in which powerful elites play Monopoly with real money. Feagin (1983:2) points out that class conflict has always been part of the dynamics of urban life:

On the one side we have the progressive city councils and the urban grass-roots peoples movements opposing unbridled growth and development. On the other side, we have the class of profit-oriented developers, bankers, landowners, and industrial executives who buy, sell, and develop land and buildings in cities just like they do with other for-profit commodities.

Developers, builders, and investment bankers are not especially interested in urban growth when it means providing housing for middle- or low-income people. This lack of interest contributes to the problem of homelessness, which will be discussed in the social policy section at the end of the chapter. These urban elites counter that the nation's housing shortage and the plight of the homeless are not their fault—and insist that they do not have the capital needed to con-

Types of Communities

Communities vary substantially in the degree to which their members feel connected and share a common identity. Ferdinand Tönnies (1988, original edition 1887) used the term *Gemeinschaft* pp. 131–32 to describe close-knit communities where social interaction among people is intimate and familiar. A small town with a single coffee shop, where when anyone enters, people stop talking, assuming they know whoever walks through the door, is a good example of a *Gemeinschaft*. A shopper at the small grocery store in this town would expect to know every employee, and probably every customer as well. By contrast, the ideal type of *Gesellschaft* describes modern urban life, in which there is little sense of commonality, and social relationships often develop as a result of interactions focused on immediate tasks, such as purchasing a product. Contemporary city life in the United States generally resembles a *Gesellschaft*.

The following sections will examine different types of communities found in the United States, focusing on the

Table 19-2 Comparing Approaches to Urbanization

	Urban Ecology	New Urban Sociology
THEORETICAL PERSPECTIVE	Functionalist	Conflict
PRIMARY FOCUS	Relationship of urban areas to their spatial setting and physical environment	Relationship of urban areas to global, national, and local forces
KEY SOURCE OF CHANGE	Technological innovations such as new methods of transportation	Economic competition and monopolization of power
INITIATOR OF ACTIONS	Individuals, neighborhoods, communities	Real estate developers, banks and other financial institutions, multinational corporations
ALLIED DISCIPLINES	Geography Architecture	Political science Economics

distinctive characteristics and problems of central cities, suburbs, and rural communities.

Central Cities

In terms of both land and population, the United States is the fourth-largest nation in the world. Yet three-quarters of the population is concentrated in a mere 1.5 percent of the nation's land area. In 1996, some 212 million people—accounting for 80 percent of the nation's population—lived in metropolitan areas. Even those who live outside central cities, such as residents of suburban and rural communities, find that urban centers heavily influence their lifestyles (Bureau of the Census 1998c:39).

Urban Dwellers

Many urban residents are the descendants of European immigrants—Irish, Italians, Jews, Poles, and others—who came to the United States in the nineteenth and early twentieth centuries. The cities socialized these newcomers to the norms, values, and language of their new homeland and gave them an opportunity to work their way up the economic ladder. In addition, a substantial number of low-income African Americans and Whites came to the cities from rural areas in the period following World War II.

Even today, cities in the United States are the destinations of immigrants from around the world—including Mexico, Ireland, Cuba, Vietnam, and Haiti—as well as

pp. 281—83 migrants from the United States commonwealth of Puerto Rico. Yet, unlike

those who came to this country 75 or 100 years ago, current immigrants are arriving at a time of growing urban decay. This makes it more difficult for them to find employment and decent housing.

Urban life is noteworthy for its diversity, so it would be a serious mistake to see all city residents as being alike. Sociologist Herbert J. Gans (1991) has distinguished between five types of people found in our cities:

1. *Cosmopolites.* Such residents remain in cities to take advantage of the unique cultural and intellectual benefits. Writers, artists, and scholars fall into this category.
2. *Unmarried and childless people.* Such people choose to live in cities because of the active nightlife and varied recreational opportunities.
3. *Ethnic villagers.* These urban residents prefer to live in their own tight-knit communities. Typically, immigrant groups isolate themselves in such neighborhoods to avoid resentment from well-established urban dwellers.
4. *The deprived.* Very poor people and families have little choice but to live in low-rent, and often run-down, urban neighborhoods.
5. *The trapped.* Some city residents wish to leave urban centers but cannot because of their limited economic resources and prospects. Gans includes the "downward mobiles" in this category—people who once held higher social positions but who are forced to live in less prestigious neighborhoods owing to loss of a job, death of a wage earner, or

Indian American residents of Chicago enjoy an outdoor ethnic festival. Many subordinate racial and ethnic groups in the United States live in close-knit urban neighborhoods.

In some cases, a neighborhood must literally defend itself. Plans for urban renewal or a superhighway may threaten to destroy an area's unique character and sense of attachment. In resisting such changes, a neighborhood may use the strategies and tactics of community organization developed by pioneering organizer Saul Alinsky (1909–1972). Like many conflict sociologists, Alinsky was concerned with the ways in which society's most powerful institutions protect the privileges of certain groups (such as real estate developers) while keeping other groups (such as slum dwellers) in a subservient position. Alinsky (1946) emphasized the need for community residents to fight for power in their localities. In his view, it was only through the achievement and constructive use of power that people could better themselves (Horwitt 1989).

old age. Both elderly individuals living alone and families may feel "trapped" in part because they resent changes in their communities. Their desire to live elsewhere may reflect their uneasiness with unfamiliar immigrant groups who have become their neighbors.

These categories remind us that the city represents a choice (even a dream) for certain people and a nightmare for others. Gans's work underscores the importance of neighborhoods in contemporary urban life. Ernest Burgess, in his study of life in Chicago in the 1920s, had given special attention to the ethnic neighborhoods of that city. Many decades later, residents in such districts as Chinatowns or Greektowns continue to feel attached to their own ethnic communities rather than to the larger unit of a city. Even outside ethnic enclaves, a special sense of belonging can take hold in a neighborhood.

In a more recent study in Chicago, Gerald Suttles (1972) coined the term *defended neighborhood* to refer to people's definitions of their community boundaries. Neighborhoods acquire unique identities because they are viewed by residents as geographically separate—and socially different—from adjacent areas. The defended neighborhood, in effect, becomes a sentimental union of similar people. Neighborhood phone directories, community newspapers, school and parish boundaries, and business advertisements all serve to define an area and distinguish it from nearby communities.

Of course, a defended neighborhood may maintain its distinctive identity by excluding those who are deemed different or threatening. In 1981, the Supreme Court upheld the right of the city of Memphis, Tennessee, to erect a barrier and close a street connecting an all-White and all-Black neighborhood. White residents requested the closure, claiming that there was too much undesirable traffic coming through their own communities. In a dissenting opinion, Justice Thurgood Marshall, the first African American to serve on the Supreme Court, called the barrier a "badge of slavery." Close to two decades later, however, defended neighborhoods with physical barriers have become more common across the United States because of the growing number of "gated communities" (see Box 19-2).

Issues Facing Cities

People and neighborhoods vary greatly within any city in the United States. Yet all residents of a central city—regardless of social class, racial, and ethnic differences—face certain common problems. Crime, air pollution, noise, unemployment, overcrowded schools, inadequate public transportation—these unpleasant realities and many more are an increasing feature of contemporary urban life.

Perhaps the single most dramatic reflection of the nation's urban ills has been the apparent "death" of entire neighborhoods. In some urban districts, business activity seems virtually nonexistent. You can walk for blocks and find little more than a devastating array of deteriorating,

The poet Robert Frost wrote that "good fences make good neighbors"; locked doors, walls, and fences have been features of shelter in the United States for generations. However, in recent decades, there has been a growing interest in isolating entire communities from those who otherwise would be neighbors. Political scientist Evan McKenzie (1994) uses the term *privatopia* to describe the emergence of a new type of artificial utopia: private communities within cities and suburbs.

In some cases, the communities are gated, sealed off from surrounding neighborhoods. There are three categories of gated communities:

- *Lifestyle communities*, including retirement communities, golf and country club leisure developments, and suburban new towns.
- *Prestige communities*, where gates symbolize distinction and stature, including enclaves of the rich and famous, developments for high-level professionals, and executive home developments for the middle class.
- *Security zones*, motivated by fear of crime and outsiders.

The private developers who build these generally "upscale" communities create homeowners' associations to establish rules and to contract for such services as security, garbage collection, and even education. The associations build community parks, recreation centers, swimming pools, and golf

courses—all of which are restricted to association members and their guests.

Some gated communities and homeowners' associations have banned display of the U.S. flag and political signs, prohibited the distribution of newspapers, and barred political meetings or rallies in public areas. Many residents of private communities defend such restrictions as essential for maintaining property values and

> The message is clear: These streets are for members only.

believe that relinquishing a bit of personal freedom is worthwhile so they may be protected from improper behavior by their neighbors.

From a conflict perspective, there is particular concern about the symbolism of gated communities, which currently house about 4 million people in the United States.

The residents of gated communities are overwhelmingly White and affluent. Gated communities are vividly separated from adjoining neighborhoods; their gates, walls, and entry doors are monitored 24 hours a day by uniformed private security guards. The message is clear: These streets are for members only.

The emergence of homeowners' associations and gated communities is troubling because it suggests an even sharper segregation of our society, with the "haves" hidden in their private fortresses and walled off from the "have-nots." Moreover, as people become isolated in private communities, they may care less and less about the deterioration of public services *outside* their communities, in nearby cities and counties. With this in mind, Evan McKenzie refers to the shift toward privatopia as "secession by the successful," with affluent individuals and families seceding from the rights and responsibilities of citizenship in a larger society.

Let's Discuss

1. Is there a gated community near you? If so, is it a lifestyle community, a prestige community, or a security zone?
2. What do you think of people who live in gated communities? Would you want to live in one yourself (or if you already do, would you want to stay)?

Sources: Blakely and Snyder 1997; Egan 1995; E. McKenzie 1994; Vanderpool 1995.

---

boarded-up, abandoned, and burned-out buildings. Such urban devastation has greatly contributed to the growing problem of homelessness, discussed in the social policy section.

Residential segregation has also been a persistent problem in cities across the United States. Such segregation has resulted from the policies of financial institutions, the business practices of real estate agents, the actions of home sellers, and even urban planning initiatives (for example, in decisions about where to locate public

housing). Sociologists Douglas Massey and Nancy Denton (1993) have used the term "American apartheid" to refer to the residential patterns of the nation. In their view, we no longer perceive segregation as a problem but rather accept it as a feature of the urban landscape. For subordinate minority groups, segregation means not only limited housing opportunities but also less access to employment, retail outlets, and medical services.

Another critical problem for the cities has been mass transportation. Since 1950, the number of cars in the

MOVE YOUR TEAM TO *OUR* CITY, AND WE'LL BUILD YOU A STADIUM!

WE'LL BUILD YOUR STADIUM, *AND* ALL YOUR INFRA-STRUCTURE!

STADIUM, INFRASTRUCTURE, AND *NO TAXES!*

NO TAXES AND... WE'LL PAY YOUR *PLAYER SALARIES!* ...WITH, AH... OUR *SCHOOL BUDGET!*

OWNERS

ST. PAUL PIONEER PRESS   KIRK —095

Although many cities claim that they do not have enough money to pay for essential public services, they nevertheless seem willing to use valuable resources to attract or keep professional sports teams.

United States has multiplied twice as fast as the number of people. As a result, there has been growing traffic congestion in metropolitan areas, and many cities have recognized a need for safe, efficient, and inexpensive mass transit systems. However, the federal government has traditionally given much more assistance to highway programs than to public transportation. Conflict theorists note that such a bias favors the relatively affluent (automobile owners) as well as corporations such as auto manufacturers, tire makers, and oil companies. Meanwhile, poor residents of metropolitan areas, who are much less likely to own cars than members of the middle and upper classes, face higher fares on public transit along with deteriorating service (Mason 1998).

In 1968, Dr. Martin Luther King Jr. observed that "urban transit systems in most American cities have become a genuine civil rights issue." An overcrowded public bus system in Los Angeles County carries 94 percent of the county's passengers—80 percent of whom are African American, Hispanic, Asian American, or Native American—yet receives less than one-third of the county's mass transit expenditures. At the same time, a lavish commuter rail system that already connects or will connect predominantly White suburbs to the downtown business district of Los Angeles carries only 6 percent of the county's passengers yet receives 71 percent of mass transit funding. Similar inequities in funding for public transportation have been challenged in New York City (Kelley 1996:18).

Ironically, while many communities are insisting that they cannot afford to maintain public services and are shifting them to the private sector, some nevertheless find substantial funds to attract professional sports franchises. According to estimates, at least $11 billion of public money was spent in the United States during the 1990s on 45 stadiums and arenas. Local politicians and business leaders claim that winning a sports franchise provides a significant boost to the local economy and enhances community spirit. But critics counter that professional sports teams build profits for a wealthy few—and offer tax write-offs to corporations that maintain lavish luxury boxes—without genuinely revitalizing neighborhoods, much less an entire city. Consequently, the use of significant public funds to attract professional sports franchises has been derided as "stadium welfare." Baltimore's highly praised Camden Yards baseball stadium produced a net gain, in terms of new jobs and tax revenue, of only $3 million a year—not much of a return on the $200 million invested (Egan 1999; Noll and Zimbalist 1997).

Suburbs

The term *suburb* derives from the Latin *sub urbe*, meaning "under the city." Until recent times, most suburbs were just that—tiny communities totally dependent on urban centers for jobs, recreation, and even water.

Today, the term **suburb** defies any simple definition. The term generally refers to any community near a large city—or, as the Census Bureau would say, any territory within a metropolitan area that is not included in the central city. By that definition, more than 138 million people, or about 51 percent of the population of the United States, lived in the suburbs in 1999. However, there are three social factors that differentiate suburbs from cities. First, suburbs are generally less dense than cities; in the newest suburbs, there are often no more than two dwellings on an acre of land. Second, the suburbs consist almost exclusively of private space. Private ornamental lawns replace common park areas for the most part.

Developers and bankers are less interested in providing affordable housing than in building new ballparks, preferably with government subsidies. Yet subsidized sports complexes rarely yield the employment opportunities they promise. Baltimore's Camden Yards, shown here, added little to the local economy compared to its cost.

Third, suburbs have more exacting building design codes than cities, and these codes have become increasingly precise in the last decade. While the suburbs may be diverse in terms of population, such design standards give the impression of uniformity (Peterson 1999).

It can also be difficult to distinguish between suburbs and rural areas. Certain criteria generally define suburbs: Most people work at urban (as opposed to rural) jobs, and local governments provide services such as water supply, sewage disposal, and fire protection. In rural areas, these services are less common, and a greater proportion of residents is employed in farming and related activities (Baldassare 1992).

Suburban Expansion

Whatever the precise definition of a suburb, it is clear that suburbs have expanded. In fact, suburbanization has been the most dramatic population trend in the United States throughout the twentieth century. Suburban areas grew at first along railroad lines, then at the termini of streetcar tracks, and by the 1950s along the nation's growing systems of freeways and expressways. The suburban boom has been especially evident since World War II.

Suburbanization is not necessarily prompted by expansion of transportation services to the fringe of a city. The 1923 earthquake that devastated Tokyo encouraged decentralization of the city. Until the 1970s, dwellings were limited to a height of 102 feet. Initially, the poor were relegated to areas outside municipal boundaries in their search for housing; many chose to live in squatter-type settlements. With the advent of a rail network and rising land costs in the central city, middle-class Japanese began moving to the suburbs after World War II (P. Hall 1977).

Proponents of the new urban sociology contend that factories were initially moved from central cities to suburbs as a means of reducing the power of labor unions. Subsequently, many suburban communities induced businesses to relocate by offering them subsidies and tax incentives. As sociologist William Julius Wilson (1996) has observed, federal housing policies contributed to the suburban boom by withholding mortgage capital from inner-city neighborhoods, by offering favorable mortgages to military veterans, and by assisting the rapid development of massive amounts of affordable tract housing in the suburbs. Moreover, federal highway and transportation policies provided substantial funding for expressway systems (which made commuting to the cities much easier), while undermining urban communities by building freeway networks through the heart of cities.

All these factors contributed to the movement of the (predominantly White) middle class out of the central cities and, as we shall see, also out of the suburbs. From the perspective of new urban sociology, suburban expansion is far from a natural ecological process; rather, it reflects the distinct priorities of powerful economic and political interests.

Diversity in the Suburbs

In the United States, race and ethnicity remain the most important factors distinguishing cities from suburbs. Nevertheless, the common assumption that suburbia includes only prosperous Whites is far from correct. The last 20 years have witnessed the diversification of suburbs in terms of race and ethnicity. For example, by 1994, 30 percent of the Black population was suburban.

But are the suburban areas recreating the racial segregation of the central cities? A definite pattern of clustering if not outright segregation is emerging. A study of

While there has been a significant increase in the proportion of African Americans living in the suburbs, African Americans remain more likely than other groups to be the victims of residential segregation in suburban communities.

suburban residential patterns in 11 metropolitan areas found that Asian Americans and Hispanics tend to reside in equivalent socioeconomic areas with Whites—that is, affluent Hispanics live alongside affluent Whites, poor Asians near poor Whites, and so on. However, the case for African Americans is quite distinct. Suburban Blacks live in poorer suburbs than Whites, even after taking into account differences in individuals' income, education, and homeownership. This Black–White disparity appears in every geographical region studied, offering strong evidence of patterns of racial segregation in suburban housing markets (Logan and Alba 1995; Palen 1995).

Again, in contrast to prevailing stereotypes, the suburbs include a significant number of low-income people from all backgrounds—White, Black, and Hispanic. Poverty is not conventionally associated with the suburbs, partly because the suburban poor tend to be scattered among more affluent people. In some instances, suburban communities in-

tentionally hide social problems so they can maintain a "respectable image." Soaring housing costs have contributed to suburban poverty, which is expected to rise at a faster rate than city poverty through 2010 (El Nasser 1999).

Sociologist Ivan Fahs, who studied homelessness in suburban Chicago, found that the lead community in finding shelter for the homeless was the suburban county seat, but neighboring communities were reluctant to even acknowledge the homeless in their midst, much less assist in easing the housing problem. Even public officials living in suburbs find it difficult to accept the diverse population living in their communities (Fahs et al. 1997; Mayor's Task Force on Homelessness 1997).

Suburban settlements have become so diverse that even the collective term *suburbs* gives undue support to the stereotype of suburban uniformity. Pollster Louis Harris has divided suburbs into four distinct categories based on income level and rate of growth. Higher-income suburbs are categorized as either affluent bedroom or affluent settled. *Affluent bedroom communities* rank at the highest levels in terms of income, proportion of people employed in professional and managerial occupations, and percentage of homeowners. *Affluent settled communities* tend to be older and perhaps even declining in population. They are more likely to house business firms and do not serve mainly as a place of residence for commuters.

Harris has recognized that certain suburban areas are composed of individuals and families with low or moderate incomes. *Low-income growing communities* serve as the home of upwardly mobile blue-collar workers who have moved from the central cities. *Low-income stagnant communities* are among the oldest suburbs and are experiencing the full range of social problems characteristic of the central cities. As is true of Gans's model of city residents, Harris emphasizes the diversity found within the general category of suburbia (*Time* 1971).

Clearly, not all suburban residents appreciate the diversity of the suburbs—especially if it means that less affluent families, or members of racial and ethnic minorities, will be moving into their communities. When the Ford Motor Company moved from Richmond, California, to Milpitas, California, the union attempted to build housing for the firm's employees—many of whom were Black. The local government of Milpitas promptly rezoned the area for industrial use (C. Larson and Nikkel 1979).

Communities enact **zoning laws,** in theory, to ensure that certain standards of housing construction are satisfied; these laws generally stipulate land use and architectural design of housing. Zoning laws can also separate industrial and commercial enterprises from residential areas. Thus, a suburb might wish to prevent a factory from moving to a quiet residential neighborhood. However, some zoning laws have served as thinly veiled efforts to keep low-income people out of a suburb and have been attacked as "snob statutes." By requiring that a person own a certain number of square feet of land before he or she can build a home—or by prohibiting prefabricated or modular housing—a community can effectively prevent the construction of any homes that lower-class families might be able to afford. The courts have generally let such exclusionary zoning laws stand, even when charges have been made that their enactment was designed to keep out racial minorities and new immigrants with large families (Salins 1996).

Some urban and suburban residents are moving to communities even more remote from the central city or to rural areas altogether. Initial evidence suggests that this move to rural areas is only furthering the racial disparities in our metropolitan areas (Bureau of the Census 1997b; Holmes 1997).

Rural Communities

As we have seen, the people of the United States live mainly in urban areas. Yet one-fourth of the population lives in towns of 2,500 people or less that are not adjacent to a city. As is true of the suburbs, it would be a mistake to view rural communities as fitting into one set image. Turkey farms, coal mining towns, cattle ranches, and gas stations along interstate highways are all part of the rural United States.

In contrast to the historic stereotype of the farmer as a White male, African Americans and women have long played a significant role in agriculture in the United States. Women actively participate in farming across the country—in large and small farms, in profitable and failing family businesses. Farming women are almost always married and generally have large families. Segregation by gender is typical of farm labor: Men are more likely to be engaged in field work, while women serve their farms as accountants, personnel and equipment managers, and purchasing agents. Many studies have documented the high degree of stress that farming women experience as they attempt to fulfill many demanding social roles (Keating and Munro 1988; Lofflin 1988).

Whereas women are involved in farming in all regions of the United States, 90 percent of African American farmers work in the South. Their farms tend to be small—an average of about 100 acres compared with the national average of 4,400 acres. Moreover, Black farmers are concentrated in areas of the country with severe economic difficulties, including limited job opportunities and few supportive services for residents. In 1950, 10 percent of people running farms in the United States were African American, but by 1997 this figure had fallen to less than 1 percent. In good part, this was not a voluntary withdrawal from farming; farm displacement and loss of land among African Americans occurs at a rate 212 times higher than the rate among White farmers (Jones 1999).

The postindustrial revolution has been far from kind to the rural communities of the United States. Despite the images portrayed in the media, agriculture accounts for only 9 percent of employment in nonurban counties. Indeed, in 1993, the Bureau of the Census calculated that farm residents accounted for only 2 percent of the nation's population—compared with 95 percent in 1790—and therefore announced that it would no longer conduct its special farm surveys. At the same time that farming has been in decline, so have mining and logging—the two nonagricultural staples of the rural economy. The manufacturing base of rural areas has been slow to participate in the growth of high-technology industries, which adds further strain to rural communities. On a more positive note, advances in electronic communication allow some people in the United States to work wherever they wish; for many concerned about quality-of-life issues, this means working at home and living in rural areas (D. Johnson 1996b; Vobejda 1993).

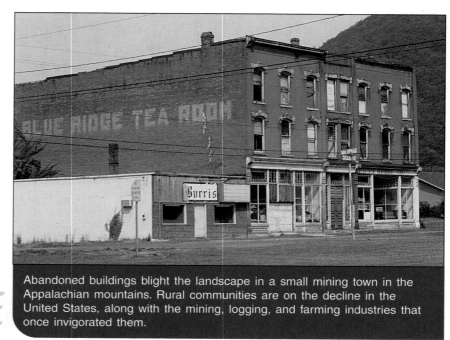

Abandoned buildings blight the landscape in a small mining town in the Appalachian mountains. Rural communities are on the decline in the United States, along with the mining, logging, and farming industries that once invigorated them.

One consequence of rural decline is that policymakers have been confronted with an unpleasant task: deciding which ailing towns and counties will be supported with funds for economic development and which rural communities will, in effect, be allowed to die. New schools, bridges, and roads can help save a declining area, but state governments are not in a position to support every area in need. At present, there are no precise data on how many small towns across the United States vanish each decade.

Rural communities that do survive may feel threatened by changes intended to provide jobs, income, and financial security. For example, the town of Postville, Iowa—with a population of only 1,512—was dying when an entrepreneur from New York City bought a run-down meat processing plant. The plant was subsequently transformed into a kosher slaughtering house, and today 10 percent of Postville's population consists of devout Hasidic Jews from the Lubavitcher sect. The new residents occupy key managerial positions in the slaughtering house, while Lubavitcher rabbis supervise the kosher processing of the meat to ensure that it is acceptable under Jewish dietary laws. Initially, there was distrust between longtime residents of Postville and their new neighbors, but gradually each group came to realize that it needed the other (Bloom 1996).

Similar tensions exist in smaller communities that experience the arrival of large discount stores such as Wal-Mart or Costco. While many residents welcome the new employment opportunities and the convenience of one-stop shopping, local merchants see their longtime family businesses endangered by a formidable 200,000-square-foot competitor with a national reputation. Even when such discount stores provide a boost to a town's economy (and this is not always the case), they can undermine the town's sense of community and identity (Curtius 1999).

No matter where people make their homes—whether in city, suburb, or country village—economic and technological change will have an impact on their quality of life. In the next section we'll see how the rise of information networks has affected a community of 34,000 people in Virginia.

Community and Technological Change: A Case Study

Like many other aspects of modern society, the concept of community is evolving in response to technological change. Many people now speak of communities or neighborhoods on the Internet, for example. We saw in our discussion of Table 19-1 that several of the changes communities and urban areas have undergone in recent years can be traced to the growth of electronic information networks. Respondents to a recent national survey of urban historians, planners, and architects predicted that the Internet will continue to be a major influence on U.S. cities over the next half century (see Table 19-3). A case in point is the city of Blacksburg, Virginia, which offers a glimpse into the future of many other cities.

Blacksburg, a college town whose population swells each year with the influx of students returning from

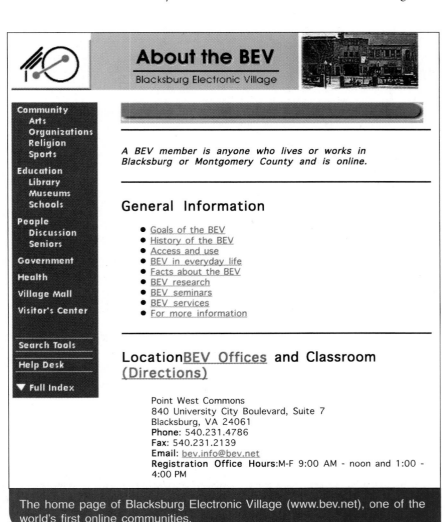

The home page of Blacksburg Electronic Village (www.bev.net), one of the world's first online communities.

summer break, lies in the Appalachian Mountain range. This rural community, at first glance no different from any other small town, has acquired an international reputation as an electronic village, one of the first of its kind. Foreigners visiting Washington, D.C., frequently seek out the town, which they expect will look something like Las Vegas. Andrew Cohill, a professor at Virginia Polytechnic Institute and State University, says he frequently hears from visitors eager to see the electronic village. He tells them there's nothing to see (Yaukey 1997).

Blacksburg Electronic Village (www.bev.net) is an online community that connects 85 percent of Blacksburg's residents and 75 percent of its businesses. The network began in 1987, when Virginia Tech invested $16 million in a high-speed voice and data network for use throughout the university. By the early 1990s university administrators were talking with Blacksburg officials and representatives of Bell Atlantic about providing affordable high-speed Internet access to everyone in town. In 1993 universal Internet access became a reality. The majority of residents have modems in their homes; schools, libraries, and the senior center offer public access to those who don't. Citizens of Blacksburg can now communicate with city hall, schools, and businesses via e-mail. Soon they will be able to pay their bills, register their cars, and license their dogs online.

The new service has had a positive effect on the town, users agree. An enhanced sense of community is the most pervasive outcome. Seniors have greeted the new service enthusiastically: The senior center houses 10 computers, and a special service tailored to the needs of elders has 180 subscribers. The strengthening of local bonds has surprised some, perhaps because it runs counter to the conventional wisdom that the Internet will unite people from around the world in a global online community. One retired physicist

Table 19-3   The City: Its Past and Its Future

The Major Influences of the Past 50 Years	The Major Influences of the Next 50 Years
1. The 1956 Interstate Highway Act and the dominance of the automobile	1. Growing disparities of wealth
2. Federal Housing Administration mortgage financing and subdivision regulation	2. Suburban political majority
3. Deindustrialization of central cities	3. Aging of the baby boomers
4. Urban renewal: downtown redevelopment and public housing projects (e.g., 1949 Housing Act)	4. Perpetual "underclass" in central cities and inner-ring suburbs
5. Levittown (the mass-produced suburban tract house)	5. "Smart Growth" environmental and planning initiatives to limit sprawl
6. Racial segregation and job discrimination in cities and suburbs	6. Internet
7. Enclosed shopping malls	7. Deterioration of the "first-ring" post-1945 suburbs
8. Sunbelt-style sprawl	8. Shrinking household size
9. Air conditioning	9. Expanded superhighway system of "outer beltways" to serve new edge cities
10. Urban riots of the 1960s	10. Racial integration as part of the increasing diversity in cities and suburbs

In a 1999 survey, urban historians, planners, and architects were asked to identify the major influences on U.S. cities over the past 50 years, and to predict the most significant influences in the next 50 years. What do you think?

Source: Fannie Mae Foundation 1999.

didn't think BEV would catch on, but was pleasantly surprised by the speed with which residents adopted it.

BEV has also brought some noticeable economic benefits to the town. Some residents, like the proprietor of Green Dreams, an online retailer of homemade vinegars, have seized the opportunity to become online entrepreneurs. And a corporate research center at the edge of town has been attracting more and more startup ventures, bringing new jobs and income to the college town. CEOs of the innovative new companies like the fresh air, low crime rate, and cutting-edge intellectual climate of Blacksburg. One, the head of Blue Ridge Interactive, an online purveyor of magazines, raves about the supportive atmosphere in the town (Clark 1999; Yaukey 1997; Zajac 1999).

The wider implications of the electronic village are only beginning to become clear. If the installation of universal high-speed access to the Internet can draw new companies away from more heavily populated areas like northern Virginia, it may contribute to the decay of older urban areas, worsening the plight of inner-city residents. And BEV users are concerned about the fact that not all families in rural Montgomery County can afford to tap into the network, which requires an in-home computer and a small monthly connection fee. Roger Ehrich, a professor of computer science at Virginia Tech, believes the best way to level the playing field is to provide Internet access to children at school, wherever they live (Zajac 1999).

Finally, the advent of the electronic community has the potential to revolutionize not just communities, but the way sociological research on communities is done. Automatic electronic monitoring of online response rates may someday replace telephone surveys and the distribution, collection, and coding of paper questionnaires. In the future, scholars may be able to visit far-flung electronic communities without leaving the comfort of their offices, and to travel safely through otherwise dangerous villages.

In the next and concluding section of this chapter, we will discuss a pressing social policy issue: the growing community of homeless people, both in the United States and abroad. What can be done to improve the lives of the homeless, who seem to have been bypassed by the Information Revolution that is benefiting so many others?

SOCIAL POLICY AND COMMUNITIES

Seeking Shelter Worldwide

In a story the press dubbed "The Prince and the Pauper," Prince Charles was surprised to run into an old classmate while visiting the office of a magazine sold by the homeless—and was even more surprised to learn that the fellow was himself homeless.

The Issue

A chance meeting brought two old classmates together. In late 1997, Prince Charles encountered Clive Harold during a tour of the offices of a magazine sold by the homeless in London. But while Prince Charles can call several palaces home, Harold is homeless. This modern-day version of the "The Prince and the Pauper" intrigued many people with its message that "it can happen to anyone." Harold had been a successful author and journalist until his marriage fell apart and alcohol turned his life inside out (*Chicago Tribune* 1997b).

The issue of inadequate shelter manifests itself in many ways, for all housing problems can be considered relative. For a middle-class family in the United States, it may mean a somewhat smaller house than they need because that is all they can afford. For a single working adult in Tokyo, it may mean having to commute two hours to a full-time job. For many people worldwide, however, the housing problem consists of merely finding shelter of any kind that they can afford, in a place where anyone would reasonably wish to live. Prince Charles of Buckingham Palace and Clive Harold, homeless person, are extreme examples of a continuum present in all communities in all societies. What can be done to ensure adequate shelter for those who can't afford it?

The Setting

Homelessness is evident in both industrialized and developing countries. According to a 1999 estimate, our nation's homeless population is at least 700,000, and may be as high as 3 million. Given the limited space in public shelters, at a minimum, hundreds of thousands of people in the United States are homeless and without shelter (Kilborn 1999; see also Jencks 1994; Snow and Anderson 1993; Snow et al. 1996).

In Great Britain, some 175,000 people are accepted as homeless by the government and are given housing. An even larger number, perhaps 1 million people, are turned away from government assistance or are sharing a household with relatives or acquaintances but want separate accommodations. While an accurate figure is not available, it is estimated that 1 percent of Western Europeans are homeless; they sleep in the streets, depend on night shelters and hostels, or live in precarious accommodations (B. Lee 1992; Platt 1993; Stearn 1993).

In Japan, the problem of homelessness is just as serious. A single protest drew roughly 6,000 homeless people to Tokyo in 1998. The Japanese usually hide such misfortune, thinking it shameful, but a severe economic downturn had victimized many formerly prosperous citizens, swelling the numbers of the homeless. A chronic space shortage in the heavily populated island nation, together with opposition to the establishment of homeless shelters in residential neighborhoods, compounds the problem (Hara 2000).

In Third World countries, rapid population growth has outpaced the expansion of housing by a wide margin, leading to a rise in homelessness. For example, estimates of homelessness in Mexico City range from 10,000 to 100,000, and these estimates do not include the many people living in caves or squatter settlements (see Box 19-1). By 1998, 600 million people around the world were either homeless or inadequately housed in urban areas alone (G. Goldstein 1998; Ross 1996).

Sociological Insights

Both in the United States and around the world, being homeless functions as a master status that largely defines a person's position within society. In this case, homelessness tends to mean that in many important respects, the individual is *outside* society. Without a home address and telephone, it is difficult to look for work or even apply for public assistance. Moreover, the master status of being homeless carries a serious stigma and can lead to prejudice and discrimination. Poor treatment of people suspected of being homeless is common in stores and restaurants, and many communities have reported acts of random violence against homeless people.

p. 178

There has been a significant change in the profile of homelessness during the last 20 years. In the past, homeless people were primarily older White males living as alcoholics in skid-row areas. However, today's homeless are comparatively younger—with an average age in the low 30s. Overall, an estimated 59 percent of homeless people in the United States are from racial and ethnic minority groups. Moreover, a 26-city survey done in 1999 found that the homeless population is growing faster than the increase in emergency food and shelter space (Burt et al. 1999; U.S. Conference of Mayors 1999).

Changing economic and residential patterns account for much of this increase in homelessness. In recent decades, the process of urban renewal has included a noticeable boom in **gentrification.** This term refers to the resettlement of low-income city neighborhoods by prosperous families and business firms. In some instances, city governments have promoted gentrification by granting lucrative tax breaks to developers who convert low-cost rental units into luxury apartments and condominiums. Conflict theorists note that although the affluent may derive both financial and emotional benefits from gentrification and redevelopment, the poor often end up being thrown out on the street.

There is an undeniable connection between the nation's growing shortage of affordable housing and the rise in homelessness (Elliot and Krivo 1991). Yet sociologist Peter Rossi (1989, 1990) cautions against focusing too narrowly on housing shortage while ignoring structural factors, such as the decline in the demand for manual labor in cities and the increasing prevalence of chronically unemployed young men among the homeless. Rossi contends that structural changes have put everyone in extreme poverty at higher risk of becoming homeless—especially poor people with an

In Japan in 1998, as many as six thousand homeless people marched on the Tokyo Metropolitan Office to protest the lack of shelter facilities. This biting cartoon from the *Japan Times* acknowledges their plight.

accumulation of disabilities (such as drug abuse, bad health, unemployment, and criminal records). Being disabled in this manner forces the individual to rely on family and friends for support, often for a prolonged period. If the strain on this support network is so great that it collapses, homelessness may result. While many researchers accept Rossi's theory, the general public often prefers to "blame the victim" for becoming homeless (B. Lee 1992).

Homeless women often have additional problems that distinguish them from homeless men. In comparison with homeless men, homeless women report more recent injuries or acute illnesses, as well as more chronic health problems. Moreover, homeless women have experienced more disruption in their families and social networks than homeless men. Anthropologist Elliot Liebow conducted a five-year, participant-observation study of single homeless women living in emergency shelters. Liebow (1995:112) concludes that

Homeless women are mainly from working-class and lower-class families that can no longer support them or from families whose members can no longer live together as husband and wife or parent and child. The weakest one (wife, mother, daughter) gets pushed out.

Sociologists attribute homelessness in developing nations not only to income inequality but also to population growth and an influx of people from rural areas and areas experiencing natural disaster, famine, or warfare.

A major barrier to constructing decent, legal, and affordable housing in the urban areas of these developing nations is the political power of large-scale landowners and small-scale land speculators—anyone buying a few lots as investment. In the view of conflict theorists, these groups conspire to enhance their own financial investment by making the supply of legally buildable land scarce. (This problem is not unknown in the cities of North America, but a World Bank survey shows that the increase in the cost of land is twice as great in developing nations as in industrial countries.) In many cases, residents who can afford building materials have no choice but to become squatters. Those who can't are likely to become homeless.

Policy Initiatives

Thus far, policymakers have often been content to steer the homeless toward large, overcrowded, unhealthful shelters. Many neighborhoods and communities have resisted plans to open large shelters or even smaller residences for the homeless, often raising the familiar cry of "Not in my backyard!" The major federal program intended to assist the homeless is the McKinney Homeless Assistance Act, passed in 1987. This act authorizes federal aid for emergency food, shelter, physical and mental health care, job training, and education for homeless children and adults. Approximately $600 to $800 million in funds are distributed annually to about 100 community-based service organizations (HUD 1999).

According to a report by the National Law Center on Homelessness and Poverty (1996), there has been a growing trend in the 1990s toward the adoption of anti-homeless public policies and the "criminalization" of homeless people. In 1995 alone, at least 29 cities enacted curbs on panhandling, sitting on sidewalks, standing near banks at automated teller machines, or other behavior sometimes evident among the homeless. At the same time, more and more policymakers—especially conservative officials—have advocated cutbacks in government funding for the homeless and argued that voluntary associations and religious organizations should assume a more important role in addressing the problem of homelessness.

By the late 1990s, the availability of low-rent housing had reached the lowest levels since surveys began in 1970. Despite occasional media spotlights on the homeless and the booming economy of the 1990s, affordable housing has become harder to find. Two out of three low-income renters receive no housing allowance, and most spend a disproportionately large share of their income to maintain their shelter. Research shows that this worsening of affordable housing stems from a substantial drop in the number of unsubsidized low-cost rental housing units in the private market and a growing number of low-income renter households. Meanwhile, federally funded rental assistance has failed to keep pace with the need (Daskal 1998).

Developing nations have special problems. They have understandably given highest priority to economic productivity as measured by jobs with living wages. Unfortunately, even the most ambitious economic and social programs may be overwhelmed by minor currency fluctuations, a drop in the value of a nation's major export, or an influx of refugees from a neighboring country. Some of the reforms implemented have included promoting private (as opposed to government-controlled) housing markets, allowing dwellings to be places of business as well, and loosening restrictions on building materials. All three of these short-term solutions have shortcomings. Private housing markets invite exploitation; mixed residential/commercial use may only cause good housing to deteriorate faster; and the use of marginal building materials leaves low-income residential areas more vulnerable to calamities such as floods, fires, and earthquakes. Large-scale rental housing under government supervision, the typical solution in North America and Europe, has been successful only in economically advanced city-states like Hong Kong and Singapore (Strassman 1998).

In sum, homeless people both in the United States and abroad are not getting the shelter they need, and they lack the political clout to corral the attention of policymakers.

Let's Discuss

1. Have you ever worked as a volunteer in a shelter or soup kitchen? If so, were you surprised by the type of people who lived or ate there? Has anyone you know ever had to move into a shelter?

2. Is gentrification of low-income housing a problem where you live? Have you ever had difficulty finding an affordable place to live?

3. What kind of assistance is available to homeless people in the community where you live? Does the help come from the government, from private charities, or both? What about housing assistance for people with low incomes, such as rent subsidies—is it available?

Summary

A *community* is a spatial or political unit of social organization that gives people a sense of belonging, based either on shared residence in a particular place or on a common identity. This chapter explains how communities originated and analyzes the process of urbanization from both the functionalist and conflict perspectives. It describes various types of communities, including the central cities, the suburbs, and rural communities, and it introduces the new concept of an electronic community. The chapter closes with an analysis of public policy toward the community of the homeless.

1. Stable communities began to develop when people stayed in one place to cultivate crops; surplus production enabled cities to emerge.

2. Gideon Sjoberg identified three preconditions of city life: advanced technology in both agricultural and nonagricultural areas, a favorable physical environment, and a well-developed social organization.

3. There are important differences between the *preindustrial city*, the *industrial city*, and the *postindustrial city*.

4. Urbanization is evident not only in the United States but throughout the world; by 1990, 43 percent of the world's population lived in urban areas.
5. The **urban ecological** approach is functionalist because it emphasizes that different elements in urban areas contribute to stability.
6. Drawing on conflict theory, **new urban sociology** considers the interplay of a community's political and economic interests as well as the impact of the global economy on communities in the United States and other countries.
7. Many urban residents are immigrants from other nations and tend to live in ethnic neighborhoods.
8. In the last three decades, cities have confronted an overwhelming array of economic and social problems, including crime, unemployment, and the deterioration of schools and public transit systems.

9. Suburbanization has been the most dramatic population trend in the United States throughout the twentieth century. In recent decades, suburbs have witnessed increasing diversity in race and ethnicity.
10. Farming, mining, and logging have all been in decline in the rural communities of the United States.
11. Technological advances like electronic information networks are changing the economy, the distribution of population, and even the concept of community. Online communities can both strengthen social ties in rural cities like Blacksburg, Virginia, and undermine the economies of the central cities.
12. Soaring housing costs, unemployment, cutbacks in public assistance, and rapid population growth have all contributed to rising homelessness around the world. Most social policy is directed toward sending the homeless to large shelters.

Critical Thinking Questions

1. How can the functionalist and conflict perspectives be used in examining the growing interest among policymakers in privatizing public services presently offered by cities and other communities?
2. How has your home community (your city, town, or neighborhood) changed over the years you have lived there? Have there been significant changes in the community's economic base and in its racial and ethnic profile? Have the community's social

problems intensified or lessened over time? Is unemployment currently a major problem? What are the community's future prospects as it approaches the twenty-first century?
3. Imagine that you have been asked to study the issue of homelessness in the largest city in your state. How might you draw on surveys, observation research, experiments, and existing sources to help you study this issue?

Key Terms

Community A spatial or political unit of social organization that gives people a sense of belonging, based either on shared residence in a particular place or on a common identity. (501)

Concentric-zone theory A theory of urban growth devised by Ernest Burgess that sees growth in terms of a series of rings radiating from the central business district. (506)

Defended neighborhood A neighborhood that residents identify through defined community borders and a perception that adjacent areas are geographically separate and socially different. (511)

Gentrification The resettlement of low-income city neighborhoods by prosperous families and business firms. (520)

Human ecology An area of study concerned with the interrelationships between people and their spatial setting and physical environment. (506)

Industrial city A city characterized by relatively large size, open competition, an open class system, and elaborate specialization in the manufacturing of goods. (503)

Megalopolis A densely populated area containing two or more cities and their surrounding suburbs. (504)

Multiple-nuclei theory A theory of urban growth developed by Harris and Ullman that views growth as emerging from many centers of development, each of which may reflect a particular urban need or activity. (507)

New urban sociology An approach to urbanization that considers the interplay of local, national, and worldwide forces and their effect on local space, with special emphasis on the impact of global economic activity. (508)

Postindustrial city   A city in which global finance and the electronic flow of information dominate the economy. (503)

Preindustrial city   A city with only a few thousand people living within its borders and characterized by a relatively closed class system and limited mobility. (502)

Squatter settlements   Areas occupied by the very poor on the fringes of cities, in which housing is often constructed by the settlers themselves from discarded material. (506)

Suburb   According to the Census Bureau, any territory within a metropolitan area that is not included in the central city. (513)

Urban ecology   An area of study that focuses on the interrelationships between people and their environment in urban areas. (506)

Urbanism   A term used by Wirth to describe distinctive patterns of social behavior evident among city residents. (503)

World systems analysis   A view of the global economic system that sees it as divided between certain industrialized nations and the developing countries that they control and exploit. (508)

Zoning laws   Legal provisions stipulating land use and architectural design of housing, often employed as a means of keeping racial minorities and low-income people out of suburban areas. (515)

Additional Readings

BOOKS

Dunier, Mitchell. 1999. *Sidewalk.* New York: Farrar, Straus and Giroux. Joined by photographer Ovie Carter, a sociologist looks at street life in New York's Greenwich Village, with a special focus on the experiences of sidewalk vendors.

Mitchell, William J. 1999. *E-topia.* Cambridge: MIT Press. A futuristic view of what the world's cities might look like in an age of cybernetics. Written by a dean of architecture, the book predicts a variety of cityscapes based on different cultural traditions, all unified by a global digital network. Visit the author's website at (http://mitpress.mit.edu/e-books/City_of_Bits/) for his companion book *City of Bits* (Cambridge: MIT Press, 1996).

Phillips, E. Barbara. 1996. *City Lights: Urban–Suburban Life in the Global Society.* New York: Oxford University Press. Drawing upon all the social sciences, a sociologist looks at the urban–global network of the twentieth century and at alternative urban–suburban futures.

Van Vliet, Willem, ed. 1998. *The Encyclopedia of Housing.* Thousand Oaks, CA: Sage Publications. This reference book has more than 500 entries arranged alphabetically from "abandonment" to "zoning."

JOURNALS

Among the journals that focus on community issues are *Journal of Urban Affairs* (founded in 1979), *Rural Sociology* (1936), *Urban Affairs Quarterly* (1965), *Urban Anthropology* (1972), and *Urban Studies* (1964).

Internet Connection

Note: While all the URLs listed were current as of the printing of this book, these sites often change. Please check our website (http://www.mhhe.com/schaefer) for updates.

1. Have you ever wondered what causes homelessness—what social forces and life circumstances separate those who have shelter from those who don't? Hobson's Choice (**http://www. realchangenews.org/hobson_intro.html**) is an online game that helps people understand this complex issue better. At the start of the game, players find themselves in a particular economic situation and are asked to make choices, each of which leads to a new situation or problem. Log on to the site and play the game four times.

   (a) In how many games were you able to escape homelessness? In how many did you find yourself on the street, without shelter?

   (b) Reflect on the choices you made. Was there a pattern to them? Which situations seemed to lead toward homelessness and which away from it?

   (c) Did you feel frustrated by the results of any of your choices? What choices would you have made differently, and why?

   (d) What is a Hobson's choice, and why it is applicable to the issue of homelessness?

   (e) What do you think are the most important social causes of homelessness? What can be done, in practical terms, to alleviate the worldwide need for shelter?

2. Gated communities have both advantages and disadvantages. Visit (**http://www.yahoo.com**) and search for the phrase "gated community." From the list of gated communities you obtain, choose two and link to their home pages. Answer the following questions for each, comparing the two communities.

   (a) Where are the two communities located? Do they appear to be geared toward a specific group in terms of age, social class, or religion? What imagery or symbolism does the name of each community convey?

   (b) What kind of housing does each community offer? How large are the houses, condominiums, or townhomes in each, and how much do they cost?

   (c) What amenities does each community offer— golf course, tennis courts, and so on?

   (d) How does a gated community differ from communities in other environments, especially urban areas?

   (e) Would you like to live in a gated community? Why or why not?

   (f) What is your opinion of Evan McKenzie's concept of "privatopia" (see Box 19-2)?

POPULATION AND
THE ENVIRONMENT

In India, pollution is becoming a controversial political issue. This billboard graphically suggests the harmful effect of pollution on public health.

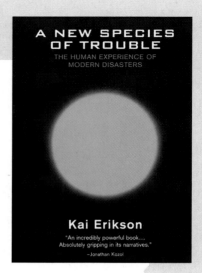

O ver the past twenty years, research errands of one kind or another have taken me to a number of communities still stunned by the effects of a recent disaster. These include a valley in West Virginia known as Buffalo Creek, devastated by a fearsome flood; an Ojibwa Indian reserve in Canada called Grassy Narrows, plagued by contamination of the waterways along which members of the band had lived for centuries; a town in South Florida named Immokalee, where three hundred migrant farm workers were robbed of the only money most of them had ever saved; a group of houses in Colorado known as East Swallow, threatened by vapors from silent pools of gasoline that had gathered in the ground below; and the neighborhoods surrounding Three Mile Island.

In one respect, at least, these events were altogether different. A flood. An act of larceny. A toxic poisoning. A gasoline spill. A nuclear accident. My assignment in each of those cases was to learn enough about the people who thought they had been damaged by the blow to appear on their behalf in a court of law, so each was a separate research effort, and each resulted in a separate research report.

In another respect, though, it was clear from the beginning that those scenes of trouble had much in common. I was asked to visit them in the first place, obviously, because the persons who issued the invitations thought they could see resemblances there. And just as obviously, I was drawn to them because they touched a corresponding set of curiosities and preoccupations in me. Moreover, common themes seemed to come into focus as I moved from one place to another, so that those separate happenings (and the separate stories told of them) began to fuse into a more inclusive whole. One of the excitements of sociological work in general is to watch general patterns—dim and shapeless at first—emerge from a wash of seemingly unconnected details. . . . *(Erikson 1994:11–12)* ■

In this passage from *A New Species of Trouble,* Kai Erikson explains how he brought his sociological imagination to bear on five seemingly unrelated disasters. Each, he realized, had been caused not by natural forces, but by human disregard for the natural world or for other human beings. But while ignorance or negligence is often thought to be at the bottom of such catastrophes, Erikson saw a larger, more sweeping process at work. Consumerism and rapid increases in population, he thought, lay at the bottom of these calamities. Economically, people and their ever-increasing wants and needs had begun to outstrip the capacity of the environment to tolerate their encroachments.

This chapter takes a sociological overview of world population and some related environmental issues. We will begin with Thomas Robert Malthus's controversial analysis of population trends and Karl Marx's critical response to it. A brief overview of world population history follows. We'll pay particular attention to the current problem of overpopulation, and the prospects for and potential consequences of stable population growth in the United States. We'll see, too, how population growth fuels the migration of large numbers of people from one area of the world to another.

Later in the chapter, we will examine the environmental problems facing the world as we enter the twenty-first century and will draw on the functionalist and conflict perspectives to better understand environmental issues. It is important not to oversimplify the relationship between population and the environment. Rising population, in itself, does not necessarily destroy the environment, while stable population growth alone is no guarantee of healthful air, water, or land. Nevertheless, as will be evident in the second half of the chapter and in the social policy section on environmentalism, increases in population can strain our environmental resources and present difficult choices for policymakers. ∎

Demography: The Study of Population

The study of population issues engages the attention of both natural and social scientists. The biologist explores the nature of reproduction and casts light on factors that affect *fertility* (the level of reproduction among women of childbearing age). The medical pathologist examines and analyzes trends in the causes of death. Geographers, historians, and psychologists also have distinctive contributions to make to our understanding of population. Sociologists, more than these other researchers, focus on the *social* factors that influence population rates and trends.

In their study of population issues, sociologists are keenly aware that various elements of population—such as fertility, *mortality* (the amount of death), and migration— are profoundly affected by the norms, values, and social patterns of a society. Fertility is influenced by people's age of entry into sexual unions and by their use of contraception—both of which, in turn, reflect the social and religious values that guide a particular culture. Mortality is shaped by a nation's level of nutrition, acceptance of immunization, and provisions for sanitation, as well as its general commitment to health care

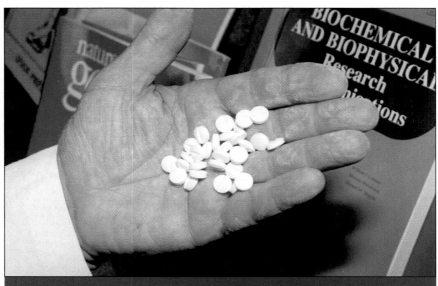

Fertility is influenced by the use of contraceptives, which is in turn affected by a population's social and religious values. For years pro-life groups blocked the distribution of this abortion pill, RU486, in the United States.

and health education. Migration from one country to another can depend on marital and kinship ties, the relative degree of racial and religious tolerance in various societies, and people's evaluations of employment opportunities.

Demography is the scientific study of population. It draws on several components of population, including size, composition, and territorial distribution, to understand the social consequences of population (see Figure 20-1). Demographers study geographical variations and historical trends in their effort to develop population forecasts. They also analyze the structure of a population—the age, gender, race, and ethnicity of its members. A key figure in this type of analysis was Thomas Malthus.

Malthus's Thesis and Marx's Response

The Reverend Thomas Robert Malthus (1766–1834) was educated at Cambridge University and spent his life teaching history and political economy. He strongly criticized two major institutions of his time—the church and slavery—yet his most significant legacy for contemporary scholars is his still-controversial *Essays on the Principle of Population,* published in 1798.

Essentially, Malthus held that the world's population was growing more rapidly than the available food supply. Malthus argued that food supply increases in an arithmetic progression (1, 2, 3, 4, and so on), whereas population expands by a geometric progression (1, 2, 4, 8, and so

The Reverend Thomas Robert Malthus suggested that the world's population was growing more rapidly than the available food supply.

on). According to his analysis, the gap between food supply and population will continue to grow over time. Even though the food supply will increase, it will not increase nearly enough to meet the needs of an expanding world population.

Malthus proposed population control as an answer to the gap between rising population and food supply, yet he explicitly denounced artificial means of birth control because they were not sanctioned by religion. For Malthus, the appropriate way to control population was to postpone marriage. He argued that couples must take responsibility for the number of children they choose to bear; without such restraint, the world would face widespread hunger, poverty, and misery (Malthus et al. 1960, original edition 1824; Petersen 1979).

Karl Marx strongly criticized Malthus's views on population. Marx saw the nature of economic relations in Europe's industrial societies as the central problem. He could not accept the Malthusian notion that rising world population, rather than capitalism, was the cause of social ills. In Marx's opinion, there was no special relationship between world population figures and the supply of resources (including food). If society were well ordered, increases in population should lead to greater wealth, not to hunger and misery.

Of course, Marx did not believe that capitalism operated under these ideal conditions. He maintained that capitalism devoted its resources to the financing of buildings and tools rather than to more equitable distribution of food, housing, and other necessities of life. Marx's work is important to the study of population because he linked overpopulation to the distribution of resources—a topic that will be taken up again later in this chapter. His concern with the writings of Malthus also testifies to the importance of population in political and economic affairs.

The insights of Malthus and Marx regarding population issues have come together in what is termed the *neo-Malthusian view.* Best exemplified by the work of Paul Ehrlich (1968; Ehrlich and Ehrlich 1990), author of *The Population Bomb,* neo-Malthusians agree with Malthus that world population growth is outstretching natural resources. However, in contrast to the British theorist, they insist that birth control measures are needed to regulate population increases. Neo-Malthusians have a Marxist flavor in their condemnation of developed nations that, despite their low birthrates, consume a disproportionately large share of world resources. While rather pessimistic about the future, these theorists stress that birth control and sensible use of resources are essential responses to rising world population (Tierney 1990; Weeks 1996; for a critique, see Commoner 1971).

Research in Action

20-1 The Demography of Islamic Nations

The 47 nations in which Islam is the dominant religion are the fastest-growing group of countries in the world. Currently, nearly one in every five human beings is Muslim. At present rates of growth, the world's Islamic population of about 1.1 billion in 1995 could almost double to 1.9 billion before the year 2020.

Sociologist and demographer John Weeks points out that "although Islam is a proselytizing religion, its proportionate increase in the modern world is much more a result of natural increase (the excess of births over deaths) than it is the conversion of non-Moslems to the Islamic faith." The Islamic nations report higher-than-average fertility, higher-than-average mortality, and rapid rates of population growth. These countries are viewed as being in the early

> Currently, nearly one in every five human beings is Muslim.

stages of demographic transition from high to low birth and death rates.

The total fertility rate (TFR) of the Islamic nations is 6.0 projected births per woman, compared with 4.5 births in other developing nations and only 1.7 births per woman in the developed nations. Islamic countries are growing at an average of 2.8 percent per year, or 22 percent faster than the world's other developing nations.

Weeks reviewed the population policies of these Islamic countries and found that there was considerable diversity in their positions regarding reproductive behavior and population growth. About half the governments of the Islamic nations reported that they were satisfied with their current rates of population growth; 40 percent stated that their current rates of growth were too high, whereas 10 percent indicated that their

growth rates were too low.

Some Islamic nations have implemented "pronatalist" policies to increase their population, only to replace those policies later with family planning programs. In 1989, Iranian officials began to encourage parents to space their children and limit themselves to three children per family. The results have been dramatic: Total fertility rates are dropping, and most Iranian women have begun to plan their families.

The diversity in the positions of Islamic nations regarding population growth is underscored in a report issued in 1992 by the Population Crisis Committee. Saudi Arabia was ranked as one of the five countries with the worst family planning records for 1991 (as was the United States), while Morocco was praised for achieving dramatic increases in contraceptive use. Other studies have included Indonesia, Turkey, Egypt, and Tunisia among the Islamic nations that have made substantial progress in promoting contraceptive use and reducing fertility rates.

Bangladesh, the world's most densely populated country and one of the largest Islamic nations, is often viewed by population experts as a notable success story. The fertility rate in Bangladesh has decreased from 7.4 births per woman in 1975 to less than 3.3 births in 1999. Nevertheless, even observers generally supportive of population

Women's right to reproductive health was an important issue at the International Conference on Population and Development in Cairo, Egypt, in 1994. These participants were discussing materials used to educate women about the reproductive process.

control have criticized Bangladesh for encouraging the sterilization of women (sometimes under unhygienic conditions) rather than less permanent methods of birth control. Even with its dramatic reduction of the fertility rate, Bangladesh could have as many as 250 million people by 2080 living in a country the size of Wisconsin.

Let's Discuss

1. In your own experience, what are the advantages of family planning techniques like the spacing of children? Do you know any families—perhaps your own—in which the children suffered because they were born too close together?

2. What other reasons can you think of for family planning? List the benefits from the point of view of the children, the parents, and society as a whole.

Sources: J. Anderson 1994; Barrett 1996; de Sherbinin 1990; Hartmann 1994; Haub and Cornelius 1999; MacFarquhar 1996; *Ms.* 1992; Omran and Roudi 1993; Roudi 1999; Weeks 1988:5, 12–13, 47.

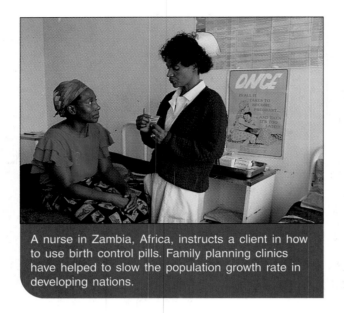

A nurse in Zambia, Africa, instructs a client in how to use birth control pills. Family planning clinics have helped to slow the population growth rate in developing nations.

terms as the "population bomb" or the "population explosion." Such striking language is not surprising, given the staggering increases in world population during the last two centuries (refer back to Table 20-1). Indeed, the

population of our planet rose from 1 billion around the year 1800 to 5.6 billion by 1999 (Haub and Cornelius 1999).

By the middle 1970s, demographers had observed a slight decline in the growth rate of many developing nations. These countries were still experiencing population increases, yet their *rates* of increase had declined as death rates could not go much lower and birthrates began to fall. It appears that family planning efforts have been instrumental in this demographic change. Beginning in the 1960s, governments in certain developing nations sponsored or supported campaigns to encourage family planning. For example, in good part as the result of government-sponsored birth control campaigns, Thailand's total fertility rate fell from 6.1 births per woman in 1970 to only 2.0 in 1998. And China's strict one-child policy resulted in a negative growth rate in some urban areas: see Box 20-2 on page 538.

Through the efforts of many governments (among them the United States) and private agencies (among them Planned Parenthood), the fertility rates of many developing countries have declined. However, some critics, reflecting a conflict orientation, have questioned why the United States and other industrialized nations are so en-

FIGURE 20-3

Population Structure of Sub-Saharan Africa and the United States, Mid-1990s

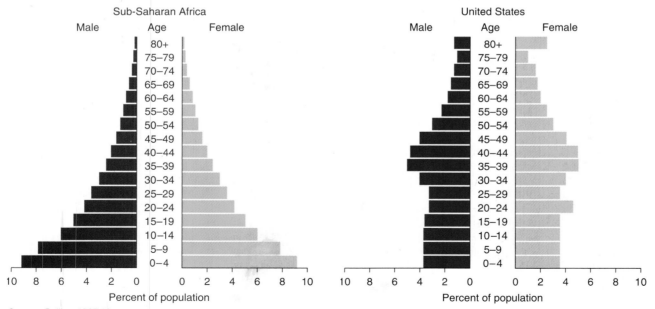

Source: Goliber 1997:10.

This figure shows the populations of sub-Saharan Africa (which includes such countries as Kenya, Nigeria, Uganda, Congo, and South Africa) and the United States. Many of the developing countries of sub-Saharan Africa have high birthrates, but mortality takes its toll quickly. The United States shows serious mortality only at older ages.

thusiastic about population control in the developing world. In line with Marx's response to Malthus, they argue that large families and even population growth are not the causes of hunger and misery. Rather, the unjust economic domination by the developed states of the world results in an unequal distribution of world resources and in widespread poverty in exploited developing nations (Fornos 1997).

Even if family planning efforts are successful in reducing fertility rates, the momentum toward growing world population is well established. The developing nations face the prospect of continued population growth, since a substantial proportion of their population is approaching childbearing years. This is evident in Figure 20-3, comparing the population pyramids of sub-Saharan Africa and the United States.

A *population pyramid* is a special type of bar chart that distributes the population by gender and age; it is generally used to illustrate the population structure of a society. As Figure 20-3 shows, a substantial portion of the population of sub-Saharan Africa (which includes such countries as Kenya, Nigeria, Uganda, Zaire, and South Africa) consists of children under the age of 15, with their childbearing years still to come. Thus, the built-in momentum for population growth is much greater in sub-Saharan Africa (and in many developing countries in other parts of the world) than in western Europe or the United States.

Consider, also, population data for India, which in 1999 had a population of 987 million. Demographers have projected that, even if India's fertility rates level off to rates near those of North America and Europe, the nation's population will still reach 1.4 billion by the year 2025. That figure is higher than the current combined total for all of North America, South America, Africa, and Europe. Sometime between the years 2030 and 2035 India's population will surpass China's. The substantial momentum for growth built into India's age structure means that the nation will face a staggering increase in population in the coming decades—even if its birthrate declines sharply (Constable 1999; Haub and Cornelius 1999).

Population growth is not a problem in all industrialized nations. A handful of countries are adopting policies that *encourage* growth. One of them is Japan, where the total fertility rate has fallen sharply. Nevertheless, a global perspective underscores the serious consequences that could result from continued population growth.

A tragic new factor has emerged in the last 15 years that will restrict worldwide population growth: the spread of AIDS. Presently, pp. 134–38 about 31 million people around the world are infected with the HIV virus. According to the United Nations, there are at least 28 developing countries (with at least 1 million population) where the number of HIV-infected adults is very high. Of the 28 countries under study, 24 are in Africa; the others are India, Thailand, Brazil, and Haiti. AIDS has lowered the aggregate life expectancy of the 24 African countries by six years. The epidemic has its greatest mortality impact in otherwise relatively robust years of life. It is estimated that in the five most affected countries, mortality during 1985–2005 will increase by 160 percent in the age group 35–49 years (compared with 33 percent for the population in general). These are exactly the ages that can contribute most to a society's economic development (United Nations Population Division 1998a).

AIDS has had a dramatic impact on the death rates in some developing countries, particularly in Africa.

20-2 Population Policy in China

In a residential district in Shanghai, a member of the local family planning committee knocks on the door of a childless couple. Why, she inquires, have they not started a family? Such a question would have been unthinkable a generation earlier, when family planning officials, in an attempt to avoid a looming population explosion, sometimes resorted to sterilization to enforce the government rule of one child per family. Since then, Shanghai's birthrate has fallen so far it is now lower than the death rate—a situation that has left the city short of workers. To remedy the shortage, the government has quietly begun to grant exceptions to the one-child policy to adults who are only children themselves. But the new leniency hasn't reversed the decline in the birthrate, as officials were hoping, for government propaganda stressing the economic benefits of fewer children seems to have changed the public's attitude toward childbearing. Stopping Chinese couples from having babies may be difficult, muses Jin Zuegong, a member of the Municipal Planning Commission in Shanghai, but persuading them to have babies may be even more difficult.

Not just Shanghai, but all of China is grappling with the unintended consequences of the draconian population control measures instituted in 1979. Nationwide, China's negative birthrate is straining its productive potential. Though employers hire rural workers to fill jobs left vacant in the shrinking cities, the relocation of rural workers only strains the economy of the

> Not just Shanghai, but all of China is grappling with the unintended consequences of the draconian population control measures instituted in 1979.

farming areas they desert. And the negative birthrate is compromising the ability of the younger generation to provide for the old—a crucial function in a country that has no old-age pension system. One of the most challenging results of the one-child policy is the so-called one-two-four household, in which a single child supports both parents and all four grandparents. That is, if a Chi-

nese woman has only one child, that child may someday have to take care of as many as six old people, explains Dr. Li Liang. And if that child marries another only child, together they may need to support as many as 12 elderly.

Chinese families are beset, too, by the unforeseen results of their attempts to circumvent the one-child policy. In the past, in an effort to ensure that their one child would be a male capable of perpetuating the family line, many couples chose to abort female fetuses, or quietly allowed female infants to die of neglect. As a result, China's sex ratio at birth (the ratio of male newborns to female newborns) is now about 114 to 100—well above the normal rate of 105 or 106 to 100. This difference in birthrates translates into 1.7 million fewer female births per year than normal—and down the line, to many fewer childbearers than normal.

In 1995 the Chinese government, alarmed by the long-term implications of sex-selected abortion and infanticide, outlawed gender screening of unborn children except when medically necessary. The government also included measures aimed at

Sources: Cardarelli 1996; Chow and Zhao 1995; Farley 1997; Longman 1999; Reuters 1995; Riley 1996; Rosenthal 1999; Wiseman 2000.

Fertility Patterns in the United States

During the last four decades, the United States and other industrial nations have passed through two different patterns of population growth—the first marked by high fertility and rapid growth (stage II in the theory of demographic transition), the second marked by declining fertility and little growth (stage III). Sociologists are keenly aware of the social impact of these fertility patterns.

The Baby Boom

The most recent period of high fertility in the United States has often been referred to as the *baby boom*. During World War II, large numbers of military personnel were separated from their spouses, but when they returned, the

annual number of births began to rise dramatically. Still, the baby boom was not a return to the large families common in the 1800s. In fact, there was only a slight increase in the proportion of couples having three or more children. The boom resulted from a striking decrease in the number of childless marriages and one-child families. Although a peak was reached in 1957, the nation maintained a relatively high birthrate of over 20 live births per 1,000 population until 1964. In 1999, by contrast, the birthrate was 15 live births per 1,000 population—or 30 percent lower than in 1964 (Bureau of the Census 1975, 1999a).

It would be a mistake to attribute the baby boom solely to the return home of large numbers of soldiers. High wages and general prosperity during the post–World War II period encouraged many married couples to have children and purchase homes. In addi-

This Chinese billboard advocates the one-child family. Note that the single, happy child is a daughter—an attempt to counter the traditional preference for male children.

come the traditional preference for boys, and the resulting negative effect on the birthrate. Still, research suggests that parental attitudes toward female children may be changing. In one study, researchers found that China's one-child policy not only increased the value Chinese parents place on their children, but that the gender of the child made no difference in parents' estimation of that value.

Chinese women have a long way to go before they equal men in status, however. Like women everywhere, they have borne the brunt of the economic dislocation caused by recent market reforms and the redistribution of rural farmland. In privatized government facto-

ries, their need for maternity benefits and child care now limits their employment opportunities; on rural farms, they struggle to cope in their husbands' absence. The female suicide rate in rural China is now the highest in the world, surpassing the rate for males. Experts think this alarming statistic reflects a fundamental lack of self-esteem among rural Chinese women. The social patterns of centuries, unlike birthrates, cannot be changed in a generation.

Let's Discuss

1. Try to imagine life in a society that is so heavily populated, basic resources like food, water, and living space are running short. Does the government of such a society have a right to sterilize people who do not voluntarily limit the size of their families? Why or why not?

2. The Chinese government's one-child policy seems to have backfired. What other policies might have worked better? Explain why.

improving the status of women in its new five-year plan. But those measures alone may not be enough to remedy the problem. Incentives, like improved educational opportunities for girls, may be needed to over-

tion, several sociologists—as well as feminist author Betty Friedan (1963)—have noted that there were pervasive pressures on women during the 1950s to marry and become mothers and homemakers (Bouvier 1980).

Stable Population Growth

Although the total fertility rate of the United States has remained low over the last two decades, the nation continues to grow in size because of two factors: the momentum built into our age structure by the postwar population boom and the continued high rates of immigration. Because of the upsurge of births beginning in the 1950s, there are now many more people in their childbearing years than in older age groups (where most deaths occur). This growth of population represents a "demographic

echo" of the baby boom generation, many of whom are now parents. Consequently, the number of people born each year in the United States continues to exceed the number who die. In addition, the nation allows a large number of immigrants to enter each year; these immigrants currently account for between one-fourth and one-third of annual growth.

Despite these trends, in the 1980s and early 1990s, some analysts projected that there would be relatively low fertility levels and moderate net migration over the coming decades. As a result, it seemed possible that the United States might reach *zero population growth (ZPG)*. ZPG is the state of a population in which the number of births plus immigrants equals the number of deaths plus emigrants. Thirty countries, most of them in Europe, are now at or approaching ZPG. In the recent past, although some nations have achieved ZPG, it has been relatively short-lived.

However, given the current international concern over world population, more nations may attempt to maintain ZPG in the early twenty-first century (Kent 1999; McFalls 1998; McFalls et al. 1984; Population Reference Bureau 1978).

What would a society with stable population growth be like? In demographic terms, it would be quite different from the United States of the 1990s. There would be relatively equal numbers of people in each age group, and the median age of the population might perhaps be as high as 38 in 2050 (compared with 35 in 1997). As a result, the population pyramid of the United States (as shown in Figure 20-3) would look more like a rectangle (Bureau of the Census 1999a:14).

There would also be a much larger proportion of older people, especially age 75 and over. They would place a greater demand on the nation's social service programs and health care institutions. On a more positive note, the economy would be less volatile under ZPG, since the number of entrants into the paid labor force would remain stable. ZPG would also lead to changes in family life. With fertility rates declining, women would devote fewer years to child rearing and to the social roles of motherhood; the proportion of married women entering the labor force would continue to rise (Spengler 1978; Weeks 1999).

According to the latest Census Bureau projections, however, the United States is *not* moving toward ZPG. Instead, the nation's population is growing faster than was expected. Previous projections indicated that the U.S. population would stabilize between 290 and 300 million by the middle of the next century, but demographers now believe that by 2050, the population of the United States will reach 391 million.

Why the new projections? The Bureau of the Census has revised its assumptions about the three basic components of a nation's population: fertility, net immigration, and mortality. Overall, U.S. fertility is on the rise because of the fertility rates among African Americans, Hispanics, and Asian Americans. Even though the fertility rates among these racial and ethnic minorities are expected to moderate, their proportion of the national population is increasing. Second, immigration rates are expected to remain high (see the social policy section in Chapter 10). Today, about one-third of the nation's population growth results from net immigration (that is, the number of immigrants entering the United States minus the number of emigrants leaving). By the year 2050, 43 percent of overall population growth will be due to immigration. Finally, despite the impact of the AIDS crisis, the nation's mortality rate is expected to decline while life expectancy will increase—from the current figure of 76 years to 82.6 years by 2050 (J. Day 1993; Pollard 1994).

Population and Migration

Along with births and deaths, migration is one of the three factors affecting population growth or decline. The term *migration* refers to relatively permanent movement of people with the purpose of changing their place of residence (Prehn 1991). Migration usually describes movement over a sizable distance, rather than from one side of a city to another.

As a social phenomenon, migration is fairly complex and results from a variety of factors. The most important tend to be economic—financial failure in the "old country" and a perception of greater economic opportunities and prosperity in the new homeland. Other factors that contribute to migration include racial and religious bigotry, dislike for prevailing political regimes, and desire to reunite one's family. All these forces combine to *push* some individuals out of their homelands and to *pull* them to areas believed to be more attractive.

International Migration

International migration—changes of residence across national boundaries—has been a significant force in redistributing the world's population during certain periods of history. For example, the composition of the United States has been significantly altered by immigrants who came here in the nineteenth and twentieth centuries. Their entry was encouraged or restricted by various immigration policies. pp. 281–83

As noted earlier, immigration into a country can become a significant factor in its population growth. In recent years, immigration has accounted for 20 to 30 percent of growth in the United States, which has led those troubled by population increases to join those opposed to an influx of foreigners in calling for serious restrictions on immigration. By contrast, however, many other countries are currently receiving a much higher proportion of immigrants. Over the last 10 years, more than 80 percent of population growth in Greece and Austria, and more than 40 percent in Canada and Australia, came from immigration (Bouvier and Grant 1994; P. Martin and Widgren 1996; Massey 1999).

In the last decade, immigration has become a controversial issue throughout much of Europe. Western Europe, in particular, has become a desirable destination for many individuals and families from former colonies or former communist-bloc countries who are fleeing the poverty, persecution, and warfare of their native lands. Currently, there are 20 million legal immigrants in western Europe, along with an estimated 2 million illegal immigrants. With the number of immigrants and refugees increasing at a time of widespread unemployment and

A street scene in Paris, in a neighborhood where many Arabic and African immigrants now live. Over the past decade, immigration has become a controversial issue in many parts of Europe.

transfers or because they believe that a particular region has better employment opportunities or a more desirable climate.

Although nations typically have laws and policies governing movement across their borders, the same is not true of internal movement. Generally, residents of a country are legally free to migrate from one locality to another. Of course, this is not the case in all nations; the Republic of South Africa historically restricted the movement of Blacks and other non-Whites through the system of segregation known as *apartheid* (refer back to Chapter 10).

We can identify three distinctive trends of recent internal migration within the United States:

1. *Suburbanization.* During the period 1980–1990, suburban counties grew in population by 14 percent while the total population of the United States rose by 10 percent. The proportion of the population living in central cities stayed constant at about one-third since 1950. Meanwhile, the share of the population living in nonmetropolitan areas declined from 44 percent in 1950 to 20 percent in 1994 (Bureau of the Census 1996b:38).

housing shortages, there has been a striking rise in antiforeign (and often openly racist) sentiment in Germany, France, and other countries. Right-wing forces in Germany (including members of the skinhead counterculture examined in Chapter 3) have mounted more than 3,500 attacks on foreigners in recent years. Immigrants from eastern Europe and Asia are often the targets, and there have been attacks as well on Germany's small Jewish community.

Developing countries in Asia and Africa are also encountering difficulties as thousands of displaced people seek assistance and asylum. For example, as of 1996, Bangladesh had received more than 300,000 refugees from Myanmar's Rohingya Muslim community; Jordan had taken in 250,000 to 300,000 Palestinians who had fled or been expelled from Kuwait; and Kenya had accepted more than 230,000 refugees fleeing war and famine in Ethiopia and Somalia. The political and economic problems of developing nations (refer back to Chapter 9) are only intensified by such massive migration under desperate conditions (Kushnick 1993; P. Martin and Widgren 1996).

Internal Migration

Migratory movements within societies can vary in important ways. In traditional societies, migration often represents a way of life, as people move to accommodate the changing availability of fertile soil and wild game. In industrial societies, people may relocate as a result of job

In Bangladesh, more than a million rural villagers—about half the country's population—have migrated to the capital city of Dhaka in search of jobs. Of all the factors that contribute to migration, the desire for greater economic opportunity is one of the most important.

2. *"Sunning of America."* There has been significant internal migration from the "snow belt" of the north central and northeastern states to the "sun belt" in the south and west. Since 1970, the sun belt has absorbed almost two-thirds of the population growth of the United States. Individuals and families move to the sun belt because of its expanding economy and desirable climate. Businesses are attracted by the comparatively inexpensive energy supplies, increased availability of labor, and relative weakness of labor unions. Since 1990, however, while internal migration to the south has remained high, migration to the west has lessened as the job boom in that region has ended (see Figure 20-4).

3. *Rural life rebound.* In the 1990s more than 71 percent of all nonmetropolitan counties gained in population. This migration to rural areas reversed a long-standing trend in internal migration in the United States. It reflected concerns about the quality of life in cities and suburbs, as well as the impact of technological advances that allow some people to work wherever they wish and rely on electronic communication to conduct business (K. Johnson 1999).

FIGURE 20-4

Where Americans Moved in the 1990s

Mapping Life NATIONWIDE

West +42,200

Northeast −2,799,815

Midwest −573,127

South +3,330,742

Note: Data for 1990–1998 were reported in 2000.

Source: Faber 2000.

The Environment

In December 1999 Julia Butterfly Hill, a 25-year-old environmental activist, agreed to climb down from the ancient redwood tree she had been living in for the past two years. Hill, who is passionately dedicated to preserving the redwoods of northern California, had braved storms, helicopters, and the privations of camping in the wild to reach a hard-won agreement with Pacific Lumber, the logging company that wanted to cut the tree down. Through the intervention of Senator Dianne Feinstein, the company had finally agreed to spare the tree and a buffer zone around it (Lappé 1999; *New York Times* 1999).

While most people would consider Hill's protest an extreme one, it demonstrated the lengths to which activists must go to reverse the wave of destruction humans have unleashed on the environment in recent centuries. With each passing year, we are learning more about the environmental damage caused by burgeoning population levels and consumption patterns. Though disasters like the ones sociologist Kai Erikson investigated are still comparatively rare, the superficial signs of despoliation can be found almost everywhere. Our air, our water, and our land are being polluted, whether we live in St. Louis, Mexico City, or Lagos, Nigeria.

Julia Butterfly Hill clings to the 200-foot-tall redwood tree she lived in for two years to keep a logging company from cutting it down.

Environmental Problems: An Overview

In recent decades, the world has witnessed serious environmental disasters. For example, Love Canal, near Niagara Falls in New York State, was declared a disaster area in 1978 because of chemical contamination. In the 1940s and 1950s, a chemical company had disposed of waste products on the site where a housing development and a school were subsequently built. The metal drums that held the chemical wastes eventually rusted out, and toxic chemicals with noxious odors began seeping into the residents' yards and basements. Subsequent investigations revealed that the chemical company knew as early as 1958 that toxic chemicals were seeping into homes and a school playground. After repeated protests in the late 1970s, 239 families living in Love Canal had to be relocated.

In 1986, a series of explosions set off a catastrophic nuclear reactor accident at Chernobyl, a part of Ukraine (in what was then the Soviet Union). This accident killed at least 32,000 people. Some 300,000 residents had to be evacuated, and the area became uninhabitable for 19 miles in any direction. High levels of radiation were found as far as 30 miles from the reactor site, and radioactivity levels were well above normal as far away as Sweden and Japan. According to one estimate, the Chernobyl accident and the resulting nuclear fallout may ultimately result in 100,000 excess cases of cancer worldwide (Shcherbak 1996).

While Love Canal, Chernobyl, and other environmental disasters understandably grab headlines, it is the silent, day-to-day deterioration of the environment that ultimately poses a devastating threat to humanity. It is impossible to examine all our environmental problems in detail, but three broad areas of concern stand out: air pollution, water pollution, and contamination of land.

Air Pollution

More than 1 billion people on the planet are exposed to potentially health-damaging levels of air pollution (World Resources Institute 1998). Unfortunately, in cities around the world, residents have come to accept smog and polluted air as "normal." Air pollution in urban areas is caused primarily by emissions from automobiles and secondarily by emissions from electric power plants and heavy industries. Urban smog not only limits visibility;

it can lead to health problems as uncomfortable as eye irritation and as deadly as lung cancer. Such problems are especially severe in developing countries. The World Health Organization estimates that up to 700,000 premature deaths *per year* could be prevented if pollutants were brought down to safer levels (Carty 1999).

We are making strides. Southern California in 1998 had three times the population and four times the number of vehicles as in 1955, yet the air was much safer. The improvement comes primarily from a law requiring new cars to be fitted with air pollution control devices beginning in 1963 and the 1970 Clean Air Act, which established minimum air quality standards for cities and industry. While these advances did require some behavioral changes, they relied for the most part on new technology. People are capable of changing their behavior, but they are also unwilling to make such changes permanent. For example, during the 1984 Olympics in Los Angeles, residents were asked to carpool and stagger work hours to relieve traffic congestion and improve the quality of air the athletes would breathe. These changes resulted in a remarkable 12 percent drop in ozone levels. However, when the Olympians left, people reverted to their normal behavior and the ozone levels climbed back up (Nussbaum 1998).

Water Pollution

Throughout the United States, streams, rivers, and lakes have been polluted through dumping of waste materials by both industries and local governments. Consequently, many bodies of water have become unsafe for drinking, fishing, and swimming. Around the world, the pollution of the oceans has become a growing concern. Such pollution results regularly from waste dumping and is made worse by fuel leaks from shipping and occasional oil spills. In a dramatic accident in 1989, the oil tanker *Exxon Valdez* ran aground in Prince William Sound, Alaska. The tanker's cargo of 11 million gallons of crude oil was lost in the sound and washed onto the shore, contaminating 1,285 miles of shoreline. About 11,000 people joined in a cleanup effort that cost over $2 billion.

Contamination of Land

Love Canal made it clear that land can be seriously contaminated by industrial dumping of hazardous wastes and chemicals. In another noteworthy case of contamination, unpaved roads in Times Beach, Missouri, were sprayed to control dust in 1971 with an oil that contained dioxin. This highly toxic chemical is a by-product of the manufacture of herbicides and other chemicals. After the health dangers of dioxin became evident, the entire community of 2,800 people was relocated (at a cost of $33

Fish poisoned by a deadly cyanide spill lie on the bank of the Tisa River in Yugoslavia. Throughout the world, industrial pollutants have rendered many water bodies unsafe for fishing, drinking, or swimming.

million) and the town of Times Beach was shut down in 1985.

A significant part of land contamination comes from the tremendous demand for landfills to handle the nation's waste. Recycling programs aimed at reducing the need for landfills are perhaps the most visible aspect of environmentalism. How successful have such programs been? In 1980, about 10 percent of urban waste was recycled; the proportion increased steadily throughout the 1980s, but started to level off at about 29 percent in 1998. Experts are beginning to revise their goals for recycling campaigns, which now appear overambitious. Yet interestingly, a new way to be green has developed: the Internet. Over-the-Net commercial transactions allow the downloading of new software, reducing the need for wasteful packaging and shipping materials, including fuel for delivery trucks. And the availability of e-mail and electronic networking encourages people to work at home rather than contribute to the pollution caused by commuting (Belsie 2000; Booth 2000).

What are the basic causes of our growing environmental problems? Neo-Malthusians such as Paul Ehrlich and Anne Erhlich (P. Ehrlich 1968; P. Ehrlich and Ehrlich 1990) see world population growth as the central factor in environmental deterioration. They argue that population control is essential in preventing widespread starvation and environmental decay. Barry Commoner (1971, 1990), a biologist, counters that the primary cause of environmental ills is the increasing use of technological innovations that are destructive to the world's environment—among them plastics, detergents, synthetic fibers, pesticides, herbicides, and chemical fertilizers. Sociologist Allan Schnaiberg (1994) is critical of both these approaches. He argues that those who own and control the means of production in advanced capitalist societies have ultimate responsibility for our environmental problems because of their need to constantly generate greater profits no matter what the environmental consequences (R. Dunlap 1993; McNamara 1992). In the following sections, we will contrast the functionalist and conflict approaches to the study of environmental issues.

Functionalism and Human Ecology

In Chapter 19 we noted that human ecology is concerned with interrelationships between people and their environment. Environmentalist Barry Commoner (1971:39) has stated that "everything is connected to everything else." Human ecologists, as we've seen, focus on how the physical environment shapes people's lives and also on how people influence the surrounding environment.

In an application of the human ecological perspective, sociologist Riley Dunlap suggests that the natural environment serves three basic functions for humans, as it does for the many animal species (Dunlap 1993; Dunlap and Catton 1983):

1. *The environment provides the resources essential for life.* These include air, water, and materials used to create shelter, transportation, and needed products. If human societies exhaust these resources—for example, by polluting the water supply or cutting down rain forests—the consequences can be dire.

2. *The environment serves as a waste repository.* More so than other living species, humans produce a huge quantity and variety of waste products—bottles, boxes, papers, sewage, garbage, to name just a few. Various types of pollution have become more common because human societies are generating more wastes than the environment can safely absorb.

3. *The environment "houses" our species.* It is our home, our living space, the place where we reside, work, and play. At times we take this for granted, but not when day-to-day living conditions become unpleasant and difficult. If our air is "heavy," if our tap water turns brown, if toxic chemicals seep into our neighborhood, we remember why it is vital to live in a healthful environment.

Dunlap (1993) points out that these three functions of the environment actually compete with one another. Human use of the environment for one of these functions will often strain its ability to fulfill the other two. For example, with world population continuing to rise, we have an increasing need to raze forests or farmland and build housing developments. But each time we do so, we are reducing the amount of land providing food, lumber, or habitat for wildlife.

The tension between the three essential functions of the environment brings us back to the human ecologists' view that "everything is connected to everything else." In facing the environmental challenges of the twenty-first century, government policymakers and environmentalists must determine how they can fulfill human societies' pressing needs (for example, for food, clothing, and shelter) while at the same time preserving the environment as a source of resources, a waste repository, and our home.

Conventional wisdom holds that concern for environmental quality is limited to the world's wealthy industrialized nations. However, the results of the 1992 Health of the Planet survey conducted in 24 countries by the Gallup International Institute show that there is *widespread* environmental concern around the planet. As Figure 20-5 shows, a higher proportion of people in the Philippines, Nigeria, Mexico, and Brazil said that they had a "great deal" of personal concern about environmental problems than did people in the United States, Great Britain, Japan, and Germany.

Conflict View of Environmental Issues

In Chapter 9, we drew on world systems analysis to show how a growing share of the human and natural resources of the developing countries is being redistributed to the core industrialized nations. This process only intensifies the destruction of natural resources in poorer regions of the world. From a conflict perspective, less affluent nations are being forced to exploit their mineral deposits, forests, and fisheries in order to meet their debt obligations. The poor turn to the only means of survival available to them: They plow mountain slopes, burn plots in tropical forests, and overgraze grasslands (Livernash and Rodenburg 1998).

Brazil exemplifies the interplay between economic troubles and environmental destruction. Each year more than 11,000 square miles of the Amazon rain forest are cleared for crops and livestock through burning. This

p. 232

FIGURE 20-5

Global Concern for the Environment

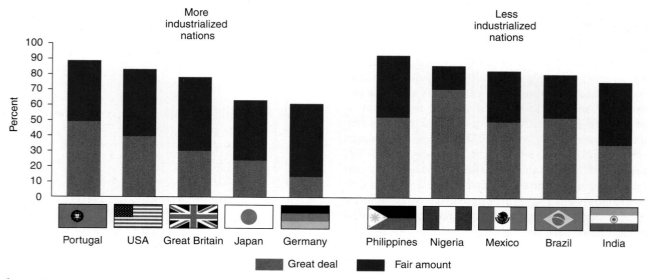

Source: Adapted from R. Dunlap 1993.

elimination of the rain forest affects worldwide weather patterns and heightens the gradual warming of the earth in a process known as the *greenhouse effect.* More than 160 nations gathered in Kyoto, Japan, in December 1997 for the Conference of the Parties on Climate Change. The preconference goal was to develop a strategy to reduce production of "greenhouse gases" by the year 2010 to pre-1900 levels. The treaty, known as the Kyoto Protocol, does call for industrial nations to reduce their emissions. However, no similar goals were established for developing countries, which, like Brazil, are struggling to move ahead economically.

These socioeconomic patterns, with harmful environmental consequences, are evident not only in Latin America but also in many regions of Africa and Asia. Conflict theorists are well aware of the environmental implications of land use policies in the Third World, but they contend that such a focus on the developing countries can contain an element of ethnocentrism. Who, they ask, is more to blame for environmental deterioration: the

poverty-stricken and "food-hungry" populations of the world or the "energy-hungry" industrialized nations (G. Miller 1972:117)?

Conflict theorists point out that Western industrialized nations account for only 25 percent of the world's

Each year more than 11,000 square miles of Brazil's Amazon rain forest are burned to clear them for crops and livestock. This contributes to the gradual warming of the earth known as the greenhouse effect.

population but are responsible for 85 percent of worldwide consumption. Take the United States alone: A mere 6 percent of the world's people consume more than half the world's nonrenewable resources and more than one-third of all the raw materials produced. Such data lead conflict theorists to charge that the most serious threat to the environment comes from "affluent megaconsumers and megapolluters" (Bharadwaj 1992; G. Miller 1972).

Allan Schnaiberg (1994) further refines this analysis by criticizing the focus on affluent consumers as the cause of environmental troubles. In his view, a capitalist system has a "treadmill of production" because of its inherent need to build ever-expanding profits. This treadmill necessitates creating an increasing demand for products, obtaining natural resources at minimal cost, and manufacturing products as quickly and cheaply as possible—no matter what the long-term environmental consequences of this approach.

Environmental Justice

Kennedy Heights, a new subdivision of Houston, attracted buyers in the late 1960s with its tidy brick façade homes and bucolic street names. But what the mostly Black buyers were not told was that the developers had constructed these homes on oil pits abandoned by Gulf Oil decades before. After experiencing periodic contaminated water supplies and a variety of illnesses, including large numbers of cancer and lupus, Kennedy Heights residents filed a class-action suit against Chevron, the company that acquired Gulf Oil. This case of environmental pollution is compounded by charges of "environmental racism," based on Gulf Oil documents in 1967 that tar-geted the area "for Negro residential and commercial development" (Verhovek 1997).

While the Kennedy Heights residents' case is still making its tortuous way through the courts, there are signs that some headway is being made in establishing *environmental justice,* a legal strategy based on claims that racial minorities are subjected disproportionately to environmental hazards. In 1998, Shintech, a chemical company, dropped plans to build a plastics plant in an impoverished Black community in Mississippi. Opponents of the plant had filed a civil rights complaint with the Environmental Protection Agency (EPA). EPA administrator Carol Browner praised Shintech's decision: "The principles applied to achieve this solution should be incorporated into any blueprint for dealing with environmental justice issues in communities across the nation" (Associated Press 1998:18).

Following reports from the EPA and other organizations documenting discriminatory locating of hazardous waste sites, President Bill Clinton issued an Executive Order in 1994 that requires all federal agencies to ensure that low-income and minority communities have access to better information about their environment and have an opportunity to participate in shaping government policies that affect their communities' health. Initial efforts to implement the policy have met widespread opposition because of the delays it imposes in establishing new industrial sites. Some observers question the wisdom of an order that slows economic development coming to areas in dire need of employment opportunities. On the other hand, there are those who point out that such businesses employ few unskilled or less skilled workers and only make the environment less livable for those left behind (Cushman 1998a; Goldman and Fitton 1994).

SOCIAL POLICY AND THE ENVIRONMENT

Environmentalism

The Issue

By the 1970s, the environment had become a major concern across the United States. In a dramatic tribute to the growing interest in environmentalism, an estimated 25 million people participated in the nation's first Earth Day on April 22, 1970. Some 2,000 communities held planned Earth Day celebrations, while environmental teach-ins took place at more than 2,000 colleges and 10,000 schools. Protest marches on behalf of environmental causes were held in many parts of the United States. The activism of the early environmentalist movement led Congress to establish the Environmental Pro-tection Agency in 1970 and to pass the Clean Air, Clean Water, and Endangered Species Acts in the early 1970s (D. Hayes 1990; Sale 1993).

A number of factors helped to mobilize the environmental movement in the 1970s. They included

1. *The activist subculture of the 1960s and early 1970s,* which encouraged people, especially the young, to engage in direct action regarding social issues.
2. *The dissemination of scientific knowledge about serious environmental problems such as oil spills and air pollution.*

3. *The growing popularity of outdoor recreation,* which increased the number of people concerned about the environment.

In this climate of wider interest in environmental issues, many existing organizations that had maintained a narrow focus on conservation of natural resources evolved into broad-based environmental groups (R. Dunlap and Mertig 1991).

The Setting

Currently it is estimated that 14 million people in the United States belong to one of the 150 nationwide environmental organizations or to one of the 12,000 grass-roots groups. The best known of the national organizations include the Sierra Club (established in 1892), the Natural Resources Defense Council (founded in 1970), and the controversial activist group Greenpeace (which gained worldwide publicity in the 1970s for its direct-action efforts to protect marine mammals by confronting whalers on the high seas). As of 1995, 63 percent of people questioned in a national Gallup survey said they consider themselves environmentalists, while 62 percent indicated that they value protection of the environment more than economic growth (R. Dunlap 1991; D. Moore 1995; Sale 1993; J. Schwartz 1990; Wapner 1994).

The contemporary environmental movement in the United States has evolved in several directions. At the local level, the number of grass-roots organizations focused on environmental hazards has markedly increased. At the same time, the largest and most powerful national organizations have become more and more bureaucratic. They are led by relatively well-paid professional management teams and often focus on particular issues such as air or water pollution, wildlife, or energy conservation. They make use of the legal and political system, primarily through educational efforts, lobbying, lawsuits, and electoral politics. By contrast, smaller environmentalist groups distrust virtually all major social institutions and sometimes resort to sabotage or other illegal tactics. The result is that the environmentalist movement is more fragmented than it was

in the 1970s (Cable and Benson 1993; R. Dunlap and Mertig 1991; McCloskey 1991; Schneider 1995).

Sociological Insights

Sociologists have focused their attention on the participants in the environmental movement and the social makeup of competing groups. Even observers who support environmentalist goals are troubled by the fact that the most powerful nationwide organizations are predominantly White, male-dominated, and affluent. One study maintains that while women are overrepresented in the environmental movement (particularly on the grass-roots level), men continue to hold most of the upper-management, high-profile positions in mainstream national organizations.

Viewed from a conflict perspective, it is significant that these major environmental organizations accept funding from oil companies, chemical giants, and other powerful corporations. Perhaps as a result, the environmentalist movement has often emphasized limited reforms rather than profound structural changes—for example, requiring cars to be more energy-efficient rather than taking steps to reduce automobile use (Dorsey 1994; Hahn-Baker 1994; Sale 1993).

Policy Initiatives

Efforts to legislate on behalf of the environment have increasingly been met by countermovements. The "wise-use" (or "sustainable-use") movement, founded in 1988, argues that we must balance our needs for clean air, unspoiled offshore waters, and pristine wilderness areas with our needs for jobs, energy, and tourist sites. Wise-use advocates hope to open *all* public lands to mining, grazing, logging, and energy development. They oppose what they view as the special "privileges" granted by the federal government through which Native Americans can control or limit development on reservation lands (Helvarg 1994; Ridgeway and St. Clair 1995; for a different view, see Callahan 1996).

The core of the wise-use movement consists of individuals and organizations who have a vested interest in opposing many of the basic tenets of environmentalism. (For example, it may be in their financial interest to cut down forest land or to dump waste products in rivers and oceans.) The wise-use movement has received financial and political support from industry associations such as the National Cattlemen's Association and the American Farm Bureau Federation. Environmentalists have criticized the self-serving nature of such "wise-use" antienvironmentalism and have expressed growing concern about the incendiary rhetoric of the wise-use movement. Some leaders openly endorse a "holy war" against those, like Julia Butterfly Hill, who "worship trees and sacrifice people." A growing campaign of intimidation and violence has been directed at environmental activists, including beatings, arsons, pet killings, and bombings (Helvarg 1994; Rowell 1996).

In sum, broad public support for environmentalism in the United States has encouraged the growth of bureaucratic organizations dedicated to environmental advocacy. While those organizations have advanced the cause of environmentalism, they have also provoked a countermovement on the part of those who stand to benefit from unrestricted development of public lands. The challenge to social policymakers is to balance the needs of future generations for clean air, land, and water against the needs of present-day business interests.

Let's Discuss

1. What is the most serious environmental problem in the area where you live? Have you ever tried to do anything about it?
2. How far should environmental activists go in promoting their goals and opposing actions that are harmful to the environment? Are they justified in resorting to illegal tactics? What is the best way to save the environment?
3. What do you think of the wise-use movement? Should lands be set aside forever as a public trust, or should all land be opened up to development? Does preserving trees hurt people?

Summary

The size, composition, and distribution of the population of the United States have an important influence on many of the policy issues that we have studied in this book. This chapter examines various elements of population, the current problem of overpopulation, the possibility of zero population growth, and the environmental problems facing our planet.

1. Thomas Robert Malthus suggested that the world's population was growing more rapidly than the available food supply and that this gap would increase over time. However, Karl Marx saw capitalism, rather than rising world population, as the cause of social ills.

2. The primary mechanism for obtaining population information in the United States and most other countries is the *census.*

3. Roughly two-thirds of the world's nations have yet to pass fully through the second stage of *demographic transition,* and thus they continue to experience significant population growth.

4. The developing nations face the prospect of continued population growth, since a substantial portion of their population is approaching the childbearing years. Some of the developed nations, however, have begun to stabilize population growth.

5. The most important factors in *migration* tend to be economic—financial failure in the "old country" and a perception of greater economic opportunities elsewhere.

6. Three broad areas of environmental concern are air pollution, water pollution, and contamination of land.

7. Using the human ecological perspective, sociologist Riley Dunlap suggests that the natural environment serves three basic functions: It provides essential resources, it serves as a waste repository, and it "houses" our species.

8. Conflict theorists charge that the most serious threat to the environment comes from Western industrialized nations.

9. *Environmental justice* is concerned with the disproportionate subjection of minorities to environmental hazards.

10. The environmental movement, which includes about 14 million people and 150 organizations in the United States alone, promotes the conservation and efficient use of natural resources and the removal of environmental hazards through activism, education, lobbying, legal action, and electoral politics.

Critical Thinking Questions

1. Select one of the social policy issues examined in this textbook and analyze in detail how the size, composition, and distribution of the population of the United States have an important influence on that issue.
2. Some European nations are now experiencing population declines. Their death rates are low and their birthrates are even lower than in stage III of the demographic transition model. Does this pattern suggest that there is now a fourth stage in the demographic transition? Even more important, what are the implications of negative population growth for an industrialized nation approaching the twenty-first century?
3. Imagine that you have been asked to study the issue of air pollution in the largest city in your state. How might you draw on surveys, observation research, experiments, and existing sources to help you study this issue?

Key Terms

Birthrate   The number of live births per 1,000 population in a given year. Also known as the *crude birthrate*. (532)

Census   An enumeration, or counting, of a population. (532)

Death rate   The number of deaths per 1,000 population in a given year. Also known as the *crude death rate*. (532)

Demographic transition   A term used to describe the change from high birthrates and death rates to relatively low birthrates and death rates. (534)

Demography   The scientific study of population. (530)

Environmental justice   A legal strategy based on claims that racial minorities are subjected disproportionately to environmental hazards. (547)

Fertility   The amount of reproduction among women of childbearing age. (529)

Growth rate   The difference between births and deaths, plus the differences between immigrants and emigrants, per 1,000 population. (533)

Infant mortality rate   The number of deaths of infants under one year of age per 1,000 live births in a given year. (532)

Life expectancy   The average number of years a person can be expected to live under current mortality conditions. (533)

Migration   Relatively permanent movement of people with the purpose of changing their place of residence. (540)

Population pyramid   A special type of bar chart that shows the distribution of population by gender and age. (537)

Total fertility rate (TFR)   The average number of children born alive to a woman, assuming that she conforms to current fertility rates. (532)

Vital statistics   Records of births, deaths, marriages, and divorces gathered through a registration system maintained by government units. (532)

Zero population growth (ZPG)   The state of a population with a growth rate of zero, achieved when the number of births plus immigrants is equal to the number of deaths plus emigrants. (539)

Additional Readings

BOOKS

Bouvier, Leon F., and Lindsey Grant. 1994. *How Many Americans? Population, Immigration, and the Environment.* San Francisco: Sierra Club. Two demographers argue that the United States cannot protect its natural environment or its way of life unless it limits both fertility and immigration.

Cohen, Joel E. 1995. *How Many People Can the Earth Support?* New York: Norton. The author—a biologist and head of the laboratory of populations at Rockefeller University in New York City—considers the different ways of calculating the constraints imposed by land, food production, and water supply.

Davis, Michael. 1998. *Ecology of Fear: Los Angeles and the Imagination of Disaster.* New York: Metropolitan Books/Henry Holt and Co. A geographer looks at the nation's second-largest metropolitan area and predicts that the future holds extreme events and abrupt changes.

Rubin, Charles T. 1994. *The Green Crusade: A History of the Environmental Idea.* New Brunswick, NJ: Transaction. A political scientist traces the emergence of the environment as a social issue in the United States.

JOURNALS

The Population Reference Bureau (1875 Connecticut Avenue, N.W., Suite 520, Washington, D.C. 20009-5728) publishes *Population Bulletin* (quarterly), *Population Today* (11 times annually), *Interchange* (quarterly), and occasionally *Teaching Modules.* These publications provide up-to-date information on population and environmental trends. The Bureau of the Census issues *Current Population Reports* that are helpful to researchers. Other journals focusing on demographic issues include *American Demographics* (founded in 1979), *Demography* (1964), and *International Migration Review* (1964).

Internet Connection

Note: While all the URLs listed were current as of the printing of this book, these sites often change. Please check our website (http://www.mhhe.com/schaefer) for updates.

1. Population change is a central theme of the online exhibit "6 Billion Human Beings" prepared by the Musée de l'Homme (Muséum National d'Histoire Naturelle). Direct your browser to (**http:// www.popexpo.net**) and select the appropriate language option. Enter your current age and work through all the sections offered to answer the following questions:

   (a) At the moment you logged on, what was the world's population, according to the website's clock? Keep track of your time online. When you are almost finished, note how many more people have been added to the world's population since you logged on. What is your reaction to the change in population?

   (b) How many people were there in the world the year you were born? How much has the world's population grown since your birth?

   (c) What percentage of the people who share your birth year are still alive? Use the map at the bottom of the screen to find how many of your cohorts are still alive in specific geographical areas. Which region has the most survivors and which the least? What social, political, biological, and environmental factors account for such differences in the survival rate?

   (d) Approximately how many people die each day the world over? How many of those people are children? What are the major causes of death?

   (e) What percentage of the world's population is currently younger than you? What percentage is older?

   (f) Considering all you have learned from this book and this website, how has your understanding of the composition of the world's population changed?

2. Environmental organizations seek to educate the public, influence legislation, and preserve natural resources. To learn more about such organizations, as well as specific environmental crises, log onto (**http://dir.yahoo.com/Society_and_Culture/ Environment_and_Nature/Organizations/**). Choose two environmental issues from the list offered. For each issue, visit one environmental organization's website and answer questions (a) through (c). Then answer questions (d) through (f).

   (a) What is the name of the organization you chose? When and why did it form?

   (b) What issue(s) is the organization most concerned with? What evidence does it provide to support its claims?

   (c) What are the organization's goals? What strategies and tactics does it use to achieve those goals? Do you believe the organization can accomplish its goals?

   (d) Are there any similarities between the two organizations you examined? If so, describe them. If not, why do you think the two organizations are so different?

   (e) What do you think is the most pressing environmental issue of all, and why?

   (f) In what specific ways could a sociologist help to alleviate environmental problems?

CHAPTER 21

COLLECTIVE BEHAVIOR AND SOCIAL MOVEMENTS

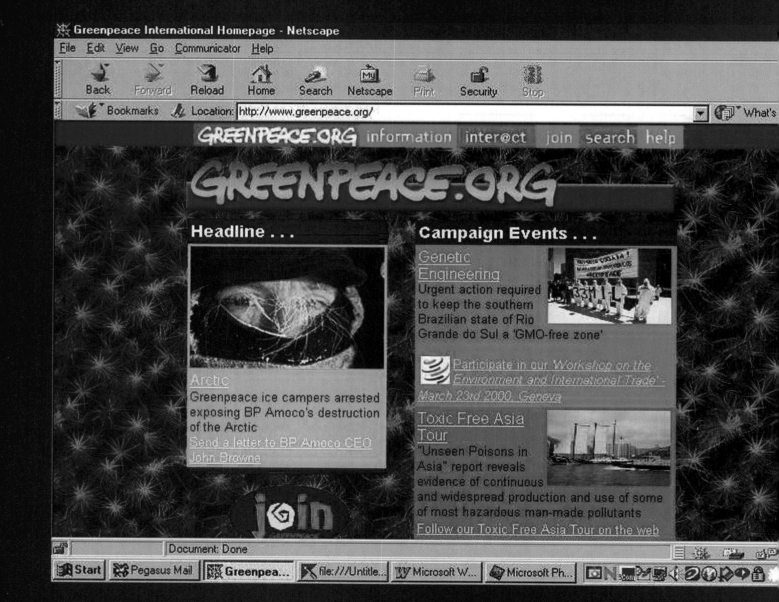

Greenpeace International Homepage - Netscape

File   Edit   View   Go   Communicator   Help

Back   Forward   Reload   Home   Search   Netscape   Print   Security   Stop

Bookmarks   Location: http://www.greenpeace.org/   What's

GREENPEACE.ORG   information   inter@ct   join   search   help

GREENPEACE.ORG

Headline . . .

Arctic
Greenpeace ice campers arrested exposing BP Amoco's destruction of the Arctic
Send a letter to BP Amoco CEO John Browne

join

Campaign Events . . .

Genetic Engineering
Urgent action required to keep the southern Brazilian state of Rio Grande do Sul a 'GMO-free zone'

Participate in our *Workshop on the Environment and International Trade'- March 23rd 2000, Geneva*

Toxic Free Asia Tour
"Unseen Poisons in Asia" report reveals evidence of continuous and widespread production and use of some of most hazardous man-made pollutants
Follow our Toxic Free Asia Tour on the web

Document: Done

Start   Pegasus Mail   Greenpea...   file:///Untitle...   Microsoft W...   Microsoft Ph...

Social activism today has gone beyond pamphlets, buttons, bumper stickers, and public service ads. Now the World Wide Web offers a new opportunity to post concerns about any social issue anywhere in the world.

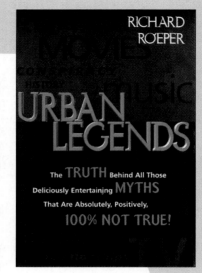

I f somebody at Bowling Green State University of Ohio had talked to somebody at the University of San Diego in California in October of 1998, both schools could have avoided a lot of unnecessary panic. Based on the stories sweeping their respective campuses at the time, a conversation between our imaginary students might have gone something like this:

Bowling Green Student: You're never going to believe what's happening here! People are freaking out.

San Diego Student: You think you're freaking out there, you should see what's going on here! . . . There's this psychic guy—he's supposed to be the most famous psychic in the world, he predicted the Oklahoma City bombing—and he went on Oprah Winfrey's show and predicted there was going to be a mass murder on Halloween at an H-shaped residence hall, and guess what, *we* have ah H-shaped residence hall at USD. . . .

(There's a long pause.)

SD: What's the matter?

BG: I don't know what you're talking about, because the psychic who was on *Oprah* didn't say anything about an H-shaped building. He said the massacre was going to take place at a state college in the Midwest and he even mentioned Bowling Green as one of the possibilities, and that's why people are freaking out here!

SD: I don't get it. Did you see the show when the guy was on?

BG: Um, no. Did you?

SD: No, I didn't see it either. What's going on here?

The reason neither of our mythological students saw the psychic's appearance is that there has never been such a segment of *Oprah*. . . .

Nevertheless, the feelings of fear on the campuses of the University of San Diego and Bowling Green State University in the fall of 1998 were very palpable. A story published on Oct. 31 in the *San Diego Union-Tribune* said that "most residents [of the H-shaped hall] were looking for somewhere else to spend the weekend" due to the spreading of a "classic urban legend." . . .

Meanwhile, similar rumors circulated through the University of Michigan, Kent State University, the University of Iowa, and the University of Illinois. Patient spokespeople for Oprah's show explained again that nothing even remotely resembling such an incident had ever happened. . . .

Students at San Diego, Bowling Green, et al., soon realized the scare was borne of pure fiction, but that certainly won't stop the class of '00 or later from going through the whole thing again. The psychic-on-the-talk-show story has been around for years. *(Roeper 1999:91–94)* ∎

ractically everyone has a tale to tell of an outlandish rumor or prank that they read about or saw on TV or learned of in an e-mail. Richard Roeper, a journalist, has collected many such stories in his book *Urban Legends*. Rumors (such as "the psychic on the talk show") and public opinion (for example, the reaction in the press and on the college campuses) are two forms of collective behavior. Practically all behavior can be thought of as collective behavior, but sociologists have given distinct meaning to the term. Neil Smelser (1981:431), a sociologist who specializes in this field of study, has defined **collective behavior** as the "relatively spontaneous and unstructured behavior of a group of people who are reacting to a common influence in an ambiguous situation."

This chapter begins with an examination of a number of theories used by sociologists to better understand collective behavior, including the emergent-norm, value-added, and assembling perspectives. Particular attention is given to certain types of collective behavior, among them crowd behavior, disaster behavior, fads and fashions, panics and crazes, rumors, public opinion, and social movements. We also look at the role communication technology plays in collective behavior. Sociologists study collective behavior because it incorporates activities that we all engage in on a regular basis. Moreover, contemporary sociology acknowledges the crucial role that social movements can play in mobilizing discontented members of a society and initiating social change. In the social policy section, we focus on the role that the social movement for lesbian and gay rights plays in promoting change. ■

Theories of Collective Behavior

In 1979, 11 rock fans died of suffocation after a crowd outside Cincinnati's Riverfront Stadium pushed to gain entrance to a concert by The Who. In 1989, when thousands of soccer fans forced their way into a stadium to see the semifinals of the English Cup, more than 90 people were trampled to death or smothered. In 1991, three young people died of suffocation *inside* an arena in Salt Lake City as a crowd surged forward to get the best vantage point to hear the heavy metal group AC/DC (J. Gross 1991; D. L. Miller 2000; see also R. Pogrebin 1996).

Collective behavior is usually unstructured and spontaneous. This fluidity makes it more difficult for sociologists to generalize about people's behavior in such situations. Nevertheless, sociologists have developed various theoretical perspectives that can help us to study—and deal with in a constructive manner—crowds, riots, fads, and other types of collective behavior.

Emergent-Norm Perspective

The early writings on collective behavior imply that crowds are basically ungovernable. However, this is not always the case. In many situations, crowds are effectively governed by norms and procedures, including queuing, or waiting in line. We routinely encounter queues when we await service, as in a fast-food restaurant or bank; or when we wish to enter or exit, as in a movie theater or football stadium. Normally, physical barriers, such as guardrails and checkout counters, help to regulate queu-

ing. When massive crowds are involved, ushers or security personnel may also be present to assist in the orderly movement of the crowd. Nevertheless, there are times when such measures prove inadequate, as the examples above and the one below demonstrate.

On December 28, 1991, people began gathering outside the City College gymnasium in New York City to see a heavily promoted charity basketball game featuring rap stars and other celebrities. By late afternoon, more than 5,000 people had gathered for the 6:00 P.M. game, even though the gym could accommodate only 2,730 spectators. Although the crowd was divided into separate lines for ticket holders and those wishing to buy tickets at the door, restlessness and discontent swept through both lines and sporadic fights broke out. The arrival of celebrities only added to the commotion and the crowd's tension.

Doors to the gymnasium were finally opened one hour before game time, but only 50 people were admitted to the lobby at a time. Once their tickets had been taken, spectators proceeded down two flights of stairs, through a single unlocked entrance, and into the gym. Those further back in the crowd experienced the disconcerting feeling of moving forward, then stopping for a period of time, then repeating this process again and again. Well past the publicized starting time, huge crowds were still outside, pressing to gain entrance to the building.

Finally, with the arena more than full, the doors to the gym were closed, As rumors spread outside the building that the game was beginning, more than 1,000 frustrated fans, many with valid tickets, poured through the

Collective behavior can sometimes have fatal results. Nine young men and women died and 29 were injured in 1991 when a crowd surged through this stairwell to gain entrance to a celebrity-studded charity basketball game at City College in New York.

idly dissolving. A new norm was simultaneously emerging: It is acceptable to push forward, even if people in front protest. Some members of the crowd—especially those with valid tickets—may have felt that this push forward was justified as a way of ensuring that they would get to see the game. Others pushed forward simply to relieve the physical pressure of those pushing behind them. Even individuals who rejected the emergent norm may have felt afraid to oppose it, fearing ridicule or injury. Thus, conforming behavior, which we usually associate with highly structured situations, was evident in this rather p. 173 chaotic crowd, as it had been at the concerts by The Who and AC/DC and at the soccer game in England. It would be misleading to assume that these fans acted simply as a united, collective unit in creating a dangerous situation.

glass doors into the building and headed for the stairs. Soon the stairwell became a horrifying mass of people surging against locked metal doors to the gym and crushed against concrete walls. The result was a tragedy: 9 young men and women eventually died, and 29 were injured through the sheer pressure of bodies against one another and against walls and doors (Mollen 1992).

Sociologists Ralph Turner and Lewis Killian (1987) have offered a view of collective behavior that is helpful in assessing a tragic event like this one. It begins with the assumption that a large crowd, such as a group of rock or soccer fans, is governed by expectations of proper behavior just as much as four people playing doubles tennis. But during the episode of collective behavior a definition of what behavior is appropriate or not emerges from the crowd. Turner and Killian call this the *emergent-norm perspective.* Like other social norms, the emergent norm reflects shared convictions held by members of the group p. 74 and is enforced through sanctions. These new norms of proper behavior may arise in what seem at first to be ambiguous situations. There is latitude for a wide range of acts, yet within a general framework established by the emergent norms (for a critique of this perspective, see McPhail 1991).

Using the emergent-norm perspective, we can see that fans outside the charity basketball game at City College found themselves in an ambiguous situation. Normal procedures of crowd control, such as orderly queues, were rap-

Value-Added Perspective

Neil Smelser (1962) proposed still another sociological explanation for collective behavior. He used the *value-added model* to explain how broad social conditions are transformed in a definite pattern into some form of collective behavior. This model outlines six important determinants of collective behavior: structural conduciveness, structural strain, generalized belief, a precipitating factor, mobilization for action, and the exercise of social control.

Initially, in Smelser's view, certain elements must be present for an incident of collective behavior to take place. He uses the term *structural conduciveness* to indicate that the organization of society can facilitate the emergence of conflicting interests. Structural conduciveness was evident in the former East Germany in 1989, just a year before the collapse of the ruling Communist party and the reunification of Germany. The government was extremely unpopular, and there was growing freedom to publicly express and be exposed to new and challenging viewpoints. Such structural conduciveness makes collective behavior possible, though not inevitable.

The second determinant of collective behavior, *structural strain,* occurs when the conduciveness of the social structure to potential conflict gives way to a perception that conflicting interests do, in fact, exist. The intense desire of many East Germans to travel to or emigrate to western European countries placed great strain on the social control exercised by the Communist party. Such structural strain contributes to what Smelser calls a *generalized belief*—a shared view of reality that redefines social action and serves to guide behavior. The overthrow of Communist rule in East Germany and other Soviet-bloc nations occurred in part as a result of a generalized belief that the Communist regimes were oppressive and that popular resistance *could* lead to social change.

Smelser suggests that a specific event or incident, known as a *precipitating factor,* triggers collective behavior. The event may grow out of the social structure, but whatever its origins, it contributes to the strains and beliefs shared by a group or community. For example, studies of race riots have found that interracial fights or arrests and searches of minority individuals by police officers often precede disturbances. The 1992 riots in South Central Los Angeles, which claimed 58 lives, were sparked by the acquittal of four White police officers charged after the videotaped beating of Rodney King, a Black construction worker.

According to Smelser, the four determinants identified above are necessary for collective behavior to occur. However, in addition to these factors, the group must be *mobilized for action.* An extended thundershower or severe snowstorm may preclude such a mobilization. People are also more likely to come together on weekends than on weekdays, in the evening rather than during the daytime.

The manner in which *social control is exercised*—both formally and informally—can be significant in determining whether the preceding factors will end in collective behavior. Stated simply, social control may prevent, delay, or interrupt a collective outburst. In some instances, those using social control may be guilty of misjudgments that intensify the severity of an outbreak. Many observers believe that the Los Angeles police did not respond fast enough when the initial rioting began in 1992, thereby creating a vacuum that allowed the level of violence to escalate.

Sociologists have questioned the validity of both the emergent-norm and value-added perspectives because of their imprecise definitions and the difficulty of testing them empirically. For example, they have criticized the emergent-norm perspective for being too vague in defining what constitutes a norm and have challenged the value-added model for its lack of specificity in defining generalized belief and structural strain. Of these two theories, the emergent-norm perspective appears to offer a more useful explanation of societywide episodes of collective behavior, such as crazes and fashions, than the value-added approach (M. Brown and Goldin 1973; Quarantelli and Hundley 1975; K. Tierney 1980).

Smelser's value-added model, however, represents an advance over earlier theories that treated crowd behavior as dominated by irrational, extreme impulses. The value-added approach firmly relates episodes of collective behavior to the overall social structure of a society (for a critique, see McPhail 1994).

Assembling Perspective

A series of football victory celebrations at the University of Texas that spilled over into the main streets of Austin came under the scrutiny of sociologists (Snow et al. 1981). Some participants actively tried to recruit passersby for the celebrations by thrusting out open palms "to get five" or by yelling at drivers to honk their horns. In fact, encouraging still further assembling became a preoccupation of the celebrators. Whenever spectators were absent, those celebrating were relatively quiet. As we have seen, a key determinant of collective behavior is mobilization for action. How do people come together to undertake collective action?

Clark McPhail, perhaps the most prolific researcher of collective behavior in the last three decades, sees people and organizations consciously responding to one another's actions. Building on the interactionist approach, McPhail and Miller (1973) introduced the concept of the assembling process. The *assembling perspective* sought for the first time to examine how and why people move from different points in space to a common location.

A basic distinction has been made between two types of assemblies. *Periodic assemblies* include recurring, relatively routine gatherings of people such as work groups, college classes, and season ticket holders of an athletic series. These assemblies are characterized by advance scheduling and recurring attendance of the majority of participants. For example, members of an introductory sociology class may gather together for lectures every Monday, Wednesday, and Friday morning at 10 A.M. By contrast, *nonperiodic assemblies* include demonstrations, parades, and gatherings at the scene of fires, accidents, and arrests. Such assemblies result from casually transmitted information and are generally less formal than periodic assemblies. One example is the organized rally at Gallaudet University in 1988 backing a deaf person for president of the school for deaf students (see the photo of the campaign leaflet).

These three approaches to collective behavior give us deeper insight into relatively spontaneous and unstructured situations. Although episodes of collective behavior may seem irrational to outsiders, norms emerge among

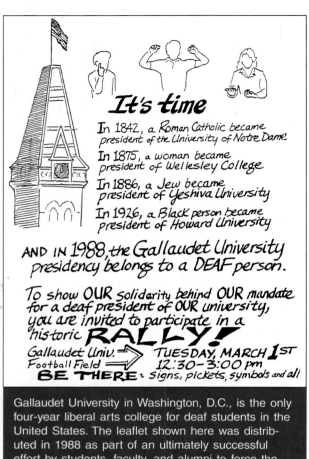

It's time

In 1842, a Roman Catholic became president of the University of Notre Dame.

In 1875, a woman became president of Wellesley College

In 1886, a Jew became president of Yeshiva University

In 1926, a Black person became president of Howard University

AND IN 1988, the Gallaudet University presidency belongs to a DEAF person.

To show OUR solidarity behind OUR mandate for a deaf president of OUR university, you are invited to participate in a historic **RALLY!**

Gallaudet Univ. ⟹ TUESDAY, MARCH 1ST
Football Field ⟹ 12:30 – 3:00 pm
BE THERE: signs, pickets, symbols and all

Gallaudet University in Washington, D.C., is the only four-year liberal arts college for deaf students in the United States. The leaflet shown here was distributed in 1988 as part of an ultimately successful effort by students, faculty, and alumni to force the board of trustees to appoint the university's first deaf president. Political demonstrations, such as the Gallaudet rally, are examples of nonperiodic assemblies (Christiansen and Barnartt 1995).

the participants and organized efforts are made to assemble at a certain time and place.

Forms of Collective Behavior

Do you remember Cabbage Patch kids? Did you collect pet rocks or *Star Wars* toys when you were young? Any bell-bottom pants lurking in your closets? These are all fads and fashions that depend on collective behavior. Using the emergent-norm, value-added, and assembling perspectives along with other aspects of sociological examination, sociologists have looked at many forms of collective behavior—not only fads and fashions but also crowds, disaster behavior, panics and crazes, rumors, public opinion, and social movements.

Crowds

Crowds are temporary groupings of people in close proximity who share a common focus or interest. Spectators at a baseball game, participants at a pep rally, and rioters are all examples of crowds. Sociologists have been interested in what characteristics are common to crowds. Of course, it can be difficult to generalize, since the nature of crowds varies dramatically. Think about how hostages on a hijacked airplane might feel as opposed to participants in a religious revival.

Like other forms of collective behavior, crowds are not totally lacking in structure. Even during riots, participants are governed by identifiable social norms and exhibit definite patterns of behavior. Sociologists Richard Berk and Howard Aldrich (1972) analyzed patterns of vandalism in 15 cities in the United States during the riots of the 1960s. They found that stores of merchants perceived as exploitative were likely to be attacked, while private homes and public agencies with positive reputations were more likely to be spared. Apparently, looters had reached a collective agreement as to what constituted a "proper" or "improper" target for destruction. Box 21-1 examines a sociological study of riots and looting in Chicago after the Chicago Bulls professional basketball team won numerous championships in the 1990s.

The emergent-norm perspective suggests that during urban rioting a new social norm is accepted (at least temporarily) that basically condones looting. The norms of respect for private property—as well as norms involving obedience to the law—are replaced by a concept of all goods as community property. All desirable items, including those behind locked doors, can be used for the "general welfare." In effect, the emergent norm allows looters to take what they regard as properly theirs (Quarantelli and Dynes 1970; see also McPhail 1991).

Disaster Behavior

Newspapers, television reports, and even rumors bring us word of many disasters around the world. The term *disaster* refers to a sudden or disruptive event or set of events that overtaxes a community's resources so that outside aid is necessary. Traditionally, disasters have been catastrophes related to nature, such as earthquakes, floods, and fires. Yet, in an industrial age, natural disasters have now been joined by such "technological disasters" as airplane crashes, industrial explosions, nuclear meltdowns, and massive chemical poisonings.

Sociologists have made enormous strides in disaster research, despite the problems inherent in this type of investigation. The work of the Disaster Research Center at the University of Delaware has been especially important.

Research in Action

21-1 The Bulls Riots in Chicago

ed by superstar Michael Jordan, the Chicago Bulls professional basketball team won six championships in the 1990s. Unfortunately, most victories were followed by a night of looting in Chicago. According to Neil Smelser's value-added model of collective behavior, the Bulls' victories would be considered precipitating factors that led to celebrations around the city after each championship, but also to looting and riots.

The most serious of these disturbances—in terms of the number of stores looted and people arrested—took place after the Bulls' victory in 1992. Hundreds of stores were looted, more than 1,000 people were arrested, and 90 police officers suffered injuries. Based on his study of the disturbances, sociologist Michael Rosenfeld concludes that the 1992 riot was the most serious because race riots in Los Angeles, which occurred six weeks earlier, aggravated underlying racial tensions in Chicago. The 1992 Los Angeles riots were the worst in the United States in the twentieth century.

In studying the Bulls riots, Rosenfeld was especially interested in whether looters targeted the establishments of particular racial and ethnic groups. An analysis of the 1992 Los Angeles riots suggested that African American participants had selectively targeted businesses owned by Korean Americans. But while that study identified the stores damaged in the riots and the race and ethnicity of their owners, it did not develop complete comparative data on stores that were *not* damaged in the riots.

With this empirical problem in mind, Rosenfeld attempted to identify the owners of *all* the stores in the African American neighborhood affected by the 1992 Bulls riot in order to assess possible targeting by race and ethnicity. He compiled data from seven distinct sources, among them a summary by Arab American merchants of their stores that were damaged and a similar summary by Korean American merchants. Rosenfeld also conducted a telephone survey of all stores damaged in the 1992 riot

> Hundreds of stores were looted, more than 1,000 people were arrested, and 90 police officers suffered injuries.

whose owners' racial and ethnic backgrounds could not be determined through other sources.

Rosenfeld found that 25 percent of stores owned by Arab Americans were looted, as compared with 15 percent of those owned by Korean Americans and only 9 percent of those owned by African Americans or others. Such data would seem to support the view that there *had* been racial and ethnic targeting, but further analysis by Rosenfeld revealed that this conclusion was misleading. Different racial and ethnic

groups in Chicago tend to own different types of businesses in ghetto neighborhoods, and these businesses have very different levels of appeal for looters. For example, African Americans own most of the restaurants in these neighborhoods, but restaurants are a poor target for looters, and most were closed during the 1992 riot. By contrast, Arab Americans own most grocery and liquor stores in Chicago's African American neighborhoods, and it is these stores (with shelves full of goods) that are an ideal target for looters.

Through careful analysis of his data, Rosenfeld found *no* evidence of selective racial or ethnic targeting during the 1992 Bulls riot. For example, grocery and liquor stores owned by Arab Americans were no more likely to be looted than similar stores owned by members of other racial and ethnic groups. Instead, the primary determinant of looting was the *type of store:* grocery and liquor stores were especially likely to be looted, while restaurants and bars were generally avoided. Rosenfeld concluded that "there was nothing inherently ethnic about the Bulls riot" in terms of the targets of looting and property damage (1997:16).

Let's Discuss

1. Have you ever been caught up in unruly crowd behavior? What triggered it? Was it targeted against some group? How was it resolved?
2. What pattern of damage and destruction did Rosenfeld find in the Bulls riot?

Sources: Rosenfeld 1997; Schaefer 1997; Tierney 1994.

The center has teams of trained researchers prepared to leave for the site of any disaster on four hours' notice. Their field kits include identification material, recording equipment, and general interview guidelines for use in various types of disasters. En route to the scene, these researchers try to get informed about the conditions they may encounter. Upon arrival, the team establishes a communication post to coordinate fieldwork and maintain contact with the center's headquarters.

Since its founding, the Disaster Research Center

has conducted more than 600 field studies of natural and technological disasters in the United States, as well as in other nations. Its research has been used to develop effective planning in such areas as delivery of emergency health care, establishment and operation of rumor-control centers, coordination of mental health services after disasters, and implementation of disaster-preparedness and emergency-response programs. The center has provided training and field research for graduate students. These students maintain a professional

21-3 Virtual Social Movements

W e are accustomed to think of social movements in terms of protest marches and door-to-door petition drives. But the World Wide Web allows for alternative ways of trying to organize people and either bring about fundamental change or resist change. The Internet itself has often been referred to as a "virtual community," and as in any community there are people who seek to persuade others to their point of view. Furthermore, the Internet serves to "bring people together"—say, by transforming the cause of the Mexican Zapatista into an international lobbying effort or linking environmentalists on every continent through Greenpeace International or e-mailing information and news from abroad to dissidents in China.

Being like-minded and in face-to-face contact, critical to conventional social movements, is not necessary on the Internet. Moreover, people can engage in their own virtual community with little impact on their everyday lives. On the Internet, for example, one can mount a petition drive to free a death row inmate without taking days and weekends away from one's job and family. Dissidents can communicate with one another using computers in Internet cafes,

with little concern for being traced or monitored by the government.

Two new studies by Matthew Zook and research by sociologist Roberta Garner examined how many websites express ideological points of view that are contentious or hostile to existing institutions. Garner looked at 542 websites that could be regarded as "ideological postings"; some reflect the inter-

> The Internet itself has often been referred to as a "virtual community," and as in any community there are people who seek to persuade others to their point of view.

ests of a particular group or organization and some are only the opinions of isolated individuals. Among the sites were postings that reflected extreme patriotic views, White racism, attachment to cults, regional separatism and new forms of nationalism, and expression of militant environmentalism.

While the Garner sample was not random and therefore may not be representa-

tive of all ideological postings, the hundreds of sites did show some consistencies, many of them also noted by Zook:

- Like conventional social movements, these sites serve as an alternative source of information, bypassing mainstream sources of opinions found in newspaper editorials.
- These nonmainstream movements enjoy legitimacy because no gate-keeper keeps them off the web. By virtue of being on a website, even an unsophisticated one, the information has the appearance of being just as legitimate as that found on a website for a *Fortune* 500 corporation or CNN news. And because the information appears on *individual* sites, it seems to be more real and even sincere than messages that come from the mass media of television or radio.
- The sites make little reference to time or specific events, except to historic moments. There is not much sense of movement along an agenda.
- The sites rely heavily on written documents, either in the form of

Sources: Calhoun 1998; Castells 1996; Garner 1999; Rosenthal 2000; Van Slambrouck 1999; Zook 1996.

Workers, many of them children, are shown in a makeshift cigarette factory in Bangladesh. New social movement theory offers a broad, global perspective on social and political activism, including dealing with exploitation of child labor in developing nations.

spreading rumors. The World Wide Web is only the latest in a wave of new communication technology that has transformed collective behavior.

How might some of the theoretical perspectives we examined earlier in the chapter evaluate technology's role in collective behavior? While Neil Smelser's value-added perspective did not explicitly refer to communication technology, his emphasis on people needing to be mobilized for action takes on new meaning today with fax machines and the Internet. With relatively little effort and expense, we can now reach a large number of people in a short period of time. Looking at the new technology from the assembling perspective, we could consider the Internet's Listservs and chatrooms as examples of nonperiodic assemblies. Without face-to-face contact or even simultaneous interaction, people can develop an identity with a large collective of like-minded people via the Internet (Calhoun 1998).

Sociology is only beginning to consider the impact of the latest technology on various forms of collective be-

manifestos or established documents such as the Constitution or the Bible. Written testimonials (such as "How I Became a Conservative") also proliferate on these websites.

- The presentations are still fairly unsophisticated. While there are glossy animated websites, most sites look like a printed page.
- Unlike conventional social movements, these virtual sites are generally not geared for action. Despite expressions of concern or foreboding (such as the site "Are You Ready for Catastrophic Natural Disasters?"), there were few calls to do anything. Sites like "Glory to the Cuban Revolution" seek to inform visitors, serve as a resource, and, perhaps, bring people around to their point of view.

Zook as well as Garner and her student researchers found that these sites often seem to define themselves by their choice of links on the web. In other words, with whom do they wish to be associated? This is particularly true of well-established social movements that have expanded to use the Inter-

net. For example, both the leading abortion rights groups and anti-abortion organizations feature links to other groups, but only to those that are like-minded.

The entire process of "links" is very important in the Internet network. How one defines one's ideology determines how a site may be located and who makes links. For example, the website of a female national socialist from Sweden boldly encourages visitors to establish a link from their website to hers as long as they are a part of the "white aryan movement on the Net." Using the term "militia" as opposed to "patriotic" would bring different people to one's site. The terms one uses are important since webpages act as recruiting tools to attract new members to a movement and may, in fact, be the only realistic way that some groups will attract followers.

People in conventional social movements commonly try to infiltrate other groups holding opposing views to learn their strategy or even disrupt their ability to function. There is a parallel to that emerging on the Internet. The term *hactivists* (a merging of "hackers" with "activists") refers to people who invade computer systems electronically, placing embarrassing information on their

enemies' webpages or, at the very least, defacing them. During the height of the 1999 NATO attacks on Yugoslavia, movements opposed to the military action bombarded the official NATO website with requests meant to overload it and paralyze its operation.

Research into virtual social movements is still exploratory. Social movement researchers such as Garner and Zook are interested in establishing the relationship between ideological websites and "real" organizations. Do these sites merely reflect a single posting? Or are they the visible manifestation of a broader consensus? And sociologists will be interested in examining a more representative sample of such sites to determine how often they explicitly call for social change.

Let's Discuss

1. What are some of the advantages of having a virtual social movement on the Internet? What might be some disadvantages?
2. If you were to create a webpage designed to attract followers to a social movement, what would it be like?

---

havior. Technology clearly plays a role in disaster research; moreover, a large number of disasters today are technological in origin. A content analysis of the coverage of disasters by *Time* magazine showed that about 40 percent were technological and 60 percent natural during the 1990s (Bernhardt 1997). (We will consider technological accidents in greater detail in the next chapter.)

We have seen that rumors fly on the Internet. One click of the "Send" button can forward messages to every person in one's address book. Multiply this by the millions of e-mail account holders to get an idea of the reach of the Internet in distributing rumors. We have seen, too, how Internet rumors can stir panics. In the same way, people can be exposed almost instantly to the latest crazes, fads, and fashions. And people are constantly being encouraged to call a telephone number or log on to a website to register their public opinion on some policy issue.

Can one be part of a "crowd" via the new communication technology? Television and the Internet, as con-

trasted with books and newspapers, often convey a false sense of intimacy reinforced by immediacy. We seem to be personally hurt by the death of Princess Diana or moved by the troubles of the Kennedy family. Therefore, the latest technology brings us together in an electronic global village to act and to react. Box 21-3 shows how virtual social movements can develop on the Web (Garner 1999).

The new communication technology is also able to create enclaves of similarly minded people. Websites are not just autonomous and independent; they are interconnected through a global electronic network. One website, in turn, lists a variety of other sites that serve as "links." For example, seeking out information on domestic partnerships may lead you to an electronic enclave on the Internet supportive of cohabitation between men and women or alternatively to an enclave that is supportive of gay and lesbian couples. Developments in communication technology have clearly broadened the way we interact with one another today (Calhoun 1998).

SOCIAL POLICY AND SOCIAL MOVEMENTS

Lesbian and Gay Rights

The Issue

Despite the large numbers of lesbians and gay men in the United States and around the world, homosexuality continues to function in many societies as a master status that carries a stigma. Amnesty International (1994) published a pioneering report documenting that lesbians and gay men suffer from governmental persecution in many parts of the world. In response to such discrimination, a social movement for lesbian and gay rights has emerged across the United States and in many diverse nations. This movement is putting pressure on policymakers to pass legislation establishing and protecting gay and lesbian rights.

The Setting

The first social movement to advance the civil rights of lesbians and gay men was founded in Germany in 1897 by physician Magnus Hirschfeld and others. The Scientific-Humanitarian Committee fought to abolish legal penalties against homosexual behavior and to educate people about gay rights and women's rights. The committee was eventually crushed by the Nazis in 1933; subsequently, at least 10,000 to 20,000 people identified as homosexuals died in Nazi concentration camps. As a result, one cherished symbol of contemporary gay activists—worn on buttons and patches—is a pink triangle, the very emblem gay prisoners were forced to wear by the Nazis (Adam 1995; Heger 1980; Lauritsen and Thorstad 1974; Plant 1986).

In the United States, the first homosexual organization was founded in Chicago in 1924, and a number of gay and lesbian groups came into existence in the 1950s. Experiences in early gay rights groups gave activists greater organizing ability—an important component of resource mobilization. In addition, there were spillover effects through involvement in other social movements of the 1950s and 1960s—such as those working for civil rights for Blacks, against the war in Vietnam, and for women's liberation. Many lesbians and gay men were forced to reflect more directly on their own oppression stemming from their sexual orientation (J. Katz 1992; see also D'Emilio 1983).

Building on earlier homosexual activism and on the growth of lesbian and gay male subcultures in major cities, the contemporary gay movement publicly began in New York City on June 28, 1969. Police raided the Stonewall Inn, an after-hours gay bar, and forced patrons onto the street. But, instead of dispersing, the patrons locked police inside the bar and rioted until official reinforcements arrived. For the next three nights, lesbians and gay men marched through the streets of New York, protesting police raids and other forms of discrimination. Within months, gay liberation groups had appeared in cities and campuses throughout the United States; within two years, similar organizations were evident in Canada, Great Britain, various western European countries, and Australia (Adam 1995; Adam et al. 1999; Garner 1996).

While many voluntary associations supporting lesbian and gay rights are primarily local in their focus, a growing number of national organizations address gay issues. Among these are the National Lesbian and Gay Task Force, which fights for gay rights on a national level while engaging in "grass-roots" organizing; the Human Rights Campaign, which lobbies Congress on gay issues and provides financial support for lesbian and gay male candidates; the Gay and Lesbian Alliance Against Defamation (GLAAD), which promotes fair and accurate representation of lesbians and gay men in the media and protests antigay stereotyping; and Parents, Families, and Friends of Lesbians and Gays (PFLAG), whose chapters in more than 380 U.S. cities and 11 countries provide support for lesbians, gay men, and their families (Brelin 1996).

In response to the AIDS crisis, self-help groups—especially in the gay communities of p. 135 major cities—have been established to care for the sick, educate the healthy, and lobby for more responsive public policies. The most outspoken AIDS activist group has been ACT-UP, which has conducted controversial protests and sit-ins in the halls of government and at scientific conferences. In the view of sociologist Barry Adam (1995), while the rise of such self-help and AIDS activist groups has siphoned away many leaders and participants from gay rights organizations, the broad reach of the AIDS crisis has mobilized new constituencies of gay men and their friends and relatives into AIDS and gay activism. Indeed, the militant and dramatic tactics of ACT-UP—which includes lesbian, gay male, and heterosexual members—contributed to the formation in the 1990s of new direct-action groups such as

Queer Nation (which attempts to combat homophobia and celebrate sexual diversity) and the Lesbian Avengers (which focuses on issues vital to lesbian survival and visibility) (M. Cunningham 1992; E. Kaplan 1990; Trebay 1990).

In the private sector, progress in alleviating discrimination has been uneven. As of 2000, more than 2,800 employers offered benefits to domestic partners (see Chapter 13). However, the many corporate mergers in recent years have sometimes hurt the gay community. For example, when Exxon and Mobil merged, the new entity announced it would end domestic partnership benefits that Mobil had previously provided (Armour 2000; Mills and Herrschaft 1999).

Sociological Insights

Despite the effort of the lesbian and gay rights movement, in 1986 the U.S. Supreme Court ruled, by a narrow 5–4 vote, that the Constitution does not protect homosexual relations between consenting adults, even in the privacy of their own homes. This decision underscored the fact that heterosexuality remains the socially approved form of sexual relations in the United States; the dominant ideology of our society promotes exclusive heterosexual norms. Sociologist Steven Seidman (1994:583) notes, "From secondary school books to public images in advertisements, movies, television shows, magazines, and newspapers, heterosexuality is presented as natural and normal." Viewed from a conflict perspective, the dominant ideology encourages antigay prejudice and discrimination by excluding positive images of lesbians and gay men while emphasizing narrow stereotypes.

By the 1990s, lesbian and gay male activists had recognized that encouraging people to "come out" could help illustrate the diversity of gay life and assist resource mobilization. Many lesbians and gay men had long felt the need to conceal their identities (remain "in the closet") out of fear that they might lose their jobs, be cut off from their families, and fall victim to prejudice and discrimination.

However, the gay movement has given many individuals the support and strength to "come out" and assert their identities publicly and proudly—as new social movements frequently do for those who are challenging dominant social norms.

Among the many lesbian, gay, and bisexual organizations in the United States and Canada, there are gay sports leagues and singing groups; professional associations, such as those of gay doctors and teachers; campus lesbian and gay male organizations; and groups of African American and Hispanic gays, some of whom have challenged White domination of the lesbian and gay movement (Brelin 1996:34).

Policy Initiatives

By the 1990s, opponents of lesbian and gay rights were focusing on statewide ballot initiatives as a key tactic. In most cases, gay rights supporters have won narrow victories. As of 2000, 10 states and 165 cities have laws that protect lesbians and gay men against workplace discrimination (ACLU 2000).

Resistance to lesbian and gay rights has also been evident in the battle over possible legalization of same-sex marriages and in the continuing controversy over gays in the military. In 1993, President Bill Clinton considered issuing an executive order against antigay discrimination within the military, but was forced to back down because of

Lesbian and gay activism is not confined to large cities like New York and San Francisco. It shows up in diverse communities across the nation, as indicated by the outreach effort of these members of the University of South Dakota's Gay, Lesbian, and Bisexual Alliance.

heated opposition from military leaders and powerful members of Congress. Under a compromise devised in 1994—known as "Don't Ask, Don't Tell"—lesbians and gay men can continue to serve in the military as long as they keep their homosexuality a secret, while commanders are prohibited from asking about a person's sexual orientation. But commanders *can* investigate and dismiss military personnel if there is evidence that they have committed homosexual acts. According to a 1998 report the military is discharging 67 percent *more* gay and lesbian troops today than before the new policy was enacted (Weiner 1998).

A common stereotype has been that lesbian and gay organizations are found only in Western industrialized nations. However, the International Lesbian and Gay Association now has about 300 member organizations in 70 countries. In 1995, Japan held its second annual gay pride march; two gay groups were formed in China; and gay groups were founded in Bolivia, Kenya, Pakistan, South Korea, and Sri Lanka. There are more than 50 gay and lesbian groups in South Africa, more than a dozen in Mexico, and at least 7 lesbian organizations in Brazil. The spread of the Internet has assisted the creation of many pioneering lesbian and gay organizations (Adam et al. 1999; Dillon 1997; *The Economist* 1996).

Let's Discuss

1. Viewed from a conflict perspective, how does the dominant ideology of our society encourage antigay prejudice and discrimination?
2. How has the AIDS crisis affected the movement for lesbian and gay rights?
3. In what ways is the social position of lesbians different from that of gay men?

Summary

Collective behavior is the relatively spontaneous and unstructured behavior of a group that is reacting to a common influence in an ambiguous situation. This chapter examines sociological theories used to understand collective behavior and forms of collective behavior, with particular attention to *social movements* and their important role in promoting social change.

1. Turner and Killian's *emergent-norm perspective* suggests that new forms of proper behavior may emerge from a crowd during an episode of collective behavior.
2. Smelser's *value-added model* of collective behavior outlines six important determinants of such behavior: structural conduciveness, structural strain, generalized belief, precipitating factor, mobilization of participants for action, and operation of social control.
3. The *assembling perspective* introduced by McPhail and Miller sought for the first time to examine how and why people move from different points in space to a common location.
4. In *crowds* people are in relatively close contact and interaction for a period of time and are focused on something of common interest.
5. Researchers are interested in how groups interact in times of disaster.

6. *Fads* are temporary patterns of behavior involving large numbers of people; *fashions* have more historical continuity.
7. The key distinction between a *panic* and a *craze* is that a panic is a flight *from* something whereas a craze is a mass movement *to* something.
8. A *rumor* is a piece of information used to interpret an ambiguous situation. It serves a social function by providing a group with a shared belief.
9. *Publics* represent the most individualized and least organized form of collective behavior. *Public opinion* is the expression of attitudes on public policy communicated to decision makers.
10. Social movements are more structured than other forms of collective behavior and persist over longer periods of time.
11. A group will not mobilize into a social movement unless there is a shared perception that its *relative deprivation* can be ended only through collective action.
12. The success of a social movement will depend in good part on how effectively it mobilizes its resources.
13. *New social movements* tend to focus on more than just economic issues and often cross national boundaries.

14. Advances in communication technology—especially on the Internet—have had a major impact on the various forms of collective behavior.

15. A growing number of organizations address national and even international concerns of lesbians and gay men.

Critical Thinking Questions

1. Are the emergent-norm, value-added, and assembling perspectives aligned with or reminiscent of functionalism, conflict theory, or interactionism? What aspects of each of these theories of collective behavior (if any) seem linked to the broader theoretical perspectives of sociology?

2. Without using any of the examples given in the textbook, list at least two examples of each of the following types of collective behavior: crowds, disasters, fads, fashions, panics, crazes, rumors, publics, and social movements. Explain why each example belongs in its assigned category. Distinguish between each type of collective behavior based on the type and degree of social structure and interaction that are present.

3. Select one social movement that is currently working for change in the United States. Analyze that movement, drawing on the concepts of relative deprivation, resource mobilization, and false consciousness.

Key Terms

Assembling perspective A theory of collective behavior introduced by McPhail and Miller that seeks to examine how and why people move from different points in space to a common location. (559)

Collective behavior In the view of sociologist Neil Smelser, the relatively spontaneous and unstructured behavior of a group of people who are reacting to a common influence in an ambiguous situation. (557)

Craze An exciting mass involvement that lasts for a relatively long period of time. (563)

Crowds Temporary gatherings of people in close proximity who share a common focus or interest. (560)

Disaster A sudden or disruptive event or set of events that overtaxes a community's resources so that outside aid is necessary. (560)

Emergent-norm perspective A theory of collective behavior proposed by Turner and Killian that holds that a collective definition of appropriate and inappropriate behavior emerges during episodes of collective behavior. (558)

Fads Temporary movements toward the acceptance of some particular taste or lifestyle that involve large numbers of people and are independent of preceding trends. (562)

False consciousness A term used by Karl Marx to describe an attitude held by members of a class that does not accurately reflect its objective position. (567)

Fashions Pleasurable mass involvements in some particular taste or lifestyle that have a line of historical continuity. (562)

New social movements Organized collective activities that promote autonomy and self-determination as well as improvements in the quality of life. (568)

Nonperiodic assemblies Nonrecurring gatherings of people that often result from word-of-mouth information. (559)

Panic A fearful arousal or collective flight based on a generalized belief that may or may not be accurate. (563)

Periodic assemblies Recurring, relatively routine gatherings of people, such as college classes. (559)

Public A dispersed group of people, not necessarily in contact with one another, who share an interest in an issue. (564)

Public opinion Expressions of attitudes on matters of public policy that are communicated to decision makers. (564)

Relative deprivation The conscious feeling of a negative discrepancy between legitimate expectations and present actualities. (566)

Resource mobilization The ways in which a social movement utilizes such resources as money, political influence, access to the media, and personnel. (567)

Rumor A piece of information gathered informally that is used to interpret an ambiguous situation. (563)

Social movements Organized collective activities to promote or resist change in an existing group or society. (565)

Value-added model A theory of collective behavior proposed by Neil Smelser to explain how broad social conditions are transformed in a definite pattern into some form of collective behavior. (558)

Additional Readings

BOOKS

Adam, Barry D., Jan Willem Duyvendak, and André Krouwel, eds. 1999. *The Global Emergence of Gay and Lesbian Politics: National Imprints of a Worldwide Movement.* Philadelphia: Temple University Press. The editors offer portraits of gay and lesbian organizing in 16 nations, including Australia, Brazil, France, Great Britain, Japan, Romania, and Spain.

Jasper, James. 1997. *The Art of Moral Protest: Culture, Biography, and Creativity in Social Movements.* Chicago: University of Chicago Press. An analysis of how social movements, ranging from nineteenth-century boycotts to contemporary antinuclear, animal rights, and environmental movements, develop and the impact they have on participants and society as a whole.

Lofland, John. 1996. *Social Movement Organizations: Guide to Research on Insurgent Realities.* New York: Aldine de Gruyter. A noted sociologist offers a handbook on studying social movement organizations.

Miller, David L. 2000. *Introduction to Collective Behavior and Collective Actions.* 2nd ed. Prospect Heights, IL: Waveland. The author, associated with the assembling perspective, covers all the major theoretical approaches of the field. He examines rumors, riots, social movements, immigration, and other forms of collective behavior.

Turner, Patricia A. 1993. *I Heard It through the Grapevine: Rumor in African-American Culture.* Berkeley: University of California Press. A scholarly examination of folktales and legends shared among African Americans.

JOURNALS

Among those journals that focus on collective behavior and social movements are the *International Journal of Mass Emergencies and Disasters* (founded in 1983), the *Journal of Gay, Lesbian, and Bisexual Identity* (1996), the *Journal of Popular Culture* (1967), and *Public Opinion Quarterly* (1937).

Internet Connection

Note: While all the URLs listed were current as of the printing of this book, these sites often change. Please check our website (http://www.mhhe.com/schaefer) for updates.

1. In the fall of 1999, Seattle was the site of mass demonstrations during the World Trade Organization conference. Learn more about this event by logging onto *Seattle Weekly*'s Special Coverage site (**http://www.seattleweekly.com/supplements/ wto/**). Be sure to read the articles and view the pictures in the "image gallery."
    (a) What themes are found in the pictures? How would you describe the interactions depicted in the photos?
    (b) What groups and organizations were involved in the events in Seattle?
    (c) What is the World Trade Organization (WTO)? When was it formed and what is its purpose?
    (d) What are some of the issues that protestors raised against the WTO?
    (e) What are the perspectives of those who support the WTO?
    (f) Which side do you most agree with and why?
    (g) What tactics and strategies did the protestors use to call attention to their views?
    (h) What was the response of city officials and President Clinton to these mass demonstrations? What is your opinion of these governmental responses?
    (i) Assume the role of a protest organizer. What would you have done differently, if anything?
    (j) Assume the role of the city's mayor. What would you have done differently, if anything?
    (k) What has been the aftermath of these days of protest in Seattle?

2. You can find links of interest to those studying gay and lesbian rights at **http://fullcoverage. yahoo.com/Full_Coverage/World/Gay_and_ Lesbian_News/**. Log on to the site and examine the following links: ACLU: Gay and Lesbian Rights and *Bowers* v. *Hardwick*. Also, visit PBS: Out of the Past (**http://www.pbs.org/outofthepast**).
    (a) What current legislation and court cases impacting gay and lesbian rights are in the news? Do the outcomes of these legal cases seem to favor or limit civil rights? How so?
    (b) Explore the timeline and facts presented on the PBS site. What role did the Stonewall Inn Riots play in the gay rights movement? What were the most surprising facts you learned about the experiences of homosexuals in world or U.S. history?
    (c) According to the ACLU site, what are the most important civil liberty issues facing gays and lesbians today?
    (d) Has your state decriminalized homosexual sexual encounters?
    (e) Does your state or city recognize domestic partnership registration?
    (f) Why are domestic partnership registrations important, according to the site?
    (g) After reading the "Model Domestic Partnerships" section, how would you summarize the ACLU's definition and requirements of domestic partnerships? What would you add or subtract from this description, and why?
    (h) What is ENDA?
    (i) What events led up to the Supreme Court case of *Bowers* v. *Hardwick*? When did the case appear before the Court?
    (j) What was the final decision? What is your opinion of the Court's decision?
    (k) Do you believe that equal rights for gay and lesbian citizens are improving or worsening in the United States? Why?

CHAPTER

22

SOCIAL CHANGE
AND TECHNOLOGY

(Artificial Intelligence)

Electronic listening music from Warp

Social change often reflects accessibility to new technology. A recent music innovation is IDM (intelligent dance music), experimental techno music made totally from electronic sources. This pixel painting appears as the cover art of the techno music compilation of England's Warp Records.

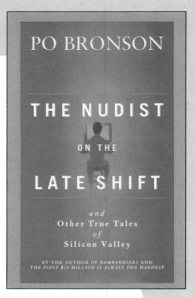

From the moment I met him, Sabeer Bhatia has given credit to the power of the idea. The idea was so powerful that when his friend and coworker Jack Smith, who was driving home to Livermore across the Dunbarton Bridge, called Sabeer on his car phone to brainstorm the pregnant thought that had just occurred to him, Sabeer heard one sentence of it and said, "Oh, my! Hang up that cellular and call me back on a secure line when you get to your house! We don't want anyone to overhear!"

It was so powerful an idea that when Jack did call Sabeer back fifteen minutes later, their minds melded as they talked, completely in sync, leaping from one ramification to the next as simultaneously as the steps of two soldiers marching side by side. It was so powerful that sleep that night was impossible for Sabeer, with the idea now in his head, exploding, autocatalytic, a bonfire of the mind. He stayed up all night, sitting at the glass-topped dining table in his small Bayside Village apartment, writing the business plan, which he took to his day job the next morning, looking so haggard that his boss stopped him and said, "You've got to cut out the partying, Sabeer." . . .

The idea came about this way: Sabeer and Jack had wanted to start a company, and they had been brainstorming possible business ideas for a few months. They wanted to e-mail each other notes, but they had been afraid that their bosses might glean their e-mail and accuse them of spending their working hours on personal projects (an accurate accusation). The budding entrepreneurs had personal America Online accounts, but these couldn't be accessed through the office network. On the evening he was driving home across the Dunbarton Bridge, Jack Smith had been frustrated all day by this problem. Then it occurred to him:

Free e-mail accounts that can be accessed anonymously, over the Web.

In getting over their own obstacle to coming up with a business idea, they came up with just that idea. . . .

It was the kind of idea that inspires legions of entrepreneurs. It was the kind of idea that spurs thousands of young people to give up their lives elsewhere and crash the Valley party. It sent the message and cc'd the entire world: to make it in Silicon Valley, you just have to come up with the right idea. . . .

Nowadays, meet Sabeer at a party and ask what he does, and he will tell you only that he works in high tech, just like hundreds of thousands of other young people in the valley. . . . Push him for more detail about his job, and he'll say he works at Hotmail. Ask if he's an engineer and he'll say no, he's the president. He's not being reclusive or coy, it just hasn't sunk in that he might be special.

What is Hotmail but e-mail on the Web? *(Bronson 1999:78–79, 80)* ∎

o Bronson specializes in writing about that hotbed of technology known as Silicon Valley. In this excerpt from his book *The Nudist on the Late Shift*, Bronson profiles the inventor of Hotmail and highlights the importance of a good idea—even so simple an idea as accessing e-mail on the Internet. Combining the convenience of e-mail with the global reach of the Web, Hotmail allows anyone in the world to communicate instantly with anyone else, as long as both have access to the Web. To appreciate the impact of this idea, drop into any cyber café—whether it be in Bangkok, Bali, or Bismarck—and observe the flurry of e-mail being sent and received by backpackers, tourists, students, and businesspeople alike.

The development of the computer as an integral part of the day-to-day life in the United States and other countries is an example of social change. ***Social change*** has been defined as significant alteration over time in behavior patterns and culture (Moore 1967). But what constitutes a "significant" alteration? Certainly the dramatic rise in formal education documented in Chapter 15 represents a change that has had profound social consequences. Other social changes that have had long-term and important consequences include the emergence of slavery as a system of stratification (see Chapter 8), the industrial revolution (Chapters 5 and 19), the increased participation of women in the paid labor forces of the United States and Europe (Chapter 11), and the worldwide population explosion (Chapter 20). In many instances, the social movements studied in Chapter 21 have played an important role in promoting social change.

This chapter examines the process of social change, with special emphasis on the impact of technological advances. Efforts to explain long-term social changes have led to the development of theories of change; we will consider the evolutionary, functionalist, and conflict approaches to change. We will see how vested interests can block changes that they see as threatening. We'll also look at various aspects of our technological future through discussion of telecommuting, the Internet, biotechnology, and technological accidents. We will examine the effects of technological advances on culture and social interaction, social control, and stratification and inequality. Taken together, the impact of these technological changes may be approaching a level of magnitude comparable to that of the industrial revolution. Finally, the social policy section will discuss the ways in which technological advances have intensified concerns over privacy and censorship. ■

Theories of Social Change

A new millennium provides the occasion to offer explanations of social change, but this is clearly a challenge in the diverse and complex world we inhabit today. Nevertheless, theorists from several disciplines have sought to analyze social change. In some instances, they have examined historical events to arrive at a better understanding of contemporary changes. We will review three theoretical approaches to change—evolutionary, functionalist, and conflict theory—and then take a look at global change today.

Evolutionary Theory

Charles Darwin's (1809–1882) pioneering work in biological evolution contributed to nineteenth-century theories of social change. According to his approach, there has been a continuing progression of successive life forms. For example, since human beings came at a later stage of evolution than reptiles, we represent a "higher" from of life. Social theorists sought an analogy to this biological model and originated ***evolutionary theory,*** which views society as moving in a definite direction. Early evolutionary theorists generally agreed that society was inevitably progressing to a higher state. As might be expected, they concluded in ethnocentric fashion that their own behavior and culture were more advanced than those of earlier civilizations.

August Comte (1798–1857), a founder of sociology, was an evolutionary theorist of change. He saw human societies as moving forward in their thinking from mythology to the scientific method. Similarly, Émile Durkheim (1933, original edition 1893) maintained that society progressed from simple to more complex forms of social organization.

The writings of Comte and Durkheim are examples of ***unilinear evolutionary theory.*** This approach contends that all societies pass through the same successive stages of evolution and inevitably reach the same end. English sociologist Herbert Spencer (1820–1903) used a similar approach: Spencer likened society to a living body with interrelated parts that were moving toward a common destiny. However, contemporary evolutionary theorists such as Gerhard Lenski are more likely to picture social change as multilinear than to rely on the more limited unilinear perspective. ***Multilinear*** *evolutionary theory* holds that change can occur in several ways and that it does not inevitably lead in the same direction (Haines 1988; J. Turner 1985).

Multilinear theorists recognize that human culture has evolved along a number of lines. For example, the theory of demographic transition graphically demonstrates that population change in developing nations has not p. 534 necessarily followed the model evident in industrialized nations. Sociologists today recognize that events do not necessarily follow in a single or several straight lines but instead are subject to disruptions—a topic we will consider later in the discussion of global social change.

Functionalist Theory

Functionalist sociologists focus on what *maintains* a system, not on what changes it. This might seem to suggest that functionalists can offer little of value to the study of social change. Yet, as the work of sociologist Talcott Parsons demonstrates, functionalists have made a distinctive contribution to this area of sociological investigation.

Parsons (1902–1979), a leading proponent of functionalist theory, viewed society as naturally being p. 14 in a state of equilibrium. By "equilibrium," he meant that society tends toward a state of stability or balance. Parsons would view even prolonged labor strikes or civilian riots as temporary disruptions in the status quo rather than as significant alterations in social structure. Therefore, according to his **equilibrium model,** as changes occur in one part of society, there must be adjustments in other parts. If this does not take place, the society's equilibrium will be threatened and strains will occur.

Reflecting an evolutionary approach, Parsons (1966) maintained that four processes of social change are inevitable. The first, *differentiation,* refers to the increasing complexity of social organization. A change from "medicine man" to physician, nurse, and pharmacist is an illustration of differentiation in the field of health. This process is accompanied by *adaptive upgrading,* whereby social institutions become more specialized in their purposes. The division of labor among physicians into obstetricians, internists, surgeons, and so forth is an example of adaptive upgrading.

The third process identified by Parsons is the *inclusion* of groups into society that were previously excluded because of such factors as gender, race, and social class background. Medical schools have practiced inclusion by admitting increasing numbers of women and African Americans. Finally, Parsons contends that societies experience *value generalization,* the development of new values that tolerate and legitimate a greater range of activities. The acceptance of preventive and alternative medicine is an example of value generalization; our society has broadened its view of health care. All four processes identified by Parsons stress consensus—societal agreement on the nature of social organization and values (B. Johnson 1975; R. Wallace and Wolf 1980).

Parsons's approach explicitly incorporates the evolutionary notion of continuing progress. However, the dominant theme in his model is balance and stability. Society may change, but it remains stable through new forms of integration. For example, in place of the kinship ties that provided social cohesion in the past, there are laws, judicial processes, and new values and belief systems.

Functionalists assume that social institutions will not persist unless they continue to contribute to the overall society. This leads functionalists to conclude that altering institutions will threaten societal equilibrium. Critics note that the

African Americans are now accepted in many exclusive golf clubs that were previously restricted, illustrating the process of *inclusion* described by Talcott Parsons. The phenomenal success of pro golfer Tiger Woods has helped the process along.

functionalist approach virtually disregards the use of coercion by the powerful to maintain the illusion of a stable, well-integrated society (Gouldner 1960).

Conflict Theory

The functionalist perspective minimizes change. It emphasizes the persistence of social life and sees change as a means of maintaining the equilibrium (or balance) of a society. By contrast, conflict theorists contend that social institutions and practices continue because powerful groups have the ability to maintain the status quo. Change has crucial significance, since it is needed to correct social injustices and inequalities.

Karl Marx accepted the evolutionary argument that societies develop along a particular path. However, unlike Comte and Spencer, he did not view each successive stage as an inevitable improvement over the previous one. History, according to Marx, proceeds through a series of stages, each of which exploits a class of people. Ancient society exploited slaves; the estate system of feudalism exploited serfs; modern capitalist society exploits the working class. Ultimately, through a socialist revolution led by the proletariat, human society will move toward the final stage of development: a classless communist society, or "community of free individuals" as Marx described it in *Das Kapital* in 1867 (see Bottomore and Rubel 1956:250).

As we have seen, Karl Marx had an important influence on the development of sociology. His thinking offered insights into such institutions as the economy, the family, religion, and government. The Marxist view of social change is appealing because it does not restrict people to a passive role in responding to inevitable cycles or changes in material culture. Rather, Marxist theory offers a tool for those who wish to seize control of the historical process and gain their freedom from injustice. In contrast to functionalists' emphasis on stability, Marx argues that conflict is a normal and desirable aspect of social change. In fact, change must be encouraged as a means of eliminating social inequality (Lauer 1982).

One conflict sociologist, Ralf Dahrendorf (1959), has noted that the contrast between the functionalist perspective's emphasis on stability and the conflict perspective's focus on change reflects the contradictory nature of society. Human societies are stable and long-lasting, yet they also experience serious conflict. Dahrendorf found that the functionalist approach and the conflict approach were ultimately compatible despite their many areas of disagreement. Indeed, Parsons spoke of new functions that result from social change, and Marx recognized the need for change so that societies could function more equitably.

Global Social Change

The end of the twentieth century is a truly dramatic period to consider global social change. Maureen Hallinan (1997), in her presidential address to the American Sociological Association, asked those present to consider just a few of the recent political events: the collapse of communism; terrorism in various parts of the world, including the United States; the dismantling of the welfare system in the United States; revolution and famine in Africa and Eastern Europe; the spread of AIDS; and the computer revolution. Just a few months after her remarks came the first verification of the cloning of a complex animal, Dolly the sheep.

In this era of massive social, political, and economic change on a global scale, is it possible to predict change? Some technological changes seem obvious, but the collapse of communist governments in the Soviet Union and Eastern Europe took people by surprise in its speed and its unexpectedness. However, prior to the Soviet collapse, sociologist Randall Collins (1986, 1995), a conflict theorist, had observed a crucial sequence of changes that most observers had missed.

In seminars as far back as 1980—and in a book published in 1986—Collins argued that Soviet expansionism in the twentieth century had resulted in an overextension of resources, including disproportionate spending on military forces. Such overextension strains a regime's stability. Moreover, geopolitical theory suggests that nations in the middle of a geographic region (like the Soviet Union) tend to fragment over time into smaller units.

Collins predicted that the coincidence of social crises on several frontiers would precipitate the collapse of the Soviet Union. The success of the Iranian revolution in 1979 led to an upsurge of Islamic fundamentalism in nearby Afghanistan and in Soviet republics with substantial Muslim populations. Moreover, there was growing resistance to communist rule throughout Eastern Europe and within the Soviet Union itself. Collins added that the rise of a dissident form of communism within the Soviet Union might facilitate the breakdown of the regime. Beginning in the late 1980s, Soviet leader Mikhail Gorbachev chose not to use military power and other types of repression to crush dissidents in Eastern Europe, offered plans for democratization and social reform of Soviet society, and seemed willing to reshape the Soviet Union into a loose federation of somewhat autonomous states. But, in 1991, six republics on the western periphery declared their independence, and within months the entire Soviet Union had formally disintegrated. (For a different course of events, see Box 22-1, which chronicles the recent, comparatively peaceful revolution in South Africa.)

In her address, Maureen Hallinan (1997) cautioned that we need to move beyond the restrictive models of

22-1 Social Change in South Africa

As recently as 10 years ago, South Africa, a nation of 43 million people, was accurately described as a country where race was the sole determinant of power. Regardless of occupation, education, or family background, White South Africans enjoyed legal rights and privileges that were denied to all people of color. Ever since 1948, when it received its independence from Great Britain, South Africa had maintained this rigid segregationist policy, known as *apartheid.*

p. 270

During the 1980s, South Africa felt increasing worldwide economic pressure. At the same time, Black South Africans were more and more vocal about their second-class citizenship. They engaged in many forms of nonviolent and violent protest, including economic boycotts, labor strikes, political demonstrations, and occasional acts of sabotage.

In a dramatic turn of events in 1990, South African prime minister F. W. de Klerk legalized 60 banned Black organizations and freed Nelson Mandela, the leader of the long-outlawed African National Congress (ANC), after 27 years of imprisonment. The following year, de Klerk and Black leaders signed a National Peace Accord, pledging themselves to the establishment of a multiparty democracy.

In 1994, South Africa held its first universal election. Nelson Mandela's ANC received 62 percent of the vote, giving him a five-year term as president. Mandela and his political party were then faced with a difficult challenge: making the transition from a liberation movement fighting for revolution to a governing party that needed to achieve political compromises. Moreover, an end to the racist policy of apartheid—while applauded around the world—was not in itself a solution to all of South Africa's serious problems. At best, one-fifth of the country's Blacks could compete in the nation's economy, while the balance formed a huge underclass.

> An end to the racist policy of apartheid—while applauded around the world—was not in itself a solution to all of South Africa's serious problems.

Some of the controversial issues facing the government are very familiar to residents of the United States:

- *Affirmative action.* Race-based employment goals and other preference programs have been proposed, yet critics insist that such efforts constitute reverse apartheid.
- *Illegal immigration.* An estimated 2 to 20 percent of South African residents are illegal immigrants, many of whom wish to escape the poverty and political turmoil of neighboring African states.

- *Medical care.* South Africa is confronting the inequities of private health care for the affluent (usually White) and government-subsidized care for others (usually people of color).
- *School integration and upgrading.* Multiracial schools are replacing the segregated school system. As of 1998, 82 percent had no media equipment (televisions or computers), and 57 percent had no electricity.

Perhaps the most difficult issue facing the government is land reform. Between 1960 and 1990, the all-White government forced 3.5 million Black South Africans from their land and frequently allowed Whites to settle on it. Under legislation adopted in 1994, these displaced citizens can now file for restitution of their land. As of 1998, more than 23,000 such claims had been filed; in many cases, there are sure to be objections from settled Whites. Even though government compensation will be offered to current landowners, bitter disputes will be inevitable.

Let's Discuss

1. How would a conflict theorist explain the relatively peaceful revolution in South Africa? What explanation might a functionalist offer?
2. Do you think other nations should use economic pressure to face social change in a country? Why or why not?

Sources: Daley 1996, 1998; Duke 1998; R. Schaefer 2000; Sidiropoulos et al. 1996; South African Institute of Race Relations 1998.

---

social change—the linear view of evolutionary theory and the assumptions about equilibrium within functionalist theory. She and other sociologists have looked to "chaos theory" advanced by mathematicians to consider erratic events as a part of change. Hallinan noted that upheavals and major chaotic shifts do occur and that sociologists must learn to predict their occurrence, as Collins did with the Soviet Union. It is not hard to imagine the dramatic nonlinear social change that will result from major innovations in the areas of communication and biotechnology, as we will see later in the chapter.

Resistance to Social Change

Efforts to promote social change are likely to meet with resistance. In the midst of rapid scientific and technological innovations, many people are frightened by the demands of an ever-changing society. Moreover, certain individuals and groups have a stake in maintaining the existing state of affairs.

Social economist Thorstein Veblen (1857–1929) coined the term *vested interests* to refer to those people or groups who will suffer in the event of social change. For example, the American Medical Association (AMA) has taken strong stands against national health insurance and p. 473 the professionalization of midwifery. National health insurance could lead to limits on the income of physicians, and a rise in the status of midwives could threaten the preeminent position of doctors as the nation's deliverers of babies. In general, those with a disproportionate share of society's wealth, status, and power, such as members of the American Medical Association, have a vested interest in preserving the status quo (Starr 1982; Veblen 1919).

Economic and Cultural Factors

Economic factors play an important role in resistance to social change. For example, it can be expensive for manufacturers to meet high standards for the safety of products and workers. Conflict theorists argue that, in a capitalist economic system, many firms are not willing to pay the price of meeting strict safety standards. They may resist social change by cutting corners within their plants or by pressuring the government to ease regulations.

Communities, too, protect their vested interests, often in the name of "protecting property values." The abbreviation "NIMBY" stands for "not in my backyard," a cry often heard when people protest landfills, prisons,

nuclear power facilities, and even group homes for people with developmental disabilities. The targeted community may not challenge the need for the facility but may simply insist that it be located elsewhere. The "not in my backyard" attitude has become so common that it is almost impossible for policymakers to find acceptable locations for such facilities as dump sites for hazardous wastes (J. Jasper 1997).

Like economic factors, cultural factors frequently shape resistance to change. William F. Ogburn (1922) distinguished between material and nonmaterial aspects of culture. *Material culture* includes investigations, artifacts, and technology; *nonmaterial culture* p. 68 encompasses ideas, norms, communication, and social organization. Ogburn pointed out that one cannot devise methods for controlling and utilizing new technology before the introduction of a technique. Thus, nonmaterial culture typically must respond to changes in material culture. Ogburn introduced the term **culture lag** to refer to the period of maladjustment during which the nonmaterial culture is still adapting to new material conditions. One example is the Internet. Its rapid uncontrolled growth raises questions about whether to regulate it and, if so, how much (see the social policy section in this chapter).

In certain cases, changes in material culture can add strain to the relationships between social institutions. For example, new techniques of birth control have been developed in recent decades. Large families are no longer economically necessary, nor are they commonly endorsed by social norms. But certain religious faiths, among them Roman Catholicism, continue to extol large families and to disapprove methods of limiting family size such as contraception and abortion. This represents a lag between aspects of material culture (technology) and nonmaterial culture (religious beliefs). Conflicts may emerge between religion and other social institutions, such as government and the educational system, over the dissemination of birth control and family-planning information (M. Riley et al. 1994a, 1994b).

"Not in my backyard!" say these demonstrators, objecting to the placement of a new incinerator in a Hartford, Connecticut, neighborhood. The phenomenon of NIMBY has become so common that it is almost impossible for policymakers to find acceptable locations for incinerators, landfills, and dump sites for hazardous wastes.

Resistance to Technology

Technological innovations are examples of changes in material culture that have often provoked

p. 133 →

resistance. The *industrial revolution,* which took place largely in England during the period 1760 to 1830, was a scientific revolution focused on the application of nonanimal sources of power to labor tasks. As this revolution proceeded, societies relied on new inventions that facilitated agricultural and industrial production and on new sources of energy such as steam. In some industries, the introduction of power-driven machinery reduced the need for factory workers and made it easier to cut wages.

Strong resistance to the industrial revolution emerged in some countries. In England, beginning in 1811, masked craft workers took extreme measures: They conducted nighttime raids on factories and destroyed some of the new machinery. The government hunted these rebels, known as *Luddites,* and ultimately banished some while hanging others. In a similar effort in France, some angry workers threw their wooden shoes (*sabots*) into factory machinery to destroy it, thereby giving rise to the term *sabotage.* While the resistance of the Luddites and the French workers was short-lived and unsuccessful, they have come to symbolize resistance to technology over the last two centuries.

Are we now in the midst of a second industrial revolution, with a contemporary group of Luddites engaged in re-

p. 133 →

sistance? Many sociologists believe that we are now living in a *postindustrial society.* It is difficult to pinpoint exactly when this era began. Generally, it is viewed as having begun in the 1950s, when for the first time the majority of workers in industrial societies became involved in services rather than in the actual manufacturing of goods (D. Bell 1973; Fiala 1992).

Just as the Luddites resisted the industrial revolution, people in many countries have resisted postindustrial technological changes. The term *neo-Luddites* refers to those who are wary of technological innovations and who question the incessant expansion of industrialization, the increasing destruction of the natural and agrarian world, and the "throw it away" mentality of contemporary capitalism with its resulting pollution of the environment. Neo-Luddites insist that whatever the presumed benefits of industrial and postindustrial technology, such technology has distinctive social costs and may represent a danger to the future of the human species and our planet (Bauerlein 1996; Rifkin 1995b; Sale 1996; Snyder 1996).

Such concerns are worth remembering as we turn now to examine aspects of our technological future and their possible impact on social change.

Technology and the Future

p. 132 →

Technology is information about how to use the material resources of the environment to satisfy human needs and desires. Technological ad-

vances—the airplane, the automobile, the television, the atomic bomb, and, more recently, the computer, the fax machine, and the cellular phone—have brought striking changes in our cultures, our patterns of socialization, our social institutions, and our day-to-day social interactions. Technological innovations are, in fact, emerging and being accepted with remarkable speed. For example, scientists at Monsanto estimated in 1998 that the amount of genetic information used in practical applications will double every year. Part of the reason for this explosion in using new technology is that it is becoming cheaper. In 1974, it cost $2.5 million to determine the chemical structure of a single gene; today that cost is $150 (Belsie 1998).

The technological knowledge with which we work today represents only a tiny portion of the knowledge that will be available in the year 2050. We are witnessing an information explosion as well: The number of volumes in

Today's version of Luddites are protesting technological innovations that they regard as destructive. This Greenpeace demonstrator in Montreal scales a giant corn "monster" in protest of genetically engineered food (see the discussion later in this chapter).

Taking Sociology to Work

LAUREL MILLER:
Executive Producer, Media Technology, McGraw-Hill Companies

When Laurel Miller got her degree from the State University of New York, Albany, in 1972, it was a time of great social change, which she admits influenced her decision to major in sociology. "I was interested in how groups of people worked, how institutions became what they are." She recalls being stimulated by writing papers on a variety of topics, such as the evolution of tennis, ballet, and a specific religious movement.

In her job at McGraw-Hill, Miller develops new media products, such as CD-ROMs and websites, for the humanities and social sciences lists, which, of course, include sociology texts. She has to keep up with the changes in technology that have come fast and furious in the last few years. She's been excited to see "the increased acceptance of technology by professors, sales representatives, and editorial staff" to the point that it is now considered the normal way of doing things in the publishing world.

Miller credits her background in sociology with giving her "a broad perspective on events and circumstances that I've been involved in." It also taught her not to jump to conclusions or to form stereotypes. She recommends that sociology students "always remain interested in what is going on around you."

---

major libraries in the United States doubles every 14 years. Individuals, institutions, and societies will face unprecedented challenges in adjusting to the technological advances soon to come (Cetron and Davies 1991; Wurman 1989).

In the following sections, we will examine various aspects of our technological future and consider their overall impact on social change, including the strains they will bring. We will focus in particular on recent developments in computer technology and biotechnology.

Computer Technology

The 1990s witnessed an explosion of computer technology in the United States and around the world. We will now examine two aspects of the technological and social changes related to computers: telecommuting and the Internet.

Telecommuting

As the industrial revolution proceeded, the factory and the office replaced the home as the typical workplace. But the postindustrial revolution has brought people home again. In 1999, at least 14 million telecommuters in the United States worked at home at least once a month. *Telecommuters* are employees of business firms or government agencies who work full-time or part-time at home rather than in an outside office. They are linked to their supervisors and colleagues through computer terminals, phone lines, and fax machines. As part of a shift toward postindustrial societies linked within a global economy, telecommuting can even cross national boundaries, oceans, and continents (Hall 1999).

Telecommuting clearly facilitates communication between a company's employees who work in different locations, including those who work at home. Telecommuting also reduces time spent on transportation and can be helpful in a family's child care arrangements. At the same time, working at home can be isolating and stressful—and even more stressful if a parent must attempt to combine working at home and caring for children. Moreover, companies still need to encourage face-to-face communication in staff meetings and social settings. Overall, while telecommuting unquestionably offers distinct advantages for many employees and companies, it also presents new challenges (Marklein 1996).

The rise of telecommuting is especially beneficial for one subordinate group in the United States: p. 123 ◄ people with disabilities. Computer terminals lend themselves to ancillary devices that make them adaptable to most types of physical impairments. For example, people who are blind can work at home using word processors that read messages in a computer voice or translate them into Braille (Nelson 1995).

By the year 2009, it is estimated that as many as half of all workers in the United States will perform their jobs partially at home through use of computer systems. The dramatic increase in use of computer networks such as the Internet has unquestionably contributed to the rise in telecommuting (Halal 1992; Rifkin 1995b).

The Internet

The Internet is the world's largest computer network. As of 1998, it was reaching some 37 million computer users, but the number of people using the Internet *doubles* each year.

The Internet actually evolved from a computer system built in 1962 by the U.S. Defense Department to

587

In our postindustrial society, computers are in use almost everywhere imaginable.

enable scholars and military researchers to continue to do government work even if part of the nation's communications system was destroyed by a nuclear attack. Until recently, it was difficult to gain access to the Internet without holding a position at a university or a government research laboratory. Today, however, virtually anyone can reach the Internet with a phone line, a computer, and a modem. And it is possible to buy and sell cars, trade stocks, auction off items, research new medical remedies, vote, track down long-lost friends—to mention just a few of the thousands of online possibilities (Reddick and King 2000).

While the rise of the Internet facilitates telecommuting and the spread of a home-based economy, much of the focus of the Internet has been on new forms of communication and social interaction. Early users established a subculture with specific norms and values. These pioneers generally resent formal rules for Internet communication, believe that access to information should be free and unlimited, and distrust efforts to centralize control of the Internet. The subculture of early Internet users also developed argot terms, such as "flaming" (hurling abuse online) and "chat rooms" (bulletin boards for people with common interests).

The expansion of the Internet has led to a proliferation of chat rooms and webpages where people can gather and exchange information on such diverse topics as artificial intelligence, baseball, the conflict in Bosnia, erotica, the Hubble space telescope, Japanese animation, and women's history in Tudor England. At the same time, the spectacular growth of the Internet has posed challenges. It is no longer possible for the Internet pioneers to enforce the informal norms that they developed. As one example of the challenge to these norms, in 1994 an attorney in Phoenix placed an advertisement for his services as a "green card" immigration lawyer on every one of a computer network's more than 5,000 discussion groups. This episode raises the danger that chat rooms could be swamped with advertising that will drown out noncommercial speech (Wiener 1994).

While the Internet has unquestionably offered exciting new possibilities for sharing information and communication, many troubling issues have been raised about day-to-day "life" on the Internet. What if anything, should be done about use of the Internet by neo-Nazis and other extremist groups who exchange messages of hatred and even bomb-making recipes? What, if anything, should be done about male domination of the Internet? And what about the issue of sexual expression on the Internet? Should there be censorship of "hot chat" and X-rated film clips? Or should there be *complete* freedom of expression? The impact of technological change on issues of privacy and censorship will be examined in the social policy section at the end of this chapter.

Most people in the United States believe that the Internet will increasingly become our primary source of information. In a national survey conducted in 1996, respondents born since 1971 (a population group that has been called the "microprocessor generation") were asked what they thought would be their main source of news in the year 2000. About 59 percent believed that they would get most of their news from the Internet, compared with 31 percent who thought it would come from radio and television and only 10 percent who thought most news would come from print media (Boeck and Staimer 1996; Bollag 1996).

While many people in the United States embrace the Internet, we should note that information is not evenly distributed throughout the population. The same people, by and large, who experience poor health and have few job opportunities also have been left off the information highway. Moreover, this pattern of inequality is global. The core nations that Immanual Wallerstein describes in his *world system analysis* have a virtual monopoly on information technology p. 232 while the developing nations of Asia, Africa, and Latin America are on the periphery, depending on the industrial giants for both the technology and the information it provides. In Box 22-2 we explore this "global disconnect" in knowledge.

Research in Action

22-2 Global Disconnect

Students in colleges in North America expect to be able to use the Internet or leave messages through voice mail. They complain when the computer is "slow" or the electronic mailbox is "full." Despite their complaints, they take these services for granted and generally do not even pay directly for them. But in much of the world, it is very different.

The United Nations has tried for years to assist the nation of Madagascar to upgrade its telephone system to be able to handle a 300 baud communication device—the slowest speed available. At this glacial rate, it would take about two minutes to transmit this page without the color and without the graphics. By comparison, in the United States, most people are *discarding* systems 50 times faster and turning to devices that transmit information 180 times faster. The irony is that it costs more per minute to use a telephone in Madagascar and much of Africa than in the United States, so we have a continent paying more per minute to transmit information much more slowly.

This is but one example of the haves and have-nots in the information age. As shown on the map on page 590, the Internet is virtually monopolized by North America and Europe and a few other industrial nations such as Australia, New Zealand, and Japan. They have the most *Internet hosts*, computers directly connected to the worldwide network of interconnected computer systems.

This inequality is not new. We also find dramatic differences in the presence of newspapers, telephones, televisions, and even radios throughout the world. For ex-

> In Madagascar, there are 3 telephone lines per 1,000 people, and for all low-income nations the average is 16.

ample, in Madagascar, there are 3 telephone lines per 1,000 people, and for all low-income nations the average is 16. In the United States, there are 644 lines per 1,000 people; for all high-income nations the average is 552. Often in developing nations, and especially their rural areas, radio and television transmission is sporadic, and the programming may be dominated by recycled information from the United States.

The consequences of the global disconnect for developing nations are far more serious than not being able to "surf the Net." Today we have the true emergence of what sociologist Manuel Castells refers to as a "global economy" because the world has the capacity to work as a single unit in real time. However, if large numbers of people and, indeed, entire nations are disconnected from the informational economy, their slow economic growth will continue with all the negative consequences it has for people. The educated and skilled will immigrate to labor markets that are a part of this global economy, deepening the impoverishment of the nations on the periphery.

Let's Discuss

1. What factors might make it difficult to remedy the global disconnect in developing nations?
2. What are some of the social and economic consequences for nations that are not "connected"?

Sources: Castells 1996; World Bank 2000; Wresch 1996.

Biotechnology

Sex selection of fetuses, genetically engineered organisms, cloning of sheep and cows—these have been among the significant and yet controversial scientific advances in the field of biotechnology in recent years. As we will see in the following sections, these advances have raised many difficult ethical and political questions.

Sex Selection

In 1978, the first baby was born as the result of conception outside the womb. Since then, advances in reproductive and screening technology have brought us closer to effective techniques for sex selection. In the United States, the prenatal test of amniocentesis has been used for 20 years to ascertain the presence of certain defects that require medical procedures prior to birth. However, such tests also identify the sex of the fetus, an outcome that has had profound social implications.

In many societies, young couples planning to have only one child will want to ensure that this child is a boy because these cultures place a premium on a male heir. In such instances, advances in fetal testing may lead to abortion if the fetus is found to be female. Kuckreja Sohoni, a social scientist from India, notes that many parents in India are "mortally afraid" of having baby girls. Well aware of the pressure on Indian women to produce sons, Sohoni (1994:96), the mother of three teenage girls, admits, "had ultrasound been available when I was having children, I shudder to think how easily I would have been persuaded to plan a sex-selected family."

Fetal testing clinics in Canada currently advertise that they can tell parents the sex of a fetus. Such advertising is particularly targeted at Asian Indian communities in both Canada and the United States. But, in the United States, the preference for a male child is hardly limited to people from India. In one study, when asked what sex they

The Global Disconnect

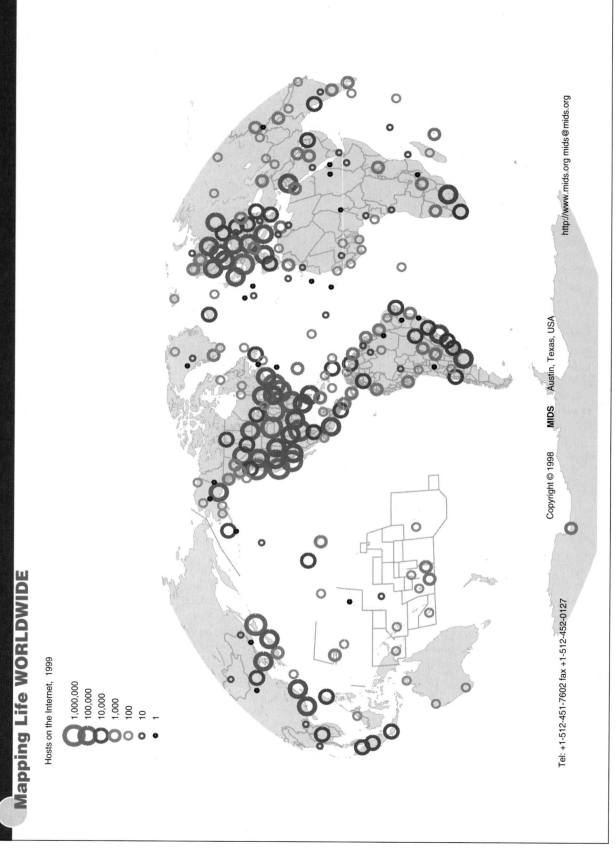

Mapping Life WORLDWIDE

Hosts on the Internet, 1999

1,000,000
100,000
10,000
1,000
100
10
1

Copyright © 1998   **MIDS**   Austin, Texas, USA

http://www.mids.org   mids@mids.org

Tel: +1-512-451-7602 fax +1-512-452-0127

Source: Matrix Information and Directory Services 1999.

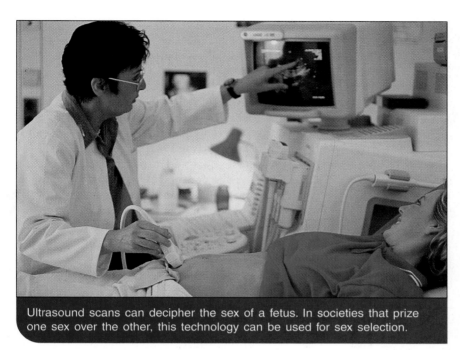

Ultrasound scans can decipher the sex of a fetus. In societies that prize one sex over the other, this technology can be used for sex selection.

Trademark Office approved 11,815 patents for genetically engineered substances. Some corporations believe that genetic engineering is a high-stakes gamble worth taking: In 1995, one company paid $20 million for an exclusive license to develop products derived from a gene that seems to play a role in obesity.

The debate on genetic engineering escalated in 1997 when scientists in Scotland announced that they had cloned a sheep. After many unsuccessful attempts, scientists finally were able to replace the genetic material of a sheep's egg with DNA from an adult sheep and thereby create a lamb that was a clone of the adult. The very next year, Japanese researchers successfully cloned cows. These developments raised the possibility that, in the near future, we may be able to clone human beings.

would prefer for an only child, 86 percent of men and 59 percent of women wanted a boy. Moreover, fetal testing to determine the sex of a child is becoming more accepted in the United States (M. Hall 1993; Sohoni 1994).

From a functionalist perspective, we can view sex selection as an adaptation of the basic family function of regulating reproduction. However, conflict theorists emphasize that sex selection may intensify the male dominance of our society and undermine the advances women have made in entering careers formerly restricted to men.

Genetic Engineering

Even more grandiose than sex selection—but not necessarily improbable—is altering human behavior through genetic engineering. Fish and plant genes have already been mixed to create frost-resistant potato and tomato crops; more recently, human genes have been implanted in pigs to provide humanlike kidneys for organ transplants.

One of the latest developments in genetic engineering is gene therapy. Geneticists in Japan have managed to disable genes in a mouse fetus that carry an undesirable trait and replace them with genes carrying a desirable trait. Such advances raise staggering possibilities for altering animal and human life forms, but gene therapy remains highly experimental and must be assessed as a long, long shot (Kolata 1999).

In 1980, the U.S. Supreme Court ruled, by a 5–4 vote, that a genetically engineered organism that cleans up oil spills constituted a new invention and could be patented. From 1981 to early 1995, the U.S. Patent and

In 1997 President Bill Clinton banned any federal support for human cloning and urged private laboratories to abide by a voluntary moratorium until the ethical issues could be carefully considered. William F. Ogburn probably could not have anticipated such scientific developments when he wrote of culture lag 70 years earlier; however, the successful cloning of sheep illustrates again how quickly material culture can change and how nonmaterial culture moves more slowly in absorbing such changes (J. Morrow 1997; Sale 1997; Wilmut et al. 1997).

July, 2018. The ethical debate, part 2,473,561

Should employees be allowed to use the office cloning machine for personal business?

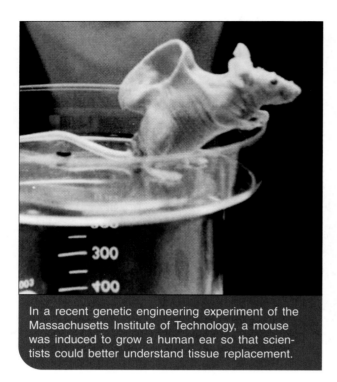

In a recent genetic engineering experiment of the Massachusetts Institute of Technology, a mouse was induced to grow a human ear so that scientists could better understand tissue replacement.

While cloning grabs the headlines, there is a growing controversy concerning food that has been genetically modified (GM). This controversy began in Europe but has since spread to other parts of the world, including the United States. The idea behind the technology is to increase food production and make agriculture more economical. Critics use the term "Frankenfood" (as in "Frankenstein") to refer to everything from breakfast cereals using genetically engineered grains to "fresh" tomatoes in the produce department. They object to tampering with nature and are concerned about the possible health effects of GM food. Supporters of the genetically modified food include not just the biotech companies but also those who see the technology as a way to help feed burgeoning populations in Africa and Asia (Golden 1999).

Technological Accidents

A carpenter who single-handedly makes a ladder has quite a different investment in the quality of the product than does a technician who develops a small part for a space shuttle. Our increasing reliance on technology has led to a growing separation between people and the outcomes of their actions.

Sociologist Charles Perrow (1999) introduced the term **normal accidents** to refer to failures that are inevitable given the manner in which human and technological systems are organized. Whether in a hospital or an aerospace program, catastrophes are often caused not by massive errors but rather by what appear to be (when considered in isolation) almost incidental human misjudgments and minor technical flaws. In studying normal accidents, engineers focus on the system design, the physical environment, and the possibility of mechanical failure; social scientists evaluate possible *human* error. Generally, 60 to 80 percent of normal accidents are attributed to human factors (Erikson 1994).

As technology continues to advance at a rapid pace, there are always new possibilities for accidents. For example, in Chapter 6 we examined the disastrous 1986 launch of the U.S. space shuttle *Challenger,* which ended in the deaths of seven astronauts. p. 152 More recently, it became apparent that electronic communication devices are vulnerable to failure. In 1998 the Galaxy IV communications satellite malfunctioned, knocking out the paging systems used by 90 percent of people in the United States. Hospitals could not page their doctors, so old-fashioned "phone trees" were established during the week of no service. The malfunction also took several broadcasters off the air, including National Public Radio. While the foul-up was ultimately corrected, this incident does underscore the possibilities for chaos in an ever-expanding electronic system (Swanson and Kirk 1998).

System accidents are uncommon, even rare. But, like the death of any individual, which occurs only once, this infrequency is not all that reassuring. Given the serious consequences of a systems failure, we can anticipate that social scientists will work even more closely with engineers to explore how better equipment, training, and organization can reduce the likelihood of normal accidents (Perrow 1999; see also Clarke 1988).

These are but a few vignettes of technological change, viewed from the vantage point of the turn of the century, that raise questions about the future. Sociologists are not fortune-tellers; the focus of the discipline is to examine the society around us, rather than to project decades ahead. But sociologists have no problem in asserting that social change (and technological change) is a given in our world. And so, they remind us, is resistance to change. We cannot know what is ahead. But the sociological imagination—with its probing and theorizing, with its careful empirical studies—can assist us in understanding the past and present and anticipating and adjusting to the future.

Technology and Society

An ATM machine that identifies a person by his or her facial structure, a small device that sorts through hundreds of odors to ensure the safety of a chemical plant, a cell phone that recognizes its owner's voice. These are real-life examples of technology that were so much science fiction a few short decades ago. Today's computer chip cannot only think but can see, smell, and hear, too (Salkever 1999).

Technological advances can dramatically transform the material culture. Word processing on computers, the pocket calculator, the photocopying machine, and the compact disc player have largely eliminated use of the typewriter, the adding machine, the mimeograph machine, and the turntable—all of which were themselves technological advances.

Technological change also can reshape *nonmaterial* culture. In the following sections, we will examine the effects of technological advances on culture and social interaction, social control, and stratification and inequality.

Culture and Social Interaction

In Chapter 3, we emphasized that language is the foundation of every culture. From a functionalist perspective, language can bring together members of a society and promote cultural integration. However, from a conflict perspective, the use of language can intensify divisions between groups and societies—just look at the battles over language in the United States, Canada, and other societies.

The Internet has often been lauded as a democratizing force that will make huge quantities of information available to great numbers of people around the world. However, while the Internet and its World Wide Web open up access to most societies, most material is transmitted in English (see Figure 22-1). Without special computer programs, documents in languages such as Chinese and Japanese cannot be transmitted in readable fashion (Colker 1996; P. Schaefer 1995).

The domination of the Internet by the English language is not surprising. English has largely become the international language of commerce and communication. Nevertheless, members of other cultures resent the way in which English is the accepted standard on the Internet. In Russia, for example, it is easier for someone to download the works of Tolstoy translated into English than it is to get Tolstoy's work as originally written in Russian (Specter 1996a).

How will social interaction *within* a culture be transformed by the growing availability of electronic forms of communication? Will people turn to e-mail, websites, and faxes rather than telephone conversations and face-to-face meetings? Certainly, the technological shift to telephones reduced the use of letter writing as a means of maintaining kinship and friendship ties. But, while it is sometimes assumed that computers and other forms of electronic communication will be socially isolating, there

FIGURE 22-1

Language Use on the Internet Worldwide, 2000

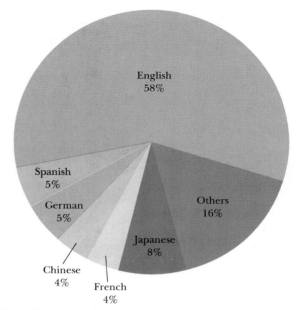

Source: Euro-Marketing Associates 2000.

are indications that computers actually put users in touch with large numbers of people on an interactive basis (L. Miller 1995). And in late 1998, the Internet was the means of putting two people together—a father and a daughter who had not seen each other in 50 years. The daughter had spent 14 years searching for her father through state and federal agencies. But after only three hours on the Internet searching the white pages (telephone directories for the entire nation), she found her father's number in Detroit. An emotional family reunion soon followed at the daughter's home in California.

Computer-mediated communication also takes place in chat rooms as well as in the more unconventional multiuser domains (MUDs), which allow people to assume new identities in role-playing games. Sociologist Sherry Turkle (1995, 1999) studied this interaction by anonymously visiting MUDs and other electronic chat rooms over a 10-year period and by conducting face-to-face interviews with more than 1,000 people who communicate by electronic mail and actively participate in MUDs. The interviews were especially important because Turkle wanted to be able to distinguish between the users' on-screen personae and their real identities. Turkle concluded that many MUD users' lives were enhanced by the opportunity to engage in role playing and "become someone else." A new sense of self emerges that is "decentered and multiple," expanding on George Herbert Mead's notion of self. At the same time, she

p. 95

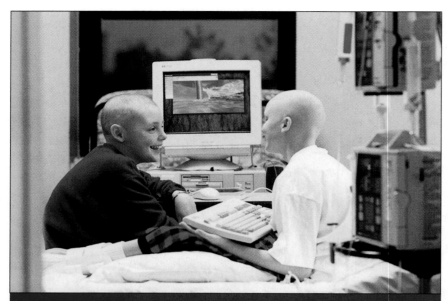

Two young patients at a New York City hospital communicate electronically with peers at a hospital in California. Electronic communication has proved useful in promoting social interaction among children who are seriously ill. The new technology, known as Starbright World, was developed with the assistance of director Steven Spielberg.

lost as people turn to e-mail and chat rooms (P. Schaefer 1995; Schellenberg 1996). A 1998 study that used survey analysis found that people in Pittsburgh who spend even a few hours a week online experience higher levels of depression and loneliness than if they had used the computer network less frequently. At least tentatively, we may conclude that as we have opened up the world to interaction, we may have reduced face-to-face interaction (R. Kraut et al. 1998).

Social Control

A data entry employee pauses to say hello to a colleague. A checker at the supermarket takes a moment to banter with a customer. A customer service telephone representative takes too much time helping callers. Each of these situations is subject to computer surveillance. Given the absence of strong protective legislation, employees in the United States are subject to increasing and pervasive supervision by computers. Supervisors have always scrutinized the performance of their workers, but with so much work now being handled electronically, the possibilities for surveillance have risen dramatically.

With Big Brother watching and listening in more and more places, computer and video technology has facilitated supervision, control, and even domination by employers or government. There is a danger that electronic monitoring of employees can become a substitute for effective management and can lead to perceptions of unfairness and intrusiveness. An American Management Association study found that 35 percent of firms keep track of their workers by recording their phone calls and voice mail, looking through their computer files, or videotaping. About a quarter of these firms said they do not inform their employees of these surveillance practices (Grimsley 1997).

In recent years, a new type of corporate surveillance has emerged. A number of Internet sites are highly critical of the operations of various corporations. On McSpotlight, one could find attacks on nutritional practices at McDonald's; on Up Against the Wal, one could study advice on how to fight plans to open new Wal-Mart stores in a community. The Internet sites of such "anticorporate vigilantes" are generally protected by the First Amend-

warns that some individuals may become so gratified by their online lives that they lose touch with their families, friends, and work responsibilities. Indeed, psychologists and therapists are giving increasing attention to what is being called "Internet addiction" (Belluck 1996).

p. 126

If electronic communication can facilitate social interaction within a community—if it can create ties among people in different communities or even countries who "meet" in chat rooms or MUDs—then is there genuinely a new interactive world known as "cyberspace"? The term *cyberspace* was introduced in 1984 by William Gibson, a Canadian science fiction writer. He came up with this term after he walked by a video arcade and noticed the intensity of the players hunched over their screens. Gibson felt that these video game enthusiasts "develop a belief that there's some kind of actual space behind the screen. Some place that you can't see but you know is there" (Elmer-DeWitt 1995:4; see also Shields 1996; Wellman et al. 1996).

The emergence of cyberspace can be viewed as yet another step away from Ferdinand Tönnies's concept of the familiar, intimate *Gemeinschaft* to the comparatively impersonal *Gesellschaft* and as yet another way in which social cohesion is being eroded in contemporary society. Critics of electronic communication question whether nonverbal communication, voice inflections, and other forms of interpersonal interaction will be

p. 131

"*Keystroke! ... Keystroke! ... Keystroke!*"

Not all the technological advances relevant to social control have been electronic in nature. DNA data banks have given police a powerful weapon in solving crimes; they have also opened the way to free wrongfully convicted citizens. A 1996 Department of Justice report noted that 28 men convicted of rape had been freed from U.S. prisons after DNA testing established their innocence. From 1996 through 1999, five death row inmates were released on the basis of DNA evidence. Efforts are under way to make such testing and other forms of DNA evidence as easily available as fingerprinting. As of mid-1996, 26 states had begun to develop DNA data banks that eventually will be linked in a nationwide network by the Federal Bureau of Investigation (FBI). While appropriate safeguards must be devised, the expansion of such DNA data banks has the potential to revolutionize law enforcement in the United States—especially in the area of sex crimes, where biological evidence is telling (Butterfield 1996; DPIC 2000c).

ment, but powerful corporations are carefully monitoring the sites in an attempt to counteract the activities of their critics (Neuborne 1996).

p. 186 ← Technological advances have also created the possibility for a new type of white-collar crime: computer crime. It is now possible to gain access to a computer's inventory without leaving home and to carry out embezzlement or electronic fraud without leaving a trace. Typically, discussions of computer crime focus on computer theft and on problems caused by computer "hackers," but widespread use of computers has facilitated many new ways of participating in deviant behavior. Consequently, greatly expanded police resources may be needed to deal with online child molesters, prostitution rings, software pirates, con artists, and other types of computer criminals. There is now a Computer Crime and Intellectual Property section of the Justice Department. The consensus of the heads of the section is that these cases are increasing and becoming more difficult (Computer Search Institute 1999).

Another connection between computer technology and social control is the use of computer databases and electronic verification of documents to reduce illegal immigration into the United States. While concerned about the issue of illegal entry, many Hispanics and Asian Americans nevertheless believe that *their* privacy, rather than that of Whites, is most likely to be infringed by government authorities (Brandon 1995). The next section of the chapter will look more fully at how technological changes can intensify stratification and inequality based on race, ethnicity, and other factors.

Stratification and Inequality

"Today we stand at the brink of becoming two societies, one largely white and plugged in and the other black and unplugged." This is how Black historian Henry Lewis Gates Jr. starkly describes today's "digital divide" (Gates 1999: A15). An important continuing theme in sociology is stratification among people. Thus far, there is little evidence to suggest that technology will reduce inequality; in fact, it may only intensify it. Technology is costly, and it is generally impossible to introduce advances to everyone simultaneously. So who gets this access first? Conflict theorists contend that as we travel further and further along the electronic frontier through advances such as telecommuting and the Internet, the disenfranchised poor may be isolated from mainstream society in an "information ghetto," just as racial and ethnic minorities have traditionally been subjected to residential segregation (Ouellette 1993).

Available data show clear differences in use of computers based on class, race, and ethnicity. A national study released in 1999 estimates that only 8 percent of households earning less than $20,000 use the Internet, compared to 60 percent of those with incomes of $75,000 or more. Moreover, in 1998, 47 percent of Asian American households and 36 percent of White households used the

Internet, compared with 30 percent of Hispanic households and 24 percent of African American households (National Telecommunications and Information Technology 1999). (See Figure 22-2.)

This issue goes beyond individual interest or lack of interest in computers. Accessibility is a major concern. According to a study by the Consumer Federation of America and the NAACP (National Association for the Advancement of Colored People), accessibility to computer networks through fiber-optic corridors (the "information superhighway") may bypass poor neighborhoods and minority populations. The researchers concluded that regional telephone companies' plans for these advanced communications networks target affluent areas and may lead to an exclusionary "electronic redlining" similar to discrimination in fields such as banking, real estate, and insurance. Industry executives counter that they have repeatedly stated their intention to deploy the information superhighway to *all* areas. Regulatory legislation has been proposed in Congress to ensure equal access to the information superhighway by mandating the wiring of schools, libraries, and hospitals. Several communities, such as Manchester, New Hampshire, and Oakland, California, have recently arranged for computer hookups in publicly built low-income housing (Lohr 1994; Lieberman 1999).

The technological advances of the present and future may not be equally beneficial to men and women. Feminist sociologists point out that technology is not necessarily gender-neutral. For example, many studies have shown that there is differential use of computers by

A satellite dish moves through a city in Pakistan on a donkey cart. Satellite television is a popular alternative to the state-run TV channels there.

FIGURE 22-2

Internet Use, 1998

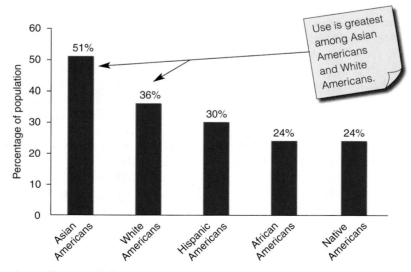

Source: Commerce Net/Nielsen Internet Demographic Study 1998.

boys and girls. Computer games, which serve as an important means of early socialization to computers, typically involve sports or skills associated with the traditional male gender role. As a result, computer camps and video arcades have become predominantly male settings. A report on "gender gaps" in schools issued by the American Association of University Women in 1998 noted that high school girls lag behind boys in technology. For example, only 17 percent of those who took the advanced placement exam in computer science in 1996 were girls. Moreover, girls tend to limit use of the computer to word processing or data entry, while boys are more likely to use it for solving problems or writing programs, preparing them in better ways for high-tech careers (Lewin 1998b).

The issue of technology and inequality is especially sensitive when viewed in a cross-cultural perspective. Although industrialization has dramatically improved the standard of living of many workers, it has allowed elites to amass untold wealth. Moreover, the activities of multinational corporations have increased the inequality between industrialized core nations (such as the United States, Germany, and Japan) and the periphery of developing countries.

p. 235

SOCIAL POLICY AND TECHNOLOGY

Privacy and Censorship in a Global Village

The Issue

In 1992, a huge explosion in a Texaco refinery in Wilmington, California, spread fire and caused panic in a nearby Hispanic community. Soon afterward, the Texaco Corporation was hit by close to 5,000 property damage claims and 14,000 claims of personal injury. Texaco promptly hired a private investigator, but not to probe the cause of the explosion. His task was to unearth compromising information about the claimants and their lawyers, whose class action suits could cost Texaco millions of dollars.

One of the claimants was 23-year-old Rossana Rivera. The private investigator didn't just learn her Social Security number, date of birth, every address where she had lived, names and numbers of present and past neighbors, the number of bedrooms in her house, her welfare history, and the employment background of her children's fathers. He also dredged up two delinquent traffic tickets, which he used to threaten her with arrest if she did not come up with damaging information about the lawyers in her case.

How did he arrive at all this information? For the most part, by buying or uncovering data in commercial databases (which most citizens are unaware of) and searching law enforcement computer files (supposedly off-limits to civilians). The Texaco investigator's actions are not at all unusual these days. According to a deputy U.S. attorney in New Jersey, "The buying and selling of information is just a huge business" (Bernstein 1997:A20). The biggest customers are companies

There are few secrets on the Internet. This naval officer faced dismissal from the Navy for acknowledging his homosexuality on a computer online service. The Navy obtained this confidential information from America Online, raising questions about how private one's online communications can be.

involved in litigation or business conflicts or just screening applicants. The suppliers in the information network include the investigators, underground information brokers, online databases, governments that sell public records, former law enforcement personnel, even former cold war spies. The means of getting information range from simple payments to computer hacking to electronic surveillance to deception in all forms.

At this point in the United States, privacy laws have so many loopholes and are so patchy that it is often difficult to distinguish between data that are obtained legally and data that are gathered illicitly. The other side of the coin is the fear that government will restrict the flow of electronic information too much, stepping over the border into censorship. Some observers, however, feel the government is fully justified in restricting pornographic information. The whole issue of privacy and censorship in this technological age is another case of culture lag, in which the material culture (the technology) is changing faster than the nonmaterial culture (norms controlling the technology).

The Setting

The typical consumer in the United States is included in at least 25 marketing databases, while some consumers are on upward of 100 databases. Overall, there are more than 15,000 specialized lists available in the United States with a total of some 2 billion consumer names. Christine Varney, former commissioner of the Federal Trade Commission (FTC), has observed, "Vast quantities of data are available easily and cheaply to business to be stored, analyzed, and re-used" (Castelli 1996:52; Horovitz 1995).

These lists may at first seem innocent enough; does it really matter if companies can buy lists for marketing with our names, addresses, and telephone numbers? Part of the problem is that computer technology has made it increasingly easy for any individual, business firm, or government agency to retrieve more and more information about any of us. For decades, information from motor vehicle offices, voter registration lists, and credit bureaus has been electronically stored, yet the incompatibility of different computer systems used to prevent access from one system to another. Today, having some information about a person has made it much easier to get other and perhaps more sensitive information (Stoll 1995).

As it becomes increasingly possible to retrieve more and more information electronically, we may be "volunteering" sensitive information about ourselves in ways

we are unaware. Point-of-sale scanning at a local grocery store or supermarket can create a data profile, revealing a person's taste in everything from candy bars to supermarket tabloids and birth control devices. Advances in DNA research suggest that it is only a matter of time before a complete genetic profile of any individual will be available. A documented finding that someone is genetically predisposed to a certain illness may be of great value to that person, but it may have interest as well for potential employers, insurers, and even would-be spouses or romantic companions. Moreover, as discussed above, this genetic information can be electronically linked with motor vehicle registrations and credit reports (Hallowell 1999).

The question of how much free expression should be permitted on the Internet relates to the issue of censorship. Pornography websites proliferate, especially after federal legislation to regulate "indecent" words and images was struck down by the Supreme Court in 1997 (as we will see later in this section). Some of the X-rated material is perfectly legal, if inappropriate for children who use the Net. Some of the sites are clearly illegal, such as those that serve the needs of pedophiles and prey on young children. Some are morally and legally elusive, such as the "upskirt" sites that post images taken by video cameras aimed under the skirts of unsuspecting women in public places. This is another area in which we can see the results of culture lag.

Sociological Insights

Functionalists can point to the manifest function of the Internet in its ability to facilitate communications. They also can identify the latent function of providing a forum for groups with few resources to communicate with literally tens of millions of people. Poorly financed groups can range from hate organizations to special interest groups vying against powerful wealthy interests. Thus, the functionalist perspective would see many aspects of technology fostering communication; the issue of censorship depends on how one views the content of the message, and the issue of privacy hinges on how information is used.

Even if computers and other forms of modern technology are peering deeper and deeper into our daily lives, some observers insist that we *benefit* from such innovations and can exist quite well with a bit less privacy. Sociologist Amitai Etzioni (1996:14A) bluntly states, "The genie is out of the bottle. We must either return to the Stone Age (pay cash, use carrier pigeons, and forget insurance) or learn to live with shrunken privacy." Etzioni adds that there are many instances in which preservation of the common good requires giving up some part of our privacy. Amnesty International, the

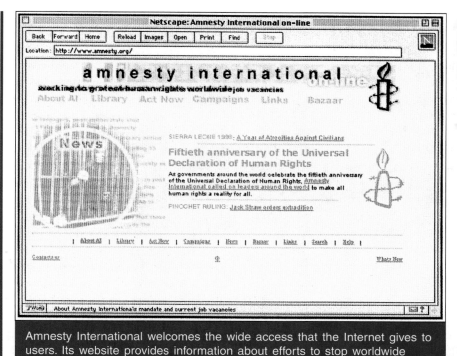

Amnesty International welcomes the wide access that the Internet gives to users. Its website provides information about efforts to stop worldwide torture and repression.

global human rights advocacy group, has applauded the expansion of the Internet. This group sees it as a means to reach a wider audience and, in the case of specific cases of torture or repression, to speedily disseminate information worldwide so that appropriate steps can be taken to end unjust situations (S. Perry 1998a).

Viewed from a conflict perspective, however, there is the ever-present danger that a society's most powerful groups will use technological advances to invade the privacy of the less powerful and thereby maintain or intensify various forms of inequality and injustice. For example, in 1989, the People's Republic of China used various types of technology to identify protestors who had participated in pro-democracy demonstrations at Tiananmen Square and elsewhere. Some protestors identified in this manner received long prison terms because of their activism. During the same period, the Chinese government intercepted the news reports, telephones calls, and facsimile messages of foreign journalists covering the demonstrations. Conflict theorists argue that control of technology in almost any form remains in the hands of those who already wield the most power, usually at the expense of the powerless and poor.

Interactionists view the privacy and censorship debate as one that parallels concerns people have in any

social interaction. Just as we may disapprove of some associations that relatives or friends have with other people, we also express concern over controversial websites and attempt to monitor people's social interaction. Obviously, the Internet facilitates interactions with a broad range of people, with minimal likelihood of detection compared to face-to-face interaction. Moreover, one can easily move a website from one country to another, avoiding not only detection but also prosecution.

Policy Initiatives

In 1986, the federal government passed the Electronic Communications Privacy Act. Wire communications—defined as use of the human voice in telephone and cordless calls—are highly protected. They cannot be subjected to surveillance unless a prosecutor obtains authorization from both the U.S. attorney general and a federal judge. By contrast, telegrams, faxes, and e-mail can be monitored simply with the approval of a judge (Eckenwiler 1995).

In 1996, the Communications Decency Act made it a federal crime to transmit "indecent" or "patently offensive" material over the Internet without maintaining safeguards to ensure that children cannot see it. Private e-mail and online chat room communications with anyone under the age of 18 were subjected to the same standard. Violations of the law could lead to up to two years in prison and a $250,000 fine (Fernandez 1996; Lappin 1996).

Civil liberties advocates insisted that such governmental action infringed on private communications between consenting adults and inevitably limited freedom of speech. They noted that at one point America Online even banned use of the term *breast,* thereby preventing any meaningful discussion of breast cancer or breast examinations. Lawsuits challenging the constitutionality of the Communications Decency Act were supported by such organizations as the American Civil Liberties Union (ACLU), the American Library Association, the American Society of Newspaper Editors, and the National Writers Union. In 1997, the Supreme Court declared that major parts of the act were unconstitutional. The Court called government

Mike Keefe, The Denver Post '97 AOL:INTOON

declared, "It is not possible for a provider to censor the Internet according to the local law, custom, or tradition. The Internet is too international and too dynamic for that. . . . Censoring the Internet has, in most cases, proved to be counterproductive" (Newsbytes News Network 1997).

While some people chastise government efforts to curb technology, others decry their *failure* to limit certain aspects of technology. The United States is developing an international reputation of being opposed to efforts to protect people's privacy. For example, the Center for Public Integrity, a nonpartisan research organization, issued a report in 1998 that critiques the U.S. government for failing to approve legislation protecting the confidentiality of medical records. In another case, America Online revealed to a U.S. Navy investigator the identity of a sailor who had described his marital status online as gay. In 1998, both the Navy and America Online were forced to reach settlements for violating the privacy of the sailor. At the same time, the United States has been vocal in opposing efforts by the 15 European Union countries to implement a tough law designed to protect citizens from computer-age invasions of privacy. The U.S. technology industry does not want to have access to information blocked, since information is vital to global commerce. While a compromise is likely, this case illustrates the fine line between safeguarding privacy and stifling the electronic flow of information (Center for Public Integrity 1998; S. Perry 1998b; Shenon 1998).

The conflict over privacy and censorship is far from over. As technology continues to advance in the twenty-first century, there are sure to be new battlegrounds.

attempts to regulate content on the Internet an attack on the First Amendment guarantee of freedom of speech (Fernandez 1996; A. Harmon 1998).

Censorship is also an issue globally. In Myanmar (or Burma), the government has ruled that fax machines and computer modems are illegal. In Saudi Arabia, access to the Internet was banned until 1999. Now all Internet connections are routed through a government hub where computers block access to thousands of sites cataloged on a rapidly expanding censorship list—for example, all gambling sites, all free-wheeling chat rooms, and all sites critical of the ruling Saudi family. By contrast, the openness of the Internet in other parts of the Middle East allows scattered Palestinian refugees to communicate with one another and establish websites that provide a history of Palestinian settlements. While China encourages expansion of the Internet, it has been wary of facilitating communication that it regards as disruptive. The government has blocked all websites related to the Falun Gong spiritual group, and in 2000 it announced that "state secrets" (very vaguely defined) were banned from the Internet (Africa News Service 1998; Jehl 1999; Rosenthal 1999, 2000; T. Wilkinson 1999).

p. 387

The international debate is not limited to societies regarded as closed to outside inspection. Consider the dilemma faced by the Internet service provider CompuServe in Germany. Because of government concern about pornography, CompuServe blocked 200 newsgroups—many of which offered valuable information unrelated to pornography. Eventually, the blocks were lifted; the German head of CompuServe spoke for many in the electronic communications community when he

Let's Discuss

1. What are some of the ways that people can obtain information about us? How do we "volunteer" information about ourselves?
2. Do you think corporations and employers have a right to monitor employees' e-mail and phone calls? Why or why not?
3. Are you more concerned about government censorship of electronic communication or about unauthorized invasion of your privacy? As a policymaker, how would you balance these concerns?

Summary

Social change is significant alteration over time in behavior patterns and culture, including norms and values. *Technology* is information about how to use the material resources of the environment to satisfy human needs and desires. This chapter examines sociological theories of social change, resistance to change, and the impact of technology on society and on social change.

1. Early advocates of evolutionary theory of social change believed that society was inevitably progressing to a higher state.
2. Talcott Parsons, a leading advocate of functionalist theory, viewed society as naturally being in a state of equilibrium or balance.
3. Conflict theorists see change as having crucial significance, since it is needed to correct social injustices and inequalities.
4. In general, those with a disproportionate share of society's wealth, status, and power have a vested interest in preserving the status quo and will resist change.
5. The period of maladjustment when the nonmaterial culture is still adapting to new material conditions is known as *culture lag.*
6. In the computer age, *telecommuters* are linked to their supervisors and colleagues through computer terminals, phone lines, and fax machines.
7. Early users of the Internet, the world's largest computer network, established a subculture with specific norms and values and with distinctive argot terms.
8. Advances in biotechnology have raised difficult ethical questions about sex selection of fetuses and genetic engineering.
9. Social scientists focus on human error in the *normal accidents* associated with increasing reliance on technology.
10. The domination of the Internet by the English language is not surprising, since English has largely become the international language of commerce and communication.
11. Computer and video technology has facilitated supervision, control, and even domination by employers or government.
12. Conflict theorists fear that the disenfranchised poor may be isolated from mainstream society in an "information ghetto," just as racial and ethnic minorities have been subjected to residential segregation.
13. Computer technology has made it increasingly easy for any individual, business firm, or government agency to retrieve more and more information about any of us and thereby infringe on our privacy; it is also easy to disseminate pornographic material to millions of people at a time. How much government should restrict access to electronic information is an import policy issue today.

Critical Thinking Questions

1. In the last few years we have witnessed phenomenal growth in the use of cellular phones in all parts of the world. Analyze this example of material culture from the point of view of culture lag. Consider how usage, government regulation, and privacy issues are being worked out to keep up with the new technology.
2. Consider one of the technological advances discussed in the section on technology and the future. Analyze this aspect of technology, focusing on whether it is likely to increase or reduce inequality in the coming decades. Whenever possible, address issues of gender, race, ethnicity, and class, as well as inequality between nations.
3. In what ways has social interaction in your college community been affected by the kinds of technological advances examined in this chapter? Are there particular subcultures that are more likely or less likely to employ new forms of electronic communication?

Key Terms

Apartheid   The former policy of the South African government designed to maintain the separation of Blacks and other non-Whites from the dominant Whites. (584)

Culture lag   A period of maladjustment during which the nonmaterial culture is still adapting to new material conditions. (585)

Equilibrium model   A functionalist view of society as tending toward a state of stability or balance. (582)

Evolutionary theory   A theory of social change that holds that society is moving in a definite direction. (581)

Luddites   Rebellious craft workers in nineteenth-century England who destroyed new factory machinery as part of their resistance to the industrial revolution. (586)

Multilinear evolutionary theory   A theory of social change that holds that change can occur in several ways and does not inevitably lead in the same direction. (582)

Normal accidents   Failures that are inevitable given the manner in which human and technological systems are organized. (592)

Social change   Significant alteration over time in behavior patterns and culture, including norms and values. (581)

Technology   Information about how to use the material resources of the environment to satisfy human needs and desires. (586)

Telecommuters   Employees of business firms or government agencies who work full-time or part-time at home rather than in an outside office and who are linked to their supervisors and colleagues through computer terminals, phone lines, and fax machines. (587)

Unilinear evolutionary theory   A theory of social change that holds that all societies pass through the same successive stages of evolution and inevitably reach the same end. (581)

Vested interests   Those people or groups who will suffer in the event of social change and who have a stake in maintaining the status quo. (584)

Additional Readings

BOOKS

Castells, Manuel. 1996, 1997. *The Information Age: Economy, Society, and Culture.* Vol. 1: *The Rise of the Network Society.* Vol. 2: *The Power of Identity.* Vol. 3: *End of Millennium.* Cambridge, MA: Blackwell Publishers. This massive work by a noted sociologist describes how global networks of both computers and people are transforming work, politics, and social relationships.

Jasper, James. 1997. *The Art of Moral Protest: Culture, Biography, and Creativity in Social Movements.* Chicago: University of Chicago Press. An analysis of how social movements, ranging from nineteenth-century boycotts to contemporary antinuclear, animal rights, and environmental movements, develop and the impact they have on participants and society as a whole.

McChesney, Robert W. 1999. *Rich Media, Poor Democracy: Communication Politics in Dubious Times.* Urbana, IL: University of Illinois Press. A look at the increasing concentration of newspapers, television stations, and radio stations in the hands of a few wealthy corporations, making the information age harmful for public life, according to the author.

Rifkin, Jeremy. 1998. *The Biotech Century: Harnessing the Gene and Remaking the World.* New York: Jeremy P. Tarcher/Putnam. A provocative examination of fundamental changes in our lives following the advent of computer technology.

Turkle, Sherry. 1995. *Life on the Screen: Identity in the Age of the Internet.* New York: Simon and Schuster. A sociologist examines the possible long-term implications of millions of people interacting electronically.

JOURNALS

Among those journals that focus on issues of social change and technology are *The Futurist* (founded in 1967), *Internet Underground* (1996), *Issues in Science and Technology* (1984), *Privacy and American Business* (1993), *Sociological Theory* (1983), *Technological Forecasting* and *Social Change* (1969), and *Technology Review* (1899).

Internet Connection

www.mhhe.com/schaefer

Note: While all the URLs listed were current as of the printing of this book, these sites often change. Please check our website (http://www.mhhe.com/schaefer) for updates.

1. Cloning has moved from the world of science fiction to the world of scientific and sociological fact. *Time* magazine offers an online interactive look at cloning, especially its potential ethical issues, at **http://www.pathfinder.com/TIME/cloning/home.html/.**
   (a) What is Dolly? Why is she important to cloning technology? What are the ramifications of her cloning?
   (c) Is it possible to clone human beings?
   (d) What potential benefits exist from cloning technology (the functions)? What are the potential drawbacks and dangers (the dysfunctions)?
   (e) Do you consider it ethical and/or beneficial to clone extinct animals? Why or why not?
   (f) Do you consider it ethical and/or beneficial to clone human beings? Why or why not?
   (g) Visit the "Ethics" section of the website and vote in the online poll. How does your opinion compare to others who have voted and to the experts who express their views on the site?
   (h) Should cloned humans be granted the same civil rights extended to us all? Why or why not?
   (i) What laws might have to be created when cloning humans becomes a reality?
   (j) How might concepts from the chapter, such as culture lag, vested interests, and normal accidents, be applied to the cloning of animals, and someday, humans?

2. The chapter discusses something you have no doubt experienced firsthand: the growth of the Internet as a tool for commerce, education, and communication. The website *24 Hours in Cyberspace* offers pictures and text about the way the Internet is changing social and personal experiences **(http://www.cyber24.com/htm3/toc.htm?about/).** Explore each of the six sections in order to engage in the following Net-based treasure hunt.
   (a) Find stories that demonstrate how the Internet has (1) brought people together who might otherwise not have interacted; (2) changed the way we shop for goods and services; (3) furthered research or education; (4) provided new opportunities for artists; (5) had an impact on medicine and health; and (6) expanded opportunities for criminal behavior.
   (b) Which of your chosen stories surprised you the most? Why?
   (c) Can you think of more ways the Internet might change social life in the future?
   (d) Using your sociological imagination, consider whether our society should be so eager to embrace the Internet. What are some of the drawbacks to the ubiquity of the Net? Does everyone have equal access? How might the extensive use of the Internet harm human relationships?

Glossary

Numbers following the definitions indicate pages where the terms were identified. Consult the index for further page references.

A

Absolute poverty   A standard of poverty based on a minimum level of subsistence below which families should not be expected to exist. (213)

Achieved status   A social position attained by a person largely through his or her own efforts. (122, 203)

Activity theory   An interactionist theory of aging that argues that elderly people who remain active will be best-adjusted. (322)

Adoption   In a legal sense, a process that allows for the transfer of the legal rights, responsibilities, and privileges of parenthood to a new legal parent or parents. (357)

Affirmative action   Positive efforts to recruit minority group members or women for jobs, promotions, and educational opportunities. (266, 459)

Ageism   A term coined by Robert N. Butler to refer to prejudice and discrimination against the elderly. (329)

Agrarian society   The most technologically advanced form of preindustrial society. Members are primarily engaged in the production of food but increase their crop yield through such innovations as the plow. (133)

Alienation   The condition of being estranged or disassociated from the surrounding society. (152, 449)

Amalgamation   The process by which a majority group and a minority group combine through intermarriage to form a new group. (270)

Anomie   Durkheim's term for the loss of direction felt in a society when social control of individual behavior has become ineffective. (13, 180)

Anomie theory of deviance   A theory developed by Robert Merton that explains deviance as an adaptation either of socially prescribed goals or of the norms governing their attainment, or both. (180)

Anticipatory socialization   Processes of socialization in which a person "rehearses" for future positions, occupations, and social relationships. (99)

Anti-Semitism   Anti-Jewish prejudice. (279)

Apartheid   The former policy of the South African government designed to maintain the separation of Blacks and other non-Whites from the dominant Whites. (270, 584)

Applied sociology   The use of the discipline of sociology with the specific intent of yielding practical applications for human behavior and organizations. (22)

Argot   Specialized language used by members of a group or subculture. (78)

Ascribed status   A social position "assigned" to a person by society without regard for the person's unique talents or characteristics. (121, 203)

Assembling perspective   A theory of collective behavior introduced by McPhail and Miller that seeks to examine how and why people move from different points in space to a common location. (559)

Assimilation   The process by which a person forsakes his or her own cultural tradition to become part of a different culture. (270)

Authority   Power that has been institutionalized and is recognized by the people over whom it is exercised. (423)

B

Basic sociology   Sociological inquiry conducted with the objective of gaining a more profound knowledge of the fundamental aspects of social phenomena. Also known as *pure sociology*. (24)

Bilateral descent   A kinship system in which both sides of a person's family are regarded as equally important. (346)

Bilingualism   The use of two or more languages in particular settings, such as workplaces or educational facilities, treating each language as equally legitimate. (82)

Birthrate   The number of live births per 1,000 population in a given year. Also known as the *crude birthrate*. (532)

Black power   A political philosophy promoted by many younger Blacks in the 1960s that supported the creation of Black-controlled political and economic institutions. (274)

Borderlands   The area of a common culture along the border between Mexico and the United States. (246)

Bourgeoisie   Karl Marx's term for the capitalist class, comprising the owners of the means of production. (207)

Bureaucracy   A component of formal organization in which rules and hierarchical ranking are used to achieve efficiency. (150)

Bureaucratization   The process by which a group, organization, or social movement becomes increasingly bureaucratic. (154)

C

Capitalism   An economic system in which the means of production are largely in private hands and the main incentive for economic activity is the accumulation of profits. (207, 445)

Castes   Hereditary systems of rank, usually religiously dictated, that tend to be fixed and immobile. (204)

Causal logic   The relationship between a condition or variable and a particular consequence, with one event leading to the other. (37)

Census   An enumeration, or counting, of a population. (532)

Charismatic authority   Max Weber's term for power made legitimate by a leader's exceptional personal or emotional appeal to his or her followers. (426)

Class   A term used by Max Weber to refer to a group of people who have a similar level of wealth and income. (207)

Class consciousness   In Karl Marx's view, a subjective awareness held by members of a class regarding their common vested interests and need for collective political action to bring about social change. (207)

Classical theory   An approach to the study of formal organizations that views workers as being motivated almost entirely by economic rewards. (156)

Class system   A social ranking based primarily on economic position in which achieved characteristics can influence mobility. (204)

Clinical sociology   The use of the discipline of sociology with the specific intent of altering social relationships and facilitating change. (24)

Closed system   A social system in which there is little or no possibility of individual mobility. (219)

Coalition   A temporary or permanent alliance geared toward a common goal. (149)

Code of ethics   The standards of acceptable behavior developed by and for members of a profession. (45)

Cognitive theory of development   Jean Piaget's theory explaining how children's thought progresses through four stages. (98)

Cohabitation The practice of living together as a male–female couple without marrying. (363)

Collective behavior In the view of sociologist Neil Smelser, the relatively spontaneous and unstructured behavior of a group of people who are reacting to a common influence in an ambiguous situation. (557)

Colonialism The maintenance of political, social, economic, and cultural dominance over a people by a foreign power for an extended period of time. (232)

Communism As an ideal type, an economic system under which all property is communally owned and no social distinctions are made on the basis of people's ability to produce. (446)

Community A spatial or political unit of social organization that gives people a sense of belonging, based either on shared residence in a particular place or on a common identity. (501)

Concentric-zone theory A theory of urban growth devised by Ernest Burgess that sees growth in terms of a series of rings radiating from the central business district. (506)

Conflict perspective A sociological approach that assumes that social behavior is best understood in terms of conflict or tension between competing groups. (17)

Conformity Going along with one's peers, individuals of a person's own status, who have no special right to direct that person's behavior. (173)

Contact hypothesis An interactionist perspective that states that interracial contact between people of equal status in cooperative circumstances will reduce prejudice. (269)

Content analysis The systematic coding and objective recording of data, guided by some rationale. (44)

Control group Subjects in an experiment who are not introduced to the independent variable by the researcher. (43)

Control theory A view of conformity and deviance that suggests that our connection to members of society leads us to systematically conform to society's norms. (176)

Control variable A factor held constant to test the relative impact of an independent variable. (40)

Correlation A relationship between two variables whereby a change in one coincides with a change in the other. (38)

Correspondence principle A term used by Bowles and Gintis to refer to the tendency of schools to promote the values expected of individuals in each social class and to prepare students for the types of jobs typically held by members of their class. (405)

Counterculture A subculture that deliberately opposes certain aspects of the larger culture. (79)

Craze An exciting mass involvement that lasts for a relatively long period of time. (563)

Creationism A literal interpretation of the Bible regarding the creation of man and the universe used to argue that evolution should not be presented as established scientific fact. (390)

Credentialism An increase in the lowest level of education required to enter a field. (403)

Crime A violation of criminal law for which formal penalties are applied by some governmental authority. (185)

Cross-tabulation A table that shows the relationship between two or more variables. (53)

Crowds Temporary gatherings of people in close proximity who share a common focus or interest. (560)

Cult Due to the stereotyping, this term has been abandoned by sociologists in favor of *new religious movements*. (386)

Cultural relativism The viewing of people's behavior from the perspective of their own culture. (81)

Cultural transmission A school of criminology that argues that criminal behavior is learned through social interactions. (182)

Cultural universals General practices found in every culture. (66, 375, 399)

Culture The totality of learned, socially transmitted behavior. (65)

Culture-bound syndrome A disease or illness that cannot be understood apart from its specific social context. (469)

Culture lag Ogburn's term for a period of maladjustment during which the nonmaterial culture is still adapting to new material conditions. (68, 585)

Culture shock The feeling of surprise and disorientation that is experienced when people witness cultural practices different from their own. (80)

D

Death rate The number of deaths per 1,000 population in a given year. Also known as the *crude death rate*. (532)

Defended neighborhood A neighborhood that residents identify through defined community borders and through a perception that adjacent areas are geographically separate and socially different. (511)

Degradation ceremony An aspect of the socialization process within total institutions, in which people are subjected to humiliating rituals. (100)

Deindustrialization The systematic, widespread withdrawal of investment in basic aspects of productivity such as factories and plants. (454)

Demographic transition A term used to describe the change from high birthrates and death rates to relatively low birthrates and death rates. (534)

Demography The scientific study of population. (530)

Denomination A large, organized religion not officially linked with the state or government. (384)

Dependency theory An approach that contends that industrialized nations continue to exploit developing countries for their own gain. (232)

Dependent variable The variable in a causal relationship that is subject to the influence of another variable. (37)

Deviance Behavior that violates the standards of conduct or expectations of a group or society. (176)

Differential association A theory of deviance proposed by Edwin Sutherland that holds that violation of rules results from exposure to attitudes favorable to criminal acts. (182)

Diffusion The process by which a cultural item is spread from group to group or society to society. (67)

Disaster A sudden or disruptive event or set of events that overtaxes a community's resources so that outside aid is necessary. (560)

Discovery The process of making known or sharing the existence of an aspect of reality. (67)

Discrimination The process of denying opportunities and equal rights to individuals and groups because of prejudice or other arbitrary reasons. (264)

Disengagement theory A functionalist theory of aging introduced by Cumming and Henry that contends that society and the aging individual mutually sever many of their relationships. (321)

Domestic partnership Two unrelated adults who have chosen to share one another's lives in a relationship of mutual caring, who reside together, and who agree to be jointly responsible for their dependents, basic living expenses, and other common necessities. (365)

Dominant ideology A set of cultural beliefs and practices that helps to maintain powerful social, economic, and political interests. (76, 209)

Downsizing Reductions taken in a company's workforce as part of deindustrialization. (455)

Dramaturgical approach A view of social interaction, popularized by Erving Goffman, under which people are examined as if they were theatrical performers. (20, 96)

Dyad A two-member group. (149)

Dysfunction An element or a process of society that may disrupt a social system or lead to a decrease in stability. (17, 151)

E

Ecclesia A religious organization that claims to include most or all of the members of a society and is recognized as the national or official religion. (383)

E-commerce Numerous ways that people with access to the Internet can do business from their computers. (455)

Economic system The social institution through which goods and services are produced, distributed, and consumed. (445)

Education A formal process of learning in which some people consciously teach while others adopt the social role of learner. (399)

Egalitarian family An authority pattern in which the adult members of the family are regarded as equals. (347)

Elite model A view of society as ruled by a small group of individuals who share a common set of political and economic interests. (433)

Emergent-norm perspective A theory of collective behavior proposed by Turner and Killian that holds that a collective definition of appropriate and inappropriate behavior emerges during episodes of collective behavior. (558)

Endogamy The restriction of mate selection to people within the same group. (351)

Environmental justice A legal strategy based on claims that racial minorities are subjected disproportionately to environmental hazards. (547)

Equilibrium model Talcott Parsons's functionalist view of society as tending toward a state of stability or balance. (582)

Established sect J. Milton Yinger's term for a religious group that is the outgrowth of a sect, yet remains isolated from society. (384)

Esteem The reputation that a particular individual has earned within an occupation. (210)

Ethnic group A group that is set apart from others because of its national origin or distinctive cultural patterns. (257)

Ethnocentrism The tendency to assume that one's culture and way of life represent the norm or are superior to all others. (80, 262)

Ethnography The study of an entire social setting through extended systematic observation. (42)

Euthanasia The act of bringing about the death of a hopelessly ill and suffering person in a relatively quick and painless way for reasons of mercy. (332, 480)

Evolutionary theory A theory of social change that holds that society is moving in a definite direction. (581)

Exogamy The requirement that people select mates outside certain groups. (351)

Experiment An artificially created situation that allows the researcher to manipulate variables. (43)

Experimental group Subjects in an experiment who are exposed to an independent variable introduced by a researcher. (43)

Exploitation theory A Marxist theory that views racial subordination in the United States as a manifestation of the class system inherent in capitalism. (268)

Expressiveness A term used by Parsons and Bales to refer to concern for maintenance of harmony and the internal emotional affairs of the family. (295)

Extended family A family in which relatives—such as grandparents, aunts, or uncles—live in the same home as parents and their children. (345)

F

Face-work A term used by Erving Goffman to refer to the efforts of people to maintain the proper image and avoid embarrassment in public. (96)

Fads Temporary movements toward the acceptance of some particular taste or lifestyle that involve large numbers of people and are independent of preceding trends. (562)

False consciousness A term used by Karl Marx to describe an attitude held by members of a class that does not accurately reflect its objective position. (207, 567)

Familism Pride in the extended family, expressed through the maintenance of close ties and strong obligations to kinfolk. (354)

Family A set of people related by blood, marriage (or some other agreed-upon relationship), or adoption who share the primary responsibility for reproduction and caring for members of society. (343)

Fashions Pleasurable mass involvements in some particular taste or lifestyle that have a line of historical continuity. (562)

Fertility The amount of reproduction among women of childbearing age. (529)

Folkways Norms governing everyday social behavior whose violation raises comparatively little concern. (73)

Force The actual or threatened use of coercion to impose one's will on others. (423)

Formal norms Norms that generally have been written down and that specify strict rules for punishment of violators. (72)

Formal organization A special-purpose group designed and structured for maximum efficiency. (150)

Formal social control Social control carried out by authorized agents, such as police officers, judges, school administrators, and employers. (175)

Functionalist perspective A sociological approach that emphasizes the way that parts of a society are structured to maintain its stability. (16)

G

Gemeinschaft A term used by Ferdinand Tönnies to describe close-knit communities, often found in rural areas, in which strong personal bonds unite members. (131)

Gender roles Expectations regarding the proper behavior, attitudes, and activities of males and females. (101, 291)

Generalized others A term used by George Herbert Mead to refer to the child's awareness of the attitudes, viewpoints, and expectations of society as a whole that a child takes into account in his or her behavior. (95)

Genocide The deliberate, systematic killing of an entire people or nation. (269)

Gentrification The resettlement of low-income city neighborhoods by prosperous families and business firms. (520)

Gerontology The scientific study of the sociological and psychological aspects of aging and the problems of the aged. (321)

Gesellschaft A term used by Ferdinand Tönnies to describe communities, often urban, that are large and impersonal with little commitment to the group or consensus on values. (131)

Glass ceiling An invisible barrier that blocks the promotion of a qualified individual in a work environment because of the individual's gender, race, or ethnicity. (265, 303)

Goal displacement Overzealous conformity to official regulations within a bureaucracy. (153)

Goal multiplication The process through which an organization expands its purpose. (160)

Goal succession The process through which an organization identifies an entirely new objective because its traditional goals have been either realized or denied. (161)

Group Any number of people with similar norms, values, and expectations who regularly and consciously interact. (125, 145)

Growth rate The difference between births and deaths, plus the difference between immigrants and emigrants, per 1,000 population. (533)

H

Hawthorne effect The unintended influence that observers or experiments can have on their subjects. (44)

Health As defined by the World Health Organization, a state of complete physical, mental, and social well-being, and not merely the absence of disease and infirmity. (471)

Health maintenance organization (HMO) An organization that provides comprehensive medical services for a preestablished fee. (491)

Hidden curriculum Standards of behavior that are deemed proper by society and are taught subtly in schools. (403)

Holistic medicine A means of health maintenance using therapies in which the health care practitioner considers the person's physical, mental, emotional, and spiritual characteristics. (485)

Homophobia Fear of and prejudice against homosexuality. (136, 292)

Horizontal mobility The movement of an individual from one social position to another of the same rank. (220)

Horticultural societies Preindustrial societies in which people plant seeds and crops rather than subsist merely on available foods. (133)

Human ecology An area of study concerned with the interrelationships between people and their spatial setting and physical environment. (506)

Human relations approach An approach to the study of formal organizations that emphasizes the role of people, communication, and participation within a bureaucracy and tends to focus on the informal structure of the organization. (156)

Human rights Universal moral rights belonging to all people because they are human. (247)

Hunting-and-gathering society A preindustrial society in which people rely on whatever foods and fiber are readily available in order to live. (132)

Hypothesis A speculative statement about the relationship between two or more variables. (37)

I

Ideal type A construct or model that serves as a measuring rod against which specific cases can be evaluated. (13, 151)

Impression management A term used by Erving Goffman to refer to the altering of the presentation of the self in order to create distinctive appearances and satisfy particular audiences. (96)

Incest taboo The prohibition of sexual relationships between certain culturally specified relatives. (351)

Incidence The number of new cases of a specific disorder occurring within a given population during a stated period of time. (477)

Income Salaries and wages. (203)

Independent variable The variable in a causal relationship that, when altered, causes or influences a change in a second variable. (37)

Industrial city A city characterized by relatively large size, open competition, an open class system, and elaborate specialization in the manufacturing of goods. (503)

Industrial society A society that depends on mechanization to produce its economic goods and services. (133, 445)

Infant mortality rate The number of deaths of infants under one year of age per 1,000 live births in a given year. (532)

Influence The exercise of power through a process of persuasion. (423)

Informal economy Transfers of money, goods, or services that are not reported to the government. (241)

Informal norms Norms that generally are understood but are not precisely recorded. (72)

Informal social control Social control carried out by people casually through such means as laughter, smiles, and ridicule. (174)

In-group Any group or category to which people feel they belong. (146)

Innovation The process of introducing new elements into a culture through either discovery or invention. (67)

Institutional discrimination The denial of opportunities and equal rights to individuals and groups that results from the normal operations of a society. (265, 299)

Instrumentality A term used by Parsons and Bales to refer to emphasis on tasks, focus on more distant goals, and a concern for the external relationship between one's family and other social institutions. (295)

Interactionist perspective A sociological approach that generalizes about fundamental or everyday forms of social interaction. (19)

Interest group A voluntary association of citizens who attempt to influence public policy. (430)

Intergenerational mobility Changes in the social position of children relative to their parents. (220)

Interview A face-to-face or telephone questioning of a respondent to obtain desired information. (41)

Intragenerational mobility Changes in a person's social position within his or her adult life. (220)

Invention The combination of existing cultural items into a form that did not previously exist. (67)

Iron law of oligarchy A principle of organizational life developed by Robert Michels under which even democratic organizations will become bureaucracies ruled by a few individuals. (154)

Issei The early Japanese immigrants to the United States. (277)

K

Kinship The state of being related to others. (346)

L

Labeling theory An approach to deviance popularized by Howard S. Becker that attempts to explain why certain people are viewed as deviants while others engaging in the same behavior are not. (183)

Laissez-faire A form of capitalism under which people compete freely, with minimal government intervention in the economy. (445)

Language An abstract system of word meanings and symbols for all aspects of culture. It also includes gestures and other nonverbal communication. (69)

Latent functions Unconscious or unintended functions; hidden purposes. (17)

Law Governmental social control. (72, 175)

Legal-rational authority Max Weber's term for power made legitimate by law. (425)

Liberation theology Use of a church, primarily Roman Catholicism, in a political effort to eliminate poverty, discrimination, and other forms of injustice evident in a secular society. (379)

Life chances Max Weber's term for people's opportunities to provide themselves with material goods, positive living conditions, and favorable life experiences. (217)

Life expectancy The average number of years a person can be expected to live under current mortality conditions. (533)

Looking-glass self A concept used by Charles Horton Cooley that emphasizes the self as the product of our social interactions with others. (94)

Luddites Rebellious craft workers in nineteenth-century England who destroyed new factory machinery as part of their resistance to the industrial revolution. (586)

M

Machismo A sense of virility, personal worth, and pride in one's maleness. (354)

Macrosociology Sociological investigation that concentrates on large-scale phenomena or entire civilizations. (16)

Manifest functions Open, stated, and conscious functions. (17)

Master status A status that dominates others and thereby determines a person's general position within society. (122)

Material culture The physical or technological aspects of our daily lives. (68)

Matriarchy A society in which women dominate in family decision making. (347)

Matrilineal descent   A kinship system that favors the relatives of the mother. (346)

McDonaldization   The process by which the principles of the fast-food restaurant have come to dominate certain sectors of society, both in the United States and throughout the world. (145)

Megachurches   Large worship centers affiliated only loosely, if at all, with existing denominations. (384)

Megalopolis   A densely populated area containing two or more cities and their surrounding suburbs. (504)

Mental illness   A disorder of the brain that disrupts a person's thinking, feeling, and ability to interact with others. (486)

Microsociology   Sociological investigation that stresses study of small groups and often uses laboratory experimental studies. (16)

Midlife crisis   A stressful period of self-evaluation that begins at about age 40. (324)

Migration   Relatively permanent movement of people with the purpose of changing their place of residence. (540)

Minority group   A subordinate group whose members have significantly less control or power over their own lives than the members of a dominant or majority group have over theirs. (257)

Modernization   The far-reaching process by which a society moves from traditional or less developed institutions to those characteristic of more developed societies. (236)

Modernization theory   A functionalist approach that proposes that modernization and development will gradually improve the lives of people in peripheral nations. (236)

Monogamy   A form of marriage in which one woman and one man are married only to each other. (345)

Monopoly   Control of a market by a single business firm. (446)

Morbidity rates   The incidence of diseases in a given population. (477)

Mores   Norms deemed highly necessary to the welfare of a society. (72)

Mortality rate   The incidence of death in a given population. (477)

Multilinear evolutionary theory   A theory of social change that holds that change can occur in several ways and does not inevitably lead in the same direction. (582)

Multinational corporations   Commercial organizations that are headquartered in one country but do business throughout the world. (234)

Multiple-nuclei theory   A theory of urban growth developed by Harris and Ullman that views growth as emerging from many centers of development, each of which may reflect a particular urban need or activity. (507)

N

Natural science   The study of the physical features of nature and the ways in which they interact and change. (9)

Negotiated order   A social structure that derives its existence from the social interactions through which people define and redefine its character. (121)

Negotiation   The attempt to reach agreement with others concerning some objective. (120)

Neocolonialism   Continuing dependence of former colonies on foreign countries. (232)

New religious movement (NRM) or **cult**   A generally small, secretive religious group that represents either a new religion or a major innovation of an existing faith. (387)

New social movements   Organized collective activities that promote autonomy and self-determination as well as improvements in the quality of life. (568)

New urban sociology   An approach to urbanization that considers the interplay of local, national, and worldwide forces and their effect on local space, with special emphasis on the impact of global economic activity. (508)

Nisei   Japanese born in the United States who were descendants of the Issei. (277)

Nonmaterial culture   Cultural adjustments to material conditions, such as customs, beliefs, patterns of communication, and ways of using material objects. (68)

Nonperiodic assemblies   Nonrecurring gatherings of people that often result from word-of-mouth information. (559)

Nonverbal communication   The sending of messages through the use of posture, facial expressions, and gestures. (19)

Normal accidents   Failures that are inevitable, given the manner in which human and technological systems are organized. (592)

Norms   Established standards of behavior maintained by a society. (72)

Nuclear family   A married couple and their unmarried children living together. (343)

O

Obedience   Compliance with higher authorities in a hierarchical structure. (173)

Objective method   A technique for measuring social class that assigns individuals to classes on the basis of criteria such as occupation, education, income, and place of residence. (210)

Observation   A research technique in which an investigator collects information through direct participation in and/or observation of a group, tribe, or community. (42)

Open system   A social system in which the position of each individual is influenced by his or her achieved status. (219)

Operational definition   An explanation of an abstract concept that is specific enough to allow a researcher to measure the concept. (36)

Organized crime   The work of a group that regulates relations between various criminal enterprises involved in the smuggling and sale of drugs, prostitution, gambling, and other activities. (186)

Out-group   A group or category to which people feel they do not belong. (146)

P

Panic   A fearful arousal or collective flight based on a generalized belief that may or may not be accurate. (563)

Patriarchy   A society in which men dominate family decision making. (347)

Patrilineal descent   A kinship system that favors the relatives of the father. (346)

Periodic assemblies   Recurring, relatively routine gatherings of people, such as college assemblies. (559)

Personality   In everyday speech, a person's typical patterns of attitudes, needs, characteristics, and behavior. (91)

Peter principle   A principle of organizational life, originated by Laurence J. Peter, according to which each individual within a hierarchy tends to rise to his or her level of incompetence. (153)

Pluralism   Mutual respect between the various groups in a society for one another's cultures, which allows minorities to express their own cultures without experiencing prejudice. (271)

Pluralist model   A view of society in which many competing groups within the community have access to governmental officials so that no single group is dominant. (435)

Political action committee (PAC)   A political committee established by an interest group—say, a national bank, corporation, trade association, or cooperative or membership association—to solicit contributions for candidates or political parties. (430)

Political socialization   The process by which individuals acquire political attitudes and develop patterns of political behavior. (426)

Political system   The social institution that relies on a recognized set of procedures for implementing and achieving the goals of a group. (423)

Politics   In Harold D. Lasswell's words, "who gets what, when, and how." (423)

Polyandry   A form of polygamy in which a woman can have several husbands at the same time. (345)

Polygamy A form of marriage in which an individual can have several husbands or wives simultaneously. (345)

Polygyny A form of polygamy in which a husband can have several wives at the same time. (345)

Population pyramid A special type of bar chart that shows the distribution of the population by gender and age. (537)

Postindustrial city A city in which global finance and the electronic flow of information dominate the economy. (503)

Postindustrial society A society whose economic system is primarily engaged in the processing and control of information. (133)

Postmodern society A technologically sophisticated society that is preoccupied with consumer goods and media images. (134)

Power The ability to exercise one's will over others. (208, 423)

Power elite A term used by C. Wright Mills for a small group of military, industrial, and government leaders who control the fate of the United States. (433)

Preindustrial city A city with only a few thousand people living within its borders and characterized by a relatively closed class system and limited mobility. (502)

Prejudice A negative attitude toward an entire category of people, such as a racial or ethnic minority. (262)

Prestige The respect and admiration that an occupation holds in a society. (210)

Prevalence The total number of cases of a specific disorder that exist at a given time. (477)

Primary group A small group characterized by intimate, face-to-face association and cooperation. (145)

Profane The ordinary and commonplace elements of life, as distinguished from the sacred. (375)

Profession An occupation requiring extensive knowledge that is governed by a code of ethics. (448)

Professional criminal A person who pursues crime as a day-to-day occupation, developing skilled techniques and enjoying a certain degree of status among other criminals. (186)

Proletariat Karl Marx's term for the working class in a capitalist society. (207)

Protestant ethic Max Weber's term for the disciplined work ethic, this-worldly concerns, and rational orientation to life emphasized by John Calvin and his followers. (379)

Public A dispersed group of people, not necessarily in contact with one another, who share an interest in an issue. (564)

Public opinion Expressions of attitudes on matters of public policy that are communicated to decision makers. (564)

Q

Qualitative research Research that relies on what is seen in the field or naturalistic settings more than on statistical data. (42)

Quantitative research Research that collects and reports data primarily in numerical form. (42)

Questionnaire A printed research instrument employed to obtain desired information from a respondent. (41)

R

Racial group A group that is set apart from others because of obvious physical differences. (257)

Racism The belief that one race is supreme and all others are innately inferior. (262)

Random sample A sample for which every member of the entire population has the same chance of being selected. (38)

Reference group Any group that individuals use as a standard in evaluating themselves and their own behavior. (148)

Relative deprivation The conscious feeling of a negative discrepancy between legitimate expectations and present actualities. (566)

Relative poverty A floating standard of deprivation by which people at the bottom of a society, whatever their lifestyles, are judged to be disadvantaged in comparison with the nation as a whole. (213)

Reliability The extent to which a measure provides consistent results. (39)

Religion According to Émile Durkheim, a unified system of beliefs and practices relative to sacred things. (375)

Religious beliefs Statements to which members of a particular religion adhere. (381)

Religious experience The feeling or perception of being in direct contact with the ultimate reality, such as a divine being, or of being overcome with religious emotion. (382)

Religious rituals Practices required or expected of members of a faith. (381)

Representative sample A selection from a larger population that is statistically found to be typical of that population. (38)

Research design A detailed plan or method for obtaining data scientifically. (40)

Resocialization The process of discarding former behavior patterns and accepting new ones as part of a transition in one's life. (99)

Resource mobilization The ways in which a social movement utilizes such resources as money, political influence, access to the media, and personnel. (567)

Rites of passage Rituals marking the symbolic transition from one social position to another. (99)

Role conflict Difficulties that occur when incompatible expectations arise from two or more social positions held by the same person. (123)

Role exit The process of disengagement from a role that is central to one's self-identity and reestablishment of an identity in a new role. (125)

Role strain Difficulties that result from the differing demands and expectations associated with the same social position. (124)

Role taking The process of mentally assuming the perspective of another, thereby enabling one to respond from that imagined viewpoint. (95)

Routine activities theory The notion that criminal victimization increases when there is a convergence of motivated offenders and suitable targets. (182)

Rumor A piece of information gathered informally that is used to interpret an ambiguous situation. (563)

S

Sacred Elements beyond everyday life that inspire awe, respect, and even fear. (375)

Sanctions Penalties and rewards for conduct concerning a social norm. (74, 171)

Sandwich generation The generation of adults who simultaneously try to meet the competing needs of their parents and their own children. (324)

Sapir-Whorf hypothesis A hypothesis concerning the role of language in shaping cultures. It holds that language is culturally determined and serves to influence our mode of thought. (71)

Science The body of knowledge obtained by methods based upon systematic observation. (8)

Scientific management approach Another name for the *classical theory* of formal organizations. (156)

Scientific method A systematic, organized series of steps that ensures maximum objectivity and consistency in researching a problem. (35)

Secondary analysis A variety of research techniques that make use of publicly accessible information and data. (44)

Secondary group A formal, impersonal group in which there is little social intimacy or mutual understanding. (145)

Sect A relatively small religious group that has broken away from some other religious organization to renew what it views as the original vision of the faith. (384)

Secularization The process through which religion's influence on other social institutions diminishes. (375)

Segregation The act of physically separating two groups; often imposed on a minority group by a dominant group. (270)

Self According to George Herbert Mead, the sum total of people's conscious perceptions of their own identity as distinct from others. (94)

Self-fulfilling prophecy The tendency of people to respond to and act on the basis of stereotypes, leading to validation of false definitions. (259)

Senilicide The killing of the aged. (332)

Serial monogamy A form of marriage in which a person can have several spouses in his or her lifetime but only one spouse at a time. (345)

Sexism The ideology that one sex is superior to the other. (299)

Sexual harassment Behavior that occurs when work benefits are made contingent on sexual favors (as a "quid pro quo") or when touching, lewd comments, or appearance of pornographic material creates a "hostile environment" in the workplace. (161)

Sick role Societal expectations about the attitudes and behavior of a person viewed as being ill. (471)

Significant others A term used by George Herbert Mead to refer to those individuals who are most important in the development of the self, such as parents, friends, and teachers. (96)

Single-parent families Families in which there is only one parent present to care for children. (358)

Slavery A system of enforced servitude in which people are legally owned by others and in which enslaved status is transferred from parents to children. (204)

Small group A group small enough for all members to interact simultaneously, that is, to talk with one another or at least be acquainted. (148)

Social change Significant alteration over time in behavior patterns and culture, including norms and values. (581)

Social constructionist perspective An approach to deviance that emphasizes the role of culture in the creation of the deviant identity. (184)

Social control The techniques and strategies for preventing deviant human behavior in any society. (171)

Social epidemiology The study of the distribution of disease, impairment, and general health status across a population. (477)

Social inequality A condition in which members of a society have different amounts of wealth, prestige, or power. (203)

Social institutions Organized patterns of beliefs and behavior centered on basic social needs. (128, 339)

Social interaction The ways in which people respond to one another. (119)

Socialism An economic system under which the means of production and distribution are collectively owned. (446)

Socialization The process whereby people learn the attitudes, values, and actions appropriate for individuals as members of a particular culture. (91)

Social mobility Movement of individuals or groups from one position of a society's stratification system to another. (219)

Social movements Organized collective activities to bring about or resist fundamental change in an existing group or society. (565)

Social network A series of social relationships that links a person directly to others and therefore indirectly to still more people. (126)

Social role A set of expectations of people who occupy a given social position or status. (122)

Social science The study of various aspects of human society. (9)

Social structure The way in which a society is organized into predictable relationships. (119)

Societal-reaction approach Another name for *labeling theory*. (184)

Society A fairly large number of people who live in the same territory, are relatively independent of people outside it, and participate in a common culture. (66)

Sociobiology The systematic study of the biological bases of social behavior. (94)

Sociocultural evolution The process of change and development in human societies that results from cumulative growth in their stores of cultural information. (132)

Sociological imagination An awareness of the relationship between an individual and the wider society. (7)

Sociology The systematic study of social behavior and human groups. (7)

Squatter settlements Areas occupied by the very poor on the fringes of cities, in which housing is often constructed by the settlers themselves from discarded material. (506)

Status A term used by sociologists to refer to any of the full range of socially defined positions within a large group or society. (121)

Status group A term used by Max Weber to refer to people who have the same prestige or lifestyle, independent of their class positions. (208)

Stereotypes Unreliable generalizations about all members of a group that do not recognize individual differences within the group. (259)

Stigma A label used to devalue members of deviant social groups. (177)

Stratification A structured ranking of entire groups of people that perpetuates unequal economic rewards and power in a society. (203)

Subculture A segment of society that shares a distinctive pattern of mores, folkways, and values that differs from the pattern of the larger society. (78)

Suburb According to the Census Bureau, any territory within a metropolitan area that is not included in the central city. (513)

Survey A study, generally in the form of interviews or questionnaires, that provides sociologists and other researchers with information concerning how people think and act. (40)

Symbols The gestures, objects, and language that form the basis of human communication. (95)

T

Teacher-expectancy effect The impact that a teacher's expectations about a student's performance may have on the student's actual achievements. (407)

Technology Information about how to use the material resources of the environment to satisfy human needs and desires. (68, 132, 586)

Telecommuters Employees of business firms or government agencies who work full-time or part-time at home rather than in an outside office and who are linked to their supervisors and colleagues through computer terminals, phone lines, and fax machines. (157, 587)

Theory In sociology, a set of statements that seeks to explain problems, actions, or behavior. (11)

Total fertility rate (TFR) The average number of children born alive to a woman, assuming that she conforms to current fertility rates. (532)

Total institutions A term coined by Erving Goffman to refer to institutions that regulate all aspects of a person's life under a single authority, such as prisons, the military, mental hospitals, and convents. (100)

Tracking The practice of placing students in specific curriculum groups on the basis of test scores and other criteria. (404)

Trade unions Organizations that seek to improve the material status of their members, all of whom perform a similar job or work for a common employer. (455)

Traditional authority Legitimate power conferred by custom and accepted practice. (424)

Trained incapacity The tendency of workers in a bureaucracy to become so specialized that they develop blind spots and fail to notice obvious problems. (152)

Triad A three-member group. (149)

U

Underclass Long-term poor people who lack training and skills. (215)

Unilinear evolutionary theory   A theory of social change that holds that all societies pass through the same successive stages of evolution and inevitably reach the same end. (581)

Urban ecology   An area of study that focuses on the interrelationships between people and their environment. (506)

Urbanism   A term used by Wirth to describe distinctive patterns of social behavior evident among city residents. (503)

V

Validity   The degree to which a scale or measure truly reflects the phenomenon under study. (39)

Value-added model   A theory of collective behavior proposed by Neil Smelser to explain how broad social conditions are transformed in a definite pattern into some form of collective behavior. (558)

Value neutrality   Max Weber's term for objectivity of sociologists in the interpretation of data. (47)

Values   Collective conceptions of what is considered good, desirable, and proper—or bad, undesirable, and improper—in a culture. (74)

Variable   A measurable trait or characteristic that is subject to change under different conditions. (37)

Verstehen   The German word for "understanding" or "insight"; used by Max Weber to stress the need for sociologists to take into account people's emotions, thoughts, beliefs, and attitudes. (13)

Vertical mobility   The movement of a person from one social position to another of a different rank. (220)

Vested interests   Veblen's term for those people or groups who will suffer in the event of social change and who have a stake in maintaining the status quo. (584)

Victimization surveys   Questionnaires or interviews used to determine whether people have been victims of crime. (190)

Victimless crimes   A term used by sociologists to describe the willing exchange among adults of widely desired, but illegal, goods and services. (187)

Vital statistics   Records of births, deaths, marriages, and divorces gathered through a registration system maintained by governmental units. (532)

Voluntary associations   Organizations established on the basis of common interest, whose members volunteer or even pay to participate. (158)

W

Wealth   An inclusive term encompassing all of a person's material assets, including land and other types of property. (203)

White-collar crimes   Crimes committed by affluent individuals or corporations in the course of their daily business activities. (186)

World systems analysis   Immanuel Wallerstein's view of the global economic system as divided between certain industrialized nations that control wealth and developing countries that are controlled and exploited. (232, 508)

X

Xenocentrism   The belief that the products, styles, or ideas of one's society are inferior to those that originate elsewhere. (81)

Z

Zero population growth (ZPG)   The state of a population with a growth rate of zero, achieved when the number of births plus immigrants is equal to the number of deaths plus emigrants. (539)

Zoning laws   Legal provisions stipulating land use and architectural design of housing and often employed as a means of keeping racial minorities and low-income people out of suburban areas. (515)

References

A

AARP. 1999. "New AARP Study Finds Boomers Vary in Their Views of the Future and Their Retirement Years." AARP News Release. June 1. Washington, DC.

ABC News. 1992. *Primetime Live: True Colors.* Transcript of November 26 episode.

Abelson, Reed. 1997. "When Waaa Turns to Why." *New York Times,* November 1, pp. C1, C6.

Abercrombie, Nicholas, and Bryan S. Turner, and Stephen Hill, eds. 1990. *Dominant Ideologies.* Cambridge, MA: Unwin Hyman.

Aberle, David F., A. K. Cohen, A. K. Davis, M. J. Leng, Jr., and F. N. Sutton. 1950. "The Functional Prerequisites of a Society." *Ethics* 60(January): 100–111.

Abowitz, Deborah A. 1986. "Data Indicate the Feminization of Poverty in Canada, Too." *Sociology and Social Research* 70(April):209–213.

Abrahams, Ray G. 1968. "Reaching an Agreement over Bridewealth in Labwor, Northern Uganda: A Case Study." Pp. 202–215 in *Councils in Action,* edited by Audrey Richards and Adam Kuer. Cambridge: Cambridge University Press.

Abrahamson, Mark. 1978. *Functionalism.* Englewood Cliffs, NJ: Prentice-Hall.

Abramson, Jeffrey. 1994. *We the Jury: The Jury System and the Ideal of Democracy.* New York: Basic Books.

Adam, Barry D. 1992. "Sociology and People Living with AIDS." Pp. 3–18 in *The Social Context of AIDS,* edited by Joan Huber and Beth E. Schneider. Newbury Park, CA: Sage.

Adam, Barry P., Jan Willem Duyvendak, and André Krouwei, eds. 1999. *The Global Emergence of Gay and Lesbian Politics: National Impact of a World-*

wide Movement. Philadelphia: Temple University Press.

Adam, Kanya. 2000. "Affirmative Action and Popular Perceptions: The Case of South Africa." *Society.* 37(February): 48–55.

Adams, Devon B. 1999. "Summary of State Sex Offender Registry Dissemination Procedures." *Bureau of Justice Statistics Fact Sheet* (August):1–8.

Addams, Jane. 1910. *Twenty Years at Hull-House.* New York: Macmillan.

———. 1930. *The Second Twenty Years at Hull-House.* New York: Macmillan.

Adler, Patricia A., and Peter Adler. 1998. *Peer Power: Preadolescent Culture and Identity.* New Brunswick, NJ: Rutgers University Press.

——— and John M. Johnson. 1992. "Street Corner Society Revisited." *Journal of Contemporary Ethnography* 21(April):3–10.

———, Steven J. Kless, and Peter Adler. 1992. "Socialization to Gender Roles: Popularity among Elementary School Boys and Girls." *Sociology of Education* 65(July):169–187.

Africa News Service. 1998. "CPJ's 10 Enemies of the Press." Accessed October 8 (www. elibrary.com/getdoc. cgi?id=113_ rydocid= 435731@ library_F+type=O~&dinst=).

Aguirre, Benigno E. 1984. "The Conventionalization of Collective Behavior in Cuba." *American Journal of Sociology* 90(3):541–566.

———, E. L. Quarantelli, and Jorge L. Mendoza. 1988. "The Collective Behavior of Fads: The Characteristics, Effects, and Career of Streaking." *American Sociological Review* 53(August):569–584.

Akers, Ronald L. 1997. *Criminological Theories: Introduction and Evaluation.* 2d ed. Los Angeles, CA: Roxbury Publishing Co.

Alain, Michel. 1985. "An Empirical Validation of Relative Deprivation." *Human Relations* 38(8):739–749.

Alam, Sultana. 1985. "Women and Poverty in Bangladesh." *Women's Studies International Forum* 8(4): 361–371.

Alba, Richard D., and Gwen Moore. 1982. "Ethnicity in the American Elite." *American Sociological Review* 47(June): 373–383.

Albas, Daniel, and Cheryl Albas. 1988. "Aces and Bombers: The Post-Exam Impression Management Strategies of Students." *Symbolic Interaction* 11(Fall): 289–302.

Alfino, Mark, John S. Carpeto, and Robin Wyngard. 1998. *McDonaldization Revisited: Critical Essays on Consumer Culture.* Westport, CT: Praeger.

Alinsky, Saul. 1946. *Reveille for Radicals.* Chicago: University of Chicago Press.

Allan, Stuart. 1999. *News Culture.* Buckingham, Great Britain: Open University Press.

Allen, Bem P. 1978. *Social Behavior: Fact and Falsehood.* Chicago: Nelson-Hall.

Allen, John L. 1996. *Student Atlas of World Politics.* 2d ed. Madison, WI: Brown and Benchmark.

Allport, Gordon W. 1979. *The Nature of Prejudice.* 25th anniversary ed. Reading, MA: Addison-Wesley.

Alonzo, Angelo A. 1989. "Health and Illness and the Definition of the Situation: An Interactionist Perspective." Presented at the annual meeting of the Society for the Study of Social Problems, Berkeley, CA.

Altman, Lawrence K. 1998. "Parts of Africa Showing H.I.V. in 1 in 4 Adults." *New York Times,* June 24, pp. A1, A6.

Alvord, Lori Arviso, and Elizabeth Cohen Van Pelt. 1999. *The Scalpel and the Silver Bear.* New York: Bantam.

Alzheimer's Association. 1999. "Statistics/Prevalence." Accessed January 10, 2000 (http://www.alz.org/facts/ stats.htm).

Amato, Paul, and Alan Booth. 1997. *A Generation at Risk.* Cambridge, MA: Harvard University Press.

American Association of Health Plans. 1998a. "Number of People in HMOs, 1976–96." Accessed August 11, 1998 (http://www.aahp.org/menus/index. cfm?cfid=64953%cftoken=32374).

———. 1998b. "Demographic Characteristics of Health Plan Enrollees." Accessed August 11, 1998 (http://www.aahp.org/menus/index.cfm?cfid=64953%cftoken=32374).

American Association of University Women. 1992. *How Schools Shortchange Girls.* Washington, DC: American Association of University Women.

American Bar Association. 1997. *Section of Individual Rights and Responsibilities. Section of Litigation (Capital Punishment).* (February). Chicago: Division for Policy Administration, ABA.

———. 1999. "Commission on Domestic Violence." Accessed July 20, 1999 (http://www.abanet.org/domviol/stats.html).

American Civil Liberties Union. 2000. "State and Local Laws Protecting Lesbians and Gay Men Against Workplace Discrimination." Accessed January 19, (http://www.aclu.org/issues/gay/gaylaws.html).

———. 1999a. "Domestic Partnerships: List of Cities, States and Counties." Accessed September 2, 1999 (http:www.aclu.org/issues/gay/dpstate.html).

———. 1999b. "School Prayer Amendment Returns." Accessed November 8, 1999 (http://www.aclu.org/action/prayer106.html).

American Humane Association. 1999. "Child Abuse and Neglect Data." Accessed July 20, 1999 (http://www.Americanhumane.org/cpfactdata.htm).

American Medical Association Council on Scientific Affairs. 1992. "Assault Weapons as a Public Health Hazard in the United States." *Journal of the American Medical Association* 267: 3067–3070.

American Sociological Association. 1993. The Sociology Major as Preparation for Careers in Business and Organizations. Washington, DC: American Sociological Association.

———. 1995a. *Careers in Sociology.* 2d ed. Washington, DC: American Sociological Association.

———. 1995b. *The Sociological Advantage.* Washington, DC: American Sociological Association.

———. 1997a. *Code of Ethics.* Washington, DC: American Sociological Association.

———. 1997b. *Style Guide.* 2d ed. Washington, DC: American Sociological Association.

———. 2000. *1999 Guide to Graduate Departments.* Washington, DC: American Sociological Association.

Ammerman, Nancy T., Jackson W. Carroll, Carl S. Dudley, and William McKinney, eds. 1998. *Studying Congregations: A New Handbook.* Nashville, TN: Abingdon Press.

Amnesty International. 1999. "Facts and Figures on the Death Penalty." Accessed August 4 (http://www.amnesty.excite.com/abolish/act500299.html).

Amnesty International and Death Penalty Information Center. 1998. *The Death Penalty: Abolitionist and Retentionist Countries.* Developed by Andrew Redey. December 30. Accessed January 30, 1999 (http:\\worldpolicy.org/americas/dp/maps-dp.html).

Amnesty International USA. 1994. *Breaking the Silence: Human Rights Violations Based on Sexual Orientation.* New York: Amnesty International.

Amnesty Now. 2000. "Mexico: Investigation into Mass Graves." 24(Winter): 8–9.

Anders, George. 1993. "McDonald's Methods Come to Medicine as Chains Acquire Physician's Practices." *Wall Street Journal,* August 24, pp. B1, B6.

Andersen, Margaret. 1997. *Thinking About Women: Sociological Perspectives on Sex and Gender.* 4th ed. Boston: Allyn and Bacon.

Anderson, Elijah. 1978. *A Place on the Corner.* Chicago: University of Chicago Press.

———. 1990. *Streetwise: Race, Class, and Change in an Urban Community.* Chicago: University of Chicago Press.

———. 1999. *Code of the Streets.* New York: Norton.

Anderson, John Ward. 1994. "Where Birth Control Is a Means of Survival." *Washington Post National Weekly Edition* 11(September):18.

——— and Molly Moore. 1993. "The Burden of Womanhood." *Washington Post National Weekly Edition* 10(March 22–28):6–7.

Andersson-Brolin, Lillemor. 1988. "Ethnic Residential Segregation: The Case of Sweden." *Scandinavian Journal of Development Alternatives* 7(March): 33–45.

Angier, Natalie. 1998. "Drugs, Sports, Body Image and G.I. Joe." *New York Times,* December 22, pp. D1, D3.

Anti-Defamation League. 1998. *Audit of Anti-Semitic Incidents, 1997.* New York: Anti-Defamation League.

Appelbaum, Richard, and Peter Dreier. 1999. "The Campus Anti-Sweatshops Movement." *The American Prospect* (September–October), pp. 71–78.

Appleby, Julie. 1999. "Rethinking Managed Care." *USA Today,* October 7, pp. A1–A2.

Arber, Sara and Jay Ginn. 1991. *Gender and Later Life: A Sociological Analysis of Resources and Constraints.* London: Sage.

Archer, Margaret. 1988. *Culture and Agency: The Place of Culture in Social Theory.* Cambridge: Cambridge University Press.

Armer, J. Michael, and John Katsillis. 1992. "Modernization Theory." Pp. 1299–1304 in *Encyclopedia of Sociology,* vol. 4, edited by Edgar F. Borgatta and Marie L. Borgatta. New York: Macmillan.

Armour, Stephanie. 2000. "Companies Work to Be More Gay-Friendly." *USA Today.* (February 28): B1.

Aronson, Elliot. 1999. *The Social Animal.* 8th ed. New York: Worth.

Associated Press. 1998a. "Environmental Test Case Averted." *Christian Science Monitor,* September 21, p. 18.

———. 1998b. "Doctors Perform Japan's First Lung Transplant from Living Donor." Accessed October 28, 1999 (http://www.ap.org).

Astin, Alexander, Kenneth C. Green, and William S. Korn. 1987. *The American Freshman: Twenty-Year Trends.* Los Angeles: Cooperative Institutional Research Program, University of California at Los Angeles.

Astin, Alexander, Sarah A. Parrott, William S. Korn, and Linda J. Sax. 1994. *The American Freshman: Thirty Year Trends.* Los Angeles: Higher Education Research Institute.

Astin, John A. 1998. "Why Patients Use Alternative Medicine: Results of a National Study." *Journal of American Medical Association* 279(May 20): 1548–1553.

Atchley, Robert C. 1976. *The Sociology of Retirement.* New York: Wiley.

———. 1985. *The Social Forces in Later Life: An Introduction to Social Gerontology.* 4th ed. Belmont, CA: Wadsworth.

Atkinson, Anthony Barnes, and John Micklewright. 1992. *Economic Transformation in Eastern Europe and the Distribution of Income.* Cambridge: Cambridge University Press.

Austin, Erica Weintraub and Bruce E. Pinkleton. 1995. "Positive and Negative Effects of Political Disaffection on the Less Experienced Voter." *Journal of Broadcasting and Electronic Media* 39(Spring):215–235.

Avni, Noga. 1991. "Battered Wives: The Home as a Total Institution" *Violence and Victims* 6(Summer):137–149.

Axtell, Roger E. 1990. *Do's and Taboos around the World.* 2d ed. New York: John Wiley and Sons.

Azumi, Koya, and Jerald Hage. 1972. *Organizational Systems.* Lexington, MA: Heath.

B

Babchuck, Nicholas, and Alan Booth. 1969. "Voluntary Association Membership: A Longitudinal Analysis." *American Sociological Review* 34(February):31–45.

Bachrach, Christine A. 1986. "Adoption Plans, Adopted Children, and Adoptive Mothers." *Journal of Marriage and the Family* 48(May):243–253.

Bachu, Amara. 1999. "Is Childlessness Among American Women on the Rise?" Working Paper No. 37, Population Division, U.S. Bureau of Census, Washington, DC.

Bailey, Susan McGee, and Patricia B. Campbell. 2000. "The Gender Wars in Education." *Wellesley Centers for Women Research Report* 20(Fall/Winter):20.

Baker, Laurence C. 1995. "Differences in Earnings between Male and Female Physicians." *New England Journal of Medicine* 334(April 11):960–964.

Baker, Linda. 1994. "Day-Care Disgrace." *The Progressive* 58(June):26–27.

Baldassare, Mark. 1992. "Suburban Communities." Pp. 475–494 in *Annual Review of Sociology,* edited by Judith Blake and John Hagan. Palo Alto, CA: Annual Reviews.

Bales, Kevin. 1999. *Disposable People: New Slavery in the Global Economy.* Berkeley, CA: University of California Press.

Barber, Benjamin R. 1995. *Jihad vs. McWorld.* New York: Times Books.

Barkey, Karen. 1991. "The Use of Court Records in the Reconstruction of Village Networks: A Corporative Perspective." *International Journal of Comparative Sociology* 32(January–April):195–216.

Barlett, Donald L., and James B. Steele. 1998. "Corporate Welfare." *Time* 152(November 9):36–39.

Barna Research Group. 1998. "The Cyberchurch Is Coming." April 20, 1998. Accessed November 10, 1999 (http://www.barna.org/cgi-bin/PagePressRelease.asp?/Press Release ID=9).

Barr, Cameron W. 1999. "Get Used to It: Japanese Steel Themselves for Downsizing." *Christian Science Monitor,* November 12, pp. 7–8.

Barrett, David B. 1996. "Worldwide Adherents of All Religions by Six Continental Areas, Mid-1995." P. 298 in *Britannica Book of the Year 1996.* Chicago: Encyclopedia Britannica.

Barron, Milton L. 1953. "Minority Group Characteristics of the Aged in American Society." *Journal of Gerontology* 8:477–482.

Barzansky, Barbara, Harry S. Jonas, and Sylvia I. Etzel. 1995. "Educational Programs in U.S. Medical Schools, 1994–1995." *Journal of the American Medical Association* 274(September 6):716–722.

Basso, Keith H. 1972. "Ice and Travel among the Fort Norman Slave: Folk Taxonomies and Cultural Rules." *Language in Society* 1(March):31–49.

Bates, Colleen Dunn. 1999. "Medicine's Gender Gap." *Shape,* October.

Bauerlein, Monika. 1996. "The Luddites Are Back." *Utne Reader* (March–April):24, 26.

Bauman, Kurt J. 1999. "Extended Measures of Well-Being: Meeting Basic Needs." *Current Population Reports,* ser. P-70, no. 67. Washington, DC: U.S. Government Printing Office.

Becerra, Rosina M. 1998. "The Mexican-American Family." Pp. 153–171 in *Ethnic Families in America: Patterns and Variations,* 4th ed., edited by Charles H. Mindel, Robert W. Habenstein, and Roosevelt Wright, Jr. Upper Saddle River, NJ: Prentice-Hall.

Becker, Howard S. 1952. "Social Class Variations in the Teacher–Pupil Rela-

tionship." *Journal of Educational Sociology* 25(April):451–465.

———. 1963. *The Outsiders: Studies in the Sociology of Deviance.* New York: Free Press.

———, ed. 1964. *The Other Side: Perspectives on Deviance.* New York: Free Press.

———. 1973. *The Outsiders: Studies in the Sociology of Deviance.* Rev. ed. New York: Free Press.

———, Blanche Greer, Everett C. Hughes, and Anselm Strauss. 1961. *Boys in White: Student Culture in Medical School.* Chicago: University of Chicago Press.

Begley, Sharon. 1998. "Why Wilson's Wrong." *Newsweek* 131(June 22):61–62.

———. 1999. "Designer Babies." *Newsweek* 132(November 9):61–62.

Belkin, Lisa. 1999. "Getting the Girl." *New York Times Magazine,* July 25, pp. 26–31, 38, 54–55.

Bell, Daniel. 1953. "Crime as an American Way of Life." *Antioch Review* 13(Summer):131–154.

———. 1999. *The Coming of Post-Industrial Society: A Venture in Social Forecasting.* With new foreword. New York: Basic Books.

Bell, Wendell. 1981a. "Modernization." Pp. 186–187 in *Encyclopedia of Sociology.* Guilford, CT: DPG Publishing.

———. 1981b. "Neocolonialism." P. 193 in *Encyclopedia of Sociology.* Guilford, CT: DPG Publishing.

Bellafante, Ginia. 1998. "Feminism: It's All About Me!" *Time* 151(June 20):54–62.

Belluck, Pam. 1996. "The Symptoms of Internet Addiction." *New York Times,* December 1, p. E5.

———. 1999. "On Assisted Suicide, Kevorkian Is Seen as 'Distraction.' " *New York Times,* March 30, p. A17.

Belsie, Laurent. 2000. "Strange Webfellows." *Christian Science Monitor.* (March 2): 15–16.

———. 1998. "Genetic Research Data Will Double Annually." *Christian Science Monitor,* July 30, p. B4.

Bendavid, Naftali. 1998. "Surge in Executions Just the Beginning." *Chicago Tribune,* January 4, pp. 1, 14.

Bender, William, and Margaret Smith. 1997. "Population, Food, and Nutrition." *Population Bulletin* 51(February).

Bendick, Marc, Jr., Charles W. Jackson, and J. Horacio Romero. 1993. *Employment*

Discrimination against Older Workers: An Experimental Study of Hiring Practices. Washington, DC: Fair Employment Council of Greater Washington.

Bendix, B. Reinhard. 1968. "Max Weber." Pp. 493–502 in *International Encyclopedia of the Social Sciences,* edited by David L. Sills. New York: Macmillan.

Benedetto, Richard. 1998. "Turncoats in Key Groups Lead Democratic Rebound." *USA Today,* November 5, p. 4A.

Benford, Robert D. 1992. "Social Movements." Pp. 1880–1887 in *Encyclopedia of Sociology,* vol. 4, edited by Edgar F. Borgatta and Marie L. Borgatta. New York: Macmillan.

Benner, Richard S. and Susan Tyler Hitchcock. 1986. *Life after Liberal Arts.* Charlottesville: Office of Career Planning and Placement, University of Virginia.

Bennet, James. 1996. "The Delegates: Where Image Meets Reality." *New York Times,* August 12, pp. A1, A11.

Bennett, Vanora. 1997. "Russia's Ugly Little Secret: Misogyny." *Los Angeles Times,* December 6, pp. A1, A9, A10.

Bennett, Vivienne. 1995. "Gender, Class, and Water: Women and the Politics of Water Service in Monterrey, Mexico." *Latin American Perspectives* 22(September):76–79.

Berger, Joan. 1988. "It's Time for Quotas to Go the Way of the Tail Fin." *Business Week* 304(March 7):60.

Berger, Peter, and Thomas Luckmann. 1966. *The Social Construction of Reality.* New York: Doubleday.

Berk, Richard A. 1974. *Collective Behavior.* Dubuque, IA: Brown.

——, and Howard E. Aldrich. 1972. "Patterns of Vandalism during Civil Disorders as an Indicator of Selection of Targets." *American Sociological Review* 37(October):533–547.

Berke, Anne C. 1995. *Body, Self, and Society: The View from Fiji.* Philadelphia: University of Pennsylvania Press.

——, and R. A. Burwell. 1999. "Acculturation and Disordered Eating in Fiji." *New Research Program and Abstracts.* Annual meeting of the American Psychiatric Association, May 3–4.

Berke, Richard L. 1994. "Defections among Men to G.O.P. Helped Insure Rout of Democrats." *New York Times,* November 11, pp. A1, A27.

Berkeley Wellness Letter. 1990. "The Nest Refilled." 6(February):1–2.

Berlin, Brent, and Paul Kay. 1991. *Basic Color Terms: Their Universality and Evolution.* Berkeley, CA: University of California Press.

Bernhardt, Todd. 1997. "Disaster Mythology: A Contest Analysis from 1985 to 1995." Presented at the annual meeting of the Midwest Sociological Society, April, Des Moines, IA.

Bernstein, Jared, Elizabeth C. McNichol, Lawrence Mishel, and Robert Zahradnik. 2000. *Pulling Apart: A State-by-State Analysis of Income Trends.* Washington, DC: Center on Budget and Policy Priorities.

Bernstein, Nina. 1997. "On Line, High-Tech Sleuths Find Private Facts." *New York Times,* September 15, pp. A1, A20.

Bernstein, Anne C. 1988. "Unraveling the Tangles: Children's Understanding of Stepfamily Kinship." Pp. 83–111 in *Relative Strangers: Studies of Step-Family* Press, edited by W. R. Beer, Totowa, NJ: Rowan and Liten Field.

Best, Fred, and Ray Eberhard. 1990. "Education for the 'Era of the Adult.' " *The Futurist* 21(May–June): 23–28.

Bettelheim, Bruno, and Morris Janowitz. 1964. *Social Change and Prejudice.* New York: Free Press.

Bharadwaj, Lakshmik. 1992. "Human Ecology." Pp. 848–867 in *Encyclopedia of Sociology,* vol. 2, edited by Edgar F. Borgatta and Marie L. Borgatta. New York: Macmillan.

Bianchi, Suzanne M., and Daphne Spain. 1996. "Women, Work, and Family in America." *Population Bulletin* 51(December).

Bielby, William T,. and Denise D. Bielby. 1992. "I Will Follow Him: Family Ties, Gender-Role Beliefs, and Reluctance to Relocate for a Better Job." *American Journal of Sociology* 97(March): 1241–1267.

Billson, Janet Mancini. 1994. "What Are Employers Looking for in BA, MA, and PhD Sociology Graduates?" *Student Sociologist* (Spring):1–3.

—— and Bettina J. Huber. 1993. *Embarking upon a Career with an Undergraduate Degree in Sociology.* 2d ed. Washington, DC: American Sociological Association.

Bjorkman, Sharon. 1999. "Doing Church: The Active Creation of Wor-ship Style." Presented at the Conference of Sociological Ethnography, February 27.

Black, Donald. 1995. "The Epistemology of Pure Sociology." *Law and Social Inquiry* 20(Summer):829–870.

Blackhall, Leslie J. et al. [5 authors]. 1995. "Ethnicity and Attitudes toward Patient Autonomy." *Journal of the American Medical Association* 274(September 13):820–825.

Blair, Jayson. 1999. "Wrongful Arrest of Actor Is Blamed on Bias." *New York Times,* July 18, p. 30.

Blakely, Earl J., and Mary Gail Snyder. 1997. *Fortress America: Gated Communities in the United States.* Washington, DC: Brookings Institution Press/Lincoln Institute.

Blanc, Ann Klimas. 1984. "Nonmarital Cohabitation and Fertility in the United States and Western Europe." *Population Research and Policy Review* 3: 181–193.

Blanchard, Fletcher A., Teri Lilly, and Leigh Ann Vaughan. 1991. "Reducing the Expression of Racial Prejudice." *Psychological Science* 2(March): 101–105.

Blanco, Robert. 1998. "The Disappearance of Mom and Dad." *USA Today*, December 17, p. D1.

Blank, Rebecca M. 1997. *It Takes a Nation: A New Agenda for Fighting Poverty.* Princeton, NJ: Princeton University Press.

Blau, Peter M. 1964. *Exchange and Power in Social Life.* New York: Wiley.

—— and Otis Dudley Duncan. 1967. *The American Occupational Structure.* New York: Wiley.

—— and Marshall W. Meyer. 1987. *Bureaucracy in Modern Society.* 3d ed. New York: Random House.

Blauner, Robert. 1964. *Alienation and Freedom.* Chicago: University of Chicago.

—— 1972. *Racial Oppression in America.* New York: Harper and Row.

Bloom, Stephan G. 1996. Strangers in a Strange Land. *Chicago Tribune Magazine* (January 28), pp. 10–15.

Bluestone, Barry, and Bennett Harrison. 1982. *The Deindustrialization of America.* New York: Basic Books.

Blumer, Herbert. 1969. *Symbolic Interactionism: Perspective and Method.* Englewood Cliffs, NJ: Prentice-Hall.

———. 1995. "Collective Behavior." Pp. 165–198 in *Principles of Sociology,* 2d ed., edited by Alfred McClung Lee. New York: Barnes and Noble.

Boaz, Rachel Floersheim. 1987. "Early Withdrawal from the Labor Force." *Research on Aging* 9(December): 530–547.

Bobo, Lawrence. 1991. "Social Responsibility, Individualism, and Redistribution Policies." *Sociological Forum* 6:71–92.

Boeck, Scott, and Marcia Staimer. 1996. "News Wire" *USA Today,* May 28, p. 1.

Bollag, Burton. 1996. "Bitter Internet Access South for Researchers Around the World." *Chronicle of Higher Education* 42(June 28): A14.

Bond, James T., Ellen Galinsky, and Jennifer E. Swanberg. 1998. The 1997 National Study of the Changing Work Force. New York: Families and Work Institute.

Booth, William. 2000. "Has Our Can-Do Attitude Peaked?" *Washington Post National Weekly Edition* 17(February 7):29.

Borman, Kathryn M. and Joel H. Spring. 1984. *Schools in Central Cities: Structure and Process.* New York: Longman.

Bornschier, Volker, Christopher Chase-Dunn, and Richard Rubinson. 1978. "Cross-National Evidence of the Effects of Foreign Investment and Aid on Economic Growth and Inequality: A Survey of Findings and a Reanalysis." *American Journal of Sociology* 84(November):651–683.

Boserup, Ester. 1977. "Preface." Pp. xi–xiv in *Women and National Development: The Complexities of Change,* edited by Wellesley Editorial Committee. Chicago: Chicago University Press.

Boston Women's Health Book Collective. 1969. *Our Bodies, Ourselves.* Boston: New England Free Press.

———. 1992. *The New Our Bodies, Ourselves.* New York: Touchstone.

Bottomore, Tom, and Maximilien Rubel, eds. 1956. *Karl Marx: Selected Writings in Sociology and Social Philosophy.* New York: McGraw-Hill.

Bouvier, Leon F. 1980. "America's Baby Boom Generation: The Fateful Bulge." *Population Bulletin* 35(April).

———, and Lindsey Grant. 1994. *How Many Americans? Population, Immigration, and the Environment.* San Francisco: Sierra Club.

Bowen, William G., and Derek Bok. 1998. *The Shape of the River: Long-Term Consequences of Considering Race in College and University Admissions.* Princeton, NJ: Princeton University Press.

Bowles, Samuel, and Herbert Gintis. 1976. *Schooling in Capitalist America: Educational Reforms and the Contradictions of Economic Life.* New York: Basic Books.

Bowles, Scott. 1999. "Fewer Violent Fatalities in Schools." *USA Today,* April 28, p. 4A.

Bracey, Gerald W. 1993. "No Magic Bullet." *Phi Delta Kappan* 74(February):495–496.

Bradley, Martin B. et al. [5 authors]. 1992. *Churches and Church Membership in the United States 1990.* Atlanta, GA: Glenmary Research Center.

Bragg, Rick. 1999. "Fearing Isolation in Old Age, Gay Generation Seeks Haven." *New York Times,* October 21, pp. A1, A16.

Brandon, Karen. 1995. "Computer Scrutiny Adds to Furor over Immigrants." *Chicago Tribune,* December 5, pp. 1, 16.

Brannigan, Augustine. 1992. "Postmodernism." Pp. 1522–1525 in *Encyclopedia of Sociology,* vol. 3, edited by Edgar F. Borgatta and Marie L. Borgatta. New York: Macmillan.

Brannon, Robert. 1976. "Ideology, Myth, and Reality: Sex Equality in Israel." *Sex Roles* 6:403–419.

Braxton, Greg. 1999. "A Mad Dash for Diversity." *Los Angeles Times,* August 9, pp. F1, F10.

Bray, James H., and John Kelly. 1999. *Stepfamilies: Love, Marriage, and Parenting in the First Decade.* New York: Broadway Books.

Brelin, Christa, ed. 1996. *Strength in Numbers: A Lesbian, Gay, and Bisexual Resource.* Detroit: Visible Ink.

Brewer, Rose M. 1989. "Black Women and Feminist Sociology: The Emerging Perspective." *American Sociologist* 20(Spring):57–70.

Bridges, George S., and Sara Steen. 1998. "Racial Disparities in Official Assessments of Juvenile Offenders: Attribu-

tional Stereotypes as Mediating Mechanisms." *American Sociological Review* 63(August):554–570.

Brint, Steven. 1998. *Schools and Societies.* Thousand Oaks, CA: Pine Forge Press.

Brodeur, Paul. 1993. "Legacy." *New Yorker* 69(June 7):114.

Bronson, P. 1999. *The Nudist in the Late Shift and Other True Tales of Silicon Valley.* New York: Random House.

Brower, Brock. 1988. "The Pernicious Power of the Polls." *Money,* March 17, pp. 144–163.

Brown, Michael, and Amy Goldin. 1972. *Collective Behavior: A Review and Reinterpretation of the Literature.* Pacific Palisades, CA: Goodyear.

Brown, Roger W. 1954. "Mass Phenomena." Pp. 833–873 in *Handbook of Social Psychology,* vol. 2, edited by Gardner Lindzey. Reading, MA: Addison-Wesley.

———. 1965. *Social Psychology.* New York: Free Press.

Brown, William J., and Michael J. Cody. 1991. "Effects of a Prosocial Television Soap Opera in Promoting Women's Status." *Human Communication Research* 18(September):114–142.

Bruce, Judith, Cynthia B. Lloyd, and Ann Leonard, with Patrice L. Engle and Niev Duffy. 1995. *Families in Focus: New Perspectives on Mothers, Fathers, and Children.* New York: Population Council.

Bruni, Frank. 1998. "A Small-But-Growing Sorority Is Giving Birth to Children for Gay Men." *New York Times,* June 25, p. A12.

Bryant, Adam. 1999. "American Pay Rattles Foreign Partners." *New York Times,* January 17, sec. 6, pp. 1, 4.

Bryson, Ken, and Lynne M-Casper. 1999. "Coresident Grandparents and Grandchildren." *Current Population Reports,* ser. P-23, no. 198. Washington, DC: U.S. Government Printing Office.

Buckley, Stephen. 1997. "Left Behind Prosperity's Door." *Washington Post National Weekly Edition,* March 24, pp. 8–9.

Buechler, Steven M. 1995. "New Social Movement Theories." *Sociological Quarterly* 36(3):441–464.

Buffalo News. 1999. "Viewpoints: We Must Continue Fight to Ban Soft Money." November 22, p. 3B.

Bulle, Wolfgang F. 1987. *Crossing Cultures? Southeast Asian Mainland.* Atlanta: Centers for Disease Control.

Bunzel, John H. 1992. *Race Relations on Campus: Stanford Students Speak.* Stanford, CA: Portable Stanford.

Bureau of the Census. 1975. *Historical Statistics of the United States, Colonial Times to 1970.* Washington, DC: U.S. Government Printing Office.

———. 1991a. "Marital Status and Living Arrangements: March 1990." *Current Population Reports,* ser. P-20, no. 450. Washington, DC: U.S. Government Printing Office.

———. 1991c. "Half of the Nation's Population Lives in Large Metropolitan Areas." Press Release, February 21.

———. 1994. *Statistical Abstract of the United States: 1994.* Washington, D.C.: U.S. Government Printing Office.

———. 1995. *Statistical Abstract of the United States, 1995.* Washington, DC: U.S. Government Printing Office.

———. 1996a. *1992 Women-Owned Businesses.* Washington, DC: U.S. Government Printing Office.

———. 1996b. *Statistical Abstract of the United States, 1996.* Washington DC: U.S. Government Printing Office.

———. 1997a. *Statistical Abstract of the United States, 1997.* Washington, DC: U.S. Government Printing Office.

———. 1997b. "Geographical Mobility: March 1995 to March 1996." *Current Population Reports,* P-20, no. 497. Washington, DC: U.S. Government Printing Office.

———. 1998a. "Race of Wife by Race of Husband." Internet Release of June 10.

———. 1998c. *Statistical Abstract of the United States, 1998.* Washington, DC: U.S. Government Printing Office.

———. 1998e. Unpub.Tables—Marital Status and Living Arrangements: March 1998 (Update). Accessed July 26, 1999 (http://www.census.gov/ prod/99pubs/ p20-514u.pdf).

———. 1998f. Voting and Registration: November 1996. Internet release date: October 17, 1997. Accessed July 17, 1998 (http://www.census.gov/ population/socdemo/voting/history/ vot01.txt).

———. 1998g. "Money Income in the United States: 1997." *Current Population Reports,* ser. P-60, No. 200. Washington, DC: U.S. Government Printing Office.

———. 1999a. *Statistical Abstract of the United States, 1996.* Washington, DC: U.S. Government Printing Office.

———. 1999b. "The Asian and Pacific Islander Population in the United States: March 1998 (Update) (PP1-113). Table 9." *Total Money Income in 1997 of Families.* Accessed August 3, 1999 (http://www.census.gov/ population/sucdemo/race/api98/ table09.txt).

———. 1999c. "American Indian Heritage Month." News release October 21.

———. 1999d. "Population Estimates for States by Race and Hispanic Origin: July 1, 1998." Accessed September 16, 1999 (http://www. census.gov/population/estimates/ state/srh/srhus98.txt).

———. 1999i. "Money Income in the United States." *Current Population Reports,* ser. P-60, no. 206. Washington, DC: U.S. Government Printing Office.

———. 2000a. "Census Bureau Projects Doubling of Nation's Population by 2100. Press release January 13.

———. 2000b. "Employment Status of the Civilian Population by Race, Sex, Age, and Hispanic Origin." Accessed January 3, 2000 (http://www.bls.gov/ news.release/empsit.102.htm).

Bureau of Labor Statistics. 1998a. "Employer-Sponsored Childcare Benefits." *Issues in Labor Statistics,* August, pp. 1–2.

———. 1998b. "Employment Status of the Civilian Population by Race, Sex, Age, and Hispanic Origin." Accessed on November 18 at http://www.bls. gen/news.release/empsit.tp2.htm.

———. 1999a. "Comparative Civilian Labor Force Statistics Ten Countries 1959–1990." Posted April 13, 1999. Accessed October 9, 1999 (ftp://ftp. bls.gov/pub/special.requests/ ForeignLabor/flslforc.txt).

———. 1999b. "What Women Earned in 1998." *Issues in Labor Statistics.* Washington, DC: U.S. Government Printing Office.

———. 2000. "Employment Status of the Civilian Population by Race, Sex, Age, and Hispanic Origin." Accessed at http://www.bls.gen/news.release.

Bureau of Primary Health Care. 1999. Home Page. Accessed January 18, 2000 (http://www.bphc.hrsa.gov/ bphcfactsheet.htm).

Burek, Deborah, ed. 1992. *Encyclopedia of Associations, 1993.* Detroit: Gale Research.

Burgess, Ernest W. 1925. "The Growth of the City." Pp. 47–62 in *The City,* edited by Robert E. Park, Ernest W. Burgess, and Roderick D. McKenzie. Chicago: University of Chicago Press.

Burns, John R. 1998. "Once Widowed in India, Twice Scorned." *New York Times,* March 29, p. A1.

Burt, Martha R. et al. 1999. *Homeless: Programs and the People They Save.* Washington, DC: Urban Institute.

Burton, Velmer S., Jr. 1990. "The Consequences of Official Labels: A Research Note on Rights Lost by the Mentally Ill, Mentally Incompetent, and Convicted Felons." *Community Mental Health Journal* 26(June):267–276.

Bush, Melanie. 1993. "The Doctor Is Out," *Village Voice* 38, June 22, p. 18.

Butler, Daniel Allen. 1998. *"Unsinkable:" The Full Story.* Mechanicsburg, PA: Stackpole Books.

Butler, Robert N. 1990. "A Disease Called Ageism." *Journal of American Geriatrics Society* 38(February): 178–180.

Butterfield, Fox. 1996. "U.S. Has Plan to Broaden Availability of DNA Testing." *New York Times,* June 14, p. A8.

C

Cable, Sherry, and Michael Benson. 1993. "Acting Locally: Environmental Injustice and the Emergence of Grassroots Environmental Organizations." *Social Problems* 40(November): 464–477.

Calhoun, Craig. 1998. "Community Without Propinquity Revisited." *Sociological Inquiry* 68(Summer): 373–397.

Callahan, Tim. 1996. "Trees and Volcanoes Cause Smog!" *Humanist* 56(January–February):29–34.

Came, Barry. 1994. "A Family Tragedy." *Maclean's* 107(November 21):40–43.

Campbell, Anne. 1991. *The Girls in the Gang.* 2d ed. Cambridge, MA: Blackwell.

Campbell, Jennifer A. 1999. "Health Insurance Coverage," *Current Population Reports Service,* P60 No. 208. Washington D.C.: U.S. Government Printing Office.

Campbell, Paul R. 1996. "Population Projections for States by Age, Sex, Race, and Hispanic Origin: 1995 to 2025." Population Division PPL-47. Washington, DC: U.S. Government Printing Office.

Camus, Albert. 1948. *The Plague*. New York: Random House.

Cancel, Cecil Marie. 1997. "The Veil." Accessed October 10, 1999 (http://about.com).

Cancian, Francesca. 1986. "The Feminization of Love." *Signs* 11(Summer): 692–708.

Cantril, Hadley. 1940. *The Invasion from Mars: A Study in the Psychology of Panic*. Princeton, NJ: Princeton University Press.

Caplan, Ronald L. 1989. "The Commodification of American Health Care." *Social Science and Medicine* 28(11): 1139–1148.

Caplow, Theodore. 1969. *Two against One: Coalitions in Triads*. Englewood Cliffs, NJ: Prentice-Hall.

Cardarelli, Luise. 1996. "The Lost Girls: China May Come to Regret Its Preference for Boys." *Utne Reader*, May–June, pp. 13–14.

Carey, Anne R., and Elys A. McLean. 1997. "Heard It Through the Grapevine?" *USA Today*, September 15, p. B1.

——— and Grant Jerding. 1999. "What Workers Want." *USA Today*, August 17, p. B1.

——— and Jerry Mosemak. 1999. "Big on Religion." *USA Today*, April 1, p. D1.

Cargan, Leonard, and Matthew Melko. 1991. "Being Single on Noah's Ark." Pp. 161–165 in *Sociological Footprints*, 5th ed., edited by Leonard Cargan and Jeanne H. Ballantine. Belmont, CA: Wadsworth.

Carlisle, David M., Barbara D. Leake, and Martin F. Shapiro. 1995. "Racial and Ethnic Differences in the Use of Invasive Cardiac Procedures among Cardiac Patients in Los Angeles County, 1986 through 1988." *American Journal of Public Health* 85(March):352–356.

Carrese, Joseph A., and Lorna A. Rhodes. 1995. "Western Bioethics on the Navaho Reservation: Benefit or Harm?" *Journal of the American Medical Association* 274(September 13): 826–829.

Carson, Rachel L. 1962. *Silent Spring*. Boston: Houghton Mifflin.

Carty, Win. 1999. "Greater Dependence on Cars Leads to More Pollution in World's Cities." *Population Today* 27(December):1–2.

Casper, Lynne M., and Loretta E. Bass. 1998. "Voting and Registration in the Election of November 1996." *Current Population Reports*, ser. P-20, no. 504. Washington, DC: U.S. Government Printing Office.

——— and Kenneth R. Bryson. 1998. "Co-resident Grandparents and Their Grandchildren: Grandparent Maintained Families." Population Divison Working Paper no. 26. Washington, DC: Bureau of the Census.

Cassidy, Claire Monod. 1982. "Protein-Energy Malnutrition as a Culture-Bound Syndrome." *Culture, Medicine, and Psychiatry* 6:325–345.

Castaneda, Jorge G. 1995. "Ferocious Differences." *Atlantic Monthly* 276(July):68–69, 71–76.

Castelli, Jim. 1996. "How to Handle Personal Information." *American Demographics* 18(March):50–52, 57.

Castells, Manuel. 1983. *The City and the Grass Roots*. Berkeley: University of California Press.

———. 1996. *The Information Age: Economy, Society and Culture*. Vol. 1, *The Rise of the Network Society*. London: Blackwell.

———. 1997. *The Power of Identity*. Vol. 1, *The Information Age: Economy, Society and Culture*. London: Blackwell.

———. 1998. *End of Millennium*. Vol. 3 of *The Information Age: Economy, Society and Culture*. London: Blackwell.

Catalyst. 1999. *1999 Catalyst Census of Women Board of Directors of the Fortune 1000*. New York: Catalyst.

Cavanagh, John, and Robin Broad. 1996. "Global Reach: Workers Fight the Multinationals." *The Nation* 262(March 18):21–24.

CBS News. 1979. Transcript of *Sixty Minutes* segment, "I Was Only Following Orders." March 31, pp. 2–8.

———. 1998. "Experimental Prison." *Sixty Minutes*. June 30.

Celis, William, III. 1993. "Suburban and Rural Schools Learning That Violence Isn't Confined to the Cities." *New York Times*, April 21, p. B11.

Center for the American Woman and Politics. 1999. *Women in Elective Office 1998*. New Brunswick, NJ: CAWP, Rutgers University.

Centers for Disease Control and Prevention. 1995. "Trends in Sexual Risk Behavior among High School Students: United States, 1990, 1991, and 1993." *Morbidity and Mortality Weekly Report* 44(February 24):124–125, 131–132.

———. 2000a. "Abortion Surveillance: Preliminary Analysis—United States, 1997." *Morbidity and Mortality Weekly Reports*, January 7, p. 2.

———. 2000b. "Commentary." *HIV/AIDS Surveillance Supplemental Report* 5, January 18, p. 1.

Center for Public Integrity. 1998. *Nothing Sacred: The Politics of Privacy*. Washington, DC: CPI.

Cetron, Marvin J., and Owen Davies. 1991. "Trends Shaping the World." *Futurist* 20(September–October):11–21.

Chaddock, Gail Russell. 1998. "The Challenge for Schools: Connecting Adults with Kids." *Christian Science Monitor*, August 4, p. B7.

———. 1999. "Can This School Make a Difference?" *Christian Science Monitor*, January 2, pp. 13, 18–19.

Chalfant, H. Paul, Robert E. Beckley, and C. Eddie Palmer. 1994. *Religion in Contemporary Society*. 3d ed. Itasca, IL: F. E. Peacock.

Chambliss, William. 1972. "Introduction." Pp. ix–xi in Harry King, *Box Man*. New York: Harper and Row.

———. 1973. "The Saints and the Roughnecks." *Society* 11(November–December):24–31.

——— and Robert B. Seidman. 1971. *Law, Order, and Power*. Reading, MA: Addison-Wesley.

Charmaz, Kathy, and Debora A. Paterniti, eds. 1999. *Health, Illness, and Healing: Society, Social Context, and Self*. Los Angeles, CA: Roxbury.

Charter, David, and Jill Sherman. 1996. "Schools Must Teach New Code of Values." *London Times*, January 15, p. 1.

Chase-Dunn, Christopher, and Peter Grimes. 1995. "World-Systems Analysis." Pp. 387–417 in *Annual Review of Sociology, 1995*, edited by John Hagan. Palo Alto, CA: Annual Reviews.

Chatzky, Jean Sherman. 1999. "The Big Squeeze." *Money* 28(October):129, 131–134, 137–138.

Cheng, Wei-yuan, and Lung-li Liao. 1994. "Women Managers in Taiwan." Pp. 143–159 in *Competitive Frontiers: Women Managers in a Global Economy,* edited by Nancy J. Adler and Dafna N. Izraeli. Cambridge, MA: Blackwell Business.

Cherlin, Andrew J. 1999. *Public and Private Families: An Introduction.* 2d ed. New York: McGraw-Hill.

——— and Frank Furstenberg. 1992. *The New American Grandparent: A Place in the Family, A Life Apart.* Cambridge, MA: Harvard University Press.

——— and ———. 1994. "Stepfamilies in the United States: A Reconsideration." Pp. 359–381 in *Annual Review of Sociology, 1994,* edited by John Hagan. Palo Alto, CA: Annual Reviews.

Chernin, Kim, 1981. *The Obsession: Reflections on the Tyranny of Slenderness.* New York: Harper and Row.

Chesney-Lind, Meda, and Noelie Rodriguez. 1993. "Women under Lock and Key." *Prison Journal* 63:47–65.

——— and Randall G. Shelden. 1998. *Girls, Delinquency, and Juvenile Justice.* 2d ed. Belmont, CA: Wadsworth.

Chicago Tribune. 1997a. "China Aborting Female Fetuses." October 17, p. 13.

———. 1997b. "In London, Prince Meets a Pauper, an Ex-Classmate." December 5, p. 19.

Chin, Ko-lin. 1996. *Chinatown Gangs: Extortion, Enterprise, and Ethnicity.* New York: Oxford University Press.

Chow, Esther Ngan-Ling, and S. Michael Zhao. 1995. "The Impact of the One-Child Policy on Parent-Child Relationships in the People's Republic of China." Presented at the annual meeting of the American Sociological Association, August, Washington, DC.

Christensen, Kathleen. 1990. "Bridges over Troubled Water: How Older Workers View the Labor Market." Pp. 175–207 in *Bridges to Retirement,* edited by Peter B. Doeringer. Ithaca, NY: IRL Press.

Christiansen, John B. and Sharon N. Barnartt. 1995. *Deaf President Now: The 1988 Revolution at Gallaudet University.* Washington, DC: Gallaudet University Press.

Cimons, Marlene. 1999. "New Data Suggest Limits to AIDS Drugs." *Los Angeles Times,* August 31, pp. A1, 12.

Civic Ventures. 1999. *The New Face of Retirement: Older Americans, Civic Engagement, and the Longevity Revolution.* Washington, DC: Peter D. Hart Research Associates.

Clark, Brian L. 1999. "Internet Life: Our Town. Online." *Money* 28(September):36.

Clark, Burton, and Martin Trow. 1966. "The Organizational Context." Pp. 17–70 in *The Study of College Peer Groups,* edited by Theodore M. Newcomb and Everett K. Wilson. Chicago: Aldine.

Clark, Candace. 1983. "Sickness and Social Control." Pp. 346–365 in *Social Interaction: Readings in Sociology,* 2d. ed., edited by Howard Robboy and Candace Clark. New York: St. Martin's.

Clark, Charles, and Jason M. Fields. 1999. "First Glance: Preliminary Analysis of Relationship, Marital Status, and Grandparents Items on the Census 2000 Dress Rehearsal." Presented at the annual meeting of the American Sociological Association, August, Chicago.

Clark, Thomas. 1994. "Culture and Objectivity." *The Humanist* 54(August):38–39.

Clarke, Lee. 1988. "Explaining Choices among Technological Risks." *Social Problems* 35(February):501–504.

Cloud, John. 1998. "Sex and the Law." *Time* 151(March 23):48–54.

Cloward, Richard A. 1959. "Illegitimate Means, Anomie, and Deviant Behavior." *American Sociological Review* 24(April):164–176.

——— and Frances Fox Piven. 1993. "The Fraud of Workfare." *The Nation* 246 (May 24):693–696.

Clymer, Adam. 2000. "College Students Not Drawn to Voting or Politics, Poll Shows." *New York Times,* January 2, p. A14.

Coatney, Caryn. 1998. "Arrest of Abortion Doctors Puts Australia Laws on Spot." *Christian Science Monitor,* March 25, p. 6.

Cockerham, William C. 1998. *Medical Sociology.* 7th ed. Upper Saddle River, NJ: Prentice-Hall.

———. 1999. *Health and Social Change in Russia and Eastern Europe.* New York: Routledge.

Coeyman, Marjorie. 1999. "Schools Question the Benefits of Tracking." *Christian Science Monitor,* September 21, p. 20.

Cohen, David, ed. 1991. *The Circle of Life: Ritual from the Human Family Album.* San Francisco: Harper.

Cohen, Lawrence E., and Marcus Felson. 1979. "Social Change and Crime Rate Trends: A Routine Activities Approach." *American Sociological Review* 44:588–608.

Cohen, Patricia. 1998. "Daddy Dearest: Do You Really Matter?" *New York Times,* July 11, p. B7.

Cole, David. 1999. *No Equal Justice: Race and Class in the American Criminal Justice System.* New York: The New Press.

Cole, Elizabeth S. 1985. "Adoption, History, Policy, and Program." Pp. 638–666 in *A Handbook of Child Welfare,* edited by John Laird and Ann Hartman. New York: Free Press.

Cole, Mike. 1988. *Bowles and Gintis Revisited: Correspondence and Contradiction in Educational Theory.* Philadelphia: Falmer.

Coleman, James William, and Donald R. Cressey. 1980. *Social Problems.* New York: Harper and Row.

Collins, Gail. 1998. "Why the Women Are Fading Away." *New York Times,* October 25, pp. 54–55.

Collins, Patricia Hill. 1991. *Black Feminist Thought: Knowledge, Consciousness, and the Politics of Empowerment.* New York: Routledge.

Collins, Randall. 1975. *Conflict Sociology: Toward an Explanatory Sociology.* New York: Academic.

———. 1979. *The Credential Society: An Historical Sociology of Education and Stratification.* New York: Academic.

———. 1980. "Weber's Last Theory of Capitalism: A Systematization." *American Sociological Review* 45(December):925–942.

———. 1986. *Weberian Sociological Theory.* New York: Cambridge University Press.

———. 1995. "Prediction in Macrosociology: The Case of the Soviet Collapse." *American Journal of Sociology* 100(May):1552–1593.

CommerceNet/Nielsen Internet Demographic Survey. 1998. "Who's on

Line." Reproduced in *USA Today*, August 25, p. D1.

Commission on Behavioral and Social Sciences Education. 1998. *Protecting Youth at Work*. Washington, DC: National Academy Press.

Commission on Civil Rights. 1976. *A Guide to Federal Laws and Regulations Prohibiting Sex Discrimination*. Washington, DC: U.S. Government Printing Office.

———. 1981. *Affirmative Action in the 1980s: Dismantling the Process of Discrimination*. Washington, DC: U.S. Government Printing Office.

Commoner, Barry. 1971. *The Closing Circle*. New York: Knopf.

———. 1990. *Making Peace with the Planet*. New York: Pantheon.

Congressional Quarterly. 1996. "Campaign Finance Reform." *CQ Research Reports*, February 9.

Conrad, Peter, ed. 1997. *The Sociology of Health and Illness: Critical Perspectives*. 5th ed. New York: St. Martin's.

——— and Joseph W. Schneider. 1992. *Deviance and Medicalization: From Badness to Sickness*. Expanded ed. Philadelphia: Temple University Press.

Constable, Pamela. 1999. "India's Clock Just Keeps on Ticking." *Washington Post National Weekly Edition* 16(August 30): 16.

Cook, P. J., and J. A. Leitzel. 1996. *Perversity, Futility, Jeopardy: An Economic Analysis of the Attack on Gun Control*. Durham, NC: Sanford Institute of Public Policy, Duke University.

Cook, Rhodes. 1991. "The Crosscurrents of the Youth Vote." *Congressional Quarterly Weekly Report* 49(June 29): 1802.

Cooley, Charles H. 1902. *Human Nature and the Social Order*. New York: Scribner.

Coontz, Stephanie. 1997. "Divorcing Realty." *The Nation* 265(November 17):21–24.

Cooper, Glenda. 1997. "Who's Right about Child Care?" *Independent*, February 4, p. 1.

Cooper, Kenneth J. 1994. "Wrong Turns on the Map?" *Washington Post National Weekly Edition* 12(January 31):14.

Cooper, Richard T. 1998. "Jobs Outside High School Can Be Costly, Report Finds." *Los Angeles Times*, November 6, p. A1.

Corning, Amy. 1993. "The Russian Referendum: An Analysis of Exit Poll Results." *RFE/RL Research Report* 2(May 7):6–9.

Coser, Lewis A. 1956. *The Functions of Social Conflict*. New York: Free Press.

Coser, Rose Laub. 1984. "American Medicine's Ambiguous Progress." *Contemporary Sociology* 13(January): 9–13.

Couch, Carl. 1996. *Information Technologies and Social Orders*. Edited with an introduction by David R. Maines and Shing-Ling Chien. New York: Aldine de Gruyter.

Council on Ethical and Judicial Affairs, American Medical Association. 1992. "Decisions Near the End of Life." *Journal of the American Medical Association* 267(April 22–29):2229–2333.

Cox, Craig. 1999. "Prime-Time Activism." *Utne Reader* (September–October), pp. 20–22.

Cox, Oliver C. 1948. *Caste, Class and Race: A Study in Social Dynamics*. Detroit: Wayne State University Press.

Cressey, Donald R. 1960. "Epidemiology and Individual Contact: A Case from Criminology." *Pacific Sociological Review* 3(Fall):47–58.

Cresson, Edith. 1995. "Roots and Wings: Remaining European in the Information Age." *New Perspectives Quarterly* 12(Fall):26–28.

Croissant, Jennifer L. 1998. "Developmental Stories for Postmodern Children." Pp. 285–300 in *Cyborg Babies: From Techno-Sex to Techno-Tots*, edited by Robbie Davis-Floyd and Joseph Dumit. New York: Routledge.

Cromwell, Paul F., James N. Olson, and D'Aunn Wester Avarey. 1995. *Breaking and Entering: An Ethnographic Analysis of Burglary*. Newbury Park, CA: Sage.

Crossette, Barbara. 1996. "'Oldest Old,' 80 and Over, Increasing Globally." *New York Times*, December 22, p. 7.

———. 1996b. "Snubbing Human Rights," *New York Times* (April 28), p. E3.

———. 1999. "The Internet Changes Dictatorship's Rules." *New York Times*, August 1, sec. 4, p. 1.

Crouse, Kelly. 1999. "Sociology of the Titanic." *Teaching Sociology Listserv*. May 24.

Counts, D. A. 1977. "The Good Death in Kaliai: Preparation for Death in Western New Britain." *Omega* 7:367–372.

Cuff, E. C., W. W. Sharrock, and D. W. Francis, eds. 1990. *Perspectives in Sociology*. 3d ed. Boston: Unwin Hyman.

Cullen, Francis T., Jr., and John B. Cullen. 1978. *Toward a Paradigm of Labeling Theory*, ser. 58. Lincoln: University of Nebraska Studies.

Cumming, Elaine, and William E. Henry. 1961. *Growing Old: The Process of Disengagement*. New York: Basic Books.

Cunningham, Kitty. 1993. "Caucus Rebuffs Clinton." *Congressional Quarterly Weekly Report* 51(June 12):1452.

Cunningham, Michael. 1992. "If You're Queer and You're Not Angry in 1992, You're Not Paying Attention." *Mother Jones* 17(May–June):60–66, 68.

Currie, Elliot. 1985. *Confronting Crime: An American Challenge*. New York: Pantheon.

———. 1998. *Crime and Punishment in America*. New York: Metropolitan Books.

Curry, Timothy Jon. 1993. "A Little Pain Never Hurt Anyone: Athletic Career Socialization and the Normalization of Sports Injury." *Symbolic Interaction* 26(Fall):273–290.

Curtis, James E., Edward G. Grabbs, and Douglas E. Baer. 1992. "Voluntary Association Membership in Fifteen Countries: A Composite Analysis." *American Sociological Review* 57(April):139–152.

Curtius, Mary. 1999. "Struggling Town Split Over Wal-Mart Plan." *Los Angeles Times*, July 5, pp. A1, A16–18.

Cushman, John H., Jr. 1998a. "Pollution Policy Is Unfair Burden, States Tell E. P. A." *New York Times*, May 10, pp. 1, 20.

———. 1998b. "Nike Pledges to End Child Labor and Apply U.S. Rules Abroad." *New York Times*, May 13, p. C1.

Cussins, Choris M. 1998. In *Cyborg Babies: From Techno-Sex to Techno-Tots*, edited by Robbie Davis-Floyd and Joseph Dumit. New York: Routledge.

D

Dahl, Robert A. 1961. *Who Governs?* New Haven, CT: Yale University Press.

Dahrendorf, Ralf. 1958. "Toward a Theory of Social Conflict." *Journal of Conflict Resolution* 2(June):170–183.

———. 1959. *Class and Class Conflict in Industrial Sociology*. Stanford, CA: Stanford University Press.

Dalaker, Joseph. 1999. "Poverty in the United States 1998." *Current Population Reports*, ser. P-60, no. 207. Washington, DC: U.S. Government Printing Office.

———— and Mary Naifeh. 1998. "Poverty in the United States: 1997." *Current Population Reports*, ser. P-60, no. 201. Washington, DC: U.S. Government Printing Office.

Daley, Suzanne. 1996. "Apartheid's Dispossessed Seek Restitution." *New York Times*, June 25, p. A3.

————. 1997. "Reversing Roles in a South African Dilemma." *New York Times*, October 26, sec. WE, p. 5.

————. 1998. "A Post-Apartheid Agony: AIDS on the March," *New York Times* (July 23), pp. A1, A10.

————. 1999. "Doctors' Group of Volunteers Awarded Nobel." *New York Times*, October 16, pp. A1, A6.

Daniels, Arlene Kaplan. 1987. "Invisible Work." *Social Problems* 34(December): 403–415.

————. 1988. *Invisible Careers*. Chicago: University of Chicago Press.

Dao, James. 1995. "New York's Highest Court Rules Unmarried Couples Can Adopt." *New York Times*, November 3, pp. A1, B2.

Dart, John. 1997. "Lutheran Women Wait Longer for Pastor Jobs, Survey Finds." *Los Angeles Times*, May 3, pp. B1, B5.

Daskal, Jennifer. 1998. *In Search of Shelter: The Growing Shortage of Affordable Rental Housing*. Washington, DC: Center on Budget and Policy Priorities.

Davidson, Robert C., and Ernest L. Lewis. 1997. "Affirmative Action and Other Special Consideration Admissions at the University of California, Davis, School of Medicine." *Journal of the American Medical Association* 278(October 8):1153–1158.

Davies, Christie. 1989. "Goffman's Concept of the Total Institution: Criticisms and Revisions." *Human Studies* 12(June):77–95.

Davis, Darren W. 1997. "The Direction of Race of Interviewer Effects Among African-Americans: Donning the Black Mask." *American Journal of Political Science* 41(January):309–322.

Davis, James. 1982. "Up and Down Opportunity's Ladder." *Public Opinion* 5(June–July):11–15, 48–51.

Davis, James Allan, and Tom W. Smith. 1998. *General Social Surveys, 1972–1998*. Storrs, CT: The Roper Center.

———— and ————. 1999. *General Social Surveys, 1972–1998* [MRDF]. Storrs, CT: The Roper Center for Public Opinion Research.

Davis, Kingsley. 1937. "The Sociology of Prostitution." *American Sociological Review* 2(October):744–755.

————. 1940. "Extreme Social Isolation of a Child." *American Journal of Sociology* 45(January):554–565.

————. 1947. A Final Note on a Case of Extreme Isolation. *American Journal of Sociology* 52(March):432–437.

————. [1949] 1995. *Human Society*. Reprint, New York: Macmillan.

———— and Wilbert E. Moore. 1945. "Some Principles of Stratification." *American Sociological Review* 10(April): 242–249.

Davis, Mike. 1998. *Ecology of Fear: Los Angeles and the Imagination of Disaster*. New York: Metropolitan Books/Henry Holt and Co.

Davis, Nanette J. 1975. *Sociological Constructions of Deviance: Perspectives and Issues in the Field*. Dubuque, IA: Wm. C. Brown.

Day, Jennifer Cheeseman. 1993. "Population Projections of the United States by Age, Sex, Race, and Hispanic Origin: 1993–2050," *Current Population Reports*, ser. P-25, no. 1104. Washington, DC: U.S. Government Printing Office.

Daycare Action Council. 2000. Interview, January 5. Chicago: Daycare Action Council of Illinois.

De Andra, Roberto M. 1996. *Chicanas and Chicanos in Contemporary Society*. Boston: Allyn and Bacon.

Death Penalty Information Center. 2000a. "The Death Penalty in 1999: Year End Report." Accessed February 13, 2000 (http://www.essential.org/dpic/yrendrpt99.html).

————. 2000b. "History of the Death Penalty. Part II." Accessed February 13, 2000 (http://www.essential.org/dpic/history3.html#Innocence).

————. 2000c. "Innocence: Freed From Death Row." Accessed March 20, 2000 (http://www.essential.org/dpic/Innocent/ist.html.)

————. 2000d. "Race of Defendants Executed Since 1976 as of February 10, 2000." Accessed February 13, 2000 (http://www.essential.org/dpic/dpicrace.html).

de Beauvoir, Simone. 1953. *The Second Sex*. New York: Knopf.

Deegan, Mary Jo, ed. 1991. *Women in Sociology: A Bio-Biographical Sourcebook*. Westport, CT: Greenwood.

DeFleur, Melvin L., and Everette E. Dennis. 1981. *Understanding Mass Communication*. Boston: Houghton Mifflin.

Deloria, Jr., Vine. 1999. *For This Land: Writings on Religion in America*. New York: Routledge.

Delriozolezzi, A. et al [6 authors]. 1995. "The HIV AIDS Epidemic and Women in Mexico." *Salud Publica De Mexico* 37(November–December): 581–591.

D'Emilio, John. 1983. *Sexual Politics, Sexual Communities*. Chicago: University of Chicago Press.

DePalma, Anthony. 1995a. "Racism? Mexico's in Denial." *New York Times*, June 11, p. E4.

————. 1995b. "For Mexico, NAFTA's Promise of Jobs Is Still Just a Promise." *New York Times*, October 10, pp. A1, A10.

————. 1995c. "Insecurity Rocks Mexico's Cradle-to-Coffin System." *New York Times*, November 13, p. A4.

————. 1996. "For Mexico Indians, New Voice but Few Gains." *New York Times*, January 13, pp. 1, 6.

————. 1999. "Rules to Protect a Culture Make for Confusion." *New York Times*, July 14, pp. B1, B2.

DeParle, Jason. 1998. "Shrinking Welfare Rolls Leave Record High Share of Minorities." *New York Times*, July 27, pp. A1, A12.

Department of Education. 1998. *Students' Reports of School Crime: 1989 and 1995*. Washington, DC: U.S. Government Printing Office.

————. 1999. *Report on State Implementation of the Gun-Free Schools Act. School year 1997–98*. Rockville, MD: Westat.

Department of Health and Human Services. 1999. "Change in TANF Caseloads (January 1993–March 1999)." Accessed September 29, 1999 (http://www.acf.dhhs.gov/news/stats/caseload.htm).

Department of Justice. 1999a. *Uniform Crime Reports, 1998.* Washington, DC: U.S. Government Printing Office.

———. 1999b. *Correctional Populations in the United States, 1996.* Washington, DC: Bureau of Justice Statistics.

Department of Labor. 1995a. *Good for Business: Making Full Use of the Nation's Capital.* Washington, DC: U.S. Government Printing Office.

———. 1995b. *A Solid Investment: Making Full Use of the Nation's Human Capital.* Washington, DC: U.S. Government Printing Office.

———. 1998. "Work and Elder Care: Facts for Caregivers and Their Employers." Accessed November 20 (http://www.dol.gov/dol/wb/public/wb_pubs/elderc.htm).

Desai, Manisha. 1996. "If Peasants Build Their Own Dams, What Would the State Have Left to Do?" Pp. 209–224 in *Research in Social Movements, Conflicts and Change,* vol. 19, edited by Michael Dobkowski and Isidor Wallimann. Greenwich, CT: JAI Press.

de Sherbinin, Alex. 1990. "Iraq." *Population Today* 18(October):12.

DeSimone, Bonnie. 2000. "Gold Tendency." *Chicago Tribune Magazine.* (February 20):9–19.

Devine, Don. 1972. *Political Culture of the United States: The Influence of Member Values on Regime Maintenance.* Boston: Little, Brown.

Devitt, James. 1999. *Framing Gender on the Campaign Trail: Women's Executive Leadership and the Press.* New York: Women's Leadership Conference.

Dickerson, Marla. 1998. "Belief in Ideas Inspires Women to Start Businesses." *Los Angeles Times,* February 24, pp. D1, D13.

Dillon, Sam. 1997. "Gay Rights, Prejudice and Politics in Mexico." *New York Times,* January 4, p. 4.

———. 1998. "Sex Bias at Border Plants in Mexico Reported by U.S." *New York Times,* January 13, p. A6.

Dinello, Dan. 1998. "Denizens of the Dark." *Chicago Tribune,* February 2, pp. C1, 7.

Dionne, Annette, Cecile, and Yvonne. 1997. "Letter." *Time,* December 1, p. 39.

Disaster Research Center. 2000. "The Disaster Research Center." Accessed January 19, 2000 (http://www.udel.eder/DRC/index2.html).

Doeringer, Peter B., ed. 1990. *Bridges to Retirement: Older Workers in a Changing Labor Market.* Ithaca, NY: ILR Press.

Dohan, Daniel, and Martin Sánchez-Jankowski. 1998. "Using Computers to Analyze Ethographic Field Data: Theoretical and Practical Considerations." Pp. 477–498 in *Annual Review of Sociology,* 1998, edited by John Hogan and Karen S. Cook.

Doig, Stephen, Reynolds Farley, William Frey, and Dan Gillman. 1993. *Blacks on the Block—New Patterns of Residential Segregation in a Multi-Ethnic Country.* Cambridge, MA: Harvard University Press.

Dolbeare, Kenneth M. 1982. *American Public Policy: A Citizen's Guide.* New York: McGraw-Hill.

Domhoff, G. William. 1978. *Who Really Rules? New Haven and Community Power Reexamined.* New Brunswick, NJ: Transaction.

———. 1998. *Who Rules America?* 3d ed. Mountain View, CA: Mayfield.

Domino, John C. 1995. *Sexual Harassment and the Courts.* New York: HarperCollins.

Donnelly, Jack. 1989. *Universal Human Rights in Theory and Practice.* New York: Cornell University Press.

Donohue, Elizabeth, Vincent Schiraldi, and Jason Ziedenberg. 1998. *School House Hype: School Shootings and Real Risks Kids Face in America.* New York: Justice Policy Institute.

Doob, Christopher Bates. 1999. *Racism: An American Cauldron.* 3d ed. New York: Longman.

Dore, Ronald P. 1976. *The Diploma Disease: Education, Qualification and Development.* Berkeley: University of California Press.

Doress, Irwin, and Jack Nusan Porter. 1977. *Kids in Cults: Why They Join, Why They Stay, Why They Leave.* Brookline, MA: Reconciliation Associates.

Dornbusch, Sanford M. "The Sociology of Adolescence." Pp. 233–259 in *Annual Review of Sociology, 1989,* edited by W. Richard Scott and Judith Blake. Palo Alto, CA: Annual Reviews.

Dorsey, Heather. 1994. "Origins of the Ecofeminist Movement." Western Illinois University, Macomb, IL. Unpublished MA thesis.

Dotson, Floyd. 1991. "Community." P. 55 in *Encyclopedic Dictionary of Sociology,* 4th ed. Guilford, CT: Dushkin.

Dougherty, John, and David Holthouse. 1999. "Bordering on Exploitation." Accessed March 5, 1999 (http://www.phoenixnewtimes.com/issues/1998-07-09/feature.html).

Dougherty, Kevin, and Floyd M. Hammack. 1992. "Education Organization." Pp. 535–541 in *Encyclopedia of Sociology,* vol. 2, edited by Edgar F. Borgatta and Marie L. Borgatta. New York: Macmillan.

Douglas, Jack D. 1967. *The Social Meanings of Swank.* Princeton, NJ: Princeton University Press.

Dowd, James J. 1980. *Stratification among the Aged.* Monterey, CA: Brooks/Cole.

Doyle, James A. 1995. *The Male Experience.* 3d ed. Dubuque, IA: Brown & Benchmark.

——— and Michele A. Paludi. 1998. *Sex and Gender: The Human Experience.* 4th ed. New York: McGraw-Hill.

Doyle, Leonard, John Sweeney, and Peter Beaumont. 1998. "Global Roll of Dishonour." *The Observer* (London), June 2, 1998.

Drucker, Peter F. 1999. "Beyond the Information Revolution." *Atlantic Monthly* 284(October):42–57.

Du Bois, W. E. B. 1909. *The Negro American Family.* Atlanta University. Reprinted 1970, Cambridge, MA: M.I.T. Press.

———. 1911. "The Girl Nobody Loved," *Social News* 2(November):3.

Duberman, Lucille. 1976. *Social Inequality: Class and Caste in America.* Philadelphia: Lippincott.

Dugger, Celia W. 1999. "Massacres of Low-Born Touch Off a Crisis in India." *New York Times,* March 15, p. A3.

Duke, Lynne. 1998. Education Is Failing the Students. *Washington Post National Weekly Edition* 15 (June 26), p. 16.

Duncan, Greg J. 1994. "Welfare Can Fuel Upward Mobility." *Profiles* 18(May):6.

——— and Ken R. Smith. 1989. "The Rising Affluence of the Elderly: How Far, How Fair, and How Frail." Pp. 261–289 in *Annual Review of Sociology, 1989,* edited by W. Richard Scott and Judith Blake. Palo Alto, CA: Annual Reviews.

——— and Wei-Jun J. Yeung. 1995. "Extent and Consequences of Welfare

Dependence among America's Children." *Children and Youth Service Review* 17(1–3):157–182.

Duneier, Mitchell. 1994a. "On the Job, but Behind the Scenes." *Chicago Tribune,* December 26, pp. 1, 24.

———. 1994b. "Battling for Control." *Chicago Tribune,* December 28, pp. 1, 8.

Dunlap, Riley E. 1991. "Trends in Public Opinion toward Environmental Issues: 1965–1990." *Society and Natural Resources* 4(July–September): 285–312.

———. 1993. "From Environmental to Ecological Problems." Pp. 707–738 in *Introduction to Social Problems,* edited by Craig Calhoun and George Ritzer. New York: McGraw-Hill.

——— and William R. Catton, Jr. 1983. "What Environmental Sociologists Have in Common." *Sociological Inquiry* 53(Spring):113–135.

——— and Angela G. Mertig. 1991. "The Evolution of the U.S. Environmental Movement from 1970 to 1990: An Overview." *Society and Natural Resources* 4(July–September):209–218.

Durand, Jorge, Emilio A. Parrado, and Douglas S. Massey. 1996. "Migradollars and Developments: A Reconsideration of the Mexican Case." *International Migration Review* 30(Summer):423–444.

Durkheim, Émile. [1893] 1933. *Division of Labor in Society.* Translated by George Simpson. Reprint, New York: Free Press.

———. [1912] 1947. *The Elementary Forms of the Religious Life.* Reprint, Glencoe, IL: Free Press.

———. [1897] 1951. *Suicide.* Translated by John A. Spaulding and George Simpson. Reprint, New York: Free Press.

———. [1845] 1964. *The Rules of Sociological Method.* Translated by Sarah A. Solovay and John H. Mueller. Reprint, New York: Free Press.

Durning, Alan B. 1990. "Life on the Brink." *World Watch* 3(March–April):22–30.

———. 1993. "Supporting Indigenous Peoples," in Lester R. Brown (ed.), *State of the World*, 1993. New York: Norton, pp. 80–100.

Dworkin, Rosalind J. 1982. "A Woman's Report: Numbers Are Not Enough." Pp. 375–400 in *The Minority Report,*

edited by Anthony Dworkin and Rosalind Dworkin. New York: Holt.

Dychtwald, Ken. 1999. *Age Power: How the 21st Century Will be Ruled by the New Old.* New York: Putnam.

Dynes, Russell R. 1978. "Interorganizational Relations in Communities under Stress." Pp. 50–64 in *Disasters: Theory and Research*, edited by E. L. Quarantelli. Beverly Hills, CA: Sage.

E

Eakin, Emily. 2000. "Bigotry as Mental Illness or Just Another Norm." *New York Times.* (January 15): A21.

Eayrs, Caroline B., Nick Ellis, and Robert S. P. Jones. 1993. "Which Label? An Investigation into the Effects of Terminology on Public Perceptions of and Attitudes toward People with Learning Difficulties." *Disability, Handicap, and Society* 8(2):111–127.

Ebaugh, Helen Rose Fuchs. 1988. *Becoming an Ex: The Process of Role Exit.* Chicago: University of Chicago Press.

Eckenwiler, Mark. 1995. "In the Eyes of the Law." *Internet World* (August):74, 76–77.

Eckholm, Erik. 1994. "While Congress Remains Silent, Health Care Transforms Itself." *New York Times,* December 18, pp. 1, 34.

———. 1999. "A Quiet Roar." *New York Times,* November 4, pp. A1, A10.

The Economist. 1990. "Thick Skins." 314(February 24):26.

———. 1994. "Parent Power." 331(May 7):83.

———. 1995. "Home Sweet Home." 336(September 9):25–26, 29, 32.

———. 1996. "It's Normal to Be Queer." (January 6), pp. 68–70.

———. 1998. "Cruel and Ever More Unusual." 346(February 14).

Eden, Dov, and Abraham B. Shani. 1982. "Pygmalion Goes to Boot Camp: Expectancy, Leadership, and Trainee Performance." *Journal of Applied Psychology* 67(April):194–199.

EDK Associates. 1993. *Men Beating Women: Ending Domestic Violence.* New York: EDK Associates.

Edmonston, Barry, and Jeff Passel. 1999. "How Immigration and Intermarriage Affect the Racial and Ethnic Composition of the U.S. Population" in *Immigration and Opportunity,*

Race, Ethnicity, and Employment in the United States, edited by Frank D. Bean and Stephanie Bell-Rose. New York: Russell Sage Foundation.

Education Week. 1999. "Home Schooling." *Education Week,* October 6.

———. 2000. "Who Should Teach? Quality Counts." Accessed February 23, 2000 (http://www.edweek.org/ sreports/qc00/).

Edwards, Harry. 1984. "The Black 'Dumb Jock,'" *College Board Review, 131*(Spring):8–13.

Efron, Sonni. 1997. "In Japan, Even Tots Must Make the Grade." *Los Angeles Times,* February 16, pp. A1, A17.

———. 1998. "Japanese in Quandary on Fertility." *Los Angeles Times,* July 27, pp. A1, A6.

Egan, Timothy. 1995. "Many Seek Security in Private Communities." *New York Times,* September 3, pp. 1, 22.

———. 1998. "New Prosperity Brings New Conflict to Indian Country." *New York Times,* March 8, pp. 1, 24.

———. 1999. "What Price the Most Expensive Diamond of All?" *New York Times,* July 17, p. A7.

Ehrenreich, Barbara, and Deidre English. 1973. *Witches, Midwives, and Nurses: A History of Women Healers.* Old Westbury, NY: Feminist Press.

Ehrlich, Paul R. 1968. *The Population Bomb.* New York: Ballantine.

——— and Anne H. Ehrlich. 1990. *The Population Explosion.* New York: Simon and Schuster.

Eisenberg, David M. et al. 1998. "Trends in Alternative Medicine Use in the United States, 1990–1997." *Journal of the American Medical Association* 280(November 11): 1569–1636.

Ekman, Paul. 1973. "Strong Evidence for Universals in Facial Expressions: A Reply to Russell's Mistaken Critique." *Psychology Bulletin* 115: 268–287.

———, Wallace V. Friesen, and John Bear. 1984. "The International Language of Gestures." *Psychology Today* 18(May):64–69.

El-Badry, Samira. 1994. "The Arab-American Market." *American Demographics* 16(January):21–27, 30.

Elias, Marilyn. 1996. "Researchers Fight Child Consent Bill." *USA Today,* January 2, p. A1.

Elliott, Helene. 1997. "Having an Olympic Team Is Their Miracle on Ice." *Los Angeles Times,* March 25, Sports section, p. 5.

Elliott, Marta, and Lauren J. Krivo. 1991. "Structural Determinants of Homelessness in the United States." *Social Problems* 38(February):113–131.

Elliott, Michael. 1994. "Crime and Punishment." *Newsweek* 123(April 18):18–22.

Ellis, Virginia, and Ken Ellingwood. 1998. "Welfare to Work: Are There Enough Jobs?" *Los Angeles Times,* February 8, pp. A1, A30.

Ellison, Ralph. 1952. *Invisible Man.* New York: Random House.

Elmer-DeWitt, Philip. 1995. "Welcome to Cyberspace." *Time* 145(Special Issue, Spring):4–11.

El Nasser, Haya. 1999. "Soaring Housing Costs Are Culprit in Suburban Poverty." *USA Today,* April 28, pp. A1, A2.

Ely, Robin J. 1995. "The Power of Demography: Women's Social Construction of Gender Identity at Work." *Academy of Management Journal* 38(3):589–634.

Ember, Carol R., and Melvin Ember. 1993. *Anthropology.* 7th ed. Englewoods Cliff, NJ: Prentice-Hall.

Emery, David. 1997. "The Kidney Snatchers." Accessed December 21, 1999 (http://urbanlegends.about.com/culture/urbanlegends/library/blkid.htm).

Engardio, Pete. 1999. "Activists Without Borders." *Business Week,* October 4, pp. 144–145, 148, 150.

Engels, Friedrich. 1884. "The Origin of the Family, Private Property and the State." Pp. 392–394, excerpted in *Marx and Engels: Basic Writings on Politics and Philosophy,* edited by Lewis Feuer. Garden City, NY: Anchor, 1959.

England, Paula. 1999. "The Impact of Feminist Thought on Sociology." *Contemporary Sociology* 28(May):263–268.

Entine, Jon, and Martha Nichols. 1996. "Blowing the Whistle on Meaningless 'Good Intentions.'" *Chicago Tribune,* June 20, sec. 1, p. 21.

Epstein, Steven. 1997. *Impure Science: AIDS, Activism, and the Politics of Knowledge.* Berkeley: University of California Press.

Ericksen, Julia A. 1999. *Kiss and Tell: Surveying Sex in the Twentieth Century.* Cambridge, MA: Harvard University Press.

Erikson, Kai. 1966. *Wayward Puritans: A Study in the Sociology of Deviance.* New York: Wiley.

———. 1986. "On Work and Alienation." *American Sociological Review* 51(February):1–8.

———. 1994. *A New Species of Trouble: The Human Experience of Modern Disasters.* New York: Norton.

Espenshade, Edward B., Jr. 1990. *Rand McNally Goode's World Atlas.* 18th ed. Chicago: Rand McNally.

Etzioni, Amitai. 1964. *Modern Organization.* Englewood Cliffs, NJ: Prentice-Hall.

———. 1985. "Shady Corporate Practices." *New York Times,* November 15, p. A35.

———. 1990. "Going Soft on Corporate Crime." *Washington Post,* April 1, p. C3.

———. 1996. "Why Fear Date Rape?" *USA Today,* May 20, p. 14A.

Euro-Marketing Associates. 2000. "Global Internet Statistics (by Language)." Accessed January 30, 2000 (http://www.glreach.com/globstats).

Evans, Peter. 1979. *Dependent Development.* Princeton, NJ: Princeton University Press.

Evans, Sara. 1980. *Personal Politics: The Roots of Women's Liberation in the Civil Rights Movement and the New Left.* New York: Vintage.

F

Faber, Carol S. 2000. "Geographical Mobility: Population Characteristic." *Current Population Reports,* ser. P-20, no. 520. Washington, DC: U.S. Government Printing Office.

Fager, Marty, Mike Bradley, Lonnie Danchik, and Tom Wodetski. 1971. *Unbecoming Men.* Washington, NJ: Times Change.

Fahs, Ivan J., Dan A. Lewis, C. James Carr, and Mark W. Field. 1997. "Homelessness in an Affluent Suburb: The Story of Wheaton, Illinois." Paper presented at the annual meeting of the Illinois Sociological Association, October, Rockford, IL.

Fairness and Accuracy in Reporting. 1990. *Lost in the Margins and the Media.* New York: FAIR.

Faison, Seth. 1997. "Chinese Happily Break the 'One-Child' Rule." *New York Times,* August 17, pp. 1, 6.

Falk, William B. 1996. "Everybody Dance." *Newsday,* February 21, p. B3.

Faludi, Susan. 1999. *Stiffed: The Betrayal of the American Man.* New York: William Morrow.

Fannie Mae Foundation. 1999. "The American Metropolis at Century's End: Past and Future Influences." Presented at 1999 Fannie Mae Foundation Annual Housing Conference, Washington, DC.

Farhi, Paul, and Megan Rosenfeld. 1998. "Exporting America." *Washington Post National Weekly Edition* 16(November 30):6–7.

Farley, Maggie. 1997. "Loophole Lets More Chinese Have 2 Children." *Los Angeles Times,* October 20, pp. A1, A14–A15.

———. 1998. "Indonesia's Chinese Fearful of Backlash." *Los Angeles Times,* January 31, pp. A1, A8–A9.

Farr, Grant M. 1999. *Modern Iran.* New York: McGraw-Hill.

Feagin, Joe R. 1983. *The Urban Real Estate Game: Playing Monopoly with Real Money.* Englewood Cliffs, NJ: Prentice-Hall.

———. 1989. *Minority Group Issues in Higher Education: Learning from Qualitative Research.* Norman: Center for Research on Minority Education, University of Oklahoma.

———, Harnán Vera, and Nikitah Imani. 1996. *The Agony of Education: Black Students at White Colleges and Universities.* New York: Routledge.

Featherman, David L., and Robert M. Hauser. 1978. *Opportunity and Change.* New York: Aeodus.

Federal Communications Commission. 1998. "Commission Finds Industry Video Programming Rating System Acceptable." Report No. GN98-3, March 12. In association with the National Association of Broadcasters, National Cable Television Association, and the Motion Picture Association. Washington, DC: U.S. Government Printing Office.

Federman, Joel. 1998. *1998 National Television Violence Study: Executive Summary.* Santa Barbara: University of California, Santa Barbara.

Federman, Maya et al. [8 authors]. 1996. "What Does It Mean to Be Poor in

America?" *Monthly Labor Review* 119(May):3–17.

Fein, Helen. 1995. "Gender and Genocide." Paper presented at the annual meeting of the American Sociological Association, Washington, D.C.

Feinglass, Joe. 1987. "Next, the McDRG." *The Progressive* 51(January):28.

Feldman, Linda. 1999. "Control of Congress in Seniors' Hands." *Christian Science Monitor.* (June 21):1–4.

Felson, Marcus. 1998. *Crime and Everyday Life: Insights and Implications for Society.* 2d ed. Thousand Oaks, CA: Pine Forge Press.

Ferman, Louis A., Stuart Henry, and Michael Hoyman, eds. 1987. *The Informal Economy.* Newbury Park, CA: Sage. Published as September 1987 issue of *The Annals of the American Academy of Political and Social Science.*

Fernandez, John R. 1999. *Race, Gender and Rhetoric.* New York: McGraw-Hill.

Fernández, Sandy. 1996. "The Cyber Cops." *Ms.* 6(May–June):22–23.

Fernea, Elizabeth. 1998. *In Search of Islamic Feminism: One Woman's Global Journey.* New York: Bantam Books.

Fernea, Elizabeth W., and Robert A. Fernea. 1997. "A Look Behind the Veil." *Human Nature.* (January).

Ferrell, Tom. 1979. "More Choose to Live outside Marriage." *New York Times,* July 1, p. E7.

Feuer, Lewis S., ed. 1959. *Karl Marx and Friedrich Engels: Basic Writings on Politics and Philosophy.* Garden City, NY: Doubleday.

Fiala, Robert. 1992. "Postindustrial Society." Pp. 1512–1522 in *Encyclopedia of Sociology,* vol. 3, edited by Edgar F. Borgatta and Marie L. Borgatta. New York: Macmillan.

Fields, Jason M., and Charles L. Clark. 1999. "Unbinding the Ties: Edit Effects of Marital Status on Same Gender Groups." Paper presented at the annual meeting of the American Sociological Assocation, August, Chicago.

Finder, Alan. 1995. "Despite Tough Laws, Sweatshops Flourish." *New York Times,* January 6, pp. A1, B4.

Findlay, Steven. 1998. "85% of American Workers Using HMOs." *USA Today,* January 20, p. 3A.

Fine, Gary Alan. 1984. "Negotiated Orders and Organizational Cultures." Pp. 239–262 in *Annual Review of Sociology,* 1984, edited by Ralph Turner. Palo Alto, CA: Annual Reviews.

Fine, Michelle, and Adrienne Asch. 1988. *Women with Disabilities: Essays in Psychology, Culture, and Politics.* Philadelphia: Temple University Press.

Finkel, Steven E., and James B. Rule. 1987. "Relative Deprivation and Related Psychological Theories of Civil Violence: A Critical Review." *Research in Social Movements* 9:47–69.

Fiore, Faye. 1997. "Full-Time Moms a Minority Now, Census Bureau Finds." *Los Angeles Times,* November 26, pp. A1, A20.

Firestone, David. 1999. "School Prayer Is Revived As an Issue In Alabama." *New York Times* (July 15), p. A14.

Firestone, Shulamith. 1970. *The Dialectic of Sex: The Case for Feminist Revolution.* New York: Bantam.

Firmat, Gustavo Perez. 1994. *Life on Hyphen: The Cuban-American Way.* Austin: University of Texas Press.

Fisher, Carolyn A., and Carol A. Schwartz. 1995. *Encyclopedia of Associations, 1996.* Detroit: Gail Research.

Fisher, Ian. 1999. "Selling Sudan's Slaves into Freedom." *New York Times,* April 25, p. A6.

Fishman, Mark, and Gray Cavender, eds. 1998. *Entertaining Crime: Television Reality Programs.* Hawthorne, NY: Aldine de Gruyter.

Flacks, Richard. 1971. *Youth and Social Change.* Chicago: Markham.

Flavin, Jeanne. 1998. "Razing the Wall: A Feminist Critique of Sentencing Theory, Research, and Policy." Pp. 145–164 in *Cutting the Edge,* edited by Jeffrey Ross. Westport, CT: Praeger.

Fletcher, Connie. 1995. "On the Line: Women Cops Speak Out." *Chicago Tribune Magazine,* February 19, pp. 14–19.

Fletcher, Robert S. 1943. *History of Oberlin College to the Civil War.* Oberlin, OH: Oberlin College Press.

Flexner, Eleanor. 1972. *Century of Struggle: The Women's Rights Movement in the United States.* New York: Atheneum.

Fornos, Werner. 1997. *1997 World Population Overview.* Washington, DC: The Population Institute.

Forsythe, David P. 1990. "Human Rights in U.S. Foreign Policy: Retrospect and Prospect," *Political Science Quarterly,* 105(3):435–454.

Fountain, Monica. 1996. "Not the Retiring Type." *Chicago Tribune,* April 14, sec. 13, p. 6.

Francis, David R. 1999. "Part-time Workers Face Full-time Problems." *Christian Science Monitor,* July 1, p. 11.

Franklin, John Hope and Alfred A. Moss, Jr. 1994. *From Slavery to Freedom.* 7th ed. New York: Knopf.

Frazee, Valerie. 1997. "Establishing Relations in Germany." *Workforce* 76(No. 4):516.

Freeman, Jo. 1973. "The Origins of the Women's Liberation Movement." *American Journal of Sociology* 78(January): 792–811.

———. 1975. *The Politics of Women's Liberation.* New York: McKay.

Freeman, Linton C. 1958. "Marriage without Love: Mate Selection in Non-Western Countries." Pp. 20–30 in *Mate Selection,* edited by Robert F. Winch. New York: Harper and Row.

Freidson, Eliot. 1970. *Profession of Medicine.* New York: Dodd, Mead.

Freire, Paulo. 1970. *Pedagogy of the Oppressed.* New York: Herder and Herder.

French, Howard W. 2000. "Women Win a Battle, But Job Bias Still Rules Japan." *New York Times,* February 26, p. A3.

Freudenheim, Milt. 1990. "Employers Balk at High Cost of High-Tech Medical Care." *New York Times,* April 29, pp. 1, 16.

———. 1998. "Aetna Is Reducing Fertility Benefits." *New York Times,* January 10, pp. A1, A8.

Fridlund, Alan. J., Paul Erkman, and Harriet Oster. 1987. "Facial Expressions of Emotion: Review of Literature 1970–1983." Pp. 143–224 in *Nonverbal Behavior and Communication,* 2d ed., edited by Aron W. Seigman and Stanley Feldstein. Hillsdale, NJ: Lawrence Erlbaum Associates.

Friedan, Betty. 1963. *The Feminine Mystique.* New York: Dell.

Friedman, Thomas L. 1999. *The Lexus and the Olive Tree: Understanding Globalization.* New York: Farrar, Straus, Giroux.

Friedrichs, David O. 1998. "New Directions in Critical Criminology and White Collar Crime." Pp. 77–91 in *Cutting the Edge,* edited by Jeffrey Ross. Westport, CT: Praeger.

Fuller, Bruce and Xiaoyan Liang. 1993. *The Unfair Search for Child Care.* Cambridge, MA: Preschool and Family Choice Project, Harvard University.
———, and Sharon Lynn Kagan. 2000. *Remember the Children: Mothers Balance Work and Child Care Under Welfare Reform.* Berkeley: Graduate School of Education, University of California.

Fullerton, Howard N., Jr., 1997. "Labor Force 2006: Slowing Down and Changing Composition." *Monthly Labor Review* (November):23–38.
———. 1999. "Labor Force Projections to 2008: Steady Growth and Changing Composition." *Monthly Labor Review* (November):19–32.

Furstenberg, Frank. 1987. "The New Extended Family: The Experience of Parents and Children After Remarriage." Pp. 42–71 in *Remarriage and Stepparenting: Current Research and Theory,* edited by K. Pasley and M. Ihinger-Tallman. New York: Guilford.
——— and Andrew Cherlin. 1991. *Divided Families: What Happens to Children When Parents Part.* Cambridge, MA: Harvard University Press.
——— et al. 1999. *Managing to Make It: Urban Families and Adolescent Success.* Chicago: University of Chicago Press.

G

Gable, Donna. 1993a. "On TV, Lifestyles of the Slim and Entertaining." *USA Today,* July 27, p. 3D.
———. 1993b. "Series Shortchange Working-Class and Minority Americans." *USA Today,* August 30, p. 3D.

Gabor, Andrea. 1995. "Crashing the 'Old Boy' Party." *New York Times,* January 8, sec. 3, pp. 1, 6.

Galant, Debra. 2000. "Finding a Substitute for Office Chitchat." *New York Times,* February 16, sec. Retirement, p. 20.

Gallup Poll. 1999. "Public Support for the Death Penalty." As reported in *New York Times,* April 3, p. A11.

Gamson, Josh. 1989. "Silence, Death, and the Invisible Enemy: AIDS Activism and Social Movement 'Newness.'" *Social Problems* 36(October): 351–367.
———. 1998. *Freaks Talk Back: Tabloid Talk Shows and Sexual Nonconformity.* Chicago: University of Chicago Press.

Gans, Herbert J. 1991. *People, Plans, and Policies: Essays on Poverty, Racism, and Other National Urban Problems.* New York: Columbia University Press and Russell Sage Foundation.
———. 1995. *The War against the Poor: The Underclass and Antipoverty Policy.* New York: Basic Books.

Ganzeboom, Harry B. G., Ruud Luijkx, and Donald J. Treiman. 1989. "Intergenerational Class Mobility in Comparative Perspective." Pp. 3–84 in *Research in Social Stratification and Mobility,* edited by Arne L. Kalleberg. Greenwich, CT: JAI Press.
———, Donald J. Treiman, and Woult C. Ultee. 1991. "Comparative Intergenerational Stratification Research." Pp. 277–302 in *Annual Review of Sociology, 1991,* edited by W. Richard Scott. Palo Alto, CA: Annual Reviews.

Gardner, Carol Brooks. 1989. "Analyzing Gender in Public Places: Rethinking Goffman's Vision of Everyday Life." *American Sociologist* 20(Spring): 42–56.
———. 1990. "Safe Conduct: Women, Crime, and Self in Public Places." *Social Problems* 37(August):311–328.
———. 1995. *Passing By: Gender and Public Harassment.* Berkeley: University of California Press.

Gardner, Marilyn. 1998. "Prime-Time TV Fare Rarely Shows a Family Life as It's Really Lived." *Christian Science Monitor,* June 10, p. 13.

Garfinkel, Harold. 1956. "Conditions of Successful Degradation Ceremonies." *American Journal of Sociology* 61(March):420–424.

Garner, Roberta. 1996. *Contemporary Movements and Ideologies.* New York: McGraw-Hill.
———. 1999. "Virtual Social Movements." Presented at Zaldfest: A conference in honor of Mayer Zald. September 17, Ann Arbor, MI.

Garreau, Joel. 1991. *Edge City: Life on the New Frontier.* New York: Doubleday.

Garza, Melita Marie. 1993. "The Cordi-Marian Annual Cotillion." *Chicago Tribune,* May 7, sec. C, pp. 1, 5.

Gates, Henry Louis, Jr. 1991. "Delusions of Grandeur." *Sports Illustrated* 75(August 19):78.
———. 1999. "One Internet, Two Nations." *New York Times,* October 31, p. A15.

Gauette, Nicole. 1998. "Rules for Raising Japanese Kids." *Christian Science Monitor,* October 14, pp. B1, B6.
———. 1999. "Japanese Suburbanites Defy Law." *Christian Science Monitor,* September 28, p. 5.

Gay Men's Health Crisis. 2000. "Facts and Statistics." Accessed February 1, 2000 (http://www.gmhc.org/basics/statmain.html).

Gearty, Robert. 1996. "Beware of Pickpockets." *Chicago Daily News,* November 19, p. 5.

Gecas, Viktor. 1981. "Concepts of Socialization." In Morris Rosenberg and Ralph H. Turner (eds.), *Social Psychology: Sociological Perspectives.* New York: Basic Books, pp. 165–199.
———. 1982. "The Self-Concept." Pp. 1–33 in *Annual Review of Sociology, 1982,* edited by Ralph H. Turner and James F. Short, Jr. Palo Alto, CA: Annual Reviews.
———. 1992. "Socialization." Pp. 1863–1872 in *Encyclopedia of Sociology,* vol. 4, edited by Edgar F. Borgatta and Marie L. Borgatta. New York: Macmillan.

Geckler, Cheri. 1995. *Practice Perspectives and Medical Decision-Making in Medical Residents: Gender Differences—A Preliminary Report.* Wellesley, MA: Center for Research on Women.

Gelles, Richard J., and Claire Pedrick Cornell. 1990. *Intimate Violence in Families.* 2d ed. Newbury Park, CA: Sage.

Gereffi, Gary, and Miguel Kovzeniewicz, eds. 1994. *Commodity Chains and Global Capitalism.* New York: Praeger.

Gerrows, Henry A. 1988. *Schooling and the Struggle for Public Life: Critical Pedagogy in the Modern Age.* Minneapolis: University of Minnesota Press.

Gerth, H. H., and C. Wright Mills. 1958. *From Max Weber: Essays in Sociology.* New York: Galaxy.

Gesensway, Deborah, and Mindy Roseman. 1987. *Beyond Words: Images from America's Concentration Camps.* Ithaca, NY: Cornell University Press.

Gest, Ted. 1985. "Are White-Collar Crooks Getting Off Too Easy?" *U.S. News & World Report* 99(July 1):43.

Geyh, Paul. 1998. "Feminism Fatale?" *Chicago Tribune,* July 26, sec. 13, pp 1 6.

Gibbs, Nancy, 1993. "Rx for Death." *Time*, May 31, pp. 34–39.

Gibson, James William. 1994. *Warrior Dreams: Paramilitary Culture in Post-Vietnam America.* New York: Hill and Wang.

Gillespie, Mark. 1999. "Poll Releases, April 6, 1999: U.S. Gun Ownership Continues Broad Decline." Accessed July 2, 2000 (http://www.gallup.com/poll/releases/pr990406.asp).

Gilliard, Darrell K., and Allen J. Beck. 1998. *Prison and Jail Inmates at Midyear 1997.* Washington, DC: U.S. Government Printing Office.

Giordano, Peggy C., Stephen A. Cernkovich, and Alfred DeMaris. 1993. "The Family and Peer Relations of Black Adolescents." *Journal of Marriage and Family* 55(May):277–287.

Giroux, Henry A. 1988. *Schooling and the Struggle for Public Life: Critical Pedagogy in the Modern Age.* Minneapolis: University of Minnesota Press.

Glascock, Anthony P. 1990. "By Any Other Name, It Is Still Killing: A Comparison of the Treatment of the Elderly in American and Other Societies." Pp. 44–56 in *The Cultural Context of Aging: Worldwide Perspectives,* edited by Jay Sokolovsky. New York: Bergen and Garvey.

Glasser, Susan B., and Juliet Eilperin. 1999. "A New Conduit for 'Soft Money': Critics Decry Big, Largely Untraceable Donations to Lawmakers' Leadership PACS." *Washington Post,* May 16, p. A1.

Glassner, Barry. 1999. *The Culture of Fear: Why Americans Are Afraid of the Wrong Things.* New York: Basic Books.

Glaub, Gerald R. 1990. "Gap between State Funding and School Spending Widens." *Illinois School Board Journal* 58(July–August):24–26.

Glauber, Bill. 1998. "Youth Binge Drinking Varies Around World." *St. Louis Post-Dispatch,* February 9, p. E4.

Gleick, James. 1999. *Faster: The Acceleration of Just About Everything.* New York: Pantheon.

Goffman, Erving. 1959. *The Presentation of Self in Everyday Life.* New York: Doubleday.

———. 1961. *Asylums: Essays on the Social Situation of Mental Patients and Other Inmates.* Garden City, NY: Doubleday.

———. 1963a. *Stigma: Notes on Management of Spoiled Identity.* Englewood Cliffs, NJ: Prentice-Hall.

———. 1963b. *Behavior in Public Places.* New York: Free Press.

———. 1971. *Relations in Public.* New York: Basic Books.

———. 1979. *Gender Advertisements.* New York: Harper and Row.

Goldberg, Carey. 1998. "Little Drop in College Binge Drinking." *New York Times,* August 11, p. A14.

——— and Janet Elder. 1998. "Public Still Backs Abortion but Wants Limits, Poll Says." *New York Times,* January 16, pp. A1, A16.

Golden, Frederic. 1999. "Who's Afraid of Frankenfood?" *Time,* November 29, pp. 49–50.

Goldman, Benjamin A., and Laura Fitton. 1994. *Toxic Wastes and Race Revisited: An Update of the 1987 Report on the Racial and Social Economic Characteristics of Communities with Hazardous Waste.* Washington, DC: Center for Policy Alternatives, United Church of Christ Commission for Racial Justice, and NAACP.

Goldman, Robert, and Stephen Papson. 1998. *Nike Culture: The Sign of the Swoosh.* London: Sage Publications.

Goldstein, Amy. 1998. "A Transfusion from Patients' Wallets May Be in Order." *Washington Post National Weekly Edition,* September 21, p. 31.

Goldstein, Greg. 1998. "World Health Organization and Housing." Pp. 636–637 in *The Encyclopedia of Housing,* edited by Willem van Vliet. Thousand Oaks, CA: Sage Publications.

Goldstein, Melvyn C., and Cynthia M. Beall. 1981. "Modernization and Aging in the Third and Fourth World: Views from the Rural Hinterland in Nepal." *Human Organization* 40(Spring): 48–55.

Gole, Nilofer. 1997. "Lifting the Veil—Reform vs. Tradition in Turkey—An Interview." *Manushi,* May 1.

Goleman, Daniel, 1991. "New Ways to Battle Bias: Fight Acts, Not Feelings." *New York Times,* July 16, pp. C1, C8.

Goliber, Thomas J. 1997. "Population and Reproductive Health in Sub-Saharan Africa." *Population Bulletin* 52(December).

Goode, Erica. 1999. "For Good Health, It Helps to Be Rich and Important." *New York Times,* June 1, pp. 1, 9.

Goode, William J. 1959. "The Theoretical Importance of Love." *American Sociological Review* 24(February):38–47.

Goodgame, Dan. 1993. "Welfare for the Well-Off." *Time* 141(February 22): 36–38.

Gottdiener, Mark, and Joe R. Feagin. 1988. "The Paradigm Shift in Urban Sociology." *Urban Affairs Quarterly* 24(December):163–187.

——— and Ray Hutchison. 2000. *The New Urban Sociology.* 2d ed. New York: McGraw-Hill.

Gottfredson, Michael, and Travis Hirschi. 1990. *A General Theory of Crime.* Palo Alto, CA: Stanford University Press.

Gottschalk, Peter, Sara McLanahan, and Gary Sandefur. 1994. "The Dynamics and Intergenerational Transmission of Poverty and Welfare Participation." Pp. 85–108 in *Confronting Poverty: Prescriptions for Change,* edited by Sheldon H. Danziger, Gary D. Sandefur, and Daniel H. Weinburg. Cambridge, MA: Harvard University Press.

Gough, E. Kathleen. 1974. "Nayar: Central Kerala." Pp. 298–384 in *Matrilineal Kinship,* edited by David Schneider and E. Kathleen Gough. Berkeley: University of California Press.

Gouldner, Alvin. 1960. "The Norm of Reciprocity." *American Sociological Review* 25(April):161–177.

———. 1970. *The Coming Crisis of Western Sociology.* New York: Basic Books.

Gove, Walter R., ed. 1980. *The Labelling of Deviance.* 2d ed. Beverly Hills, CA: Sage.

———. 1987. "Sociobiology Misses the Mark: An Essay on Why Biology but Not Sociobiology Is Very Relevant to Sociology." *American Sociologist* 18(Fall):258–277.

Gramsci, Antonio. 1929. "Selections from the Prison Notebooks." In Quintin Hoare and Geoffrey Nowell Smith, eds. London: Lawrence and Wishort.

Greeley, Andrew M. 1989. "Protestant and Catholic: Is the Analogical Imagination Extinct?" *American Sociological Review* 54(August):485–502.

Green, Dan S., and Edwin D. Driver. 1978. "Introduction." Pp. 1–60 in *W. E. B. DuBois on Sociology and the Black Community,* edited by Dan S. Green and Edwin D. Driver. Chicago: University of Chicago Press.

Greenburg, Jan Crawford. 1999. "Sampling for Census Restricted." *Chicago Tribune,* January 26, pp. 1, 10.

Greene, Jay P. 1998. "A Meta-Analysis of the Effectiveness of Bilingual Education." Sponsored by the Toms River Policy Initiative. Accessed July 1 (http://data.Fas.harvard.edu/pepg/biling.htm).

———, William G. Howell, and Paul E. Peterson. 1997b. *Lessons from the Cleveland Scholarship Program.* Cambridge, MA: Harvard University's Program on Education Policy and Governance.

———, Paul E. Peterson, and Jiangtro Du. 1997a. *Effectiveness of School Choice: The Milwaukee Experiment.* Cambridge, MA: Harvard University's Program on Education Policy and Governance.

Greenhouse, Linda. 1998a. "High Court Ruling Says Harassment Includes Same Sex." *New York Times,* March 5, pp. A1, A17.

———. 1998b. "Overturning of Late-Term Abortion Ban Is Let Stand." *New York Times,* March 24, p. A13.

———. 2000. "Justices Uphold Ceiling of $1,000 on Political Gifts." *New York Times,* January 25, pp. A1, A18.

Greenhouse, Steven. 1994. "State Dept. Finds Widespread Abuse of World's Women," *New York Times* (February 3), pp. A1, A9.

———. 1998. "Equal Work, Less-Equal Perks." *New York Times* (March 30), p. c1.

Greenwood, Ernest. 1957. "Attributes of a Profession." *Social Work* 2(July):45–55.

Greif, Mark. 2000. "Potemkin Villages." *The American Prospect* 11(January 3):54–57.

Grimsley, Kirstin Downey. 1997. "Big Boss May Be Watching—and Listening." *Washington Post National Weekly Edition,* June 2, p. 20.

Grob, Gerald N. 1995. "The Paradox of Deinstitutionalization." *Society* 32(July–August):51–59.

Gross, Jane. 1991. "Surge of Rock Fans, Then Death, Grief, Anger." *New York Times,* January 25, pp. A1, A16.

Grossman, David C. et al. 1997. "Effectiveness of a Violence Prevention Curriculum among Children in Elementary School." *Journal of the American Medical Association* 277(May 28):1605–1617.

Groves, Martha. 1999. "New Adoptions Open Up the Family Circle." *Los Angeles Times,* August 8, p. A3.

Groza, Victor, Daniela F. Ileana, and Ivor Irwin. 1999. *A Peacock or a Crow: Stories, Interviews, and Commentaries on Romanian Adoptions.* Euclid, OH: Williams Custom Publishing.

Guillemin, Jeanne. 1999. *Anthrat: The Investigation of a Deadly Outbreak.* Berkeley: University of California Press.

Guralnik, Jack M. et al. [5 authors]. 1993. "Educational Status and Active Life Expectancy among Older Blacks and Whites." *New England Journal of Medicine* 329(July 8):110–116.

Gutiérrez, Gustavo. 1990. "Theology and the Social Sciences," in Paul E. Sigmund, *Liberation Theology at the Crossroads: Democracy or Revolution?* New York: Oxford University Press, pp. 214–225.

Gwynne, S. C., and John F. Dickerson. 1997. "Lost in the E-Mail." *Time* 149(April 21):88–90.

H

Hacker, Andrew. 1964. "Power to Do What?" Pp. 134–146 in *The New Sociology,* edited by Irving Louis Horowitz. New York: Oxford University Press.

Hacker, Helen Mayer. 1951. "Women as a Minority Group." *Social Forces* 30(October):60–69.

———. 1973. "Sex Roles in Black Society: Caste versus Caste." Presented at the annual meeting of the American Sociological Association, August 30, New York City.

———. 1974. "Women as a Minority Group, Twenty Years Later." Pp. 124–134 in *Who Discriminates against Women?,* edited by Florence Denmark. Beverly Hills, CA: Sage.

Hahn, Harlan. 1993. "The Political Implications of Disability Definitions and Data." *Journal of Disability Policy Studies* 4(2):41–52.

Hahn, Robert A. 1985. "Culture-Bound Syndromes Unbound." *Social Science and Medicine* 21(2):165–171.

Hahn-Baker, David. 1994. "Rocky Roads to Consensus." *Americus Journal* 16(Spring):41–43.

Haines, Valerie A. 1988. "Is Spencer's Theory an Evolutionary Theory?" *American Journal of Sociology* 93(March):1200–1223.

Halal, William E. 1992. "The Information Technology Revolution." *Futurist* 26(July–August):10–15.

Halbfinger, David M. 1998. "As Surveillance Cameras Peer, Some Wonder if They Also Pry." *New York Times,* February 22, p. A1.

Hall, Cindy, and Grant Jerding. 1999. "Grandparents' Nests Not Empty." *USA Today,* April 5, p. A1.

Hall, Kay. 1999. "Work From Here." *Computer User.* 18(November):32.

Hall, Mimi. 1993. "Genetic-Sex-Testing a Medical Mine Field." *USA Today,* December 20, p. 6A.

Hall, Peter. 1977. *The World Cities.* London: Weidenfeld and Nicolson.

Hall, Robert H. 1982. "The Truth about Brown Lung." *Business and Society Review* 40(Winter 1981–82):15–20.

Haller, Max, Wolfgang Konig, Peter Krause, and Karin Kurz. 1990. "Patterns of Career Mobility and Structural Positions in Advanced Capitalist Societies: A Comparison of Men in Austria, France, and the United States." *American Sociological Review* 50(October):579–603.

Halliday, M. A. K. 1978. *Language as Social Semiotic.* Baltimore: University Park Press.

Hallinan, Maureen T. 1997. "The Sociological Study of Social Change." *American Sociological Review* 62(February):1–11.

Hallowell, Christopher. 1999. "Playing the Odds." *Time,* January 11, p. 60.

Hamm, Mark S. 1993. *American Skinheads: The Criminology and Control of Hate Crime.* Westport, CT: Greenwood.

Haney, Craig, and Philip Zimbardo. 1998. "The Past and Future of U.S. Prison Policy: Twenty-Five Years after the Stanford Prison Experiment." *American Psychologist* 53(July):709–727.

Hani, Yoko. 1998. "Hot Pots Wired to Help the Elderly." *Japan Times Weekly International Edition,* April 13, p. 16.

Hansell, Saul. 1999. "Amazon's Risky Christmas." *New York Times,* November 3, sec. 3, pp. 1, 15.

Hara, Hiroko. 2000. "Homeless Desperately Want Shelter, Jobs." *Japan Times International* 40(January 16), p. 14.

Harap, Louis. 1982. "Marxism and Religion: Social Functions of Religious Belief." *Jewish Currents* 36(January): 12–17, 32–35.

Hare, A. Paul. 1992. "Group Size." Pp. 788–791 in *Encyclopedia of Sociology,* vol. 2, edited by Edgar F. Borgatta and Marie L. Borgatta. New York: Macmillan.

Harlow, Harry F. 1971. *Learning to Love.* New York: Ballantine.

Harmon, Amy. 1998. "The Law Where There Is No Land." *New York Times,* March 16, pp. C1, C9.

Harrah's Entertainment. 1996. *Harrah Survey of Casino Entertainment.* Memphis, TN: Harrah's Entertainment.

Harrington, Michael. 1980. "The New Class and the Left." Pp. 123–138 in *The New Class,* edited by B. Bruce-Briggs. Brunswick, NJ: Transaction.

Harris, Chauncy D., and Edward Ullman. 1945. "The Nature of Cities." *Annals of the American Academy of Political and Social Science* 242(November):7–17.

Harris, David. 1999. *Driving While Black: Racial Profiling on Our Nation's Highways.* New York: American Civil Liberties Union.

Harris, Judith Rich. 1998. *The Nurture Assumption: Why Children Turn Out the Way They Do.* New York: Free Press.

Harris, Marvin. 1997. *Culture, People, Nature: An Introduction to General Anthropology.* 7th ed. New York: Longman.

Hartjen, Clayton A. 1978. *Crime and Criminalization.* 2d ed. New York: Praeger.

Hartmann, Betsy. 1994. "What Success Story?" *New York Times,* September 29, p. A25.

Haub, Carl, and Deana Cornelius. 1999. *1999 World Population Data Sheet.* Washington, DC: Population Reference Bureau.

Hauser, Robert M., and David B. Grusky. 1988. "Cross-National Variation in Occupational Distributions, Relative Mobility Chances, and Intergenerational Shifts in Occupational Distributions." *American Sociological Review* 53(October):723–741.

Haviland, William A. 1999. *Cultural Anthropology (Case Studies in Cultural Anthropology).* 9th ed. Ft. Worth: Harcourt Brace.

Hayes, Denis. 1990. "Earth Day 1990: Threshold of the Green Decade." *Natural History* 99(April):55–58, 67–70.

Hayward, Mark D., William R. Grady, and Steven D. McLaughlin. 1987. "Changes in the Retirement Process." *Demography* 25(August):371–386.

Health Care Financing Administration. 1999. *National Health Expenditure Projections 1998–2008.* Washington, DC: HCFA.

Healy, Melissa. 1997. "Child Care to Get Brief Spotlight at a Crucial Time." *Los Angeles Times,* October 23, pp. A1, A16.

Heckert, Druann, and Amy Best. 1997. "Ugly Duckling to Swan: Labeling Theory and the Stigmatization of Red Hair." *Symbolic Interaction* 20(No. 4):365–384.

Hedges, Chris. 1993. "A Sickness in Egypt: Swooning." *New York Times,* April 18, p. 13.

Hedley, R. Alan. 1992. "Industrialization in Less Developed Countries." Pp. 914–920 in *Encyclopedia of Sociology,* vol. 2, edited by Edgar F. Borgatta and Marie L. Borgatta. New York: Macmillan.

Heger, Heinz. 1980. *The Men with the Pink Triangle.* London: Gay Men's Press.

Heikes, E. Joel. 1991. "When Men Are the Minority: The Case of Men in Nursing." *Sociological Quarterly* 32(3):389–401.

Heise, Lori, M. Ellsberg, and M. Gottemuelle. 1999. "Ending Violence Against Women." *Population Reports,* ser. L, no. 11. Baltimore: Johns Hopkins University School of Public Health.

Helvarg, David. 1994. *The War against Greens: The "Wise Use" Movement, the New Right and Anti-Environment Violence.* San Francisco: Sierra Club.

Henley, Nancy, Mykol Hamilton, and Barrie Thorne. 1985. "Womanspeak and Manspeak: Sex Differences and Sexism in Communication, Verbal and Nonverbal." Pp. 168–185 in *Beyond Sex Roles,* 2d ed., edited by Alice G. Sargent. St. Paul, MN: West.

Henly, Julia R. 1999. "Challenges to Finding and Keeping Jobs in the Low-Skilled Labor Market." *Poverty Research News* 3(No. 1):3–5.

Henneberger, Melinda. 1995. "Muslims Continue to Feel Apprehensive." *New York Times,* April 14, p. B10.

Henry, Mary E. 1989. "The Function of Schooling: Perspectives from Rural Australia." *Discourse* 9(April):1–21.

Herman, Andrew. 1999. *The "Better Angels" of Capitalism: Rhetoric, Narrative, and Moral Identity Among Men of the American Upper Class.* Boulder, CO: Westmer Press.

Herman, Edward S., and Gerry O'Sullivan. 1990. *The "Terrorism" Industry: The Experts and Institutions That Shape Our View of Terror.* New York: Pantheon.

Herrmann, Andrew. 1994. "Survey Shows Increase in Hispanic Catholics." *Chicago Sun-Times,* March 10, p. 4.

Hersch, Patricia. 1998. *A Tribe Apart: A Journey into the Heart of the American Adolescence.* New York: Fawcett Books.

Hershey, Robert D., Jr. 1988. "Underground Economy Is Not Rising to the Bait." *New York Times,* January 24, p. E5.

Herskovits, Melville J. 1930. *The Anthropometry of the American Negro.* New York: Columbia University Press.

———. 1941. *The Myth of the Negro Past.* New York: Harper.

———. 1943. "The Negro in Bahia, Brazil: A Problem in Method." *American Sociological Review* 8(August):394–402.

Hess, John L. 1990. "Confessions of a Greedy Geezer." *The Nation* 250(April 2):451–455.

Hetherington, E. Mavis. 1979. "Divorce: A Child's Perspective." *American Psychologist* 34(October): 851–858.

Hewlett, Sylvia Ann, and Cornel West. 1998. *The War Against Parents.* Boston: Houghton Mifflin.

Heyck, Dennis Lynn Daly. 1994. *Barrios and Borderlands: Cultures of Latinos and Latinas in the United States.* New York: Routledge.

Hill, Robert B. 1972. *The Strengths of Black Families.* New York: Emerson.

———. 1987. "The Future of Black Families." *Colloqui* (Spring):22–28.

Hillery, George A. 1955. "Definitions of Community: Areas of Agreement." *Rural Sociology* (2):111–123.

Hirschi, Travis. 1969. *Causes of Delinquency.* Berkeley: University of California Press.

Hochschild, Arlie Russell. 1973. "A Review of Sex Role Research." *American Journal of Sociology* 78(January): 1011–1029.

———. 1990. "The Second Shift: Employed Women Are Putting in Another Day of Work at Home." *Utne Reader* 38(March–April):66–73.

———. 1997. *Time Bind: When Work Becomes Home and Home Becomes Work.* New York: Metropolitan Books, Henry Holt.

———, with Anne Machung. 1989. *The Second Shift: Working Parents and the Revolution at Home.* New York: Viking Penguin.

Hockstader, Lee. 1996. "Moscow Moppets Meet the Muppets: Russian Television Produces a Homegrown 'Sezam' Street." *Washington Post,* October 23, p. A1.

Hodge, Robert W., and Peter H. Rossi. 1964. "Occupational Prestige in the United States, 1925–1963." *American Journal of Sociology* 70(November): 286–302.

Hodson, Randy, and Teresa A. Sullivan. 1995. *The Social Organization of Work.* 2d ed. Belmont, CA: Wadsworth.

Hoebel, E. Adamson. 1949. *Man in the Primitive World: An Introduction to Anthropology.* New York: McGraw-Hill.

Hoffman, Adonis. 1997. "Through an Accurate Prism." *Los Angeles Times,* August 8, p. M1.

Hoffman, Donald L., and Thomas P. Novak. 1998. "Bridging the Racial Divide on the Internet." *Science* 200(April 17):390–391.

Hoffman, Lois Wladis. 1985. "The Changing Genetics/Socialization Balance." *Journal of Social Issues* 41(Spring):127–148.

Hofstede, Geert. 1997. *Cultures and Organizations: Software of the Mind.* Rev. ed. New York: McGraw-Hill.

Holcomb, Betty, Shaun Dreisbach, and Sarah Hutter. 1999. "Child Care: How Does Your State Rate?" *Working Mother* website. Accessed July 30, 1999 (http://www.workingmother.com/staterate/index.html).

Holden, Constance. 1980. "Identical Twins Reared Apart." *Science* 207(March 21):1323–1328.

———. 1987. "The Genetics of Personality." *Science* 257(August 7):598–601.

Hollingshead, August B. 1975. *Elmtown's Youth and Elmtown Revisited.* New York: Wiley.

Holloway, Lynette. 1998. "Pupils Using Vouchers Had Better Scores, Study Finds." *New York Times,* October 28, p. B12.

Holmes, Steven A. 1999. "Black Groups in Florida Split Over School Voucher Plan." *New York Times,* May 30, p. 15.

———. 1997. "Leaving the Suburbs for Rural Areas." *New York Times,* October 19, p. 34.

———. 1998a. "Court Voids Plan to Use Sampling for 2000 Census." *New York Times,* August 25, pp. A1, A12.

Holt, Pat M. 1999. "Mexico's Dramatically Shrinking Families." *Christian Science Monitor,* June 22, p. 9.

Homans, George C. 1979. "Nature versus Nurture: A False Dichotomy." *Contemporary Sociology* 8(May):345–348.

Hondagneu-Sotelo, Pierrette. 1994. "Regulating the Unregulated? Domestic Workers' Social Networks." *Social Problems* 41(February):50–64.

Honey, Martha. 1994. "Mexico's Open Secret: Illegal Abortions." *The Nation* 259(September 26):312.

Horgan, John. 1993. "Eugenics Revisited." *Scientific American* 268(June): 122–128, 130–133.

Horn, Jack C., and Jeff Meer. 1987. "The Vintage Years." *Psychology Today* 21(May):76–77, 80–84, 88–90.

Horne, A. D. 1995. "Women Face 'Global Glass Ceiling.' U.N. Says." *Washington Post,* August 18, pp. A27–A28.

Horovitz, Bruce. 1995. "Marketers Tap Data We Once Called Our Own." *USA Today,* December 19, pp. A1, A2.

Horowitz, Helen Lefkowitz. 1987. *Campus Life.* Chicago: University of Chicago Press.

Horowitz, Irving Louis. 1983. *C. Wright Mills: An American Utopia.* New York: Free Press.

Horwitt, Sanford D. 1989. *Let Them Call Me Rebel: Saul Alinsky—His Life and Legacy.* New York: Knopf.

Hosokawa, William K. 1969. *Nisei: The Quiet Americans.* New York: Morrow.

Houseman, John. 1972. *Run Through.* New York: Simon and Schuster.

Housing and Urban Development. 1999. *Stuart B. McKinney Homeless Programs.* Washington, DC: U.S. Government Printing Office.

Hout, Michael. 1988. "More Universalism, Less Structural Mobility: The American Occupational Structure in the 1980s." *American Journal of Sociology* 91(May):1358–1400.

Howard, Michael C. 1989. *Contemporary Cultural Anthropology.* 3d ed. Glenview, IL: Scott, Foresman.

Howell, James C. 1998. "Youth Gangs: An Overview." *Juvenile Justice Bulletin* (August):1–19.

Huang, Gary. 1988. "Daily Addressing Ritual: A Cross-Cultural Study." Presented at the annual meeting of the American Sociological Association, Atlanta.

Huber, Bettina J. 1985. *Employment Patterns in Sociology: Recent Trends and Future Prospects.* Washington, DC: American Sociological Association.

Huddy, Leonie, Joshua Billig, John Bracciodieta, Lois Hoeffler, Patrick J. Moynihan, and Patricia Pugliani. 1997. "The Effect of Interviewer Gender on the Survey Response." *Political Behavior* 19(September):197–220.

Huffstutter, P. J., Tini Tran, and David Reyes. 1999. "Pirates of the High-Tech Age." *Los Angeles Times,* July 25, pp. A1, A28–A29.

Hughes, Everett. 1945. "Dilemmas and Contradictions of Status." *American Journal of Sociology* 50 (March): 353–359.

Hunt, Geoffrey et al. 1993. "Changes in Prison Culture: Prison Gangs and the Case of the 'Pepsi Generation.'" *Social Problems* 40(August):398–409.

Hunter, Herbert, ed. 2000. *The Sociology of Oliver C. Cox: New Perspectives: Research in Race and Ethnic Relations,* vol. II. Stanford, CT: JAI Press.

Hunter, James Davison. 1991. *Culture Wars: The Struggle to Define America.* New York: Basic Books.

Hurh, Won Moo, and Kwang Chung Kim. 1998. "The 'Success' Image of Asian Americans: Its Validity, and Its Practical and Theoretical Implications." *Ethnic and Racial Studies* 12(October):512–538.

———. 1994. *Korean Immigrants in America: A Structural Analysis of Ethnic Confinement and Adhesive Adaptation.* Rutherford, NJ: Fairleigh Dickinson University Press.

———. 1998. *The Korean Americans.* Westport, CT: Greenwood Press.

Hurn, Christopher J. 1985. *The Limits and Possibilities of Schooling.* 2d ed. Boston: Allyn and Bacon.

Hurst, Erik, Ming Ching Luoh, and Frank P. Stafford. 1996. "Wealth Dynamics of American Families, 1984–1994." Institute for Social Research, University of Michigan, Ann Arbor, MI. Unpublished paper.

I

Ibarra, Herminia. 1995. "Race, Opportunity, and Diversity of Social Circles in Managerial Networks." *Academy of Management Journal* 38(3):673–703.

Illinois Coalition Against the Death Penalty. 2000. "Basic Facts on the Death Penalty in Illinios." Accessed February 17, 2000 (http://www. keynet/nicadp/).

Immigration and Naturalization Service. 1997. *1996 Statistical Yearbook of the Immigration and Naturalization Service.* Washington, DC: U.S. Government Printing Office.

———. 1998. *1997 Statistical Yearbook of the Immigration and Naturalization Service.* Washington, DC: U.S. Government Printing Office.

———. 1999a. *Legal Immigration, Fiscal Year 1998.* Washington, DC: U.S. Government Printing Office.

———. 1999b. *1997 Statistical Yearbook of the Immigration and Naturalization Service.* Washington, DC: U.S. Government Printing Office.

Institute of International Education. 1998. "Foreign Students in U.S. Institutions 1997–98." *Chronicle of Higher Education* 45(December 11):A67.

Instituto del Tercer Mundo. 1997. *The World Guide 1997/98.* Oxford: New International Publications.

Inter-Parliamentary Union. 1999. "Women in National Parliaments. Situation as of 30 September 1999." Accessed October 3, 1999 (http://www. ipu.org/wmn-e/classif.htm). Geneva, Switzerland: Inter-Parliamentary Union.

———. 2000. "Women in National Parliaments." (http://www.ipu.org).

Irwin, Katherine. 1998. "Getting a Tattoo: Self Transformation and Defining Deviance Down." Presented at the annual meeting of the American Sociological Association, San Francisco.

———. 1999a. "Getting a First Tattoo: Techniques of Legitimation and Social Change." University of Colorado, Boulder, CO. Unpublished paper.

———. 1999b. "Body Deviant's Subculture." University of Colorado, Boulder, CO. Unpublished paper.

J

Jackson, Elton F., Charles R. Tittle, and Mary Jean Burke. 1986. "Offense-Specific Models of the Differential Association Process." *Social Problems* 33(April):335–356.

Jackson, Kenneth T. 1996. "America's Rush to Suburbia." *New York Times,* June 9, p. E15.

Jackson, Philip W. 1968. *Life in Classrooms.* New York: Holt.

Jacobson, Jodi. 1993. "Closing the Gender Gap in Development." Pp. 61–79 in *State of the World,* edited by Lester R. Brown. New York: Norton.

Janovsky, Michael. 1999. "New Mexico Bans Creationism from State Curriculum." *New York Times,* October 9, p. A7.

———. 2000. "Parents Lead Way As States Debate School Vouchers." *New York Times,* January 31, pp. A1, A21.

Japan Times Staff. 1998. "Practical Alternatives to Donor Organs Decades Away." *Japan Times Weekly* 38(October 26), p. 11.

———. 1999. "80% Back Capital Punishment." *Japan Times International Edition* 14(December 7):8.

Jasper, James M. 1997. *The Art of Moral Protest: Culture, Biography, and Creativity in Social Movements.* Chicago: University of Chicago.

Javna, John. 1986. *Cult TV.* New York: St. Martin's.

Jehl, Douglas. 1999. "The Internet's 'Open Sesame' Is Answered Warily." *New York Times,* March 18, p. A4.

Jencks, Christopher. 1994. *The Homeless.* Cambridge, MA: Harvard University Press.

Jenkins, Richard. 1991. "Disability and Social Stratification." *British Journal of Sociology* 42(December):557–580.

Jennings, M. Kent, and Richard G. Niemi. 1981. *Generations and Politics.* Princeton, NJ: Princeton University Press.

Johannesburg Mail and Guardian. 1997. "The Millennium's Closing Down." February 7.

Johnson, Anne M., Jane Wadsworth, Kaye Wellings, and Julie Field. 1994. *Sexual Attitudes and Lifestyles.* Oxford: Blackwell Scientific.

Johnson, Benton. 1975. *Functionalism in Modern Sociology: Understanding Talcott Parsons.* Morristown, NJ: General Learning.

Johnson, Chip. 1994. "LAPD Lingo." *Los Angeles Times,* December 19, pp. B1, B8.

Johnson, Dirk. 1993. "More and More, the Single Parent Is Dad." *New York Times,* August 31, pp. A1, A15.

———. 1996b. "Rural Life Gains New Appeal, Turning Back a Long Decline." *New York Times,* September 23, pp. A1, B6.

Johnson, George. 1999. "It's a Fact: Faith and Theory Collide Over Evolution." *New York Times,* August 15, sec. 4, pp. 1, 12.

Johnson, Kenneth M. 1999. "The Rural Rebound." *Reports on America* 1(September).

Johnson, Kevin, and Lori Sharn. 1997. "Attacks on Clinics Expose Raw Emotion on Both Sides," *USA Today* (January 23), pp. A1–A2.

Johnson, Peter. 1997. "Crime Wave Sweeps Networks." *Newscasts,* February 13, p. 3D.

Johnson, Richard A. 1985. *American Fads.* New York: Beech Tree.

Johnston, David Cay. 1994. "Ruling Backs Homosexuals on Asylum." *New York Times,* June 17, p. A12.

———. 1996. "The Divine Write-Off." *New York Times* (January 12), pp. D1, D6.

Joint Center for Political and Economic Studies. 1997a. *National Roster of Black Elected Officials.* Washington, DC.

———. 1997b. "House Rejects National School Vouchers Bill." *Focus Magazine* 25(November):2.

Jolin, Annette. 1994. "On the Backs of Working Prostitutes: Feminist Theory and Prostitution Policy." *Crime and Delinquency* 40(No. 2):69–83.

Jones, Charisse. 1999. "Minority Farmers Say They've Been Cheated." *USA Today,* January 5, p. 9A.

Jones, James T., IV. 1988. "Harassment Is Too Often Part of the Job." *USA Today,* August 8, p. 5D.

Jones, Stephen R. G. 1992. "Was There a Hawthorne Effect?" *American Journal of Sociology* 98(November):451–568.

Juhasz, Anne McCreary. 1989. "Black Adolescents' Significant Others." *Social Behavior and Personality* 17(2): 211–214.

K

Kagay, Michael R. 1994. "Poll on Doubt of Holocaust Is Corrected." *New York Times,* July 8, p. A10.

———. 1996. "Experts Say Refinements Are Needed in the Polls." *New York Times,* December 15, p. 34.

Kahn, Jeremy. 1999. "Global 5 Hundred: the World's Largest Corporations." *Fortune* 140(August 2):144–145, F1–F24.

Kail, Barbara Lynn, and Eugene Litwak. 1989. "Family, Friends and Neighbors: The Role of Primary Groups in Preventing the Misuse of Drugs." *Journal of Drug Issues* 19(2):261–282.

Kaiser Family Foundation. 1999. *Fact Sheet: The HIV/AIDS Epidemic in the U.S.* New York: Kaiser Family Foundation.

Kalb, Claudia. 1999. "Our Quest to Be Perfect." *Newsweek* 134(August 9): 52–59.

Kalish, Richard A. 1985. *Death, Grief, and Caring Relationships.* 2d ed. Monterey, CA: Brooks/Cole.

Kalleberg, Arne L. 1988. "Comparative Perspectives on Work Structures and Inequality." Pp. 203–225 in *Annual Review of Sociology, 1988,* edited by W. Richard Scott and Judith Blake. Palo Alto, CA: Annual Reviews.

Kanagae, Haruhiko. 1993. "Sexual Harassment in Japan: Findings from Survey Research." Presented at the annual meeting of the Pacific Sociological Association, Portland, OR.

Kanellos, Nicholás. 1994. *The Hispanic Almanac: From Columbus to Corporate America.* Detroit: Visible Ink Press.

Kang, Mee-Eun. 1997. "The Portrayal of Women's Images in Magazine Advertisements: Goffman's Gender Analysis Revisited." In *Sex Roles* 37(December): 979–996.

Kapferer, Jean-Noel. 1992. "How Rumors Are Born." *Society* 29(July–August): 53–60.

Kaplan, Esther. 1990. "A Queer Manifesto." *Village Voice,* August 14, p. 36.

Kasarda, John D. 1990. "The Jobs–Skills Mismatch." *New Perspectives Quarterly* 7(Fall):34–37.

Katovich, Michael A. 1987. Correspondence. June 1.

Katz, Jonathan Ned. 1992. *Gay American History: Lesbians and Gay Men in the United States.* Rev. ed. New York: Meridian.

Katz, Michael. 1971. *Class, Bureaucracy, and the Schools: The Illusion of Educational Change in America.* New York: Praeger.

Kay, Paul, and Willett Kempton. 1984. "What Is the Sapir-Whorf Hypothesis?" *American Anthropologist* 86(March):65–79.

Kearl, Michael C. 1989. *Endings: A Sociology of Death and Dying.* New York and Oxford: Oxford University Press.

Keating, Noah and Brenda Munro. 1988. "Farm Women/Farm Work." *Sex Roles* 19(August):155–168.

Kelley, Robin D. G. 1996. "Freedom Riders (the Sequel)." *The Nation* 262(February 5):18–21.

Kelley, Tina. 1999. "Candidate on the Stump Is Surely on the Web." *New York Times* (October 19), pp. A1, A15.

Kelly, Katy, and Doug Levy. 1995. "HMOs Dogged by Issue of Cost vs. Care." *USA Today,* October 17, pp. D1, D2.

Kelsoe, John R. et al. [12 authors]. 1989. "Re-evaluation of the Linkage Relationship between Chromosome LTP Loci and the Gene for Bipolar Affective Disorder in the Old Order Amish." *Nature* 342(November 16): 238–243.

Kemper, Vicki, and Viveca Novak. 1991. "Health Care Reform: Don't Hold Your Breath." *Washington Post National Weekly Edition* 8(October 28):28.

Kennedy, Bruce P., Ichiro Kawachi, and Deborah Prothrow-Stith. 1996. "Income Distribution and Mortality: Cross Sectional Ecological Study of the Robin Hood Index in the United States." *British Medical Journal* 312(April 20):1004–1007.

Kennickell, Arthur B., Martha Starr-McCluer, and Brian J. Surette. 2000. "Recent Changes in U.S. Family Finances: Results from the 1998 Survey of Consumer Finances." *Federal Reserve Bulletin* (January):1–29.

Kent, Mary Mederios. 1999. "Shrinking Societies Favor Procreation." *Population Today* 27(December):4–5.

Kephart, William M., and William M. Zellner. 1998. *Extraordinary Groups: An Examination of Unconventional Life-Styles.* 6th ed. New York: St. Martin's.

Kerbo, Harold R. 1996. *Social Stratification and Inequality: Class Conflict in Historical and Comparative Perspective.* 3d ed. New York: McGraw-Hill.

——— and John A. McKinstry. 1998. *Modern Japan.* Boston, MA: McGraw-Hill.

Kerr, Clark. 1960. *Industrialization and Industrial Man: The Problems of Labor and Management in Economic Growth.* Cambridge, MA: Harvard University Press.

Kidron, Michael and Ronald Segal. 1995. *The State of the World Atlas.* 5th ed. London: Penguin.

Kifner, John. 1994a. "Pollster Finds Error on Holocaust Doubts." *New York Times,* May 20, p. A20.

———. 1994b. "Gunman Kills 2 at Abortion Clinics in Boston Suburb." *New York Times,* December 31, pp. 1, 8.

Kilborn, Peter T. 1999. "Gimme Shelter: Same Song, New Time." *New York Times,* December 5, p. 5.

Kim, Kwang Chung. 1999. *Koreans in the Hood: Conflict with African Americans.* Baltimore: Johns Hopkins University Press.

King, Anthony. 1998. "London Mayor Is Casualty of Voters' Apathy." *The Daily Telegraph* (London), May 19, p. 12.

King, Leslie. 1998. "'France Needs Children': Pronatalism, Nationalism, and Women's Equity." *Sociological Quarterly* 39(Winter):33–52.

——— and Madonna Harrington Meyer. 1997. "The Politics of Reproductive Benefits: U.S. Insurance Coverage of Contraceptive and Infertility Treatments." *Gender and Society* 11(February):8–30.

King, Sharon A. 1999. "Mania for 'Pocket Monsters' Yields Billions for Nintendo." *New York Times,* April 26, pp. A1, A18.

Kinkade, Patrick T., and Michael A. Katovich. 1997. "The Driver Adaptations and Identities in the Urban Worlds of Pizza Delivery Employees." *Journal of Contemporary Ethnography* 25(January):421–448.

Kinsey, Alfred C., Wardell B. Pomeroy, and Clyde E. Martin. 1948. *Sexual Behavior in the Human Male.* Philadelphia: Saunders.

———, ———, and Paul H. Gebhard. 1953. *Sexual Behavior in the Human Female.* Philadelphia: Saunders.

Kinzer, Stephen. 1993. "German Court Restricts Abortion, Angering Feminists and the East." *New York Times,* May 29, pp. 1, 3.

Kirk, Margaret O. 1995. "The Temps in the Gray Flannel Suits." *New York Times,* December 17, p. F13.

Kirp, David L. 1994. "Freedom's Not Enough." *Tikkun* 9 (November–December):72–74.

Kitchener, Richard F. 1991. "Jean Piaget: The Unknown Sociologist." *British Journal of Sociology* 42(September): 421–442.

Kleinknecht, William. 1996. *The New Ethnic Mobs: The Changing Face of Organized Crime in America.* New York: Free Press.

Knowles, James, Jere R. Behrman, Benjamin E. Dikono, and Keith McInnes. 1998. "Key Issues in the Financing of Viet Nam's Social Services." In *Financing of Social Services Project: Report to the Government of Viet Nam and the Asian Development Bank.* Bethesda, MD: Abt Associates.

Koenig, Frederick W. 1985. *Rumor in the Marketplace.* Dover, MA: Auburn House.

Kohn, Alfie. 1988. "Girltalk, Guytalk." *Psychology Today* 22(February): 65–66.

Kohn, Melvin L. 1970. "The Effects of Social Class on Parental Values and Practices." Pp. 45–68 in *The American Family: Dying or Developing,* edited by David Reiss and H. A. Hoffman. New York: Plenum.

Kolata, Gina. 1997. "Clinics Selling Embryos Made for 'Adoption.'" *New York Times,* November 25, pp. 1, 18.

———. 1998. "Infertile Foreigners See Opportunity in U.S." *New York Times,* January 4, pp. 1, 12.

———. 1999. *Clone: The Road to Dolly and the Path Beyond.* New York: William Morrow.

———. 2000. *Clone. The Road to Dolly, and the Path Ahead.* New York: William Morrow.

———. 2000. "Web Research Transforms Visit to the Doctor." *New York Times.* (March 6): A1, A18.

Komarovsky, Mirra. 1991. "Some Reflections on the Feminist Scholarship in Sociology." Pp. 1–25 in *Annual Review of Sociology, 1991,* edited by W. Richard Scott and Judith Blake. Palo Alto, CA: Annual Reviews.

Kopinak, Kathryn. 1995. "Gender as a Vehicle for the Subordination of Women Maquiladora Workers in Mexico." *Latin American Perspectives* 22(Winter):30-48.

Kortenhaus, Carole M., and Jack Demarest. 1993. "Gender Role Stereotyping in Children's Literature: An Update." *Sex Roles* 28(3–4):219–232.

Kourvetaris, George. 1999. "The Greek-American Family: A Generational Approach." Pp. 68–101 in *Ethnic Families in America: Patterns and Variations,* 4th ed., edited by Charles H. Mindel, Robert W. Habenstein, and Roosevelt Wright, Jr. Upper Saddle River, NJ: Prentice-Hall.

Koval, John, Roberta Garner, Judith Bootcheck, Kenneth Fidel, and Noel Barker. 1996. "Motorola in Harvard: A Microcosm of Social Change." Proposal to the National Science Foundation, DePaul University, Chicago.

Kovaleski, Serge F. 1999. "Choosing Alternative Medicine by Necessity." *Washington Post National Weekly Edition* 16(April 5):16.

Kozol, J. 1991. *Savage Inequalities.* New York: Crown.

Krach, Constance A., and Victoria A. Velkoff. 1999. "Centenorians in the United States 1990." *Current Population Reports,* ser. P-23, no. 199RV. Washington, DC: U.S. Government Printing Office.

Kraut, Robert et al. 1998. "Internet Paradox: A Social Technology That Reduces Social Involvement and Psychological Well-Being." *American Psychologist* 55(September): 1017–1031.

Kristof, Nicholas D. 1995. "Japanese Say No to Crime: Tough Methods, at a Price." *New York Times,* May 14, pp. 1, 8.

———. 1995c. "Japan's Invisible Minority: Better Off Than in Past, but Still Outcasts," *New York Times* (November 30), p. A18.

———. 1996. "In Japan, Nothing to Fear but Fear Itself." *New York Times,* May 19, p. E4.

———. 1997. "The Communist Dynasty Had Its Run, Now What?" *New York Times,* February 23, sec. 4, pp. 1, 3.

———. 1998. "As Asian Economies Shrink, Women Are Squeezed Out." *New York Times,* June 11, pp. A1, A12.

Kroeber, Alfred L. 1923. *Anthropology: Culture Patterns and Processes.* New York: Harcourt Brace and World.

Kübler-Ross, Elisabeth. 1969. *On Death and Dying.* New York: Macmillan.

Kunii, Irene M. 1997. "Where the Heart Isn't: Pressure from the Medical Community May Force Japan to Make Transplants Easier—and Save Lives." *Times International,* May 12, p. 20.

Kunkel, Dale et al. 1999. *Sex on TV: A Biennial Report to Kaiser Family Foundation.* Santa Barbara, CA: University of California, Santa Barbara.

Kuptsch, Christine, and David M. Mazie. 1999. "Social Protection." Pp. 316–318 in *Enyclopedia Britannica Yearbook 1999.* Chicago: Encyclopedia Britannica.

Kurtz, Lester R., ed. 1999. *Encyclopedia of Violence, Place and Conflict.* San Diego, CA: Academic Press.

Kushnick, Louis. 1993. "Internal Migration." Pp. 252–253 in *1993 Encyclopedia Britannica Book of the Year.* Chicago: Encyclopedia Britannica.

Kwong, Peter, and JoAnn Lum. 1988. "Chinese-American Politics: A Silent Minority Tests Its Clout." *The Nation* 246(January 16):49–50, 52.

Kyodo News International. 1998a. "More Japanese Believe Divorce Is Acceptable." *Japan Times* 38(January 12), p. B4.

———. 1998b. "62% of Japanese Want Increased 'Koban' Police Patrol." March 28.

———. "Second Transplant Recipients Listed in Stable Conditions." *Japan Times International,* May 16, p. 4.

L

Labaree, David F. 1986. "Curriculum, Credentials, and the Middle Class: A Case Study of a Nineteenth Century High School." *Sociology of Education* 59(January):42–57.

Ladner, Joyce. 1973. *The Death of White Sociology.* New York: Random Books.

La Ganga, Maria L. 1999. "Trying to Figure the Beginning of the End." *Los Angeles Times*, October 15, pp. A1, A28, A29.

———. 2000. "The Age of the Aging Electorate." *Los Angeles Times*, January 13, pp. A1, A17.

Lancaster, John. 1992. "Does Anyone Allow Gays to Serve in the Military?" *Washington Post National Weekly Edition* 9(December 7):14.

Landers, Robert K. 1988. "Why America Doesn't Vote." *Editorial Research Reports* (*Congressional Quarterly*) 8 pt. 1, pp. 82–95.

Landre, Rick, Mike Miller, and Dee Porter. 1997. *Gangs: A Handbook for Community Awareness.* New York: Facts on File.

Landtman, Gunnar. 1968. *The Origin of Inequality of the Social Class.* New York: Greenwood (original edition 1938, Chicago: University of Chicago Press).

Lang, Eric. 1992. "Hawthorne Effect." Pp. 793–794 in *Encyclopedia of Sociology,* vol. 2, edited by Edgar F. Borgatta and Marie L. Borgatta. New York: Macmillan.

Lappé, Anthony. 1999 "There Is No Average Day When You Live in a Tree." *New York Times Magazine* (December 12), p. 29.

Lappin, Todd. 1996. "Aux Armes, Netizens!" *The Nation* 262(February 26): 6–7.

Larson, Calvin J., and Stan R. Nikkel. 1979. *Urban Problems: Perspectives on Corporations, Governments, and Cities.* Boston: Allyn and Bacon.

Larson, Jan. 1996. "Temps Are Here to Stay." *American Demographics* 18(February):26–31.

Lassey, Marie L., William R. Lassey, and Martin J. Jinks. 1997. *Health Care Systems around the World: Characteristics, Issues, Reforms.* Upper Saddle River, NJ: Prentice-Hall.

Lasswell, Harold D. 1936. *Politics: Who Gets What, When, How.* New York: McGraw-Hill.

Lauer, Robert H. 1982. *Perspectives on Social Change.* 3d ed. Boston: Allyn and Bacon.

Laumann, Edward O., John H. Gagnon, and Robert T. Michael. 1994a. "A Political History of the National Sex Survey of Adults." *Family Planning Perspectives* 26(February):34–38.

———, ———, ———, and Stuart Michaels. 1994b. *The Social Organization of Sexuality: Sexual Practices in the United States.* Chicago: University of Chicago Press.

Lauritsen, John, and David Thorstad. 1974. *The Early Homosexual Rights Movement (1864–1935).* New York: Times Change.

Leacock, Eleanor Burke. 1969. *Teaching and Learning in City Schools.* New York: Basic Books.

Leavell, Hugh R., and E. Gurney Clark. 1965. *Preventive Medicine for the Doctor in His Community: An Epidemiologic Approach.* 3d ed. New York: McGraw-Hill.

Lee, Alfred McClung. 1978. *Sociology for Whom?* New York: Oxford University Press.

Lee, Barrett A. 1992. "Homelessness." Pp. 843–847 in *Encyclopedia of Sociology,* vol. 2, edited by Edgar F. Borgatta and Marie L. Borgatta. New York: Macmillan.

Lee, Felicia R. 1996. "Infertile Couples Forge Ties within Society of Their Own." *New York Times,* January 9, pp. A1, A7.

Lee, Heon Cheol. 1999. "Conflict Between Korean Merchants and Black Customers: A Structural Analysis." Pp. 113–130 in *Koreans in the Hood: Conflict with African Americans,* edited by Kwang Chung Kim. Baltimore: Johns Hopkins University Press.

Lee, Taeku. 1998. "The Backdoor and the Backlash: Campaign Finance and the Politicization of Chinese-Americans." Research Roundtable Series, Harvard University, Cambridge, MA. Unpublished paper.

Leeman, Sue. 1999. "Increased Drug Use Blamed. HIV's Devastating Effects." *USA Today,* November 24, p. 6A.

Le Feber, Walter. 1999. *Michael Jordan and the New Global Capitalism.* New York: W. W. Norton.

Legato, Marianne J. 1998. "Research on the Biology of Women Will Improve Health Care for Men, Too." *Chronicle of Higher Education* 44(May 15): B4–B5.

Lehne, Gregory K. 1995. "Homophobia among Men: Supporting and Defining the Male Role." Pp. 325–336 in *Men's Lives,* edited by Michael S. Kimmel

and Michael S. Messner. Boston: Allyn and Bacon.

Leicht, Kevin T., and Mary L. Fennell. 1997. "The Changing Organizational Context of Professional Work." Pp. 215–231 in *Annual Review of Sociology 1997,* edited by John Hagan. Palo Alto, CA: Annual Reviews.

Lemann, Nicholas. 1991. "The Other Underclass." *Atlantic Monthly* 268(December):96–102, 104, 107–108, 110.

———. 1999. *The Big Test: The Secret History of the American Meritocracy.* New York: Farrar, Straus and Giroux.

Lemkow, Louis. 1987. "The Employed Unemployed: The Subterranean Economy in Spain." *Social Science and Medicine* 25(2):111–113.

Lengermann, Patricia Madoo, and Jill Niebrugge-Brantley. 1998. *The Women Founders: Sociology and Social Theory, 1830–1930.* Boston: McGraw-Hill.

Lennon, Mary Clare, and Sarah Rosenfield. 1994. "Relative Fairness and the Division of Housework: The Importance of Options." *American Journal of Sociology* 100(September):506–531.

Lenski, Gerhard. 1966. *Power and Privilege: A Theory of Social Stratification.* New York: McGraw-Hill.

———, Jean Lenski, and Patrick Nolan. 1995. *Human Societies: An Introduction to Macrosociology.* 7th ed. New York: McGraw-Hill.

Leo, John. 1987. "Exploring the Traits of Twins." *Time* 129(January 12):63.

Leon, Sy. 1996. *None of the Above: Why Non-Voters Are America's Political Majority.* San Francisco: Fox and Wilkes.

Letkemann, Peter. 1973. *Crime as Work.* Englewood Cliffs, NJ: Prentice-Hall.

Levin, Jack. 1999. *Sociological Snapshots 3.* Thousand Oaks, CA: Pine Forge Press.

——— and William C. Levin. 1980. *Ageism.* Belmont, CA: Wadsworth.

Levinson, Arlene. 1984. "Laws for Live-In Lovers." *Ms.* 12(June):101.

Levinson, Daniel J. 1978. *The Seasons of a Man's Life.* With Charlotte N. Darrow et al. New York: Alfred A. Knopf.

———. 1996. *The Seasons of a Woman's Life.* In collaboration with Judy D. Levinson. New York: Alfred A. Knopf.

Lewin, Tamar. 1992. "Hurdles Increase for Many Women Seeking Abortions." *New York Times,* March 15, pp. 1, 18.

———. 1997. "Abortion Rate Declined Again in '95, U.S. Says, but Began

Rising Last Year." *New York Times*, December 5, p. A10.

———. 1998. "Report Finds Girls Lagging Behind Boys in Technology." *New York Times*, October 14, p. B8.

Lewis, Anthony. 1999. "Abroad at Home: Something Rich and Strange," *New York Times* (October 12): accessed at *The New York Times on the Web*.

Liao, Youlian, Daniel L. McGee, Guichan Cao, and Richard S. Cooper. 2000. "Quality of the Last Year of Life of Older Adults: 1986–1993." *Journal of American Medical Association* 283(January 26):512–518.

Lieberman, David. 1999. "On the Wrong Side of the Wires." *USA Today*, October 11, pp. B1, B2.

Liebow, Elliot. 1993. *Tell Them Who I Am: The Lives of Homeless Women*. New York: Free Press.

Light, Ivan. 1996. "A Self-Help Solution to Fight Urban Poverty." *American Enterprise Magazine* 7(July/August): 50–52.

———. 1999. "Comparing Incomes of Immigrants." *Contemporary Sociology* 28(July):382–384.

Lillard, Margaret. 1998. "Olympics Put Spotlight on Women's Hockey." *Rocky Mountain News*, February 1, p. 8C.

Lilliston, Ben. 1994. "Corporate Welfare Costs More Than Welfare to the Poor, Group Reports." *The Daily Citizen*, January 18, p. 8.

Lin, Na, and Wen Xie. 1988. "Occupational Prestige in Urban China." *American Journal of Sociology* 93(January):793–832.

Lindholm, Charles. 1999. "Isn't Romantic?" *Culture Front Online* Spring:1–5.

Lindner, Eileen, ed. 1998. *Yearbook of American and Canadian Churches, 1998*. Nashville: Abingdon Press.

Lines, Patricia M. 1985. "A Briefing on Tuition Vouchers and Related Plans." *Footnotes* 22(Spring):5–7.

Link, Bruce G. 1987. "Understanding Labeling Effects in the Area of Mental Disorders: An Assessment of the Effects of Expectations of Rejection." *American Sociological Review* 52(February):96–112.

———, Frances T. Cullen, Elmer Struening, and Patrick E. Shrout. 1989. "A Modified Labeling Theory Approach to Mental Disorders." *American Sociological Review* 54(June):400–423.

Linn, Susan, and Alvin F. Poussaint. 1999. "Watching Television: What Are Children Learning About Race and Ethnicity?" *Child Care Information Exchange* 128(July):50–52.

Linton, Ralph. 1936. *The Study of Man: An Introduction*. New York: Appleton-Century.

Lipset, Seymour Martin. 1990. *Continental Divide: The Values and Institutions of the United States and Canada*. New York: Routledge.

———. 1996. *American Exceptionalism: A Double-Edged Sword*. New York: Norton.

Lipson, Karen. 1994. "'Nell' Not Alone in the Wilds." *Los Angeles Times*, December 19, pp. F1, F6.

Liska, Allen E., and Steven F. Messner. 1999. *Perspectives on Crime and Deviance*. 3d ed. Upper Saddle River, NJ: Prentice-Hall.

Little, Kenneth. 1988. "The Role of Voluntary Associations in West African Urbanization." Pp. 211–230 in *Anthropology for the Nineties: Introductory Readings*, edited by Johnnetta B. Cole. New York: Free Press.

Livernash, Robert, and Eric Rodenburg. 1998. "Population Change, Resources, and the Environment." *Population Bulletin* 53(March).

Llanes, José. 1982. *Cuban Americans: Masters of Survival*. Cambridge, MA: Abt Books.

Lofflin, John. 1988. "A Burst of Rural Enterprise." *New York Times*, January 3, sec. 3, pp. 1, 23.

Lofland, John. 1981. "Collective Behavior: The Elementary Forms," Pp. 441–446 in *Social Psychology: Sociological Perspectives*, edited by Morris Rosenberg and Ralph Turner. New York: Basic Books.

———. 1985. *Protest: Studies of Collective Behavior and Social Movements*. Rutgers, NJ: Transaction.

Lofland, Lyn H. 1975. "The 'Thereness' of Women: A Selective Review of Urban Sociology." Pp. 144–170 in *Another Voice*, edited by M. Millman and R. M. Kanter. New York: Anchor/Doubleday.

Logan, John R., and Richard D. Alba. 1995. "Who Lives in Affluent Suburbs? Racial Differences in Eleven Metropolitan Regions." *Sociological Focus* 28(October):353–364.

Lohr, Steve. 1994. "Data Highway Ignoring Poor, Study Charges." *New York Times*, May 24, pp. A1, D3.

London, Kathryn A. 1991. *Cohabitation, Marriage, Marital Dissolution, and Remarriage: United States, 1988*. Washington, DC: National Center for Health Statistics.

Longman, Phillip. 1999. "The World Turns Gray." *U.S. News & World Report* 126(March 1):30–35.

Longworth, R. C. 1993. "UN's Relief Agendas Put Paperwork before People." *Chicago Tribune*, September 14, pp. 1, 9.

———. 1996. "Future Shock: The Graying of the Industrial World." *Chicago Tribune*, September 4, pp. 1, 20.

Lopreato, Joseph. 1992. "Sociobiology and Human Behavior." Pp. 1195–2000 in *Encyclopedia of Sociology*, vol. 4, edited by Edgar F. Borgatta and Marie L. Borgatta. New York: Macmillan.

Lorber, Judith. 1994. *Paradoxes of Gender*. New Haven, CT: Yale University Press.

Lott, John R., Jr. 1998. *More Guns, Less Crime: Understanding Crime and Gun Control Laws*. Chicago: University of Chicago Press.

Lowe, Marcia D. 1992. "Alternatives to Shaping Tomorrow's Cities." *The Futurist* 26(July–August):28–34.

Lowry, Brian, Elizabeth Jensen, and Greg Braxton. 1999. "Networks Decide Diversity Doesn't Pay." *Los Angeles Times*, July 20, p. A1.

Lukacs, Georg. 1923. *History and Class Consciousness*. London: Merlin.

Luker, Kristin. 1984. *Abortion and the Politics of Motherhood*. Berkeley: University of California Press.

———. 1996. *Dubious Conceptions: The Politics of Teenage Pregnancy*. Cambridge, MA: Harvard University Press.

———. 1999. "Is Academic Sociology Politically Obsolete?" *Contemporary Sociology* 28(January):5–10.

Lum, Joann, and Peter Kwong. 1989. "Surviving in America: The Trials of a Chinese Immigrant Woman." *Village Voice* 34(October 31):39–41.

Luo, Michael. 1999. "Megachurches Search for Ideas to Grow Again." *Los Angeles Times*, June 7, pp. B1, B3.

Luster, Tom, Kelly Rhoades, and Bruce Haas. 1989. "The Relation between Parental Values and Parenting Behavior: A Test of the Kohn Hypothesis."

Journal of Marriage and the Family 51(February):139–147.

Lustig, Myron W., and Jolene Koester. 1999. *Intercultural Competence.* 3d ed. New York: Longman.

Lyotard, Jean François. 1993. *The Postmodern Explained: Correspondence, 1982–1985.* Minneapolis: University of Minnesota Press.

M

MacCoun, Robert J. 1989. "Experimental Research on Jury Decision-Making." *Science* 244(June 2):1046–1050.

MacFarquhar, Neil. 1996. "With Iran Population Boom, Vasectomy Receives Blessing." *New York Times,* September 8, pp. 1, 14.

———. 1999. "For First Time in War, E-Mail Plays a Vital Role." *New York Times,* March 29, p. A12.

Mack, Raymond W., and Calvin P. Bradford. 1979. *Transforming America: Patterns of Social Change.* 2d ed. New York: Random House.

MacKinnon, Catharine A. 1998. "Harassment Law under Siege." *New York Times,* March 5, p. A25.

MacLeod, Alexander. 1996. "The World Rushes to Speak and Write 'American' English." *Christian Science Monitor,* September 4, p. 10.

Magnier, Mark. 1999. "Equality Evolving in Japan." *Los Angeles Times,* August 30, pp. A1, A12.

Maguire, Brendan. 1988. "The Applied Dimension of Radical Criminology: A Survey of Prominent Radical Criminologists." *Sociological Spectrum* 8(2):133–151.

Maines, David R. 1977. "Social Organization and Social Structure in Symbolic Interactionist Thought." Pp. 235–259 in *Annual Review of Sociology, 1977,* edited by Alex Inkles. Palo Alto, CA: Annual Reviews.

———. 1982. "In Search of Mesostructure: Studies in the Negotiated Order." *Urban Life* 11(July):267–279.

Malcolm, Andrew H. 1974. "The 'Shortage' of Bathroom Tissue: A Classic Study in Rumor." *New York Times,* February 3, p. 29.

Malcolm X, with Alex Haley. 1964. *The Autobiography of Malcolm X.* New York: Grove.

Malthus, Thomas Robert. 1798. *Essays on the Principle of Population.* New York: Augustus Kelly, Bookseller; reprinted in 1965.

———, Julian Huxley, and Frederick Osborn. [1824] 1960. *Three Essays on Population.* Reprint, New York: New American Library.

Manson, Donald A. 1986. *Tracking Offenders: White-Collar Crime.* Bureau of Justice Statistics Special Report. Washington, DC: U.S. Government Printing Office.

Marcuse, Peter. 1991. *Missing Marx: A Personal and Political Journal of a Year in East Germany, 1989–1990.* New York: Monthly Review Press.

Marklein, Mary Beth. 1996. "Telecommuters Gain Momentum." *USA Today,* June 18, p. 6E.

Marks, Alexandra. 1998. "Key Swing Vote in 1998: Women," *Christian Science Monitor,* July 14, p. 3.

Markson, Elizabeth W. 1992. "Moral Dilemmas." *Society* 29(July–August):4–6.

Marquis, Julie, and Dan Morain. 1999. "A Tortuous Path for the Mentally Ill." *Los Angeles Times,* November 21, pp. A1, A22, A23.

Marsden, Peter V. 1992. "Social Network Theory." Pp. 1887–1894 in *Encyclopedia of Sociology,* vol. 4, edited by Edgar F. Borgatta and Marie L. Borgatta. New York: Macmillan.

Marshall, Victor W., and Judith A. Levy. 1990. "Aging and Dying." Pp. 245–260 in *Handbook of Aging and the Social Sciences,* edited by Robert H. Binstock and Linda K. George. San Diego: Academic Press.

Martelo, Emma Zapata. 1996. "Modernization, Adjustment, and Peasant Production." *Latin American Perspectives* 23(Winter):118–130.

Martin, Joyce A., and Melissa M. Park. 1999. "Trends in Twin and Triplet Births: 1980–97." *National Vital Statistics Reports* 47(September 14).

Martin, Marvin. 1996. "Sociology Adapting to Changes." *Chicago Tribune,* July 21, sec. 18, p. 20.

Martin, Philip, and Elizabeth Midgley. 1999. "Immigrants to the United States." *Population Bulletin* 54(June):1–42.

Martin, Philip, and Jonas Widgren. 1996. "International Migration: A Global Challenge." *Population Bulletin* 51(April).

Martin, Susan E. 1994. "Outsider Within the Station House: The Impact of Race and Gender on Black Women Politics." *Social Problems* 41(August):383–400.

Martineau, Harriet. 1896. "Introduction" to the translation of *Positive Philosophy* by Auguste Comte. London: Bell.

———. [1837] 1962. *Society in America.* Edited, abridged, with an introductory essay by Seymour Martin Lipset. Reprint, Garden City, NY: Doubleday.

Martinez, Elizabeth. 1993. "Going Gentle into That Good Night: Is a Rightful Death a Feminist Issue?" *Ms.* 4(July–August):65–69.

Martinez, Valerie, Kay Thomas, and Frank R. Kenerer. 1994. "Who Chooses and Why: A Look at Five School Choice Plans." *Phi Delta Kappan* 75(May):678–681.

Martyna, Wendy. 1983. "Beyond the He/Man Approach: The Case for Nonsexist Language." Pp. 25–37 in *Language, Gender and Society,* edited by Barrie Thorne, Cheris Kramorae, and Nancy Henley. Rowley, MA: Newly House.

Marx, Karl, and Friedrich Engels. [1847] 1955. *Selected Work in Two Volumes.* Reprint, Moscow: Foreign Languages Publishing House.

Masaki, Hisane. 1998. "Hashimoto Steps Down." *The Japan Times* 38 (July 20):1–5.

Mascia-Lees, Frances E., and Patricia Sharp, eds. 1992. *Tattoo, Torture, Mutilation, and Adornment: The Denaturalization of the Body in Culture and Text.* Albany: State University of New York Press.

Masland, Tom. 1992. "Slavery." *Newsweek* 119(May 4):30–32, 37–39.

Mason, J. W. 1998. "The Buses Don't Stop Here Anymore." *American Prospect* 37(March):56–62.

Mason, Marie K. 1942. "Learning to Speak after Six and One-Half Years of Silence." *Journal of Speech Disorders* 7(December):295–304.

Massey, Douglas S. 1998. "March of Folly: U.S. Immigration Policy After NAFTA." *The American Prospect* (March–April):22–33.

——— 1999. "International Migration at the Dawn of the Twenty-First Century:

The Role of the State." *Population and Development Review* 28(June):303–322.

——— and Nancy A. Denton. 1993. *American Apartheid: Segregation and the Making of the Underclass.* Cambridge, MA: Harvard University Press.

Matloff, Norman. 1998. "Now Hiring! If You're Young." *New York Times*, January 26, p. A21.

Matrix Information and Directory Services. 1999. "Current World Map of the Internet." Austin, TX: MIDS. Also accessible online (http://www.mids.org/mapsale/world/index.html).

Matsushita, Yoshiko. 1999. "Japanese Kids Call for a Sympathetic Ear." *Christian Science Monitor*, January 20, p. 15.

Mauro, Tony. 1999. "Will Every Childish Taunt Turn Into a Federal Case?" *USA Today*, May 25, pp. A1, A2.

——— and Jim Drinkard. 1999. "Review Could Jeopardize Campaign-Finance Laws." *USA Today*, October 6, p. A6.

Maxwell, Joe. 1992. "African Megachurch Challenged over Teaching." *Christianity Today* 36(October 5):58.

Mayer, Karl Ulrich, and Urs Schoepflin. 1989. "The State and the Life Course." Pp. 187–209 in *Annual Review of Sociology, 1989,* edited by W. Richard Scott and Judith Blake. Palo Alto, CA: Annual Reviews.

Mayor's Task Force on Homelessness. 1997. *Report to Wheaton City Council on the Mayor's Task Force on Homelessness.* Wheaton, IL: Mayor's Task Force on Homelessness.

Maze, Brian, M. Cathey Maze, and Judith Glasser. 1997. "Assessing Alcoholism and Codependency in St. Kitts: Inappropriate Standards and Culture-Bound Syndromes." Presented at the annual meeting of the American Sociological Association, Toronto.

McAdam, D. 1989. "The Biographical Consequences of Activism." *American Sociological Review* 54(October): 744–760.

McCaghy, Charles H. 1980. *Crime in American Society.* New York: Macmillan.

McCarthy, Terry. 1999. "Inside the Falun Gong." *Time* 154(August 9):48–50.

McChesney, Robert W. 1999. *Rich Media, Poor Democracy: Communication Politics in Dubious Times.* Urbana, IL: University of Illinois Press.

McCloskey, Michael. 1991. "Twenty Years of Change in the Environmental Movement: An Insider's View." *Society and Natural Resources* 4(July–September):273–284.

McClung, H. Juhling, Robert D. Murray, and Leo A. Heitlinger. 1998. "The Internet as a Source for Current Patient Information." *Pediatrics* 10(June 6): electronic edition.

McCormick, John, and Claudia Kalb. 1998. "Dying for a Drink." *Newsweek*, June 15, pp. 30–31, 33–34.

McCreary, D. 1994. "The Male Role and Avoiding Femininity." *Sex Roles* 31: 517–531.

McDermott, Kevin. 1999. "Illinois Bill Would Repeal Law Requiring Listing of Campaign Donors on Internet." *St. Louis Post-Dispatch*, November 25, p. A1.

McDonald, Kim A. 1999. "Studies of Women's Health Produce a Wealth of Knowledge on the Biology of Gender Differences." *Chronicle of Higher Education* 45(June 25):A19, A22.

McDonald's. 1999. *The Annual.* Oak Brook, IL: McDonald's.

McDonnell, Patrick J., and Maki Becker. 1996. "7 Plead Guilty in Sweatshop Slavery Case." *Los Angeles Times*, February 10, p. A1.

McEnroe, Jennifer. 1991. "Split-Shift Parenting." *American Demographics* 13(February):50–52.

McFalls, Joseph A., Jr. 1998. "Population: A Lively Introduction." *Population Bulletin* 53(September).

———, Brian Jones, and Bernard J. Gallegher III. 1984. "U.S. Population Growth: Prospects and Policy." *USA Today*, January, pp. 30–34.

McGue, Matt, and Thomas J. Bouchard Jr. 1998. "Genetic and Environmental Influence on Human Behavioral Differences." Pp. 1–24 in *Annual Review of Neurosciences.* Palo Alto, CA: Annual Reviews.

McGuire, Meredith B. 1981. *Religion: The Social Context.* Belmont, CA: Wadsworth.

———. 1992. *Religion: The Social Context.* 3d ed. Belmont, CA: Wadsworth.

McKenzie, Evan. 1994. *Privatopia: Homeowner Associations and the Rise of Residential Private Government.* New Haven, CT: Yale University Press.

McKinlay, John B., and Sonja M. McKinlay. 1977. "The Questionable Contribution of Medical Measures to the Decline of Mortality in the United States in the Twentieth Century." *Milbank Memorial Fund Quarterly* 55(Summer):405–428.

McKinley, James C., Jr. 1999. "In Cuba's New Dual Economy, Have-Nots Far Exceed Haves." *New York Times*, February 11, pp. A1, A6.

McKinney, Kathleen. 1990. "Sexual Harassment of University Faculty by Colleagues and Students." *Sex Roles* 23(October):421–438.

McLane, Daisann. 1995. "The Cuban-American Princess." *New York Times Magazine*, February 26, pp. 42–43.

McLaughlin, Abraham. 1998. "Tales of Journey from Death Row to Freedom." *Christian Science Monitor*, November 16, p. 2.

McMahon, Colin. 1995. "Mexican Rebels' Struggle in Chiapas Is 'about the Future.'" *Chicago Tribune,* January 1, p. 6.

McNamara, Robert S. 1992. "The Population Explosion." *The Futurist* 26 (November–December):9–13.

McPhail, Clark. 1991. *The Myth of the Madding Crowd.* New York: De Gruyter.

———. 1994. "The Dark Side of Purpose in Riots: Individual and Collective Violence." *Sociological Quarterly* 35(January):i–xx.

——— and David Miller. 1973. "The Assembling Process: A Theoretical and Empirical Examination." *American Sociological Review* 38(December): 721–735.

McPherson, J. Miller, and Lynn Smith-Lovin. 1986. "Sex Segregation in Voluntary Associations." *American Sociological Review,* 51(February):61–79.

Mead, George H. 1930. "Cooley's Contribution to American Social Thought." *American Journal of Sociology* 35(March):693–706.

———. 1934. In *Mind, Self and Society,* edited by Charles W. Morris. Chicago: University of Chicago Press.

———. 1964a. In *On Social Psychology,* edited by Anselm Strauss. Chicago: University of Chicago Press.

———. 1964b. "The Genesis of the Self and Social Control." Pp. 267–293 in *Selected Writings: George Herbert Mead,* edited by Andrew J. Reck. Indianapolis: Bobbs-Merrill.

Mead, Margaret. [1935] 1963. *Sex and Temperament in Three Primitive Societies.* Reprint, New York: Morrow.

———. 1973. "Does the World Belong to Men—Or to Women?" *Redbook* 141(October):46–52.

Mechanic, David, and David Rochefort. 1996. "Comparative Medical Systems." Pp. 475–494 in *Annual Review of Sociology, 1996,* edited by John Hagan. Palo Alto, CA: Annual Reviews.

Mehren, Elizabeth. 1999. "Working 9 to 5 at Age 95." *USA Today,* May 5, pp. A1, A21–A22.

——— and Robert A. Rosenblatt. 1995. "For AARP a Reversal of Fortune." *Los Angeles Times,* August 23, pp. A1, A10–A11.

Melia, Marilyn Kennedy. 2000. "Changing Times." *Chicago Tribune,* January 2, sec. 17, pp. 12–15.

Melson, Robert. 1986. "Provocation or Nationalism: A Critical Inquiry into the Armenian Genocide of 1915." Pp. 61–84 in *The Armenian Genocide in Perspective,* edited by Richard G. Hovannisian. Brunswick, NJ: Transaction.

Mendez, Jennifer Brikham. 1998. "Of Mops and Maids: Contradictions and Continuities in Bureaucratized Domestic Work." *Social Problems* 45(February):114–135.

Merton, Robert K. 1968. *Social Theory and Social Structure.* New York: Free Press.

——— and Alice S. Kitt. 1950. "Contributions to the Theory of Reference Group Behavior." Pp. 40–105 in *Continuities in Social Research: Studies in the Scope and Method of the American Soldier,* edited by Robert K. Merton and Paul L. Lazarsfeld. New York: Free Press.

———, G. C. Reader, and P. L. Kendall. 1957. *The Student Physician.* Cambridge, MA: Harvard University Press.

Messner, Michael A. 1997. *Politics of Masculinities: Men in Movements.* Thousand Oaks, CA: Sage.

Meyer, David S., and Nancy Whittier. 1994. "Social Movement Spillover." *Social Problems* 41(May):277–298.

Meyers, Thomas J. 1992. "Factors Affecting the Decision to Leave the Old Order Amish." Presented at the annual meeting of the American Sociological Association, Pittsburgh.

Michael, Robert T., John H. Gagnon, Edward O. Laumann, and Gina Kolata. 1994. *Sex in America: A Definitive Survey.* Boston: Little, Brown.

Michels, Robert. 1915. *Political Parties.* Glencoe, IL: Free Press (reprinted 1949).

Mifflin, Lawrie. 1999. "Many Researchers Say Link Is Already Clear on Media and Youth Violence." *New York Times,* May 9, p. 23.

Migration News. 1998a. "Canada: Immigration, Diversity Up." 5(January). Accessed May 22 (http://migration.ucdavis.edu).

———. 1998b. "Immigration in EU, France: New Law, Australia: Immigration Unchanged." 5(May). Accessed May 6 (http://migration.ucdavis.edu).

———. 1999a. "Japan: Korean Illegals." *Migration News* 6(March).

———. 1999b. "Mexico: Demography, Remittances." *Migration News* 6(July).

———. 1999c. "Mexico: NAFYTA" 6(November):16–17.

Milgram, Stanley. 1963. "Behavioral Study of Obedience." *Journal of Abnormal and Social Psychology* 67(October):371–378.

———. 1975. *Obedience to Authority: An Experimental View.* New York: Harper and Row.

Miller, David L. 1973. *George Herbert Mead: Self, Language, and the World.* Chicago: University of Chicago Press.

———. 2000. *Introduction to Collective Behavior and Collective Action.* 2d ed. Prospect Heights, IL Waveland Press.

——— and Richard T. Schaefer. 1993. "Feeding the Hungry: The National Food Bank System as a Non-Insurgent Social Movement." Presented at the annual meeting of the Midwest Sociological Society, Chicago.

——— and ———. 1998. "Promise Keepers and Race: The Stand in the Gap Rally, Washington, DC, 1997." Paper presented at the annual meeting of the Midwest Sociological Society, April, Kansas City, MO.

Miller, Greg. 1999. "Internet Fueled Global Interest in Disruptions." *Chicago Tribune,* December 2, p. A24.

Miller, G. Tyler, Jr. 1972. *Replenish the Earth: A Primer in Human Ecology.* Belmont, CA: Wadsworth.

Miller, Leslie. 1995. "MIT Prof Taps into Culture of Computers." *USA Today,* November 7, pp. D1, D2.

———. 1998. "Finding On-Line Faithful Revives Religious Groups." *USA Today,* March 25, pp. D1, D2.

Miller, Michael. 1998. "Abortion by the Numbers." *The Village Voice* 43, January 27, p. 58.

Miller, Reuben. 1988. "The Literature of Terrorism," *Terrorism,* 11(1):63–87.

Millett, Kate. 1970. *Sexual Politics.* New York: Doubleday.

Mills, C. Wright. 1956. *The Power Elite.* New York: Oxford University Press.

———. 1959. *The Sociological Imagination.* London: Oxford University Press.

Mills, Kim I., and Daryl Henschaft. 1999. *The State of the Workplace for Lesbian, Gay, Bisexual and Transgendered Americans 1999.* Washington, DC: Human Rights Campaign Foundation.

Milton S. Eisenhower Foundation. 1999. *To Establish Justice, To Insure Domestic Tranquility: A Thirty Year Update of the National Commission on the Causes and Prevention of Violence.* Washington, DC: Milton S. Eisenhower Foundation.

Mindel, Charles, Robert W. Habenstein, and Roosevelt Wright, Jr. 1998. *Ethnic Families in America: Patterns and Variations.* 4th ed. Upper Saddle River, NJ: Prentice Hall.

Miner, Horace. 1956. "Body Ritual Among the Nacirema." *American Anthropologist* 58(June):503–507.

Mingle, James R. 1987. *Focus on Minorities.* Denver: Education Commission of the States and the State Higher Education Executive Officers.

Mitchell, William J. 1996. *City of Bits.* Cambridge, MA: MIT Press.

———. 1999. *E-topia.* Cambridge, MA: MIT Press.

Mitofsky, Warren J. 1998. "The Polls-Review. Was 1996 a Worse Year for Polls than 1948?" *Public Opinion Quarterly* 62(Summer):230–249.

Mizrahi, Terry. 1986. *Getting Rid of Patients.* New Brunswick, NJ: Rutgers University Press.

Moffatt, Susan. 1995. "Minorities Found More Likely to Live Near Toxic Sites." *Los Angeles Times,* August 30, pp. B1, B3.

Mogelonsky, Marcia. 1996. "The Rocky Road to Adulthood." *American Demographics* 18(May):26–29, 32–35, 56.

Mollen, Milton. 1992. *"A Failure of Responsibility": Report to Mayor David N. Dinkins on the December 28, 1991, Tragedy at City College of New York.* New York: Office of the Deputy Mayor for Public Safety.

Monaghan, Peter. 1993. "Sociologist Jailed Because He 'Wouldn't Snitch' Ponders the Way Research Ought to

Be Done." *Chronicle of Higher Education* 40(September 1):A8, A9.

Money. 1987. "A Short History of Shortages." 16(Fall, special issue):42.

Monmaney, Terence. 1995. "Ethnicities' Medical Views Vary, Study Says." *Los Angeles Times,* September 13, pp. B1, B3.

Monteiro, Lois A. 1998. "Ill-Defined Illnesses and Medically Unexplained Symptoms Syndrome." *Footnotes* 26(February):3, 6.

Montgomery, Marilyn J., and Gwendolyn T. Sorrell. 1997. "Differences in Love Attitudes Across Family Life Stages." *Family Relations* 46:55–61.

Moore, David A. 1995. "Public Sense of Urgency about Environment Wanes." *Gallup Poll Monthly* (April), pp. 17–20.

———. 1999. "Americans Oppose General Legalization of Marijuana." Poll Released April 9. Accessible online (http://www.gallup.com/poll/releases/pr990409b.asp).

Moore, Kristin A. 1995. *Report to Congress on Out-of-Wedlock Childbearing.* Washington, DC: Child Trends.

Moore, Thomas S. 1996. *The Disposable Work Force: Worker Displacement and Employment Instability in America.* New York: Aldine de Gruyter.

Moore, Wilbert E. 1967. *Order and Change: Essays in Comparative Sociology.* New York: Wiley.

———. 1968. "Occupational Socialization." Pp. 861–883 in *Handbook of Socialization Theory and Research,* edited by David A. Goslin. Chicago: Rand McNally.

Morehouse Medical Treatment and Effectiveness Center. 1999. *A Synthesis of the Literature: Racial and Ethnic Differences in Acccess to Medical Care.* Menlo Park, CA: Henry J. Kaiser Family Foundation.

Morehouse Research Institute and Institute for American Values. 1999. *Turning the Corner on Father Absence in Black America.* Atlanta: Morehouse Research Institute and Institute for American Values.

Morello, Carol. 1997. "Opponents Chip Away at Prop. 209." *USA Today,* November 17, pp. A1–A2.

Morin, Richard. 1993. "Think Twice before You Say Another Word." *Washington Post National Weekly Edition* 10, January 3, p. 37.

———. 1997. "An Airwave of Crime." *Washington Post National Weekly Edition,* August 18, p 34.

———. 1999. "Not a Clue." *Washington Post National Weekly Edition* 16(June 14):34.

Morland, John, Jr. 1996. "The Individual, the Society, or Both? A Comparison of Black, Latino, and White Beliefs about the Causes of Poverty." *Social Forces* 75(December):403–422.

Morris, Bonnie Rothman. 1999. "You've Got Romance! Seeking Love on Line." *New York Times,* August 26, p. D1.

Morris, Charles. 1996. *The AARP: America's Most Powerful Lobby and the Clash of Generations.* New York: Times Books/ Random House.

Morrison, Denton E. 1971. "Some Notes toward Theory on Relative Deprivation, Social Movements, and Social Change." *American Behavioral Scientist* 14(May–June):675–690.

Morrow, David J. 1999. "A Movable Epidemic." *New York Times,* August 9, p. C1.

Morrow, John K. 1997. "Of Sheep Cloning and Cold Fusion." *Chicago Tribune,* March 7, p. 23.

Morse, Arthur D. 1967. *While Six Million Died: A Chronicle of American Apathy.* New York: Ace.

Mortimer, Jeylan E., and Roberta G. Simmons. 1978. "Adult Socialization." Pp. 421–454 in *Annual Review of Sociology, 1978,* edited by Ralph H. Turner, James Coleman, and Renee C. Fox. Palo Alto, CA: Annual Reviews.

Moseley, Roy. 1999. "Dutch Euthanasia Plan Lets Kids Make Choice." *Chicago Tribune,* August 26, p. 1, 22.

Moser, Nancy. 1998. "Wishing for Maybes." Pp. 158–164 in *Generation to Generation: Reflections on Friendships Between Young and Old,* edited by Sandra Martz and Shirley Coe. Watsonville, CA: Papier-Mache Press.

Moskos, Charles C., Jr. 1991. "How Do They Do It?" *New Republic* 205(August 5):20.

Mosley, J., and E. Thomson. 1995. Pp. 148–165 in *Fatherhood: Contemporary Theory, Research and Social Policy,* edited by W. Marsiglo. Thousand Oaks, CA: Sage.

MOST. 1999. MOST Quarterly. Internet vol. 1. Accessed July 19, 1999 (http://www.mostonline.org/qtrly/qtrly-index.htm).

Ms. Magazine. 1992. "Family Planning Policies: 1991's Winners and Losers." 2(March–April):10.

Mulcahy, Aogan. 1995. "'Headhunter' or Real Cop? Identity in the World of Internal Affairs Officers." *Journal of Contemporary Ethnography* 24(April):99–130.

Murdock, George P. 1945. "The Common Denominator of Cultures." Pp. 123–142 in *The Science of Man in the World Crisis,* edited by Ralph Linton. New York: Columbia University Press.

———. 1949. *Social Structure.* New York: Macmillan.

———. 1957. "World Ethnographic Sample." *American Anthropologist* 59(August): 664–687.

Murphy, Caryle. 1993. "Putting Aside the Veil." *Washington Post National Weekly Edition* 10, April 12–18, pp. 10–11.

Murphy, Dean E. 1997. "A Victim of Sweden's Pursuit of Perfection." *Los Angeles Times,* September 2, pp. A1, A8.

N

Nader, Laura. 1986. "The Subordination of Women in Comparative Perspective." *Urban Anthropology* 15(Fall–Winter):377–397.

Nagel, Joanne. 1996. *American Indian Ethnic Renewal: Red Power and the Resurgence of Identity and Culture.* New York: Oxford University Press.

Naifeh, Mary. 1998. "Trap Door? Revolving Door? Or Both? Dynamics of Economic Well-Being, Poverty 1993–94." *Current Population Reports,* ser. P-70, no. 63. Washington, DC: U.S. Government Printing Office.

Nakao, Keiko, Robert W. Hodge, and Judith Treas. 1990. *On Revising Prestige Scores for All Occupations.* Chicago: NORC.

——— and Judith Treas. 1990. *Computing 1989 Occupational Prestige Scores.* Chicago: NORC.

——— and ———. 1994. "Updating Occupational Prestige and Socioeconomic Scores: How the New

Measures Measure Up." Pp. 1–72 in *Sociological Methodology, 1994,* edited by Peter V. Marsden. Oxford: Basil Blackwell.

Nash, Manning. 1962. "Race and the Ideology of Race." *Current Anthropology* 3(June):285–288.

National Abortion and Reproductive Rights Action League. 1999. "House Passes HR2436, The So-Called 'Unborn Victims of Violence Act.'" Accessed October 9, 1999 (http://www.naral.org/publications/press/99sep/093099b.htm).

———. 1999b. "NARAL Factsheets: Public Funding for Abortion." Accessed October 9, 1999 (http://www.naral.org/publications/facts/1999/public_funding.html).

National Advisory Commission on Criminal Justice. 1976. *Organized Crime.* Washington, DC: U.S. Government Printing Office.

National Alliance for Caregiving. 1997. *The NAC Comparative Analysis of Caregiver Data for Caregivers to the Elderly, 1987 and 1997.* Bethesda, MD: National Alliance for Caregiving.

National Alliance for the Mentally Ill. 2000. "What Is Mental Illness?" Accessed January 18, 2000 (http://www.nami.org/disorder/whatis.html).

National Center for Educational Statistics. 1997. "Digest of Education Statistics 1997." Washington, DC: U.S. Government Printing Office. Accessed September 29, 1999 (http://nces.ed.gov/pubs).

———. 1998. *Students' Report of School Crime: 1989 and 1995.* Washington, DC: U.S. Government Printing Office.

———. 1999. *Digest of Education Statistics, 1998.* Washington, DC: U.S. Government Printing Office.

National Center for Health Statistics. 1974. *Summary Report: Final Divorce Statistics, 1974.* Washington, DC: U.S. Government Printing Office.

———. 1990. *Annual Survey of Births, Marriages, Divorces, and Deaths: United States, 1989.* Washington, DC: U.S. Government Printing Office.

———. 1997a. *U.S. Deceased Life Tables for 1989–91.* Washington, DC: U.S. Government Printing Office.

———. 1997b. "Births and Deaths: United States, 1996." *Monthly Vital Statistics Report* 46(September 11).

———. 1998. "Births, Marriages, Divorces, and Deaths: Provisional Data for July 1998." *Monthly Vital Statistics Report* 47(November 27):1–2.

———. 1998. "Expectation of Life at Single Years of Age, by Race and Sex." *National Vital Statistics Report* 47(December 24):10.

———. 1999. "Infant, Neonatal, and Postnatal Mortality Rates by Race and Sex." *National Vital Statistics Report* 47(June 30):86–87.

———. 2000. "Births, Marriages, Divorces, and Deaths: Provisional Data for January 1999." *Monthly Vital Statistics Reports* 48(January 25):1–2.

National Center on Elder Abuse. 1998. *The National Elder Abuse Incidence Study.* Washington, DC: American Public Human Services Association.

National Center on Women and Family Law. 1996. *Status of Marital Rape Exemption Statutes in the United States.* New York: National Center on Women and Family Law.

National Conference of State Legislatures. 2000. *Limits on Contributions to Candidates.* Washington, DC: NCSL.

National Gay and Lesbian Task Force. 1999. *Hate Crime Laws in the United States.* Accessed September 7, 2000 (http://www.ngltf.org).

National Homeschool Association. 1999. *Homeschooling Families: Ready for the Next Decade.* Accessed November 19, 2000 (http://www.n-h-a.org/decade.htm).

National Institute of Mental Health. 1999. *The Numbers Count: Mental Illness in America.* Washington, DC: U.S. Government Printing Office.

National Institute on Aging. 1999a. *Early Retirement in the United States.* Washington, DC: U.S. Government Printing Office.

———. 1999b. *The Declining Disability of Older Americans.* Washington, DC: U.S. Government Printing Office.

National Law Center on Homelessness and Poverty. 1996. *Mean Sweeps: A Report on Anti-Homeless Laws, Litigation, and Alternatives in 50 United States Cities.* Washington, DC: National Law Center on Homelessness and Poverty.

National Organization for Men Against Sexism (NOMAS). 1999. "Statement of Principles." Accessed October 11, 1999 (http://www.nomas.org/statemt_of_prin-ciples.htm).

National Partnership for Women and Families. 1998. *Balancing Acts: Work/Family Issues on Prime-Time TV. Executive Summary.* Washington, DC: The National Partnership for Women and Families.

National Telecommunications Information Administration. 1999. *Falling through the Net: Defining the Digital Divide.* Washington, DC: U.S. Government Printing Office.

Navarro, Mineya. 1998. "Group Forced Illegal Aliens into Prostitution, U.S. Says." *New York Times,* April 24, p. A10.

Navarro, Vicente. 1984. "Medical History as Justification Rather Than Explanation: A Critique of Starr's *The Social Transformation of American Medicine.*" *International Journal of Health Services* 14(4):511–528.

Neary, Tom. 1997. "Burakumin in Contemporary Japan." Pp. 50–78 in *Japan's Minorities: The Illusion of Homogeneity,* edited by Michael Weiner. London: Routledge.

Negushi, Mayumi. 1998. "A Matter of Life and Death." *Japan Times Weekly* 38(October 26):10–11.

Nelson, Jack. 1995. "The Internet, the Virtual Community, and Those with Disabilities." *Disability Studies Quarterly* 15(Spring):15–20.

Nelson, Mariah Burton. 1994. *The Stronger Women Get, the More Men Love Football.* New York: Avon.

Neuborne, Ellen. 1996. "Vigilantes Stir Firms' Ire with Cyber-antics." *USA Today,* February 28, pp. A1, A2.

Newman, Katherine S. 1999. *No Shame in My Game: The Working Poor in the Inner City.* New York: Alfred A. Knopf and Russell Sage Foundation.

Newman, William M. 1973. *American Pluralism: A Study of Minority Groups and Social Theory.* New York: Harper and Row.

Newport, Frank. 2000. "Americans Remain Very Religious, But Not Necessarily in Conventional Ways." *Emerging Trends* 22(January):2–3.

Newsbytes News Network. 1997a. "Groups Want Intervention in CompuServe/Gernig Case." March 25. Accessed October 8, 1998 (http://www.elibrary.com/getdoc.cg1?id=

113_ydocid=1183038@library_d&dty pe=O~o&dinst=).

Newsday. 1997. "Japan Sterilized 16,000 Women." September 18, p. A19.

New York Times. 1992. "Californians Confront Wave of Earthquake Rumors." July 20, p. A8.

———. 1993a. "Child Care in Europe: Admirable but Not Perfect, Experts Say." February 15, p. A13.

———. 1993b. "Dutch May Broaden Euthanasia Guidelines." February 17, p. A3.

———. 1995b. "Reverse Discrimination of Whites Is Rare, Labor Study Reports." March 31, p. A23.

———. 1997. "Slave Trade in Africa Highlighted by Arrests." August 10, p. 5.

———. 1998. "2 Gay Men Fight Town Hall for a Family Pool Pass Discount." July 14, p. B2.

———. 1999a. "Woman Strikes Deal to Quit Redwood Home." (December 19), p. 33.

———. 1999b. "Cult in Gas Attack Apologizes, But the Japanese Are Skeptical," (December 2), p. A8.

NHTSA (National Highway Traffic Safety Administration). 1996. *Fatal Accident Reporting System.* Washington, DC: NHTSA.

———. 1997. *Fatal Accident Reporting System.* Washington, DC: NHTSA.

Nie, Norman H. 1999. "Tracking Our Techno-Future." *American Demographics* (July):50–52.

——— and Lutz Eybring. 2000. "Study of the Social Consequences of the Internet." Accessible online (http://www.stanford.edu/group/sigss/). Palo Alto, CA: Stanford Institute for the Quantitative Study of Society.

Nielsen, François. 1994. "Sociobiology and Sociology." Pp. 267–303 in *Annual Review of Sociology, 1994,* edited by John Hagan. Palo Alto, CA: Annual Reviews., pp. 267–303.

NIHCD. 1999a. "Higher Quality Care Related to Less Problem Behavior." Accessed July 28, 1999 (http://www.nih.gov/nichd/docs/news/DAYCAR99.htm).

———. 1999b. "Child Outcomes When Child Care Center Classes Meet Recommended Standards for Quality." *American Journal of Public Health* 89(July):1072–1077.

Nixon, Howard L., II. 1979. *The Small Group.* Englewood Cliffs, NJ: Prentice-Hall.

Noble, Holcomb B. 1998. "Struggling to Bolster Minorities in Medicine." *New York Times,* September 29.

Nock, Steven L., James D. Wright, and Laura Sanchez. 1999. "America's Divorce Problem." *Society* 36(May/June):43–52.

Nolan, Patrick and Gerhad Lenski. 1999. *Human Societies: An Introduction to Macrosociology.* New York: McGraw-Hill.

Noll, Roger G., and Andrew Zimbalist. 1997. *Sports, Jobs and Taxes: The Economic Impact of Sports Teams and Stadiums.* Washington, DC: The Brookings Institution.

NORC (National Opinion Research Center). 1994. *General Social Surveys 1972–1994.* Chicago: National Opinion Research Center.

Norman, Jim. 1996. "At Least 1 Pollster Was Right on Target." *USA Today,* November 7, p. 8A.

North Carolina Abecedarian Project. 2000. *Early Learning, Later Success: The Abecedarian Study.* Chapel Hill, NC: Frank Porter Graham Child Development Center.

Novak, Tim, and Jon Schmid. 1999. "Lottery Picks Split by Race, Income." *Chicago Sun-Times,* June 22, pp. 1, 24, 25.

Novick, Peter. 1999. *The Holocaust in American Life.* Boston: Houghton Mifflin.

Nussbaum, Daniel. 1998. "Bad Air Days." *Los Angeles Times Magazine*, July 19, pp. 20–21.

O

Oakes, Jeannie. 1985. *Keeping Track: How Schools Structure Inequality.* New Haven, CT: Yale University Press.

Obermiller, Tim Andrew. 1994. "Sex by the Numbers." *University of Chicago Magazine* 87(October):34–37.

Oberschall, Anthony. 1973. *Social Conflict and Social Movements.* Englewood Cliffs, NJ: Prentice-Hall.

O'Donnell, Mike. 1992. *A New Introduction to Sociology.* Walton-on-Thames, United Kingdom: Thomas Nelson and Sons.

O'Donnell, Rosie. 1998. Statement at the National Partnership for Women and Families Annual Luncheon, June 10.

OECD. 1995. *Trends in International Migration: Continuing Reporting System on Migration, Annual Report 1994.* Paris: OECD.

———. 1998. "Annual National Accounts: Gross Domestic Product." Accessed April 21, 1998 (http://www.oecd.olrg/std/gdp.htm).

Office of Justice Programs. 1999. "Transnational Organized Crime." *NCJRS Catalog* 49(November/December):21.

Office of the Federal Register. 1997. *United States Government Manual, 1997–1998.* Washington, DC: U.S. Government Printing Office.

Ogburn, William F. 1922. *Social Change with Respect to Culture and Original Nature.* New York: Huebsch (reprinted 1966, New York: Dell).

——— and Clark Tibbits. 1934. "The Family and Its Functions." Pp. 661–708 in *Recent Social Trends in the United States,* edited by Research Committee on Social Trends. New York: McGraw-Hill.

O'Hare, William P., and Brenda Curry-White. 1992. "Is There a Rural Underclass?" *Population Today* 20(March):6–8.

O'Hearn, Claudine Chiawei, ed. 1998. *Half and Half: Writers on Growing Up Biracial and Bicultural.* New York: Pantheon Books.

Okano, Kaori, and Motonori Tsuchiya. 1999. *Education in Contemporary Japan: Inequality and Diversity.* Cambridge: Cambridge University Press.

Oliver, Melvin L., and Thomas M. Shapiro. 1995. *Black Wealth/White Wealth: New Perspectives on Racial Inequality.* New York: Routledge.

Omran, Abdel R., and Farzaneh Roudi. 1993. "The Middle East's Population Puzzle." *Population Bulletin* 48(July).

O'Rand, Angele M. 1996. "The Precious and the Precocious: Understanding Cumulative Disadvantage and Cumulative Advantage Over the Life Course." *The Gerontologist* 36(No. 2):230–258.

Orum, Anthony M. 1989. *Introduction to Political Sociology: The Social Anatomy of the Body Politic.* 3d ed. Englewood Cliffs, NJ: Prentice-Hall.

Orwell, George. 1949. *1984.* New York: Harcourt Brace Jovanovich.

OSHA (Occupational Safety and Health Administration). 1999. "One Size Doesn't Fit All Approach." National News Release: USDL 99–333. Washington, DC: U.S. Department of Labor.

Ostling, Richard N. 1993. "Religion." *Time International,* July 12, p. 38.

Ouellette, Laurie. 1993. "The Information Lockout." *Utne Reader,* September–October, pp. 25–26.

P

Paddock, Richard C. 1999. "Republic Stirs Debate by Allowing for Multiple Wives." *Los Angeles Times,* August 15, pp. A27–A28.

Pagani, Steve. 1999. "End the 'Culture of Death,' Pope Tells America." Reuters Wire Service, January 23.

Page, Charles H. 1946. "Bureaucracy's Other Face." *Social Forces* 25 (October):89–94.

Palen, J. John. 1995. "The Suburban Revolution: An Introduction." *Sociological Focus* 28(October):347–351.

Pamuk, E., D. Makui, K. Heck, C. Rueben, and K. Lochren. 1998. *Health, United States 1998 with Socioeconomic Status and Health Chartbook.* Hyattsville, MD: National Center for Health Statistics.

Pappas, Gregory et al. [4 authors]. 1993. "The Increasing Disparity in Mortality between Socioeconomic Groups in the United States, 1960 and 1986." *New England Journal of Medicine* 329(July 8):103–109.

Park, Robert E. 1916. "The City: Suggestions for the Investigation of Human Behavior in the Urban Environment." *American Journal of Sociology* 20(March):577–612.

———. 1936. "Succession, an Ecological Concept." *American Sociological Review* 1(April):171–179.

Parker, Suzi. 1998. "Wedding Boom: More Rings, Tuxes, Bells, and Brides." *Christian Science Monitor,* July 20, pp. 1, 14.

Parsons, Talcott. 1951. *The Social System.* New York: Free Press.

———. 1966. *Societies: Evolutionary and Comparative Perspectives.* Englewood Cliffs, NJ: Prentice-Hall.

———. 1972. "Definitions of Health and Illness in the Light of American Values

and Social Structure." Pp. 166–187 in *Patients, Physicians and Illness,* edited by Gartley Jaco. New York: Free Press.

———. 1975. "The Sick Role and the Role of the Physician Reconsidered." *Milbank Medical Fund Quarterly, Health and Society* 53(Summer):257–278.

——— and Robert Bales. 1955. *Family, Socialization, and Interaction Process.* Glencoe, IL: Free Press.

Pasternak, Judy. 1998. "'Edge City' Is Attempting to Build a Center." *Los Angeles Times,* January 1, p. A5.

Pate, Antony M., and Edwin E. Hamilton. 1992. ("Formal and Informal Deterrents to Domestic Violence: The Dade County Spouse Assault Experiment." *American Sociological Reviews* 57(October):691–697.

Patterson, Orlando. 1998. "Affirmative Action." *Brookings Review* 16(Spring): 17–23.

Patton, Carl V., ed. 1988. *Spontaneous Shelter: International Perspectives and Prospects.* Philadelphia: Temple University Press.

Paul, Angus. 1987. "Why Does Terrorism Subside? Researchers Offer Preliminary Theories," *Chronicle of Higher Education,* 34 (September 23):A10.

Pavalko, Ronald M., ed. 1972. *Sociological Perspectives on Occupations.* Itasca, IL: F. E. Peacock.

———. 1988. *Sociology of Occupations and Professions.* 2d ed. Itasca, IL: F. E. Peacock.

Payer, Lynn. 1988. *Medicine and Culture: Varieties of Treatment in the United States, England, West Germany, and France.* New York: Holt.

Pear, Robert. 1983. "$1.5 Billion Urged for U.S. Japanese Held in War." *New York Times,* June 17, pp. A1, D16.

———. 1996. "Clinton Endorses the Most Radical of Welfare Trials." *New York Times,* May 19, pp. 1, 20.

———. 1997a. "New Estimate Doubles Rate of H.I.V. Spread." *New York Times,* November 26, p. A6.

———. 1997b. "Now, the Archenemies Need Each Other." *New York Times,* June 22, sec. 4, pp. 1, 4.

———. 1999. "House Rejects Doctor-Assisted Deaths." *Chicago Tribune,* October 23, p. 4.

Pelton, Tom. 1994. "Hawthorne Works' Glory Now Just So Much Rubble." *Chicago Tribune,* April 18, pp. 1, 6.

Perkins, Craig, and Patsy Klaus. 1996. *Criminal Victimization 1994.* Washington, DC: U.S. Government Printing Office.

Perlez, Jane. 1996. "Central Europe Learns about Sex Harassment." *New York Times,* October 3, p. A3.

Perrow, Charles. 1999. *Normal Accidents: Living with High Risk Technologies.* Updated edition. New Brunswick, NJ: Rutgers University Press.

———. 1986. *Complex Organizations.* 3d ed. New York: Random House.

Perruci, Robert. 1974. *Circle of Madness: On Being Sane and Institutionalized in America.* Englewood Cliffs, NJ: Prentice-Hall.

Perry, Suzanne. 1998a. "Human Rights Abuses Get Internet Spotlight." Reuters, February 4.

———. 1998b. "U.S. Data Companies Oppose Primary Laws." Reuters, March 19.

Pescovitz, David. 1999. "Sons and Daughters of HAL Go on Line." *New York Times,* March 18, pp. D1, D8.

Pestello, Frances, Stanley Saxton, Dan E. Miller, and Patrick G. Donnelly. 1996. "Community and the Practice of Sociology." *Teaching Sociology* 24(April):148–156.

Peter, Laurence J., and Raymond Hull. 1969. *The Peter Principle.* New York: Morrow.

Petersen, William. 1979. *Malthus.* Cambridge, MA: Harvard University Press.

Peterson, Deb. 1996. "Kinship Support Differences between African Americans and Whites: Results from an Analysis." Paper presented at the annual meeting of the Midwest Sociological Society, Chicago.

Peterson, Paul E., Jay P. Greene, and William Howell. 1998. *New Findings from the Cleveland Scholarship Program: A Reanalysis of Data from the Indiana University School of Education Evaluation.* Cambridge, MA: Harvard University, Program on Education Policy and Governance.

Phelan, Michael P., and Scott A. Hunt. 1998. "Prison Gang Members' Tattoos as Identity Work: The Visual Comments of Moral Careers." *Symbolic Interaction* 21(No. 3):277–298.

Phillips, E. Barbara. 1996. *City Lights: Urban–Suburban Life in the Global Society.* New York: Oxford University Press.

Piaget, Jean. 1954. *The Construction of Reality in the Child.* Translated by Margaret Cook. New York: Basic Books.

Pillemer, Karl, and David Finkelhor. 1988. "The Prevalence of Elder Abuse: A Random Sample Survey." *The Gerontologist* 28(February):51–57.

Pinderhughes, Dianne. 1987. *Race and Ethnicity in Chicago Politics: A Reexamination of Pluralist Theory.* Urbana: University of Illinois Press.

——. 1996. "The Impact of Race on Environmental Quality: An Empirical and Theoretical Discussion." *Sociological Perspectives* 39(Summer):231–248.

Pipher, Mary. 1994. *Reviving Ophelia: Saving the Selves of Adolescent Girls.* New York: Ballantine.

Plant, Richard. 1986. *The Pink Triangle: The Nazi War against Homosexuals.* New York: Henry Holt.

Platt, Kevin. 1999. "China vs. Mass Spiritual Thirst." *Los Angeles Times,* August 3, pp. 1, 10.

Platt, Steve. 1993. "Without Walls." *Statesman and Society* 6(April 2):5–7.

Plimmer, Martin. 1998. "This Demi-Paradise: Martin Plummer Finds Food in the Fast Lane Is Not to His Taste." *Independent* (London), January 3, p. 46.

Plomin, Robert. 1989. "Determinants of Behavior." *American Psychologist* 44(February):105–111.

Plotnick, Robert D., Eugene Smolensky, Eirik Evenhouse, and Siobhan Reilly. 1998. "Identity and Poverty in the United States: The Twentieth Century Record." *Focus* 19(Summer–Fall):7–14.

Pogrebin, Letty Cottin. 1981. *Growing Up Free: Raising Your Child in the 80's.* New York: McGraw-Hill.

Pogrebin, Robin. 1996. "Hard-Core Threat to Health: Moshing at Rock Concerts." *New York Times,* May 9, pp. B1, B9.

Polk, Barbara Bovee. 1974. "Male Power and the Women's Movement." *Journal of Applied Behavioral Sciences* 10(July):415–431.

Pollack, Andrew. 1996. "It's See No Evil, Have No Harassment in Japan." *New York Times,* May 7, pp. D1, D6.

Pollack, William. 1998. *Real Boys: Rescuing Our Sons from the Myths of Boyhood.* New York: Henry Holt.

Pollard, Kelvin M. 1994. "Population Stabilization No Longer in Sight for U.S." *Population Today* 22(May):1–2.

—— and William P. O'Hare. 1999. "America's Racial and Ethnic Minorities." *Population Bulletin* 54(September).

Ponczek, Ed. 1998. "Are Hiring Practices Sensitive to Persons with Disabilities?" *Footnotes* 26(No. 3):5.

Poole, Teresa. 1998. "Population: China: Draconian Family Planning Has Desired Effect." *The Independent* (London), January 12, p. 11.

Popenoe, David, and Barbara Dafoe Whitehead. 1999. *Should We Live Together? What Young Adults Need to Know About Cohabitation Before Marriage.* Rutgers, NJ: The National Marriage Project.

Population Reference Bureau. 1978. "World Population: Growth on the Decline." *Interchange* 7(May):1–3.

——. 2000. "More Youths Take Alternative Route to Finish High School." *Population Today* 28(January):7.

Porter, Rosalie Pedalino. 1997. "The Politics of Bilingual Education." *Society* 34(No. 6):31–40.

Power, Carla. 1998. "The New Islam." *Newsweek* 131(March 16):34–37.

Power, Richard. 1999. "1999 CSI/FBI Computer Curve and Security Survey." *Computer Security Issues and Trends* 5(Winter):1–15.

Powers, Mary G., and Joan J. Holmberg. 1978. "Occupational Status Scores: Changes Introduced by the Inclusion of Women." *Demography* 15(May):183–204.

Prehn, John W. 1991. "Migration." Pp. 190–191 in *Encyclopedia of Sociology,* 4th ed. Guilford, CT: Dushkin.

Preston, Julia. 1998. "Both Carrot and Stick Fail in Chuapas." *New York Times,* May 17, p. 6.

Prince, Raymond. 1985. "The Concept of Culture-Bound Syndromes: Anorexia Nervosa and Brain-Fog." *Social Science and Medicine* 21(2):197–203.

Princeton Religious Research Center. 1998. "U.S. Far Less Protestant Than Half-Century Ago." *Emerging Trends* 20:1.

Pritchard, Peter. 1987. *The Making of McPaper: The Inside Story of USA Today.* Kansas City, MO: Andrews, McMeel and Parker.

Public Interest Research Groups. 1999. *Running for the Money: An Analysis of the 2000 Presidential Wealth Primary.* Boston, MA: PIRG.

Pula, James S. 1995. *Polish Americans: An Ethnic Community.* New York: Twayne.

Purnick, Joyce. 1996. "G.O.P. Quest to Narrow Gender Gap." *New York Times,* November 14, p. B1.

Pyle, Amy. 1998. "Opinions Vary on Studies That Back Bilingual Classes." *Los Angeles Times,* March 2, pp. B1, B3.

Q

Quadagno, Jill. 1999. *Aging and the Life Course: An Introduction to Social Gerontology.* New York: McGraw-Hill.

Quarantelli, Enrico L. 1957. "The Behavior of Panic Participants." *Sociology and Social Research* 41(January):187–194.

——. 1992. "Disaster Research." Pp. 492–498 in *Encyclopedia of Sociology,* vol. 2, edited by Edgar F. Borgatta and Marie L. Borgatta. New York: Macmillan.

—— and Russell R. Dynes. 1970. "Property Norms and Looting: Their Patterns in Community Crises." *Phylon* 31(Summer):168–182.

—— and James R. Hundley, Jr. 1975. "A Test of Some Propositions about Crowd Formation and Behavior." Pp. 538–554 in *Readings in Collective Behavior,* edited by Robert R. Evans. Chicago: Rand McNally.

Quinney, Richard. 1970. *The Social Reality of Crime.* Boston: Little, Brown.

——. 1974. *Criminal Justice in America.* Boston: Little, Brown.

——. 1979. *Criminology.* 2d ed. Boston: Little, Brown.

——. 1980. *Class, State and Crime.* 2d ed. New York: Longman.

R

Radosh, Mary Flannery. 1984. "The Collapse of Midwifery: A Sociological Study of the Decline of a Profession." Southern Illinois University, Carbondale. Unpublished Ph.D. dissertation.

Radosh, Polly F. 1986. "Midwives in the United States: Past and Present." *Population Research and Policy Review* 5:129–145.

Ramet, Sabrina. 1991. *Social Currents in Eastern Europe: The Source and Meaning of the Great Transformation.* Durham, NC: Duke University Press.

Raybon, Patricia. 1989. "A Case for 'Severe Bias.'" *Newsweek* 114(October 2):11.

Read, Jen'nan Ghazal, and John P. Bartkowski. 1999. "To Veil or Not to Veil? A Case Study of Identity Negotiation Among Muslim Women in Austin, Texas." Presented at the annual meeting of the American Sociological Association, August, Chicago.

Reddick, Randy, and Elliot King. 2000. *The Online Student: Making the Grade on the Internet.* Fort Worth: Harcourt Brace.

Reese, William A., II, and Michael A. Katovich. 1989. "Untimely Acts: Extending the Interactionist Conception of Deviance." *Sociological Quarterly* 30(2):159–184.

Reiman, Jeffrey H. 1984. *The Rich Get Richer and the Poor Get Prison.* 2d ed. New York: Wiley.

Reinharz, Shulamit. 1992. *Feminist Methods in Social Research.* New York: Oxford University Press.

Reiss, Ira L. 1995. "Is This the Definitive Sexual Survey?" *Journal of Sex Research* 22(1):77–85.

Religion Today.com. 2000. "Promise Keepers Takes Its Message to Latin America." Accessed February 11, 2000 (http://www.religiontoday.com/Archive/FeatureStory/view.cgi?File=20000113.s1.html).

Religion Watch. 1991. "Current Research: New Findings in Religious Attitudes and Behavior." 6(September):5.

———. 1995. "European Dissenting Movement Grows among Laity Theologians." 10(October):6–7.

Remnick, David. 1998. *King of the World.* New York: Random House.

Rennison, Callie Marie. 1999. "Criminal Victimization 1998. Changes 1997–98 with Trends 1993–98." *Bureau of Justice Statistics National Crime Victimization Survey* (July).

Rensberger, Boyce. 1994. "Damping the World's Population." *Washington Post National Weekly Edition* 12(September 18):10–11.

Reskin, Barbara, and Irene Padavic. 1994. *Women and Men at Work.* Thousand Oaks, CA: Pine Forge Press.

Retsinas, Joan. 1988. "A Theoretical Reassessment of the Applicability of Kübler-Ross's Stages of Dying." *Death Studies* 12:207–216.

Reuters. 1995. "New Chinese Law Prohibits Sex-Screening of Fetuses." *New York Times,* November 15.

Rheingold, Harriet L. 1969. "The Social and Socializing Infant." Pp. 779–790 in *Handbook of Socialization Theory and Research,* edited by David A. Goslin. Chicago: Rand McNally.

Richardson, James T. 1993. "Definitions of the Cult: From Sociological-Technical to Popular-Negative." *Review of Religious Research* 34(June).

——— and Barend van Driel. 1997. "Journalists' Attitudes Toward New Religious Movements." *Review of Religious Research* 39(December):116–136.

Richburg, Keith B. 1985. "Learning What Japan Has to Teach." *Washington Post National Weekly Edition* 3, November 4, p. 9.

Richey, Warren. 1998. "Counting the People: Court to Settle Dispute." *Christian Science Monitor,* November 30, p. 2.

Richman, Joseph. 1992. "A Rational Approach to Rational Suicide." *Suicide and Life-Threatening Behavior* 22(Spring):130–141.

Rideout, Victoria J., Ulla G. Foehr, Donald F. Roberts, and Mollyann Brodie. 1999. *Kids & Media @ the New Millennium.* New York: Kaiser Family Foundation.

Ridgeway, Cecilia L. 1987. "Nonverbal Behavior, Dominance, and the Basis of Status in Task Groups." *American Sociological Review* 52(October):683–694.

Ridgeway, James, and Jeffrey St. Clair. 1995. "Where the Buffalo Roam." *Village Voice* 40, July 11, p. 14.

Riding, Alan. 1993. "Women Seize Focus at Rights Forum," *New York Times* (June 16), p. A3.

———. 1998. "Why 'Titanic' Conquered the World." *New York Times,* April 26, sec. 2, pp. 1, 28, 29.

Ries, Lynn M. 1992. "Social Mobility." Pp. 1872–1880 in *Encyclopedia of Sociology,* vol. 4, edited by Edgar F. Borgatta and Marie L. Borgatta. New York: Macmillan.

Rifkin, Jeremy. 1995a. *The End of Work: The Decline of the Global Labor Force and the Dawn of the Post-Market Era.* New York: Tarcher/Putnam.

———. 1995b. "Afterwork." *Utne Reader* (May–June):52–62.

———. 1996. "Civil Society in the Information Age." *The Nation* 262(February 26):11–12, 14–16.

———. 1998. *The Biotech Century: Harnessing the Gene and Remaking the World.* New York: Tarcher/Putnam.

Riley, John W., Jr. 1992. "Death and Dying." Pp. 413–418 in *Encyclopedia of Sociology,* vol. 1, edited by Edgar F. Borgatta and Marie L. Borgatta. New York: Macmillan.

Riley, Matilda White, Robert L. Kahn, and Anne Foner. 1994a. *Age and Structural Lag.* New York: Wiley Inter-Science.

——— and ———, in association with Karin A. Mock. 1994b. "Introduction: The Mismatch between People and Structures." Pp. 1–36 in *Age and Structural Lag,* edited by Matilda White Riley, Robert L. Kahn, and Ann Foner. New York: Wiley Inter-Science.

Riley, Nancy E. 1996. "China's 'Missing Girls:' Prospects and Policy." *Population Today* (February):pp. 4–5.

Rimer, Sara. 1998. "As Centenarians Thrive, 'Old' Is Redefined." *New York Times,* June 22, pp. A1, A14.

Ringel, Cheryl. 1997. *Criminal Victimization 1996.* Washington, DC: U.S. Government Printing Office.

Ritzer, George. 1977. *Working: Conflict and Change.* 2d ed. Englewood Cliffs, NJ: Prentice-Hall.

———. 1995a. *Modern Sociological Theory.* 4th ed. New York: McGraw-Hill.

———. 1995b. *The McDonaldization of Society.* Rev. ed. Thousand Oaks, CA: Pine Forge Books.

———. 1996. *The McDonaldization of Society.* Rev. ed. Thousand Oaks, CA: Pine Forge Press.

———. 1998. *The McDonaldization Thesis: Explorations of Extensions.* Thousand Oaks, CA: Sage Publications.

———. 2000. *The McDonaldization of Society.* New Century Edition. Thousand Oaks, CA: Pine Forge Press.

Roan, Shari. 1995. "Under Pressure, Isolation: Jury Stress Sparks Concerns." *Los Angeles Times,* September 22, pp. A1, A28.

Robberson, Tod. 1995. "The Mexican Miracle Unravels." *Washington Post National Weekly Edition,* January 6, p. 20.

Robbins, Catherine C. 1999. "A Zoo in Peril Stirs a Debate About Navajo Tradition." *New York Times,* March 28, p. 63.

Roberts, D. F. 1975. "The Dynamics of Racial Intermixture in the American Negro—Some Anthropological Considerations." *American Journal of Human Genetics* 7(December): 361–367.

———, Lisa Henriksen, Peter G. Christenson, and Marcy Kelly. 1999. "Substance Abuse in Popular Movies and Music." Accessible online (http://www.whitehousedrugpolicy. gov/news/press/042899.html). Washington, DC: Office of Juvenile Justice.

Roberts, Keith A. 1995. *Religion in Sociological Perspective.* 3d ed. Belmont, CA: Wadsworth.

Roberts, Sam. 1994. "Hispanic Population Now Outnumbers Blacks in Four Major Cities as Demographics Shift." *New York Times,* October 9, p. 34.

Robertson, Roland. 1988. "The Sociological Significance of Culture: Some General Considerations." *Theory, Culture, and Society* 5(February): 3–23.

Robey, Bryant, Shea O. Rutstein, and Leo Morris. 1993. "The Fertility Decline in Developing Countries." *Scientific American* 269(December):60–67.

Robinson, James D., and Thomas Skill. 1993. "The Invisible Generation: Portrayals of the Elderly on Television." University of Dayton. Unpublished paper.

Rocks, David. 1999. Urger Giant Does as Europeans Do." *Chicago Tribune,* January 6, sec. 3, pp. 1, 4.

Rodberg, Simon. 1999. "Woman and Men at Yale." *Culturefront Online.* Accessed September 9, 1999 (http://www. culturefront.org/culturefront/ magazine/99/spring/article.5.html).

Rodgers, Harrell R., Jr. 1987. *Poor Women, Poor Families.* Armonk, NY: Sharpe.

Roeper, Richard. 1999. *Urban Legends.* Franklin Lakes, NJ: Career Press.

Roethlisberger, Fritz J., and W. J. Dickson. 1939. *Management and the Worker.* Cambridge, MA: Harvard University Press.

Romero, Mary. 1988. "Chicanas Modernize Domestic Service." *Qualitative Sociology* 11:319–334.

Rosario, Ruben, and Tony Marcano. 1989. "A Killer Is Freed." *New York Daily News,* April 1, p. 2.

Rose, Arnold. 1951. *The Roots of Prejudice.* Paris: UNESCO.

Rose, Lowell C., and Alec M. Gallup. 1999. "The 31st Annual Phi Delta Kappa/Gallup Poll." Accessed November 23, 1999 (http://www.pdkintl.org/ kappan/kpol9909.htm).

Rose, Peter I., Myron Glazer, and Penina Migdal Glazer. 1979. "In Controlled Environments: Four Cases of Intense Resocialization." Pp. 320–338 in *Socialization and the Life Cycle,* edited by Peter I. Rose. New York: St. Martin's.

Rosenbaum, Lynn. 1996. "Gynocentric Feminism: An Affirmation of Women's Values and Experiences Leading Us toward Radical Social Change." *SSSP Newsletter* 27(1):4–7.

Rosenberg, Douglas H. 1991. "Capitalism." Pp. 33–34 in *Encyclopedic Dictionary of Sociology,* 4th ed., edited by Dushkin Publishing Group. Guilford, CT: Dushkin.

Rosenfeld, Michael. 1997. "Celebration, Politics, Looting and Riots: A Micro Level Analysis of the Bulls Riot of 1992 in Chicago." *Social Problems* 44:483–502.

Rosenthal, Elizabeth. 1998. "For One-Child Policy, China Rethinks Iron Hand." *New York Times*, November 1, pp. 1, 16.

———. 1999a. "Women's Suicides Reveal Rural China's Bitter Roots." *New York Times*, January 24, pp. A1, A8.

———. 1999b. "Web Sites Bloom in China, and Are Waded." *New York Times*, December 23, pp. A1, A10.

———. 2000. "China Lists Controls to Restrict the Use of E-Mail and Web." *New York Times*, January 27, pp. A1, A10.

Rosenthal, Robert, and Elisha Y. Babad. 1985. "Pygmalion in the Gymnasium." *Educational Leadership* 45(September):36–39.

——— and Lenore Jacobson. 1968. *Pygmalion in the Classroom.* New York: Holt.

Rosman, Abraham, and Paula G. Rubel. 1994. *The Tapestry of Culture: An Introduction to Cultural Anthropology.* 5th ed. Chapter 1, Map. P. 35. New York: McGraw-Hill.

Rosnow, Ralph L. 1991. "Inside Rumor: A Personal Journey." *American Psychologist* 46(May):484–496.

——— and Gary L. Fine. 1976. *Rumor and Gossip: The Social Psychology of Hearsay.* New York: Elsevier.

Ross, Andrew. 1999. *The Celebration Chronicles.* New York: Ballantine Books.

Ross, John. 1996. "To Die in the Street: Mexico City's Homeless Population

Booms as Economic Crisis Shakes Social Protections." *SSSP Newsletter* 27(Summer):14–15.

Rossi, Alice S. 1968. "Transition to Parenthood." *Journal of Marriage and the Family* 30(February):26–39.

———. 1984. "Gender and Parenthood." *American Sociological Review* 49(February):1–19.

Rossi, Peter H. 1987. "No Good Applied Social Research Goes Unpunished." *Society* 25(November–December): 73–79.

———. 1989. *Down and Out in America: The Origins of Homelessness.* Chicago: University of Chicago Press.

———. 1990. "The Politics of Homelessness." Presented at the annual meeting of the American Sociological Association, Washington, DC.

Rossides, Daniel W. 1997. *Social Stratification: The Interplay of Class, Race, and Gender.* 2d ed. Upper Saddle River, NJ: Prentice-Hall.

Roszak, Theodore. 1969. *The Making of a Counterculture.* Garden City, NY: Doubleday.

———. 1998. *America the Wise.* Boston: Houghton Mifflin.

Rotella, Sebastin. 1999. "A Latin View Of American-Style Violence." *Los Angeles Times* (November 25), p. A1.

Roth, Jeffrey A., and Christopher S. Koper. 1999a. "Impacts of the 1994 Assault-Weapons Ban: 1994–96." *National Institute of Justice Research in Brief* (March).

——— and ———. 1999b. *Impact Evaluation of the Public Safety and Recreational Firearms Use Protection Act of 1994.* Washington, DC: Urban Institute.

Rothman, David. 1971. *The Discovery of the Asylum.* Boston: Little, Brown.

Roudi, Farzaneh. 1999. "Iran's Revolutionary Approach to Family Planning." *Population Today* 27(July/August): 4–5.

Rourke, Mary. 1998. "Redefining Religion in America." *Los Angeles Times*, June 21, p. A1.

Rowell, Andy. 1996. "Global Warming: Wise Use Reinvents Itself as an International Environmental Movement." *Village Voice* 41, October 15, pp. 22, 24.

Roxane Laboratories. 2000. *Daily Dosing of Available Antiretroviral Agents.*

Roy, Donald F. 1959. "'Banana Time': Job Satisfaction and Informal

Interaction." *Human Organization* 18(Winter):158–168.

Rubin, Alissa J. 1998. "Where Are We Now?" *Los Angeles Times*, January 22, pp. E1, E4.

Russakoff, Dale. 1998. "In the Jungle of Kids' TV." *Washington Post National Weekly Edition* 16(December 21): 20–21.

Russell, Cheryl. 1995. "Murder is All-American." *American Demographics* 17(September):15–17.

Russo, Nancy Felipe. 1976. "The Motherhood Mandate." *Journal of Social Issues* 32:143–153.

Ryan, William. 1976. *Blaming the Victim.* Rev. ed. New York: Random House.

S

Saarinen, Thomas F. 1988. "Centering of Mental Maps of the World." *National Geographic Research* 4(Winter): 112–127.

Sabini, John. 1992. *Social Psychology.* New York: Norton.

Sadker, Myra Pollack, and David Sadker. 1985. "Sexism in the Schoolroom of the '80s." *Psychology Today* 19(March): 54–57.

———. 1995. *Failing at Fairness: How America's Schools Cheat Girls.* New York: Touchstone.

Safire, William. 1996. "Downsized." *New York Times Magazine,* May 26, pp. 12, 14.

Sagarin, Edward, and Jose Sanchez. 1988. "Ideology and Deviance: The Case of the Debate over the Biological Factor." *Deviant Behavior* 9(1): 87–99.

Saldaña, Lori. 1999. "Tijuana's Toxic Waters." *NACLA Report on the Americas* 33(November/December):30–35.

Sale, Kirkpatrick. 1993. "The U.S. Green Movement Today." *The Nation* 257(July 19):92–96.

———. 1996. *Rebels against the Future: The Luddites and Their War on the Industrial Revolution* (with a new preface by the author). Reading, MA: Addison-Wesley.

———. 1997. "Ban Cloning? Not a Chance." *New York Times*, March 7, p. A17.

Salem, Richard, and Stanislaus Grabarek. 1986. "Sociology B.A.s in a Corporate Setting: How Can They Get There and

of What Value Are They?" *Teaching Sociology* 14(October):273–275.

Salholz, Eloise. 1990. "Teenagers and Abortion." *Newsweek* 115(January 8): 32–33, 36.

Salinger, Adrienne. 1999. *Living Solo.* Kansas City, MO: Andrews McMeel.

Salins, Peter D. 1996. "How to Create a Real Housing Crisis." *New York Times*, October 26, p. 19.

Salkever, Alex. 1999. "Making Machines More Like Us." *Christian Science Monitor,* December 20, electronic edition.

Samuelson, Paul A., and William D. Nordhaus. 1998. *Economics.* 16th ed. New York: McGraw-Hill.

Samuelson, Robert J. 1996a. "Are Workers Disposable?" *Newsweek* 127, February 12, p. 47.

———. 1996b. "Fashionable Statements," *Washington Post National Weekly Edition* 13, March 18, p. 5.

Sandberg, Jared. 1999. "Spinning a Web of Hate." *Newsweek* 134(July 19): 28–29.

Sandnabba, N. Kenneth, and Christian Ahlberg. 1999. "Parents' Attitudes and Expectations About Children's Cross-Gender Behavior." *Sex Roles* 40(Nos. 3/4):249–263.

Sapir, Edward. 1929. "The Status of Linguistics as a Science." *Language* 5(4): 207–214.

Sappenfield, Mark. 1999. "School Equity Fight Gets 'Smarter.'" *Christian Science Monitor,* August 9, pp. 1, 10.

Sassen, Saskia. 1999. *Guests and Aliens.* New York: The New Press.

Saukko, Paula. 1999. "Fat Boys and Goody Girls." In *Weighty Issues: Fatness and Thinness as Social Problems,* edited by Jeffrey Sobal and Donna Maurer. New York: Aldine de Gruyter.

Sawyer, Tom. 2000. "Antiretrovira Drug Costs." Correspondence to author from Roxane Laboratories, Cincinnati, OH, January 19.

Sax, Linda J., A. W. Astin, W. S. Korn, and K. M. Mahoney. 1999. *The American Freshman: National Norms for Fall 1999.* Los Angeles: Higher Education Research Institute.

Scarce, Rik. 1994. "(No) Trial (But) Tribulations: When Courts and Ethnography Conflict." *Journal of Contemporary Ethnography* 23(July):123–149.

———. 1995. "Scholarly Ethics and Courtroom Antics: Where Researchers Stand in the Eyes of the Law." *American Sociologist* 26(Spring):87–112.

Scarr, Sandra. 1997. "New Research on Day Care Should Spur Scholars to Reconsider Old Ideas." *Chronicle of Higher Education* 43(August 8):A48.

Schaefer, Peter. 1995. "Destroy Your Future." *Daily Northwestern,* November 3, p. 8.

Schaefer, Richard T. 1997. "Placing the Los Angeles Riots in Their Social and Historical Context." *Journal of American Ethnic History,* forthcoming.

———. 1998a. "Differential Racial Mortality and the 1995 Chicago Heat Wave." Presentation at the annual meeting of the American Sociological Association, August, San Francisco.

———. 1998b. *Alumni Survey.* Chicago, IL: Department of Sociology, DePaul University.

———. 2000. *Racial and Ethnic Groups.* 8th ed. Upper Saddle River, NJ: Prentice-Hall.

Schaefer, Sandy. 1996. "Peaceful Play." Presentation at the annual meeting of the Chicago Association for the Education of Young Children, Chicago.

Schaller, Lyle E. 1990. "Megachurch!" *Christianity Today* 34(March 5):10, 20–24.

Scheer, Robert. 1998. "The Dark Side of the New World Order." *Los Angeles Times*, January 13, p. B7.

Scheff, Thomas J. 1999. *Being Mentally Ill: A Sociological Theory.* 3d ed. New York: Aldine de Gruyter.

Schellenberg, Kathryn, ed. 1996. *Computers in Society.* 6th ed. Guilford, CT: Dushkin.

Schiraldi, Vincent. 1999. "Juvenile Crime Is Decreasing—It's Media Coverage That's Soaring." *Los Angeles Times,* November 22, p. B7.

Schlenker, Barry R., ed. 1985. *The Self and Social Life.* New York: McGraw-Hill.

Schmetzer, Uli. 1999. "Modern India Remains Shackled to Caste System." *Chicago Tribune,* December 25, p. 23.

Schmid, Carol. 1980. "Sexual Antagonism: Roots of the Sex-Ordered Division of Labor." *Humanity and Society* 4(November):243–261.

Schmidt, William E. 1990. "New Vim and Vigor for the Y.M.C.A." *New York Times,* July 18, pp. C1, C10.

Schmitt, Eric. 1998. "Day-Care Quandary: A Nation at War with Itself." *New York Times*, January 11, sec. 4, pp. 1, 4.

Schnaiberg, Allan. 1994. *Environment and Society: The Enduring Conflict.* New York: St. Martin's.

Schnaiberg, Lynn. 1999a. "Study Finds Home Schoolers Are Top Achievers on Tests." *Education Week* 18(March 31):5.

———. 1999b. "Home Schooling Queries Spike After Shootings." *Education Week* 18(June 9):3.

Schneider, Howard. 1997. "Canada's Culture War Questioned in Battle with U.S., Arsenal of Federal Protections Called Needless." *Washington Post*, February 15, p. A29.

Schneider, Keith. 1995. "As Earth Day Turns 25, Life Gets Complicated." *New York Times*, April 16, p. E6.

Schur, Edwin M. 1965. *Crimes without Victims: Deviant Behavior and Public Policy.* Englewood Cliffs, NJ: Prentice-Hall.

———. 1968. *Law and Society: A Sociological View.* New York: Random House.

———. 1985. "'Crimes without Victims': A 20 Year Reassessment." Paper presented at the annual meeting of the Society for the Study of Social Problems.

Schwab, William A. 1993. "Recent Empirical and Theoretical Developments in Sociological Human Ecology." Pp. 29–57 in *Urban Sociology in Transition,* edited by Ray Hutchison. Greenwich, CT: JAI Press.

Schwartz, Howard D., ed. 1987. *Dominant Issues in Medical Sociology.* 2d ed. New York: Random House.

Schwartz, Joe. 1990. "Earth Day Today." *American Demographics* 12(April): 40–41.

———. 1991. "Why Japan's Birthrate Is So Low." *American Demographics* 13(April):20.

Sciolino, Elaine. 1993. "U.S. Rejects Notion That Human Rights Vary with Culture," *New York Times* (June 15), pp. A1, A18.

Scott, Alan. 1990. *Ideology and the New Social Movements.* London: Unwin Hyman.

Scott, Ellen Kaye. 1993. "How to Stop the Rapists? A Question of Strategy in Two Rape Crisis Centers." *Social Problems* 40 (August):343–361.

Scott, Hilda. 1985. *Working Your Way to the Bottom: The Feminization of Poverty.* London: Routledge.

Second Harvest. 1997. *1997 Annual Report.* Chicago, IL: Second Harvest.

Secretan, Thierry. 1995. *Going into Darkness: Fantastic Coffins from Africa.* London, Eng.: Thames and Hudson.

Segall, Alexander. 1976. "The Sick Role Concept: Understanding Illness Behavior." *Journal of Health and Social Behavior* 17(June):163–170.

Segall, Rebecca. 1998. "Sikh and Ye Shall Find." *Village Voice* 43(December 15): 46–48, 53.

Seidman, Steven. 1994. "Heterosexism in America: Prejudice against Gay Men and Lesbians." Pp. 578–593 in *Introduction to Social Problems,* edited by Craig Calhoun and George Ritzer. New York: McGraw-Hill.

Selig, Josh. 1998. "Muppets Succeed Where Politicians Haven't." *New York Times,* March 29, p. C45.

Senior Action in a Gay Environment (SAGE). 1999. *One Family All Ages.* New York: SAGE.

Serrano, Richard A. 1996. "Militias: Ranks Are Swelling." *Los Angeles Times,* April 18, pp. A1, A6.

Shaheen, Jack G. 1999. "Image and Identity: Screen Arabs and Muslims." In *Cultural Diversity: Curriculum, Classrooms, and Climate Issues,* edited by J. Q. Adams and Janice R. Welsch. Macomb, IL: Illinois Staff and Curriculum Development Association.

Shapiro, Isaac, and Robert Greenstein. 1999. *The Widening Income Gulf.* Washington, DC: Center on Budget and Policy Priorities.

Shapiro, Joseph P. 1993. *No Pity: People with Disabilities Forging a New Civil Rights Movement.* New York: Times Books.

Sharma, Hari M., and Gerard C. Bodeker. 1998. "Alternative Medicine." In *Britannica Book of the Year 1998.* Chicago: Encyclopaedia Britannica, pp. 228–229.

Shaw, Marvin E. 1981. *Group Dynamics: The Psychology of Small Group Behavior.* 3d ed. New York: McGraw-Hill.

Shaw, Susan. 1988. "Gender Differences in the Definition and Perception of Household Labor." *Family Relations* 37(July):333–337.

Shcherbak, Yuri M. 1996. "Ten Years of the Chernobyl Era." *Scientific American* 274(April):44–49.

Sheehy, Gail. 1995. *New Passages: Mapping Your Life across Time.* New York: Random House.

———. 1999. *Understanding Men's Passages: Discovering the New Map of Men's Lives.* New York: Ballantine Books.

Shelley, Louise I. 1992. "Review of Crime and Justice in Two Societies." Pacific Grove, CA: Brooks/Cole.

Shenon, Philip. 1995. "New Zealand Seeks Causes of Suicides by Young." *New York Times,* July 15, p. 3.

———. 1998. "Sailor Victorious in Gay Case on Internet Privacy." *New York Times,* June 12, pp. A1, A14.

Sherman, Arnold K., and Aliza Kolker. 1987. *The Social Bases of Politics.* Belmont, CA: Wadsworth.

Sherman, Lawrence W., Patrick R. Gartin, and Michael D. Buerger. 1989. "Hot Spots of Predatory Crime: Routine Activities and the Criminology of Place." *Criminology* 27: 27–56.

Sherrill, Robert. 1995. "The Madness of the Market." *The Nation* 260(January 9–16):45–72.

Sherwin, Susan. 1992. *No Longer Patient: Feminist Ethics and Health Care.* Philadelphia: Temple University Press.

Shibutani, Tamotshu. 1966. *Improvised News: A Sociological Study of Rumor.* Indianapolis: Bobbs-Merrill.

Shields, Rob, ed. 1996. *Cultures of Internet: Virtual Spaces, Real Histories, Living Bodies.* London: Sage.

Shilts, Randy. 1987. *And the Band Played On: Politics, People, and the AIDS Epidemic.* New York: St. Martin's.

Shinkai, Hiroguki, and Uglješa Zvekic. 1999. "Punishment." Pp. 89–120 in *Global Report on Crime and Justice,* edited by Graeme Newman. New York: Oxford University Press.

Shioiri, Toshiki, Toshiguki Someya, Daigo Helmeste, and Siu Wa Tang. 1999. "Misinterpretation of Facial Expression: A Cross-Cultural Study." *Journal of Psychiatry and Clinical Neurosciences* 24(March).

Shogan, Robert. 1998. "Politicians Embrace Status Quo as Nonvoter Numbers Grow." *Los Angeles Times*, May 4, p. A5.

Shogren, Elizabeth. 1994. "Treatment against Their Will." *Los Angeles Times*, August 18, pp. A1, A14–A15.

Short, Kathleen, Thesia Garner, David Johnson, and Patricia Doyle. 1999. "Experimental Poverty Measures: 1990 to 1997." *Current Population Reports*, ser. P-60, no. 205. Washington, DC: U.S. Government Printing Office.

Shorten, Lynda. 1991. *Without Reserves: Stories from Urban Natives*. Edmonton, Can.: NeWest Press.

Shuit, Douglas P. 1995. "Disparity Found in Heart Care for Minorities." *Los Angeles Times*, March 29, pp. A3, A27.

Shupe, Anson D., and David G. Bromley. 1980. "Walking a Tightrope." *Qualitative Sociology* 2:8–21.

Siddiqi, Mohammad A. 1993. "The Portrayal of Muslims and Islam in the U.S. Media." Presented at the conference on The Expression of American Religion in the Popular Media, Indianapolis.

Sidel, Ruth, and Victor Sidel. 1984. "Toward the Twenty-First Century." Pp. 267–284 in *Reforming Medicine,* edited by V. Sidel and R. Sidel. New York: Pantheon.

Sidiropoulos, Elizabeth et al. 1996. *South Africa Survey 1995/96.* Johannesburg: South African Institute of Race Relations.

Sigelman, Lee, Timothy Bledsoe, Susan Welch, and Michael W. Combs. 1996. "Making Contact? Black–White Social Interaction in an Urban Setting." *American Journal of Sociology* 5(March):1306–1332.

Silicon Valley Cultures Project. 1999. The Silicon Valley Cultures Project Website. Accessed July 30, 1990 (www.sjsv.edu/depts/anthrology/svcp).

Sills, David L. 1957. *The Volunteers: Means and Ends in a National Organization.* Glencoe, IL: Free Press.

———. 1968. "Voluntary Associations: Sociological Aspects." Pp. 362–379 in *International Encyclopedia of the Social Sciences,* vol. 16, edited by D. L. Sills. New York: Macmillan.

Silver, Ira. 1996. "Role Transitions, Objects, and Identity." *Symbolic Interaction* 19(1):1–20.

Simmel, Georg. 1950. *Sociology of Georg Simmel.* Translated by K. Wolff. Glencoe, IL: Free Press (originally written in 1902–1917).

Simmons, Ann M. 1998. "Where Fat Is a Mark of Beauty." *Los Angeles Times*, September 30, pp. A1, A12.

Simon, Joshua M. 1999. "Presidential Candidates Face Campaign Finance Issue." *Harvard Crimson,* July 2.

Simon, Stephanie. 1999. "In Insular Iowa Town, a Jolt of Worldliness." *Los Angeles Times*, January 25, pp. A1, A8.

Simons, John. 1999. "Are Web Political Polls Reliable? Yes? No? Maybe?" Accessed April 13, 1999 (http://deseretnews.com/dn/view/0,1249,75003756,00.html).

Simons, Marlise. 1996. "African Women in France Battling Polygamy." *New York Times*, January 26, pp. A1, A6.

———. 1989. "Abortion Fight Has New Front in Western Europe." *New York Times*, June 28, pp. A1, A9.

———. 1996c. "U. N. Court, for First Time, Defines Rape as War Crime," *New York Times* (June 28), pp. A1, A10.

———. 1997. "Child Care Sacred as France Cuts Back the Welfare State." *New York Times*, December 31, pp. A1, A6.

Simpson, Sally. 1993. "Corporate Crime." Pp. 236–256 in *Introduction to Social Problems,* edited by Craig Calhoun and George Ritzer. New York: McGraw-Hill.

Sjoberg, Gideon. 1960. *The Preindustrial City: Past and Present.* Glencoe, IL: Free Press.

Skafte, Peter. 1979. "Smoking Out Secrets of the Mysterious 'Snakers' in India." *Smithsonian* 10(October):120–127.

Skees, Suzanne. 1995. "The Last of the Shakers?" *Ms.* 5(March–April):40–45.

Sly, Liz. 1998. "China's Voluntary One-Child Policy Birthing New Revolution." *Chicago Tribune*, May 24, pp. 1, 14.

Smart, Barry. 1990. "Modernity, Postmodernity, and the Present." Pp. 14–30 in *Theories of Modernity and Postmodernity,* edited by Bryan S. Turner. Newbury Park, CA: Sage.

Smelser, Neil. 1962. *Theory of Collective Behavior.* New York: Free Press.

———. 1963. *The Sociology of Economic Life.* Englewood Cliffs, NJ: Prentice-Hall.

———. 1981. *Sociology.* Englewood Cliffs, NJ: Prentice-Hall.

Smith, Christian. 1991. *The Emergence of Liberation Theology: Radical Religion and Social Movement Theory.* Chicago: University of Chicago Press.

Smith, Dan. 1999. *The State of the World Atlas.* 6th ed. Brighton, England: Penguin.

Smith, David A. 1995. "The New Urban Sociology Meets the Old: Rereading Some Classical Human Ecology." *Urban Affairs Review* 20(January):432–457.

——— and Michael Timberlake. 1993. "World Cities: A Political Economy/Global Network Approach." Pp. 181–207 in *Urban Sociology in Transition,* edited by Ray Hutchison. Greenwich, CT: JAI Press.

Smith, James F. 2000. "Little by Little, Breathing Easier in Mexico City." *Los Angeles Times,* January 15, p. A2.

Smith, Michael Peter. 1988. *City, State, and Market.* New York: Basil Blackwell.

Smith, Patricia K. 1994. "Downward Mobility: Is It a Growing Problem?" *American Journal of Economics and Sociology* 53(January):57–72.

Smith, Tom W. 1996. *A Survey of the Religious Right: Views on Politics, Societies, Jews and Other Minorities.* New York: American Jewish Committee.

Smothers, Ronald. 1990. "For Black Farmers, Extinction to Be Near." *New York Times,* August 3, p. A10.

Snell, Tracy L. 1997. *Capital Punishment 1996.* Washington, DC: U.S. Government Printing Office.

Sniderman, Paul M., and Edward G. Carmines. 1997. *Reaching beyond Race.* Cambridge, MA: Harvard University Press.

Snow, David A., and Leon Anderson. 1993. *Down on Their Luck: A Study of Homeless Street People.* Berkeley, CA: University of California Press.

———, Louis A. Zurcher, Jr., and Robert Peters. 1981. "Victory Celebrations as Theater: A Dramaturgical Approach to Crowd Behavior." *Symbolic Interaction* 4:21–42.

———, Thercn Quist, and Daniel Cress. 1996. "The Homeless as Bricoleurs: Material Survival Strategies on the Streets." Pp. 86–96 in *Homelessness in America: A Reference Book,* edited by Jim Baumohl. Phoenix: Oryx Press.

Snyder, Thomas D. 1996. *Digest of Education Statistics 1996.* Washington, DC: U.S. Government Printing Office.

Sociological Abstracts. 1998. *Sociological Abstracts* 44:1–6. San Diego, CA: Sociological Abstracts.

Sohoni, Neera Kuckreja. 1994. "Where Are the Girls?" *Ms.* 5(July–August):96.

Son, In Soo, Suzanne W. Model, and Gene A. Fisher. 1989. "Polarization and Progress in the Black Community: Earnings and Status Gains for Young Black Males in the Era of Affirmative Action." *Sociological Forum* 4(September):309–327.

Son, Johanna. 1996. "Religion's TV Diet Needs More Local Flavor." *Inter Press Service*, July 17.

Sørensen, Annemette. 1994. "Women, Family and Class." Pp. 27–47 in *Annual Review of Sociology, 1994,* edited by Annemette Sørensen. Palo Alto, CA: Annual Reviews.

Sorokin, Pitirim A. 1959. *Social and Cultural Mobility.* New York: Free Press (original edition 1927, New York: Harper).

Sorrentino, Constance. 1990. "The Changing Family in International Perspective." Monthly Labor Review 113(March):41–56.

South African Institute of Race Relations. 1998. *South Africa Survey 1997/1998.* Johannesburg: SAIRR.

Spain, Daphene. 1992. *Gendered Spaces.* Chapel Hill, NC: The University of North Carolina Press.

Spanier, Graham B. 1983. "Married and Unmarried Cohabitation in the United States 1980." *Journal of Marriage and the Family* 45(May):277–288.

Spear, Allan. 1967. *Black Chicago: The Making of a Negro Ghetto.* Chicago, IL: University of Chicago Press.

Specter, Michael. 1996a. "World, Wide, Web: 3 English Words." *New York Times,* April 14, pp. E1, E5.

———. 1996b. "Russian Polls: Mostly Wrong, but the Only Game in Town," *New York Times* (May 15), pp. A1, A6.

———. 1998a. "Population Implosion Worries a Graying Europe." *New York Times,* July 10, pp. A1, A6.

———. 1998b. "Doctors Powerless as AIDS Rakes Africa." *New York Times,* August 6, pp. A1, A7.

Spengler, Joseph J. 1978. *Facing Zero Population Growth: Reactions and Interpretations, Past and Present.* Durham, NC: Duke University Press.

Spielman, Peter James. 1992. "11 Population Groups on 'Endangered' List," *Chicago Sun-Times* (November 23), p.12.

Spitzer, Steven. 1975. "Toward a Marxian Theory of Deviance." *Social Problems* 22(June):641–651.

Spradley, James P., and David W. McCurdy. 1980. *Anthropology: The Cultural Perspective.* 2d ed. New York: Wiley.

Sproull, Lee, and Sara Kiesler. 1991. *Connections: New Ways of Working in the Networked Organization.* Cambridge, MA: M.I.T. Press.

Squire, Peverill. 1988. "Why the 1936 Literary Digest Poll Failed." *Public Opinion Quarterly* 52(Spring):125–133.

St. John, Eric. 1997. "A Prescription for Participation." *Black Issues in Higher Education* 14(December 11):18–23.

Staggenborg, Suzanne. 1988. "Consequences of Professionalization and Formalization." *American Sociological Review* 53(August):585–606.

———. 1989a. "Stability and Innovation in the Women's Movement: A Comparison of Two Movement Organizations." *Social Problems* 36(February): 75–92.

———. 1989b. "Organizational and Environmental Influences on the Development of the Pro-Choice Movement." *Social Forces* 68(September):204–240.

Stammer, Larry B. 1999. "Former Baptists Leader Seeks a Dialogue with Gay Church." *Los Angeles Times,* July 27, pp. B1, B5.

Stanley, Alessandra. 1995. "Rich or Poor, Russian Mothers Go It Alone." *New York Times,* October 22, pp. 1, 5.

Stark, Rodney, and William Sims Bainbridge. 1979. "Of Churches, Sects, and Cults: Preliminary Concepts for a Theory of Religious Movements." *Journal for the Scientific Study of Religion* 18(June):117–131.

———. 1985. *The Future of Religion.* Berkeley: University of California Press.

——— and Laurence R. Iannaccone. 1992. "Sociology of Religion." Pp. 2029–2037 in *Encyclopedia of Sociology,* vol. 4, edited by Edgar F. Borgatta and Marie L. Borgatta. New York: Macmillan.

Starr, Kevin. 1999. "Building from Within." *Los Angeles Times,* March 7, p. 1.

Starr, Paul. 1982. *The Social Transformation of American Medicine.* New York: Basic Books.

Stavenhagen, Rodolfo. 1994. "The Indian Resurgence in Mexico." *Cultural Survival Quarterly,* Summer–Fall, pp. 77–80.

Stearn, J. 1993. "What Crisis?" *Statesmen and Society* 6(April 2):7–9.

Stedman, Nancy. 1998. "Learning to Put the Best Shoe Forward." *New York Times,* October 27.

Stein, Leonard. 1967. "The Doctor–Nurse Game." *Archives of General Psychiatry* 16:699–703.

Stein, Peter J. 1975. "Singlehood: An Alternative to Marriage." *Family Coordinator* 24(October):489–503.

———, ed. 1981. *Single Life: Unmarried Adults in Social Context.* New York: St. Martin's.

Steinfeld, Edward S. 1999. "Beyond the Transition: China's Economy at Century's End." *Current History* 98(September):271–275.

Stenning, Derrick J. 1958. "Household Viability among the Pastoral Fulani." Pp. 92–119 in *The Developmental Cycle in Domestic Groups,* edited by John R. Goody. Cambridge, Eng.: Cambridge University Press.

Stern, Kenneth S. 1996. *A Force upon the Plain: The American Militia Movement and the Politics of Hate.* New York: Simon and Schuster.

Sternberg, Steve. 1999. "Virus Makes Families Pay Twice." *USA Today,* May 24, p. 6D.

Sterngold, James. 1992. "Japan Ends Fingerprinting of Many Non-Japanese," *New York Times* (May 21), p. A11.

Stevens, Ann Huff. 1994. "The Dynamics of Poverty Spells: Updating Bane and Ellwood." *American Economic Review* 84(May):34–37.

Stevenson, David, and Barbara L. Schneider. 1999. *The Ambitious Generation: America's Teenagers, Motivated but Directionless.* New Haven: Yale University Press.

Stevenson, Robert J. 1998. *The Boiler Room and Other Telephone Sales Scams.* Urbana, IL: University of Illinois Press.

Stoeckel, John, and N. L. Sirisena. 1988. "Gender-Specific Socioeconomic Impacts of Development Programs in

Sri Lanka." *Journal of Developing Areas* 23(October):31–42.

Stolberg, Sheryl. 1995. "Affirmative Action Gains Often Come at a High Cost." *Los Angeles Times*, March 29, pp. A1, A13–A16.

———. 1997. "U.S. Publishes First Guide to Treatment of Infertility." *New York Times*, December 19, p. A14.

Stolberg, Sheryl Gay. 2000. "Alternative Care Gains a Foothold." *New York Times* (January 31): A1, A16.

Stoll, Clifford. 1995. *Silicon Snake Oil: Second Thoughts on the Information Superhighway*. New York: Anchor/Doubleday.

Stone, Brad. 1999. "Get a Life?" *Newsweek* 133(June 7):68–69.

Stoughton, Stephanie, and Leslie Walker. 1999. "The Merchants of Cyberspace." *Washington Post National Weekly Edition* 16(February 15):18.

Strassman, W. Paul. 1998. "Third World Housing." Pp. 589–592 in *The Encyclopedia of Housing,* edited by Willem van Vliet. Thousand Oaks, CA: Sage Publications.

Straus, Murray A. 1994. "State-to-State Differences in Social Inequality and Social Bonds in Relation to Assaults on Wives in the United States." *Journal of Comparative Family Studies* 25(Spring):7–24.

———. 1999. *Violence in Intimate Relationships*. Thousand Oaks, CA: Sage.

Strauss, Anselm. 1977. *Negotiations: Varieties, Contexts, Processes, and Social Order*. San Francisco: Jossey Bass.

Strom, Stephanie. 1999. "In Japan, From a Lifetime Job to No Job at All." *New York Times,* February 3, p. A1.

———. 2000a. "In Japan, the Golden Years Have Lost Their Glow." *New York Times* (February 16): 7.

———. 2000b. "Tradition of Equality Fading in New Japan." *New York Times,* January 4, pp. A1, A6.

Struck, Doug. 2000. "A Violent Crime Wave Hits Japan." *Washington Post National Weekly Edition* 17(February 14):12.

Strum, Charles. 1993. "Schools' Tracks and Democracy." *New York Times,* April 1, pp. B1, B7.

Sugimoto, Yoshio. 1997. *An Introduction to Japanese Society*. Cambridge, Eng.: Cambridge University Press.

Sumner, William G. 1906. *Folkways*. New York: Ginn.

Surgeon General. 1999. *Surgeon General's Report on Mental Health*. Washington, DC: U.S. Government Printing Office.

Sutherland, Edwin H. 1937. *The Professional Thief*. Chicago: University of Chicago Press.

———. 1940. "White-Collar Criminality." *American Sociological Review* 5(February):1–11.

———. 1949. *White Collar Crime*. New York: Dryden.

———. 1983. *White Collar Crime: The Uncut Version*. New Haven, CT: Yale University Press.

——— and Donald R. Cressey. 1978. *Principles of Criminology*. 10th ed. Philadelphia: Lippincott.

Suttles, Gerald D. 1972. *The Social Construction of Communities*. Chicago: University of Chicago Press.

Swanson, Stevenson, and Jim Kirk. 1998. "Satellite Outage Felt by Millions." *Chicago Tribune,* May 21, pp. 1, 26.

Swartz, Leslie. 1985. "Anorexia Nervosa as a Culture-Bound Syndrome." *Social Science and Medicine* 20(7):725–730.

Swiss, Deborah, and Judith Walker. 1993. *Women and the Work/Family Dilemma: How Today's Professional Women Are Finding Solutions*. New York: Wiley.

Szasz, Thomas S. 1971. "The Same Slave: An Historical Note on the Use of Medical Diagnosis as Justificatory Rhetoric." *American Journal of Psychotherapy* 25(April):228–239.

———. 1974. *The Myth of Mental Illness* (rev. ed.). New York: Harper and Row.

T

Taeuber, Cynthia M. 1992. "Sixty-Five Plus in America." *Current Population Reports,* ser. P-23, no. 178. Washington, DC: U.S. Government Printing Office.

Tagliabue, John. 1996. "In Europe, a Wave of Layoffs Stuns White-Collar Workers." *New York Times,* June 20, pp. A1, D8.

Takahara, Kanako. 1999. "Preventing an AUM Comeback. Will Bills Save Society from Cult's Menace?" *The Japan Times* (November 18), p. 3.

Takezawa, Yasuko I. 1995. *Breaking the Silence: Redress and Japanese American Ethnicity*. Ithaca, NY: Cornell University Press.

Talbot, Margaret. 1998. "Attachment Theory: The Ultimate Experiment." *New York Time Magazine,* May 24, pp. 4–30, 38, 46, 50, 54.

Tannen, Deborah. 1990. *You Just Don't Understand: Women and Men in Conversation*. New York: Ballantine.

———. 1994a. *Talking from 9 to 5*. New York: William Morris.

———. 1994b. *Gender and Discourse*. New York: Oxford University Press.

Tashman, Billy. 1992. "Hobson's Choice: Free-Market Education Plan Vouches for Bush's Favorite Class." *Village Voice* 37(January 21): educational supplement, pp. 9, 14.

Taylor, Carl S. 1993. *Girls, Gangs, Women, and Drugs*. East Lansing: Michigan State University Press.

Taylor, Humphrey, and George Terhanian. 1999a. "Heady Days Are Here Again: Online Polling Is Rapidly Coming of Age." *Public Perspectives* 10(June/July):20–23.

———. 1999b. "No Witchcraft Here." *Public Perspective* 10(August/September):42–43.

Telecommunications and Information Administration. 2000. Falling Through the Net. Washington, DC: U.S. Government Printing Office.

Telsch, Kathleen. 1991. "New Study of Older Workers Finds They Can Become Good Investments." *New York Times,* May 21, p. A16.

Tenner, Edward. 1996. *Why Things Bite Back: Technology and the Revenge of Unintended Consequences*. New York: Vintage Books.

Terhanian, George. 2000. Correspondence to author, January 7.

Terkel, Studs. 1974. *Working*. New York: Pantheon.

———. 1999. "Looking Toward Cyberspace: Beyond Grounded Sociology." *Contemporary Sociology* 28(November):643–654.

Theberge, Nancy. 1997. "'It's Part of the Game'—Physicality and the Production of Gender in Women's Hockey." *Gender and Society* 11(February): 69–87.

Third International Mathematics and Science Study. 1998. *Mathematics and Science Achievement in the Final Year of Secondary School.* Boston, MA: TIMSS International Study Center.

Third World Institute. 1997. *Third World Guide 97/98.* Toronto, Ontario: Garamond Press.

Thirlwall, A. P. 1989. *Growth and Development.* 4th ed. London: Macmillan.

Thomas, Gordon, and Max Morgan Witts. 1974. *Voyage of the Damned.* Greenwich, CT: Fawcett Crest.

Thomas, Jim. 1984. "Some Aspects of Negotiating Order: Loose Coupling and Mesostructure in Maximum Security Prisons." *Symbolic Interaction* 7(Fall): 213–231.

Thomas, Robert McG., Jr. 1995. "Maggie Kuhn, 89, the Founder of the Gray Panthers, Is Dead." *New York Times,* April 23, p. 47.

Thomas, William I. 1923. *The Unadjusted Girl.* Boston: Little, Brown.

Thompson, Linda, and Alexis J. Walker. 1989. "Gender in Families: Women and Men in Marriage, Work, and Parenthood." *Journal of Marriage and the Family* 51(November):845–871.

Thomson, Elizabeth, and Ugo Colella. 1992. "Cohabitation and Marital Stability: Quality or Commitment?" *Journal of Marriage and the Family* 54(May):259–267.

Thornton, Russell. 1987. *American Indians Holocaust and Survival: A Population History Since 1492.* Norman: University of Oklahoma Press.

Tiano, Susan. 1987. "Gender, Work, and World Capitalism: Third World Women's Role in Development." Pp. 216–243 in *Analyzing Gender: A Handbook of Social Science Research,* edited by Beth B. Hess and Myra Marx Ferree. Newbury Park, CA: Sage.

Tierney, John. 1990. "Betting the Planet." *New York Times Magazine,* December 2, pp. 52–53, 71, 74, 76, 78, 80–81.

Tierney, Kathleen. 1980. "Emergent Norm Theory as 'Theory': An Analysis and Critique of Turner's Formulation." Pp. 42–53 in *Collective Behavior: A Source Book,* edited by Meredith David Pugh. St. Paul, MN: West.

———. 1994. "Property Damage and Violence: A Collective Behavior Analysis." Pp. 149–173 in *The Los Angeles Riots: Lessons for the Urban Future,* edited by Mark Baldassare. Boulder, CO: Westview.

Tilly, Charles. 1993. *Popular Contention in Great Britain 1758–1834.* Cambridge, MA: Harvard University Press.

Time. 1971. "Suburbia: The New American Plurality." 97(March 15):14–20.

Tobin, Jacqueline, and Raymond Dobard. 1999. *Hidden in Plain View: The Secret Story of Quilts and the Underground Railroad.* New York: Doubleday.

Tonkinson, Robert. 1978. *The Mardudjara Aborigines.* New York: Holt.

Tönnies, Ferdinand. [1887] 1988. *Community and Society.* Rutgers, NJ: Transaction.

Topolnicki, Denise M. 1993. "The World's 5 Best Ideas." *Money* 22(June):74–83, 87, 89, 91.

Touraine, Alain. 1974. *The Academic System in American Society.* New York: McGraw-Hill.

Treas, Judith. 1995. "Older Americans in the 1990s and Beyond." *Population Bulletin* 50(May).

Trebay, Guy. 1990. "In Your Face." *Village Voice* 35, August 14, pp. 14–39.

Treiman, Donald J. 1977. *Occupational Prestige in Comparative Perspective.* New York: Academic.

Trubisky, Paula. 1995. "Congressional Briefing Highlights Sexual Behavior Survey." *Footnotes* 23(January):1.

Tuchman, Gaye. 1992. "Feminist Theory." Pp. 695–704 in *Encyclopedia of Sociology,* vol. 2, edited by Edgar F. Borgatta and Marie L. Borgatta. New York: Macmillan.

Tumin, Melvin M. 1953. "Some Principles of Stratification: A Critical Analysis." *American Sociological Review* 18(August):387–394.

———. 1985. *Social Stratification.* 2d ed. Englewood Cliffs, NJ: Prentice-Hall.

Ture, Kwame, and Charles Hamilton. 1992. *Black Power: The Politics of Liberation.* Rev. ed. New York: Vintage Books.

Turkle, Sherry. 1995. *Life on the Screen: Identity in the Age of the Internet.* New York: Simon and Schuster.

———. 1999. "Looking Toward Cyberspace: Beyond Grounded Sociology," *Contemporary Sociology* 28 (November):643–654.

Turner, Bryan S., ed. 1990. *Theories of Modernity and Postmodernity.* Newbury Park, CA: Sage.

Turner, Craig. 1998. "U.N. Study Assails U.S. Executions as Biased." *Los Angeles Times,* March 4, p. A1.

Turner, J. H. 1985. *Herbert Spencer: A Renewed Application.* Beverly Hills, CA: Sage.

Turner, Margery Austin, and Felicity Skidmore, eds. 1999. *Mortgage Lending Discrimination: A Review of Existing Evidence.* Washington, DC: Urban Institute.

Turner, Ralph, and Lewis M. Killian. 1987. *Collective Behavior.* 3d ed. Englewood Cliffs, NJ: Prentice-Hall.

Twaddle, Andrew. 1974. "The Concept of Health Status." *Social Science and Medicine* 8(January):29–38.

Tyler, Charles. 1991. "The World's Manacled Millions." *Geographical Magazine* 63(1):30–35.

Tyler, Patrick E. 1995a. "As Deng Wanes, a Backlash Stalls His Last Big Reform," *New York Times* (June18), pp. 1, 7.

———. 1995b. "For China's Girls, Rural Schools Fail." *New York Times,* December 31, p. 5.

Tyler, William B. 1985. "The Organizational Structure of the School." Pp. 49–73 in *Annual Review of Sociology, 1985,* edited by Ralph H. Turner. Palo Alto, CA: Annual Reviews.

U

Uchitelle, Louis. 1996. "More Downsized Workers Are Returning as Rentals." *New York Times,* December 8, pp. 1, 34.

———. 1998. "Downsizing Comes Back, but the Outcry Is Muted." *New York Times,* December 7, p. A1.

———. 1999. "Divising New Math to Define Poverty." *New York Times,* October 18, pp. A1, A14.

United Nations. 1995. *The World's Women, 1995: Trends and Statistics.* New York: United Nations.

United Nations Development Programme. 1995. *Human Development Report 1995.* New York: Oxford University Press.

———. 1996. *Human Development Report 1996.* New York: Oxford University Press.

United Nations Human Rights Commission. 1997. "U.N. Human Rights Commission Acts on Texts." M2 Press-Wire. 4/9.

United Nations Population Division. 1998a. "Demographic Input of HIV/AIDS." Accessed (http://www.undp.org/popin/wdtrends/demoimp.htm).

———. 1998b. *World Abortion Policies.* New York: Department of Economic and Social Affairs, UNPD.

———. 1998c. *World Population Projections to 2150,* February 1, 1998. Accessed August 10, 1998 (http://www.undp.org/popin/wdtrends/execsum.htm).

———. 1999. *The World at Six Billion.* New York: UNPA.

USA Today. 1998. "Did Tobacco Company Money Kill the Anti-smoking Bill?" June 22, p. 16A.

U.S. Conference of Mayors. 1999. *A Status Report on Hunger and Homelessness in America's Cities.* Washington: U.S. Conference of Mayors.

U.S. English. 1999. "States with Official English Laws." Accessed July 27, 1999 (http://www.us-english.org/states.htm).

University of New Hampshire. 2000. "Kentucky Fried Chicken Hoax." Accessed January 20, 2000 (http://www.unh.edu/BoilerPlate/kfc.html).

Utt, Ronald D. 1998. *Cities in Denial: The False Promises of Subsidized Tourist and Entertainment Complex.* Washington, DC: Heritage Foundation.

Utter, Jack. 1993. *American Indians: Answers to Today's Questions.* Lake Ann, MI: National Woodlands Publishing.

Uttley, Alison. 1993. "Who's Looking at You, Kid?" *Times Higher Education Supplement* 30(April 30):48.

V

Vallas, Steven P. 1999. "Rethinking Post-Fordism: The Meaning of Workplace Flexibility." *Sociological Theory* 17(March):68–101.

van den Berghe, Pierre. 1978. *Race and Racism: A Comparative Perspective.* 2d ed. New York: Wiley.

Vanderpool, Tim. 1995. "Secession of the Successful." *Utne Reader* (November–December):32, 34.

Vanneman, Reeve, and Lynn Weber Cannon. 1987. *The American Perception of Class.* Philadelphia: Temple University Press.

Van Slambrouck, Paul. 1998. "In California, Taking the Initiative—Online." *Christian Science Monitor,* November 13, pp. 1, 11.

———. 1999. "Netting a New Sense of Connection." *Christian Science Monitor,* May 4, pp. 1, 4.

———. 1999. "Newest Tool for Social Protest: The Internet." *Christian Science Monitor,* June 18, p. 3.

van Vucht Tijssen, Lieteke. 1990. "Women between Modernity and Postmodernity." Pp. 147–163 in *Theories of Modernity and Postmodernity,* edited by Bryan S. Turner. London: Sage.

Vaughan, Diane. 1996. *The Challenger Launch Decision: Risky Technology, Culture, and Deviance at NASA.* Chicago: University of Chicago Press.

———. 1999. "The Dark Side of Organizations: Mistake, Misconduct, and Disaster." Pp. 271–305 in *Annual Review of Sociology,* edited by Karen J. Cook and John Hagan. Palo Alto: Annual Reviews.

Veblen, Thorstein. 1919. *The Vested Interests and the State of the Industrial Arts.* New York: Huebsch.

Vega, William A. 1995. "The Study of Latino Families: A Point of Departure." Pp. 3–17 in *Understanding Latino Families: Scholarship, Policy, and Practice,* edited by Ruth E. Zambrana. Thousand Oaks, CA: Sage.

Velkoff, Victoria A., and Valerie A. Lawson. 1998. "Gender of Aging." *International Brief,* ser. IB, no. 98–3. Washington, DC: U.S. Government Printing Office.

Venkatesh, Sudhir Alladi. 1997. "The Social Organization of Street Gang Activity in an Urban Ghetto." *American Journal of Sociology* 103(July):82–111.

Ventura, Stephanie J., Sally C. Curtin, and T. J. Mathews. 1998a. *Teenage Births in the United States: National and State Trends, 1990–96.* Washington, DC: National Vital Statistics System.

———, T. J. Mathews, and Sally C. Curtin. 1999. "Declines in Teenage Birth Rates, 1991–98: Update of National and State Patterns." *National Vital Statistics Reports* 47(October 25).

Verhovek, Sam Howe. 1997. "Racial Tensions in Suit Slowing Drive for 'Environmental Justice,'" *New York Times,* September 7, pp. 1, 16.

———. 1999. "Oregon Reporting 15 Deaths in Year Under Suicide Law." *New York Times,* February 18, pp. A1, A17.

Vernon, Glenn. 1962. *Sociology and Religion.* New York: McGraw-Hill.

Vernon, Jo Etta A. et al. [4 authors]. 1990. "Media Stereotyping: A Comparison of the Way Elderly Women and Men Are Portrayed on Prime-Time Television." *Journal of Women and Aging* 2(4):55–68.

Vladimiroff, Christine. 1998. "Food for Thought." *Second Harvest Update* (Summer):2.

Vobejda, Barbara. 1993. "U.S. Ends Survey of Its Dwindling Farm Population." *Chicago Sun-Times,* October 9, p. 6.

———, and Judith Havemann. 1997. "Experts Say Side Income Could Hamper Reforms." *Washington Post* (November 3), p. A1.

W

Wacquant, Loïc J. D. 1993. "When Cities Run Riot." *UNESCO Courier* (February), pp. 8–15.

Wages for Housework Campaign. 1999. *Wages for Housework Campaign.* Circular. Los Angeles.

Wagley, Charles and Marvin Harris. 1958. *Minorities in the New World: Six Case Studies.* New York: Columbia University Press.

Waitzkin, Howard. 1986. *The Second Sickness: Contradictions of Capitalist Health Care.* Chicago: University of Chicago Press.

Waldron, Arthur. 1998. "Why China Could Be Dangerous." *The American Enterprise* 9 (July/August):40–43.

Wallace, Ruth A., and Alison Wolf. 1980. *Contemporary Sociological Theory.* Englewood Cliffs, NJ: Prentice-Hall.

Wallerstein, Immanuel. 1974. *The Modern World System.* New York: Academic Press.

———. 1979. *Capitalist World Economy.* Cambridge, Eng.: Cambridge University Press.

———. 1999. *The End of the World As We Know It: Social Science for the Twenty-first Century.* Minneapolis: University of Minnesota Press.

Wallis, Claudia. 1987. "Is Mental Illness Inherited?" *Time* 129(March 9):67.

Walzer, Susan. 1996. "Thinking about the Baby: Gender and Divisions of Infant Care." *Social Problems* 43(May):219–234.

Wapner, Paul. 1994. "Environmental Activism and Global Civil Society." *Dissent* 41(Summer):389–393.

Waring, Marilyn. 1988. *If Women Counted: A New Feminist Economics.* San Francisco: Harper and Row.

Warner, Judith. 1996. "France's Anti-abortion Movement Gains Momentum." *Ms.* 7(September–October): 20–21.

Washington Transcript Service. 1999. "Hillary Rodham Clinton Holds News Conference on Her New York Senatorial Bid." November 23.

Watts, Jerry G. 1990. "Pluralism Reconsidered." *Urban Affairs Quarterly* 25(June):697–704.

Weber, Max. 1922. *Wirtschaft und Gesellschaft.* Tübingen, Ger.: J. C. B. Mohr.

———. [1913–1922] 1947. *The Theory of Social and Economic Organization.* Translated by A. Henderson and T. Parsons. New York: Free Press.

———. [1904] 1949. *Methodology of the Social Sciences.* Translated by Edward A. Shils and Henry A. Finch. Glencoe, IL: Free Press.

———. [1904] 1958a. *The Protestant Ethic and the Spirit of Capitalism.* Translated by Talcott Parsons. New York: Scribner.

———. [1916] 1958b. *The Religion of India: The Sociology of Hinduism and Buddhism.* New York: Free Press.

Wechsler, Henry et al. 2000. What Colleges Are Doing About Student Binge Drinking A Survey of College Administrators. *Journal of American College Public Health* (April). Accessed at www.hsph.harvard.edu/cas/alcohol.surveyrpt2.html.

Weeks, John R. 1988. "The Demography of Islamic Nations." *Population Bulletin* 43(December).

———. 1996. *Population: An Introduction to Concepts and Issues.* 6th ed. Belmont, CA: Wadsworth.

———. 1999. *Population: An Introduction to Concepts and Issues.* 7th ed. Belmont, CA: Wadsworth.

Weigard, Bruce. 1992. *Off the Books: A Theory and Critique of the Underground Economy.* Dix Hills, NY: General Hall.

Weil, Frederick D. 1987. "Cohorts, Regimes, and the Legitimization of Democracy: West Germany since 1945." *American Sociological Review* 52(June):308–324.

Weiner, Tim. 1998. "Military Discharges of Homosexuals Soar." *New York Times*, February 12, p. A21.

Weinstein, Deena. 1999. *Knockin' The Rock: Defining Rock Music as a Social Problem.* New York: McGraw-Hill/Primis.

———. 2000. *Heavy Metal: The Music and Its Culture.* Cambridge, MA: Da Capo.

Weisman, Steven R. 1992. "Landmark Harassment Case in Japan." *New York Times*, April 17, p. A3.

Weiss, Rick. 1998. "Beyond Test-Tube Babies." *Washington Post National Weekly Edition* 15(February 16):6–7.

Welfare to Work Partnership. 1998. "Survey of Businesses." News Release. April 9. Washington, DC: Welfare to Work Partnership.

———. 1999. "Member Survey: Promotion and Partnership." Accessed September 29, 1999 (http://www.welfaretowork.org).

Wellman, Barry et al. [6 authors]. 1996. "Computer Networks as Social Networks: Collaborative Work, Telework, and Virtual Community." Pp. 213–238 in *Annual Review of Sociology, 1996,* edited by John Hagan. Palo Alto, CA: Annual Reviews.

West, Candace, and Don H. Zimmerman. 1983. "Small Insults: A Study of Interruptions in Cross Sex Conversations between Unacquainted Persons." Pp. 86–111 in *Language, Gender, and Society,* edited by Barrie Thorne, Cheris Kramarae, and Nancy Henley. Rowley, MA: Newbury House.

——— and ———. 1987. "Doing Gender." *Gender and Society* 1(June): 125–151.

Whyte, William Foote. 1981. *Street Corner Society: Social Structure of an Italian Slum.* 3d ed. Chicago: University of Chicago Press.

———. 1989. "Advancing Scientific Knowledge through Participatory Action Research." *Sociological Forum* 4(September):367–385.

Wickham, DeWayne. 1998. "Affirmative Action not in Real Jeopardy." *USA Today,* April 7, p. 13A.

Wickman, Peter M. 1991. "Deviance." Pp. 85–87 in *Encyclopedic Dictionary of Sociology*, 4th ed., by Dushkin Publishing Group. Guilford, CT: Dushkin.

Wiener, Jon. 1994. "Free Speech on the Internet." *The Nation* 258(June 13): 825–828.

Wilford, John Noble. 1997. "New Clues Show Where People Made the Great Leap to Agriculture." *New York Times*, November 18, pp. B9, B12.

Wilhelm, Anthony. 1998. *Buying into the Computer Age: A Look at Hispanic Families.* Claremont, CA: The Thom's Rivera Policy Institute.

Wilkinson, Tracy. 1999 "Refugees Forming Bonds on Web." *Los Angeles Times*, July 31, p. A2.

Williams, Carol J. 1995. "Taking an Eager Step Back." *Los Angeles Times*, June 3, pp. A1, A14.

Williams, Christine L. 1992. "The Glass Escalator: Hidden Advantages for Men in the 'Female' Professions." *Social Problems* 39(3):253–267.

———. 1995. *Still a Man's World: Men Who Do Women's Work.* Berkeley: University of California Press.

Williams, David R., and Chiquita Collins. 1995. "U.S. Socioeconomic and Racial Differences in Health: Patterns and Explanations." Pp. 349–386 in *Annual Review of Sociology, 1995,* edited by John Hagan. Palo Alto, CA: Annual Reviews.

Williams, J. Allen, Jr., Nicholas Batchuk, and David R. Johnson. 1973. "Voluntary Associations and Minority Status: A Comparative Analysis of Anglo, Black and Mexican Americans." *American Sociological Review* 38(October): 637–646.

Williams, Patricia J. 1997. "Of Race and Risk." *The Nation*. Digital Edition. Accessed December 12, 1999 (http://www.thenation.com).

Williams, Robin M., Jr. 1970. *American Society.* 3d ed. New York: Knopf.

———, in collaboration with John P. Dean and Edward A. Suchman. 1964. *Strangers Next Door: Ethnic Relations in American Communities.* Englewood Cliffs, NJ: Prentice-Hall.

Williams, Simon Johnson. 1986. "Appraising Goffman." *British Journal of Sociology* 37(September):348–369.

Williams, Wendy M. 1998. "Do Parents Matter? Scholars Need to Explain What Research Really Shows." *Chronicle of Higher Education* 45(December 11): B6–B7.

Wilmut, Ian et al. [5 authors]. 1997. "Viable Offering Derived from Fetal and Adult Mammalian Cells." *Nature* 385(February 27):810–813.

Wilson, Edward O. 1975. *Sociobiology: The New Synthesis.* Cambridge, MA: Harvard University Press.

———. 1978. *On Human Nature.* Cambridge, MA: Harvard University Press.

Wilson, John. 1973. *Introduction to Social Movements.* New York: Basic Books.

———. 1978. *Religion in American Society: The Effective Presence.* Englewood Cliffs, NJ: Prentice-Hall.

Wilson, Warner, Larry Dennis, and Allen P. Wadsworth, Jr. 1976. "Authoritarianism Left and Right." *Bulletin of the Psychonomic Society* 7(March):271–274.

Wilson, William Julius. 1980. *The Declining Significance of Race: Blacks and Changing American Institutions.* 2d ed. Chicago: University of Chicago Press.

———. 1987. *The Truly Disadvantaged: The Inner City, the Underclass and Public Policy.* Chicago: University of Chicago Press.

———. 1988. "The Ghetto Underclass and the Social Transformation of the Inner City." *The Black Scholar* 19(May–June):10–17.

———, ed. 1989. *The Ghetto Underclass: Social Science Perspectives.* Newbury Park, CA: Sage.

———. 1996. *When Work Disappears: The World of the New Urban Poor.* New York: Knopf.

———. 1999a. "Towards a Just and Livable City: The Issues of Race and Class." Address at the Social Science Centennial Conference, April 23, 1999. Chicago, IL: DePaul University.

———. 1999b. *The Bridge Over the Racial Divide: Rising Inequality and Coalition Politics.* Berkeley: University of California Press.

Winerip, Michael. 1998. "Schools for Sale." *New York Times Magazine*, July 14, pp. 42–48, 80, 86, 88–89.

Winsberg, Morton. 1994. "Specific Hispanics." *American Demographics* 16(February):44–53.

Winter, J. Alan. 1977. *Continuities in the Sociology of Religion.* New York: Harper and Row.

Wirth, Louis. 1928. *The Ghetto.* Chicago: University of Chicago Press.

———. 1931. "Clinical Sociology." *American Journal of Sociology* 37(July):49–66.

———. 1938. "Urbanism as a Way of Life." *American Journal of Sociology* 44(July):1–24.

Wiseman, Paul. 2000. "China's Little Emperors:' The Offspring of Policy." *USA Today*, February 23, p. 10D.

Witt, Matt. 1999. "Missing in Action: Media Images of Real Workers." *Los Angeles Times*, August 30, pp. E1, E3.

Wolf, Naomi. 1991. *The Beauty Myth.* New York: Anchor Books.

———. 1992. *The Beauty Myth: How Images of Beauty Are Used against Women.* New York: Anchor.

Wolf, Richard. 1996. "States Can Expect Challenges after Taking over Welfare." *USA Today*, October 1, p. 8A.

———. 1998. "States Slow to Plunge into Covenant Marriage." *USA Today*, June 16, p. 3A.

Wolff, Edward N. 1999. "Recent Trends the Distribution of Household Wealth Ownership." In *Back to Shared Prosperity: The Growing Inequality of Wealth and Income in America*, edited by Ray Marshall. New York: M.E. Sharpe.

Wolinsky, Fredric P. 1980. *The Sociology of Health.* Boston: Little, Brown.

Wolraich et al. 1998. "Guidance for Effective Discipline." *Pediatrics* 101(April):723–728.

Women's International Network. 1995. "Working Women: 4 Country Comparison." *WIN News* 21(September 9): 82.

Wood, Daniel B. 1999. "In Mexico, U.S. Industry Finds Uncertainty." *Christian Science Monitor*, November 1, p. 3.

———. 2000. "Minorities Hope TV Deals Don't Just Lead to 'Tokenism.'" *Christian Science Monitor*, January 19.

Woodard, Colin. 1998. "When Rate Learning Fails against the Test of Global Economy." *Christian Science Monitor*, April 15, p. 7.

Wooden, Wayne. 1995. *Renegade Kids, Suburban Outlaws: From Youth Culture to Delinquency.* Belmont, CA: Wadsworth.

World Bank. 1990. *World Development Report 1990: Poverty.* New York: Oxford University Press.

———. 1992. *Housing: Enabling Markets to Work: A World Bank Policy Paper.* Washington, DC: World Bank.

———. 1995. *World Development Report 1994: Workers in an Integrating World.* New York: Oxford University Press.

———. 1996. *World Development Report 1996: From Plan to Market.* New York: Oxford University Press.

———. 1997a. *World Development Indicators 1997.* Washington, DC: International Bank for Reconstruction and Development/The World Bank.

———. 1997b. *World Development Report 1997: The State in a Changing World.* New York: Oxford University Press.

———. 1999a. *World Development Report 1998/99: Knowledge for Development.* New York: Oxford University Press.

———. 1999b. *World Development Indicators 1999.* New York: Oxford University Press.

———. 2000. *World Development Report 1999/2000: Entering the 21st Century.* New York: Oxford University Press.

World Development Forum. 1990. "The Danger of Television." 8(July 15):4.

World Health Organization. 1998. *Unsafe Abortion: Global and Regional Estimates of Incidence of and Mortality Due to Unsafe Abortion.* Geneva: WHO.

World Resources Institute. 1998. *1998–99 World Resources: A Guide to the Global Environment.* New York: Oxford University Press.

———. The United Nations Environment Programme, United Nations Development Program, The World Bank. 1996. *World Resources, 1996–1997.* New York: Oxford University Press.

Wresch, William. 1996. *Disconnected: Haves and Have-Nots in the Information Age.* New Brunswick, NJ: Rutgers University Press.

Wright, Eric R., William P. Gronfein, and Timothy J. Owens. 2000. "Deinstitutionalization, Social Rejection, and the Self-Esteem of Former Mental Patients." *Journal of Health and Social Behavior* (March).

Wright, Erik Olin, David Hachen, Cynthia Costello, and Joy Sprague. 1982.

"The American Class Structure." *American Sociological Review* 47(December):709–726.

Wright, Gerald C., and Dorothy M. Stetson. 1978. "The Impact of No-Fault Divorce Law Reform on Divorce in the American States." *Journal of Marriage and the Family* 40:575–580.

Wright, James D. 1995. "Ten Essential Observations on Guns in America." *Society* 32(March/April):63–68.

Wright, Robin. 1995. "The Moral Animal: Why We Are the Way We Are." *Science of Evolutionary Psychology.* Reprint edition. New York: Vintage Books.

Wurman, Richard Saul. 1989. *Information Anxiety.* New York: Doubleday.

Wuthnow, Robert, and Marsha Witten. 1988. "New Directions in the Study of Culture." Pp. 49–67 in *Annual Review of Sociology, 1988,* edited by W. Richard Scott and Judith Blake. Palo Alto, CA: Annual Reviews.

X

Xinhua News Agency. 1997. "IDB Okays Financing for Child Care in Ecuador." November 19.

Y

Yamagata, Hisashi, Kuang S. Yeh, Shelby Stewman, and Hiroko Dodge. 1997. "Sex Segregation and Glass Ceilings: A Comparative Statistics Model of Women's Career Opportunities in the Federal Government over a Quarter Century." *American Journal of Sociology* 103(November):566–632.

Yap, Kioe Sheng. 1998. "Squatter Settlements." Pp. 554–556 in *The Encyclopedia of Housing,* edited by Willem van Vliet. Thousand Oaks, CA: Sage Publications.

Yaukey, John. 1997. "Blacksburg, VA: A Town That's Really Wired." *Gannett News Service,* April 8, pp. 1–3.

Yax, Laura K. 1999. "National Population Projections." Accessed October 30, 1999 (http://www.census.gov/population/www/projections/natprog.html).

Yglesias, Linda. 1996. "Splitting Hairs." *New York Daily News,* February 18, pp. 50–51.

Yinger, J. Milton. 1970. *The Scientific Study of Religion.* New York: Macmillan.

———. 1974. "Religion, Sociology of." In *Encyclopaedia Britannica,* vol. 15. Chicago: Encyclopaedia Britannica, pp. 604–613.

Young, Gay. 1993. "Gender Inequality and Industrial Development: The Household Connection." *Journal of Comparative Family Studies* 124(Spring):3–20.

Z

Zajac, Andrew. 1999. "Notes from a Wired Community." *Chicago Tribune,* April 5, pp. C3–C4.

Zald, Mayer N. 1970. *Organizational Change: The Political Economy of the YMCA.* Chicago: University of Chicago Press.

Zaslow, M. 1988. "Sex Differences in Children's Response to Parental Divorce: 1. Research Methodology and Postdivorce Family Forms." *American Journal of Orthopsychiatry* 58(July):355–378.

———. 1989. "Sex Differences in Children's Response to Parental Divorce: 2. Samples, Variables, Ages, and Sources." *American Journal of Orthopsychiatry* 59(January):118–141.

Zelizer, Gerald L. 1999. "Internet Offers Only Fuzzy Cyberfaith, Not True Religious Experiences." *USA Today,* August 19, p. 13A.

Zellner, William M. 1978. "Vehicular Suicide: In Search of Incidence." Western Illinois University, Macomb. Unpublished M.A. thesis.

Zhou, Xueguang, and Liren Hou. 1999. "Children of the Cultural Revolution: The State and the Life Course in the People's Republic of China." *American Sociological Review* 64(February): 32–36.

———. 1995. *Countercultures: A Sociological Analysis.* New York: St. Martin's.

Zia, Helen. 1990. "Midwives: Talking about a Revolution." *Ms.* 1(November–December):91.

———. 1993. "Women of Color in Leadership." *Social Policy* 23(Summer):51–55.

Zimbardo, Philip G. 1972. "Pathology of Imprisonment." *Society* 9(April):4, 6, 8.

———. 1992. *Psychology and Life.* 13th ed. New York: HarperCollins.

———, Craig Haney, W. Curtis Banks, and David Jaffe. 1974. "The Psychology of Imprisonments: Privation, Power, and Pathology." In *Doing Unto Others: Joining, Molding, Conforming, Helping, and Loving,* edited by Zick Rubin. Englewod Cliffs, NJ: Prentice-Hall.

Zimmer, Lynn. 1988. "Tokenism and Women in the Workplace." *Social Problems* 35(February):64–77.

Zimmerman, Mary K. 1987. "The Women's Health Movement: A Critique of Medical Enterprise, and the Position of Women." Pp. 442–472 in *Analyzing Gender: A Handbook of Social Science Research,* edited by Beth B. Hess and Myra Marx Ferree. Newbury Park, CA: Sage.

Zola, Irving K. 1972. "Medicine as an Institution of Social Control." *Sociological Review* 20(November):487–504.

———. 1983. *Socio-Medical Inquiries.* Philadelphia: Temple University Press.

Zook, Matthew A. 1996. "The Unorganized Militia Network: Conspiracies, Computers, and Community." *Berkeley Planning Journal* 11:1–15.

Zweigenhaft, Richard L., and G. William Domhoff. 1998. *Diversity in the Power Elite: Have Women and Minorities Reached the Top?* New Haven: Yale University Press.